Y0-ENM-082

The Book of Daniel

Bible in
History

Bible in History focuses on biblical interpretation in different ages and countries and is a series dedicated to studies of biblical exegesis as well as to research about principles of interpretation relevant to interpreters of the Bible. The series is open to studies focusing on philological and theological aspects of particular Bible passages but it also welcomes publications in the field of history of biblical interpretation that study the development of new ideas and their impact on interpretation of the text. Editions of textual variants as well as of influential old and modern commentaries are also within the scope of this series.

Ayant pour but l'étude de l'interprétation biblique à travers les époques et dans des pays différents, *la Bible dans l'Histoire* est une collection consacrée à la recherche exégétique ainsi qu'à l'étude des principes qui déterminent la compréhension des commentateurs. Etant ouverte à l'exégèse biblique dans son aspect philologique et théologique, cette collection cherche par ailleurs à promouvoir les publications dans le domaine de l'histoire d'interprétation, ainsi que celles étudiant comment l'introduction des nouveaux principes a permis l'ajustement de l'ancien sens à la réalité d'aujourd'hui. L'édition des variantes textuelles ainsi que des commentaires anciens et modernes correspondent aussi au but fixé à cette collection.

The series accepts publications in French and English.
La collection accueille des ouvrages en langue française et anglaise.

Collection publiée sous la direction de /
Series published by
Joseph Alobaidi

PETER LANG
Bern · Berlin · Bruxelles · Frankfurt am Main · New York · Oxford · Wien

Joseph Alobaidi

The Book of Daniel

The Commentary of R. Saadia Gaon
Edition and Translation

PETER LANG
Bern · Berlin · Bruxelles · Frankfurt am Main · New York · Oxford · Wien

Bibliographic information published by Die Deutsche Bibliothek
Die Deutsche Bibliothek lists this publication in the Deutsche National-bibliografie; detailed bibliographic data is available on the Internet at ‹http://dnb.ddb.de›.

British Library and Library of Congress Cataloguing-in-Publication Data:
A catalogue record for this book is available from *The British Library*, Great Britain, and from *The Library of Congress*, USA.

ISSN 1422-5972
ISBN 3-03910-811-5
US-ISBN 0-8204-8028-2

© Peter Lang AG, European Academic Publishers, Bern 2006
Hochfeldstrasse 32, Postfach 746, CH-3000 Bern 9, Switzerland
info@peterlang.com, www.peterlang.com, www.peterlang.net

All rights reserved.
All parts of this publication are protected by copyright.
Any utilisation outside the strict limits of the copyright law, without the permission of the publisher, is forbidden and liable to prosecution.
This applies in particular to reproductions, translations, microfilming, and storage and processing in electronic retrieval systems.

Printed in Germany

To Adrian Sckenker, OP
In acknowledgement of
the professor
the scholar
and the priest

"At that time there shall arise Michael, the great prince, guardian of your people; it shall be a time unsurpassed in distress since nations began until that time. At that time your people shall escape, everyone who is found written in the book. Many of those who sleep in the dust of the earth shall awake; some shall live forever, others shall be an everlasting horror and disgrace. But the wise shall shine brightly like the splendor of the firmament, and those who lead the many to justice shall be like the stars forever."

Daniel 12:1–3.

Table of Contents

The Judeo-Arabic Text of R. Saadia Gaon's Commentary on the Book of Daniel

Raabi Saadia's Commentary on the Book of Daniel

Transliteration

ا	א	د	ד	ض	ץ̇ צ̇	ك	ך כ
ب	ב	ذ	ד̇	ط	ט	ل	ל
ت	ת	ر	ר	ظ	ט̇	م	ם מ
ث	ת̇	ز	ז	ع	ע	ن	ן נ
ج	ג	س	ס	غ	ג̇	ه	ה
ح	ח	ش	ש	ف	ף פ	و	ו
خ	ך̇ כ̇	ص	ץ צ	ق	ק	ي	י

Symbols and Abreviations

> D	Missing because of a damage in the manuscript.
> L	Missing because laking in the manuscript.
+	Added.
[ ]	Enclose word or words, added by the editor, necessary for the full understanding of the author's expression.
{ }	Enclose word or words from the Bible to complete the author's quotation.
Italics	Are used for the translation of Hebrew and Aramaic word or words in the Judeo-Arabic text, with the exception of proper names and Hebrew or Aramaic word or words to which the Arabic definite article, אל, is added.

Preface

The edition of R. Saadia's commentary on Daniel was a project dear to Fr. Dominique Barthélemy, who died three years before its completion. His passion for the Judeo-Arabic exegetical literature, for R. Saadia Gaon and the Karaite Yefet ben Eli in particular, was so inspiring that the span of a lifetime would not be enough to edit all the commentaries he unearthed and amply employed in his monumental project *Critique Textuelle de l'Ancien Testament*. His dedication to teaching at the *Ecole Biblique* of Jerusalem and the University of Fribourg, can only be paralleled to his exhaustless effort to gather microfilms of manuscripts relating to the Old Testament text and exegesis. Of major interest for him was the first period of "modern" Jewish exegetes that reshaped biblical interpretation by avoiding midrashic and moralistic exposition of the Hebrew Bible. This period represents, at the same time, the golden age of Judeo-Arabic writings, mainly occasioned by Rabbanite-Karaite polemic.

Because of its apocalyptic nature, the Book of Daniel enjoyed the favor of the commentators, since it allowed them to foresee the end of the Jewish exile and the re-appropriation of the lost homeland and past glory. It is a surprise for no one, then that R. Saadia Gaon, Salmon ben Yeruham and Yefet ben Eli, while commenting this Book, were in fact displaying two different visions of Judaism and its future. R. Saadia was the first of the three to write a *tafsir* on Daniel. The two others followed him, reacting to what he wrote, and opposing the Orthodox Judaism that he symbolized. Their work would be misunderstood, and their thinking partially grasped, if there were no edition of the Gaon's commentary. Little is known about the commentary on Daniel by Salmon ben Yeruham, outside the reference made in Yefet ben Eli's commentary on Daniel (p. 153 of D. S. Margoliouth's edition, in *Anecdota Oxoniensia* L 3b, 1889) to Salmon's refutation of R. Saadia. Such refutation may very well be part of a polemical writing against the Rabbanite and not a commentary on the whole Book of Daniel. Thus, a particular place is given to the only other commentary at that time: Yefet ben Eli's commentary on Daniel. Writing one century, roughly, after R. Saadia, he is our first witness to the Gaon's understanding of this Book.

My deepest appreciation goes to Fr. Stephen Ryan OP, who exercised patience and knowledge in reading the first draft of the English translation, and to Fr. Benedict Viviano OP, whose judicious remarks were of great help.

The Manuscripts

1. Antonin

A. Andrei Ivanovich Kapustin (1817–1894) was a Russian archimandrite who from 1865 until his death lived in Jerusalem. He acquired, while visiting Cairo, 1189 Geniza Fragments that later passed into the possession of Leningrad / Petersburg Saltykov-Shchedrin Library.[1]

B. Antonin's manuscript three folios are of 32 or 33 lines of a regular and stylish handwriting. The right and left lower angles of the folios are cut in a triangular form at the level of the twenty-first or the twenty-second lines. The last folio is having a hole in its midst. The shadings represent the missing or damaged parts of the folios.

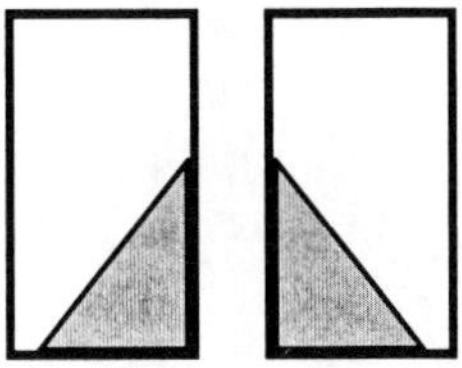

C. The folios start at the end of R. Saadia's commentary on Dn 1:21. Then continues to cover Dn 2 partially. Only the first Hebrew or Aramaic word of every verse is written before the Judeo-Arabic translation of the verse. Ms Antonin discloses R. Saadia's commentary on

1. The end of Dn 1:21.
2. Dn 2:1–2.
3. Dn 2:8–17.
4. Dn 2:22–27.
5. Dn 2:29.

1 This brief biographical notice, plus the catalogs where the list of Antonin's collection could be found, are mentioned in Benjamin RICHLER, *Guide to Hebrew Manuscript Collections*. The Israel Academy of Science and Humanities. Jerusalem 1994, p. 8.

2. BM.Or.5554a. (British Museum)

A. BM.Or.5554a is part of the manuscript of R. Saadia's commentary transmitted by Yeirin. Similar to all the other folios in the facsimile edition of R. Saadia's commentary on Daniel by Yeirin, the two folios of British Museum bring us the text of Dn 7:19–22, its translation and the beginning of the commentary on the same passage. Each folio is of 22 lines with regular and stylish handwriting.

B. *1st folio:* BM.Or.5554a.9 (5th folio in Yeirin's edition. Pp. 215–216).
r. text and translation of Dn 7:19–22 with the beginning of the commentary.
v. commentary on Dn 7:22.
2nd folio: BM.Or.5554a.10 (5th folio in Yeirin's edition. Pp. 217–218).
r. continuation of the commentary of Dn 7:22.
v. continuation of the commentary of Dn 7:22.

C. The two folios are heavily damaged. While the first folio is cut of its last third of each page, the second is damaged by holes in its middle. The shaded parts illustrate the damages of the folios.

1

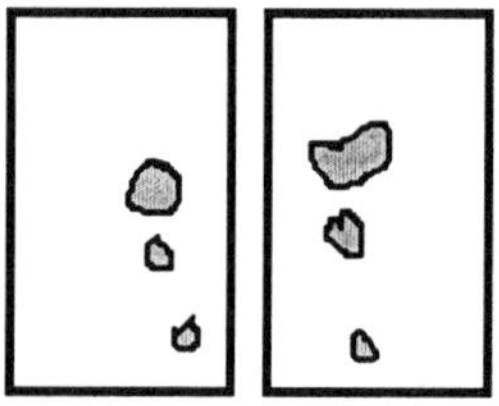

2

D. The text of Daniel. Minor differences between the masoretic text of Daniel and the text transmitted by the manuscript published by Yeirin can be clearly seen. The reason can be found in the passage to the Babylonian vocalization, which does not cover all the vowels designated by the masoretic vocalization. The other reason is the passage in some cases from a short vowel to a long vowel. The meaning is not strongly affected by such minor variations. The material state of the manuscript makes it difficult to write the Babylonian vocalization. In fact the uncut and undamaged parts of the manuscript are not free of ink and moisture stains transforming the transcription of the vocalization into uncertain approximation. However, since the differences are confined to the field of vocalization, but also represented by adding or subtracting a letter or more, here are the words written differently in the two texts, the masoretic and the text transmitted by BM.Or.5554a.9 and 10:

Dn 7:19	ומדקה	MT	מַדֱּקָה
Dn 7:20	בראשׂיה		בְּרֵאשַׁהּ
	קדמיהי		קֳדָמַיְהּ
	ופום ממליל		וּפֻם מְמַלִּל
Dn 7:21	דכין		דִּכֵּן
Dn 7:22	אתא		אֲתָה
	יהיב		יְהִב

A summary of all the differences between the masoretic text of Daniel and the text of the one manuscript, found in different libraries, could be found under Yeirin.

3. Bud.Kauf.222. (Budapest, Hungarian Academy of Science, MS Kaufmann)

A. Bud. Kauf. 222 is part of the manuscript of R. Saadia's commentary transmitted by Yeirin.[2] While the second of the two folios in the possession of the Hungarian Academy of Science is almost complete, with few stains of ink, the first folio is cut lengthwise, taking away more than half of the two pages that compose the folio.

B. *1st folio:* MS Kaufmann 222 (9th folio in Yeirin edition. Pp. 222–223).
r. part of the commentary on Dn 7:22.
v. continuation of the commentary on Dn 7:22 with partial text of Dn 7:26–27.
2nd folio: MS Kaufmann 222 (10th folio in Yeirin edition. Pp. 224–225).
r. part of the translation of Dn 7:28 with text and translation of Dn 7:28 followed by the commentary.
v. text, translation and commentary on Dn 8:1 with the first three words of the text of Dn 8:2.

2 The question could be asked whether it is a pure coincidence that the number of Kaufmann's manuscript is 222 or whether such number was given because the facsimile edition of the manuscript starts at p. 222 in Yeirin's edition.

C. The folios are cut and damaged as represented by the shaded parts.

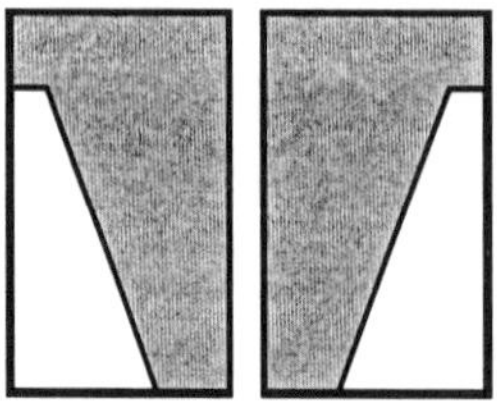

1

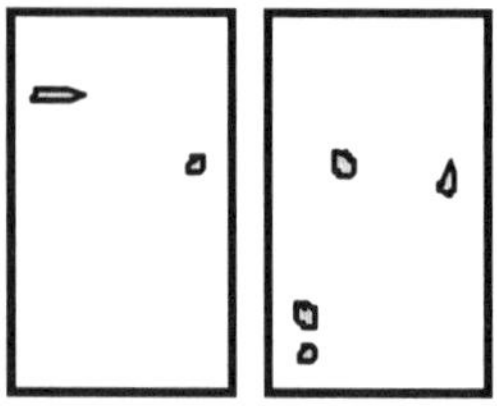

2

D. The text of Daniel. The only readable part of the text is Dn 8:1 with the following variant with masoretic text.

Dn 8:1 בלשׁצר MT בלשׁאצר

4. GE.GN.82. 1.2 (Bibliothèque publique et universitaire de Genève)

A. Two folios discovered by the author of this line and never noticed before in the Bibliothèque publique et Universitaire de Genève (GE), in its Geniza collection of manuscript (GN). They are important because they cover passages that otherwise would remain unintelligible, since other manuscripts dealing with the same passages are heavily damaged.

B. *1st folio:* GE.GN.82. 1.
r. the end of the commentary of on the passage on Dn 2:29–45.
v. continuation of the commentary on Dn 2:29–45 with the translation and the beginning of the commentary on Dn 2:46.
2nd folio: GE.GN.82.2.
r. continuation of the commentary following Dn 3:16.
v. continuation of the same commentary as in recto.

C. While the first folio is readable in his entirety the second folio is heavily damaged.

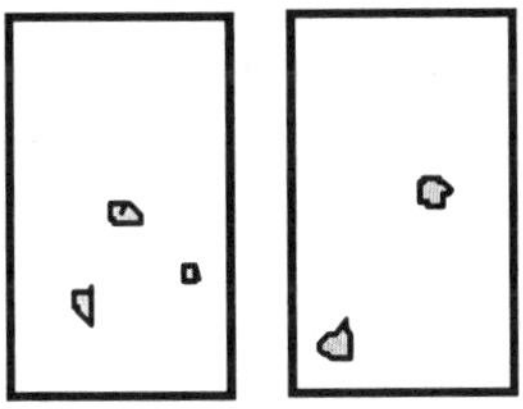

1

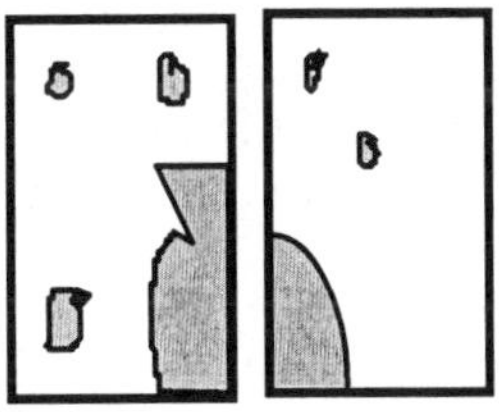

2

D. The text of Daniel. The first Aramaic word of the only verse translated in the two folios, Dn 2:46, is written. It has no vocalization and it is followed by its Judeo-Arabic translation. Thus, no comparison is possible with masoretic text of Daniel.

5. JTS.ENA.3462.5 (Jewish Theological Seminary of America)

A. JTS.ENA.3462.5 is part of the manuscript of R. Saadia's commentary published by Yeirin.

B. *One folio:* (5th folio in Yeirin's facsimile edition. Pp. 215–216).
r. text and translation of Dn 5:13–17.
v. text and translation of Dn 5:18–23.

C. The exterior angles of the two pages are cut. The upper angles are cuts in the middle of the first two lines and the last quarter of the line four, five and six. The lower angles have a cut that damage the last three lines. The damage is in the following shape:

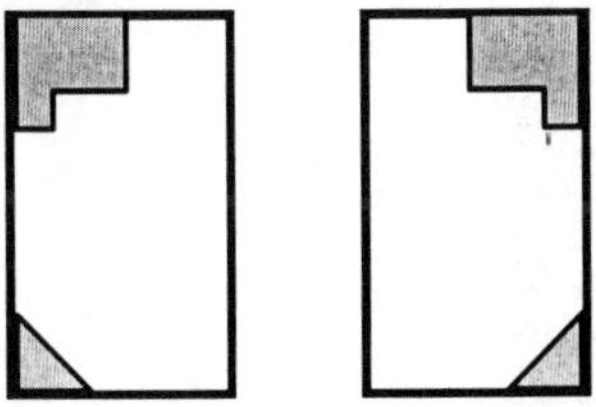

D. The text of Daniel. Being part of one manuscript published by Yeirin, JTS.ENA.3462.5 present the same differences with the masoretic text of Daniel in common with the other parts of the same manuscript.

Dn 5:13	הייתי	MT	הֲיְתִי
Dn 5:14	ושמעית		וְשִׁמְעֵת
	עלך		עֲלָיךְ
	וסכלתנו		וְשָׂכְלְתָנוּ
Dn 5:15	הועלו		הֻעַלּוּ
	כתבא		כְתָבָה
	ופשריה		וּפִשְׁרֵהּ
Dn 5:16	ואנא		וַאֲנָה
	שמעית		שִׁמְעֵת
	עלך		עֲלָיךְ
	תכל		תִּוכֻל
	למשרי		לְמִשְׁרֵא
	תכול		תִּוכֻל
	למקרי		לְמִקְרֵא
	ופשרא		וּפִשְׁרֵהּ
	והמניכא		וְהַמְוֺנְכָא
	צורך		צַוְּארָךְ
	ותולתא		וְתַלְתָּא
Dn 5:17	אהודעיניה		אֲהוֹדְעִנֵּהּ
Dn 5:18	עילאה		עִלָּיאָ
Dn 5:19	ליה		לֵהּ
	ולישניא		וְלִשָּׁנַיָּא
	זיעין		זָאֲעִין
	קטיל		קָטֵל
	צבי		צָבֵא
	צבי		צָבֵא
Dn 5:20	לבביה		לִבְבֵהּ
	ורוחיה		וְרוּחֵהּ
	תיקפת		תִּקְפַת
	כרסי		כָּרְסֵא
	מלכות[יא]		מַלְכוּתֵהּ
	ויקרא		וִיקָרָה
	מניה		מִנֵּהּ
Dn 5:21	אינשא		אֱנָשָׁא

	ולבביה	וְלִבְבֵהּ
	מדוריה	מְדוֹרֵהּ
	יטעמוניה	יְטַעֲמוּנֵּהּ
	גשמיה	גִּשְׁמֵהּ
	> אלהא	אֱלָהָא
	אינשא	אֲנָשָׁא
Dn 5:22	השפילת	הַשְׁפֵּלְתְּ
Dn 5:23	מרי	מָרֵא

6. Morag

A. The facsimile edition by Shelomo Morag of a Babylonian-Yemenite manuscript of R. Saadia translation, that belongs to Rabbi J. Qafih. (יוסף קאפח הרב) covers, with few exceptions, all the Judeo-Arabic translation of Book of Daniel, without R. Saadia's commentary. Morag's edition has the odd particularity that the name of R. Saadia does not appear neither in the title nor in the subtitle.[3] Seven pages (VIII–XV) in English present an abbreviation of Morag's long Hebrew introduction (pp. 13–66).

B. The text of Morag's edition is formed by two distinct manuscripts: The old, written in the fourteenth century, and the new one written at the end of the nineteenth-beginning of the twentieth century, supplementing the missing part in the old Ms.[4] While the new Ms is a replica of the MT, the old Ms, by its Babylonian vocalization and its many variations in comparison with the MT, offers interesting new readings of the Book of Daniel.[5] The two manuscripts divide the Book of Daniel as follow:

The old Ms.	The New Ms.
--------------	Dn 1:1–2:11.
Dn 2:11–29.	---------------

3 Shelomom MORAG, *The Book of Daniel.* A Babylonian-Yemenite Manuscript. Jerusalem 1973. Pp. XV (English) + 153.

4 MORAG, op. cit. p. viii.

5 It is useless to repeat here the Morag's findings here. The variants he studied in his introduction refer to the text (interchange of letters, addition or omission of letters and words, grammatical variants) and to its vocalization. There are also grammatical variants, in the Hebrew and the Aramaic text.

--------------	Dn 2:29–38.
Dn 2:38–3:26.	---------------
--------------	Dn 3:26–4:16.
Dn 4:16–32.	---------------
--------------	Dn 4:32–5:6.
Dn 5:6–6:8	---------------
--------------	Dn 6:8–7:2.
Dn 7:2–9:10.	---------------
--------------	Dn 9:11–18.
Dn 9:18–10:6.	---------------
--------------	Dn 10:6–15.
Dn 10:15–12:13.	

The old Ms is erased and damaged in many places.[6] Otherwise, it represents a fine handwriting.

C. No attempt had been made by Morag to study the Judeo-Arabic of the two manuscripts. Here are some distinctive marks of the two manuscripts.

1. while the old Ms is constant in omitting the marks of pronunciation,[7] (short. vowels and "tashdid"), the new Ms writes frequently the marks of short vowels on the letters, (the thammah or the short o and the fethah or the short a), but never the "kessrah" or the short i that should be written under the letter.
2. the "tashdid" or the doubling the pronunciation value of a letter is never marked by the old Ms. It is often marked in the new Ms, but inconstantly. Sometime it is written with the repetition of the letter in writing (like in Dn 1:4.8), which makes the writing of the "tashdid" useless. Sometime the "tashdid" is written without writing the same letter two times (like in Dn 1:5). Sometime the "tashdid" is not written, it should be, like אלכ̇זאן in Dn 1:11. Sometime the same word is written with two different spellings. We have תחג̇יר in Dn 2:9, but we have the same verb written differently, יתג̇ייר, in Dn 3:27.
3. while the old Ms writes בלטשׁצר the new Ms writes constantly this same name in two words בלט שׁצר.
4. the new Ms shortens beyond reason the ends of the letters ב and כ, which makes possible the confusion between these two letters and the נ. The same can be said of the letters ד and ר. Another possible confusion is between

6 Dn 2:41. 7:19; 23; 25; 27; are erased. An ink stain damages Dn 7:28. A hole damages Dn 8:2-3; 6-7.

7 With the exception of a short o in Dn 11:4.

these two letters and the ך. The old Ms distinctively writes the letters. However, a light tendency of confusing the כ and the פ, can be observed.

7. Oxf. 2486 (University of Oxford, England)

A. This Oxford manuscript contains 175 folios, of twenty short lines each, when unaltered. It deals with the translation and commentary of R. Saadia on the Book of Daniel. Contrary to the major part of the manuscripts utilized in this edition, the vocalization is not Babylonian and usually follows the masoretic vocalization. The material state of the manuscripts, damaged and unclear in its major part, discourages any attempts for a through study of the vocalization. If undertaken, such attempt will equate a guessing game. In fact, the large number of the folios is damaged, either by stains of moisture, or by cuts in their extremities.

B. Oxf.2486 should be read as follow (→ refers to a number of a folio in discontinuation with the consecutive numbering. Whenever it occurs, such discontinuation is underlined by a footnote):

9–26 → 31 → 27–29 → 32–38 → 41–44 → 39–40 → 45–54 → 55b–55a → 57–60 → 61b–61a → 62–64 → 56 → 65–81 → 7–8 → 82 → 30 → 83–90 → 175 → 91–108 → 117–122 → 109–116 → 123–140 → 149–150 → 141–142 → 147–148 → 167 → 155 → 151–154 → 143–146 → 156–166 → 172 → 170 → 168–169 → 171 → 173–174.

C. The book of Daniel is translated and commented in Oxf.2486 according to the following order:

Dn 2:31–49:	ff.9a–19b.
Dn 3:1–33:	ff.19b–26b.31ab.27a–29b.32a.
Dn 4:1–34:	ff.32a–38b.41a–44b.39a–40b.45a–48a.
Dn 5:1–30:	ff.48a–54b.55b–55a.57a–58b.
Dn 6:1–29:	ff.58b–60b.61b–61a.62a–64b.56ab.65a–68a.
Dn 7:1–28:	ff.68a–81b.7a–8b.82ab.30ab.83a–90b.175ab.91a–92b.
Dn 8:1–27:	ff.92b–108b.117a–118b.
Dn 9:1–27:	ff.118b.–122b.109a–116b.123a–132b.
Dn 10:1–21:	ff.132b–140b.149a–150b.141a–142b.147a.
Dn 11:1–45:	ff.147a.–148b.167ab.155ab.151a–155b.143a–146b.156a–166b.172ab.170a.
Dn 12:1–4:	ff. 17b.168a–169b.171ab.173a–174b.

D. The text of the Book of Daniel. The physical state of the manuscript does not allow a full comparison with the masoretic text. However, few clear passages, much less pages or folios, show that the text of Daniel according to Oxf.2486 follows the Tiberien vocalization of the masoretic text. Finally, Oxf.2486 is lacking the translation and the commentary on the beginning and the end of the Book of Daniel: Dn 1:1–2:30 and 12:5–13.

8. Oxf.2628. (University of Oxford, England)

A. This manuscript of five folios give us R. Saadia translation of Dn 9:26–11:20. No commentary is included.

B. The pages are small, well preserved, with regular handwriting. They are of fourteen, fifteen or sixteen lines.

C. The text of Daniel. The Hebrew text of Daniel is partially vocalized, according to the Tiberien vocalization. Accents for reading are also partially written. There are many small differences with the masoretic text.

Dn 9:26	שׁוממות	MT	שֹׁמֵמוֹת
Dn 9:27	שׁומם		שֹׁמֵם
Dn 10:1	בלטשאצר		בֵּלְטְאשַׁצַּר
Dn 10:2	שׁבועים		שָׁבֻעִים
Dn 10:3	שׁלושת שׁבועים		שְׁלֹשֶׁת שׁבֻעִים
Dn 10:4	לחודשׁ		לַחֹדֶשׁ
Dn 10:5	חגורים		חֲגֻרִים
Dn 10:6	וזרועתיו ומרגלותיו		וּזְרֹעֹתָיו וּמַרְגְּלֹתָיו
	נחושת		נְחֹשֶׁת
Dn 10:7	גדולה		גְדֹלָה
Dn 10:10	חמודות		חֲמֻדוֹת
Dn 10:11	חמודות		חֲמֻדוֹת
	דובר עליךָ ועמוד על		דֹּבֵר אֵלֶיךָ וַעֲמֹד עַל
	עומדיךָ		עָמְדֶיךָ
Dn 10:13	עומד		עֹמֵד
Dn 10:16	נוגיע		נֹגֵעַ
	העומד		הָעֹמֵד
Dn 10:19	חמודות		חֲמֻדוֹת

Dn 11:2	עומדים	עֹמְדִים
	עושר	עֹשֶׁר
Dn 11:6	יעמוד	יַעֲמֹד
	והיולדה	וְהַיֹּלְדָהּ
Dn 11:8	יביא	יָבִא
	יעמוד	יַעֲמֹד
Dn 11:10	וישוב	וְיָשֹׁב
Dn 11:12	ורם	ירום°
	רבואותו	רִבֹּאותו
Dn 11:15	וזרועות	וּזְרֹעוֹת
	יעמודו	יַעֲמֹדוּ
Dn 11:16	ויעמוד	וְיַעֲמֹד
Dn 11:17	בתוקף	בְּתֹקֶף
	תעמוד	תַּעֲמֹד

9. Oxf.2629. (University of Oxford, England)

A. A valuable and much damaged manuscript assembling different writings. The part related to this work contains three kinds of writings by four different hands.

1. An introduction, written in Judeo-Arabic, to a commentary on the Song of Songs. It is the first page of the beginning of the manuscript.
2. R. Saadia's commentary on Dn 1:1–2,21–2:1–2,35–45 written with the same handwriting. The handwriting is regular and stylish in pages of nineteen lines each. This part of R. Saadia's commentary is contained in folios 37–40. A second part of R. Saadia's commentary, on Dn 10:8–21, in folios 43–44 of the same manuscript. The handwriting is totally different from the partial commentary on Dn 1–2. The folios 43–44 are big pages of thirty-three lines, in small letters and unpolished handwriting. The two folios are heavily damaged.
3. One page of thirty lines, heavily damaged, of a commentary, in Judeo-Arabic. It probably deals with Dn 3 (his name occurs in the line 20) where his friends are thrown to the furnace, since there is a discussion in the upper third of the page about the nature of fire.

B. All the pages, but one, are damaged. Some are damaged beyond any possible use. Here is a visual description of the damage in Oxf.2629.

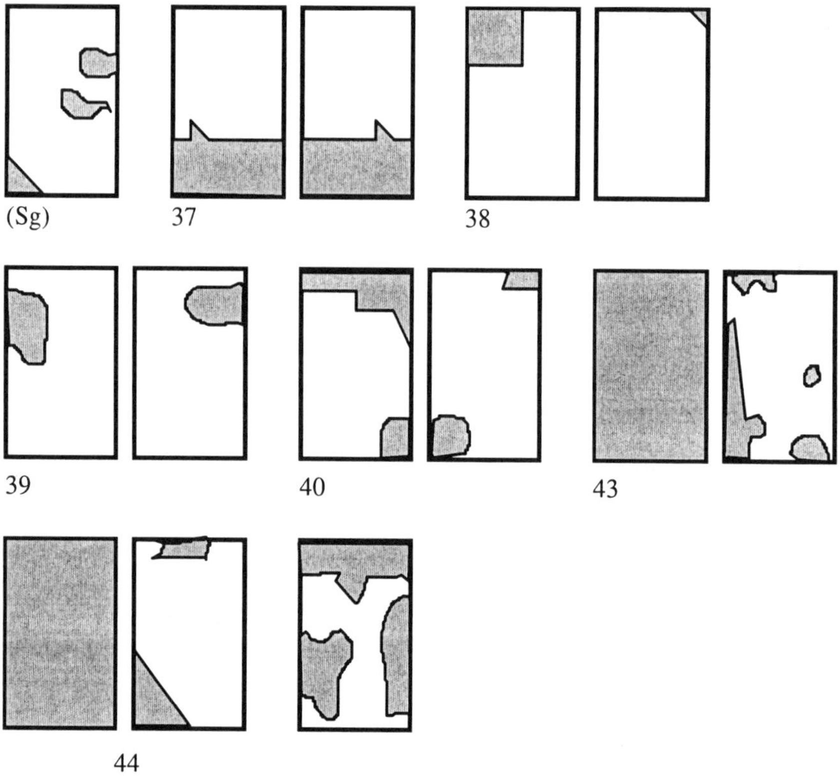

C. The text of Daniel. The first one or two words alone of the masoretic text are mentioned, followed by the Judeo-Arabic translation.

10. Oxf.2652 (University of Oxford, England)

A. Two big folios of beautiful handwriting that are part of the same manuscript as TS.Ar.51; TS.Ar.28.102 and TS.Ar.28.102. Pages have twenty-four or twenty-five regular lines. They are uncut and with the exception of the ink density between the upper part (darker) and the lower part (lighter) they are undamaged.

B. Oxf. 2652.54 (r. v.) deals with the commentary on Dn 7:10.

Oxf. 2652.55 (r. v.) deals with the end of the commentary on Dn 8:14 and the translation of Dn 8:15–21.

C. Only the first Aramaic and Hebrew words of the masoretic text are written, followed by the Judeo-Arabic translation.

11. Oxf.2652.B. (University of Oxford, England)

Two folios of short lines and small pages. Each has eight lines of Daniel text alone, followed by R. Saadia's translation. The Aramaic text has Babylonian vocalization. The folios have the text and the translation of Dn 4:11–14. There is the translation of Dn 4:11 alone. Here are the differences with the masoretic text:

Dn 4:12	שׁורשׁוהי	MT	שָׁרְשׁוֹהִי
	שׁבוקו		שְׁבֻקוּ
	ובאיסור		וּבֶאֱסוּר
	בדתאה		בְּדִתְאָא
Dn 4:13	לביה		לִבְבֵהּ
Dn 4:14	עירן		עִירִין
	שׁאילתא		שְׁאֵלְתָא
	עילאה		עִלָּיא
	אינשׁא		אֱנוֹשָׁא
	יצבי		יִצְבֵּא
	יתנינה		יִתְּנִנַּהּ

12. Oxf.2659 (University of Oxford, England)

A. The four folios of Oxf. 2659 are undoubtedly part of a manuscript containing all the commentary of R. Saadia on Daniel. The other part can be found in the central part of Oxf. 2629 (fol. 37–40). The pages are of eighteen (Oxf.2659.42–43) or nineteen lines (Oxf.2659.40–41). While the handwriting of Oxf.2659.42–

43 is stylish with larger letters, the handwriting of Oxf.2659.40–41 is regular, without being stylish.

B. The four folios are of two handwritings. The first and second folios are of the same handwriting. The third and the fourth folios are of a handwriting other than the handwriting of the first two folios.
2nd folio: (Oxf.2659.40)
r. continuation of the commentary on Dn 11:36–45.
v. continuation of the commentary on Dn 11:36–45.
1st folio: (Oxf.2659.41)
r. continuation of the commentary on Dn 12:1.
v. continuation of the commentary on Dn 12:1.
3rd folio: (Oxf.2659.42)
r. continuation of the commentary on Dn 9:24–27.
v. continuation of the commentary on Dn 9:24–27.
4th folio: (Oxf.2659.43)
r. partial translation of Dn 10:6 with the full translation of Dn 10:7–8 followed by the commentary on Dn 10:4–8.
v. continuation of the commentary on Dn 10:4–8.

C. Only the first Hebrew words of the masoretic text are written, followed by the Judeo-Arabic translation.

13. Oxf.3109. (University of Oxford, England)

A. One folio of eleven lines on each page containing R. Saadia's translation of Dn 11:40–12:4. The folio is well preserved in spite of many stains of moistures and two erased words. However, the folio is easily readable.

B. Only the first Hebrew words of the masoretic text are written, followed by the Judeo-Arabic translation.

14. Spiegel[8]

A. The booklet of Dr. H. Spiegel is the edition of a Berlin manuscript[9] containing R. Saadia's translation of the Book of Daniel, without his commentary.

B. No study was tempted by H. Spiegel other than a brief presentation of less than one page, p. 15, in which he lists the following particularities:

1. the short alif is replaced by a long alif: חתי and אדי, for example, are written חתא and אדי.
2. the "tashdid" or the doubling of a letter, represented by a small "w" over a letter, is generally omitted. There are two exceptions to this particularity: when the letters are ו and י. However, these two letters are not always written with the "tashdid." The "tashdid" may appear simply by writing the same letter two times. Hens, we have הייה instead of היה.
3. there is a confusion between the accusative and the nominative plural. For example we have nouns ending with ין instead of ון.
4. another particularity could be seen in Spiegel's edition, not systematically in the manuscript, is the replacement of the letter ט by the letter צ in עיטים for example, that becomes עיצים. It is a particularity of many Yemenite manuscripts. This explain the many agreement between Spiegel edition and the facsimile edition of a Yemenite manuscript by Morag. Nevertheless, Spiegel spells the words containing ט correctly in his footnotes.
5. as a reference to his edition of R. Saadia's translation, and similar to this edition, Spiegel chooses Yefet ben Eli's translation of the Book of Daniel.

C. H. Spiegel's edition covers R. Saadia's translation of the whole book of Daniel. The translation alone is given.

8 *Saadia al-Fajjumi's arabische Danielversion.* Nach einem Manuscript der kgl. Bibliothek in Berlin zum ersten Male herausgegeben, mit Einleitung und Anmerkungen versehen. Von Dr. H. Spiegel. Druck von H. Itzkowiski, Gipsstr. 9. 1906. (pp. 17 + XXXV).

9 According to H. Spiegel (p. 15) the manuscript has the number 1203 following Steinschneider's catalog.

16. Str.BNU.5138.

A. Two pages from different folios. They are part of the manuscript published by Yeirin in his facsimile edition. Thus they partake in the characteristics of the same manuscript.

B. This is s visual portrayal of the two pages, cut and heavily damaged in their major part, is as follow:

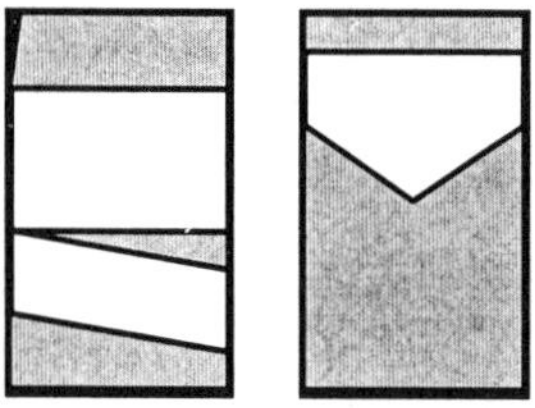

C. the partial Aramaic text of Dn 7:15 with Babylonian vocalization, presents the following differences with the masoretic text:

Dn 7:15	אתכריאת	אֶתְכְּרִיַּת
	אנא	אֲנָה
	יבהלונני	יְבַהֲלֻנַּנִי

17. TS.Ar.1b.88. (Cambridge University Library)

A. TS Ar.1b.88 along with TS.Ar.23.11. and TS.Ar.26.6. are fragments of a very important manuscript. This part covers R. Saadia's commentary of Dn 7:5 until the middle of his commentary on Dn 7:7. Their pages are long (23–24 lines) with small handwriting containing many abbreviations. While heavily damaged it remains with the other two fragments one of the longest and most valuable manuscript for the project of editing this commentary.

B. *One folio:* r. the end of R. Saadia's commentary on Dn 7:5, plus the translation and the whole commentary on Dn 7:6.
v. the translation and half of the commentary on Dn 7:7.

C. The folio is damaged according to the following representation:

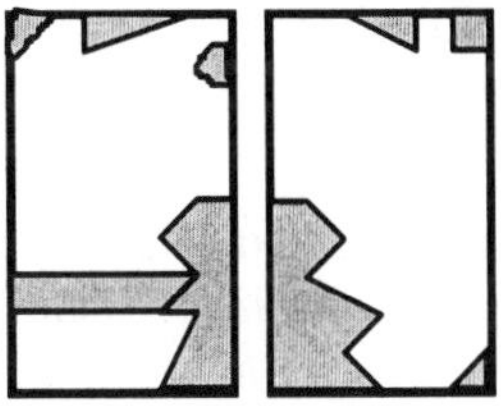

D. Daniel's masoretic text is mentioned by its first one or two words, without vocalization, followed by the Judeo-Arabic translation.

17. TS.Ar.b1.90. (Cambridge University Library)

A. Two folios of a manuscript heavily damaged. The handwriting is regular to elegant when in parts easy to read. The pages are long, of thirty-two lines.

B. *1st folio:* r. R. Saadia's commentary on Dn 4:11–20.
v. R. Saadia's commentary on Dn 4:20–33.
2nd folio: r. R. Saadia's commentary on Dn 6:18–28.
v. R. Saadia's commentary on Dn 6:29–7:1.

C. The folios could be represented as follow:

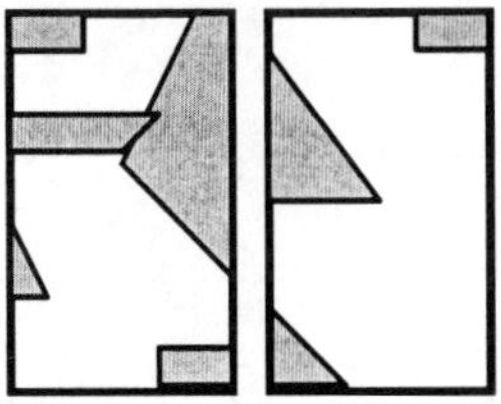

1

2

C. The two folios do not contain a full verse of either Dn 4 or Dn 6. However, the biblical quotations inside the commentary are not vocalized.

18. TS.Ar.b1.101. (Cambridge University Library)

A. This Cambridge manuscript is first published by Yeirin. It is part of a single manuscript dispersed in five different Libraries in Europe and the United States. This is the fourth of four parts in the possession of Cambridge University Library, three of which are published by Yeiriin's edition.

B. *1st folio:* (4th folio in Yeirin's facsimile edition. Pp. 213–214).
r. text, translation of Dn 5:4–8.
v. text, translation of Dn 5:9–13.
2nd folio: (11th folio in Yeirin's facsimile edition Pp. 226–227).
r. text and translation of Dn 8:2–6 plus the partial text of Dn 8:7
v. end of the text and translation of Dn 8:7 plus the beginning of the commentary on Dn 8:1–7.
3rd folio: (12th folio in Yeirin's facsimile edition. Pp. 228–229).
r. text and translation of Dn 8:13–14 followed by the commentary.
v. continuation of the commentary on Dn 8:14.
4th folio: (13th folio in Yeirin's facsimile edition. Pp. 230–231).
r. continuation of the commentary on Dn 8:14 and the beginning of the text of Dn 8:15.
v. text and translation of Dn 8:15–23.
5th folio: (14th folio in Yeirin's facsimile edition. Pp. 232–233).
r. text, translation and the beginning of the commentary on Dn 9:17–19.
v. continuation of the commentary on Dn 9:19.

C. The folios are slightly damaged in various places.

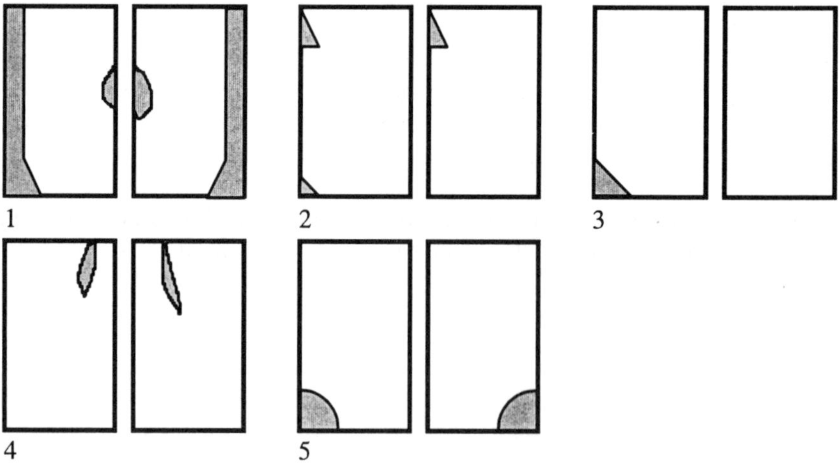

D. The text of Daniel. Being part of one manuscript published by Yeirin, JTS.ENA.3462.5 present the same differences with the masoretic text of Daniel in common with the other parts of the same manuscript.

Dn 5:4	אשתיאו	MT	אִשְׁתִּיו
Dn 5:5	נפקא		נְפַקָו
	אינישׁ		אֱנָשׁ
	לקביל		לָקֳבֵל
	גרא		גִּירָא
	כותל		כְּתַל
	חזי		חָזֵה
Dn 5:6	ורעיניהי		וְרַעְיֹנֹהִי
	יבהלניה		יְבַהֲלוּנֵּהּ
	[חר]ציה		חַרְצֵהּ
	וארכבתיה		וְאַרְכֻבָּתֵהּ
Dn 5:7	בחייל		בְּחַיִל
	כסדאי		כַּשְׂדָּיֵא
	עני		עָנֵה
	והמניכא		וְהַמְוּנְכָא
	צוריה		צַוּארֵהּ
Dn 5:8	למקרי		לְמִקְרֵא
Dn 5:9	סגיא		שַׂגִּיא
	מתבהיל		מִתְבְּהַל
Dn 5:10	לקביל		לָקֳבֵל
	[י]שׁתני		יִשְׁתַּנּוֹ
Dn 5:11	ביה		בֵּהּ
	כסד[אין]		כַּשְׂדָּאִין
Dn 5:12	וסכלתנ[ו]		וְשָׂכְלְתָנוּ
	ומשׁרי		וּמְשָׁרֵא
	ביה		בֵּהּ
	שׁמיה		שְׁמֵהּ
	ופשׁריה יהחויה		וּפִשְׁרָה יְהַחֲוֵה
Dn 5:13	הייתי		הַיְתִי

19. TS.Ar.21.35. (Cambridge University Library)

A. It is a manuscript of a folio and a half page containing Dn 12:2–13 masoretic text, plus R. Saadia's translation. It may well be part of a lost manuscript that consists of the masoretic text of Daniel, R. Saadia's translation and commentary. In fact the last four words of TS.Ar.21.35 are the following: תם דניאל קרא ותפסיר that could be translated as "the reading and the commentary of Daniel is achieved." This obvious meaning of the final sentence has to pass, yet, the scrutiny forged by the experience of the editions of R. Saadia's commentaries of the Bible. First, the word תפסיר may also mean "rendition" or "translation." Secondly, it seems methodologically incoherent to start Dn 12 by separate and long commentaries on the first four verses of this chapter, then to have a commentary on the nines remaining verses all together. Thirdly, and most logically, such commentary, if exists, should have been following the translation of Dn 12:5–13 immediately.

B. *1st folio:* r. Daniel-s masoretic text and R. Saadia's translation of Dn 12:5–7.
v. Daniel-s masoretic text and R. Saadia's translation of Dn 12: 8–10.
2nd folio: r. (Half a page of eight lines) Daniel-s masoretic text and R. Saadia's translation of Dn 12:11–13.

C. The recto page of the folio is damaged in different places, as following:

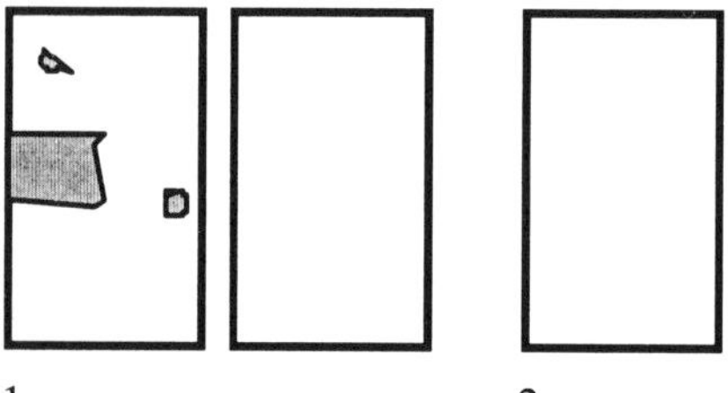

1 2

D. The text of Daniel transmitted by TS.Ar.21.39 is similar to the masoretic text with the particularity that very few words are vocalized. Furthermore, such words are only partially vocalized. Some signs suggest that there is confusion between the masoretic and Babylonian vocalization. It is also possible that some signs for readers were added.

20. TS.Ar.21.49. (Cambridge University Library)

A. It is a manuscript of five folios of which the first half of the first folio and the second half of the last folio are missing. Pages are of twenty-three lines of an irregular and hardly elegant handwriting. The letters are totally or partially erased in many places and stains of moister are present in all the pages.

B. *1st folio:* r. missing.
v. R. Saadia's translation of Dn 3:23–29.
2nd folio: r. R. Saadia's translation of Dn 3:33–4:10.
v. R. Saadia's translation of Dn 4:14–23.
3rd folio: r. R. Saadia's translation of Dn 4:24–33.
v. R. Saadia's translation of Dn 4:34–5:9.
4th folio: r. R. Saadia's translation of Dn 5:10–19.
v. R. Saadia's translation of Dn 5:20–6:1.
5th folio: r. R. Saadia's translation of Dn 6:2–12.
v. missing.

C. Most the folios are damaged in various places:

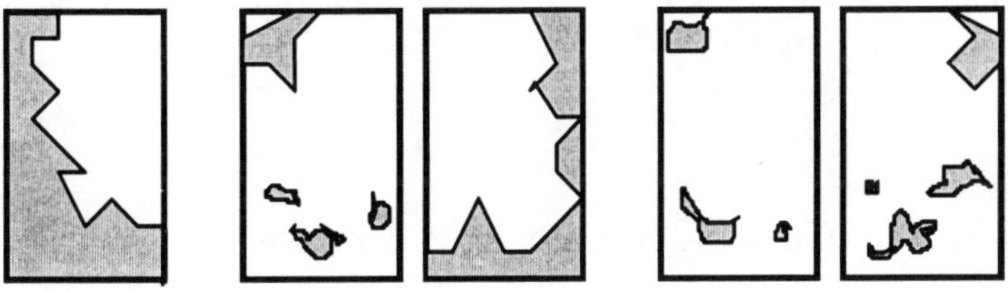

1 2 3

4 5

D. Only the first word of the masoretic text of Daniel, without vocalization, is written followed by the Judeo-Arabic translation of R. Saadia.

20. TS.Ar.22.104. (Cambridge University Library)

A. A folio of twenty-two lines each page of a distinctive and elegant handwriting. It is unfortunate that the material quality made it difficult to preserve such impression because of the many damages resulting from a poor ink and papers quality, in addition to the stains of moisture.

B. *One folio:* r. continuation of R. Saadia's commentary on Dn 6:19–29.
v. end of the commentary on Dn 6:19–29 and the first two lines plus the first three words of the masoretic text of Dn 7:1.

C. The folio is heavily damaged in more than one place.

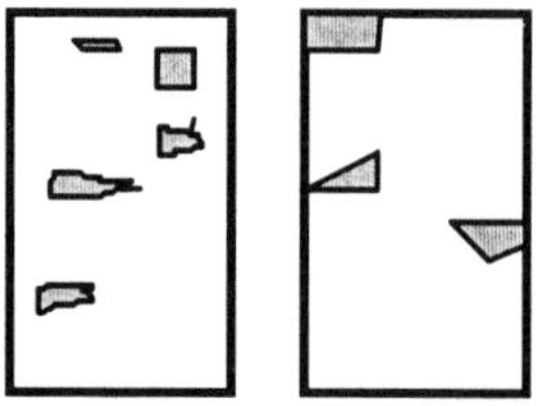

D. The first three words of Dn 7:1 show a Hebrew text, without vocalization, similar to the masoretic text of Daniel.

21. TS.Ar.23.11. (Cambridge University Library)

A. TS.Ar.23.11. along with TS Ar.1b.88 and TS.Ar.26.6. are fragments of the same manuscript. This part covers R. Saadia's commentary on most of Dn 7 and the beginning of Dn 8. Big portion of each folio is made unreadable because of stains of moisture. The handwriting uses many abbreviations. Nevertheless, the fine handwriting, combined with big size of the pages (of twenty-four or twenty-three lines) made this manuscript valuable.

B. *1st folio:* r. the end of the commentary on Dn 7:7; the translation and the beginning of the commentary on Dn 7:8.
v. end of the commentary on Dn 7:8; the translation and the beginning of the commentary on Dn 7:9–10.
2nd folio: r. the continuation of the commentary on Dn 7:9–10.
v. the continuation of the commentary on Dn 7:9–10.

3rd folio: r. continuation of the commentary on Dn 7:9–10.
v. the continuation of the commentary on Dn 7:9–10 with the translation and the beginning of the commentary on Dn 7:11–12.
4th folio: r. the end on the commentary on Dn 7:11–12; the translation and the beginning of the commentary on Dn 7:13–14.
v. the end of the commentary on Dn 7:13–14; the translation and the commentary on Dn 7:15–16.
5th folio: r. the translation and the commentary on Dn 7:17–18; translation and the beginning of the commentary on Dn 7:19–22. At the seventh line from the bottom continues the commentary on Dn 8:4–7.
v. the end of the commentary on Dn 8:4–7.
6rh folio: r. the end of the commentary on Dn 7:19–22 with the translation and the beginning of the commentary on Dn 7:23–25.
v. the continuation of the commentary on Dn 7:23–25.
7th folio: r. the end of the commentary on Dn 7:23–25; the translation of Dn 7:26–27.
v. the translation and the commentary on Dn 7:28–8:1.
8th folio: r. the end of the translation of Dn 8:3 and the translation and the beginning of the commentary on Dn 8:4–7. (The continuation of the commentary is at the seventh line from bottom of the 5th folio, recto.)
v. the end of the commentary on Dn 8:4–7; the translation and the beginning of the commentary on Dn 8:8–12.

C. All the folios are damaged in their opposite angles at the top and the bottom.

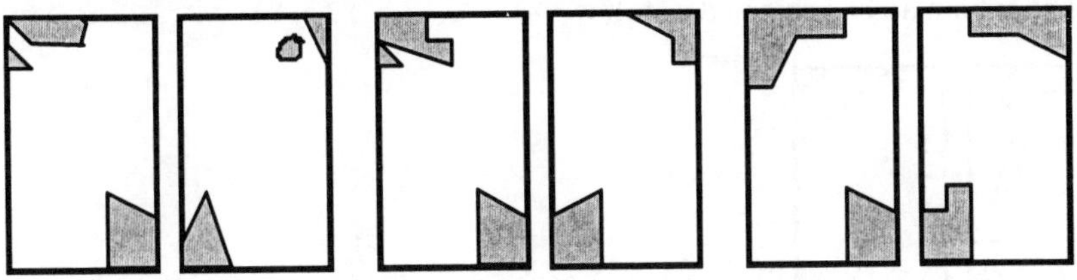

1 2 3

4 5 6

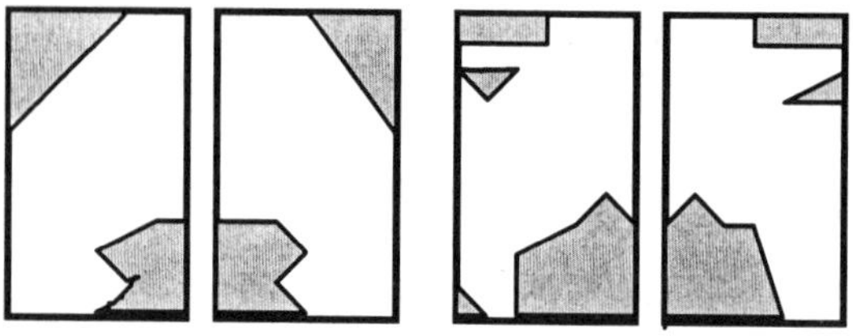

7 8

D. With the exception of the first one or two words, without vocalization, the masoretic text of Daniel is not written. Some quotations inside the commentary are partially vocalized.

22. TS.Ar.23.29

A. One folio heavily damaged and covering a small part of R. Saadia's translation and commentary on Dn 10. The handwriting, while regular, can not be described as elegant.

B. *One folio:* r. the commentary on Dn 10:5–8; the translation of Dn 10:9–10.
v. the translation of Dn 10:11–21.

C. The folio may be presented as follow:

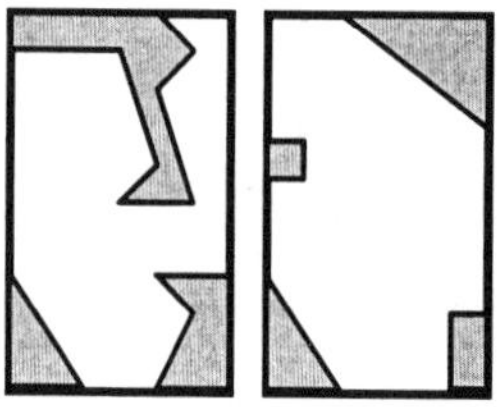

D. The text of Daniel is mentioned by the first one or two words, vocalized, followed by the translation. The damaged state of the folio makes it impossible to undertake any comparison between the masoretic text and the text of TS.Ar.23.29.

23. TS.Ar.24.22. (Cambridge University Library)

A. Two folios that give us R. Saadia's commentary and translation, starting by the end of the commentary on Dn 12:2 followed by the translation and commentary on Dn 12:3–4 and finishing by the translation of Dn 12:5–10. Its value comes from the fact that it continues the main Oxford manuscript (2486). With exception of one, all the pages, of twenty-seven or twenty-eight lines, are damaged.

B. *1st folio:* r. the translation and the beginning of the commentary on Dn 11:13–15.
v. the continuation of the commentary on Dn 11:13–15.
2nd folio: r. the end of the commentary on Dn 12:2, plus the translation and the commentary on Dn 12:3.
v. the end of the commentary on Dn 12:3, plus the translation and the commentary on Dn 12:4 with the translation of Dn 12:5–10.

C. While one page is heavily damaged the rest of the two folios are hardly damaged.

a b c d

D. The text of Daniel is mentioned by the first Hebrew word, without vocalization, followed by R. Saadia's Judeo-Arabic translation.

25. TS.Ar.26.6. (Cambridge University Library)

A. Three folios, part of the same manuscript as TS.Ar.1b.88 and TS.Ar.23.11. lightly damaged, the pages, of twenty-three lines, shows a regular handwriting, without refinement, that brings us R. Saadia's commentary and translation of two different parts of the book of Daniel: Dn 4 and Dn 7.

B. *1st folio:* r. the translation of Dn 4:7–22.
v. the translation of Dn 4:23–43, followed by the beginning of the commentary on Dn 4.
2nd folio: r. the end of the commentary on Dn 7:1, the translation of Dn 7:2 followed by its commentary.
v. the end of the commentary on Dn 7:2, the translation of Dn 7:3 followed by its commentary.
3rd folio: r. the end of the commentary on Dn 7:3, the translation of Dn 7:4 followed by its commentary.
v. the end of the commentary on Dn 7:4, the translation and the beginning of the commentary on Dn 7:5.

C. The three folios are slightly damaged. Yet, they remain readable, with the exception of very few words.

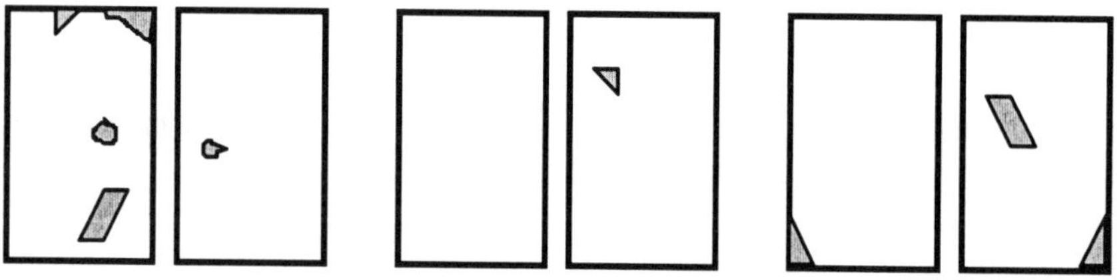

1 2 3

D. The text of Daniel is mentioned by the first Hebrew word, without vocalization, followed by R. Saadia's Judeo-Arabic translation.

26. TS.Ar.26.54. (Cambridge University Library)

A. This Cambridge manuscript is first published by Yeirin. It is part of a single manuscript dispersed in five different Libraries in Europe and the United States. This is the first of four parts in the possession of Cambridge University Library, three of which are published by Yeirin's edition.

B. *1st folio:* (1st folio in Yeirin's facsimile edition. Pp. 207–208).
r. the final part of the introduction to the whole commentary.
v. the end of the introduction to the whole commentary, plus text, translation and the beginning of the commentary on Dn 1:1.

2nd folio: (2nd folio in Yeirin's facsimile edition Pp. 209–210).
r. the end of the commentary on Dn 1:1 plus text, translation and the beginning of the commentary on Dn 1:2.
v. the continuation of the commentary on Dn 1:2.

C. The folios are slightly damaged in various places.

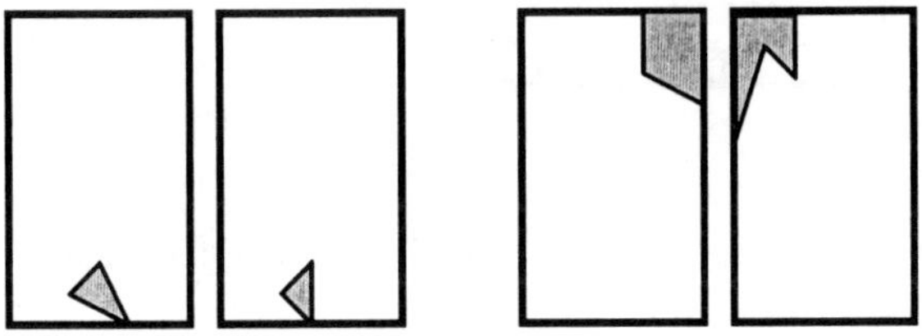

1 2

D. The two folios deal with the final part of R. Saadia's introduction to his commentary on the Book of Daniel with the text, the translation and the commentary on Dn 1:1–2. No significant difference with the masoretic text is found.

Dn 1:1 נבוכדנצר TM נְבוּכַדְנֶצַּאר

27. TS.Ar.26.62. (Cambridge University Library)

A. Two folios of unequal length (the verso is longer than the recto) that bring us R. Saadia's partial translation and commentary on Dn 9. While regular, with large letters, the handwriting affects no tendency for being stylish.

B. *1st folio:* r. (thirteen lines). The translation of Dn 9:19 followed by the beginning of the commentary on the section Dn 9:5–19 that R. Saadia translates as one section, without interruption by a commentary on any individual verse.
v. (sixteen lines). Continuation of the commentary on the section Dn 9:5–19.
2nd folio: r. (twelve lines). The translation of Dn 9:20–23.
v. (sixteen lines). The end of the translation of Dn 9:23 and the beginning of the commentary on the section Dn 9:20–23.

C. The two folios are slightly damaged in many places.

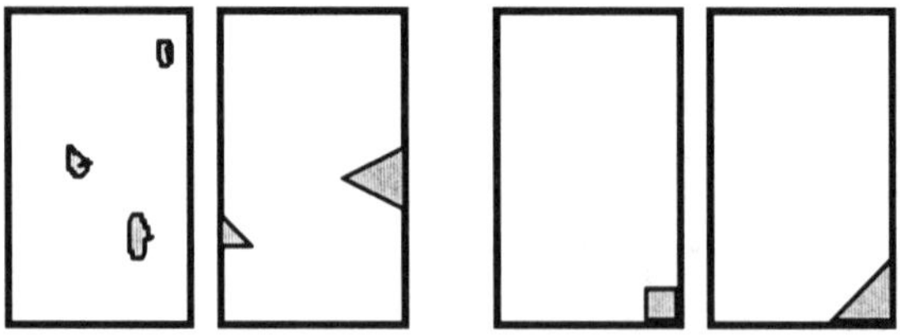

1 2

D. There is no masoretic text of Daniel appearing in this in any of the pages of the two folios.

28. TS.Ar.27.35. (Cambridge University Library)

A. Two big pages with small handwriting and unequal length. They bring us R. Saadia's translation and commentary on the beginning of Dn 7. The hand writing is similar to TS.Ar.28.155 that appears to complete TS.Ar.27.35. It seems possible to conclude that both are part of the same manuscript. However, the lines in TS.Ar.27.35 are shorter that the line in TS.Ar.28.155 which may well indicate the existence of two manuscripts written by the same copyist.
B. *The first page:* The end of the commentary on Dn 7:3 with the translation and the commentary on Dn 7:4.
The second page: The end of the commentary on Dn 7:4: the translation and the commentary of Dn 7:5–6, and the translation of Dn 7:7 with the first line of its commentary.

C. The two pages are very damaged by cuts and stains of moisture that affect the density, and the visibility, of the letters.

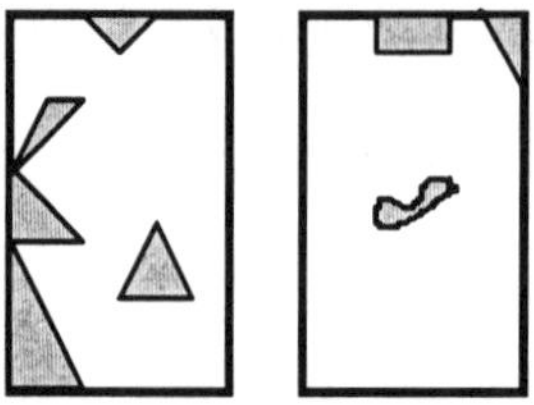

1 2

D. Only the first word, or the first two words, without vocalization, of the masoretic text of Daniel is written, followed by the Judeo-Arabic translation.

29. TS.Ar.28.1. (Cambridge University Library)

A. The four folios of TS.Ar.28.1. are part of the same manuscript as TS.Ar.51.3; TS.Ar.28.102; Oxf.2659. The very regular and stylish handwriting is the mark of this manuscript. It brings us two distinctive parts: The end of the commentary on Dn 11 with the translation and the beginning of the commentary on Dn 12; the end of the translation and commentary on Dn 9 with the beginning of the translation and commentary on Dn 10.

B. *1st folio:* r. the commentary on Dn 11:30–41.
v. the commentary on Dn 11:42–43.
2nd folio: r. the commentary on Dn 11:44–45.
v. the end of the commentary on Dn 11:45 with the translation and the beginning of the commentary on Dn 12:1.
3rd folio: r. the commentary on Dn 9:26–27.
v. the continuation of the commentary on Dn 9:27.
4th folio: r. the end of the commentary on Dn 9:27. The translation and the beginning of the commentary on Dn 10:1.
v. the continuation of the commentary on Dn 10:1.

C. While some parts are very well preserved, others are heavily damaged by stains of moisture (in particular, the verso of the second folio) or deep cuts in the upper parts f the folios.

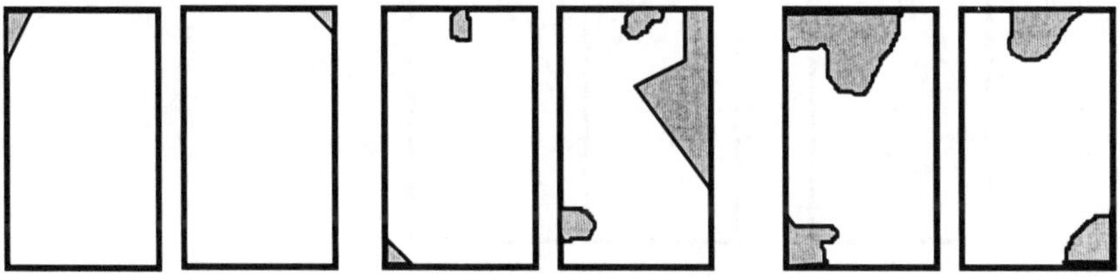

1 2 3

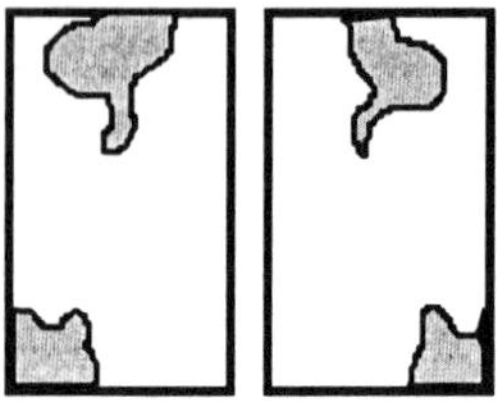

4

D. Only the first word, or the first two words, without vocalization, of the masoretic text of Daniel is written, followed by the Judeo-Arabic translation.

30. TS.Ar.28.76. (Cambridge University Library)

A. Two folios cut in a regular form in their upper half. They bring us the end of R. Saadia's commentary on Dn 4; all the translation and the beginning of the commentary on Dn 5. The handwriting is regular and elegant.

B. *1st folio:* r. the end of the commentary on Dn 4:34 with the translation of Dn 5:1–11.
v. the translation of Dn 5:12–21.
2nd folio: r. the translation of Dn 5:22–30 with the beginning of the commentary on all Dn 5. (Dn 5:1–4).
v. the continuation of the commentary on Dn 5. (Dn 5:5–11).

C. The two folios are cut in a similar way.

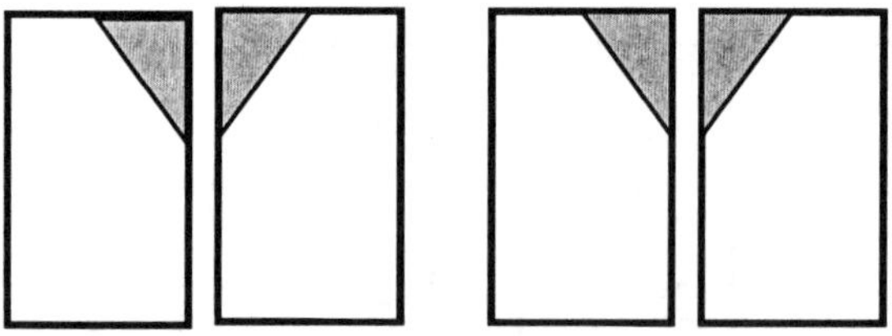

1 2

D. Only the first word, or the first two words, without vocalization, of the masoretic text of Daniel is written, followed by the Judeo-Arabic translation.

31. TS.Ar.28.102. (Cambridge University Library)

A. One folio. The four folios of TS.Ar.28.102 are part of the same manuscript as TS.Ar.28.1; TS.Ar.51.3 and Oxf.2659. It partakes in the same characteristic of elegant handwriting in small pages of eighteen lines.

B. One folio: r. the continuation of the commentary on Dn 8:6.
v. the commentary on Dn 8:7 and the translation of Dn 8:8–12.

C. The folio is well preserved with the exception of some stains of moisture that do not forbid the reading.

1 2

D. Only the first word, or the first two words, without vocalization, of the masoretic text of Daniel is written, followed by the Judeo-Arabic translation.

32. TS.Ar.28.155. (Cambridge University Library)

A. Two pages of thirty-two lines preserved without significant damages. They bring us R. Saadia's partial translation and commentary on Dn 7.

B. *1st page:* The commentary on Dn 7:7 and the translation of Dn 7:8.
2nd page: The commentary on Dn 7:8; the translation and the beginning of the commentary on Dn 7:9–10.

C. The two pages are damaged by stains of moisture that erase some letters without making the making the manuscript unreadable.

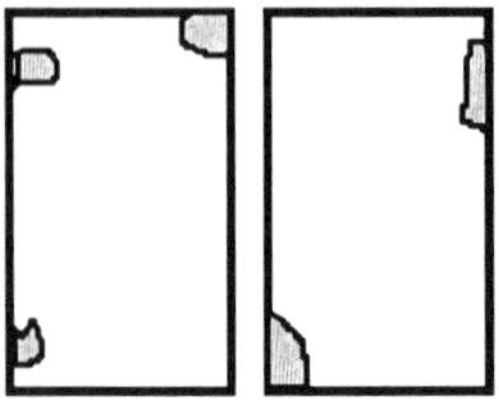

1 2

D. Only the first word, or the first two words, without vocalization, of the masoretic text of Daniel is written, followed by the Judeo-Arabic translation.

33. TS.Ar.28.165. (Cambridge University Library)

A. Two big folios of regular and elegant handwriting that bring us two distinctive sections of R. Saadia's commentary on the book of Daniel. The first, deals with the commentary of Dn 2; the second deals with Dn 7.

B. *1st folio:* r. the commentary on Dn 2:33,39–34.
v. the commentary on Dn 2:34–35,44.
2nd folio: r. the end of the commentary on Dn 7:2; the translation and the commentary on Dn 7:3; the translation of Dn 7:4.
v. the end of the commentary on Dn 7:4 with the translation and the commentary on Dn 7:5.

C. Both folios are heavily damaged by many cuts.

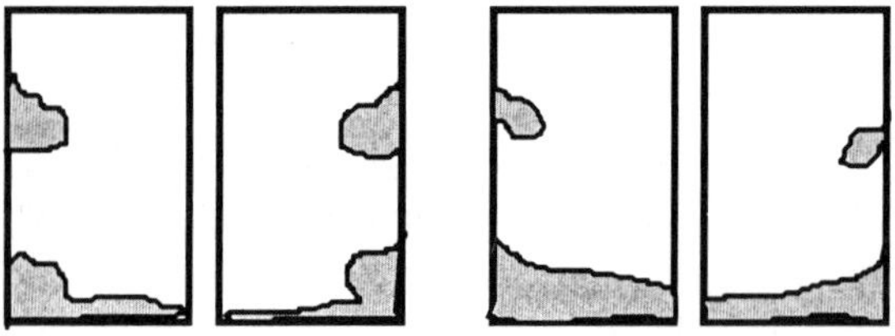

1 2

D. Only the first word, or the first two words, without vocalization, of the masoretic text of Daniel is written, followed by the Judeo-Arabic translation.

34. TS.Ar.51.3. (Cambridge University Library)

A. Two pages that are part of the same manuscript as TS.Ar.28.1 The four folios of TS.Ar.28.102 and Oxf.2659. They bring us R. Saadia's translation and commentary on Dn 7.

B. *1st page:* The translation and the commentary on Dn 7:15–16.
2nd page: The end of the commentary on Dn 7:16 with the translation and the beginning of the commentary on Dn 7:17–18.

C. The two pages are well preserved in spite of a small cut and stains of moisture in the upper angles.

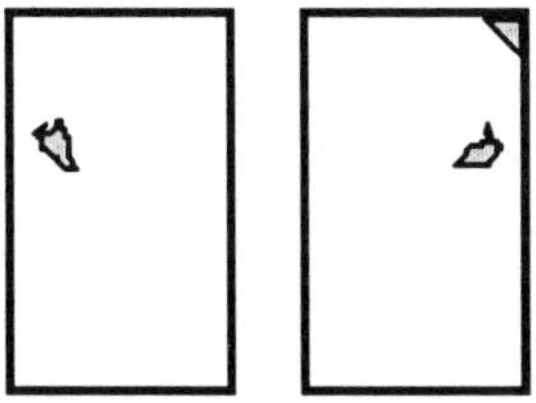

1 2

D. Only the first word, or the first two words, without vocalization, of the masoretic text of Daniel is written, followed by the Judeo-Arabic translation.

35. TS.Misc.5. (Cambridge University Library)

A. This Cambridge manuscript is first published by Yeirin. It is part of a single manuscript dispersed in five different Libraries in Europe and the United States. This is the third of four parts in the possession of Cambridge University Library, three of which are published by Yeirin's edition.

B. *One folio:* (3rd folio in Yeirin's facsimile edition. Pp. 209–210)
r. text, translation and the commentary on Dn 2:11–13.
v. the end of the commentary on Dn 2:13 plus text and translation of Dn 2:14–20 with the beginning of the text of Dn 2:21.

C. The folio is uncut. It contains, however, many stains of moisture that do not prohibit clear reading of the text.

D. Here are the differences with masoretic text and its Tiberien vocalization.

Dn 2:11	ומילתא	MT	וּמִלְּתָא
	שׁאיל		שָׁאֵל
	יקירא		יַקִּירָה
	להין		לָהֵן
	אילהין		אֱלָהִין
Dn 2:12	דנא		דְּנָה
	להובדא		לְהוֹבָדָה
Dn 2:14	עיטא		עֵטָא
	וטעים		וּטְעֵם
Dn 2:15	ענה דניאל ואמר		עָנֵה וְאָמַר
	שׁליטא		שַׁלִּיטָה
	מהחצפא		מְהַחְצְפָה
Dn 2:16	ינתין ליה		יִנְתֶּן לֵהּ
Dn 2:17	לביתיה		לְבַיְתֵהּ
	חברוהי הודע		חַבְרוֹהִי מִלְּתָא הוֹדַע
Dn 2:18	למבעי		לְמִבְעֵא
	דנא		דְּנָה
Dn 2:20	אילהא		אֱלָהָא
	ליה		לֵהּ

36. TS.NS.105. (Cambridge University Library)

A. Two pages (fifteen and sixteen lines) of R. Saadia's translation alone. They deal with the end of Dn 6 and the beginning of Dn 7. Without being elegant the handwriting is clear and regular.

B. *1st page:* The end of the masoretic text of Dn 6:25 until the beginning of the translation of Dn 6:27.
2nd page: The end of the translation of Dn 6:27 until the beginning of the translation of Dn 7:2.

C. The two pages are marked by big stains that darken their lower parts without making it unreadable.

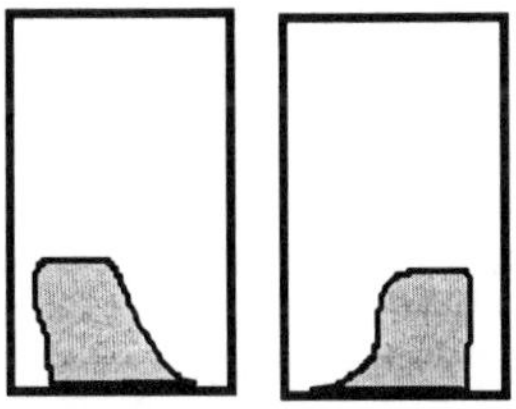

1 2

D. This is a manuscript that has the masoretic text, with small differences, followed by the Judeo-Arabic translation. The masoretic text is partially vocalized: Not all the letters in one word, nor all the words in one verse. These are the differences between the masoretic text of Daniel and its transcription by the TS.NS.105.23:

Dn 6:26	דירין	MT	דָאְרִין
Dn 6:29	פרסאה		פרְסָיאְ

37. TS.NS.285.21. (Cambridge University Library)

A. Tow big folios, very damaged, in a small, regular handwriting. The cuts in all the directions make it hard to know precisely the real size, or the number of lines, of each folio.

B. *1st folio:* r. the end of the commentary on Dn 1 with the translation and the commentary of Dn 2:1–13 followed by the translation of Dn 2:14–24.
v. the translation and the commentary of Dn 2:25–28 and the translation of Dn 2:29–30.
2nd folio: r. the translation and the commentary of Dn 3:24–30.
v. the continuation of the commentary on Dn 3:24–30.

C. The folios are heavily damaged in their ends.

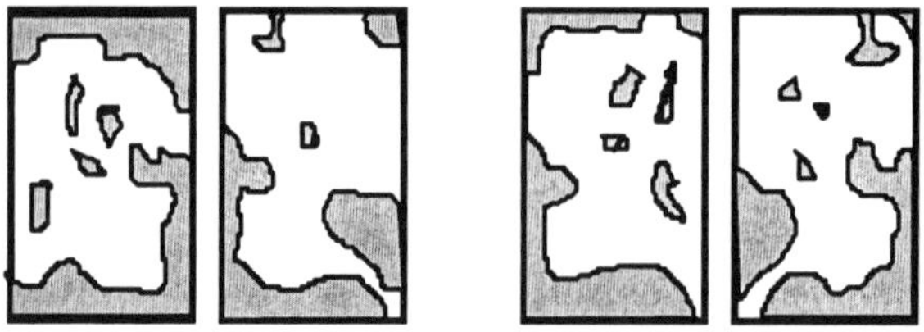

1.c a 2.b d.

D. Only the first word, or the first two words, without vocalization, of the masoretic text of Daniel is written, followed by the Judeo-Arabic translation.

38. TS.NS. 318.6. (Cambridge University Library)

A. Two pages of twenty-two lines, with elegant handwriting, unreadable, yet, because many letters and words are erased in the middle of each page. The two pages deal with the end of R. Saadia's commentary on Dn 1 and the beginning of Dn 2.

B. *1st page:* The commentary on Dn 1:18–21.
2nd page: The end of the commentary on Dn 1:21 and the translation with the commentary on Dn 2:1–2.

C. The two pages are damaged in their middle and their lower part. The damage was not inflicted by cuts, but by the poor ink quality that comes off the paper, once it is dry.

1 2

D. The text of Dn 2:1–2 is written with the Babylonian vocalization. Many of the vowels are illegible because of the physical condition of the manuscript. Here are the only two words that differ from the masoretic text:

Dn 2:2	לקרוא לחרטומים	MT	לִקְרֹא לַחַרְטֻמִּים

39. Yeirin

A. Here is a list of the words, written differently from the masoretic text of Daniel. They are taken from the manuscripts utilized in this edition and are listed according to the division in chapters of the book of Daniel.

Dn 1:1	נבוכדנצר	MT	נְבוּכַדְנֶצַּאר
Dn 2:11	ומילתא		וּמִלְּתָא
	שׁאיל		שָׁאֵל
	יקירא		יַקִּירָה
	להין		לָהֵן
	אילהין		אֱלָהִין
Dn 2:12	דנא		דְּנָה
	להובדא		לְהוֹבָדָה
Dn 2:14	עיטא		עֵטָה
	וטעים		וּטְעֵם
Dn 2:15	ענה דניאל ואמר		עָנֵה וְאָמַר
	מהחצפא		מְהַחְצְפָה
Dn 2:16	ינתין ליה		יִנְתֵּן לֵה
Dn 2:17	לביתיה		לְבַיְתֵהּ
	חברוהי הודע		חַבְרוֹהִי מִלְּתָא הוֹדַע
Dn 2:18	למבעי		לְמִבְעֵא
	דנא		דְּנָה
Dn 2:20	אילהא		אֱלָהָהּ
	ליה		לֵהּ
Dn 5:4	אשתיאו		אִשְׁתִּיו
Dn 5:5	נפקא		נְפַקוּ
	איניש		אֱנָשׁ
	לקביל		לָקֳבֵל
	גרא		גִּירָא
	כותל		כְּתַל
	חזי		חָזֵה
Dn 5:6	ורעיניהי		וְרַעְיֹנֹהִי

	יבהלניה	יְבַהֲלוּנֵּהּ
	[חר]ציה	חַרְצֵהּ
	וארכבתיה	וְאַרְכֻבָּתֵהּ
Dn 5:7	בחייל	בְּחַיִל
	כסדאי	כַּשְׂדָּיֵא
	עני	עָנֵה
	יהמניכא	וְהַמְונְכָא
	צוריה	צַוְּארֵהּ
Dn 5:8	למקרי	לְמִקְרֵא
Dn 5:9	סגיא	שַׂגִּיא
	מתבהיל	מִתְבָּהַל
Dn 5:10	לקביל	לָקֳבֵל
	[י]שתני	יִשְׁתַּנּוֹ
Dn 5:11	ביה	בֵּהּ
	כסד[אין]	כַּשְׂדָּאִין
Dn 5:12	וסכלתנ[ו]	וְשָׂכְלְתָנוּ
	ומשרי	וּמְשָׁרֵא
	ביה	בֵּהּ
	שמיה	שְׁמֵהּ
	ופשריה יהחויה	וּפִשְׁרָה יְהַחֲוֵה
Dn 5:13	הייתי	הַיְתִי
Dn 5:14	שמעיתעלך	וְשִׁמְעֵת עֲלָיךְ
	וסכלתנו	וְשָׂכְלְתָנוּ
Dn 5:15	הועלו	הֻעַלּוּ
	כתבא	כְּתָבָה
	ופשריה	וּפִשְׁרֵהּ
Dn 5:16	ואנא	וַאֲנָה
	שמעיתעלך	שִׁמְעֵת עֲלָיךְ
	תכל	תוּכֻל
	למשרי	לְמִשְׁרֵא
	תכל	תוּכֻל
	למקרי ופשרא	לְמִקְרֵא וּפִשְׁרֵהּ
	והמניכא	וְהַמְונְכָא
	צורך ותולתא	צַוְּארָךְ וְתַלְתָּא
Dn 5:17	אהודעיניה	אֲהוֹדְעִנֵּה
Dn 5:18	עילאה	עִלָּיָא
Dn 5:19	ליה	לֵהּ
	לישניא	וְלִשָּׁנַיָּא

	זיען	זָאְעִין
	קטיל	קָטֵל
	צבי	צָבֵא
	צבי	צָבֵא
Dn 5:20	לבביה ורוחיה תיקפת	לִבְבֵהּ וְרוּחֵהּ תִּקְפַת
	כרסי מלכות[יא] ויקרא	כָּרְסֵא מַלְכוּתֵהּ וִיקָרָה
	מניה	מִנֵּהּ
Dn 5:21	אינשא	אֲנָשָׁא
	לבביה	וְלִבְבֵהּ
	מדוריה	מְדוֹרֵהּ
	טעמוניה	יְטַעֲמוּנֵּהּ
	גשמיה	גִּשְׁמֵהּ
	אלהא >	אֱלָהָא
	אינשא	אֲנָשָׁא
Dn 5:22	השפילת	הַשְׁפֵּלְתְּ
Dn 5:23	מרי	מָרֵא
Dn 7:15	אתכריאת	אֶתְכְּרִיַּת
	אנא	אֲנָה
	יבהלונני	יְבַהֲלֻנַּנִי
Dn 7:19	ומדקה	מַדֱּקָה
Dn 7:20	בראשיה	בְּרֵאשַׁהּ
	קדמיהי	קֳדָמַיהּ
	פום ממליל	וּפֻם מְמַלִּל
Dn 7:21	דכין	דִּכֵּן
Dn 7:22	אתא	אֲתָה
Dn 7:28	כא	כָּה
	אנא	אֲנָה
	סגי	שַׂגִּיא
	נטית	נִטְרֵת
Dn 8:1	בלשצר	בֵּלְאשַׁצַּר
Dn 8:3	האובל	הָאֻבָל
	באחרונה	בָּאַחֲרֹנָה
Dn 8:6	האובל	הָאֻבָל
Dn 8:13	שומם	שֹׁמֵם
Dn 8:16	בן	בֵּין
	הבין	הָבֵן
Dn 8:17	ובבואו	וּבְבֹאוֹ
	הבין	הָבֵן

Dn 8:18	ויעמדני		וַיַּעֲמִידֵנִי
Dn 8:23	הפושעים		הַפֹּשְׁעִים
Dn 9:18	וראה את שממותינו		וּרְאֵה שֹׁמְמֹתֵינוּ
Dn 9:19	כי שמך על עירך		כִּי שִׁמְךָ נִקְרָא עַל עִירְךָ

B. Manuscripts not utilized in this edition

1. Collection of Juda Levy Nahum

Dn 7:13	אינש	MT	אֱנָשׁ
	אתי [הוא]		אָתֵה הֲוָא
	מטא		מְטָה
Dn 7:14	וליה		וְלֵהּ
	שולטן		שָׁלְטָן
	אומיא		אֻמַיָּא
	ליה		לֵה
	שולטניה		שָׁלְטָנֵה
	יעידי		יֶעְדֵּה
	ומלכותיה		וּמַלְכוּתֵה
Dn 7:15	אתכריאת		אֶתְכְּרִיַּת
	אנא		אֲנָה
	נדנא		נִדְנֶה
	רישי		רֵאשִׁי
Dn 7:16	קמיא		קָאֲמַיָּא
	אבעי מיניה		אֶבְעֵא מִנֵּהּ
	יהודעינני		יְהוֹדְעִנַּנִי
Dn 7:26	יתיב		יִתִּב
	שולטניה		וְשָׁלְטָנֵהּ
	להשמדא		לְהַשְׁמָדָא
	ולהובדא		וּלְהוֹבָדָה
Dn 7:27	ושולטנא		וְשָׁלְטָנָא
	מלכותיה		מַלְכוּתֵהּ
	שילטוניא ליה		שָׁלְטָנַיָּא לה
Dn 7:28	עד־כא		עַד־כָּה
	אנא		אֲנָה
	נטרית		נִטְרֵת
Dn 8:1	בלשצר		בֵּלְאשַׁצַּר
Dn 8:2	בראותי		בִּרְאֹתִי
Dn 8:3	האובל		הָאֻבָל
	ולא		וְלוֹ

	גבוהות		גְבֹהוֹת
	והגבוהה עולה		וְהַגְּבֹהָה עֹלָה
Dn 8:4	וצפנה		וְצָפוֹנָה

2. Alliance israélite universelle

Dn 3:32	אילהא	MT	אֱלָהָא
	עלאה		עִלָּיאָ
	להחואה		לְהַחֲוָיָה
Dn 3:33	מלכותיה		מַלְכוּתֵהּ
	ושולטניה		וְשָׁלְטָנֵהּ
Dn 4:1	אנא		אֲנָה
Dn 4:2	חלים		חֵלֶם
Dn 4:3	טעים		טְעֵם
	להנעלא		לְהַנְעָלָה
Dn 10:3	חמודות		חֲמֻדוֹת
Dn 11:8	יעמוד		יַעֲמֹד
Dn 11:10	יתגרה		יִתְגָּרוּ
	מעוזו		מָעֻזֹּה

3. Cambridge MS T.S.K 24,26.

Dn 5:14	עלך	MT	עֲלָיךְ
	אילהין		אֱלָהִין
	ושוכלתנו		וְשָׂכְלְתָנוּ
	יתירא		יַתִּירָה
Dn 6:3	מינהון		מִנְּהוֹן
Dn 6:4	קביל		קֳבֵל
	ביה		בֵּהּ
	להקמותיה		לַהֲקָמוּתֵהּ
Dn 6:5	להשכחא		לְהַשְׁכָּחָה
	קביל		קֳבֵל
	שׁלה		שָׁלוּ

4. The collection of Jacques Mosseri and his family

Dn 2:36	ופשריה נימר	MT	וּפִשְׁרֵהּ נֵאמַר
Dn 2:37	אילה		אֱלָהּ
	חוסנא ותוקפא		חִסְנָא וְתָקְפָּא
Dn 2:38	דירין		דָאְרִין
	אינשא		אֲנָשָׁא
Dn 2:43	אינשׂא		אֲנָשָׁא

	דנא		דִּנָה
Dn 2:44	אילהא		אֱלָהּ
	אוהרן		אָחֳרָן
	תשׁתביק תדיק		תִשְׁתְּבִק תַּדִּק
	אילין		אִלֵּין

5. The Bodleian Library, MS Heb. d. 28. Fol. 25b.

Dn 4:12	שׁורשׁוהי	MT	שָׁרְשׁוֹהִי
	שׁבוקו		שְׁבֻקוּ
	ובאיסור		וּבֶאֱסוּר
	בדתאה		בְּדִתְאָא
	חלקיה		חֲלָקֵהּ
Dn 4:13	לביה		לִבְבֵהּ
	אינשׂא		אֲנָשָׂא
	ליה		לֵהּ
Dn 4:14	שׁאילתא		שְׁאֵלְתָא
	עילאה		עִלָּיָא
	אינשׂא		אֲנָשָׂא
	יצבי יתנינה		יִצְבֵּא יִתְּנִנַּהּ
	עלה		עֲלַיַהּ
Dn 4:15	אנא		אֲנָה
	ואנתא		וְאַנְתְּה
	אימר		אֱמַר
Dn 5:12	ופשׂרא יהחוא		וּפִשְׁרָה יְהַחֲוֵה

6. Cambridge University. MS T.-S. Ar.1b1.

Dn 3:12	עלךְ	MT	עֲלָיךְ
	לאלהךְ		לֵאלָהָיךְ
	ולצלים		וּלְצֶלֶים
	הקימתא		הֲקֵימְתָּ
Dn 3:13	לחיתיא		לְחַיְתָיָה
Dn 3:14	לאילהי		לֵאלָהַי
	ולצלים		וּלְצֶלֶים
Dn 3:15	בעידנא		בְּעִדָּנָא
	סבכא		שַׂבְּכָא
	תיפלון		תִּפְּלוּן
	עבדית		עַבְדֵת
Dn 3:20	בחיליה		בְּחַילֵהּ

Dn 3:21	פשטיהון	פַּטְּישֵׁיהוֹן
	לבושיהון	וּלבֻשֵׁיהוֹן
	לגו	לְגוֹי
	יקידתא	יָקִדְתָּא
Dn 3:22	קביל	קֳבֵל
	מחצפא	מַחְצְפָה
	אילך	אִלֵךְ
	קטול	קַטִּל
Dn 3:23	תלתיהון	תְּלָתֵהוֹן
Dn 3:24	תלתה	תְּלָתָא

Synopsis of Manuscripts for R. Saadia's Commentary on the Book of Daniel

MSS or editions marked by * contain R. Saadia's translation alone, without his commentary on the Book of Daniel

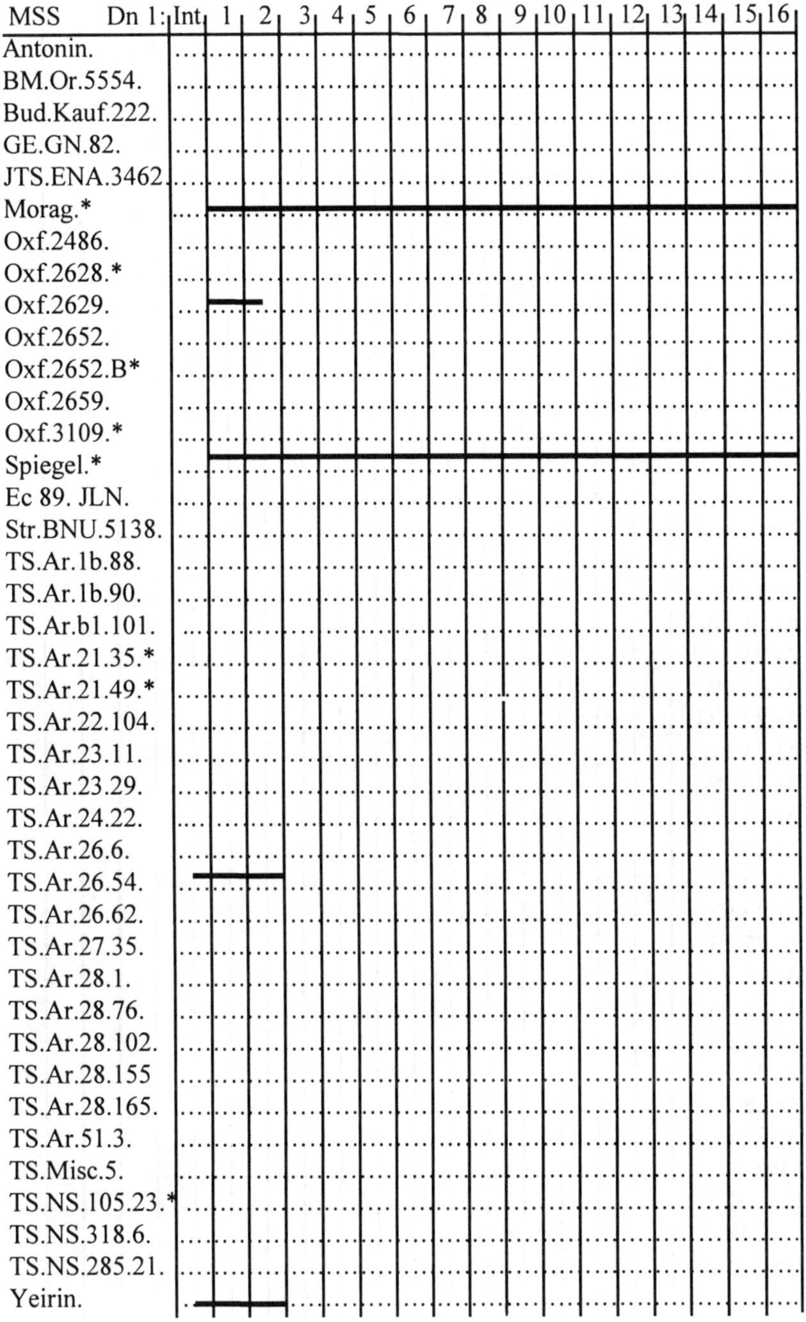
MSS
Dn 1:
Int
1
2
3
4
5
6
7
8
9
10
11
12
13
14
15
16
Antonin.
BM.Or.5554.
Bud.Kauf.222.
GE.GN.82.
JTS.ENA.3462
Morag.*
Oxf.2486.
Oxf.2628.*
Oxf.2629.
Oxf.2652.
Oxf.2652.B*
Oxf.2659.
Oxf.3109.*
Spiegel.*
Ec 89. JLN.
Str.BNU.5138.
TS.Ar.1b.88.
TS.Ar.1b.90.
TS.Ar.b1.101.
TS.Ar.21.35.*
TS.Ar.21.49.*
TS.Ar.22.104.
TS.Ar.23.11.
TS.Ar.23.29.
TS.Ar.24.22.
TS.Ar.26.6.
TS.Ar.26.54.
TS.Ar.26.62.
TS.Ar.27.35.
TS.Ar.28.1.
TS.Ar.28.76.
TS.Ar.28.102.
TS.Ar.28.155
TS.Ar.28.165.
TS.Ar.51.3.
TS.Misc.5.
TS.NS.105.23.*
TS.NS.318.6.
TS.NS.285.21.
Yeirin.

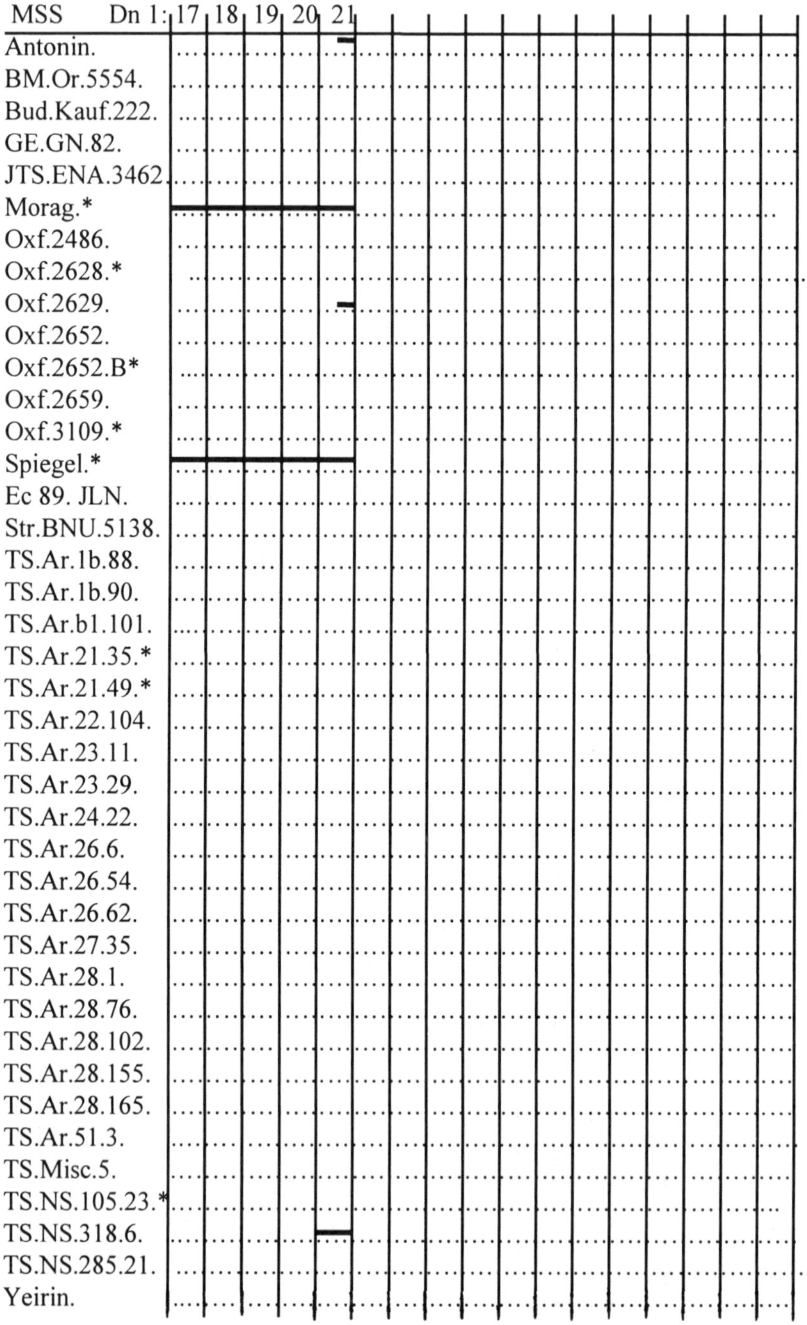
MSS
Dn 1:
17
18
19
20
21
Antonin.
BM.Or.5554.
Bud.Kauf.222.
GE.GN.82.
JTS.ENA.3462
Morag.*
Oxf.2486.
Oxf.2628.*
Oxf.2629.
Oxf.2652.
Oxf.2652.B*
Oxf.2659.
Oxf.3109.*
Spiegel.*
Ec 89. JLN.
Str.BNU.5138.
TS.Ar.1b.88.
TS.Ar.1b.90.
TS.Ar.b1.101.
TS.Ar.21.35.*
TS.Ar.21.49.*
TS.Ar.22.104.
TS.Ar.23.11.
TS.Ar.23.29.
TS.Ar.24.22.
TS.Ar.26.6.
TS.Ar.26.54.
TS.Ar.26.62.
TS.Ar.27.35.
TS.Ar.28.1.
TS.Ar.28.76.
TS.Ar.28.102.
TS.Ar.28.155.
TS.Ar.28.165.
TS.Ar.51.3.
TS.Misc.5.
TS.NS.105.23.*
TS.NS.318.6.
TS.NS.285.21.
Yeirin.

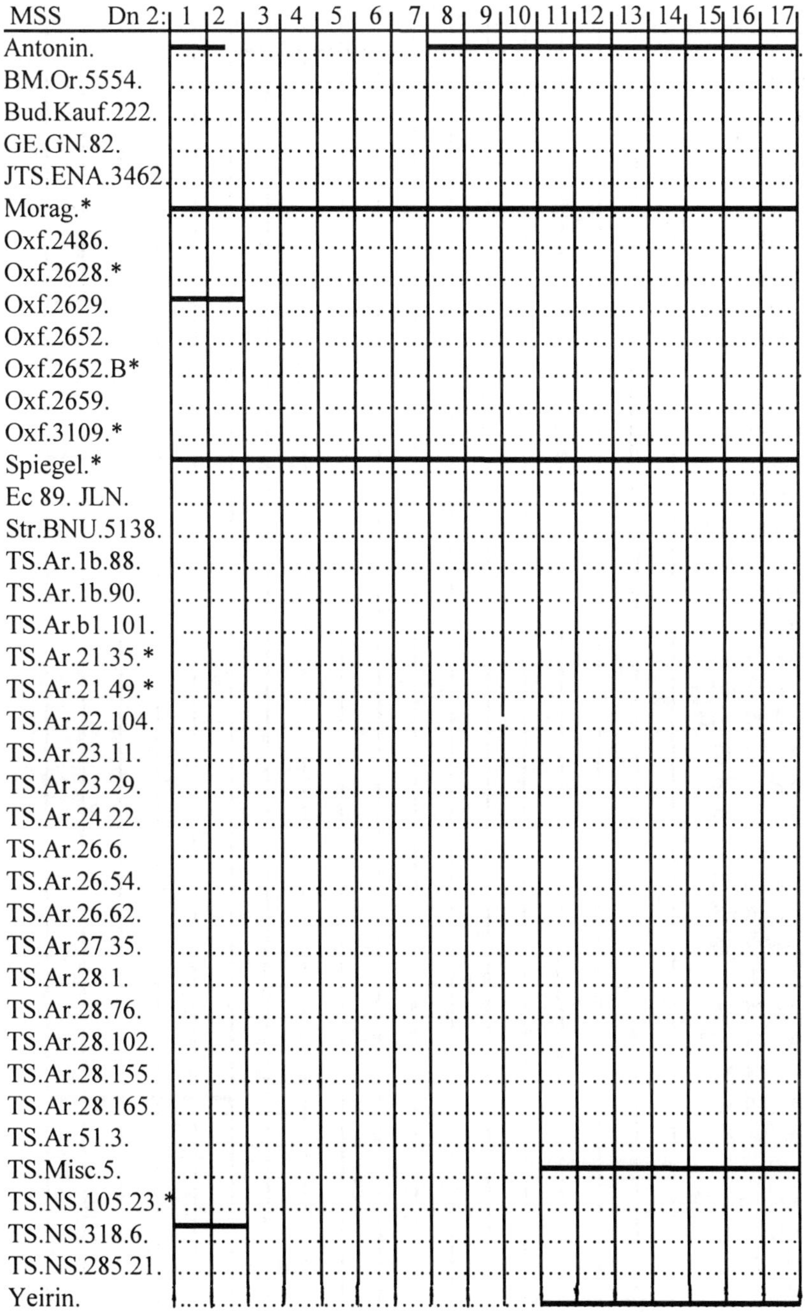
MSS Dn 2: 1 2 3 4 5 6 7 8 9 10 11 12 13 14 15 16 17
Antonin.
BM.Or.5554.
Bud.Kauf.222.
GE.GN.82.
JTS.ENA.3462
Morag.*
Oxf.2486.
Oxf.2628.*
Oxf.2629.
Oxf.2652.
Oxf.2652.B*
Oxf.2659.
Oxf.3109.*
Spiegel.*
Ec 89. JLN.
Str.BNU.5138.
TS.Ar.1b.88.
TS.Ar.1b.90.
TS.Ar.b1.101.
TS.Ar.21.35.*
TS.Ar.21.49.*
TS.Ar.22.104.
TS.Ar.23.11.
TS.Ar.23.29.
TS.Ar.24.22.
TS.Ar.26.6.
TS.Ar.26.54.
TS.Ar.26.62.
TS.Ar.27.35.
TS.Ar.28.1.
TS.Ar.28.76.
TS.Ar.28.102.
TS.Ar.28.155.
TS.Ar.28.165.
TS.Ar.51.3.
TS.Misc.5.
TS.NS.105.23.*
TS.NS.318.6.
TS.NS.285.21.
Yeirin.

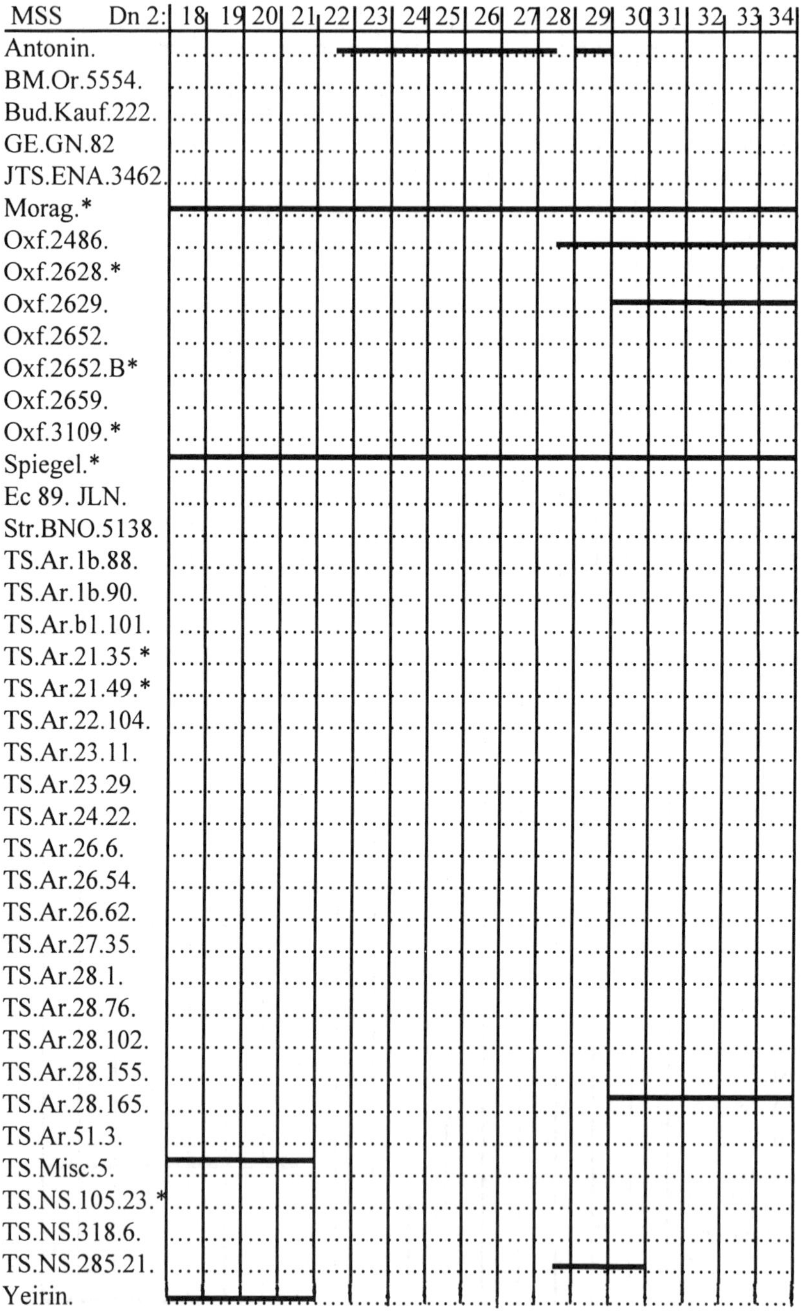
MSS
Dn 2:
18
19
20
21
22
23
24
25
26
27
28
29
30
31
32
33
34
Antonin.
BM.Or.5554.
Bud.Kauf.222.
GE.GN.82
JTS.ENA.3462.
Morag.*
Oxf.2486.
Oxf.2628.*
Oxf.2629.
Oxf.2652.
Oxf.2652.B*
Oxf.2659.
Oxf.3109.*
Spiegel.*
Ec 89. JLN.
Str.BNO.5138.
TS.Ar.1b.88.
TS.Ar.1b.90.
TS.Ar.b1.101.
TS.Ar.21.35.*
TS.Ar.21.49.*
TS.Ar.22.104.
TS.Ar.23.11.
TS.Ar.23.29.
TS.Ar.24.22.
TS.Ar.26.6.
TS.Ar.26.54.
TS.Ar.26.62.
TS.Ar.27.35.
TS.Ar.28.1.
TS.Ar.28.76.
TS.Ar.28.102.
TS.Ar.28.155.
TS.Ar.28.165.
TS.Ar.51.3.
TS.Misc.5.
TS.NS.105.23.*
TS.NS.318.6.
TS.NS.285.21.
Yeirin.

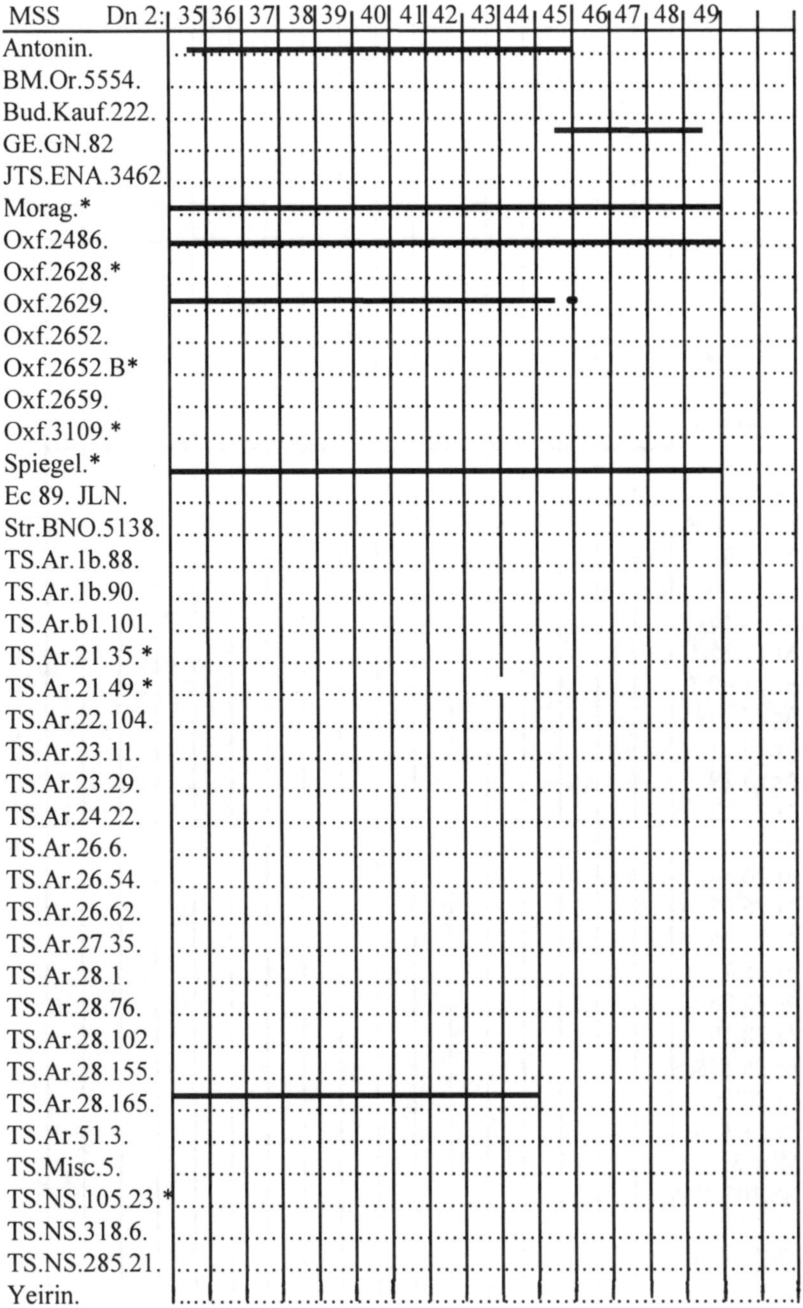
MSS
Dn 2:
35 36 37 38 39 40 41 42 43 44 45 46 47 48 49
Antonin.
BM.Or.5554.
Bud.Kauf.222.
GE.GN.82
JTS.ENA.3462.
Morag.*
Oxf.2486.
Oxf.2628.*
Oxf.2629.
Oxf.2652.
Oxf.2652.B*
Oxf.2659.
Oxf.3109.*
Spiegel.*
Ec 89. JLN.
Str.BNO.5138.
TS.Ar.1b.88.
TS.Ar.1b.90.
TS.Ar.b1.101.
TS.Ar.21.35.*
TS.Ar.21.49.*
TS.Ar.22.104.
TS.Ar.23.11.
TS.Ar.23.29.
TS.Ar.24.22.
TS.Ar.26.6.
TS.Ar.26.54.
TS.Ar.26.62.
TS.Ar.27.35.
TS.Ar.28.1.
TS.Ar.28.76.
TS.Ar.28.102.
TS.Ar.28.155.
TS.Ar.28.165.
TS.Ar.51.3.
TS.Misc.5.
TS.NS.105.23.*
TS.NS.318.6.
TS.NS.285.21.
Yeirin.

MSS Dn 3:	1	2	3	4	5	6	7	8	9	10	11	12	13	14	15	16	17
Antonin.	…	…	…	…	…	…	…	…	…	…	…	…	…	…	…	…	…
BM.Or.5554.	…	…	…	…	…	…	…	…	…	…	…	…	…	…	…	…	…
Bud.Kauf.222.	…	…	…	…	…	…	…	…	…	…	…	…	…	…	…	…	…
GE.GN.82	…	…	…	…	…	…	…	…	…	…	…	…	…	…	…	…	…
JTS.ENA.3462.	…	…	…	…	…	…	…	…	…	…	…	…	…	…	…	…	…
Morag.*	…	…	…	…	…	…	…	…	…	…	…	…	…	…	…	…	…
Oxf.2486.	…	…	…	…	…	…	…	…	…	…	…	…	…	…	…	…	…
Oxf.2628.*	…	…	…	…	…	…	…	…	…	…	…	…	…	…	…	…	…
Oxf.2629.	…	…	…	…	…	…	…	…	…	…	…	…	…	…	…	…	…
Oxf.2652.	…	…	…	…	…	…	…	…	…	…	…	…	…	…	…	…	…
Oxf.2652.B*	…	…	…	…	…	…	…	…	…	…	…	…	…	…	…	…	…
Oxf.2659.	…	…	…	…	…	…	…	…	…	…	…	…	…	…	…	…	…
Oxf.3109.*	…	…	…	…	…	…	…	…	…	…	…	…	…	…	…	…	…
Spiegel.*	…	…	…	…	…	…	…	…	…	…	…	…	…	…	…	…	…
Ec 89. JLN.	…	…	…	…	…	…	…	…	…	…	…	…	…	…	…	…	…
Str.BNO.5138.	…	…	…	…	…	…	…	…	…	…	…	…	…	…	…	…	…
TS.Ar.1b.88.	…	…	…	…	…	…	…	…	…	…	…	…	…	…	…	…	…
TS.Ar.1b.90.	…	…	…	…	…	…	…	…	…	…	…	…	…	…	…	…	…
TS.Ar.b1.101.	…	…	…	…	…	…	…	…	…	…	…	…	…	…	…	…	…
TS.Ar.21.35.*	…	…	…	…	…	…	…	…	…	…	…	…	…	…	…	…	…
TS.Ar.21.49.*	…	…	…	…	…	…	…	…	…	…	…	…	…	…	…	…	…
TS.Ar.22.104.	…	…	…	…	…	…	…	…	…	…	…	…	…	…	…	…	…
TS.Ar.23.11	…	…	…	…	…	…	…	…	…	…	…	…	…	…	…	…	…
TS.Ar.23.29.	…	…	…	…	…	…	…	…	…	…	…	…	…	…	…	…	…
TS.Ar.24.22.	…	…	…	…	…	…	…	…	…	…	…	…	…	…	…	…	…
TS.Ar.26.6.	…	…	…	…	…	…	…	…	…	…	…	…	…	…	…	…	…
TS.Ar.26.54.	…	…	…	…	…	…	…	…	…	…	…	…	…	…	…	…	…
TS.Ar.26.62.	…	…	…	…	…	…	…	…	…	…	…	…	…	…	…	…	…
TS.Ar.27.35.	…	…	…	…	…	…	…	…	…	…	…	…	…	…	…	…	…
TS.Ar.28.1.	…	…	…	…	…	…	…	…	…	…	…	…	…	…	…	…	…
TS.Ar.28.76.	…	…	…	…	…	…	…	…	…	…	…	…	…	…	…	…	…
TS.Ar.28.102.	…	…	…	…	…	…	…	…	…	…	…	…	…	…	…	…	…
TS.Ar.28.155.	…	…	…	…	…	…	…	…	…	…	…	…	…	…	…	…	…
TS.Ar.28.162.	…	…	…	…	…	…	…	…	…	…	…	…	…	…	…	…	…
TS.Ar.51.3.	…	…	…	…	…	…	…	…	…	…	…	…	…	…	…	…	…
TS.Misc.5.	…	…	…	…	…	…	…	…	…	…	…	…	…	…	…	…	…
TS.NS.105.23.*	…	…	…	…	…	…	…	…	…	…	…	…	…	…	…	…	…
TS.NS.318.6.	…	…	…	…	…	…	…	…	…	…	…	…	…	…	…	…	…
TS.NS.285.21.	…	…	…	…	…	…	…	…	…	…	…	…	…	…	…	…	…
Yeirin.	…	…	…	…	…	…	…	…	…	…	…	…	…	…	…	…	…

MSS Dn 3:	18	19	20	21	22	23	24	25	26	27	28	29	30	31	32	33	
Antonin.	…	…	…	…	…	…	…	…	…	…	…	…	…	…	…	…	…
BM.Or.5554.	…	…	…	…	…	…	…	…	…	…	…	…	…	…	…	…	…
Bud.Kauf.222.	…	…	…	…	…	…	…	…	…	…	…	…	…	…	…	…	…
GE.GN.82	—	…	…	…	…	…	…	…	…	…	…	…	…	…	…	…	…
JTS.ENA.3462	…	…	…	…	…	…	…	…	…	…	…	…	…	…	…	…	…
Morag.*	—	—	—	—	—	—	—	—	—	—	—	—	—	—	—	—	…
Oxf.2486.	—	—	—	—	—	—	—	—	—	—	—	—	—	—	—	—	…
Oxf.2628.*	…	…	…	…	…	…	…	…	…	…	…	…	…	…	…	…	…
Oxf.2629.	…	…	…	…	…	…	…	…	…	…	…	…	…	…	…	…	…
Oxf.2652.	…	…	…	…	…	…	…	…	…	…	…	…	…	…	…	…	…
Oxf.2652.B*	…	…	…	…	…	…	…	…	…	…	…	…	…	…	…	…	…
Oxf.2659.	…	…	…	…	…	…	…	…	…	…	…	…	…	…	…	…	…
Oxf.3109.*	…	…	…	…	…	…	…	…	…	…	…	…	…	…	…	…	…
Spiegel.*	—	—	—	—	—	—	—	—	—	—	—	—	—	—	—	—	…
Ec 89. JLN.	…	…	…	…	…	…	…	…	…	…	…	…	…	…	…	…	…
Str.BNO.5138.	…	…	…	…	…	…	…	…	…	…	…	…	…	…	…	…	…
TS.Ar.1b.88.	…	…	…	…	…	…	…	…	…	…	…	…	…	…	…	…	…
TS.Ar.1b.90.	…	…	…	…	…	…	…	…	…	…	…	…	…	…	…	…	…
TS.Ar.b1.101.	…	…	…	…	—	—	—	…	…	…	…	…	…	…	…	…	…
TS.Ar.21.35.*	…	…	…	…	…	…	…	…	…	…	…	…	…	…	…	…	…
TS.Ar.21.49.*	…	…	…	…	—	—	—	—	—	—	—	—	—	…	…	—	…
TS.Ar.22.104.	…	…	…	…	…	…	…	…	…	…	…	…	…	…	…	…	…
TS.Ar.23.11.	…	…	…	…	…	…	…	…	…	…	…	…	…	…	…	…	…
TS.Ar.23.29.	…	…	…	…	…	…	…	…	…	…	…	…	…	…	…	…	…
TS.Ar.24.22.	…	…	…	…	…	…	…	…	…	…	…	…	…	…	…	…	…
TS.Ar.26.6.	…	…	…	…	…	…	…	…	…	…	…	…	…	…	…	…	…
TS.Ar.26.54.	…	…	…	…	…	…	…	…	…	…	…	…	…	…	…	…	…
TS.Ar.26.62.	…	…	…	…	…	…	…	…	…	…	…	…	…	…	…	…	…
TS.Ar.27.35.	…	…	…	…	…	…	…	…	…	…	…	…	…	…	…	…	…
TS.Ar.28.1.	…	…	…	…	…	…	…	…	…	…	…	…	…	…	…	…	…
TS.Ar.28.76.	…	…	…	…	…	…	…	…	…	…	…	…	…	…	…	…	…
TS.Ar.28.102.	…	…	…	…	…	…	…	…	…	…	…	…	…	…	…	…	…
TS.Ar.28.155.	…	…	…	…	…	…	…	…	…	…	…	…	…	…	…	…	…
TS.Ar.28.165.	…	…	…	…	…	…	…	…	…	…	…	…	…	…	…	…	…
TS.Ar.51.3.	…	…	…	…	…	…	…	…	…	…	…	…	…	…	…	…	…
TS.Misc.5.	…	…	…	…	…	…	…	…	…	…	…	…	…	…	…	…	…
TS.NS.105.23.*	…	…	…	…	…	…	…	…	…	…	…	…	…	…	…	…	…
TS.NS.318.6.	…	…	…	…	…	…	…	…	…	…	…	…	…	…	…	…	…
TS.NS.285.21.	…	…	…	…	…	…	—	—	—	—	—	—	—	…	…	…	…
Yeirin.	…	…	…	…	…	…	…	…	…	…	…	…	…	…	…	…	…

MSS Dn 4:	1	2	3	4	5	6	7	8	9	10	11	12	13	14	15	16	17
Antonin.	...	...	...	...	...	...	...	...	...	...	...	...	...	...	...	...	...
BM.Or.5554.	...	...	...	...	...	...	...	...	...	...	...	...	...	...	...	...	...
Bud.Kauf.222.	...	...	...	...	...	...	...	...	...	...	...	...	...	...	...	...	...
GE.GN.82	...	...	...	...	...	...	...	...	...	...	...	...	...	...	...	...	...
JTS.ENA.3462.	...	...	...	...	...	...	...	...	...	...	...	...	...	...	...	...	...
Morag.*	...	...	...	...	...	...	...	...	...	...	...	...	...	...	...	...	...
Oxf.2486.	...	...	...	...	...	...	...	...	...	...	...	...	...	...	...	...	...
Oxf.2628.*	...	...	...	...	...	...	...	...	...	...	...	...	...	...	...	...	...
Oxf.2629.	...	...	...	...	...	...	...	...	...	...	...	...	...	...	...	...	...
Oxf.2652.	...	...	...	...	...	...	...	...	...	...	...	...	...	...	...	...	...
Oxf.2652.B*	...	...	...	...	...	...	...	...	...	...	...	...	...	...	...	...	...
Oxf.2659.	...	...	...	...	...	...	...	...	...	...	...	...	...	...	...	...	...
Oxf.3109.*	...	...	...	...	...	...	...	...	...	...	...	...	...	...	...	...	...
Spiegel.*	...	...	...	...	...	...	...	...	...	...	...	...	...	...	...	...	...
Ec 89. JLN.	...	...	...	...	...	...	...	...	...	...	...	...	...	...	...	...	...
Str.BNO.5138.	...	...	...	...	...	...	...	...	...	...	...	...	...	...	...	...	...
TS.Ar.1b.88.	...	...	...	...	...	...	...	...	...	...	...	...	...	...	...	...	...
TS.Ar.1b.90.	...	...	...	...	...	...	...	...	...	...	...	...	...	...	...	...	...
TS.Ar.b1.101.	...	...	...	...	...	...	...	...	...	...	...	...	...	...	...	...	...
TS.Ar.21.35.*	...	...	...	...	...	...	...	...	...	...	...	...	...	...	...	...	...
TS.Ar.21.49.*	...	...	...	...	...	...	...	...	...	...	...	...	...	...	...	...	...
TS.Ar.22.104.	...	...	...	...	...	...	...	...	...	...	...	...	...	...	...	...	...
TS.Ar.23.11.	...	...	...	...	...	...	...	...	...	...	...	...	...	...	...	...	...
TS.Ar.23.29.	...	...	...	...	...	...	...	...	...	...	...	...	...	...	...	...	...
TS.Ar.24.22.	...	...	...	...	...	...	...	...	...	...	...	...	...	...	...	...	...
TS.Ar.26.6.	...	...	...	...	...	...	...	...	...	...	...	...	...	...	...	...	...
TS.Ar.26.54.	...	...	...	...	...	...	...	...	...	...	...	...	...	...	...	...	...
TS.Ar.26.62.	...	...	...	...	...	...	...	...	...	...	...	...	...	...	...	...	...
TS.Ar.27.35.	...	...	...	...	...	...	...	...	...	...	...	...	...	...	...	...	...
TS.Ar.28.1.	...	...	...	...	...	...	...	...	...	...	...	...	...	...	...	...	...
TS.Ar.28.76.	...	...	...	...	...	...	...	...	...	...	...	...	...	...	...	...	...
TS.Ar.28.102.	...	...	...	...	...	...	...	...	...	...	...	...	...	...	...	...	...
TS.Ar.28.155.	...	...	...	...	...	...	...	...	...	...	...	...	...	...	...	...	...
TS.Ar.28.165.	...	...	...	...	...	...	...	...	...	...	...	...	...	...	...	...	...
TS.Ar.51.3.	...	...	...	...	...	...	...	...	...	...	...	...	...	...	...	...	...
TS.Misc.5.	...	...	...	...	...	...	...	...	...	...	...	...	...	...	...	...	...
TS.NS.105.23.*	...	...	...	...	...	...	...	...	...	...	...	...	...	...	...	...	...
TS.NS.318.6.	...	...	...	...	...	...	...	...	...	...	...	...	...	...	...	...	...
TS.NS.285.21.	...	...	...	...	...	...	...	...	...	...	...	...	...	...	...	...	...
Yeirin.	...	...	...	...	...	...	...	...	...	...	...	...	...	...	...	...	...

MSS Dn 4:	18	19	20	21	22	23	24	25	26	27	28	29	30	31	32	33	34
Antonin.	…	…	…	…	…	…	…	…	…	…	…	…	…	…	…	…	…
BM.Or.5554.	…	…	…	…	…	…	…	…	…	…	…	…	…	…	…	…	…
Bud.Kauf.222.	…	…	…	…	…	…	…	…	…	…	…	…	…	…	…	…	…
GE.GN.82.	…	…	…	…	…	…	…	…	…	…	…	…	…	…	…	…	…
JTS.ENA.3462.	…	…	…	…	…	…	…	…	…	…	…	…	…	…	…	…	…
Morag.*	—	—	—	—	—	—	—	—	—	—	—	—	—	—	—	—	—
Oxf.2486.	—	—	—	—	—	—	—	—	—	—	—	—	—	—	—	—	—
Oxf.2628.*	…	…	…	…	…	…	…	…	…	…	…	…	…	…	…	…	…
Oxf.2629.	…	…	…	…	…	…	…	…	…	…	…	…	…	…	…	…	…
Oxf.2652.	…	…	…	…	…	…	…	…	…	…	…	…	…	…	…	…	…
Oxf.2652.B*	…	…	…	…	…	…	…	…	…	…	…	…	…	…	…	…	…
Oxf.2659.	…	…	…	…	…	…	…	…	…	…	…	…	…	…	…	…	…
Oxf.3109.*	…	…	…	…	…	…	…	…	…	…	…	…	…	…	…	…	…
Spiegel.*	—	—	—	—	—	—	—	—	—	—	—	—	—	—	—	—	—
Ec 89. JLN.	…	…	…	…	…	…	…	…	…	…	…	…	…	…	…	…	…
Str.BNU.5138.	…	…	…	…	…	…	…	…	…	…	…	…	…	…	…	…	…
TS.Ar.1b.88.	…	…	…	…	…	…	…	…	…	…	…	…	…	…	…	…	…
TS.Ar.1b.90.	—	—	—	—	—	—	—	—	—	—	—	—	—	—	…	…	…
TS.Ar.b1.101.	…	…	…	…	…	…	…	…	…	…	…	…	…	…	…	…	… -
TS.Ar.21.35.*	…	…	…	…	…	…	…	…	…	…	…	…	…	…	…	…	…
TS.Ar.21.49.*	—	—	—	—	—	—	—	—	—	—	—	—	—	—	—	—	—
TS.Ar.22.104.	…	…	…	…	…	…	…	…	…	…	…	…	…	…	…	…	…
TS.Ar.23.11.	…	…	…	…	…	…	…	…	…	…	…	…	…	…	…	…	…
TS.Ar.23.29.	…	…	…	…	…	…	…	…	…	…	…	…	…	…	…	…	…
TS.Ar.24.22.	…	…	…	…	…	…	…	…	…	…	…	…	…	…	…	…	…
TS.Ar.26.6.	—	—	—	—	—	—	—	—	—	—	—	—	—	—	—	—	—
TS.Ar.26.54.	…	…	…	…	…	…	…	…	…	…	…	…	…	…	…	…	…
TS.Ar.26.62.	…	…	…	…	…	…	…	…	…	…	…	…	…	…	…	…	…
TS.Ar.27.35.	…	…	…	…	…	…	…	…	…	…	…	…	…	…	…	…	…
TS.Ar.28.1.	…	…	…	…	…	…	…	…	…	…	…	…	…	…	…	…	…
TS.Ar.28.76.	…	…	…	…	…	…	…	…	…	…	…	…	…	…	…	…	…
TS.Ar.28.102.	…	…	…	…	…	…	…	…	…	…	…	…	…	…	…	…	…
TS.Ar.28.155.	…	…	…	…	…	…	…	…	…	…	…	…	…	…	…	…	…
TS.Ar.28.165.	…	…	…	…	…	…	…	…	…	…	…	…	…	…	…	…	… -
TS.Ar.51.3.	…	…	…	…	…	…	…	…	…	…	…	…	…	…	…	…	…
TS.Misc.5.	…	…	…	…	…	…	…	…	…	…	…	…	…	…	…	…	…
TS.NS.105.23.*	…	…	…	…	…	…	…	…	…	…	…	…	…	…	…	…	…
TS.NS.318.6.	…	…	…	…	…	…	…	…	…	…	…	…	…	…	…	…	…
TS.NS.285.21.	…	…	…	…	…	…	…	…	…	…	…	…	…	…	…	…	…
Yeirin.	…	…	…	…	…	…	…	…	…	…	…	…	…	…	…	…	…

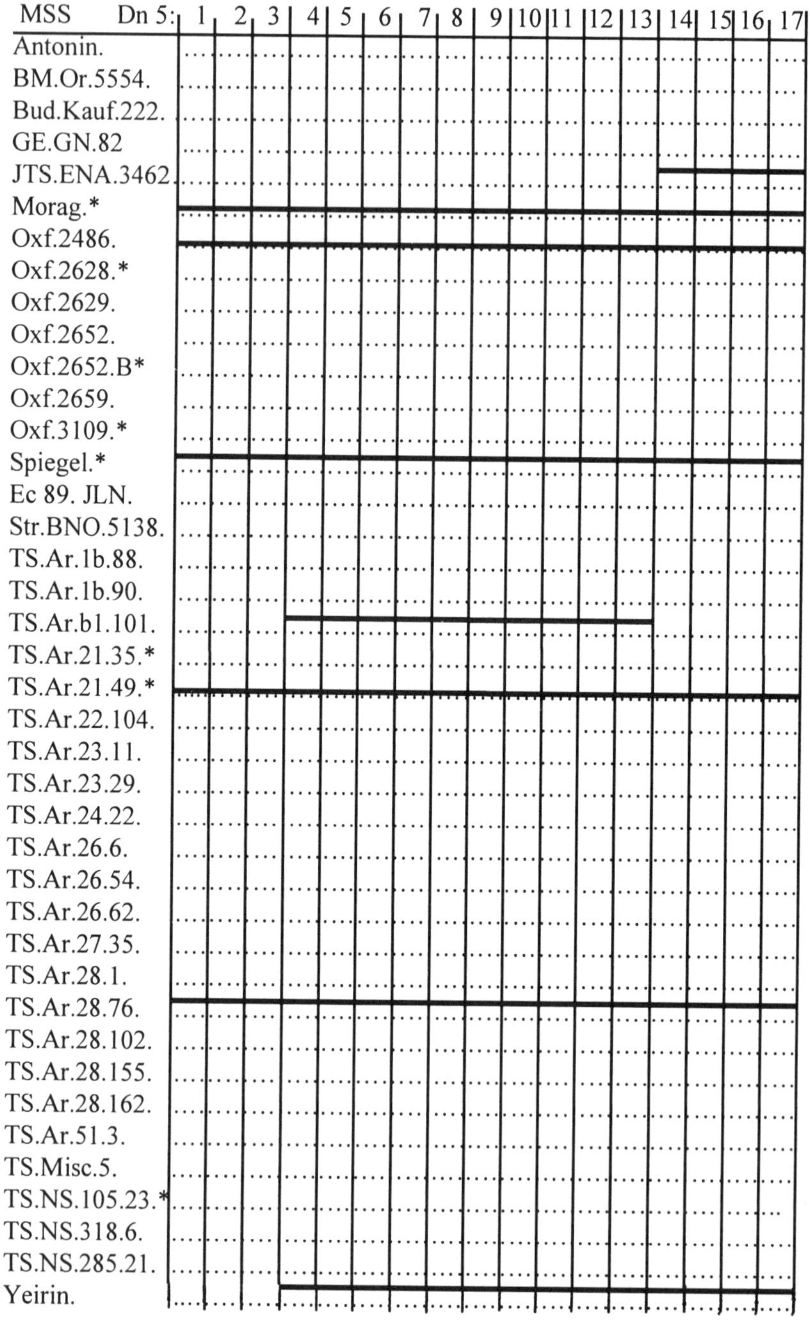
MSS
Dn 5:
1
2
3
4
5
6
7
8
9
10
11
12
13
14
15
16
17
Antonin.
BM.Or.5554.
Bud.Kauf.222.
GE.GN.82
JTS.ENA.3462
Morag.*
Oxf.2486.
Oxf.2628.*
Oxf.2629.
Oxf.2652.
Oxf.2652.B*
Oxf.2659.
Oxf.3109.*
Spiegel.*
Ec 89. JLN.
Str.BNO.5138.
TS.Ar.1b.88.
TS.Ar.1b.90.
TS.Ar.b1.101.
TS.Ar.21.35.*
TS.Ar.21.49.*
TS.Ar.22.104.
TS.Ar.23.11.
TS.Ar.23.29.
TS.Ar.24.22.
TS.Ar.26.6.
TS.Ar.26.54.
TS.Ar.26.62.
TS.Ar.27.35.
TS.Ar.28.1.
TS.Ar.28.76.
TS.Ar.28.102.
TS.Ar.28.155.
TS.Ar.28.162.
TS.Ar.51.3.
TS.Misc.5.
TS.NS.105.23.*
TS.NS.318.6.
TS.NS.285.21.
Yeirin.

MSS Dn 5:	18	19	20	21	22	23	24	25	26	27	28	29	30			
Antonin.																
BM.Or.5554.																
Bud.Kauf.222.																
GE.GN.82.																
JTS.ENA.3462.																
Morag.*																
Oxf.2486.																
Oxf.2628.*																
Oxf.2629.																
Oxf.2652.																
Oxf.2652.B*																
Oxf.2659.																
Oxf.3109.*																
Spiegel.*																
Ec 89. JLN.																
Str.BNU.5138.																
TS.Ar.1b.88.																
TS.Ar.1b.90.																
TS.Ar.b1.101.																
TS.Ar.21.35.*																
TS.Ar.21.49.*																
TS.Ar.22.104.																
TS.Ar.23.11.																
TS.Ar.23.29.																
TS.Ar.24.22.																
TS.Ar.26.6.																
TS.Ar.26.54.																
TS.Ar.26.62.																
TS.Ar.27.35.																
TS.Ar.28.1.																
TS.Ar.28.76.																
TS.Ar.28.102.																
TS.Ar.28.155.																
TS.Ar.28.165.																
TS.Ar.51.3.																
TS.Misc.5.																
TS.NS.105.23.*																
TS.NS.318.6.																
TS.NS.285.21.																
Yeirin.																

MSS Dn 6:	1	2	3	4	5	6	7	8	9	10	11	12	13	14	15	16	17
Antonin.	…	…	…	…	…	…	…	…	…	…	…	…	…	…	…	…	…
BM.Or.5554.	…	…	…	…	…	…	…	…	…	…	…	…	…	…	…	…	…
Bud.Kauf.222.	…	…	…	…	…	…	…	…	…	…	…	…	…	…	…	…	…
GE.GN.82	…	…	…	…	…	…	…	…	…	…	…	…	…	…	…	…	…
JTS.ENA.3462.	…	…	…	…	…	…	…	…	…	…	…	…	…	…	…	…	…
Morag.*	…	…	…	…	…	…	…	…	…	…	…	…	…	…	…	…	…
Oxf.2486.	…	…	…	…	…	…	…	…	…	…	…	…	…	…	…	…	…
Oxf.2628.*	…	…	…	…	…	…	…	…	…	…	…	…	…	…	…	…	…
Oxf.2629.	…	…	…	…	…	…	…	…	…	…	…	…	…	…	…	…	…
Oxf.2652.	…	…	…	…	…	…	…	…	…	…	…	…	…	…	…	…	…
Oxf.2652.B*	…	…	…	…	…	…	…	…	…	…	…	…	…	…	…	…	…
Oxf.2659.	…	…	…	…	…	…	…	…	…	…	…	…	…	…	…	…	…
Oxf.3109.*	…	…	…	…	…	…	…	…	…	…	…	…	…	…	…	…	…
Spiegel.*	…	…	…	…	…	…	…	…	…	…	…	…	…	…	…	…	…
Ec 89. JLN.	…	…	…	…	…	…	…	…	…	…	…	…	…	…	…	…	…
Str.BNO.5138.	…	…	…	…	…	…	…	…	…	…	…	…	…	…	…	…	…
TS.Ar.1b.88.	…	…	…	…	…	…	…	…	…	…	…	…	…	…	…	…	…
TS.Ar.1b.90.	…	…	…	…	…	…	…	…	…	…	…	…	…	…	…	…	…
TS.Ar.b1.101.	…	…	…	…	…	…	…	…	…	…	…	…	…	…	…	…	…
TS.Ar.21.35.*	…	…	…	…	…	…	…	…	…	…	…	…	…	…	…	…	…
TS.Ar.21.49.*	…	…	…	…	…	…	…	…	…	…	…	…	…	…	…	…	…
TS.Ar.22.104.	…	…	…	…	…	…	…	…	…	…	…	…	…	…	…	…	…
TS.Ar.23.11.	…	…	…	…	…	…	…	…	…	…	…	…	…	…	…	…	…
TS.Ar.23.29.	…	…	…	…	…	…	…	…	…	…	…	…	…	…	…	…	…
TS.Ar.24.22.	…	…	…	…	…	…	…	…	…	…	…	…	…	…	…	…	…
TS.Ar.26.6.	…	…	…	…	…	…	…	…	…	…	…	…	…	…	…	…	…
TS.Ar.26.54.	…	…	…	…	…	…	…	…	…	…	…	…	…	…	…	…	…
TS.Ar.26.62.	…	…	…	…	…	…	…	…	…	…	…	…	…	…	…	…	…
TS.Ar.27.35	…	…	…	…	…	…	…	…	…	…	…	…	…	…	…	…	…
TS.Ar.28.1.	…	…	…	…	…	…	…	…	…	…	…	…	…	…	…	…	…
TS.Ar.28.76.	…	…	…	…	…	…	…	…	…	…	…	…	…	…	…	…	…
TS.Ar.28.102.	…	…	…	…	…	…	…	…	…	…	…	…	…	…	…	…	…
TS.Ar.28.155.	…	…	…	…	…	…	…	…	…	…	…	…	…	…	…	…	…
TS.Ar.28.162.	…	…	…	…	…	…	…	…	…	…	…	…	…	…	…	…	…
TS.Ar.51.3.	…	…	…	…	…	…	…	…	…	…	…	…	…	…	…	…	…
TS.Misc.5.	…	…	…	…	…	…	…	…	…	…	…	…	…	…	…	…	…
TS.NS.105.23.*	…	…	…	…	…	…	…	…	…	…	…	…	…	…	…	…	…
TS.NS.318.6.	…	…	…	…	…	…	…	…	…	…	…	…	…	…	…	…	…
TS.NS.285.21.	…	…	…	…	…	…	…	…	…	…	…	…	…	…	…	…	…
Yeirin.	…	…	…	…	…	…	…	…	…	…	…	…	…	…	…	…	…

MSS Dn 6:	18	19	20	21	22	23	24	25	26	27	28	29					
Antonin.	…	…	…	…	…	…	…	…	…	…	…	…	…	…	…	…	…
BM.Or.5554.	…	…	…	…	…	…	…	…	…	…	…	…	…	…	…	…	…
Bud.Kauf.222.	…	…	…	…	…	…	…	…	…	…	…	…	…	…	…	…	…
GE.GN.82.	…	…	…	…	…	…	…	…	…	…	…	…	…	…	…	…	…
JTS.ENA.3462.	…	…	…	…	…	…	…	…	…	…	…	…	…	…	…	…	…
Morag.*	—	—	—	—	—	—	—	—	—	—	—	—	…	…	…	…	…
Oxf.2486.	…	…	…	…	…	…	…	…	…	…	…	…	…	…	…	…	…
Oxf.2628.*	…	…	…	…	…	…	…	…	…	…	…	…	…	…	…	…	…
Oxf.2629.	…	…	…	…	…	…	…	…	…	…	…	…	…	…	…	…	…
Oxf.2652.	…	…	…	…	…	…	…	…	…	…	…	…	…	…	…	…	…
Oxf.2652.B*	…	…	…	…	…	…	…	…	…	…	…	…	…	…	…	…	…
Oxf.2659.	…	…	…	…	…	…	…	…	…	…	…	…	…	…	…	…	…
Oxf.3109.*	…	…	…	…	…	…	…	…	…	…	…	…	…	…	…	…	…
Spiegel.*	—	—	—	—	—	—	—	—	—	—	—	—	…	…	…	…	…
Ec 89. JLN.	…	…	…	…	…	…	…	…	…	…	…	…	…	…	…	…	…
Str.BNU.5138.	…	…	…	…	…	…	…	…	…	…	…	…	…	…	…	…	…
TS.Ar.1b.88.	…	…	…	…	…	…	…	…	…	…	…	…	…	…	…	…	…
TS.Ar.1b.90.	—	—	—	—	—	—	—	—	—	—	—	—	…	…	…	…	…
TS.Ar.b1.101.	…	…	…	…	…	…	…	…	…	…	…	–	…	…	…	…	…
TS.Ar.21.35.*	…	…	…	…	…	…	…	…	…	…	…	…	…	…	…	…	…
TS.Ar.21.49.*	…	…	…	…	…	…	…	…	…	…	…	…	…	…	…	…	…
TS.Ar.22.104.	…	…	…	…	…	…	…	…	…	…	…	–	…	…	…	…	…
TS.Ar.23.11.	…	…	…	…	…	…	…	…	…	…	…	…	…	…	…	…	…
TS.Ar.23.29.	…	…	…	…	…	…	…	…	…	…	…	…	…	…	…	…	…
TS.Ar.24.22.	…	…	…	…	…	…	…	…	…	…	…	…	…	…	…	…	…
TS.Ar.26.6.	…	…	…	…	…	…	…	…	…	…	…	…	…	…	…	…	…
TS.Ar.26.54.	…	…	…	…	…	…	…	…	…	…	…	…	…	…	…	…	…
TS.Ar.26.62.	…	…	…	…	…	…	…	…	…	…	…	…	…	…	…	…	…
TS.Ar.27.35.	…	…	…	…	…	…	…	…	…	…	…	…	…	…	…	…	…
TS.Ar.28.1	…	…	…	…	…	…	…	…	…	…	…	…	…	…	…	…	…
TS.Ar.28.76.	…	…	…	…	…	…	…	…	…	…	…	…	…	…	…	…	…
TS.Ar.28.102.	…	…	…	…	…	…	…	…	…	…	…	…	…	…	…	…	…
TS.Ar.28.155.	…	…	…	…	…	…	…	…	…	…	…	…	…	…	…	…	…
TS.Ar.28.165.	…	…	…	…	…	…	…	…	…	…	…	…	…	…	…	…	…
TS.Ar.51.3.	…	…	…	…	…	…	…	…	…	…	…	…	…	…	…	…	…
TS.Misc.5.	…	…	…	…	…	…	…	…	…	…	…	…	…	…	…	…	…
TS.NS.105.23.*	…	…	…	…	…	…	…	—	—	—	—	—	…	…	…	…	…
TS.NS.318.6.	…	…	…	…	…	…	…	…	…	…	…	…	…	…	…	…	…
TS.NS.285.21.	…	…	…	…	…	…	…	…	…	…	…	…	…	…	…	…	…
Yeirin.	…	…	…	…	…	…	…	…	…	…	…	…	…	…	…	…	…

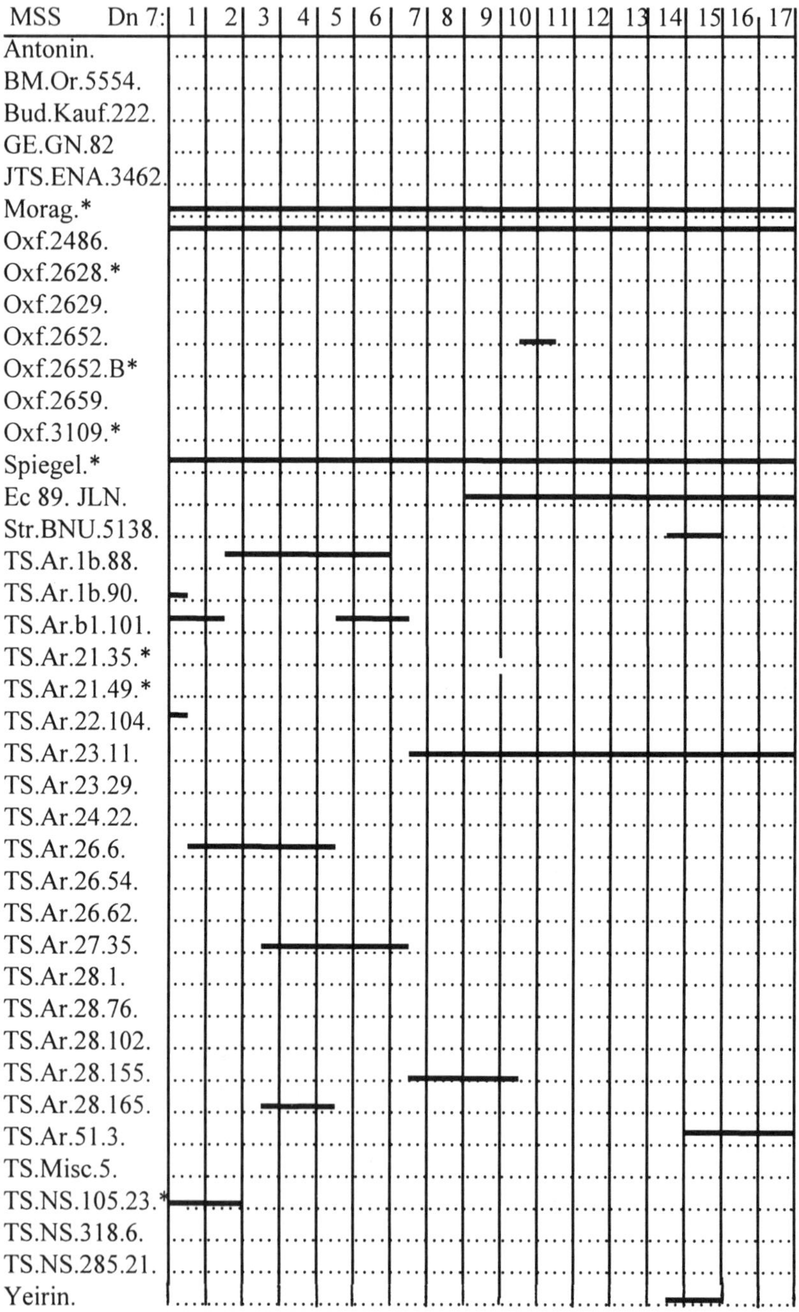
MSS
Dn 7:
1
2
3
4
5
6
7
8
9
10
11
12
13
14
15
16
17
Antonin.
BM.Or.5554.
Bud.Kauf.222.
GE.GN.82
JTS.ENA.3462.
Morag.*
Oxf.2486.
Oxf.2628.*
Oxf.2629.
Oxf.2652.
Oxf.2652.B*
Oxf.2659.
Oxf.3109.*
Spiegel.*
Ec 89. JLN.
Str.BNU.5138.
TS.Ar.1b.88.
TS.Ar.1b.90.
TS.Ar.b1.101.
TS.Ar.21.35.*
TS.Ar.21.49.*
TS.Ar.22.104.
TS.Ar.23.11.
TS.Ar.23.29.
TS.Ar.24.22.
TS.Ar.26.6.
TS.Ar.26.54.
TS.Ar.26.62.
TS.Ar.27.35.
TS.Ar.28.1.
TS.Ar.28.76.
TS.Ar.28.102.
TS.Ar.28.155.
TS.Ar.28.165.
TS.Ar.51.3.
TS.Misc.5.
TS.NS.105.23.*
TS.NS.318.6.
TS.NS.285.21.
Yeirin.

MSS	Dn 7: 18	19	20	21	22	23	24	25	26	27	28
Antonin.											
BM.Or.5554.		—	—	—	—						
Bud.Kauf.222.								—	—	—	—
GE.GN.82.											
JTS.ENA.3462.											
Morag.*	—	—	—	—	—	—	—	—	—	—	—
Oxf.2486.	—	—	—	—	—	—	—	—	—	—	—
Oxf.2628.*											
Oxf.2629.											
Oxf.2652.											
Oxf.2652.B*											
Oxf.2659.											
Oxf.3109.*											
Spiegel.*	—	—	—	—	—	—	—	—	—	—	—
Ec 89. JLN.								—	—	—	—
Str.BNU.5138.											
TS.Ar.1b.88.											
TS.Ar.1b.90.											
TS.Ar.b1.101.											
TS.Ar.21.35.*											
TS.Ar.21.49.*											
TS.Ar.22.104.											
TS.Ar.23.11	—	—	—	—	—	—	—	—	—	—	—
TS.Ar.23.29.											
TS.Ar.24.22.											
TS.Ar.26.6.											
TS.Ar.26.54.											
TS.Ar.26.62.											
TS.Ar.27.35.											
TS.Ar.28.1.											
TS.Ar.28.76.											
TS.Ar.28.102.											
TS.Ar.28.155.											
TS.Ar.28.165.											
TS.Ar.51.3.	—										
TS.Misc.5.											
TS.NS.105.21.*											
TS.NS.318.6.											
TS.NS.285.21.											
Yeirin.		—	—	—	—			—	—	—	—

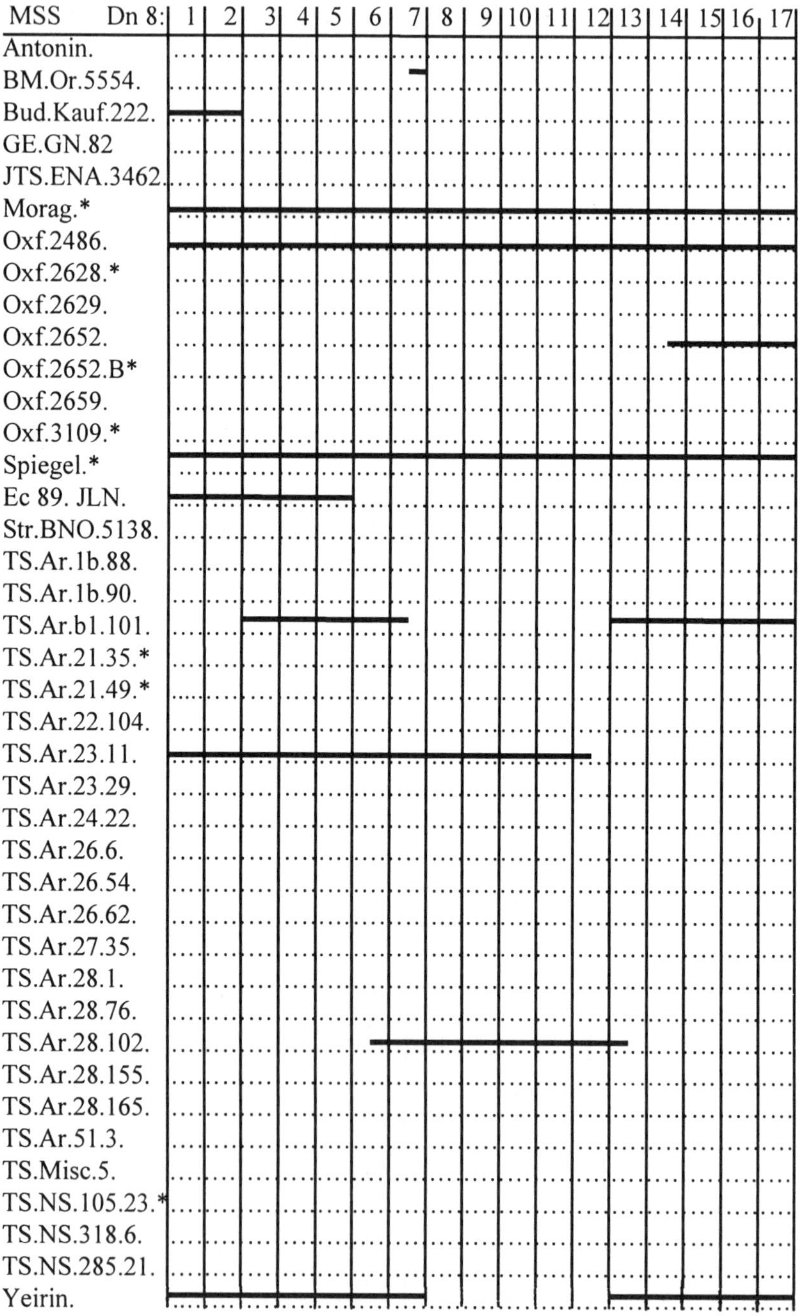
MSS
Dn 8:
1
2
3
4
5
6
7
8
9
10
11
12
13
14
15
16
17
Antonin.
BM.Or.5554.
Bud.Kauf.222.
GE.GN.82
JTS.ENA.3462.
Morag.*
Oxf.2486.
Oxf.2628.*
Oxf.2629.
Oxf.2652.
Oxf.2652.B*
Oxf.2659.
Oxf.3109.*
Spiegel.*
Ec 89. JLN.
Str.BNO.5138.
TS.Ar.1b.88.
TS.Ar.1b.90.
TS.Ar.b1.101.
TS.Ar.21.35.*
TS.Ar.21.49.*
TS.Ar.22.104.
TS.Ar.23.11.
TS.Ar.23.29.
TS.Ar.24.22.
TS.Ar.26.6.
TS.Ar.26.54.
TS.Ar.26.62.
TS.Ar.27.35.
TS.Ar.28.1.
TS.Ar.28.76.
TS.Ar.28.102.
TS.Ar.28.155.
TS.Ar.28.165.
TS.Ar.51.3.
TS.Misc.5.
TS.NS.105.23.*
TS.NS.318.6.
TS.NS.285.21.
Yeirin.

MSS Dn 8:	18	19	20	21	22	23	24	25	26	27							
Antonin.																	
BM.Or.5554.																	
Bud.Kauf.222.																	
GE.GN.82.																	
JTS.ENA.3462.																	
Morag.*	—	—	—	—	—	—	—	—	—	—							
Oxf.2486.	—	—	—	—	—	—	—	—	—	—							
Oxf.2628.*																	
Oxf.2629.																	
Oxf.2652.	—	—	—	—													
Oxf.2652.B*																	
Oxf.2659.																	
Oxf.3109.*																	
Spiegel.*	—	—	—	—	—	—	—	—	—	—							
Ec 89. JLN.																	
Str.BNU.5138.																	
TS.Ar.1b.88.																	
TS.Ar.1b.90.																	
TS.Ar.b1.101.	—	—	—	—	—	—											
TS.Ar.21.35.*																	
TS.Ar.21.49.*																	
TS.Ar.22.104.																	
TS.Ar.23.11.																	
TS.Ar.23.29.																	
TS.Ar.24.22.																	
TS.Ar.26.6.																	
TS.Ar.26.54.																	
TS.Ar.26.62.																	
TS.Ar.27.35.																	
TS.Ar.28.1.																	
TS.Ar.28.76.																	
TS.Ar.28.102.																	
TS.Ar.28.155.																	
TS.Ar.28.165.																	
TS.Ar.51.3.																	
TS.Misc.5.																	
TS.NS.105.23.*																	
TS.NS.318.6.																	
TS.NS.285.21.																	
Yeirin.	—	—	—	—	—	—											

MSS Dn 9:	1	2	3	4	5	6	7	8	9	10	11	12	13	14	15	16	17
Antonin.	...	...	...	...	...	...	...	...	...	...	...	...	...	...	...	...	...
BM.Or.5554.	...	...	...	...	...	...	...	...	...	...	...	...	...	...	...	...	...
Bud.Kauf.222.	...	...	...	...	...	...	...	...	...	...	...	...	...	...	...	...	...
GE.GN.82	...	...	...	...	...	...	...	...	...	...	...	...	...	...	...	...	...
JTS.ENA.3462.	...	...	...	...	...	...	...	...	...	...	...	...	...	...	...	...	...
Morag.*	...	...	...	...	...	...	...	...	...	...	...	...	...	...	...	...	...
Oxf.2486.	...	...	...	...	...	...	...	...	...	...	...	...	...	...	...	...	...
Oxf.2628.*	...	...	...	...	...	...	...	...	...	...	...	...	...	...	...	...	...
Oxf.2629.	...	...	...	...	...	...	...	...	...	...	...	...	...	...	...	...	...
Oxf.2652.	...	...	...	...	...	...	...	...	...	...	...	...	...	...	...	...	...
Oxf.2652.B*	...	...	...	...	...	...	...	...	...	...	...	...	...	...	...	...	...
Oxf.2659.	...	...	...	...	...	...	...	...	...	...	...	...	...	...	...	...	...
Oxf.3109.*	...	...	...	...	...	...	...	...	...	...	...	...	...	...	...	...	...
Spiegel.*	...	...	...	...	...	...	...	...	...	...	...	...	...	...	...	...	...
Ec 89. JLN.	...	...	...	...	...	...	...	...	...	...	...	...	...	...	...	...	...
Str.BNO.5138.	...	...	...	...	...	...	...	...	...	...	...	...	...	...	...	...	...
TS.Ar.1b.88.	...	...	...	...	...	...	...	...	...	...	...	...	...	...	...	...	...
TS.Ar.1b.90.	...	...	...	...	...	...	...	...	...	...	...	...	...	...	...	...	...
TS.Ar.b1.101.	...	...	...	...	...	...	...	...	...	...	...	...	...	...	...	...	...
TS.Ar.21.35.*	...	...	...	...	...	...	...	...	...	...	...	...	...	...	...	...	...
TS.Ar.21.49.*	...	...	...	...	...	...	...	...	...	...	...	...	...	...	...	...	...
TS.Ar.22.104.	...	...	...	...	...	...	...	...	...	...	...	...	...	...	...	...	...
TS.Ar.23.11.	...	...	...	...	...	...	...	...	...	...	...	...	...	...	...	...	...
TS.Ar.23.29.	...	...	...	...	...	...	...	...	...	...	...	...	...	...	...	...	...
TS.Ar.24.22.	...	...	...	...	...	...	...	...	...	...	...	...	...	...	...	...	...
TS.Ar.26.6.	...	...	...	...	...	...	...	...	...	...	...	...	...	...	...	...	...
TS.Ar.26.54.	...	...	...	...	...	...	...	...	...	...	...	...	...	...	...	...	...
TS.Ar.26.62.	...	...	...	...	...	...	...	...	...	...	...	...	...	...	...	...	...
TS.Ar.27.35.	...	...	...	...	...	...	...	...	...	...	...	...	...	...	...	...	...
TS.Ar.28.1.	...	...	...	...	...	...	...	...	...	...	...	...	...	...	...	...	...
TS.Ar.28.76.	...	...	...	...	...	...	...	...	...	...	...	...	...	...	...	...	...
TS.Ar.28.102.	...	...	...	...	...	...	...	...	...	...	...	...	...	...	...	...	...
TS.Ar.28.155.	...	...	...	...	...	...	...	...	...	...	...	...	...	...	...	...	...
TS.Ar.28.165.	...	...	...	...	...	...	...	...	...	...	...	...	...	...	...	...	...
TS.Ar.51.3.	...	...	...	...	...	...	...	...	...	...	...	...	...	...	...	...	...
TS.Misc.5.	...	...	...	...	...	...	...	...	...	...	...	...	...	...	...	...	...
TS.NS.105.23.*	...	...	...	...	...	...	...	...	...	...	...	...	...	...	...	...	...
TS.NS.318.6.	...	...	...	...	...	...	...	...	...	...	...	...	...	...	...	...	...
TS.NS.285.21.	...	...	...	...	...	...	...	...	...	...	...	...	...	...	...	...	...
Yeirin.	...	...	...	...	...	...	...	...	...	...	...	...	...	...	...	...	...

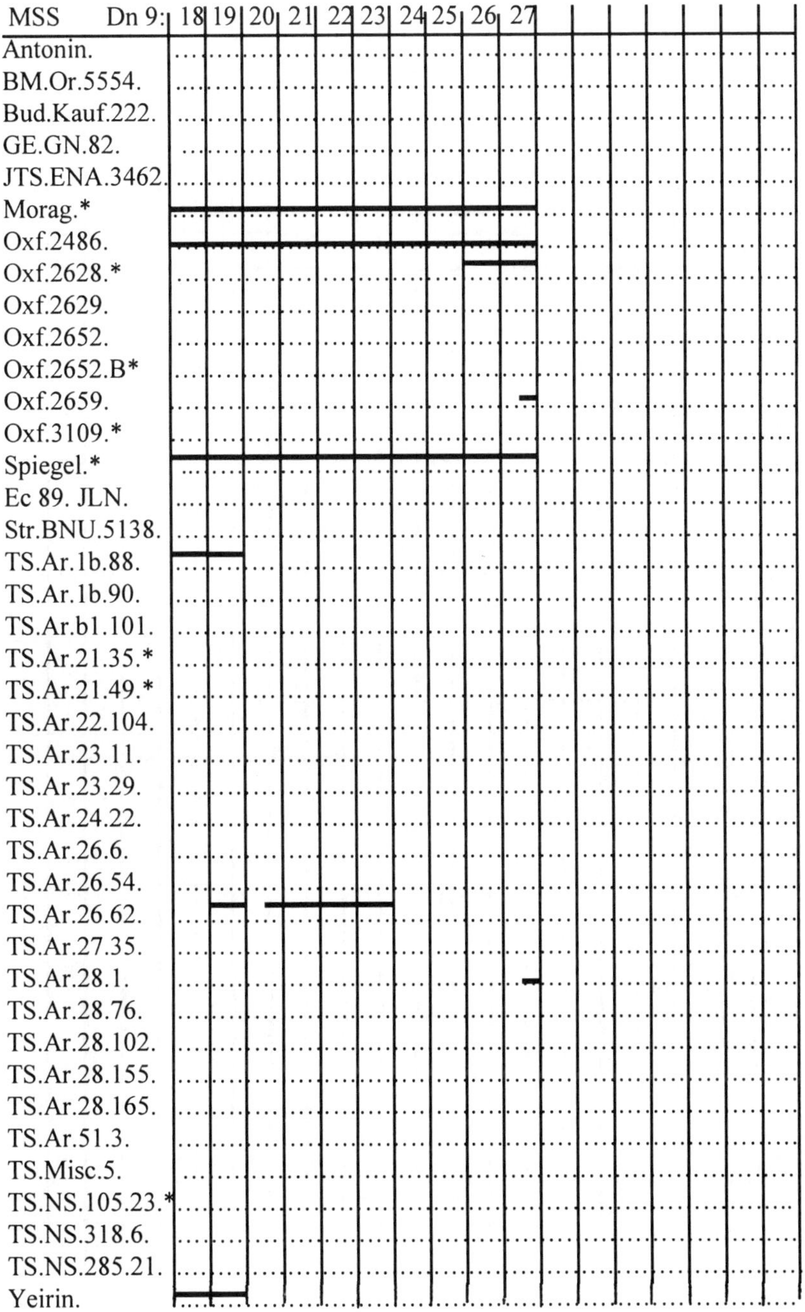
MSS Dn 9: 18 19 20 21 22 23 24 25 26 27
Antonin.
BM.Or.5554.
Bud.Kauf.222.
GE.GN.82.
JTS.ENA.3462.
Morag.*
Oxf.2486.
Oxf.2628.*
Oxf.2629.
Oxf.2652.
Oxf.2652.B*
Oxf.2659.
Oxf.3109.*
Spiegel.*
Ec 89. JLN.
Str.BNU.5138.
TS.Ar.1b.88.
TS.Ar.1b.90.
TS.Ar.b1.101.
TS.Ar.21.35.*
TS.Ar.21.49.*
TS.Ar.22.104.
TS.Ar.23.11.
TS.Ar.23.29.
TS.Ar.24.22.
TS.Ar.26.6.
TS.Ar.26.54.
TS.Ar.26.62.
TS.Ar.27.35.
TS.Ar.28.1.
TS.Ar.28.76.
TS.Ar.28.102.
TS.Ar.28.155.
TS.Ar.28.165.
TS.Ar.51.3.
TS.Misc.5.
TS.NS.105.23.*
TS.NS.318.6.
TS.NS.285.21.
Yeirin.

MSS Dn 10:	1	2	3	4	5	6	7	8	9	10	11	12	13	14	15	16	17
Antonin.																	
BM.Or.5554.																	
Bud.Kauf.222.																	
GE.GN.82																	
JTS.ENA.3462.																	
Morag.*																	
Oxf.2486.																	
Oxf.2628.*																	
Oxf.2629.																	
Oxf.2652.																	
Oxf.2652.B*																	
Oxf.2659.																	
Oxf.3109.*																	
Spiegel.*																	
Ec 89. JLN.																	
Str.BNO.5138.																	
TS.Ar.1b.88.																	
TS.Ar.1b.90.																	
TS.Ar.b1.101.																	
TS.Ar.21.35.*																	
TS.Ar.21.49.*																	
TS.Ar.22.104.																	
TS.Ar.23.11.																	
TS.Ar.23.29.																	
TS.Ar.24.22.																	
TS.Ar.26.6.																	
TS.Ar.26.54.																	
TS.Ar.26.62.																	
TS.Ar.27.35.																	
TS.Ar.28.1.																	
TS.Ar.28.76.																	
TS.Ar.28.102.																	
TS.Ar.28.155.																	
TS.Ar.28.165.																	
TS.Ar.51.3.																	
TS.Misc.5.																	
TS.NS.105.23.*																	
TS.NS.318.6.																	
TS.NS.285.21.																	
Yeirin.																	

MSS Dn 10:	18	19	20	21
Antonin.				
BM.Or.5554.				
Bud.Kauf.222.				
GE.GN.82.				
JTS.ENA.3462.				
Morag.*				
Oxf.2486.				
Oxf.2628.*				
Oxf.2629.				
Oxf.2652.				
Oxf.2652.B*				
Oxf.2659.				
Oxf.3109.*				
Spiegel.*				
Ec 89. JLN.				
Str.BNU.5138.				
TS.Ar.1b.88.				
TS.Ar.1b.90.				
TS.Ar.b1.101.				
TS.Ar.21.35.*				
TS.Ar.21.49.*				
TS.Ar.22.104.				
TS.Ar.23.11.				
TS.Ar.23.29.				
TS.Ar.24.22.				
TS.Ar.26.6.				
TS.Ar.26.54.				
TS.Ar.26.62.				
TS.Ar.27.35.				
TS.Ar.28.1.				
TS.Ar.28.76.				
TS.Ar.28.102.				
TS.Ar.28.155.				
TS.Ar.28.165.				
TS.Ar.51.3.				
TS.Misc.5.				
TS.NS.105.23.*				
TS.NS.285.6.				
TS.NS.318.21.				
Yeirin.				

MSS Dn 11:	1	2	3	4	5	6	7	8	9	10	11	12	13	14	15	16	17
Antonin.	…	…	…	…	…	…	…	…	…	…	…	…	…	…	…	…	…
BM.Or.5554.	…	…	…	…	…	…	…	…	…	…	…	…	…	…	…	…	…
Bud.Kauf.222.	…	…	…	…	…	…	…	…	…	…	…	…	…	…	…	…	…
GE.GN.82	…	…	…	…	…	…	…	…	…	…	…	…	…	…	…	…	…
JTS.ENA.3462.	…	…	…	…	…	…	…	…	…	…	…	…	…	…	…	…	…
Morag.*	▬	▬	▬	▬	▬	▬	▬	▬	▬	▬	▬	▬	▬	▬	▬	▬	▬
Oxf.2486.	▬	▬	▬	▬	▬	▬	▬	▬	▬	▬	▬	▬	▬	▬	▬	▬	▬
Oxf.2628.*	▬	▬	▬	▬	▬	▬	▬	▬	▬	▬	▬	▬	▬	▬	▬	▬	▬
Oxf.2629.	…	…	…	…	…	…	…	…	…	…	…	…	…	…	…	…	…
Oxf.2652.	…	…	…	…	…	…	…	…	…	…	…	…	…	…	…	…	…
Oxf.2652.B*	…	…	…	…	…	…	…	…	…	…	…	…	…	…	…	…	…
Oxf.2659.	…	…	…	…	…	…	…	…	…	…	…	…	…	…	…	…	…
Oxf.3109.*	…	…	…	…	…	…	…	…	…	…	…	…	…	…	…	…	…
Spiegel.*	▬	▬	▬	▬	▬	▬	▬	▬	▬	▬	▬	▬	▬	▬	▬	▬	▬
Ec 89. JLN.	…	…	…	…	…	…	…	…	…	…	…	…	…	…	…	…	…
Str.BNO.5138.	…	…	…	…	…	…	…	…	…	…	…	…	…	…	…	…	…
TS.Ar.1b.88.	…	…	…	…	…	…	…	…	…	…	…	…	…	…	…	…	…
TS.Ar.1b.90.	…	…	…	…	…	…	…	…	…	…	…	…	…	…	…	…	…
TS.Ar.b1.101.	…	…	…	…	…	…	…	…	…	…	…	…	…	…	…	…	…
TS.Ar.21.35.*	…	…	…	…	…	…	…	…	…	…	…	…	…	…	…	…	…
TS.Ar.21.49.*	…	…	…	…	…	…	…	…	…	…	…	…	…	…	…	…	…
TS.Ar.22.104.	…	…	…	…	…	…	…	…	…	…	…	…	…	…	…	…	…
TS.Ar.23.11.	…	…	…	…	…	…	…	…	…	…	…	…	…	…	…	…	…
TS.Ar.23.29.	…	…	…	…	…	…	…	…	…	…	…	…	…	…	…	…	…
TS.Ar.24.22.	…	…	…	…	…	…	…	…	…	…	…	…	▬	▬	▬	…	…
TS.Ar.26.6.	…	…	…	…	…	…	…	…	…	…	…	…	…	…	…	…	…
TS.Ar.26.54.	…	…	…	…	…	…	…	…	…	…	…	…	…	…	…	…	…
TS.Ar.26.62.	…	…	…	…	…	…	…	…	…	…	…	…	…	…	…	…	…
TS.Ar.27.35.	…	…	…	…	…	…	…	…	…	…	…	…	…	…	…	…	…
TS.Ar.28.1.	…	…	…	…	…	…	…	…	…	…	…	…	…	…	…	…	…
TS.Ar.28.76.	…	…	…	…	…	…	…	…	…	…	…	…	…	…	…	…	…
TS.Ar.28.102.	…	…	…	…	…	…	…	…	…	…	…	…	…	…	…	…	…
TS.Ar.28.155.	…	…	…	…	…	…	…	…	…	…	…	…	…	…	…	…	…
TS.Ar.28.165.	…	…	…	…	…	…	…	…	…	…	…	…	…	…	…	…	…
TS.Ar.51.3.	…	…	…	…	…	…	…	…	…	…	…	…	…	…	…	…	…
TS.Misc.5.	…	…	…	…	…	…	…	…	…	…	…	…	…	…	…	…	…
TS.NS.105.23.*	…	…	…	…	…	…	…	…	…	…	…	…	…	…	…	…	…
TS.NS.318.6.	…	…	…	…	…	…	…	…	…	…	…	…	…	…	…	…	…
TS.NS.285.21.	…	…	…	…	…	…	…	…	…	…	…	…	…	…	…	…	…
Yeirin.	…	…	…	…	…	…	…	…	…	…	…	…	…	…	…	…	…

MSS Dn 11:	18	19	20	21	22	23	24	25	26	27	28	29	30	31	32	33	34
Antonin.																	
BM.Or.5554.																	
Bud.Kauf.222.																	
GE.GN.82.																	
JTS.ENA.3462.																	
Morag.*																	
Oxf.2486.																	
Oxf.2628.*																	
Oxf.2629.																	
Oxf.2652.																	
Oxf.2652.B*																	
Oxf.2659.																	
Oxf.3109.*																	
Spiegel.*																	
Ec 89. JLN.																	
Str.BNU.5138.																	
TS.Ar.1b.88.																	
TS.Ar.b1.101.																	
TS.Ar.1b.90.																	
TS.Ar.21.35.*																	
TS.Ar.21.49.*																	
TS.Ar.22.104.																	
TS.Ar.23.11.																	
TS.Ar.23.29.																	
TS.Ar.24.22.																	
TS.Ar.26.6.																	
TS.Ar.26.54.																	
TS.Ar.26.62.																	
TS.Ar.27.35.																	
TS.Ar.28.1.																	
TS.Ar.28.76.																	
TS.Ar.28.102.																	
TS.Ar.28.155.																	
TS.Ar.28.165.																	
TS.Ar.51.3.																	
TS.Misc.5.																	
TS.NS.105.23.*																	
TS.NS.318.6.																	
TS.NS.285.21.																	
Yeirin.																	

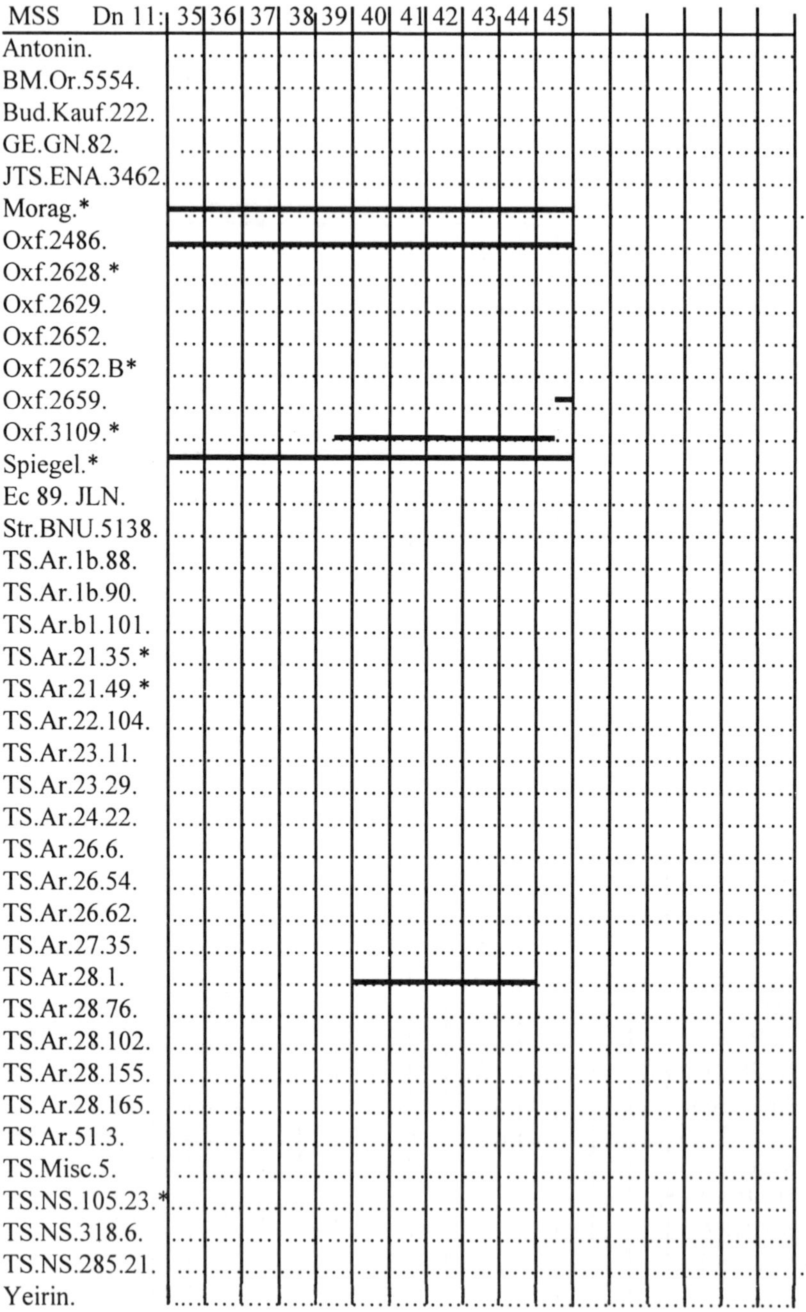
MSS Dn 11: 35 36 37 38 39 40 41 42 43 44 45
Antonin.
BM.Or.5554.
Bud.Kauf.222.
GE.GN.82.
JTS.ENA.3462.
Morag.*
Oxf.2486.
Oxf.2628.*
Oxf.2629.
Oxf.2652.
Oxf.2652.B*
Oxf.2659.
Oxf.3109.*
Spiegel.*
Ec 89. JLN.
Str.BNU.5138.
TS.Ar.1b.88.
TS.Ar.1b.90.
TS.Ar.b1.101.
TS.Ar.21.35.*
TS.Ar.21.49.*
TS.Ar.22.104.
TS.Ar.23.11.
TS.Ar.23.29.
TS.Ar.24.22.
TS.Ar.26.6.
TS.Ar.26.54.
TS.Ar.26.62.
TS.Ar.27.35.
TS.Ar.28.1.
TS.Ar.28.76.
TS.Ar.28.102.
TS.Ar.28.155.
TS.Ar.28.165.
TS.Ar.51.3.
TS.Misc.5.
TS.NS.105.23.*
TS.NS.318.6.
TS.NS.285.21.
Yeirin.

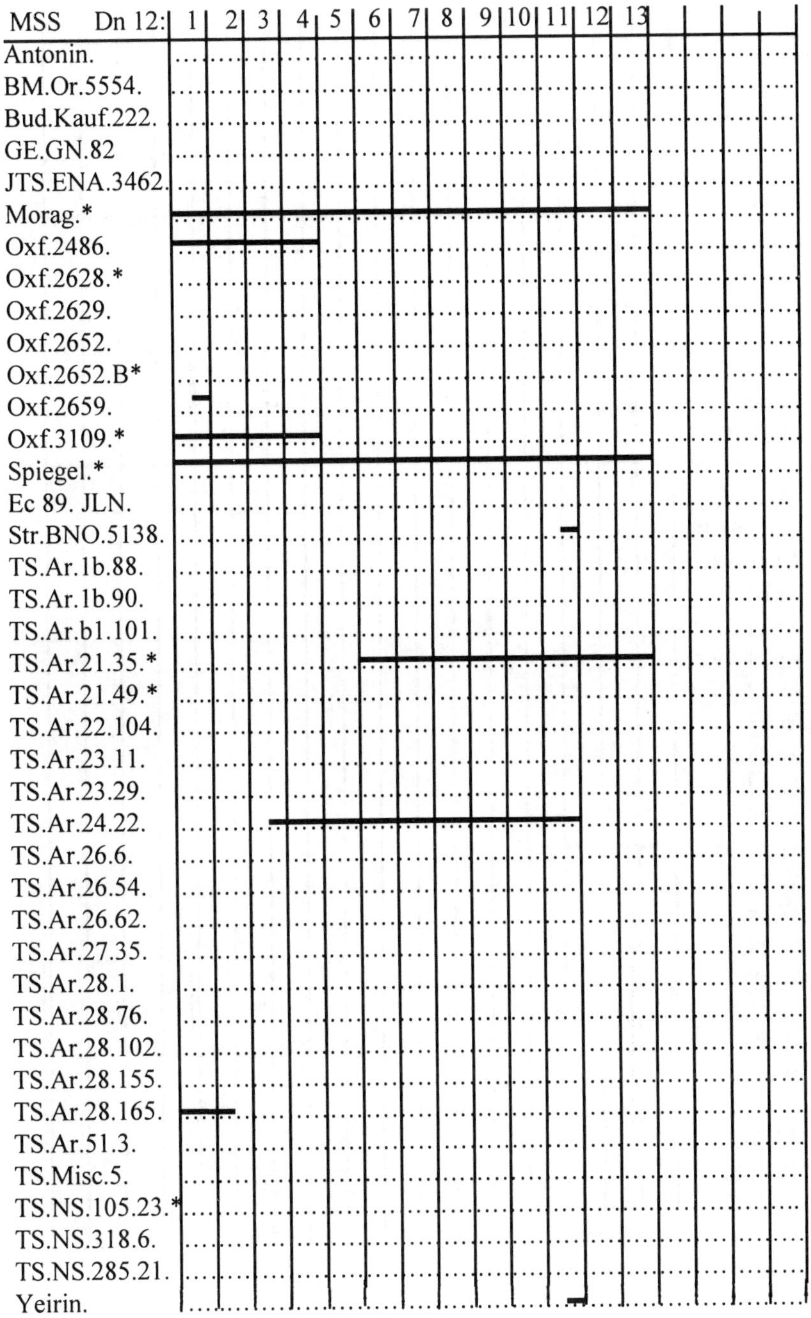
MSS Dn 12: 1 2 3 4 5 6 7 8 9 10 11 12 13
Antonin.
BM.Or.5554.
Bud.Kauf.222.
GE.GN.82
JTS.ENA.3462.
Morag.*
Oxf.2486.
Oxf.2628.*
Oxf.2629.
Oxf.2652.
Oxf.2652.B*
Oxf.2659.
Oxf.3109.*
Spiegel.*
Ec 89. JLN.
Str.BNO.5138.
TS.Ar.1b.88.
TS.Ar.1b.90.
TS.Ar.b1.101.
TS.Ar.21.35.*
TS.Ar.21.49.*
TS.Ar.22.104.
TS.Ar.23.11.
TS.Ar.23.29.
TS.Ar.24.22.
TS.Ar.26.6.
TS.Ar.26.54.
TS.Ar.26.62.
TS.Ar.27.35.
TS.Ar.28.1.
TS.Ar.28.76.
TS.Ar.28.102.
TS.Ar.28.155.
TS.Ar.28.165.
TS.Ar.51.3.
TS.Misc.5.
TS.NS.105.23.*
TS.NS.318.6.
TS.NS.285.21.
Yeirin.

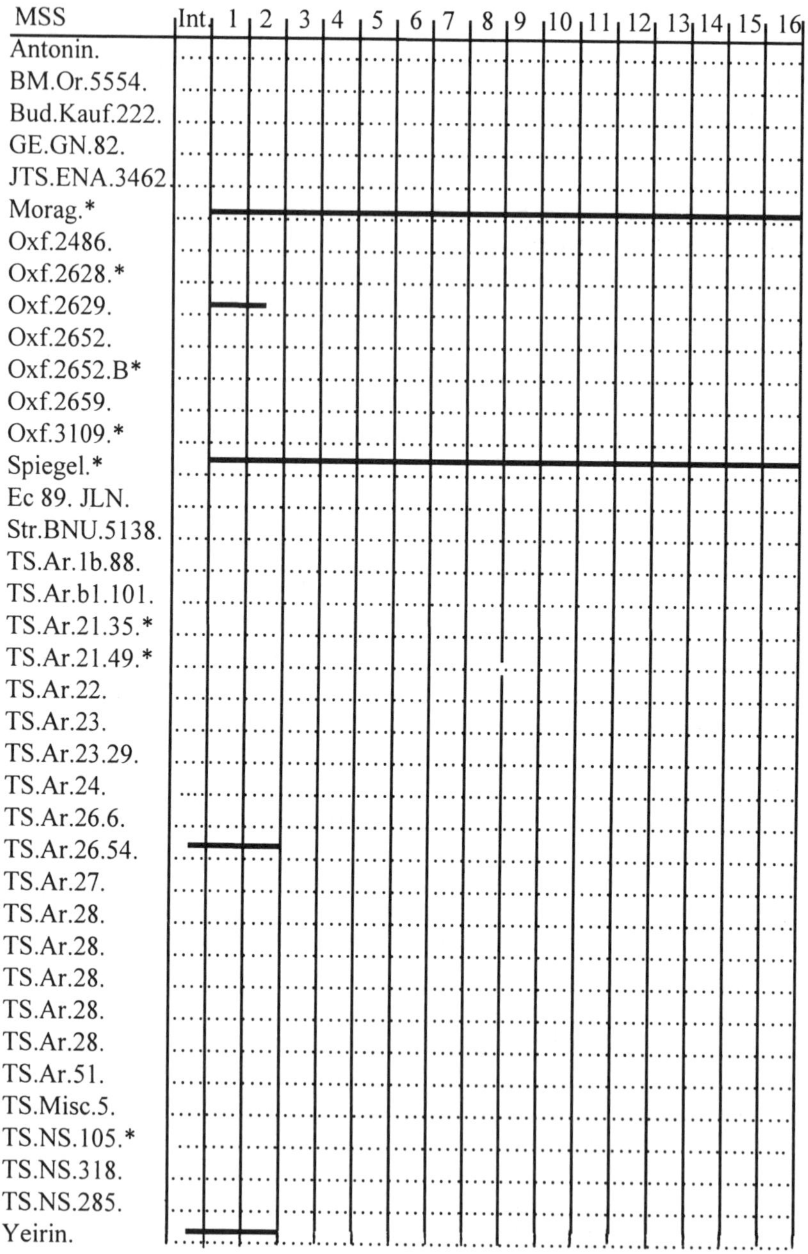
MSS
Int
1
2
3
4
5
6
7
8
9
10
11
12
13
14
15
16
Antonin.
BM.Or.5554.
Bud.Kauf.222.
GE.GN.82.
JTS.ENA.3462
Morag.*
Oxf.2486.
Oxf.2628.*
Oxf.2629.
Oxf.2652.
Oxf.2652.B*
Oxf.2659.
Oxf.3109.*
Spiegel.*
Ec 89. JLN.
Str.BNU.5138.
TS.Ar.1b.88.
TS.Ar.b1.101.
TS.Ar.21.35.*
TS.Ar.21.49.*
TS.Ar.22.
TS.Ar.23.
TS.Ar.23.29.
TS.Ar.24.
TS.Ar.26.6.
TS.Ar.26.54.
TS.Ar.27.
TS.Ar.28.
TS.Ar.28.
TS.Ar.28.
TS.Ar.28.
TS.Ar.28.
TS.Ar.51.
TS.Misc.5.
TS.NS.105.*
TS.NS.318.
TS.NS.285.
Yeirin.

The Judeo-Arabic Text of R. Saadia Gaon's Commentary on the Book of Daniel

[...] ישׂראל[1] ומשיחם אדֹ קאל **כה אמר יוי למשיחו לכורש וג׳** (יש׳ 45:1) וסאיר אלקצה. פלמא מלך כורש ואמר[2] בבנא אלבית וגב עליהם אלתעדיק בכל פנון אלישועה. כדֹאך חנביש **מלך הצפון ומלך הנגב** וסאיר מא אנצֹאף אליהא איאת לנא באלגמלה עלי אלישועה ובאלתפעיל בעצֹהא עלי בעץ. פכאן אדֹא גאזת אלחאדתֹה אלאולא כמא קאל אלמלך דלת עלי באקי צחת אלחוادתֹ ואלישועה. ואדֹא ואפת אלחאדתֹה אלתֹאניה במא קאל איצֹא חצל לנא דלילין עלי באקי אלחואדתֹ. ואדֹא אנקצֹת אלחאדתֹה אל גֹ צח לנא גֹ דלאיל עלי באקי אלחואדתֹ ואלישועה. וכל מא מר אלזמאן כתֹרת אלדלאיל עלי אלישועה אלי אן תואפי הי בעינהא. פיך גמיע מא תקדם ואלישועה אדלה עלי מא יך פי דאר אלאכֹרה מע אלאיאת אלחאדתֹה פי זמאן אלישועה כמא קאל **השמש יהפך לחשך והירח לדם לפני בא יום יוי הגדול והנורא** (יואל 3:4).

פקד תבין אן מנאפע הדֹא אלספר לא תחצא בסרעה והי פי נצה ינקסם אלי יׄ אקסאם. הׄ מנהא פי אמור אלמלכותֹ ואלהׄ אלאכֹר פי מנאפע ומצאלח ללאמה. ולדֹלך געלנאהא יׄ אגזא. אלגז אלאול פי כיפיה אלגללות ופי אלמאכל ואלמשקי מן יד אלגוים. ואלגז אלבֹ פימא כשף לנבוכדנצר מן דׄ מלכיות ותמתֹילהא בצורה קבל אן יכשף לדניאל מא יכֹצה הו נֹבֹ סנה. ואלגז אלגֹ פי אלאמתנאע מן עבאדה אלאצנאם. ואלגז אלדֹ פי כיפיה[3] אלאפה[4] אלתי חלת בבלשאצר. ואלגז אלהׄ פי כיפיה קתל בלשצר. ואלגז אלוׄ פי אלתמסך באלצלואת פי אלגלות. ואלזׄ גמל מן אלקול פי תמתֹיל אלממאלך באלוחש. ואלגז אלחׄ גמל מן אלקול אלמוצוף. ואלגז אלטֹ תפציל אלסבעין אסבוע אלתי לבין אלביאון[5] ואלעמר אלתֹאני. ואלגז אליׄ פי מלאחם אלמלוך ומקדאר אלקץ אלאכֹרין.

[1] ישׂראל Beginning of Yeirin 207 (Camb. TS Ar.26. 54a)

[2] אמ[ר] Yeirin 207 > D

[3] כיפיה End of Yeirin 207

[4] אלאפה Beginning of Yeirin 208 (Camb. TS Ar.26.54b)

[5] Uncertain lesson

פהדֿה אלדֿ אגזא אלאכֿרה מן אלגז אלבֿ הי אלהֿ אלתי ללמלכיות. ואלהֿ[6] אלבואקי פי אסתעבאראת ומצאלח לנא ואדֿ קד קדמת אסמאהא[7] [א]אכֿדֿ[8] פי נצוצהא ומעאניהא ואסתעין באלרחמון. נץ אלגז אלאול.

Dn 1:1

בשנת שלוש למלכות יהויקים מלך יהודה בא נבוכדנאצר מלך בבל ירושלם ויצר עליה.

פי אלסנה אלתֿאלתֿה[9] מן מלך יהויקים מלך יהודה[10] ואפא[11] בכֿתנצר[12] מלך באבל ירושלם[13] פחאצרהא.

אול מא ינבגֿי אן נפחץ ענה מא מעני קולה **בשנת שלוש**[14] (דניאל 1:1). ודֿלך אן אלכתאב[15] קד נץ פי ספר מלכי[16] אן יהויקים מלך יֿאֿ סנה. פאן כאן קד תסלמה נבוכֿדנצר מן אלסנה אלתֿאלתֿה[17] פכיף מלך יֿאֿ ? בל לם ימלך אלא גֿ סנין פקט. תֿם נפחץ איצֿא[18] ונקול והל כאן אבתדי מלך נבוכֿדנצר[19] פי אלסנה אלתֿאלתֿה[20] ליהויקים או ליס אנמא אבתדי מלכה[21] פי אלסנה אלראבעה[22] ליהויקים כמא קאל[23] **הדבר אשר היה אל ירמיהו על כל עם יהודה בשנה**

[6] ואלה Beginning of Oxf 2629.40a
[7] אל[באקי] פי [אלאסתעבאדא]ת ... קד קד[מת אסמאה אאכד פי נ]צוצהא Oxf 2629.40a >D
[8] אכד Yeirin 208
[9] אלג Yeirin 208
[10] יהודא Oxf 2629.40a
[11] ואפי Yeirin 208
[12] בכת נצר Morag
[13] ירושלאם Oxf 2629.40a
[14] ש Oxf 2629.40a
[15] אלכת[אב] Oxf 2629.40a > D
[16] ע׳ מל״ב 23:36.
[17] אלג Yeirin 208
[18] איצ Oxf 2629.40a
[19] נבוכד Oxf 2629.40a
[20] אלג Yeirin 208
[21] במלכה Oxf 2629.40a
[22] אלד Yeirin 208
[23] לי[הויקים] כק Yeirin 208

הרביעית ליהויקים בן[24] **יאשיהו מלך יהודה היא השנה הראשנית לנבוכדנצר מלך בבל**[25] (ירמ' 25:1).

ונגיב ען אלמסאלתין גמיעא ונקול[26] אן אול מלך נבוכׄדנצר[27] כאן פי אלסנה אלראבעה[28] ליהויקים[29] ואן[30] יהויקים מלך יׄאׄ סנה גׄ[31] מנהא[32] קבל נבוכדנצר וחׄ בעדה. ולדׄלך קאל ען יכניה אבנה[33] **ויקח**[34] **אתו**[35] **מלך בבל בשנת שמנה למלכו**[36] (מל"ב 24:12) [...][37] סנין בעד מא עצאה וכׄאלף עליה כׄקׄ **ויהי לו יהויקים עבד שלש שנים וישב וימרד בו** (מל"ב 24:1). אדׄאׄ[38] אגתמעת לנבוכדנצר סנתאן קבל אלטׄפר וגׄ סנין[39] טאעה וגׄ סנין עציאן צארת[40] חׄ. ואדׄאׄ זיד[41] עליהא ליהויקים אלגׄ אלמתקדמה צארת יׄאׄ סנה.[42] תׄם קאל

Dn 1:2

ויתן אדני בידו את יהויקים מלך יהודה ומקצת כלי בית האלהים ויביאם ארץ שנער בית אלהיו ואת הכלים הביא אוצר אלוהיו.

[24] ירמיהו ... ליהויקים בן Yeirin 208 > L

[25] לנב מׄ בׄ Oxf 2629.40a

[26] [גמיעא ונקו]ל Yeirin 208 > D

[27] נבוכד Oxf 2629.40a

[28] אלד Yeirin 208

[29] [ליה]ויקים Oxf 2629.40a > D

[30] לאן Oxf. 2629.40a

[31] End of Yeirin 208 (Camb. TS Ar.26.54b)

[32] Beginning of Yeirin 209 (Camb. TS Ar.26.54c)

[33] אבנה | ען יכניה אבנה Yeirin 209 > D

[34] ויקח End of the readable part of Oxf 2629.40a

[35] אתו Beginning of Oxf 2629.40b

[36] שמ[נה] ל[מ]ל[כו] Yeirin 209 > D

[37] ול[...] Yeirin 209 > D

[38] בבל ... אדׄאׄ Oxf 2629.40b > D

[39] סנתאן קבל אלטפר וגׄ סנין Oxf 2629.40b > D

[40] צא[רת] Yeirin 209 > D

[41] צארת ... זיד Oxf 2629.40b > D

[42] [אלמתקדמה צ]רת יׄ[אׄ סנה] Oxf 2629.40b > D

פאטֹפרה[43] אללה[44] ביהויקים מלך יהודה ובבעץ[45] אנית בית אללה[46] פאתי[47] בהא[48] בלד שנער בית מעבודה ואלאניה אתי[49] בהא כֹזאנה מעבודה.[50]

קולה[51] **ויתן אדני בידו** (דניאל 1:2) ולם יקול **וינהו אמיתהו** אדֹא גמענא הדֹא אלקול מע קולה הנאך **ויאסרהו בנחשתים**[52] **להוליכו בבלה** (דה״ב 36:6) ולם יקול **ויוליכהו בבלה**[53] דלא גמיעא עלי[54] אנה כמא[55] קידה[56] ליחמלה מאת פי קידה[57] ואמר בסחבה והו בעד פי חדוד[58] ירושלם כמא קאל[59] הנאך **קבורת חמור**[60] **יקבר**[61] **סחוב והשלך מהלאה לשערי ירושלם**[62] (ירמ׳ 22:19). ומנע מן דפנה כמא קאל[63] **ונבלתו תהיה משלכת לחורב ביום ולקרח בלילה** (ירמ׳ 36:30). ולמוצֹע מא[64] דֹכר[65] אלכתאב דֹלך לם יגוז אן ידפן אבדא[66] עלאמה מן אלעקובה למא אחרק אלמגלה. וקולה **ומקצת כלי**

[43] פאצֹפרה Spiegel + Yeirin 209 + Morag
[44] [פאטפרה אלל]ה Oxf 2629.40b > D
[45] ובעץ Yeirin 209 + Oxf 2629.40b
[46] [אל]לה Oxf 2629.40b > D
[47] פאתא Yeirin 209 + Morag
[48] פא[תי ב]הא Oxf 2629.40b > D
[49] אתא Spiegel + Morag
[50] ואלאניה ... מעבודה Oxf 2629.40b > L
[51] [קו]לה Oxf 2629.40b > D
[52] בנחש Oxf 2629.40b
[53] בבלה Oxf 2629.40b > L
[54] עלי Oxf 2629.40b > L
[55] כ[מא] Oxf 2629.40b > D
[56] קיידה Yeirin 209
[57] בקידה Yeirin 209
[58] חדו[ד] Oxf 2629.40b > D
[59] כמק Oxf 2629.40b | כק Yeirin 209
[60] קבורת חמור Oxf 2629.40b > D
[61] וג׳ + Oxf 2629.40b
[62] סחוב ... ירושלם Oxf 2629.40b > L
[63] כמק Oxf 2629.40b | כק Yeirin 209
[64] מא Yeirin 209 > L
[65] [תהיה ... מא] ד[כ]ר Oxf 2629.40b > D | וכר Yeirin 209
[66] [לם יגוז] יד[פן אב]דא Oxf 2629.40b > D

בית האלהים[67] (דניאל 1:2) כם עדדהא. פנקול אלף ת̇צ̇ט̇[68]. והד̇ה שעבה תשעבת לנא מן ד̇כר אלכתאב לעדד אלכלים פי וקת רדהא כורש. וד̇לך[69] [...][70] גמלתהא[71] ה̇ אלאף ת̇ והי מקסומה ג̇ אקסאם [...].[72] והד̇א[73] תפצילהא. **אגרטלי זהב שלשים** (עזרא 1:9) והי [...].[74] **אגרטלי כסף אלף** (עזרא 1:9) והי מת̇להא. **מחלפים כ̇ט̇**[75] (עזרא 1:9) והי סכאכין [...][76] פי אלמשנה **בית החליפות ששם גונזין את הסכינין** (מידות IV:7) **כפורי זהב שלשים** (עזרא 1:10) והי דרוג. **כפורי כסף משנים ת̇י̇**[77] (עזרא 1:10) הי מת̇להא פד̇לך אלף ת̇צ̇ט̇.

ת̇ם אלף אניה מגמלה ג̇יר מפצלה והי קולה **כלים אחרים אלף** (עזרא 1:10) והו אלקסם אלת̇אני. ת̇ם מא בקי לתתמה ה̇ אלף ת̇ לקו̇ **כל כלים לזהב ולכסף ה̇ אלפים ת̇**[78] (עזרא 1:11) ועדדהא אלפין ת̇ת̇ק̇א̇ ולם פצלהא מנה והו מגמל. פלמא תאמלנא מא פי אלכתאב מן חמל אניה אלקדס אלי באבל וגדנא ד̇לך פי ג̇ דפעאת. אלאולי מע יהויקים כק̇ **ומכלי בית האלהים הביא נבוכדנצר ויתנם בהיכלו בבל** (דה״ב 36:7). ואלב̇ מע יכוניה. ואלג̇ מע צדקיה. קאל פיה **וכל כלי בית האלהים הגדולים והקטנים ואוצרות בית יוי ואוצרות בית האלהים המלך ושריו הכל הביא בבל** (דה״ב 36:18). פקלנא יסתקים אן תלך אלכלים אלמבסוטה **ואלה מספרם** (עזרא 1:9) הי אלתי מע יהויקים. ובאלגמלה אלת̇אניה **כלים אחרים אלף** (עזרא 1:10) הי אלתי מע יכניהו ובאקי אלה̇ אלף ת̇ הי אלתי מע צדקיהו. פלד̇לך לם יגמע אלגמלתין אד̇ המא פי דפעתין. וק̇ **ויביאם ארץ שנער בית אלהיו** (דניאל 1:2)

[67] אלים Oxf. 2629.40b

[68] תצט End of Oxf 2629.40b

[69] ודלך End of Yeirin 209

[70] [...] Yeirin 210 > D

[71] [ג]מלתהא Beginning of the readable part of Yeirin 210 (TS Ar 26.54d)

[72] [...]לה Yeirin 210 > D

[73] וה[ד]א Yeirin 210 > D

[74] [...] Yeirin 210 > D

[75] תשעה ועשרים MT

[76] [...] Yeirin 210 > D

[77] ארבע מאות ועשרה MT

[78] וארבע מאות MT

ען ישראל אלדׄין כאנו מע יהויקים וען אלכלים ידל אנהם מן אן יכון אלכלים אתי בהא מע אלסבי.[79]

Dn 1:3

ויאמר המלך לאשפנז רב סריסיו להביא מבני ישראל ומזרע המלוכה ומן הפרתמים.

ואמר[80] אלמלך אשפנז רייס כׄדמה באן יאתי[81] מן בני אסראיל ומן נסל אלמלך ואלבטארקה.

Dn 1:4

ילדים אשר אין בהם כל מאום וטובי מראה ומשכילים בכל חכמה וידעה דעת ומביני מדע ואשר כח בהם לעמד בהיכל המלך וללמדם ספר ולשון כשדים.

בשבאב ליס פיהם שיא[82] מן אלעיב וחסני[83] אלמנטׄר[84] וקד אטלעו פי כל עלם ויעלמון אלמערפה ויפהמונהא ומן פיהם קווה אן[85] יקימו פי היכל אלמלך ואן יעלמהם כׄט אלכסדאניין ולגׄתהם.

Dn 1:5

וימן להם המלך דבר יום ביומו צפת בג המלך ומיין משתיו ולגדלם שנים שלש ומקצתם יעמדו לפני המלך.

ווצׄף[86] להם אלמלך גאריא[87] יום ביום מן כׄבזה ואומה וכׄמר שרבה, ואן ירבון[88] כדׄאך תׄלאתׄ סנין פאדׄא אנקצׄת יקפון בין ידי אלמלך.

[79] אלסבי End of Yeirin 210 (TS Ar 26.54d)
[80] פאמר Spiegel
[81] יאתו Spiegel
[82] שי Spiegel
[83] וחסנא Spiegel
[84] אלמנצר Spiegel + Morag
[85] אן Spiegel > L
[86] פוצף Spiegel
[87] גארי Morag
[88] ירבו Spiegel

Dn 1:6
ויהי בהם מבני יהודה דניאל חנניה מישאל ועזריה.

פכאן פיהם מן בני יהודה דניאל חנניה מישאל ועזריה.

Dn 1:7
וישם להם שר הסריסים שמות ווישם לדניאל בלטשאצר ולחנניה שדרך ולמישאל מישך ולעזריה עבד נגו.

פלקבהם רייס אלכֿדם אלקאבא, פאמא דניאל בלטשצר[89] וחנניה שדרך ומישאל מישך ועזריה עבד[90] נגו.

Dn 1:8
וישם דניאל על לבו אשר לא יתגאל בפת בג המלך וביין משתיו ויבקש משר הסריסים אשר לא יתגאל.

פוצֿע דניאל פי נפסה אן לא יתלוותֿ בשי מן כֿבז אלמלך וארמה וכֿמר שרבה, פאלתמס מן רייס אלכֿדם אן לא ילזמה דֿלך.[91]

Dn 1:9
ויתן האלהים את דניאל לחסד ולרחמים לפני שר הסריסים.

פרזקה אללה חטֿא[92] ורחמה ענדה.

Dn 1:10
ויאמר שר הסריסים לדניאל ירא אני את אדני המלך אשר מנה את מאכלכם ואת משתיכם אשר למה יראה את פניכם זעפים מן הילדים אשר כגילכם וחיבתם את ראשי למלך.

[89] בלט שאצר Spiegel
[90] עביד Morag
[91] דאלך Spiegel
[92] חצאא Spiegel + Morag

פקאל רייס אלכ̇דם לדניאל כ̇איף אנא מן סיידי אלמלך אלד̇י וצ̇ף[93] מאכלכם ומשרובכם אלד̇י[94] ינט̇ר וגוהכם עאבסין[95] מן אלשבאב אלד̇י הם אקראנכם פתכ̇אטרו בראסי ללמלך.[96]

Dn 1:11

ויאמר דניאל אל המלצר אשר מנה שר הסריסים על דניאל חנניה מישאל ועזריה.

פקאל[97] דניאל ללכ̇זאן[98] אלד̇י ולאה ריס[99] אלכ̇דם עלי דניאל חנניה מישאל ועזריה.

Dn 1:12

נס נא את עבדיך ימים עשרה ויתנו לנו מן הזרעים ונאכלה ומים ונשתה.

אמתחן עבידך עשרה איאם יעטונא פיהא מן אלחבוב מא נאכל ומן אלמא מא נשרב.

Dn 1:13

ויראו לפניך מראינו ומראה הילדים האוכלים את פת בג המלך וכאשר תראה עשה עם עבדיך.

פתתביין לך סחנתנא וסחנה אלשבאב אכלי טעאם[100] אלמלך וארמה[101] ובחסב[102] מא תראה אסתעמלה מע עבידך.

Dn 1:14

וישמע להם לדבר הזה ויסם ימים עשרה.

[93] וצף Spiegel
[94] לם + Spiegel
[95] עאבסה Spiegel
[96] לאלמלך Spiegel + Morag
[97] וקאל Spiegel
[98] לאלכזאן Spiegel + Morag
[99] רייס Spiegel
[100] טעאים Spiegel
[101] ואדמה Spiegel
[102] ואדמה וחסאב Spiegel

פקבל מנהם קולהם הד̇א[103] ואמתחנהם עשרה איאם.

Dn 1:15
ומקצת ימים עשרה נראה מראיהם טוב ובריאי בשר מן כל הילדים האכלים את פת בג המלך.

פלמא אנקצ̇ת עשרה איאם תביינת סחנתהם צביחה ואבדאנהם צ̇כ̇מה אכת̇ר מן אלשבאב אכלי טעאם אלמלך וארמה.[104]

Dn 1:16
ויהי המלצר נשא את פת בגם ויין משתיהם ונתן להם זרענים.

פכאן[105] אלכ̇זאן יאכ̇ד̇ לנפסה כ̇בזהם וארמהם[106] וכ̇מר שרבהם ויעטיהם[107] חבובא.

Dn 1:17
והילדים האלה ארבעתם נתן להם האלהים מדע והשׂכל בכל ספר וחכמה ודניאל הבין בכל חזון וחלמות.

והאולי[108] אלשבאב אלארבעה רזקהם אללה מערפה ועקל פי כל כתאב וחכמה ויפצ̇להם דניאל בכל[109] חלם ורויא.

Dn 1:18
ולמקצאת הימים אשר אמר המלך להביאם ויביאם שר הסריסים לפני נבוכדנצר.

ולמא אנקצ̇ת אלאיאם אלד̇י אגלהם אלמלך אלי אן יחצ̇רו פאחצ̇רהם ראייס אלכ̇דם בין ידיי[110] בכ̇תנצר.

[103] הדא Spiegel > L
[104] ואדמה Spiegel
[105] וכאן Spiegel
[106] ואדמהם Spiegel + Morag
[107] ויעטהם Morag
[108] והולאי Spiegel
[109] פי כל Spiegel
[110] ידי Spiegel

Dn 1:19

וידבר אתם המלך ולא נמצא מכלם כדניאל חנניה מישאל ועזריה ויעמדו לפני המלך.

פכלמהם אלמלך ולם יגד פי[111] גמיעהם מת̇ל דניאל חנניה מישאל ועזריה פאלזמהם חצ̇רתה.

Dn 1:20

וכל דבר חכמת בינה אשר בקש מהם המלך וימצאם עשר ידות על כל החרטמים האשפים אשר בכל מלכותו.

וכל אמר וחכמה ופהם אלתמסה מנהם אלמלך וגדהם פיה עשרה אצ̇עאף עלי[112] סאיר[113] אלחכמא ואלמנגמין אלד̇י[114] פי גמיע ממלכתה.

Dn 1:21

ויהי דניאל עד שנת אחת לכורש המלך.

פאקאם דניאל אלי סנת אחדי[115] עשר[116] לכורש[117] אלמלך.

[....][118] **שאלתם**[119] **וישלח רזון בנפשם** (תה׳ 106:15). כד̇אך כאנו **הילדים היהודים האוכלים**[120] **את פת בג המלך** (ע׳ דניאל 1:15). והאולי אלד̇ יאכלון חבובא [...][121] אכת̇ר מנהם כלהם. וקולה **ולמקצת הימים אשר אמר**[122] **המלך להביאם** (דניאל 1:18) יעני בה אלג̇ אלסנין אלתי געלהא אגלא כק̇ **ולדגלם שנים שלש ומקצתם יעמדו לפני המלך** (דניאל 1:5).

[111] יוגד מן Spiegel

[112] גמיע + Spiegel

[113] סאיר > L Spiegel

[114] אלדין Spiegel

[115] אחד Spiegel

[116] עשר > L Spiegel

[117] לכרש Spiegel

[118] [...] TS NS 318.6a > D

[119] שאלתם Beginning of TS NS 318.6a | [ש]אלתם TS NS 318.6a > D

[120] ו[האוכ]לים TS NS 318.6a > D

[121] [...] TS NS 318.6a > D

[122] אמר TS NS 318.6a > D

וקד ינבגי אן נשרח מא נאל[123] אללוים [אלדי] יחתאגון אלי הֹ סנין תמאמא תֹם יכֹדמון כקֹ **מבן עשׂרים וחמש שנה ומעלה יבא לצבא צבאו** (במד׳ 8:24). וקאל **מבן שלשים שנה**[124] **ומעלה, יבוא**[125] **לעבוד** (במד׳ 4:47). והאולי [... ...][126] פנקול [...][127] הדֹא אכֹתיאר אלמלך בגֹיר תחריף.[128] תֹם נקול אללוים [...][129] לעבודה [...][130] קבל אלהֹ אלסנין [... ...][131] אלדֹ אלחכמה קבל אלגֹ סנין כקֹ **ומשׂכילים בכל חכמה** (דניאל 1:4).

וימצאם עשר ידות (דניאל 1:20) יעני בה אצֹעאפא כתֹירה לא [... ...][132] ודֹלך אן אלחרטמים כל ואחד מנהם קד בלגֹ מבלגֹא פי אלעלם. פאדֹא כאנת מבלגֹתהם גֹיר מתסאניה לם יגוז אן תכון אצֹעאפא[133] מתסאויה. תֹם נקול [... ...][134] דניאל [...][135] אלי גֹ סנין מן מלך כורש כמא יקול[136] **בשנת שלש לכורש מלך פרס דבר נגלה לדניאל**[137] (דניאל 10:1). פכיף[138] יקול ההנא[139] **ויהי דניאל לשנת**[140] **אחת לכורש המלך** (דניאל 1:21). פאגיב[141] ען דֹלך גואבין. אחדהמא אנה אקאם פי בבל[142] אלי אלסנה אלאולי מן מלך כורש ובעד דֹלך [...][143] ואלתֹאני אן יכון אקאם[144] פי כֹדמה אלסלטאן אלי סנה אחדי[145]

123 נאל Uncertain lesson
124 ש[נה] TS NS 318.6a > D
125 הבא MT
126 [... ...] TS NS 318.6a > D
127 [...] TS NS 318.6a > D
128 תחריך Another possible reading
129 ל[...] TS NS 318.6a > D
130 [..]ל[..]תה TS NS 318.6a > D
131 [... ...] TS NS 318.6a > D
132 עש[... ...] TS NS 318.6a > D
133 א[צ]עאפא TS NS 318.6a > D
134 [... ...] TS NS 318.6a > D
135 [...] TS NS 318.6a > D
136 [י]קול TS NS 318.6a > D
137 לדניאל Beginning of the readable part of Oxf 2629.39a | לנ׳ Oxf 2629.39a
138 וכיף TS NS 318.6a
139 הא[הנא] TS NS 318.6a > D
140 שנת TS NS 318.6a
141 לשנת ... פאגיב Oxf 2629.39a > D
142 [אנה ...ב]בל Oxf 2629.39a > D
143 [...] Oxf 2629.39a > D

לכורש לאנה נזול מלכות[146] בבל כאן ת̇אבתא[147] עלי [... ...][148] לה נבוכ̇דנצר[149] אד̇ יקול[150] **בשנה שלוש לבלשצר**[151] (דניאל 8:1) **ואקום ואעשה**[152] **את מלכת המלך**[153] (דניאל 8:27). ודריוש זאדה[154] פגעלה[155] **שליט תלתא**[156] **במלכותא**[157] (ע׳ דניאל 5:7.16). אלי אן גא כורש פאזאלה. ואלת̇אני אן יכון אקאם פי בבל אלי **שנת ג̇ לכורש**.[158] תם אלגזא אלאול.

144 [אחדהמא … א]קאם TS NS 318.6a > D

145 [סנה אח]די TS NS 318.6a > D

146 [נזול מלכו]ת TS NS 318.6a > D

147 [ת]בתא TS NS 318.6a > D

148 [… …] TS NS 318.6a and Oxf 2629.39a > D

149 נבוכד Beginning of Antonin 1

150 [אד] יק[ול] TS NS 318.6a > D

151 בשנת … לבלשצר Oxf 2629.39a > D

152 וג̇ +Antonin 1

153 ואקום … המלך Antonin 1 > D

154 זאדה End of TS NS 318.6a

155 Beginning of TSNS 318.6b

156 תלתא Antonin 1 > L

157 במלכותה Antonin 1

158 ואלתאני…לכורש TSNS 318.6a and Oxf 2629.39a > L

נץ אלגזא אלת'אני.

Dn 2:1

ובשנת שתים למלכות נבוכדנצר חלם נבוכדנצר חלמות ותתפעם רוחו ושנתו נהיתה עליו.

ופי[1] אלסנה אלת'אניה[2] מן מלך בכ'תנצר[3] ראי[4] חלמא פכרב רוחה ותנג'ץ נומה.

Dn 2:2

ויאמר המלך לקרא לחרטומים ולאשפים ולמכשפים ולכשדים להגיד למלך חלמתיו ויבאו ויעמדו לפני המלך.

פאמר באן ידעא באלחכמא ואלמנגמין ואלסחרה ואלכסדאניין[5] ליערפונה[6] רויאה[7] פגאו ווקפו[8] בין ידיה.

אול[9] מא נפחץ ענה קולה[10] **ובשנת שתים**[11] **למלכות נבוכדנצר**[12] (דניאל 2:1). פנקול אד' קד תביין אן נבוכ'דנצר[13] כאן אול מלכה פי אלסנה אלראבעה[14]

[1] פי Spiegel
[2] אלב Antonin 1 + TS NS 318.6b
[3] בכתנ' Antonin 1 ו נבוכדנצר TS NS 318.6b
[4] ראא Morag
[5] ואלכסדאנין Antonin 1
[6] ליערפוה Antonin 1 + Spiegel + TS NS 318.6b
[7] ריאה TS NS 318.6b
[8] פוקפו Oxf 2629.39a + Antonin 1
[9] אול TS NS 318.6b < D
[10] קול Oxf 2629.39a
[11] ש Oxf 2629.39a
[12] נבו' וג' Oxf 2629.39a ו נבו' חלם Antonin 1
[13] נבוכדנ' Oxf 2629.39a ו נבוכ' Antonin 1
[14] אלס[נה אלראבעה] TS NS 318.6b < D

ליהויקים. ואנמא[15] סבי דניאל ומן מעה פי סנה יאׄ[16] ליהויקים[17] והי[18] אלסנה אלח̇[19] למלכה. פכיף כאנו ענדה פי אלסנה אלת̇אניה[20] מן מלכה ולם יסבהם[21] בעד בל[22] לם[23] יטיעה[24] יהויקים בעדא. פנקול הד̇ה **שנה שתים לחרבות ירושלם** (ע' דניאל 9:2)[25] לאן[26] אלכתאב[27] כמא וגדנאה יורך̇ לבבל כד̇אך יורך̇[28] לירושלם. וכאן חיניד̇ לדניאל ענדה יג̇ סנה עלי מא יוגבה אלחסאב. ולד̇לך געלנא פי ענואן הד̇א אלכתאב[29] אעני[30] אלתפסיר אן פיה חואדת̇ אלף ש̇פ̇ו̇. אד̇ אול כשף אלחואדת̇ מן **שנת שתים לחרבות ירושלם**[31] (ע' דניאל 9:2). ולד̇לך[32] נ̇ת̇[33] קבל[34] **אשרי המחכה** (דניאל 12:12).

וקולה[35] **חלם נבוכדנצר**[36] **חלמות**[37] (דניאל 2:1) הי רויא ואחדה.[38] לכנהא למא אנקסמת ארבעה[39] אקסאם סמאהא **חלמות**.[40] ותעדידה[41] ללכשׂדים[42] מע צנוף

[15] ואמא Antonin 1
[16] אחדי עשר TS NS 318.6b
[17] ליהויק Antonin 1
[18] ופי TS NS 318.6b
[19] אלתמנה Oxf 2629.39a
[20] אלב Antonin 1
[21] אלסנה אלתאיה מן מלכה ולם יסבהם TS NS 318.6b > D
[22] בל Antonin 1 > D
[23] לא Antonin 1
[24] [יט]עה Antonin 1 > D
[25] ודלך ב[יי]ן קבל דשרת המחכ[ה] + Oxf 2629.39a
[26] End of Oxf 2629.39a
[27] Beginning of Oxf.2629.39b
[28] לחרבות +Antonin 1
[29] אלכת Antonin 1
[30] אלכתאב אעני Oxf 2629.39b > L
[31] ירו Antonin 1
[32] לחר ירושלם [...לחרבות ירושלם] ולדלך TS NS 318.6b > L homeoteleuton
[33] בנ̇ TS NS 318.6b
[34] תאריך + Oxf 2629. 39b
[35] וקול TS NS 318.6b + Oxf 2629. 39b
[36] ובוכד Antonin 1 | Oxf 2629.39b נבו̇
[37] חלומות Oxf 2629.39b
[38] [וא]חד[ה] TS NS 318.6b
[39] ד Antonin 1 + Oxf 2629.39b
[40] חלומות Oxf 2629. 39b | [חלמות ו]תעדידהא ללכסדים TS NS 318.6b
[41] [ות]עדי[דה] TS NS 318.6b | ותעדידדה Antonin 1
[42] ללכסדים TS NS 318.6b

אלעלמא ידל עלי אן הד׳א אלאסם כאן יקום[43] להם מקאם אלאסם אלעלמי כקולך אצחאב אלרואק. וקולה[44] **להגיד**[45] **למלך חלומתיו**[46] (דניאל 2:2) עלי פציח[47] מא טאלבהם בה[48] לאנה לם ילתמם מנהם תאוילא[49] פקט, בל נפס אלרויה, מא הי. ולא[50] מן אגל אנה נסיהא. לכנה אמתחנהם[51] בד׳לך. לאנה לו כאן נסיהא לם[52] יאמן אן יכ׳ילו לה רויא מא[53] פתתשבה[54] לה[55] אן[56] לעלהם[57] אן יצדקוה[58] פלא יתבין צדקהם. ולכן[59] באלג׳ פי מחנתהם. וענד[60] אלתצפח וגדנא הולא אלג׳ מלוך כל ואחד באלג׳ פי מדנה[61] אלעלמא פי אמר אלרויא[62] אכת׳ר מן אלאכ׳ר. אמא פרעה פקאל להם אלרויא ואלתמס אלתפסיר כמא קאל[63] **ויספר פרעה להם את חלמו** (בר׳ 41:8). ואמא נבוכ׳דנצר[64] פאסתקל[65] אלתאויל[66] ואלתמס ד׳את[67] אלרויא[68] כק׳[69] **להגיד למלך**[70] **חלומותיו** (דניאל

[43] יקום TS NS 318.6b

[44] וקול Oxf 2629.39b

[45] א[צחאב ... להג]יד TS NS 318.6b > D | וקו להן[גיד] Antonin 1 > D

[46] חל Oxf 2629.39b

[47] [פצי]ח TS NS 318.6b > D

[48] טאלבהם בה TS NS 318.6b > D

[49] [מנהם תא]וילא TS NS 318.6b > D

[50] פקט בל נפס אלרויא מא הי לא TS NS 318.6b > D

[51] אמת[חנהם] Antonin 1 > D

[52] לם TS NS 318.6b > D

[53] יקולו ... מא TS NS 318.6b > D

[54] פתשתבה TS NS 318.6b

[55] פתתש[בה לה] Antonin 1 | או + Antonin 1

[56] אן Antonin 1and TS NS 318.6b > D

[57] ל[ה] לעלה[ם] TS NS 318.6b > D

[58] יצ[דקוה] TS NS 318.6b > D | יצדקוה End of the readable part of TS NS 318.6b

[59] ולכנה Antonin 1

[60] מחנ[תהם וענד] Antonin 1> D

[61] מדינה אלעליל Antonin 1

[62] א[מר אלרויא] Antonin 1

[63] כמק Oxf 2629.39b | כמ[א קאל] Antonin 1

[64] נבו Antonin 1

[65] אלתפסיר + Antonin 1

[66] אלתאויל Antonin 1 > L

[67] ואלת[מס ד׳את] Antonin 1 > D

[68] אל[רוי]א Oxf 2629.39b > D

[69] כמק Oxf 2629.39b

[70] למלך End of Oxf 2629.39b

2:2). אלי אן [...][71] דׄלך [...][72] לדניאל אדׄא מאכוד [...][73] פאסתקאל אלתאויל. בל דׄאת אלרויה. פטאלב [...][74] אל רגלא מן א..... מא ירא במנאם מן קבל אן יראהא, ולמא לם [... ...][75] נכות פי דׄלך אלוקת אסתעמל שמואל חילה באבא מן אלטיף פקאל לה מא שגׄל קלבה ... אכׄד פכרה חתי תעלק בה פראה. והו אן קאל [...][76] וידכׄלה אלי בית רוחה פיה מן אלכׄוף. [... ...][77]

Dn 2:3
ויאמר להם המלך חלום חלמתי ותפעם רוחי לדעת את החלום.

פקאל להם אלמלך קד ראית רויא פכרב רוחי אלי אן אערפה.

Dn 2:4
וידברו הכשדים למלך ארמית מלכא לעלמין חיי אמר חלמא לעבדיך ופשרא נחוא.

פכלמוה באלאנבטייה[78] אטאל אללה בקא אלמלך קל אלרויא לעבידך ונכׄברך[79] בתפסירהא.

Dn 2:5
ענה מלכא ואמר לכשדיא מלתא מני אזדא הן לא תהודעונני חלמא ופשרה הדמין תתעבדון ובתיכון נולי יתשמון.

אגאבהם וקאל[80] קד גר מני אלאמר באנכם אן לם תערפוני אלרויא ותפסירהא אעצׄא[81] תפעלון וביותכם צואפי יתציירון.[82]

71 [..]פי כנא Antonin 1 > D
72 [... ...] Antonin 1 > D
73 [...] Antonin 1 > D
74 [...] Antonin 1 > D
75 [... ...] Antonin 1 > D
76 [...] Antonin 1 > D
77 אלכׄוף End of the readable part of Antonin 1
78 באלנבטיה Spiegel
79 נכברך Spiegel
80 פקאל Spiegel
81 אעצאא Spiegel
82 תציירון Spiegel

Dn 2:6

והן חלמא ופשריה תהחון מתנן ונבזבה ויקר שגיא תקבלון מן קדמי להן חלמא ופשרה החוני.

ואן אלרויה ותפסירהא תכׄברון[83] הבאת וגואיז ווקאר[84] ועז כביר[85] תרפעון מן קדאמי לדׄלך אלרויא ותפסירהא אכׄברוני.

Dn 2:7

ענו תנינות ואמרין מלכא חלמא יאמר לעבדוהי ופשרה נהחוה.

אגאבוה תׄאניה וקאלו אלמלך יקול אלרויא[86] לעבידה[87] פנכׄברה[88] בתפסירהא.

Dn 2:8

ענה[89] מלנא ואמר מן יציב ידע אנה די עדנא אנתון זבנין כל קבל די חזיתון די אזדא מני מלתא.

אגאבהם פקאל[90] אנני[91] לאעלם[92] יקינא אנכם תשתרון סאעתכם ודׄאך[93] למא ראיתם גר אלאמר מני.

Dn 2:9

די הן חלמא לא תהודענני חדא היא דתכון ומלה כדבה ושחיתה הזמנתון למימר קדמי עד די עדנה ישתנה להן חלמא אמרו ואנדע די פשרה תהחונני.

83 תכברוני Spiegel
84 ווקר Spiegel
85 ווקר ועז כתׄיר Spiegel
86 לעבודה + Spiegel
87 לעבידה L < Morag ׀ לעבודה Spiegel
88 פנכברה Spiegel
89 ענה Beginning of Antonin 2
90 וקאל Spiegel
91 אני Antonin 2 + Spiegel
92 לא אעלם Antonin 2
93 ודאלך Spiegel

באנכם אן לם תערפוני אלרויא פסבילכם ואחד[94] ואנמא אעתדתם[95] כלאם כדֿב וזור[96] אן תקולוה בין ידי אלי אן תתגֿיר[97] אלסאעה ותנגלי לכן קולו לי דֿאת אלרויה חתי אעלם אנכם צאדקין פי אכֿבארי בתפסירהא.[98]

Dn 2:10

ענו כשדיא קדם מלכא ואמרין לא איתי אנש על יבשתא די מלת מלכא יוכל להחויה כל קבל די כל מלך רב ושליט מלה כדנה לא שאל לכל חרטם ואשף וכשדי.

אגאבוה אלכסדאניין[99] בחצֿרה אלמלך וקאלו ליס אנסאן[100] עלי אלארץֿ יקדר אן יכֿבר במא קאל אלמלך ודֿלך[101] אן כל מלך גליל וסלטאן[102] לם יסאל[103] קט מתֿל הדֿא אלקול[104] לאי חכים או מנגם או כסדאני.

Dn 2:11

ומלתא[105] די מלכא שאל יקירה ואחרן לא איתי די יחוינה קדם מלכא להן אלהין די מדורהון אם בסרא לא איתוהי.

ואלאמר אלדֿי יסאל[106] ענה אלמלך עזיז וליס אכֿר סואנא[107] יקדר אן יכֿבר במא[108] קאל אלמלך[109] אלא[110] אלמלאיכה אלדֿי[111] ליס מסכנהם מע אלנאס.

[94] ואחדא Spiegel | ואחדה Antonin 2
[95] אעדדתם Antonin 2
[96] אלכדב ואלזור Spiegel
[97] תתגֿייר Spiegel
[98] ותפסירהא Spiegel
[99] אגאבו אלכסדאניין Spiegel | אגאב אלכסדאנין Antonin 2
[100] אנסן Antonin 2
[101] ודאלך Spiegel + Morag
[102] עצים + Spiegel
[103] יסל Antonin 2
[104] אלאמר Spiegel
[105] Beginning of Yeirin 211 (Camb. MS TS Misc. 5.128)
[106] יסל Antonin 2
[107] איצֿ + Yeirin 211 and Spiegel
[108] יכברה במא Yeirin 211 + Spiegel | יכברה בהא Antonin 2
[109] אלמלך > L Antonin 2 and Spiegel
[110] אלי Yeirin 211
[111] אלתי Antonin 2 + Yeirin 211

Dn 2:12

כל קביל דנא מלכא בנס וקצף סגי ואמר להובדא לכל חכימי בבל.

פענד ד̇לך[112] שאט אלמלך וסכ̇ט[113] גדא ואמר בקתל[114] גמיע חכאם באבל.

Dn 2:13

ודתא נפקת וחכימיא מתקטלין ובעו דניאל וחברוהי להתקטלה.

וכ̇רג אלתוקיע בד̇לך[115] והוד̇א יקתלון אלחכמא וכאד דניאל ואצחאבה אן יקתלו.[116]

גמיע הד̇ה אלמכ̇אטבאת אלתי[117] גרת בין אלמלך ואלחכמא ט̇אהרה[118] בינה מסתג̇ניה[119] ען אן נעוד עליהא בשרח ולא סימא אנא[120] קד צ̇מננאהא[121] חרופא

קד דלת עלי אג̇ראצ̇הא. ואעט̇ם[122] מא פיהא כלאם נבטי יסתעסר[123] עלי מן ליס לה[124] בה דרבה. וליס למת̇לה אכ̇ר גנא[125] הד̇א אלתפסיר. ומע ד̇אך פנקול אי ש̇י בין גואב אלקום אלד̇י אחדהמא **אימר חלמא לעבדך ופשרא נחוא**[126] (דניאל 2:4) ואלאכ̇ר **מלכא חלמא יאמר לעבדוהי ופשרה נהחוא**[127] (דניאל 2:7) פנקול אנהם[128] אולא[129] כ̇אטבוה באסתקבאל עלי אמר יכ̇צה. ובעד ד̇לך

[112] דאלך Spiegel + Morag

[113] וצכט Morag

[114] באבאדה Antonin 2 + Yeirin 211 + Spiegel

[115] בדאלך Spiegel + Morag

[116] יקתלון Spiegel

[117] אלדי Antonin 2

[118] טאהרא Antonin 2

[119] ביינה מסתג̇נייה Yeirin 211

[120] אנה Antonin 2

[121] צמננהא Antonin 2

[122] ואעצם Yeirin 211

[123] יסתער Yeirin 211

[124] לה Yeirin 211 > L

[125] אכרגנא Another possible lesson

[126] ופש נחוה Antonin 2

[127] ופש נהחוה Antonin 2

[128] אלי + Yeirin 211

[129] אולא Yeirin 211 > L

כּאטבוה בלא אסתקבאל יענונה אן הדׄא סביל כל מלך[130] אן יקץ אלרויה ותפסר לה. ונקול איצׄא[131] לם בדאהם[132] באלסיה קבל אלחסנה? אעני **הן לא תהודעונני**[133] **חלמא** (דניאל 2:5) קבל[134] **והן חלמא ופשריה תהחון**[135] (דניאל 2:6)? פנקול אן אלאצל[136] מטאלבתהם[137] אנמא כאנת מחנה מנה להם. ואמא **ובעו** (דניאל 2:13) ״וכאד״[138] פהו[139] פי[140] לגׄה אלתרגום במנזלה[141] **והאניה חשבה להשבר** (יונה 1:4) פי לפט[142] אלמקרא[143] ומתרגם[144] **ואלפא בעיא לאתברא**[145] אלדׄי תפסירה ״כאדת אן תכסר״.[146] תׄם קאל

Dn 2:14

באדין דניאל התיב עטא וטעם לאריוך רב טבחיא די מלכא די נפק לקטלא לחכימי בבל.

חיניד רפע דניאל אלקצה[147] אלי אריוך רייס[148] סיאפי אלמלך אלדׄי נפד[149] אן יקתל חכמא באבל.[150]

[130] יך + Yeirin 211
[131] איצׄ Antonin 2
[132] בד[א]הם Yeirin 211 > D
[133] תהודע Antonin 2
[134] ובעדה + Yeirin 211
[135] ופשׄ תהחונן Antonin 2
[136] [אן אל]אצל Antonin 2 > D
[137] מ[..]ל[...]הם Yeirin 211
[138] וכאד Antonin 2 > D
[139] פאנה Antonin 2
[140] פי Yeirin 211 > D
[141] כמנזלה Yeirin 211
[142] לפץ Yeirin 211
[143] אלמקרא End of Yeirin 211
[144] ומתרגם Beginning of Yeirin 212 (Camb. MS TS Misc. 5.128)
[145] אלמקרא ... לאתברא Antonin 2 > D
[146] תנכסר Yeirin 212
[147] קצה Spiegel + Yeirin 212 | [חיניד... אלקצ]ה Antonin 2 > D
[148] ריס Antonin 2
[149] פי + Antonin 2
[150] חכמא באבל Antonin 2 > D

Dn 2:15

עני ואמר לאריוך שליטא די מלכא על מה דתא מהחצפה מן קדם מלכא אידין מלתא הודע אריוך לדניאל.

יסאלה[151] ויקול עלי מאדא אלאמר חאת מן ענד אלמלך, חיניד ערפה אריוך אלקצה.[152]

Dn 2:16

ודניאל על ובעא מן מלכא די זמן ינתן ליה ופשרא להחואה למלכא.

פתסבב דניאל אלי אן סאל אלמלך אן ינטרה[153] אגלא חתי יערפה[154] אלרויה[155] ותפסירהא.

Dn 2:17

באידין דניאל לביתיה אזל ולחנניה מישאל ועזריה חברוהי מילתא הודע.

חיניד צאר דניאל אלי ביתה וערף חנניה מישאל[156] ועזריה אצחאבה אלקצה.[157]

Dn 2:18

ורחמין למבעי מן קדם אלה שמיה על רזא רנא די לא יהובדון דניאל וחברוהי עם שאר חכימי בבל.

ואגתמעו אן ילתמסו אלרחמה מן ענד אלרב[158] פי הדא[159] אלסר לאלא[160] יהלכון דניאל ואצחאבה מע באקי חכמא באבל.

[151] יסלה Antonin 2

[152] [חיניד.... אלק]צה Antonin 2 > D

[153] ינצרה Spiegel + Morag

[154] [אן ינטרה ... יערפ]ה Antonin 2 > D

[155] אלרויא Antonin 2 + Yeirin 212 + Spiegel

[156] [דניאל ... מי]שאל Antonin 2 > D

[157] אלקצה End of the readable part of Antonin 2

[158] אללה Yeirin 212

[159] הדי Morag

[160] ללא Yeirin 212 + Morag ׀ לילא Spiegel

Dn 2:19
אדין לדניאל בחזוה די ליליא רזא גלי אדין דניאל בריך לאלה שמיא.

חיניד׳ כשף אללה ד׳לך[161] אלסר לדניאל פי רויה אלליל פסבח דניאל רב אלסמא.

Dn 2:20
עני דניאל ואמר להוי שמיא די אלהא מברך מן עלמא ועד עלמא די חוכמתא וגבורתא די ליה היא.

באן קאל יכון אסם אללה מבארכא מן אול[162] אלעאלם אלי אכ׳רה אלד׳י אלחכמה ואלגברות[163] לה.

Dn 2:21
והוא מהשני עידניא[164] וזמניא מהעדה מלכין ומהקים מלכין יהיב חכמתא לחכימין ומנדעה לידעי בינה.

והו מג׳ייר אלאוקאת ואלאזמאן עאזל מלוך ונאצב מלוך מעטי אלחכמה ללחכמא ואלעלם לעארפי אלפהם.

Dn 2:22
והוא[165] גלי עמיקתא ומסתרתא ידע מא בחשוכא ונהורא עמיה שרי.

והו כאשף אלעמיקאת ואלמסתוראת יעלם מא פי אלט׳למאת[166] ואלנור סאכן ענדה.

Dn 2:23
לך אלה אבהתי מהודי משכח אנא די חכמתא וגבורתא יהבת לי וכען הודעתני די בעינא מינך די מלת מלכא הודעתנא.

לך יא אלאה אבאינא[167] שאכר מסבח[168] למא קד[169] רזקתני מן אלחכמה ואלגברת[170] ואלאן ערפתני מא סאלתך והי מסאלה אלמלך.

[161] דאלך Spiegel + Morag
[162] אוול Spiegel
[163] ואלגברווה Morag + Spiegel | ואלגברוה Yeirin 212
[164] עידניא End of Yeirin 212
[165] והוא Beginning of Antonin 3
[166] אלצלמאת Spiegel + Morag
[167] אלה אבאיי אנא Antonin 3

Dn 2:24

כל קביל דנא דניאל על אריוך די מני מלכא להיובדא לחכימי בבל אזל וכין אמר לה וכין אמר ליה לחכימי בבל אל תהובד העילני קדם מלכא ופשרא למלכא אחוי.

פענד[171] דׄלך[172] צאר דניאל אלי אריוך אלדׄי ולאה אלמלך ליביד חכמא באבל פקאל לה[173] לא תהלך[174] אחדא מנהם אדכׄלני אלי אלמלך אערפה אלרויה ותפסירהא.

Dn 2:25

אידין אריוך בהתבהלא הנעל לדניאל קדם מלכא וכין אמר ליה כי השכיחית גבר די מן בני גלותא די יהודי די פשרא למלכא יהודע.

חיניׄד אריוך[175] במבאדרה אדכׄל דניאל אלי אלמלך וקאל לה אני[176] וגדת רגלא[177] מן אהל גלוה[178] אליהוד ודׄכר[179] אנה יערף אלמלך אלרויה ותפסירהא.

Dn 2:26

עני מלכא ואמר לדניאל די שמיא בלט שצר האיתךכהיל להודעותני חלמא די חזית ופשריה.

פאבתדאה[180] אלמלך וקאל יא דניאל אלדׄי לקבך[181] בלטשצאר הל תקדר אן תערפני אלרויא אלתי[182] ראיתהא ותפסירהא.

168 מ[ס]בח Morag > D ו ומסבח Spiegel
169 קד Antonin 3 > L
170 ואלגברווה Spiegel + Morag ו ואלגבורה Antonin 3
171 ענד Spiegel
172 דאלך Spiegel + Morag
173 פקאל לה Spiegel > L
174 תביד Antonin 3 + Spiegel
175 אמיוך Antonin 3
176 קד Antonin 3 and Spiegel +
177 רגל Spiegel + Morag
178 אלגלוה Morag
179 ידכר Antonin 3 + Spiegel
180 אבתדאה Spiegel
181 דניאל אלדי לקבך Antonin 3 and Spiegel > L
182 אלדי Spiegel

Dn 2:27
ענה דניאל קדם מלכא ואמר לזה די מלכא שאיל לא חכימין אשפין חרטומין גזרין יכלין להחואה למלכא.

אגאב דניאל וקאל אלסר אלדׄי אלתמס[183] אלמלך לא אלחכמא ואלמנגמין ואלכסראניין[184] יקדרון אן יכׄברון בה.

Dn 2:28
ברם איתי אלה בשמיה גלי רזין והודע למלכא נבוכדנצר מה דא להוי באחרית יומיא חלמך וחזוי רישך על משכבך דנא הוא.

לכן[185] אללה[186] אלדׄי[187] פי אלסמא[188] וכאשף[189] אלאסראר ערף בכׄתנצר מא[190] סיכון פי אכׄר[191] אלזמאן לרויאך ומא נטׄרתה עינאך[192] עלי מצׄגעך הו הדׄא[193] אלדׄי אקולה.

פסרת **התיב עטא וטעם** (דניאל 2:14) ״רפע[194] קצה.״ מתׄל קולה[195] פי **רחום בעל טעם** (עזרא 4:8) אנה רפע קצה. ואנמא[196] זאד פי אמר דניאל **התיב** (דניאל 2:14) אדׄ הו מן חאשיה[197] אלמלך וקד ישאר[198] אליהם בהדׄה אללפטׄה אדׄ יקול **חכם עצל בעיניו**[199] **משבעה משיבי טעם**[200] (משלי 26:16). ומסלתה

[183] ילתמסה Antonin 3 ׀ אלתמסה Spiegel
[184] ואלכסדאנין Antonin 3
[185] לא כן Spiegel
[186] אללאה Morag ׀ אלאלאה Spiegel
[187] אלדׄי > L Antonin 3
[188] לכן פי אלסמא רב Antonin 3
[189] כאשף Spiegel ׀ יכשף Antonin 3
[190] אלמלך בכׄתנצר אלמלך במא Spiegel ׀ בכׄתנצר אלמלך מא Antonin 3
[191] אלאכׄר Spiegel
[192] נצׄרתה עינאך Morag ׀ נצׄרא עיניך Spiegel ׀ נטׄרא עינאך Antonin 3
[193] הדׄי Spiegel + Morag
[194] רפע TS NS > D ׀ [רפ]ע Beginning of the readable part of TS NS 285.21c 285.21c
[195] קׄו Antonin 3
[196] ואמא TS NS 285.21c
[197] התׄ[יב... חאשיה] TS NS 285.21c > D
[198] ישאר TS NS 285.21c > D
[199] וג׳ + TS NS 285.21c
[200] מי׳ משיבי טע Antonin 3

לה **על מה דתא מהחצפה**[201] (דניאל 2:15) ידל[202] עלי אן אריוך לם יכן יבין למן[203] יקתלה מן אלעלמא אי שי דׄנבה אדׄ לם ידכׄלן כלהם אלי אלמלך. וקולה[204] פי גׄ מואצׄע מן[205] הדׄה אלקצה **פשרה** פקט[206] עני **חלמא ופשרה** (דניאל 2:5.6). ואנמא אכׄתצר. והי **זמן ינתן לה**[207] **ופשרא** (דניאל 2:16), **העלני**[208] **קדם מלכא ופשרא למלכא אחוי** (דניאל 2:24), **ודי פשרא למלכא יהודע** (דניאל 2:25).[209] לכן אלתחציל חין[210] וקע בין ידי אלמלך קאל **חלמא די חזית ופשרה**[211] (דניאל 2:26). ונקול[212] [למדׄא] גסר[213] דניאל עלי מסלת אלתאגיל והו לא יעלם הל ינכשף לה אלסר[214] אם לא. פנגיב ען דׄלך[215] לסבבין. אחדהמא אסתדפאע אלמאלה אלעאגל. ואלתׄאני[216] אלתכלאן עלי רבה.

ואמא תסמיה רבה פי הדׄא אלספר ופי עזרא **אלה**[217] **שמיא** (דניאל 2:19) **אלהי השמים** (עזרא 1:2) פהו עלי מא עאדתנא[218] אן נעללה באן אמתנא קבל[219] אן תציר כתׄרה[220] כאנת תסמי אללה **אלהי השמים**. כקולה[221] **אלהי השמים אשר**[222] **לקחני**[223] (בר׳ 24:7). פלמא צארת גמאעה קאלת[224] **אלהי**

[201] מהתחצפא TS NS 285.21c

[202] ידל TS NS 285.21c > D

[203] יכ[ן יבין למ]ן TS NS 285.21c > D

[204] וק Antonin 3

[205] [מ]ן TS NS 285.21c > D

[206] אלק[צה פשרא פקט] TS NS 285.21c > D

[207] ליה Morag

[208] העילני Morag

[209] והי ... יהודע TS NS 285.21c > L

[210] אלת[חציל חין] Antonin 3 > D

[211] ופשרא TS NS 285.21c

[212] ונק[ול] Antonin 3 > D

[213] ו[נקול ... גס]ר TS NS 285.21c > D

[214] אלסר Antonin 3 > D

[215] ען דלך Antonin 3 > D

[216] אלמ[סלה אלעאגל ואלתׄאני] Antonin 3 > D

[217] אלספר ופי עזרא אלה Antonin 3 > D

[218] [עאד]תנה TS NS 285.21c > D

[219] נעללה באן אמתנא קבל TS NS 285.21c > D

[220] כ[תׄרה] TS NS 285.21c > D

[221] כק Antonin 3

[222] אל[הי השמים אשר] Antonin 3 > D

[223] כקולה ... לקחני TS NS 285.21c > L

השמים ואלהי הארץ. פלמא[225] גלת[226] ותבדדת רד[227] אלאשארה אלי **אלהי השמים ואלה שמיא**. פנקול דניאל ונחמיה וכורש וארתחשסתא[228] וגֹירהם וכדֹלך תסביח[229] דניאל בהדֹה אלחֹ מעאני הי עלי מא ישאכל חאל[230] אלגלות[231] וחאל אלחאגה. ועלי אן מעאני[232] שתי תתנאזעהא לאן[233] אלארץֹ משאבה אלחאגה ואלגלות. פיכון קולה **מהשני עידניא וזמניא** (דניאל 2:21) באזא מא שאהד מן תבדיל זמאן דולה בני אסראיל בדולה אלכסדאנין. ויכון קולה **מהעדא מלכין ומהקים מלכין** (דניאל 2:21) למא שאהד מן חול צדקיה[234] ותמליך נבוכֹדנצר. ויכון קולה **יהב חכמה לחכימין**[235] (דניאל 2:21) יעני בה האולא אלדֹי נאשדהם חכימין הו אלדֹי אלזמהם[236] חכמה צארו בהא חכימין פי אלחאל אלתֹאניה. כקול אלקאיל[237] בנית הדֹה אלדאר ליס יעני אנה בנאהא והי דאר. ואנמא יעני אנה בנא בקעה[238] פצארת דארא פי אלחאל אלתֹאניה. וכקול[239] אליפז **ובגדי ערומים תפשיט** (איוב 22:6) מן אין ללעראיא תֹיאב, לכן יסלךֹ תֹיאב[240] אללאבסין פיצירון עראיא פי אלחאל אלתֹאני.[241] וכדֹלך יקול[242] עמוס **ולעות מאזני מרמה** (עמוס 8:5). ופסר אלמיזאן פיציר **מרמה** פי[243] אלחאל אלתֹאני.[244] וכדֹלך קול ישעיה[245] **נותן**

[224] קאל Antonin 3

[225] אלהי ... פלמא Antonin 3 > D

[226] גלת TS NS 285.21c > D

[227] רד TS NS 285.21c > D

[228] וארתחשסת Antonin 3

[229] [ת]סביח TS NS 285.21c > D

[230] תסביח ... חאל Antonin 3 > D

[231] אלגלות End of the readable part of Antonin 3

[232] מעני TS NS 285.21c

[233] לא אן TS NS 285.21c

[234] צדק[יה] TS NS 285.21c > D

[235] לח TS NS 285.21c

[236] אלזמהם Beginning of Antonin 4 | [אל]זמהם TS NS 285.21c > D

[237] א...ת + TS NS 285.21c

[238] יע[ני אנה] בנא [בקעה] TS NS 285.21c > D

[239] [אלתאניה וכק]ול TS NS 285.21c > D

[240] תיאב, לכן יסלך תיאב TS NS 285.21c > D

[241] אלב Antonin 4

[242] יקול Antonin 4 > L

[243] ופסר ... מרמה TS NS 285.21c > D

[244] אלב Antonin 4

[245] ישעיהו Antonin 4

נשמה לעם עליה (יש׳ 42:5) פי אחואלהם אלתٌואני. **ומנדעה לידעי בינה** (דניאל 2:21) יעני[246] מן יחסן[247] יפהם לנפסה ויפהם גֹירה. אדֹ אלפהם ואלאפהאם מתסאויאן פי לפטֹ אלעבראני. אדֹ יקול פי אלפהם **ויבן עלי** (שמ״א 3:8). ופי אלאפהאם[248] **ויבן וידבר עמי אותי**[249] (דניאל 9:22) וינבגֹי אן נבין ההנא מא כאן[250] מעני[251] דניאל פי **חכמתא ומנדעא** (ע׳ דניאל 2:21). פנקול **חכמתא** הו מא יקום[252] פי[253] אלכאינאת **ומנדעא** מא יאת מן אלכאינאת.[254] ועאדתנא[255] נבין אן אלחכמה[256] למא מצٌי[257] כקולה[258] **כל זה נסיתי בחכמה** (קהלת 7:23), **רחוק מה שהיה וגׄ** (קהלת 7:24). ואן בינה למא יאתי כקולה[259] **ובאתי להבינך את**[260] **אשר יקרא**[261] (דניאל 10:14). ואלהٌ **הוא**[262] **גלי**[263] **עמיקתא** (דניאל 2:22) יעני בה מא פי קלוב אלנאס כקׄ[264] **וקרב איש ולב עמוק** (תה׳ 64:7). ואלו[265] **ומסתרתא**[266] (דניאל 2:22) יעני [267]בה מא תחת אלתٌרא כקולה[268] **מי יתן בשאול תצפנני** (איוב 14:13). ומא פי

[246] ומנדעה ... יעני TS NS 285.21c > D
[247] אן + Antonin 4
[248] [אד אלפהם ואלאפהאם ... ויבן עלי] פי אלאפהאם TS NS 285.21c > L
[249] אותי Antonin 4 > L
[250] וינבגי ... כאן TS NS 285.21c > D
[251] [מענ]א TS NS 285.21c > D
[252] תקום Antonin 4
[253] מן Antonin 4
[254] ומנדעא ... אלכאינאת TS NS 285.21c > D
[255] אן + Antonin 4
[256] חכמה Antonin 4
[257] מצא TS NS 285.21c
[258] כק Antonin 4
[259] בחכמ]ה וג׳ ... כקול]ה TS NS 285.21c > D
[260] את וגׄ Antonin 4
[261] אשר יקרא Antonin 4 > L
[262] והו Antonin 4
[263] גלא MT ׀ גלה Antonin 4
[264] מא ... כק TS NS 285.21c > D
[265] ואלסאדס Antonin 4
[266] יריד + Antonin 4
[267] יעני Antonin 4 > L
[268] אלתٌרי כק Antonin 4

אלבחאר איצׄא כקולה[269] **ואם**[270] **יסתרו מנגד עיני בקרקע הים**[271] (עמוס 9:3). ואלדׄ **ידע מה בחשוכא** (דניאל 2:22) עלי טׄאהרה. ואלחׄ **ונהורא עמה שרא**[272] (דניאל 2:22) יריד בה מעין כאלנור מן אנארה[273] אלאבצאר[274] ואלעקול ועלי מא קאל פי אלמתׄל אלממתׄל[275] בה **מצות יוי ברה** (תה" 19:9). וינבגׄי[276] אן נעלם איצׄא[277] לם קרן **חכמתא**[278] **וגבורתא** (דניאל 2:23) אלי[279] וצף[280] אללה אדׄ קאל **די חכמתא וגבורתא די ליה היא**[281] (דניאל 2:20). ופי וצף נפסה אדׄ קאל **די חכמתא וגבורתא יהבת לי**[282] (דניאל 2:23). פנקול אמא פי וצף אללה גל גלאלה פלאנה גׄאלב כאלחכים כקולה **כי בכל חכמי הגוים ובכל מלכותם מאין כמוך**[283] (ירמ' 10:7). ואמא פי וצף נפסה[284] פלאן[285] חכמתה[286] גׄלבת עלי גמיע חכמא אלמלך כקאלה[287] **ולא**[288] **נמצא מכלם כדניאל חנניה מישאל ועזריה**[289] (דניאל 1:19). פלדׄלך אתבעה בקולה **וכען הודעתני די בעינא מנך**[290] (דניאל 2:23) יעני **חלמא ופשרה** (ע' דניאל 23:5.6). פאמא **חלמא** פהו[291] למא מצׄא לאנה קד[292] כאן פסמאה **חכמה**

[269] איצׄ כק Antonin 4 | [תצפנני ... כקו]לה TS NS 285.21c > D
[270] אם TS NS 285.21c
[271] עיני ... הים Antonin 4 > L
[272] עמה שרא MT | עמיה שרי Morag | עמה שרה Antonin 4
[273] ונהורא ... אנארה TS NS 285.21c > D
[274] ואנארה + Antonin 4
[275] ואלממתׄל Antonin 4
[276] ינבגׄי TS NS 285.21c
[277] איצׄ Antonin 4
[278] [איצׄא ...חכמת]א TS NS 285.21c > D
[279] פי Antonin 4
[280] [וצ]ף Antonin 4 > D
[281] די ליה היא Antonin 4 > L
[282] די [חכמתא וגבורת]א יהבת לי TS NS 285.21c > D
[283] ומכל מלכותם מאין TS NS 285.21c > D
[284] [וצף נפסה אדׄ...] וצף נפסה פנקול Antonin 4 > L homeoteleuton
[285] Beginning of Oxf 2486.9a
[286] חכמתה Oxf 2486.9a > D
[287] כמא קאל Oxf 2486.9a
[288] כקולה ולם TS NS 285.21c | כק ולא Antonin 4
[289] כ[דניאל חנניה מישאל ועזריה] TS NS 285.21c > D | חנׄ מיׄ ועזׄ Antonin 4
[290] מינך Morag
[291] פהו Antonin 4 > D
[292] [למא מצׄי לאנה ק]ד TS NS 285.21c > D

(דניאל 2:21). ואמא **פשרה** פהו ללמסתקבל לאנה[293] לם יכן בעד פסמאה
בינה (דניאל 2:24). ואמא וצלה **כל קבל** (דניאל 2:24) בין[294] כל קצה וקצה
פמחץ̇ אללפט̇ה[295] באזא. פלמא לם ינתט̇ם פי אלתכ̇ריג קלנא "ענד ד̇לך".
ואמא [... ...][296] קבל[297] אן[298] יקול שיא **לא**[299] **חכימין אשפין חרטמין גזרין**
יכלין להחניא למלכא (דניאל 2:27). פהו[300] ישאכל למא עאדה אלאנביא[301]
אן יפעלוה[302] מן[303] קבל אן יתׄבתו[304] קול אלנבוה[305] יעגזון אקואל
אלמתברטין[306] כמא[307] שרחנא פי קצה[308] **מפר אתת**[309] **בדים**[310] (יש' 44:25)
ת̇ם **מקים דבר עבדו** (יש' 44:26) וסאיר אלפואסק.[311] פלמא עגזהם[312] רד
אלקדרה אלי רבה[313] כקולה[314] **ברם איתי**[315] **אלה בשמיה וג̇** (דניאל 2:28).
ת̇ם קאל לה[316]

Dn 2:29

אנתא מלכא רעיונך על משכבך סליקו מא די להוי אחרי דנה וגלא רזיא הודעך מא די להוה.

[293] לאנה Antonin 4 > D
[294] פאמ[א וצלה כל קבל ב]ין TS NS 285.21c > D
[295] אללפצה Antonin 4
[296] תק[... ...]אל Oxf 2486.9a > D
[297] [...קב]ל Antonin 4 and TS NS 285.21c > D
[298] אן Oxf 2486.9a > L
[299] שיא לא Oxf 2486.9a > D
[300] גזרין יכלין. פהו Oxf 2486.9a > L ׀ גזרין. פהו Antonin 4 > L
[301] [למא עאדה אלנ]ביא Antonin 4 > D
[302] אן יפעלוה Antonin 4 > L
[303] קול + Oxf 2486.9a
[304] [אלאנביא ... ית]בתו TS NS 285.21c > D
[305] אלנב[וה] Oxf 2486.9a > D ׀ אלנביה Antonin 4
[306] אלמתדרסין TS NS 285.21c ׀ אלמתכרטין Antonin 4
[307] כמא Oxf 2486.9a > D
[308] כמא ... קצה Antonin 4 > D
[309] אותות Oxf 2486.9a ׀ אתת TS NS 285.21c ׀ אתות Antonin 4
[310] ב[ד]ים Oxf 2486.9a > D ׀ בדים End of the readable part of Oxf 2486.9a
[311] [מקים ... אל]פואסק TS NS 285.21c > D
[312] אלפואסק ... עגזה]ם Antonin 4 > D
[313] רבהא Antonin 4
[314] בק Antonin 4 ׀ כקולה Beginning of Oxf 2486.9b
[315] ברם איתי TS NS 285.21c > D
[316] בשמיה ... לה Antonin 4 > D and TS NS 285.21c > D

יא איהא[317] אלמלך[318] כאנת[319] אפכארך קבל נומך חאלת[320] פי מא יכון בעד הדֿא אלאיאם[321] פאסעפך[322] כאשף אלאסראר[323] באן[324] ערפך דֿלך.[325]

Dn 2:30

ואנה לא בחכמה די איתי בי מן כל חייא רזא דנה גלילי להן על דברת די פשרא למלכא יהודעון ורעיוני לבבך תנדע.

ואני[326] פליס לאני[327] אחכם[328] אלנאס כשף לי הדֿא אלסר לכן בסבב אלדֿי[329] יערפון אלמלך[330] אלתפסיר ולכי תערף מראד[331] נפסך.[332]

Dn 2:31

אנחה מלכא חזה הוית ואלו צלם חד שגיא צלמא דכן רב וזווה יתיר קאם לקבלך ורוה דחיל.

יא איה[333] אלמלך ראית כאנך מתבצר פאדֿא[334] בצנם עטֿים[335] ודֿלך[336] אלצנם כביר לה בהגה כתֿירה והו קאים אמאמך ולה רועה האילה.

[317] יא איה Spiegel | יאיהא Antonin 4

[318] יא איהא אלמלך > D TS NS 285.21c

[319] כאן Antonin 4 + Spiegel + Morag

[320] חארת Spiegel

[321] [נו]מך חאל[ת ... אלאי]אם > D TS NS 285.21c | [חאלת ... אלאיא]ם > D Antonin 4

[322] נומך ... אלאיאם > D Oxf 2486.9b | חאל[ת ... אלאיאם] > D TS NS 285.21c | [חאלת ... אלאיא]ם > D Antonin 4

[323] End of TS NS 285.21c

[324] End of the readable part of Antonin 4

[325] דאלך + Spiegel + Morag

[326] ואנא + Spiegel + Oxf 2486.9b

[327] לאני > L Morag

[328] אחכם Beginning of Oxf 2629.38a

[329] אללדין Oxf 2486.9b | אלדין Oxf 2629.38a

[330] יערפ[ון אלמלך] > D Oxf 2486.9b

[331] כאשף (2:29) ... מ]דאר (2:30) > D TS NS 285.21c | מדאר End of the readable part of TS NS 285.21c

[332] [תערף מראד נפס]ך > D Oxf 2486.9b

[333] יאיהא Oxf 2629.38a + Oxf 2486.10a | Beginning of Oxf 2486.10a

[334] פאדי Morag

[335] עצים Spiegel + Morag

[336] דאך Morag | דאלך Spiegel

Dn 2:32
הוא צלמא ראשה די דהב טב חדוהי ודרעוהי די כסף מעוהי וירכתיה די נחש.

ד̇לך[337] אלצנם ראסה מן ד̇הב[338] כ̇אלץ צדרה וד̇ראעיה[339] מן פצ̇ה בטנה ואפכ̇אד̇ה[340] מן[341] נחאס.

Dn 2:33
שקוהי די פרזל רגלוהי מנהון די פרזל ומנהון די חסף.
סאקיה[342] מן חדיד ורגליה[343] בעץ̇ אגזאהא מן חדיד ובעצ̇הא מן כ̇זף.[344]

Dn 2:34
חזה[345] הוית עד די התגזרת אבן די לא בידין ומחת לצלמא על רגלוהי די פרזלא וחספא והדקת המון.

ת̇ם ראית כאן חגר קד[346] אנקטע[347] לא ביד אחד[348] פצ̇רב ד̇לך[349] אלצנם אלי רגליה אלד̇י מן אלחדיד ואלכ̇זף[350] פדקהא[351] פסקט.

Dn 2:35
באדין דקו כחדה פרזלא חספא נחשא כספא ודהבא והון כעור מן אדרי קיט ונשא המון רוחא וכל אתר לא השתכח להון ואבנא די מחת לצלמאהות לטור רב ומלאת כל ארעא.

337 דאלך Spiegel + Morag
338 דה[ב] Oxf 2629.38a > D
339 ודראעאה Oxf 2486.10a | ודראעה Oxf 2629.38a
340 ופכדאה Oxf 2629.38a + Oxf 2486.10a
341 מן Oxf 2486.10a > L
342 סאקאה Oxf 2629.38a + Oxf 2486.10a
343 רגלאה Spiegel + Morag + Oxf 2629.38a
344 כ[זף] Oxf 2486.10a > D | כזף End of Oxf 2486.10a
345 חזה Beginning of Oxf 2486.10b
346 קד Oxf 2486.10b > L
347 אנקטעת Spiegel
348 לא ביד אחד Spiegel > L
349 דאלך Spiegel + Morag
350 אלתי הי מן חדיד וכזף Oxf 2629.38a + Oxf 2486.10b | אלתי מן חדיד וכזף Spiegel
351 פדקהמא Spiegel + Oxf 2486.10b | פדקתהמא Oxf 2629.38a |

חיניד̇[352] אנדקו אגמעין אלחדיד ואלכ̇זף ואלנחאס]ואלפצ̇ה ואלד̇הב וצארו כהשים[353] מן בואד̇ר[354] אלציף ת̇ם חמלהם אלריח ולם יוגד להם את̇רא אלבתה[355] ת̇ם אן אלחגר אלד̇י[356] צ̇רב אלצנם צאר גבלא עט̇ימא[357] ומלא גמיע[358] תלך אלארץ̇.[359]

Dn 2:36

דנה[360] חלמא ופשרה נאמר קדאם מלכא.

ואד̇ הד̇א[361] אלרויא נקול תפסירהא בין ידיי[362] אלמלך.

Dn 2:37

אנתה מלכא מלך מלכיא די אלה שמיא מלכותא חסנא ותקפא ויקרא יהב לך.

יא איה[363] אלמלך אנת מלך אלמלוך[364] אד̇ רב אלסמא אלמלך ואלות̇אק[365] ואלתאייד ואלכרם רזקך.

Dn 2:38

ובכל די דארין בני נשא חיות ברא ועוף שמיא יהב בידך והשלטך בכלהון אנתא הוא רושה די דהבא.

וחית̇ יאוי גמיע אלנאס וחיואן[366] אלצחרי[367] וטאיר אלסמא סלמה אליך וסלטך[368] עלי גמיעהם[369] פאנת[370] הו אלממת̇ל בראס[371] אלד̇הב.

[352] חינ̇ Oxf 2629.38a
[353] כאלהשים Oxf 2629.38a + Oxf 2486.10b
[354] ביאדר Oxf 2629.38a
[355] בתה Oxf 2486.10b | אלבתה Beginning of Antonin 5
[356] אלדי אלדי Morag
[357] עטים Oxf 2486.10b | עטימא Spiegel > L
[358] ומ[לא ג]מי[ע] Antonin 5 > D
[359] אלארץ End of Oxf 2486.10b
[360] דנה Beginning of Oxf 2486.11a
[361] הדה Oxf 2486.11a
[362] ידי Antonin 5 + Spiegel + Oxf 2629.38a + Oxf 2486.11a
[363] יאיהא Antonin 5 + Oxf 2486.11a | יא[...] Oxf 2629.38a > D
[364] מלוך Oxf 2486.11a
[365] אלות̇אק Morag
[366] וח[יוא]ן Oxf 2486.11a > D

Dn 2:39

ובתרך תקום מלכו אוחרי ארע מינך ומלכו תליתאה אוחרי די נחשא[372] די[373] תשלט בכל ארעא.

ובעדך תקום מ̇מלכה[374] אכ̇רי[375] אדון מנך ואלממלכה אלת̇אלת̇ה[376] תשבה אלנחאס ותתסלט[377] עלי גמיע[378] אלארץ̇.

Dn 2:40

ומלכו רביעאה תהוי תקיפא כפרזלא כל קביל די פרזלא מהדיק וחשיל כולא וכפרזלא די מרעע כל אילין תדק ותרוע.

ואלממלכה אלראבעה[379] תכון צלבה כאלחדיד כמא[380] אן[381] אלחדיד ידק אלכל ויסחקה וירצ̇ה[382] כד̇אך[383] תדק אלכל ותרצ̇ה.[384]

Dn 2:41

ודי חזית רגליא ואצבעתא מנהון חסף די פחר ומנהון פרזלא מלכו פליגה תהוה ומן נצבתא די פרזלא להוי בה כל קבל די חזיתא פרזלא מערב בחסף טינא.

367 אלצחרא Antonin 5 + Spiegel + Oxf 2629.38a + Oxf 2486.11a

368 וצלטך Morag

369 [גמי]עהם Morag > D

370 אנת Spiegel

371 באלראס Antonin 5 + Oxf 2629.38a + Oxf 2486.11a

372 נחשא End of Oxf 2486.11a

373 די Beginning of Oxf 2486.11b

374 ממלכה End of Oxf 2629.38a

375 אכרי Beginning of Oxf 2629.38b

376 אלג̇ Antonin 5

377 ותתצלט Morag

378 [אלת̇אלת̇ה ... ג]מיע Oxf 2629.38b > D

379 אלד Antonin 5 + Oxf 2486.11b

380 וכמא Antonin 5 + Oxf 2486.11b

381 ואלממלכה ... אן Oxf 2629.38b > D

382 וירצ̇צה Antonin 5 + Oxf 2486.11b | ידק ... וירצה Oxf 2629.38b > D

383 הי + Spiegel

384 תדק ... ותרצה Oxf 2629.38b > D

ואמא מא ראית מן[385] אלקדמין ואלאצאבע בעץ׳ אגזאה[386] כ׳זף מפכ׳ר ובעצ׳הא חדיד פיכון ד׳אך מלכא מנקסמא ופיה[387] מן[388] אצל[389] אלחדיד באיזא[390] מא ראיתה יכ׳אלט אלכ׳זף ואלטין.[391]

Dn 2:42

ואצבעת רגליא מנהון פרזל ומנהון חסף מן קצת מלכותא תהוי תקיפא ומנה תהוי תבירא.

ותאויל אלאצאבע אלתי מנהא חדיד ומנהא כ׳זף אן יד[392] בעץ׳ אלממלכה צלבה[393] ובעצ׳הא מנכסרא.[394]

Dn 2:43

די חזיתא פרזלא מערב בחסף טינה מתערבין להון בזרע אנשא ולא להון דבקין דנא עם דנאהא פרזלא לא מתערב בחסף טינא.

ואמא מא ראית מן אכ׳תלאטהא[395] פתאוילה אן יכ׳תלטו הולאי[396] באלמנאסלה ולא יכ׳תלטו באלכליה[397] כמא[398] אן[399] אלחדיד לא יכ׳תלט באלכ׳זף.[400]

Dn 2:44

וביומיהון די מלכיא אלין יקים אלה שמיא מלכו די לעלמין לא תתחבל מלכותא לעם אחרן לא תשתביק תדיק ותסיף כל אילין מלכותא והיא תקום[401] לעלמיא.[402]

[385] אן Antonin 5 + Oxf 2486.11b

[386] אגזאיהא Antonin 5 + Oxf 2486.11b

[387] פיהא Spiegel

[388] מן End of Oxf 2486.11b

[389] אצל Beginning of Oxf 2486.12a

[390] חדיד באיזא Spiegel

[391] אלטין Antonin 5 + Oxf 2486.12a | ואמא ... ואלטין < D Oxf 2629.38b

[392] יכון Spiegel + Oxf 2486.12a | אן יכן Antonin 5

[393] צלבא Antonin 5 + Spiegel + Oxf 2486.12a

[394] מנכסרה Antonin 5 | ותאויל ... מנכסרא < D Oxf 2629.38b

[395] אכתלאטהמא Antonin 5 + Spiegel + Oxf 2486.12a

[396] האולי Oxf 2486.12a

[397] ילתקון באלכליה Oxf 2486.12a | יכתלטו באלכליה Antonin 5 + Spiegel

[398] כמא Morag < L | יכתלטו ... כמא < D Oxf 2629.38b

[399] ואמא ... הולאי < D Oxf 2629.38b

[400] יכאלט אלכ׳זף Oxf 2629.38b + Antonin 5 + Oxf 2486.12a

ובעד[403] מדת[404] התין אלממלכתין[405] יקים אלאה[406] אלסמא ממלכה לא תפסד אלי אלדהור[407] ולא יתרך[408] מלכא לאמה אכ̇רי פהי תדק גמיע[409] הד̇ה אלממאלך ותסיפהא והי תת̇בת אלי אלדהור.

Dn 2:45

כל קבל די חזיתא די מאורא התגזלת אבן די לא בידיין והדיקת פרזלא נחשא חספא כספא ודהבא אלה רב הודע למלכא מא די להוא אחרי דנא ויציב חלמא ומהימן פשריה.

וד̇אך[410] באיזא[411] מא ראית אן חגרא אנקטע מן אלגבל לא ביד[412] פדק אלחדיד ואלנחאס ואלכ̇זף[413] ואלפצ̇ה ואלד̇הב גמלה אלאמר אן אללה אלכביר ערף אלמלך מא יכון[414] פי אכ̇ר אלאיאם פאלרויא צחיחה[415] ותפסירהא[416] צאדק.[417]

תקדימה לה **רעיונך על משכבך**[418] **סליקו** (דניאל 2:29) ליס הו[419] ליצ̇עף פי[420] נפסה אלרויא.[421] וד̇לך אנא נקול אן ללרויא ד̇[422] אסבאב. ג̇[423] מא גא

[401] תקום End of Oxf 2486.12a

[402] לעלמיא Beginning of Oxf 2486.12b

[403] וכעד Spiegel

[404] מדה Antonin 5 + Spiegel + Oxf 2629.38b + Oxf 2486.12b

[405] [אל]מ[מלכ]תין Oxf 2629.38b > D

[406] רב Antonin 5 + Spiegel + Oxf 2629.38b + Oxf 2486.12b

[407] אלדהר Oxf 2486.12b

[408] מעהא Antonin 5 and Spiegel and Oxf 2629.38b and Oxf 2486.12b

[409] גמיע Oxf 2629.38b > D

[410] ודלך Spiegel

[411] באזא Antonin 5 + Oxf 2629.38b + Oxf 2486.12b

[412] אחד Spiegel

[413] אלכזן Oxf 2486.12b ׀ ואלכזף Antonin 5 > L

[414] יכן Antonin 5

[415] צחיח Spiegel + Morag

[416] ותפסירה Morag + Oxf 2486.12b ׀ ואלתפס Oxf 2629.38b

[417] ואלתפס [צא]דק Oxf 2629.38b ׀ [צ]אדק End of Oxf 2629.38b

[418] מש[כבך] Antonin 5

[419] הו Oxf 2486.12b > L

[420] פי Antonin 5 > L

[421] נפס[ה אלרויא] Antonin 5 > D

[422] ג̇ Antonin 5

[423] ג̇ Antonin 5 > L

מנהא[424] פאסד[425] ויקאל לה[426] אלאצ׳גאת׳. ואלראבע[427] הו מא סלם מן אלג׳ והו אלצחיח. פאול אלג׳ מא כאן מן[428] כת׳רה אלאפכאר וכד אלרוח. ואליה יבאהי[429] אלמת׳ל פי אלאבטאל כמא קאל קהלת[430] **כי בא החלום ברב ענין וקול כסיל**[431] **ברב דברים**[432] (קהלת 5:2). ואלת׳אני[433] מא כאן סבבה כת׳רת אלגד׳א[434] וקלתה.[435] ואליה איצ׳א[436] יסנד אלמת׳ל פי אלאבטאל כמא קאל[437] ישעיהו **והיה כאשר**[438] **יחלם הרעב והנה**[439] **אכל והקיץ וריקה נפשו וכאשר יחלם הצמא והנה שתה והקיץ והנה עיף ונפשו שוקקה כן יהיה המון כל הגוים הצבאים על הר ציון**[440] (יש׳ 29:8). ואלת׳אלת׳[441] מא יכון[442] סבבה אלאוגאע ואלאלאם פהו איצ׳א[443] פאסד כמא קאל[444] איוב **כי אמרתי תנחמני ערשי אשא**[445] **בשיחי משכבי וחתתני בחלמות ומחזיונות תבעתני**[446] (איוב 7:13–14). ומא כ׳לץ מן הד׳ה אלת׳לאת׳ה[447] פהו מן ענד אללה

[424] מנהא End of Oxf 2486.12b
[425] פסאד Beginning of Oxf 2486.13a
[426] ויק[אל לה] Antonin 5 > D
[427] ואלד Antonin 5
[428] כאן מן Antonin 5 > D
[429] ינתהי Antonin 5
[430] אלאב[טאל כמא קאל קהלת] Antonin 5 > D
[431] כמיל וג׳ Antonin 5
[432] [ברב דברים] וג׳ Antonin 5 > L
[433] ואלב Antonin 5
[434] סבבה כתרה אלגד׳א Antonin 5 > D
[435] או קלתה Antonin 5
[436] איצ Antonin 5
[437] כק Antonin 5
[438] כק [ישעיהו והיה כאשר] Antonin 5 > D
[439] וג׳ + Antonin 5
[440] [אכל ... ציון] וג׳ Antonin 5 > L
[441] ואלג׳ Antonin 5
[442] כאן Antonin 5
[443] אלאו[גאע ... איצא] Antonin 5 > D
[444] כק Antonin 5
[445] ישׂא MT
[446] [אשׂא ... תבעתני] וג׳ Antonin 5 > D
[447] אלג׳ Antonin 5

כמא קאל **בחלום חזיון לילה בנפל תרדמה על אנשים** (איוב 33:15) **ובמוסרם יחתם**[448] **אז יגלה אזן**[449] **אנשים**[450] (איוב 33:16)[451] וסאיר אלקול כמא פי כתאב אלאמאנאת. פלמא[452] כאן[453] נבוכׄדנצר[454] מן קבל נומה תפכר פי מן ימלך בעדה וכאן הדׄא אלתפכר ענד אלעלמא ממא יפסד אלרויא[455] ויגעלהא[456] אצׄגׄאתׄ אחתאג אן יקדם לה דניאל דׄלך פיקול לה ליס אלרויא פאסדה ועלי אנך תפכרת פי מתׄלהא בל הי צחיחה ולולא דׄאך לם אפסרהא לך. פהדׄא מעני אלחאקה פי אלקול **ויציב חלמא ומהומן פשרה** (דניאל 2:45). ותעלילה כשף אלסר בסבב **די פשרא למלכא יהודעון** (דניאל 2:30). יעני האולי[457] אלבאיסין אלדׄין[458] כאנו יערפון אלמלך אלתפסיר אברא[459] לילא[460] יהלכון והם פקד אענו באלחכמה.

פסרת **חדוהי** (דניאל 2:32) "צדרה" לאן תרגום **חזה**[461] **התנופה** (במד׳ 6:20) **חדיא דארמותא**.[462] ופסרת[463] **כעור מן אדרי קיט** (דניאל 2:35) "השימא" לאנה תרגום **כמוץ**. ופסרת[464] **וחשל** (דניאל 2:40) "יסחק" לאן אלאצל פיה יצׄעף כמא קאל **כל הנחשלים אחריך** (דבר׳ 25:18). ופסרת[465] **מרעע** (דניאל 2:40) "ירץׄ" לאנה תרגום **קנה רצוץ**.

448 בחלום ...] וג׳ Antonin 5 > D
449 אזן וג׳ [אנשים] Antonin 5 > L
450 אנשים Antonin 5 > L
451 A reversed quotation of Jb 33:16.
452 פלמא End of Oxf 2486.13a
453 פי כתאב ... כאן Antonin 5 > D | כאן Beginning of Oxf 2486.13b
454 נבוכׄ Antonin 5
455 [בעד... אלרוי]א Antonin 5 > D
456 ויגעלהא End of thr readable part of Antonin 5
457 האולי Beginning of Antonin 6 | [ה]אולי Antonin 6 > D
458 אלדׄין Oxf 2486.13b | אלדׄי Antonin 6
459 אברא Uncertain lesson
460 [ל]ילא Antonin 6 > D
461 ח[זה] Antonin 6 > D
462 דארמות[א] Oxf 2486.13b > D
463 ופס Antonin 6
464 ופס Antonin 6
465 ופס Antonin 6

פאמא צורה אלצנם נפסה פמערופה מן אלנץ תתצור[466] פי[467] אלוהם נכֿתצר[468] דון אעאדתהא, אעני אלצורה, לילא נטיל.[469] ולכן אלדֿי יחתאג אליה אן יבין[470] תפסיר אלרויא ביאנא גידא. ונקול אמא קולה[471] לה **אנת מלכא מלך מלכיא** (דניאל 2:37) ולם יקל **מלכא די מלכיא** לאנה מלך מלוך כמא קאל[472] יחזקאל **נבוכדנצר מלך בבל מצפון מלך מלכים** (יח׳ 26:7). וליס הו מלך אלמלוך אדֿ הדֿא אלאסם לרב אלעאלמין. וקולה **ובכל די דארין**[473] (דניאל 2:38) הו נטֿיר מא קאל ירמיהו **ועתה אנכי נתתי כל הארצות האלה**[474] **ביד נבוכדנצר מלך בבל עבדי וגם עת חית השדה נתתי לו**[475] (ירמ׳ 27:6). וזאד ההנא[476] **ועוף שמיא** (דניאל 2:38) שרחא. וליס עלי סביל אלאגלאל קאל לה דניאל דֿלך, לכן עלי סביל אלחכמה אן יבתדא כל תקסים מן אלראס. ונקול ההנא[477] ומא וגה אלחכמה פי אן ירי נבוכֿדנצר מא יכון[478] לסאיר אלממאלך? פנקול לאנה סלט עליהם אגמע[479] פצארו לה כמנילה.[480] פכמא ירא אלואחד[481] למנזלה כדֿאך ירי להם. ולדֿלך וצל דניאל[482] **ובכל**[483] **די דארין** (דניאל 2:38). ואיצֿא[484] ליכֿרג כֿבר רויאה אלי[485] גמיע אלאפאק.[486] ויויד דֿלך מא גרי מן תעגיז אלחכמא ומן קתלהם פהו אוכד לאדֿאעה אלכֿבר.

[466] תתצור End of Oxf 2486.13b
[467] פי Beginning of Oxf 2486.14a
[468] פנכלתצר Antonin 6
[469] נטול Antonin 6
[470] נבין Antonin 6
[471] קו Antonin 6
[472] כק Antonin 6
[473] וג׳ + Antonin 6
[474] וג׳ + Antonin 6
[475] ביד ... לו Antonin 6 > L
[476] האהנא Oxf 2486.14a
[477] האהנא Oxf 2486.14a
[478] יכן Antonin 6
[479] סלטאן עלי גמיעהם Antonin 6
[480] כמנזלה Antonin 6
[481] ירן[י ...אל]אחד Antonin 6 > D
[482] דניאל End of Oxf 2486.14a
[483] ובכל Beginning of Oxf 2486.14b
[484] [וא]יצ׳ Antonin 6 > D
[485] לי Antonin 6
[486] אלמכלוקין

ואמא אלמלך אלצג'יר פאנמא ירי לממלכתה פקט כמא ראי פרעה **לארץ מצרים וארץ כנען** פקט.[487] ואמא אלפראד פיאליתה[488] יצדק פימא יראה[489] לאהל ביתה. לכן[490] אלנבי יסתקים אן ירי לגמיע אהל אלעאלם[491] אד' צאחבה רב אלעאלמין מאלך[492] אלכל. ת'ם נקול מא וגה אלחכמה פי תמת'יל אלאמם בצנם[493] ותמת'יל ישראל בחגר?[494] ונגיב באן אלצנם מן צנעה אלנאס. כד'אך[495] מלכהם תדביר דניאיי. ואמא[496] אלחגר פמן כ'לק אללה. וכד'אך מלכהם, אעני מלך ישראל,[497] דיאני וכמא קאל[498] פי אלגמיע **מושל באדם**[499] **צדיק מושל**[500] **יראת אלהים** (שמ"ב 23:3). ומא לאנתפאע[501] פי אגתמאע מעאניהם[502] כלהא אלי אעצ'א גסם ואחד? פנקול לאנה[503] שעבוד ואחד[504] עלינא אתפקו הם אם תפרקו,[505] הם כמבעות[506] ואחד.[507] אלא תרי אן[508] אלתוראה[509] תסמי אעדאנא כלהם **איבך, בלשון יחיד** פי **משנה תורה**.[510] ולם לם יקל לה **ובתרך**

[487] פקט Antonin 6 > D
[488] אלפראא[ד פיא]ליתה Antonin 6 > D
[489] ירי Antonin 6
[490] לכן Antonin 6 > D
[491] לגמי[ע אהל אלעא]לם Antonin 6 > D
[492] מאלך Antonin 6 > D
[493] באלצנם Antonin 6
[494] ותמ[ת'יל ישראל בח]גר Antonin 6 > D
[495] כד'א[ך] Antonin 6 > D
[496] תדבי[ר דניאיי ואמ]א Antonin 6 > D
[497] אעני מלך ישראל Antonin 6 > L
[498] כק Antonin 6
[499] אל[גמיע מושל באד]ם Antonin 6 > D
[500] מושל Oxf 2486.14b > L
[501] אלפאידה Antonin 6
[502] [אגתמאע מעאני]הם Antonin 6 > D
[503] פאנה נקול פיה Antonin 6
[504] מעבוד ואחד Antonin 6 > D
[505] אפתרקו Antonin 6
[506] כמבעות End of Oxf 2486.14b
[507] ואחד Beginning of Oxf 2486.15a
[508] ואחד ... אן Antonin 6 > D
[509] אלתוריה Antonin 6
[510] יחיד ... תורה Antonin 6 > D

תקום מלכו אחרי די כספא ארע מנך[511] כמא קאל[512] לה **אנת**[513] **הוא ראשא די דהבא** (דניאל 2:38)? פנקול לאן ארבע מלוך אלפרס אללדין כאנו[514] בעקב מלך בבל כאנו רון כתיר. ואלדליל עלי דלך תגלב אצחב סלטאנהם[515] עליה. פאשארו[516] עלי[517] דריוש במא לם יכן לה בד מן קבולה. ואראד אן יתכלץ דניאל מן ידהם פלם ימכנה כמא סנשרח.

ואמא מלך באבל פכאן ינפד אמרה כמא ירי, כמא קאל **די**[518] **הוה צבא הוה מרים ודי**[519] **הוה צבא הוה משפיל**[520] (דניאל 5:19). ואמא אלממלכה אלתאלתה[521], אעני **יון**, פטואהא טיא ולם יקל פי אמרהא אכתר מן **תשלט בכל ארעה** (דניאל 2:39). והדא ממא ידלנא[522] אן גרצה לם יכן[523] אחדי אלג ממאלך.[524] ואנמא כאן גרצה אנקסאם אלראבעה. וכמא סיקול בעד הדא **אדין צבית**[525] **ליצבא על חיותא**[526] **רביעיתא**[527] (דניאל 7:19). כדאך פי תפסירה לנבוכדנצר[528] אכתצר פי וצף אלג ממאלך[529] ואתסע פי אלראבעה.[530] פקאל אולא אנהא תכון בראסהא מדה טוילה באזא מא קאל[531] **שקוהי די פרזל** (דניאל 2:33) מפרד. תם תשארכהא[532] לאדום אלממלכה אלאכרי מדה הי אקל

[511] אחרי ... מנך Antonin 6 > D
[512] כק Antonin 6
[513] את Oxf 2486.15a
[514] [פנקול ... כא]נו Antonin 6 > D
[515] [כתיר ... סל]טאנהם Antonin 6 > D
[516] פאשארו Antonin 6 > L
[517] עלי End of the readable part of Antonin 6
[518] די Beginning of TS Ar 28.165a | [קד]מחא די TS Ar 28.165a > D
[519] וג׳ + TS Ar 28.165a
[520] ודי ... משפיל TS Ar 28.165a > L
[521] אלג TS Ar 28.165a
[522] יבין לנא TS Ar 28.165a
[523] יך TS Ar 28.165a
[524] אלממאלך TS Ar 28.165a
[525] אד[ין צבי]ת TS Ar 28.165a > D
[526] וג׳ + TS Ar 28.165a | חיותא End of Oxf 2486.15a
[527] רביעיתא TS Ar 28.165a > L | רביעיתא Beginning of Oxf 2486.15b
[528] לנבו TS Ar 28.165a
[529] וצף אלג ממאלך TS Ar 28.165a > D
[530] אלד TS Ar 28.165a
[531] מדה ... קאל TS Ar 28.165a > D
[532] שארכהא TS Ar 28.165a

מן דֿאך[533] במקדאר מסאחה אלקדם מן מסאחה אלסאק לקולה[534] **רגלוהי מנהין די פרזל ומנהין די חסף** (דניאל 2:33). וליס מענאה[535] אן אחדי[536] אלקדמין חדיד ואלאכֿרי כֿזף. ואנמא יריד אן בעץֿ אגזא כל קדם[537] חדיד ובעץֿ אגזאיהא כֿזף. ועלי הדֿה אלנסבה מן אלמסאחה כֿלץ אלמלך[538] לאדום תֿקנֿ סנה. תֿם ישארכה שריכא[539] בעד דֿלך שֿנֿ סנה שמסיה באלתקריב.[540] פתכון נסבה שֿנֿ מן תֿקנֿ כנסבה סבעה אגזא[541] מן יֿאֿ גזא. כמא אן מקדאר[542] אלקדם מן מקדאר אלסאק סבעה[543] אגזא מן יֿא[544] פתכון אלנסבה כלהא מן יֿחֿ.[545] ואמא תעדידה לתֿלתֿה[546] אפעאל אלחדיד אלדֿי מתֿלהא בה **מהדק וחשל ומרעע**[547] (דניאל 2:40) פאנא נקול בחסב[548] אכֿתלאף[549] אלתסלט עלי אלאמם. אמא אלאמה אלתי תסתגֿרק[550] דינהא חתי יבטל פהי[551] כאלשי אלדֿי יברדה אלחדיד והו פעל[552] **חשל**. ואלאמה אלתי[553] תפרק שמלהא פי אלאפאק פהי אלממתֿלה[554] באלמדקוק אלדֿי קד[555] תפרקת אגזאוה. ואלאמה אלתי תקמעהא תחת טאעתהא פקט פהי[556] אלממתֿלה באלמרצֿוץֿ. ועלי מא הדֿה

[533] אלמ[מלכה אל]אכֿרי מ[דה הי אקל מן דאך] TS Ar 28.165a > D
[534] לקו TS Ar 28.165a
[535] מ[ענאה] TS Ar 28.165a > D
[536] אחד TS Ar 28.165a
[537] אגזא כל קדם TS Ar 28.165a > D
[538] אלמסאח[ה כלץ אלמלך] TS Ar 28.165a > D
[539] תשארכהא שריכה TS Ar 28.165a
[540] [שנֿ סנה שמסיה באלת]קריב TS Ar 28.165a > D
[541] ז אגזא TS Ar 28.165a
[542] יֿאֿ כמא אן מקדאר TS Ar 28.165a > D
[543] ז אגזא TS Ar 28.165a
[544] גזו + TS Ar 28.165a
[545] אלנסבה כלהא מן יֿחֿ TS Ar 28.165a > D
[546] לגֿ TS Ar 28.165a
[547] [מהדק ... ומ]רעע TS Ar 28.165a > D
[548] בחסב End of Oxf 2486.15b
[549] אכֿתלאף Beginning of Oxf 2486.16a
[550] אמ[א אלאמה אלתי תסתגרק TS Ar 28.165a > D
[551] פהו TS Ar 28.165a
[552] פעל TS Ar 28.165a > L
[553] אלדֿי Oxf Oxf 2486.16a
[554] אלממתלה TS Ar 28.165a > D
[555] קד TS Ar 28.165a > L
[556] ט[אעתהא פקט] TS Ar 28.165a > D

אלממלכה[557] מוצופה בהדֹה אלקוי אלגֹ פאן ישֹראל אלמוצופין באקוי מנהא אדֹ קאל פיהם **תדק ותסף כל אלין מלכותא** (דניאל 2:44). פליס אלעגב מן חדיד יבדד דֹהבא[558] ופצֹה ונחאסא[559], אנמא[560] אלעגב מן חגר ידק חדיד ומא מעה חתי יפניה.

ואמא תשביהה לשריכה אדום באלכֹזף פליס לאנה אדון פי חסבהא או[561] נסבהא[562] או סלטאנהא ולכן[563] באזא תרתיב אלנאס ללאואני. פאנהם יקדמון אלדֹהב ובעדה אלפצֹה ובעדה אלנחאס ובעדה אלחדיד ובעד אלכל אלכֹזף.[564] כדֹאך למא כאן תרתיב הדֹה אלממאלך ואחדה בעד[565] אכֹרי[566] שבההם בהדֹה אלמשבהאת. ומעני געלה[567] ללכֹזף גֹ מנאזל **חסף** (דניאל 2:33) סתם, **וחסף די פחר** (ע׳ דניאל 2:41) **וחסף טינא** (ע׳ דניאל 2:41.43) פנקול כמא אן[568] אלמעמול מן אלטין עלי גֹ צֹרוב, אמא רטב לא מגפף ולא משוי ואמא מגפף[569] לא משוי ואמא משוי איצֹא.[570] כדֹאך אלקום גֹ מנאזל מן לם ידכֹל פי אלדין בתה[571] ומן דכֹל פיה עלי שריטה[572] או שראיט ומן דכֹל פי דינהם עלי אלכמאל.[573] ואיצֹא[574] אדֹא כאן אסאס אלצנם עלי כֹזף פכלה קאים במשיה מקימה חתי[575] שא כסרה באהון סעי וכמא קאל[576] **הנה כחסר ביד**[577] **היוצר**

[557] אדום + TS Ar 28.165a
[558] דהב TS Ar 28.165a
[559] ונחאס TS Ar 28.165a
[560] ואנמא TS Ar 28.165a
[561] או TS Ar 28.165a > L
[562] ונסבהא TS Ar 28.165a
[563] לכן TS Ar 28.165a
[564] ובע[אלכל] TS Ar 28.165a > D
[565] בעד End of Oxf Oxf 2486.16a
[566] אכרי Beginning of Oxf Oxf 2486.16b
[567] ומעני געלה TS Ar 28.165a > D
[568] טינה ... אן TS Ar 28.165a > D
[569] מגפ[ף ... מגפף] TS Ar 28.165a > D
[570] איצ TS Ar 28.165a
[571] מנאז[ל ... בתה] TS Ar 28.165a > D
[572] שרוטה TS Ar 28.165a
[573] [שריט] ומן [דכל ... אלכמאל] TS Ar 28.165a > D
[574] ואיצ TS Ar 28.165a
[575] פכל[ה ... חתי] TS Ar 28.165a > D
[576] וכק TS Ar 28.165a
[577] ביד End of the readable part of TS Ar 28.165a

כן אתם בידי בית ישראל (ירמ׳ 18:6) וסאיר אלקצה. ואיצׄא לכי יכון אלקדם אדׄא תכסר סקטת אלגתׄה כלהא פתכסרת. ואיצׄא ליטבק **באדין דקו כחדא וגׄ** (דניאל 2:35). ואמא קולה **מתערבין להון בזרע אנשא ולא להון דבקין דנה עם דנה** (דניאל 2:43) פהו מא ישאהד מן אלתזויג ואלתסרי בעץׄ מן בעץׄ מן חית לא תכׄתלט[578] אלאמתאן[579] פתציר ואחדה.

וקולה **וביומהון** (דניאל 2:44) יעני בעד **יומיהון** כמא קאל הנאך **בשבעתיכם** (במד׳ 28:26) יעני בעד **שבעתיכם**. וקולה **די מלכיא אנון** (דניאל 2:44) יעני **תרתין מלכותא אנון אדום** ושריכתהא. ומגאז דׄלך כמא סנבין **ארבעה מלכין יקומון מן ארעה** (דניאל 7:17). אנה יעני **ארבע מלכין יקומון מן ארעה**. וקולה **תדק ותסף כל אלין מלכותא** (דניאל 2:44) ליס יעני לאתׄנתין פקט בל אלכׄמסה כלהא. וקולה **ומלכותא לעם אכרון לא תשתבק** (דניאל 2:44) בעד[580] זואל אלארבעה[581] ידל אן אלאולי יבקא מנהא ענד אבתדי אלתׄאניה. וכדׄאך מן אלתׄאניה[582] ענד דולה אלתׄאלתׄה.[583]

ואמא תקדימהא פי אלתאויל **פרזלא נחשא חספא** פהו מעני תמשי אלתכסיר[584] ומן אספל אלי פוק בכׄלאף אלאעאדה. ולדׄלך קדם **נחשא** עלי **חספא**. ופי קולה[585] **והדקת המון** (דניאל 2:34) כלמה מצׄמרה והי **ונפל**[586] **צלמא באדין דקו**[587] (דניאל 2:35). וקולה[588] **והון כעור מן אדרי קיט** (דניאל 2:35) נטׄיר מא ימתׄל[589] אמרא[590] אלכפאר[591] באלמוץ אדׄ יקול **ורדף כמוץ הרים לפני רוח וכגלגל לפני סופה**[592] (ישׁ׳ 17:13). וזיאדתה דׄכר אלציף לאן

[578] תכתלט End of Oxf 2486.16b
[579] אלאמתאן Beginning of Oxf 2486.17a
[580] בעד Beginning of TS Ar 28.165b
[581] אלראבעה TS Ar 28.165b
[582] אלב TS Ar 28.165b
[583] אלגׄ TS Ar 28.165b
[584] אלתכסיר TS Ar 28.165b > D
[585] קו TS Ar 28.165b
[586] ונפל TS Ar 28.165b > D
[587] כחדא + TS Ar 28.165b
[588] וק TS Ar 28.165b
[589] ימתל End of Oxf 2486.17a
[590] אמרא Beginning of Oxf 2486.17b
[591] ימתל ... אלכפאר TS Ar 28.165b
[592] לפני ... סופה TS Ar 28.165b > L

אלמוץ פי אלשתי[593] יתרטב ברטובה אלהוא פלא יחמלה אלריח בסרעה.[594] וקולה[595] **וכל אתר**[596] **לא השתכח להון** (דניאל 2:35) הו[597] נט̇יר קולה[598] **ושאר חיותא העדיו שלטנהון**[599] (דניאל 7:12). וכ̇תם אלקצה עלי[600] **ואבנא**[601] **די מחת לצלמא הות לטור רב**[602] (דניאל 2:35) הו תפסירה **יקים**[603] **אלה שמיא מלכו די לעלמין לא תתחבל** (דניאל 2:44). ושבההא בחגר לאנה כ̇ליקתה[604] הו. וכד̇י יש̇ראל צניעתה וג̇רסה **נצר מטעי מעשה ידי להתפאר**[605] (יש׳ 60:21).

ומלך יש̇ראל פקד מת̇לה[606] באלחגר אלצלד אלת̇אבת כמא קאל[607] **הנני יסד בציון אבן** (יש׳ 28:16). ווצפה בסתה אוצאף[608] **אבן בחן פנת יקרת מוסד מוסד** (יש׳ 28:16). פאמא וגה תמת̇ילה **באבן** פכמא קלנא.[609] ומעני[610] **בחן** פהו צנאם[611] אקוי מן אלחגר אלמטלק ומת̇להא **הקימו בחוניו**[612] (יש׳ 23:13). ומעני **פנת** הו אן אלבנאיין יכ̇תארון אלחגארה אלקויה[613] ללזואיא[614] אד̇

[593] אל[ציף ... אלש]תי TS Ar 28.165b > D
[594] אל[ריח בסרעה] TS Ar 28.165b > D
[595] וק TS Ar 28.165b
[596] אתר TS Ar 28.165b > D
[597] להון הו TS Ar 28.165b > D
[598] מא סיקול TS Ar 28.165b
[599] שלטנהון TS Ar 28.165b > L
[600] עלי TS Ar 28.165b > L
[601] וג̇ + TS Ar 28.165b
[602] מחת ... רב TS Ar 28.165b > L
[603] [הו ... י]קים TS Ar 28.165b > D
[604] [לאנה כליקת]ה TS Ar 28.165b > D
[605] י׳ להת TS Ar 28.165b > L
[606] [ומלך ... מת]לה TS Ar 28.165b > D
[607] כק TS Ar 28.165b
[608] [ווצפה בסתה אוצא]ף TS Ar 28.165b > D
[609] באבן ... קלנא TS Ar 28.165b > D
[610] ואמא TS Ar 28.165b
[611] אלצנאם TS Ar 28.165b
[612] ומ[תלהא ... בחוניו] TS Ar 28.165b > D
[613] אלקויה End of Oxf 2486.17b
[614] ללזואיא Beginning of Oxf 2486.18a

אכתֿר[615] אלעמל עליהא. בל אעלאהא אותֿק[616] כמא קאל[617] הנאך **אבן מאסו הבנים היתה לראש פנה**[618] (תה׳ 118:22). ומעני **מוסד** ״בנא״ לאן אלחגר אן לם יבן פליס יסאוי[619] שיא. ומעני **מוסד** מאסס לאן אלבנא אן לם יכן לה אסאס לם יסאוי שיא.[620] פלפטֿתא אלבנא ואלאסאס **בלשון יסודה**.[621] אלא אן אלאסאס עלי אכתֿרהא יכון[622] דגֿש כקולך **ויסדו הבנים**[623] **היכל יוי**[624] (עזרא 3:10). וקולה **די לא בידין**[625] (דניאל 2:34) יקצד בדֿלך אלתכסיר והו[626] מא סיקול **ובאפס יד ישבר** (דניאל 8:25). וקולה[627] **ומלאת כל ארעה**[628] (דניאל 2:35) אמא פי רויא מן ירי[629] פתלך אלארץֿ אלתי בחצֿרתה כֿאצה. ואמא עלי[630] אלתאויל פגמלה אלארץֿ עאמה. והו מא ועד פי בסט יד מלך משיח פי אלעאלם כלה כמא קאל[631] **ומשלו מים עד ים**[632] **ומנהר עד אפסי ארץ**[633] (זכ׳ 9:10). וקאל איצֿא[634] **וירד מים עד ים וג׳, לפניו**[635] **יכרעו ציים ואיביו עפר ילחכו**[636]**, מלכי תרשיש**[637] **ואיים**[638] **מנחה ישיבו מלכי שבא וסבא**

[615] ללזואיא ... אכתֿר TS Ar 28.165b > D
[616] אותֿק TS Ar 28.165b > L
[617] כק TS Ar 28.165b
[618] לרא פ TS Ar 28.165b > L
[619] יבנא לם יסוא TS Ar 28.165b
[620] ומעני מוסד מאסס ... שיא TS Ar 28.165b > L
[621] בל[שון יסירה] TS Ar 28.165b > D
[622] יכן TS Ar 28.165b
[623] וג׳ + TS Ar 28.165b
[624] היכל יוי TS Ar 28.165b > L
[625] [וקולה ... בי]דין TS Ar 28.165b > D
[626] נטֿיר + TS Ar 28.165b
[627] וק TS Ar 28.165b
[628] ארעא MT
[629] ראי TS Ar 28.165b
[630] סביל + TS Ar 28.165b
[631] כמא קאל TS Ar 28.165b > D
[632] וג׳ + TS Ar 28.165b
[633] ומנהר ... ארץ TS Ar 28.165b > L
[634] איצֿ TS Ar 28.165b
[635] וג׳ + TS Ar 28.165b
[636] יכרעו ... ילחכו TS Ar 28.165b > L
[637] וג׳ + TS Ar 28.165b | תרשיש End of Oxf 2486.18a
[638] ואיים Beginning of Oxf 2486.18b

אשכר יקריבו[639]**, וישתחוו לו כל**[640] **מלכים כל גוים יעבדוהו**[641] (תה׳ 72:8-11).

ואעלם עלמך אללה אן ליס אנתפאענא בהדֹה אלקצה אן נעלם אמור ארבע[642] מלכיות ואלישועה פקט בל הי איה עטֹימה מן איאת בני[643] ישׂראל. ודֹלך אן אלאבא אתֹבתו נבוה דניאל הדֹה והם לא חילה להם אלי אן יעלמו כם ממלכה תקום[644] פי אלארץֹ.[645] אממלכה ואחדה או עשרה או כֹמסין[646] או מא זאד. ואעגב מנה[647] משארכה שריכה אדום להא והי אלראבעה. ואעגב מנה אנהא ליס מן אול דולתהא[648] תשארכהא. ואנמא תשארכהא פי[649] אכֹר אלדולה. ואעגב מן אלכל כיף חצל להם אן מדה אלמשארכה[650] יכון[651] מקדארהא כסבעה[652] אגזא מן יֹא גזא מן מדה אנפראד אדום והו[653] מקדאר[654] נסבה **רגלוהי** מן **שקוהי** (דניאל 2:33). פאני לא[655] אעלם אכבארא פי אלארץֹ[656] אעגב[657] ואבהר מן הדֹה[658] ולא וגה לתחצילהא[659] עלי גמיע[660] אסבאב אלא מן טריק אלנבוה. בל לו לם יכן מן[661] אלתאריךֹ אלא תֹ סנה. פקט כאן אלעגב

[639] ואיים ... יקריבו TS Ar 28.165b > L
[640] וג׳ + TS Ar 28.165b
[641] מלכים ... יעבדוהו TS Ar 28.165b > L
[642] אלד TS Ar 28.165b
[643] בני TS Ar 28.165b > D
[644] יעלמו ... תקום TS Ar 28.165b > D
[645] בעד אלבאבליין + TS Ar 28.165b
[646] או י׳ או נ׳ TS Ar 28.165b
[647] או מא ... מנה TS Ar 28.165b > D
[648] [מנה ... דולתה]א TS Ar 28.165b > D
[649] פי TS Ar 28.165b > D
[650] [ואעגב ... אלמשארכ]ה TS Ar 28.165b > D
[651] יכן TS Ar 28.165b
[652] כז׳ TS Ar 28.165b
[653] גזא ... והו TS Ar 28.165b > D
[654] כמקדאר TS Ar 28.165b
[655] לא Beginning of GE.EN.82.1a
[656] אעלם ... אל]ארץ TS Ar 28.165b > D | אלארץ End of Oxf 2486.18b
[657] אעגב Beginning of Oxf 2629.43a line 23
[658] אעגב ולא אכתֹר ולא אעגב TS Ar 28.165b
[659] [...]להא TS Ar 28.165b > D
[660] וגה ... גמיע Oxf 2629.43a > D | גמיע End of the readable part of TS Ar 28.165b
[661] לגֹתנא ולא מן Oxf 2629.43a uncertain lesson

אלעגיב כיף[662] נעלם אנה ענד[663] אנקצ̇י דולה בעצ̇הם[664] תט̇הר דולה[665] אלמשארכה ותקים[666] אלמדה אלד̇י[667] ד̇כרנאהא.[668] פכיף אן אלתאריך̇ פי הד̇ה אלנבוה אלף ד̇ סנה וכסר. פלו תאמל סאיר אלאמם הד̇ה [...][669] ואנצפו לאטבקו[670] כלהם עלי אלתצדיק בהא פסבחאן מן בצרנא ועלמנא ושרפנא[671] ולם יכ̇לינא מן עלמה. ת̇ם לא יגוז[672] אן נתוהם אן ממלכה אכ̇רא[673] תתבעהם לאן אלסאקין ואלקדמין לא עצוא אכ̇ר בעדהמא[674] פי אלצורה.[675] ומן וגה אכ̇ר לא יגוז אן נתוהם ד̇לך̇ לאנה קד אסתעברנא מן בני יפת[676] ושם ואברהאם[677] אד̇ כלהם **אבות גוים**. פמלכות בבל ברסם חם, חסב קולה[678] פי נמרוד **ותהי ראשית ממלכתו בבל** (בר׳ 10:10.22). ומלכותי מדי ברסם שם כקולה **בני שם עילם ואשור** (בר׳ 10:22). וקאל[679] דניאל[680] **ואני בשושן הבירה אשר בעילם המדינה** (דניאל 8:2). **ומלכות יון** ברסם יפת כמק̇ **בני יפת גמר ומגוג**[681] (בר׳ 10:2. דה״א 1:5) ומלכות אדום וישמעל גמיעא מן בני אברהם[682] כמק̇ **אלה**[683] **תלדות יצחק בן אברהם** (בר׳ 25:19). ואדום הו עש̇ו בן יצחק ראסהם אד̇ הו **אב המון גוים**. פלם יבקא ואחד יקאל לה אבות גוים ג̇יר האולא.[684] ת̇ם קאל[685]

[662] Oxf 2629.43a > D [...]
[663] Oxf 2629.43a > D [...]
[664] Oxf 2629.43a > D [... ...]
[665] Oxf 2629.43a > D [...]
[666] Oxf 2629.43a > D [...]
[667] אלתי Oxf 2629.43a
[668] Oxf 2629.43a > D [... ...]
[669] אל[...]ור GE.GN.82.1a ׀ [...] Oxf 2629.43a > D
[670] Oxf 2629.43a > D [...]
[671] Oxf 2629.43a > D [...]
[672] יגוז GE.GN.82.1a > L
[673] אכ̇רי GE.GN.82.1a
[674] Oxf 2629.43a > D [...]
[675] אלאצנאם Oxf 2629.43a
[676] [..]יפת Oxf 2629.43a > D
[677] ואברהאם Oxf 2629.43a > D
[678] כמא קאל GE.GN.82.1a
[679] End of GE.GN.82.1a
[680] Beginning of GE.GN.82.1b
[681] ברסם...ומגוג Oxf 2629.43a > D
[682] ברסם בני אברהאם GE.GN.82.1b
[683] ואלה.MT
[684] ברסם אברה .... האולא Oxf 2629.43a > D

Dn 2:46
באידין מלכא נבוכדנצר נפל על אפוהי ולדניאל סגיד ומנחה וניחחין אמר לנסכה ליה.

חיניד̇ וקע אלמלך בכ̇תנצר עלי וגהה וסגד לדניאל ואמר באן תקרב לה הדאיא ושמאים.[686]

Dn 2:47
עני מלכא לדניאל ואמר מן קשוט די אלהכון הוא אלה אלהין ומרי מלכין וגלי רזין די יכילתא למגלי רזא הדין.

ת̇ם[687] קאל לה מן אלחק אלצחיח[688] אן רבכם הו אלאה[689] אלאלהה[690] וסיד[691] אלמלוך וכאשף אלאסראר[692] אד̇ מכנך אן תכשף הד̇א[693] אלסר.[694]

Dn 2:48
אדין מלכא לדניאל רבי ומתנן רברן סגיאן יהבליה והשלטיה על כל מדינת בבל ורב סגנין על כל חכימי בבל.

חיניד̇ כת̇ר אלמלך דניאל ווהב לה עטאיא[695] נפיסה גלילה וסלטה[696] עלי גמיע מדינה באבל ומרה עלי גמיע חכמא באבל.[697]

[685] קאל End of the readable part of 2629.43a line 33
[686] חיניד וקע בכתנצר אלמלך [ע]ל[י] וגהה פסגד לדניאל ואמר אן תקרב קדאמה הדאיא ושמאים. GE.GN.82.1b
[687] תם Beginning of Oxf 2486.19a
[688] אל[צח]יח Oxf 2486.19a > D
[689] אלה Oxf 2486.19a
[690] אלאלאהאת Spiegel
[691] וסייד Spiegel + Morag
[692] אלסראיר Morag
[693] כשפת הדי Morag
[694] אלס[ר] Oxf 2486.19a > D | תם קאל לה מן אלחק אלצחיח אן אלהכם הו אלה אלאלאהאת וסיד אלמלך וכאשף אלסראיר אד מכנך מן כשף הדא אלסר GE.GN.82.1b
[695] עניאיא Morag
[696] וצלטה Morag
[697] חיניד שרף אלמלך דניאל ווהב להעטאיא נפיסא גלילה וסלטה עלי גמיע מדינה בבל וומרה עלי גמיע חכמא בבל GE.GN.82.1b

Dn 2:49
ודניאל בעא מן מלכא ומני על עבידתא די מדינת בבל לשרך מישך ועביד נגו ודניאל בתרע מלכא.

תֿם אן דניאל[698] סאל אלמלך אן יולי[699] עלי אעמאל[700] מדינה[701] באבל[702] שדרך מישך ועביד נגו ואקאם[703] הו בבאב אלמלך.

ואמא אלסגוגד[704] אלדֿי בדלה[705] נבוכֿדנצר[706] [... ...][707] פי קבולה לה[708] מנה[709] שיא. אדֿ גאיז פי שריעתנא יסגד בעצֿנא לבעץֿ סגוד אגלאל לא סגוד עבאדה כמא הו משרוח פי תפסיר אלמגלה. ואמא אלקראבין פלם יקבלהא. ולדֿלך אוקע פי אלנץ **אמר לנסכא לה** (דניאל 2:46). פיכון דֿלך באלקול לא באלפעל. ונקלת תפסיר **די יכלת למגלא רזה דנה** (דניאל 2:47) מן פעל דניאל אלי פעל אלכֿאלק פקלת "אלדֿי מכנך" לאן אלשכר לה לא יקע אלא עלי פעלה. ופסרת **ורב סגנין** (דניאל 2:48) "אמרה" אדֿ **סגנים** "כֿלפא" פיכון כבירהם אסירא. תם שרח אלגז אלתֿאני.

[698] תֿם אן דניא]ל Oxf 2486.19a > D
[699] בה + Oxf 2486.19a | יולי Spiegel
[700] אעמל Spiegel
[701] אעמל מדינה Oxf 2486.19a > D
[702] בבל GE.GN.82.1b
[703] ש]דר[ך]מישך ... ואק[אם Oxf 2486.19a > D
[704] ואמא אלסגוד Oxf 2486.19a > D
[705] בדלה Oxf 2486.19a uncertain lesson
[706] End of GE.GN.82.1b
[707] [... ...] Oxf 2486.19a > D
[708] לה End of Oxf 2486.19a
[709] מנה Beginning of 2486.19b

ונץ אלגז אלת̇אלת̇

Dn 3:1

נבוכדנצר מלכא עבד צלם די דהב רומיה אמין שתין פתייה אמין שית אקימיה בבקעת דורא במדינת בבל.

ת̇ם אן בכ̇ת נצר[1] אלמלך אצלח[2] צנמא[3] מן[4] ד̇הב רפעה סתין ד̇ראע וערצ̇ה סתה ונצבה פי בקעת[5] דורא פי מדינת[6] באבל.

Dn 3:2

ונבוכדנצר מלכא שלח למכנש לאכשדרפניא סגניא ופחוותא אדרגזריא גדבריא דתבריא תפתיא וכל שלטוני מדינתא למיתי לחנוכת צלמא די הקים נבוכדנצר מלכא.

ת̇ם אנה בעת̇ ליחשר אלבטארקה ואלאמרא ואלכ̇לפא ואלחכאם ואלעמאל[7] ואלכתאב ואלשרטיין וסאיר ס[8]לאטין אלבלדאן[9] אלי וכארה[10] אלצנם אלדי נצבה.

Dn 3:3

באידין מתכנשין אחשדרפניא סגניא לפחוותא אדרגזריא גדבריא רתבריא תפתאי וכל שלטוני מדינתא לחנוכת צלמא די הקים נבוכד נצר מלכא וזימין לקביל צלמא די הקים נבוכד נצר.

[1] בכ̇תנצר Spiegel + Oxf 2486.19b

[2] אצלח End of the readable part of Oxf 2486.19b

[3] צנמא Oxf 2486.19b > D

[4] מן Beginning of Oxf 2486.20a

[5] בקעה Spiegel + Oxf 2486.20a

[6] מדינה Spiegel + Oxf 2486.20a

[7] ואל[ע]מאל Oxf 2486.20a > D

[8] צלאטין Morag

[9] אלמדן Spiegel | פיגו + Oxf 2486.20a

[10] וכרה Spiegel

חיניד[11] אגתמעו אלבטארקה ואלאמרא[12] ואלכ̇לפא[13] ואלחכאם ואלעמאל ואלכתאב ואלשרטיין וסאיר סלאטין[14] אלבלדאן אלי וכארת[15] אלצנם אלד̇י נצבה בכ̇ת נצר[16] ווקפו בין ידיה.

Dn 3:4
וכרוזא קרי בחיל לכון אמרין עממיה אומיה ולישניא.

ואלמנאדי ינאדי בקוה[17] לכם[18] יא מעאשר[19] אלשעוב ואלאמם ואהל אללג̇את.

Dn 3:5
בעידנא די תשמעון קל קרנא משרוקיתא קתרוס סבכא פסנתירין סמפוניה וכל זני זמרא תפלון ותסגדון לצלם דהבא די הקים נבוכד נצר מלכא.

פי וקת אן[20] תסמעון צות אלבוק ואלצפארה ואלדף ואלטבל ואלצנג ואלנאי[21] וסאיר אנואע אלמלאהי תכ̇רו[22] ותסגדו לצנם אלד̇הב אלד̇י נצבה בכ̇תנצר אלמלך.[23]

Dn 3:6
ומן די לא יפל ויסגוד בה שעתא[24] יתרמי[25] לגו אתון נורא יקירתא.

ומן מנכם לם[26] יכ̇ר ויסגד[27] לה מן קאעתה ירמא בה אלי אתון אלנאר אלמתווקד.[28]

[11] חיניד Oxf 2486.20a > D
[12] אלאמרא End of Oxf 2486.20a
[13] ואלכלפא Beginning of Oxf 2486.20b
[14] צלאט[א]ן Oxf 2486.20b > D
[15] וכרה Spiegel
[16] בכת נצר Oxf 2486.20b > D
[17] בקווה Spiegel + Morag
[18] יקאל + Spiegel and Oxf 2486.20b
[19] יא מעאשר Spiegel > D
[20] אן Oxf 2486.20b > L
[21] ואלינאי Oxf 2486.20b
[22] תכר Spiegel
[23] אלמלך Spiegel and Oxf 2486.20b > L
[24] שעתא End of Oxf 2486.20b
[25] יתרמי Beginning of Oxf 2486.21a

Dn 3:7

כל קביל דנא בה זמנא כדי שמעין כל עממיא קל קרנא משרוקיתא קתרוס סבכא פסנתידין וכל מני זמרא נפלין כל עממיא אומיא ולישניא סגדין לצלים דהבא די הקים נבוכד נצר מלכא.

פענד דֹלך[29] כמא כאן יסמע גמיע אלשעוב צות אלבוק ואלצפארה ואלדף ואלטבל ואלצנג[30] וסאיר אנואע אלמלאהי מן וקתה יכֹרון גמיע אלשעוב ואלאמם ואהל אללגֹאת פיסגדון ללצנם אלדֹהבי[31] אלדֹי נצבה בכֹתנצר אלמלך.

Dn 3:8

כל קביל דנא בה זימנא קריבו גלכרין כסדאין ואכלו קרציהון די יהודאי.[32]

וענד[33] דֹאלך[34] מן וקתה תקדם קום כסדאניין[35] פסעו[36] וגֹמזו[37] באליהוד.

Dn 3:9

ענו ואמרין לנבוכד נצר מלכא מלכא לעולמין חיי.

באן אבתדו וקאלו[38] לבכֹתנצר אלמלך אטאל אללה בקא אלמלך.

Dn 3:10-11

אנתא מלכא שמתה טעים די כל אנש די ישמע קל קרנא משרוקיתא קתדוס סבכא פסנתירין וסומפוניא וכל זני זמרא יפול ויסגוד לצלים דהבא. ומן די לא יפול ויסגוד יתרמי לגו אתון נורא יקידתא.[39]

[26] לא Spiegel + Oxf 2486.21a

[27] פיסגד Oxf 2486. 21a

[28] אלמתוקד Spiegel + Oxf 2486. 21a

[29] דאלך Spiegel + Morag

[30] ואלנאי Spiegel +

[31] ללצנם אלדהב Morag | לצנם אלדהב Spiegel

[32] יהודיא End of Oxf 2486.21a

[33] וענד Beginning of Oxf 2486.21b

[34] דלך Oxf 2486.21b

[35] כסד[...] Oxf 2486.21b | כסאדניין Spiegel

[36] פמחלו Oxf 2486.21b | פלעו Spiegel

[37] וגֹמזו Oxf 2486.21b > L

[38] פקאלו Oxf 2486.21b

[39] Dn 3:10-11 are considered one verse by Morag

יא[40] איה[41] אלמלך אנת אמרת באן כל אנסאן יסמע צות אלבוק ואלצפארה ואלדף ואלטבל ואלצנג ואלנאי וסאיר אנואע אלמלאהי[42] ומן לם יכ̇ר פיסגד ללצנם אלד̇הב, ומן לם יכ̇ר ויסגד[43] פירמא[44] בה[45] אלי[46] אתון אלנאר אלמתוקד.[47]

Dn 3:12

איתי גוברין יהודאין די מניתא יתהון[48] על[49] עבידת מדינת בבל שדרך משך ועביד נגו גובריא אלך לא שמו עלך מלכא טעים לאלהך לא פלחין ולצלים דהבא די הקימתא לא סגדין.

מוגוד[50] קום יהוד אלד̇ין ואליתהם עלי אעמאל מדינה באבל שדרך משך[51] ועבד נגו אולאיך קום לם יקבלו ללמלך[52] אמרה מעבודה[53] לא יעבדון ואלצנם[54] אלד̇הב אלד̇י נצבתה[55] לא יסגדון לה.[56]

Dn 3:13

באדין נבוכדנצר ברגז ובחמה אמר להיתאה לשדרך משך ועביד נגו באידין גובריא אליך היתו קדם מלכא.

חיניד̇ אמר בכ̇תנצר[57] ברגז וחמיה[58] אן יחצ̇ר שדרך משך ועבד נגו חיניד̇[59] אחצ̇רו[60] בין ידיה.

40 יא Spiegel > L
41 יאיהא Oxf 2486.21b
42 ואלנאי וסאיר אנואע אלמלאהי Oxf 2486.21b > L
43 פיסגד Oxf 2486.21b
44 ורמי Oxf 2486.21b | ירמה Spiegel
45 פי Spiegel + Oxf 2486.21b
46 אלי Spiegel and Oxf 2486.21b > L
47 אלמתווקד Morag
48 יתהון End of Oxf 2486.21b
49 על Beginning of Oxf 2486. 22a
50 פמוגוד Oxf 2486.22a
51 ומישך Oxf 2486.22a | מישך Spiegel
52 לאמלד Spiegel
53 מעבודך Spiegel
54 וללצנם Oxf 2486.22a | ולאלצנם Spiegel
55 נצבתהא Spiegel
56 לה Spiegel and Oxf 2486.22a > L
57 בכתנצר Beginning of TS Ar b1 B1a

Dn 3:14
ענה נבוכד נצר ואמר להון הצדא שדרך משך ועביד נגו לאלהי לא איתיכון פלחין ואלצלים דהבא די הקימית לא סגדין.[61]

פאבתדי[62] וקאל̇ להם איקינא יא שדרך משך[63] ועבד נגו למעבודי[64] ליס אנתם עאבדון[65] ולצנם[66] אלד̇הב[67] אלד̇י נצבתה ג̇יר סאגדין.[68]

Dn 3:15
כען הן איתיכון עתידין די בעידנא די תשמעון קל קדנא משרוקיתא קתרוס סבכא פסנתירין וסומפוניא וכל זני זמרא תפלון ותסגדון לצלמא די עבדית והן לא תסגדון בה שעתא תתרמון לגו אתון נורא[69] יקידתא ומן הו אלה די ישוזבינכון מן ידי.

אלאן[70] כונו[71] מסתעדין פי וקת תסמעון צות[72] אלבוק ואלצפארה ואלדף ואלטבל ואלצנג ואלנאי וסאיר אנואע אלמלאהי תכ̇רון ותסגדון ללצנם אלד̇י צנעתה ואן לם תסגדון[73] מן סאעתכם ירמא[74] בכם אלי אתון אלנאר אלמתווקד[75] ואי ד̇א רב יכ̇לצכם מן ידי.

[58] וחמייה Spiegel + Morag
[59] חיניד Spiegel and Oxf 2486.22a > L
[60] פאחצרו Spiegel + Oxf 2486.22a | נג[ו ... אח]צרו TS Ar b1 B1a > D
[61] סגדין End of Oxf 2486.22a
[62] פאבתדא Spiegel + TS Ar b1 B1a | פאבתדי Beginning of Oxf 2486.22b
[63] ומישך Oxf 2486.22b | מישך Spiegel + TS Ar b1 B1a
[64] מעבודי Spiegel + TS Ar b1 B1a + Oxf 2486.22b
[65] עאבדין Spiegel + Oxf 2486.22b | עאבדון Beginning of TS Ar b1 B1b
[66] עאבדון ולצנם TS Ar b1 B1b > D | וללצנם Oxf 2486.22b | ולאלצנם Spiegel
[67] [אל]ד[ה]ב TS Ar b1 B1b > D
[68] נצבתה ... סאגדין TS Ar b1 B1b > D
[69] נורא End of TS Ar b1 B1b
[70] ואלאן Spiegel
[71] כנו Oxf 2486.22b
[72] צות Oxf 2486.22b > L
[73] תסגדו Oxf 2486.22b
[74] ירמי Oxf 2486.22b
[75] אלמתוקד Spiegel + Oxf 2486.22b

Dn 3:16

ענו שדרך מישך ועבד נגו ואמרין[76] למלכא[77] נבוכד נצר לא חשחין אנחנא על דנא פתגם להתבותך.

אגאבוה וקאלו יא בכ֗תנצר אלמלך[78] לא נחתאג אן נג֗יבך ען[79] הד֗א[80] בכלמה.

Dn 3:17

הן איתי אלהנא די אנחנא פלחין ליה יכיל לשיזבותנא מן אתון נורא יקידתא ומן ידך מלכא ישיזיב.

אד֗ רבנא אלד֗י נעבדה יסתטיע אן יכ֗לצנא מן אתון אלנאר אלמתוקד[81] ומן ידך יא איהא[82] אלמלך יכ֗לצנא.

Dn 3:18

והן לא ידיע להוי לך מלכא די לא להך לא איתנא פלחין ולצלם דהבא די הקימתא לא נסגור.

ואן לם יכ֗לצנא פאעלם[83] יא איהא[84] אלמלך אנא[85] לא נעבד מעבודך ולא נסגד לצנם[86] אלד֗הב[87] אלד֗י נצבתה.

Dn 3:19

באדין נבוכד נצר התמלי חמא וצלים אנפוהי השתני על שדרך מישך ועבד נגו[88] עני[89] ואמר למזא לאתונא חד שבעה על די חזי למיזי.

[76] ואמרין End of Oxf 2486.22b

[77] למלכא Beginning of Oxf 2486.23a

[78] אלמלך Spiegel and Oxf 2486.23a > L

[79] עלי Spiegel

[80] הדי Morag

[81] אלמתווקד Morag

[82] יאיהא Oxf 2486.23a | יא אייה Spiegel

[83] פאעלם Spiegel > L

[84] יאיהא Oxf 2486. 23a | יא אייה Spiegel

[85] אן Morag

[86] ללצנם Oxf 2486.23a

[87] אלדהב Spiegel > L

[88] נגו End of Oxf 2486.23a

[89] עני Beginning of Oxf 2486.23b

חיניד̇ אמתלא בכ̇תנצר חמייה וסחנת[90] וגהה תג̇יירת עלי שדרך משך ועביד נגו[91] פאמר באן יסגר אלאתון ללואחד[92] סבעה עלי מא ינבג̇י לה[93] אן יסגר.

Dn 3:20
ולגוברין גיברי חיל די בחיליה אמר לכפתא לשדרך משך ועבד נגו למרמי לגו אתון נורא יקידתא.

ואמר קומא גבארין מן גישה אן יכפתון[94] שדרך משך[95] ועב[96] נגו לירמי[97] בהם פי אתון אלנאר אלמתוקד.[98]

Dn 3:21
באדיין גובריא אליך כפיתו בסרבליהון[99] פטשיהון[100] וכרבלתהון ולבושיהון ורמיו לגו אתון נורא יקידתא.

חיניד̇ כפתו[101] אולאיך אלקום בסראוילאתהם[102] וקמצאנהם ומשמאלהם[103] וסאיר לבאסהם ורמי בהם פי וסט אתון אלנאר[104] אלמתוקד.[105]

Dn 3:22
כל קביל דנה מן די מלת מלכא מהחצפא ואתונא איזיה יתירא גובריא אליך די הסיקו לשדרך מישך ועבד נגו קתילהמון שביבא די נורא.

[90] חמייה וסחנה Spiegel + Oxf 2486.23b
[91] ומישך ועבד נגו Oxf 2486.23b ׀ מישך ועבד נגו Spiegel
[92] ללואחד Spiegel > L
[93] לה Spiegel > L
[94] יכפתו Spiegel + Oxf 2486.23b
[95] ומישך Oxf 2486.23b ׀ מישך Spiegel
[96] ועביד Spiegel
[97] לירמא Morag
[98] אלמתווקד Morag
[99] בסרבליהון End of Oxf 2486.23b
[100] פטשיהון Beginning of Oxf 2486.24a
[101] כתף Oxf 2486.24a
[102] בסראוילתהם Oxf 2486. 24a ׀ בסראוי לאתהם Spiegel
[103] ומשאמלהם Spiegel + Oxf 2486. 24a
[104] אלי וסט אלנאר Oxf 2486. 24a ׀ פי אתון אלנאר Spiegel
[105] אלמתווקד Morag

פממא[106] כאן אלאמר[107] חאתא ואלאתון סגר פצ̇לא[108] אלקום אלד̇ין[109] גאזו[110] בשדרך מישך[111] ועבד[112] נגו קתלהם והג אלנאר.[113]

Dn 3:23

וגובריא אלין תלתיהון שדרך מישך ועביד נגו נפלו לגו אתון נורא[114] יקידתא מכפתין.[115]

ואלנפר[116] אלת̇לאת̇ה[117] שדרך משך ועביד[118] נגו פוקעו פי וסט אתון אלנאר אלמתווקד מכפותין.[119]

Dn 3:24

אדין[120] נבוכד נצר מלכא תוה וקם בהתבהלא עני ואמר להדברוהי הלא גוברין תלתה רמינא לגו נורא מכפתין ענין ואמרין[121] למלכא יציבא מלכא.

חיניד̇ קלק בכ̇תנצר[122] אלמלך וקאם מבאדרא פאבתדא[123] וקאל לקואדה אליס ת̇לאת̇ה נפר רמינא[124] בהם אלי וסט אלנאר[125] מכפותין[126] אגאבוה וקאלו יקינא יא איהא[127] אלמלך.[128]

106 פממא Beginning of TS Ar b1 B1c | פכמא TS Ar b1 B1c

107 אמר אלמלך TS Ar b1 B1c + Oxf 2486. 24a

108 פצ̇לא Beginning of TS Ar 21.49a

109 אולאיך אלדי Spiegel

110 זגו Spiegel + TS Ar 21.49a + Oxf 2486. 24a | יגו TS Ar b1 B1c

111 בש מ̇ TS Ar 21.49a

112 ועביד Spiegel | מ̇ וע נגו TS Ar b1 B1c

113 וע[בד ... אלנאר] TS Ar 21.49a > D

114 נורא Beginning of the readable part of TS Ar b1 B1d

115 מכפתין TS Ar b1 B1d > D

116 ואולאיך אלנפר Spiegel

117 אלג̇ Oxf 2486.24a

118 ועבד נגו Spiegel + Oxf 2486.24a

119 מכפותין End of Oxf 2486.24a

120 אדין Beginning of Oxf 2486.24b

121 ואמרין End of TS Ar b1 B1d

122 נ̇ TS Ar 21.49a

123 פאבתדי Oxf 2486.24b | מבאדרא פאבתדי TS Ar 21.49a > D

124 רמינא Beginning of the radable part of TS NS 285.21b

125 וסט אלנאר TS Ar 21.49a > D

126 מכתפין Oxf 2486.24b | TS Ar 21.49a | [מכ]תפין TS NS 285.21b > D

Dn 3:25

עני מלכא ואמר הא אנא חזה גוברין ארבעה שרין מהלכין בגו נורא וחבל לר איתי בהון וריויה די רביעה דמי לבר אלהין.

אגאבהם וקאל הודי[129] אנטׄר[130] ארבעה[131] מחללין[132] יתמשון פי וסט אלנאר וליס[133] פיהם שייא[134] מן אלפסאד וחלית[135] אלראבע תשבה אלמלאיכה.[136]

Dn 3:26

באידיין קריב נבוכד נצר לתרע אתון נורא יקידתא עני ואמר שדרך מישך[137] ועבד[138] נגו עבדוהי די אלהא עליא פקו ואתו באדין נפקין שדרך ועבד נגו מן גוא נורא.

חיניד[139] תקדם בכת נצר[140] אלי באב אתון אלנאר[141] אלמתוקד[142] פנאדא יא שדרך מישך ועבד נגו[143] עביד[144] אלאלאה אלעאלי[145] אכׄרגו ותעאלו חיניד[146] שדרך מישך ועבד נגו[147] כׄרגו[148] מן[149] וסט[150] אלנאר.

[127] יאיהא TS Ar 21.49a + Oxf 2486.24b ׀ איהא TS NS 285.21b ׀ יא אייה Spiegel

[128] אל[מלך] TS Ar 21.49a > D

[129] אגאבהם ... הודי TS Ar 21.49a > D

[130] אנצׄר Spiegel + Morag ׀ האנא נאטׄר Oxf 2486. 24b

[131] ד נפר TS Ar 21.49a + Oxf 2486. 24b

[132] [אגבהם ... מחל[לין TS NS 285.21b > D

[133] ית[משון ... אלנאר] TS Ar 21.49a > D ׀ אל[נא]ר ול[יס] TS NS 285.21b > D

[134] שיא TS Ar 21.49a + Oxf 2486.24b ׀ שי Spiegel + TS NS 285.21b

[135] וחליה TS NS 285.21b + TS Ar 21.49a + Oxf 2486.24b ׀ וחלייה Spiegel

[136] אלרא[בע ... אלמלאיכה] TS Ar 21.49a > D

[137] מישך End of Oxf 2486.24b

[138] ועבדו Beginning of Oxf 2486.25a

[139] חיניד TS NS 285.21b > D

[140] נׄ TS Ar 21.49a

[141] אל[נאר] TS NS 285.21b > D

[142] אלמתוקד Morag > L

[143] וע עביד TS NS 285.21b > L

[144] אלמתוקד ... ועבד נגו TS Ar 21.49a > D ׀ שד מיש ועב נגו Morag

[145] עבד Spiegel

[146] אלעלי Oxf 2486. 25a ׀ אלעאליי Spiegel

[147] שד מיש ועב נגו Morag ׀ שׄ מׄ וע TS Ar 21.49a

[148] חיניד כרג שדרך ומישך ועבד נגו Oxf 2486. 25a

[149] שדרך ... מן TS NS 285.21b > D

[150] מן וסט TS Ar 21.49a > D ׀ וצט Morag

Dn 3:27

ומתכנשין אחשדרפניא סגניא ופחותא והדברי מלכא חזין לגובריא אלך די לא שלט נורא בגשמהון ושער ראשהון לא התחרך וסרבליהון לא שנו וריח נור לא עדת בהון.

ואגתמע[151] אלבטארקה ואלאמרא ואלכ̇לפא[152] וקואד[153] אלמלך פנט̇רו[154] אוליך[155] אלקום ותעגבו כיף[156] לא[157] יתסלט[158] אלנאר עלי[159] אגסאמהם[160] ושער רוסהם[161] לם יתשוט[162] ולבאסהם לם יתג̇ייר[163] וראיחה אלדכאן[164] לם תעבק בהם.[165]

Dn 3:28

ענה[166] נבוכדנצר ואמר בריך אלההון די שדרך ומישך ועבד נגו די שלח מלאכיה ןשיזיב לעבדוהי די התרחיצו עלוהי ומלאת מלכא שניו ויהבו גשמיהון די לא יפלחון ולא יסגדון לכל אלה להן לאלההון.

ת̇ם אבתדא[167] בכתנצר[168] וקאל[169] תבארך אלאה[170] שדרך ומישך ועבד נגו[171] אלד̇י בעת̇ במלכה[172] וכ̇לץ עבידה אלד̇י[173] תוכלו עליה וג̇יירו[174] אמר

[151] ואגתמע TS NS 285.21b > D | ואגתמעו Spiegel
[152] ואל[אמרא ואל]כלפא TS Ar 21.49a > D
[153] ואלקואד TS Ar 21.49a
[154] פנצ̇רו Morag | ונצ̇רו Spiegel | אלי + TS NS 285.21b
[155] אליך TS Ar 21.49a
[156] ותעגבו כיף TS NS 285.21b > D
[157] ותע[גבו ... לא] TS Ar 21.49a > D | לם Spiegel
[158] לם תתסלט TS NS 285.21b
[159] פי TS NS 285.21b
[160] אגסא[מה]ם TS NS 285.21b > D
[161] רווסהם Oxf 2486. 25a
[162] לם יתשוט TS Ar 21.49a > D | יתשווט
[163] יתג̇יר Spiegel + TS Ar 21.49a + Oxf 2486. 25a
[164] [אלד]כאן TS NS 285.21b > D
[165] תע[בק בהם] TS Ar 21.49a> D | בהם TS NS 285.21b> D | End Oxf 2486. 25a
[166] ענה Beginning of Oxf 2486.25b
[167] אבתדי TS Ar 21.49a + Oxf 2486. 25b
[168] נ̇ TS Ar 21.49a
[169] ת̇ם [אבתדא] קאל בכתנצר TS NS 285.21b > L
[170] אלה Oxf 2486. 25b | תבאר[ך אל]לה TS NS 285.21b > D
[171] שד̇ מיש̇ ועב̇ נגו Morag | ש̇ מ̇ וע̇ TS Ar 21.49a + TS NS 285.21b > L

אלמלך[175] ובד̇לו[176] אגסאמהם דון אן יעבדון או[177] יסגדון[178] לאלאה[179] סוא
אלאההם.[180]

Dn 3:29

ומני שים טעם די כל עם אמה ולשן די יאמר שלה על אלההון די שדרך ומישך ועבד נגו הדמין יתעביד וביתה נזלי ישתוה כל קבל די לא איתי אלה אחרן די יכל להצלה כרנה.

והוד̇א[181] אמר באמר אן יכון[182] אי קביל או אמה או[183] ד̇ו לג̇ה[184] יתקוול[185] אלמחאל עלי[186] אלאה[187] שדרך ומישך ועבד נגו[188] אן יגעל אעצ̇אא[189] ומנזלה נכאלא אד̇ לא[190] יוגד אלאה[191] אכ̇ר יסתטיע[192] יכ̇לץ כד̇אלך.

Dn 3:30

נאדין מלכא הצלח לשדרך מישך ועבד נגו במדינת בבל.

ת̇ם אן אלמלך אצלח[193] חאל שדרך ומישך ועבד נגו פי מדינת בבל.[194]

[172] אלדי ... במלכה TS Ar 21.49a > D ׀ מלכה TS NS 285.21b
[173] אלדין Spiegel + TS NS 285.21b + TS Ar 21.49a + Oxf 2486. 25b
[174] וג̇ירו TS Ar 21.49a + Oxf 2486. 25b ׀ א[.]רו TS NS 285.21b > D
[175] אלמ[לך] TS NS 285.21b > D
[176] אמר ... ובדלו TS Ar 21.49a > D
[177] ואן Spiegel
[178] יעבדו או יסגדו TS Ar 21.49a + Oxf 2486. 25b
[179] לאלה סוי אלההם Oxf 2486. 25b ׀ לאללה סוא אלאההם Spiegel
[180] לאללה ... אלאההם TS Ar 21.49a > D ׀ [יעבדון א]ו יסג[דון לאלא]ה סוא אלההם TS NS 285.21b > D
[181] ואנא TS NS 285.21b
[182] אי יכון TS NS 285.21b > D
[183] אי ... או TS Ar 21.49a > D
[184] או לסאן TS NS 285.21b
[185] יתקול TS NS 285.21b + TS Ar 21.49a + Oxf 2486. 25b
[186] אלמח[אל ע]לי TS Ar 21.49a > D
[187] אלה TS Ar 21.49a ׀ אללה TS NS 285.21b ׀ אלה End of the readable part of TS Ar 21.49a
[188] שד מיש ועב Morag ׀ שדרך מישף ועביד נגו Spiegel
[189] ש[דרך.. נגו] אן [א]ע[צ̇]א TS NS 285.21b > D ׀ אעצ̇אא End of Oxf 2486. 25b
[190] ליס TS NS 285.21b
[191] אללה TS NS 285.21b
[192] יסת[טיע] TS NS 285.21b > D ׀ אן + TS NS 285.21b and Spiegel

אול מא אנתפענא בה מן הד̇ה אלקצה אן עלמנא[195] אן אסם אללה אד̇א כאן ללמעבוד פהו ג̇ [...][196] אם [...][197] אמא קיאם וסגוד. פכמא קאל הונא **לחנכת צלמא** (דניאל 3:2.3) קימין וסגדין. ואמא קרבאן פכמא קאל הנאך [...][198] יכן לח...לו[199] רד ואי שי מן אלנפע פי הד̇א אלעלם. פנקול אן אלכתאב ד̇כר ען אלאבא אנהם עמלו פי זמאן[200] שלמה [... ...][201] **חג הסכות.** וכמא קאל **כי חנכת המזבח עשו שבעת**[202] **ימים** (דה״ב 7:9). פמן לם יקע **חנכה** ג̇יר אלאכל [... ...][203] ויאכלו אלקום ושרבו **יום כיפור** אלדאכ̇ל פי אלז̇ איאם [......][204] אן אלסבעת איאם כאנת מנפצלה[205] מן [...][206] בעצ̇הא[207] מן בעצ̇ ביום. פאד̇ קד אנפתח לנא [...] הד̇א אלקול[208] מעני **חנכה** קיאם וסגוד וקרבאן אסתג̇נינא ען תפריק ז̇ מן ז̇ או בעצ̇ סבעה מן בעצ̇ [... ...][209] קרבאן אגמע יגוז פי אלכפור.

ופסרת **לא שמו עליך מלכא טעם** (דניאל 3:12) ״לם יקבלון אמרך [... ...][210] **עליהון טעם מינך**. והד̇א מת̇ל **כל העובר על הפקודים** (שמ׳ 30:13) **העומדים על הפקודים** (במד׳ 7:2) [... ...][211] **נרפא [נגע] הצרוע מן הצרעת** (ע׳ ויק׳ 14:3).[212] ומת̇ל **פן מצא לו ערים בצורות והציל עיננו**

[193] אצלח TS NS 285.21b

[194] חאל ... באבל TS NS 285.21b > D

[195] עלמ[נ]א TS NS 285.21b > D

[196] א[...] TS NS 285.21b > D

[197] אם [...] TS NS 285.21b > D

[198] [...] TS NS 285.21b > D

[199] ר[...] יכן לח[...]א TS NS 285.21b > D

[200] ז[מאן] TS NS 285.21b > D

[201] חנ[... ...]ם TS NS 285.21b > D

[202] שבעת TS NS 285.21b > D

[203] א[... ...] TS NS 285.21b > D

[204] אי[... ...] TS NS 285.21b > D

[205] מנפצלה TS NS 285.21b

[206] [...] TS NS 285.21b > D

[207] [בעצ̇ה]א TS NS 285.21b > D

[208] [... ...]דא אלק[ול] TS NS 285.21b > D

[209] [... ...] TS NS 285.21b > D

[210] ל[... ...] TS NS 285.21b > D

[211] [...] [...] TS NS 285.21b > D

[212] נרפא נגע הצרעת מן הצרוע (ויק׳ 14:3)

(שמ״ב 20:6). [... ...] **באש**[213] **מקדשיך** (תה׳ 74:7) חאצלה **שלחו אש בקדשיך**. וכד̇לך **מבצריהם**[214] **תשלח באש**[215] (מל״ב 8:12). ופסרת **הצדא** (דניאל 3:14) מת̇ל **אזדא** (דניאל 2:5) פגעלתה ״גדא״ ו״יקינא״ אד̇ האד̇אן אלחרפאן[216] ינוב אחדהמא ען אלאכ̇ר פי אלאבדאל. ופסרת **חשחין** (דניאל 3:16) ״נחתאג״ לאנהא ג̇ כלמאת הכד̇א פי אלכסדאני[217] **לא**[218] **חשחין** (דניאל 3:16) **ומן**[219] **חשחן** (ע׳ עזרא 6:9) **ושאר חשחות בית אלהיך**[220] (עזרא 7:20). ופי קולהם לה ״לא נחתאג אן נגיבך ען הד̇א״ וגוהא[221]. מנהא לאן הד̇א שיא מסלם אן[222] רב אלעאלמין הו אלמעבוד.[223] ואיצ̇א לאן[224] אלמחדת̇ ואלמצנוע ליס במעבוד. ואיצ̇א לאן אלקאדר[225] עלי כל שיא יקדר עלי כ̇לאצנא. ומנהא אנה[226] לא נדרי יכ̇לצנא באלפעל או לא, אד̇ רבמא אמתחן אוליאה. ולכנא[227] נגיבך ען אלקסמין[228] גמיעא.[229] כ̇לץ אם[230] לם יכ̇לץ נחן ללצנם לא נסגד.[231]

וזיאדתהם **ומן ידך מלכא**[232] (דניאל 3:17) יענון בה גמיע אנואע[233] אלעד̇אב. אי[234] ליס מן אלנאר וחדהא[235] יכ̇לצנא בל מן אלחבס ואלקיד ואלסיף ואלסבאע

[213] [בא]ש TS NS 285.21b > D
[214] מבצריהם Beginning of Oxf 2486. 26a
[215] תש[לח באש] TS NS 285.21b > D
[216] [אד ה]דין אלחרפין TS NS 285.21b > D
[217] לאנה[א ג̇ כלמאת הכד̇א פי אלכ]סדאני TS NS 285.21b > D
[218] לא TS NS 285.21b > L
[219] ומן TS NS 285.21b > L | ומה MT
[220] [ושאר] תשחות [בית אלהיך] TS NS 285.21b > L
[221] וגוה Oxf 2486. 26a
[222] [לאן ... א]ן TS NS 285.21b > D
[223] ומנהא אן + TS NS 285.21b
[224] ואיצ̇א לאן TS NS 285.21b > L
[225] ואיצ̇א לאן אלקאדר TS NS 285.21b > D
[226] אנה TS NS 285.21b > L
[227] אמתחן ... ולכנא TS NS 285.21b > D
[228] עלי קסמין TS NS 285.21b
[229] גמיעא TS NS 285.21b > L
[230] או TS NS 285.21b
[231] פאנא לא נסגד ללצנם TS NS 285.21b
[232] ישיזב + TS NS 285.21b
[233] יע[נון בה גמיע אנואע] TS NS 285.21b > D
[234] אד̇ TS NS 285.21b
[235] וחדה TS NS 285.21b

ואלעדׄאב וסאיר מא[236] תנאל[237] יד אלסלטאן אן יסתעמלה מע מן יסכׄט עליה. ופי קולה **והן לא**[238] **ידיע להוי לך מלכא**[239] (דניאל 3:18) אעתבאראן.[240] אחדהמא אנה יגב עלינא בדׄל[241] נפוסנא דון עבאדה אלאצנאם. והו באב מן גׄ אבואב יגב עלינא בדׄל נפוסנא[242] ולא נצׄמנהא. פאולהא עבאדה[243] גׄיר רבנא כמא[244] פי הדׄה אלקצה. ואלבׄ ארתכאב אלמחארם[245] כמא פי קצה[246] יוסף **ואיך אעשה הרעה הגדולה הזאת וחטאתי לאלהים**[247] (בר' 39:9). וקד כׄאטר[248] בנפסה אדׄ כאן פי מכנה סידתה אן תקתלה. ואלגׄ ספך אלדמא[249] כמא פי[250] קצה שאול **ולא אבו עבדי המלך**[251] **לשלח את ידם**[252] **לפגע בכהני יוי**[253] (שמ"א 22:17). וקד כאן פי מכנתה אן יקתלהם פכׄאטרו[254] בנפוסהם.[255] פהדׄה אלגׄ[256] **עבדה זרה וגילוי עריות ושפיכות דמים**[257] הי אלתי ילזמנא[258] אן נמד אענאקנא[259] ללקתל אדׄא תחראם[260] אלכפאר בדׄלך

236 מא End of Oxf 2486. 26a ׀ וסאיר מא TS NS 285.21b > D
237 תדרכה TS NS 285.21b ׀ תנאל Beginning of Oxf 2486. 26b
238 + וג' Oxf 2486. 26b
239 ידיע להוה לך מלכא Oxf 2486. 26b > L
240 אעתבאראן TS NS 285.21b > D
241 [בדׄ]ל TS NS 285.21b > D
242 עלי[נא בדל נפוסנא] TS NS 285.21b > D
243 + אלאצנאם כקולה TS NS 285.21b
244 גׄיר רבנא כמא TS NS 285.21b > L
245 מחארם Beginning of GE.GN.82.2a
246 אלמחא[רם כמא פי קצה] TS NS 285.21b > D
247 הגׄ הזׄ וחט לאלהים Oxf 2486. 26b ׀ וחטאתי לאלהים TS NS 285.21b > L ׀ וחטאתי לשלהים GE.GN.82.2a >
248 וקד באן כׄאטר GE.GN.82.2a
249 תקת[לה ואלגׄ ספך אלדמא] TS NS 285.21b > D
250 פי TS NS 285.21b > D
251 עבדי שאול GE.GN.82.2a
252 לשלח ידם Oxf 2486. 26b ׀ לשלוח את ידם TS NS 285.21b
253 לפגע בכהני יוי TS NS 285.21b > L
254 א[ן יקתלהם פכׄאטרו] TS NS 285.21b > D
255 באנפסהם GE.GN.82.2a
256 פהדה אלגׄ TS NS 285.21b > D
257 ושפיכות דמים TS NS 285.21b > L
258 הי אן ילזמנא GE.GN.82.2a
259 ילזמנא … אענאקנא TS NS 285.21b > D
260 תהדדונא GE.GN.82.2a

ולא[261] נפעלה.[262] ואמא סאיר אלשראיע אלסמעיה[263] פאן ראינא[264] קצד אלמתהד̇ר אכ̇ראגנא ען דיננא כאנת סבילהא[266] סביל הד̇ה אלג̇. ואן כאן קצד[267] אלמתהד̇ר[268] מנפעה נפסה לם נבד̇ל[269] נפוסנא עלי נפעה ומת̇אל ד̇לך כאן כאפר[270] עלק[271] ביהודי יום אלסבת פקאל לה אקטע[272] לי רטבה ואלא קתלתך.[273] פאן ראי קצדה עלף דאבתה[274] פליקטע לה. ואן קאל לה ארם בהא אלי אלנהר פלא[275] יקטע לה. ואלפאידה אלת̇אניה[276] אן אלמומן אד̇א בד̇ל[277] נפסה עלי אחד הד̇ה[278] אלג̇[279] אן הו[280] אעתקד[281] לא בד[282] מן אן יכ̇לצה רבה פליס הד̇ה בד̇ל[283] תאם.[284] בל ליס הו בד̇ל[285] בתה, ולכנה יעתקד[286] אלבד̇ל ועלי[287] אנה ליס יכ̇לצה.[288]

[261] ולא GE.GN.82.2a
[262] תחראם ... נפעלה TS NS 285.21b > D
[263] ואןמא] סאיר אלש[ראיע אלסמעיה] Oxf 2486.26b > D ו אלסמעןיה] TS NS 285.21b > D ו אלשראיע אלעקליה GE.GN.82.2a
[264] ראינא End of Oxf 2486. 26b
[265] קצד Beginning of Oxf 2486.31a
[266] אכראגנא ען[.. ...] פסבילהא GE.GN.82.2a
[267] פאן ראינא ... קצד TS NS 285.21b > D
[268] אלמתהדר End of the readable part of TS NS 285.21b
[269] כאן ק[... ...] לם נבדל GE.GN.82.2a
[270] ומ[... ...] כאפר GE.GN.82.2a
[271] חבס GE.GN.82.2a
[272] אל[... ...] אקטע GE.GN.82.2a
[273] ואלא קתלתך GE.GN.82.2a L >
[274] פאן כאן ק[... ...] דאבתה GE.GN.82.2a
[275] ואן [... ...] בריא ? פלא GE.GN.82.2a
[276] ואלפאידה אלת̇אניה GE.GN.82.2a D >
[277] בדל Beginning of TS NS 285.21c
[278] ע[... ...] GE.GN.82.2a D > ו End of GE.GN.82.2a
[279] Beginning of GE.GN.82.2b
[280] אנה GE.GN.82.2b
[281] אחד ... אעתקאד TS NS 285.21c > D
[282] אעתקד אנה לא בד GE.GN.82.2b
[283] פ[..] הדא ב[..]ל GE.GN.82.2b
[284] פליס ... תאם TS NS 285.21c > D
[285] [...]ל GE.GN.82.2b
[286] [י]עתקד TS NS 285.21c > D
[287] עלי TS NS 285.21c
[288] ול[...] יעתק[..] אלבדל עלי אן לא וכלץ GE.GN.82.2b

ואדׄא חדדנא[289] כלאם חנניה ומישאל ועזריה[290] הדׄא וגדנאה[291] כדׄאך. לאנהם פי באב אלכׄלאץ[292] דׄכרו קדרה רבהם[293] פקאלו[294] **יכיל לשיזבותנא** (דניאל 3:17) ולם יקלו[295] אנה יכׄלצהם[296] באלפעל. ולדׄלך אוקע אלחביס אלשך[297] פי אמר אלמוחדין.[298] ליכון[299] בעצׄהם יכׄלצהם מן יד אלכפאר[300] ובעצׄהם[301] לא יכׄלצהם[302] חתי יתם[303] בדׄלהם לנפוסהם.[304] לאנהם[305] לו ותׄקו באנה יכׄלצהם[306] דאימא[307] בטל בדׄלהם באלכליה. והדׄא איצׄא[308] כמא נסל[309] פי אמר אברהם ויצחק.[310] ויקאל לנא[311] אדׄא כאן קד ותׄק אברהם[312] בחיוה[313] יצחק[314] ואנסאלה[315] בקולה לה[316] **כי ביצחק יקרא**[317] **לך זרע** (בר׳ 21:12)

[289] [אנה ... חדד]נא TS NS 285.21c > D | חדדנא GE.GN.82.2b > D
[290] ח מ וע TS NS 285.21c ׀ [ח]נניה מישאל ועזריה GE.GN.82.2b
[291] לוגדנאה GE.GN.82.2b
[292] לאנהם אנמא דכרו אלכלאץ TS NS 285.21c
[293] [רב]הם Oxf 2486. 31a > D ׀ ד[..]רו [..]רה ר[..]הם GE.GN.82.2b
[294] קדר[ה ר]בהם כקולה חן אית[...]ה TS NS 285.21c > D
[295] יקולון TS NS 285.21c
[296] [..]לם [...]לו [... ...]צהם GE.GN.82.2b
[297] אוקע ... אלשך GE.GN.82.2b D >
[298] אלמומן GE.GN.82.2b
[299] [ל]יכון TS NS 285.21c > D ׀ אן יכון GE.GN.82.2b
[300] [בעצהם] יכל[צ]הם מן יד אלכפ[אר] Oxf 2486. 31a > D ׀ אל[כפא]ר TS NS > D 285.21c ׀ אלכפאר End of Oxf 2486. 31a
[301] ובעצהם Beginning of Oxf 2486. 31b
[302] י[..]לץ ב[..]צהם ובעצהם לא GE.GN.82.2b
[303] יצח TS NS 285.21c
[304] [... ...]דלהם [...]סהם GE.GN.82.2b
[305] נפוסהם אנהם לו TS NS 285.21c ׀ אנהם GE.GN.82.2b
[306] יכלצהם GE.GN.82.2b D >
[307] ד[אימא] TS NS 285.21c > D ׀ [..]מא GE.GN.82.2b
[308] [והדא איצ]א TS NS 285.21c > D ׀ והדא איצא GE.GN.82.2b D >
[309] נסאל GE.GN.82.2b
[310] אבראהים ואסחאק TS NS 285.21c
[311] ויקאל אנה GE.GN.82.2b D >
[312] אבר[אהים] TS NS 285.21c > D ׀ [..]א כאו אללה אועד אברהם GE.GN.82.2b
[313] בחיה GE.GN.82.2b
[314] אסחאק TS NS 285.21c
[315] ואנסאלה TS NS 285.21c > L ׀ יצחק ואנסאלה GE.GN.82.2b D >
[316] לה GE.GN.82.2b L >
[317] יקרא GE.GN.82.2b D >

פאנמא בדׄלא גמיעא[318] אמר אלעקידה[319] אתכאלא[320] עלי הדׄא אלמיתׄאק.[321]
ונחן נגיב פנקול[322] קד[323] ימכן[324] אן יתם אלדׄבח עלי[325] יצחק[326] לו אמר בה[327]
תׄם יחייה רבה[328] וינסל. ולהדׄה אלעלה איצׄא[329] אדׄא[330] סאל אלממתחן לרבה
לם אבלאה[331] יגיבה בגואב אכׄר ולם יקל[332] לה לאעוצׄך[333] לילא יקל צברה ענד
אלנאס כמא אגאב משה חין קאל **למה הרעות**[334] **לעם הזה וג׳**[335] (ש׳ 5:22)
עתה תראה אשר אעשה לפרעה[336] (ש׳ 6:1). וכמא אגאבה איצׄא[337] חין קאל
למה הרעות לעבדך (במד׳ 11:11) **אספה לי שבעים איש** (במד׳ 11:16).
וכמא אגאב איוב חין קאל **הודיעני**[338] **עלמה**[339] **תריבני** (איוב 10:2) **איפה
היית**[340] **ביסדי ארץ** (איוב 38:4) וסאיר[341] אלקצתין.[342]

וליס תצדירהם בקול **נבוכדנצר**[343] **לא חשחין** (דניאל 3:16) אסתכׄפאפא בה
לאנא נגדהם[344] יסמונה מלכא. לכן קולהם נבוכדנצר[345] כאן מכאן קולהם

[318] נכ[... ...] גמיעא GE.GN.82.2b
[319] א[...] אלעקובה GE.GN.82.2b
[320] אתכאלא < GE.GN.82.2b L
[321] הדׄא אלמיתׄאק < GE.GN.82.2b D
[322] [ונחן נ]גיב פנ[קול] < TS NS 285.21c D
[323] קד < TS NS 285.21c L
[324] באן ימכן TS NS 285.21c | נ[..]ב ונקול קד כאן GE.GN.82.2b
[325] אן יתם אלדׄבח עלי < GE.GN.82.2b D
[326] [...]חק GE.GN.82.2b
[327] + בבל GE.GN.82.2b
[328] תׄם יחייה רבה < GE.GN.82.2b D
[329] איצׄא < TS NS 285.21c L | איצׄא < GE.GN.82.2b L
[330] End of GE.GN.82.2b
[331] א[לממתחן] לר[בה לם א]בלאה < TS NS 285.21c D
[332] ולא יקול TS NS 285.21c
[333] לא[עיצׄך] < TS NS 285.21c D
[334] משה ... הר]עות < TS NS 285.21c D| הרעתה MT
[335] וג׳ < TS NS 285.21c L
[336] אשׁ אעׂ [לפרעה] TS NS 285.21c | לפ[רע]ה < Oxf 2486.31b D
[337] איצׄא < TS NS 285.21c L
[338] הודיעני End of Oxf 2486.31b
[339] עלמה Beginning of Oxf 2486.27a
[340] אספ[ה ... איפה] < TS NS 285.21c D
[341] [וסא]יר < Oxf 2486.27a D
[342] וסאיר אלקצתין < TS NS 285.21c D
[343] נבׂ נצׂ TS NS 285.21c
[344] אסת[כׄפאפא בה לא]נא נגדה[ם] < TS NS 285.21c D

אלמלך. אד̇ הו לקב ללכסדאניין[346] ולאסם ג̇ירה. וקולה **וגבריא אלך די הסיקו**[347] **לשדרך מישך ועבד נגו**[348] (דניאל 3:22) ידל עלי אנה אנמא טרחהם אלי[349] אלנאר במנגניק כמא נרי[350] אלמתחארבין יצנעון[351] דאימא. וקול נבוכדנצר **הא אנה חזה**[352] **גברין ארבעה**[353] (דניאל 3:25) ידל עלי אן חנניה ומישאל ווזריה כאנו יסירון[354] בין ידי אלמלאך פי אלנאר והו וראהם אד̇ לם יקל[355] **ורוה**[356] **די קדמאה**. ומנהא נקול אן מרתבה אלצאלחין אעלי מן[357] מרתבת אלמלאיכה. ולה נט̇איר כת̇ירה נכ̇תצר[358] דון ד̇כרהא האהנא. ולד̇לך קאל נבוכדנצר[359] **די שלח מלאכה ושיזב לעבדוהי**[360] (דניאל 3:28). וינבג̇י אן נערף כיף כ̇לצהם. וד̇לך אן לכ̇לאצהם[361] וגהין. אמא[362] אן יברד אלנאר ואמא אן יוקיהם[363] בערץ̇. פאן קלנא אנה ברד[364] אלנאר פליס הד̇א בעגב. לאנא נעלם אן אלשיא[365] אלבארד לא יחרק אחדא. ולכן תרך אלנאר עלי טביעתהא ווקאהם[366] בערץ̇ אלא[367] תעמל פיהם. הד̇ה[368] הי[369] אלאיה אלבאהרה.[370]

345 נב נצ TS NS 285.21c

346 אלכסדאנין TS NS 285.21c

347 ג̇יר[ה וקולה וגב]ריא אלך [די] TS NS 285.21c > D

348 לש̇ מ̇ וע̇ TS NS 285.21c

349 טרחהם אלי TS NS 285.21c > D

350 נרי TS NS 285.21c > L

351 יצנעאן Oxf 2486. 27a

352 הא אנה הזה TS NS 285.21c > D

353 ד TS NS 285.21c

354 [חנניה ומישאל ועזריה] כאנו [יסירון] TS NS 285.21c > D

355 אד לם יקל TS NS 285.21c > D

356 וריוה TS NS 285.21c

357 [אלצאלחין ... מרתב]ת TS NS 285.21c > D

358 אלכתצרת TS NS 285.21c

359 נב נצר TS NS 285.21c

360 מלאכה ... לעבדוה TS NS 285.21c > D

361 וינבג̇י ... וגהין Oxf 2486. 27a > D | וגהין End of Oxf 2486. 27a

362 אמא Beginning of Oxf 2486. 27b

363 יוקיה[ם] Oxf 2486. 27b > D | יקויהם TS NS 285.21c

364 בערץ ... ברד TS NS 285.21c > D

365 אלשי[א] Oxf 2486. 27b > D | אלשיא TS NS 285.21c > D

366 אל[נאר ... ווקאהם] TS NS 285.21c > D

367 לילא TS NS 285.21c

368 הד̇ה TS NS 285.21c > L

369 והי TS NS 285.21c

370 אלבאהרה TS NS 285.21c > L

וקדמת פי כל תפסיר **פחוהא** (דניאל 3:27) עלי **סגניא** (דניאל 3:27) אד̇ **פחה** "אמיר" כקולה **פחת יהודה** (חגי 1:1) **וסגן** כ̇ליפה כקולהם[371] ר̇ חנניה **סגן הכהנים** (פסחים I.6).

ת̇ם נטלע ההנא מסלה ונקול קד צח לנא[372] אן חנניה ומישאל ועזריה[373] לם יסגדו ללצנם פמא[374] תקול פי סאיר גלות[375] בבל או פי סאיר[376] ישראל, סגדו לה[377] אם לא? פאן כאנו כלהם סגדו פמציבה[378] או ליס פיהם אנביא.[379] ואן כאנו לם יסגדו פיגב אן יכונו קד אחרקו. ת̇ם נגיב ונקול אן נבוכדנצר לם[380] ילזם גמיע אלנאס[381] אלסגוד למעבודה א[נ]מא אלזם ד̇לך אצחאב[382] אלסלטאן[383] פקט.[384] ולד̇לך בסט תעדידהם פקאל **אחשדרפניא**[385] **סגניא ופחותא אדרגזריא גבריא דתבריא תפתיא** (דניאל 3:2.3). ת̇ם אלחק בהם[386] **וכל שלטוני מדינתא** (דניאל 3:3). ועלי אנה יד̇כר פי וסט[387] אלקצה **עממיא אמיא ולישניא** (דניאל 3:4). פאנמא[388] יריד בד̇לך אן האולי אלסלאטין[389] הן מן אמם מכ̇תלפה ולג̇את שתי. ואמא אלעאמה[390] מן[391] כל מלה פלם יטאלבהם באלסגוד ללצנם[392] בל לא[393] באלחצ̇ור בתה. ואנמא וקעת

[371] כקול TS NS 285.21c

[372] מסל[ה ק]ד צח [לנא] TS NS 285.21c > D

[373] ומ̇ וע̇ TS NS 285.21c

[374] מא TS NS 285.21c

[375] גלוב Oxf 2486. 27b

[376] סאיר TS NS 285.21c > L

[377] סגדו TS NS 285.21c > L

[378] כאנו ... פמציבה TS NS 285.21c > D

[379] פאנה כאן פיהם אנביא TS NS 285.21c

[380] אן ... לם TS NS 285.21c > D

[381] [גמיע אלנא]ס TS NS 285.21c > D

[382] אנמא ... אצחאב Oxf 2486. 27b > D

[383] אלסלטאן End of Oxf 2486. 27b

[384] ולדלך Beginning of the readable part of Oxf 2486. 28a

[385] [תעדידהם ... אחש]דרפניא Oxf 2486. 28a > D

[386] ת̇ם ... בהם TS NS 285.21c > D

[387] ועלי ... וסט TS NS 285.21c > D

[388] פאמא Oxf 2486. 28a

[389] הולא אלסלטאניין TS NS 285.21c

[390] ולא̇[ת א]לעאמה TS NS 285.21c > D

[391] מן TS NS 285.21c > L

[392] ללצנם TS NS 285.21c > L

[393] לא TS NS 285.21c > L

אלמטאלבה עלי חנניה ומישאל ועזריה באלסגוד[394] לה לעלה אנהם מן אצחאב אלסלטאן כמא קדם אולא **ומני על עבידתא די מדינת בבל לשדרך מישך ועבד נגו**[395] (דניאל 2:49).

ובסבב ראיסתהם[396] סעו בהם אלכסדאניין. ולעל אלסעאה כאנו מן[397] אצחאב אלסלטאן פחסדוהם עלי תקדמהם או עלי חכמתהם או עלי שכר אלנאס להם. פמנהא[398] קאלו לה[399] **די מנית**[400] **יתהון על עבידת מדינת בבל**[401] (דניאל 3:12). פאן[402] קד תבין אן אלרעיה לם יטאלבו בדׄלך ואנמא[403] טולב בה אצחאב אלסלטאן סקטת[404] אלמסאלה[405] מן אצלהא ולם יבק פיהא אלא שעבה ואחדה והי אן יסאל[406] ען דניאל הל טולב[407] איצׄא באלסגוד אם לא. פאן כאן[408] טולב לאנה מן אצחאב אלסלטאן כמא קדם **והשלטה על כל**[409] **מדינת בבל** (דניאל 2:48) ולא שך פי אנה[410] קד אמתנע פלם לם ילק פי אלנאר?[411] פנקול אן דניאל כאן ענד נבוכׄדנצר מעבוד מן אלמעבודאת אדׄ לים מנכר ענד אלכפאר אן יעבדו אלהה כתׄירה.[412] וענד בעצׄהם[413] אן אלכׄאלק יחל נורה פי כל עצׄה פי כל ואחד מן אלנאס או פי כתׄירא מנהם. פאן חל פיה דׄלך אלנור פוגב אן יעבד. פלמא סמע בחתנצר חכמה דניאל סגד לה ואמר באלתקריב לה עלי מא וצפנא.

[394] חנ[ניה ... באלסגוד TS NS 285.21c > D
[395] די ... נגו TS NS 285.21c > L
[396] לאסתהם TS NS 285.21c
[397] אלכס[דאניין ... מן] TS NS 285.21c > D
[398] מנה TS NS 285.21c
[399] לה End of the readable part of Oxf 2486. 28a
[400] [קאלו ... מ]נית TS NS 285.21c > D
[401] על ... בבל TS NS 285.21c > L
[402] פאו Beginning of Oxf 2486.28b | פאד TS NS 285.21c
[403] ואמא TS NS 285.21c > D
[404] אל[סלטאן סקט]ת TS NS 285.21c > D
[405] אלמסלה TS NS 285.21c + Oxf 2486.28b
[406] יסל TS NS 285.21c + Oxf 2486.28b
[407] טלב TS NS 285.21c
[408] אם ... כאן TS NS 285.21c > D
[409] כל Oxf 2486.28b > L
[410] שך פי אנה TS NS 285.21c > D
[411] [אמתנע ...אל]תון TS NS 285.21c > D
[412] [דניאל ... נבוכד]נצר מעצ[ור ... כתירה] TS NS 285.21c > D
[413] בעצה[ם] TS NS 285.21c > D | בעצהם End of the readable part of TS NS 285.21c

ולעלנא כנא נשך[414] פי פעל נבוכֿדנצר הדֿא הל הו עבאדה.[415] פקאל[416] אנה אנמא סמאה בלטשצר באסם מעבודה ואן עלתה פי דֿלך הי אן פיה רוח אללה אלמקדסה כמא קאל **ועד אחרן על קדאמי דניאל די שמה בלטשצר כשום אלהי ודי רוח אלהין קדישין בה** (דניאל 4:5) תבין לנא אן אלסגוד ואלאמר באלתקריב לה אנמא כאנא מנה עלי סביל אלעבאדה. ואדֿא כאן דאניאל ענד נבוכֿדנצר מעבוד מתֿל אלצנם פליס יגיז לה אן יטאלב מעבוד באלסגוד למעבוד אכֿר אדֿ המא פי אלחאל סיאן. תֿם נשרח כיף צאר אסם בלטשצר ישבה אסם מעבודה וגמיע אלעלה והי אן פיה רוח אללה מסתורה. פנקול קד עלמנא אן **בל** אסם מעבוד בבל כמא קאל **ופקדתי על בל בבבל** (ירמ׳ 51:44). וקאל איצֿא **כרע בל קרס נבו** (יש׳ 46:1). וקאל איצֿא **אמרו נכלדה בבל הוביש בל חת מרודך הובישו עצביה חתו גלוליה** (ירמ׳ 50:2). פגעל נבוכֿדנצר [... ...][417] כמא[418] נגעל נחן אסם רבנא אן פי אויל אלאסמא פנקול אלעזר אלחנן אלגבר. ונקול יהורם יהושע ומא שאכל דֿלך. תֿם אצֿאף אליה כלמתין נבטיתין **טשא צר**. פאמא **טשא** פהו "סתר וכֿפי" לא מחאלה. ואמא **צר** פהו שד וותֿאק לא מחאלה. פכאנה יקול אן אלהה מכֿפי מותֿק פי גסם דניאל. ולולא אן נבוכדנצר קאל **די שמה בלטשאצר כשום אלהי** (דניאל 4:5) לם יקע לנא שיא מן דֿלך. פקד איצֿחנא אלגואב ען הדֿה אלשעבה איצֿא.

וקד כאן בעץֿ אלקדמא יגיב באן בעץֿ ישׂראל סגדו לה מן גֿיר ניה ולדֿלך אפזעו באלקתל עלי עהד המן מן גֿיר יקין. אלא אן הדֿא אלגואב מחדד אדֿ לם תחצר דעותה אמה מן אלאמם בל לא ימכן גמע אלנאס. אלא תרי אנא פי חאל אלנעמה עבדנא אלאצנאם[419] [... ...][420]. **מסכה**[421] **מכספם כתבונם עצבים** (הושע 13:2). בל כאנו יחנון אליהא כחנין אלאב אלי ולדה כמא קאל **כזכר בניהם מזבחותם** (ירמ׳ 17:2).[422] פלמא וקע בנא אלשעבוד תאדבנא פאכֿתרנא אלאחתראק באלנאר עלי עבאדתהא. והדֿא ידכֿל פי תמתֿיל **פתחתי אני לדודי ודודי חמק עבר נפשי יצאה בדברו** (ש"הש׳ 5:6) וסאיר אלקצה. ואמא כתבה **די יאמר שלו שלה** (דניאל 3:29) יעני ולא זלה ואחמדה. יקאל אנה זלה

[414] נ[ש]ך Oxf 2486.28b > D
[415] עבאדה End of the readable part of Oxf 2486.28b
[416] [פק]אל Beginning of the readable part of Oxf 2486.29a
[417] [... ...] One line Oxf 2486.29a > D
[418] כמא Beginning of Oxf 2486. 29b
[419] אלאצנאם End of the readable part of Oxf 2486.29b
[420] [... ...] One line Oxf 2486.29b > D
[421] מסכה Beginning of Oxf 2486.32a
[422] Uncertain lesson of Jeremy quotation

ונטׄיר מא קאל **ומה שמץ דבר נשמע בו** (איוב 26:14). ואמא קולה **באדין מלכא הצלח לשדרך מישך ועבד נגו במדינת בבל** (דניאל 3:30) ופסרנאה ״אצלח חאלהם״ פאן אלסבב פי דׄלך אן אלכסדאניין אכׄדׄו פי אן ירוהם בעין מן כׄאלף אמר אלמלך. ועלי אן אלאיה קד תׄבתת להם פאחתאג נבוכדנצר אן יאמרהם באמור דניאייה כתירה. יתבין ללכסדאניין אדׄאהם באליהוד.[423] [...][424] עליהא אנהם גׄיר[425] [...] מכׄלפין[426] עלי אלמלך חתי [...][427] חאלהם ענדהם פלם יכׄאלפו עליהם. וכדׄלך אלקול פי **דניאל דנה הצלח** (דניאל 6:29). תׄם אלגז אלתׄאלתׄ.[428]

[423] אדׄאהם באליהוד Uncertain lesson
[424] [...] Oxf 2486.32a > D
[425] גׄיר End of Oxf 2486.32a
[426] מכׄלפין Beginning of Oxf 2486.32b
[427] [...] Oxf 2486.32a > D
[428] Dn 3:31-33 are considered part of Dn 4 by R. Saadia

ונץ אלגז אלראבע. נסכ֗ה כתאב כתבה נבוכדנצר אלי גמיע אלאפאק במא גרי לה אורדהא אלאבא אלנאקלין ללכתב אלמקדסה פי כתאב דניאל למא צח ענדהם אן גמיע מא את֗בת פיהא הו חק. ועלי אן מנשיי אלכתב ללמלוך קד יזידון פי אלכ֗בר אלחאדת֗ וקד ינקצונה וקד ינסקונה ויזכ֗רפונה. אלא אן הד֗ה אלנסכה לם ילחקהא שיא מן ד֗לך. ונגד גמיע כלאמהא מנסוב אליה מא[1] כלא פואסיק פי וסטהא והי נפס הליל[2] [...][3] גמלה[4] אלנסכ֗ה[5] מעאני נד֗כרהא בעד אלאסתתמאם בעון אלרחמאן ומשיתה. פאול אלנסכ֗ה

Dn 3:31

נבוכדנצר מלכא לכל עממיא אמיא ולשיא די דארין בכל ארעה שלמכון ישׂגא.

ת֗ם אן בכ֗תנצר[6] אלמלך[7] כתב אלי גמיע אלשעוב ואלאמם וד֗וי אללג֗את אלמקימין פי גמיע אלבלדאן[8] סלאם אללה[9] עליכם וברכאתה.[10]

Dn 3:32

אתיא ותמהיא די עבד עמי אלהא עליה שפר קדמי להחויה.

אלאיאת ואלאעגובאת אלד֗י[11] צנעהא מעי אללה[12] אלעאלי[13] ראית אן אכ֗ברכם בהא.

[1] מא Uncrtain lesson
[2] הליל Uncertain lesson | End of the readable part of Oxf 2486.32b
[3] [...] Oxf 2486.33a > D
[4] גמלה Uncrtain lesson
[5] אלנסכה Beginning of the readable part of Oxf 2486.33a
[6] נבוכדנצר Oxf 2486.33a
[7] אלמלך Spiegel > D
[8] אלבלאד Oxf 2486.33a
[9] אללה Spiegel and Oxf 2486.33a > L
[10] וברכאת אללה Spiegel + Oxf 2486.33a
[11] אלתי Spiegel + Oxf 2486.33a
[12] אלאלאה Spiegel

Dn 3:33

אתוהי כמא רברבין ותמהוהי כמא תקיפין מלכותיה ושלטאנה עם דר ודר.[14]

איאתה[15] פמא אכתֿרהא ואעגובאתה[16] פמא[17] אשדהא[18] מלכה מלך אלעאלם וסלטאנה פי כל גיל ואגיאל.[19]

Dn 4:1

אנה נבוכדנצר שלה הוית בביתי ורענן בהיכלי.

אנא בכֿתנצר[20] כנת סאליא פי מנזלי[21] ומטמאנא פי היכלי.[22]

Dn 4:2

חלם חזית וידחלנני והרהרין על משכבי וחזוי ראשי יבהלנני.[23]

חתי ראית[24] חלמא[25] פאפזעני ואפכארי עלי מצֿגעי ורויאי[26] ידֿערני.[27]

Dn 4:3

ומני שים מעם להנעלא קדאמי לכל חכימי בבל די פשר חלמא יהודענני.

פאמרת באחצֿאר[28] אליי[29] גמיע חכמא באבל[30] ליערפוני תפסיר דֿלך.[31]

[13] אלעלי Oxf 2486.33a

[14] ודר End of the readable part ofOxf 2486.33a

[15] Beginning of TS Ar 21.49b

[16] איאתה ... ואעגובאתה Oxf 2486.33a > D

[17] פמא Beginning of Oxf 2486.33b

[18] [איאתה ... אשד]הא TS Ar 21.49b > D

[19] פי ... ואגיאל TS Ar 21.49b > D

[20] אנא בכֿתנצר TS Ar 21.49b > D

[21] פי מנזלי Spiegel > L

[22] פי היכלי TS Ar 21.49b > D

[23] Dn 4:1-2 are considered one verse by Oxf 2486.33b

[24] חתי ראית TS Ar 21.49b > D

[25] רויא Spiegel

[26] ורויאיי Oxf 2486.33b

[27] מצגעי ... ירויאי TS Ar 21.49b > D

[28] פאחצר Spiegel + TS Ar 21.49b + Oxf 2486.33b

[29] אלי Oxf 2486.33b

Dn 4:4

באדין עללין חרטמיא אשפיא כשדיא וגזריא וחלמא אמר אנא קדמיהון ופשרה לא מהודעין לי.

חיניד̇ חצ̇רו[32] אלחכמא ואלמנגמין[33] ואלכסדאניין[34] ואלחכאם פקצצת[35] עליהם אלרויא ולם יערפוני[36] תאוילהא.[37]

Dn 4:5

ועד אחרין על קדאמי דניאל די שמה בלטשצר כשם אלהי ודי רוח אלהין קדישין בה וחלמא קדמוהי אמרת.

ואלי[38] אן[39] חצ̇ר בין ידיי[40] אכ̇רהם[41] דניאל אלד̇י[42] אסמה[43] בלט שצר[44] באסם[45] מעבודי ולאן פיה רוח אללה אלמקדס[46] פקצצתהא עליה.

Dn 4:6

בלטשאצר רב חרטמיא די אנה ידעת די רוח אלהין קדשין בך וכל רז לא אנס לך חזוי חלמי די חזית ופשרה אמר.

וקלת לה יא בלטשצר[47] רייס[48] אלחכמא[49] אלד̇י אעלם מנך אן פיך רוח אללה אלמקדס[50] וכל סר[51] פמא יעוזך[52] ואלד̇י קאל לי אנפא אלרויא[53] ותפסירהא.

[30] גמיע ... באבל] TS Ar 21.49b > D

[31] דאלך Spiegel + Morag

[32] חצר Oxf 2486.33b

[33] חצרו ... ואלמנגמין] TS Ar 21.49b > D

[34] ואלכסד TS Ar 21.49b > L

[35] פקצצתהא TS Ar 21.49b ׀ פקצצת End of the readable part of Oxf 2486.33b

[36] ואלחכאם...יערפוני Oxf 2486.33b > D ׀ עליהם יערפוני] TS Ar 21.49b > D

[37] תאוילהא Beginning of Oxf 2486.34a

[38] אלי TS Ar 21.49b + Oxf 2486.34a

[39] אן Spiegel > L

[40] ידי TS Ar 21.49b + Oxf 2486.34a

[41] אכדהם Spiegel

[42] אכרהם ... אלד̇י TS Ar 21.49b > D

[43] אסמיתה Spiegel + TS Ar 21.49b + Oxf 2486.34a

[44] בלט TS Ar 21.49b

[45] כאסם Spiegel

[46] אללה אלמקדס TS Ar 21.49b > D

[47] בלטש TS Ar 21.49b ׀ בלטשאצר Spiegel

[48] ריס Oxf 2486.34a

Dn 4:7

וחזוי ראשי על משכבי חזה הוית ואלו אילן בגו ארעא ורומה שׂגיא.[54]

רויאי[55] אלאן[56] עלי[57] מצ̇געי ראית כאן שגרה[58] וסט[59] אלארץ̇[60] ואסעה רפעהא[61] כת̇יר.[62]

Dn 4:8

רבה אילנא ותקף רוממה ימטא לשמיא וחזותה לסוף כל ארעא.

חתי[63] כברת[64] ועט̇מת[65] ובלג̇[66] רפעהא אלי דוין[67] אלסמא[68] ושעבהא אלי גמיע[69] תלך אלארץ̇.[70]

Dn 4:9

עפיה שפיר ואנבה שגיא ומזון לכלא ביה תחתוהי תטלל חיות ברא ובענפוהי ידרון צפרי שמיא ומניה יתזין כל בשרא.

49 [רייס א]לחכמא TS Ar 21.49b > D

50 אן רוח אללה אלמקדס פיך Spiegel + TS Ar 21.49b + Oxf 2486.34a

51 ס[ר] Oxf 2486.34a > D

52 יעייך Oxf 2486.34a | [סר פמא י]עדך TS Ar 21.49b > D

53 רויאיי Oxf 2486.34a | אלרויאי Spiegel

54 שׂגיא End of Oxf 2486.34a

55 רויאיי Beginning of Oxf 2486.34b

56 רויאי אלאן TS Ar 21.49b > D

57 עלו Spiegel

58 כאן שגרה Oxf 2486.34b > D | פי + Spiegel

59 וצט Morag

60 ארץ TS Ar 21.49b

61 רפ[עהא] Oxf 2486.34b > D | [ואסעה רפ]עהא TS Ar 21.49b > D

62 ורפעהא עצים Spiegel

63 Beginning of the readable part of TS Ar 26.6a

64 ואן תלך אלשגרה כת̇רת Spiegel

65 ועצמת Spiegel + Morag | פעטמת TS Ar + TS Ar 21.49b + Oxf 2486.34b 26.6a

66 ובלג̇ Spiegel > L

67 דון Spiegel + Oxf 2486.34b

68 אל[ס]מא TS Ar 21.49b > D

69 אקצא Spiegel +

70 רפעהא ... אלארץ TS Ar 26.6a > D

ואגֿצאנהא[71] חסאן ותֿמרהא כתֿיר וקות[72] ללכל[73] פיהא ותחתהא[74] יסתטֿל[75] חיואן אלצחרא[76] ופי אגֿצאנהא יאוי טאיר אלסמא[77] ומנהא ימאן כל בשרי[78] הנאך.[79]

Dn 4:10
חזה הוית בחזוי ראשי על משכבי ואלו עיר וקדיש מן שמיא נחת.[80]

תֿם ראית תמאם[81] רויאיי[82] פי אלליל כאן[83] מלך קדוס[84] מן אלסמא קד נזל מן אלסמא.[85]

Dn 4:11
קרא בחיל וכן אמר גדו אילנא וקציצו ענפוהי אתרו עפיה ובדרו אנבה תנור חיותא מן תחתוהי וצפריא מן ענפוהי.

ינאדי[86] בקוה[87] והכדֿא[88] יקול גדֿו[89] אלשגרה[90] וקצו[91] אגֿצאנהא ואכֿרטו ורקהא ובדֿרו[92] תֿמרהא יזול אלוחש מן תחתהא ואלטאיר[93] מן אגֿצאנהא.

71]ואגֿצאנ[הא TS Ar 21.49b > D
72 וקוה TS Ar 21.49b | ותמר]הא ... וקו[ת TS Ar 26.6a > D
73 לאלכל Spiegel + Morag
74 פיהא ותחתהא TS Ar 26.6a > D
75 יסתצל Spiegel + Morag | ותחתהא יסתטל TS Ar 21.49b > D | פי]הא ... יסתטל TS Ar 26.6a > D
76 אלארץ אלצ]חרא[TS Ar 26.6a > D | אלארץ אלצחרא TS Ar 21.49b
77 אלסמא TS Ar 26.6a > D
78 בשרי TS Ar 26.6a > D
79 הנאך Spiegel > L
80 נחת End of the readable part of Oxf 2486.34b
81 תם ... תמאם TS Ar 21.49b > D
82 אלרויאי Morag | רויאי Spiegel
83 באן Spiegel + TS Ar 26.6a
84 קדיס TS Ar 21.49b | מלך קדוס TS Ar 26.6a > D
85 תם ... נזל Oxf 2486.34b > D | קד נזל מן אלסמא TS Ar 21.49b | נזל ... אלסמא TS Ar 21.49b > D | מן אלסמא Morag > D
86 ינאדי TS Ar 21.49b > D
87 בקווה Morag
88 והכדי TS Ar 26.6a
89 ב]קוה ... גד[ו TS Ar 21.49b > D
90 אלשגרה End of the readable part of TS Ar 21.49b
91 וקצו Spiegel

Dn 4:12

ברם עקר שרשוהי בארעא שבוקו ובאסור די פרזל ונחש בדתאא גי ברא ובטל שמיא יצטבע ועם חיותא חלקה בעשב ארעא.

לכן[94] סנך̇ אצולהא אתרכוה פי אלארץ̇ ושדוה בות̇אק מן חדיד ונחאס[95] פי כ̇לא[96] אלצחרא ומן נדא אלסמא ינצבג̇[97] וקותה מע אלבהאים מן עשב אלצחרא.

Dn 4:13

לבבה מן אנושא ישנון ולבב חיוה יתיהב לה ושבעה עדנין יחלפון עלוהי.

ותמייזה[98] יג̇יר[99] מן חאל אלנאס ותכ̇יל[100] אלבהאים יגעל לה וסבעה[101] אחואל תמצ̇י עליה כד̇לך.[102]

Dn 4:14

בגזירת עירין פתגמא ומאמר קדישין שאלתא על דבראת די ינדעון חייא די שליט עליא במלכות אנושא ולמן די.

וכאן[103] אלקול בחתם אלמלאיכה[104] וגואב[105] מסאלה[106] בקול אלקדוסין[107] לכי יעלם אלנאס אן אלעאלי[108] מסלט עלי מלך אלנאס[109] למן שא אעטאה[110] ומן שא[111] ינצבה להם[112] ויגוז אן ינצב לה[113] אלוצ̇יע מנהם.[114]

[92] [אג̇]צאנהא ואן[כר]טו [ורקהא ו]ב]דדו TS Ar 26.6a > D
[93] ואלטיר Spiegel
[94] לא Spiegel
[95] אלחדיד ואלנחאס Spiegel
[96] כ̇לאי Spiegel
[97] אלסמא ינצבג̇ TS Ar 26.6a > D
[98] [ותמ]ייזה TS Ar 26.6a > D
[99] יג̇ייר Spiegel
[100] ותכ̇ייל Spiegel | מן ... ותכ̇יל TS Ar 26.6a > D
[101] וז̇ TS Ar 26.6a
[102] כד̇לך TS Ar 26.6a > L | כד̇אלך Morag | כד̇אך Spiegel
[103] [וכא]ן TS Ar 26.6a > D | וכאן Beginning of TS Ar 21.49c
[104] אלמליכה TS Ar 21.49c
[105] [אלמלאיכה וגו]אב TS Ar 26.6a > D
[106] אלמסלה TS Ar 26.6a | אלמ[סאלה] TS Ar 21.49c > D
[107] אלקדיסין TS Ar 26.6a | אלק[דיסון] TS Ar 21.49c > D

Dn 4:15

דנה חלמא חזית אנה מלכא נבוכדנצר ואנתה בלטשאצר פשרא אמר כל קבל די כל חכימי מלכותי לא יכלין פשרא להדעותני ואנתה כהל די רוח אלהין קדישין בך.

הכדׄא אלרויא נטׄרת[115] אנא אלמלך בכׄתנצר[116] ואנת יא בלטשצר[117] תפסירהא[118] קל לאגל[119] חכמא ממלכתי לם יסתטיעו תפסירהא לתעריפי[120] ואנת תסתטיע לאן מוגוד פיך רוח אללה אלמקדס.[121]

Dn 4:16

אדין דניאל די שמא בלטשאצר אשתומם בשעה חדה ורעצהי יבהלנה ענה מלכא ואמר בלטשאצר חלמא ופשרא אל יבהלך ענה כל טשאצר ואר מראי חלמא לשנאיך ופשרה לעריך.

חיניׄד אטרק דניאל אלמסמא בלטשצר[122] נחו סאעה[123] ואכׄדׄת[124] אפכארה אן[125] תדהשה חתי אבתדי[126] אלמלך[127] וקאל[128] יא בלטשצר[129] לא יהולך

[108] [אן אלע]אלי TS Ar 26.6a > D

[109] מלכהם Spiegel + TS Ar 26.6a | מ[לך אלנא]ס TS Ar 21.49c > D

[110] למן שא אעטאה Spiegel and TS Ar 26.6a and Ar 21.49c > L

[111] שא TS Ar 21.49c > D | ישא Spiegel + TS Ar 26.6a

[112] לה TS Ar 26.6a and Ar 21.49c

[113] להם Spiegel

[114] ויגוז ... מנהם TS Ar 26.6a and TS Ar 21.49c > L

[115] נצרת Spiegel + Morag

[116] בכתנצר Beginning of Oxf 2486.35a | אנא בכתנצר אלמלך Spiegel

[117] בלטשאצר Spiegel

[118] ערפני תפסירה אד ליס פי חכמא ממלכתי מן יקדר ואנת תערפני לאן פיך עלמא מן אלקדיסין Oxf 2486.35a

[119] אן גמיע + Spiegel

[120] לתערפוני Spiegel

[121] דניאל 4:15 TS Ar 26.6a and TS Ar 21.49c > L

[122] אלמסמא בלטשצר TS Ar 26.6a and TS Ar 21.49c > L | בלטשאצר Spiegel

[123] ואחדה + Ar 21.49c | [...]דה + TS Ar 26.6a

[124] וכאדת Spiegel + Morag

[125] אן TS Ar 26.6a and Ar 21.49c and Oxf 2486.35a > L

[126] אבתדא Spiegel

[127] אבתדי אלמלך TS Ar 21.49c > D

[128] פקאל לה TS Ar 26.6a + TS Ar 21.49c + Oxf 2486.35a

[129] בלטשאצר Spiegel | בלטש TS Ar 26.6a

אלרויא[130] ותפסירהא[131] פאגאבה[132] וקאל[133] יא סיידי[134] אלרויא לשאניך ותפסירהא[135] לעדוך.[136]

Dn 4:17

אילנא די חזית די רבא ותקיף ורומיה ימטי לשמיא וחיזותיה לכל ארעא.

תאויל[137] אלשג̇רה אלתי ראיתהא קד[138] כברת ועט̇מת[139] ובלג̇ ארתפאעהא[140] דון[141] אלסמא[142] ושעבהא[143] אלי[144] אקצי[145] תלך[146] אלארץ̇.

Dn 4:18

עופיה שפיר ואנביה שגיא ומזון לכולא ביה תחותוהי תדור חיות ברא ובענפוהי ישכנן ציפרי שמיא.

ואג̇צאנהא חסאן ות̇מרהא כת̇יר וקות אלכל מנהא[147] ותחתהא יאוי[148] וחש אלצחרי[149] ופי אג̇צאנהא יסכן טאיר אלסמא.

Dn 4:19

אנתא הוא מלכא די רביתא ותקיפתא ורבותך רבת ומטת לשמיא ושולטנך לסוף ארעה.

[130] אלרוי[א] TS Ar 26.6a > D

[131] ותאוילהא TS Ar 26.6a + Oxf 2486.35a | ותאויל[הא] TS Ar 21.49c > D

[132] אגאבה Spiegel + Morag | פאגאבה TS Ar 21.49c > D

[133] פקאל Spiegel

[134] סידי TS Ar 21.49c + TS Ar 26.6a + Oxf 2486.35a

[135] ותאוילהא TS Ar 26.6a

[136] ותאויל[הא לעדוך] TS Ar 21.49c > D | לעדווך Spiegel + Morag

[137] [תאוי]ל TS Ar 26.6a > D

[138] קד End of the readable part of Oxf 2486.35a

[139] כברת ועטמת TS Ar 21.49c > D | ועצמת Spiegel + Morag

[140] אלי + Spiegel

[141] דוין TS Ar 26.6a + TS Ar 21.49c

[142] כברת ... אלסמא Oxf 2486.35a > D

[143] ושעבהא Beginning of Oxf 2486.35b

[144] אלי TS Ar 21.49c and Oxf 2486.35b > L

[145] אקאצי Spiegel | אקצא Morag

[146] וש[עבהא אלי אקצי תלך] TS Ar 26.6a > D

[147] מנה Oxf 2486.35b

[148] [יאו]י TS Ar 26.6a > D

[149] אלצחרא Spiegel + TS Ar 26.6a + TS Ar 21.49c + Oxf 2486.35b

אנת הו יא איהא[150] אלמלך אלדׄי כברת ועטׄמת[151] ועלת ריאסתך פדאנת[152]
אלסמא ובלג̇ סלטאנך[153] אלי אקטאר אלארץׄ.

Dn 4:20

ודי חזא מלכא עיר וקדיש נחית משמיא ואמר גדו אילנא וחבלוהי ברם עיקר שורשוהי בארעא שבוקו ובאיסור די פרזל ונחש בדתאה די ברא ומטל שמיא[154] יצטבע ועם חיות ברא חולקיה עד די שבעה עידנין יחלפון עלוהי.[155]

ואמא[156] מא ראי[157] אלמלך מלכא קדיסא[158] נזל מן אלסמא[159] פקאל גדׄו
אלשגרה ואקטעוהא לכן סנך̇[160] אצלהא[161] אתרכוה[162] פי אלארץׄ מותׄוקא
בחדיד[163] ונחאס פי כׄלא אלצחרא[164] מן[165] נדא[166] אלסמא ינצבג̇[167] ומע וחש[168]
אלצחרא[169] קותה[170] אלי[171] אן[172] תמצׄי עליה ז[173] אחואל.[174]

[150] יאיהא TS Ar 26.6a + Oxf 2486.35b ׀ יא אייה Spiegel
[151] ועצמת Spiegel + Morag
[152] ועטמ[ת ... פדא]נת TS Ar 26.6a > D
[153] צלטאנך Morag
[154] שמיא Beginning of Oxf 2652b
[155] עלוהי End of Oxf 2486.35b
[156] ואמא Beginning of Oxf 2486.36a
[157] מא ראי TS Ar 26.6a > D
[158] מלך קדוסא Morag ׀ מלך קדוס Spiegel
[159] אל[סמא] TS Ar 21.49c > D
[160] סנך TS Ar 26.6a > D
[161] אצולהא Spiegel + TS Ar 26.6a + TS Ar 21.49c ׀ [אצ]ולהא Oxf 2486.36a > D
[162] אתרכו Spiegel + Morag
[163] ושדוה בותׄאק מן חדיד Oxf 2652b
[164] אלצחרי Morag
[165] אלצחרא ומן Spiegel + TS Ar 26.6a + TS Ar 21.49c + Oxf 2486.36a
[166] נדי TS Ar 26.6a + TS Ar 21.49c
[167] אלסמא ינצבג̇ TS Ar 26.6a > D
[168] וחוש TS Ar 26.6a
[169] אלצחרי Morag
[170] וקותה מע אלבהאים מן עשב אלצחרא Spiegel + Oxf 2652b
[171] [א]ל[י] TS Ar 26.6a > D
[172] [א]ן Morag
[173] סבעה Spiegel
[174] אלי ... אחואל Oxf 2652b > L ׀ End of Oxf 2652b

Dn 4:21

דנא פשרא מלכא וגזירת עילאה היא די מטת על מרי מלכא.

פהד֗א[175] תאוילה[176] יא איה[177] אלמלך והו חכם אלעאלי אלד֗י[178] חכם[179] עלי סידי[180] אלמלך.

Dn 4:22

ולך טרדין מן אנשא ועם חיות ברא להוי מדורך ועסבא כתורא לך יטעמון ומטל שמיא לך מצבעין ושבעה עידנין יחלפון עלך עד די תנדע די שליט עילאה במלכות אנשא ולמן די יצבי יתנינה.

באן ינפא[181] מן בין אלנאס ויאוי[182] מע[183] וחש[184] אלצחרי[185] פיג֗תד֗י אלעשב[186] כאלבקר וינצבג֗[187] מן טל אלסמא[188] ותמצ֗י עליה[189] סבעה[190] אחואל כד֗אך[191] חתי תעלם אן אלעאלי[192] מסלט[193] עלי מלך אלנאס[194] למן שא[195] יעטיה.

175 פהדי Morag | [פהד]א D < TS Ar 21.49c

176 תאוילהא TS Ar 26.6a

177 יאיהא TS Ar 26.6a + Oxf 2486.36a | יא אייה Spiegel

178 קד + Oxf 2486.36a

179 [והו ... על]י D < TS Ar 21.49c

180 סיידי Spiegel + Morag

181 באן ינפא D < TS Ar 26.6a

182 ויאוי D < Oxf 2486.36a

183 [ויא]וי [מ]ע D < TS Ar 26.6a

184 וחש End of the readable part of Oxf 2486.36a

185 וח[ש אלצ]חרא D < TS Ar 21.49c | אלצחרא Spiegel + TS Ar 26.6a

186 אלע[ש]ב D < TS Ar 21.49c

187 כאל[בקר וינצבג֗] D < TS Ar 26.6a | וינצ[בג֗] D < TS Ar 21.49c

188 אלסמ[א] D < TS Ar 21.49c

189 עליך Spiegel

190 ז֗ TS Ar 26.6a + TS Ar 21.49c

191 כדאך Beginning of Oxf 2486.36b | [כד֗א]ך D < TS Ar 26.6a

192 אלעלי TS Ar 21.49c

193 מצלט Morag | מסל[ט] D < TS Ar 21.49c | מסלט End of the readable part of TS Ar 26.6a

194 [אלנ]אס Beginning of TS Ar 26.6b

195 ישא TS Ar 21.49c

Dn 4:23

ודי אמרו למשבק עקר שרשיהי די אילנא מלכותך לך קימא מן די תנדע די שליטין שמיא.

ואמא[196] מא קאלו[197] מן תרך סנךׄ[198] אצל[199] אלשגרה פתאוילה[200] אן מלכך
סיעוד[201] אליך[202] בעד אן[203] תעתרף[204] בסלטאן[205] צאחב[206] אלסמא.

Dn 4:24

להן מלכא מלכי ישפר עלך וחטאך בצדקה פרוק ועויתך במחן ענוין הן תהוי ארכא לשלותך.

ולכן[207] יא איה[208] אלמלך תחסן[209] משורתי ענדך פתפך[210] כׄטיתך[211]
בצדקה[212] ודׄנובך בראפה אלצׄעפי[213] פלעל[214] אן תכון מוהלה[215] לנעמתך.[216]

Dn 4:25

כולא מטא על נבוכדנצר מלכא.

[196] ואמא TS Ar 26.6b
[197] קאלו D < TS Ar 21.49c ׀ קאל Spiegel
[198] סנוך TS Ar 21.49c
[199] אצול Spiegel + TS Ar 26.6b + TS Ar 21.49c + Oxf 2486.36b
[200] תאוילה TS Ar 21.49c ׀ תאויל]ה ... מלכך[D < TS Ar 26.6b
[201] סי]עוד[D < TS Ar 21.49c
[202] עליך TS Ar 26.6b + TS Ar 21.49c
[203] אן End of TS Ar 21.49c
[204]]ת[עתרף Beginning of TS Ar 21.49d ׀]תע[תרף D < TS Ar 26.6b
[205] בצלטאן Morag ׀ בס]לט[אן TS Ar 21.49d
[206] בסלטאן צאחב D < TS Ar 26.6b
[207] וליכן TS Ar 26.6b ׀ לכן Spiegel
[208] יאיהא TS Ar 26.6b + Oxf 2486.36b ׀ יא]א[יה TS Ar 21.49d ׀ יא אייה Spiegel
[209] אל]מלך]ת[חסן D < TS Ar 21.49d ׀]אלמלך תח[סן D < TS Ar 26.6b
[210] פתפך D < TS Ar 26.6b
[211] כׄטייתך Morag ׀ כׄטייך Spiegel
[212] באלצדקה TS Ar 26.6b + Oxf 2486.36b ׀]בא[לצד]קה[D < TS Ar 21.49d
[213] אלצׄעפא Spiegel
[214] פלעל D < TS Ar 26.6b
[215] מהלה Spiegel + TS Ar 26.6b + Oxf 2486.36b
[216]]מהלה ל[נעמתך TS Ar 21.49d ׀ פי דלך + TS Ar 21.49d and Oxf 2486.36b and TS Ar 26.6b

אלכל[217] חל פי[218] בכ̇תנצר[219] אלמלך.[220]

Dn 4:26

לקצת[221] ירחין תרי עשר על היכל מלכותא די בבל מהליך הוה.

בעד[222] את̇נא עשר[223] שהרא[224] כאן יתמשי[225] עלי היכל אלמלך פי באבל.[226]

Dn 4:27

עני מלכא ואמר הלא דא היא בבל רבתא די אנא בניתה לבית מלכו בתקוף חוסני וליקר הדרי.

פאבתדי[227] וקאל אלא[228] אן הד̇ה[229] באבל[230] אלכברי[231] אלתי בניתהא[232] למנבר[233] אלמלך בשדה[234] ות̇אקי[235] וכרמי[236] ובהאיי.[237]

Dn 4:28

עוד מילתא בפום מלכא קל מן שמיא נפל לך אמרין נבוכ דנצר מלכא מלכותא עדת מינך.

[217] פכל TS Ar 26.6b + TS Ar 21.49d

[218] אלכל חל פי Oxf 2486.36b > D

[219] בבכ̇תנצר TS Ar 26.6b + Oxf 2486.36b + Spiegel | בנ̇ TS Ar 21.49d | בבכ̇תנצר End of the readable part of Oxf 2486.36b

[220] אלכל ... אלמלך Oxf 2486.36b > D | End of Oxf 2486.36b

[221] לקצת Beginning of Oxf 2486.37a

[222] [בע]ד TS Ar 21.49d > D

[223] יב TS Ar 26.6b + TS Ar 21.49d | את̇ני עשר Spiegel

[224] שהרא TS Ar 26.6b > D | שהר TS Ar 21.49d

[225] יתמשא Spiegel + Morag

[226] באבל TS Ar 21.49d > D

[227] פאבתדא Spiegel

[228] אלא Spiegel + Morag > L

[229] הדא Spiegel

[230] בבל TS Ar 21.49d

[231] אלכ[ברי] Oxf 2486.37a > D | אלכברי TS Ar 26.6b > D | כברי Spiegel

[232] בנית[הא] TS Ar 21.49d

[233] מנבר TS Ar 26.6b + Oxf 2486.37a | לי מנבר Spiegel

[234] בש[דה] TS Ar 26.6b > D

[235] ו[ת̇א]ק[י] Oxf 2486.37a

[236] וכרמי Spiegel > L

[237] לכרמי ובהאי TS Ar 26.6b + TS Ar 21.49d | לכרמי ובהאיי Oxf 2486.37a

בינמא[238] אלכלמה פי פיה[239] חתי ורד[240] צות מן אלסמא לך יקאל יא בכֿתנצר[241] אלמלך אלמלך[242] קד זאל ענך.[243]

Dn 4:29

ומן אנשא לך טרדין ועם חיות[244] ברא מדורך ועסבא כתורא לך יטעמון ושבעה עידנין יחלפון לך עד די יתנדע לשליט עלאה במלכות אנשא ולמן די יצבי יתנינה.[245]

ומן בין אלנאס תנפי[246] ומע וחש אלצחרי[247] תאוי פתגֿחדי אלעשב כאלבקר ותמצי עליך[248] ז[249] אחואל בדֿאך חתי[250] תעלם אן[251] אלעלי מסלט[252] עלי מלך אלנאס למן שא[253] יעטיה.[254]

Dn 4:30

בה שעתא מילתא ספת על נבוכד נצר ומן אנשא טריד ועסבא כתורין ייכל ומטל שמיא גשמיה יצטבע עד די שעריה כנשרין רבא וטופרוהי כצפרין.

מן[255] סאעתה חל אלאמר[256] בבכֿתנצר[257] ומן בין אלנאס נפי וצאר יאכל אלעשב[258] כאלבקר[259] וינצבגֿ[260] מן נדא[261] אלסמא אלי אן כתֿר שערה שביה בריש אלנסור[262] ואטֿפארה[263] כאלגוארח.

[238] בינאה Morag ו בינא Oxf 2486.37a ו בין מא Spiegel

[239] פיה D < TS Ar 26.6b ו פאה Morag ו פמה Spiegel

[240] אד וקע Spiegel

[241] יא נֿ TS Ar 21.49d ו בכת TS Ar 26.6b

[242] אלמלך L < D < TS Ar 26.6b

[243] קד זאל אלמלך ענך TS Ar 26.6b + TS Ar 21.49d + Oxf 2486.37a

[244] חיות End of the readable part of Oxf 2486.37a

[245] יתנינה Beginning of Oxf 2486.37b

[246] תנפא Spiegel

[247] אלצחרא Spiegel + TS Ar 26.6b + TS Ar 21.49d + Oxf 2486.37b

[248] אלבק[ר ותמצי ע]ליך D < TS Ar 26.6b

[249] סבעה Spiegel

[250] חתי L < Morag

[251] כדאך תערף באן TS Ar 26.6b + TS Ar 21.49d + Oxf 2486.37b

[252] מצלט Morag

[253] ישא TS Ar 21.49d

[254] יש[א יעטיה] D < TS Ar 26.6b

[255] ומן Morag

Dn 4:31

ולקצת יומיא אנא נבוכד נצר עיני לשמיא נטלית ומנדעי עלי יתוב ולעליא בריכת ולחי עולמא שבחית והדרת די שולטניא[264] שולטן עלם ומלכותיה עם דר ודר.[265]

פלמא אנקצ̇ת[266] תלך אלאיאם[267] רפעת עיניי[268] אנא בכ̇ת נצר[269] אלי אלסמא ורגעת עליי[270] עקלי פחמדת אלעאלי[271] וסבחת ומגדת[272] חי[273] אלעאלם אלד̇י סלטאנה סלטאן[274] אלעאלם ומלכה מע גיל ואגיאל.[275]

Dn 4:32

וכל דירי ארעא בלא חשיבין וכמצבי עביד בחיל שמיא ודיירי ארעא ולא איתי די ימחי בידיה ויימר ליה מא עבדתא.

וגמיע אהל[276] אלארץ̇ לא כשי מחסובין[277] והו מראדה יצנעה בג̇יש[278] אלסמא ואהל אלארץ̇ וליס[279] מן יצ̇רב עלי ידה ולא[280] יקול[281] לה מאד̇א צנעת.[282]

[256] אלאמ[ר] TS Ar 21.49d > D
[257] בנ̇ TS Ar 21.49d | בבכ̇ת TS Ar 26.6b
[258] עשב Spiegel
[259] כאלבק[ר] TS Ar 21.49d > D | כאלב[קר] TS Ar 26.6b > D
[260] ויצבג̇ TS Ar 26.6b + TS Ar 21.49d | ואנצבג̇ Spiegel
[261] נדי TS Ar 26.6b + TS Ar 21.49d
[262] [אלנס]ר TS Ar 21.49d > D | אלנסר Oxf 2486.37b
[263] ואצ̇פארה Spiegel + Morag
[264] שולטניא End of the readable part of Oxf 2486.37b
[265] ודר Beginning of Oxf 2486.38a
[266] תמת Oxf 2486.38a
[267] אלאאם TS Ar 21.49d
[268] עיני TS Ar 26.6b + TS Ar 21.49d + Oxf 2486.38a
[269] נ̇ TS Ar 21.49d | בכ̇ת TS Ar 26.6b
[270] פרגע אליי Oxf 2486.38a | פרגע עליי TS Ar 26.6b + TS Ar 21.49d | ורגע עלי Spiegel
[271] אלעליי Oxf 2486.38a
[272] ומ[גדת] TS Ar 21.49d > D
[273] חי Spiegel > L
[274] צלטאנה צלטאן אלעאלם Morag | סלטאן אלעאלם Spiegel + Oxf 2486.38a
[275] סל[טאן] ומלכה [מע גי]ל ואג[יאל] TS Ar 21.49d > D
[276] א[ה]ל TS Ar 26.6b > D
[277] בש[י מחסו]בין TS Ar 21.49d > D
[278] כג̇יש Morag

Dn 4:33

בה זמנא מנדעי יתוב עלי וליקר מלכותי הדרי וזיוי יתוב עלי ולי הדברי ורברבני יבעון ועל מלכותי התקנת ורבו יתירא הוספת לי.

פי[283] דׄלך אלוקׄת עאד אליי עקלי ווקאר מלכי ובהגתי[284] ובהאי תראגע אליי ולי אלקואד[285] ואלרוסא[286] יטלבון ותׄבתת[287] פי מלכי וזיד[288] לי שרף[289] כתׄיר.

Dn 4:34

כען[290] אנה נבוכד נצר משבח ומרומם ומהדר למלך שמיא די כל מעבדוהי קשט וארחתה דין ודי מהלכין בגוה יכל להשפלה.

אלאן[291] אנא בכׄת נצר[292] מסבח ומרפע ומבגל[293] למלך אלאמם אלדׄי[294] גמיע[295] צנעה אלחק[296] וסבלה[297] אלחכם ומן יסיר בין ידיה[298] באקתדאר יקדר אן יחטה. כאן תצדיק כתאבנא למא[299] אנשאה אלכאתב[300] מן הדׄה[301] אלנסכׄה בתצדיקה אלקרעה אלתי אוקעהא יהושע בקולה[302] **ונקרבתם בבקר**

279 ולי[ס] TS Ar 26.6b > D

280 מן + Oxf 2486.38a

281 יקל TS Ar 26.6b + TS Ar 21.49d

282 מא צנעת TS Ar 26.6b + TS Ar 21.49d

283 פי End of the readable part of Oxf 2486.38a

284 ובהגתי TS Ar 21.49d > L

285 אלוקאר Spiegel

286 אלרוסא Beginning of Oxf 2486.38b | אלרויסא Morag

287 ותתבת Oxf 2486.38b | ותׄבחת Spiegel

288 וזוד TS Ar 21.49d

289 [שר]ף TS Ar 21.49d > D

290 כען End of TS Ar 21.49d

291 אלאן Beginning of TS Ar 21.49e

292 נׄ TS Ar 21.49e | בכׄת TS Ar 26.6b

293 ובגל TS Ar 21.49e | [...]בגל TS Ar 26.6b > D

294 [אל]סמא אל[די] TS Ar 21.49e > D

295 גמע Oxf 2486.38b

296 אלדי חק Oxf 2486.38b

297 וסבילה Spiegel

298 יסיר ... ידיה TS Ar 21.49e > D | ידי Spiegel

299 ל[מ]א TS Ar 26.6b > D

300 אלכתׄ TS Ar 26.6b

301 הדה TS Ar 26.6b > L

302 בקול Oxf 2486.38b | בקו TS Ar 26.6b

לשבטיכם[303] (יהושע 7:14) **והיה הנלכד**[304] **בחרם** (יהושע 7:15). ולולא דֿאך כאנת גֿיר מצדקה. ואנמא חכמהא עלי אלקום לעלמה אנהא תקע עלי חקיקה.

ואול[305] מא אבתדי אצֿמר[306] כלמה **נבוכדנצר**[307] **מלכא** כתב[308] **לכל עממיה**[309] (דניאל 3:31). ופסרת[310] **ורענן** (דניאל 4:1)[311] ״מטמאנה״[312] מן אלמעני[313] עלי אנהא מפרדה. ולמא וצף אנה אחצֿר אלעלמא לם ילתמס מנהם אן[314] יכֿברונה באלרויה ותאוילהא גמיעא למעניין. אחדהמא לאנה קד אמתחנהם במתֿל דֿלך פי אלמרה אלאולי פעגזו ענה. ואלתֿאניה לשגֿל קלבה באלדֿהול ואלדֿעור אלתי נאלתה פי הדֿה אלרויה כמא קאל **חלם חזית וידחלנני** (דניאל 4:2) וכאנה נסבה אלי נפסה. ולדֿלך לם יתמאלך אן יטאלב דניאל באכֿבארה בהא ובתפסירהא גמיעא. פאדֿא כאן אלאמר הכדֿא וקד קץ נבוכֿדנצר אלרויה עלי אלחכמא פמא באלהם וקפו ען תאוילהא לה ותאוילהא משהור ענד כתֿיר[315] מן אעואם אלנאס פצֿלא עלי כֿואצהם, לאנהם יעלמון אן אלאנסאן אלגליל אלדֿי יעיש פי כנפה כתֿירא מן אלנאס ישבה שגרה יסתכן אלחיואן אלי פיהא ויעשש אלטאיר פי אגֿצאנהא ויגֿתדֿו כתֿירין[316] מן תֿמרהא. ואיצֿא[317] [... ...][318] אי[319] גֿירהא בנבות יחזקאל עלי מלך צור ותשביהה לה במלך אשור אלמשבה בשגרה הדֿה אחואלהא. פקד וקף עלי דֿלך וקאפא[320] כונה מן חאל אלתשריף לה ותכברה פי נפסה וחטיטתה אדֿ קאל פי דֿלך אגמע **הנה אשור ארז בלבנון יפה ענף וחרש מצל וגבה קומה ובין עבותים היתה צמרתו. מים גדלוהו תהום רוממתהו את נהרתיה הלך**

[303] לשבטיכם TS Ar 26.6b > L
[304] הלנכד TS Ar 26.6b
[305] אול Oxf 2486.38b
[306] אבת[די] א[צמ]ר Oxf 2486.38b > D
[307] נבוכ TS Ar 26.6b
[308] [מ]ל[כא כתב] Oxf 2486.38b > D
[309] עממ TS Ar 26.6b
[310] [ופ]סרת Oxf 2486.38b > D | ופסר TS Ar 26.6b
[311] בהיכלי + TS Ar 26.6b | ורעון End of Oxf 2486.38b
[312] מטמטנה Beginning of Oxf 2486.41a
[313] Uncertain lesson
[314] אן End of TS Ar 26.6b
[315] כתֿירא Oxf 2486.41a
[316] כתֿיר[ין] Oxf 2486.41a > D
[317] End of the readable part of Oxf 2486.41a
[318] [... ...] Oxf 2486.41a > D
[319] אי Beginning of Oxf 2486.41b
[320] Uncertain lesson

גדלוהו תהום רוממתהו את נהרתיה הלך סביבות מטעה ואת תעלותיה שלחה אל כל עצי השדה. על כן גבהא קומתו מכל עצי השדה ותרבינה סרעפתיו ותארכנה פארתיו ממים רבים בשלחו. בסעפתיו קננו כל עון השמים ותחת פארתיו ילדו כל חית השדה ובצלו ישבו כל גוים רבים (יחז׳ 31:3–6). וקאל פי באב אלתעט̇ם **יען אשר גבהת בקומה ויתן צמרתו אל בין עבותים ורם לבבו בגבהו** (יחז׳ 31:10). וקאל פי באב אלעקובה **ויכרתהו זרים עריצי גוים ויטשהו אל ההרים**[321] **ובכל**[322] **גיות**[323] **נפלו דליותיו ותשברנה פארתיו בכל אפיקי הארץ וירדו מצלו כל עמי הארץ ויטשהו** (יחז׳ 31:12).

ולאסימא אן רויה נבוכדנצר הד̇ה תנאדי באן תאוילהא לאנסאן בל למלך בל הו פי נצהא. פאמא אנסאן פמן קולה **ובאסור די פרזל ונחש** (דניאל 4:12) פכיף תות̇ק אלשגרה בקיד מן חדיד ונחאס? ואיצ̇א **ובטל שמיא יצטבע** (דניאל 4:12). פאן אלט̇ל צאלח ללשגרה [...][324] שיא מנכר פיהא. ואיצ̇א כיף יגעל ג̇דאה אלעשב והי נבאת? ואיצ̇א **לבבה מן אנשא ישנון** (דניאל 4:13). אליס הד̇א פציח אן צאחב אלרויה אנסאן? ואלבאב אלאעט̇ם קולה **די שליט עלאה במלכות אנשא** (דניאל 4:14). אי שיא יכון אבין מן הד̇א אלקול אנה מלך מסלט. פאד̇א כאנת הד̇ה אליצ̇אחאת קד גרת אי שיא אעתאץ̇ עלי אלחכמא מן תאויל הד̇ה אלרויה? פנקול אלאקרב אן יכון תוקפהם ליס מן אלעגז[325] לכן מן היבה אלמלך. פאנהם[326] [...][327] אן[328] יגאבהוה[329] פאן מלכה יזול. ולאסימא אנהם קד שאהדו אנה אמר בקתלהם תחת באלחגר בסבב מא לם יבלגוה שהותה פי **חלמא ופשרה**. פכיף בסבב זואל מלכה! ואיצ̇א ימכן אן יסתריב בהם פיקול אנהם אנמא תאולו עליה הד̇ה אלתאויל אלרדיא בסבב מא כאן אמר פיהם. וכמא וגדנא **שארית הגולה** אסתראבו באצחאב[330] ירמיהו למא סבק פקאלו לה **כי ברוך בן נריה מסית אותך בנו למען לתת אותנו ביד הכשדים להמית אותנו ולהגלות אותנו בבל** (ירמ׳ 43:3). אלא תרי אן דניאל

[321] זרים ... ההרים Oxf 2486.41b > D
[322] ובכל End of Oxf 2486.41b
[323] גיות Beginning of Oxf 2486.42a | גאיות MT
[324] ‏וא[..] Oxf 2486.42a > D
[325] ‏אלע[...] Oxf 2486.42a > D
[326] פאנהם End of Oxf 2486.42a
[327] [...] Oxf 2486.42a > D
[328] אן Beginning of Oxf 2486.42b
[329] יגבהוה Oxf 2486.42b
[330] ב[...]אב Oxf 2486.42b > D

איצ׳א קד אטרק מקדאר סאעה ימיז כיף יכון אלגואב חתי סאלה נבוכדנצר בקולה **חלמא ופשרה אל יבהלך** (דניאל 4:16).

ת׳ם נתסלם פי תחדיד אלרויא ונקול אד׳א כאן אנמא נזל מן אלסמא מלך ואחד[331] פלמן יקול **גדו וקציצו אתרו**[332] (דניאל 4:11). פיקול למלאיכה[333] אכ׳רין[334] נזלו[335] מעה כמא סיד׳כרהם[336] פיקול **עירין**[337] **וקדישין**[338] (דניאל 4:14). ונקול איצ׳א אית מסאלה[339] גרת פי נפס אלרויא חתי קאל **ומאמר קדישין שאלתא**[340] (דניאל 4:14)? פנקול אלמסלה ען אלעלה. כאן אלמלך אלואחד אלפאצ׳ל למא אמר[341] אלבאקיין במא אמר סאלוה פקאלו ״ולאית עלה נצנע באלשגרה הד׳א אלצניע״. פאגאבהם ״לעלה אן יעתבר אלנאס״. והו קולה[342] **עד דברת די ינדעון חייא וג׳** (דניאל 4:14). ויגוז אן ינצ׳אף אלי הד׳ה אלמסלה גז מן אכ׳ר אלרויא והו[343] מקדאר אלמדה. כאנהם יסאלונה אלי כם תקים אלשגרה הכד׳א. פאגאבהם וקאל **עדי שבעה עדנין יחלפון עלוהי** (ע׳ דניאל 4:13.20).

וקולה לה **חזוי חלמי די חזית ופשרה אמר** (דניאל 4:6) הו מקאם[344] **אֱמַר** בפתחתין. יעניה אנך אלד׳י קלת לי **חלמא ופשרה** תלך אלמדה פאני אלאן ליס אכלפך אלא אלתפסיר פקט והו אכ׳ף עליך.[345] ופסרת **וחזותה** (דניאל 4:8) ״שעבה״ מת׳ל **קרן חזות**[346] (דניאל 8:5) **ותעלינה**[347] **חזות ארבע**[348] (דניאל

331 ואחד Beginning of the readable part of TS Ar 1b 90a

332 [...] D < Oxf 2486.42b

333 פיקול למלאיכה D < TS Ar 1b 90a

334 א[כ׳ר]ין D < TS Ar 1b 90a | [א]כ׳רין D < Oxf 2486.42b

335 נזלו D < Oxf 2486.42b

336 [כמא סידכ]רהם D < Oxf 2486.42b

337 עירין End of Oxf 2486.42b

338 וקדישין Beginning of Oxf 2486.43a | וקדישין D < TS Ar 1b 90a

339 מסלה Oxf 2486.43a

340 ומאמר ... שאלתא D < TS Ar 1b 90a

341 אלפאצל ...אמר D < TS Ar 1b 90a

342 קולך TS Ar 1b 90a

343 גז ... והו D < TS Ar 1b 90a

344 [אלי ... מ]קאם D < TS Ar 1b 90a

345 אכ[לפך ... עליך] D < TS Ar 1b 90a

346 קרן חזות D < TS Ar 1b 90a | ק[רן חזו]ת D < Oxf 2486.43a

347 ותצלי[נה] D < Oxf 2486.43a | ותצלינה D < TS Ar 1b 90a | ותעלינה End of the readable part of Oxf 2486.43a

348 וג׳ + TS Ar 1b 90a

8:8). ופסרת **לבבה מן**[349] **אנשא** (דניאל 4:13). [... ...].[350] ופסרת **לבב חיוה** (דניאל 4:13) תכ̇ייל אלבהאים עלי מא אוגבה[351] אלתחציל. וד̇לך[352] אן אלעלמא יתׄבתון ללאנסאן תמייזא ולא יתׄבתון ללבהאים[353] תמייזא. ואנמא יתׄבתון להא תכ̇יילא. אן יתכ̇יל להא אלאסד ואלנסר[354] ואלנאר ואלג̇ד̇א ואלמא וסאיר דואעיהא וד̇ואעׄרהא.[355] ואד̇ קד[356] קדמת הד̇ה אלמקדמאת פקד[357] תבין תפסיר אלרויה כיף[358] הו ועלי מא קאל דניאל.[359] ונחתאג[360] אלאן אן נתבין מן אלחאדתׄה[361] אלתי חדתׄת עלי נבוכדנצר. וד̇לך אן כתׄירא מן אלנאס יתוהמון אנה[362] מסך̇ מן אלנאס פצאר בהימה. ואכ̇רון זאדו עלי ד̇לך[363] פקאלו בל[364] מסך̇ אנתׄי לתקע[365] בה מע ד̇אך ד̇לה אלג̇שיאן.

ואכ̇רון זאדו[366] פקאלו בל כאן[367] יתבדל[368] פי כל חול או פי כל שהר או פי כל יום[369] מן שכ̇ץ אלי שכ̇ץ. וכל תעלק בשבה.[370] וקצדו פרט אד̇לאל אלמתעטׄמין[371] בין ידי אללה ואלמתכברין. ואלצחיח[372] הו אן צורה[373]

[349] לבבה מן Beginning of the readable part of Oxf 2486.43b
[350] [... ...] TS Ar 1b 90a > D
[351] אוגבת Oxf 2486.43b > D
[352] [אלתחציל ו]דלך TS Ar 1b 90a > D
[353] ללבהאים TS Ar 1b 90a > D
[354] ואלנהר TS Ar 1b 90a
[355] ודואערהא Oxf 2486.43b > D
[356] ואד קד TS Ar 1b 90a > D
[357] פקד Oxf 2486.43b > D
[358] כיף TS Ar 1b 90a > D
[359] ועלי ... דניאל Oxf 2486.43b > D
[360] פנחתאג TS Ar 1b 90a
[361] אלחא[דתׄה אל]תי TS Ar 1b 90a > D
[362] יתוה[מון] TS Ar 1b 90a > D
[363] פי דלך TS Ar 1b 90a
[364] פקאלו בל TS Ar 1b 90a > D
[365] [אנתׄי] ל[תק]ע TS Ar 1b 90a > D
[366] ואכ̇רון זאדו TS Ar 1b 90a > D
[367] כאן TS Ar 1b 90a > D
[368] יבתדל TS Ar 1b 90a
[369] או פי כל יום TS Ar 1b 90a > D
[370] בשבהה TS Ar 1b 90a
[371] וקצדו ... אלמתעטמין TS Ar 1b 90a > D
[372] ואלמ[תכברין ואלצחיח] Oxf 2486.43b > D
[373] ה[ו אן צ]ורה Oxf 2486.43b > D | צורה End of the readable part of Oxf 2486.43b

נבוכ׳דנצר לם תתג׳ייר[374] ואנמא תג׳ייר עליה עקלה. וד׳לך כמא ערץ׳ לשאול[375] **ובעתתו**[376] **רוח רעה מאת יוי** (שמ״א 16:14) ולם יתג׳יר[377] שיא[378] מן צורה גסמה. אלא אן[379] עלה שאול כאנת כ׳פיפה[380] חתי אן אללחון[381] ואלתדביר אללטיף כאן יסכנהא כמא הו משרוח פי קצתה.[382] ואמא עלה נבוכ׳דנצר פעט׳ימה והו זואל עקל אלאנסאן ענה באלכליה.[383] ולד׳לך קאל פי אכ׳ר אלקצה **ומנדעי עלי יתוב**[384] (דניאל 4:31) **מנדעי**[385] **עלי יתוב**[386] (דניאל 4:33). ובלג׳ מן אמרה[387] אלי אן האם מן בין אלנאס כמא קאל[388] **ומן אנשא טריד** (דניאל 4:30). וסאח פי[389] אלצחארי ואלגבאל אלא אן רבנא צנע[390] לה איאת מעגזאת חתי חפט׳ בהא רוחה תלך אלמדד.

פאלאיה אלאולי אנה[391] כאן יאכל אלעשב פיגדוה כמא יגדו אלבקר לקולה[392] **ועשׂבה כתורין**[393] **יאכל** (דניאל 4:30) ומוצ׳ע אלאיה אן אלאנסאן לו ראם אן יג׳תד׳י בעשב מדה מא[394] לם יתם לה ד׳לך. בל אלחב נפסה לא יאכל מנה אלא אלמכ׳תאר כאלחנטה ואלשעיר.[395] בל אלמכ׳תאר נפסה לא יאכל ניא.[396] בל[397]

[374] תת[ג׳יר] TS Ar 1b 90a > D
[375] לשאול Beginning of Oxf 2486.44a
[376] ובעתתו TS Ar 1b 90a > D
[377] [יתג׳י]ר TS Ar 1b 90a > D
[378] שי TS Ar 1b 90a
[379] אן TS Ar 1b 90a > D
[380] כ׳פיפה TS Ar 1b 90a > D
[381] אלאלחאן TS Ar 1b 90a
[382] [יסכנה ... ק]צתה TS Ar 1b 90a > D
[383] [פעטימה ... ב]לכליה TS Ar 1b 90a > D | ענה + TS Ar 1b 90a
[384] אלקצה ... יתוב TS Ar 1b 90a > D
[385] ומנדעי TS Ar 1b 90a
[386] יתוב End of TS Ar 1b 90a
[387] אמרהם Beginning of the readable part of TS Ar 1b 90b
[388] [אלנאס] כק TS Ar 1b 90b > D
[389] ומן ... פי TS Ar 1b 90b > D
[390] צנע TS Ar 1b 90b > D
[391] אנה TS Ar 1b 90b > D
[392] כק TS Ar 1b 90b
[393] ועשׂבה כתורין TS Ar 1b 90b > D
[394] יג׳ת[די ... מא] TS Ar 1b 90b > D
[395] [אלא ... ואלש]עיר TS Ar 1b 90b > D
[396] End of Oxf 2486.44a
[397] Beginning of Oxf 2486.44b

אלמטחון ואלמעגון לא יאכלהמא[398] חתי יכ̇בזאן.[399] בל חתי ינצ̇גאן.[400] ובאלחרי טעאם אלמלוך ובכ̇אצה נבוכ̇דנצר אד̇[401] כאן אגלהם.[402] פאלעגב אלכביר כיף לם יהלך מן אכל אלעשב[403] תלך אלמדד ומן ד̇לך אלערי וד̇לך אן מעני קולה אן גסמה[404] ינצבג̇ באלנדא.[405] אי לא יכון עליה לבאס. וסביל אלנאס[406] לא יחתמלון אלערי פי אלחצ̇ר[407] פכיף פי אלצחרא[408] פכיף מלך מנהם, פכיף נבוכ̇דנצר[409] אלד̇י הו אגל מלוכהם. פפיה ג̇איה אלעגב כיף חפט̇ רוחה מע עריה[410] מן אלחר ואלברד ומא אנטוי מעהמא. ומן ד̇לך חפט̇ה מן אלסבאע[411] אלא תפתרסה ולא סימא אד̇א שאהדת גסמה לם תר פי אלצחרא[412] מת̇לה מעהא[413] קט. פאיקאע היבתה עליהא אחרי אלאיאת.[414] ומן[415] ד̇לך חפט̇ה מן אלנאס אלד̇ין[416] יקתלון אלוחש פלם יקתלוה. ומא ד̇לך[417] אלא באיה שביהה במא קאל[418] **וישם יוי לקין אות לבלתי הכות אתו**[419] **כל מוצאו** (בר׳ 4:15).

ובאצ̇עאף הד̇ה[420] אלחט̇וט̇[421] תגב לנא[422] פי אלגלות. לו[423] לם יכן אלא עלי[424] סביל אלאעתבאר אד̇א כאן אחד אלכפאר למא סכ̇ט̇[425] עליה פחבס וועד

[398] אלמטחון ... יאכלהמא TS Ar 1b 90b > D
[399] יכבזן TS Ar 1b 90b
[400] ינצג TS Ar 1b 90b
[401] טעאם ... אד TS Ar 1b 90b > D
[402] אגלהם TS Ar 1b 90b > D
[403] אלכביר ... אלעשב TS Ar 1b 90b > D
[404] [אלערי ... גס]מה TS Ar 1b 90b > D
[405] בנדי אלסמא TS Ar 1b 90b
[406] עליה ... אלנאס TS Ar 1b 90b > D
[407] אלצחרא TS Ar 1b 90b
[408] פכיף פי אלצחרא TS Ar 1b 90b > L
[409] מ[לך ... נבוכדנצר] TS Ar 1b 90b > D
[410] כיף ... עריה TS Ar 1b 90b > D
[411] ומן ... אלסבאע TS Ar 1b 90b > D
[412] גס[מה ... אלצחרא] TS Ar 1b 90b > D
[413] מעהא מתלה TS Ar 1b 90b
[414] אלא[יא]ת TS Ar 1b 90b > D
[415] ומן TS Ar 1b 90b > D
[416] אללדין Oxf 2486.44b
[417] יק[תלוה ומא דלך] TS Ar 1b 90b > D
[418] אלדין + TS Ar 1b 90b
[419] לבלתי ... אתו TS Ar 1b 90b > D
[420] הד-ה End of Oxf 2486.44b

באטלאקה חפט̇ אללה[426] נפסה מן כל מהלך.[427] פכיף נחן צפותה וכ̇אצתה אד̇ אלקאנא פי אלשעבוד[428] וועד ברדנא ואן יחפט̇נא מן[429] כל מהלך. פכיף ולנא בד̇לך[430] נצוץ פציחה. אד̇א שבהנא גולאננא פי אלשעבוד בדוראן אלחנטה פי[431] אלג̇רבאל פלא יסקט מנה ד̇רה עלי[432] אלארץ̇ כמא קאל[433] **כי**[434] **הנה**[435] **אנכי מצוה והניעתי בכל הגוים**[436] **את**[437] **בית ישׂראל כאשר ינוע בכברה ולא יפול צרור ארץ**[438] (עמ׳ 9:9). ואד̇[439] שבה ד̇לך באלקאנא בין אלאסד פתאכל אלאסד בעצ̇הא בעצ̇א[440] ונסלם נחן כמא קאל[441] **כל חיתו שׂדא**[442] **אתיו**[443] **לאכל כל חיתו**[444] **ביער**[445] (יש׳ 56:9).

ואד̇א שבה ד̇לך באלקאנא[446] פי אלמא ויחפט̇נא[447] מן אלג̇רק כמא קאל[448] **כי תעבור במים אתך אני ובנהרות**[449] **לא ישטפוך**[450] (יש׳ 43:2). ואד̇ שבה ד̇לך

[421] אלחטוט Beginning of Oxf 2486.39a | אלחטט TS Ar 1b 90b
[422] פעל בנא TS Ar 1b 90b
[423] אל[גלות לון] TS Ar 1b 90b > D
[424] אלי עליי TS Ar 1b 90b
[425] למא סכט TS Ar 1b 90b > D
[426] אלה TS Ar 1b 90b
[427] מהלך TS Ar 1b 90b > D
[428] שעבוד TS Ar 1b 90b > D
[429] יחפטנ[א מ]ן TS Ar 1b 90b > D
[430] אן לנא פי דאלך TS Ar 1b 90b
[431] אלחנטה פי TS Ar 1b 90b > D
[432] אלי TS Ar 1b 90b
[433] כק TS Ar 1b 90b
[434] כי Oxf 2486.39a > L
[435] הנה TS Ar 1b 90b > D
[436] כל Oxf 2486.39a +
[437] את Oxf 2486.39a > D
[438] כאשר ... ארץ TS Ar 1b 90b > L
[439] [וא]ד TS Ar 1b 90b > D
[440] בעץ TS Ar 1b 90b
[441] כק TS Ar 1b 90b
[442] שדי MT
[443] התיו Oxf 2486.39a | אתיו TS Ar 1b 90b > L
[444] וג׳ TS Ar 1b 90b +
[445] ביער TS Ar 1b 90b > D
[446] [בא]לקאנא TS Ar 1b 90b > D
[447] פיחפטנא TS Ar 1b 90b
[448] כק TS Ar 1b 90b

באלקאנא פי אלנאר[451] ויחפט̇נא[452] מן אלחרק כמא קאל[453] **כי תלך במו אש לא תכוה**[454] **ולהבה לא תבער בך**[455] (יש׳ 43:2). וכיף לכל מולם ממתחן אן יכונו[456] מת̇לנא[457] מחבוסין אלי אן יבלג̇[458] אלוקת פיטלקון וכמא קאל **לאמר**[459] **לאסורים**[460] **צאו לאשר בחשך הגלו** (יש׳ 49:9). וקד תמני איוב אן יחבס פי אלארץ̇ מדה אלי אן יגיזה וקת אלנכ̇בה פיכ̇רג חיניד̇ אלי אלנעמה פלם יגב וד̇אך קולה **מי יתן בשאול תצפנני תסתירני עד שוב אפך תשית לי חק ותזכרני** (איוב 14:13).

ומא כנא נתוהם אן תאויל **ברם עקר שרשוהי בארעא שבוקו** (דניאל 4:12) אלא תבקיה אלמלך לנסל נבוכ̇דנצר דונה חתי פסרה לה אנה רגוע מלכה אליה כמא קאל **ודי אמרו למשבק עקר שרשיהי די אילנא מלכותך לך קימא** (דניאל 4:23). וקולה **די שַלִּטִן שמיא** (דניאל 4:23) תסויג̇ לנא כלמא ידעוה אלרבונין בעצ̇הם לבעץ̇ בלפצ̇ה **שמיא** וכאנה **לשון רבים**. פמסתקים כלה והו קולהם **נטרוהי מן שמיא וקימוהי וגברוהי**[461] **לן[...]**[462] **שולטן ואשמן[..]ת [...]לך**.[463] וקבל ד̇לך קול ר̇ חנניה בן תרדיון **מן השמים ירחמו**. והד̇א אצל אן יכון כל אסם יקאל ללרחמן בכל לג̇ה. פמן חלף בה ילזמה ד̇לך. כמא וגדנא מן סבח בה מת̇אבא.

ואמא משורתה עליה באלצדקה עלי אלצ̇עפי יסתדפע בהא מעאגלה אלעקובה. פהי משורה אן כאן לקנהא דניאל פסביל ד̇אך ואלא יכון אסתעמאלה[464] אלמשורה מן חית̇ וגד אלמעאגלה פי אלתוראה עלי ט̇לם אלצ̇עיפי אד̇ קאלת

449 וג׳ + TS Ar 1b 90b
450 לא ישטפוך > D TS Ar 1b 90b
451 אלנאר End of Oxf 2486.39a
452 ויחפטנא Beginning of Oxf 2486.39b
453 כק TS Ar 1b 90b
454 וג׳ + TS Ar 1b 90b
455 ולהבה … בך > D TS Ar 1b 90b
456 יכון TS Ar 1b 90b
457 מתלנ]נא[> D TS Ar 1b 90b
458]יב[לג̇ > D TS Ar 1b 90b
459]פיטלבון … לא[מר > D TS Ar 1b 90b
460 לאסורים End of TS Ar 1b 90b
461 וגברוהי End of Oxf 2486.39b
462 לן[…] | Beginning of Oxf 2486.40a > D Oxf 2486.40a
463 ואשמן[…] […]לך > D Oxf 2486.40a
464 יכון אסתעמאלה Uncertain lesson

והיה כי יצעק עלי ושמעתי כי חנון אני (ש׳ 22:26). וכדֹלך **והיה כי יקרא אלי וחנותיו כי חנון אני** (?). ולדֹלך כדר אלחנינה פי מוצׄע אלעקובה.

[...]יד[465] אן ננטׄר הל [...][466] קבל נבוכדֹנצר משורתה אם לא. [... ...][467] תֹאניה עשרה[468] כמא קאל **לקצת ירחין תרי עשר** (דניאל 4:26) פלו לא [...][469] קבלהא לם ימהלה לה. והדֹא[470] [......][471] מעאגלה[472] אפה אסתדפענאהא באלצדקה ואלמערוף. תֹם ערפנא אן אלאפה קארנת קול תעטֹם גרי לנבוכדֹנצר והו קולה **הלא דא היא בבל וג׳** (דניאל 4:27).

ופי הדֹא לנא אלאעתבאר אלאעטֹם אלא נתעטֹם בין ידי רבנא כמא קאל אלחכים **אל תבהל על פיך ולבך אל ימהר להוציא דבר לפני האלהים כי האלהים בשמים ואתה על הארץ על כן יהיו דבריך מעטים** (קהלת 5:1). וגדנא פרעה עוקב עלי קול תעטֹם כמא קאל **והיתה ארץ מצרים לשממה וחרבה וידעו כי אני יוי יען אמר יאור לי ואני עשׂיתי** (יחז׳ 29:9). וכדֹלך מלך ארם עלי קולה **אם ישפק עפר שמרון לשעלים לכל העם אשר ברגלי** (מל״א 20:10). וכדֹלך סנחריב עלי קולה **בכח ידי עשיתי ובחכמתי כי נבונתי** (יש׳ 10:13) וסאיר אלקול. וכדֹלך **נגיד צור** עלי קולה מתעטֹמא[473] **יען גבה לבך ותאמר אל אני מושב**[474] **אלהים**[475] **ישבתי בלב ימים** (יחז׳ 28:2). וכדֹלך סאיר אלמתעטֹמין תסרע עליהם אלאפה וכמא קאל לאיוב והו יצף פעלה אלרבובי **עדה נא גאון וגבה והוד והדר תלבש הפץ עברות אפך וראה כל גאה והשפילה ראה כל גאה הכניעהו והדך רשעים תחתם טמנם בעפר יחד פניהם חבוש בטמון** (איוב 40:10–13) ובאלשרוח אלתי דֹכרנאהא פי תפסיר **כי גאה גאה** (ש׳ 15:2).

465 [...]יד Oxf 2486.40a > D
466 [...] Oxf 2486.40a > D
467 [..]ל [..]פה תא[..]ת Oxf 2486.40a > D
468 ת[...]ה Oxf 2486.40a > D
469 א[..]ק Oxf 2486.40a > D
470 והדֹא End of the readable part of Oxf 2486.40a
471 First line of Oxf 2486.40b
472 מעאגלה Beginning of the readble oart of Oxf 2486.40b
473 מתעטמה End of the readable part of Oxf 2486.40b
474 יעו ... מושב Oxf 2486.40b > D
475 אלהים Beginning of Oxf 2486.45a

כמא סארעת נבוכֿדנצר אד̇ קאל **עוד מלתא בפֻם מלכא** (דניאל 4:28). ולאבד מן אן יכון קומא כת̇ירין קד סמעו אלצות אלד̇י קרע סמע נבוכדנצר חתי תתבין אלאיה. ולאבד איצ̇א מן אן יכון צות מן מצות והו מלך מן אלמלאיכה. ופסרת **עד די שעריה כנשרין רבה** (דניאל 4:30) "כבעץ̇ ריש אלנסור" אד̇ לא ישבה שער אלנאס ללנסר ואן כת̇ר. ופסרת איצ̇א **וטפרוהי כצפרין** (דניאל 4:30) "כאלגוארח" אד̇ ליס כל אלטאיר לה מכֿאליב, ואנמא הי ללמפתרס מנהא[476] פקט.[477]

ת̇ם נקול אן הד̇ה אלפואסיק אלמתוסטה ללקצה **אשתומם כשעה** (דניאל 4:16) הד̇ה אלי **וטפרוהי כצפרין** (דניאל 4:30) ליס הי מורדה עלי לסאן נבוכדנצר באלאשארה אליה אן יקול **מהלך הוה ענה מלכא ואמר הלא דא היא** (דניאל 4:26–27) ואמת̇אל ד̇לך. פאול מא נקדם מגאז אללגֿה אלמסתעמל. אן יקוי ראובן מת̇אלא פעל ראובן וצנע. וגזא אללה ראובן כידא והו יעני נפסה. כקול שמואל **וישלח יוי את ירבעל ואת בדן ואת יפתח ואת שמואל** (שמ"א 12:11). וכקול דויד **קחו עמכם את עבדי אדניכם** (מל"א 1:33). וכקול אכשורוש **כתבו על היהודים כטוב בעיניכם בשם המלך וחתמו בטבעת המלך** (אסתר 8:8). וכקול למך **נשי למך האזנה אמרתי** (בר' 4:23). וכקול[478] בלעם **נאם בלעם בנו בעור** (במד' 24:3). וכקול דויד **נאם דוד בן ישי** (שמ"ב 23:1). והד̇ה אלאסתשהאדאת נחתאג אליהא פי כל פסוק יתכרר פיה אסם רבנא גל ועז כקולך **ויוי המטיר על סדום[479] מאת[480] יוי** (בר' 19:24).

וימכן אן יכון להד̇ה אלפואסיק אלתי לם תנסב אלי נבוכֿדנצר מעני אכֿר והו אן אלכתאב אלמנשיין אסתחו אן ינסבוהא אליה. בל לם יחסן ד̇לך עלי וגה. ולהא מעני אכֿר אקוי מן אלגמיע והו אן אלאפה אלתי ורדת עליה למא גֿירת עקלה לם ימכנה אן יקטע אלשהאדה, כיף חלת ולא מתי חלת ולא מתי זאלת. כמא לא יעלם אלמצרוע מאד̇א יכון מנה. פאלד̇י לא בד מן אן יכון גֿיר מנסוב אלי נבוכֿדנצר הו קולה **בה שעתא מלתא ספת על נבוכדנצר** (דניאל 4:30). פסבק בה מן אול אלתפסיר עלי מא וצפנא. פלמא אנקצ̇ת הד̇ה אלפואסיק עאד אלאשארה אלי נבוכֿדנצר פקאל **ולקצת יומיא אנא נבוכדנצר וג̇** (דניאל 4:31). ויעני בקולה **ולקצת יומיא** (דניאל 4:31) **אלשבעה עדנין** (דניאל 4:29)

476 מנהא End of Oxf 2486.45a
477 פקט Beginning of Oxf 2486.45b
478 בקול Oxf 2486.45b
479 סדום End of Oxf 2486.45b
480 מאת Beginning of Oxf 2486.46a

אלמקדם ד׳כרהא. יקול למא אנקצ׳ת רגע אליה עקלה ועאד אלי מלכה ואג׳תמע אליה אלאמרא ואלקואד וסאיר אלאתבאע.

וגעל לנא פי[481] הד׳ה[482] איצ׳א אעתבארא פי שעבודנא, עלי כל נכתה ד׳כרהא נבוכ׳דנצר אן יכון לנא מת׳להא באלאוכד. פבאזא **עיני לשמיא נטלת** (דניאל 4:31) קאל לנא **שאי אליו כפיך על נפש עולליך** (איכה 2:19). ונט׳יר **ומנדעי עלי יתוב** (דניאל 4:31), **וידעו תעה רוח בניה** (יש׳ 29:24). ונט׳יר קולה **וליקר מלכותי** (דניאל 4:33), **וראו גוים צדקך וכל מלכים כבודך** (יש׳ 62:2). ונט׳יר קולה **הדרי וזיוי** (דניאל 4:33), **כי כליל הוא בהדרי אשר שמתי עליך** (יחז׳ 16:14). ואיצ׳א **בהדרי קדש מרחם משחר** (תה׳ 110:3). ונט׳יר קולה **ולי הדברי ורברבני יבעון** (דניאל 4:33), **והיה אדירו ממנו ומשלו מקרבו יצא** (ירמ׳ 30:21). ונט׳יר קולה **ועל מלכותי התקנת** (דניאל 4:33), **וכוננתי את כסא ממלכתו עד עולם** (שמ"ב 7:13). ונט׳יר קולה **ורבו יתירא הוספת לי** (דניאל 4:33), **והיטיבך והרבך מאבתיך** (דב׳ 30:5). ונט׳יר קולה **משבח ומרומם ומהדר** (דניאל 4:34), **הריעו ליוי כל הארץ פסחו**[483] **ורננו**[484] **וזמרו** (תה׳ 98:4). פסבחאן מן געל אכת׳ר גז...ארת[485] אלסאלפה תקויה לקלובנא פי אמר אלישועה.

ואכ׳ד לפט׳ה **די מהלכין בגוה יכל להשפלה** (דניאל 4:34) ליטבק עליהא קצת באלשאצר לאנהא תשאבההא פי הד׳ה אלבאב אד׳ קאל דניאל **ואנת בריה בלשצר לא השפלתא לבבך כל קבל די כל דנה ידעת** (דניאל 5:22). ליס אן בלשאצר מלך בעקב מות נבוכדנצר לאן אלאמר לו כאן כד׳אך לבטל קול אלנבי **ועדו אתו כל הגוים ואת בנו ואת בן בנו** (ירמ׳ 27:7). פלמא לם יך בד מן תמאם הד׳א וגב אן יכון אויל מרודך מלך בעקב מות נבוכ׳דנצר והו אבנה חתי יציר בלשצר אבן אבנה. ומנה אנקטע מלכהם. ומע ד׳אך פלם ינץ אלכתאב מן ספר מן אלספור כם מלך אויל מרודך ולא כם מלך נבוכ׳דנצר איצ׳א. אלא אנה נסתכ׳רג אלגמיע מן אלחסאב ונקול למא נץ אלכתאב אן אויל מרודך ימלך[486] פי[487] סנה לז׳ לגלות יכניה וכאן יכניה גלא פי סנה ח׳ לנבוכדנצר עלי מא בינגא וגב אן יכון נבוכ׳דנצר מלך מה׳ סנה. ולמא כאן אלמפרוץ׳ למלך בבל ע׳ סנה

481 פי End of Oxf 2486.46a
482 הדה Beginning of Oxf 2486.46b | פי הדה Oxf 2486.46b
483 פסחו End of Oxf 2486.46b
484 ורננו Beginning of Oxf 2486.47a | [ורנ]נו Oxf 2486.47a > D
485 גז[...]ארת Oxf 2486.47a > D
486 ימלך End of Oxf 2486.47a
487 פי Beginning of Oxf 2486.47b

כמא קאל **ועבדו הגוים האלה את מלך בבל שבעים שנה** (ירמ׳ 25:11) וכאן כ̇רג מן אולהא לנבוכ̇דנצר מד̇ תאמה ובעץ̇ סנה וכ̇רג מן אכ̇רהא לבלשצר ג̇ סנין נאקצה בקי אלצ̇רורה לאויל מרודך פי וסט מג̇ נא̇ נאקצה. וכמא שרחנא אן מעני תסמיתה בלטשצאר תקדים ד̇כר מעבודה פי אלאסם כד̇לך אלקול פי בלשצר. וכד̇לך אלקול פי מרדוך בלאדין מקדמא ופי אויל מרודך מואכ̇רא. ופי נבוכ̇דנצר ופי נבוזרדאן ונבושזבן מקדמא וסמגרנבו מואכ̇רא. אד̇ הד̇אן אלאסמאן אעני מרדך[488] ונבו המא אסמא[489] מעבודין כמא אן בל אסם[490] מעבוד.[491] תם[492] אלגז אלראבע.

[488] מרדך Beginning of TS Ar 28.76a | מר[ד]ך > D TS Ar 28.76a
[489] אסמ[א] TS Ar 28.76a and Oxf 2486.47b > D
[490] מעבודין ... אסם TS Ar 28.76a > D
[491] מעבוד End of Oxf 2486.47b
[492] תם Beginning of Oxf 2486.48a

ונץ אלגז אלכ̇אמס

Dn 5:1

בלשאצר מלכא עבד לחם רב לרברבנוהי אלף ולקבל אלפא חמרא שתה.

ת̇ם אן בלשצר[1] אלמלך אצלח טעאמא כת̇ירא לאלף[2] ריס[3] מעה וגלס[4] חד̇אהם[5] ישרב[6] כ̇מרא.[7]

Dn 5:2

בלשצר אמר בטעם חמרא להיתיה למאני דהבא וכספא די הנפק נבוכדנצר אבוהי די בירושלם וישתון בהון מלכא ורברבונוהי שגל תה ולחנתה.

פלמא מלכה[8] ראי אלכ̇מר[9] אמר אן[10] תחצ̇ר אניה[11] אלד̇הב[12] ואלפצ̇ה אלתי[13] אכ̇ד̇הא[14] בכ̇תנצר[15] אביה[16] מן אלהיכל אלד̇י פי מדינת[17] אלסלאם[18] ולישרב[19] בהא אלמלך ואלרויסא[20] וחראריה[21] וסראריה.[22]

[1] תם אן בלשצר TS Ar 28.76a and TS Ar 21.49e > D ׀ בלשאצר Spiegel
[2] [אצלח ... לא]לף TS Ar 28.76a > D
[3] רייס TS Ar 28.76a + Morag
[4] וגלס TS Ar 21.49e > D
[5] וגל[ס] חדאיהם TS Ar 28.76a
[6] ישוב TS Ar 28.76a ׀ שארבא Spiegel
[7] אלכמר TS Ar 21.49e + Oxf 2486.48a ׀ כמרא TS Ar 28.76a > D
[8] פלמא מלכה TS Ar 28.76a > D
[9] פלמא ... אלכמר TS Ar 21.49e > L
[10] באן TS Ar 21.49e
[11] נייה Spiegel
[12] [אלד]הב TS Ar 21.49e > D
[13] אלדי Oxf 2486.48a
[14] [אלדהב ... אכר]הא TS Ar 28.76a > D ׀ אכרגהא TS Ar 21.49e
[15] נ̇ TS Ar 21.49e
[16] אבוה TS Ar 21.49e

Dn 5:3

באדין[23] היתיו מאני דהבא די הנפקו מן היכלא די בית אלהא די בירושלם ואשתיו בהון מלכא ורברבנוהי שגלתה ולחנתה.

חיניד̇ אחצ̇רת[24] אניה[25] אלד̇הב[26] אלד̇י[27] אכ̇רגוהא[28] מן היכל בית אללה אלד̇י[29] פי ירושלם[30] וטפק[31] אן ישרב בהא אלמלך ואלרויסא[32] וחראירה וסראריה.[33]

Dn 5:4

אשתיו[34] חמרא ושבחו לאלהי דהבא וכספא פרזלא אעה ואבנא.

אכ̇ד̇ו[35] אן ישרבו בהא[36] כ̇מרא וסבחו לאלהה[37] אלד̇הב ואלפצ̇ה[38] ואלנחאס ואלחדיד[39] ואלכ̇שב ואלחגארה.[40]

[17] [מדינ]ת TS Ar 21.49e > D
[18] אלסלם Oxf 2486.48a | אלסלאם Spiegel > L
[19] [פי ... לישר]ב TS Ar 28.76a > D
[20] אלריסא TS Ar 28.76a + TS Ar 21.49e + Oxf 2486.48a | אלרוסא Spiegel
[21] וחר[אירה] Oxf 2486.48a > D | ו[חר]אירה TS Ar 28.76a > D
[22] וסראירה TS Ar 28.76a > D | וסראירה End of the readable Oxf 2486.48a
[23] באדין Beginning of Oxf 2486.48b
[24] אחצרה Morag
[25] אנייה Spiegel
[26] ואלפצה + Spiegel
[27] אלתי Spiegel + TS Ar 21.49e
[28] אכרגו[הא] Oxf 2486.48b > D | אכרגוה Spiegel
[29] אלתי Morag
[30] דאר אלסלם Oxf 2486.48b | ירוש TS Ar 21.49e
[31] וספק TS Ar 21.49e
[32] ואלריסא TS Ar 21.49e + Oxf 2486.48b | אלרוסא Spiegel
[33] דניאל 5:3 TS Ar 28.76a > D
[34] אשתיו Beginning of Yeirin 213 (MS TS Ar 1b.101)
[35] [א]כדו TS Ar 28.76a
[36] בהא Yeirin 213 and TS Ar 28.76a and TS Ar 21.49e and Oxf 2486.48b > D
[37] לאלאהה Spiegel + TS Ar 28.76a | לאלה TS Ar 21.49e
[38] אלפצה ואלדהב Spiegel
[39] [אלדהב ... ואלנ]חאס [ו]אלחד[י]ד TS Ar 28.76a > D
[40] ואלחגר Yeirin 213 + TS Ar 28.76a + TS Ar 21.49e + Oxf 2486.48b

Dn 5:5

בה שעתא נפקו אצבען די יד אנש וכתבן לקביל נברשתא על גירא די כחל היכלא די מלכא ומלכא חזה פס ידא די כתבה.

מן סאעתה חצ֗רת[41] אצאבע[42] בצורה[43] יד אנסאן[44] פכתבת בחד֗א אלמנארה[45] עלי[46] אספידאג[47] חאיט היכל[48] אלמלך ואלמלך[49] ינט֗ר[50] אלכף[51] והי תכתב.[52]

Dn 5:6

אדין מלכא זיוהי שנהי ורעיונוהי יבהלוניה וקטרי חרציה משתרין וארכובתיה דא לדא נקשן.

חיניד֗ תג֗ירת[53] סחנתה ואד֗ערתה[54] אפכארה[55] וכאן[56] כ֗רז צלבה[57] תחללת ואקבלת[58] רכבתאה[59] תנצך[60] ואחדה מע אלאכ֗רי.[61]

[41] טהרת TS Ar 21.49e + Oxf 2486.48b ׀ [חצ\טה]רת TS Ar 28.76a

[42] אלאצאבע Yeirin 213 + Morag

[43] בצורת Morag

[44] אלנאס Yeirin 213 + TS Ar 28.76a ׀ אלאנסאן Spiegel

[45] פכת[בת בחדא] אל[מנא]רה Yeirin 213 > D ׀ פכת[בת ... אלמנא]רה TS Ar 28.76a

[46] עלא Morag ׀ עלי End of Oxf 2486.48b

[47] אספידאג Beginning of Oxf 2486.49a ׀ אספיראג Yeirin 213 > D ׀ אספירג TS Ar 28.76a

[48] היכל Spiegel > L

[49] ואלמ[לך] TS Ar 28.76a > D

[50] ינצ֗ר Morag ׀ ירי Yeirin 213 + TS Ar 21.49e + Oxf 2486.48b ׀ ירא Spiegel

[51] ואלמלך ... אלכף TS Ar 28.76a > D

[52] והי תכתב Yeirin 213 > D

[53] תג֗יירת Spiegel + Morag ׀ [חיניד֗ תג֗י]רת Yeirin 213

[54] וארדעתה Yeirin 213 + TS Ar 21.49e + Oxf 2486.49a ׀ ואדערתה TS Ar 28.76a > D

[55] [א]פכאר[ה] TS Ar 28.76a > D

[56] וכאן TS Ar 28.76a > D

[57] צ[לב]ה TS Ar 21.49e > D

[58] [צלבה תח]ללת וא[קבל]ת Yeirin 213 > D

[59] רכבה TS Ar 21.49e ׀ רכבאתה Spiegel

[60] תצטך TS Ar 28.76a + Oxf 2486.49a

[61] [ואחדה מע אל]אכ֗רי TS Ar 28.76a > D ׀ אככרי TS Ar 21.49e

Dn 5:7

קרי מלכא בחיל לאעלא קדמוהי לאשפיא כסדאי וגזריא עני ואסר לחכימי בבל די כל אנש די יקריה כתבא דנא ופשריה יחוונני ארגונא ילבש והמניכה די דהבא על צוריה ותלתי במלכותא ישלט.

פנאדא[62] בקוה[63] באחצ̇אר אלמנגמין[64] ואלכסראניין[65] ואלחכאם פאבתדי וקאל להם אי אנסאן אחסן אן יקרא[66] הד̇א[67] אלכתאב[68] ויערפני[69] תפסירה[70] פלילבס[71] אלחמרה[72] ויטוק[73] בטוק אלד̇הב ויל̇י[74] ת̇לת̇ אלממלכה.[75]

Dn 5:8

אדין[76] עלין כל חכימי מלכא ולא כהלין כתבא למקרי ופסריה להודעא למלכא.

חיניד̇ חצ̇ר גמיע חכמא[77] אלממלכה[78] פלם יטיקו אן יקרו אלכתאב[79] פצ̇לא עלי[80] אן יערפו אלמלך תפסירה.[81]

[62] פנאדי Oxf 2486.49a ׀ נאדי TS Ar 21.49e ׀ נאדא TS Ar 28.76a ׀ נא[די] Yeirin 213

[63] בקווה Spiegel + Morag

[64] באחצא[ר אל]מנגמין TS Ar 21.49e > D

[65] ואלכס[ד]א[ניין] TS Ar 21.49e > D ואלכסד[אניין] TS Ar 28.76a > D

[66] [י]ק[רא] TS Ar 28.76a > D

[67] הדי Morag

[68] אלכת TS Ar 28.76a

[69] ויערפ[ני] TS Ar 21.49e > D

[70] תפסירהא Spiegel

[71] לילבס Yeirin 213 ׀ ילבס Spiegel

[72] חמרה Yeirin 213 + TS Ar 28.76a + TS Ar 21.49e

[73] ויטווק Spiegel + Morag

[74] ויולי Yeirin 213 + TS Ar 21.49e + Oxf 2486.49a

[75] אלממלכה End of Oxf 2486.49a

[76] אדין Beginning of Oxf 2486.49b

[77] חכמי Morag ׀ חכמא TS Ar 28.76a > D

[78] באבל Spiegel

[79] אלכת TS Ar 28.76a

[80] פצל[א עלי] Morag > L

[81] תפסירהא End of Yeirin 213 ׀ Morag

Dn 5:9

אדין[82] מלכא בלשצר שׂגיא מתבהיל וזיוהי שנין עלוהי ורברבנוהי משתבשין.

חיניד̇ תחייר בלשצר[83] אלמלך[84] כת̇ירא[85] ותג̇יר[86] לונה עליה ואלריסא[87] אלד̇ין[88] מעה מתשושין.[89]

Dn 5:10

מלכתא לקביל מילי מלכא ורברבנוהי לבית משתיא עלת ענת מלכתא ואמרת מלכא לעלמא חיי אל יבהלך רעיונך וזיונך לא ישתני.

ענד כלאם[90] אלמלך ואלריסא[91] דכ̇לת אלמלכה אלי אלמגלס[92] פאבתדאת וקאלת אטאל אללהו[93] בקא אלמלך לא[94] תד̇הלך[95] אפכארך ולא[96] יתג̇ייר[97] לונך.[98]

Dn 5:11

איתי[99] גבר במלכותך די רוח אלהין קדישין ביה וביומי אבוך נהירו וסוכלתנו וחכמה כחכמת אלהין השתסחת ביה ומלכא נבוכדנצר אבוך רב חרטומין אשפין בסראין גזרין הקימיה אבוך מלכא.

[82] Beginning of Yeirin 214 (MS TS Ar 1b.102)

[83] בלשצר TS Ar 28.76a > L ! בלשאצר Spiegel + Yeirin 214 ׀ בלשצר End of TS Ar 21.49e

[84] אלמלך Beginning of TS Ar 21.49f ׀ אלמלך באלשצר Morag

[85] כעירא TS Ar 21.49f

[86] ותג̇ייר Spiegel + Morag

[87] ואלרייסא Morag ׀ אלריוסא TS Ar 28.76a

[88] אלדי Spiegel + TS Ar 28.76a ׀ אללדין Oxf 2486.49b

[89] מתשו[שי]ן TS Ar 21.49f > D

[90] כלם TS Ar 28.76a

[91] אלרייסא Morag ׀ אלרוסא Spiegel + Yeirin 214

[92] [אלי אלמ]גלס TS Ar 21.49f > D ׀ אלמגל[ס] Yeirin 214 > D ׀ מגלס Spiegel

[93] ו[ק]ל[ת] א[טאל אל]לה TS Ar 28.76a > D

[94] ל[א] Yeirin 214 > D

[95] [לא תדה]לך TS Ar 21.49f > D

[96] ולא Oxf 2486.49b > D

[97] יתג̇יר TS Ar 28.76a + TS Ar 21.49f + Oxf 2486.49b

[98] לונך End of Oxf 2486.49b

[99] איתי Beginning of Oxf 2486.50a

מוגוד פי ממלכתך[100] רגל[101] מן[102] פיה רוח אללה[103] אלמקדס[104] מן איאם[105] אביך[106] אלאיצ̇אח[107] ואלעקל ואלחכמה[108] כחכמה אלמלאיכה[109] מוגודה פיה[110] ולד̇לך[111] נצבה אביך[112] בכ̇תנצר אסתאד̇ אלחכמא[113] ואלמנגמין ואלכסדאניין[114] ואלחכאם.

Dn 5:12

כל קביל[115] די רוח יתירא ומנדע וסוכלתנו ומפשר חלמין ואחוית אחידון ומשרי קטרין והשתכחת ביה בדניאל די מלכא שם שמיה בלטשצר כען דניאל יתקרי ופשרא יהחוי.

לאגל[116] מא פיה[117] מן[118] אלראי אלפאצ̇ל[119] ואלמערפה ואלעקל יפסר[120] אלאחלאם וירוי[121] ג̇לאחאדית̇[122] ויחלל[123] אלעקד אלכל[124] מוגוד פי דניאלא

[100] מן[מ]לכתך TS Ar 21.49f > D
[101] רגל Spiegel > L
[102] מן TS Ar 21.49f and Oxf 2486.50a > L
[103] [אל]לה TS Ar 28.76a > D
[104] אלמקדס Yeirin 214 > D
[105] [אי]אם TS Ar 28.76a > D
[106] אבוך Spiegel + Yeirin 214 + Morag
[107] איצ̇אח TS Ar 28.76a
[108] וחכמה TS Ar 28.76a + Oxf 2486.50a
[109] ואלחכ[מה] כחכמ[ה אלמלאיכה] Yeirin 214 > D ׀ אלמליכה TS Ar 21.49f
[110] פיה TS Ar 21.49f > D
[111] ולדאלך Spiegel + Morag ׀ לדלך Oxf 2486.50a ׀ ודלך Yeirin 214
[112] בכתנצר + Morag
[113] לאלחכמא Spiegel
[114] ואלכסד TS Ar 21.49f ׀ [ואלכס]דאניין Yeirin 214
[115] קביל TS Ar 28.76a
[116] לאגל TS Ar 28.76b
[117] פי[ה] TS Ar 28.76b > D
[118] מן Morag > L
[119] אלרוח אלפאצ̇לה TS Ar 28.76b
[120] ואלמערפה ... יפסר TS Ar 28.76b > D
[121] ורויא Spiegel
[122] אלחדית Yeirin 214 + TS Ar 28.76b + TS Ar 21.49f + Oxf 2486.50a
[123] ויחל TS Ar 21.49f
[124] כל TS Ar 28.76b + TS Ar 21.49f + Oxf 2486.50a

אלדׄי[125] אסמאה[126] אלמלך בלטשצר[127] אלאן[128] ידעי בה חתי יערפך[130] אלתפסיר.[131]

Dn 5:13

באידין[132] דניאל הועל קדם מלכא[133] ואמר לדניאל אנתא הוא דניאל די מן בני גלותא די יהוד די היתי מלכא אבי מן יהוד.

חיניד[134] תצׄר[135] דניאל בין ידי אלמלך[136] פאבתדאה[137] וקאל לה אנת הו דניאל[138] אלדׄי מן[139] גלוה[140] אליהוד[141] אלדׄי סבאהם אבי[142] מן אלשאם.

Dn 5:14

ושמעת עלך די רוח אלהין בך ונהירו וסוכלתנו וחכמה יתיוא השתכחת בך.[143]

וסמעת[144] ענך אן מוגוד פיך רוח אללה[145] ואיצׄאח[146] ועקל וחכמה פאצׄלה וגדת[147] פיך.

[125] ויחל[ל ... אלדי] TS Ar 28.76b > D | אלדי End of Oxf 2486.50a

[126] אסמאה Beginning of Oxf 2486.50b

[127] בלשאצר Spiegel + Yeirin 214 | בלשט TS Ar 21.49f

[128] אלא TS Ar 21.49f

[129] אדע Morag | ידעא Spiegel + Yeirin 214

[130] יכׄברך TS Ar 21.49f + Oxf 2486.50b | אלאן ... יערפך TS Ar 28.76b > D

[131] באלתפסיר TS Ar 28.76b + TS Ar 21.49f + Oxf 2486.50b

[132] באידין End of Yeirin 214

[133] מלכא Beginning of the readable part of Yeirin 215 (MS ENA 3462.5)

[134] [חיני]ד TS Ar 28.76b > D

[135] אחצר Spiegel + Oxf 2486.50b

[136] דניאל ... אלמלך TS Ar 28.76b > D

[137] פאבתד[אה] Yeirin 215 > D | פאבתדא Spiegel

[138] [לה ... דני]אל Yeirin 215 > D

[139] אהל + Spiegel

[140] גלות Morag

[141] דניאל ... אליהוד TS Ar 28.76b > D

[142] אלמלך + TS Ar 28.76b

[143] דניאל 5:14-15 TS Ar 21.49f > L

[144] אלדי סמעת Oxf 2486.50b

[145] [וסמעת ...] אלהה אלמקדסה פיך TS Ar 28.76b > D

[146] ואלאיצׄאח TS Ar 28.76b | ואיצׄאת Spiegel

[147] ועקל ... וגדת TS Ar 28.76b > D

Dn 5:15

וכען הועלו קדמי חכימיא אשפיא די כתבא דנא יקרון ופשריה להודעתני ולא כהלין פשר מילתא להחויא.[148]

ואלאן[149] פאצעדי אליי[150] אלחכמא ואלמנגמין ליקרו[151] הד̇י[152] אלכתאב ויערפוני תפסירה[153] ולם יסתטיעו[154] תפסיר לפט̇ה[155] לאכ̇באר.[156]

Dn 5:16

ואנא שמעית עלך די תיכול פשרין למפשר וקשרין למשרי כען הן תוכל כתבא לקרי ופשרא להודעתני ארגונא תלבש והמניכא די דהבא על צורך ותלתא במלכותא תשלט.

פאנא[157] קד סמעת ענך אנך[158] תסתטיע אן תפסר[159] אלתפאסיר[160] ותחלל אלעקד[161] אלאן[162] אן[163] אמכנך אן תקרא הד̇א[164] אלכתאב[165] ותערפני[166] תפסירה תלבס אלחמרה[167] ותטוק[168] בטוק אלד̇הב[169] ותלי ת̇לת̇ אלממלכה.

[148] להחויא End of Oxf 2486.50b

[149] ואלאן Beginning of Oxf 2486.51a | (דניאל 5:15) ולאן פקד אדכלו אלי חצ̇רתי חכמא ומנגמין עלי אן יקרון הדא אלכתאב ויערפוני תפסירה פלם יטיקו עלי ביאן כלמה ואחדה.

[150] ולאן קד דכלו בין TS Ar 28.76b | אלאן אצעדו בין ידי Spiegel | ואלאן אצעדו קדאמי Yeirin 215

[151] [אלחכמא ואלמנגמין] אנהם יקראו TS Ar 28.76b > D | לאן יקרון Yeirin 215 | אן יקרון Spiegel

[152] הדה TS Ar 28.76b | הדא Spiegel + Yeirin 215

[153] תפסירה Yeirin 215 > L

[154] יטיקו Yeirin 215

[155] לפצ̇ה Spiegel + Morag

[156] תפס[ירה ... לאכבאר] TS Ar 28.76b > D

[157] פאני TS Ar 21.49f

[158] אן TS Ar 28.76b

[159] תפסר Oxf 2486.51a > D

[160] תפסר אלתפאסיר TS Ar 28.76b > D

[161] אלעקוד TS Ar 28.76b

[162] אלא[ן] TS Ar 21.49f > D

[163] אן Spiegel > L

[164] הדי Morag | [ה]דא Yeirin 215 > D

[165] אלכת TS Ar 21.49f

[166] אלכתאב ותערפני TS Ar 28.76b > D

[167] אלחומרה TS Ar 28.76b

[168] ותטוק Yeirin 215 + TS Ar 28.76b + TS Ar 21.49f + Oxf 2486.51a

[169] בט[וק אלדהב] TS Ar 28.76b > D | [אלד]הב Yeirin 215 > D

Dn 5:17

באדין ענה דניאל ואמר קדם מלכא מתנתך לך להיון ונבזבזתך לאחרן הב ברם כתבא אקרי למלכא ופשרא אהודעיניה.

חיניד[170] אגאבה דניאל וקאל[171] אמא[172] עטאיאך[173] פתבקא[174] ענדך ואמא גואיזך הבהא[175] לג̇ירי לכני[176] אקרא ללמלך אלכתאב[177] ואערפה[178] תפסירה.[179]

Dn 5:18

אנתא מלכא[180] אלהא עלאה מלכותא ורבותא ויקרא והדרא יהב לנבוכדנצר אבוך.

ואקדם קבל ד̇לך[181] אנת[182] יא איה אלמלך[183] תעלם אן[184] אללה אלעאלי[185] אעטא בכ̇תנצר[186] אבוך[187] אלמלך[188] ואלשרף[189] ואלוקאר[190] ואלבהא.[191]

[170] חינ[י]ד TS Ar 21.49f > D
[171] דני[אל וקאל] TS Ar 28.76b > D
[172] דנ[יאל וקאל] אמ[א] TS Ar 21.49f > D
[173] עטאי[אך] Oxf 2486.51a | [דניאל ... עטאי]אך Yeirin 215 > D | עטא[יאך] TS Ar 21.49f | עטאיאך End of the readable part of Oxf 2486.51a
[174] תבקא TS Ar 28.76b
[175] פהב[הא] TS Ar 28.76b > D
[176] פה[הא לג̇ירי לכ]ני TS Ar 21.49f > D
[177] אקרא אלכת ללמל[ך] Yeirin 215 + TS Ar 28.76b + TS Ar 21.49f | אלכת TS Ar 21.49f
[178] ואערפה TS Ar 21.49f > D | ואערפך TS Ar 28.76b
[179] תפסירה End of Yeirin 215
[180] מלכא Beginning of Yeirin 216 (MS ENA 3462.6)
[181] ד̇אלך Spiegel + Morag
[182] אנת Spiegel > L
[183] איה אלמלך TS Ar 21.49f > D | ואקד[ם ... אלמלך] Yeirin 216 > D | אלמלך Beginning of the readable part of Oxf 2486.51b
[184] תעלם אן Oxf 2486.51b > D | אן Yeirin 216 > D
[185] אלעלי Oxf 2486.51b
[186] נ̇ TS Ar 21.49f
[187] אביך Spiegel + TS Ar 28.76b | אבאך TS Ar 21.49f
[188] אבוך אלמלך Oxf 2486.51b > D
[189] אלמלך ואלשרף Yeirin 216 > D
[190] ואלהיבה + TS Ar 28.76b
[191] ואלבהי Oxf 2486.51b

Dn 5:19

ומן רבותא די יהיב ליה כל עממיא אומיא ולשניא הוו זיעין ודחלין מן קדמוהי די הוה צבי הוה קטיל ודי הוה צבי הוה משפיל.

ומן שרף מא אעטאה כאן[192] גמיע אלשעוב ואלאמם ואהל[193] אללגֿאת יתקונה ויכֿאפונה[194] פמן שא קתל ומן שא[195] אסתבקא[196] ומן שא רפע[197] ומן שא חט.[198]

Dn 5:20

וכדי רים ליביה ורוחיה תקיפת להזרא הונחת מן כורסי מלבותיה ויקריה העדיו מיניה.[199]

ולמא עטֻם[200] קלבה ועלת[201] נפסה אלי אלאתקאה[202] חט[203] מן כרסי[204] מלכה[205] ווקארה זאל[206] ענה.

Dn 5:21

ומן בני אנשא טריד וליביה עם חיותא שוי ועם ערודיא מדוריה עסבא בתורא יטעמוניה ומטל שמיא גשמיה יצטבע עד די ידע די שליט אלהא עלאה במלכות אנשא ולמן די יצבי יהקים עלה.

192 מן TS Ar 28.76b | באן Spiegel + Yeirin 216

193 ואהל Yeirin 216 > L

194 יתוקונה ויכפוה TS Ar 21.49f

195 שא End of TS Ar 21.49f

196 אסתבקא Beginning of TS Ar 21.49g

197 ומן … רפע Oxf 2486.51b > D

198 חט End of the readable part of Oxf 2486.51b

199 מנה Beginning of Oxf 2486.52a

200 עצֻם Spiegel + Yeirin 216 + Morag

201 ו[ע]לת TS Ar 21.49g > D

202 אלאתקאה Oxf 2486.52a > D | אלתוקא TS Ar 21.49g | אלתוקה TS Ar 28.76b + Spiegel + Yeirin 216

203 אחט Spiegel + Morag

204 [מן כרס]י TS Ar 21.49g > D

205 מולכה TS Ar 21.49g

206 [ז]אל TS Ar 21.49g > D

ומן בין אלנאס נפי[207] וצאר ראיה[208] מע וחש[209] אלצחרא[210] ומאואה מע אלעראביד[211] יגֿתדי[212] אלעשב כאלבקר[213] וינצבגֿ מן טל אלסמא[214] חתי אעתרף באן אללה[215] מסלט[216] עלי מלך אלנאס למן שא[217] אעטאה ויגוז לה אן ינצב[218] אלוצֿיע מנהם.[219]

Dn 5:22

ואנתא בריה בלשצר לא השפילתא לבבך כל קביל די כל דנה ידעתא.

ואנת[220] יא בלשצר[221] אבנה לם תתצֿע[222] מעמא[223] קד וקפת עלי[224] גמיע דֿלך.[225]

Dn 5:23

ועל[226] מרי שמיא[227] התרוממת ולמניא די ביתיה היתיו קדמך ואנתא ורברבניך שגילתך ולחינתך חמרא שתין בהון ולאלהי כספא ודהבא

207 [אל]נ[אס נפי] TS Ar 21.49g > D

208 ראיה וצאר Oxf 2486.52a

209 אלוחש TS Ar 21.49g + Oxf 2486.52a

210 אלצחרא Oxf 2486.52a > L | אלצחרי Morag

211 אלערבד Yeirin 216 + Oxf 2486.52a | אלערביד TS Ar 28.76b | [אלער]בד D < TS Ar 21.49g

212 ויתגֿדי TS Ar 28.76b

213 כאל[בקר] Oxf 2486.52a > D

214 אלס[מא] TS Ar 21.49g > D

215 אלעאלי + TS Ar 21.49g and TS Ar 28.76b and Oxf 2486.52a

216 מצלט Morag

217 ינצבה להם + Spiegel

218 אן ינצב לה Yeirin 216 + TS Ar 21.49g + TS Ar 28.76b + Oxf 2486.52a

219 אעטאה ... מנהם Spiegel > L

220 [ואנ]ת Oxf 2486.52a > D

221 בלש TS Ar 21.49g | בלשצאר Spiegel | בלשצר End of TS Ar 28.76b

222 תתואצֿע TS Ar 21.49g + Oxf 2486.52a | ת[ת]ואצ[ע] Yeirin 216 | תתוצֿע Spiegel

223 [מעמ]א Beginning of the readable part of TS Ar 28.76c | מעמא Oxf > D 2486.52a | כמא TS Ar 21.49g

224 מעמא ... עלי Yeirin 216 > D

225 [מעמ]א ... דלך TS Ar 28.76c > D | דאלך Spiegel + Morag | דלך End of Oxf 2486.52a

226 ועל Beginning of Oxf 2486.52b

227 שמיא End of the readable part of Yeirin 216

נחשא פרזלא אעא ואבנא די לא חזין ולא שמעין ולא ידעין שבחתא ולאלהי די נשמתך בידיה וכל אורחתן ליה לא הדרת.

ולכנך[228] תרפעת[229] עלי רב אלסמא פאחצ̇רת בין ידיך אניה ביתה ושרבת[230] אנת[231] ואלרייסא[232] וחראריך וסראריך אלכ̇מר[233] בהא וסבחת[234] לאלהה[235] אלד̇הב ואלפצ̇ה ואלנחאס ואלחדיד ואלכ̇שב[236] ואלחגר[237] אלתי לא[238] תבצר ולא תסמע ולא[239] תעלם[240] שיא[241] ולא[242] תבגל[243] אללה אלד̇י נסמתך פי ידה[244] וגמיע אחואלך לה.[245]

Dn 5:24

באדין מן קדמוהי שליח פסא די ידא וכתבא דנא רשים.

חיניד̇ בעת̇[246] מן חצ̇רתה בהד̇א[247] אלכף פרסמת[248] הד̇א[249] אלכתאב.[250]

[228] לכנך TS Ar 21.49g + Oxf 2486.52b
[229] ולכנך תרפעת TS Ar 28.76c > D
[230] [ידיך ... ושר]בת TS Ar 28.76c > D
[231] א[נת] TS Ar 21.49g > D
[232] ואלריסא TS Ar 28.76c + TS Ar 21.49g + Oxf 2486.52b | אלרוסא Spiegel
[233] אלכמרא Spiegel
[234] וס[בח]ת TS Ar 21.49g > D
[235] אלהה TS Ar 21.49g + Oxf 2486.52b | [אלכמר ... לאל]אה TS Ar 28.76c > D
[236] [ו]אלכשב TS Ar 21.49g > D
[237] ואלחגאר Spiegel + Morag | [אלח]גר TS Ar 28.76c > D | [אל]חגר TS Ar 21.49g > D
[238] אלדי לם Spiegel
[239] ול[א] TS Ar 21.49g > D | ולם Spiegel
[240] [תע]לם Oxf 2486.52b > D
[241] שייא Morag
[242] ולם TS Ar 21.49g
[243] [תעלם ... תבג]ל TS Ar 28.76c > D
[244] פידה TS Ar 28.76c
[245] לה TS Ar 28.76c > D
[246] [חיניד בע]ת TS Ar 28.76c > D
[247] בהדה Oxf 2486.52b + Morag
[248] [פר]סמת TS Ar 21.49g > D
[249] הדי Morag
[250] אלכתאב TS Ar 28.76c > D

Dn 5:25
ודנא כתבא די רשים מנא מנא תקיל[251] ופרסין.[252]

והדֹא[253] הו[254] אלכתאב אלמרסום[255] אחצא אחצא[256] וזן וזן וכסר כסר.

Dn 5:26
דנא פשר מילתא מנא מנא אלהא מלכותך והשלמה.

והדֹא[258] תפסיר הדֹה אלכלמאת[259] אמא[260] אלאחצא[261] פאן[262] אללה קד אחצא[263] מדת מלכך ותממהא.[264]

Dn 5:27
תקיל תקילת במאזניא והשתכחת חסיר.

ואמא[265] אלוזן[266] פאנך[267] וזנת פי מיזאן פוגדת נאקצא.[268]

Dn 5:28
פרס פרסית מלכותיך ויהיבת למדי ופרס.

ואמא[269] אלכסר פקד[270] כסר מלכך וסלם[271] אלי מדי ופרס.

[251] תקיל End of Oxf 2486.52b
[252] ופרסין Beginning of Oxf 2486.53a
[253] והדי Morag | [והד]א TS Ar 28.76c > D
[254] הו Spiegel > L
[255] [הו ... אלמ]רסום TS Ar 21.49g > D | אלמרסום Morag > L
[256] אחצי אחצי Morag | אחצ[... אחצ]א TS Ar 21.49g > D | אחצא אחצי Spiegel
[257] וזן ... כסר TS Ar 28.76c > D
[258] והדי Morag
[259] אלבלמאת TS Ar 28.76c
[260] [והדא ... אמ]א TS Ar 21.49g > D
[261] אלאחצי TS Ar 21.49g
[262] אמא ... פאן TS Ar 28.76c > D
[263] אחצי Oxf 2486.53a
[264] אללה ... ותממהא TS Ar 21.49g > D | ותמאמהא TS Ar 28.76c
[265] [וא]מא TS Ar 21.49g > D
[266] [ואמא ... אלו]זן TS Ar 28.76c > D
[267] פאנך Morag > L | קד + TS Ar 28.76c
[268] מיז[אן פוג]דת נאק[צא] TS Ar 21.49g > D
[269] ואמא TS Ar 28.76c > D

Dn 5:29

באדין אמר בלשצר והולבישו לדניאל ארגונא והמניכא די דהבא על צוריה והכריזו עלוהי די להוי שליט תלתא במלכותא.[272]

חיניד[273] אמר בלשצר[274] פאלבסו[275] דניאל אלחמרה[276] וטוקה[277] בטוק אלדׄהב[278] ונאדו עליה באן[279] ילי תׄלתׄ אלממלכה.

Dn 5:30

ביה בליליא קטיל בלשצר מלכא כסראה.

פי[280] תלך אללילה קתל[281] בלשצר[282] אלמלך[283] אלכסדאני.[284]

אול מא לנא מן אלתאדיב פי הדׄה אלקצה אלא[285] ננאל מן אלשראב מא יגׄלב עלי עקולנא פימלכנא. אדׄ קד תבيננא[286] אן[287] אלסבב אלדׄי[288] חמל[289] בלשצר עלי מא פעל ראי אלנביד̇ כמא קאל **בטעם**[290] **חמרא** (דניאל 5:2). וכדׄלך מא חמל אחשורש עלי[291] מא פעל פי אמר ושתי[292] אלא[293] ראי אלנביד̇ כמא

[272] במלכותא End of Oxf 2486.53a

[273] חיניד Beginning of Oxf 2486.53b | [חי]ניד > D TS Ar 28.76c

[274] בלשצר > D TS Ar 21.49g | בלשצאר Spiegel

[275] פאלבס Morag | באלבסו TS Ar 21.49g

[276] חמרה TS Ar 28.76c + Morag

[277] וטווקה Morag | וטוק TS Ar 28.76c

[278] [אלדה]ב > D TS Ar 28.76c

[279] ב[אן] > D TS Ar 21.49g

[280] ופי TS Ar 21.49g + Oxf 2486.53b

[281] קתל > D TS Ar 28.76c

[282] בלש TS Ar 21.49g | בלשצאר Spiegel

[283] אלמלך > D TS Ar 28.76c

[284] אלכסדאניא Spiegel

[285] אלא > D TS Ar 28.76c

[286] תבין TS Ar 28.76c

[287] אן > L TS Ar 28.76c

[288] אלי TS Ar 28.76c

[289] [חמ]ל > D Oxf 2486.53b

[290] כק בעעם TS Ar 28.76c

[291] אחשורוש פי מא TS Ar 28.76c

[292] והו + TS Ar 28.76c

[293] אלא > L TS Ar 28.76c

קאל[294] **ביום השביעי כטוב לב המלך**[295] **ביין** (אסתר 1:10). וכדׄלך מא חמל פלשתים עלי אחצׄאר שמשון לילעב[296] להם וכאן סבב[297] הלאכהם אלא[298] ראי אלנביד̇ כמא קאל[299] **ויהי כטוב לבם ויאמרו**[300] (שופ׳ 16:25). וכדׄלך מא שגׄל אמנון ען אלתחרז מן אן יקתלה אבשלון אלא חמל אלנביד̇ כמא קאל **ויצו**[301] **אבשלום**[302] **את נעריו לאמר ראו כטוב לב אמנון ביין ואמרתי אליכם הכו את אמנון והמתם אתו**[303] (שמ״ב 13:28). וכדׄלך אלה[304] בן בעשא קתל **והוא בתרצה**[305] **שותה שכור** (מל״א 16:9). וכדׄלך בן הדד גׄלב[306] **והוא שותה הוא והמלכים בסכות** (מל״א 20:12). וכדׄלך לוט לם יגר[307] פי אמרה[308] מא גרי אלא בסבב אלסכר כמא קאל[309] **לכה נשקה את אבינו יין** (בר׳ 19:32). וכדׄלך נוח לם יגרי מא גרי מן אמרה כמא קאל **ויחל נוח וג׳** (בר׳ 9:20) אלא והו **שכור**[310] ומן מאתׄל האולי.

תׄם נתאדב באן כל סכראן[311] יגני[312] גנאיה. פאנה[313] ילזמה חכם[314] עקובתהא כאלצאחי לא פרק.[315] כמא צח לנא אן בלשצר פעל אפעאלא[316] בסכר ועאקבה

[294] כק TS Ar 28.76c
[295] המׄ TS Ar 28.76c
[296] ילעב TS Ar 28.76c
[297] לסבב TS Ar 28.76c
[298] אלא TS Ar 28.76c > L
[299] כמא קאל TS Ar 28.76c > L
[300] ויאמרו TS Ar 28.76c > L | End of Oxf 2486.53b
[301] וכדלך … ויצו Oxf 2486.53b > D
[302] אבשלום Beginning of the readable part of Oxf 2486.54a
[303] לאמור … אתו TS Ar 28.76c > L
[304] אילא Oxf 2486.54a
[305] בתרצה והוא TS Ar 28.76c
[306] גׄלב TS Ar 28.76c
[307] יגרי מא גרי עליה TS Ar 28.76c
[308] אמרה TS Ar 28.76c > L
[309] כק TS Ar 28.76c
[310] כמא קאל … שכור Oxf 2486.54a > L
[311] End of TS Ar 28.76c
[312] Beginning of TS Ar 28.76d
[313] פאנה TS Ar 28.76d > L
[314] לחכ[ם] TS Ar 28.76d > D
[315] עקובתהא … פרק TS Ar 28.76d > D
[316] אפעלא Oxf 2486.54a

אללה[317] עליה. וכדׄאך נגד פי אלפקה אן אלסכר ליס[318] הו עדׄר[319] בתה לכן **שכור מקחו מקח וממכרו ממכר עבד עבידה שיש**[320] **בה מיתה ממיתין אתו מלקות מלקין ואתו**[321] **כללו של דבר הרי הוא כפקח לכל דבריו אלא שפטור מן התפלה**[322] (עירובין 65a). ואמא בדל בלשצר[323] למן יפתיה **ארגונא** (דניאל 5:7). [...][324] ואדׄא קאלו לבס אלחמרה פקד באלגׄו וכמא יקול אלערב פי[325] [...][326] הדׄא קד לבס אלסואר ואסמה ענד גׄיר [...][327] וכמא נפסר קולה **במרכבה הרושנה סוסים אדומים** (זכ׳ 6:2) יעני **מלכות בבל**.[328]

ואמא עגז חכמא בבל ען קראה אלכתאב פלאנה כאן[329] עבראניא ובאלצׄרורה פקד וקף אלקום ען תפסירה.[330] ואמא אלסתה[331] אוצאף אלתי[332] וצפת בהא אלמלכה[333] לדניאל והי[334] **רוח יתירא ומנדע ושוכלתנו ומפשר חלמין ואחוית אחידון ומשרא קטרין**[335] (דניאל 5:12) פיכון שרחהא עלי מא[336] נצו[337] באכׄתצאר. אמא **רוח יתירא**[338] (דניאל 5:12) פאן אלחכמא[339] אגתמעו

[317] אפעאלא ... אללה TS Ar 28.76d > D
[318] אלפקה ... ליס TS Ar 28.76d > D
[319] עדר הו TS Ar 28.76d
[320] שיש End of the readable part of Oxf 2486.54a
[321] [מלקות מלקין] וא[תו] TS Ar 28.76d > D
[322] דבריו ... התפלה TS Ar 28.76d > D
[323] בלשצר Beginning of the readable part of Oxf 2486.54b
[324] [...] TS Ar 28.76d and Oxf 2486.54b > D
[325] יקול ... פי TS Ar 28.76d > D
[326] TS Ar 28.76d and Oxf 2486.54b > D
[327] [...] TS Ar 28.76d and Oxf 2486.54b > D
[328] יעני ... בבל TS Ar 28.76d > D
[329] אל[כתאב ... כאן] TS Ar 28.76d > D
[330] ען תפסירה TS Ar 28.76d > D
[331] אלו TS Ar 28.76d
[332] אלדי TS Ar 28.76d
[333] אלממלכה Oxf 2486.54b
[334] אל[ממלכה לדניאל והי] TS Ar 28.76d > D
[335] ואחוית ... קטרין TS Ar 28.76d > D
[336] עלי מא TS Ar 28.76d > D
[337] אצף TS Ar 28.76d
[338] ית TS Ar 28.76d
[339] אל[חכמ]א TS Ar 28.76d > D | אלח[כמא] Oxf 2486.54b > D

עלי[340] אן הדׄא אלתדביר ליס הו אלי גׄ וגוה [...][341] הו וגהא ראבעא. ואמא **ומנדע** (דניאל 5:12) פהו[342] אסתכׄראג מא יכון כמא כאן כקולך[343] **ואנדע די פשרה תהחונני** (דניאל 2:9). ואמא **שכלתנו** (דניאל 5:12) פהו[344] קוה[345] אלנטׄר ואלתאמל[346] כקולך[347] **משתכל הוית בקרניא**[348] (דניאל 7:8). ומעני[349] **מפשר חלמין**[350] (דניאל 5:12) פהו[351] אסתמדאד אמתׄאל אלאחלאם מן דׄ עלל, אלעלה אלענצריה ואלצוריה ואלפאעלה ואלתמאמיה. וזאד[352] עליהא אלכׄבר ואלשרע. ומעני **אחוית אחידון** (דניאל 5:12) אלדי הו רויא[353] אלאחאדית, תקריב[354] אלמעאני חתי תציר באלאכׄבאר אלמתקדמה ואלמתאכׄרה כקולה[355] **להבין משל ומליצה דברי חכמים וחידותם**[356] (משלי 1:6). ומעני[357] **ומשרא קטרין** (דניאל 5:12) הו אדׄא תעקד[358] אלאמר ולם יגד אלמשירין לה מן חל.[359] כאנהם יקולון יכרה אלבאב[360] אלפלאני מן גהה כדׄי ואלבאב אלפלאני מן גהה כדׄי. וחל דניאל ואחדה מנהא בלטיף פהמה כמא יצנע אלנאטׄרון באחכאם אלאקסאם[361] אדׄ יקולון לא יכלו מן כדׄי וכדׄי. וזאדת עליהא באב סאבעה[362] והו **נהירו**[363] (דניאל 5:14) ומענאה אלאיצׄאח אן יכון כלאמה מסמועא מפהומא

[340] עלי End of the readable part of Oxf 2486.54b

[341] [...] TS Ar 28.76d > D

[342] Beginning of the readable part of Oxf 2486.<u>55b</u>

[343] כק TS Ar 28.76d

[344] פי TS Ar 28.76d

[345] תקויה TS Ar 28.76d

[346] [ואל]תאמול TS Ar 28.76d > D

[347] כק TS Ar 28.76d

[348] משת[כל] [ח]יות [בקרניא] TS Ar 28.76d > D

[349] ומע TS Ar 28.76d > D

[350] חלמ[ין] TS Ar 28.76d > D

[351] פהו TS Ar 28.76d > D

[352] ויזדאד TS Ar 28.76d

[353] ירוי TS Ar 28.76d

[354] בתקריב TS Ar 28.76d

[355] כקו TS Ar 28.76d

[356] דברי ... וחידותם TS Ar 28.76d > L

[357] ומע TS Ar 28.76d

[358] [תע]קד Oxf 2486.55b > D

[359] אלחל TS Ar 28.76d

[360] אלבאב End of the readable part of Oxf 2486.55b

[361] אלאקסאם Beginning of Oxf 2486.55a | אקסאם TS Ar 28.76d

[362] באבא זׄ TS Ar 28.76d

[363] נהירו End of TS Ar 28.76d

ואצלא אלי קלב סאמעיה באחכאם אללפט ואלתאני ואלנטֹאם. פהדֹה אלדֹ מעאני אלתי אכֹתצרתהא לו חתי תגמע שרוחהא ותגעל כתאבא לכאן באדעא פי פנון אלחכמה.

ופסרת **נברשתא** (דניאל 5:5) "סראגא" לאני וגדת גמעה תרגום **נרות**. ודֹאך קולה **אחפש את ירושלם בנרות** (צפניה 1:12). פתרגומה **אפקיד בלושין ויבלשון ית יתיב ירושלם** כמא **דבלשין בנברשאתא**. ואמא אלכף אלדֹי טֹהרת פהי כף מלאך לא מחאלה. וסימא לקולה **וידי אדם מתחת כנפיהם** (יח" 1:8). פכאן אלמלאך מכֹפי [..]נה[364] אלא כפה כמא [... ...][365] חסן אלא[366] [...][367] **מן**[368] **שמיא נפל** (דניאל 4:28). ואמא קול דניאל לבלשצר **ולאלהי די נשמתך בידיה** (דניאל 5:23) פהו אבתדא תלויח בקתלה לאנה אדֹא כֹאלפה קבץֹ עלי רוחה. ואמא קולה לה **וכל ארחתך לה** (דניאל 5:23) פיעני בהא אמור אלדניא מן צחה ומרץֹ וולאד ועקם ואיסאר ופקר ועז ודֹל ונצר וכֹדֹלאן ואשבאה דֹלך. תֹם נקול ומא מעני הדֹה אלגֹ אלפאטֹ אלתי חכית בהא מציבה נבוכֹדנצר (?) בלשצר? פנקול לאן אלתחציל אלעאמי יכון בגֹ פנון באלוזן ובאלעדד [ו]באלכיל. פחכי רבנא גל גלאלה תהדידה למדד דול אלמלוך בתֹלתֹהא. וכמא קאל עלמאנא פי אכֹראג אלתרומה **המונה משובח והמודד משובח ממנו והשוקל משובח משניהם** (?) (תרומות 6:6). פעלי הדֹה אלאצול קאל **מנה תקל פרס** (ע' דניאל 5:25) [... ...][369] מנהא לשון[370]. [...][371] לם[372] ידכֹל אלמכיאל. ואיצֹא לאן דולה תאמה ליס תחצל לואחד בל למד ופרס. וגעל לנא פי דֹלך אעתבאר. אמא פי מתֹל **מנה** (דניאל 5:25) פנעלם אנה יחדד מדד אלדול. אלא תדכֹל ואחדה פי אלאכֹרי עלי מא אוגבת אלחכמה אן יחצי אעמאר אלנאס וכמא קאל **גלמי ראו עיניך ועל ספרך כלם יכתבו ימים יצרו ולא אחד בהם** (תה' 139:16). ומן מתֹל **תקל** (דניאל 5:25) אנה יזן באלחכם אעמאל אלנאס וזנא ויכאפיהם עלי זיאדתהא ונקצאנהא כמא קאל **פלס ומאזני משפט ליוי מעשיה כל אבני כיס** (משלי 16:11). וקאל אלולי אלאכֹר **ישקלני במאזני צדק וידע אלוה תמתי** (איוב 31:6). ומן מתֹל **פרס** (דניאל 5:25) אנה

364 [..]נה Oxf 2486.55a > D
365 [...] Oxf 2486.55a > D
366 אלא End of the readable part of Oxf 2486.55a
367 [...] Oxf 2486.55a > D
368 מן Beginning of of Oxf 2486.57a
369 ול[..] לן[..] Oxf 2486.57a > D
370 End of the readable part of Oxf 2486.57a
371 [...] Oxf 2486.57a > D
372 לם Beginning of Oxf 2486.57b

ידך אלמתעטֿמין דכא כמא קאל **וזרוע רמה תשבר** (איוב 38:15). וקאל איצֿא **מגביה פתחו מבקש שבר** (משלי 17:19). תֿם נשיע הדֿה [... ...][373] אלתי פיהא[374] [...][375] אין[376] צח לבלשצר וקומה אן דניאל קד אחסן אן יקרא אלכתאב וקד צדק פי תפסירה. פלעלה צנע בהם כמא יצנע אלמחתאלון, אן יצברו פלא יקוֹלו שיא חתי יסתופון אכֿר מא ענד אלחאצֿרין כלהם פאדֿא אסתגרקו מא ענדהם פעגזו אדעוהם אלוקוף עליה בחיתֿ לא יכון אחד אן יכדֿבהם בעד קולה אנה לא עלם לה בתה בה. פלעל דניאל פעל מתֿל האולי. קלנא אן אלמעני אלצֿרורי יבטל הדֿא אלוהם עלי דניאל. והו אן אלכתאב לם יזל טֿאהרא אלי אן קראה דניאל ופסרה. פלמא קראה ופסרה גֿאב ען חסהם. ואלעלה פי דֿלך אנה רסול מן ענד אלכֿאלק יבשר בלשצר במא יסוה כמא קאל **באדין מן קדמוהי שליח פסא די ידא** (דניאל 5:24). ומן הו רסול פלא בד אן ילבתֿ אלי אן יבלגֿ אלרסאלה[377] [...][378] פלא מעני למקא[... ...][379] [...][380] דניאל[381] לגאז יקים סנה וסנין. פלמא אוגב אלנטֿר אן ירתפע בעד קראה דניאל לה ותפסירה וגב עלי אלקום למא שאהדו גֿיבה אלכתאב בעד תמאם כלאם דניאל אן יעתקדו אנה קד אחסן קראתה וקד צדק ען תפסירה בלא שך. ואמא זיאדתה **מלכא כשׂדיא** (דניאל 5:30) פהי ליערפנא אן דולה אלכסדאניין כאנת אלי האהנא ואנקטעת כמא עאדתה אן יזיד כלאמא פי אלנהאיאת כמא אקול פי **עוד עצור מפני שאול בן קיש** (דהי״א 12:1) אנה אכֿרהא. ופי **ועוד לו אך המלוכה** (שמ״א 18:8) אנה אכֿרהא. ופי **ועדנו עצור בחצר המטרה** (ירמ׳ 33:1) אנה אכֿרהא ומא מאתֿל דֿלך. תם תפסיר אלגז אכֿאמס.

373 [… …] Oxf 2486.57b > D

374 פיהא End of the readable part of Oxf 2486.57b

375 […] Oxf 2486.58a > D

376 אין Beginning of Oxf 2486.58a

377 אלר[סאלה] Oxf 2486.58a > D

378 […] Oxf 2486.58a > D

379 למק[… …] Oxf 2486.58a > D | End of the readable part of Oxf 2486.58a

380 […] Oxf 2486.58b > D

381 Beginning of Oxf 2486.58b

ונץ אלגז אלסאדס[1]

Dn 6:1

ודריוש מדאה קביל מלכותא כבר שנין[2] שתין ותרתין.

תׄם צאר אלמלך אלי דרויש[3] אלמדי[4] והו שביה באבן אתׄנין וסתין[5] סנה.

Dn 6:2

שפר קדם דרויש והקים על מלכותא לאחשדרפניא מאה ועסרין די להון בכל מלכותא.

וראי מן ראיה אן ינצב[6] פי ממלכתה מאיה ועשרין[7] בטריקא יתצרפון[8] פי גמיעהא.

Dn 6:3

ועילא מנהון סרכין תלתא די דניאל חר מנהון די להון אחשדרפניא אליך יהבין להון טעמא ומלכא לא להוי נזיק.

ופוקהם[9] תׄלאתׄה[10] וזרא לדׄי דניאל ואחד מנהם[11] לכי יכון אולאיך[12] אלוזרא[13] יעטׄונהם[14] אלראי[15] ולא יתאדׄי[16] אלמלך.

1 אלסאדס End of the readable part of Oxf 2486.58b
2 שנין Beginning of Oxf 2486.59a
3 דארא TS Ar 21.49g + Oxf 2486.59a | דריוש Spiegel | דארא End of TS Ar 21.49g
4 אלמאדי Oxf 2486.59a | [אלמ]אדי Beginning of TS Ar 21.49h > D | אלמאדי Spiegel
5 [ב]אבן סב TS Ar 21.49h > D
6 [וראי] מן ראיה [אן ינצב] TS Ar 21.49h > D
7 קב TS Ar 21.49h
8 ית[צרפון] TS Ar 21.49h > D
9 ופוקהם TS Ar 21.49h > D
10 ג׳ TS Ar 21.49h + Oxf 2486.59a
11 [מנה]ם TS Ar 21.49h > D

Dn 6:4

אדין דניאל הוה[17] מתנצה[18] על סרכיא[19] ואחשדרפניא כל קביל די רוח יתירא ביה ומלכא עשית להקמותיה על[20] כל מלכותא.[21]

חיניד כאן דניאל[22] מתג̇לב[23] עלי אלוזרא[24] ואלבטארקה לעלה[25] אן פיה פצ̇ל ראי ואלמלך[26] עאזם אן ינצבה לג̇מיע אלממלכה.

Dn 6:5

אדין סרכיא ואחשדרפניא הוו בען עלה להשכחא לדניאל מצד מלכותא וכל עלה ושחיתה לא יכלין להשכחא כל קביל די מהימן הוא וכל שלו ושחיתה לא השתכחת עלוהי.

חיניד̇ כאנו[27] אלוזרא ואלבטארקה יטלבון[28] עלה יג̇דונהא עלי דניאל פי[29] ג̇הה אלממלכה לם[30] ימכנהם אן יג̇דו[31] אית[32] עלה או ג̇נאיה מן אג̇ל אנה אלאמין פלא[33] זלה ולא ג̇לטה[34] תוג̇ד עליה.

[12] אליך TS Ar 21.49h
[13] אלוזרא Morag > L
[14] יעטונה Oxf 2486.59a | יעטונהא Spiegel
[15] אלראי TS Ar 21.49h > D
[16] יתאדא TS Ar 21.49h
[17] דוה Oxf 2486.59a
[18] מתנצה Oxf 2486.59a > D
[19] מריכא End of the readable part of Oxf 2486.59a
[20] על Beginning of Oxf 2486.59b
[21] מלכותא Oxf 2486.59b > D
[22] דניאל TS Ar 21.49h > D
[23] מתג̇לבא Oxf 2486.59b
[24] על אלרוסא Spiegel
[25] לעל Spiegel
[26] [ראי וא]למלך TS Ar 21.49h > D
[27] באנו Morag
[28] איה + Spiegel
[29] מן Spiegel
[30] פלם TS Ar 21.49h + Oxf 2486.59b | ולם Spiegel
[31] עליה + Spiegel
[32] אוית Morag
[33] ולא Morag
[34] ג̇למה Spiegel

Dn 6:6

אדין גובריא אליך אמרין די לא נהשכח לדניאל דנא על כל[35] עלה להן אשכחנא[36] עלוהי בדת אלהיה.

חיניד קאל אולאיך[37] אלקום אד[38] לא נגד עלי[39] דניאל הדא[40] שיא[41] מן אלעלל לכנא[42] נגד[43] עליה פי סנה דינה.

Dn 6:7

אדין סרכיא ואחשדרפניא שלין הרגישו על מלכא וכן אמרין ליה דרויש מלכא לעמין חיי.

חיניד[44] צאר[45] אולאיך[46] אלוזרא ואלבטארקה אלי אלמלך וקאלו[47] לה[48] אטאל אללה[49] בקא דרויש אלמלך.[50]

Dn 6:8

אתיעטו כל סרכי מלכותא סגניא ואחשדרפניא הדבריא ופחותא לקיימא קים[51] מלכא ולתקפא איסר כל די יבעי בעו מן כל אלה ואנוש עד יומין תלתין להן מינך מלכא יתרמא לגב אריותא.

קד אשארו[52] גמיע אגלא אלממלכה ואלאמרא[53] ואלבטארקה ואלרויסא[54] ואלכלפא באן יעהד אלמלך עהדא[55] ויחטר חטרא[56] אן יכון[57] כל מן טלב[58]

[35] לדניאל... כל Oxf 2486.59b > D

[36] אשכחנו End of the readable part of Oxf 2486.59b

[37] אליך TS Ar 21.49h

[38] הודא Spiegel

[39] עלי Beginning of Oxf 2486.60a

[40] הדי Morag ו עלי הדא דניאל Oxf 2486.60a

[41] שי Morag

[42] ולכנא TS Ar 21.49h

[43] דלך + TS Ar 21.49h ו דאלך + Spiegel

[44] כאטב + Morag

[45] צארו TS Ar 21.49h + Spiegel

[46] צאר אולאיך Morag > L ו אליך TS Ar 21.49h

[47] פקאלו Oxf 2486.60a

[48] לה Morag > L

[49] אללה Morag > L ו יה + Oxf 2486.60a

[50] אלי ... אלמלך TS Ar 21.49h > L

[51] קדם Morag

[52] אשאר TS Ar 21.49h + Oxf 2486.60a

טלבה מן אי[59] מעבוד ואי אנסאן[60] סוי[61] אלמלך אלי תֿלאתֿין[62] יומא[63] ירמא[64] בה אלי גב אלאסד.[65]

Dn 6:9

כען[66] מלכא תקים אסרא ותרשם כתבה די להשניא כדת מרי ופרס די לא תעדא.

נריד אלאן יא איהא[67] אלמלך אן תקים הדֿא אלחטֿר[68] ותרסמה פי כתאב ואן לא יגֿייר כסנן מאהאת[69] ופארס[70] אלתי[71] לא תזול.

Dn 6:10

כל קבל דנא מלכא דריוש כתבא ואמרא.

פענד דֿלך[72] רסם דריוש אלמלך אלכתאב באלחטֿר.[73]

53 אלאמרא TS Ar 21.49h + Oxf 2486.60a

54 ואלרואסא Oxf 2486.60a | ואלרוסא Spiegel + TS Ar 21.49h

55 עהד Spiegel

56 ויחצר חצרא Spiegel + Morag | חט[ר]א TS Ar 21.49h > D

57 יכון Spiegel > L

58 יטלב Spiegel

59 טלבה מן אי Oxf 2486.60a > D

60 ואי אנסאן TS Ar 21.49h > D

61 סוא Spiegel

62 ל TS Ar 21.49h

63 יום Spiegel

64 ירמי TS Ar 21.49h

65 אנס[אן ... אלאסד] Oxf 2486.60a > D | אנס[אן] End of the readable part of Oxf 2486.60a

66 כען Beginning of Oxf 2486.60b

67 יאיהא TS Ar 21.49h + Oxf 2486.60b | יא אייה Spiegel

68 אלחצר Spiegel + Morag

69 מדי TS Ar 21.49h + Oxf 2486.60b

70 ופרס TS Ar 21.49h + Oxf 2486.60b

71 אלדי Spiegel + TS Ar 21.49h

72 דאלך Spiegel

73 דניאל TS Ar 21.49h > L 6:10 | באלחצר Spiegel + Morag

Dn 6:11

ודניאל כדי ידע די רשים כתבא על לביתה וכוין פתיחן לה בעליתה נגד ירושלם וזמנין תלתה ביומא הוא ברך על ברכוהי ומצלא ומורא קדם אלהה כל קבל די הוא עבד מן קדמת דנא.

פלמא[74] עלם דניאל אן[75] אלכתאב קד רסם צאר אלי מנזלה[76] ולה כוי[77] מפתוחה[78] פי ג̇רפה חד̇א[79] ירושלם[80] ות̇לאת̇[81] מראת[82] פי כל יום הו יג̇ת̇י עלי רכבתיה[83] ויצלי וישכר[84] רבה[85] עלי מא כאן[86] סבילה אן יצנע[87] קבל ד̇לך.[88]

Dn 6:12

אדין גבריה אלך הרגישו והשכחו לדניאל בעה ומתחנן קדם אלהה.

חיניד̇ תחסס[89] אולאיך[90] אלקום עלי דניאל[91] פוגדוה יתחנן ויטלב[92] מן[93] בין ידי רבה.

[74] פלמא TS Ar 21.49h > D

[75] באן Oxf 2486.60b

[76] [רסם ... מנ]זלה Oxf 2486.60b > D

[77] כוא Morag ׀ כוין Spiegel

[78] מ[פתו]חה TS Ar 21.49h > D

[79] בחדי TS Ar 21.49h

[80] [פי ... ירוש]לם Oxf 2486.60b > D

[81] ותלת Oxf 2486.60b ׀ וג̇ TS Ar 21.49h

[82] מראר Spiegel + Morag

[83] רכבתאה Spiegel + Morag ׀ [רכב]תיה TS Ar 21.49h > D

[84] [פי ... ויצ]לי וי[שכר] Oxf 2486.60b > D ׀ וישכר End of Oxf 2486.60b

[85] רבה Beginning of Oxf 2486.61b ׀ [וי]צלי ויש[כר רבע] TS Ar 21.49h > D

[86] עלי סביל מא כאן צאנעא Oxf 2486.61b

[87] אן יצנע TS Ar 21.49h > D ׀ מן + TS Ar 21.49h

[88] דל[ך] TS Ar 21.49h > D

[89] תחכר Spiegel

[90] אלאיך TS Ar 21.49h

[91] אל[קום] ע[לי דניאל] TS Ar 21.49h > D

[92] יטלב ויתחננן Oxf 2486.61b + TS Ar 21.49h ׀ [ו]יתחנן TS Ar 21.49h > D

[93] מן Spiegel and TS Ar 21.49h and Oxf 2486.61b > L

Dn 6:13

באדיו קרבו ואמרין קדם מלכא על אסר מלכא חלא אסר רשמתא די כל אנש די יבעא מן כל אלה ואנש עד יומין תלתין להן מנך מלכא יתרמא לגוב אריותא. ענה מלכא ואמר יציבא מלתא בדת מדי ופרס די לא תעדא.

חיניד̇ תקדמו פכלמו[94] אלמלך בסבב חט̇רה[95] אליס קד רסמת אלחט̇ר[96] אנה אי אנסאן טלב[97] מן אי מעבוד[98] ואי אנסאן סוא[99] אלמלך אלי ת̇לאת̇ין[100] יומא ירמא[101] בה אלי[102] גב אלאסד. אגאבהם אלמלך[103] פקאל אלאמר יקינא[104] כסנן מאהאת ופארס[105] אלתי[106] לא תזול.

Dn 6:14

באדין ענו ואמרין קדם מלכא די דניאל די מן בני גלותא די יהודלא שם עליך מלכא טעם ועל אקרא די רשמת וזמנין תלתה ביומא בעא בעותה.

חיניד̇[107] אגאבו בין ידי אלמלך וקאלו אן[108] דניאל אלד̇י מן אהל גלות אליהוד לם[109] יקבל ללמלך אמרא ולם[110] ילתפת אלי אלחט̇ר[111] אלד̇י רסמתה[112] ות̇לאת̇ מראר[113] פי כל יום יטלב[114] טלבתה.

[94] וכלמו Spiegel
[95] חצרה Spiegel + Morag | אלחטר Oxf 2486.61b
[96] אלחצר Spiegel + Morag
[97] אנס[אן ט]לב TS Ar 21.49h > D
[98] ומן + Oxf 2486.61b
[99] אנסאן סוא Oxf 2486.61b > D
[100] תלתין End of the readable part of Oxf 2486.61b
[101] ירמי TS Ar 21.49h > D
[102] [א]לי TS Ar 21.49h > D
[103] אלמלך TS Ar 21.49h > L
[104] יקינא End of TS Ar 21.49h
[105] פרס Beginning of Oxf 2486.61a
[106] אלדי Spiegel
[107] חיניד Oxf 2486.61a > L
[108] פאן Oxf 2486.61a
[109] ליס Oxf 2486.61a
[110] ולא Oxf 2486.61a
[111] אלחצר Spiegel + Morag
[112] רסמתאה Morag
[113] ותלת מראת Oxf 2486.61a
[114] לטלב Oxf 2486.61a

Dn 6:15

אדין מלכא כדי מלתא שמע שגיא באש עלוהי ועל דניאל שם בל לשיזבותה ועד מעלי שמשא הוא משתדר להצלותה.

חיניד̇ למא סמע אלמלך הד̇א אלאמר שק[115] עליה גדא ורד באלה פי תכ̇ליץ[116] דניאל ולם יזאל חריצא[117] עלי תכ̇ליצה[118] אלי מג̇יב[119] אלשמס.

Dn 6:16

באדין גבריא אלך הרגישו על מלכא יאמרין[120] למלכא דע מלכא די דת למדי ופרס די כל אסר וקים די מלכא יהקים לא להשניה.

חיניד̇ שג̇בו[121] אולאיך[122] אלוזרא ואלבטארקה[123] עלי אלמלך וקאלו לה יעלם אלמלך אן מן סנן מדי ופרס[124] אן יכון כל חט̇ר[125] ורסם אן[126] יקימה אלמלך לא יג̇יר.[127]

Dn 6:17

באדין מלכא אמר והיתיו לדניאל ורמו לגבא די אריותאענה מלכא ואמר לדניאל אלהך די אנתה פלח לה בתדירא הוא ישיזבנך.

חיניד̇ אמר אלמלך פאתי[128] בדניאל ורמי[129] בה פי[130] גב אלאסד[131] פאבתדא[132] וקאל לה אלהך[133] אלד̇י תעבדה דאימא הו יכ̇לצך.

[115] [ש]ק Oxf 2486.61a > D
[116] תכלץ Oxf 2486.61a
[117] ולם ... חריצא Oxf 2486.61a > D
[118] תכלצה Oxf 2486.61a
[119] מג̇יב End of the readable part of Oxf 2486.61a
[120] יאמרין Beginning of Oxf 2486.62a
[121] שג̇ב Oxf 2486.62a
[122] אלקום + Spiegel
[123] אלוזרא ואלבטארקה Spiegel > L
[124] מאהאת ופארס Morag
[125] חצר Spiegel + Morag
[126] אן Spiegel and Oxf 2486.62a > L
[127] יג̇ייר Spiegel + Morag
[128] פגי Spiegel + Oxf 2486.62a
[129] פרמי Oxf 2486.62a
[130] אלי Oxf 2486.62a
[131] אלאסוד Spiegel

Dn 6:18

והיתית אבן חדא ושמת על פם גבא וחתמה מלכא בעזקתה ובעזקאת רברבנוהי די לא תשנא צבו בדניאל.

תֹם אתי[134] בחגר עטים[135] פוצֹע עלי פם אלגב וכֹתמה אלמלך בכֹאתמה וכֹואתם[136] אלרויסא[137] לאלא[138] יתֹגיר[139] ראיה פי דניאל.

Dn 6:19

אדין אזל מלכא להיכלה ובת טות ורחון לא הנעל קדמוהי ושנתה נדת עלוהי.

חיניד̇ צאר אלי היכלה ובאת[140] טאויא ולם יחצֹר כֹואנא בין[141] ידיה פארק נומה.

Dn 6:20

באדין מלכא בשפרפרא יקום בנגהא ובהתבהלה לגבא די אריותא אזל.

חיניד̇ קאם אלמלך ענד מטלע אלפגר וצאר אלי גב אלאסד[142] מבאדרא.

Dn 6:21

וכמקרבה לגבא לדניאל בקל עציב זעיק ענה מלכא ואמר לדניאל דניאל עבד אלהא חיא אלהיך די אנתה פלח לה בתדירא היכל לשיזבותך מן אריותא.

פלמא קרב מנה צות לדניאל[143] צות חזין וקאל לה יא דניאל עבד אללה אלחי[144] אלהך אלד̇י תעבדה דאימא[145] הל אמכן כֹלאצה[146] לך מן אלאסד.[147]

[132] פאבתדי Oxf 2486.62a | פאבתדאה Spiegel
[133] אלאהר Morag | אלאהך Spiegel
[134] גי Spiegel + Oxf 2486.62a
[135] עצ̇ים Spiegel + Morag
[136] [וכתמה ... וכו]אתם D < Oxf 2486.62a
[137] אלרויסא End of the readable part of Oxf 2486.62a
[138] ללא Morag | כלא Beginning of Oxf 2486.62b | כלא Oxf 2486.62b
[139] יתג̇ייר Spiegel + Morag
[140] פבאת Spiegel + Oxf 2486.62b
[141] בן Morag
[142] אלגב Spiegel + Morag
[143] בדניאל Spiegel + Oxf 2486.62b

Dn 6:22
אדין דניאל אמ מלכא מלל מלכא לעלמין חיי.

חיניד̇ כ̇אטב דניאל אלמלך וקאל לה[148] אטאל אללה בקא אלמלך.

Dn 6:23
אלהי שלח מלאכה וסגר פם אריותא ולא חבלוני כל קבל די קדמוהי זכו השתכחת לי ואף קדמיך מלכא חבולה לא עבדת.

רבי[149] בעת̇ במלכה פסד פם אלאסד חתי לם תוד̇יני[150] וד̇לך[151] למא חצ̇רני בין ידיה מן אלחסנאת[152] ואיצ̇א בחצ̇רתך יא איה[153] אלמלך לם אעמל סיה.[154]

Dn 6:24
באדין מלכא שׂגיא טאב עלוהי ולדניאל אמר להנקמה מן גבא והסק דניאל מן גבא וכל חבל לא השתכח בה די הימן באלהה.

חיניד̇ למא סמע אלמלך הד̇א אלאמר סרה גדא ואמר באצעאד דניאל מן אלגב פאצעד ולם יוגד פיה שיא[155] מן אלפסאד למא אמן ברבה.[156]

Dn 6:25
ואמר מלכא והיתיו גבריא אלך די אכלו קרצוהי די דניאל ולגוב אריותא רמו אנון בניהון ונשיהון ולא מטו לארעית גבא עד די שליטו[157] בהון אריותא וכל גרמיהון.

[144] אלאלה אלחי Morag
[145] דא[ימא] End of the readable part of Oxf 2486.62b
[146] כלאצה Beginning of Oxf 2486.63a
[147] אסד Spiegel
[148] לה Spiegel and Oxf 2486.63a > L
[149] [רב]י Oxf 2486.63a > D
[150] תודני Oxf 2486.63a
[151] ודאלך Spiegel
[152] אלחסנא Morag
[153] יאיהא Oxf 2486.63a + יא אייה Spiegel
[154] סאיה Morag ׀ סייה Spiegel ׀ סיה End of the readable part of Oxf 2486.63a
[155] שי Spiegel
[156] ברן[בה] Beginning of Oxf 2486.63b
[157] Beginning of TS NS 105.23a

ואמר אלמלך פאתי[158] באולאיך[159] אלדׄין[160] מהלו[161] בדניאל ורמי[162] בהם פי גב אלאסד[163] ובניהם[164] ונסאנם פמא וצלו אלי קערה חתי תסלטת[165] עליהם[166] אלאסד[167] פדקת גמיע עטׄאמהם.[168]

Dn 6:26

באדין דריוש מלכא כתב לכל עמאיא אמיא ולשניא די דארין בכל ארעא שלמכון ישגא.

חיניד̇ כתב דריוש[169] אלמלך אלי גמיע אלשעוב ואלאמם ודׄוי אללגׄאת אלמקימין[170] פי גמיע[171] אלבלדאן סלאם[172] אללה עליכם וברכאתה.[173]

Dn 6:27

מן קדמי שׂים טעם די בכל שלטן מלכותי[174] להון זאעין ודאכלין מן קדם אלהה די דניאל די הוא אלהא חיא וקים לעאלמין ומלכותיה די לא תתחבל ושלטאניה עד סופה.[175]

קד[176] אמרת באמר פי גמיע סלטנה ממלכתי אן יכונו מתקיין פאזעין[177] מן אלאה דניאל אדׄ הו[178] אלאלאה[179] אלחי אלקיום אלי אלאבד[180] ומלכה[181] לא יזול וסלטאנה[182] אלי אכׄר אלעאלם.

[158] פגי Oxf 2486.63b | פגאו Spiegel + TS NS 105.23a

[159] באוליך Oxf 2486.63b

[160] אללדין Oxf 2486.63b | אלדי Spiegel + TS NS 105.23a

[161] גׄמזו TS NS 105.23a

[162] רמו Spiegel

[163] אלאסוד TS NS 105.23a | הם + Spiegel

[164] ובבניהם TS NS 105.23a

[165] תסלטו Oxf 2486.63b

[166] עליהם Morag > L

[167] אלאסודה Oxf 2486.63b

[168] עצאמהם Morag | עצמהם Spiegel

[169] דריוש Oxf 2486.63b > D

[170] ואלאמם ... אלמקימין Oxf 2486.63b > D

[171] שעוב + Spiegel

[172] סלם Oxf 2486.63b

[173] סלאם עליכם וברכאת אללה Spiegel | וברכאת[ה] TS NS 105.23a > D

[174] מלכותי End of the readable part of Oxf 2486.63b

[175] ושלטאניה Beginning of the readable part of Oxf 2486.64a

[176] קד Oxf 2486.64a > D

[177] פזעין Oxf 2486.64a

Dn 6:28

משיזב ומציל ועבד אתין ותמהין בשמיא ובארעא די שיזב לדניאל מן יד אריותא.

והו[183] אלמנגי ואלמכ̇לץ̇ וצאנע[184] איאת ואעגובאת פי אלסמא ואלארץ̇ אד̇ כ̇לץ̇ דניאל[185] מן יד[186] אלאסד.[187]

Dn 6:29

ודניאל דנה הצלח במלכות דריוש ובמלכות כורש פרסיא.

ת̇ם אצלח חאל[188] דניאל פי מלך דריוש וכורש אלפארסי.[189]

אול מא ינבג̇י אן נכשף ענה פי הד̇ה אלפואסיק מא אלפאידה פי תאריכ̇ה כם מ[..][190] מן אלסנין אלי אן מלך[191] [...][192] למא[193] רדדנא אלסנין אלי וראהא [...][194] הד̇א אלתאריך̇ וגדנא סנה ולד דריוש הי סנה דכ̇ול נבוכ̇דנצר אלי אלקדס פי זמאן יהויכין. וקאל פיה **ויצא משם את** {**כל**} **אצרות בית ייי ואת אצרות בית המלך ויקצץ את כלי הזהב אשר עשה שלמה** (מל״ב 24:13).

וכד̇לך̇ אלקול פי **יהוידע הכהן**. לם ישרח מן בין סאיר אלכהנים אלא עמרה אד̇ קאל **ויזקן יהוידע וישבע ימים וימת בן מאה ושלשים שנה במתו**

178 הוא Morag

179 אללה Oxf 2486.64a

180 אלאבד End of TS NS 105.23a

181 ומלכה TS NS 105.23b

182 וסולטאנה TS NS 105.23b

183 הו TS NS 105.23b

184 צאנע TS NS 105.23b

185 לדניאל TS NS 105.23b

186 יד TS NS 105.23b > L

187 אלאסוד TS NS 105.23b

188 חאל Spiegel > L

189 ודניאל הד̇א צלח חאלה פי מלך דריוש אלמלך ומלך כורש אלפארסי TS NS 105.23b

190 מן[..] Oxf 2486.64a > D

191 מלך End of the readable part of Oxf 2486.64a

192 [...] Oxf 2486.64a > D

193 למא Beginning of Oxf 2486.64b

194 [...] Oxf 2486.64b > D

(דה״ב 24:15). פנקול אנא רדדנא אלסנין מן הדֿא אלתאריךֿ אלי ורא פבלגֿת אלי סתה סנין קבל חדותֿ אלתכֿליט בעד ופאה שלמה. פיכון ולאד אלמצלח קבל חדותֿ מא יחתאג אלי אלצלאח [...][195] סנין. וכדֿלך תאריךֿ [... ...][196] וערים עשרין [...][197] מקאלה[198] פי מוצֿע אכֿר[199] [...][200] דבר[201] ישראל יגֿ סנה ודֿלך אלי וקת באיעו בית יהודה לדויד והי סבע סנין מן אכֿר אלעשרין. ואלתֿאניה אן אלסנתין אלמורכֿתין למלך שאול סנתין עלי אלחקיקה והי מע שמואל. פיכון אלתדביר כֿלץ לשמואל יאֿ סנה. ואיצֿא אן יכון בית ישראל אקאמו כֿמס סנין בלא מלך איש בשת אנמא מלך עליהם סנתין מן הדֿה אלסבעה.

וקולה **די להון אחשדרפניא אלין** (דניאל 6:3) הו מקאם קולה **די להון סרכיא אלך** .ולדֿלך פסרתה אלוזרא. ואנמא לקב האולי בהאולי למגאנבה אלריאסה. כמא לקב **מלכיה, נביאיה** מן גהה אלתרייס אדֿ קאל **קשר נביאיה בתוכה כארי שאג טרף טרף נפש אכלו חסן ויקר יקחו אלמנותיה הרבו בתוכה** (יחז׳ 22:25) ואנמא מענאה **קשר מלכיה בתוכה**. וכמא לקב **חֵרֵש** עור אדֿ קאל **מי עִוֵּר כִּמְשֻׁלָּם ועור כעבד יוי** (יש״ 42:19) אדֿ תגאנסא מן אגל אלעאהה. ואנמא [מתֿל] דֿלך כתֿיר[202] לא[203] אטיל אלמתֿאלאת.

וקולה **ומלכא עשׂת**[204] **להקמותה** (דניאל 6:4) ידל עלי אן שעורהם כמאלה פי נפס אלמלך מן אלתרתיב ממא זאדהם חסדא לה עלי מא בהם. ושביה במא כאנת מחבה יעקב ליוסף **ועשׂה לו כתנת פסים** (בר׳ 37:3). וכדֿלך איצֿא **חלומותיו** (בר׳ 37:8) [מ]מא זאדת אכֿותה חסדא לה עלי מא בהם. וסבב אלחסד אלמתקדם מן אלגמיע פצֿל אלמערפה.

ופי הדֿה אלקצה **הרגישו** גֿ ופסרתהא תֿלתֿ תפאסיר עלי מא יחסן בכל ואחד. פאלאול אלדֿי מע משורה, פסרתה ״מכֿאטבה״ (דניאל 6:7). ואלתֿאני אלדֿי

195 Oxf 2486.64b > D [...]
196 Oxf 2486.64b > D [... ...]
197 Oxf 2486.64b > D [...]
198 מקא[ל]ה Oxf 2486.64b > D
199 אכֿר End of the readable part of Oxf 2486.64b
200 Oxf 2486.64b > D [...]
201 דבר Beginning of Oxf 2486.56a
202 כתֿיר End of the readable part of Oxf 2486.56a
203 לא Beginning of Oxf 2486.56b
204 עשית :MT

יקארן אלוקוף עלי צלוה דניאל, פסרתה "תחססה" (דניאל 6:12). ואלת̇אלת̇ אלד̇י יקארנה מטאלבה אלמלך בעקובה דניאל, פסרתה "שגבה" (דניאל 6:16). ונחתאג אן נקרב כיף סאג̇ להם אן ישירו עלי אלמלך במנע אלנאס מן [...][205] ואלמס[א]לה ת̇לת̇ין יום [... ...][206] קול כאנהם אוקעו[207] תהמה[208] או תהמא עלי קום באנהם לא ינצחון אלסלטאן. ת̇ם געלו אסתכשאף ד̇לך אלנדא בהד̇א אלאמר. פימכן אן יכון קבל להד̇א אלתקריב.

ואסתפדנא מן הד̇ה אלקצה פואידא כת̇ירה ללצלוה. פאולהא אן אלצלואת אלדאימה ת̇לת̇ה לקולה **וזמנין תלתה ביומא** (דניאל 6:11.14). ואיצ̇א אן וגוב הד̇ה אלצלואת פי ארץ̇ ישראל ופי אלגלות באלסוא לקולה **כל קבל די הוה עבד מן קדמת דנה** (דניאל 6:11). ואיצ̇א אנהא צלואת מתפרקה פי ג̇ ארכאן מן אלליל ואלנהאר לקולה **ביומא** (דניאל 6:11.14). פנצפא אלנהאר מערופאן פיהמא צלותאן. ואד̇ לא יערף נצף אלליל פאלצלוה אלת̇אלת̇ה נצפה אלאול. ואיצ̇א אן ד̇את אלצלוה הי מסאיל וטלבאת כ̇אצה לאנה תרגמהא פקאל **בעת בעותה** (דניאל 6:14) והו קולה **חננו השיבנו סלח לנו רפאנו** ומא אנצ̇ם

אליהא. ואיצ̇א אן אלמצלי יגב [...][209] מאכ̇ר אלתחנן[210] [...][211] **בעה**[212] **ומתחנן קדם אלהה** (דניאל 6:12). ואיצ̇א אן אמצלי יגב אן ינחני מראת פי צלותה כמא קאל **הוא ברך על ברכוהי** (דניאל 6:11) עלי אנה ג̇ת̇וא. פאן אלעבראניין יסתעמלונה פי אלאנחני כמא קאל **כי עשה שלמה כיור נחשת ויתנהו בתוך העזרה חמש אמות ארכו וחמש אמות רחבו ואמות שלוש קומתו ויעמד עליו ויברך על ברכיו** (דה"ב 6:13). פלא יגתמע **ויעמד** מע **ויברך** אלא עלי סביל אלאנחנא. ובעד אסתתמאם באב אלטלבאת יגב שכר אללה כמא קאל **ומצלא ומודא קדם אלהה** (דניאל 6:11). והו כמא יקאל בעד אלטלבאת **מודים אנחנו לך** (דה"א 29:13), ויכתם **הטוב לך להודות**. ואיצ̇א יגב אן תכון אלצלוה פי **חוצה לארץ** באסתקבאל ארץ̇ ישראל כמא קאל **שלמה, והתפללו דרך ארצם** (דה"ב 6:38). ופי ארץ̇ ישראל באסתקבאל

[205] אל[..] Oxf 2486.56b > D

[206] [... ...] Oxf 2486.56b > D

[207] אוקעו End of Oxf 2486.56b

[208] תהמה Beginning of Oxf 2486.65a

[209] [...] Oxf 2486.65a > D

[210] אלתחנ[ן] Oxf 2486.65a > D ׀ אלתחנן End of the readable part of Beginning of Oxf 2486.65a

[211] [...] Oxf 2486.65a > D

[212] בעה Beginning of Oxf 2486.65b

ירושלם כמא קאל **והעיר אשר בחרת** (דהי״ב 6:38). ופי ירושלם באסתקבאל אלקדס כמא קאל **והבית**[213] **אשר**[214] **בניתי לשמך** (דהי״ב 6:38). ופי אלבית נפסה באסתקבאל אלמגׄרב כמא קאל **אשר יתפללו אל המקום הזה** (דהי״ב 6:21). אללהם אלא אן יכון אלכׄט אלמכׄרג אלי ארץׄ ישראל ואלי ירושלם ואחדא מסתקימא כמא קאל פי דניאל **וכוין פתיחן לה בעליתה נגד ירושלם** (דניאל 6:11). תׄם נקול ואדׄא כאנת אלצלוה גאיזה פי בית לא כוי פיה לם קאל **וכוין פתיחן לה** (דניאל 6:11)? פנקול ליטבק עליה **הרגישו והשכחו לדניאל בעא ומתחנן** (דניאל 6:12). כאן אלכוי כאנת אלסבב או אחד אלאסבאב.

וקולה **ועל דניאל שׂם בל לשיזבותה** (דניאל 6:15). ידל עלי אנה כאן יחמל[215] כלאמהם אמכאנאת ליכׄלץ בהא דניאל אלי אן פנו[216] אלגאיז מן קולה. ומע דׄלך פאכׄד אן ידאפעהם אלי אן שגׄבו[217] עליה[218] פלם יטקהם.[219] ומא מעני **והיתית אבן חדא ושמת על פם גבא וחתמה מלכא בעזקתה ובעזקאת רברבנוהי** (דניאל 6:18) אנמא[220] כאן סביל מן יטרח[221] פי דׄלך[222] אלגב אן תמוקה[223] אלאסד[224] מן סאעתה, פאי נפע[225] פי כתׄם אלגב? פנקול לילא יתגׄיר[226] ראי אלמלך פיכׄרג דניאל מנה. והל הדׄא אלא כאלעבתׄ?[227] פנקול הדׄא ידל עלי[228] אן אלגב נפסה כאלדהליז למוצׄע[229] אלאסד. ואלאסד אנפסהא פהי[230] פי מטׄמורה

[213] והבית End of Oxf 2486.65b

[214] אשר Beginning of Oxf 2486.66a

[215] יחמל Uncertain lesson

[216] פנו \ פני Uncertain lesson

[217] שגׄבו Beginning of TS Ar 1b 90c

[218] על[יה] TS Ar 1b 90c > D

[219] יטק[הם] TS Ar 1b 90c > D

[220] מעני ... אנמא TS Ar 1b 90c > D

[221] מ[ן יטרח] TS Ar 1b 90c > D

[222] דאלך TS Ar 1b 90c | דלך End of the readable part of Oxf 2486.66a

[223] תמ[וזקה] Oxf 2486.66a > D

[224] אלאסד Beginning of Oxf 2486.66b

[225] תמ[... נפ]ע TS Ar 1b 90c > D

[226] לילא יתגׄיר TS Ar 1b 90c > D

[227] דני[אל מנה והל הדא] אלא כאל[ע]בתׄ TS Ar 1b 90c > D

[228] על[י] TS Ar 1b 90c > D

[229] נפסה ... למוצׄע TS Ar 1b 90c > D

[230] פהי TS Ar 1b 90c > L

ידכׄל[231] אליהא מן דׄלך אלגב.[232] פלמא אלקי דניאל פי אלגב בחצׄרתהם וראי אן אלאסד לם תתׄר[233] פתכׄרג עליה נסבו דׄלך אלי שבע מנהא. וראו אן יתרכוה מכאנה[234] אלי אן תגוע[235] אלאסד. לכנהם[236] יכׄתמון ראס אלגב לילא יבדו ללמלך פירקיה[237] מנה.[238] פלמא אלתמסו דׄלך אגאבהם אלי אן יכׄתמוה[239] בכׄאותימהם לכי יברו[240] אלמלך מן אכׄראגה. ואצׄאף אלי דׄלך[241] אן יכׄתמה הו בכׄאתמה לאלא[242] תקע בדניאל חילה מנהם.[243] ולדׄלך קאל **די לא תשנא צבו**[244] **בדניאל**[245] (דניאל 6:18). ואמא קולה **ובת טות** (דניאל 6:19) פמענאה אנה[246] טוא אלליל מע אלנהאר בלא גדׄא.[247] ואמא **ודחון** (דניאל 6:19) פקד יפסר כׄואנאת[248] ליוכל[249] בין ידיה. וקד יוגד מתׄל הדׄה אללפטׄה[250] פי **תוספת כלים** יקול פיהא **כליי**[251] **הדחונות שאוכלין עליהון** (תוספת כלים B, m V.3). וקד יפסר "מסאמרין ומחאדתׄין"[252] מן גהה **יחוון**[253] **ויהתוון**[254] באלגמלה. יראד בהא[255] מא יזיל[256] אלנום ענה.[257]

[231] וידכל TS Ar 1b 90c
[232] [אליהא ... אלג]ב TS Ar 1b 90c > D
[233] וראי ... תתׄר TS Ar 1b 90c > D
[234] וראו ... מכאנה TS Ar 1b 90c > D
[235] תגוע TS Ar 1b 90c > D
[236] ליכן TS Ar 1b 90c
[237] [יכתמון ... פירקי]ה TS Ar 1b 90c > D
[238] מנהא TS Ar 1b 90c
[239] דלך ... יכתמוה TS Ar 1b 90c > D
[240] יבין TS Ar 1b 90c
[241] [אכראגה ... ד]לך TS Ar 1b 90c > D
[242] לילא Oxf 2486.66b
[243] תק[ע ... מנהם] TS Ar 1b 90c > D
[244] ציבו TS Ar 1b 90c
[245] Beginning of TS Ar 22.104a
[246] אנה TS Ar 22.104a > D
[247] ואמא [קולה גדא] ואמא TS Ar 1b 90c > homeuteleuton
[248] כואנאת End of Oxf 2486.66b
[249] ליוכל Beginning of Oxf 2486.67a
[250] [מתל] הדה [אללפטה] TS Ar 1b 90c > D
[251] כילים [יקול פיהא כלי] TS Ar 1b 90c > D
[252] ומח[אדתי]ן TS Ar 1b 90c > D
[253] יחון TS Ar 1b 90c
[254] ויהתוון Uncertain lesson
[255] בה TS Ar 22.104a > D
[256] [יריד בהא] מ[א יז]יל TS Ar 1b 90c > D
[257] מנה TS Ar 1b 90c

וקול דניאל **אלהי שלח מלאכה**[258] **וסגר פם**[259] **אריותא ולא חבלוני**[260] (דניאל 6:23) עלי אלאצל אלאול אנה לא יזיל טבע אלשי. ואנמא יחגב[261] ען פעלה כמא דֹכרנא פי קצה **אתון נורא יקדתא**[262] (דניאל 3:26). וקולה **ואף קדמך**[263] **מלכא חבולא לא עבדת**[264] (דניאל 6:23) תוביכֿא[265] לה אד̇ לם יסתחק מנה עקובה. ופי קולה **ואמר מלכא והיתיו לגבריא**[266] **אלך וג̇** (דניאל 6:25) מא אקרבה אן יכון[267] עדד אלאסד[268] שׂתֹו אד̇ אלקום קֹכ̇ב̇ ולמוצׂע אצׂאפתה **בניהון ונשיהון** (דניאל 6:25) יציר[269] מתֹאלהם באלתקריב[270] זאיד מע נאקץ.[271] וקד גמע[272] אלמלוך מתֹל הד̇א ואכתֹר.[273]

ואמא קול דריוש[274] **ועבד אתין**[275] **ותמהין**[276] **בשמיא**[277] **ובארעא** (דניאל 6:28) יעני[278] נזול[279] אלמלך מן אלסמא ותכ̇ליצה[280] דניאל פי אלארץ̇,[281]

258 מלאכיה TS Ar 1b 90c
259 פם TS Ar 1b 90c > D
260 ולא חבלוני TS Ar 1b 90c > L
261 וחגב TS Ar 1b 90c > D ׀ ואנמא ... יחגב TS Ar 22.104a > D
262 יקדתא TS Ar 1b 90c > L
263 [ו]אף קד[מך] TS Ar 1b 90c > D
264 חבולא ... עבדת TS Ar 1b 90c > L
265 עבד[ת ... תו]ביכא TS Ar 22.104a > D
266 גבריא TS Ar 1b 90c
267 [יכ]ון TS Ar 22.104a > D
268 אלאס[ד] TS Ar 1b 90c > D
269 בניה[ם [ונסאי]הם [יציר] TS Ar 1b 90c > D
270 [בא]לתקריב TS Ar 22.104a > D
271 זאיד מע נאקץ TS Ar 22.104a > D
272 ג[מע] TS Ar 1b 90c > D
273 ואכתֹאר TS Ar 1b 90c
274 דרי[וש] TS Ar 1b 90c > D
275 [את]ין TS Ar 1b 90c > D
276 ותמהין End of TS Ar 22.104a
277 בשמיא Beginning of TS Ar 22.104b
278 יע[ני] TS Ar 22.104b > D
279 טול TS Ar 1b 90c
280 ותכלצה TS Ar 22.104b
281 אל[אר]ץ TS Ar 22.104b > D

כמא[282] קאל[283] **אלהי שלח מלאכה**[284] **וג'**[285] (דניאל 6:23). וכדׄלך[286] קול נבוכׄדנצר[287] **וכמצבי**[288] **עביד בחיל שמיא ודיירי ארעא**[289] (דניאל 4:32) לחאל **עיר וקדיש מן שמיא נחת**[290] (דניאל 4:10), **קרא**[291] **בחיל וכן אמר וג'** (דניאל 4:11). וכׄתם אלקצה[292] בקולה[293] **ודניאל דנה**[294] **הצלח וג'**[295] (דניאל 6:29). ידל עלי אן כורש[296] דריוש סבב[297] לה אמורא תבינת[298] טאעתה[299] לה פיהא לילא ירונה אהל[300] אלממלכה בעין[301] אנה כׄאלף עלי[302] אלמלך פיזרו בה ובאלמלך איצׄא יזרון אדׄא[303] ראוה יכׄדמה מעמא[304] קד וקפו עלי מכׄאלפתה לה וכאלתדביר[305] אלדׄי דברנאה[306] לחנניה ומישאל ועזריה[307] אניפא.

282 כמא End of the readable part of Oxf 2486.67a

283 כק TS Ar 1b 90c | כמא [קאל] TS Ar 22.104b > D

284 מלאכה Beginning of Oxf 2486.67b

285 מלאכיה [וג'] TS Ar 22.104b + TS Ar 1b 90c

286 וכ דׄא[לך] TS Ar 1b 90c > D

287 נבכׄדנצר TS Ar 1b 90c | נבוכ TS Ar 22.104b

288 וכמצביה TS Ar 22.104b + TS Ar 1b 90c

289 ודיירי ארעה TS Ar 1b 90c > L | ודיירי ארעה TS Ar 22.104b > D

290 נתית TS Ar 1b 90c

291 נתת קרא TS Ar 22.104b > D

292 וג' ... אלקצה TS Ar 1b 90c > D

293 בקול[ה] TS Ar 22.104b > D

294 דנא TS Ar 1b 90c | דנה TS Ar 22.104b > D

295 וג' TS Ar 22.104b > D and TS Ar 1b 90c > D

296 כורש TS Ar 22.104b > L

297 [כורש] דר[יוש ס]בב TS Ar 1b 90c > D

298 ת[בינת] TS Ar 1b 90c > D

299 ת[בינת טאעת]ה TS Ar 22.104b > D

300 לילא ... אהל TS Ar 1b 90c > D

301 בע[ין] TS Ar 1b 90c > D | בעין End of the readable part of TS Ar 1b 90c

302 עלי TS Ar 22.104b > D

303 אדׄא Beginning of the readable part of TS Ar 1b 90d

304 יכׄ[דמה מע]מא TS Ar 1b 90d > D | [יכׄדמה מע]מא TS Ar 22.104b > D

305 על[י ... וכאלתדביר] TS Ar 22.104b > D

306 [וקפו ... וכ]אלתדבי אל]דׄי [דברנ]אה TS Ar 1b 90d > D

307 ומישאל ועזריה TS Ar 1b 90d > D

ואד׳ קד אכ׳תצרנא שרוח[308] הד׳ה אלסתה אגזא[309] פנחן מעדין אן[310] נתתבע[311] מא פי שרוח אלארבעה[312] אגזא[313] אלבאקיה באכת׳ר[314] מן הד׳ה אלשרוח לשדה אלחאגה[315] אלי תערף שרוח אלקצים ומסתעמל אללג׳ה ומן אלרחמן אלמעונה.[316] תם[317] אלגז אלסאדס.[318]

[308] שרוח D < TS Ar 1b 90d | שרח TS Ar 22.104b
[309] אלאגזא TS Ar 22.104b + Oxf 2486.67b
[310] פנחן מעדין אן D < TS Ar 1b 90d
[311] נתבע TS Ar 1b 90d
[312] אלד TS Ar 22.104b
[313] אלאגזא TS Ar 22.104b + Oxf 2486.67b | אגזא L < TS Ar 1b 90d
[314] באכ[תר] D < TS Ar 1b 90d | בא[כתר] D < TS Ar 22.104b
[315] [אלי]הא פצלא D < TS Ar 1b 90d | אליהא פצלא TS Ar 22.104b
[316] אלי תערף ... אלמעונה L < TS Ar 22.104b + TS Ar 1b 90d | אלמעונה End of Oxf 2486.67b
[317] תם Beginning of Oxf 2486.68a
[318] אלו TS Ar 1b 90d | תם ... אלסאדס L < TS Ar 22.104b

ונץ[1] אלגז אלסאבע מן כתאב דניאל ידֿכר פיה מקדמאת[2] אלארבע[3] ממאלך אלמתוסטה[4] **בין גלוה בני**[5] **ישראל**[6] **ואבותהם**.[7] קאל אול דֿלך[8]

Dn 7:1

בשנת חדה לבלאשצר מלך[9] **בבל דניאל חלם חזה וחזוי ראשה על משכבה באדין חלמא כתב ראש מלין אמר.**

פי אלסנה אלאולי[10] מן מלך בלשצר[11] מלך באבל[12] ראי דניאל חלמא כמא[13] תרא[14] עינאה[15] והו פי מצֿגעה[16] חיניד כתב דֿלך[17] אלחלם וקאל פי אול[18] אלכלאם.[19]

נקול פימא יחתאג אליה[20] מן שרח דֿלך אן הדֿה אלארבעה[21] אגזא אלאכֿירה מורכֿה לתֿלתֿ מלוך, אתֿנין[22] מנהא לבלשאצר. ואחד פי אלסנה אלאולי מן

[1] ונץ ... אלסאבע TS Ar 1b.90d > D ׀ ונץ TS Ar 22.104b > L
[2] פיה מקדמאת TS Ar 22.104b > D
[3] אלד TS Ar 22.104b + TS Ar 1b.90d
[4] [אלממאלך] אלמתוסט[ה] TS Ar 22.104b > D
[5] ממאל[ך ... בני] TS Ar 1b.90d > D
[6] אסראיל Oxf 2486.68a ׀ אסראיל וא[בותי]הם TS Ar 22.104b
[7] ואובתהם TS Ar 1b.90d
[8] קאל ... דלך TS Ar 1b.90d > D
[9] מלך End of TS Ar 22.104b
[10] אלאולא Spiegel
[11] פי ... מלך TS Ar 1b.90d > D ׀ בלשצאר TS NS 105.23b + Oxf 2486.68a
[12] בבל TS Ar 1b.90d
[13] כמ[א] TS NS 105.23b > D
[14] תרי Oxf 2486.68a
[15] עינה Spiegel + Oxf 2486.68a ׀ עינ[ה] TS NS 105.23b > D
[16] מוצעה TS NS 105.23b
[17] חלמא ... דלך TS Ar 1b.90d > D ׀ דאלך Spiegel + TS Ar 1b.90d
[18] אוול Spiegel + Morag
[19] וקאל ... אלכלאם TS NS 105.23b > L
[20] אול ... אליה TS Ar 1b.90d > D

מלכה[23] [ואלת'אני פי אלסנה] אלג'[24] מן מלכה. ומנהא את'נין[25] לדריוש וכורש. ואחדה[26] פי אלסנה אלאולי מן[27] מלך הד'א[28] ואלאכ'ר[29] פי אלסנה אלג' מן מלך הד'א. ואלסבב פי ד'לך הו אן[30] בלשאצר[31] כאן[32] אכ'ר מלוך באבל ודריוש כאן אול מלוך מדי וכורש[33] כאן אול מלוך אלפרס.[34] פערף דניאל[35] הד'ה אלעלום אלג'יביה[36] פי אבתדי[37] מלך כל ואחד מן האולי[38] ופי אכ'רה. ולד'לך[39] קאל **בשנת חדה**[40] **לבלאשצר מלך בבל** (דניאל 7:1), **בשנת**[41] **שלוש למלכות בלשצר המלך**[42] (דניאל 8:1), **בשנת אחת לדריוש** (דניאל 9:1), **בשנת**[43] **שלוש**[44] **לכורש מלך פרס** (דניאל 10:1).

וקולה[45] **דניאל חלם חזה** (דניאל 7:1) עלי מא קדמנא[46] אן האהנא חלמא והו נבוה[47] ובאלעלאמאת אלתי רסמנאהא פי צדר[48] הד'א אלכתאב באלקול[49]

[21] אלד TS Ar 1b.90d

[22] אלאכר[ה] ... את'נין TS Ar 1b.90d > D

[23] מלכה End of the readable part of Oxf 2486.68a

[24] אלג' Beginning of Oxf 2486.68b

[25] ב TS Ar 1b.90d

[26] א TS Ar 1b.90d

[27] פי ... מן TS Ar 1b.90d > D

[28] הד'א TS Ar 1b.90d > D

[29] ואלאכר TS Ar 1b.90d

[30] ואלסבב ... אן TS Ar 1b.90d > D

[31] בלשצר TS Ar 1b.90d

[32] [כא]ן TS Ar 1b.90d > D

[33] וכורש TS Ar 1b.90d > D

[34] א[ול] מלך [אלפ]רס TS Ar 1b.90d > D

[35] דניאל TS Ar 1b.90d > D

[36] אלג'איבה TS Ar 1b.90d

[37] אול TS Ar 1b.90d

[38] [מן הא]ולי TS Ar 1b.90d > D

[39] פלד'לך TS Ar 1b.90d

[40] ק[אל חדה] TS Ar 1b.90d > D

[41] [בש]נת TS Ar 1b.90d > D

[42] בלשצר המלך TS Ar 1b.90d > D

[43] ב[שנ]ת TS Ar 1b.90d > D

[44] שלש TS Ar 1b.90d

[45] פרס וקולה TS Ar 1b.90d > D

[46] קד[מנא] TS Ar 1b.90d > D

[47] חל[מא והו נבוה] TS Ar 1b.90d > D

[48] פ[י צ]דר TS Ar 1b.90d > D

אלמגמל. וסנבינהא איצ̇א פי וסט אלמקאלה בקול מפצל. וקולה[50] **וחזוי ראשה על משכבה** (דניאל 7:1) פסרנאה[51] רויה עיניה למא כאנת[52] לג̇ת אלערב[53] לא תטלק אלרויא עלי[54] אלראס[55] כמא תטלק לג̇ה[56] אלכסדאניין ואנמא[57] תנסבה אלי אלעין. והד̇א[58] מן אכ̇ראגנא[59] מת̇למא נכ̇רג **ושׂמחת**[60] **עולם על ראשם** (יש' 35:10) "ופרח אלדהר פי קלובהם"[61] למא כאנת[62] לג̇ה אלערב לא תטלק אלפרח עלי אלראס[63] כמא[64] תטלקה לג̇ה אלעבראניין. ולם אחתיג בעד קולה **חלם**[65] **חזה** (דניאל 7:1) אלי אן[66] יקאל **וחזוי ראשה על משכבה** (דניאל 7:1)? ליערפנא אן אלחלם עלי[67] צ̇רבין. מנהא מא סבבה כ̇ארג ען נפס[68] אלאנסאן והי[69] אלג̇ צ̇רוב[70] אלד̇י[71] ד̇כרנאהא,[72] אעני מא הו קבל אלכימוס[73] ואלגד̇א ואלכד.[74] ומנהא מא סבבה דאכ̇ל פי נפס אלאנסאן והו מא תקתבסה מן נור אלחכמה אלד̇י[75] פוקהא. ואעטינא אלפרק[76] אלפארק בינהמא והו אן אלד̇י מן

[49] באל[קול] TS Ar 1b.90d > D

[50] אלמק[אלה] ב[קו]ל [מפצ]ל וקול[ה] TS Ar 1b.90d > D

[51] [משכבה] פסר[נ]אה TS Ar 1b.90d > D

[52] [עיניה למא] כא[נת] TS Ar 1b.90d > D

[53] לג̇ה אלערב Oxf 2486.68b > D

[54] עלי End of Oxf 2486.68b

[55] אלראס Beginning of Oxf 2486.69a

[56] כמ[א תט]לק [לג̇ה] TS Ar 1b.90d > D ׀ לג̇ה Beginning of TS Ar 26.6c

[57] לג̇ה ... ואנמא TS Ar 26.6c > D

[58] ו[הדא] TS Ar 26.6c > D

[59] מן אכ̇ראגנא TS Ar 1b.90d > D ׀ [אכ̇]ראגנא TS Ar 26.6c > D

[60] [וש]מ[חה] TS Ar 26.6c > D

[61] [אלדהור פי קל]לובהם TS Ar 1b.90d > D

[62] כאנת TS Ar 26.6c > D

[63] [אלפרח] עלי אל[ראס] TS Ar 26.6c > D

[64] [אלפרח ... כ]מא TS Ar 1b.90d > D

[65] א[חתיג בעד] קו[לה חלם] TS Ar 1b.90d > D

[66] אן TS Ar 26.6c > D

[67] משכ[בה ... עלי] TS Ar 1b.90d > D

[68] מנהא ... נפס TS Ar 1b.90d > D ׀ כ̇ארג] ען [נ]פס TS Ar 26.6c > D

[69] והו TS Ar 1b.90d

[70] ג̇ צ̇רוב TS Ar 1b.90d ׀ ג̇ אלצ̇רוב TS Ar 26.6c

[71] אלתי TS Ar 1b.90d

[72] ד̇כר[נאהא] TS Ar 1b.90d > D ׀ ד̇כרנאהא End of the readable part of TS Ar 1b.90d

[73] אלכימוט TS Ar 26.6c

[74] אלכד TS Ar 26.6c > D

[75] אלתי TS Ar 26.6c

מעדן אלנפס מוצ̇וע עלי אמת̇אל אלחכמה אלמעקול מנא ואלמכתוב. ומא ליס מן מעדן אלנפס[77] פהו בתכ̇ליט ועלי ג̇יר נט̇אם.[78] הד̇א[79] אלפרק סוי[80] מא יד̇כרה אלאנסאן מן אלאסבאב אלסאבקה לרויאה.[81] פלמא כאן הד̇א אלחלם[82] אלד̇י ראה דניאל הו מן מעדן אלנפס וגוהר אלחכמה קדם פי צדרה **וחזוי ראשה** (דניאל 7:1). יעני אן הד̇א אלרויה מן אלד̇את והו צחיחה[83] מת̇ל מא קדם פי חלמי נבוכ̇דנצר[84] אלמתקדמין.

וקולה[85] **באדין חלמא כתב** (דניאל 7:1) יעני בה אנה את̇בתה מן וקתה ולם יעתקדה נבוה[86] חתי ראי פי אליקט̇ה ד̇אך אלשכ̇ץ אלד̇י פסרה לה פי אלמנאם כמא סנבין פי קולה[87] **קרבת על חד מן קאמיא**[88] (דניאל 7:16). וקולה[89] **ראש מלין** (דניאל 7:1) אמר יחתמל ג̇ מעאני. אלאול, והו אדונהא, אן יכון יומי[90] בהד̇א אלקול אלי **וארו**[91] **ארבע רוחי שמיא מגיחן לימא רבא** (דניאל 7:2). אי אנה אנמא אסתקאם[92] לה אן ישבה אלעאלם כלה באלבחר בעד אן ראי אלארבע גהאת מנצ̇מה אלי אלבחר[93] פיכון **מגיחן**[94] **לימא רבא** (דניאל 7:2) הו **ראש**[95] **מלין**[96] (דניאל 7:1). ויכון **סלקן מן ימא**[97] (דניאל 7:3) הו[98] **סוף**

[76] [אל]פ[ר]ק TS Ar 26.6c > D
[77] מוצע ... אלנפס TS Ar 26.6c > L homeoteleuton
[78] נטאם End of the readable part of Oxf 2486.69a
[79] ה[דא] TS Ar 26.6c > D
[80] סוי Beginning of Oxf 2486.69b
[81] ללרויה TS Ar 26.6c
[82] אלרויא Oxf 2486.69b
[83] צחיח Oxf 2486.69b
[84] נבוכד TS Ar 26.6c
[85] וקו TS Ar 26.6c
[86] נביא TS Ar 26.6c
[87] ופי קו TS Ar 26.6c
[88] קאמיא TS Ar 26.6c
[89] וקו TS Ar 26.6c
[90] אומי TS Ar 26.6c
[91] ואלו TS Ar 26.6c
[92] אסתק TS Ar 26.6c
[93] מנצמה אלי אלבחר Oxf 2486.69b > D
[94] מגיטן TS Ar 26.6c
[95] ריש TS Ar 26.6c
[96] רבא ... מלין Oxf 2486.69b > D
[97] ימא End of Oxf 2486.69b
[98] הו Beginning of Oxf 2486.70a

מלין. ואלת̇אני,[99] והו אגל מנה, אן יכון קולה **ראש**[100] **מלין** (דניאל 7:1) אצלא וקאנונא לגמלה[101] אלקצה. יעני אנה ליס ישרח מן אחואל כל ממלכה פרוע אכ̇בארהם ומא יכון למלך מלך מנהא או פי סנה סנה לטול ד̇לך וכ̇רוגה ען אחתמאל אלתכליף. ואנמא ישרח מן אחואל כל ממלכה אצולא ועיונא וגמלא תטיף באכת̇ר[102] מלכהא בחסב מקדאר אחתמאל אלסאמע ואלמסמע. ואלת̇אלת̇[103] אן יכון קולה[104] **ראש**[105] **מלין** (דניאל 7:1) יומי בה אלי חאשיה אלקצה אלאולי פיקול אני אנמא אשרח מן קצתי הד̇ה חאשיתהא, פי קצה אלשעבוד וכמיה אלדול. ואמא חאשיתה אלאכ̇ירה[106] אלתי הי כמיה אלקץ ועיון אלישועה[107] והי **סוף**[108] **מלין** פלא וליס אנה אהמל הד̇א אלבאב אלאכ̇יר באלכליה. לכנה קאלה קולא מדמגא[109] ליס יתבין באלקול אלאול אד̇ קאל **עד עדן ועדנין ופלג עידן** (דניאל 7:25). וקאל[110] איצ̇א[111] **ומלכותא**[112] **ושלטנה**[113] **ורבותא די מלכות**[114] **תחות כל שמיא יהבת לעם קדישי עליונין** (דניאל 7:27). ת̇ם[115] קאל

Dn 7:2

ענה דניאל ואמר חזה חוית בחזוי עם ליליא וארו ארבע רוחי שמיא מגיחן לימא רבא.

אבתדי[116] דניאל וקאל[117] ראית פימא יראה[118] פי אלליל כאן[119] ארבע[120] גהאת אלסמא מצדרה מנצ̇מה אלי אלבחר אלכביר.

[99] ואלב TS Ar 26.6c
[100] ריש TS Ar 26.6c
[101] הדה + TS Ar 26.6c
[102] באסתר Oxf 2486.70a
[103] ואלג̇ TS Ar 26.6c
[104] קו TS Ar 26.6c
[105] ריש TS Ar 26.6c
[106] אלג̇ TS Ar 26.6c
[107] [אליש]ועה TS Ar 26.6c > D
[108] סנה TS Ar 26.6c
[109] מדגמא Oxf 2486.70a
[110] וקאל End of the readable part of Oxf 2486.70a
[111] איצ̇ End of TS Ar 26.6c | TS Ar 26.6c
[112] ומלכותא Beginning of TS Ar 26.6d
[113] ושלטנה Beginning of Oxf 2486.70b
[114] [די מל]כות TS Ar 26.6d > D
[115] תם TS Ar 26.6d > D
[116] אבתדא Beginning of TS NS | TS NS 105.23b

פסרת קולה[121] **ענה דניאל ואמר** (דניאל 7:2) "אבתדי" אד̇ ליס הו גואב לכלאם תקדמה.[122] וזיאדתה פי אלקול **חזה חוית בחזוי** (דניאל 7:2) יריד בה רויא כ̇אץ לה וחדה לם יסמע באן אנסאנא ראי קט מת̇ל הד̇ה[123] אלרויא. ונחן איצ̇א[124] אד̇א סמענאהא יקע לנא מת̇ל ד̇לך. קולה[125] **וארו ארבע רוחי שמיא מגיחן לימא רבה**[126] (דניאל 7:2) יכ̇ץ בחר אלשאם[127] מן בין סאיר אלבחאר.[128] לאן גמלה אלקצה[129] פי סבב אלקום אלכ̇ואץ ואלבלד אלכ̇אץ. ואלאנצ̇מאם[130] אלד̇ גהאת אליה[131] ג̇[132] מעאני. אחדהא אן גמיע מא סיד̇כרה לכל אמה מן אלמלך ליס יריד בה מא תמלכה פי אטראף אלעאלם ונואחיה[133] ואנמא יריד בה מא תמלכה פי בלד אלשאם כ̇אצה. וד̇לך אן אלבאבליין[134] כאן להם מלך עט̇ים אלסנין אלכת̇ירה מן קבל אן ימלכו אלשאם. ואנמא קיל אנהם מלכו סבעין[135] סנה פקט עלי בלד אלשאם כ̇אצה. וכד̇לך אלפרס אנמא קיל אנהם מלכו את̇נין וכ̇מסין סנה עלי בלד אלשאם כ̇אצה.[136] ואמא קבל ד̇לך ובעד ד̇לך פמלכו סנין כת̇ירה פי נואחי אכ̇ר.[137] וכד̇לך אלקול פי אליונאניה ואלרום וג̇ירהם. ואלת̇אני[138] אן כל אמה יחכם להא בדולה עלי בלד אלשאם לא תבקא אמה פי חואלי ד̇לך אלבלד אלא ותכון תחת ידהא פי וקת סלטאנהא עלי בלד אלשאם. ואלג̇ אנה לא יגוז אן יתוהם בני יש̇ראל אן קד בקית ממלכה אכ̇רי

117 אבתדי דניאל וקאל TS Ar 26.6d > D

118 רואיי Oxf 2486.70b ו רויאיי TS Ar 26.6d ו רויאי Spiegel + TS NS 105.23b

119 End of TS NS 105.23b

120 ד TS Ar 26.6d + Oxf 2486.70b

121 פס קו TS Ar 26.6d

122 תקדמהו Oxf 2486.70b

123 הדא Oxf 2486.70b

124 איצ TS Ar 26.6d

125 וקו TS Ar 26.6d

126 מגיחן לימא רבה TS Ar 26.6d > L

127 אלשאם Oxf 2486.70b > D

128 אלבחור Oxf 2486.70b

129 אלק[צה] Oxf 2486.70b > D ו אלקצה TS Ar 26.6d > D

130 [אלכאץ ואלאנצ]מאם Oxf 2486.70b > D

131 אליה End of Oxf 2486.70b

132 ג̇ Beginning of Oxf 2486.71a

133 ונואחיה TS Ar 26.6d > D

134 אלבאבלין TS Ar 26.6d

135 ע TS Ar 26.6d

136 וכדלך אלפרס ... כאצה TS Ar 26.6d > L

137 וכדלך אלפרס ... כאצה TS Ar 26.6d +

138 ואלב̇ TS Ar 26.6d

תסלט עליהם[139] סוי[140] הדֿה אלמדֿכורה. כמא אנה לם תבק גהה[141] אלא וקד ראהא דניאל מחיטה באלבחר. ואמא כיף יתצור לנא אן דניאל ראי אלדֿ גהאת[142] מחיטה באלבחר פנקול כאנה ראי אן גהה אלמשרק מע אלבחר סוא, ליס בינהמא מדינה ולא קריה ולא גבל ולא גֿיר דֿלך. וכדֿאך פי גהה אלגנוב ואלשמאל ואלמגֿרב. וימכן אן יכון ראי מא הו אגל מן הדֿא כאן אלכואכב אלגנוביה ואלשמאליה[143] ואלטאלע באינמא[144] כאן ואלכֿאבע כלהא מנצֿמה[145] אלי אלבחר. ולא שט אלא מקדאר מקאם דניאל ואלאשכֿאץ פקט. לכן בעד מגי[146] אלחאכם אלדֿי סידֿכרה אדֿ[147] אלכרסי יצאגֿ לה עאד אלמחיט באלארץֿ אלי אתסאעה אלטביעי[148] וזאל אנצֿגֿאטה מע אלבחר חתי אמכן אן ירי **נהר די נור,**[149] **ואלף אלפין, ורבו רבון** (דניאל 7:10) וסאיר מא וצפה מע דֿלך. תֿם קאל[150]

Dn 7:3

וארבע[151] חיון רברבן סלקן מן ימא שנין דא מן דא.

וכאן ארבע[152] אשכֿאץ עטֿימה[153] צאעדה מן אלבחר כל ואחד מתגֿיר[154] מן אלאכֿר.

פסרת[155] **חיון** (דניאל 7:3) "אשכֿאץ" אדֿ לם יחסן אן אקול[156] "חיואנאת".[157] וקד יגוז[158] אן נקול "וחוש". וזיאדתה[159] פי אלקול[160] **רברבן** (דניאל 7:3)

[139] אכֿ[רי ... עליהם] Oxf 2486.71a > D | עליהם End of Oxf 2486.71a

[140] סוי Beginning of Oxf 2486.71b

[141] גהה TS Ar 26.6d > D

[142] אלגהאת TS Ar 26.6d

[143] אלשמאליה ואלגנוביה TS Ar 26.6d

[144] באין מא Oxf 2486.71b

[145] מוצֿמה Oxf 2486.71b | מצֿממה TS Ar 26.6d

[146] מגי Beginning of TS Ar 28.165c

[147] אן Oxf 2486.71b

[148] אלטביע TS Ar 28.165c + TS Ar 26.6d

[149] [די נ]ור Oxf 2486.71b > D

[150] קאל End of Oxf 2486.71b

[151] וארבע Beginning of Oxf 2486.72a

[152] ד TS Ar 26.6d

[153] עצֿימה Spiegel + Morag

[154] מתגֿייר Spiegel + Morag

[155] פס TS Ar 28.165c + TS Ar 26.6d

[156] אק[ול] TS Ar 26.6d > D | אקול End of TS Ar 26.6d

מענאה אן ליס תפסירהא סנין[161] כמא ראי פרעה **שבע**[162] **פרות** (בר׳ 41:36). ולא תפסירהא[163] ״רגל״. כמא ראי[164] יוסף **אחד עשׂר כוכבים** (בר׳ 37:9) בל[165] הי ממאלך עט̇אם כמא[166] פסר לה אלמלאך[167] פקאל **ארבעה**[168] **מלאכין יקומון מן ארעה** (דניאל 7:17). ולו אמסך עלי הד̇א[169] אלקול לכאנו[170] ארבעה[171] רגאל מלוך. לכנה קאל בעדה אנהא אסם ליס רגאל אחאד.[172] וד̇לך[173] קולה[174] **מלכו רבריעא**[175] **תהוא בארעא די תשנא**[176] **מן כל מלכותא**[177] (דניאל 7:23) עלמנא אן אלראבעה ואלת̇אלת̇ה[178] אלתי קבלהא[179] כלהא אמם וממאלך[180] להא דול[181] וסלאטן.[182] ותחת קולה[183] **שנין**[184] **דא מן דא** (דניאל 7:3) מעאני[185] כת̇ירה[186] מנהא אכ̇תלאף

[157] חיואנאת Beginning of TS Ar 26.6e
[158] ו[קד יגו]ז TS Ar 26.6e > D
[159] וזיאד TS Ar 28.165c
[160] [פי אלקו]ל TS Ar 26.6e > D
[161] סנון TS Ar 26.6e
[162] ז̇ TS Ar 28.165c
[163] תפסי[ר]הא Oxf 2486.72a
[164] כ[מא רא]י TS Ar 26.6e > D
[165] [ב]ל TS Ar 26.6e > D
[166] כמ TS Ar 26.6e > D ׀ כ TS Ar 28.165c
[167] אלמל[אך] TS Ar 28.165c > D
[168] ד TS Ar 28.165c + TS Ar 26.6e
[169] ה[ד̇א] TS Ar 26.6e > D
[170] כאנו TS Ar 26.6e
[171] ד TS Ar 26.6e ׀ לכא[נו ארבעה] TS Ar 28.165c > D
[172] אלד + TS Ar 26.6e
[173] אן + TS Ar 26.6e
[174] קו TS Ar 26.6e ׀ וד̇לכ[ך קולה] TS Ar 28.165c > D
[175] רביעיא TS Ar 26.6e
[176] תשנא Oxf 2486.72a > D ׀ וג׳ + TS Ar 28.165c
[177] מן כל מלכותא TS Ar 28.165c and TS Ar 26.6e > L
[178] אלרא[בעה ואלת̇אלת̇ה] Oxf 2486.72a > D ׀ אל[ראבעה ואלת̇אלת̇ה] D > TS Ar 28.165c
[179] [קב]להא Oxf 2486.72a > D
[180] ממאלך Oxf 2486.72a > D
[181] דול Oxf 2486.72a > D ׀ דול Beginning of TS Ar 27.35a
[182] וסלטאן End of the readable part of Oxf 2486.72a
[183] קולה Beginning of Oxf 2486.72b ׀ קולה TS Ar 27.35a > L ׀ קו TS Ar 26.6e
[184] ו[תחת קולה שנין] TS Ar 28.165c > D
[185] [דא ... מ]עאני TS Ar 27.35a > D

בלדאנהם.[187] לאן אלבאבליין[188] מנסובין[189] אלי גהה[190] אלשמאל כמא קאל[191] **כי הנני**[192] **קרא לכל**[193] **משפחות ממלכות**[194] **צפונה**[195] (ירמ׳ 1:15). ואלפרס ועלי אנהם קד[196] ינסבון אלי גהה אלשמאל כמא קאל[197] **כי הנה**[198] **אנכי**[199] **מעיר ומעלה**[200] **על בבל קהל גוים גדלים מארץ צפון**[201] (ירמ׳ 50:9) פאן[202] גהה[203] אלמשרק תשארכהם כמא נשאהד[204] אליונאניין, פהם מן אלמגׄרב[205] כמא[206] סיקול **והנה צפיר העזים**[207] **בא**[208] **מן המערב**[209] (דניאל 8:5). וכמא נעלם אן אתיניה[210] וסקליה ופרנגה פי[211] גהה אלמגׄרב. ואדום

186 כתירא TS Ar 27.35a

187 בלדאנ[הם] TS Ar 27.35a > D

188 אלבאבלין TS Ar 26.6e | [אלב]א[ב]לין TS Ar 28.165c > D | אלבבלין TS Ar 27.35a

189 מ[נס]ובין TS Ar 26.6e > D | אלמנסובין TS Ar 27.35a > D

190 גהה TS Ar 27.35a > D

191 כק TS Ar 26.6e + TS Ar 28.165c | כקולה TS Ar 27.35a

192 הנה Oxf 2486.72b

193 [לכ]ל TS Ar 27.35a > D

194 ממל[כו]ת TS Ar 27.35a > D

195 לכל ... צפונה TS Ar 28.165c and TS Ar 26.6e > L | צ[פ]ונ[ה] TS Ar 27.35a > D

196 [ו]אלפרס [ו]עלי [אנהם קד] TS Ar 27.35a > D

197 כק TS Ar 28.165c | כקולה TS Ar 27.35a

198 כק כי הנה TS Ar 26.6e > D | הנני TS Ar 27.35a

199 אנכי TS Ar 27.35a > L

200 מ[עיר ומעל[ה] TS Ar 27.35a > D | וג׳ + TS Ar 28.165c and TS Ar 26.6e and TS Ar 27.35a

201 על ... צפון TS Ar 27.35a and TS Ar 28.165c and TS Ar 26.6e > D

202 פאנה TS Ar 27.35a

203 מן + TS Ar 27.35a

204 תשאר[כה]ם כמא [נשא]הד TS Ar 27.35a > D

205 אלמג̇[ר]ב TS Ar 27.35a > D

206 כמׄ TS Ar 26.6e | כ TS Ar 28.165c

207 וג׳ + TS Ar 28.165c

208 ו[ה]נה צפיר [העזים ב]א TS Ar 27.35a > D

209 בא מן הערב TS Ar 27.35a and TS Ar 28.165c and TS Ar 26.6e > L

210 אוניניה TS Ar 28.165c + TS Ar 26.6e

211 וסקל[יה] ופר[נגה פי] TS Ar 27.35a > D

פי[212] גהה[213] אלגנוב כמא קאל[214] **והיה לכם פאת נגב ממדבאר**[215] **צין על ידי אדום**[216] (במד׳ 34:3). ולהם אכ̇תלאף איצ̇א[217] פי[218] אדיאנהם[219] ומקאלאתהם[220] כמא[221] עלמנא[222] אן[223] הד̇ה תסמי שינוי[224] אד̇ יקול[225] פי[226] יש̇ראל[227] **ודתיהם שונות**[228] **מכל**[229] **עם**[230] (אסתר 3:8). ויכ̇תלפון[231] איצ̇א[232] פי זיהם[233] מא בין[234] אלחמרה ואלביאצ̇[235] ואלצפרה[236] ואלסואד כק̇[237] **אשר בא**[238] **הסוסים השחרים**[239] **יצאים**[240] **אל ארץ צפון והלבנים יצאים**

212 ואלרום מן TS Ar 27.35a
213 גהה TS Ar 27.35a > D
214 כק TS Ar 28.165c + TS Ar 26.6e | כקולה TS Ar 27.35a
215 וג׳ + TS Ar 28.165c
216 צין ... אדום TS Ar 28.165c and TS Ar 26.6e > L | נגב ... אדום TS Ar 27.35a > L
217 איצ̇ TS Ar 28.165c + TS Ar 26.6e
218 אי TS Ar 28.165c | אן TS Ar 27.35a
219 אד[יאנה]ם TS Ar 26.6e > D | אדי[אנה]ם TS Ar 27.35a > D
220 ומקאלתהם TS Ar 27.35a
221 כמ̇ TS Ar 26.6e | כ TS Ar 28.165c
222 נעלם TS Ar 27.35a
223 פי TS Ar 26.6e
224 [שי]נוי TS Ar 26.6e > D | הד[ה תסמי שינוי] TS Ar 27.35a > D
225 קיל TS Ar 27.35a
226 ארץ + TS Ar 28.165c
227 י[ש̇רא]ל TS Ar 26.6e > D
228 וג׳ + TS Ar 28.165c
229 שונות מכל TS Ar 26.6e > D
230 מכל עם TS Ar 28.165c > D | ע[ם] TS Ar 27.35a > D
231 [ויכ]תלפון TS Ar 27.35a > D
232 איצ̇ TS Ar 28.165c + TS Ar 26.6e
233 מן + TS Ar 27.35a
234 מא בין TS Ar 27.35a > D
235 ואלביאצ̇ TS Ar 28.165c and TS Ar 26.6e > L
236 אל[חמ]רה [ואלבי]אצ̇ ואלצפ[רה] TS Ar 27.35a > D
237 כמא קאל Oxf 2486.72b > D | כקולה TS Ar 27.35a
238 בה TS Ar 27.35a
239 השחרים End of Oxf 2486.72b | [אשר בא] הסוסים [השחרים] TS Ar 26.6e > D
240 יצאים Beginning of Oxf 2486.73a

אחריהם והברדים יצאו אל ארץ התימן[241] (זכר׳ 6:6). ויכ̇תלפון איצ̇א[242] פימא יגירון עלי[243] ישׂראל. פאמא בבל פגירת[244] אלסגוד ללצנם. ומדי אלא תצלי[245] צלוה.[246] ופרס **להשמיד להרג ולאבד**[247] (אסתר 3:13). ויון[248] פמנעת אלסבת ואלכ̇תאנה.[249] ואדום[250] פטאלבת באלכ̇רוג מן[251] גמלה אלדין[252] ואלא[253] תקרא אלתוראה.[254] פמן[255] הד̇ה[256] אלאמור[257] ואשבאההא[258] קאל **שנין דא מן**[259] **דא** (דניאל 7:3). ת̇ם קאל[260]

Dn 7:4

קדמייתא כאריה וגפין די נשר ליה חזי הוית עד די מריטו גפיה ונטילת מן ארעא ועל רגלין כאנש הוקימת ולבב אנש יהיב לה.

אלשכ̇ל אלאול[261] ישבה אלאסד ולה אגנחה**[262]** כאלנסר[263] ת̇ם ראית כאן אגנחתה קד[264] אנתתפת[265] ורפע מע ד̇לך[266] מן אלארץ̇ ת̇ם[267] אקים עלי רגלין[268] מת̇ל אנסאן[269] ואעטי עקל אלנאס.[270]

[241] יצאים ... התימן TS Ar 27.35a > L | יצאים וג׳ TS Ar 28.165c | אל ... התימן L > TS Ar 28.165c and TS Ar 26.6e
[242] איצ̇א TS Ar 28.165c and TS Ar 26.6e > L
[243] אי[צ̇א] פ[ימא יגז̇רון על]י TS Ar 27.35a > D
[244] עליהם + TS Ar 27.35a
[245] יצלון TS Ar 27.35a
[246] צלוה TS Ar 28.165c > D | צ[לוה] TS Ar 27.35a > D
[247] [ופר]ס [להש]מיד להרג אל[אבד] TS Ar 27.35a > D
[248] אלמנע ען + TS Ar 27.35a
[249] ואלכ̇תאנה TS Ar 28.165c and TS Ar 26.6e > L | ואלמילה TS Ar 26.6e + TS Ar 28.165c
[250] ואדום TS Ar 28.165c > D | ואלאדום TS Ar 27.35a
[251] פעלת לא[... מן] TS Ar 27.35a > D
[252] אלדין TS Ar 27.35a > L
[253] ולא TS Ar 26.6e + TS Ar 28.165c | ואן לא TS Ar 27.35a
[254] אלתוריה TS Ar 26.6e
[255] ומן TS Ar 27.35a
[256] [ה]דה TS Ar 27.35a > D
[257] אלתו[ראה פמן הדה אלאמור] TS Ar 28.165c > D
[258] וא[אשבאה]הא TS Ar 27.35a > D
[259] דא מן TS Ar 27.35a > D
[260] תם קאל TS Ar 27.35a > L
[261] תם ... אלאול TS Ar 28.165c > D | אלאוול Spiegel + Morag
[262] אגנחא TS Ar 27.35a
[263] כ[אלנס]ר TS Ar 27.35a > D

הד̇א[271] אלשכ̇ץ ואלאת̇נאן אלאכ̇ראן[272] למא לם יפסר אלמלך[273] לדניאל מן[274] הם ולא שרח[275] לה כל נכתה[276] מן[277] אוצאפהם ואחואלהם אחתגנא[278] אלי אן נשרח ד̇לך[279] ונבינה. ולם ידע אלמלאך[280] אן[281] ד̇לך בכ̇לא ולכן אכ̇תצארא.[282] ולאן דניאל סאלה[283] מסאלה[284] מגרדה ען[285] כל נכתה מן אחואל[286] אלשכ̇ץ. לד̇אך[287] שרחה לה ובינה. פנקול אן הד̇א אלשכ̇ץ[288] אלמשבה באלאסד הו ממלכה בבל, כמא קאל פי נבוכ̇דנצר[289] **עלה אריה מסבכו** (ירמ׳ 4:7). ולה סרעה[290] כחרכה[291] אגנחה אלנסר, כמא[292] קאל[293]

264 קד TS Ar 27.35a > D | קד Spiegel > L
265 כאל[נסר ... אנתתפת] TS Ar 28.165c > D | ואנתפת TS Ar 27.35a
266 מע דלך TS Ar 27.35a > L | דאלך Spiegel | דלך End of the readable part of TS Ar 28.165c
267 תם TS Ar 27.35a > D
268 רגלאן Spiegel + Morag | אלרגלין TS Ar 27.35a
269 אלאנסאן TS Ar 27.35a
270 אלנאס End of Oxf 2486.73a | אנסאן Spiegel
271 הדא Beginning of Oxf 2486.73b | הד[א אלשכ̇ץ] TS Ar 27.35a > D
272 ואלב אלאכרין TS Ar 27.35a
273 אלמלאך TS Ar 27.35a
274 ומן TS Ar 27.35a
275 [ש]רח TS Ar 27.35a > D
276 כ[ל נכתה] TS Ar 27.35a > D
277 מן TS Ar 26.6e > L
278 אחת[גנא] TS Ar 27.35a > D
279 [ד]לך TS Ar 27.35a > D
280 ולם ידע אלמלאך TS Ar 27.35a > D
281 אן TS Ar 27.35a > D
282 לאן אכ̇תצרה TS Ar 27.35a
283 [סא]ל[ה] TS Ar 27.35a > D
284 מסלה TS Ar 27.35a + TS Ar 26.6e + Oxf 2486.73b
285 עלי TS Ar 27.35a
286 נכ[תה מן אחואל] TS Ar 27.35a > D
287 לדך TS Ar 27.35a
288 פנק[ול אן הדא אלשכ̇]ץ TS Ar 27.35a > D
289 ממלכה ... נבוכדנצר TS Ar 27.35a > D | נבוכד TS Ar 26.6e
290 [ו]לה סרע[ה] TS Ar 27.35a > D
291 כסרעה TS Ar 26.6e
292 כחרכה ... כמא TS Ar 27.35a > D
293 כק TS Ar 26.6e | יקול TS Ar 27.35a

ישא יווי[294] **עליך גוי מרחוק מקצה הארץ כאשר ידאה הנשר**[295] (דבר' 28:49). וקאל איצ̇א[296] **אל חכך שופר כנשר אל בית יווי**[297] (הושע 8:1).

וקולה **חזי הוית**[298] **עד די מריטו גפה ונטילת מן ארעא** (דניאל 7:4) הו תמאם אלעגז[299] ען[300] אלחרכה. ודלך[301] אן הד̇א אלמלך אעטי[302] אולא קואים כאלאסד ואגנחה כאלנסר.[303] פאן[304] שא[305] משי[306] ואן שא טאר. פלמא נתפת[307] אגנחתה[308] לו תרך קאימה עלי[309] אלארץ̇[310] לכאן ימשי בארגלה.[311] או לו כאן למא רפע מן אלארץ̇ בקית[312] לה[313] אגנחתה[314] לטאר בהא. ולכן[315] אלאפתין גמיעא[316] אגתמעת עליה: נתף רישה פמנע[317] אלטיראן ורפע מן אלארץ̇ פמנע אלמשי. ותפסיר הד̇א מא גרי[318] עלי נבוכ̇דנצר[319] מן אכ̇תלאט

[294] ישא יוי TS Ar 26.6e > D
[295] מקצה ... הנשר TS Ar 26.6e > D ׀ ישא ... הנשר TS Ar 27.35a > D
[296] איצ̇ TS Ar 26.6e
[297] כנשר ... יוי TS Ar 26.6e > D
[298] [שופר ... ה]וית TS Ar 27.35a > D
[299] [גפה ... תמאם] אלעג[ז] TS Ar 27.35a > D
[300] ען Oxf 2486.73b > L
[301] אלחרכ[ה ודלך] TS Ar 27.35a > D
[302] אלמל[ך א]עטי TS Ar 27.35a > D
[303] כאלנסר End of TS Ar 26.6e ׀ ואג[נחתה כאלנסר] TS Ar 27.35a > D
[304] פאן Beginning of TS Ar 26.6f ׀ [פ]א[ן] TS Ar 26.6f > D
[305] שא End of Oxf 2486.73b
[306] משא TS Ar 27.35a
[307] אנתפת TS Ar 27.35a
[308] אגנחתה Beginning of the readable part of Oxf 2486.74a ׀ פלמ[א ... אגנחתה] TS Ar 26.6f > D ׀ [אגנ]חתה TS Ar 27.35a > D
[309] לו ... עלי Oxf 2486.74a > D
[310] אלא[רץ̇] TS Ar 27.35a > D
[311] [ימ]שי ברגל[ה] TS Ar 27.35a > D ׀ [באר]גלה TS Ar 26.6f > D
[312] מן ... בקית TS Ar 26.6f > D
[313] לה TS Ar 27.35a > L
[314] א[גנח]תה TS Ar 26.6f > D
[315] לכן TS Ar 27.35a
[316] אלאפ[תין גמי]עא TS Ar 27.35a > D ׀ גמיעא TS Ar 26.6f > D
[317] רישה פמנע TS Ar 26.6f > D ׀ פמנע עו TS Ar 27.35a
[318] גרא TS Ar 27.35a
[319] נבוכד TS Ar 26.6f ׀ נבנצר TS Ar 27.35a

עקלה והימאנה[320] פי אלצחרא תלך[321] אלמדה[322] אלמדׄכורה.[323] פסלב מלכה וסלטאנה ותדבירה[324] עלי מא[325] שרחנא פצאר[326] לא[327] כחאל אלנאס ולא כחאל אלבהאים. וקולה[328] **ועל רגלין**[329] **כאנש**[330] **הקימת ולבב**[331] **אנש יהיב לה**[332] (דניאל 7:4) תפסירה[333] רגוע עקל[334] נבוכׄדנצר[335] אליה חתי[336] עאד אלי מלכה ואגתמע[337] אליה אמראוה[338] וקואדה[339] עלי מא שרח ובין **בה זמנא מנדעי**[340] **יתוב עלי וליקר מלכותי הדרי וזיוי יתוב עלי ולי הדברי ורברבני יבעון**[341] (דניאל 4:33). ולדׄלך פסרנא **לבב**[342] **אנש**[343] (דניאל 7:4) ״עקל אלנאס״.[344] ומתׄל דׄלך כתׄיר[345] פי **משלי** יסמי אלחכמה[346] **לב**.[347]

[320] עקל[ה ו]הימאנ[ה] TS Ar 27.35a > D
[321] אל[צח]ארי תל[ך] TS Ar 27.35a > D
[322] אלמדה Beginning of TS Ar 28.165d
[323] אל[מ]דה TS Ar 28.165d > D | אל[מ]דה אלמדכור[ה] TS Ar 27.35a > D
[324] מלכה ... ותדבירה TS Ar 26.6f > D | ות[דביר]ה TS Ar 27.35a > D
[325] עלי מא TS Ar 27.35a > D
[326] פצאר TS Ar 28.165d > D
[327] [פ]צאר [לא] TS Ar 27.35a > D
[328] וקו TS Ar 28.165d + TS Ar 26.6f | לקולה TS Ar 27.35a
[329] וע[ל] רגלי[ן] TS Ar 27.35a > D
[330] כאנש TS Ar 26.6f > D | וג׳ + TS Ar 28.165d
[331] [כא]נש הקימ[ת] ולב[ב] TS Ar 27.35a > D
[332] הקימת ... לה TS Ar 28.165d and TS Ar 26.6f > L
[333] תפס TS Ar 28.165d + TS Ar 26.6f
[334] [ע]קל TS Ar 27.35a > D
[335] נבוכד TS Ar 28.165d + TS Ar 26.6f
[336] ח[תי] TS Ar 27.35a > D
[337] ו[אג]תמע [אליה] TS Ar 27.35a > D
[338] אמראה TS Ar 28.165d + TS Ar 26.6f
[339] [וקו]אדה TS Ar 26.6f
[340] ומנד[עי] TS Ar 26.6f > D
[341] יתוב ... יבעון TS Ar 28.165d + TS Ar 26.6f > L | עלי ... יבעון TS Ar 27.35a > L
[342] ולבב TS Ar 27.35a
[343] ל[בב אנש] Oxf 2486.74a > D | א[נ]ש TS Ar 27.35a > D
[344] אלנאס End of Oxf 2486.74a | [ע]קל אר[נא]ס TS Ar 27.35a > D
[345] כ[תיר] TS Ar 27.35a > D
[346] אלחכ TS Ar 27.35a
[347] לב Beginning of the readable part of Oxf 2486.74b

ועלי[348] אן קצה נבוכ̇דנצר[349] כאנת קד אנקצ̇ת קבל[350] וקת תאריכ̇ הד̇ה[351]
אלרויא. לכנה[352] למא כאן אלקצד[353] אט̇האר דניאל[354] עלי אכבאר אלממאלך[355],
עלי נט̇אמנא, אבתדי[356] לה ממא[357] מצ̇י[358] חתי ינסק לה עליה מא יאתי[359]
מת̇ל קולה[360] **ויאמר**[361] **לו אלהים שמך**[362] **יעקב**[363] (בר׳ 35:10) חתי יטבק
עליה[364] **לא יקרא שמך**[365] **עוד יעקב**[366] (בר׳ 35:10). ומת̇ל קול אלמלאך[367]
לזוגה מנוח **הנה נא את עקרה**[368] **ולא ילדת** (שופטים 13:3) חתי יטבק
עליה[369] **והרית וילדת בן**[370] (שופטים 13:3) ומא[371] אשבה[372] ד̇לך. ת̇ם קאל

Dn 7:5

וארו חיוא אוחרי תנינא דמי לדוב ולסטר חד הוקימת ותלת עלעין בפומה בין שניה וכין אמרין לה קומי אכולי בשר סגי.

[348] אל[חכמה לב עלי] TS Ar 26.6f > D
[349] נבוכד TS Ar 28.165d + TS Ar 26.6f
[350] נבוכ[דנצר ... קבל] TS Ar 27.35a > D
[351] הדא TS Ar 28.165d + TS Ar 26.6f | [תאריך ה]דה TS Ar 27.35a > D
[352] לכנה TS Ar 27.35a > D
[353] קצד TS Ar 27.35a
[354] קצד דניאל אטהאר TS Ar 27.35a
[355] [אלמ]מאלך TS Ar 26.6f > D | [אלממ]אלך TS Ar 27.35a > D
[356] אבתדא TS Ar 27.35a
[357] [עליה ממ]א TS Ar 27.35a > D
[358] מ[צי] TS Ar 26.6f > D | מצא TS Ar 27.35a
[359] [מא יא]תי TS Ar 26.6f > D
[360] קו TS Ar 28.165d + TS Ar 26.6f
[361] מא ... ויאמר TS Ar 27.35a > D
[362] שמך TS Ar 28.165d > D
[363] [ש]מך [יעק]ב TS Ar 27.35a > D
[364] יטבק עליה TS Ar 27.35a > D
[365] שמך End of the readable part of TS Ar 27.35a
[366] לא ... יעקב TS Ar 26.6f > D
[367] [קול אלמ]לאך TS Ar 28.165d > D
[368] עקרה Beginning of the readable part of TS Ar 27.35b
[369] עלי TS Ar 26.6f
[370] וילדת בן TS Ar 26.6f > L | וילד[ת בן] TS Ar 27.35b > D
[371] [והרית ... בן] ו[מא] TS Ar 28.165d > D
[372] שבה TS Ar 27.35b

וכאן[373] שכ̇ץ אכ̇ר ת̇אני ישבה[374] אלדב[375] וקד[376] אקים אלי[377] גאנב ואחד וכאן פי פיה[378] ג̇[379] אצ̇לאע מתעלקה בין[380] אסנאנה[381] והכד̇א[382] יקאל[383] לה קם פכל אללחם אלכת̇יר.[384]

תפסיר[385] הד̇א אלשכ̇ץ אלת̇אני[386] ממלכה אלפרס[387] ושבההא באלדב לאנה אדון[388] מן[389] אלאסד. ועלי מא תקדם **ובתרך יקום מלכו אחרי ארע מנך** (דניאל 2:39). וקולה[390] **ולשׂטר**[391] **חד הקימת**[392] (דניאל 7:5) לאן אלמלך לם יכן[393] כ̇אלצא ללפארסין[394] בל קד כאן אלהמדאניין[395] משארכין להם כמא קאל[396] **חיל פרס ומדי** (אסתר 1:3). וקאל איצ̇א[397] **למלכי מדי**[398] **ופרס** (אסתר 10:2). וגדנא[399] אלמלוך[400] ד̇.[401] ב̇[402] משרוחין לפרס,[403] המא[404]

[373] ואלאן Spiegel
[374] ת̇אני ישבה TS Ar 27.35b > D | שביה Spiegel
[375] [ישבה אל]דב TS Ar 28.165d > D | אלדוב TS Ar 27.35b
[376] ישבה ... וקד TS Ar 26.6f > D
[377] עלי TS Ar 27.35b
[378] פאה Morag | פמה Spiegel
[379] תלאת Morag | תלאתה Spiegel
[380] אצאלע מעלקה פי TS Ar 27.35b
[381] אסנאנה End of Oxf 2486.74b
[382] והכדא Beginning of Oxf 2486.75a | והכדי Morag | והכ[דא] Oxf 2486.75a > D
[383] קיל TS Ar 27.35b
[384] וה[כדא ... אלכת̇יר] Oxf 2486.75a > D | לחמא כת̇ירא TS Ar 27.35b
[385] תפס TS Ar 26.6f
[386] אלב TS Ar 28.165d + TS Ar 26.6f
[387] פרס TS Ar 26.6f
[388] דון TS Ar 27.35b
[389] מן TS Ar 27.35b > L
[390] וקו TS Ar 28.165d + TS Ar 26.6f
[391] ולסטר TS Ar 27.35b
[392] [הקי]מת TS Ar 27.35b > D
[393] י[כן] TS Ar 27.35b > D
[394] ללפארסיין Oxf 2486.75a
[395] אלהמדאנין TS Ar 28.165d
[396] כק TS Ar 28.165d + TS Ar 26.6f | כקולה TS Ar 27.35b
[397] איצ TS Ar 28.165d + TS Ar 26.6f | א[יצ]א TS Ar 27.35b > D
[398] מ[די] TS Ar 27.35b > D
[399] ו[ו]ג[ד]נא TS Ar 28.165d > D
[400] אלמל[וך] TS Ar 26.6f > D
[401] ארבעה TS Ar 28.165d + TS Ar 26.6f

כורש[405] וארתחששתא.[406] ואכ̇ר משרוח[407] למדי, והו דריוש.[408] ואלראבע קריבא[409] אן יכון למדי והו אחשורוש.[410] ואן לם יד[411] ד̇לך פציחא. פמנהא[412] קאל **ולש̇טר חד הקימת** (דניאל 7:5). מדי[413] פי אלסטר ופרס פי אלסטר.[414] ומעני **ותלת̇**[415] **עלעין בפמה בין שנה** (דניאל 7:5) מעני[416] עגיב. ותכ̇ילה[417] אולא[418] באן סבע[419] קאים פי פמה ג̇[420] אצ̇לאע[421] מן אלפריסה והי מתעלקה בין[422] אסנאנה,[423] לא[424] הי מאכולה אד̇ לם יבלעהא[425] ולא[426] הי[427] מטרוחה אד̇ לם ירם[428] בהא. ולכנהא מתוסטה[429] בין ד̇לך. ותפסירהא[430] אן ממלכה[431]

[402] את̇נין Oxf 2486.75a
[403] המדי + TS Ar 27.35b
[404] המא TS Ar 27.35b > L
[405] כ[ור]ש TS Ar 28.165d > D
[406] וארתחששת TS Ar 26.6f ׀ וארתחש TS Ar 28.165d
[407] מש[רו]ח TS Ar 27.35b > D
[408] [דרי]וש TS Ar 27.35b > D
[409] ואלד קריב TS Ar 27.35b
[410] אחשורש TS Ar 26.6f
[411] יכן TS Ar 27.35b + TS Ar 28.165d
[412] [פמ]נהא TS Ar 27.35b > D
[413] מ[די] TS Ar 27.35b > D
[414] מדי פי אלש̇טר ופארס פי אלש̇טר TS Ar 28.165d ׀ אלש̇טר ... אלש̇טר TS Ar 27.35b
[415] וג̇ TS Ar 27.35b
[416] אן + TS Ar 28.165d ׀ [מ]ע[ני] TS Ar 27.35b > D
[417] ותכ̇יילה Oxf 2486.75a
[418] תכ̇יל[ה אולא] TS Ar 27.35b > D
[419] באו סבע TS Ar 27.35b > D
[420] תלתה Oxf 2486.75a
[421] אצ̇לאע TS Ar 28.165d > D
[422] מעלקה מן TS Ar 27.35b
[423] [מעלקה] בין [אסנאנה] TS Ar 26.6f > D ׀ אסנאנה End of Oxf 2486.75a
[424] אלא TS Ar 27.35b
[425] יבתלעהא TS Ar 27.35b
[426] אד לם יבלעהא ולא TS Ar 28.165d > D ׀ ולא TS Ar 27.35b > D
[427] הי Beginning of the readable part of Oxf 2486.75b
[428] ירמי TS Ar 27.35b
[429] ירן[מ ... מטרוחה] TS Ar 26.6f > D
[430] ותפסירה TS Ar 27.35b
[431] מתיס[טה ... ממלכה] TS Ar 28.165d > D

אלפרס יכון בינהא ובין ממלכה[432] אלרום ג̇[433] בלדאן ג̇יר חאצלה[434] להד̇א[435] ולא להד̇א. בל פי[436] וקת יג̇לב עליהא[437] אלרום ופי וקת יג̇לב עליהא אלפרס.

ואסמא הד̇ה[438] אלמדן לא יוצל[439] אליהא אלא[440] מן גהה אלנקל.[441] והי חראן ונציבין[442] ושהרזור, כמא נקל אלקדמא **ותלת**[443] **עלעין בפמה בין שנה** (דניאל 7:5), **זו**[444] **חרן חדיב ונציבין**[445] **שפעמים פילטתן**[446] **מלכות**[447] **הרשעה ופעמים מולכת עליהן**[448] (קדושין 72a). ופי לג̇ה אלאבא קד תסמי[449] נואחי אלארץ̇ **צלעות** אלד̇י תרגומהא[450] **עלעין** (דניאל 7:5) כמא תקול **ולצלע המשכן** (שמ׳ 26:20). ותקול איצ̇א[451] **ושמעי הלך**[452] **בצלע ההר** (שמ״ב 16:13). ואמא[453] קולה[454] **וכן**[455] **אמרין**[456] **לה**[457] **קומי אכולי בש̇ר ש̇גיא**[458]

[432] ו[בין ממלכה] TS Ar 26.6f > D
[433] תלת Oxf 2486.75b
[434] חאצלה End of TS Ar 26.6f | חא[צל]ה TS Ar 27.35b > D
[435] להד̇א Beginning of the readable part of TS Ar 1b.88a
[436] אלר[ום ... פי] TS Ar 28.165d > D
[437] [ולא ... ע]ליהא TS Ar 1b.88a > D
[438] וקת ... הד̇ה TS Ar 1b.88a > D
[439] וקת ... יוצל TS Ar 28.165d > D | ולם יצל TS Ar 27.35b
[440] End of TS Ar 28.165d
[441] [אל]נקל TS Ar 27.35b > D
[442] מן ... ונציבין TS Ar 1b.88a > D
[443] וג̇ TS Ar 27.35b
[444] אלקדמא ... זו TS Ar 1b.88a > D | והר TS Ar 27.35b
[445] חרוב ונצבין TS Ar 27.35b
[446] [ונציבין שפעמים] פי[לט]תן TS Ar 1b.88a > D
[447] הר + TS Ar 1b.88a and TS Ar 27.35b
[448] [הרשעים ... עלי]הן TS Ar 1b.88a > D
[449] תסמי TS Ar 1b.88a > D
[450] אלתי תרגמת TS Ar 27.35b | תרג[ומהא] TS Ar 1b.88a > D
[451] איצ̇ TS Ar 1b.88a
[452] הולך TS Ar 27.35b
[453] ואמא TS Ar 27.35b > L | ואמא TS Ar 1b.88a > D
[454] וקולה TS Ar 27.35b | וקו TS Ar 1b.88a
[455] וכין Morag
[456] אמרין TS Ar 1b.88a > D
[457] וכן ... לה TS Ar 27.35b > L
[458] בש ש TS Ar 1b.88a

(דניאל 7:5) פאן תפסירה כמא[459] קאל[460] חסן לאחשורש אן יהלך בני ישראל[461] לאן **בשר שגיא**[462] (דניאל 7:5) הם ישׂראל[463] כמא קאל[464] **ויהי**[465] **שם לגוי גדול עצום**[466] **ורב** (דב׳ 26:5) ומא שאבה[467] דׄלך. ומעני **קומי אכולי**[468] (דניאל 7:5) אפנא אלקום והלאכהם[469] כמא קאל[470] **ואכלת את כל העמים**[471] (דב׳ 7:16). וקאל איצׄא[472] **כי אכלו את יעקב ואכלוהו ויכלהו**[473] (ירמ׳ 10:25). ומעׄני **אמרין לה** (דניאל 7:5) הו אן אחשורש[474] לם יקצד אן[475] יפעל דׄלך מן תלקא[476] נפסה. ואנמא המן אלדׄי אשאר עליה בדׄלך כמא קאל[477] **ויאמר המן**[478] **למלך אחשורוש**[479] **ישנו עם אחד**[480] (אסתר 3:8) **אם על המלך טוב יכתב לאבדם**[481] (אסתר 3:9). ולם ינץ פי אלרויא אנה אכל שיא. ואנמא קיל[482] אן קאילא קאל לה[483] "קם פכל אללחם אלכתׄיר" פקט. וכדׄלך

[459] פאן תפסירה כמא L > TS Ar 27.35b | תפס TS Ar 1b.88a
[460] קול TS Ar 27.35b | כק TS Ar 1b.88a
[461] יס TS Ar 1b.88a
[462] בני ... שׂגיא L > TS Ar 27.35b | שׂגיא D > TS Ar 1b.88a
[463] יש TS Ar 1b.88a
[464] קאל End of Oxf 2486.75b | כקולה TS Ar 1b.88a | כק TS Ar 27.35b
[465] ויהי Beginning of Oxf 2486.76a
[466] ג׳ עצ TS Ar 1b.88a
[467] שם ... שאבה D > Oxf 2486.76a
[468] אכ TS Ar 1b.88a
[469] אל[קום] ו[אה]לאכהם D > TS Ar 1b.88a
[470] כקולה ... כקולה homeoteleuton L > TS Ar 27.35b | כק TS Ar 1b.88a
[471] הע TS Ar 1b.88a
[472] ואיצׄא קולה TS Ar 27.35b | איצ TS Ar 1b.88a
[473] ואכלוהו ויכלהו L > TS Ar 27.35b | ואכ ויכ TS Ar 1b.88a
[474] אמרין רחשורש D > Oxf 2486.76a
[475] אן L > TS Ar 27.35b
[476] דאת TS Ar 27.35b
[477] כקולה TS Ar 27.35b | כק TS Ar 1b.88a
[478] [ויא]מר ה[מן] D > TS Ar 1b.88a
[479] אחש TS Ar 1b.88a
[480] ישנו עם אחד L > TS Ar 1b.88a and Oxf 2486.76a
[481] יכתב לאבדם L > TS Ar 27.35b
[482] אכל ... קיל D > TS Ar 27.35b
[483] קאל לה L > TS Ar 27.35b

לם יתם[484] עלי ישׂראל אן יקתלהם אחשורוש.[485] ואנמא קיל לה אן יקתלהם פקט. תֹם קאל[486]

Dn 7:6
בתר דנא חזי הוית וארו אוחרי כנמר ולה גפין ארבע די עוף על גבה וארבעה ראשין לחיותא ושולטן יהיב לה.

ובעד דֹלך[487] ראית[488] כאן שכֹצא[489] אכֹר כאלנמר ולה ארבע מן אגנחה אלטאיר[490] עלי[491] טֹהרה[492] ולה ארבעה[493] רוס וקד דפע אליה סלטאן.[494]

תפסיר[495] דֹלך אלממלכה[496] אלתֹאלתֹה[497] שבההא באלנמר[498] והי ממלכה אליונאניה לאן מעהא צברא ותֹבאתא ולזומא כאלנמר, כמא קאל[499] **נמר שקד על עריהם** (ירמ׳ 5:6). ותפסיר אלדֹ אגנחה[500] אלתי פוק טֹהרה[501] אלתפרק[502] אלדֹי[503] תפרקת הדֹה אלממלכה[504] בעד מות אלאסכנדר דֹ פרק. וולי[505] כל

[484] יתןם] TS Ar 1b.88a > D
[485] ישׂ אן יקתלהם אחש TS Ar 1b.88a
[486] פקט וכדלך ... פקט תֹם קאל TS Ar 27.35b > L
[487] דאלך Spiegel + Morag
[488] ובעד ... ראית TS Ar 1b.88a > D
[489] שכֹץ Spiegel + TS Ar 27.35b + Morag | שבץ TS Ar 1b.88a
[490] טאיר Spiegel
[491] עלי End of Oxf 2486.76a
[492] צהרה Spiegel + Morag | ו[לה ... אגנח]ה כאל[טאיר עלי ט]הרה TS Ar 27.35b > D
[493] ד TS Ar 1b.88a + TS Ar 27.35b
[494] צלטאן Morag | [וקד ... סלט]אן TS Ar 1b.88a > D
[495] תפסיר Beginning of the readable part of Oxf 2486.76b | תפס TS Ar 1b.88a
[496] אלממל[כה] TS Ar 27.35b > D
[497] אלגֹ TS Ar 1b.88a + TS Ar 27.35b
[498] ישבהה[א] באל[נמר] TS Ar 1b.88a > D
[499] כקולה TS Ar 27.35b | כק TS Ar 1b.88a
[500] ד אגנחתה TS Ar 27.35b | ותפסיר אלד אגנחה TS Ar 1b.88a > D
[501] טהרהא TS Ar 27.35b
[502] אל[תפר]ק TS Ar 1b.88a > D
[503] אלתי TS Ar 27.35b
[504] אלממלכה TS Ar 1b.88a > L
[505] וולא TS Ar 27.35b

פרקה ריס[506] מן אלנאס. והד̇א אלאנקסאם קד ד̇כר פי הד̇א[507] אלכתאב[508] פי ג̇ מואצ̇ע אכ̇ר **ותעלינה חזות ארבע תחתיה**[509] **לארבע רוחות השמים**[510] (דניאל 8:8). ותפסירה[511] **וארבעה ראשין**[512] **לחיותא**[513] (דניאל 7:6) עלי מא[514] שוהד[515] מן אחואל אליונאניה אנה כאן להם ארבע[516] מנאבר פי מדתהם.[517] ואחד פי רומיה. ואכ̇ר פי אנטאכיה. ואכ̇ר[518] פי אלאסכנדריה. ואכ̇ר[519] פי בית אלמקדס. לאן אלאנתצאב[520] פי מואצ̇ע שתי[521] יקאל לה פי לג̇ה אבאנא[522] **ראשים** כמא קאל[523] **ויצא**[524] **המשחית ממחנה פלשתים**[525] **שלשה**[526] **ראשים הראש האחד**[527] **יפנה**[528] **אל דרך עפרה אל ארץ שועל והראש**[529] **האחד יפנה דרך בית חורן והראש אחד יפנה דרך**[530] **הגבול הנשקף**[531] **על גי הצבעים המדברה**[532] (שמ"א 13:17–18). וקולה[533]

506 רייס TS Ar 27.35b
507 [ד פרק ... ד̇כר] פי [הד̇]א TS Ar 1b.88a > D
508 אלכת̇ TS Ar 1b.88a
509 [מואצ̇ע ... תחתי]ה TS Ar 1b.88a > D | וג' + TS Ar 1b.88a
510 לארבע ... השמים TS Ar 1b.88a > L
511 ארבע ... ותפסירה TS Ar 27.35b > L
512 ראשין TS Ar 27.35b
513 והד̇א אלדי + TS Ar 27.35b
514 עלי מא TS Ar 27.35b > L
515 שהד TS Ar 27.35b | [שו]הד TS Ar 1b.88a > D
516 להא ד TS Ar 27.35b | מן ... ארבע TS Ar 1b.88a > D
517 [מנ]אבר פי [מד]תהם TS Ar 1b.88a > D
518 ותאלת̇ TS Ar 27.35b
519 וראבע TS Ar 27.35b | ואכר פי אלאסכנדריה ואכר TS Ar 1b.88a > D
520 אלאנתסאב TS Ar 27.35b
521 שתא TS Ar 27.35b
522 פי ... אבאנא Oxf 2486.76b > L
523 כקולה TS Ar 27.35b
524 אבאנא ... ויצא TS Ar 1b.88a > D
525 פלשתים End of Oxf 2486.76b
526 שלשה Beginning of Oxf 2486.77a | שמנה TS Ar 27.35b
527 אחד TS Ar 1b.88a + TS Ar 27.35b
528 ראשים ... יפנה Oxf 2486.77a > D
529 עפ[רה ... והראש Oxf 2486.77a > D
530 אל ד[... דר]ך TS Ar 1b.88a > D
531 וג' + TS Ar 1b.88a
532 אל דרך ... המדברה TS Ar 27.35b > L | על גי ... המדברה TS Ar 1b.88a > L
533 וקו̇ TS Ar 1b.88a

ושלטן[534] **יהיב לה** (דניאל 7:6) יריד[535] בה[536] סלטאנא תאמא כמא קאל[537] אולא[538] **ומלכו תליתאה**[539] **אחרי די נחשא די תשלט בכל ארעא**[540] (דניאל 2:39). וקד עלמנא[541] אן דֿא אלקרנין[542] מלך אכתֿר אלעמארה.[543] תֿם קאל[544]

Dn 7:7

בתר דנאחזי הוית בחזוי ליליא וארו חיוא רביעאה דחילא ואימתני ותקיפא יתירא ושנין די פרזל ליה רברבן אכלא ומדקא ושארא ברגליה רפסא והיא משניא מן כל חיותא די קדמיה וקרנין עשר לה.

בעד דֿלך[545] ראית פי רויא אלליל כאן[546] שכֿץ ראבע פזיע[547] היוב שדיד[548] גדא ולה אסנאן[549] כבאר מן חדיד יאכל בהא וידק[550] ואלבאקי ידוסה[551] ברגליה והו מתגֿיר ען סאיר[552] אלאשכֿאץ אלדֿי[553] קבלה[554] ולה עשרה[555] קרון.[556]

תפסיר[557] דֿלך אלממלכה אלראבעה והי מלכות[558] אדום[559] שבההא[560] בגסם עטֿים גדא.[561] ולם יחד[562] מא הו כמא חד[563] פי אלגֿ אלממאלך אלאול[564]

534 ושלטן TS Ar 27.35b > L
535 יר[יד] TS Ar 27.35b > L
536 בהם TS Ar 27.35b | בה TS Ar 1b.88a > L
537 כקולה TS Ar 27.35b
538 אולא TS Ar 27.35b > L
539 סל[טאנא ... תליתאה] TS Ar 1b.88a > D
540 בכל ארעא Oxf 2486.77a > D | תש[לט ... ארעה] TS Ar 27.35b > L
541 על[מנא] TS Ar 27.35b > D
542 [וקד ... קר]נין TS Ar 1b.88a > D
543 אלע[מאר]ה Oxf 2486.77a > D | אלעמארה End of TS Ar 1b.88a
544 ק[אל] Oxf 2486.77a > D | תם קאל TS Ar 27.35b > L
545 דאלך Spiegel + Morag
546 כאן Beginning of the readable part of TS Ar 1b.88b
547 פזע Morag | זרי + TS Ar 1b.88b
548 פזיעא היובא שדידא TS Ar 27.35b
549 היוב ... אסנאן TS Ar 1b.88b > D
550 [ו]ידק TS Ar 27.35b > D
551 ידוסה End of Oxf 2486.77a | [יאכל ... ידוס]ה TS Ar 1b.88b > D
552 סאיר Beginning of the readable part of Oxf 2486.77b
553 אלתי TS Ar 27.35b
554 קבלה TS Ar 27.35b > D
555 י TS Ar 27.35b
556 [ק]ר[ו]ן TS Ar 27.35b > D
557 תפס TS Ar 1b.88b

אנהן[565] כּאלאסד ואלדב[566] ואלנמר. לכנה עטֿמה ופכֿמה[567] פקט.[568] פכאנה[569] יומי אלי אנה[570] ישבה אלפיל. פנקול עלא הדֿא[571] אלימא,[572] פאן[573] כאן ישבה אלפיל פחאל בני יסראל[574] מעה תשבה[575] אלכרכדן אלדֿי הו[576] אהול ואעטֿם מנה אצֿעאפא כמא קאל[577] **אל מוציאם ממצרים כתועפת**[578] **ראם לו**[579] (במ׳ 23:22). ועז בנ֗ יסראל וקותהם ממתֿלה בקרון אלכרכדן כמא קאל[580] **וקרני ראם קרניו בהם עמים ינגח**[581] (דב׳ 33:17). וסמאהא **תועפת**[582] באסם אלגבאל אלעאליה ואלשאהקה[583] כמא קאל[584] **אשר בידו מחקרי ארץ ותועפת**[585] **הרים**[586] **לו**[587] (תה׳ 95:4).

[558] אלד והי מלכ TS Ar 27.35b
[559] א[דו]ם TS Ar 27.35b > D
[560] אלרא[בעה] מל[כות אד]ום [משא]בהא TS Ar 1b.88b > D
[561] גדא TS Ar 27.35b > D
[562] יח[ד] End of the readable part of TS Ar 27.35b
[563] Beginning of TS Ar 28.155a
[564] אלאואיל TS Ar 1b.88b | אלאכר TS Ar 28.155a
[565] אנהן TS Ar 1b.88b > D | אנהם TS Ar 28.155a
[566] אלדוב Oxf 2486.77b | [כאל]אסד [וא]לדב TS Ar 1b.88b > D
[567] עטֿים ופכם TS Ar 28.155a
[568] פקט TS Ar 28.155a > L
[569] כאנה TS Ar 28.155a
[570] אן TS Ar 28.155a
[571] [הד]א TS Ar 1b.88b > D
[572] אלאימא TS Ar 28.155a > L
[573] אן TS Ar 28.155a
[574] יס TS Ar 1b.88b | ישראל TS Ar 28.155a
[575] תתשבה TS Ar 28.155a
[576] הו TS Ar 28.155a > L
[577] כק TS Ar 1b.88b | כקולה TS Ar 28.155a
[578] כתוע TS Ar 1b.88b
[579] כתועפת ראם לו TS Ar 28.155a > L
[580] כק TS Ar 1b.88b | כקולה TS Ar 28.155a
[581] קרניו ... ינגח TS Ar 1b.88b > L | בהם ... ינגח TS Ar 28.155a > L
[582] תועפות TS Ar 28.155a
[583] אלעא[ליה ואלש]הקה TS Ar 1b.88b > D
[584] כק TS Ar 1b.88b | כקולה TS Ar 28.155a
[585] ותועפות TS Ar 28.155a + MT
[586] ה TS Ar 28.155a
[587] ארץ ... לו TS Ar 1b.88b > L

ויכון מעני וצפה להא[588] באנהא[589] **דחילה ואימתני**[590] (דניאל 7:7) אלדׄין[591] המא תרגומי[592] **נורא ואיום** יריד בהמא[593] אנהא[594] תפוק ממלכת באבל אלדׄי קאל[595] פיהא[596] **איום ונורא הוא ממנו משפטו ושׂאיתו יצא**[597] (חבקוק 1:7). ויכון מעני[598] קולה[599] **ותקיפה** (דניאל 7:7) אלדׄי הו תרגום **חזקה** יריד בה[600] אנהא תפוק[601] ממלכה אלפרס אלדׄי קיל פיהא **לכורש אשר החזקתי בימינו לרד לפניו גוים ומתני מלכים אפתח**[602] (יש׳ 45:1). ויכון מעני קולה[603] **יתירה** (דניאל 7:7) יריד בה[604] אנהא תפוק ממלכה[605] אליונאניה אלדׄי[606] קיל פיהא **ותגדל יתר אל הנגב ואל המזרח ואל הצבי**[607] (דניאל 8:9). הדׄה אלמעאני בעד[608] צפאת מתׄלהא פי גסמהא. יכון מעני **דחילה**[609] (דניאל 7:7) שיא[610] יתבין פי אלעינין מן קוה וקצד. ומעני **אימתני**[611] (דניאל 7:7) וחשה פי שכלהא[612] ותכׄטיטהא.[613] ומעני **תקיפא** (דניאל 7:7) צלאבה ותׄכׄאנה פי

[588] מע וצפה לה TS Ar 28.155a
[589] באנהא TS Ar 28.155a > L
[590] ו[אי]מתני TS Ar 1b.88b > D | ואמתני TS Ar 28.155a
[591] אללדין Oxf 2486.77b | אלדי[ן] TS Ar 28.155a > D
[592] הן תרגום TS Ar 28.155a
[593] בהמא End of Oxf 2486.77b
[594] אנהא Beginning of Oxf 2486.78a
[595] קיל TS Ar 28.155a
[596] באבל ... פיהא Oxf 2486.78a > D
[597] משפטו ... יצא TS Ar 28.155a > L
[598] מעני TS Ar 28.155a > D
[599] קולה TS Ar 28.155a > L
[600] בהא TS Ar 28.155a
[601] תפוק ממלכה ... תפוק ממלכה TS Ar 1b.88b > L homeoteleuton
[602] בימינו ... אפתח TS Ar 1b.88b > L | לרד ... אפתח TS Ar 28.155a > L
[603] ויך מעני קו TS Ar 1b.88b
[604] יריד בה TS Ar 28.155a > L
[605] ממלכה TS Ar 28.155a and TS Ar 1b.88b > L
[606] אלתי TS Ar 1b.88b
[607] ואל המזרח ואל הצבי TS Ar 1b.88b > L | הצבי TS Ar 28.155a > L
[608] בעד TS Ar 28.155a > D
[609] [דחי]לה TS Ar 1b.88b > D
[610] שי TS Ar 28.155a + TS Ar 1b.88b
[611] המיתני TS Ar 1b.88b
[612] עלי [אנ]ה וחש[ה] פי [שכל]הא TS Ar 1b.88b > D
[613] ותכטיטהא TS Ar 28.155a > D

אעצ׳איהא.[614] ומעני[615] **יתירה** (דניאל 7:7) זיאדה[616] עלי מא גרת בה אלעאדאת[617] אלמתעארפה.[618]

ותפסיר[619] אלאנסאן קוה ותאיד. וכונהא מן חדיד אשד להא ואות׳ק.[620] ומוצ׳ע[621] תמת׳יל ד׳לך קולה[622] **אלהים**[623] **הרס שנימו בפימו**[624] **מלעתות**[625] **כפירים נתץ**[626] **יוי** (תה׳ 58:7). וקאל[627] קבלה **שני רשעים שברת**[628] (תה׳ 3:8) ומא שאבה ד׳לך. וזאד פי קצץ אלרויא עלי אלמלאך לאן[629] אלמכ׳אליב[630] מן נחאס. ד׳אך קולה[631] **וטפריה**[632] **די נחש** (דניאל 7:19). פעלמנא אן הד׳א אלקול כאן פי אלאצל ואנמא אכ׳תצרה. ותפסיר ד׳לך גראה[633] ואקדאם ובטש[634] כמא קאל[635] פי אלתמת׳יל הנאך **קומי ודשי בת ציון כי קרנך אשים ברזל ופרסותיך אשים נחושה והדקות עמים רבים**[636] (מיכה 4:13). ותפסיר **אכלה ומדקה**[637] (דניאל 7:7) יריד בה אסתג׳ראק מא יחצל פי ידהא מן סלב אלאעדא ונהבהם.[638]

[614] אעטאיהא TS Ar 28.155a
[615] ומעני תקיפה ... ומעני יתירה TS Ar 1b.88b > L homeoteleuton | ומענא TS Ar 28.155a
[616] [זי]אדה TS Ar 1b.88b > D
[617] גרת בה אלעאדאת TS Ar 1b.88b > D
[618] אלמתעארפ[ה] TS Ar 28.155a > D
[619] ותפס TS Ar 1b.88b | ותפסר TS Ar 28.155a
[620] אשד לה ואותק TS Ar 1b.88b > D | ואו[ת]ק TS Ar 28.155a > D
[621] ומעני TS Ar 1b.88b
[622] קולה End of Oxf 2486.78a | קולה TS Ar 28.155a > L
[623] אלים TS Ar 28.155a
[624] ב[פימו] TS Ar 1b.88b > D | שנימ[ו בפימו] TS Ar 28.155a > D
[625] [מלעתו]ת Beginning of the readable part of Oxf 2486.78b
[626] מלעתות ... נתץ TS Ar 28.155a and TS Ar 1b.88b > L
[627] וקול[ה] TS Ar 28.155a > D
[628] רשעים שברת TS Ar 1b.88b > D
[629] אן TS Ar 28.155a + TS Ar 1b.88b
[630] אן אלמכליב Oxf 2486.78b
[631] אל[מכאלב ... קולה] TS Ar 1b.88b > D | [ו]דאך [ק]ול[ה] TS Ar 28.155a > D
[632] וטפרה TS Ar 28.155a + TS Ar 1b.88b
[633] גרה Oxf 2486.78b | אלאצל ... גראה TS Ar 1b.88b > D
[634] בט[ש] TS Ar 28.155a > D
[635] כק TS Ar 1b.88b | כקולה TS Ar 1b.88b
[636] כי ... רבים TS Ar 28.155a > L
[637] קוצי ... ומדקה TS Ar 1b.88b > D
[638] כקולה + TS Ar 28.155a

ושביה במא קאל לישׂראל[639] **יאכל גוים**[640] **צריו ועצמתיהם יגרם**[641] (במ׳ 24:8). ותפסיר[642] **ושארא ברגליה רפסה** (דניאל 7:7) מא יתבקא מן אמואל אלקרי ואלמלוך אלמחארבה[643] להא ממן[644] לם יפתח בין ידיהא ולם יטעהא.[645] פהי אמא אן תצׄרבה באלנאר[646] ואמא אן[647] תגׄרקה באלמא או תתלפה[648] באחד[649] וגוה[650] אלאתלאף. והדׄא כמא[651] קאל[652] לישׂראל פי קצה **ואם**[653] **לא תשלים עמך**[654] (דב׳ 20:12) אלי[655] אכׄרהא. וקד יכון איצׄא[656] יחתמל[657] קולה[658] **ושארא**[659] **ברגלה**[660] **רפסה**[661] (דניאל 7:7) עלי סביל אלבדׄל ואלבטר כמא קאל[662] **המעט מכם המרעה הטוב**[663] **תרעו ויתר מרעיכם תרמסו ברגליכם ומשקע מים תשתו ואת הנותרים ברגליכם תרפסון**[664]

639 ושביה ... לישׂראל TS Ar 28.155a > L

640 ונה[בהם ... גו]ים TS Ar 1b.88b > D

641 ועצמתיהם יגרם TS Ar 28.155a and TS Ar 1b.88b > L

642 ותפס TS Ar 1b.88b

643 ואלמחארבה TS Ar 28.155a

644 אמו[אל ... ממן] TS Ar 1b.88b > D

645 יעטהא TS Ar 1b.88b | יעדמא אלסאעה TS Ar 28.155a

646 או + TS Ar 28.155a

647 ואמא אן TS Ar 28.155a > L

648 תצׄרבה ... תתלפה TS Ar 1b.88b > D

649 באחד End of Oxf 2486.78b | באחדי TS Ar 1b.88b

650 וגוה Beginning of Oxf 2486.79a

651 כמא End of the readable part of TS Ar 1b.88b

652 אלא[תלאף ... קאל] Oxf 2486.79a > D

653 אם Oxf 2486.79a

654 עמך TS Ar 28.155a > L

655 אלי Beginning of TS Ar 23.11a

656 יכן איצ TS Ar 23.11a

657 י[חתמ]ל Oxf 2486.79a > D

658 קול TS Ar 28.155a | קו TS Ar 23.11a

659 ושארה TS Ar 23.11a

660 [ב]רג[לה] TS Ar 23.11a > D

661 רפסא TS Ar 23.11a

662 כקולה TS Ar 28.155a | אל[ב]ד[ך ואלבטר כמא קאל] TS Ar 23.11a > D

663 המֹ טוב TS Ar 28.155a

664 ויתר ... תרפסון TS Ar 28.155a > L | הטוב ... תרפסון TS Ar 23.11a > L

(יחז' 34:18). ותפסיר[665] **והיא**[666] **משניא מן כל**[667] **חיותא**[668] **די קדמה**[669] (דניאל 7:7) מכׄאלפה פי מדׄאהב[670] אדיאנהם ולבאסהם ואבניתהם ומא[671] יזרון עלי אלאמה כמא קדמנא.[672] ויחתמל איצׄא[673] אן יצרף אלי מדה מקאמהא. אי אנהא תטול[674] אלי אכתׄר מן מדד אלתׄלתׄ[675] ממלך אלמתקדמה[676] מגמועהא.[677] ודׄלך אן[678] מדד אלגׄ מגמועה תכון שׄ סנה וסנתין. מנהא סבעין[679] לבבל, נבׄ ללפרס,[680] וקׄפׄ[681] ליון. וממלכה אדום אכתׄר מן הדׄא אלמגמוע לאנהא אקאמת[682] כׄמס מאיה אתׄנין וכׄמסין[683] סנה.

ותפסיר[684] **וקרנין עשׂר**[685] **לה**[686] (דניאל 7:7) אולה ובדיהתה[687] מלוך כמא[688] פסר אלמלאך[689] לדניאל וקאל **וקרניא עשר**[690] **מנה מלכותא עשׂרה מלכין**[691]

[665] ותפס TS Ar 23.11a
[666] היא TS Ar 28.155a
[667] מכל TS Ar 23.11a + TS Ar 28.155a + Oxf 2486.79a
[668] [חיו]תא TS Ar 23.11a > D
[669] קדמא TS Ar 28.155a
[670] מדאהב TS Ar 23.11a > L
[671] ובמא TS Ar 28.155a
[672] אל[אמה] כמׄ קדמ[נא] TS Ar 23.11a > D
[673] י[חתמ]ל איצׄ TS Ar 23.11a > D
[674] תטיל TS Ar 23.11a
[675] אלגׄ TS Ar 23.11a + TS Ar 28.155a
[676] אלמת[קדמ]ה TS Ar 28.155a > D | אל[מתקדמ]ה TS Ar 23.11a > D
[677] מגמועה TS Ar 23.11a + TS Ar 28.155a
[678] ודלך TS Ar 23.11a > D
[679] עׄ TS Ar 23.11a + TS Ar 28.155a
[680] לפרס TS Ar 23.11a + Oxf 2486.79a
[681] קפ TS Ar 23.11a + Oxf 2486.79a
[682] קאמת TS Ar 28.155a
[683] תקנׄב TS Ar 23.11a + TS Ar 28.155a
[684] ותפס TS Ar 23.11a
[685] עשׂר End of Oxf 2486.79a
[686] ל[ה] Beginning of Oxf 2486.79b
[687] ובדיה TS Ar 28.155a | ובדיהתה TS Ar 23.11a
[688] כמׄ TS Ar 23.11a
[689] [אולה ... אלמ]לאך Oxf 2486.79b > D
[690] וקאל ... עשׂר Oxf 2486.79b > D
[691] מלׄ TS Ar 28.155a

יקומון[692] (דניאל 7:24). ועלי מא קאל **שם אצמי**[693] **קרן לדויד**[694] (תה׳ 132:17). וקאל[695] איצ̇א[696] **וירם**[697] **קרן משיחו** (שמ״א 2:10). פאן קאל קאיל פקד[698] קאם לאדום פי הד̇ה אלסנין אלמד̇כורה[699] אכת̇ר מן ל̇ מלך קלנא יסתקים אן יכון[700] אומי [701] אלי אלאגלא מנהם ותרך אלבאקי. וימכן אן יכון[702] קצד אלי[703] אלאבא מנהם אלד̇ין הם אבתדי ותרך[704] אלבנין. וימכן אן יכון קצד אלד̇ין[705] כאנו מן עשאיר מכ̇תלפה ותרך אללד̇ין[706] מן עתרה ואחדה. פאי פן מן הד̇ה אלג̇ פנון[707] אכ̇רגנאה מן אלגמלה כאן אלבאקי[708] עשר[709] מלוך פקט. ויחתמל מע ד̇אך אן[710] יכון ישיר בהד̇ה אלקרון אלי בלדאן[711] חצינה ות̇יקה כמא וגדנא אלמוצ̇ע אלצלב יסמי קרן [712] אד̇ קאל **כרם היה לידידי**[713] **בקרן**[714] **בן**[715] **שמן** (יש׳ 5:1). פיכון[716] תפסיר **וקרנין עשר לה** (דניאל 7:7) אן אדום[717]

692 יקומון TS Ar 23.11a > L | מלכותא ... יקומון TS Ar 28.155a > L

693 שם אצמיח TS Ar 23.11a > D

694 לדוד TS Ar 28.155a | לד TS Ar 23.11a

695 כמא קאל TS Ar 28.155a

696 איצ̇ TS Ar 23.11a

697 וְיָרֶם TS Ar 23.11a

698 פאדא קד TS Ar 28.155a

699 אלסנין אלמדכורה TS Ar 23.11a > D

700 יכן TS Ar 23.11a

701 אלי אן יומי TS Ar 28.155a

702 אשאר + TS Ar 28.155a | יכן TS Ar 23.11a

703 קצד אלי TS Ar 23.11a > D

704 אבתדי ותרך TS Ar 28.155a > D

705 אללד̇ין Oxf 2486.79b

706 אללד̇ין Oxf 2486.79b

707 אלסנין Oxf 2486.79b

708 אל[בא]קי TS Ar 23.11a > D

709 י̇ TS Ar 23.11a

710 אן TS Ar 28.155a > L

711 אלקרון אלי בלדאן TS Ar 28.155a > D

712 אלסלב וסמי קרנא TS Ar 28.155a

713 כרם ... לידידי TS Ar 28.155a > L

714 [ב]קרן TS Ar 28.155a > D

715 ב TS Ar 23.11a

716 פיכן TS Ar 23.11a

717 אלאדום TS Ar 28.155a

תפתח עשר[718] בלדאן עט̇ימה.[719] והד̇א שיא[720] ענינא בה[721] חתי[722] סאלנא[723] ענה מן[724] נת̇ק בה[725] וחסבנאהא[726] פוגדנאהא[727] כד̇אך. פאן קאל קאיל איצ̇א[728] פאן[729] תחת יד[730] אדום בלדאנא[731] כת̇ירה אכת̇ר[732] מן קנ̇ בלד עט̇ים[733] קלנא יסתקים אן יכון[734] אראד אלט̇אהרה[735] אלמחיטה באלחדוד ותרך מא בין ד̇לך. כמא[736] נקול[737] אן יהושע אנמא אחצי[738] מן בלד אלשאם אלקרי ואלמדן אלמחיטה באלחדוד[739] ותרך מא בין[740] ד̇לך כמא קאל[741] **וערי מבצר הצדים**[742] **צר**[743] **וחמת רקת וכנרת**[744] (יהושע 19:35). ת̇ם קאל[745]

[718] י׳ TS Ar 23.11a + TS Ar 28.155a
[719] ות̇יקה + TS Ar 28.155a
[720] ובדא שי TS Ar 23.11a
[721] בה End of Oxf 2486.79b
[722] חתי Beginning of Oxf 2486.80a
[723] סלנא TS Ar 23.11a
[724] ענה מן TS Ar 28.155a > D
[725] סאלנא ... בה Oxf 2486.80a > D
[726] וח[סבנאהא] TS Ar 23.11a > D
[727] ווג[דנאהא] TS Ar 28.155a > D
[728] איצ̇ TS Ar 23.11a
[729] אן TS Ar 28.155a
[730] אידי Oxf 2486.80a | יד TS Ar 28.155a | ידי TS Ar 23.11a
[731] אלרום בלדאן TS Ar 28.155a
[732] אכת̇ר TS Ar 23.11a
[733] בלדא עצ̇ימא TS Ar 28.155a
[734] תכון TS Ar 28.155a | יך TS Ar 23.11a
[735] אלט̇אהרה אלמחיטה TS Ar 28.155a > D
[736] כמ̇ TS Ar 23.11a
[737] כקולה וערי כמא נקול TS Ar 28.155a
[738] אחצא TS Ar 23.11a + TS Ar 28.155a
[739] באלחד[וד] TS Ar 23.11a
[740] מ[א ב]ין TS Ar 23.11a > D
[741] כקולה TS Ar 28.155a
[742] דלך ... הצדים TS Ar 23.11a > D
[743] וג׳ + TS Ar 23.11a
[744] ותמת ... וכנרת TS Ar 23.11a > D
[745] ותמת ... קאל TS Ar 28.155a > L

Dn 7:8

משׂתכיל הוית בקרניא ואלו קרן אוחרי זעירא סליקת ביניהון ותלת מן קרניא קדמיתא אתעקרא מן קדמיא ואלו עינין כעיני אנשא בקרנא דא ופום ממליל רברבן.

ובינמא[746] אנא מתפרס[747] פי תלך אלקרון פאדֹא[748] בקרן[749] צגֹיר[750] קד נבת פימא[751] בינהא[752] ותֹלאתֹה[753] מן אלקרון אלאולי[754] אנקלעת[755] מן בין ידיה וכאן[756] לה[757] עיון[758] כעיון אלנאס פי[759] דֹלך[760] אלקרין[761] ופם יתכלם באלכבאיר.[762]

תפסיר[763] הדֹא[764] אלקרין אלצגֹיר אלאמה אלאכֹרי[765] אלתי תשארך[766] אדום[767] ותמלך[768] תבעהא בלד אלשאם. פקולנא[769] ״תשארך אדום״[770] לקולה

[746] ובין מא Morag | פבין Spiegel
[747] מתפסר Morag | מתפכר Spiegel
[748] פאדי Morag
[749] בקרין TS Ar 28.155a | בקרין אכר Spiegel
[750] סגֹיר Spiegel
[751] פימא TS Ar 28.155a > L | מת[פרס ... פימא] TS Ar 23.11a > D | פי מא Spiegel
[752] בינהמא Morag
[753] ותלתה Oxf 2486.80a | וגֹ TS Ar 23.11a + TS Ar 28.155a
[754] אלאולי Morag > L | אלאול Oxf 2486.80a
[755] קד אנקדת TS Ar 28.155a
[756] וכאן Morag > L
[757] לה Spiegel and TS Ar 28.155a and Oxf 2486.80a > L
[758] עיונא TS Ar 28.155a
[759] בי[ן יד]יה [וכאן ... פי] TS Ar 23.11a > D
[760] דֹאך TS Ar 23.11a + Oxf 2486.80a | תלך TS Ar 28.155a
[761] אלקרון TS Ar 28.155a
[762] באלכבאיר End of Oxf 2486.80a | דניא 7:8 TS Ar 23.11a > L
[763] תפס TS Ar 23.11a
[764] הדא TS Ar 23.11a > D
[765] אלאכֹ[י]רה TS Ar 28.155a | [אלצגֹיר ... אלאכֹ]רי TS Ar 23.11a > D
[766] תשארך End of TS Ar 28.155a
[767] אלרום Beginning of TS Ar 28.155b
[768] ותמלך Beginning of the readable part of Oxf 2486.80b
[769] קלנא TS Ar 23.11a + TS Ar 28.155b
[770] אדום TS Ar 28.155b > L

האהנא[771] **ביניהון** (דניאל 7:8). וקולנא[772] "תבעהא" לקולה[773] הנאך **יקום אחריהן** (דניאל 7:24). וזיאדתה[774] פי אלוצף **משׂתכל** (דניאל 7:8) ופסרנאה "בינמא".[775] יריד בה אן[776] אדום אסר ומא כאנת ואקד עינא[777] חתי תגׄלב עליהא אלאמה. ושביה בהדׄא קיל לאדום[778] **אם גנבים באו לך אם שדדי לילה איך נדמית הלא יגנבו דים**[779] (עבדיה 5). ויכון[780] מעני **ותלת מן קרניא קדמיתא אתעקרו**[781] (דניאל 7:8) עלי[782] אלתפסיר אלאול,[783] אן[784] הדׄה אלממלכה[785] תטׄפר מן אדום בתׄלת[786] מלוך. ועלי אלתפסיר אלתׄאני[787] אנהא תפתח מן בלדאנהא[788] גׄ בלדאן. והדׄא משאהד[789] לאנהא פתחת ממא[790] פי יד אדום[791] בלד אלשאם ובלד[792] מצר[793] ובלד אפריקיה.[794] ואמא[795] סאיר[796]

[771] הנאך TS Ar 28.155b
[772] [תשארך ... וקו]לנא TS Ar 23.11a > D
[773] לקו TS Ar 23.11a
[774] אחרי[הן] וזיאד[תה] TS Ar 28.155b > D
[775] ופסרנתה בינהמא TS Ar 28.155b
[776] פי ... אן TS Ar 23.11a > D
[777] אן אסד מא כאנת אדום ואטקד עינא TS Ar 23.11a
[778] אלאמה ... לאדום TS Ar 23.11a > D
[779] אם שדדי ... דים TS Ar 23.11a and TS Ar 28.155b > L
[780] ויכן TS Ar 23.11a | End of TS Ar 23.11a
[781] אתעקרה TS Ar 28.155b
[782] עלי Beginning of the readable part of TS Ar 23.11b
[783] [אלתפסיר אלאו]ל TS Ar 23.11b > D
[784] מן TS Ar 28.155b
[785] [אלממ]לכה TS Ar 23.11a > D
[786] בגׄ TS Ar 23.11b + TS Ar 28.155b
[787] אלתפסיר אלתׄאני TS Ar 23.11b > D
[788] תפתח מן בלדאנהא TS Ar 23.11b > D
[789] מ[שא]הד TS Ar 23.11a > D
[790] מא TS Ar 28.155b
[791] אלאדום TS Ar 28.155b | אדום TS Ar 23.11a > D
[792] אלרום + TS Ar 28.155b
[793] מצר TS Ar 28.155b > L
[794] אל[שאם ובלד מצר ובלד אפ]רקיה TS Ar 23.11b > D
[795] ואמא TS Ar 28.155b > L
[796] וסאיר TS Ar 28.155b

אלבלדאן פמן יד אלפרס אכ̇דתהא.[797] פאן ט̇ן[798] ט̇אן אן הד̇א[799] אלתפסיר[800] אלב̇, אן אלקרון בלדאן הו[801] מכ̇אלף למא פסרה אלמלאך פקאל **ותלתה**[802] **מלכין יהשפל**[803] (דניאל 7:24) קלנא לאנה קד סמי[804] אלממאלך מלוכא אד̇ קאל **וארבעה**[805] **מלכין** (דניאל 7:17). וקאל **מלכו רביעה תהוא**[806] **בארעא די משנא מן כל מלכותא**[807] (דניאל 7:23).

ותפסיר[808] **ואלו**[809] **עינין כעיני**[810] **אנשא בקרנא דא** (דניאל 7:8)[811] אלעיון עלם ופקה ואחכאם וחכמה כמא קאל[812] **החכם עיניו בראשו** (קהלת 2:14). וקאל איצ̇א פי תמת̇יל אלחכמה[813] באלעיון **וטוב לעינים לראות את**[814] **השמש**[815] (קהלת 11:7). וקאל איצ̇א[816] פי[817] תמת̇יל אלנביין באלעיון **כי נסך עליכם יוי**[818] **רוח תרדמה ויעצם את עיניכם**[819] **את הנביאים**[820] (יש׳

[797] [אכ̇דתה]א TS Ar 23.11b > D
[798] [ט̇]ן TS Ar 23.11b > D
[799] הד̇א End of Oxf 2486.80b ׀ [אן הד̇]א TS Ar 23.11b > D
[800] אלתפסיר Beginning of Oxf 2486.81a
[801] אלת̇אני ... הו Oxf 2486.81a > D
[802] ותלתה TS Ar 23.11b > D
[803] יהש TS Ar 28.155b ׀ יהשפל TS Ar 23.11b > L
[804] סמא TS Ar 28.155b
[805] ארבעה TS Ar 28.155b ׀ וד TS Ar 23.11b
[806] תהוא TS Ar 23.11b > D
[807] די ... מלכותא TS Ar 28.155b > L ׀ בארעה ... מלכותא TS Ar 23.11b > L
[808] ותפסיר TS Ar 23.11b > D
[809] ואלן TS Ar 28.155b
[810] כעינין TS Ar 23.11b
[811] בקרנא דא TS Ar 23.11b > L
[812] כקולה TS Ar 28.155b ׀ כק TS Ar 23.11b
[813] [וקאל ...פ]י ת[מת̇י]ל [אלח]כמה TS Ar 23.11b > D
[814] את Oxf 2486.81a > L
[815] לראות את השמש TS Ar 23.11b > L
[816] וקאל איצ̇א TS Ar 28.155b > L ׀ איצ TS Ar 23.11b
[817] ופי TS Ar 28.155b
[818] יוי עליכם TS Ar 28.155b ׀ עליכם יוי TS Ar 23.11b > D
[819] תרד ויע א עי׳ TS Ar 23.11b
[820] רוח ... הנביאים TS Ar 28.155b > L ׀ את הניביאים TS Ar 23.11b > L

29:10). ותפסיר[821] **ופם**[822] **ממלל רברבן** (דניאל 7:8) כלאם שנע וטען יתכלם בהא[823] אלכפאר[824] מן אדום ותאבעיהא[825] עלי רב[826] בני אסראיל[827] ועליהם. לאן אלכלאם[828] באלעטׄאים הדׄא[829] מענאה כמא קאל[830] **יכרת יוי כל שׂפתי חלקות לשון מדברת גדולות**[831] (תה׳ 12:4). וכדׄלך אלכלאם באלשואמךׄ הדׄא מענאה כמא קאל[832] **אל תרבו תדברו**[833] **גבוהה**[834] **גבוהה**[835] **יצא עתק מפיכם**[836] (שמ״א 2:3). תׄם קאל

Dn 7:9

חזי[837] היות עד די כורסון רמיו ועתיק יומין יתיב לבושיה כתלג חיור ושער ראשיה כעמר נקי כורסיה שביבין די נור גלגלוהי נור דליק.

תׄם ראית כאן[838] כראסי[839] קד[840] טרחת וכאן שיכׄא קד גלס פוקהא[841] לבאסה[842] כאלתׄלג אלאביץׄ[843] ושער ראסה אביץׄ כאלצוף וכרסיה[844] מן נאר[845] להא[846] שעאע ולואלבה נאר משתעלה.

[821] ותפס[יר] TS Ar 28.155b > D ׀ ותפס TS Ar 23.11b

[822] פם Oxf 2486.81a

[823] בה TS Ar 23.11b

[824] אל[כפאר] TS Ar 23.11b > D

[825] ותאבעיהא TS Ar 28.155b > L

[826] אלעאלמין + TS Ar 23.11b

[827] בני אסראיל TS Ar 23.11b > L

[828] צול[...] או[...] TS Ar 28.155b

[829] הדה TS Ar 23.11b

[830] כקולה TS Ar 28.155b ׀ כמק TS Ar 23.11b

[831] לשון ... גדולות TS Ar 28.155b > L ׀ לש מד גד TS Ar 23.11b

[832] כקולה TS Ar 28.155b ׀ כק TS Ar 23.11b

[833] תדברו TS Ar 23.11b > D

[834] גבוהה End of Oxf 2486.81a

[835] גב וג׳ TS Ar 23.11b

[836] יצא ... מפיכם TS Ar 23.11b and TS Ar 28.155b > L

[837] חזי Beginnig of the readable part of Oxf 2486.81b

[838] כאן Morag > L

[839] כרסיא TS Ar 28.155b

[840] קד TS Ar 28.155b > L

[841] עליהא TS Ar 23.11b

[842] ולבאסה Spiegel + TS Ar 23.11b

[843] אביץׄ כאלתׄלג TS Ar 23.11b + TS Ar 28.155b

[844] וכראסיה Morag

[845] מן נאר Morag > L ׀ אלנאר TS Ar 23.11b

Dn 7:10

נהר די נור נגיד ונפיק מן קדמוהי אלף אלפין ישמשוניה ורבו רבון קדמוהי יקומון דינא יתיב וספרין פתיחו.

ונהר מן נאר יגרי[847] ויכ̇רג[848] מן[849] בין ידיה[850] ואלף אלוף יכ̇דמונה[851] ורבוה רבואת[852] יקומון[853] מן[854] בין ידיה וקד וצ̇ע אלחכם ונשרת אלדואוין.[855]

אקול פי תפסיר[856] הד̇ין אלפסוקין אנה למא[857] כאן פיהמא ד̇כר כרסי ניראן[858] וחכם[859] ודואוין[860] תוהם קום מן אמתנא[861] אנהא אוצאף אלכ̇אלק תברך[862] ותעאלי מן ג̇יר תשניע.[863] וקום[864] מן ג̇יר אמתנא שנעו[865] עלינא בד̇לך[866] וגעלוהא[867] תשביהא ותגסימא.[868] וקום[869] אכ̇רון תאולוה[870] עלי אמה

[846] לה Spiegel + TS Ar 28.155b

[847] יגר TS Ar 23.11b

[848] ויכרג Spiegel and TS Ar 23.11b and TS Ar 28.155b > L

[849] מן TS Ar 23.11b and TS Ar 28.155b > L

[850] ויכרג Spiegel and TS Ar 23.11b and TS Ar 28.155b +

[851] יכדמונה Morag > L

[852] ורבואת רבואת Spiegel + TS Ar 23.11b + TS Ar 28.155b

[853] יקומו TS Ar 23.11b

[854] מן Spiegel and TS Ar 23.11b and TS Ar 28.155b > L

[855] אלדיאוין Spiegel + Morag | אלדאין TS Ar 28.155b

[856] פי תפסיר TS Ar 28.155b > L | תפס TS Ar 23.11b

[857] ל[מא] אן פ[יהמ]א ד[כ]ר כ[רס]י Oxf 2486.81b > D

[858] וניראן End of Oxf 2486.81b

[859] וחכם Beginning of Oxf 2486.7a

[860] ודואין TS Ar 28.155b

[861] ק[ום מ]ן א[מתנא] TS Ar 23.11b > D

[862] תבארך TS Ar 23.11b + TS Ar 28.155b

[863] תשנוע TS Ar 23.11b

[864] וקומא Oxf 2486.7a | וקום TS Ar 28.155b > L

[865] [ש]נעו TS Ar 28.155b > D

[866] דלך TS Ar 28.155b > L

[867] ו[גע]לה TS Ar 28.155b > D | עלינא ... וגעלוהא TS Ar 23.11b > D

[868] [ותג]סימא TS Ar 23.11b > D

[869] וקומא Oxf 2486.7a

[870] תאולה TS Ar 28.155b | תוהמוה TS Ar 23.11b

בני יסראיל[871] וגעלו הדׄה[872] אוצאפה. פנקול[873] ובאללה נסתעין[874] אמא נסב הדׄה אלקצה אלי בני אסראיל פאנה[875] גׄיר מסתקים מן אגל אן ולי[876] הדׄה[877] אלקצה[878] יסלם[879] אלמלך ויעקדה ללמושיע אלדׄי ננתטׄרה[880] אדׄ הו אעלי מנה.

פלא יגוז[881] אן תכון[882] אלאמה[883] תולי אלמושיע[884] הדׄה אלולאיה אדׄ הי אדון מנה ותחת ידה.[885] ובאלחרי אן יכון נסב הדׄה אלקצה[886] אלי אלכׄאלק גל ועז אלי טריק אלתגסים ואלתשביה[887] גׄיר[888] מסתקים אדׄ הו כׄאלק כל גסם וכל גוהר וכל ערץׄ. פלא[889] יגוז אן יכון פיה שיא[890] ממא כׄלקה. וממא דלת אלכתב[891] עלי אנה לא שיא[892] ישבהה ממא פי אלסמא[893] קולהא[894] **כי מי**[895] **בשחק יערך**[896] **ליוי**[897] **ידמה ליוי בבני אלים**[898] (תה׳ 89:7). ולא[899] שיא[900]

871 ישׂראל TS Ar 28.155b
872 הדא TS Ar 28.155b
873 וגעל[ו ... פנקול] TS Ar 23.11b > D
874 אלתופיק TS Ar 23.11b + TS Ar 28.155b
875 ישׂראל אנה TS Ar 28.155b
876 ולי TS Ar 28.155b
877 בני יסראיל ... הדה TS Ar 23.11b > D
878 אל[קצ]ה TS Ar 28.155b > D
879 וסלם TS Ar 28.155b
880 נחן מנתטריה TS Ar 23.11b
881 [אד ... י]גוז TS Ar 23.11b > D
882 תכן TS Ar 23.11b
883 [אלא]מה TS Ar 23.11b > D
884 ללמושיע ... אלמושיע TS Ar 28.155b > L homeoteleuton
885 ידה ... אלקצה TS Ar 23.11b > D
886 אלקצה TS Ar 28.155b > D | ידה ... אלקצה TS Ar 23.11b > D
887 אלתשביה ואלתגסים TS Ar 23.11b
888 גׄ[יר] TS Ar 23.11b > D and TS Ar 28.155b > D
889 [מסתקים ... פ]לא TS Ar 23.11b > D
890 שי TS Ar 23.11b
891 ערץ ... אלכתאב TS Ar 28.155b > L
892 ו[ממא ... שיא] TS Ar 28.155b > D
893 [אלס]מא TS Ar 23.11b > D
894 קולהא End of the readable part of TS Ar 23.11b
895 כי מי Oxf 2486.7a > D
896 [יער]ך Oxf 2486.7a > D | ויערך End of Oxf 2486.7a
897 ליוי Beginning of Oxf 2486.7b | ל[יוי] Oxf 2486.7b > D
898 ידמה ... אלים TS Ar 28.155b > L
899 ולא Beginning of TS Ar 23.11c

ישבהה ממא פי אלארץ̇ ד̇אך[901] קולה[902] **ואל מי תדמיון אל ומה דמות תערכו לו**[903] (יש׳ 40:18). ועלי אן גמיע אלאעראץ̇ מנפיה[904] ענה ד̇אך[905] קולה[906] **לא ייעף ולא ייגע ואין חקר לתבונתו**[907] (יש׳ 40:28). ואיצ̇א קולה[908] **הנה**[909] **לא ינום ולא יישן שומר ישראל**[910] (תה׳ 121:4). ועלי אנה כ̇פי מן גהה אלרויא[911] וט̇אהר[912] מן גהה אלפעל לקולהא[913] **אכן**[914] **אתה אל מסתתר אלהי ישראל מושיע**[915] (יש׳ 45:15). פקולה **מסתתר**[916] ישיר[917] אלי אלד̇את וקולה[918] **מושיע** ישיר אלי אלפעל.

ולכן[919] אלקול אלצחיח[920] אן אלשכ̇ץ̇ אלמד̇כור פי הד̇ה אלקצה הו נור אבתדאה[921] אלכ̇אלק לידל נביה בה עלי אן הד̇ה אלאקואל הי מן ענדה. והד̇א אלמעני[922] יצח[923] למלתמסה בארבע[924] מקדמאת. אלמקדמה אלאולי[925] אן[926]

[900] ולא שי Oxf 2486.7b > D
[901] דאך TS Ar 23.11c > L
[902] וכקולה TS Ar 23.11c | קו TS Ar 23.11c
[903] ומה ... לו TS Ar 28.155b > L | אל ... לו TS Ar 23.11c > L
[904] ומה ... מנפיה TS Ar 23.11c > D
[905] דאך TS Ar 23.11c > L
[906] אערא[ץ] מנפי[ה ענה] כק[ולה] TS Ar 28.155b > D | קו TS Ar 23.11c
[907] ואין חקר לתבונתו TS Ar 23.11c and TS Ar 28.155b > L
[908] ואיצא קולה TS Ar 28.155b > L | ואיצ קו TS Ar 23.11c
[909] והנה TS Ar 28.155b
[910] שומר ישראל ועלי TS Ar 28.155b > L
[911] הנה ... אלרויה TS Ar 23.11c > D | אלרו[י]א TS Ar 28.155b > D
[912] ושאהד TS Ar 28.155b
[913] קולהא TS Ar 23.11c + TS Ar 28.155b
[914] אכן TS Ar 28.155b > D
[915] אלהי ... מושיע TS Ar 28.155b > L
[916] פקולה מסתתר TS Ar 23.11c > L
[917] אלהי ... ישיר TS Ar 23.11c > D
[918] אל[ד]את וקולה TS Ar 23.11c > D
[919] ולכון TS Ar 28.155b
[920] [אל]צחיח TS Ar 28.155b
[921] הו ... אבתדאה TS Ar 23.11c > D
[922] אלמענא TS Ar 28.155b | אלמע[ני] TS Ar 23.11c > D
[923] יצף TS Ar 28.155b
[924] יצח ... בארבע TS Ar 23.11c > D | בד TS Ar 28.155b
[925] אלא[ולי] TS Ar 28.155b > D
[926] יכון + TS Ar 28.155b

כל נבי יחתאג אלי עלאמה יצח לה בהא אן[927] אלכלאם אלדׄי[928] יסמעה[929] הו מן ענד אללה. פאמא אן תכון אלעלאמה[930] אסטואנה[931] מן סחאב[932] מנתצבה בלאקרב מע אן[933] סאיר[934] אלגו נקי והדׄא[935] הו **עמוד ענן** כמא יקול[936] פי משה ואהרון ושמואל[937] **בעמוד ענן ידבר אלהים**[938] (תה׳ 99:7). ואמא אן תכון אלעלאמה נורא עמומיא[939] ליס הו מן אלשמס ולא מן[940] אלקמר[941] ולא מן סאיר אלניראת אלמתערפה[942] כמא משרוח פי כתׄיר מן אלאנביא אנהם ראו[943] **כבוד יוי**. ואן תכון תלך אלעלאמה תבתדי[944] מע אבתדא[945] אלכלאם ותנקצׄי מע אנקצׄאיה. פלא ישך אלנבי חינידׄ פי אנהא אנמא טׄהרת לה ליצח ענדה[946] אן אלצות אלדׄי סמעה הו מן ענד רבה.[947]

ואלמקדמה אלבׄ הי אן אלנבי או אלגמאעה אדׄא ראו דׄלך אלנור יקולון ראינא אללה פי מגאז לגׄה אלעבראניין וליס יענון אנהם ראו דׄאת אלכׄאלק. אדׄ לא וצלה בין דׄאתה ובין אלאכׄאר.[948] ואנמא יענון בכלאמהם דׄאך אנהם ראו איאתה ושאהדו דלאילה. כמא וגדנא אלתורה תקול פי אלמגאז ען

[927] אן TS Ar 28.155b > L

[928] אל[די] TS Ar 28.155b > D

[929] בהא ... יסמעה TS Ar 23.11c > D

[930] [אן תכון] אל[ע]ל[אמה] Oxf 2486.7b > D

[931] [אן תכ]ו]ן אלעל[אמה אסטואנה] TS Ar 28.155b > D

[932] סחאב End of Oxf 2486.7b

[933] א[ן] TS Ar 28.155b > D

[934] מע אן סאיר TS Ar 23.11c > D

[935] והדה TS Ar 23.11c

[936] כ יק TS Ar 23.11c

[937] וש[מו]אל TS Ar 28.155b > D

[938] יד אל TS Ar 23.11c

[939] עטׄימא TS Ar 28.155b | עמימא TS Ar 23.11c

[940] ולא מן TS Ar 23.11c > L

[941] ואלקמר TS Ar 23.11c

[942] אלמתעארפה TS Ar 23.11c

[943] אנהם ראו TS Ar 28.155b > D

[944] א[לעלאמ]ה ת[בת]די TS Ar 23.11c > D

[945] אבתדי TS Ar 23.11c

[946] אנקצא[יה ... ענ]דה TS Ar 28.155b > D

[947] רבה End of the readable part of TS Ar 28.155b

[948] אלאכׄגאר TS Ar 23.11c

אלמלאיכה[949] אנהם ראו אלכֹאלק. תֹם תבין בעד דֹלך פי אלתוריה[950] [...][951] אן ראו מגדה, דֹאך קו̇ **ויעל משה ואהרן**[952] **ונדב ואביהוא ושבעים מזקני**[953] **ישׂראל ויראו את אלהי ישׂראל**[954] (שמ׳ 24:9-10). תֹם קאלת[955] פי שרח דֹלך **ומראה כבוד יוי** (שמ׳ 24:17). ועלי הדֹא קאל [... ...][956] וקאל מיכה **ראיתי את**[957] **יוי** (מל״א 22:19).

ואלמקדמה אלגֹ אן הדֹא אלנור [... ...][958] בצורה חיואן כמא שרחנא פי קולה[959] **ומראה כבוד יוי כאש אכלת** (שמ׳ 24:17). וקאל איצֹא[960] [... ...][961] וקד ישא פי בעץֹ אלאוקאת אן יטֹהרה בצורה אנסאן תחתה [... ...][962] ועליה[963] תֹיאב מן נור כמא[964] קאל[965] **ושוליו**[966] **מלאים**[967] **את ההיכל**[968] (יש׳ 6:1). ולא יכון דֹיל אלא למלבוס. ואלממתֹל באלדֹיל פהו[969] שעאע לדֹלך אלנור. כמא מתֹל אן ללשמס כנף או אכנאף[970] אדֹ קאל **וזרחה לכם יראי שמי שמש**

[949] Uncertain reading

[950] אלתור]יה[TS Ar 23.11c > D

[951] [...] TS Ar 23.11c > D

[952] ואהרן TS Ar 23.11c > L

[953] וש̇ מז̇ TS Ar 23.11c

[954] ישׂראל ... ישׂראל TS Ar 23.11c > D

[955] ק]אל[ת TS Ar 23.11c > D

[956] [... ...] TS Ar 23.11c > D

[957] א TS Ar 23.11c

[958] [... ...]רא TS Ar 23.11c > D

[959] כֹ שרחנא פי קו̇ TS Ar 23.11c

[960] וק]ו[ ]אי[צֹ TS Ar 23.11c > D

[961] [... ...] TS Ar 23.11c > D

[962] [... ...] TS Ar 23.11c > D

[963] ועליה Beginning of the readable part of Oxf 2486.8a

[964] כמא Beginning of Oxf 2652.54a

[965] כק TS Ar 23.11c

[966]]כמא ... ושול[יו Oxf 2486.8a > D

[967] מ̇ TS Ar 23.11c

[968] את ההיכל TS Ar 23.11c > D

[969] למלבוס ... פהו TS Ar 23.11c > D | פהו Oxf 2486.8a > D

[970] אי אכנאף Oxf 2652.54a

צדקה ומרפא בכנפיה (מלאכי 3:20). וקד[971] יט̇הר[972] איצ̇א[973] מלאיכה ען ימין ד̇לך אלכרסי[974] ויסארה כמא קאל מיכה **וכל צבא השמים עומד עליו מימינו ומשמול** (מל"א 22:19). וקד יט̇הר[975] איצ̇א ערשא[976] תחת ד̇לך אלכרסי וארבעה[977] אשכ̇אץ מן אלמלאיכה תחמלהא כמא קאל יחזקאל **ודמות על ראשי[978] החיה[979] רקיע[980]** (יחז' 1:22). וקאל[981] בעדה **וממעל לרקיע אשר על ראשם כמראה[982] אבן ספיר דמות כסא[983]** (יחז' 1:26). וקד יכ̇אטב ד̇לך אלשכ̇ץ אלאנביא כמא קאל **ויאמר[984] עלי[985] בן אדם עמד[986] על רגלך[987] ואדבר אותך[988]** (יחז' 2:1). וענד גמיע אלאנביא אן[989] גמלה הד̇ה אלאשכ̇אץ[990] אלתי מן[991] נור מחדת̇ה[992] אד̇ כאן כל מן כ̇אטב[993] נביא סוי מוסי פהו מחדת̇ כמא כ̇צתה אלתוריה בכ̇אציה והי[994] **אשר ידעו יוי פנים אל פנים[995]** (דב' 34:10). וכמא כאן אלאמר ענד אלאנביא אן כל רויא מנסובה אלי אלכ̇אלק[996]

971 אכנ]אף ... וקד TS Ar 23.11c > D

972 יצהר Oxf 2652.54a

973 איצ TS Ar 23.11c

974 אל[כרסי] TS Ar 23.11c > D ׀ אלכרסי End of the readable part of TS Ar 23.11c

975 יצהר Oxf 2652.54a

976 ערשה Beginning of the readable part of TS Ar 23.11d

977 ארבע Oxf 2486.8a ׀ וד TS Ar 23.11d

978 מן ... ראשי TS Ar 23.11d > D

979 תחיוה TS Ar 23.11d

980 רקיע TS Ar 23.11d > L

981 כ קאל Oxf 2652.54a

982 כמר[אה] Oxf 2486.8a > D

983 אשר ... כסא TS Ar 23.11d > L

984 [יכאטב ... ויאמ]ר TS Ar 23.11d > D

985 אלי TS Ar 23.11d

986 וג' + TS Ar 23.11d

987 רגליך End of Oxf 2486.8a

988 על ... אותך TS Ar 23.11d > L

989 אן Beginning of the readable part of Oxf 2486.8b

990 אן ... אלאשכאץ TS Ar 23.11d > D

991 אלתי מן Oxf 2486.8b > D

992 מ[ח]דת[ה] TS Ar 23.11d > D

993 כאטב Oxf 2486.8b > D

994 כצתה ... והי TS Ar 23.11d > D ׀ והי Oxf 2652.54a > L

995 פ TS Ar 23.11d

996 רויה ... אלכאלק TS Ar 23.11d > D

פאנמא הי רויא נור מחדת֗[997] לא רויא אלד֗את כ֗דאך כאן אלאמר [998] ענד סלף אלאמה ואלאמנא[999] עלי דינהא לאנהם תרגמו לנא **ויראו את אלהי**[1000] **ישראל**[1001] (שמ׳ 24:10), **וחזו ית יקר אלהא דישראל**. ותרגמו[1002] איצ֗א[1003] **ואראה את יוי** (יש׳ 6:1) וכד֗לך **ראיתי את יוי** (מל״א 22:19), **חזיתי ית יקרא דיוי**. אלא אן הד֗א כאן אלשכ֗ץ אלד֗י מן נור כיף כאף לא יט֗הר אלא מחדת֗א[1004] עלי מא וצפנא.

ואלמקדמה אלראבעה[1005] אן הד֗א אלנור לם יכן[1006] אחד מן אלאנביא[1007] ימכנה אן ינט֗ר[1008] אלי אואילה. אד֗ קוה כל נור פי מסתקבלה[1009] עלי אלעאדה. פאן תאמל אנסאן אואילה אנחל תרכיבה. וענה יקול אללה למשה **וראית את אחרי**[1010] **ופני לא יראו**[1011] (שמ׳ 33:23). וליס יגוז אן יכון[1012] אראד אלכ֗אלק ד֗אתה בהד֗א אלקול. אד֗ אלרויה[1013] אלי ד֗אתה ג֗יר גאיז, לא עלי[1014] סביל אן יעיש אלאנסאן ולא עלי סביל אן ימות.[1015] ואנמא אראד בהד֗א[1016] אלקול ד֗לך אלנור אלמחדת֗ אלד֗י אלרויה[1017] עליה גאיזה.[1018] ואנמא בקי אן נעלם[1019] הל

[997] מ[חד]ת TS Ar 23.11d > D

[998] איצא + Oxf 2652.54a and TS Ar 23.11d

[999] [אלאמ]ה ואל[אמ]נא TS Ar 23.11d > D

[1000] אל TS Ar 23.11d

[1001] ישראל TS Ar 23.11d > L

[1002] ותרג[מו] TS Ar 23.11d > D

[1003] איצ TS Ar 23.11d

[1004] לא יצהר אלא מחדודא Oxf 2652.54a

[1005] אלד TS Ar 23.11d

[1006] יך TS Ar 23.11d

[1007] אלאנביא End of Oxf 2486.8b

[1008] ינצר Oxf 2652.54a

[1009] [מס]תקבל[ה] TS Ar 23.11d > D

[1010] אחורי TS Ar 23.11d

[1011] יר TS Ar 23.11d

[1012] יכן TS Ar 23.11d

[1013] אלרויא Oxf 2652.54a

[1014] [ע]לי TS Ar 23.11d > D

[1015] עלי סביל אן ימות אלאנסאן ולא עלי סביל אן יעיש Oxf 2652.54a

[1016] ב[הדא] TS Ar 23.11d > D

[1017] אלרוי[ה] TS Ar 23.11d > D ׀ אלרויא Oxf 2652.54a

[1018] עלי[ה גאיז]ה Oxf 2652.54a > D

[1019] [ואנמא בקי] אן [נ]על[ם] TS Ar 23.11d > D

יעיש אלאנסאן אלד׳י יראה או ימות. פערפנא[1020] אן אלאנסאן אן הו ראי[1021] אויל ד׳לך אלנור או אסתקבלה אנחל תרכיבה ומאת,[1022] בקולה[1023] **לא תוכל לראות את פני כי לא יראני האדם**[1024] **וחי**[1025] (שמ׳ 33:20). לכן[1026] אד׳א אראד[1027] אלבארי באנסאן אן ירי[1028] ד׳לך אלנור אלמחדת׳[1029] פיעיש סתר בג׳מאמה או מא שאבההא חתי[1030] יסיר אול אלנור פיבעד ענה.[1031] ת׳ם יכשף ענה אלג׳מאמה פירי אואכ׳רה פיעיש כמא[1032] צנע במשה **רבינו** אד׳ קאל לה **והסרתי**[1033] **את כפי וראית וג׳** (שמ׳ 33:23). ואתת סאיר אלכתב[1034] במת׳ל התין אלחאלין, אנה מן ינט׳ר[1035] אויל אלנור יהלך. אד׳ קאל חבקוק **ונגה כאור תהיה וג׳**[1036] (חבקוק 3:4), **לפניו ילך דבר**[1037] (חבקוק 3:5). ומן ינט׳ר[1038] אואכ׳רה[1039] יסלם[1040] כמא קאל[1041] ישעיהו **מלך ביפיו תחזינה עיניך תראנה ארץ מרחקים** (יש׳ 33:17). יעני כמא תרי אלבלאד אלבעיד.[1042]

1020 פ[ער]פנא TS Ar 23.11d > D
1021 אלאנסאן ... ראי TS Ar 23.11d > D
1022 ומאת TS Ar 23.11d > D
1023 בקו׳ TS Ar 23.11d
1024 י[ר]אני [ה]אדם וחי Oxf 2652.54a > D
1025 וחי End of Oxf 2652.54a
1026 לכן Beginning of Oxf 2652.54b
1027 תו[כל] ל[רא]ות ... ארא]ד TS Ar 23.11d > D
1028 יר TS Ar 23.11d
1029 אל[נור] אל[מ]חדת׳ TS Ar 23.11d > D
1030 סתר ... חתי TS Ar 23.11d > D
1031 [פיב]עד ע[נה] TS Ar 23.11d > D
1032 אלג[׳מאמה ... כמא] TS Ar 23.11d > D
1033 והסירות TS Ar 23.11d
1034 ורא[ית וג׳ ... אלכתב] TS Ar 23.11d > D
1035 ינצ׳ר Oxf 2652.54b
1036 קאל ... וג׳ TS Ar 23.11d > D
1037 דבר TS Ar 23.11d > L
1038 ינצ׳ר Oxf 2652.54b
1039 אואלהה TS Ar 23.11d
1040 י[ס]ל[ם] TS Ar 23.11d > D
1041 כק TS Ar 23.11d
1042 מ[לך ... אלבעי]ד TS Ar 23.11d > D

פאד[1043] קד פרג̇נא מן הד̇ה אלד̇ מקדמאת ותביין אן אלאנואר אלתי תט̇הר[1044] ללאנביא מחדת̇ה[1045] ואנהא קד תט̇הר[1046] בצורה אנסאן[1047] פי בעץ̇ אלאוקאת פיסתקים איצ̇א אן[1048] תכון פי וקת בצורה שיך̇ פוק כרסי.[1049] והו מא קאל דניאל ההנא **עד די כורסון רמיו ועתיק יומין יתיב** (דניאל 7:9). ויכון[1050] וגה אלחכמה פי ט̇הורה[1051] שיכ̇א לעלה אנה סיסלם אלמלך אלי אלמושיע תסלים מן הו אעלי[1052] כמא[1053] סיקול **וקדמוהי הקרבוהי ולה יהב שלטן**[1054] (דניאל 7:13–14). וכאן אלמושיע ישבה באלנאמי ואלנאשי ואלמבתדא[1055] כמא קאל[1056] **ויצא חטר מגזע ישי** (יש׳ 11:1). וקאל **והקימתי לדוד צמח צדיק**[1057] (ירמ׳ 23:5). וקאל **מראש ינקתיו רך אקטף** (יחז׳ 17:22) ומא[1058] אשבה ד̇לך.

קדם אול אלקול פגעל מן יריסה[1059] וישרפה[1060] כאלשיך̇ ואלעתיק[1061] ואלקדים חתי[1062] יגעלה הו כאלשאב פיקול **כבר אנש אתה הוה** (דניאל 7:13) לתקאבל[1063] אלמת̇אלאת בעצ̇הא בעצ̇. פיולי[1064] אלשיך̇ ללשאב כמשה

[1043] [פא]ד TS Ar 23.11d > D
[1044] תצהר Oxf 2652.54b
[1045] ותביין ... מחדת̇ה TS Ar 23.11d > D
[1046] תצהר Oxf 2652.54b
[1047] א[נסאן] TS Ar 23.11d > D | אנסאן End of the readable part of TS Ar 23.11d
[1048] אן Beginning of TS Ar 23.11e
[1049] כרסי TS Ar 23.11e > D
[1050] דניאל ... ויכון TS Ar 23.11e > D
[1051] צהורה Oxf 2652.54b
[1052] לע[לה ... אעלי] TS Ar 23.11e > D
[1053] כמ̇ TS Ar 23.11e
[1054] [של]טן TS Ar 23.11e > D
[1055] וכאן ... ואלמבתדא TS Ar 23.11e > D
[1056] כק TS Ar 23.11e
[1057] צדיק TS Ar 23.11e > L
[1058] [מראש ינ]קת[יו רך אקטף ומא] TS Ar 23.11e > D
[1059] ירוסה TS Ar 23.11e
[1060] ישרנה TS Ar 23.11e
[1061] ואלע[תי]ק TS Ar 23.11e > D
[1062] ח[תי] TS Ar 23.11e > D
[1063] ל[ת]אקבל TS Ar 23.11e > D
[1064] בעצ̇הא ... פיולי TS Ar 23.11e > D

ליהושע, כשמואל לדוד וכדוד לשלמה ומא אשבה דׄלך. ואמא קולה[1065] **כרסון** (דניאל 7:9) בלפטה[1066] גמע ולם יקל "כרסיא" בלפט[1067] פראד פימכן אן יכון[1068] דׄלך לאן אלכרסי[1069] אגזאא ופצול. פאדׄא אגתמעת קטעהא צארת ואחדא[1070] כמא קאל[1071] פי וסט אלפסוק **כורסיה שביבין די נור** (דניאל 7:9) ולם יקל[1072] **כרסותיה**. פאדׄ קד בינא תאויל **כרסון ועתיק** (דניאל 7:9) פינבגׄי אן נקול[1073] תפסיר[1074] **לבושה כתלג חור** (דניאל 7:9) אן טׄאהרה[1075] יקתצׄי **נור** (דניאל 7:9). והו[1076] כמא קאל[1077] הנאך **ושוליו מלאים את ההאיכל** (יש' 6:1). ומתׄל קולה איצׄא **והחצר מלאה את נגה כבוד יוי**[1078] (יחז' 10:4). וקולה[1079] קבל דׄלך **וכבוד יוי מלא את המשכן**[1080] (שמ' 40:34). ותאוילה מא ועד[1081] בני אסראל[1082] מן טׄהור[1083] אלנור[1084] פי וקת אלישועה[1085] אלדׄי יכון עלי בית אלמקדס. מנתצבא[1086] מן אלארץׄ אלי אלסמא יסיר אלאמם אליה כׄק **קומי אורי** (יש' 60:1), **והלכו גוים לאורך**[1087] (יש' 60:3). ותאויל **ושער ראשו**

[1065] ואמא קולה TS Ar 23.11e > D
[1066] בלפצה Oxf 2652.54b
[1067] בלפצ Oxf 2652.54b
[1068] יך TS Ar 23.11e
[1069] [אלכר]סי TS Ar 23.11e
[1070] וא[חדא] TS Ar 23.11e > D
[1071] כק TS Ar 23.11e
[1072] יקל TS Ar 23.11e
[1073] נקול TS Ar 23.11e > L
[1074] תפס TS Ar 23.11e
[1075] טוהרה TS Ar 23.11e | צאהרה Oxf 2652.54b
[1076] והו Oxf 2652.54b > L
[1077] כק TS Ar 23.11e
[1078] את ההיכל … וכבוד יוי TS Ar 23.11e > L
[1079] וקולה TS Ar 23.11e > L | מתל + TS Ar 23.11e
[1080] מ[לא] את [המשכן] Oxf 2652.54b > D | את המשכן TS Ar 23.11e > L
[1081] בה + TS Ar 23.11e
[1082] אסר TS Ar 23.11e
[1083] צהור Oxf 2652.54b
[1084] אל[נור] Oxf 2652.54b > D | אלנור End of Oxf 2652.54b
[1085] אליש[וע]ה TS Ar 23.11e > D
[1086] אלמק[דס מנתצב]א TS Ar 23.11e > D
[1087] לא TS Ar 23.11e > L

כעמר נקא[1088] (דניאל 7:9) [...][1089] אן גמיע ד̇נוב אלאמה וכ̇טאיאהא חתי תציר כאנהא סואדא [...][1090] אביצ̇ת מת̇ל אלצוף אלנקי כ̇ק̇ הנאך **אם יהיו חטאיכם כשנים כשלג**[1091] **ילבינו** (יש׳ 1:18) [...][1092] יצל עמך [...][1093] **וטהרתים מכל עונם** (ירמ׳ 33:8). ותאויל **כורסיה שביבין די נור גלגלוהי**[1094] (דניאל 7:9), הו מא [... ...][1095] [...][1096] מן אלחאל אלשדידה כאנהא ניראן תשתעל קד [... ...][1097] **כי הנה יוי באש יבא** (יש׳ 66:15) **כי באש יוי נשפט** (יש׳ 66:16). וקאל **ואני** [...][1098] קאל לג̇ירנא חין [...][1099] **וגלגליו כסופה** (יש׳ 5:28). וד̇אך עלי עאדה [... ...][1100] אלאנתקאם ואלקדום.

ויכון תפסיר[1101] **נהר די נור** (דניאל 7:9) ״עקובאת״ [... ...][1102] עלי אלכפאר ואלט̇אלמין כאלסיל אלמנגר כ̇ק̇ הנאך **הנה סערת יוי** (ירמ׳ 23:19) [... ...][1103] ויכון מעני ט̇אהר ק̇ו **אלף אלפין** (דניאל 9:10) פימא סנצף מן אלנט̇ר [... ...][1104] ומעני **ורבו רבון קדמ[והי]** (דניאל 7:10) בלא כ̇דמה חתי אד̇א תצרף [... ...][1105] לילא תכ̇לו חצ̇רתה.[1106] **עתיק**[1107] **יומין** (דניאל 7:9) נט̇יר מא קאל הנאך **וכל צבא השמים עמד עליו וג׳** (מל״א 22:19) [... ...][1108] מן אקבאל

[1088] רא[שו כ]עמר [נ]ק[א] TS Ar 23.11e > D
[1089] [...] TS Ar 23.11e > D
[1090] [...] TS Ar 23.11e > D
[1091] חט כש כש TS Ar 23.11e
[1092] [...] TS Ar 23.11e > D
[1093] כל[...] TS Ar 23.11e > D
[1094] [די נור ג]לגל[והי] TS Ar 23.11e > D
[1095] יא[...]ה TS Ar 23.11e > D
[1096] [...]קאן TS Ar 23.11e > D
[1097] [... ...] TS Ar 23.11e > D
[1098] [...] TS Ar 23.11e > D
[1099] [...] TS Ar 23.11e > D
[1100] [... ...] TS Ar 23.11e > D
[1101] תפס TS Ar 23.11e
[1102] [... ...] TS Ar 23.11e > D
[1103] [... ...] TS Ar 23.11e > D
[1104] [... ...] TS Ar 23.11e > D
[1105] [... ...] TS Ar 23.11e > D
[1106] חצרתה End of the readble part of TS Ar 23.11e
[1107] עתיק Beginning of the readable part of TS Ar 23.11f
[1108] [... ...] TS Ar 23.11f > D

אלאלוף ואלרבואת מן אלאמם [... ...].[1109] כק **הן גוי לא תדע** (יש׳ 55:5). וקאל **להביא אליך חיל וג׳** (יש׳ 60:11). וקאל **כל צאן קדר וג׳** (יש 60:7). וקאל **והיו מלכים אומניך** (יש׳ 49:23). ומא שאכל דלך. ומעני **דינא יתיב** (דניאל 7:10) ליס הו למחאסבה אלנאס אגמעין אד[1110] וקת אלישועה ליס הו יום אלקיאמה. ואנמא דלך למחאסבה אלאמם עלי מא [... ...][1111] והו מא קאל יואל פיהא[1112] משרוחא **יערו ויעלו וג׳** (יואל 4:12). ומעני **וספרין פתיחו** (דניאל 7:10), [...] חסנאת[1113] כל אלעבאד וסיאתהם אד דלך אנמא יכון פי דאר אלאכרה. כמא[1114] נצת אלאנביא עלי אן[1115] אלכאלק חאפט לאעמאל עבאדה כאלמחפוט ענדנא פי כתאב[1116] ודיואן אד קאל **ויכתב ספר זכרון לפניו ליראי יוי**[1117] (מלאכי 3:16). וקאל איצא[1118] **הנה כתובה** (יש׳ 65:6). וקאל אלולי **ספר כתב איש ריבי** (איוב 31:35) ומא שאכל דלך. ולכן תלך אלכתב[1119] ואלדואוין אלתי דכרת ההנא **וספרין פתיחו** (דניאל 7:10) מא צנע אלקום בישראל ליכאפיהם עליה פי אלדניא כק להם **ואם גמלים אתם עלי** (יואל 4:4). וקאל איצא **ושלמתי לבבל ולכל יושבי כשדים**[1120] (ירמ׳ 51:24). וקאל **כעל גמלות** (יש׳ 59:18) ומא שאכל דלך. ואלדליל עלי הדה אלכתב ואלחסאב אלדי יתולאה **עתיק יומין** (דניאל 7:9) אנמא הו ללממאלך ואלאמם עלי מא צנעתה באיאם[1121] דולתהם אנה קאל בעדה אן אלמחאסבה[1122] למא וקעת אסתחק בעץ אלממאלך[1123] אלקתל ואלאראק ואלפנא. ואסתחק[1124] אלבאקון זואל אלמלך ואלבקא. דאך[1125] קולה[1126] פי נץ הדא אלפצל[1127]

[1109] [... ...] D < TS Ar 23.11f

[1110] [אלנ]אס א[גמ]ע[ין א]ד D < TS Ar 23.11f

[1111] [... ...] D < TS Ar 23.11f

[1112] [פי]הא D < TS Ar 23.11f

[1113] [חסנ]את D < TS Ar 23.11f Uncertain lesson

[1114] כמ TS Ar 23.11f

[1115] ע[לי א]ן D < TS Ar 23.11f

[1116] כת TS Ar 23.11f

[1117] לפ ליר יוי TS Ar 23.11f

[1118] איצ TS Ar 23.11f

[1119] ול[כן ת]לך אלכ[תב] D < TS Ar 23.11f

[1120] יושבי כשדים L < TS Ar 23.11f

[1121] צנ[עת ב[אי]אם D < TS Ar 23.11f

[1122] אלמ[חאס]בה D < TS Ar 23.11f

[1123] א[סת]חק בע[ץ] אל[מ]מאלך D < TS Ar 23.11f

[1124] אסתחק Beginning of the readable part of Oxf 2486.82a | אסת[חק] D < Oxf 2486.82a

[1125] אלבאקין ... דאך D < Oxf 2486.82a

Dn 7:11

חזי הוית באידין מן קל מדיא רברתאדי קדנא ממללאחזי היות עד די קטילת חיותא והובד גשמיה ויהיבת ליקידת אשא.

תֹם ראית כאן מן אגל[1128] תלך אלכלמאת אלעטֹימה[1129] אלתי[1130] כאנת אלקרן[1131] תתכלם[1132] בהא אסתחק גמלה אלשכֹץ אן[1133] יקתל[1134] ובאד גסמה וגעל וקידא ללנאר.[1135]

Dn 7:12

ושאר חיותא העדיו שלטניהון וארכא בחיין יהיבת עד זמן ועדן.

ואמא באקי אלאשכֹאץ פזאל סלטאנהם[1136] ואעטו מהלה מן חיותה[1137] אלי וקת וזמאן.[1138]

כנא שרחנא אן אלקריין תפסיר[1139] אלאמה אלמתצלה באלממלכה[1140] [... ...][1141] אנמא יקולוה אלכפאר מנהא פי אללה[1142] ופי אמתה מחאלא.[1143] פבין ההנא אן אללה יחאסבהם ויטאלבהם[1144] בה פיהלכהם. ודֹאך מא אכֹבר באנה יסוק אלמסרפין מנהם אלי גבל בית אלמקדס חתי יהלכון[1145] הנאך בעץֹ

[1126] קו TS Ar 23.11f

[1127] [אל]פ[צל] TS Ar 23.11f > D | אל[פצל] Oxf 2486.82a > D

[1128] אגל Spiegel > L

[1129] אלעצימה Spiegel + Morag | תלך ... אלעטֹימה TS Ar 23.11f > D

[1130] אלדי Spiegel

[1131] תלך ... אלקרן] TS Ar 23.11f > D | אלקרין Spiegel

[1132] יתכלם Spiegel

[1133] [א]ן Oxf 2486.82a > D

[1134] קתל Spiegel + Morag | י[קת]ל TS Ar 23.11f > D

[1135] גסמה ... ללנאר TS Ar 23.11f > D | לאלנאר Spiegel + Morag

[1136] סלטאנהם End of Oxf 2486.82a | צלטאנהם Morag

[1137] פי חיותהם Spiegel

[1138] ח[יותה ... וזמאן] TS Ar 23.11f > D

[1139] תפס TS Ar 23.11f

[1140] באלממל[כה ...] TS Ar 23.11f > D

[1141] [...] TS Ar 23.11f > D

[1142] אללה Beginning of the readable part of Oxf 2486.82b

[1143] מחא[לא] TS Ar 23.11f > D

[1144] פבין ... יטאלבהם TS Ar 23.11f > D

[1145] אלי ... יהלכון TS Ar 23.11f > D

באלנאר ובעץ[1146] באלמא כמא קאל[1147] **ונשפטתי אתו בדבר ובדם**[1148] **וגשם שוטף ואבי אלגביש ואש**[1149] **וגפרית**[1150] (יחז' 38:22). ובעץ מאסי[1151] לחומהם ואעצ̇איהם[1152] כמא קאל[1153] **וזאת תהיה המגפה אשר יגף יוי את כל העמים אשר צבאו על ירושלם המק בשרו**[1154] (זכריה 14:12). חתי אן אחדהם ימד ידה ליעתצ̇ד ביד אלאכ̇ר פתגי ידה מעה מנפצלה[1155] כמא קאל[1156] **והחזיקו איש יד רעיהו ועלתה ידו אל יד רעהו**[1157] (זכריה 14:13). ואמא[1158] אלבאקי[1159] [... ...][1160] לם[1161] יסרפו פי אלכלאם פי אללה ופי אמתה במהאלך [...][1162] ויכון[1163] פי אלמושיע כק̇ לוליה **שאל ממני** (תה' 2:8). פבעצ̇הם[1164] [... ...][1165] תקולה **ועתה מלכים השכילו, עבדו את יוי ביראה**[1166] (תה' 2:10–11). וקאל [...][1167] **כי הגוי**[1168] **והממלכה אשר לא** (יש' 60:12). ופצח באן אלבאקין ידכ̇לון פי אלדין ויסתקבלון אלקבלה[1169]

[1146] וב[עץ] TS Ar 23.11f > D
[1147] כק TS Ar 23.11f
[1148] ובדם Oxf 2486.82b > L
[1149] אש MT
[1150] בדבר ... וגפרית TS Ar 23.11f > L
[1151] ב[.]מאסי Oxf 2486.82b > D
[1152] וב[עץ ... ואעצ̇איהם] TS Ar 23.11f > D
[1153] כק TS Ar 23.11f
[1154] אשר ... בשרו TS Ar 23.11f > L
[1155] ליעתצד ... מנפצלה TS Ar 23.11f > D
[1156] כק TS Ar 23.11f
[1157] ועלתה ... רעהו TS Ar 23.11f > L
[1158] ואמ[א] TS Ar 23.11f > D | ואמא End of the readable part of TS Ar 23.11f
[1159] אלבאקי End of Oxf 2486.82b
[1160] [... ...] TS Ar 23.11f > D
[1161] לם Beginning of TS Ar 23.11g
[1162] [...] TS Ar 23.11g > D
[1163] ויכ[ון] TS Ar 23.11g > D
[1164] פבע[צהם] TS Ar 23.11g > D
[1165] [... ...] TS Ar 23.11f > D
[1166] ביר[אה] TS Ar 23.11g > D
[1167] [...] TS Ar 23.11g > D
[1168] כי הגוי TS Ar 23.11g > D
[1169] אלק[ב]לה TS Ar 23.11g > D

ויחגון פי כל סנה אלי בית אלמקדס[1170] כק **והיה כל הנותר מכל הגוים** (זכריה 14:16). תם קאל

Dn 7:13
חזי חוית בחיזו ליליא וארו עם ענני שמיא כבר אנש אתי הוה ועד עתיק יומיא מטא וקדמוהי הקרבוהי.

תם ראית פימא ירא[1171] פי[1172] אלליל כאן שאבא מקבל מע אלסחאב חתי בלג אלי מוצע אלשיך פקדמה[1173] בין[1174] ידיה.

Dn 7:14
וליה יהיב שולטאן ויקר ומלכו וכל עממיא ואמיא ולישניא ליה יפלחון שולטניא שולטן עלם די לא יעדי ומלכותיה די לא תתחבל.

פאעטאה אלסלטאן[1175] ואלוקאר ואלמלך[1176] וגמיע אלשעוב ואלאמם ואהל אללגאת[1177] לה יטיעון[1178] סלטאנה[1179] סלטאן[1180] אלעאלם[1181] אלדי לא יזול ומלכה לא יתגיר.[1182]

תפסיר[1183] הדא **באר אנש** (דניאל 7:13) אלדי דכרה ההנא הו אלמושיע. ואנמא מתלה באלשאב למא קדמנא מן נשוה ונמוה ונגמה ונגבה. ולהדה אלעלה איצא[1184] ירי אלמשרפה ואלמעטמה שיכא חתי תתקאבל אלאמתאל.

[1170] אלמק[דס] TS Ar 23.11g > D
[1171] תם ... ירא TS Ar 23.11g > D
[1172] מן Spiegel
[1173] וקדמה Spiegel
[1174] פקדמה בין TS Ar 23.11g > D
[1175] אלצלטאן Morag
[1176] ואלמלוך TS Ar 23.11g
[1177] וא[ה]ל [א]לל[גאת] TS Ar 23.11g > D
[1178] יטיע[ון] TS Ar 23.11g > D
[1179] פסלטאנה TS Ar 23.11g
[1180] צלטאנה צלטאן Morag | אבדי + TS Ar 23.11g | אבדא + Spiegel
[1181] אלעאלם Spiegel and TS Ar 23.11g > L
[1182] יתגייר Spiegel + Morag
[1183] תפס TS Ar 23.11g
[1184] איצ TS Ar 23.11g

ולתקאבלהא איצׄא[1185] אן אלשאב[1186] אלמשיע קיל[1187] לה **בר**[1188] **אנש** (דניאל 7:13) אדׄ אלשיךׄ אלאול מלאך[1189] מן אלמלאיכה. ופי לגׄה אלכסדאניין יסמון אלמלאך **בר אלהין**. פאסמי הדׄא באזא דׄאך **בר אנש** (דניאל 7:13).

ואלסבב[1190] אן[1191] אלשאב[1192] לם יטׄהר מע אלשיךׄ[1193] מן אול אלקצה, חתי יגלס אלשיךׄ פיחאסב[1194] ויעאקב וינגל אלדניא וימהרהא ללשאב ויטויהא[1195] אדׄ[1196] הדׄא מלאך[1197] והדׄא אנסאן ממא פצח אלנבי[1198] וקאל **הנני שלח מלאכי ופנה דרך לפני ופתאם יבא אל היכלו האדון אשר אתם מבקשים ומלאך הברית אשר**[1199] **אתם חפצים הנה בא אמר יוי צבאות**[1200] (מלאכי 3:1). תׄם שבהה בשיין מצלחין. אחדהמא[1201] פי אעטׄם אלאחואל, והי אלנאר אלתי תסבך.[1202] ואלאכׄר פי חאל קריבה,[1203] והי אלאשנאן אלדׄי יגׄסל[1204] כמא קאל[1205] בעדה **ומי מכלכל את יום בואו ומי העמד בהראותו כי הוא כאש מצרף וכברית מכבסים**[1206] (מלאכי 3:2). פהו **כאש מצרף**[1207] (מלאכי 3:2)

1185 איצׄ TS Ar 23.11g
1186 אל[שא]ב TS Ar 23.11g > D
1187 קיל Beginning of Oxf 2486.30a
1188 [ב]ר Oxf 2486.30a > D
1189 מלך TS Ar 23.11g
1190 פי + TS Ar 23.11g
1191 אן TS Ar 23.11g > L
1192 אלש[א]ב TS Ar 23.11g > D
1193 [יטׄהר מע אל]שיך TS Ar 23.11g > D
1194 פיחא[סב] Oxf 2486.30a > D | ויחאסב TS Ar 23.11g
1195 ו[יטויה]א TS Ar 23.11g > D
1196 א[ד] Oxf 2486.30a > D
1197 מלך TS Ar 23.11g
1198 אל[נבי] TS Ar 23.11g > D
1199 [אש]ר Oxf 2486.30a > D
1200 ופנה ... צבאות TS Ar 23.11g > L
1201 [מצלחין אחד]המא TS Ar 23.11g > D
1202 ת[ס]בך TS Ar 23.11g > D
1203 [קרי]בה TS Ar 23.11g > D
1204 [אלאשנאן אלדי יגׄס]ל TS Ar 23.11g > D
1205 כק TS Ar 23.11g
1206 את ... מכבסים TS Ar 23.11g > L | וכב[רי]ת [כבסים] Oxf 2486.30a > D
1207 [כא]ש [מ]צרף Oxf 2486.30a > D | ו[כא]ש [מצ]רף TS Ar 23.11g > D

ללמסרפין[1208] מן[1209] אלאמם כמא קאל[1210] האהנא **ויהבת ליקדת אשא**[1211] (דניאל 7:11). ומן אמה[1212] בני אסראל איצֿא[1213] כמא קאל[1214] להם **ואצרף כבור סיגיך ואסירה כל בדיליך** (יש׳ 1:25). והו **כברית מכבסים**[1215] (מלאכי 3:2) ללמדֿנבין[1216] אלדֿין[1217] לם יסרפו מן אלאתֿם[1218] כמא קאל[1219] פיהם **והסרתי דמיו מפיו ושקציו מבין שניו** (זכריה 9:7). ומן אמה יסראיל[1220] איצֿא[1221] כמא קאל[1222] **אם**[1223] **רחץ יוי צאת בנות ציון ואת דמי ירושלם ידיח מקרבה**[1224] (יש׳ 4:4). פאדֿא אנתטֿמת הדֿה אלאמור [... ...].[1225] ואלמעני כונה[1226] פי[1227] אלסחאב וגוה. מנהא אלתשריף כמא[1228] שרח[1229] אליהו[1230] חין[1231] קאל[1232] **ויעל אליהו בסערה השמים**[1233] (מל״ב 2:11). ומנהא ללסרעה מע אלתנגיל כמא קאל[1234] **מי אלה כעב תעופנה**[1235] (יש׳

1208 ללמסרפין] End of Oxf 2486.30a
1209 מן] Beginning of Oxf 2486.30b
1210 כק TS Ar 23.11g
1211 האהנא ... אשא TS Ar 23.11g > D
1212 [ומ]ן [א]מה TS Ar 23.11g > D
1213 איצ TS Ar 23.11g
1214 כק TS Ar 23.11g
1215 [ואצרף ... מכב]סים TS Ar 23.11g > D
1216 ללמד[נבין] TS Ar 23.11g > D
1217 אללדין Oxf 2486.30b
1218 אלאמם Oxf 2486.30b
1219 כק TS Ar 23.11g
1220 [פיהם ... יסראי]ל TS Ar 23.11g > D
1221 איצ TS Ar 23.11g
1222 כק TS Ar 23.11g
1223 אם TS Ar 23.11g > D
1224 צאת ... מקרבה TS Ar 23.11g > L
1225 [... ...] Oxf 2486.30b > D
1226 [אלאמור ... כו]נה TS Ar 23.11g > D | מע + TS Ar 23.11g
1227 פי TS Ar 23.11g > L
1228 שרף + TS Ar 23.11g
1229 שרח TS Ar 23.11g > L
1230 אֶלִיָּהו TS Ar 23.11g
1231 ח[ין] TS Ar 23.11g > D
1232 קאל Oxf 2486.30b > L
1233 השמימה Oxf 2486.30b | [ויעל ... השמי]ם TS Ar 23.11g > D
1234 כק TS Ar 23.11g
1235 תע TS Ar 23.11g

60:8). ומנהא לאן מעה אלג̇פראן כמא קאל **מחיתי**[1236] **כעב**[1237] **פשעיך וכענן חטאותיך**[1238] (יש׳ 44:22). ומנהא[1239] לאן מעה ט̇הור אלוחי **בעמוד ענן ידבר אליהם** (תה׳ 99:7) וט̇הור אלשכינה כמא קאל **והענן מלא את בית יוי** (מל״א 8:10) ומא נחי[1240] הד̇א אלנחו מן אלתמת̇ילאת.[1241]

ומעני[1242] **ועד עתיק יומיא מטא** (דניאל 7:13) לידל אנה סאר בקוה[1243] הי ג̇יר קותה וג̇יר קוה אלשך̇ חתי וצל אלי מוצ̇עה. והי קוה רב אלעאלמין כמא קאל ללאמה[1244] **וגברתים ביוי ובשמו יתהלכו נאם יוי**[1245] (זכריה 10:12). ומעני **וקדמוהי הקרבוהי** (דניאל 7:13) אולאיך אלד̇ין[1246] יכ̇דמונה יסתקבלו[1247] אלשאב[1248] ״פקדמוה בין ידיה״ ליסלם אליה אלמלך כמא קאל[1249] בעדה **וליה יהיב שלטאן וג׳** (דניאל 7:14). ומעני[1250] **וכל עממיא ואמיא ולשניא לה יפלחון**[1251] (דניאל 7:14) הו מא וצפנא מן טאעה כל אלנאס לה אלס̇[1252] ואלאויל. ואלת̇מאנין[1253] אלמד̇כורה[1254] פי אלתוראה[1255] ומן בעדהם מן אלקבאיל ואלעשאיר עלי מא שרחנא[1256] פי תפסיר **ואלה תולדות**[1257] **בני**

[1236] מחיתי End of Oxf 2486.30b | ומנהא ... מחיתי TS Ar 23.11g > D
[1237] כעב Beginning of Oxf 2486.83a
[1238] פשע]יך ... חטותיך[TS Ar 23.11g > D
[1239]]ומנ[הא TS Ar 23.11g > D
[1240] ידבר ... נחי TS Ar 23.11g > D
[1241] אל]תמתילאת[TS Ar 23.11g > D
[1242]]ומ[עני TS Ar 23.11g > D | מעני End of TS Ar 23.11g
[1243] בקוה Beginning of the readable part of TS Ar 23.11h
[1244] ו]הי ... ללאמ[ה TS Ar 23.11h > D
[1245] ובשמו ... יוי TS Ar 23.11h > L
[1246] אללדין Oxf 2486.83a
[1247]]י[סתקבלו Oxf 2486.83a > D
[1248] אלדין ... אלשאב TS Ar 23.11h > D
[1249] כק TS Ar 23.11h
[1250]]וליה ... ומע[ני TS Ar 23.11h > D
[1251] ולשניא ... יפלחון TS Ar 23.11h > L
[1252] ל מה + Oxf 2486.83a
[1253] ואלתמאנין End of Oxf 2486.83a
[1254] אלמדכורה Beginning of Oxf 2486.83b |]אלאויל ... אלמד[כורה TS Ar > D 23.11h
[1255] אלתוריה TS Ar 23.11h
[1256] שרח TS Ar 23.11h
[1257]]תפסיר תולדו[ת TS Ar 23.11h > D

נח[1258] (בר׳ 10:1). ומעני **ומלכותה**[1259] **מלכות עלם** (ע׳ דניאל 7:14) הו תאביד[1260] אלמלך אלדׄי ועדה בה רבנא אד[1261] קאל **ישראל נושע ביוי תשועת עולמים**[1262] (יש׳ 45:17). ואנה לא יזול מא קאמת אלדניא[1263] כמא קאל[1264] **לא יבא עוד שמשך וירחך**[1265] **לא יאסף כי יוי יהיה לך לאור עולם ושלמו ימי אבלך**[1266] (יש׳ 60:20) ומא שאבה דׄלך.

פאמא קול דניאל ען אלשאב **וכל עממיא**[1267] **ואמיא ולשניא**[1268] **לה**[1269] **יפלחון**[1270] (דניאל 7:14) פהו שי יראה פי מנאמה. ואמא[1271] קולה[1272] **שלטניא שלטן עלם וג׳**[1273] (דניאל 7:14) פליס הו[1274] שי יקע עליה אלבצר ולכנה קול סמעה[1275] פי מנאמה[1276] וקאל **שלטניא**[1277] **שלטן עלם**[1278] (דניאל 7:14) פלמא אנקצׄת אלרויא[1279] ערפנא[1280] כיף פסר לה בעץׄ אלמלאיכה מעאניהא פקאל[1281]

[1258] [נ]ח TS Ar 23.11h > D
[1259] מלכותה TS Ar 23.11h
[1260] [ת]אביד TS Ar 23.11h > D
[1261] וע[דנא ... א]ד TS Ar 23.11h > D
[1262] תשועת עולמים TS Ar 23.11h > D
[1263] מא קאמת אלדניא TS Ar 23.11h > L
[1264] כק TS Ar 23.11h
[1265] ויר TS Ar 23.11h
[1266] לא ... אבלך TS Ar 23.11h > L
[1267] [עממ]יא TS Ar 23.11h > D
[1268] ולשניא Beginning of Yeirin 217 (Strasb BNU MS 5138)
[1269] ליה Yeirin 217
[1270] ואמיא ... יפלחון TS Ar 23.11h > L
[1271] ואמא Yeirin 217 > D
[1272] קו TS Ar 23.11h
[1273] וג׳ Yeirin 217 and TS Ar 23.11h > L
[1274] הו TS Ar 23.11h > L
[1275] [סמ]עה TS Ar 23.11h > D
[1276] מנאמר TS Ar 23.11h
[1277] [ש]ל[טנ]יה TS Ar 23.11h > D
[1278] עלם TS Ar 23.11h > D
[1279] פליס ... אלרויא Yeirin 217 > D | אלרויא End of Oxf 2486.83b
[1280] ערפנא Beginning of Oxf 2486.84a
[1281] אלמלאיכ[ה ... פקאל] Yeirin 217 > D

Dn 7:15
אתכריאת רוחי אנא דניאל בגוא נדנא וחזוי ראשי יבהלונני.

פלמא[1282] כרב רוחי[1283] אנא דניאל[1284] פי גסמי ורויא[1285] עיני[1286] אדהשני.

Dn 7:16
קריבת על חד מן קאמיא ויציבא אבעי מיניה על כל דנא ואמר לי ופשר מליא יהודעינני.

תקדמת אלי ואחד מן אלוקוף ואלתמסת[1288] מנה אלצחיח פי גמיע ד̈לך[1289] פקאלה[1290] לי[1291] וערפני תפסיר[1292] אלאמור.

אמא לפט̇ה[1293] **אתכרית** (דניאל 7:15) פהי תרגמה **ותפעם**[1294] **רוחי**.[1295] ולם יתפק[1296] אן תדכ̇ל[1297] הד̇ה אללפט̇ה פי מוצ̇ע אכ̇ר[1298] מן אלמקרא. ומחץ̇ **בגוא נדנה** (דניאל 7:15) "פי גוף אלג̇מר" כמא קאל[1299] הנאך **וישב חרבו**[1300] **אל נדנה**[1301] (דהי"א 21:27). וגסד אלרוח פהו אלגסם[1302] לדלך[1303]

[1282] פלמא Beginning of TS Ar 51.3a

[1283] רוח[י] Yeirin 217 > D ׀ רוחי End of the readable part of Yeirin 217

[1284] דנ̇ TS Ar 51.3a

[1285] וריא TS Ar 51.3a

[1286] עיניי קד Morag

[1287] ידהשני TS Ar 51.3a ׀ אדהשתני Spiegel

[1288] ואלת[מס]ת TS Ar 23.11h > D

[1289] דאלך Spiegel + Morag

[1290] פקאל Spiegel + Morag

[1291] לה TS Ar 51.3a

[1292] תפס TS Ar 51.3a ׀ דאלך + Morag

[1293] אמא לפטה TS Ar 23.11h > D

[1294] ות[פעם] TS Ar 23.11h > D

[1295] רוחן Oxf 2486.84a

[1296] יתפ[ק] TS Ar 23.11h > D

[1297] [תדכ]ל TS Ar 23.11h > D

[1298] א[כר] TS Ar 23.11h > D

[1299] כק TS Ar 23.11h ׀ כמק TS Ar 51.3a

[1300] [הנאך וי]שב [חרבו] TS Ar 23.11h > D

[1301] אל נדנה TS Ar 23.11h > L

[1302] אלגסם TS Ar 23.11h > D

[1303] פלדלך TS Ar 51.3a

פסרתה[1304] ״גסמי״.[1305] ומנה וקע אשתקאק **לא ידון רוחי**[1306] **באדם**[1307] (בר׳ 6:3), ״לא ינגסד״.[1308] יעני[1309] לא ית̇בת.[1310] ויכון[1311] איצ̇א[1312] יפסר **בגוא**[1313] **נדנה**[1314] (דניאל 7:15) פי וסט אלאמר ואלתחריך ואלאצ̇טראב, מת̇ל[1315] **נעונד, והתנודדה**[1316] (יש׳ 24:20) ומא אשבהה.[1317]

וקולה[1318] **וחזוי ראשי** (דניאל 7:15) הו רויא אלעין עלי מא גאז[1319] פי לג̇ה[1320] אלתרגום. וקולה[1321] **קרבת**[1322] **על חד** (דניאל 7:16) הו מקאם קולה[1323] **קרבת לחד**, כמא יבתדל **אל ועל** גמיעא. וקולה[1324] **מן קאמיא**[1325] (דניאל 7:16) יעני[1326] בה אלוקוף בין ידי אלשיך̇ כמא קאל[1327] **ורבו רבון קדמוהי יקומון**[1328] (דניאל 7:10). והם אשרף מן אלד̇ין[1329] **ישמשנה**[1330] (דניאל 7:10). ויקאל אן

[1304] פסרתה End of Oxf 2486.84a | פסרתר TS Ar 23.11h
[1305] גסמי Beginning of Oxf 2486.84b
[1306] [וקע ... ידון] ר[ו]חי TS Ar 23.11h > D
[1307] באדם TS Ar 23.11h > L | בא TS Ar 51.3a
[1308] ל[א יצ]מך TS Ar 23.11h > D Uncertain lesson
[1309] יע TS Ar 51.3a
[1310] י[ת̇בת] TS Ar 23.11h > D
[1311] וימכן TS Ar 23.11h + TS Ar 51.3a
[1312] איצ̇ אן TS Ar 23.11h + TS Ar 51.3a
[1313] בגוי TS Ar 51.3a
[1314] יפ[סר בגו]א נד[נה] TS Ar 23.11h > D
[1315] פי ... מת̇ל TS Ar 23.11h > D
[1316] והתנו[דדה] TS Ar 23.11h > D
[1317] שאבהה TS Ar 23.11h > D
[1318] וקו TS Ar 23.11h
[1319] ריא עיני עלי מגאז TS Ar 51.3a
[1320] ראשי ... לג̇ה TS Ar 23.11h > D
[1321] וקו TS Ar 23.11h + TS Ar 51.3a
[1322] ק[רב]ת TS Ar 23.11h > D
[1323] קול TS Ar 51.3a | קולה TS Ar 23.11h > L
[1324] הו ... וקולה TS Ar 23.11h > D | וקו TS Ar 51.3a
[1325] [קא]מיא TS Ar 23.11h > D
[1326] יע TS Ar 51.3a
[1327] כק TS Ar 23.11h | כמק TS Ar 51.3a
[1328] ק יק TS Ar 51.3a
[1329] אללד̇ין Oxf 2486.84b
[1330] רבון ... ישמשנה TS Ar 23.11h > D | ישמשניה TS Ar 51.3a

אלמלאך אלמדכור ההנא[1331] הו מיכאל לקול גבראל פימא[1332] בעד **והנה מיכאל אחד**[1333] **השׂרים הראשנים**[1334] (דניאל 10:13). והו קריב. וקולה[1335] **אבעא** (דניאל 7:16) וקולה[1336] **יהודעינני** (דניאל 7:16) כאנהמא מסתאנפין והמא מאצ׳יין[1337] נחו[1338] קולה[1339] **אלוה מתימן יבוא**[1340] (חבקוק 3:3). וקולה[1341] **יעשו**[1342] **עגל בחרב** (תה׳ 106:19)[1343], **תפתח ארץ ותבלע דתן** (תה׳ 106:17) ומא שאבה דלך.[1344] תם קאל[1345] פי[1346] אלתפסיר[1347]

Dn 7:17
אלין חיותא וברברתא די אנין ארבע ארבעה מלכיא יקומון מן ארעה.

הדה אלאשכאץ אלעטאם[1348] אלתי[1349] הי ארבע[1350] ממאלך תקום פי[1351] אלארץ.

Dn 7:18
ויקבלון מלכותא קדישי עליונין ויחסנון מלכותא עד עלמא ועד עלם עלמיא.

[1331] האהנא Oxf 2486.84b | ההונא TS Ar 51.3a
[1332] פימ TS Ar 51.3a
[1333] פימא ... אחד TS Ar 23.11h > D
[1334] השׂ הרא TS Ar 51.3a
[1335] וקו TS Ar 51.3a + TS Ar 23.11h
[1336] וקולה TS Ar 23.11h > D | וקו TS Ar 51.3a
[1337] יהודע[ני ... מאצ׳יין] TS Ar 23.11h > D
[1338] נחו End of TS Ar 51.3a
[1339] קו Beginning of TS Ar 51.3b
[1340] יבוא End of Oxf 2486.84b | אלוה ... יבוא TS Ar 23.11h > D
[1341] וקולה Beginning of Oxf 2486.85a | וקו TS Ar 51.3b
[1342] וקו [יעש]ו TS Ar 23.11h > D
[1343] בחרב TS Ar 23.11h > L
[1344] ארץ ... דלך TS Ar 23.11h > D
[1345] קאל End of TS Ar 23.11h
[1346] פי Beginning of TS Ar 23.11i
[1347] אלתפס TS Ar 51.3b
[1348] אלעצאם Spiegel + Morag
[1349] אלדי Spiegel
[1350] הי ארבע הי ארבע Morag | לארבע TS Ar 51.3b
[1351] אלעטאם ... פי TS Ar 23.11i > D

תׄם יתסלם[1352] אלמלך אלקדוסין[1353] אלמתעאליין[1354] וירתׄונה אלי אלדהר ודהר[1355] אלדהור.[1356]

הדׄא מא כנא קדמנאה,[1357] אן[1358] **ארבעה**[1359] **מלכין** (דניאל 7:17), ״ארבע[1360] ממאלך״[1361] וליס הי ארבע אנאס פקט. ותאיד[1362] דׄלך מן קולה[1363] בעדה[1364] **מלכו**[1365] **רביעיא** (דניאל 7:23) ולם יקל **מלכו רביעאה**. ואחכם אלאמר ההנא[1366] אנה[1367] לא יגוז אן יסתעבד בני אסראיל[1368] ממלכה אכׄרי סוי[1369] הדׄה[1370] אלממאלך. אדׄ קאל בעדה[1371] **ויקבלון מלכותא קדישי עליונין**[1372] (דניאל 7:18) והם ישׂראל[1373] אלדׄי[1374] שרפו בהדׄין[1375] אללפטׄתין אדׄ קאל להם **ולתתך עליון, ולהיותך עם קדו**][1376] (דב׳ 26:19). וקאל איצׄא[1377] **ונתנך**[1378] **יוי אלהיך**[1379] **עליון**[1380] (דב׳ 28:1), **יקימך יוי לו לעם קדו** ז[1381] (דב׳ 28:9).

[1352] יתסלמון Spiegel + TS Ar 23.11i + Morag
[1353] אלקדיסיין Morag ׀ אלקדיסון Spiegel
[1354] אלמתעאליון Spiegel
[1355] ו[ד]הר Morag > D
[1356] [אלקדוסין ... אל]דהור TS Ar 23.11i > D ׀ ודהר אלדהור Spiegel > L
[1357] מן TS Ar 23.11i +
[1358] אן TS Ar 23.11i > L
[1359] ד TS Ar 23.11i
[1360] ד TS Ar 51.3b + TS Ar 23.11i
[1361] ממ[א]לך Oxf 2486.85a > D
[1362] ממאלך ... ותאיד TS Ar 23.11i > D
[1363] קולה TS Ar 23.11i > D
[1364] בעדה End of Oxf 2486.85a
[1365] מלכו Beginning of Oxf 2486.85b
[1366] האהנא Oxf 2486.85b
[1367] [ואחכם ... א]נא TS Ar 23.11i > D
[1368] אסרא TS Ar 23.11i ׀ אסר TS Ar 51.3b
[1369] סוא TS Ar 51.3b + TS Ar 23.11i
[1370] האולי TS Ar 51.3b + TS Ar 23.11i
[1371] בעדהם Oxf 2486.85b ׀ ק[אל בעדה] TS Ar 23.11i > D
[1372] קדישי עליונין TS Ar 23.11i > L ׀ קד על TS Ar 51.3b
[1373] יש TS Ar 51.3b
[1374] אללדין Oxf 2486.85b
[1375] בהאתין TS Ar 23.11i
[1376] ולהיתך עם קדש TS Ar 23.11i > L
[1377] איצ TS Ar 51.3b + TS Ar 23.11i
[1378] ונתתך TS Ar 23.11i > D
[1379] אלה[יך] TS Ar 23.11i > D

וקד שרחנא פי תפסיר מגלת[1382] אסתר[1383] אן אבא אלאמם ד̇, שם וחם ויפת כמא קאל[1384] **שלשה אלה[1385] בני נח ומאלה נפצה כל הארץ**[1386] (בר׳ 9:19). ואברהם איצ̇א[1387] כמא קאל[1388] **כי אב המון גוים[1389] נתתיך**[1390] (בר׳ 17:5). פאול מן אסתעבדנא מן כאן[1391] בית מלכה לחם והו נבוכ̇דנצר[1392] מלך בבל. כמא קאל[1393] פי נמרוד בן כוש בן חם **ותהי ראשית[1394] ממלכתו[1395] בבל**[1396] (בר׳ 10:10). ואלת̇אני[1397] מן כאן בית מלכה[1398] בלד עילם בן שם והם אלפרס כמא קאל[1399] **ואני בשושן הבירה אשר בעילם המדינה**[1400] (דניאל 8:2). ואלת̇אלת̇[1401] אליונאניין אלד̇ין[1402] פצ̇חת אלתוריה[1403] באנהם מן בני יפת אד̇ קאלת **בני יפת גמר ומגוג ומדי ויון**[1404] (בר׳ 10:2). ואלראבע[1405]

1380 עליון TS Ar 23.11i > L

1381 לעם קדוש TS Ar 23.11i > L | קד TS Ar 51.3b

1382 אלמגלה TS Ar 23.11i

1383 אסתר TS Ar 23.11i > L

1384 כמק TS Ar 51.3b

1385 כמא ... אלה TS Ar 23.11i > D

1386 כ הא TS Ar 23.11i

1387 איצ̇א TS Ar 23.11i > L | איצ̇ TS Ar 51.3b

1388 כק TS Ar 23.11i

1389 גו̇ TS Ar 23.11i

1390 נתתיך TS Ar 23.11i > L | נ̇ TS Ar 51.3b

1391 אסתעבדנא מן כאן TS Ar 23.11i > D

1392 נבוכד TS Ar 23.11i | נבוכדנ̇ TS Ar 51.3b

1393 כק TS Ar 23.11i | כמק TS Ar 51.3b

1394 ראש TS Ar 23.11i

1395 רא ממ̇ TS Ar 23.11i | ממ̇ TS Ar 51.3b

1396 בבל End of Oxf 2486.85b

1397 ואלת̇אני Beginning of Oxf 2486.86a | אלב TS Ar 23.11i

1398 מלכה End of TS Ar 51.3b

1399 כק TS Ar 23.11i

1400 אשר ... המדינה TS Ar 23.11i > L

1401 ואלג̇ TS Ar 23.11i

1402 אללד̇ין Oxf 2486.86a

1403 אל[תו]ריה TS Ar 23.11i > D

1404 ומג̇ ומד ויון TS Ar 23.11i

1405 ואלד TS Ar 23.11i

אדום וישמעאל אלד̇ין[1406] הם מן בני אברהם. ואבתדי באדום[1407] לאנה[1408] מן ולד אברהם ויסחק גמיעא. ולא יגוז אן נתוהם אן ממלכה אכ̇רי קד תבקת[1409] תסתעבדנא אד̇ לם יבק[1410] מן אבא[1411] אלאמם אחד. פמן[1412] קאל ההנא[1413] בעד **ארבעה מלכין** (דניאל 7:17), **ויקבלון מלכותא קדישי עליונין** (דניאל 7:18). ת̇ם קאל[1414]

Dn 7:19
אדין צבית ליצבא על חיותא רביעיתא די הות שניה מן כלהון דחילא ואימתני יתירה שניא די פרזל וטופרהא די נחש[1415] אכלה מדקא ושארא[1416] ברגלהא רפסא.[1417]

חיניד̇ ארדת אן[1418] אסתת̇בת[1419] אמר[1420] אלשכ̇ץ אלראבע[1421] אלד̇י כאן[1422] מג̇ירא[1423] מן אלגמיע פהו[1424] מפזוע[1425] גדא[1426] אסנאנה[1427] מן חדיד ואט̇פארה[1428] מן נחאס יאכל[1429] וידק ואלבאקי ידוסה ברגליה.[1430]

[1406] אללדין Oxf 2486.86a
[1407] ב[אד]ום TS Ar 23.11i > D
[1408] לאנהם TS Ar 23.11i
[1409] [תבק]ת TS Ar 23.11i > D
[1410] יבקא TS Ar 23.11i
[1411] א[בא] TS Ar 23.11i > D
[1412] פמנהא TS Ar 23.11i
[1413] האהנא Oxf 2486.86a
[1414] ת̇ם קאל TS Ar 23.11i > D
[1415] נחש Beginning of Yeirin 218 (BM Or.5554a.9a)
[1416] ושא[רא] End of the readable part of Oxf 2486.86a
[1417] רפסא Beginning of Oxf 2486.86b
[1418] ארדת אן Morag > L
[1419] אסתת̇[ב]ת TS Ar 23.11i > D
[1420] [אן ... א]מר Yeirin 218 > D
[1421] אלראבע Morag > D | אלד Yeirin 218
[1422] כאן TS Ar 23.11i > D
[1423] מג̇יירא Spiegel + Yeirin 218 + Morag | [מג̇]ירא TS Ar 23.11i > D
[1424] פה Spiegel
[1425] [מפז]ע Yeirin 218 > D
[1426] [אלגמיע ... גד]א TS Ar 23.11i > D
[1427] [גדא אסנא]נה Morag > D
[1428] ואצפארה Spiegel + Morag | [ואט̇]פארה TS Ar 23.11i > D
[1429] בהא + Spiegel

Dn 7:20

ועל קרניא עשר די ברישיה ואוחרי די סליקת ונפלו מן קדמיה תלת וקרנא די בין ועינין לה ופם ממליל רברבן וחזוה רב מן חברתה.

ואמא[1431] אלעשר[1432] קרון[1433] אללואתי[1434] פי ראסה ולאכ̇ר אלד̇י[1435] נבת וסקט מן בין ידיה ת̇לאת̇ה[1436] ואלקרן מנתצב[1437] ולה[1438] עיון[1439] ופם יתכלם[1440] באלכבאיר וצאר מנט̇רה[1441] אכת̇ר[1442] מן נט̇ראיה.[1443]

Dn 7:21

חזי הוית וקרנא דכן עבדא קרב עם קדישין ויכלא להון.[1444]

וכנת[1445] ראית[1446] כאן[1447] ד̇לך[1448] אלקרן[1449] יחארב אלקדוסין[1450] ויט̇פר[1451] בהם.[1452]

[1430] וידק ... ברגליה TS Ar 23.11i < D ׀ ברגלה Oxf 2486.86b + Yeirin 218 ׀ ברגלאה Spiegel

[1431] ואמר TS Ar 23.11i

[1432] אלי̇ TS Ar 23.11i

[1433] אלקרון אלעשרה Morag ׀ אלעשר אלקרון Spiegel

[1434] אלאוליאת Morag ׀ אלאואיל אללואתי Spiegel

[1435] אלד Yeirin 218

[1436] ג̇ Oxf 2486.86b

[1437] [אלדי ... מנתצ]ב TS Ar 23.11i < D

[1438] ולה Spiegel and Yeirin 218 and Morag < L

[1439] אלעיון Spiegel + Yeirin 218 + Morag ׀ עינין TS Ar 23.11i

[1440] י[תכ]לם TS Ar 23.11i < D

[1441] מנצ̇רה Spiegel + Morag

[1442] אכבר Yeirin 218 + Oxf 2486.86b

[1443] נצ̇ראיה Spiegel + Morag ׀ נט̇אריה Yeirin 218 ׀ מנטרה ... נטראיה TS Ar 23.11i < D

[1444] להון End of Oxf 2486.86b

[1445] וכנת Beginning of Oxf 2486.87a

[1446] וכ[נת ר]אית Morag < D

[1447] באן TS Ar 23.11i + Morag

[1448] דאלך Spiegel + Morag

[1449] אלקרין Spiegel + Morag

[1450] אלקדיסין Yeirin 218 + TS Ar 23.11i

[1451] ויצפר Spiegel + Morag

[1452] [בה]ם Morag ׀ ויטפר בהם TS Ar 23.11i < D

Dn 7:22

עד די אתא עתיק יומיא ודינא יהיב לקדישי עליונין וזמנא מטא ומלכותא החסינו קדישין.

אלי אן גא אלשיך[1453] פצאר[1454] אלחכם ללקדוסין[1455] אלמתעאליין ודני[1456] אלאגל וורתֿ אלמלך אלקדוסין.[1457]

זאד דניאל[1458] ההנא[1459] גֿ נכת לם יכן[1460] דֿכרהא פי נץ אול[1461] אלרויא. פתממהא[1462] ההנא[1463] פי מוצֿע אלתמאם ואלתפסיר.[1464] אמא אלנכתה אלאולי פאן אלשכֿץ אלראבע לה אטֿפאר מן[1465] נחאס[1466] כמא קאל[1467] **וטפרהא די נחש**[1468] (דניאל 7:19). והדֿא[1469] אלשאן פי אלבהאם, זיאדה[1470] קוה פי[1471] דוס אלשי[1472] ורפסה.[1473] פהו אסתעאנה עלי **ושארא ברגלהא רפסא** (דניאל 7:19). פאדֿא אנתקל הדֿא[1474] אלשאן[1475] באלתאויל אלי אלנאס כאן מעני אלאטֿפאר אלכתאבה ואלתֿבאת. ואדֿ אלחאל מדֿמומה[1476] פתכן[1477]

[1453] אלי ... אלשיך TS Ar 23.11i > D
[1454] [פ]צאר Yeirin 218
[1455] לאלקדוסין Spiegel + Morag | ללקדיסין Yeirin 218 + TS Ar 23.11i
[1456] ודנא Spiegel + Oxf 2486.87a + Morag
[1457] אלקדיסיין Morag | אלקדיסין Yeirin 218
[1458] [אלמלך ...ד]ניאל TS Ar 23.11i > D | [ד]ניאל Yeirin 218 > D
[1459] האהנא Oxf 2486.87a
[1460] יכון Yeirin 218
[1461] אול Yeirin 218 > L
[1462] פתמהא TS Ar 23.11i
[1463] האהנא Oxf 2486.87a
[1464] ההנא ... ואלתפסיר TS Ar 23.11i > D | אלתפסיר Yeirin 218
[1465] אלש[כֿץ ... מן] Yeirin 218 > D
[1466] חדיד Oxf 2486.87a
[1467] כק Yeirin 218
[1468] מן ... נחש TS Ar 23.11i > D
[1469] ו[ה]דא TS Ar 23.11i > D
[1470] וטפראה ... זיאדה Yeirin 218 > D
[1471] פי End of the readable part of Yeirin 218
[1472] אל[שאן ... אלשי] TS Ar 23.11i > D
[1473] ורפסה End of the readable part of TS Ar 23.11i
[1474] הדא End of Oxf 2486.87a
[1475] אלשאן Beginning of Oxf 2486.87b
[1476] מדמומה Beginning of the readable part of TS Ar 23.11j
[1477] פתכון TS Ar 23.11j

אלכתאבה חקדא ללדׄנוב[1478] וחפטׄא ללגרום. ותכן אלצפח ען[1479] שי כמא קאל והו[1480] ימתׄל **חטאת יהודה כתובה בעט ברזל בצפרן שמיר**[1481] (ירמ׳ 17:1). ואלנכתה אלתׄאניה[1482] מא דׄכר ען[1483] אלקרין אלצגׄיר[1484] אנה צאר[1485] מנטׄרה אכבר[1486] מן אצחאבה אדׄ קאל[1487] **וחזוה רב מן חברתה** (דניאל 7:20) והו אלמשאהד מן אן אלממלכה אלראבעה[1488] לאדום עטׄמת[1489] אכתׄר מנהא. ואלנכתה אלגׄ מחארבה בני אסראיל כמא קאל[1490] **וקרנא דכן עבדא קרב עם קדישין**[1491] (דניאל 7:21). פלא תזל טׄאפרה בהם אלי אן יואפי וקת אלישועה כקׄ **אכלא להון** (דניאל 7:21) **עד**[1492] **די אתה עתיק יומין** (דניאל 7:22).

וקד עלמנא אן קולה[1493] **ודינה יהב** (דניאל 7:22) אנמא כאן[1494] **לעתיק יומיא** (ע׳ דניאל 7:22) והו אן ינטׄר[1495] פי מטׄאלם[1496] אלנאס. פכיף קאל האהנא[1497] **ודינא**[1498] **יהיב לקדישי עליונין** (דניאל 7:22) וישׂראל לם ינטׄרו[1499] פי שיא[1500] מנהא? פנקול ליס יעני אנהם ינטׄרון פי מטׄאלם גׄירהם.[1501] ואנמא יריד

[1478] [לל]דנ[וב] TS Ar 23.11j > D

[1479] ען Beginning of Yeirin 219 (BM Or.5554a.9b)

[1480] וחפטא ... והו TS Ar 23.11j > D

[1481] כתובה ... שמיר TS Ar 23.11j > L | שמיר Yeirin 219 > L

[1482] אלב TS Ar 23.11j

[1483] עלי Yeirin 219

[1484] [אלצ]גׄי[ר] TS Ar 23.11j > D

[1485] [צ]אר Yeirin 219

[1486] [אנה ... אכ]בר TS Ar 23.11j > D

[1487] קאל End of the readable part of Oxf 2486.87b

[1488] [אלמשאהד ... אלראב]עה TS Ar 23.11j > D

[1489] עצמת Yeirin 219

[1490] אסר כק TS Ar 23.11j > D

[1491] עם קדישין TS Ar 23.11j > L

[1492] אכלא ... עד TS Ar 23.11j > D

[1493] קוׄ TS Ar 23.11j

[1494] כאן Beginning of Oxf 2486.88a

[1495] יומיא ... ינטר TS Ar 23.11j > D | נטר Yeirin 219

[1496] מצלם Yeirin 219

[1497] האהנא Oxf 2486.88a

[1498] דינה TS Ar 23.11j

[1499] י[נט]רו TS Ar 23.11j > D

[1500] שי Yeirin 219 + TS Ar 23.11j

[1501] אנהם ליס ינטרון גׄירהם TS Ar 23.11j

אן אלשיך ינט̇ר פי מט̇אלמהם הם פיחכם[1502] להם עלי[1503] מן ט̇למהם כמא[1504] שרחנא **ונשפטתי עמם שם על עמי ונחלתי ישׂראל**[1505] (יואל 4:2). ועלי מא עלמנאה קאל לאברהם **וגם את הגוי אשר יעבדו דן אנכי**[1506] (בר׳ 15:14). וקאל למשה **וגם**[1507] **ראיתי את הלחץ אשר מצרים לחצים**[1508] **אתם**[1509] (שמ׳ 3:9). וקאל ען מלכות בבל **קצפתי על עמי חללתי נחלתי**[1510] **ואתנם בידך ולא שׂמת להם רחמים**[1511] (יש׳ 47:6). וקאל ען[1512] מלכות פרס[1513] **וקצף גדול אני קצף**[1514] **על הגוים השאננים אשר אנכי**[1515] **קצפתי מעט**[1516] **והמה עזרו לרעה**[1517] (זכריה 1:15). וקאל[1518] פי[1519] סאיר אלאמם **כי ידין יוי עמו ועל עבדיו יתנחם** (דב׳ 32:36). וקאל איצ̇א **אשיב נקם לצרי ולמשנאי אשלם** (דב׳ 32:41), ואיצ̇א **כי דם עבדיו יקום ונקם ישיב לצריו**[1520] (דב׳ 32:43). ת̇ם אג̇אב[1521] אלג̇ואב בעד אלסואל פקאל

Dn 7:23

כן אמר חיותא רביעיתא מלכו רביעאה תהוא בארעא די תשנא מן כל מלכותא ותאכל כל ארעא ותדושנה ותדקנה.

[1502] פיח[כם] TS Ar 23.11j > D

[1503] עלי Yeirin 219 > L

[1504] כמ TS Ar 23.11j

[1505] עמי ... ישׂראל TS Ar 23.11j > L

[1506] יע[בדו ... אנוכי] TS Ar 23.11j > D

[1507] וגם Yeirin 219 > D

[1508] לוחצים Yeirin 219

[1509] אשר ... אתם TS Ar 23.11j > L

[1510] ען ... נחלתי Yeirin 219 > D

[1511] חללתי ... רחמים TS Ar 23.11j > L

[1512] וק[אל ען] TS Ar 23.11j > D

[1513] [בידך ... פר]ס Yeirin 219 > D

[1514] א[ני] ק[צ]ף TS Ar 23.11j > D

[1515] אני MT

[1516] מעט Oxf 2486.88a > L | [גדול ... מע]ט Yeirin 219 > D | מעט End of the readable part of Yeirin 219

[1517] על ... לרעה TS Ar 23.11j > L

[1518] וקאל End of Oxf 2486.88a

[1519] פי Beginning of Oxf 2486.88b

[1520] ועל עבדיו ... לצריו TS Ar 23.11j > L

[1521] א[גא]ב TS Ar 23.11j > D

הכד׳י[1522] קאל תפסיר אלשכ׳ץ אלראבע[1523] ממלכה ראבעה[1524] תכון[1525] פי אלארץ׳ תג׳יר[1526] מא תקדם מן אלממאלך וכאנהא תאכל[1527] גמיע אלבלאד ותדוסה ותדקה.

Dn 7:24

וקרניא עשר מינה מלכותא עשרה מלכין יקומון [ואחרן] יקום אחריהון והוא ישני מן קדמיא ותלתא מלכין יהשפיל.[1528]

ותפסיר[1529] אלעשרה[1530] קרון[1531] מן תלך אלממלכה[1532] יקום עשרה[1533] מלוך ואכ׳ר יקום בעדהם פהו יג׳יר[1534] מא תקדם מן אלאולין[1535] ויצ׳ע ת׳לאת׳ה[1536] מלוך.[1537]

Dn 7:25

ומלין לצר עלאה ימלל ולקדישי עליונין יבלא ויסבר להשניא זמנין ודת ויתיהבון בידה עד עידן ועידנין ופלג עידן.

וכלאם[1538] יתקולה[1539] עלי אלעאלי[1540] ויכ׳לק לקדוסין[1541] אלמתעאליין[1542] ויאמל[1543] אן יג׳יר[1544] אעיאדהם וסננהם[1545] ויסלמון פי ידה אלי מדה[1546] ומדתין ונצף.[1547]

[1522] הכדא Spiegel
[1523] אלד TS Ar 23.11j
[1524] ד TS Ar 23.11j
[1525] תכן Oxf 2486.88b | [ת]כון TS Ar 23.11j > D
[1526] תגוהר Oxf 2486.88b | תג׳ייר Spiegel
[1527] הכדי קאל אל[תפסיר אלשכ]ץ אלרא[בע אלממ]לכה ראבעה תכון פי אל[ארץ תג׳ייר מא [תקדם מן אלממא]לך וכאנהא תא[כל] Morag > D
[1528] יהשפיל End of Oxf 2486.88b
[1529] ותפסיר Beginning of Oxf 2486.89a
[1530] אלי׳ TS Ar 23.11j | אלעשר Spiegel + Oxf 2486.89a
[1531] אלקרון Spiegel + Morag
[1532] אלממל[כה] TS Ar 23.11j > D
[1533] י׳ TS Ar 23.11j
[1534] יג׳ייר Spiegel + Morag
[1535] אלאוולין Spiegel + Morag
[1536] ג׳ Oxf 2486.89a | תלאת[ה] Morag > D | תלאת Spiegel
[1537] [ויצע ג׳ מל]וך TS Ar 23.11j > D
[1538] וכלא[ם] TS Ar 23.11j > D
[1539] יתקו[לה] Morag > D | יתקוולה Spiegel
[1540] אלעלי Oxf 2486.89a

תצדירה[1548] בקול **כן אמר** (דניאל 7:23) ליס יעני בה **עתיק יומין**. ועלי אנה מתצל בדׄכרה[1549] לאן **עתיק יומין** לם יפסר לדניאל שיא. ואנמא יעני **בכן אמר** (דניאל 7:23) דׄלך אלמלאך[1550] אלדׄי הו **חד מן קמאיא** (דניאל 7:16) אלדׄי אלתמס מנה אלתפסיר. אעני[1551] מעאני[1552] **חיותא רביעיתא** (דניאל 7:23) וקד סבק אתׄבאתנא לגמיע דׄלך,[1553] אעני **ותאכל כל ארעא**[1554] **ותדושנה ותדקנה**[1555] (דניאל 7:23). **וקרניא**[1556] **עשר** (דניאל 7:24) וכל מא בעדה חכאה באכׄתצאר[1557] עלי מא צלח ועלי מא לם[1558] יגז אן נתסע[1559] פיה באכתׄר מן דׄלך. ולכנה זאד ההנא[1560] שרחא פי אחואל אלממלכה[1561] אלמתצלה באדום תפסירא ללנכתה אלתי זאדהא[1562] פקאל **עבדא קרב**[1563] **עם קדישין ויכלה להון**[1564] (דניאל 7:21). פערפנא אי שי הו[1565] אלסבב פי אלמחארבה[1566] פקאל

1541 אלקדוסיין Morag | אלקדיסין TS Ar 23.11j + Oxf 2486.89a
1542 אל[מת]עאליין Morag
1543 וי[אמל] TS Ar 23.11j > D | ויאמל End of TS Ar 23.11j dealing with this passage
1544 יגׄייר Spiegel + Morag
1545 אע[יאדהם וסננהם] Morag > D
1546 י[דה עלי מ]דה Morag > D
1547 ו[נצ]ף Morag > D
1548 תצדירה Beginning of the readable part of TS Ar 23.11L
1549 [לי]ס [יעני ... בדכרה] TS Ar 23.11L > D
1550 [ואנמא ... אלמל]אך TS Ar 23.11L > D
1551 אעני End of Oxf 2486.89a
1552 מנה ... מעאני TS Ar 23.11L > D | מעאני Beginning of Oxf 2486.89b
1553 וקד ... ד לך Oxf 2486.89b > D
1554 ארע[ע]ם TS Ar 23.11L > D
1555 [ארע]ה ותדו[שנ]ה ותדק[נה] Oxf 2486.89b > D | ותדושנה ותדקנה TS Ar 23.11L > L
1556 וקרניא Oxf 2486.89b > D
1557 בא[כתצאר] Oxf 2486.89b > D
1558 [עלי] מא [צח ... לם] TS Ar 23.11L > D
1559 לם ... נתסע Oxf 2486.89b > D
1560 האהנא Oxf 2486.89b
1561 [שרחא ... אלממ]לכה TS Ar 23.11L > D
1562 זא[דהא] Oxf 2486.89b > D
1563 עבדא קרב TS Ar 23.11L > D
1564 עם ... להון TS Ar 23.11L > L
1565 הו TS Ar 23.11L > L
1566 אל[מחאר]בה TS Ar 23.11L > D

אן ד̇לך לאכ̇ראגהם ען דינהם[1567] ואלט̇אהר מנה אעיאדהם[1568] וסננהם. והו מא קאל **ויסבר להשניה זמנין ודת** (דניאל 7:25).

פאמא **ויסבר**[1569] (דניאל 7:25) פהו תרגום **ראה פניך לא פללתי**[1570] (בר׳ 48:11), **לא סברית**.[1571] ואמא[1572] **זמנין** (דניאל 7:25) פהי אלאעיאד כמא קאל[1573] **תלת זמנין**, תרגום **שלש**[1574] **פעמים**[1575] (שמ׳ 23:17). ואמא **דת** (ע׳ דניאל 7:25) פהי סנן[1576] אלתוראה[1577] כמא[1578] קאל[1579] **מימינו אש דת למו** (דב׳ 33:2). וקאל עדוהם **ודתיהם שונות מכל עם**[1580] (אסתר 3:8). וקאל צדיקהם[1581] לעזרא **בדת אלהיך די בידך** (עזרא 7:14). פירום[1582] תג̇ייר רסומהם הד̇ה בעד אן יכ̇לקהם באלשנאעאת אלסו[1583] ואלאד̇י כמא קאל[1584] **ולקדישי עליונין יבלא**[1585] (דניאל 7:25).

ולמוצ̇ע מא כאן קד קדם מן קולה **וזמנא מטא** (דניאל 7:22) והו אלאגל, אעני אלקץ שרחה לה ההנא[1586] כם הו פקאל **ויתיהבון בידה עד עדן ועדנין ופלג עדן**[1587] (דניאל 7:25). ולהד̇א ד̇ תפאסיר כלהא תתפק ותכ̇רג אלי נקטה ואחדה. תפסירין מנהא[1588] אגתמע[1589] פיהמא מדה אלממלכה[1590]

[1567] דינ[הם] TS Ar 23.11L > D

[1568] אעיא[דה]ם TS Ar 23.11L > D

[1569] [ויסבר ... פאמא] ויסבר TS Ar 23.11L > D homeoteleuton

[1570] לא פללתי TS Ar 23.11L > L

[1571] Uncertain lesson

[1572] אמא TS Ar 23.11L

[1573] כק TS Ar 23.11L

[1574] רגלים + TS Ar 23.11L

[1575] פעמים TS Ar 23.11L > L

[1576] סנן Oxf 2486.89b > D

[1577] אלתוריה TS Ar 23.11L

[1578] כמא End of Oxf 2486.89b

[1579] אלתוריה כק TS Ar 23.11L | קאל Beginning of Oxf 2486.90a

[1580] ש[ונות מכל עם] TS Ar 23.11L > D

[1581] צדיקיהם TS Ar 23.11L

[1582] [פי]רום TS Ar 23.11L > D

[1583] ואלסו TS Ar 23.11L

[1584] כק TS Ar 23.11L

[1585] עליונין יבלא TS Ar 23.11L > L

[1586] האהנא Oxf 2486.90a

[1587] עדן ... עדן TS Ar 23.11L > L

[1588] נקטה ... מנהא TS Ar 23.11L > D

אלאכ̇ירה[1591] מע אלממאלך אלמתקדמה. פיקול **ויתיהבון בידה**[1592] (דניאל 7:25) אלי תמאם **עדן ועדנין ופלג עדן**[1593] (דניאל 7:25) ליס כלהא פי יד אלאכ̇ירה. לכנהא מן אול אלי אכ̇ר. פיכון[1594] פי אלתפסיר אלאול מנהמא[1595] מקדאר[1596] **עדן**[1597] (דניאל 7:25) ת̇[1598] סנה נט̇יר אלשעבוד אלד̇י אקאם אלקום במצר.[1599] וד̇לך אן **קץ וזמן ועדן**[1600] כלהא מתגאנסה[1601] פי אנהא מדד ואוקאת. פיכון מקדאר **עדן**[1602] (דניאל 7:25) ת̇ סנה ומקדאר[1603] **עדנין**[1604] (דניאל 7:25) ת̇ת̇ סנה ומקדאר[1605] **ופלג עדן** (דניאל 7:25) ר̇ סנה.[1606] פד̇לך אלף ת̇ סנה. ויכון דלך מן **גלוה**[1607] **יכניה** אלי וקת אלישועה. וד̇לך אן הד̇א אלקול קיל[1608] לדניאל[1609] **בשנת חדה לבלאשצר** (דניאל 7:1).

וכאן לגלוה[1610] יכניה חיניד̇[1611] נ̇ב̇[1612] סנה לאן **גלוה יכניה**[1613] כאנת פי סנה ת̇מן מן מלך נבוכדנצר כמא קאל[1614] **ויקח אתו מלך בבל בשנת שמנה**

[1589] תגתמע TS Ar 23.11L
[1590] אל[ממ]לכה TS Ar 23.11L > D
[1591] אלאכרי TS Ar 23.11L
[1592] אלממאלך ... בידה TS Ar 23.11L > D
[1593] ופ ע TS Ar 23.11L
[1594] יד ... פיכון TS Ar 23.11L > D
[1595] מנהמא TS Ar 23.11L > L
[1596] מקדאר End of Oxf 2486.90a | מקד[אר] TS Ar 23.11L > D
[1597] עדן Beginning of Oxf 2486.90b
[1598] ת Oxf 2486.90b > D
[1599] סנה ... במצר TS Ar 23.11L > D
[1600] ו[עד]ן TS Ar 23.11L > D
[1601] מת[גאנ]סה TS Ar 23.11L > D
[1602] פי ... עדן TS Ar 23.11L > D
[1603] ומקדאר TS Ar 23.11L > L
[1604] ועדנין TS Ar 23.11L
[1605] ומקדאר TS Ar 23.11L > L
[1606] סנה TS Ar 23.11L > D
[1607] אל[לף ... גלוה] TS Ar 23.11L > D
[1608] קיל Beginning of the readable part of Yeirin 222a (MS Kaufmann 222)
[1609] ל[דני]אל TS Ar 23.11L > D
[1610] בשנת ... גולה TS Ar 23.11L > D
[1611] לדניאל ... חיניד Yeirin 222a > D
[1612] נ̇ב̇ TS Ar 23.11L > D
[1613] [יכ]ניה TS Ar 23.11L > D
[1614] סנ[ה ... קאל] Yeirin 222a > D

למלכו[1615] (מל״ב 24:12). ונבוכדנצר[1616] מלך[1617] מהׄ, בקי מן מלכה לחׄ. ואויל מרודך אבנה מלך[1618] כׄגׄ ובלשאצר[1619] אבן אבנה סנה ואחדה. פדׄלך סׄבׄ סנין. ובקי[1620] מן מלך בלשאצר[1621] סנתין מדאכׄלה. ואחדה למלך כורש,[1622] צארת[1623] סׄגׄ ומלך כורש[1624] סנתין[1625] פצארת סׄהׄ.[1626] תׄם קיל[1627] לדניאל פי אלסנה אלתׄאלתׄה מן מלך כורש אן[1628] קד בקי ללישועה אלף שׄלׄהׄ צאר אלכל[1629] אלף וארבע מאיה.[1630] ויכון[1631] פי אלתפסיר אלתׄאני[1632] מן אלתפסירין אללדׄין[1633] יגמעאן[1634] אלשעבוד מן אולה אלי אכׄרה מקדאר **עדן**[1635] **ועדנין**[1636] **ופלג עדן**[1637] (דניאל 7:25) מתׄל קולה[1638] **כי למועד מועדים וחצי**[1639] (דניאל 12:7). ויכון[1640] אלוא[1641] אלזאידה[1642] פי קולה[1643]

[1615] פי ... מלכו TS Ar 23.11L > D
[1616] ונבוכד TS Ar 23.11L
[1617] מלך End of the readable part of TS Ar 23.11L אתו ... מלך > D Yeirin 222a
[1618] מלך Beginning of TS Ar 23.11m
[1619] ב]קי ... ובלשאצר] Yeirin 222a > D
[1620] וקד בקי Yeirin 222a. קד בקי Probable homeoteleuton with the following
[1621] אב]נה ... בלשאצר] TS Ar 23.11m > D
[1622] מ]דא]כלה ו]אחד]ה למלך כור[ש] Oxf 2486.90b > D | כורש End Oxf 2486.90b
[1623] צארת Beginning of Oxf 2486.175a | [צ]ארת Oxf 2486.175a > D
[1624] ומל[ך] כו[רש] Oxf 2486.175a > D
[1625] אב]נה ... סנתין] Yeirin 222a > D | צארת .. פצארת Probablz homeoteleuton
[1626] כור[ש ...ס]ה TS Ar 23.11m > D
[1627] קיל TS Ar 23.11m > D
[1628] סה ... אן Yeirin 222a > D
[1629] ת סנה + TS Ar 23.11m
[1630] אלף וארבע מאיה TS Ar 23.11m > L
[1631] ויכן TS Ar 23.11m
[1632] אלב TS Ar 23.11m
[1633] ויכון ... אללדין Yeirin 222a > D | אלדין TS Ar 23.11m
[1634] י[גמעא]ן TS Ar 23.11m > D
[1635] [אול]ה [אלי ...מ]קדאר [עדן] TS Ar 23.11m > D
[1636] אל[שעבוד ... ועדנין] Yeirin 222a > D
[1637] ופ ע TS Ar 23.11m
[1638] קו TS Ar 23.11m
[1639] וחצי TS Ar 23.11m > L
[1640] פיכן TS Ar 23.11m | מ[תל ... ויכון] Yeirin 222a > D
[1641] לוא Yeirin 222a
[1642] אלזא[ידה] TS Ar 23.11m > D
[1643] קו TS Ar 23.11m

ועדנין (דניאל 7:25) תעקיבא[1644] מתׄלהא פי קולה[1645] **ובני אלה וקנז** (דה"א 4:15) ופי קולה[1646] **ועפר וישעי** (דה"א 5:24) ופי קולה[1647] **וחמש עשרה אמה**[1648] **קלעים לכתף** (שמ' 27:14). ויכון[1649] אלכׄאלץ **עד עדן ועדנין ופלג עדן**[1650] (דניאל 7:25) פהו מתׄל **למועד**[1651] **מועדים וחצי** (דניאל 12:7) סוא. ויציר **מועד** אלאול כׄאדמא[1652] פי אלכלאם[1653] כקולך[1654] באגל נׄ יום ועלי[1655] מא סנפסר הדׄא אלפסוק פי מוצׄעה.[1656] ונקול אן **מועדים**[1657] (דניאל 12:7) הי מדה דולה ישׂראל מנדׄ כׄרגו[1658] מן מצר[1659] אלי כׄראב[1660] אלקדס,[1661] ודׄלך תׄתׄצׄ סנה.[1662] מנהא תׄפׄ אלי אן בני[1663] בית אלמקדס. ומנהא תׄיׄ[1664] מקדאר מא עמר אלבית. ונצף הדׄה אלמדה תׄמׄהׄ. פדׄלך אלף שׂלׄהׄ סנה[1665] והי אלמדה אלמכתובה[1666] פי פסוק **אשרי המחכה** (דניאל 12:12). פיקימון ישׂראל תחת יד הדׄא **אחרן יקום אחריהון**[1667] (ע' דניאל 7:24) אלי תמאם מא בקי מן מקדאר **מועדים וחצי** (דניאל 12:7) מן אול שעבודהם.

[1644] תעקיבא Uncertain lesson | תעקיבא TS Ar 23.11m > L
[1645] קו TS Ar 23.11m
[1646] קו TS Ar 23.11m
[1647] קו TS Ar 23.11m
[1648] וע[פר ... אמה] Yeirin 222a > D
[1649] וחמש ... ויכון TS Ar 23.11m > D | ויך Yeirin 222a
[1650] ופ ע TS Ar 23.11m
[1651] מועד TS Ar 23.11m
[1652] וי[ציר ... כאדמא TS Ar 23.11m > D
[1653] אלכלאץ ... אלכלאם Yeirin 222a > D
[1654] כקך TS Ar 23.11m
[1655] עלי Yeirin 222a
[1656] מא ... מו[צעה Yeirin 222a > D
[1657] ונקול אן מועדים TS Ar 23.11m > D
[1658] [מדה דו]לה [ישרא]ל מ[נ]ד כ[ר]גו Oxf 2486.175a > D
[1659] מדה ... מצר Yeirin 222a > D | מצר End of Oxf 2486.175a
[1660] כראב Beginning of the readable part of Oxf 2486.175b
[1661] אלק[דס] TS Ar 23.11m > D
[1662] סנה Oxf 2486.175b > D
[1663] ת[תצ ...בני] Yeirin 222a > D
[1664] תׄיׄ End of the readable part of Yeirin 222a
[1665] סנה Oxf 2486.175b > L
[1666] אל[מכת]ובה TS Ar 23.11m > D
[1667] אחריהון TS Ar 23.11m > L

ואלתפסירין אלאכׄרין המא יכׄצאן אלשעבוד אלדׄי יכון[1668] תחת יד הדׄא אלאכׄיר וחדה. פאחדהמא והו אלתפסיר[1669] אלתׄאלתׄ[1670] הו[1671] אן יכון[1672] מקדאר **עדן** (דניאל 7:24) מאיה[1673] סנה ואחדה **ועדנין** (דניאל 7:24) מאיתי[1674] סנה **ופלג עדן**[1675] (דניאל 7:24) נׄ סנה. פדׄלך שנׄ סנה[1676] והו באלתקריב מקדאר מא יבקא[1677] מן אלף שׄלׄהׄ אלדׄי לא[1678] **אחרן יקום**[1679] **אחריהון** (ע׳ דניאל 7:24). ואלתׄאני[1680] מן אלתפסירין אלכׄאצין אן יכון[1681] תפסיר **עדן** (דניאל 7:24) מדה דולה מלך[1682] בבל והו סבעין[1683] סנה. **ועדנין** (דניאל 7:24) מדתי[1684] דולה[1685] למלך[1686] אלפרס ומלך[1687] אליונאניה והי[1688] מאתין אתׄנין ותׄלתׄין.[1689] ודׄלך אן מלך אלפרס נׄבׄ[1690] ואבתדי[1691] מלך אליונאניה וצפא דולתהם[1692] מאיה ותׄמאנין[1693] סנה. פדׄלך שׄ וסנתין. ומקדאר **פלג עדן**[1694] (ע׳ דניאל 7:24) נצף[1695] אלמדה[1696] אלאולי אלתי הי מלך בבל והי כׄמסה ותׄלאתׄין סנה. פצאר אלגמיע[1697] איצׄא[1698] קריב מן שׄמׄ עלי אלגמלה. פאי[1699] ואחד מן

[1668] אלתי תכן TS Ar 23.11m
[1669] אלתפס TS Ar 23.11m
[1670] וג׳ ודאך + TS Ar 23.11m
[1671] הו > L TS Ar 23.11m
[1672] יכן TS Ar 23.11m
[1673] ק TS Ar 23.11m
[1674] ד TS Ar 23.11m
[1675] ופ ע TS Ar 23.11m
[1676] סנה > L Oxf 2486.175b
[1677] והו ... יבקא > D TS Ar 23.11m
[1678] לה TS Ar 23.11m
[1679] אחרן יקום Beginning of the readable part of Yeirin 222b
[1680] ואלב TS Ar 23.11m
[1681] [יקום ... יכו]ן > D Yeirin 222b
[1682] אלכאצין ... מלך > D TS Ar 23.11m
[1683] ע TS Ar 23.11m
[1684] מד[תי] > D Oxf 2486.175b ׀ מדתי End of Oxf 2486.175b
[1685] [עדן ... דול]ה > D Yeirin 222b ׀ דולה Beginning of Oxf 2486.91a
[1686] למלך > L TS Ar 23.11m
[1687] ו[מ]ל[ך] > D Oxf 2486.91a
[1688] ו[הי] > D Oxf 2486.91a
[1689] אלפרס ... ותלתין > D Yeirin 222b
[1690] ומלך אליונאניה ... נׄבׄ > D TS Ar 23.11m
[1691] ו[אבת]די > D TS Ar 23.11m
[1692] [מלך ... דולתה]ם > D Yeirin 222b
[1693] ק פ Yeirin 222b
[1694] דולתהם ... עדן > D TS Ar 23.11m
[1695] [נצ]ף > D TS Ar 23.11m

אלגמיע[1697] איצ̇א[1698] קריב מן ש̇מ̇ עלי אלגמלה. פאי[1699] ואחד מן הד̇ה אלארבע[1700] תפאסיר קיל כאן גאיזא[1701] מסתקימא. ועלי אן בעצ̇הא,[1702] והו אלת̇אני,[1703] אשד תחקקא מן בעצ̇. ת̇ם קאל[1704]

Dn 7:26

ודינה יתיב[1705] ושלטנה יתעדון להשמדא ולהובדא עד סופא.

ולמא[1706] וצ̇ע אלחכם[1707] אזיל[1708] סלטאנה[1709] וצאר[1710] אלי אלנפאד̇ ואלאבאדה[1711] אלי[1712] אכ̇ר אלזמאן.[1713]

Dn 7:27

ומלכותא[1714] ושלטנ̇ה ורבותא די מלכות[1715] תחות כל שמיא יהיבת לעם קדישי עליונין[1716] מלכותיא מלכות עלם וכל שלטוניה ליה פלחון וישתמעון.[1717]

[1696] [פדלך ... אלמד]ה Yeirin 222b > D
[1697] אלתי ... אלגמיע Yeirin 222b > D | הי ... אלגמיע TS Ar 23.11m > D
[1698] איצ TS Ar 23.11m
[1699] [אלגמלה] פ[אי] TS Ar 23.11m > D
[1700] שמ ... אלארבע Yeirin 222b > D
[1701] הדה ... גאיזא TS Ar 23.11m > D
[1702] קיל ... בעצהא Yeirin 222b > D
[1703] אלב TS Ar 23.11m
[1704] תחקקא ... קאל TS Ar 23.11m > D
[1705] [אשד ... יתי]ב Yeirin 222b > D
[1706] [ול]מא Yeirin 222b > D
[1707] אל[ח]כם Oxf 2486.91a > D
[1708] ואזיל Spiegel + Morag
[1709] סלטאנה End of the readable part of TS Ar 23.11m | צלטאנה Morag
[1710] [וצ]אר Oxf 2486.91a > D
[1711] נפאד ואבאדה Morag
[1712] סלטאנה ... אלאבאדה אלי Yeirin 222b > D
[1713] [אלז]מאן Oxf 2486.91a > D | אלזמאן End of Oxf 2486.91a
[1714] ומלכותא Beginning of Oxf 2486.91b
[1715] ומלכותא ... מלכות Yeirin 222b > D
[1716] [יהיבת ... עליו]ן Yeirin 222b > D
[1717] וכל ... וישתמעון Yeirin 222b > D

ואלמלך ואלסלטאן[1718] ואלשרף אלדין[1719] למלך גמיע מא תחת אלסמא[1720] סלמת אלי אלקום[1721] אלקדוסין[1722] אלמתעאליין פמלכהם[1723] מלך אלדהר[1724] וגמיע אלסלאטין להם[1725] יסמעון[1726] ויטיעון.

Dn 7:28

עד כא סופה די מלתא אנא דניאל שגיא רעיוני יבהונני וזיוי ישתנון עלי ומלתא בלבי נטרית.

אלי ההנא[1727] אכ̇ר אלקצה ואנא[1728] דניאל אדהשתני אפכארי כת̇ירא ותג̇יירת[1729] סחנתי עליי וחפט̇ת[1730] אלקצה[1731] פי קלבי.

פאמא קולה **ודינה יתיב ושלטנה**[1732] **יתעדון**[1733] (דניאל 7:26) פהו מא וצפנא אן אלחכם למא[1734] וצ̇ע זאל סלטאן[1735] גמיע אלממאלך והו מת̇ל מא קאל **והפכתי כסא ממלכות**[1736] **והשמדתי**[1737] **חזק**[1738] **ממלכות הגוים** (חגי

[1718] ואלצלטאן Morag

[1719] אללדין Oxf 2486.91b

[1720] אלדין ... אלסמא Yeirin 222b > D

[1721] אלקום Morag > L

[1722] אלקדוסיין Morag ׀ אלקדיסין Yeirin 222b + Oxf 2486.91b

[1723] מלכהם Spiegel

[1724] אלמתעאליין ... אלדהר Yeirin 222b > D

[1725] להם End of Yeirin 222b

[1726] יסמעון Beginning of Yeirin 222c (Budapest, MS Kaufmann 222c)

[1727] ההנא Beginning of the readable part of TS Ar 23. 11n ׀ [הה]נא TS Ar > D b23. 11n ׀ [אלי הא]הנא Oxf 2486.91b > D

[1728] ו[אנא] Morag > D

[1729] ותג̇ירת Oxf 2486.91b

[1730] וחפצת Spiegel + Yeirin 222c + Morag

[1731] אפכארי ... אלקצה TS Ar 23. 11n > D

[1732] ושלטנה End of Oxf 2486.91b ׀ ושולטנה Yeirin 222c

[1733] יתעדון Beginning of Oxf 2486.92a

[1734] יתיב ... ולמא TS Ar 23. 11n > D

[1735] אלסלטאן Oxf 2486.92a

[1736] ו[הפכתי ... מלכו]ת TS Ar 23. 11n > D

[1737] והשבתי Oxf 2486.92a

[1738] חזק TS Ar 23. 11n > D

2:22) ומא אשבה דֿלך. ואמא קולה[1739] **ומלכותא ושלטנא**[1740] **ורבותא די מלכות תחות כל שמיא יהיבת**[1741] **לעם קדישי עליונין** (דניאל 7:27) פהו[1742] מתֿל מא קאל **והיתה ליוי המלכוה**[1743] (עבדיה 21), **והיה יוי למלך על כל הארץ**[1744] **ביום ההוא והיה יוי אחד ושמו אחד**[1745] (זכריה 14:9). וקולה[1746] **עד כה סופה די מלתא**[1747] (דניאל 7:28) יעני בה[1748] אן הדֿה אלנבוה[1749] וסאיר[1750] נבואת[1751] אלאנביא[1752] אקצאהא[1753] ונהאיאתהא[1754] אלי איאם אלישועה. ואמא שרוח[1755] מא יכון פי דאר[1756] אלאכֿרה פלם יבין[1757] לנא בעד. וכמא קאל[1758] אלחכמים, זכרם לברכה,[1759] **כל הנביאים כולן**[1760] **לא נתבאו**[1761] **אילא**[1762] **לימות המשיח אבל העולם**[1763] **הבא**[1764] (ברכות 34b),

[1739] קו TS Ar 23. 11n | בקולה Yeirin 222c
[1740] ושל TS Ar 23. 11n
[1741] [יה]יבת D < Yeirin 222c
[1742] ורבותא ... פהו L < TS Ar 23. 11n
[1743] המלכה Oxf 2486.92a | המל TS Ar 23. 11n
[1744] וג׳ + Yeirin 222c
[1745] על ... אחד L < TS Ar 23. 11n | ביום ... אחד L < Yeirin 222c
[1746] וקו TS Ar 23. 11n | וקולה L < Yeirin 222c
[1747] די מלתא L < TS Ar 23. 11n
[1748] [יע]ני ב[ה] D < TS Ar 23. 11n
[1749] אלנבווה Yeirin 222c
[1750] אן ... וסאיר D < TS Ar 23. 11n
[1751] אלנבואת TS Ar 23. 11n
[1752] אלאנביא L < TS Ar 23. 11n
[1753] אנקצאהא TS Ar 23. 11n
[1754] ונהאיא[תהא] Oxf 2486.92a | ונהאיתהא TS Ar 23. 11n
[1755] ואמ[א שרוח] D < Oxf 2486.92a
[1756] [ואמא ...ד]אר D < TS Ar 23. 11n
[1757] יב[ין] D < Oxf 2486.92a | יכון Yeirin 222c
[1758] וכק TS Ar 23. 11n | וכמא קאלו Yeirin 222c
[1759] זכ לב TS Ar 23. 11n | זל Yeirin 222c
[1760] כולון Yeirin 222c
[1761] לא נתבאו D < TS Ar 23. 11n
[1762] אלא TS Ar 23. 11n
[1763] העולם End of Oxf 2486.92a | ה[עו]לם D < TS Ar 23. 11n
[1764] הבא Beginning of Oxf 2486.92b

עין לא ראתה אלהים זולתך[1765] **יעשה למחכה לו**[1766] (יש' 64:3). ואנמא
תתבין שרוח מא[1767] יכון פי דאר אלאכ̇רה[1768] פי וקת אלישועה כמא קאל[1769]
והיה אכרי כן אשפך את רוחי על כל בשר ונבאו בניכם ובנותיכם[1770]
(יואל 3:1) וסאיר אלקצה. תם תפסיר[1771] אלגז אלז̇.

[1765] זולתיך Yeirin 222c
[1766] אלהים ... לו TS Ar 23. 11n > L
[1767] מ[א] TS Ar 23. 11n > D
[1768] ד[אר] אלאכ[רה] TS Ar 23. 11n > D
[1769] כק Yeirin 222c + TS Ar 23. 11n
[1770] על ... ובנותיכם TS Ar 23. 11n > L
[1771] אלתפסיר Yeirin 222c

תפסיר[1] אלגז אלת̇מן[2] מן הד̇א אלכתאב אלד̇י פיה שרוח כאנת תבקת פימא[3] בין פצול[4] אלד̇ ממאלך אלמד̇כורה. קאל דניאל פי צדרה

Dn 8:1
בשנת שלש למלכות בלשצר המלך חזון נראה אלי אני דניאל אחרי הנראה אלי בתחלה.

פי אלסנה אלת̇אלת̇ה[5] מן מלך באלשצר[6] אלמלך[7] אורי[8] לי רויא אנא[9] דניאל בעד מא ארי[10] לי אולא.[11]

אלחאקה[12] באלקול **אחרי הנראה אלי בתחלה**[13] (דניאל 8:1). ונחן נעלם אנה בעדה אד̇[14] כאן אלאול **בשנת חדה**[15] (דניאל 7:1) והד̇א **בשנת שלוש** (דניאל 8:1).[16] ולאכנה[17] אראד בקולה[18] **אחרי הנראה אלי בתחלה** (דניאל 8:1) אן עיון הד̇א אלחלם דאכ̇לה פי ד̇לך אלמעאני כל ואחדה מן תלך אלאדנין

[1] תפסיר TS Ar 23. 11n > D
[2] אלת̇ Yeirin 222c + TS Ar 23. 11n
[3] פי מא End of the readable part of Yeirin 222c
[4] פצול Beginning of Yeirin 222d
[5] אלג̇ Yeirin 222d+ TS Ar 23. 11n
[6] בלשאצר Spiegel + Oxf 2486.92b | בלשאצר End of Oxf 2486.92b
[7] אלמלך Beginning of Oxf 2486.93a
[8] ארי Spiegel + TS Ar 23. 11n
[9] פאנא Spiegel
[10] אורי Yeirin 222d
[11] אוולא Morag | אולה Yeirin 222d
[12] אלחאק[ה] TS Ar 23. 11n > D
[13] בתחלה TS Ar 23. 11n > L
[14] בע[ד]ה [אד̇] TS Ar 23. 11n > D
[15] ח[דה] Oxf 2486.93a > D | חדא Yeirin 222d
[16] שלש Yeirin 222d
[17] של[וש] [ו]ל[כנ]ה TS Ar 23. 11n > D
[18] בקו Yeirin 222d+ TS Ar 23. 11n

כל ואחדה מנהא[19] אלי אלאכרא תתממהא. ומעני אכ̇ר לקולה **אחרי הנראה אלי בתחלה**[20] (דניאל 8:1) והי[21] מסאלמה[22] האולי[23] אלאמם לבני[24] אסראיל בעד מא[25] כאנו יוחשונהם ויפזעונהם.[26] וד̇לך אן אלרויא אלאולי שבהת אלממאלך פיהא באלאסד ואלדב ואלנמר ואלפיל. והד̇ה כלהא[27] ד̇ואער.[28] ואלרויא אלב̇[29] שבהת[30] פיהא באלכבש ואלתיס. והד̇אן עפיפאן סלימאן. וד̇אך מא[31] ועד אלאמה באן[32] ילין[33] להא אעדאיהא[34] ויעפפהא כמא קאל[35] **ויתן אתם לרחמים לפני כל שוביהם** (תה׳ 106:46). וקאל פי[36] מלך בבל **ואתן**[37] **לכם**[38] **רחמים ורחם**[39] **אתכם**[40] (ירמ׳ 42:12). וקאל[41] פי[42] מלך אלפרס **מי אתה הר הגדול**[43] **לפני זרבבל למישור**[44] (זכריה 4:7). וקאל קולא מגמלא[45]

[19] כל ואחדה מנהא Uncertain reading
[20] בתחלה [אן ... בתחלה] והי TS Ar 23. and Oxf 2486.93a > D homeoteleuton 11n
[21] והו Yeirin 222d
[22] [מסא]למה TS Ar 23. 11n > D
[23] הדה Yeirin 222d
[24] לב[ני] TS Ar 23. 11n > D
[25] ב[עד מ]א TS Ar 23. 11n > D
[26] כאנו ... ויפזעונהם TS Ar 23. 11n > D
[27] באלא[סד ... כלהא] TS Ar 23. 11n > D
[28] דאערה (דוערה) Yeirin 222d + TS Ar 23. 11n
[29] אלת̇אניה TS Ar 23. 11n
[30] שבהת TS Ar 23. 11n > D
[31] באלכבש ... מא TS Ar 23. 11n > D
[32] [בא]ן TS Ar 23. 11n > D
[33] ילון Yeirin 222d
[34] אעדאהא Yeirin 222d
[35] כק Yeirin 222d
[36] אעדא[יהא ... פי] TS Ar 23. 11n > D
[37] להם + Yeirin 222d
[38] אתם Yeirin 222d > L
[39] לכם ... ורחם TS Ar 23. 11n > D | אותם + Yeirin 222d
[40] אתכם Yeirin 222d > L
[41] וקאל End of Oxf 2486.93a
[42] פי Beginning of Oxf 2486.93b
[43] וקאל ... הגדול TS Ar 23. 11n > D
[44] זר למי̇ TS Ar 23. 11n
[45] מג[מלה] TS Ar 23. 11n > D

אנהא לו שאבהת אלנאר או אלמא לכאן רבנא יוקינא[46] חרהא וברדהא כמא קאל[47] **כי תעבר במים אתך אני[48] ובנהרות לא ישטפוך כי תלך במו אשלא תכוה ולהבה[49] לא תבער בך** (יש׳ 43:2). תֹם קאל

Dn 8:2

ואראה בחזון ויהי[50] בראותי[51] ואני בשושן הבירה אשר בעילם המדינה ואראה בחזון ואני הייתי על אובל אולי.

וראית[52] פי אלמנאם כאנני[53] פי סוס אלגוסק אלדֹי[54] פי בלד כֹוזסתאן[55] ואנא עלי שט[56] נהר אולי.[57]

Dn 8:3

ואשא עיני ואראה והנה איל אחד עומד לפני האובל ולו קרנים והקרנים גבוהות והאחת גבהה מן השנית[58] והגבוהה[59] עולה באחרונה.

פמדדת בצרי פראית[60] כאן כבש קאים[61] עלי אלשט[62] ולה[63] קרנאן ואלקרנאן עטֹימאן[64] אחדהמא אעטֹם[65] מן אלאכֹר ואעטֹמהמא[66] אלדֹי נבת אכֹרא.[67]

[46] שא[בהת ... יוקינא] TS Ar 23. 11n > D
[47] כק Yeirin 222d + TS Ar 23. 11n
[48] אני End of the readable part of TS Ar 23. 11n
[49] ול[הבה] Yeirin 222d > D
[50] ויהי End of Yeirin 222d
[51] בראותי Beginning of Yeirin 226 (TS Ar. b1. 101i)
[52] פראית Yeirin 226 + Oxf 2486.93b
[53] כאני Spiegel + Yeirin 226
[54] כא[נני ... אלדֹי] Morag > D
[55] כזוזסתאן Spiegel
[56] שאטי Yeirin 226 ׀ שאט Spiegel
[57] עלי ... אולי Morag > D
[58] השנית End of Oxf 2486.93b
[59] והגבוהה Beginning of Oxf 2486.94a
[60] וראית Spiegel
[61] [קאי]ם Yeirin 226 > D
[62] אלשאט Spiegel
[63] לה Spiegel + Morag
[64] עטימאן Beginning of TS Ar 23. 11o ׀ עצימאן Spiegel + Morag
[65] אעצם Spiegel + Morag ׀ [אע]צם Yeirin 226 > D
[66] ואעצמהמא Spiegel + Morag ׀ ואעצמהא TS Ar 23. 11o ׀ הו + Oxf 2486.94a and Yeirin 226

Dn 8:4

ראיתי את האיל מנגח ימה וצפנה ונגבה וכל חיות לו יעמדו לפניו ואין מציל מידו ועשׂה כרצונו והגדיל.

ראיתה[68] ינטח[69] מן[70] וגד ג̇רבא ושמאלא וגנובא[71] וגמיע אלוחוש[72] לא יקפו[73] בין[74] ידיה[75] ולא[76] מכ̇לץ מן ידה[77] פיצנע[78] בהם[79] רצ̇אה[80] ואסרף.

Dn 8:5

ואני הייתי מבין והנה צפיר העזים בא מן המערב על פני כל הארץ ואין נוגע בארץ והצפיר קרן חזות בין עינין.[81]

פבינמא[82] אנא מתפהם פאד̇א[83] בתיס קד אקבל[84] מן[85] אלמג̇רב יעדו[86] עלי וגה אלארץ̇ וליס[87] ימסהא מן שדה[88] אלעדו ולה קרן[89] מתשעב[90] בין עיניה.[91]

67 אכ̇ירא Oxf 2486.94a

68 ראית Spiegel

69 אלדי ... ינטח TS Ar 23. 11o > D | מא + TS Ar 23. 11o | ינטח Yeirin 226 > D

70 מן TS Ar 23. 11o > L

71 וגנו[בה] Morag > D

72 אלוחש Yeirin 226 + Oxf 2486.94a

73 יקפון Spiegel + Oxf 2486.94a | יקף TS Ar 23. 11o

74 בין Yeirin 226 > D

75 וליס Morag +

76 ולא Morag > L

77 ידיה Oxf 2486.94a

78 וגמי[ע ... פיצנע] TS Ar 23. 11o > D

79 מרצ̇א נפסה TS Ar 23. 11o +

80 רצ̇אה TS Ar 23. 11o > L

81 עינין End of Oxf 2486.94a

82 פבינמא Beginning of Oxf 2486.94b | ובין מא Morag | פבין מא Yeirin 226

83 פאדי Morag

84 [קד א]קבל Yeirin 226 > D

85 פב[ינמא ... מן] TS Ar 23. 11o > D

86 יעדוא Spiegel

87 ולא TS Ar 23. 11o > D

88 שדת Morag | [שד]ה Yeirin 226 > D

89 ול[ה קרן] Morag > D

90 משעב Spiegel

91 אלעדו ... עיניה TS Ar 23. 11o > D | עינאה Spiegel + Yeirin 226 + Morag

Dn 8:6

ויבא עד האיל בעל הקרנים אשר ראיתי עמד לפני האאבל וירץ אליו בחמת כחו.

פוצל אלי אלכבש דו֗[92] אלקרנין[93] אלד֗י ראיתה[94] ואקפא[95] עלי אלשט[96] פעדא[97] עליה[98] בקוה[99] חמיתה.[100]

Dn 8:7

וראיתיו מגיע אצל האיל ויתמרמר אליו ויך את האיל וישבר את שני קרניו ולא היה כח לאיל לעמד לפניו וישלכהו ארצה[101] וירמסהו[102] ולא היה מציל לאיל מידו.

וראיתה[103] למא[104] וצל אליה אחתד[105] עליה פצ֗רבה[106] וכסר[107] קרנאה[108] ולם תך[109] פיה קוה[110] אן יקף בין ידיה פטרחה[111] עלי[112] אלרץ֗[113] ודאסה[114] ולם יך[115] לה מכ֗לץ מן ידה.[116]

92 די TS Ar 23. 11o + Oxf 2486.94b

93 אלקרנאן Spiegel

94 [אלקרנין ... רא]יתה Morag > D

95 [ואקפ]א Yeirin 226 > D

96 אלשאט Spiegel ׀ פותב + Oxf 2486.94b

97 פעדא Oxf 2486.94b > L

98 אל[שט ... עליה] TS Ar 23. 11o > D

99 בקווה Spiegel

100 על[יה ... חמיתה] Morag > D ׀ חמייתה Spiegel

101 ארצה End of Yeirin 226

102 וירמסהו Beginning of Yeirin 227 (TS Ar.1b. 101j)

103 ורא[ית]ה TS Ar 23. 11o > D ׀ פראיתה Yeirin 227

104 למ[א] Yeirin 227 > D

105 פאחתד TS Ar 23. 11o ׀ אחתר Spiegel + Morag

106 וצרבה TS Ar 23. 11o

107 וכסר TS Ar 23. 11o > D

108 קרניה Yeirin 227 + TS Ar 23. 11o + Oxf 2486.94b

109 יכון Morag ׀ ת[כ]ן Yeirin 227 > D ׀ תכון Spiegel

110 קווה Spiegel + Morag

111 וטרחה TS Ar 23. 11o ׀ אלי + Yeirin 227

112 עלי End of Oxf 2486.94b ׀ עלי Yeirin 227 > L

113 אלארץ Beginning of Oxf 2486.95a

114 פדאסה Spiegel + Yeirin 227 + Oxf 2486.95a ׀ ו[דאס]ה TS Ar 23. 11o > D

115 יכן Oxf 2486.95a ׀ יכון Spiegel + Yeirin 227

צדר הדׄא אלכלאם ידל עלי אן דניאל כאן באלחקיקה פי בבל.[117] ואנמא ראי כאנה[118] פי כוזסתאן כמא ירי מן הו בבגׄדאד[119] כאנה באלבצרה.[120] **ואובל אולי**[121] (דניאל 8:2) פאצחאבנא[122] מגמעין עלי אנה נהר.[123] לכנהם יבדלון אלאלפאטׄ. פמנהם מן יגעל **אובל** אסם[124] אלשט[125] **ואולי** אסם אלנהר. ומנהם מן יגעל **אובל**[126] אסמ אלנהר[127] **ואולי** אסם אלשט.[128] ואמא[129] מן תרך אן יקול אנה נהר וכׄרג אלי אן קאל[130] אבניה אואן[131] וטאקאת פהו שאדׄ לא נדׄכרה מע אלגמאעה.

ואסתמדאד תאויל[132] הדׄה[133] אלרויא איצׄא[134] מן אלתפסיר אלדׄי פסרה גבריאל לדניאל: אן אלכבש הו מלוך[135] מדי ופרס כמא[136] סיקול **האיל אשר ראית בעל**[137] **הקרנים**[138] **מלכי מדי ופרס**[139] (דניאל 8:20). פראי דניאל הדׄה[140]

[116] ולק[ם ... מכלץ] מ[ן י]דה TS Ar 23. 11o > D
[117] פי בבל Yeirin 227 > L
[118] [ואנמא ... כ]אנה TS Ar 23. 11o > D
[119] בב[גׄד]אד TS Ar 23. 11o > D
[120] פי אלבצרה TS Ar 23. 11o
[121] אלי TS Ar 23. 11o
[122] פאצ[חאבנא] TS Ar 23. 11o > D
[123] נ[הר] TS Ar 23. 11o > D
[124] א[סם] TS Ar 23. 11o > D
[125] שט TS Ar 23. 11o
[126] [אוב]ל TS Ar 23. 11o > D
[127] אל[נה]ר TS Ar 23. 11o > D
[128] אל[ש]ט TS Ar 23. 11o > D
[129] אסם אלשט [ואולי ... אסם אלשט] ואמא Yeirin 227 > L homeoteleuton
[130] אל[י אן קאל] TS Ar 23. 11o > D
[131] ואיואן TS Ar 23. 11o ׀ איואן Yeirin 227
[132] תאויל TS Ar 23. 11o > L
[133] [ה]ד[ׄה] TS Ar 23. 11o > D
[134] איצׄ TS Ar 23. 11o
[135] מלך Yeirin 227 + TS Ar 23. 11o
[136] כמׄ TS Ar 23. 11o
[137] בעל End of Oxf 2486.95a
[138] הקרנים Beginning of Oxf 2486.95b ׀ הק TS Ar 23. 11o
[139] מלכי מדי ופרס TS Ar 23. 11o > L
[140] הדׄ Yeirin 222f

אלרויא פי סנה זואל[141] מלך באלשצר[142] אלדׄי הו אכׄר מלוך באבל ואבתדי מלך אלפרס.[143] ומעני[144] וקוף אלכבש עלי שאטי[145] אלנהר לא[146] עלי[147] אלבחר אלכביר כמא ראי פי אלאולי **מגיחן לימא רבה**[148] (דניאל 7:2) הו מתׄל מא קדמנאה[149] מן תכׄפיפה אלעול אלדׄי[150] להם עלי בני אסראיל[151] חתי אנה יגעלה כחאל[152] עבור אלנהר בעד[153] מא כאן כחאל רכוב אלבחר.

ואלקרנין[154] איצׄא פתאוילהמא[155] ריאסה ושרף כמא[156] פסרנא[157] פי אלרויא אלאולי. וכמא לבני[158] אסראיל[159] פי **שבע קרנות** אלתי תגעל **עשר קרנות** עלי סביל אלאגרה פהו קרן ישׂראל[160] כמא[161] יקול[162] **וירם קרן**[163] **לעמו** (תה׳ 148:14). וקרן נבוה[164] כמא יקול[165] **חזה המלך בדברי האלהים להרים**[166] **קרן**[167] (דבהי ״א 25:5). **וקרן לויה** כמא קאל **רמה**[168] **קרני**[169] **ביוי**[170] (שמ״א

[141] [ס]נ[ה] ז[וא]ל TS Ar 23. 11o > D

[142] בלשאצר Oxf 2486.95b

[143] [בא]בל [ואבתדי מלך אל]פרס TS Ar 23. 11o > D

[144] ו[מע]ני TS Ar 23. 11o > D

[145] אל[כבש ע]לי [שאטי] TS Ar 23. 11o > D ׀ שא[וי] Yeirin 227 > D

[146] יולי + Yeirin 227

[147] עלי Yeirin 227 > L

[148] ראי ... רבה TS Ar 23. 11o > D

[149] ק[דמנאה] TS Ar 23. 11o > D

[150] אל[די] Yeirin 227 > D

[151] ישׂראל Yeirin 227

[152] כמאל Yeirin 227

[153] [עלי ... ב]עד TS Ar 23. 11o > D ׀ בעד Yeirin 227 > D

[154] ואלקרנאן Oxf 2486.95b

[155] פתאוילה[מא] Yeirin 227 > D

[156] כמא Yeirin 227 > D

[157] [ואלקרנין ... פ]סרנא TS Ar 23. 11o > D

[158] [וכמא] ל[בני] Yeirin 227 > D

[159] אס TS Ar 23. 11o

[160] פי ... ישׂראל TS Ar 23. 11o > D ׀ י[שׂראל] Yeirin 227 > D

[161] Back to the last five lines of TS Ar.23. 11j

[162] כק TS Ar. 23. 11j

[163] ק[ר]ן Yeirin 227 > D

[164] נב[ו]ה TS Ar. 23. 11j

[165] כק TS Ar.23. 11j

[166] להרים End of Oxf 2486.95b

[167] קרן Beginning of Oxf 2486.96a

2:1). **וקרן כהנה**[171] כמא קאל[172] **וברצונך**[173] **תרום קרנינו**[174] (תה' 89:18). **וקרן מלוכה** כמא קאל[175] **ובשמי תרום קרנו**[176] (תה' 89:25). **וקרן צדיקים** כמא קאל[177] **תרוממנה קרנות צדיק** (תה' 75:11). **וקרן המקדש** כמא קאל[178] **כרם היה לידידי**[179] **בקרן בן שמן**[180] (יש' 5:1). וקד תזאד[181] עליהא ג̇[182] ליס מן פנהא. **קרן**[183] **אברהאם** לחאל **נאחז בסבך בקרניו**[184] (בר' 22:13). **וקרן משה**[185] לחאל **והנה קרן אור פניו** (שמ' 34:30). **וקרן המזבח**[186] עלי אלתסמיה[187] ואן לם תקם[188] עלי אלנטׄר.[189]

וכיף יסוג̇ בעדמא קאל **והקרנים גבהות**[190] (דניאל 8:3) אן יקול[191] **והאחת גבהה מן השנית** (דניאל 8:3)? פנקול כמא סאג̇ בעד[192] קולה[193] **ויעש אלהים**

[168] בדברי ... רמה TS Ar. 23. 11j > D ׀ כ[מא ... רמה] Yeirin 227 > D ׀ [רמה] End of Yeirin 227

[169] קרני Beginning of Yeirin 220 (MS Or. 5554a)

[170] בי[וי] Yeirin 220

[171] כהונה TS Ar.23. 11j

[172] כק TS Ar.b 23. 11j ׀ כ[מא קאל] Yeirin 220 > D

[173] וברצ[ונ]ך TS Ar.23. 11j > D

[174] קרננו Oxf 2486.96a

[175] כק Yeirin 220

[176] וקרן מלוכה ... קרנו TS Ar.23. 11j > D ׀ [ובשמי ת]רו[ם] קרנ[ו] Yeirin 220 > D

[177] כק Yeirin 220 + TS Ar.23. 11j

[178] כק Yeirin 220

[179] לי[די]די Yeirin 220 > D

[180] המק[דש ... שמן] TS Ar.23. 11j > D ׀ שמן Yeirin 220 > D

[181] יזאד Oxf 2486.96a

[182] תלאתה Oxf 2486.96a

[183] פנ[הא ק]רן TS Ar.23. 11j > D ׀ [פ]נה[א] קר[ן] Yeirin 220 > D

[184] [בקרנ]יו Yeirin 220 > D

[185] נאחז .. משה TS Ar.23. 11j > D ׀ למשה Yeirin 220

[186] והנה ... המזבח TS Ar.23. 11j > D

[187] אלת[סמ]יה TS Ar.23. 11j > D ׀ אלתסמיה End of the readable part of TS Ar. 23. 11j

[188] תסק אכ[ר עלי] Yeirin 220 > D

[189] אלנצׄר Yeirin 220

[190] גבוהות Yeirin 220

[191] יק[ו]ל Yeirin 220 > D

[192] בעד Beginning of TS Ar.23. 11k ׀ כמא ... בעד Yeirin 220 > D

[193] קו̇ TS Ar.23. 11k

את שני[194] **המאורת**[195] **הגדולים** (בר׳ 1:16) אן יקול **את**[196] **המאור הגדול לממשלת**[197] **היום ואת המאור הקטן**[198] **לממשלת**[199] **הלילה**[200] (בר׳ 1:16). ועלי מא נמת̇ל לד̇לך כאנהא[201] גמאעה הי[202] אלף אנסאן ובינהא[203] שיכ̇אן אכבר מן פי אלגמאעה. ת̇ם אן אחד מן אלשיכ̇ין אכבר[204] מן אלאכ̇ר, אד̇ הד̇א אבן[205] מאיה[206] סנה[207] והד̇א אבן תסעין[208] סנה. פהכד̇א[209] כאן סביל מלוך מדי ופרס.[210] ותפסיר[211] קולה[212] **והגבוהה עולה באחרונה**[213] (דניאל 8:3) אן כורש[214] אלד̇י כאן[215] מנהם בעד[216] דריוש כאן אקוי[217] שוכה[218] ואוסע דולה מן דריוש.[219] אד̇ ד̇אך מלך סנתין והד̇א ת̇לאת̇ה.[220] ואן ארתחשסתא[221] אלד̇י הו

194 ש[ני] Yeirin 220 > D
195 המאורות Yeirin 220
196 הגדולי[ם ... את] Yeirin 220 > D
197 לממשל[ת] Yeirin 220 > D
198 הקטן End of Oxf 2486.96a
199 לממשלת Beginning of Oxf 2486.96b
200 המ[אור ... ה]ליל[ה] Yeirin 220 > D
201 ה[מאורת ... כאנה] TS Ar.23. 11k > D
202 והי TS Ar.23. 11k | הו Yeirin 220
203 פבינהמא TS Ar.23. 11k
204 שיכאן אכבר ... אלשיכין אכבר TS Ar.23. 11k > D
205 בן TS Ar.23. 11k | הד[א א]בן Yeirin 220 > D
206 ק Yeirin 220 + TS Ar.23. 11k
207 סנה TS Ar.23. 11k > D | ס[נה] Yeirin 220 > D
208 צ Yeirin 220 + TS Ar.23. 11k
209 ס[נה ... פהכדא] Yeirin 220 > D
210 מדי ופרס Yeirin 220 > D
211 פה[כדא ... ותפסיר] TS Ar.23. 11k > D
212 קו TS Ar.23. 11k > D
213 [והגבוהה ... ב]אחרונה Yeirin 220 > D
214 [כו]רש Yeirin 220 > D
215 [כ]אן TS Ar.23. 11k > D
216 בעד Yeirin 220 > D
217 כאן אקוי Yeirin 220 > D
218 [בעד ... אקוי] שוכ[ה] TS Ar.23. 11k > D
219 אחשורש TS Ar.23. 11k | ואו[סע ד]ולה מ[ן דרי]וש Yeirin 220 > D
220 דאך מלך [סנתין ... דאך מלך] יד homeoteleuton TS Ar.23. 11k > D | ג̇ Yeirin 220
221 [ואן א]ר[ת]חש[סתא Yeirin 220 > D

בעד אחשורוש[222] כאן אשד שוכה[223] ואוסע[224] מדה[225] מן אחשורוש אד̇[227] ד̇אך[228] מלך יד̇ והד̇א מלך[229] לד̇.[230]

ותפסיר קולה[231] **ראיתי את**[232] **האיל מנגח**[233] (דניאל 8:4) הי מחארבה מלוך אלפרס לסאיר מלוך אלעאלם[234] כמא[235] פצח פי הד̇א אלכתאב[236] **ובעת**[237] **קץ יתנגח**[238] **עמו מלך הנגב**[239] (דניאל 11:40). ועלי[240] מא קאל[241] לישׂראל[242] **בהם**[243] **עמים ינגח**[244] **יחדו**[245] (דב׳ 33:17) ועלי מא קאלו הם **בך צרינו ננגח**[246] (תה׳ 44:6) ומא[247] אשבה[248] ד̇לך.[249] ואמא אכ̇תצארה מן אלד̇ גהאת

[222] [אח]שורש Yeirin 220 > D
[223] ואטול + Yeirin 220
[224] ואוסע Yeirin 220 > L
[225] [ואוסע דולה ...] ואוסע מדה homeoteleuton TS Ar.23. 11k > D
[226] אחשורוש Yeirin 220
[227] הד[א] + Yeirin 220
[228] דאך Yeirin 220 > L
[229] מלך TS Ar.23. 11k > D
[230] סנה + Yeirin 220
[231] ותפס קו TS Ar.23. 11k | קו Yeirin 220
[232] [ר]איתי [את] Yeirin 220 > D
[233] ראיתי ... מנגח TS Ar.23. 11k > D
[234] אלעאל[ם] Yeirin 220 > D
[235] כמ̇ TS Ar.23. 11k | [כ]מא Yeirin 220 > D
[236] אלכתאב End of Oxf 2486.96b
[237] ובעת Beginning of Oxf 2486.97a
[238] הד[א ... יתנגח] TS Ar.23. 11k > D
[239] מלך הנגב TS Ar.23. 11k > L
[240] ה[נגב] וע[לי] Yeirin 220 > D
[241] קיל Yeirin 220 + TS Ar.23. 11k
[242] ליש TS Ar.23. 11k
[243] ב[ה]ם TS Ar.23. 11k > D
[244] י[נג]ח TS Ar.23. 11k > D
[245] יח TS Ar.23. 11k | יחדו Yeirin 220 > D
[246] [ב]ך צרי[נו נ]נגח Yeirin 220 > D
[247] הם ... ומא TS Ar.23. 11k > D
[248] אשבה End of Yeirin 220
[249] דלך Beginning of Yeirin 221 (MS Or. 5554a)

עלי ג̇[250] אד̇ קאל **מנגח ימה וצפונה**[251] **ונגבה** (דניאל 8:4) ולם[252] יקל **ומזרחה** פאלסבב פי ד̇לך הו אן מוכד אלכבש פי אלמשרק[253] פליס יגוז[254] אן ינטח[255] מסתדברה. ואנמא ינטח[256] מסתקבלה וימנה ויסרה. וקולה[257] **וכל חיות לא יעמדו לפניו** (דניאל 8:4) וסאיר אלפסוק[258] תאוילה אלתמכין[259] אלד̇י[260] געלה[261] אללה לארבעה[262] מלוך אלפרס. כמא[263] עלמנא אנה קאל פי דריוש **כתב לכל עמאיא**[264] **אמיא ולשניא**[265] **די דירין בכל ארעא שלמכון ישׂגיא**[266] (דניאל 6:26) כמת̇ל מא קאל פי[267] נבוכ̇דנצר.[268] וקאל פי תפצ̇יל[269] כורש **לרד לפניו גוים ומתני מלכים אפתח**[270] **לפתח**[271] **לפניו דלתים ושערים לא יסגרו**[272] (יש׳ 45:1). וקאל הו **כל ממלכות**[273] **הארץ נתן לי יוי אלהי השמים**[274] (עזרא 1:2). וקאל פי[275] אחשורוש **וישׂם המלך אחשורוש**[276]

[250] אלג̇ TS Ar.23. 11k
[251] צפונה Yeirin 221
[252] ו[צפונה ... ולם TS Ar.23. 11k > D
[253] אלמ[שר]ק TS Ar.23. 11k > D
[254] פלם יגז TS Ar.23. 11k
[255] ינטח TS Ar.23. 11k
[256] מן הו + TS Ar.23. 11k | מן + Yeirin 221
[257] וקו TS Ar.23. 11k
[258] לפניו ... אלפסוק TS Ar.23. 11k > L
[259] אלתמכן TS Ar.23. 11k
[260] אלדי TS Ar.23. 11k > D
[261] ו[געׄ]לה TS Ar.23. 11k
[262] לארבע TS Ar.23. 11k | לד Oxf 2486.97a
[263] ומא TS Ar.23. 11k
[264] עממיא TS Ar.23. 11k
[265] ולישניא Yeirin 221
[266] אמיא ... ישגיא TS Ar.23. 11k > L | יסגיא Yeirin 221
[267] פי TS Ar.23. 11k > L
[268] [נבו[כדנ]צר Yeirin 221 > D
[269] אלתפצ̇יל TS Ar.23. 11k
[270] אפתח End of Oxf 2486.97a | ומ[תני אפ]תח Yeirin 221 > D
[271] לפתח Beginning of Oxf 2486.97b
[272] לפניו ... יסגרו TS Ar.23. 11k > L | דלת[ים וש]ערים ל[א י]סגרו Yeirin 221 > D
[273] וקאל ... ממלכ]ות Yeirin 221 > D
[274] נתן ... השמים TS Ar.23. 11k > L
[275] וקאל פי Yeirin 221 > D
[276] אחש TS Ar.23. 11k

מס על הארץ ואיי[277] **מים**[278] (אסתר 10:1). וקאל פי אלראבע[279] **ארתחשסתא**[280] **מלך מלכיא** (עז' 7:12) שביהא במא[281] קאל[282] פי נבוכדנצר **הנני מביא**[283] **אל צר נבוכדנצר מלך בבל מצפון מלך**[284] **מלכים**[285] (יח' 26:7).

ומעני קולה **ואני**[286] **הייתי**[287] **מבין**[288] (דניאל 8:5) אנה[289] כאן מתאמלא[290] מן בעד כיף יקבל מנאוש אלכבש. ודאת[291] **צפיר העזים**[292] (דניאל 8:5) הו אול מלך קאם לליונאניה,[293] כמא[294] פסר לה[295] גבריאל **והצפיר השעיר מלך יון** (דניאל 8:21). וקולה **בא מן**[296] **המערב** (דניאל 8:5) לאן אקבאל אליונאניה[297] כאן מן אלמגרב. אעני[298] מן בלד פרנגה ונואחיהא מע[299] נואחי[300] אנדלס,[301] ואלי אפריקיה, ואלי סקליה,[302] ואלי אתיניה[303] בלד[304] אלחכמא. ומן בקי מנהם

277 ואי Yeirin 221 > D
278 על ... מים TS Ar.23. 11k > L
279 אלד TS Ar.23. 11k
280 א[ארחת]]שסתא TS Ar.23. 11k > D ו ארחתש[ס]תא Yeirin 221 > D
281 במ TS Ar.23. 11k
282 שביה[א ... קאל] Yeirin 221 > D
283 מ[בי]א TS Ar.23. 11k > D
284 מלן ... מ]לך Yeirin 221 > D
285 נבוכדנצר ... מלכים TS Ar.23. 11k > L
286 ואני Beginning of TS Ar 28. 102a
287 קו ואני היתי TS Ar.23. 11k
288 [מבי]ן Yeirin 221 > D
289 ואנה Oxf 2486.97b
290 מתאמל Oxf 2486.97b ו [מ]תאמלא Yeirin 221 > D
291 [וד]את Oxf 2486.97b > D
292 מנ[אוש ... ה]ע[זי]ם TS Ar.23. 11k > D
293 לליונאנייה Yeirin 221+ TS Ar.23. 11k
294 כמ TS Ar.23. 11k
295 פסרה Yeirin 221
296 והצפיר ... מן TS Ar.23. 11k > D
297 אליונאנייה Yeirin 221+ TS Ar.23. 11k
298 אע[ני] Yeirin 221 > D
299 מע TS Ar 28. 102a > L
300 מ[ע נו]אחי Yeirin 221 > D
301 מן ... אנדלס TS Ar.23. 11k > D
302 סקלייה Yeirin 221
303 אתיניה End of Oxf 2486.97b ו אתוניה TS Ar 28.102a
304 בלד Beginning of Oxf 2486.98a

אלי אלאן פהו פי[305] פרנגה.[306] וקולה[307] **על פני כל הארץ**[308] (דניאל 8:5) הד̇ה חאל עט̇ימה פי אלחצאר ואלעדו אנה כל אלארץ̇ ענדה[309] באלסוא: אלסהל ואלגבל ואלואדי ואלראביה ואלהותה[310] ואלבקעה וג̇יר ד̇לך̇. ליס יקפה שיא[311] מנהא[312] ולא יבטי[313] בסרעה חצ̇ארה. ומעני קולה[314] **ואין נוגע בארץ** (דניאל 8:5) כאנה ליס̇ ימס אלארץ̇ מן שדה[315] אלחצ̇אר. כמא[316] יקאל אן כ̇טוה אלגמאז לא תתבין פי אלארץ̇ מן אג̇ל סרעתהא. וד̇לך אנה יקאל[317] אנהא תסיר[318] פי יום ארבעין[319] פרסך̇. ופסרת[320] **קרן הזות** (דניאל 8:5) "משעבה" מת̇ל מא קיל פי אלשגרה אלתי ראהא נבוכ̇דנצר[321] **וחזותה לסוף כל ארעא** (דניאל 4:8) עלי מא בינא.

וקולה[322] **ויבא עד האיל** (דניאל 8:6), **וראיתיו מגיע אצל האיל וג'**[323] (דניאל 8:7) תאויל[324] גמיע[325] ד̇לך הו מא ט̇פר מלך אליונאניין[326] אלאול,[327] אעני אלאסכנדר, במכלכה אלפרס. פתאויל **ויך את האיל** (דניאל 8:7) אלהזימה[328]

[305] [פ]י Yeirin 221 > D
[306] אלחכמא ... פרנגה TS Ar.23. 11k > D
[307] וקו TS Ar.23. 11k
[308] הארץ End of Yeirin 221
[309] פי ... ענדה TS Ar.23. 11k > D
[310] ואלהותם TS Ar.23. 11k
[311] שי[א] TS Ar 28.102a > D
[312] [ואלבקעה ... מנ]הם TS Ar.23. 11k > D
[313] [יב]טי TS Ar.23. 11k > D
[314] קו TS Ar.23. 11k | ומע קול TS Ar 28.102a
[315] בארץ ... שדה TS Ar.23. 11k > D
[316] כמ TS Ar.23. 11k
[317] [אלארץ ... יק]אל TS Ar.23. 11k > D
[318] תס[יר] TS Ar.23. 11k > D
[319] מ̇ TS Ar.23. 11k | אליום מ̇ TS Ar 28.102a
[320] ופסרת End of the readable part of TS Ar.23. 11k
[321] נבוכדנ̇ TS Ar 28.102a | נבוכד Back to the the third line from the bottom TS Ar.23. 11o
[322] וקול TS Ar 28.102a
[323] וג' End of Oxf 2486.98a
[324] תאויל Beginning of Oxf 2486.98b
[325] ארן[עה ... גמיע] TS Ar.23. 11o > D
[326] אליונאנייה End of TS Ar 28.102a
[327] אלאול Beginning of TS Ar 28.102b
[328] מל[ך ... אלה]זימה TS Ar.23. 11o > D | פאלהזימה TS Ar 28.102b

להם.[329] ותאויל **וישבר את שני**[330] **קרניו**[331] (דניאל 8:7) מא כסר מן עסאכרהם. ותאויל **וישלכהו ארצה** (דניאל 8:7) הו מא בדד מן שמלהם. ותאויל **וירמסה** (דניאל 8:7) הו מא אדל מן בקי מנהם. ותאויל[332] **ולא היה מציל**[333] **לאיל מידו**[334] (דניאל 8:7) אנהם[335] קד תערצו[336] אן תכון להם נגדה פלם תכן אד לם יקל[337] **ואין מציל** ואנמא[338] קאל **ולא היה**[339] **מציל** (דניאל 8:7). תֿם קאל[340]

Dn 8:8
וצפיר העזים הגדיל עד מאד וכעצמו נשברה הקרן הגדלה ותעלינה חזות ארבע תחתיה לארבע רוחות השמים.

תֿם ראית אלתיס קד אסרף[341] גדא[342] פענד[343] תעטׄמה[344] אנכסר[345] אלקרן אלאכבר[346] פנבת מכאנה ארבע[347] שעב בחדֿא ארבע[348] גהאת אלסמא.[349]

Dn 8:9
ומן האחת מהם יצאה קרן אחת מצעירה ותגדל יתר אל הנגב ואל המזרח ואל הצבי.

[329] להם End of the readable part of TS Ar.23. 11o
[330] שתי TS Ar 28.102b
[331] הו + TS Ar 28.102b
[332] תאויל Beginning of TS Ar.23. 11p ו [אלתא]ויל TS Ar.23. 11p > D
[333] מצל TS Ar.23. 11p
[334] לאיל מידו TS Ar.23. 11p > L
[335] ואנהם TS Ar.23. 11p
[336] ת[ערצו TS Ar.23. 11p > D
[337] יקול TS Ar 28.102b
[338] [אן ... אנ]מא TS Ar.23. 11p > D
[339] ול[א] ה[יה] TS Ar 28.102b > D
[340] תם קאל TS Ar.23. 11p > D
[341] א[סרף] TS Ar 28.102b > D
[342] גדא End of Oxf 2486.98b ו תם ... גדא TS Ar.23. 11p > D
[343] פענד Beginning of Oxf 2486.99a
[344] תעצמה Spiegel + Morag
[345] אנכסל TS Ar.23. 11p
[346] אלקרין אלכביר Spiegel
[347] ד TS Ar 28.102b ו ארבע Spiegel > L
[348] ד TS Ar 28.102b + Oxf 2486.99a
[349] פנבת ... אלסמא TS Ar.23. 11p > D

ומן ואחד מנהם[350] נבת קרין צגׄיר פעטֹם[351] פצֹלא[352] מן[353] גהה מהב אלגנוב ואלמשרק ואלשאם[354] יעני[355] אלשמאל.

Dn 8:10

ותגדל עד צבא השמים ותפל ארצה מן הצבא ומן הכוכבים ותרמסם.

תֹם עלת[356] אלי נגום אלסמא חתי אוקעת[357] עלי אלארץׄ[358] מן[359] אלנגום ואלכואכב ודאסתהא.[360]

Dn 8:11

ועד שׂר הצבא הגדיל וממנו הורס התמיד והשלך מכון מקדושו.[361]

ואלי[362] ריס[363] אלנגום עלת חתי רפע מנה אלשי אלדאים[364] וטרח[365] מהייא[366] מקדסה.[367]

Dn 8:12

וצבא תנתן על התמיד בפשע ותשלך אמת ארצה ועשתה והצליחה.

[350] אחדהם Morag

[351] פעצם Spiegel + Morag | פתעטם TS Ar 28.102b

[352] פ[צלא] TS Ar.23. 11p > D | פי + TS Ar.23. 11p TS Ar 28.102b and and Oxf 2486.99a

[353] מן TS Ar 28.102b and TS Ar.23. 11p and Oxf 2486.99a > L

[354] [ואל]שאם TS Ar.23. 11p > D

[355] יע TS Ar 28.102b

[356] עלית Oxf 2486.99a

[357] וקעת Morag | אלי + Spiegel and Oxf 2486.99a | [נגום ... אוקע]ת TS Ar. > D 23. 11p

[358] עלי Spiegel and Oxf 2486.99a > L

[359] אל[ר]ץ מן TS Ar.23. 11p > D

[360] פדאסתהא Spiegel

[361] מקרשו End of Oxf 2486.99a

[362] ואלי Beginning of Oxf 2486.99b

[363] רייס Spiegel + TS Ar.23. 11p + Morag

[364] [עלת ... אלד]אים TS Ar.23. 11p > D

[365] מנה + Spiegel

[366] מהייא Oxf 2486.99b > D | מהיא TS Ar.23. 11p + TS Ar 28.102b

[367] מקד[סה] TS Ar 28.102b > D

ווצֿעת אלנגום בסבב אלשיא אלדאים פי גרם[368] אנהא אן[369] קד[370] טרחת אלחק עלי אלארץ[371] פעמלת[372] עמלהא ואנגחת[373] פיה עאגלא.[374]

תצדירה פי הדֿא אלקול[375] **וצפיר**[376] **העזים**[377] **הגדיל**[378] **עד מאד**[379] (דניאל 8:8) הו באב אלאסראף. ערפנא[380] בדֿלך[381] אן סבב אלאנתקאם[382] מן כל מסלט[383] וממכן הו אסראפה כמא קאל[384] פי נבוכֿדנצר[385] **וכדי רם לבבה ורוחה תקפת להזרה הנחת מן כרסא מלבותה ויקרה העדיו מנה**[386] (דניאל 5:20). וכמא קאל פי סנחריב[387] **והיה**[388] **כי יבצע יוי את**[389] **כל**[390] **מעשׂהו בהר ציון ובירושלם אפקד על פרי גדל לבב מלך אשור ועל תפארת רום עיניו**[391] (יש׳ 10:12). ופי סאיר אלנאס[392] **במלאת ספקו**[393] **יצר לו כל יד עמל תבאנו**[394] (איוב 20:22) ומא שאכל[395] דֿלך. ותאויל **וכעצמו נשברה**[396]

[368] אלשיא ... גרם TS Ar.23. 11p > D

[369] אן Spiegel + Morag > L | הי + TS Ar.23. 11p

[370] קד TS Ar 28.102b and TS Ar.23. 11p and Oxf 2486.99b > L

[371] אלי אלארץ Morag

[372] עמלת TS Ar 28.102b + TS Ar.23. 11p + Oxf 2486.99b | ועמלת Spiegel

[373] ואנגחת TS Ar 28.102b > D

[374] עאגלה Morag | עא[ג]ל[א] TS Ar.23. 11p > D

[375] אלק[ו]ל TS Ar.b 23. 11p > D

[376] השעיר + TS Ar.23. 11p

[377] העזים TS Ar.23. 11p > L

[378] הגדיל Oxf 2486.99b > D | הגדיל End of TS Ar 28.102b

[379] עד מאד TS Ar.23. 11p > D

[380] ער[פנ]א TS Ar.23. 11p > D

[381] פי דלך TS Ar.23. 11p

[382] אל[אנתקאם] TS Ar.23. 11p > D

[383] מ[ס]לט TS Ar.23. 11p > D

[384] כמא קאל Oxf 2486.99b > D | כק TS Ar.23. 11p

[385] [נבוכדנצ]ר TS Ar.23. 11p > D

[386] ורוחה ... מנה TS Ar.23. 11p > L

[387] סנחריב TS Ar.23. 11p > D

[388] והיה TS Ar.23. 11p > L

[389] את End of Oxf 2486.99b

[390] כל Beginning of Oxf 2486.100a

[391] את ... עיניו TS Ar.23. 11p > D

[392] אל[א]מ[ם] TS Ar.23. 11p > D

[393] במלאות יספקו TS Ar.23. 11p

[394] יצר ... תבאנו TS Ar.23. 11p > L

[395] [... שאכ]ל TS Ar.23. 11p > D

הקרן הגדלה ותעלנה חזות ארבע תחתיה[397] (דניאל 8:8) אן יכון[398] בעד מותה תזול[399] ריאסה אליונאניין,[400] אן תכון לרגל ואחד ויצירו[401] ארבע[402] פרק[403] להם רואסא ארבעה[404] עלי מא סישרח פי אלגז[405] אלעאשר מן הדֹא[406] אלכתאב. ולעל[407] אן יכון[408] אלאסכנדר[409] אנמא אסמי[410] דֹא אלקרנין לקול[411] דניאל **בעל הקרנים**[412] (דניאל 8:6.20). ולכנה לם יקל דֹלך למלך ואחד[413] בעינה ואנמא[414] קאלה פי גמיע מלוכהם.[415] ווגדנא גמיע[416] מלוך אליונאניין תֹמניה.[417] פקד ימכן[418] אן יכונא[419] אתֹנין[420] מן כל קביל[421] מן בלד מן ארבע[422] גהאת אלארץֹ כמא קאל **לארבע רוחות השמים**[423] (דניאל 8:8). וימכן[424] אן[425] יכון[426] אקל או אכתֹר בעד[427] אן תפרק אלחֹ פתציר מן ארבע גהאת אלארץֹ.

[396] וכן[עצ]מו נ[שב]רה TS Ar.23. 11p > D
[397] הקרן ... תחתיה TS Ar.23. 11p > L
[398] תכון TS Ar.23. 11p
[399] ת[זו]ל TS Ar.23. 11p > D
[400] ריאסה אליונאניה TS Ar.23. 11p
[401] ל[ר]גל [וא]חד ויצי[רו] TS Ar.23. 11p > D
[402] ד TS Ar.23. 11p
[403] [פר]ק TS Ar.23. 11p > D
[404] ד רוסא TS Ar.23. 11p
[405] אלגז TS Ar.23. 11p > L
[406] [ה]דא TS Ar.23. 11p > D
[407] ולעלה TS Ar.23. 11p
[408] יכן TS Ar.23. 11p
[409] אל[אסכנדר] TS Ar.23. 11p > D
[410] סמי TS Ar.23. 11p
[411] לקו TS Ar.23. 11p
[412] ב[על ה]ק[רנים] TS Ar.23. 11p > D
[413] ואחד TS Ar.23. 11p > D
[414] ב[עינ]ה [ואנמ]א TS Ar.23. 11p > D
[415] מלו[כהם] TS Ar.23. 11p > D
[416] ווגדנא גמיע TS Ar.23. 11p > D
[417] אליונאנין ח TS Ar.23. 11p
[418] י[מכ]ן TS Ar.23. 11p > D
[419] יכונו TS Ar.23. 11p
[420] יכונו ב TS Ar.23. 11p
[421] [קבי]ל TS Ar.23. 11p > D
[422] ד TS Ar.23. 11p
[423] גהאת ... השמים TS Ar.23. 11p > D
[424] וימכן End of Oxf 2486.100a
[425] אן Beginning of Oxf 2486.100b

וקולה **ומן האחת**[428] **מהם יצא קרן אחת מצעירה**[429] (דניאל 8:9) תאוילה[430] גסקלגס אלמלך וכיף כאן צ̇עפה פי אול אמרה. וקולה **ותגדל יתר** (דניאל 8:9) הו מא קוית חאלה[431] פי אכ̇ר אמרה. ואמא ד̇כרה לג̇ גהאת, אד̇ קאל **אל הנגב ואל המזרח ואל הצבי** (דניאל 8:9) ולם יקל **ואל המערב**, כאן[432] אלסבב פיה הו אנה קאים מן אלמג̇רב כמא קאל פי אול קצתה **והנה צפיר העזים בא מן המערב** (דניאל 8:5). פאנמא[433] וצ̇ע[434] אלקצד ימנה ויסרה ומסתקבל לא מסתדבר, כמא שרחנא פי קולה **ראיתי את האיל מנגח** (דניאל 8:4). וקולה **ואל הצבי**[435] (דניאל 8:9) הי גהה אלשאם[436] כמא קאל **צבי היא לכל הארצות** (יח' 20:6) והי גהה אלשמאל [...][437] כמא קאל **הר ציון ירכתי**[438] **צפון**[439] (תה' 48:3). [...][440] עלי אלאמם.[441]

[...][442] ותאויל **עד צבא השמים** (דניאל 8:10) אלי יש̇ראל אלממת̇לין באלכואכב כמא קאל **והנכם היום ככוכבי השמים לרב** (דב' 1:10). וקולה **ותפל ארצה** (דניאל 8:10) הו באב אלאד̇לאל להם ואלקמע כמא שרחנא **וישליכהו ארצה וירמסה** (דניאל 8:7). והו נט̇יר קולה **השליך משמים ארץ תפארת יש̇ראל** (איכה 2:1). וקולה **ותרמסם** (דניאל 8:10) זיאדה פי אלד̇ל, שביה בקולה **ברגלים תרמסנה עטרת גאות** (יש' 28:3). וקולה פי מואב **תרמסנה רגל רגלי עני פעמי דלים** (יש' 26:6). ושביה במא קאל דויד **ואשחקם כעפר על פני ארץ כטיט חוצות אריקם** (תה' 18:43). ויכון עלי

[426] יכן TS Ar.23. 11p
[427] [אכ]תר בע[ד] TS Ar.23. 11p > D
[428] בע[ד ... האחת] TS Ar.23. 11p > D
[429] יצא ... מצעירה TS Ar.23. 11p > L
[430] תאויל TS Ar.23. 11p
[431] [וכיף ... מא] ק[ו]ית [ח]אלה TS Ar.23. 11p > D
[432] ואמ[א ... המ]ערב [כא]ן TS Ar.23. 11p > D
[433] א[נה ... פאנמא] TS Ar.23. 11p > D
[434] [וצ̇]ע TS Ar.23. 11p and Oxf 2486.100b > D
[435] וי[סרה ... הצ]בי TS Ar.23. 11p > D
[436] אלש[אם] TS Ar.b 23. 11p > D | אלשאם End of the readable part of TS Ar.23. 11p
[437] [...] Oxf 2486.100b > D
[438] ירכתי End of Oxf 2486.100b
[439] צפון Beginning of Oxf 2486.101a | [צפ]ון Oxf 2486.101a > D
[440] [...] Oxf 2486.101a > D
[441] י[סראיל תא]מר עלי אלאמם Oxf 2486.101a > D
[442] [...] Oxf 2486.101a > D

הדׄה אלתפסיר מעני קולה **מן הצבא** (דניאל 8:10) "עואם אלאמה" כקולה **ויואב אל כל הצבא ישׂראל** (שמ״ב 20:23). ויכון קולה **הכוכבים**[443] (דניאל 8:10) כמא[444] קאל **דרך כוכב מיעקב וקם שבט מישׂראל** (במ׳ 24:17).

וקולה **ועל שׂר הצבא הגדיל** (דניאל 8:11) אמא פי טׄאהר אלרויא פאלי אלשמס אדׄ הי אעטׄם. או אלי זחל אדׄ הו אעלאהא. ואמא תאוילה פאן אפת גסקלגס וצלת אלי ראייס ישׂראל. ויכׄץ מן רוסהם **כהן גדול** לתתמת אלפסוק בקול **וממנו הורס התמיד** (דניאל 8:11). יעני ארתפע ען **כהן גדול קרבן תמיד** וגׄירה. ומעני **והשלך מכון מקדושו** (דניאל 8:11) נקץׄ אלמדׄבח אלדׄי הו **מכון התמיד** ומוצׄעה אלמהיא לה. פאתצל באלרויא מא ליס מתׄלה פי אליקטׄה והו אן יכון ללשמס מכאן ינקץׄ. ואנמא הו מתׄל מצׄרוב **לכהן גדול**. ומעני אלתמיד אלדׄי קאל ענה אן אלאמה וקעת פי גרם בסבבה או פי דׄנב אן קאל **וצבא תנתן על התמיד בפשע**[445] (דניאל 8:12) פיה[446] אלקרבאן כקולך **עולת התמיד** (במ׳ 28:10). ויתבעה סאיר אלשראיע לאן תלאיתהא דאימא אדׄ קאל **והגית בו יומם ולילה** (יהושע 1:8). וקאל **תמיד לא יחשו** (יש׳ 62:6) ומא שאכל דׄלך. וכיף וקעת אלאמה בדׄנב בסבב אלתמיד? כאן צאר אלכפאר יקולון להא אן תרכת דינהא אלחק אפלחת אמור דניאהא, הו קולהא **ותשלך אמת ארצה** (דניאל 8:11). יריד בה אלתוראה כמא קאל **ותוראתך אמת** (תה׳ 119:142) ואלחכמה איצׄא ואלאדב כמא קאל **אמת קנה ואל תמכר חכמה ומוסר ובינה** (תה׳ 23:23). ומעני **ועשתה והצליחה** (דניאל 8:12) פהי[447] אמור אלדניא כמא קאם[448] נבוכׄדנצר חנניה ומישאל ועזריה אלסגוד ללצנם. וקאם אצחאב דריוש דניאל [...][449] אלצלוה וקאל ניקנור ליוחנן **סב חזירא ונכוס על פרכה**[450] **ולבוש**[451] **די מלכא ורכוב על סוסיא די מלכא וכחד מן רחמי מלכא ההוא** (בית המדרש, כרך 6:5-6). והו מן אליונאניין. תׄם קאל.

[443] הכוכבים End of the readable part of Oxf 2486.101a
[444] כמא Beginning of Oxf 2486.101b
[445] בפשע End of Oxf 2486.101b
[446] פיה Beginning of Oxf 2486.102a
[447] פ[הי] Oxf 2486.102a > D
[448] קאם Uncertain lesson
[449] [...] Oxf 2486.102a > D
[450] פרכה End of Oxf 2486.102a
[451] ולבוש Beginning of Oxf 2486.102b

Dn 8:13
ואשמעה אחד קדוש מדבר ויאמר אחד[452] **קדוש לפלמוני המדבר עד מתי החזון התמיד והפשע שמם תת וקדש וצבא מרמס.**

תֹם סמעת ואחדא מן אלמלאיכה יתכלם[453] פקאל[454] מלך[455] אכׄר[456] ללפלאני[457] אלמתכלם אלי מתי[458] אלרויא אלדאים[459] ואלדׄנב ואלוחשה תגעל[460] ואלקדס וגישה רוסא.

Dn 8:14
ויאמר עלי עד ערב בקר אלפים ושלש מאות ונצדק קדש.

פקאל לי אלי[461] אלפין ותׄלאתׄ[462] מיאה ליל ונהאר יזכו אלקדס ויפלג.[463]

תפסיר דׄלך קולה **ואשמעה אחד**[464] **קדוש**[465] **מדבר** (דניאל 8:13) יעני בה מלאך[466] לאן אלמלאיכה[467] הכדׄא תסמי באלעבראניה[468] כמא קאל[469] **ובא יוי אלהי כל**[470] **קדשים עמך**[471] (זכריה 14:5). ובאלכסדאניה[472] כמא קאל[473] **ואלו**

[452] אחד Beginning of Yeirin 228 (TS Ar 1b.101c)
[453] פסאל + Spiegel and Yeirin 228
[454] פקאל < L Spiegel
[455] אלמלך Oxf 2486.102b
[456] יתכלם + Spiegel
[457] לאלפלאני Morag | לפלאני + Yeirin 228 Spiegel
[458] מ[תי] Yeirin 228 | מתא Spiegel
[459] ללדאים Oxf 2486.102b
[460] פגעל Oxf 2486.102b
[461] אלי < L Oxf 2486.102b
[462] ותלת Oxf 2486.102b | וש Yeirin 228
[463] ויזכו Oxf 2486.102b
[464] אחד End of Oxf 2486.102b
[465] קדוש Beginning of Oxf 2486.103a
[466] מלך Yeirin 228
[467] אלמלאכים Oxf 2486.103a
[468] ובאלעבראנייה Yeirin 228
[469] כק Yeirin 228
[470] וכל Yeirin 228
[471] עמו Yeirin 228
[472] ובאלכסדאנייה Yeirin 228
[473] כקו Yeirin 228

עיר וקדיש מן שמיא נחית[474] (דניאל 4:10). והדׄא אלקדוש אלאול הו אלאסתאדׄ לאנה אלמסאול. ואלקדוש[475] אלתׄאני הו דונה לאנה אלסאיל[476] לה ולם ישרח אי שיא כאן יקול. ואנמא קאל **מדבר** (דניאל 8:12) פקט.[477] פאלאקרב פי הדׄא אן יכון מסבחא לאן אלכלאם[478] אלסתם[479] אלמערוף ללמלאיכה[480] הו תסביח[481] כמא קאל[482] **וקרא זה על זה ואמר קדוש קדוש קדוש יוי צבאות מלא כל הארץ כבודו**[483] (יש׳ 6:3). ואלמלאך אלתׄאני פהו[484] דונה ולדׄלך[485] סאלה ען אלקץ[486] אדׄ קאל **ויאמר אחד קדוש** (דניאל 8:13). וקולה **לפלמוני** (דניאל 8:13) הי כלמה מגמועה מן כלמתין. ודׄלך אן[487] פי לגׄה אלעבראניין[488] אדׄא[489] הם אראדו אן יקולו פלאן אלפלאני בתכׄציץ יקולון **פלני אלמני**, כמא פי קול דויד (ע׳ שמ״א 21:3), ופי[490] קול[491] בעז[492] (ע׳ רות 4:1), ופי קצה אלישע (ע׳ מל״ב 6:8). וקד יגוזו[493] אן יכׄתצרו[494] אלכלמתין פי ואחדה פיקולון **פלמוני**.

[474] נחי[ת] Yeirin 228 > D
[475] ואל[ק]דוש Yeirin 228 > D
[476] אלסאל Yeirin 228
[477] פקט Oxf 2486.103a > L
[478] אלכלאם Yeirin 228 > L
[479] סתם Oxf 2486.103a
[480] ללמלא[יכה] Oxf 2486.103a > D
[481] אלתסביח Yeirin 228 | מן + Yeirin 228
[482] כמא קאל Yeirin 228 > L
[483] קדוש ... כבודו Yeirin 228 > L
[484] פהו Beginning of Oxf 2652.55a
[485] ו[לד]לך Yeirin 228 > D
[486] אלק[ץ] Yeirin 228 > D
[487] ודל[ך] א[ן] Yeirin 228 > D
[488] אלעבראניין End of Oxf 2486.103a
[489] אדׄא Beginning of Oxf 2486.103b
[490] ופי Oxf 2652.55a and Yeirin 228 > L
[491] קול Yeirin 228 > L | וקול Oxf 2652.55a
[492] ובעז Yeirin 228
[493] [יגו]ז Yeirin 228 > D
[494] יכתצר Yeirin 228

והדׄה אלאפאטׄ אלתי סאלה[495] ענהא הי דׄ[496] מעאני. **החזון**[497] (דניאל 8:13) פי[498] הדׄה אלרויא עלי מא קדם פי אולהא **ואראה בחזון** (דניאל 8:2). וקאל פי וסטהא **כי לעת קץ**[499] **החזון** (דניאל 8:17).[500] והו[501] **תרגום המראה**. פפי הדׄה[502] אלרויה דׄ אשיא. קצה אלתמיד ותפסירהא ארתפאע[503] אלקראבין כמא קאל[504] **וממנו הורס התמיד** (דניאל 8:11). וקצה אלפשע והי מא תטאלב[505] אלאמה באלכׄרוג[506] ען אלדין כמא קאל[507] **וצבא תנתן על התמיד בפשע** (דניאל 8:12). וקצה **שומם** והי וחשה אלבלאד וכׄראבהא.[508] וקצה **קדש וצבא מרמס** (דניאל 8:13) והו תבדל אלקדס[509] ודׄל[510] אלאמה. פגמע אלסאיל[511] הדׄה אלאחואל כלהא פסאל ענהא וקאל אלי כם תבקי. פקאל לה אלמגיב אלי[512] ״אלפין[513] ותׄלאתׄ מאיה ליל ונהאר״. פאדׄא גמעתהמא, אעני אלליל ואלנהאר[514] וגב אן תאכׄדׄ נצפהא עלי שרט **ויהי ערב ויהי בקר יום אחד** (בר׳ 1:5). ודׄלך אן פי[515] גמלה הדׄא אלספר גׄ מקאדיר. מקדאר הו אלף ומאיתין ותסעין,[516] מוצוף באיאם[517] **ימים אלף מאתים ותשעים** (דניאל 12:11).

[495] [ס]אלה Yeirin 228
[496] ד > L Yeirin 228
[497] + הי Yeirin 228
[498] פי > L Yeirin 228
[499] קץ > L Oxf 2652.55a and Oxf 2486.103b
[500] החזון End of Yeirin 228
[501] והו Beginning of Yeirin 229 (TS Ar 1b.101d)
[502] הדא Yeirin 229
[503] א[רת]פאע > D Yeirin 229
[504] כק Yeirin 229
[505] תטלב Yeirin 229
[506] באל[כר]וג > D Yeirin 229
[507] כקו Yeirin 229
[508] וכ[ראבהא] > D Oxf 2652.55a
[509] אלקדס End of Oxf 2486.103b
[510] ודל Beginning of Oxf 2486.104a
[511] אלסאל + Oxf 2652.55a Yeirin 229
[512] + אללפט Oxf 2652.55a
[513] ש + Oxf 2652.55a Yeirin 229 ׀ אלפין > L Oxf 2652.55a
[514] ואלנהאר > L Yeirin 229
[515] פי > L Oxf 2486.104a
[516] רצ + Oxf 2652.55a Yeirin 229
[517] באיא[ם] > D Yeirin 229

ומקדאר הו אלף שׁלֹה, מוצוף **בימים לימים אלף**[518] **שלש מאות שלשים וחמשה**[519] (דניאל 12:12). פלו כאו ההנא[520] קאל[521] איצֿא[522] **עד ימים אלפים ושלש מאות** (ע׳ דניאל 8:14) כאנת[523] אלפין[524] ותֿלתֿ מאיה[525] סנה, עלי אלסם אן אלסנה יקאל להא ימים, כמא נצת[526] אלתוראה[527] פי בעץֿ אלביוע **ימים תהיה גאלתו** (ויקר׳ 25:29). ואיצֿא[528] **ואם לא יגאל עד מלאת לו שנה תמימה**[529] (ויקר׳ 25:30). פלמא גֿיר[530] ההנא[531] עאדה **ימים** פקאל מכאנהא[532] **ערב בקר** (דניאל 8:14) אללדֿין המא גזא[533] אלאיאם[534] וגב אן יכון אלמאכֿוד נצפהא[535] לאן[536] אדֿא[537] כאנת גמלה אלליל ואלנהאר[538] אלפין וש̇[539] פגמלה אלאיאם אלתי תגמעהמא[540] אלף ומאיה וכֿמסין[541] לא מחאלה. פיגב מן הדֿא[542] אלקול אן תכון[543] אלמדה מן וקת חדותֿ הדֿה אלחאדתֿה[544] עלי

[518] שׂהל Oxf 2652.55a
[519] שלש מאות שלשים וחמשה L < Oxf 2652.55a
[520] האהנא Oxf 2486.104a
[521] קאל ההנא Oxf 2652.55a
[522] איצֿא L < Oxf 2486.104a
[523] כאנ[ת] D < Oxf 2486.104a
[524] ש̇ Yeirin 229
[525] ותֿלתֿ מאיה L < Yeirin 229
[526] נצ[ת] D < Oxf 2486.104a
[527] אלתוריה Oxf 2652.55a + Yeirin 229
[528] ואיצֿא L < Oxf 2652.55a + Yeirin 229
[529] וג׳ + Yeirin 229
[530] גֿיר End of Oxf 2486.104a
[531] האהנא Beginning of Oxf 2486.104b
[532] מכאנה Yeirin 229
[533] גזוי Yeirin 229 | גזוא Oxf 2652.55a
[534] אלאיהאם Yeirin 229
[535] נצפהמא Oxf 2652.55a + Yeirin 229
[536] לאן L < Oxf 2652.55a
[537] אד Oxf 2652.55a
[538] אלנהאר ואלליל Oxf 2652.55a
[539] ש̇ Oxf 2652.55a + Yeirin 229
[540] תגמעה Yeirin 229 | תגמעהא Oxf 2652.55a
[541] אלפין ונ̇ Yeirin 229 | אלף וקנ̇ Oxf 2652.55a
[542] הדה Yeirin 229
[543] [תכ]ון D < Yeirin 229
[544] [חדותֿ ... אל]חאדתֿה D < Oxf 2652.55a

אלאמה, אעני **התמיד והפשע ושומם ומרמס** אלי אן ינקצׄי גמיע דׄלך[545] אלף סנה[546] ומאיה וכׄמסין[547] סנה. ויכון אבתדי הדׄה אלחואדתׄ[548] מגתמעה[549] בעד אלוקת אלדׄי[550] קיל פיה לדניאל **אשרי המחכה**[551] (דניאל 12:12) במאיה[552] סנה[553] כׄמסה[554] ותׄמאנין סנה.[555] ודׄלך פי דולה אליונאניין חיתׄ[556] תכון הדׄה אלסנין אדׄא סירת בלגׄת נהאיתהא אלי נקטה מן אלזמאן מואפקה מדה **אשרי המחכה** (דניאל 12:12) בלא זיאדה[557] ולא[558] נקצאן.

וקד[559] כאנת ללאמה חאדתׄה פי אלתמיד פקט פי סנה לבׄ מן מלך ארתחשסתא[560] והי בעד אלוקת[561] אלדׄי קיל פיה **אשרי המחכה**[562] (דניאל 12:12) בכׄמס[563] וארבעין[564] סנה. קאל פיה **ומעת הוסר התמיד אלף**[565] **ומאתים ותשעים**[566] (דניאל 12:11) חתי אדׄא סירת הדׄה אלמדה איצׄא[567] אנתהת מן[568] אלסנה[569] אל אן מואפקה[570] לנהאיה תלך אלגמלה. פאדׄא תמת

545 אלמדה ... דלך Yeirin 229 > L
546 קנׄ + Oxf 2652.55a and Yeirin 229
547 ומאיה וכׄמסין Oxf 2652.55a and Yeirin 229 > L
548 אל[ח]ואד[תׄ] Oxf 2652.55a > D
549 מגת[מע]ה Yeirin 229 > D
550 א[לוק]ת א[ל]די Oxf 2652.55a > D
551 [המ]חכה Yeirin 229 > D
552 [ב]מאיה Yeirin 229 > D | במאיה End of Yeirin 229
553 סנה End of Oxf 2652.55a
554 ופה Beginning of Yeirin 230 (TS Ar 1b.101g) | Beginning of Oxf 2652.55b
555 כמסה ותמאנין סנה Oxf 2652.55b > D
556 חת Yeirin 230 | חתי Oxf 2652.55b
557 זיאדה End of Oxf 2486.104b
558 ולא Beginning of Oxf 2486.105a
559 [ו]קד Yeirin 230 > D
560 ארתחשתסתא Yeirin 230
561 אלקול Oxf 2486.105a
562 במהׄ + Yeirin 230
563 בכמסה Oxf 2486.105a
564 בכמס וארבעין סנה Yeirin 230 > L
565 רצׄ + Oxf 2652.55b and Yeirin 230
566 ומאתים ותשעים Oxf 2652.55b and Yeirin 230 > L
567 א[יצא] Yeirin 230 > D
568 אלז[מא]ן + Yeirin 230 | אלזמאן + Oxf 2652.55b
569 אלסנה Oxf 2652.55b and Yeirin 230 > L
570 מופקה Oxf 2652.55b

הדֿה אלאלף וקנֿ[571] סנה מן אול וקתהא יכון **ונצדק קדש** (דניאל 8:14).[572] ומכן[573] אן יכון תפסירה פלגא[574] מן[575] אלחגה[576] ללמומנין כמא קאל[577] **וכל לשון תקום אתך למשפט תרשיעי** (יש׳ 54:17). ויגוז אן תכון[578] זכוה וצלאה כמא קאל[579] **קרוב צדקי**[580] (יש׳ 51:5), **ועמך כל צדיקים** (יש׳ 60:21) ומא[581] נחי הדֿא אלנחו.

ואתצל בי אן[582] מן[583] אלמפסרין מן[584] געל הדֿה אלמדה אלפין[585] ותֿלתֿ מאיה[586] סנה תאמה. וגעל אבתדאהא לעשרין[587] סנה[588] קבל כֿרוג אלקום מן[589] מצר. והו ענדה **וימת מלך מצרים ויאנחו**[590] **בני ישראל**[591] (שמ׳ 2:23) חתי יכֿרג אלי אכֿרהא מע אכֿד **אשרי המחכה**[592] (דניאל 12:12). ואן בעצֿהם איצֿא יגעלהא הם אלפין[593] ותֿלתֿ מאיה[594] סנה, אלא[595] אנה יגעל אולהא מן וקת קאל אללה לאברהאם **ולישמעאל שמעתיך** (בר׳ 17:20) ואכֿרהא אלי

571 וכמסין Oxf 2486.105a
572 ויסתקים + Oxf 2652.55b and Yeirin 230
573 ומכן L < Oxf 2652.55b and Yeirin 230
574 פי + Yeirin 230
575 מן L < Yeirin 230
576 א[לחג]ה D < Yeirin 230
577 כק Yeirin 230
578 יכון Oxf 2652.55b and Yeirin 230
579 כק Yeirin 230
580 וג׳ Yeirin 230
581 מא Yeirin 230
582 בעץ + Oxf 2652.55b and Yeirin 230
583 מן L < Oxf 2652.55b and Yeirin 230
584 מן L < Oxf 2652.55b and Yeirin 230
585 ש + Oxf 2652.55b and Yeirin 230
586 תלת מאיה L < Oxf 2652.55b and Yeirin 230
587 לעשרין End of Oxf 2486.105a
588 סנה Beginning of Oxf 2486.105b
589 אלקום מן L < Oxf 2652.55b
590 וג׳ + Oxf 2652.55b
591 בני ישראל L < Oxf 2652.55b
592 וגעל אבתדאהא ... המחכה L < Yeirin 230
593 ש + Oxf 2652.55b and Yeirin 230
594 ותלת מאיה L < Oxf 2652.55b and Yeirin 230
595 אלי Yeirin 230

וקת[596] אבתדי[597] מלכות[598] ישמאל. ומן אלנאס מן יגעלהא איאמא מחצ'ה[599] פתכון[600] סת סנין ויקול[601] אנהא מדה[602] גסקלגס. ומנהם[603] מן יאכ'ד נצפהא עלי שביה במא ד'כרנא[604] מן תחציל **ערב ובקר** (דניאל 8:14). אלא[605] אנהא יגעלהא איאמא

מחצ'ה[606] פתכון ג' סנין ויזעם אנהא מדה מא גזר[607] גסקלגס עלי אלאמה. ואלד'י ארצ'אה[608] הו אלתפסיר אלד'י קדמת שרחה.[609] תֿם חכי תפסיר אלקצה פקאל[610]

Dn 8:15

ויהי[611] בראותי אני[612] דניאל[613] את החזון ואבקשה בינה והנה עמד לנגדי כמראה גבר.

פלמא ראית[614] אנא דניאל הד'ה[615] אלרויא טלבת אן אתפהמהא[616] פכאן שכ'ץ[617] קאים חד'אי[618] כמנט'ר[619] רגל.

[596] וקת Yeirin 230 > L

[597] אבתדי Yeirin 230

[598] מלך Oxf 2652.55b

[599] מחצאה Yeirin 230

[600] ו + Oxf 2652.55b and Yeirin 230

[601] ויקולון Yeirin 230

[602] מ[דה] Oxf 2652.55b > D

[603] [ומנ]הם Oxf 2486.105b > D

[604] [במא ד]כרנא Oxf 2486.105b > D

[605] אלא Oxf 2486.105b > D

[606] מחציה Oxf 2652.55b

[607] גזר Oxf 2486.105b > D

[608] ארתצאה Yeirin 230

[609] שרחה Oxf 2486.105b > D

[610] פקאל End of Oxf 2486.105b

[611] ויהי Beginning of Oxf 2486.106a

[612] אני End of Yeirin 230

[613] דניאל Beginning of Yeirin 231 (TS Ar 1b.101h)

[614] ר[אי]ת Yeirin 231

[615] הדי Morag | הדא Spiegel

[616] אתפהם Morag | אתפהמ[הא] Yeirin 231 > D | אסתפהמה Spiegel

[617] פאדי בשכ'ץ Morag

[618] חדאיי Oxf 2652.55b + Oxf 2486.106a

[619] כמנצר Spiegel + Morag

Dn 8:16

ואשמע קול אדם בן אולי ויקרא ויאמר גבריאל הבן להלז את המראה.

ת̇ם[620] סמעת כצות[621] אנסאן[622] פי גהה[623] אלנהר פנאדי[624] במן קאל לה יא גבריל אפהם ד̇אך תפסיר אלרויא.[625]

Dn 8:17

ויבא אצל עמדי ובבאו נבעתי ואפלה על פני ויאמר אלי הבן בן אדם כי לעת קץ החזון.

פגא ענד מוקפי פמע[626] מגייה[627] האלני פוקעת[628] עלי[629] וגהי פקאל לי אפהם יא אבן[630] אדם[631] תפסיר אלרויא פאנה אלי וקת אלאגל.

Dn 8:18

ובדברו עמי נרדמתי על פני ארצה ויגע בי ויעמדני על עמדי.

פלמא כלמני[632] אסבתת[633] עלי וגהי[634] עלי אלארץ̇[635] פדני[636] חתי אוקפני עלי וקפי.

Dn 8:19

ויאמר הנני מודיעך את אשר יהיהבאחרית הזעם כי למועד קץ.

[620] ת[ם] Yeirin 231 > D

[621] צות Spiegel

[622] אנ[סא]ן Yeirin 231 > D

[623] גהת Morag

[624] פנאדא Spiegel + Morag

[625] תפ[סיר אלר]ויא Yeirin 231 > D

[626] פמ[ע] Yeirin 231 > D

[627] מגיה Oxf 2652.55b + Oxf 2486.106a ׀ מגיוה Yeirin 231

[628] פוקעת End of Oxf 2486.106a

[629] עלי Beginning of Oxf 2486.106b

[630] בן Oxf 2652.55b

[631] אד[ם] Yeirin 231 > D ׀ אדם Spiegel

[632] כלמת Yeirin 231

[633] אס[ב]תת Yeirin 231

[634] וגה Spiegel

[635] עלי אלארץ Spiegel > L

[636] פדנא Morag ׀ פדאנא בי Spiegel

וקאל[637] האנא מערפך מא יכון[638] פי אכ̇ר הד̇א[639] אלזג̇ם[640] פאנה אלי וקת אלאג̇ל.

Dn 8:20
האיל אשר ראית בעלה הקרנים מלכי מדי ופרס.

אלכבש אלד̇י ראיתה ד̇א[641] אלקרנין[642] מלוך[643] מאהאת[644] ופארס.

Dn 8:21
והצפיר השעיר מלך יון והקרן הגדולה אשר בין עיניו הוא המלך הראשון.

ואלתיס פהו מלוך[645] אליונאניין[646] ואלקרן אלעט̇ים[647] אלד̇י בין עיניה[648] הו אלמלך אלאול[649] מנהם.

Dn 8:22
והנשברת ותעמדנה ארבע תחתיה ארבע מלכיות מגוי יעמדנה ולא בכחו.

ואלמנכסרה אלד̇י נבת[650] מכאנהא ארבע הי ארבע[651] ממאלך תקום[652] מן אמה ואחדה[653] לא בקותהא.[654]

[637] וקאל Spiegel + לי ׀ Morag
[638] יך Morag
[639] הד̇א Oxf 2486.106b > D ׀ הדי Morag
[640] אלרגם Spiegel
[641] דו Spiegel + Morag
[642] הו + Morag
[643] מלוך End of Oxf 2486.106b
[644] מאהאת Beginning of Oxf 2486.107a ׀ מהאת Yeirin 231
[645] מלך Morag
[646] אליונאניה Oxf 2652.55b
[647] אלעצים Spiegel + Oxf 2652.55b + Yeirin 231 + Morag ׀ End of Oxf 2652.55b
[648] עינאה Spiegel + Morag
[649] אלאוול Spiegel
[650] אלתי נבתת Morag
[651] ארבעה הי ארבע Oxf 2486.107a ׀ ד הי ד Yeirin 231
[652] תקום Morag > L ׀ ת[ק]ום Yeirin 231
[653] תקף + Morag

Dn 8:23

ובאחרית מלכותם כהתם הפשעים[655] יעמד מלך עז פנים ומבין חידות.

ופי אכ̇ר מלכהם ענד כמאל אלגרום[656] יקום מלך צפיק אלוגה יפהם אלאחאדית̇.[657]

Dn 8:24

ועצם[658] כחו ולא בכחו ונפלאות ישחית והצליח ועשה והשחית עצומים ועם קדושים.

פתעט̇ם קוותה[659] ולא[660] בקותה[661] ויפסד פסאדא[662] עגיבא ויתם לה אן יצנעה ויהלך אלעט̇מא[663] ואלקום אלקדוסין.[664]

Dn 8:25

ועל שׂכלו והצליח מראה בידו ולבבו יגדיל ובשלוה ישחית רבים ועל שׂר שׂרים יעמד ובאפס יד ישבר.

ומע כ̇בת̇ה[665] תמאם[666] אלמכר[667] פי ידה פיכבר קלבה ויהלך[668] אלכת̇ירין פיהדו[669] ואלי ראייס אלרייסא[670] יקום[671] וענד כ̇לו אלמקדרה[672] ינכסר.

[654] בקוותהא Spiegel + Yeirin 231 + Morag
[655] הפושעים End of Yeirin 231
[656] אלגרם Spiegel + Morag
[657] אלאחאדית End of Oxf 2486.107a
[658] ועצם Beginning of Oxf 2486.107b
[659] פתעצם קוותה Spiegel + Morag
[660] לא Oxf 2486.107b
[661] בקוותה Morag | בקווה Spiegel
[662] פאסדא Spiegel
[663] אלעצמא Spiegel + Morag
[664] אלקדיסין Oxf 2486.107b
[665] ומע כבתה Oxf 2486.107b > D
[666] יתם Spiegel
[667] יתם אלאמר Oxf 2486.107b
[668] [קלבה ויה]לך Oxf 2486.107b > D
[669] פי הדו Spiegel
[670] אלרייסא Oxf 2486.107b > D | יחצר + Oxf 2486.107b
[671] יקום Oxf 2486.107b > L
[672] אלקדרה Oxf 2486.107b

Dn 8:26
ומראה הערב והבקר אשר נאמר אמת הוא ואתה סתום החזון כי לימים רבים.[673]

ורויא[674] מדת אלליל ואלנהאר אלתי[675] קילת פהי[676] חק ואנת פאחפט[677] אלרויא פאנהא[678] אלי[679] דהר[680] טויל.

Dn 8:27
ואני דניאל נהייתי ונהליתי ימים רבים ואקום ואעשה את מלאכת המלך ואשתומם על המארה ואין מבין.

ואנא דניאל אגׄתממת[681] פמרצׄת איאמא אלי אן קמת פעמלת עמל אלמלך פכנת מטרקא פי אלתפכר פי אלרויא פלם[682] אגד מפהמא.

אמא תקדימה **ואבקשה בינה** (דניאל 8:15) ליערפנא אנה כמא אכׄתלג בקלבה אלתמאס אלתפסיר טׄהר לה אלשכׄץ אלדׄי קאל ענה **כמראה גבר** (דניאל 8:15). פכמא טׄהר לה אלשכׄץ סמע צות ישבה צות אנסאן ליאמר אלשכׄץ בתעריף דניאל אלתפסיר כמא קאל **ואשמע קול אדם** (דניאל 8:16). והדׄא אלדׄי סמע צותה[683] אגל[684] מן אלשכׄץ וקריב [...][685] במנזלה **עתיק יומין** (דניאל 7:9) ענד **בר אנש** (דניאל 7:13) וכמנזלה **פלמוני המדבר** (דניאל 8:13) ענד **אחד קדוש** (דניאל 8:13). אלא אן דניאל ראי **עתיק יומין** ולם יר **פלמוני** ולא הדׄא אלאדם. ואנמא סמע צותיהמא פקט. ומעני **ויקרא** (דניאל 8:16) נאדי פקאל יא גבריאל. ומעני קולה **ויאמר, הבן להלז** (דניאל 8:16) יעני דניאל.

673 רבים End of Oxf 2486.107b
674 ורויא Beginnng of Oxf 2486.108a
675 אלדׄי קלת Spiegel
676 פהו Spiegel + Morag
677 פאחפץ Spiegel + Morag
678 פאנה Morag
679 וקת + Spiegel
680 דהר > L Spiegel
681 אגׄתמת Spiegel + Morag
682 ולם Spiegel
683 צותה End of Oxf 2486.108a
684 אגל Beginning of Oxf 2486.108b
685 [...] Oxf 2486.108b > D

ומעני **בין אולי** (דניאל 8:16) מן גהה אלנהר לתשאבה הדׄה [...][686] קצה **אשר ממעל למימי היאר** (דניאל 12:6). [...][687] סיצף פי אלמסתאנף. [...][688] פי סואל בעץׄ אלמלאיכה [... ...][689] אלקץ. ופי אמר בעצׄהם [...][690] שפה לדניאל ליעזז ענדנא [...][691] אלקול אצולה ופרועה ויפסרהא אדׄא סמענא [...][692] מעאני יסל ענהא אלמלאיכה [...][693] אשר[694] [...].

[...][695] **את**[696] **הארץ ביד רעים** (יח' 30:12) ומא אשבה דׄלך. פסרת קולה **עז פנים** (דניאל 8:23) אנה לא ירחם ולא יהאב, כמא קאל **גוי עז פנים אשר לא ישׂא פנים לזקן ונער לא יחן** (דב' 28:50). ומעני **ומבין חידות** (דניאל 8:23) אנה יערף [...][697] אלמלוך אללדׄין מן קבלהם וסירהם. פהו יחתאג לכל פעל יפעלה מן חיתׄ שא, כיף שא ויקול פעלת כמא פעל פלאן אלמלך.

ועצם כחו ולא בכחו (דניאל 8:24) מתׄל מא שרחנא פימא תקדם. ומעני **ונפלאות ישחית** (דניאל 8:24) הו מא יתעגב מן אפסאדה אדׄא גרת אשיא לם יר מתׄלהא לאן הדׄא אלעגב מא לם יר מתׄלהא אעני מרתין. ומעני **והשכית עצומים ועם קדושים** (דניאל 8:24) אנה יקתל מן כׄואץ בני יסראיל ומעני **ועל שׂכלו והצליח מרמה בידו** (דניאל 8:25) [...][698] בעקל צחיח, לאן[699] אלעקל[700] אלצחיח הו מא אמר באלעדל. ולאכנה תעאקל ותחאכם כמא יקול **חכמים המא להרע** (ירמ' 4:22). ולדׄלך פסרתה "כבתא". וכמא פסרת כל

[686] Oxf 2486.108b > D [...]
[687] Oxf 2486.108b > D א[...]
[688] Oxf 2486.108b > D מה[...]
[689] Oxf 2486.108b > D [... ...]
[690] Oxf 2486.108b > D [...]
[691] Oxf 2486.108b > D [...]
[692] Oxf 2486.108b > D [...]
[693] Oxf 2486.108b > D [...]
[694] אשר End of Oxf 2486.108b
[695] The commentary of דניאל 8:14-22 is missing in Oxf 2486.108b
[696] את Beginning of Oxf 2486.117a
[697] א[...]אד Oxf 2486.117a > D
[698] [בידו ...] Oxf 2486.117a > D
[699] לאן End of Oxf 2486.117a
[700] אלעקל Beginning of Oxf 2486.117b

הצליח (דניאל 8:24.25) פי הדֹא אלמוצֹע ״תמאם״ ולם אפסרה ״אצלאחא״ אד̇ אלמכר לא יכון אצלאחא. ומעני **ובשלוה ישחית גוים**[701] **רבים** (דניאל 8:25) אנה יעטי ישׂראל אלאמאן חתי יהדו ויטמאנו. תֹם יעטף עליהם פיהלך מנהם. ולעלה אן יפעל בג̇ירהם כדֹאך. ומעני **ועל שׂר שׂרים יעמד** (דניאל 8:25) קד יכון פי אלארצֹין פיקצד אגל אלמלוך או אגל אלאמרא, אי **כהן גדול** או מן שאבההם. וקד יכון פי אלמסמין. פכאנה יקצד באלכלאם אלדעוי אמא מיכאל ואמא גבריאל או מן אשבאההמא. ומעני **ובאפס יד ישבר** (דניאל 8:25) פהו[702] וקת[703] פנא מתֹלה ומקדרתה כמא מתֹל למואב פקאל **כי אפס**[704] **חציר כלה דשא ירק לא היה** (יש׳ 15:6). וקאל איצֹא **כי אפס המעכלה שד תמו רמס מן הארץ** (יש׳ 16:4) ומא לאאם דֹלך.

ומעני **ואתה סתם החזון** (דניאל 8:26) ליס הו ״אכֹתמוה״ לאנה לו כאן כדֹאך לם יגז דניאל אן יתֹבתה וידונה. ואנמא הו ״אחפטֹה״ ״ואכנזה״ ״ואדֹכֹרה״ כמא קאל **ובסתום חכמה תודיעני** (תה׳ 51:8) ועלי מא סנקול פי אכֹר הדֹא אלבתאב. ותצריף **ונהייתי** (דניאל 8:27) קד יכון מן **נהי** וקד יכון מן **הוה** ויראד באלגמיע גֹמ והם. ואלחאקה בהדֹא אלקול **ואקום ואעשׂה את מלאכת המלך** (דניאל 8:27) יריד בה אנה לולא צֹרורה עמל אלסלטאן לם יפק מן גֹמה ודֹאך לעטֹם מא גרי לה. וקולה **ואשתומם על המארה ואין מבין** (דניאל 8:27) ליס יעני תפסיר אלרויא לאן גבריאל קד אפהמה[705] איאהא[706] כמא קאל לה **הבן בן אדם** (דניאל 8:17). ואנמא יעני בדֹלך אנה ליס יעלם הל הו נבי אם לא חתי טֹהר לה גבריאל פי אליקטֹה בעד דֹלך כמא סישרח פימא יסתאנף. פארתגע מעתקדא אן הדֹה אלרויא נבוה כאנת. פדֹלך תמאם שרח אלגז אלתֹאמן.

[701] גוים > L Oxf 2486.117b
[702] פהו End of Oxf 2486.117b
[703] וקת Beginning of Oxf 2486.118a
[704] יבש MT
[705] אפהמה End of Oxf 2486.118a
[706] איאהא Beginning of Oxf 2486.118b

Dn 9:1

בשנת אחת לדריוש בן אחשורוש מזרע מדי אשר המלך על מלכות כשׂדים.

ופיי[1] סנת אחדי לדריוש בן[2] אחשורוש[3] מן נסל אלמדיין אלדׄי נצב מלכא בעקב מלך אלכסדאניין.

קולה הדׄא יתצל במא כאן קד קדמה קבלה מן אן באלשאצר למא קתל[4] קאם[5] בעדה דריוש כמא קאל **ביה בליליא קטל בלשצר** (דניאל 5:30), **ודריוש מדאה קבל מלכותא** (דניאל 6:1). ולם ישרח תׄם אבן מן הו פשרח האהנא אבן אחשורוש וליס הדׄא הו אחשורש צאחב המן. בל קד בקי מן אלסנין אלי אול מלך אחשורוש צאחב המן ד̇ סנין ואלי אכׄר מלכה יח̇ סנה לאנה אקאם יד̇ סנה. ולכן הדׄא אחשורוש צאחב המן ד̇ סנין ואלי אכׄר מלכה יח̇ סנה לאנה אקאם יד̇ סנה. ולכן הדׄא אחשורש אכׄר לם יוצף אנה מלך או עאמי בוגה. תׄם קאל

Dn 9:2

בשנת אחת למלכו אני דניאל לבינתי בספרים מספר השנים אשר היה דבר יהוה אל ירמיהו הנביא למלאות לחרבות ירושלם שבעים שנה.

פי תלך סנה אחדי[6] מן מלכה אנא[7] דניאל תבינת[8] פי אלכתב[9] עדד אלסנין אלדׄי

[1] פי Spiegel
[2] אבן Spiegel
[3] אחשורש Oxf 2486.118b
[4] קתל End of Oxf 2486.118b
[5] קאם Beginning of Oxf 2486.119a
[6] אחדא Morag
[7] אני Spiegel
[8] תביינת Spiegel + Morag
[9] אלכתאב Spiegel + Morag

אוחי בה[10] אללה אלי ירמיה אלנבי ענד תמאם[11] סבעין[12] סנה לכ׳ראב ירושלם.[13]

Dn 9:3
ואתנה את פני אל יהוה האלהים לבקש תפלה ותחנונים בצום ושק ואפר.

פקצדת אללה רבי טאלבא[14] צלוה ותחננא בצום ומסח ורמאד.

אבתדי אולא באלעלה אלתי אוגבת קצדה אלדעא פי תלך אלסנה פי בנא אלקדס. פערפנא אנה למא חסב חסאב אלסבעין ווקע לה אנהא קד תמת וקע לה אן אלקץ יחתאג אלי תחריך בדעא וצלוה. פפעל ד׳לך כמא חרך אלקץ צראך׳ אלקום אד׳ קאל **ויאנחו בני ישראל מן העבדה ויזעקו ותעל שועתם אל האלוהים מן העבדה** (שמ׳ 2:23). ועלי אנה קד נסב אלחסאב האהנא אלי **חרבות ירושלם** (דניאל 9:2). פינבג׳י אן[15] נעלם[16] אנה אנמא הו **למלכות בבל** לאן ירמיהו הכד׳י קאל אללה לה **כי לפי מלאות לבבל שבעים שנה אפקד אתכם** (ירמ׳ 29:10). פרגא דניאל אן יכון אול אלסבעין אול מלך נבוכ׳דנצר. פקאל עלי הד׳א אלחסאב קד תמת אלסבעין סנה. וד׳לך אן נבוכ׳דנצר מלך כ׳מסה וארבעין סנה ואבנה מרודך ת׳לת׳ ועשרין סנה ואבן אבנה בלשאצר ת׳לת׳ סנין. פד׳לך סבעין סנה. ומן אין לנא אן נבוכ׳דנצר מלך כ׳מסה וארבעין סנה? מן קול אלכתאב אן אויל מרודך מלך פי סנה סבעה ות׳לת׳ין מן **גלות יכניה** אד׳ קאל **ויהי בשלשים ושבעה שנה לגלות יהויכין מלך יהודה, נשׂא הויל מרודך בשנת מלכו** (מל״ב 25:27). ופי וקת **גלות יכניה** כאן קד מצ׳י מן מלך נבוכדנצר ח׳ סנין כמא קאל **ויצא יהויכין מלך יהודה על מלך בבל הוא ואמו ועבדיו ושׂריו[17] וסוריסיו[18] ויקח אתו מלך בבל בשנת שמנה למלכו** (מל״ב 24:12). וד׳לך יואפק מא נץ אלכתאב אן נבוכ׳דנצר מלך פי אלסנה אלראבעה ליהויקים אד׳ קאל **הדבר אשר היה על ירמיהו על כל עם יהודה בשנת הרביעית ליהויקים בן יאשיהו מלך יהודה היא השנת הראשנית**

10 בהא Morag

11 תמאם End of Oxf 2486.119a

12 סבעין Beginning of Oxf 2486.119b

13 סנה ... ירושלם Oxf 2486.119b > D

14 טאלב Morag

15 אן End of Oxf 2486.119b

16 נעלם Beginning of Oxf 2486.120a

17 ושריו End of Oxf 2486.120a

18 וסורסיסיו Beginning of Oxf 2486.120b

לנבוכדנצר מלך בבל (ירמ׳ 25:1). פקד תבין אן מלך נבוכֿדנצר כֿמסה וארבעין סנה ומלך בלשאצר תֿלתֿ סנין לקול דניאל **בשנת שלש למלכות בלשצר המלך** (דניאל 8:1). מא תקדם ובאלצֿרורה פלא בד מן אן יכון מלך לאויל מרודך בין נבוכדנצר ובלשאצר לקול ירמיהו **ועבדו הגוים האלה את מלך בבל שבעים שנה** (ירמ׳ 25:11). וקאל איצֿא **ועבדו אתו כל הגוים ואת בנו ואת בן בנו** (ירמ׳ 27:7). פבנו הו אויל מרודך **ובן בנו** הו בלשאצר עלי מא שרחנא.

ועלי תאריךֿ אלסנין[19] אלנואקץ[20] תכון **שנת אחת לדריוש** (ע׳ דניאל 9:1) סנה אחד וסבעין לבבל. ולדֿלך קבלהא[21] בסנה אטֿהר בלשאצר אניה אלקדס כמא שרחנא. לאנה כאן ענדה אן אלקץ קד אנקצֿי ובטל רדהא[22] אלי אלקדס. ועלי אסקאט אלסנה אלנאקצה תציר **שנת אחת לדריוש** (ע׳ דניאל 9:1) סנה סבעין. ולדֿלך אדי[23] לכורש כמא קאל **ובשנת אחת לכורש מלך פרס לכלות דבר ייי בפי ירמיהו** (עזרא 1:1). ואלסבב פי דֿלך סקוט גֿ סנין מן אלחסאב. סנה בין נבוכדנצר ואויל, וסנה בין אויל ובלשאצר, וסנה בין בלשאצר ודריוש. פואפי תמאם אלסבעין **בשנת אחת לכורש** (עזרא 1:1). ולם יכן אלבנא אלתאם, לאן אלבנא אלתאם אנמא צמן ענד תמאם סבעין **לחרבות ירושלם** (דניאל 9:2).

ואמא ענד תמאם סבעין לבבל פאנמא צֿמן ללקום פקידה פקט כמא קאל **אפקד אתכם** (ירמ׳ 29:10). ובין סבעין[24] לבבל[25] וסבעין **לחרבות ירושלם** (דניאל 9:2) יחֿ סנה כמא קאל **ובחדש החמישי בעשור לחדש היא שנת תשע עשרה שנה למלך נבוכדנצר מלך בבל** (ירמ׳ 52:12), **וישרף את בית ייי** (ירמ׳ 52:13). והדֿה אליטֿ תסתגֿרק תֿלתֿ סנין מלך כורש וארבע עשרה סנה מלך אחשורוש ואלי סנתין מן מלך ארתחשסתא אלמסמי דריוש כמא מנצוץ **בשנת שתים לדריוש** (חגי 1:1. זכריהו 1:1) פי נבוה חגי וזכריה. ויקאל אן אחשורוש איצֿא חסב עלי חסאב בלשאצר פקאל אנני ארי פימא חסבה בלשאצר גֿלטא חֿ סנין ולדֿלך עוגל באלקתל.[26] והי אלחֿ סנין אלתי מן אול מלך

[19] אלסנין End of Oxf 2486.120b
[20] אלנואקץ Beginning of Oxf 2486.121a
[21] Uncertain lesson
[22] Uncertain lesson
[23] Uncertain lesson
[24] סבעין End of Oxf 2486.121a
[25] לבבל Beginning of Oxf 2486.121b
[26] Uncertain lesson

נבוכדנצר אלי **גלות יכניה** כמא שרחנא נחן. פראי אחשורוש אנהא קד תמת **בשנת שלוש למלכו** (אסתר 1:3). ודלך סנתין לדריוש ותלתה לכורש ותלתה לאחשורוש בכסור אלסנה, פדלך סבעין. פלדלך **עשה משתה לכל שריו**[27] (אסתר 1:3) סרורא[28] בבטלאן קץ ישראל, ועלי מא שרחנא פי מגלה אסתר. וגרי עליה מא גרי.

ויקאל איצא אן חנניה בן עזור חסב הדא אלחסאב קבל אלגמיע. וגלט פיה לאנה געל אול אלסבעין בעד סנה כמסה ותלתין מן מלך מנשה והו אלוקת אלדי בסטת פיה ידה עלי ישראל כמא קאל **ויבא ייי עליהם את שרי הצבא אשר למלך אשור** (דה״ב 33:11). וקאל **ויוליכהו בבלה** (דה״ב 33:11). פבקי עשרין מן מלך מנשה וסנתין לאמון וליאשיהו אחד ותלתין וליהויקים אחד עשרה. פלמא מצת ארבע סנין לצדקיה, כמא קאל **ויהי בשנה ההיא ברשית ממלכת צדקיה מלך יהודה בשנת הרבעית בחדש החמישי אמר אלי חנניה בן עזור הנביא** (ירמ׳ 28:1), **בעוד שנתים ימים אני משיב אל המקום הזה את**[29] **כל**[30] **כלי בית יוי** (ירמ׳ 28:3) ודלך תמאם סת סנין לצדקיה עלי והמה אן אלסבעין קד תמת. פקאל אלאן דניאל: למא רגות מואפאה אלקץ אכדת פי תחריכה בדעא וצלוה. וגעלהא כמסה פנון: **תפלה, ותחנונים, וצום, ושק ואפר**.

פאמא **תפלה**, פהי אעאדה פצול אלפריצה עלי גהתהא נאפלה עלי אלמתעלם. ואמא **תחנונים** פהו אלדעא ואלתחנן אלדי יסתעמלאה אלמומנין בעד צלואתהם כמא קאל **והתפללו והתחננו לפניך בבית הזה** (מל״א 8:33). ואמא אלצום פלה מעאני אלתי שרחנאהא פי שרוע **יום הכפורים**. ואמא **ושק ואפר** פהי אלעלל אלתי בינאהא פי תפסיר **קינה** ופי תפסיר **מגלה אסתר**. והדה כלהא לא תנפע שיא אלא באכלאץ מן אלעבד לתצדירה קבלהא **ואתנה את פני** (דניאל 9:3), והו אלקצד.[31]

Dn 9:4

ואתפללה ליהוה ואתודה ואמרה אנא אדני האל הגדול והנורא שמר הברית וחסד לאהביו ולשומרי מצותיו.

[27] שריו End of Oxf 2486.121b

[28] סרורא Beginning of Oxf 2486.122a

[29] את End of Oxf 2486.122a

[30] כל Beginning of Oxf 2486.122b

[31] אלקצד End of Oxf 2486.122b | דניאל 9:4-12 Missing in Oxf 2486

ולמא צלית ללה רבי אקררת בדׄנובי וקלת אללהם יא רבי אלטאיק אלכביר אלמהיוב חאפץׄ אלעהד ואלפצׄל למחביה וחאפצׄי וצאיאה.

Dn 9:5

חטאנו ועוינו והרשענו ומרדנו וסור ממצותיך וממשפטיך.

קד אכׄטינא[32] ואדׄנבנא וטׄלמנא[33] ועצינא וזלנא מן שראיעך[34] ואחכאמך.

Dn 9:6

ולא שמענו אל עבדיך הנביאים אשר דברו בשמך אל מלכינו ושרינו ואבותינו ואל כל עם הארץ.

ולם נקבל מן רסלאך אלאנביא[35] אלדׄי כׄאטבו ענך מלוכנא וריאסנא ואבאינא[36] וסאיר אלעאמה.

Dn 9:7

לך יהוה הצדקה ולנו בשת הפנים בהיום הזה לאיש יהודה ולישבי ירושלם ולכל ישראל הקרובים והרחקיםבכל הארצת אשר הרחקתם שם במעלם אשר מעלו בך.

לך יא רב אלעדל ולנא אלכׄזא יומנא הדׄא לאל יהודה ולאל ירושלם לסאיר[37] בני אסראיל אלקריבין ואלבעידין פי גמיע אלבלדאן אלדׄי דחית בהם תׄם בנכתׄהם אלדׄי נכתׄו בטאעתך.

Dn 9:8

יהוה לנו בשת הפנים למלכינו ולשׂארינו ולאבותינו אשר חטאנו לך.

וכמא לנא אלכׄזיא רב[38] כדׄאך למלוכנא וריסאנא[39] ואבאנא אדׄ אכׄטאנא לך.

[32] אלכטינא Spiegel
[33] וצלמנא Spiegel + Morag
[34] שראיען Spiegel
[35] אלאנבי Spiegel
[36] ואבאנא Morag
[37] וסאיר Spiegel
[38] אלכדא יא רבנא Spiegel
[39] וראייסנא Morag

Dn 9:9

לאדני אלהינו הרחמים והסליחות כי מרדנו בו.

ועלי אנה ללה[40] רבנא אלרחמה ואלמגׇפרה עלי[41] אנא קד עצינאה.

Dn 9:10

ולא שמענו בקול יהוה אלהינו ללכת בתורתו אשר נתן לפנינו ביד עבדיו הנביאים.

ולם נקבל אמר רבנא לנסיר פי שראיעה אלתי תלאהא עלינא רסלאה אלאנביא.

Dn 9:11

וכל ישראל עברו את תורתך וסור לבלתי שמוע בקלך ותתך עלינו האלה והשבעה אשר כתובה בתורת משה עבד האלהים כי חטאנו לו.

וסאיר אל אסראיל[42] תגאוזו תוראתך וזאלו ולם[43] יקבלו אמרך חתי אנצב עלינא מא[44] מכתוב[45] פי תוראת מוסי רסול אללה[46] אלדׇי[47] אכׇטאנא לה.

Dn 9:12

ויקם את דבריו אשר דבר עלינו ועל שפטינו אשר שפטונו להביא עלינו רעה גדולה אשר לא נעשׂתה תחת כל השמים כאשר נעשׂתה בירושלם.

פואפא בועדה[48] אלדׇי תואעדנא[49] וחכאמנא אלדׇי ולונא אן ינזל בנא בלייה[50] עטׇימה[51] מא לם תצנע תחת אלסמא כמא צנעת פי [52] ירושלם.

[40] אללה Morag
[41] ועלי Spiegel
[42] אלאסראיל Spiegel
[43] וזאלוא פלם Spiegel
[44] פי אלחרג ואלימין + Spiegel
[45] אלמכתוב Spiegel
[46] ממא + Spiegel
[47] אלדי > L Spiegel
[48] בועדה Spiegel
[49] בה + Spiegel
[50] בלייה Beginning of Oxf 2486.109a
[51] עצימה Spiegel + Morag
[52] [פ]י > D Oxf 2486.109a

Dn 9:13
כאשר בתוב בתורה משה את כל הרעה הזאת באה עלינו ולא חלינו את פני יהוה אלהינו לשוב מעוננו ולהשׂכיל באמתך.

כמא[53] מכתוב פי תוראת מוסי לאן גמיע דׄלך[54] חל בנא ולם[55] נבתהל אלי אללה רבנא פנתוב אליה מן דׄנובנא ונעקל חקאיקה.

Dn 9:14
וישקד יהוה על הרעה ויביאה עלינו כי צדיק יהוה אלהינו על כל מעשיו אשר עשׂה ולא שמענו בקלו.

פחתם[56] אללה עלי אלבלייה[57] ואתי[58] בהא עלינא אדׄ הו אלעדאל פי גמיע צנאיעה[59] אלדׄי צנע[60] ונחן אלדׄין[61][62] לם[63] נקבל אמרה.

Dn 9:15
ועתה אדני אלהינו אשר הוצאת את[64] עמך[65] מארץ מצרים ביד חזקה ותעש לך שם כיום הזה כטאנו רשענו.

ולאן[66] יא אללה רבנא אלדׄי אכׄרגת קומך[67] מן בלד מצר ביד שדידה וצנעת לך אסם עטׄימא[68] פאנא[69] יומנא הדׄא קד אכׄטאנא וטׄלמנא.[70]

[53] בעדמא Spiegel + Oxf 2486.109a
[54] דאלך Spiegel
[55] ולא Oxf 2486.109a
[56] פחכם Morag
[57] אלבליה Oxf 2486.109a
[58] ואתא Spiegel
[59] צנעה Oxf 2486.109a
[60] צנעה Oxf 2486.109a
[61] אללדין Oxf 2486.109a
[62] ונחן אלדיו Spiegel > L
[63] ולם Spiegel
[64] את End of Oxf 2486.109a
[65] עמך Beginning of Oxf 2486.109b
[66] ואללא Spiegel
[67] קומנא Morag ׀ שעבך Spiegel
[68] עצימא Spiegel + Morag
[69] פאננא Oxf 2486.109b
[70] וצלמנא Spiegel + Morag

Dn 9:16

אדני ככל צדקתיך ישב נא אפך וחמתך מעירך ירושלם הר קדשך כי בחטאינו ועונות אבותינו ירושלם ועמך לחרפה לכל סביבותינו.

אללהם כגמיע אחסאנך אסאלך[71] אן תרד גֹצׄבך וחמיתך[72] ען מדינתך ירושלם[73] גבל קדסך פאנהא בכׄטאינא ודׄנוב אבאינא קד צארת הי וקומך מעיירה[74] לגמיע אלמחיטין בנא.[75]

Dn 9:17

ועתה שמע אלהינו אל תפלת עבדך[76] ואל[77] תחנוניו והאר פניך מקדושך השמם[78] למען אדני.

ואלאן אסמע יא רבנא צלוה[79] עבדך ותחננה ואקבל נור וגהך אלי קדסך אלוחשי[80] כמא אנת אהלה.

Dn 9:18

הטה אלהי אזנך ושמע פקח עיניך וראה שוממותינו והעיר אשר נקרא שמך עלי כי לא על צדקיתינו אנחנו מפילים תחנונינו ולפניך כי על רחמיך הרבים.

ואסמע לנא סמעא תאמא ואנטׄר[81] אלינא[82] נטׄרא[83] כאמלא[84] ולוחשתנא[85] ואלקריה אלתי נסבת אלי אסמך פאנה לים עלי[86] צלאחנא נחן מוקעין[87] תחננא

[71] אסלך Oxf 2486.109b
[72] וחמייתך Spiegel + Morag
[73] [יר]ושלם Oxf 2486.109b > D
[74] מעיירה Oxf 2486.109b > L
[75] בנא Spiegel > L
[76] עבדך End of Oxf 2486.109b
[77] ואל Beginning of Oxf 2486.110a
[78] השמם Beginning of Yeirin 232 (TS Ar 1b.101e)
[79] צלות Yeirin 232
[80] אלוחש Yeirin 232
[81] ואנצׄר Spiegel + Morag
[82] לנא Spiegel + Oxf 2486.110a
[83] נצׄרא Spiegel + Morag
[84] כאמלה Spiegel
[85] ואלוחשתנא Spiegel
[86] על Spiegel

בין ידיך לכן[88] עלי[89] רחמתך אלואסעה.

Dn 9:19

אדני שמעה אדני צלחה אדני הקשיבה[90] ועשה[91] אל תאחר למענך אלהי כי שמך נקרא על עירך ועל עמך.

אללהם אסמע לנא אללהם אגׄפר לנא אללהם אגבנא ואקץׄ חואיגנא ולא תואכׄרהא[92] במא אנת אהלה יא רבי[93] אדׄ נסב אליך מדינתך וקומך.

ואדׄ[94] קד תרגמנא פואסיק הדׄה אלצלוה פינבגׄי[95] אן נעוד עליהא[96] בשרוח[97] מעאני באכׄתצאר. ונקול אולא כיף[98] צאר אלואחד מן אלצאלחין ישפע פי גמאעה או פי אמה וירגו קבול[99] דׄלך.[100] פאמא אן כאן **כהן** פלא עגב מן דׄלך לאן רבנא גל[101] ועז[102] נצבה[103] להדׄא אלשאן[104] כמא[105] קאל[106] **בין האולם ולמזבח[107] יבכו הכהנים משרתי יוי[108] ויאמרו חוסה יוי על עמך ואל תתן נחלתך לחרפה[109] למשל[110] בם גוים למה יאמרו בעמים איה אלהיהם[111]**

[87] מוקעי Yeirin 232 ׀ מוקע Oxf 2486.110a
[88] ולכן Spiegel Spiegel
[89] עלי > L
[90] הקשיבה End of Oxf 2486.110a
[91] ועשה Beginning of Oxf 2486.110b
[92] תוכרהא Beginning of TS Ar 26.62a
[93] יא רבי > L Morag ׀ יא רב TS Ar 26.62a
[94] אד TS Ar 26.62a
[95] פונבגׄי TS Ar 26.62a
[96] ע[ל]יהא > D TS Ar 26.62a
[97] בשרח TS Ar 26.62a
[98] וכיף + Oxf 2486.110b Yeirin 232
[99] קבל TS Ar 26.62a
[100] ק[בו]ל [דלך] > D Yeirin 232
[101] לאן ... גל > D Yeirin 232 ׀ גלאלה + Yeirin 232
[102] ועז > L Yeirin 232
[103] נ[צ]בה > D Yeirin 232
[104] אד + TS Ar 26.62a
[105] כמא > L TS Ar 26.62a
[106] כק Yeirin 232
[107] [האולם ולמז]בח > D Yeirin 232
[108] יב[כו] הכ[הנים] מש[רתי] יוי L TS Ar 26.62a
[109] לחרפה End of Oxf 2486.110b

(יואל 2:17). ולכן מן ליס הו מן[112] אלכהנים כיף ירגו אן יגאב דעאה פי אלאמה? פנקול[113] אליס[114] קד תקדמת מנה[115] שרוח[116] באן[117] ההנא[118] אפעאלא[119] תגב עלי גמיע אלאמה. פאי פראד סבק אליהא פקד[120] נאב ענהא כמא צנע פינחס פי אלשטים. פיכון אלדעא איצֿא[121] כדֿלך מע בעץֿ תובה או אנכסאר. פמנהא קאל דניאל **ואתפללה ואתודה**[122] (דניאל 9:4). ולם קאל **האל הגדול**[123] **והנורא** (דניאל 9:4) ולם יקל[124] **הגבור**?[125] וכדֿלך קאל ירמיהו **האל הגדול והגבור**[126] (ירמ׳ 32:18) ולם יקל[127] **והנורא**? ועזרא יקול **האלהים הגדול**[128] (נחמיה 8:6) ולם יקל[129] **הגבור**[130] ולא **הנורא**.[131] ואמא[132] **משה רבינו** פקאל **האל הגדול**[133] **הגבור והנורא**[134] (דב׳ 10:17). פלדֿלך גואבאן, אחדהמא[135] כלי[136] והו[137] אן הדֿה כלהא אדֿ הי אוצאף רבנא תבארך[138] אסמה.

[110] למשל Beginning of Oxf 2486.111a

[111] ויאמרו ... אלהים L > TS Ar 26.62a and Yeirin 232

[112] מן ליס הו מן D > Yeirin 232

[113] [פי ... פ]נקול D > Yeirin 232

[114] אוליס Oxf 2486.111a | אן ליס Yeirin 232

[115] מנא Yeirin 232

[116] שרוח End of Yeirin 232

[117] באן)TS Ar 1b.101f(Beginning of Yeirin 233

[118] האהנא Oxf 2486.111a

[119] פעאלא Yeirin 233

[120] אליה פהד TS Ar 26.62a

[121] איצ׳ TS Ar 26.62a

[122] ואֿ[ת]ודה TS Ar 26.62a

[123] הג׳ TS Ar 26.62a

[124] יקול TS Ar 26.62a + Yeirin 233

[125] והנורא + Yeirin 233

[126] הג׳ והג׳ TS Ar 26.62a

[127] יקול TS Ar 26.62a

[128] [האלהים הגדו]ל D > TS Ar 26.62a

[129] יקול TS Ar 26.62a

[130] הג׳ TS Ar 26.62a

[131] וכדלך ... ולא הנורא L > Yeirin 233

[132] פאמא Yeirin 233

[133] [רבינו ... האל ה]ג׳ D > TS Ar 26.62a

[134] הג׳ הג׳ והנו׳ TS Ar 26.62a

[135] אחדהמא End of TS Ar 26.62a

[136] כלי Beginning of TS Ar 26.62b | בלכלי Yeirin 233 | [בל]כלי פי TS Ar 26.62b

[137] והו L > TS Ar 26.62b and Yeirin 233

פאי ואחד או את̇נין[139] או[140] ת̇לת̇ה[141] קילת[142] מנהא פהי מקאם אלכל. ואלת̇אני[143] גזוי והו אן יכון דניאל כ̇צץ כלאמה בנורא למא כאנת מסלתה בנא בית אלמקדס. וקד קיל[144] פיה **מה נורא המקום הזה** (בר׳ 28:17). ולסבבה קיל[145] **נורא אלהים**[146] **ממקדשך**[147] (תה׳ 68:36). וקאל איצ̇א[148] **נורא**[149] **יוי**[150] **עליהם כי רזה את כל אלהי הארץ**[151] (צפניה 2:11). ואמא ירמיהו פכ̇צץ כלאמה בגבור לאנה אלתמס אלאנתקאם אלמחאצרין[152] ללבלד בקולה[153] **הנה הסוללת**[154] **באו העיר ללכדה**[155] (ירמ׳ 32:24). וקד קיל[156] פי מת̇ל ד̇לך **יוי כגבור יצא כאיש מלחמות יעיר קנאה**[157] **יריע**[158] **אף יצריח על איביו יתגבר**[159] (יש׳ 42:13). ואמא **משה רבינו** פכאן קצדה אכ̇באר קומה באן אלכ̇אלק[160] אזלי פקאל **הגדול** לאן אלכביר אלסן מן אלנאס למא[161] כאן ענדנא[162] יקאל לה **הגדול**[163] כאנת אלגדולה לא תזאל[164] תרתקי[165] אלי[166] אן

[138] תב TS Ar 26.62b
[139] ב TS Ar 26.62b
[140] או End of Oxf 2486.111a
[141] תלתה Beginning of Oxf 2486.111b | ג׳ TS Ar 26.62b + Yeirin 233
[142] קיל TS Ar 26.62b
[143] ואב TS Ar 26.62b + Yeirin 233
[144] קאל Yeirin 233
[145] קאל TS Ar 26.62b
[146] אלים TS Ar 26.62b
[147] ממקדשיך Yeirin 233
[148] איצ TS Ar 26.62b
[149] נירא Yeirin 233
[150] יוי TS Ar 26.62b > D
[151] כי ... הארץ TS Ar 26.62b > L
[152] ללמחאצרין Yeirin 233
[153] בקו̇ TS Ar 26.62b
[154] הסללות TS Ar 26.62b
[155] וקו̇ קול + Yeirin 233
[156] וקד Yeirin 233 > L
[157] כא[יש] מל[חמות] יע[יר] TS Ar 26.62b > L
[158] ירע Yeirin 233
[159] יריע ... יתגבר TS Ar 26.62b > L
[160] באן אלכ̇אלק Yeirin 233 > D
[161] אלנאס למא Yeirin 233 > D
[162] ענ[דנ]א TS Ar 26.62b > D | ענדנא End of TS Ar 26.62b
[163] גדול Yeirin 233
[164] תזאל End of Oxf 2486.111b

תבלג̇ אלי אלאזלי אלד̇י לא אול לה. וקצד אכ̇בארהם[167] באנה מעאקב[168] ומת̇יב פקאל **גבור ונורא**[169] עלי מא שרחנא. ואמא עזאר פאד̇ לם יקצד ת̇ואבא ולא עקאבא ואנמא כאן יתלו אלתוראה ואלחכמה פהי אול אלמכ̇לוקין כמא קאלת **יוי קנני ראשית דרכו** (מש' 8:22) והי לא תזול אד̇ לא תנט̇ר. פלד̇לך קאל **הגדול** (נחמיה 8:6) פקט.

וד̇אך קולה **חטאנו ועוינו והרשענו ומרדנו** (דניאל 9:5) פהי צ̇רוב אלכ̇טא ועלי נט̇אמהא מן אלאדון פאלאדון כמא שרחנא פי תפסיר אחרי **וסור ממצותיך** (דניאל 9:5) אלסמעיה **וממשפטיך** (דניאל 9:5) אלעקליה. ופסרת **בשמך** (דניאל 9:6) עלי מא הו מעלום אן אקסאם **שם** אלי ארבע מעאני. ואמא **כיום הזה** (דניאל 9:7) אלד̇י פי פסוק **לך יוי הצדקה** (דניאל 9:7). יכתב **כהיום** לאנה יסתקים אן ישיר אלי ארבע[170] פואסיק[171] פיהא **כהיום** כל ואחד מנהא ישאבה קטעה מן הד̇א אלדעא. פאמא אלאול **ויהי כהיום הזה ויבא הביתה לעשות מלכות** (בר' 39:11) ישאבה **בושת הפנים** (דניאל 9:7) אלמד̇כורה האהנא. ועלי מא קאל **הובישו כי תועבה עשו** (ירמ' 6:15). ואלת̇אני **לחיותנו כהיום הזה** (דב' 6:24) ישאבה **לך יוי הצדקה** (דניאל 9:7) אד̇ בעדה **וצדקה תהיה לנו** (דב' 6:25). ואלת̇אלת̇ פי אבתדא מלך שאול **כי אתו כהיום תמצאון אתו** (שמ"א 9:13) ישאבה מא קאל **למלכינו ולשארינו ולאבתינו** (דניאל 9:8). ואלראבע **ותהי ארצכם לחרבה לשמה ולשרקה מאין יושב כהיום הזה** (ירמ' 44:22) ישאבה קולה **מקדשך השמם** (דניאל 9:17), **וראה שוממתינו** (דניאל 9:18). ובעד אלארבעה ספר כ̇לה **כהיום** (עזרא 9:7.15) והו כתאב עזרא אד̇ פיה בני **בית שני**. וקולה **הקרבים** (דניאל 9:7) מת̇ל **גלות בבל ומצרים**.[172] **והחרקים**[173] (דניאל 9:7) מת̇ל **לחלח וחבור וגוזן**.

ואעאדתה **יהוה לנו בשת הפנים למלכינו** (דניאל 9:8) יריד בד̇לך כ̇ואץ אלקום, פאן אלגנאיה תתצ̇אעף עליהם. וקולה **לאדני אלהינו הרחמים**

[165] תרתקי Beginning of Oxf 2486.112a
[166] לא ... אלי Yeirin 233 > D
[167] וקצד אכבארהם Yeirin 233 > D
[168] מועאקב Yeirin 233
[169] גב[ור] ונ[ורא] Yeirin 233 > D | נורא End of the readable part of Yeirin 233
[170] ארבע End of Oxf 2486.112a
[171] פואסיק Beginning of Oxf 2486.112b
[172] ומצרים End of Oxf 2486.112b
[173] והרחיקם Beginning of Oxf 2486.113a

והסליחות יעני (דניאל 9:9) ועלי אן כ̇טאנא עט̇ימא פרחמתך אעטם מנה. וכמא נגד פי אקואל אלאנביא **ואשמתנו גדלה עד לשמים** (עזרא 9:6), **כי גדול מעל שמים חסדך** (תה׳ 108:5). וקולה **אשר לא נעשׂתה תחת כל השמים כאשר נעשׂתה בירושלם** (דניאל 9:12) יעני בה קצה מא אכל אלבנון לחום אלאבא וכמא קאל יחזקאל **לכן אבות יאכלו בנים בתוכך ובנים יאכלו אבותם** (יח׳ 5:10). לאן אכל אלאבא לחום אביהם קד כאן מת̇לה פי שמרון פי עצר יהורם בן אחאב. ועלי אנה קד כאן יגוז אן יכון אלקולאן מבאלגה̇ מן שדה אלגוע. אלא אנה למא וגדנא **אבות**[174] **יאכלו**[175] **בנים** (יח׳ 5:10) כאן מפעולא צאר איצ̇א **בנים יאכלו אבותם** (יח׳ 5:10) מפעולא.

וקולה **לא חלינו** (דניאל 9:13) יעני פי ד̇לך אלוקת כמא קאל הנאך (דניאל 9:14) **שכלתי אבדתי את עמי מדרכיהם לא שבו** (ירמ׳ 15:7). וקולה **וישקד יהוה על הרעה** (דניאל 9:14) ופסרנאה "חתמא" למא ראינאה תהדדהם זמאנא טוילא. פלמא לם יקבלו חתם עליהם ד̇לך. ומע ד̇לך **כי צדיק יהוה אלהינו** (דניאל 9:14). הו אלע[א]דל והו אלמחסן אד̇ אחסן עליהם בתסביק **גלות יכניה** יח̇ סנה יבנון להם ויג̇רסון להם כמא קאל **בנו בתים ושבו ונטעו גנות** (ירמ׳ 29:5) וחתי יגז פינילו עלי אקרבאיהם ואהלהם לא תשתד וחשתהם.

ואמא תוסלה בקצה **אשר הוצאת את עמך מארץ מצרים ביד חזקה** (דניאל 9:15) ובינהם אקל מן אלף סנה פאנה יריד בד̇לך אן קדרתך לא תתג̇יר ואן טאל אלזמאן. ואקראנה[176] בהא[177] **יוי ככל צדקתך** (דניאל 9:16) שביה במא קאל שמואל **את כל צדקות יוי אשר עשׂה אתכם ואת אבותיכם** (שמ״א 12:7), **כאשר בא יעקב מצ[רים]** (שמ״א 12:8). ומראדה בקולה **והאר פניך מקדשך** (דניאל 9:17) אן יאד̇ן פי בנא אלקדס וירד אליה אלשכינה אלתי הי **אור** כמא קאל יחזקאל **והארץ האירה מכבודו** (יח׳ 43:2). וכמא יקול פי וקת אלישועה פי קצה **קומי אורי כי בא אורך** (יש׳ 60:1) אלי אכרה. וקולה **למען יוי** (דניאל 9:17) מקאם קולה **למענך יוי** מת̇ל קולה **אליך יוי אקרא ואל יוי אתחנן** (תה׳ 30:9) מקאם **ואליך יוי אתחנן** ואמת̇אל ד̇לך כת̇יר.

[174] אבות End of Oxf 2486.113a
[175] יאכלו Beginning of Oxf 2486.113b
[176] ואקראנה End of Oxf 2486.113b
[177] בהא Beginning of Oxf 2486.114a

ופסרת **הטה אלהי אזנך ושמע** (דניאל 9:18) ״אסמע לנא סמעא תאמא״ כמא וגדת עאדה אלנאס ימילון אדאנהם אדֿא קצדו אסתיפא אלסמע. ופסרת איצֿא **פקח עיניך וראה** (דניאל 8:18) ״ואנטֿר לנא נטֿרא כאמלא״. כמא וגדת עאדתהם אדֿא אראדו אלתאמל[178] יתזידון[179] אבצארהם. ושפעה בקולה **כי שמך נקרא** (דניאל 9:19) הו בטריק אלנסבה כמא שפע יהושע וקאל **ומה תעשׂה לשמך הגדול** (יהושע 7:9). אדֿ קד נסב אלקום ואלבלד אליך. פאן לם תרחמהם תבדֿלת אלאמם אסמך. ולם יזל אלאנביא יתוסלון בהדֿא אלמעני חתי קאל אללה ליחזקאל **לא למענכם אני עשׂה בית ישׂראל כי אם לשם קדשי חללתם בגוים אשר באתם שם** (יח׳ 36:22), **וקדשתי את שמי הגדול המחולל בגוים** (יח׳ 36:23). וקאל איצֿא **ואת שם קדשי אודיע בתוך עמי ישׂראל ולא אחלל את שם קדשי** (יח׳ 39:7). תֿם[180] קאל

Dn 9:20

ועוד אני מדבר ומתפלל ומתודה חטאתי וחטאת עמי ישראל ומפיל תחנתי לפני יהוה אלהי על הר קדש אלהי.

ואיצֿא[181] אנא מדעי[182] ומצלי[183] ומקר בכֿטיתי[184] וכֿטאיא[185] קומי בני אסראיל[186] ומוקע תחנני בין ידי אללה רבי[187] עלי גבל קדסה.

קול דניאל הדֿא ידל[188] עלי אנה לם יתֿבת ההנא[189] גמיע מא צלי בה ודעי בה. ואנמא אתֿבת מן גמלה דֿלך עיונא הי כאלאצול ואלאקטאב[190] לדֿלך. ואן אלדֿי

[178] אלתאמל End of Oxf 2486.114a
[179] יתזידון Beginning of Oxf 2486.114b
[180] ותם Beginning of TS Ar 26.62c
[181] ואיצ TS Ar 26.62c
[182] דאע Oxf 2486.114b ׀ [ד]אע TS Ar 26.62c ׀ דאעי Spiegel
[183] ומצלי TS Ar 26.62c > L
[184] בכטיתי End of Oxf 2486.114b ׀ בכטייתי Spiegel + Morag
[185] וכטאיא Beginning of Oxf 2486.115a ׀ וכטא Spiegel
[186] אסרא TS Ar 26.62c ׀ אל יסראיל Spiegel
[187] רבי Spiegel + Morag > L
[188] דאל TS Ar 26.62c
[189] האהנא Oxf 2486.115a
[190] ואלאקט[א]ב TS Ar 26.62c

ידעו[191] בה ללקום וללקדס אצֹעאף הדֹא[192] מן קולה **ועוד** (דניאל 9:20). תֹם קאל

Dn 9:21

ועוד אני מדבר בתפלה והאיש גבריאל אשר ראיתי בחזון בתחלה מועף ביעף נגע אלי כמנחת ערב.

ובינמא[193] אנא[194] פי אלדעא[195] בעד אלצלוה פאדֹא[196] בגבריאל[197] אלמלאך[198] אלדֹי ראיתה פי אלרויא[199] אלאולא[200] טאירא בסרעה[201] וצל[202] אליי[203] ענד צלוה אלמגֹרב.[204]

Dn 9:22

ויבן[205] וידבר עמי ויאמר דניאל עתה יצאתי להשכילך בינה.

פפהמני אדֹ[206] כֹאטבני[207] וקאל יא דניאל[208] אלאן כֹרגת לאעלמך[209] אלפהם.

Dn 9:23

בתחלת תחנוניך יצא דבר ואני באתי להגיד לך כי חמודות אתה ובין בדבר והבן במראה.

[191] דעי TS Ar 26.62c
[192] א[צע]אף [הד]א TS Ar 26.62c > D
[193] ובין מא Spiegel + Morag | ובינא TS Ar 26.62c
[194] אנא TS Ar 26.62c > L
[195] אלדעי TS Ar 26.62c
[196] פאדי Morag
[197] בגב[רי]אל TS Ar 26.62c > D
[198] אלמלך Spiegel + TS Ar 26.62c + Morag
[199] אבתדאא TS Ar 26.62c +
[200] אלאולי Spiegel + TS Ar 26.62c + Oxf 2486.115a > L
[201] בס[רעה] TS Ar 26.62c > D
[202] ואצל TS Ar 26.62c | Spiegel + Oxf 2486.115a ואצלא
[203] אלי TS Ar 26.62c
[204] אלמגֹיב Spiegel + TS Ar 26.62c | אלמגֹרב End of Oxf 2486.115a
[205] ויבן Beginning of Oxf 2486.115b
[206] כדי Morag +
[207] כאט[בני] TS Ar 26.62c > D
[208] אלכאץ TS Ar 26.62c and Oxf 2486.115b +
[209] לאעלאמך TS Ar 26.62c | לאעלך Spiegel

וד̇לך[210] אן[211] מן אבתדי[212] תחננך[213] כ̇רג לך אמר ואנא גית לאכ̇ברך בה אד̇[214] אנת[215] אלכ̇אץ פאפהם אלאמר ותאמל אלמנט̇ר.[216]

קולה[217] **ועוד אני מדבר בתפלה** (דניאל 9:21) ידל עלי אנה אגיב קבל אן יתם דעאה כשרוט אלצאלחין **עוד הם מדברים ואני אשמע** (יש׳ 65:24). ועלי מא עלמנא מן **משה רבינו** אן אללה קאל לה **מה תצעק אלי דבר אל בני ישׂראל**[218] **ויסעו**[219] (שמ׳ 14:15). ומן אליעזר אלד̇י קיל פיה **ויהי**[220] **הוא**[221] **טרם כלה לדבר** (בר׳ 24:15) ומא שאבההמא. וקולה[222] **והאיש גבריאל אשר ראיתי**[223] **בחזון בתחלה** (דניאל 9:21) ידל עלי אנה אעתקד אלאן אן אלד̇י כאן ראה אולא פי אלנום הו נבוה אד̇ ט̇הר לה פי אליקט̇ה אלשכ̇ץ אלד̇י כאן [... ...][224] אלנום עלי שרוט רויא[225] [...][226] כג̇רץ[227] אלרסאלה והי אגאבה דעאה פי אלקום ואלקדס. וערפה מאד̇א יכון מן אמרהם מן כ̇ראב אלבית אלאול אלי כ̇ראב אלבית אלת̇אני. ומא בין ד̇לך מדה ארבע מאיה ותסעין סנה. פקאל

Dn 9:24

שבועים שבעים נחתך על עמך ועל עיר קדשך לכלא הפשע ולחתם חטאת ולכפר עון ולהביא צדק עולמים ולחתום חזון ונביא ולמשח קדש קדשים.

210 ודאלך Spiegel + Morag

211 אן End of the readable part of TS Ar 26.62c

212 מ[ן אבתדי] TS Ar 26.62c > D | אבתדא Spiegel

213 תחננך Beginning of TS Ar 26.62d

214 אנא + Oxf 2486.115b

215 אנת Oxf 2486.115b > L | אלמשתה[ר] + TS Ar 26.62d

216 אלמנצר Spiegel + Morag

217 וקולה TS Ar 26.62d

218 ישׁ TS Ar 26.62d

219 דבר ... ויסעו Oxf 2486.115b > L

220 ויהי TS Ar 26.62d > D

221 הוא End of Oxf 2486.115b

222 וקול TS Ar 26.62d

223 [אש]ר רא[יתי] TS Ar 26.62d > D

224 [... ...] TS Ar 26.62d > D

225 רויא End of the readable part of TS Ar 26.62d

226 [...] TS Ar 26.62d > D | טרם כלה ... כג̇רץ Oxf 2486 > L

227 כג̇רץ Beginning of Oxf 2486.116a

והי[228] סבעין אסבוע קד[229] קטעת עלי קומך[230] ועלי קריה קדסך לפנא אלגרם ואלכֿטייה[231] וגֿפראן אלדֿנב ומגי עדל אלדהור[232] וכֿתם אלוחי ואלנבוה[233] ומסח כֿאץ אלאקדאס.

Dn 9:25

ותדע ותשׂכיל מן מוצא דבר להשיב ולבנות ירושלם עד משיח נגיד שבועים[234] שבעה ושבועים ששים ושנים תשוב ונבנתה[235] רחוב וחרוץ ובצוק העתים.

ותעלם ותפהם מנד[236] כֿרג אלאמר אלי אלרגוע ובנא ירושלם מע אלממסוח ואלמדבר סבעה[237] אסאביע תֿם אתֿנין וסתין אסבועא תעוד ותבנא רחאבהא ופצולהא ויך[238] רנין[239] פי אוקאת מנהא.

Dn 9:26

ואחרי השבועים ששים[240] ושנים יכרת משיח ואין לו והעיר והקדש ישחית עם נגיד הבא וקצו בשטף ועד קץ מלחמה נחרצת שוממות.

ובעד אלאתֿנין[241] ואלסתין[242] אלאסבוע ינקטע[243] אלממסוח מן אלמוצֿע[244] פליס לה ואלקריה[245] ואלקדס יפסדהמא[246] קום אלמדבר אלמקבל ואגלה באלגֿרק

[228] והי D > Oxf 2486.116a | הי Spiegel
[229] קד L > Spiegel
[230] קומך D > Oxf 2486.116a | קוומך Spiegel
[231] ואלכטיי]ה D > Oxf 2486.116a
[232] אלדהור D > Oxf 2486.116a
[233] ואלנבווה Morag + Spiegel
[234] שבועים End of the readable part of Oxf 2486.116a
[235] ונבנתה Beginning of Oxf 2486.116b
[236] מד Spiegel
[237] אלמדבר סבע Oxf 2486.116b
[238] ויכון Oxf 2486.116b + Spiegel | דבק + Spiegel
[239] רנה Oxf 2486.116b | רנין L > Spiegel
[240] ששים Beginning of Oxf 2628.49b
[241] אתֿנין Spiegel
[242] וסתין Oxf 2486.116b + Spiegel | אלטב Oxf 2628.49b
[243] ינק[טע] D > Oxf 2486.116b
[244] אלמרצע Spiegel | מן אלמוצֿע L > Oxf 2628.49b
[245] ואל[קריה] D > Oxf 2486.116b | ואלקריה L > Spiegel
[246] יפסדהא Spiegel

ואלי אגל אלחרב תנבתר עלי[247] וחשאת.[248]

Dn 9:27

והגביד[249] ברית לרבים שבוע אחד וחצי השבוע ישבית זבח ומנחה ועל כנף שקוצים משמם ועד כלה ונחרצה תתך על שמם.

ויתֿבת[250] אלעהד ללגמאעה[251] אסבועא ואחדא לכנה[252] פי נצפה ינכתֿ פי עטל[253] אלדֿבח ואלבר ומע בסטה אלרגס[254] וחשה חתי[255] אן פנא ואנבתר[256] ינצבון[257] עלי אלוחשה.

[...][258] סנין[259] אדֿ קאל **וספרת לך שבע שבתת שנים** (ויק׳ 25:8). ואיצֿא **והיו לך ימי שבע שבתות השנים** (ויק׳ 25:8). פפי אלתוראה אסתתֿני **שבועים ימים** עלי מא וצפנא. וקולה **על עמך** (דניאל 9:24) לם ירד בדֿלך אלאמה כלהא אלתי הי קום דניאל אלכלי. ואנמא אראד **שבט יהודה ובנימן** אללדֿין הם קום דניאל אלגזוי אדֿ דניאל מן יהודה. ודֿלך עלי אן מסלה דניאל, ועלי אנהא כאנת כליה ען אלאמה פי לפטֿה וטויתה אלא אן אלגֿרץֿ למא כאן הו בנא אלבית אלתֿאני ופי אלקום אלראגעין אליה וכאן אכתֿרהם אנמא הו מן בני יהודה ובנימן, עלי מא הו משרוח פי ספר עזרא, עאד אלגואב אלי אלתכֿציץ יכֿץ קום דניאל אלגזוין. והכֿדי משרוח פי עזרא **אלה בני המדינה[260] העלים[261] משבי הגולה אשר הגלה נבוכדנצר מלך בבל לבבל** (עזרא 2:1). ותגדה יחצי עדדהם פיכון פי אלתפציל תֿלתֿין אלף. ויציר פי אלפדלכה מבֿ אלפא וכסר.

[247] ואלי ... עלי Oxf 2486.116b > D

[248] וחשאת End of Oxf 2486.116b

[249] דניאל 9:27 Missing in Oxf 2486

[250] ויעצם Spiegel | ויתֿבת Spiegel > L

[251] לאלגמאעה Spiegel + Morag

[252] ואחדה ליכון Spiegel

[253] מעטל Oxf 2628.49b

[254] אלגרם Oxf 2628.49b

[255] וחתי Spiegel

[256] אלאנפנא ואלאנבתאר Spiegel

[257] ינצבאן Oxf 2628.49b

[258] [...] Oxf 2486.116b > D

[259] סנין Beginning of Oxf 2486.123a

[260] המדינה End of Oxf 2486.123a

[261] העלים Beginning of Oxf 2486.123b

פהדֿא ידל עלי אן אלמעדודין פי אלתפציל מן יהודה ובנימן ואלמזאד עליהם פי אלגמלה מן סאיר אלאבסאט.

ואדֿ קד כשפנא אלגואב ען הדֿה אלמסלה אלכבירה פנרי אן נציף אליהא גואבא ען מסלה אכֿרי כבירה. והי אן נחמיה יעיד אחצא אלקום אלדֿין[262] דֿכרהם עזרא אולא פנגדהם בזיאדה ונקצאן. וקום דֿכרהם עזרא לם ידֿכרהם נחמיה. וקום דֿכרהם נחמיה לם ידֿכרהם עזרא. ומע דֿלך פיקול נחמיה **ויתן אלהי אל לבי ואקבצה את ההרים ואת הסגנים ואת**[263] **העם**[264] **להתיחש ואמצא ספר היחש העלים בראשנה ואמצא כתוב בו** (נחמיה 7:5). פכאנה יקתצי ופאקא והו יוגד כֿלאפא. פנקול אנה ינבגי אן יכון מצֿמרא.[265] **ואמצא** מן **הכתוב בו** בני פלאן בחאלהם[266] ובני פלאן זאדו ובני פלאן נקצו ובני פלאן אצֿמחלו. ופלאן אלדֿי לם יכן לה דֿכר פי אלאול וגדה נחמין פי וקתה. ודֿלך אן בין וקת נחמיה אלי וקת עזרא סתה ותֿלתֿין סנה. אדֿ תאריך עזרא **בשנת אחד לכרש** (עזרא 1:1). ובינה ובין אבתדא[267] ארתחשסתא סתה עשר סנה. ותאריך נחמיה **שנת עשרים לארתחשסת המלך** (נחמיה 2:1). פפי הדֿה אלסתה ותֿלתֿין סנה עאש קום ומאת אכֿרון וזאד קום ונקץ אכֿרון. פקד תבין אן קולה **על עמך** (דניאל 9:24) יעני בית יהודה ובנימן גמיעא כֿאצה.

וגעל חואדתֿ הדֿה[268] אלסבעין[269] אסבוע תגמע אשיא [...][270] מנהא סארה ומנהא גֿאמה והי סבע חואדתֿ **לכלא הפשע ולהתם חטאת ולכפר עון ולהביא צדק עולמים** (דניאל 9:24). הדֿה אלארבעה סארה. ומנה **לחתום חזון ונביא ולמשח קדש קדשים** (דניאל 9:24). והדֿה אלתֿלאתֿה גֿאמה. וליס יריד בקולה **צדק עולמים** (דניאל 9:24) שיא מנבדֿא לא ינקטע למוצֿע לפטֿה **עולמים** אלתי תומי אלי דהור ועואלם. לכנה יריד בדֿלך דהרא כֿאצא ועאלמא מעלומא מן אלזמאן. והי מדה מא אקאם להם אלעדל פי אלבית אלתֿאני. וענד אלבחתֿ וגדנא **עולמים** זמאנא מתקצֿיא כמא קאל קהלת **יש דבר שיאמר ראה**

[262] אלדֿין Oxf 2486.123b
[263] את End of Oxf 2486.123b
[264] העם Beginning of Oxf 2486.124a
[265] מצמ[רא] Oxf 2486.124a > D
[266] בחאל[ה]ם Oxf 2486.124a > D
[267] א[בתדא] Oxf 2486.124a > D
[268] הדה End of Oxf 2486.124a
[269] אלסבעין Beginning of Oxf 2486.124b
[270] [...] Oxf 2486.124b > D

זה חדש הוא כבר היה לעולמים אשר היו מלפנינו (קהלת 1:10). פלמא כאן אלזמאן אלדׄי כאן קבלנא קד[271] תקצׄי תבין[272] אן לפטׄה **עולמים** קד תקע עלי זמאן גזוי. ואקול ולדׄלך יקול פי אלתאביד **עד עולמי עד** (יש׳ 45:17) ומא שאבה דׄלך. פפי בעץׄ הדׄה אלתצׄ סנה כאן לבית יהודה מא ועדהם **לכלה הפשע ולהתם חטאת ולכפר עון** (דניאל 9:24). והו מא ועדהם בה עלי קול ירמיהו **כה אמר יוי אלהי ישראל כתנים הטבת האלה כן אכיר את גלות יהודה אשר שלחתי מן המקום הזה ארץ כשדים ושמתי עיני עליהם לטובה והשבתים אל הארץ הזאת ובניתים ולא אהרס ונטעתים ולא אתוש ונתתי להם לב לדעת אותי כי אני יוי והיו לי לעם ואני אהיה להם לאלהים כי ישובו אלי בכל לבם** (ירמ׳ 7–24:5). ודׄלך פי אול בנא אלבית אלתׄאני. ופי דׄלך אלוקת ופי עצר[273] נחמיה[274] צח להם **ולהביא צדק עולמים** (דניאל 9:24). כמא עלמת אן אלחכם ואלעדל טׄהרא עלי עהד עזרא כמא קאל **ואנתה עזרא כחכמת אלהך די בידך מני שפטין ודינין** (עזרא 7:25), **וכל די לא להוה עבד די דת די אלהך** (עזרא 7:26) וסאיר אלקצה. ווצף נחמיה איצׄא מן עדלה ואחסאנה ללקום **ואני לא עשיתי כן מפני יראת אלהים** (נחמיה 5:15). ואיצׄא **זכרה לי אלהי לטובה כל אשר עשיתי עם[275] העם הזה** (נחמיה 5:19).

ופי בעץׄ אלתׄצ סנה ואפאהם אנקטאע אלנבוה וכׄתם אלוחי והו קולה **ולחתום חזון ונביא** (דניאל 9:24) כמא קאל יחזקאל **כי חזון אל כל המונה לא ישוב** (יח׳ 7:13). וקאל איצׄא **גם נביאיה לא מצאו חזון מיוי** (איכה 2:9). ודׄלך בעד סבעין סנה ללבנא. ופי אכׄרהא. ואפאהם אנקטאע אלמסוחיה והו[276] קולה[277] **ולמשח קדש קדשים** (דניאל 9:24). פלם יבק אחד מן **אל הרון** ממסוח ליכון **כהן גדול וכהן הדיוט**, גמיעא יקאל להמא **קדש קדשים** כמא קאל **ובני עמרם אהרון ומשה ויבדל אהרן להקדישו קדש קדשים הוא ובניו עד עולם להקטיר לפני יוי לשרתו ולברך בשמו עד עולם** (דה״א 23:13). פגמע גבריאל הדׄה אלחואדתׄ כלהא פקאל לדניאל מדתהא תצׄ סנה עלי מא בינא.

[271] קד End of Oxf 2486.124b | תקמ + Oxf 2486.124b

[272] תבין Beginning of Oxf 2486.125a

[273] עצר End of Oxf 2486.125a

[274] נחמיה Beginning of Oxf 2486.125b

[275] על MT

[276] והו End of Oxf 2486.125b

[277] קולה Beginning of Oxf 2486.126a

תֿם אנה קסם לה בעד דֿלך אלסבעין אסבוע תֿלתֿה אקסאם. אלקסם אלאול סבע אסאביע והו קולה **ותדע ותשׂכיל מן מוצא דבר להשיב ולבנות ירושלם עד משיח נגיד שבעים שבעה** (דניאל 9:25). ואלקסם אלתֿאני אתֿנין וסתין אסבוע קאל לה ענהא **ושבעים ששים ושנים תשוב ונבנתה רחוב**[278] **וחרוץ**[279] (דניאל 9:25). ואלקסם אלתֿאלתֿ אסבוע ואחד קאל לה ענה **והגביר ברית לרבים שבוע אחד** (דניאל 9:27). פדֿלך סבעין אסבוע. לכנה אסתתֿני בנצף אלאסבוע אלאכֿיר פקאל **וחצי השבוע ישבית זבח ומנחה** (דניאל 9:27) חתי לא יזיד שיא עלי אלסבעין. וסנשרח הדֿה אלתֿלתֿה אקסאם שרחא שאפיא.

פאמא שרח אלקסם אלאול אלדֿי הו סבע אסאביע פאן גבריאל געלה **מן מוצא דבר** (דניאל 9:25) אלי וקת **ולהשיב ולבנות ירושלם** (דניאל 9:25). פקולה **מן מוצא דבר** (דניאל 9:25) לם ירד בה **מוצא דבר יוי לדניאל**. אעני קול גבריאל לה **בתחלת תחנוניך יצא דבר** (דניאל 9:23). לאן הדֿא וקת מכֿאטבתה לה. ולכנה יריד בה **מן מוצא דבר יוי אל ירמיהו** בסבב רגועהם. והו מא קאל להם **כי לפני מלאת לבבל שבעים שנה אפקד אתכם**[280] **והקמתי**[281] **עליכם את דברי הטוב** (ירמ׳ 29:10). פקולה **דברי הטוב** (ירמ׳ 29:10) הו **מוצא דבר** (דניאל 9:25). וכאן דֿלך קבל כֿראב אלבית אלאול אלי אלוקת אלדֿי אדֿן פיה כורש **להשיב ולבנות ירושלם** (דניאל 9:25) כֿמסין סנה עלי מא בינּא אנפא פי **מספר השנים** (דניאל 9:2). ועלי אן סבע אסאביע אנמא תכון תסעה וארבעין סנה. לכנה לם ירד אלסנה אלזאידה אדֿ ליס הי נצף אסבוע. פפי סנה אחד וכֿמסין מלך כורש ונאדי **להשיב ולבנות** (דניאל 9:25) בקולה **יוי אלהיו עמו ויעל ירושלם אשר ביהודה ויבן את בית יוי** (עזרא 1:3). ויחתמל קולה **עד משיח נגיד** (דניאל 9:25) אן יכון אראד בה אי ואחד מן אלראיסין, אלאמר ואלמאמור. אעני כורש ויהושע בן יהוצדק. פאמא יהושע בן יהוצדק פיסמי **משיח** אדֿ הו **כהן גדול** כמא קאל **אם הכהן המשיח**[282] (ויק׳ 4:3), **ולקח**[283] **הכהן המשיח** (ויק׳ 4:5), **והכהן המשיח תחתיו מבניו** (ויק׳ 6:15). ויסמי **נגיד** (דניאל 9:25) כמא קאל **יהוידע הנגיד לאהרון** (דה״א 12:28). וקאל[284]

[278] רחוב End of Oxf 2486.126a

[279] וחרוץ Beginning of Oxf 2486.126b

[280] אתכם End of Oxf 2486.126b

[281] והקמתי Beginning of Oxf 2486.127a

[282] המשיח End of Oxf 2486.127a

[283] ולקח Beginning of Oxf 2486.127b

[284] וקאל Beginning of Oxf 2659.42a

איצ̇א[285] **ועזריהו נגיד בית האלהים** (דה״ב 31:13). ואמא כורש[286] פיסמי[287] **משיח** כמא יסמי כל מלך ינצב,[288] מסח או לם ימסח כמא[289] קאל למלך צר[290] **את כרוב ממשח הסוכך**[291] (יח׳ 28:14). ויסמי **נגיד** (דניאל 9:25) כמא[292] קיל[293] ליחזקאל **בן אדם אמר**[294] **לנגיד צר**[295] **כה אמר יוי אלהים יען גבה לבך**[296] (יח׳ 28:2). וקד עלמת אן אללה קאל לאליהו **ובאת ומשחת את חזאל**[297] **למלך על ארם**[298] (מל״א 19:15). ולם נגדה ולא אלישע מסחה. ואנמא[299] קאל לה אלישע קולא **הראני יוי אתך מלך על ארם** (מל״ב 8:13).

פקד תבין אן לפט̇ה **משיחה** תקע עלי כל ריאסה **בישראל ובגוים**.[300] וקד קאל איצ̇א[301] ען אברהם יצחק ויעקב[302] **אל תגעו במשיחי**[303] **ולנביאי אל תרעו**[304] (תה׳ 105:15) ולם[305] ימסחהם[306] אחד בדהן ולא ג̇ירה. ויסתקים אן יקאל[307] אן כורש כ̇אצה קד פצח באן אללה ריסה[308] וסמאה **משיחו** אד̇ קאל **כה אמר יוי**[309] **למשיחו לכורש**[310] (יש׳ 45:1). ועלי אנה קד יחתמל תוגיהאן אכ̇ראן.[311]

[285] איצא D < Oxf 2486.127b | איצ Oxf 2659.42a
[286] כרש Oxf 2659.42a
[287] [פיס]מי D < Oxf 2486.127b | פי[סמי] D < Oxf 2659.42a
[288] ונצב Oxf 2486.127b
[289] מסח ... כמא D < Oxf 2486.127b
[290] צור Oxf 2659.42a
[291] את ... הסוכך D < Oxf 2486.127b
[292] [כמ]א D < Oxf 2486.127b
[293] כמק כקו Oxf 2659.42a
[294] אמר D < Oxf 2486.127b
[295] וג׳ + Oxf 2659.42a
[296] כה ... לבך L < Oxf 2659.42a
[297] חזהאל Oxf 2486.127b
[298] א[רם] D < Oxf 2486.127b | למ על א Oxf 2659.42a
[299] ו[אנמ]א D < Oxf 2486.127b
[300] פי ישראל וגוים Oxf 2659.42a
[301] איצ Oxf 2659.42a
[302] יצ ויע Oxf 2659.42a
[303] במש וג׳ Oxf 2659.42a
[304] ולנביאי אל תרעו L < Oxf 2659.42a
[305] ולם End of Oxf 2486.127b
[306] ימסחהם Beginning of Oxf 2486.128a
[307] יקול Oxf 2486.128a
[308] רוסה Oxf 2659.42a
[309] א יוי Oxf 2659.42a

אחדהמא אן יומי במשיחו אלי ישעיהו אד̇ הו נבי כסאיר אלאנביא פיקול לה ען כורש כד̇י וכד̇י. ואלאכ̇ר[312] אן יומי בקולה **משיחו** אלי אלגואל אלד̇י ננתצ̇רה[313] ויט̇מר[314] **אות למשיחו**. פכאנה קד געל קצה כורש איה וברהאנא עלי אמור אלישועה. כמא צחת הד̇ה תצח הד̇ה[315] ועלי מא בינא פי תפסיר[316] ישעיהו.[317]

ושרח[318] אלקסם אלת̇אני אלד̇י הו את̇נין וסתין[319] אסבוע קאל[320] פי נצה **ושבעים ששים ושנים תשוב ונבנתה**[321] (דניאל 9:25) יכון מקדאר ד̇לך ארבע מאיה וארבעה[322] ות̇לת̇ין[323] סנה. פלו אמסך עלי ד̇לך כאן אלבית אלת̇אני יעמר ארבע מאיה וארבעה[324] ות̇לת̇ין[325] סנה. פלמא אלחק בה **רחוב וחרוץ ובצוק העתים** (דניאל 9:25) ואמכן אן יכון לד̇לך תפסיראן. אחדהמא אן יכון **רחוב וחרוץ** (דניאל 9:25) רחבה אלמדינה ופצולהא. וקטעהא[326] עלי תצריף **חריצי הברזל** (שמ״ב 12:31) **וחריצי החלב** (שמ״א 17:18) ואמת̇אלהא. ואלאכ̇ר אן יכון אלבנא מרה פי סעה ומרה פי אנבתאר. ואטבק עלי ד̇לך **ובצוק העתים** (דניאל 9:25). ויכון צ̇יק ודנק פי אוקאת וגב אלא תכון הד̇ה אלת̇לד̇ סנה כלהא בבנא תאמא. לכנה יכון פימא בינהא אנקטאע ואנבתאר וצ̇יק ודנק פי אוקאת והו מא קאל **באדין בטלת עבידת בית אלהא די בירושלם עד שנת תרתין [למלכות] דריוש מלכא [פרס]** (עזרא 4:24). פב..טל (?) אלבנא סנינא הי מן

[310] וג׳ + Oxf 2659.42a
[311] אכראן Oxf 2486.128a > L
[312] אלאסר Oxf 2659.42a
[313] ויעמד + Oxf 2659.42a
[314] ויצמר Oxf 2659.42a > L
[315] תצח הדה Oxf 2486.128a > D
[316] תפס Oxf 2659.42a
[317] ישעיהו End of Oxf 2659.42a
[318] ושרח Beginning of Oxf 2659.42b
[319] סב Oxf 2659.42b
[320] וקאל Oxf 2659.42b
[321] וש תש ונב Oxf 2659.42b
[322] [וא]רבעה Oxf 2486.128a > D | וארבעה End of Oxf 2486.128a
[323] ותלתין Beginning of Oxf 2486.128b | ת̇ולד̇ Oxf 2659.42b
[324] [ו]ארבעה Oxf 2486.128b > L
[325] ת̇ולד̇ Oxf 2659.42b
[326] וק[טע]הא Oxf 2486.128b > D

גהה[327] סת עשר[328] סנה והי מן גהה[329] יח̇ בדכ̇ול סנין[330] נואקץ עלי מא שרחנא[331] פי **מספר השנים** (דניאל 9:2).

וערפנא אן בעד הד̇ה אלסבֿ אסבוע ינקטע אלמסח ולא יכון ד̇לך לאחד מן אלנאס בקולה[332] **יכרת משיח ואין לו** (דניאל 9:26). לא מן אל הרון ולא מן דאוד. לאן קולה[333] **יכרת משיח** (דניאל 9:26) מקאם קאלה[334] **יכרתו כל המשוחים**. וליס יומי[335] בה אלי שכ̇ץ ואחד פי ד̇אתה. ויסתדל עלי ד̇לך במשאכלה אול אלקצה אד̇ קאל **לכלה הפשע ולחתם חטאת ולכפר עון** (דניאל 9:24). וליס עלי אלחקיקה הו **פשע** ואחד ו**חטאת** ואחדה **ועון** ואחד. ואנמא יעני **כל פשעים וכל חטאות וכל עונות**. ובקולה איצ̇א **ולחתום חזון ונביא** (דניאל 9:24) ליס יעני **חזון** ואחד **ונביא** ואחד. ואנמא יעני **כל חזיונות וכל נביאים**. ובקולה **ישבית זבח ומנחה** (דניאל 9:27) יעני כל **הזבחים** וכל **המנחות** וליס הו **זבח** ואחד[336]. כד̇אך[337] קולה **יכרת משיח** (דניאל 9:25) ליס מענאה **משיח** ואחד ואנמא יריד כל **המשוחים**. ופי לג̇ה אלעבראניין מן הד̇א מא לא יחצא בסרעה ולא סימא פי אלחאל מן אד̇ יקולו **סוס ורכבו רמה בים** (שמ׳ 15:1). והם ירידון **כל סוסים וכל רכבים רמה בים**. ויקולון **כי נשמרה מבנימין אשה** (שפטים 21:16) והם יענון כל **הנשים** לא אמראה וחדה. ויקולון **הבישו אכרים הלילו כרמים על חטה ועל שערה** (יואל 1:11) והם יענון כל **החטאים** וכל **השערים**. ומתל הד̇א כת̇יר. פאלקום אלד̇ין תעלקו בהד̇ה אלקצה פנסבוהא אלי צאחבהם לם יג̇אבהו[338] אלי הד̇ה אלדלאיל מן אצולהא. נעם, ואחמלו איצ̇א אלתחציל אן לפט̇ה **יכרת** (דניאל 9:26) לא תקע אלא עלי מן יסתחק אלאבאדה כמא קאל **כי נפש כל בשר דמו הוא כל אכליו יכרת** (ויקר׳ 17:14). ואיצ̇א **הכרת תכרת הנפש ההיא**[339] **עונה**[340] **בה** (במ׳ 15:31).

327 מן גהה > D Oxf 2486.128b
328 יו̇ Oxf 2659.42b
329 [גה]ה > D Oxf 2486.128b
330 סנין Beginning of the readable part of Oxf 2486.129a
331 שר[חנא] > D Oxf 2486.129a
332 בקו Oxf 2659.42b
333 קו Oxf 2659.42b
334 קו Oxf 2659.42b
335 ול[יס] יו[מ]י > D Oxf 2659.42b | יומי End of Oxf 2659.42b
336 ואחד End of Oxf 2486.129a
337 כדאך Beginning of the readable part of Oxf 2486.129b
338 [יג]בהו Oxf 2486.129b uncrtain
339 ההיא End of Oxf 2486.129b

ואיצֿא למא ראו אן צאחבהם כאן קבל כֿראב אלבית אלתֿאני במאיה וכֿמסה ותֿלתֿין סנה געל אול הדֿה אלתֿצֿ סנה מן וקת קילת לדניאל. פגמעו אלכֿמסין אלסנה אלמאצֿיה קבל דֿלך אלי מאיה [ו]כֿמסה ותֿלתֿין אלבאקיה בעד כון צאחבהם. פצאר אלגמיע שביה במאיתי סנה פזאדוהא פי אלתאריךֿ בין מלך אלפרס ובין אליונאניה. וזעמו אנה מן וקת קיל הדֿא לדניאל אלי אול מלך דֿי אלקרנין מאיתי סנה וניף וארבעין. ומא כפאהם דֿאך חתי אדעו עלינא אנא אסקטנא מן אלחסאב מאיתי סנה תעצבא עלי צאחבהם. וכדֿלך צנעו פי תאריךֿ **בראשית**. ודֿלך אנהם סמעו סמאעא אן אלמסיח יגי פי אלאלף אלכֿמסה ללכֿלוקה. פלמא חסבו וגדו כון צאחבהם פי אלאלף אלראבעה זאדו פי אלתאריךֿ אלף[341] סנה[342] חתי יציר להם פי אלאלף אלכֿאמס. אסתקרינאהם פוגדנאהם יקולון עאש אדם מאיתין ותֿלתֿין סנה חתי ולד לה שת. ועאש מאיתין וכֿמס סנין חתי ולד לה אנוש. ועאש אנוש קצֿ סנה חתי ולד לה קינון. ועאש קינון קעֿ סנה חתי ולד לה מהללאל. וכדֿלך יזידון שביהא אלף סנה מן אדם אלי אלמבול. ואעטֿם מן דֿלך ידעון עלינא אנא נחן אלדֿין נקצנאהם תעצבא עלי צאחבהם. **יוי הצילה נפשי**[343] **משׂפת שקר**[344] **מלשון רמיה**[345] (תה׳ 120:2). ואעגב מן דֿלך אן גמיע נסךֿ אלתוראה אלדֿין[346] מעהם תואריכֿהא כתואריכנא. ואנמא ידעון[347] אנהם וגדו נסכֿה בהדֿא אלתאריךֿ פי כֿזאנה בטלמיוס[348] הרשע[349] בגֿיר נאקלין ינקלונהא. ולא יצלחון נסכֿהם עלי מא פיהא. פהם[350] פי עמא מא ידעון.

וקולה[351] **והעיר והקדש**[352] **ישחית**[353] **עם**[354] **נגיד הבא** (דניאל 9:26) תצפחנא

340 עונה Beginning of Oxf 2486.130a
341 אלף End of Oxf 2486.130a
342 סנה Beginning of Oxf 2486.130b
343 נפשי Beginning of TS Ar 28.1e
344 משׂ ש וג׳ TS Ar 28.1e
345 מלשון רמיה TS Ar 28.1e > L
346 וא[עגב ... אלדין] TS Ar 28.1e > D ׀ אללדין Oxf 2486.130b
347 כ[תואריכנא ... ידעו]ן TS Ar 28.1e > D
348 אלתא[ריך ... בטלמיוס] TS Ar 28.1e > D
349 הרשע Oxf 2486.130b > L
350 יצ[לחון ... פהם] TS Ar 28.1e > D
351 וקו TS Ar 28.1e
352 והקדש End of Oxf 2486.130b
353 ישחית Beginning of Oxf 2486.131a
354 [והעיר ... ע]ם TS Ar 28.1e > D

הד̇א פוגדנאה כ̇בר טיטוס אלרומי[355] לאנה נגיד[356] עלי תסמיה סאיר אלמלוך. והם דניאל יקול[357] ענהם **וגם נגיד ברית**[358] (דניאל 11:22). והו אלד̇י ואפי[359] פאכ̇רב אלמדינה[360] ואלקדס עלי מא חמלת את̇אר אמתנא. וקולה[361] **וקיצו בשטף** (דניאל 9:26) יריד בה אן גישה יג̇רקון אלבלד ג̇רקא כמא קאל[362] פי פרעה **הנה מים עלים מצפון והיו**[363] **לנחל שוטף וישטפו ארץ ומלואה עיר וישבי בה**[364] (ירמ׳ 47:2). וקאל אן מלך אשור **וחלף ביהודה שטף ועבר**[365] **עד צואר יגיע**[366] (יש׳ 8:8). ופי קול דניאל[367] מן הד̇ה אללפט̇ה כת̇יר, **וזרעות השטף ישטפו מלפניו**[368] (דניאל 11:22) ומא אשבההא.

וקולה[369] **ועד קץ מלחמה נחרצת שוממות**[370] (דניאל 9:26) תצפחנא אלאכ̇באר איצ̇א[371] פוגדנא **קץ מלחמה** (דניאל 9:26) ג̇ סנין ונצף. והו מקדאר נצף אסבוע. מעני[372] **נחרצת** (דניאל 9:26) לאן אלחרב תנבתר[373] לצ̇רבין.[374] אמא ללקום ואמא עליהם. פכאן אנפצאל הד̇ה אלחרוב עליהם[375] לא להם בל עלי איחאש בלדהם וכ̇ראבה.

[355] פוגד[נאה ... אלרו]מי TS Ar 28.1e > D
[356] נ[גי]ד TS Ar 28.1e > D
[357] אלמ[לוך וה]ם [דניאל י]קול TS Ar 28.1e > D
[358] ברית TS Ar 28.1e > D
[359] ואפא TS Ar 28.1e
[360] אל[מד]ינה TS Ar 28.1e > D
[361] וקול TS Ar 28.1e
[362] כמק TS Ar 28.1e
[363] וג׳ + TS Ar 28.1e
[364] לנחל ... בה TS Ar 28.1e > L
[365] וג׳ + TS Ar 28.1e
[366] עד ... יגיע TS Ar 28.1e > D
[367] דני TS Ar 28.1e
[368] מלפניו TS Ar 28.1e > D
[369] וקו TS Ar 28.1e
[370] נ ש TS Ar 28.1e
[371] איצ TS Ar 28.1e
[372] מע TS Ar 28.1e
[373] תובתד[ין] Oxf 2486.131a > D | ת[בתדי... אמא] TS Ar 28.1e > D | תובתדי End of Oxf 2486.131a
[374] לצרבין Beginning of Oxf 2486.131b
[375] הדה ... עליהם TS Ar 28.1e > D

וקולה **והגביר**[376] **ברית לרבים שבוע אחד** (דניאל 9:27) יעני[377] בה אנה יהאדנהם[378] ויעאהדהם עלי אסבוע ואחד.[379] לכנה יג'דר בהם פי[380] נצף ד'לך אלאסבוע פיחארבהם וימנעהם מן קרבאן אללחם ואלבר[381] והי ואחדה ובטל **התמיד**. וקולה **ועל כנף שקוצים**[382] **משומם**[383] (דניאל 9:27) יריד בה אלצנם אלד'י אדכ'לוה אלי אלקדס כקולה **ולמלך**[384] **שקוץ בני עמון** (מל"א' 11:7), **ותראו את שקוציהם** (דב' 29:16) ואמת'אלהא. וכמא[385] עדד איצ'א פי אלגזירות **והעמיד צלם בהיכל**. וחכאיתה[386] לד'לך בלפט'ה **כנף** (דניאל 9:27) יריד בה אנה בסטה פאכתנף[387] אלמוצ'ע והו מת'ל קולה **והיו מטות כנפיו** (יש' 8:8). וד'לך אן הד'א אלאסם עלי[388] כ'מס[389] מעאני. אולהא עלי ט'אהרה, גנאח,[390] **כל צפור כל כנף**[391] (בר' 7:14). ואלת'אני,[392] זאויה[393] מן אלבית כקולך **בארבע כנפות הבית**[394] (איוב 1:19). וכד'לך פי גמלה אלארץ' כקולה **מכנף הארץ** (יש' 24:16), **מארבע כנפות הארץ** (יש' 11:12). וכד'לך פי אלאזאר **על ארבע כנפות כסותך** (דב' 22:12), **וצרת אותם בכנפיך** (יח' 5:3). ואלת'אלת, שעאע אלשמס כמא קאל **צדקה ומרפא בכנפיה** (מלאכי 3:20). ואלראבע, לואחאת אלפגר כקולך **אשא**[395] **כנפי שחר** (תה' 139:9). ואלכ'אמס, מא יבסטה

[376] וכ[ראבה ... והגביר] TS Ar 28.1e > D
[377] ש א יע TS Ar 28.1e
[378] יהאד[נהם] TS Ar 28.1e > D | יהאדנהם End of the readable part of TS Ar 28.1e
[379] ואחד Beginning of TS Ar 28.1f
[380] וא[חד ... פי] TS Ar 28.1f > D
[381] מן ... אלבר TS Ar 28.1f > D
[382] וקולה ... שקוצים TS Ar 28.1f > D
[383] מש TS Ar 28.1f
[384] אד[כל]וה [אלי ... אלמלו]ך TS Ar 28.1f > D
[385] שקוצי[הם ... וכ]מא TS Ar 28.1f > D
[386] והעמ[יד ... חכ]איתה TS Ar 28.1f > D
[387] [בסטה] פ[אכת]נף TS Ar 28.1f > D
[388] עליה TS Ar 28.1f
[389] כמס TS Ar 28.1f > L
[390] גנאח עלי טאהרה TS Ar 28.1f
[391] כנף End of Oxf 2486.131b
[392] ואלתאני Beginning of Oxf 2486.132a
[393] זואיא Oxf 2486.132a
[394] בארבע פנות הבית (איוב 1:19) and ארבע כנפות הארץ (יח' 7:2) Confusion
[395] אל[פגר ... אש]א TS Ar 28.1f > D

אלבאסט **ועל כנף**[396] **שקוצים** (דניאל 9:27). וקד יסתעאר אלכנף פיוצף בה סתר אללה[397] לאוליאה כמא קאל[398] **באברתו יסך לך**[399] **ותחת כנפיו תחסה**[400] (תה׳ 91:4) ואשבאה ד̇לך.

ותתמתה[401] אלקול **ועד כלה ונחרצה**[402] **תתך**[403] **על שומם** (דניאל 9:27). יעני[404] בקולה **כלה** (דניאל 9:27) אלסיף, אלסוט. **ונחרצה**[405] (דניאל 9:27) אלובא. פיקול אן הד̇ין[406] יגתמעאן עלי אלבלד מע וחשתה. והם[407] פי קול דניאל יסמו אלסיף **כלה, ויעמד**[408] **בארץ**[409] **הצבי**[410] **וכלה בידו**[411] (דניאל 11:16). ואמא **ונחרצה** (דניאל 9:27), ובא, פהו[412] כקולה **אם חרוצים ימיו**[413] (איוב 14:5). פלא יזאל[414] עלי הד̇ה אלחאל אלי אן ידפעהמא אללה ען[415] אלבלד כמא קאל[416] **וישבו בה וחרם לא יהיה עוד וישבה ירושלם לבטח**[417] (זכריה 14:11). תם אלגזא אלתאסע מן אלכתיב.

[396] [אלבאסט ... כנ]ף TS Ar 28.1f > D
[397] פיוצף ... אללה TS Ar 28.1f > D
[398] כמק TS Ar 28.1f
[399] וג׳ + TS Ar 28.1f
[400] ותחת ... תחסה TS Ar 28.1f > L
[401] [ואשבאה ... ות]תמתה TS Ar 28.1f > D
[402] ונחרצה End of TS Ar 28.1f
[403] תתך Beginning of TS Ar 28.1g
[404] שו̇ יע̇ בקו̇ TS Ar 28.1g
[405] כלה ... ונחרצה TS Ar 28.1g > D
[406] פנקול אן הד̇אן TS Ar 28.1g
[407] ע[לי ... ו]הם TS Ar 28.1g > D
[408] ויעמד End of Oxf 2486.132a
[409] בארץ Beginning of Oxf 2486.132b
[410] כ[לה ... הצב]י TS Ar 28.1g > D
[411] בי̇ TS Ar 28.1g
[412] פהו TS Ar 28.1g > L
[413] כ[קולה ... ימיו] TS Ar 28.1g > D
[414] יזל Oxf 2486.132b
[415] [אן ... ע]ן TS Ar 28.1g > D
[416] כמק TS Ar 28.1g
[417] יהיה ... לבטח TS Ar 28.1g > D

ונץ אלגז אלעאשר

Dn 10:1

בשנת שלש לכורש מלך פרס דבר נגלה לדניאל אשר נקרא שמו בלטשצר ואמת הדבר וצבא גדול ובין את הדבר ובינה לו במראה.

פי אלסנה[1] אלת̇אלת̇ה[2] לכורש[3] מלך אלפרס[4] אמר[5] ט̇הר[6] לדניאל[7] אלד̇י אסמה[8] בלטשצר[9] ואלאמר חק ואלמראד[10] לה[11] כביר וקד פהם אלאמר[12] ואפהם[13] אלמנט̇ר.[14]

אול מא יחתאג אלי שרחה[15] מן הד̇א אלפסוק, אי ש̇י[16] מעני[17] קולה לה[18] ההנא[19] **אשר נקרא שמו בלטשצר**[20] (דניאל 10:1). פנקול[21] אן הד̇א אלאסם

[1] אלסנה TS Ar 28.1g > D
[2] אלג̇ Oxf 2628.49b
[3] אלתלאתה לכרש Spiegel
[4] אלפרס End of Oxf 2628.49b ׀ אלמלך אלפארסי Spiegel
[5] אמר Beginning of Oxf 2628.50a
[6] צ̇הר Spiegel + Morag
[7] לדני̇ TS Ar 28.1g
[8] אסמי TS Ar 28.1g
[9] בלטשאצר Spiegel + Oxf 2628.50a + Oxf 2486.132b
[10] ואלמראד End of Oxf 2486.132b
[11] לה Beginning of Oxf 2486.133a ׀ לה Spiegel > L
[12] ותאמל Spiegel +
[13] ואפהם Spiegel > L
[14] אלמנצ̇ר Spiegel + Oxf 2628.50a + Morag
[15] שרח Oxf 2486.133a
[16] איש TS Ar 28.1g
[17] [מ]עני TS Ar 28.1g > D
[18] לה TS Ar 28.1g > L
[19] האהנא Oxf 2486.133a ׀ ההונא TS Ar 28.1g
[20] בלטש TS Ar 28.1g
[21] [פ]נקול TS Ar 28.1g

ועלי אנה שריף ענד נבוכדנצר[22] אד̇ פיה אסם **בל** מעבודה. ולד̇לך שרף בה[23] דניאל כמא קאל[24] **די שמה בלטשצר כשם אלהי**[25] (דניאל 4:5). פאן אליהוד ואלמלאיכה[26] לם יכנו[27] יסמוה אלא דניאל.[28] כמא סיצף פי וסט אלקצה[29] אן גבריאל קאל לה יא דניאל מראת[30] כת̇ירה. וד̇לך אנה פי אלרויא[31] אלאולי[32] אנמא קיל לה[33] סתם[34] **הבן להלז את המראה** (דניאל 8:16). ואיצ̇א[35] **הבן בן אדם** (דניאל 8:17). ת̇ם נקול,[36] ואי שיא[37] מעני קולה **ואמת הדבר** (דניאל 10:1). תראה[38] לו קאל כלאמא[39] מרסלא הל כנא נשך פי אנה[40] **אמת**[41] (דניאל 10:1). ולכן קולה[42] **ואמת הדבר** (דניאל 10:1) יעני[43] בה אנה לא שרט פיה ולא אסתת̇ני.[44] לאנך תעלם אן כת̇ירא מן אלנבואת לא יפצח פיה באסתת̇ני.[45] ויכון עליה אסתדלאל[46] פי אלמעקול או פי אלמחכום בה שרט[47] או שרוט כקצה **עוד ארבעים יום ונניוה נהפכת**[48] (יונה 3:4).

22 נבוכדנ̇ TS Ar 28.1g
23 שר[ף בה] TS Ar 28.1g > D
24 כמק TS Ar 28.1g
25 שמיה בלטש̇ בש̇ אל̇ TS Ar 28.1g
26 אלי[הוד ואלמלאיכה] TS Ar 28.1g > D
27 יכונו TS Ar 28.1g
28 דני̇ TS Ar 28.1g
29 סי[צף ... אל]קצה TS Ar 28.1g > D
30 דניא[ל מראת] TS Ar 28.1g > D
31 אלריא TS Ar 28.1g
32 אלאולי End of the readable part of TS Ar 28.1g
33 לה Beginning of TS Ar 28.1h
34 סתם TS Ar 28.1h > L
35 לה[לז ... איצ̇א] TS Ar 28.1h > D
36 נ[קול] TS Ar 28.1h > D
37 שי TS Ar 28.1h
38 [מעני ... תר]אה TS Ar 28.1h > D
39 אלכלאם Oxf 2486.133a
40 אנה End of Oxf 2486.133a
41 אמת Beginning of Oxf 2486.133b | מרסלא ... אמת TS Ar 28.1h > D
42 קולה TS Ar 28.1h > L
43 יע̇ TS Ar 28.1h
44 [לא ... אסת]תנא TS Ar 28.1h > D
45 [אלנבואת ... ב]אסתתני TS Ar 28.1h > D
46 אסתדלאל Oxf 2486.133b > L | אסת[דלאל] TS Ar 28.1h > D
47 [או ... שר]ט TS Ar 28.1h > D
48 ונ̇ נה TS Ar 28.1h

ופסרת[49] **וצבא** (דניאל 10:1), "אראדה", לאני[50] אצרפהא[51] מן **לשון תרגום, די לא**[52] **תשנא צבו בדניאל**[53] **צבית ליצבא. ולמן די יצבא**[54] ואשבאה דׄלך. ונעתה ללמראד באנה כביר לאנה יגמע אחואל ארבע[55] מלכיות. ושרח אלקץ וגׄרץׄ אלישועה **ותחית המתים** ותׄואב **העולם**[56] **הבא**. פיאלך מן נבוה גמעת הדׄה אלאמור. ותכראר[57] אלקול **ובין את הדבר ובינה לו במראה** (דניאל 10:1) יעני[58] אן אכתׄר אלקצה פהמהא[59] מן דׄאתה. ואמא בעצׄהא פלם יפהמה הו חתי אפהמה[60] איאה[61] גבריאל כמא סיקול אכׄרהא[62] **ואני שמעתי**[63] **ולא אבין** (דניאל 12:8) חתי בין לה אלמלאך בעד דׄלך. ולדׄלך וצׄעת[64] פי אלנץ "ופהם" "ואפהם". תׄם קאל

Dn 10:2

בימים ההם אני דניאל הייתי מתאבל שלשה שבועים ימים.

פי[65] דׄלך[66] אלוקת[67] אקמת[68] אנא דניאל[69] מתחזנא[70] תׄלתׄ[71] אסאביע איאם.

[49] [ופסר]ת TS Ar 28.1h > D
[50] לאנה TS Ar 28.1h
[51] צרפתהא TS Ar 28.1h
[52] ת[רגום די ל]א TS Ar 28.1h > D
[53] בדניאל Oxf 2486.133b > L ׀ בדנׄ TS Ar 28.1h
[54] יצ[בא] TS Ar 28.1h > D
[55] א[רב]ע TS Ar 28.1h > D
[56] העול[ם] TS Ar 28.1h > D
[57] ו[תכ]רא[ר] TS Ar 28.1h > D
[58] במרא יע TS Ar 28.1h
[59] [אל]קצה [פהמה]א TS Ar 28.1h > D
[60] אפהמה End of Oxf 2486.133b ׀ [הו ... אפהמ]ה TS Ar 28.1h > D
[61] איאהא Beginning of Oxf 2486.134a
[62] אכׄרהא Oxf 2486.134a > D
[63] ואני שמעתי TS Ar 28.1h > D
[64] [דלך ...ו]צעת TS Ar 28.1h > D
[65] ופי Oxf 2628.50a + Oxf 2486.134a
[66] דׄאלך Spiegel
[67] כנת + Morag
[68] אקמת Morag > L
[69] דניאל End of TS Ar 28.1h
[70] מתחזננא Morag
[71] גׄ Spiegel + Oxf 2628.50a

Dn 10:3
לחם חמדת לא אכלתי ובשר ויין לא בא אל פי וסוך לא סכתי עד מלאת שלשת שבועים ימים.

טעאמא[72] לדידא[73] לם אכל ולחם ושראב לם ידכׄלא פאי[74] ולם אדהן דהנא אלי אן תמת תׄלאתׄה[75] אסאביע איאם.

אלמקדם פי עלה תחזונה הדׄה אלמרה[76] הו[77] אנה למא כאן דעי וצלי פי **שנת אחת לדריוש** (דניאל 9:1) ואגיב **בשבעים שבעים** (דניאל 9:24). וראי אן פי אלסנה אלתׄאניה נאדי כורש פי בנא אלבית ופי אלסנה אלתי בעדהא עטל אלבנא. וכמא שרחנא אן הדׄה אלסנין נואקץ כלהא ואן סנתי דריוש ותׄלתׄ סני כורש, הדׄה אלכׄמסה מע תׄלתׄ סנין בלשצר מקאם כׄמס פקט. פלמא וקעת אלעטלה בעד אלבנא חזן דניאל ומנהא קאל **הייתי מתאבל** (דניאל 10:2). כמא קאל נחמיה חין סמע מא גמה בסבב אלקדס **ויהי כשמעי את הדברים ישבתי ואבכה ואתאבלה** (נחמיה 1:4) וסאיר אלקצה.

וקולה **לחם חמדות לא אכלתי ובשר ויין** (דניאל 10:3) יכשף לנא אן ישׂראל פי אלגלות ליס יחרם עליהם אכל אללחם ולא שרב אלכׄמר ולא אלמלאדׄ אלחלאל מן אגל כׄראב אלקדס.[78] ולו כאנת אלתוראה אחרמת דׄלך[79] עליהם[80] לכאן דניאל ונטׄראיה אולי מן ימתתׄלהא. פלמא וגדנאה פרד אחד ועשרין יומא לם יאכל פיהא מן הדׄה אלאשיא עלמנא אנה כאן יאכלהא קבל אחד ועשרין יומא ובעדהא. ולאסימא לתחדירה **עד מלאת** (דניאל 10:3). וכדׄלך אלדהן איצׄא ומא אשבהה. וקריב אן יכון **לחם חומדות** (דניאל 10:3) טעאם אלסלאטין כקול נחמיה **לחם הפחה לא אכלתי** (נחמיה 5:14). ודׄלך תאוכׄד פי אלאטלאק. וקד יטׄן אן הדׄה אלאחד ועשרין יומא אלתי מן **שבעה עשר** בתמוז אלי **תשעה** באב. והדׄא טׄן כׄטא מן גהאת אולהא לאן **שבעה עשר** בתמוז **ותשעה** באב

[72] טעאם Morag
[73] לדיד Spiegel + Morag
[74] פי Oxf 2628.50a + Oxf 2486.134a
[75] ג׳ Oxf 2628.50a + Oxf 2486.134a
[76] אלמדה End of Oxf 2486.134a
[77] הו Beginning of Oxf 2486.134b
[78] אלקדס End of Oxf 2486.134b
[79] ולו ... דלך Restored by by Margoliouth in Yefet ben Eli-s commentary on Daniel, p. vii, n. 5
[80] עליהם Beginning 0f the readable part of Oxf 2486.135a

אנמא הי מן רסום כ̇ראב אלבית אלת̇אני. ואמא אלבית אלאול פאן רסום כ̇ראבה תסעה פי תמוז ועשרה פי אב לאן **בתשעה**[81] [...][82] (ירמ' 52:6), **ובחדש**[83] **החמישי בעשור לחדש** (ירמ' 52:12), **וישרף את בית יוי** (ירמ' 52:13) בינהמא ת̇לת̇ין יום. וקאל ענה **וביום עשרים וארבעה לחדש הראשון ואני הייתי על [יד] [ה]נהר** (דניאל 10:4) כ̇בר (?). פקד תבין אמא ועשרין אלשהר מן בעד ג̇ פי ניסאן ואלי הד̇א אליום אלמשרוח. פאן דכ̇לת איאם מועד אלפסח פי גמלתהא פג̇יר מנכר. ת̇ם קאל

Dn 10:4

וביום עשרים וארבעה לחדש הראשון ואני הייתי על יד הנהר הגדול הוא הדקל.

ופי[84] אליום אלראבע ואלעשרין[85] מן אלשהר אלאול[86] כנת ואקפא עלי שט[87] אלנהר אלכביר הו[88] אלדגלה.[89]

Dn 10:5

ואשא את עיני ואראה והנה איש אחד לבוש בדים ומתניו חגורים בכתם אופז.[90]

פמדדת בצרי[91] פראית[92] פאד̇א[93] במלך בצורה[94] רגל לאבס עשר ומשדודה[95] חקויה בפצוץ מן[96] אלפאיז.[97]

[81] בתשעה End of Oxf 2486.135a
[82] [... ...] Oxf 2486.135b > D
[83] ובחדש Beginning of the readable part of Oxf 2486.135b
[84] ומן Oxf 2628.50a + Oxf 2486.135b
[85] אלד וכ Oxf 2628.50a
[86] אלאוול Spiegel
[87] שאט Spiegel + Oxf 2628.50a + Oxf 2486.135b
[88] הי Spiegel
[89] דגלה Oxf 2486.135b
[90] אופז End of Oxf 2486.135b
[91] ואני + Spiegel
[92] ראית Spiegel
[93] פאדי Morag
[94] בצרה Beginning of the readable part of Oxf 2486.136a
[95] ומשד[ודה] Oxf 2486.136a > D
[96] מן End of Oxf 2628.50a
[97] אלפאיז Beginning of Oxf 2628.50b

Dn 10:6

וגויתו כתרשיש ופניו כמראה ברק ועיניו כלפידי אש וזרועותיו ומרגלותיו כעין נחשת קלל וקול דבריו כקול המון.

וראית[98] גתתה כאלאזרק מן אלגוהר ווגהה כרויא אלברק ועינאה[99] כפלאיל[100] נאר[101] וידאה ורגלאה[102] כלון אלנחאס אלמגלי[103] וצות כלאמה כצות גמהור.

Dn 10:7

וראיתי אני דניאל לבדי את המראה והאנשים אשר היו עמי לא ראו את המראה אבל חרדה גדלה נפלה עליהם ויברחו בהחבא.[104]

וראית אנא דניאל וחדי הדׄא אלמנטׄר[105] ואלקום אלדׄי כאנו מעי[106] לם ירוה ולכן וקע[107] בהם אנזעאג עטׄים[108] חתי הרבו[109] פאכׄתבו.

Dn 10:8

ואני נשארתי לבדי ואראה את המראה הגדלה הזאת ולא נשאר בי כח והודי נהפך עלי למשחית ולא עצרתי כח.

פבקית אנא וחדי וראית הדׄא אלמנצׄר אלעצׄים[110] ולם תבק[111] בי[112] קוה[113] ובהגי אנקלב עליי[114] מתגׄירא[115] ולם אחבס קותי.[116]

[98] ודאת Spiegel + Oxf 2486.136a

[99] ועיניה Oxf 2628.50b

[100] פליל Spiegel + Oxf 2628.50a + Oxf 2486.136a

[101] אלנאר Spiegel

[102] ורגלאת Spiegel

[103] מגלו Beginning of Oxf 2659.43a | אלמגׄל Spiegel

[104] בהחבה End of Oxf 2486.136a

[105] אלמנצר Spiegel + Oxf 2628.50b + Morag

[106] מעי Beginning of the readable part of Oxf 2486.136b | [מ]עי Oxf 2486.136b

[107] ול[כן וקע] Oxf 2486.136b > D | ולך Oxf 2628.50b

[108] עצים Spiegel + Morag

[109] הרבו Oxf 2486.136b > D

[110] אלמנצר אלעצים Spiegel + Morag

[111] תבקא Morag | יבק Spiegel | תבק End of Oxf 2628.50b

[112] פיי Beginning of Oxf 2628.51a | פיי Oxf 2659.43a + Oxf 2486.136b | פי Spiegel

[113] קווה Spiegel + Morag

[114] עלי Spiegel + Oxf 2659.43a

אול מא נקול כיף סמי אלכתאב[117] אלדגלה **הנהר הגדול** (דניאל 10:4) ופי אלתוראה[118] **הנהר הגדול**[119] **נהר פרת** (בר׳ 15:18). פנקול אן פי אלתוראה[120] ופי **ספר יהושע** אנמא ינסב אלפראת אלי בלד אלשאם והו אכבר נהר יג̇אור בלד אלשאם. אד̇ סאיר[121] אלאנהאר[122] הנאך צג̇אר מת̇ל אלארדן[123] ואלירמוך וברדא ואלפיג̇ה ואלארנט וג̇יחאן וג̇ירהם. ואמא דניאל[124] פאנה נסב אלדג̇לה אלי בלד אלעראק והי אכבר נהר באלעראק עלי מא וצף. ת̇ם וצף חליה אלמלאך אלד̇י ראה[125] ולם יד̇כ̇ר אנה מתעלק פוק[126] מא[127] אלדג̇לה. ולכנה שרח ד̇לך פי אכ̇ר אלקצה[128] פקאל **אשר**[129] **ממעל למימי היאר** (דניאל 12:6.7) מרתין. ווצפה לה באנה[130] **לבוש בדים** (דניאל 10:5) ליס אן עליה[131] ת̇יאב מן[132] אלעשר עלי אלחקיקה. ולכן עליה נור ישבה בעין אלעשר.[133] ומעני[134] **ומתניו חגורים**[135] (דניאל 10:5) עלאמה אנה רסול[136] מבעות̇ אלי דניאל[137] כמא[138] ישד אוסאטהם אלפיוג[139] ואלפראנקיון.

[115] מתג̇יירא Oxf 2628.51a | מג̇יירא Spiegel

[116] קוותי Spiegel + Morag

[117] סמא אלכת̇ Oxf 2659.43a

[118] אלתוריה מכת̇ Oxf 2659.43a

[119] הג̇ Oxf 2659.43a

[120] אלתוריה Oxf 2659.43a

[121] סאיר End of Oxf 2486.136b

[122] אלאנהאר Beginning of Oxf 2486.137a

[123] אלא[רדן] Oxf 2486.136b > D

[124] דני׳ Oxf 2659.43a

[125] ראה Beginning of Oxf 2629.44a | [רא]ה Oxf 2629.44a > D

[126] [מת]עלק פ[וק] Oxf 2629.44a > D

[127] מא Oxf 2629.44a > L

[128] אלקצה Oxf 2629.44a > L

[129] א[שר] Oxf 2629.44a > D

[130] אלה לאנה Oxf 2629.44a

[131] [ליס] אן עלי[ה] Oxf 2629.44a > D

[132] מן Oxf 2629.44a > L

[133] ולכן ... אלעשר Oxf 2659.43a > L

[134] ומע Oxf 2659.43a | אלעשר[עלי ... אלעשר] ומעני Oxf 2629.44a > D homeoteleuton

[135] ומתנ[יו חגורים] בכתם או[פז] Oxf 2629.44a > D

[136] רסול Oxf 2629.44a > L

[137] דני׳ Oxf 2659.43a

[138] במא Oxf 2629.44a

[139] פיוג Oxf 2629.44a

ואמא תגזיתה לאעצֿאה[140] באלואן כתֿירה[141] אד[142] קאל **וגויתו**[143] **בתרשיש וג׳**[144] (דניאל 10:6). פאלסבב[145] פי דֿלך לתתבין[146] אלאגזא[147] אד[148] תלון כל גז בלון מא. פדֿאת אלגסם נאר אסמאנגוניה[149] בלון אלזרקה[150] לקולה[151] **וגויתו**[152] **בתרשיש וג׳**[153] (דניאל 10:6). יעני[154] **תרשיש**[155] אלגוהרה. ואלוגה מן נאר צפרא לקולה[156] **ופניו כמראה ברק** (דניאל 10:6). ואלעינאן מן נאר חמרא[157] לקולה[158] **ועיניו כלפידי**[159] **אש** (דניאל 10:6). ואלידאן ואלרגלאן כלון אלצפר[160] אלבראק[161] לקולה[162] **וזרועתיו ומרגלותיו כעין נחשת**[163] **קלל**[164] (דניאל 10:6). והדֿה אלתשכילאת ואלתכֿאטיט משאבהה[165] פי[166] אלתגֿייר

[140] לאעצֿאיה Oxf 2629.44a
[141] כ[תֿיר]ה D < Oxf 2659.43a | כתירה End of Oxf 2659.43a
[142] אד Beginning of Oxf 2659.43b
[143] [קאל וגו]יתו D < Oxf 2629.44a
[144] וג׳ L < Oxf 2629.44a and Oxf 2659.43b
[145] פאלסב[ב] D < Oxf 2629.44a
[146] אלאעצֿא באלואן כתֿ[ירה] + Oxf 2629.44a
[147] אלאגז[א] Oxf 2659.43b
[148] אלאגזא אד L < Oxf 2629.44a
[149] אסמנגוניה End of Oxf 2486.137a
[150] נאר זרקא אסמאנגונ[יה] Oxf 2629.44a
[151] לקולה Beginning of the readable part of Oxf 2486.137b | לקול Oxf 2659.43b | [לק]ו D < Oxf 2629.44a
[152] [וגו]יתו D < Oxf 2659.43b | וגיותו Oxf 2629.44a
[153] בתרשי[ש וג׳] D < Oxf 2629.44a | וג׳ L < Oxf 2659.43b
[154] יע Oxf 2659.43b
[155] תר[שיש] D < Oxf 2629.44a
[156] לקול Oxf 2659.43b | לקו Oxf 2629.44a
[157] ואלעינא[ן מן] נאר [חמרא] D < Oxf 2629.44a
[158] לקו Oxf 2629.44a + Oxf 2659.43b
[159] כ[לפיד]י D < Oxf 2629.44a | Beginning of TS Ar 23.29a
[160] אלצפאר Oxf 2629.44a
[161] אלברא[ק] D < Oxf 2629.44a | ואלידאן ... אלבראק D < TS Ar 23.29a
[162] לקו Oxf 2659.43b | כקו Oxf 2629.44a
[163] כע נֿ Oxf 2659.43b | נחש[ת] Oxf 2629.44a
[164] וזרועתיו ... קלל D < TS Ar 23.29a
[165] [אל]תשכילאת ואלתכט[יט] משאבה[ה] D < Oxf 2629.44a
[166] ו[ה]דה אל[תשכילאת ... פי] D < TS Ar 23.29a

לתג'ייר[167] אגזא אלחיות ואלאופנים ואלרקיע[168] ואלכסא[169] **ומראהו**[170] **אדם** וסאיר אלדואיר אלתי ראהא[171] יחזקאל.[172] פאן גמיע[173] ד̇לך אנמא[174] כ̇לק לה מתג'ירא לירתסם[175] לה פי אלרויא[176] ופי[177] אלפכר ופי אלחכאיה.[178] ונכ̇תצר[179] דון[180] שרח שיא[181] מן ד̇לך ההנא.[182] ואמא **וקול דבריו**[183] **כקול**[184] **המון** (דניאל 10:6) פמענאה[185] אנה אד̇א תכלם יתשבה[186] ללסאמע[187] כאן[188] גמאעה יתכלמון. ונט̇יר[189] מא[190] קאל יחזקאל[191] ען צות[192] אגנחה[193] אלחיות **קול**[194] **המולה כקול**[195] **מחנה**[196] (יח' 1:24).

[167] לתג'יר Oxf 2629.44a

[168] [אל]תג'ייר [לתג'יר ... אלר]קיע TS Ar 23.29a > D

[169] ו[אל]כסא Oxf 2629.44a > D

[170] ומראה TS Ar 23.29a > D

[171] ראה[א] Oxf 2629.44a > D

[172] [אל]דואי[ר] אלתי רא[הא יחז]קאל TS Ar 23.29a > D | יחזקאל Oxf > L 2629.44a

[173] גמ[יע] Oxf 2629.44a > D

[174] אנמא TS Ar 23.29a > D

[175] מת[ג'יר] ליתֹ[ר]סם TS Ar 23.29a > D

[176] אלרויא Oxf 2629.44a | פי אלראויא TS Ar 23.29a > L

[177] ופי Oxf 2629.44a > L

[178] [ואלחכ]אי[ה] Oxf 2629.44a > D

[179] [אלח]כאיה ו[נ]כ[תצ]ר TS Ar 23.29a > D

[180] [דו]ן Oxf 2629.44a > D

[181] שי TS Ar 23.29a + Oxf 2629.44a + Oxf 2659.43b

[182] האהנא Oxf 2486.137b | הא[הנא] Oxf 2629.44a > D

[183] [דב]ריו TS Ar 23.29a > D

[184] כקו[ל] Oxf 2629.44a > D

[185] פמענא[ה] Oxf 2629.44a > D

[186] תכל[ם י]תשבה TS Ar 23.29a > D

[187] לאלסאמע Oxf 2486.137b | לסמאע כצות + TS Ar 23.29a

[188] כאן TS Ar 23.29a > L

[189] ונ[טי]ר Oxf 2629.44a > D

[190] נטיר מא TS Ar 23.29a > D

[191] יחז' Oxf 2629.44a

[192] צות End of Oxf 2486.137b | צ[ו]ת TS Ar 23.29a > D

[193] אגנחה Beginning of Oxf 2486.138a | א[גנ]חת Oxf 2629.44a > D

[194] כקול Oxf 2629.44a

[195] המולה כקול TS Ar 23.29a > D

[196] מחנה Oxf 2486.138a > D | מח[נה] Oxf 2629.44a > D

ואלאקרב אן יכונו **והאנשים אשר היו**[197] **עמי**[198] (דניאל 10:7) חנניה[199] ומישאל ועזריה. וממא[200] ידל עלי[201] אן מנט̇רה[202] הד̇א הו פי[203] אליקט̇ה אעגאבה[204] באנה[205] **לא ראו**[206] **את המראה**[207] (דניאל 10:7). ולו[208] כאן ד̇לך[209] פי[210] אלמנאם מן לא[211] יעלם[212] אן[213] עשרה פי בית[214] ירי כל ואחד מנהם שיא פי מנאמה[215] מא לא יראה אלתסעה[216] אלאכ̇ר.[217] ואיצ̇א[218] לו כאן ד̇לך[219] פי אלמנאם[220] לם יקם[221] אלקום[222] פיהרבון[223] לאנהם לם יכנו[224] ישערון[225] במא ראה דניאל. כמא אן[226] רובן[227] לו ראי[228] פי מנאמה[229] כאנה יצ̇רב באלמקארע לם[230] ישער שמעון[231] בד̇לך.[232] וקולה[233] **ולא**[234] **נשאר בי**

[197] א[ן … היו] Oxf 2629.44a > D
[198] עמו Oxf 2659.43b
[199] [וה]אנשים [אשר … חנניה] TS Ar 23.29a > D
[200] וממ[א] Oxf 2629.44a > D
[201] [יד]ל [ע]לי TS Ar 23.29a > D
[202] מנ[ט]רה Oxf 2659.43b > D
[203] הדא הו פי Oxf 2629.44a > D
[204] אע[גאבה] Oxf 2629.44a > D | מנטרה … אלי]קצה אעגא[בה] TS Ar 23.29a > D
[205] באנהם Oxf 2629.44a + TS Ar 23.29a
[206] רא[ו] Oxf 2629.44a > D
[207] [המר]אה TS Ar 23.29a > D
[208] ולו Oxf 2659.43b > D
[209] כדלך Oxf 2629.44a
[210] פי End of Oxf 2659.43b
[211] אל[מנאם מן לא] Oxf 2629.44a > D
[212] יע[ל]ם TS Ar 23.29a > D
[213] יעל[ם] א[ן י] Oxf 2629.44a > D
[214] אלבית ירי Oxf 2629.44a
[215] פי מנאמה [שי]א Oxf 2629.44a
[216] אלט̇ ? TS Ar 23.29a > D
[217] יראה … אלאכר Oxf 2629.44a > D | אלד[י] מעה + TS Ar 23.29a
[218] וא[יצ]א Oxf 2629.44a > D | וא[י]צ[א] TS Ar 23.29a > D
[219] דאך TS Ar 23.29a
[220] [אל]מנאם Oxf 2629.44a > D
[221] יקום TS Ar 23.29a
[222] אלק[ו]ם Oxf 2629.44a > D
[223] פיהר[בון] TS Ar 23.29a > D
[224] לאנה[ם ל]ם יכונ[ו] Oxf 2629.44a > D
[225] ישערון Oxf 2629.44a > D | [י]שערו TS Ar 23.29a > D
[226] כ[מ]א רא[ה] Oxf 2629.44a > D
[227] ראוב[ן] Oxf 2629.44a > D | ראובן TS Ar 23.29a

באלמקארע לם[230] ישער שמעון[231] בדׄלך.[232] וקולה[233] **ולא**[234] **נשאר בי כח**[235] (דניאל 10:8) באלקוה[236] עלי טריק אלתבאלג.ׄ[237] **והודי נהפך**[238] **עלי למשחית**[239] (דניאל 10:8) דיבאגה וגהה.[240] **ולא עצרתי**[241] **כח** (דניאל 10:8) באלפעל.[242] תׄם קאל[243]

Dn 10:9

ואשמע[244] **את קול דבריו וכשמעי את קול דבריו ואני הייתי נרדם על פני ופני ארצה.**

תׄם[245] סמעת כלאמה[246] וכסמאעי כׄטאבה ואנא כנת מסבחא עלי וגהי ווגהי עלי אלארץ.[247]

Dn 10:10

והנה יד נגעה בי ותניעני על ברכי וכפות ידי.

[228] ראןין D < Oxf 2629.44a ו ראי D < TS Ar 23.29a

[229] מנאמה D < Oxf 2629.44a

[230] יצרןב] בןאלמןקאןרע לם] D < Oxf 2629.44a

[231] שמשון Oxf 2629.44a

[232] [כ]אנ[ה [יצרב] באלמ[קארע לם ישער] שמ[עון ב]דלך D < TS Ar 23.29a

[233] וקו Oxf 2629.44a

[234] לא Oxf 2629.44a

[235] נשאר בי כח D < Oxf 2629.44a

[236] באלקום Oxf 2629.44a

[237] ול[א ... אלת]באל[ג] D < TS Ar 23.29a

[238] טרי[ק ... נהפך] D < Oxf 2629.44a

[239] למשחי[ת] Oxf 2629.44a D ו [והודי ... למ]ש[חית] D < TS Ar 23.29a

[240] וגה[ה] D < Oxf 2629.44a ו וג[הה] D < TS Ar 23.29a

[241] עצר[ת]י D < Oxf 2629.44a

[242] [ולא ... בא]לפעל D < TS Ar 23.29a

[243] קאל End of Oxf 2486.138a ו תׄם קאל L < Oxf 2629.44a

[244] ואשמע Beginning of Oxf 2486.138b ו [ואשמ]ע D < Oxf 2486.138b

[245] את ... תׄם D < TS Ar 23.29a

[246] כלאמה End of the readable part of TS Ar 23.29a

[247] ... פכמא סמעת וקעת עלי וגהי עלי אלארץ כאלמסבות Oxf + Oxf 2486.138b 2628.51a ו פכמא סמעת [וקעת] עלי וגהי [עלי אלארץ] כאלמסבות D < Oxf 2629.44a

פאדׄי קד למסתני יד פכמא מסחני אסותני[248] עלי רכבתי וכפי.[249]

Dn 10:11

ויאמר אלי דניאל איש חמדות הבן בדברים אשר אנכי דבר אליך ועמד על עמדך כי עתה שלחתי אליך ובדברו עמי את הדבר הזה עמדתי מרעיד.

פקאל לי יא דניאל אלכׄאץ[250] אפהם אלכלאם אלדׄי אקולה לך וקם עלי רגליך[251] פאני[252] קד ארסלת אליך פלמא כלמני[253] בהדׄא אלכלאם[254] וקפת[255] מרתעדא.[256]

Dn 10:12

ויאמר אלי אל תירא דניאל כי מן היום הראשון אשר נתת את לבך להבין ולהתענות לפני אלהיך נשמעו דבריך ואני באתי בדבאריך.

וקאל[257] לי[258] לא[259] תכׄאף[260] יא דניאל[261] אדׄ[262] מן אליום אלאול[263] אלדׄי רדדת באלך לאלתפטן ותעבד קדאם אלאהך סמע כׄטאבך ואנא אתית בכׄטאבך.[264]

[248] אסותני Beginning of TS Ar 23.29b ו [אסות]ני TS Ar 23.29b > D

[249] פאדא ביד מסתני פסותני עלי רכבתיי וכפיי Oxf 2486.138b ו פאדא ביד מסתני פחרכתני עלי רכבתי וכפי Oxf 2628.51a ו פא[דא] ביד מסתני פ[סות]ני [ע]לי רכ[ב]תי וכפיי Oxf 2629.44a > D ו [פאדא ... אסות]ני על[י] רוכבתי וכפיי TS > D Ar 23.29b ו פאדא ביד קד לאמסתני פכמא מסכתני אסותני עלי רכבתיי ועלי כפיי Spiegel

[250] פקאל ... אלכׄאץ TS Ar 23.29b > D

[251] [אלדׄי ... ו]קם על[י] רג[לי]ך TS Ar 23.29b ו וקף עלי וקפך Spiegel ו רגלאך Morag

[252] פאנני TS Ar 23.29b

[253] כלמני End of Oxf 2486.138b ו בדלך Beginning of Oxf 2486.139a ו בדלך קמת + Oxf 2628.51a and Oxf 2486.139a ו [ב]דלך [ק]מת TS Ar 23.29b > D

[254] בהדׄא אלכלאם TS Ar 23.29b and Oxf 2628.51a and Oxf 2486.139a > L

[255] וקפת TS Ar 23.29b and Oxf 2628.51a and Oxf 2486.139a > L

[256] [אפהם] אלכלאם אלדׄי אק[ול]ה לך [ו]קם עלי רגל[יך] פאנ[י ק]ד ארסלת פלמא כ[למני בהדׄא אלכלאם וק]פת מרתעד[א] Oxf 2629.44a > D

[257] תם קאל Oxf 2629.44a and Oxf 2628.51a and Oxf 2486.139a ו פקאל Spiegel

[258] לי End of Oxf 2628.51a ו לי Spiegel > L

[259] לא Beginning of Oxf 2628.51b ו וקאל ... לא TS Ar 23.29b > D

[260] תכׄף Oxf 2486.139a ו לא תכׄף Oxf 2629.44a > D

[261] פאן + Oxf 2486.139a ו פאנא + Oxf 2628.51b ו פ[אנא] + Oxf 2629.44a

Dn 10:13

ושׂר מלכות פרס עמד לנגדי עשרים ואחד יום והנה מיכאל אחד השׂרים הרישנים בא לעזרני ואני נותרתי שם אצל מלכי פרס.

ורייס ממלכת פארס ואקף חדׄאי הודׄא ואחד ועשרין יומא ואדׄא[265] מיכאל אחד אלרויסא אלאואיל[266] גא[267] לנצרי[268] ואנא[269] פצלת[270] תׄם לזק מלוך פארס.[271]

Dn 10:14

ובאתי[272] להבינך את אשר יקרה לעמך באחרית הימים כי עוד חזון לימים.

פאתית לאפטנך מא יצאדף קומך פי אכׄר אלזמאן אדׄ בקי וחי לאלזמאן.[273]

[262] אד Oxf 2629.44a and Oxf 2628.51b and Oxf 2486.139a > L | אד TS Ar 23.29b > L

[263] אלאוול Spiegel

[264] אלדי קצדת פיה אלתובה ואלצום בין ידי רבך אגאב דעאך ואני גית לדעאיך Oxf 2628.51b + 2486.139a | ואגאב דעאך ונא ואנא Oxf 2486.139a | גית לדאעיך Oxf 2628.51b | אלדי ק[צדת פיה אלת]וב[ה] ואלצו[ם בין] ידין רבך [אג]אב דעאך ואנא גית לד[עאיך] D > Oxf 2629.44a | [אלדי ק]צדת פיה אלתובה ו[אל]צום בין ידי רבך [אג]ב דועאך ואנא גית לדעאיך D > TS Ar 23.29b | אלדי ציירת קלבך לתתוב ותצום קדאם אלהך קד סמע כטאבך ואנא אתית בה Spiegel

[265] ואדי Spiegel

[266] אלריסא אלאוולין Spiegel

[267] ליעיבני + Spiegel

[268] לנצרי Spiegel > L

[269] תבקית + Spiegel

[270] פצלת Spiegel > L

[271] ולכן אלמלך אלמוכל בממלכה אלפרס כאן ואקפא חדאיי אחד ועשרין יומא חתי ופי מיכאל אחד אלמלאיכה אלאואיל יעאונני למא כנת קד בקית וחדי מע מלוך אלפרס Oxf 2486.139a | ולכן אלמלך אלמוכל בממלכה אלפרס כאן ואקפא חדאיי כׄא יומא חתי ואפא אחד אלמלאיכה אלאואיל יעאונני למא כנת בקית וחדי מע מלוך אלפרס Oxf 2628.51b | ולכ[ן אלמ]לאך אלמוכל בממלכ[ה] אלפרס כאן ואקפא חדאי כׄא יומ[א] חתי ואפא [א]חד אלמלאיכה אלאוא[יל] למעאונתי למא [כנת] בקית וחד[י מע מלוך אלפרס] D > Oxf 2629.44a | ולכ[ן] אלמלך אלמוכל [ב]ממלכה אלפארס כאן ואק[פא חדאיי כׄא יומא ח[ת]י ואפא [מיכאל] אחד אלמלאיכ[ה] אלאואיל יעאנני למא כנת בקית וחדי מע מולך [א]לפ[רס] D > TS Ar 23.29b | אלפרס End of Oxf 2486.139a

[272] ובאתי Beginning of Oxf 2486.139b

[273] וגית לאפהמך מא סילקא קומך פי אכׄר הדה אלאיאם אד [קד + Oxf 2628.51b] בקית אליהא נבואת Oxf 2628.51b + Oxf 2486.139b | Oxf 2629.44a illegible |

Dn 10:15

ובדברו עמי כדברים יאלה נתתי פני ארצה ונאלמתי.

פלמא כלמני בהד̇א[274] אלכלאם אנחנית עלי[275] אלארץ̇[276] וסבתת.[277]

Dn 10:16

והנה כדמות בן אדם נגע על שפתי ואפתח פי ואדבר ואמרה[278] אל[279] העומד לנגדי אדני במראה נהפכו צירי עלי ולא עצרתי כח.

פאד̇א[280] בשכ̇ץ אנסאן קד דנא בשפתיי[281] פפתחת פאי[282] וקלת[283] ללד̇י[284] כאן [285] קאים חד̇אי[286] יא[287] סידי[288] מן רויא הד̇א[289] אלשכ̇ץ[290] קד[291] אכ̇ד̇ני[292] אלמכ̇אץ̇ ולם אחבס קותי.[293]

וגית לאפהמך מא סילקא [קומ]ך פי אכר הדה אלא[יאם] אד קד בקי[ת] אליה[א] נבואת TS Ar 23.29b > D | פאתית לתפטינך מא יואפי שעבך פי אכר אלאיאם אד קד בקי וחי אלזמאן Spiegel

274 בהדי Morag | בהד[א] TS Ar 23.29b > D

275 אלי Oxf 2628.51b | אלכלאם ... עלי TS Ar 23.29b > D | עלי Spiegel > D

276 וכרסת + Oxf 2486.139b + Oxf 2628.51b | וכוריסת TS Ar 23.29b > D

277 וסבתת Oxf 2628.51b and Oxf 2486.139b > L | Oxf 2629.44a illegible

278 ואמרה End of Oxf 2628.51b

279 אל Beginning of Oxf 2628.52a

280 פאדי Morag | פי אדא | פאדא Beginning of Oxf 2629.44b

281 פאדא ביד [בן אדם + Oxf 2628.52a] כאידי אלנאס קד מסת שפתי Oxf 2629.44b + Oxf 2628.52a + 2486.139b

282 פיי Oxf 2486.139b | פי Oxf 2628.52a

283 למן + Oxf 2629.44b and Oxf 2628.52a and 2486.139b

284 ללדי Oxf 2629.44b and Oxf 2628.52a and Oxf 2486.139b > L | לאלדי Spiegel

285 ואקפא + Oxf 2629.44b

286 חדאיי Oxf 2628.52a + Oxf 2486.139b

287 ואקפא חדאי יא Oxf 2629.44b > D

288 סיידי Spiegel + Morag

289 הדי Morag

290 אד + Morag

291 קד Morag > L

292 אכדתני Oxf 2629.44b

293 ק[ות]י Oxf 2486.139b > D | קותי End of Oxf 2486.139b | ביד כיאדי [א]לנאס קד מסת שפת[א]יי פפתחת פאיי וקלת למן כאן קאים חדאיי יא [ס]ידי אן רויא הדא אלשכץ קד אכדני אלמכאץ ולם אחבס [קותי] TS Ar 23.29b > D | קוותי Spiegel

Dn 10:17
ואיך[294] יוכל עבד אדני זה לדבר עם אדני ואני מעתה לא יעמוד בי כחונשמה לא נשארה בי.

פכיף יסתטיע[295] עבד[296] סידי[297] הד̇א[298] אן[299] יכ̇אטב[300] ואנא[301] מן[302] רויתה לם תת̇בת בי[303] קוה[304] ותכ̇אד[305] אלא[306] תבקא פיי[307] נסמה.[308]

Dn 10:18
ויוסף ויגע בי כמראה אדם ויחזקני.

פעאוד אלמלך[309] בצורה[310] אנסאן[311] פמסני[312] ושדדני.[313]

Dn 10:19
ויאמר אל תירא איש חמודות שלום לך חזק וחזק ובדברו עמי החזקתי ואמרה ידבר אדני כי חזקתני.

294 ואיך Beginning of Oxf 2486.140a
295 וכיף יקדר Oxf 2629.44b
296 עב[ד] Oxf 2629.44b > D
297 סיידי Spiegel + Oxf 2628.52a + Morag
298 הדי אן יכ̇אטב סיידי הדי Morag | [ה]ד̇א Oxf 2629.44b > D
299 ליתכלם מע סיידי הד̇א + TS Ar 23.29b
300 אן יכ̇אטב Spiegel and Oxf 2628.52a > L | יכ̇אטבה Oxf 2629.44b | יכ̇אטב L > TS Ar 23.29b
301 לאנא Oxf 2628.52a
302 מן Spiegel > L
303 פיי Oxf 2628.52a + Oxf 2486.140a
304 קווה Spiegel + Morag
305 וכאד Morag | ויכ̇אד Spiegel
306 אן לא Spiegel + Morag
307 פי Oxf 2629.44b | בי Spiegel
308 [מן רוי]תה לם ת[ת̇ב]ת פי קווה [ות]כא[ד אלא תבקא] פיי נסמ[תה] TS Ar > D 23.29b
309 אלמלאך Oxf 2629.44b
310 בצורת Morag | [בצור]ת TS Ar 23.29b > D
311 אנסאן Spiegel > L
312 פדנא בי + Spiegel and Morag | פמסני Spiegel and Morag > L
313 וקואני Oxf 2629.44b | פמסנ[י] פשדדני TS Ar 23.29b > D

וקאל[314] לא תכ̇אף יא איה אלרגל אלכ̇אץ אלסלאם לך תשדד ותאייד פלמא כלמני בד̇לך תשדדת וקלת יכלמני סידי במא שא פאנך קד שדדתני.[315]

Dn 10:20

ויאמר הידעת למה באתי אליך ועתה אשוב להלחם[316] עם שׂר פרס ואני יוצא והנה[317] שׂר[318] יון בא.

פקאל[319] הל עלמת[320] לם[321] גית[322] אליך[323] פאעלם[324] אני[325] סאעוד[326] אלי אלמחארבה[327] מע[328] אלמלך[329] אלמוכל[330] באלפרס[331] ת̇ם אנצרף[332] ויקבל[333] אלמלך אלמווכל באליונאניה.[334]

314 פקאל Spiegel

315 וקאל לא תכאף יא רגל כאץ אלסלם לך אשתד ותאיד ולמא כאטבני בדלך תשדדת וקלת יתכלם סידי אד קד שדדתני Oxf 2486.140a | וקאל לא תכשא יא רג[ל] אלמתמנאאת סלאמה לך אשתד ושדד פקלת יתכלם סיידי אד קוויתני Oxf 2628.52a | פקאל לא תכאף יא רגל אלכאץ סלאמא לך תשדד ותאייד פלמא כלמני בדלך תשדדת פקלת יכלמני סיידי במן שא פאנך קד שדדתני Spiegel | דניאל 10:19 Oxf > L | שדדתני TS Ar 23.29b and 2629.44b End of the readable part of Oxf 2486.140a

316 להלחם Beginning of the readable part of Oxf 2486.140b

317 והנה End of Oxf 2628.52a

318 שׂר Beginning of Oxf 2628.52b

319 [פקא]ל Oxf 2486.140a > D

320 אעלמת Oxf 2629.44b + Oxf 2628.52b + Oxf 2486.140a

321 למא Spiegel + Oxf 2629.44b

322 [פקאל הל על]מת לם [ג]ית TS Ar 23.29b > D

323 פאנני + Oxf 2629.44b

324 [פאע]לם TS Ar 23.29b > D

325 אנני Oxf 2629.44b + Oxf 2628.52b + Oxf 2486.140b | פאעלם אני Oxf 2629.44b > L

326 אליך + Morag | סאעוד Oxf 2486.140b > D

327 [אני ... אלמחא]רבה TS Ar 23.29b > D

328 דאלך + Morag

329 אלמלאך Oxf 2629.44b | אל[מ]לך TS Ar 23.29b > D

330 אלמווכל Morag

331 [ב]אל[פר]ס Oxf 2486.140b > D | אלמוכל באלפרס TS Ar 23.29b > D

332 וינצרף + Oxf 2628.52b

333 ויקבל Oxf 2628.52b > L | [א]נצר[ף] ויק[בל] TS Ar 23.29b > D

334 באליונאנייה Morag

Dn 10: 21

אבל אגיד לך את הרשום בכתב אמת ואין אחד מתחזק עמי על אלה כי עם מיכאל שרכם.

ולכני אכ̇ברך[335] במא[336] קד[337] רסם[338] פי[339] כתאב אלחק וליס אחד[340] עאונני עלי האולי[341] אלא[342] מיכאל אלמוכל[343] בכם.

נעוד בשרח[344] עלי מא פי[345] הד̇ה[346] אלקצה ונקול[347] קד כאן[348] דניאל קאל אולא **וקול דבריו כקול המון** (דניאל 10:6) ולם יקע[349] עלי וגהה. פאי שיא מעני[350] קולה **וכשמעי את קול דבריו ואני[351] הייתי נרדם על פני[352] וג'** (דניאל 10:9)? פנקול אולא קד יגוז אן יכון קולה אלת̇אני שרחא[353] ללאול. וקד ימכן אן יכון אלצות אלאול לם יקצדה בה פלד̇לך לם ירעה. פלמא קצדה באלמכ̇אטבה אראעה ואד̇הלה. ואלמעני[354] פי אן יד אלמלאך אצלחתה עלי רכבתיה וכפיה לתותי לה אלקיאם[355] אד̇[356] יתוכי[357] עלי אלארץ̇ בכפיה[358]

[335] אלמוכל (דניאל 10:20) ... אכברך TS Ar 23.29b > D
[336] [במ]א D < Oxf 2486.140b | במא End of the readable part of TS Ar 23.29b
[337] ק[ד] D < Oxf 2629.44b
[338] עלי + Spiegel
[339] פי L < Spiegel
[340] אח[ד] D < Oxf 2486.140b
[341] הולאי Morag + Spiegel | הולי Oxf 2629.44b
[342] אלא D < Oxf 2486.140b
[343] אלמווכל Morag
[344] בעוד באלשרח Oxf 2629.44b
[345] פי D < Oxf 2486.140b
[346] הדא Oxf 2629.44b
[347] אן + Oxf 2629.44b
[348] [ק]ד כא[ן] D < Oxf 2486.140b
[349] ול[ם י]קע D < Oxf 2486.140b
[350] [פ]א[י שי מע]ני D < Oxf 2486.140b | מענא Oxf 2629.44b
[351] דבריו ואני D < Oxf 2486.140b | ואני L < Oxf 2629.44b
[352] פני End of the readable part of Oxf 2486.140b
[353] שרחא Beginning of Oxf 2486.149a
[354] ואלמענא Oxf 2629.44b
[355] אן + Oxf 2629.44b
[356] אד L < Oxf 2629.44b
[357] י[ת]וכי D < Oxf 2629.44b
[358] [ב]כפיה D < Oxf 2629.44b

ורכבתיה ויניהץ̇. ולד̇לך קאל לה **ועמד על**[359] **עמדך**[360] (דניאל 10:11). ופסרת **דניאל איש חמדות**[361] (דניאל 10:11) ״אלכ̇אץ̇״ עלי מא קדמת מן תצריף[362] **ההר חמד אלהים**[363] **לשבתו** (תה׳ 68:17). ופסרת[364] **להבין** (דניאל 10:12) ״תובה״[365] עלי מעני **ולבבו יבין ושב** (יש׳ 6:10). ופסרת **ולהתענות** (דניאל 10:12) ״צומא״ עלי כ̇אלץ̇ **ועניתם**[366] **את נפשתיכם** (ויק׳ 16:31). וקול[367] אלמלאך לה **כי מן**[368] **היום הראשון, נשמעו דבריך** (דניאל 10:12) יעני אן[369] דעאך אסתגיב מן אולה.[370] ובעת̇ בי[371] פי אגאבתה ולכני[372] תאכ̇רת הד̇ה אלאחד ועשרין[373] יומא פי מצלחה **שׂר פרס**. פלמא קצ̇יתהא גיתך.

ונחתאג[374] אן[375] נגרד האהנא ג̇ מסאיל. אלמסלה אלאולי לם תאכ̇ר גבריאל ען דניאל אחד ועשרין יומא[376] והו קד ארסל אליה מן אליום אלאול? ואלת̇אניה, הל[377] לכל אמה מלך פי אלסמא ינצרהא[378] ויקויהא? פאן כאן כד̇לך[379] פתקויה[380] דינהא וכפרהא[381] מן ענד[382] אלכ̇אלק.[383] ואלת̇אלת̇,[384] והל

359 רגליך + Oxf 2629.44b
360 עמדך Oxf 2629.44b > L
361 איש חמדות Oxf 2629.44b > D
362 תצרי[ף] Oxf 2629.44b > D
363 אלים Oxf 2629.44b
364 ופסר[ת] Oxf 2629.44b > D
365 [ופסרת] להב[ין תובה] Oxf 2629.44b > D
366 צומ[א] עלי כ̇[אלץ] ועני[תם] Oxf 2629.44b > D
367 וקיל Oxf 2629.44b
368 מ[ן] Oxf 2629.44b > D
369 [ד]ברי[ך] יעני א[ן] Oxf 2629.44b > D
370 אול[ה] Oxf 2629.44b > D
371 בי Oxf 2629.44b > L
372 לכן Oxf 2629.44b
373 אל[כא] Oxf 2629.44b > D
374 ונחתאג End of Oxf 2486.149a
375 אן Beginning of Oxf 2486.149b
376 הד̇ה אלאחד ועשרין יומא [... אחד ועשרין יומא] הו Oxf > D homeoteleuton 2629.44b
377 ואלת̇א[נ]י [ה]ל Oxf 2629.44b > D
378 [ינ]צ[רהא] Oxf 2629.44b > D
379 כדאל[ך] Oxf 2629.44b > D
380 תלך יבעת̇הא + Oxf 2629.44b
381 דינהא וכפרהא Oxf 2629.44b > L
382 אללה + Oxf 2629.44b

האולי[385] אלמלאיכה ימאנע בעצ̇הם[386] בעץ[387] ויחארב בעצ̇הם בעץ?[388] פאן כאן כד̇אך[389] פבאמר רבהם או באכ̇תיארהם?[390] פנגיב ען אלמסלה אלאולי ונקול[391] אן גבריאל[392] למא[393] קאל **שׂר מלכות פרס עמד לנגדי עשרים ואחד יום**[394] (דניאל 10:13) דלנא עלי[395] אן רבה אועז אליה[396] גואב דניאל מן אליום[397] אלאול. וקאל לה לא תודה[398] אליה אלא בעד[399] מא[400] תסתתם[401] מא אמרתך פי מלך[402] אלפרס. פמכת̇ גבריאל פי ד̇לך[403] אחד ועשרין[404] יומא. וכאן ד̇לך במקדאר[405] מא[406] תברע[407] בה[408] דניאל צומא וצלוה.[409] ונגיב ען

[383] אלכאלק Oxf 2629.44b < L
[384] ואלג̇ Oxf 2629.44b
[385] הולי Oxf 2629.44b
[386] [ימ]אנע בע[צהם] Oxf 2629.44b < D
[387] בעצא Oxf 2629.44b
[388] יחארב בעצהם בעץ Oxf 2629.44b < L
[389] כדלך Oxf 2629.44b
[390] פבאמ[ר רבהם] או באלכתיארה[ם] Oxf 2629.44b < D
[391] ו[נ]קול Oxf 2486.149b < D
[392] אן גבריאל Oxf 2629.44b < L
[393] ולמא Oxf 2629.44b
[394] מלכ̇ פרס ע[מד] לנגד[י כ̇]א [יומא] Oxf 2629.44b < D
[395] עלי Oxf 2629.44b < L
[396] או[עז א]ליה Oxf 2629.44b < D
[397] אליום Oxf 2629.44b < D
[398] תודיה Oxf 2629.44b
[399] אן + Oxf 2629.44b
[400] מא Oxf 2629.44b < L
[401] פי אמר אלפרס + Oxf 2629.44b
[402] מא אמרתך פי מלך Oxf 2629.44b < L
[403] דלך[ך] Oxf 2629.44b < D
[404] כא̇ Oxf 2629.44b
[405] במק[ד]א[ר] Oxf 2629.44b < D
[406] מא End of Oxf 2486.149b
[407] תברע Beginning of Oxf 2486.150a | תב[ר]ע Oxf 2629.44b < D
[408] ב[ה] Oxf 2629.44b < D
[409] וצלאה Oxf 2629.44b

אלמסאלה[410] אלת̇אניה ונקול אנה[411] אית אמה[412] אכ̇רגת אלי אלנאס[413] אוגבת אלחכמה אן[414] ינצב להא רב אלעאלמין[415] מלכא מן אלמלאיכה ישדד[416] אמרהא ויודהא[417] מן אול דולתהא אלי אכ̇ר מדתהא.

וכמא קאל[418] גבריאל לדניאל **ואני בשנת אחד לדריוש המדי עמדי למחזיק ולמעוז לו** (דניאל 11:1). יעני אן רבה אוקפה ליויד אמרה. ומעני **בשנת אחד** (דניאל 11:1) יריד בה **מן שנת אחד**, אי מן אול[419] מא געל[420] לה דולה. וכד̇אך לסאיר[421] אלאמם. והד̇ה[422] מן ענד[423] אללה תקויה למלכהא לא תקויה לדינהא.[424] כמא אנה יעטי אלמלוך קוה למלכהם לא לכפרהם.[425] וכמא ענד אלנאס כלהם אלאסתטאעה לאכ̇תיארהם ולא יפרד ד̇לך ויקאל אנה קואהם עלי[426] [...][427] תלך[428] אלטאעה לא ג̇ירהא. ונגיב ען אלמסלה אלת̇אלת̇ה ונקול אן הד̇ה אלמחארבה אלמד̇כורה בין אלמלאיכה ליסת תנאזע ותג̇לב חתי יט̇פר מן יט̇פר. ולכנהא צרף מן בעצ̇הם לבעץ̇ באמר אללה חתי תבקי אלאמה אלמצרופה בג̇יר מלך יודהא פתכמל אמורהא ותבטל דולתהא. ואנמא סמי ד̇לך **מלחמה** (דניאל 10:20) עלי מגאז אלקול ואסתעארתה מן אפעאל אלמלוך ואלסלאטין. אלא תרי אן מת̇ל הד̇א קד קיל פי אפעאל אללה. מנהא במצר: **יוי**

[410] אלמסלה Oxf 2629.44b + Oxf 2486.150a

[411] אנה Oxf 2629.44b > L

[412] אי אומה Oxf 2629.44b

[413] אכרגת אלי אלנאס Oxf 2629.44b > D

[414] פאן אלחכמה אוגבת אן Oxf 2629.44b

[415] [ר]ב אלעאל[מי]ן Oxf 2629.44b > D

[416] מ[ן ... אלמלאיכה ישדד] Oxf 2629.44b > D

[417] ואן יודהא Oxf 2629.44b

[418] אלי אכר מדתהא וכמא קאל Oxf 2629.44b > D

[419] עמדי ... מן אול Oxf 2629.44b > D

[420] געל Oxf 2629.44b > D

[421] וכדלך סאיר Oxf 2629.44b

[422] נובא ? Oxf 2629.44b

[423] ענד Oxf 2629.44b > D

[424] תק[ויה למלכהא לא תקויה] Oxf 2629.44b > D

[425] לכ[פרהם] Oxf 2629.44b > D | לכפרהם End of the readable part of Oxf 2629.44b

[426] עלי End of the readable part of Oxf 2486.150a

[427] [...] Oxf 2486.150a > D

[428] תלך Beginning of Oxf 2486.150b

ילחם לכם (שמ׳ 14:14). ופי עצר יהושע: **כי יוי נלחם לישׂראל** (יהושע 10:14). וקאל נחמיה **אלהינו ילחם לנו** (נחמיה 4:14). וקאל זכריה **ויצא יוי ונלחם בגוים ההם כיום הלחמו ביום קרב** (זכריה 14:3). וקאל לנא וקת טרדנא מן אלבלד **ונלחמתי**[429] **אני אתכם ביד נטויה ובזרוע חזקה ובאף**[430] **ובחמה ובשטף גדול** (ירמ׳ 21:5). פכמא אן הדׂה אלמלחמות אלמנסובה אלי אלכׂאלק ליסת מגאחשה ולא מחארבה ואנמא כׂאלץ מעאניהא צרף ותמכן קום כדׂאך הדׂה אלמלחמות אלמנסובה אלי אלמלאיכה אנמא הי צרף אמה ותמכין אמה.

ואדׂ קד אגבנא ען הדׂה אלמסאיל אלתׂלאתׂה נאכׂדׂ פי תמאם שרוח אלקצה. ונקול קול גבריאל לדניאל **ושׂר מלכות פרס עמד לנגדי עשרים ואחד יום** (דניאל 10:13) ידל עלי אן רבה קאל לה אגב דניאל בעד אסתתמאמך מא אמרתתך פי פרס. וקולה לה **והנה מיכאל אחד השׂרים הראשנים בא לעזרני** (דניאל 10:13) ידל עלי אן מיכאל עאונה באמר רבה עלי אכׂתר אמור אלקום. ותסמיתה לה **אחד השׂרים הראשנים** (דניאל 10:13) ידל בדׂלך אנה מן **שׂרי ישׂראל**. מתׂל אלמלאך אלדׂי טׂהר ליעקב[431] וסמאה ישׂראל.[432] ולמשה,[433] **וירא מלך יוי אליו בלבת אש** (שמ׳ 3:2). וליהושע, **כי אני שׂר צבא יוי עתה באתי** (יהושע 5:14) וסאיר אלמלאיכה אלדׂין טׂהרו לנביאי ישׂראל. וקד יגוז אן יכונו כתׂירין, וקד יגוז אן יכון הו ואחד. וקולה לה **השׂרים הראשנים** (דניאל 10:13) לטׂהורה פי אעצאר מכׂתלפה ובצור מכׂתלפה.

וקולה לה **את אשר יקרה לעמך באחרית הימים** (דניאל 10:14) יעני פי אכׂר אלשעבוד אלדׂי אבתדי אולה פי וקת דניאל ונחן פי אכׂרה אלי אלאן. וקד יכתב **יקרה** (דניאל 10:14) אלדׂי הו יערץׂ בהי ובאלף כמא קאל יעקב **את אשר יקרא אתכם** (בר׳ 49:1). והדׂא מתׂל **וקרהו** (בר׳ 44:29) **וקראהו** (בר׳ 42:38), ואלגמיע גאיז. וקול דניאל **נתתי פני ארצה ונאלמתי** (דניאל 10:15) לם יעני אנה וקע עלי וגהה כׂאלמרה אלאולי. לכנה אנחני עלי אלארץׂ וסבת חתי אידה אלמלאך. ומעני **כמראה אדם** (דניאל 10:18), **וכדמות בני אדם** (דניאל 10:16)

429 ונלחמתי End of the readable part of Oxf 2486.150b
430 ובאף Beginning of Oxf 2486.141a
431 ל[יע]קב Oxf 2486.141a > D
432 יש[רא]ל Oxf 2486.141a > D ׀ ישראל End of Oxf 2486.141a
433 ולמשה Beginning of Oxf 2486.141b

ליונסה[434] אד[435] לא יאנס אלאנסאן אלא אלי [...][436] וצורתה. וקולה **במראה נהפכו צירי וג׳** (דניאל 10:16), **והיך יוכל וג׳** (דניאל 10:17) יעני אדׄא כאן רויה אלמלאך אראעתה הדׄא אלרוע אלעטׄים פכיף מן מכׄאטבתה.

ופסרת **חֲזַק וַחֲזָק** (דניאך 10:19) מקאם **חזק ואמץ** (דב׳ 31:7) למוצׄע תכראר. וקולה לה פי אלכׄטאב אלתׄאני **הידעת למא באתי אליך** (דניאל 10:20) וקד כאן ערפה פי אלכׄטאב אלאול **ובאתי להבינך אשר יקרה לעמך באחרית הימים** (דניאל 10:14)? אלסבב פי דׄלך אנה למא ראה מרתעדא כמא קאל **עמדתי מרעיד** (דניאל 10:11) וקע לה לעל דניאל לם יפהם אלכלאם. פאחתאג אן יקול לה **הידעת למא באתי אליך** (דניאל 10:20) חתי אן כאן לם יחפטׄ אלקול אעאדה עליה. ודׄלך אן אלמלאיכה לם תעלם מא פי קלוב אלנאס. ואנמא יעלם דׄלך אלכׄאלק נפסה כמא קאל **כי אתה לבדך ידעת את לבב בני האדם**[437] (דהי״ב׳ 6:30). פלמא[438] אמסך דניאל עלי דׄלך או לעלה קד קאל לה נעם ואכׄתצר אתׄבאתה תמם לה גבריאל אלקצה פקאל **ועתה אשוב להלחם עם שׂרי פרס** (דניאל 10:20) למוצׄע מא כאן בקי מן אמור אלקום חתי ינצרף גבריאל ען אלמעאונה ותאתי דולה אליונאניין. דׄאך קולה **ואני יוצא והנה שׂר יון בא** (דניאל 10:20). וקולה לה **אבל אגיד לך את הרשים בכתב אמת** (דניאל 10:21), עלי מא פסרנא פי קולה **אמת הדבר** (דניאל 10:1). יריד בה אנה לא בשרט ולא אסתתׄני ודׄאך כקולה לדויד **נשבע יוי לדויד אמת לא ישוב ממנה** (תה׳ 132:11). אמא ולדך אלאול פהו יכׄלפך בלא אססתתׄני עליה, **מפרי בטנך אשית לכסה לך** (תה׳ 132:11) והו שלמה. ואמא מן בעדה פאן כאנו עלי טאעתה כמא קאל בעדה **אם ישמרו בניך בריתי ועדתי זו אלמדם גם בניהם עדי עד ישבו לכסה לך** (תה׳ 132:12). ולדׄלך למא אכׄטא שלמה לם[439] ינקץ[440] הו שיא ונקץ ולדה דׄלך. וכדׄלך אהל **בית שני** טׄמן להם אלרגוע אלי אלבלד בגׄיר אסתתׄני כמא קאל **ונטעתים בארץ הזאת באמת** (ירמ׳ 32:41). וכדׄלך נחן טׄמן לנא אלישועה בלא אסתתׄני כמא קאל **תתן אמת ליעקב** (מיכה 7:20). וכדׄלך קאל אלמלאך לדניאל **את הרשים בכתב אמת**

[434] ליונסה End of Oxf 2486.141a

[435] אד Beginning of Oxf 2486.142a

[436] מ...ה Oxf 2486.142a > D

[437] האדם End of Oxf 2486.142a

[438] פלמא Beginning of Oxf 2486.142b | פל[מ]א Oxf 2486.142b > D

[439] לם End of Oxf 2486.142b

[440] ינקץ Beginning of Oxf 2486.147a

(דניאל 10:21). וכדׄלך קאל פי תחקיק אלישועה **בי נשבעתי יצא מפי צדקה דבר ולא ישוב כי לא תכרע כל ברך ותשבע כל לשון** (יש׳ 45:23). ואיצׄא **ביוי לי אמר צדקות ועוז** (יש׳ 45:24) וסאיר אלקצה. תׄם קאל לה גבריאל

תֿם קאל לה גבריאל

Dn 11:1
ואני בשנת אחד לדריוש המדי עמדי למחזיק ולמעוז לו.

ואנא מן אלסנה אלאולי לדריוש אלמדי[1] אוקפת לאשדדה[2] ולאעזה.[3]

הדֿא אלקטב אלדֿי ידל עלי נצב **שׂרים** לכל אמה לישדד אמורהא[4] [...][5] פהו[6] כמא קאל יחזקאל **וחזקתי את זרעות מלך בבל** (יח׳ 30:24). ואמא **ולמעוז** (דניאל 11:1) פהו כמא קאל ישעיהו **ומלך עז ימשָׁל בם** (יש׳ 19:4). פלם יזל גבריאל משירא ומוידא מלכות פרס ואכֿר דֿלך פי יומא אלדֿי וקף **שׂר פרס** בין ידיה. פכאנה כאן יעלמה פיהא ויבצרה ויפתח לה טרק אלאיד. פלמא ואפי מיכאל סלם גבריאל **שׂר פרס** אליה ליעלמה ויודה הו. וצאר הו אלי דניאל פערפה אלגואב כמא קאל לה **בא לעזרני** (דניאל 10:13), **ובאתי להבינך** (דניאל 10:14). פלמא תמם לה אלגואב רגע יעון **שׂר פרס** פי מחארבתה לאעדאיה כמא קאל **ועתה אשוב להלחם עם שׂר פרס** (דניאל 10:20). ודֿאך כקולה **התלך עמי**[7] **למלחמה רמות גלעד** (מל״א׳ 22:4). פלמא אנקצֿת דולה אלפרס כֿרג גבריאל ען אלמעאונה כמא קאל **ואני יוצא והנה שׂר יון בא** (דניאל 10:20) אדֿ לם יאמר במעאונה[8] אליונאניין, ואנמא אמר[9] במעאונה[10] אלפרס עלי מא שרחנא.

[1] אלמאדי Oxf 2628.52b + Oxf 2486.147a
[2] לאשדה Oxf 2628.52b
[3] ואעזה Oxf 2628.52b + Oxf 2486.147a
[4] אמורהא End of the readable part of Oxf 2486.147a
[5] [...] Oxf 2486.147a > D
[6] פהו Beginning of Oxf 2486.147b
[7] אתי MT
[8] יאמר במעונה Uncertain lesson
[9] אמר End of Oxf 2486.147b
[10] במעונה Beginning of Oxf 2486.148a

ואעלם[11] עלמך אללה אנא קד וצלנא אלי [...][12] גֹרץ̇ הדֹא אלגז אלעאשר והו אכֿבאר אלמלוך אלתי תקום פי אלארץ̇ מן וקת דניאל אלי וקת אלישועה. וליס הי גמיע אלחואדתֿ אלתי תכון פי אלף סנה שֹלֹהֹ סנה. לאנך לו גמעת חואדת סנה ואחדה עלי אלתקצי למלאת אלדפאתר. ולכנהא עיון אלחואדתֿ ואצול מן אלאכֿבאר אחתיג אלי מערפתהא. ופיהא חאדתֿה פימא בין עשרין סנה וחאדתֿה פימא בין תסעין סנה ואכתֿר ואקל. אלא אן גמלה דֿלך מצֿמן סבעה וארבעין פסוק. מנהא אלפסוק אלאול פי אואכֿר אמור מלוך אלפרס. תֿם יגֿ פסוק פי מלוך אליונאניה. תֿם עשרין פסוק פי מלוך אדום. תֿם עשרה פואסיק פי מלוך ישמעאל. פדֿלך ארבעה[13] וארבעין[14] פסוק. ותבקא אלגֿ פואסיק אלאכֿירה. אחדהא פי אלישועה והו **ובעת ההיא יעמד מיכאל וג׳** (דניאל 12:1) ואלבֿ פי תחיה **המתים** והו **ורבים מישׁנה אדמת וג׳** (דניאל 12:2). ואלתֿאלתֿ פי תֿואב אלאכֿרה והו **והמשׂכילים יזהירו כזהר הרקיע וג׳** (דניאל 12:3).

ואנמא אחתאג אלי תקדים הדֿא אלכלאם לאן עואם אלנאס יתוהמון אן גבריאל לם יבק חאדתֿה תכון פי זמאן אלשעבוד חתי כשפהא לדניאל, מן כבירה אלי צגֿירה. פאקול אן ליס אלאמר כמא תוהמו. ולו אסתופי לה חואדתֿ סנה ואחדה לכאנת כשיעור אלמקרא או אכתֿר. ואיצֿא אכֿתצר דֿלך ליכון משאכלא למא פי אלתוראה. כמא עלמת אן חואדתֿ אלף סנה תֿרנֿהֿ גמעת פי פרשה ואחדה. ואיצֿא חואדתֿ תֿלתֿ מאיה וארבעין[15] סנה[16] גמעת פי אלפרשה אלתֿאניה. וכדֿלך חואדתֿ מצר לם יתקדם מנהא אלא בפסוקין פקט המא נפס אלחאגה. כדֿאך פי אמור האולי אלמלוך לם ירסם לנא אלא עיונא מן חואדתֿהם. פבעצֿהא לנא בהא תעלק מתֿל **ומשׂכילי עם יבינו לרבים ונכשלו בחרב ובלהבה בשבי ובבזה ימים** (דניאל 11:33). ומתֿלה **ובני פריצי עמך ינשׂאו להעמיד חזון ונכשלו** (דניאל 11:14). ובעצֿהא לתכון לנא איאת עלי מא יבשרנא בה מתֿל מא כאנת קצה כורש איה לישועה. כדֿאך קצה **ותחץ לארבע רוחות השמים** (דניאל 11:4). וקצה **ואלה ימלטו מידו אדום ומואב וראשית בני עמון** (דניאל 11:41). וקצה **ולובים וכושים במצעדיו** (דניאל 11:43). הדֿה ואמתֿאלהא עלי מא סאשרחהא איאת לבני

[11] [ואעו]לם Oxf 2486.148a > D

[12] [...] Oxf 2486.148a > D

[13] ארבעה End of Oxf 2486.148a

[14] ארבעין Beginning of Oxf 2486.148b

[15] וארבעין End of Oxf 2486.148b

[16] סנה Beginning of Oxf 2486.167a

אסראיל עלי צחה אלישועה ואלנחמות אדֹא שאהדוהא. ואנמא אתסע גבריאל פי אכֹבאר אלמלוך פקאל[17] פיהא[18] ארבעה וארבעין פסוקא. ואכֹתצר פי אמר אלישועה פלם יקאל פיהא אלא תֹלתֹה פואסיק פקט. לאן אלישועה קד תכלמת אלאנביא פי אמרהא אלכלאם אלטויל אלואסע. ודֹלך כמא קאל ישעיהו וירמיהו ויחזקאל וגֹירהם. ואמא אמור **ארבע מלכיות** פלם תכלמת אלאנביא פיהא אלא באלאימא. פלדֹלך אתסע גבריאל פימא אכֹתצר קבלה ואכֹתצר פימא אתסע בה קבלה.

ואדֹ קד קדמת אלפואסיק הדֹה אלמקדמאת פארי אן אקדם איצֹא אלפאטֹא גֹריבה תסתעמל פי הדֹה אלקצה עלי אלאכתֹר. פאפסרהא ליסתעאן בהא עלי שרח גמלה אלקצה. ואסתשהד לתפסירי להא במא יקע מתֹלה פי סאיר אלמקרא. ואחצי מנהא יגֹ לפטֹה. פמנהא תסמיה אלולד **אחרית**. קאל האהנא **ולא**[19] **לאחריתו**[20] (דניאל 11:4). ותחדיד אללפטֹה ״כֹלף״ ״ועקב״. ודֹאך כקול עמוס **ואחריתכן בסירות דוגה** (עמוס 4:2). וקאל אלמתרגם **ובנתכון**. וכקול יחזקאל **ואכריתך בחרב תפול** (יח׳ 23:25). וכקול ירמיהו **ובאחריתו יהיה נבל** (ירמ׳ 7:11). ואלתֹאני תסמיה אלחצן **מעוז** אד קאל **וישב ויתגרה עד מעוזו** (דניאל 11:10). ודֹאך כקול עמוס **והורד ממך עזך** (עמוס 3:11). ואלתֹאלתֹ תסמיה אלסיף **כלה** אדֹ קאל **ויעמד בארץ הצבי וכלה בידו** (דניאל 11:16). ודֹאך כקולה **כלה ונחרצה** (דניאל 9:27). ואלראבע **בת** גמאעה אדֹ קאל **ובת מלך הנגב תבוא** (דניאל 11:6) ודֹאך כקול **בת ציון** (יש׳ 1:8), **בת צידון** (יש׳ 23:12), **בת בבל** (תה׳ 137:8), **בת כשדים** (יש׳ 47:1) ואשבאההא. ואלכֹאמס **נשים** (דניאל 11:37) ״מדן״ (?) **נשים שאננות קומה שמענה קולי בנות בוטחות האזנה אמרתי**[21] (יש׳ 32:9). ואלסאדס[22] **רבים ישראל**. ודֹאך קולה **יבינו לרבים** (דניאל 11:33), **ומצדיקי הרבים** (דניאל 12:3). ואלסאבע **מישירים**, צלח אדֹ קאל **לעשות מישרים** (דניאל 11:6). וצרף מנה **ישירים**, מסתאמנין, אדֹ קאל **וישירים עמו יעשה** (דניאל 11:17). ודֹאך כקול אכיש לדויד **כי ישר אתה** (של״א׳ 29:6). וקאל **מיום נפלו** (של״א׳ 29:3). ואלתאמן **חלקות** (דניאל 11:32) **וחלקלקות** (דניאל 11:21.34), חיל, מקאם **תחבלות** עלי מא סנדֹכר. ואלתאסע **שטיפה**, סיח גיש פי אלבלאד, והי

[17] פ[ק]א]ל] Oxf 2486.167a > D ׀ פקאל End of Oxf 2486.167a

[18] פיהא Beginning of Oxf 2486.167b

[19] ולא End of Oxf 2486.167b

[20] לאחריתו Beginning of Oxf 2486.155a

[21] אמרתי End of Oxf 2486.155a

[22] ואלסאדס Beginning of Oxf 2486.155b

כת̇ירה אלאסתעמאל פי אלקצה. והי מת̇ל **וכלף ביהודה שטף ועבר** (יש׳ 8:8). ואלעאשר **עתים**, משורה, אד̇ יקול **ומחזיקה בעתים** (דניאל 11:6). וד̇אך כקולה **ויאמר המלך לחכמים ידעי העתים** (אסתר 1:13). ואליא̇ **חרפה**, סבי, ד̇אך קולה **בלתי חרפתו ישיב לו** (דניאל 11:18). והו מת̇ל קולה **אשר נשאר מן השבי שם במדינה ברעה גדולה ובחרפה וחומת ירושלם**[23] **מפורצת**[24] **ושעריה אֻכלו באש** (נחמיה 1:3). ואליב̇ **נשיאה**, ספי ואנתסאף, אד̇ יקול **ונשא ההמון** (דניאל 11:12). והו מת̇ל **ונשא אתכם בצנות** (עמוס 4:2). ואליג̇ **כזב**, מא לא יג̇י מנה שיא. ד̇אך קולה **ועל שלחן אחד כזב ידברו** (דניאל 11:27). והו מת̇ל קול מיכיהו **הנה נתן ייי רוח שקר בפי נביאיך אלה** (מל״א׳ 22:23). פהד̇ה אליג̇ לפט̇ה מסתעמלה פי הד̇ה אלקצה כאנהא אנמא פרדת להא כ̇אצה. וד̇אך כאסתעמאל קהלת **תחת השמש** (קהלת 1:3) מקאם **תחת השמים**. וכאסתעמאל אליהו לפט̇ה **אור** מקאם לפט̇ה **מטר**. ואסתעמאל אלתוראה **שלה** (בר׳ 49:10) **ושליתה** (דב׳ 28:57) מקאם **בנו ובנה**. וסאיר מא יכ̇ץ בה ספר מן אללפט̇ אמא עלי אלתכ̇ציץ ואמא עלי אלתכת̇יר. פאד̇ קד קדמת הד̇ה אלאלפאט̇ אלמסתכ̇דמה פי אלקצה אבתדי[25] באלפסוק[26] אלאול אלד̇י הו פי אכ̇ר ממלכה אלפרס ואקול קאל לה גבריאל

Dn 11:2

ועתה אמת אגיד לך הנה עוד שלשה מלכים עמדים לפרס והרביעי יעשיר עשר גדול מכל וכחזקתו בעשרו יעיר הכל את מלכות יון.

ואלאן חקא אקול לך[27] קד בקי ללפרס[28] ג̇[29] מלוך ואלראבע[30] יסתג̇ני ג̇נא עט̇ים[31] מן גמיעהם פאד̇א[32] תמכן מן יסארה אט̇הר[33] אלכל מלך[34] אליונאניין.

23 ירו[שלם] Oxf 2486.155b > D | ירושלם End of Oxf 2486.155b

24 מפורצת Beginning of Oxf 2486.151a

25 אבתדי End of Oxf 2486.151a

26 באלפסוק Beginning of Oxf 2486.151b

27 הודא + Spiegel

28 לאלפרס Spiegel + Morag

29 תלת Oxf 2486.151b | תלאת Spiegel

30 ואלד Oxf 2628.52b

31 עצמא Spiegel + Morag

32 פאדי Spiegel + Morag

33 אצהר Spiegel + Morag

34 מלוך Spiegel

אול הד׳א אלרסם מן **דריוש המדי**. פכאן הו אלמלך אלאול ללפרס עלי בלד אלשאם. ובעדה ג׳ מלוך אכ׳ר, כורש ואחשורוש וארתחשסתא, עלי מא שרחנא פי **ספר השנים** (דניאל 9:2). ואלראבע אלד׳י ייסר אכת׳ר[35] מן[36] אלת׳לת׳ה[37] הו ארתחשסתא. ולד׳לך קיל לה **מלך מלכיא** (עזרא 7:12) כמא קיל לנבוכדנצר **מלך מלכים** (יח׳ 26:7). והד׳א אלרביעי הו **שלישי** מן אלבאקיין. והו **רביעי לדריוש המדי**. ובהד׳א אלקול יבטל קול מן זעם אן בין מלך אלכסדאניין ומלך אליונאניין אכ׳תר מן ארבעה מלוך ללפרס. לאן דריוש אלאול מסנד מע מלוך אלכסדאניין אד׳ קאל פיה **אשר המלך על מלכות כשדים** (דניאל 9:1). ואלראבע מסתנד עליה מלך אליונאניין כמא קאל **וכחזקתו בעשרו יעיר הכל את מלכות יון** (דניאל 11:2). פהד׳א רדא עלי אלנצארי ובעץ׳ אלמכ׳אלפין אלד׳ין ידעון יז׳ מלכא ללפרס. וקולה **יעיר הכל** (דניאל 11:2) ליס יעני אנה בעץ׳ אלאמרא ואלגיוש ירון נצב אליונאני בל כלהם אגמעין בג׳יר כ׳לף אחד. וד׳לך בעד ארבעה ות׳לת׳ין סנה כמא שאהדנא[38] אלמלך.[39] ת׳ם לארתחשסתא אלד׳ סנה. ולם יד׳כר האהנא אן תמאם בנא אלבית אלת׳אני יכון פי זמאנה לאנה קד שרחה פי קצה **שבועים שבעים** (דניאל 9:24) פי אלגז אלתאסע שרחא תאמא.

ת׳ם אד׳כר נצוץ הד׳ה אלת׳לאת׳ה וארבעין פסוקא אלד׳י יג׳ מנהא לליונאניין, כ׳ לאדום, עשרה לישמעאל. ואקול אן פי ראס כל דולה יד׳כר **ועשׂה כרצונו** (דניאל 11:3.16.36). כמא כאן ד׳כר פי אלכסדאני **די הוה צבא הוה קטל וג׳** (דניאל 5:19). וכמא כאן ד׳כר פי אבתדי מלכות פרס **ראיתי את האיל מנגח, ועשׂה כרצונו והגדיל** (דניאל 8:4). כד׳אך פי אול אליג׳ אלפסוק אלתי לליונאניין **ועמד מלך גבור ומשל ממשל רב ועשה כרצנו** (דניאל 11:3), [**ועשה כרצונו**] **המלך ויתרומם וג׳** (דניאל 11:36). ואד׳ קד קדמת הד׳א איצ׳א פאבתדי אלאן[40] בפואסיק[41] אליונאניין ואקול אולהא

Dn 11:3

ועמד מלך גבור ומשל ממשל רב ועשׂה כרצנו.

[35] אכת[ר] Oxf 2486.151b > D

[36] מן End of Oxf 2486.151b

[37] אלתלתה Beginning of Oxf 2486.152a

[38] שאהדנא End of Oxf 2486.152a

[39] אלמלך Beginning of Oxf 2486.152b

[40] אלאן End of Oxf 2486.152b

[41] בפואסיק Beginning of Oxf 2486.153a

פיקום להם מלך גבאר ויתסלטן סלטאנא[42] עטֿימא[43] ויעמל מא ירצֿאה.

Dn 11:4

וכעמדו תשבר מלכותו ותחץ לארבע רוחות השמים ולא לאחריתו ולא כמשלו אשר משל כי תנתש מלכותו ולאחרים מלבד אלה.

וענד[44] תמאם קיאמה תנכסר מלכותה ותנקסם לארבע גהאת אלסמא ולא תכון[45] לעקבה ולא[46] לסלטאנה[47] אלדֿי[48] תסלט[49] לכן ממלכתה תתשדֿב ותציר לאכֿרין סוי[50] הולאי.[51]

Dn 11:5

ויחזק מלך הנגב ומן שריו ויחזק עליו ומשל ממשל רב ממשלתו.[52]

וישתד[53] מלך אלגנוב ובעץֿ רוסאה[54] תֿם יקוי[55] עליה ויתסלט מן סלטאנה סלטאן[56] עטֿים.[57]

קולה **ועמד מלך גבור** (דניאל 11:3), תצפחנא מא כאן פוגדנאה דֿא אלקרנין, אעני אלאכסנדרוס. וקולה **ומשל ממשל רב** (דניאל 11:3) יריד בה אכתֿר אלעאלם. וקולה **ועשה כרצנו** (דניאל 11:3) אן יהדם ויבני וינקל אמם מן בלד אלי בלד. ושביה במא קאל סנחריב **ואסיר גבולת עמים ועתידתיהם**

[42] ויתצלטן צלטאנא Morag

[43] עצימא Spiegel + Morag

[44] פענד Spiegel

[45] תכן Oxf 2486.153a

[46] תכון + Spiegel

[47] בסלטאנה Oxf 2486.153a ׀ כסלטאנה Oxf 2628.53a

[48] אלתי Oxf 2628.53a + Oxf 2486.153a

[49] תסלט Morag

[50] סוא Spiegel + Oxf 2628.53a

[51] האולי Oxf 2486.153a ׀ הולי Oxf 2628.53a

[52] ממשלתו End of Oxf 2486.153a

[53] וישתד Beginning of Oxf 2486.153b

[54] רייסאה Morag ׀ ריסאה Spiegel ׀ חתי + Morag

[55] יקוא Spiegel

[56] ויצלט מו צלטאנה צלטאו Morag

[57] עצים Spiegel + Morag

שׁמתיו[58] **ואריד כביר** (יש׳ 10:13). וקולה **וכעמדו** (דניאל 11:4) יריד בעד תמאם **עמדו**, והו בעד מותה. וכאן דׄלך אתנאעשר סנה. תׄם **תשבר מלכותו** (דניאל 11:4) ותנקסם ארבע אקסאם והי עלי ארבע גהאת מן בלד אלשאם לאנהא אלמדׄכורה פי אלקצה. וכדׄלך **והבאתי אל עילם ארבע רוחות מארבע קצות השמים**[59] (ירמ׳ 49:36) מן[60] בלד עילם. ולא תכון מנהא חצה ואחדה לולדה לקולה **ולא לאחריתו** (דניאל 11:4). והו עקבה עלי מא קדמנא מן שרח אלאלפאטׄ. ומעני **ולא כמשלו אשר משל** (דניאל 11:4), :ולא לואחד מן מדׄהבה ולא מן סירתה״. וקולה **כי תנתש מלכותו** (דניאל 11:4) יעני ולא בלדה איצׄא כקולה **ויתשם ייי מעל אדמתם** (דב׳ 29:27). וקולה **ולאחרים מלבד אלה** (דניאל 11:4) יעני ולא אלדׄין סידׄכרהמא והמא **מלך הצפון ומלך הנגב**. פינקסם אלמלך אלי אתׄנין אכׄרין סוי הדׄין והמא **מלך המזרח ומלך המערב**, לם תשרחהמא פיציר אלגמיע דׄ. פאמא **מלך המזרח ומלך המערב** פלא תטול מדתהמא. ולכן **מלך הנגב** יתׄבת בעדהמא לקולה **ויחזק מלך הנגב** (דניאל 11:5). והדׄא כקולה **ויחזק העם אשר אחרי תבני בן גינת** (מל״א׳ 16:22). פאדׄא אקאם[61] מדה[62] כדׄאך הו ובעץׄ אצחאבה וחדהם טׄהר עליה מלך הצפון לתמאם אלפסוק **ויחזק עליו ומשל** (דניאל 11:5) **משל** רגל קוי יכון **ממשל רב ממשלתו** (דניאל 11:5). פיתׄבת אלמלכאן וחדהמא, **מלך הנגב**, מלך אלשאם **ומלך הצפון**, מלך אלעראק. תׄם קאל

Dn 11:6

ולקץ שנים יחדו יתחברו ובת מלך הנגב תבוא אל מלך הצפון לעשות מישרים ולא תעצר כח הזרוע ולא יעמד וזרועו תנתן היא ומביאיה והולידה ומחזיקה בעתים.

ואלי מדה[63] סנין יתאלפאן[64] וגמאעה מלך[65] אלשאם תציר[66] אלי מלך אלעראק[67] לתעמל[68] צלחא ווטאה[69] ולא תחבס קוה[70] דׄראעהא ולא[71] תתׄבת

[58] שושתי TM
[59] השמים End of Oxf 2486.153b
[60] מן Beginning of Oxf 2486.154a
[61] אקאם End of Oxf 2486.154a
[62] מדה Beginning of Oxf 2486.154b
[63] ואלא מדת Spiegel
[64] יאתלפאן Oxf 2486.154b
[65] מלוך Oxf 2486.154b
[66] תסיר Spiegel
[67] אלערק Spiegel

גמאעתה ולא קותה[72] ותסלם הי ומדאכ̇להא[73] ואסתאד̇הא[74] ומוידיהא[75] באלמשורה.[76]

Dn 11:7

ועמד[77] מנצר שרשיה כנו ויבא אל החיל ויבא במעוז מלך הצפון ועשה בהם והחזיק.

ת̇ם יקום[78] מן פרע אצולהא[79] עלי מנברה וידכ̇ל[80] גיש מלך[81] אלעראק וידכ̇ל[82] חצנה[83] ויצנע באהלהא מא יריד ויתמכן מנהא.

Dn 11:8

וגם אלהיהם עם נסיכיהם עם כלי חמדתם כסף וזהב בשבי יבא מצרים והוא שנים יעמד ממלך הצפון.

ת̇ם[84] מעבודאתהם מע כ̇ואצהם מע אניתהם[85] אלמנא מן פצ̇ה וד̇הב ידכ̇להא[86] אלי מצר סביא והו יעיש סנינא[87] בעד מלך אלעראק.

[68] עליה חצא + Morag | עליה וטאה + Spiegel
[69] צלחא ווטאה Spiegel and Morag > L
[70] קווה Spiegel + Morag
[71] אלשאם + Morag
[72] קוותה Spiegel + Morag
[73] ומדכליהא אלעראק Oxf 2628.53a + Oxf 2486.154b | ומדאכליהא ומדליהא Spiegel
[74] ואסתאדהמא Oxf 2628.53b | ואסתאדיהא Spiegel
[75] ומאיידיהא Morag | ומאידהא Spiegel
[76] באלמשורה End of Oxf 2486.154b
[77] ועמד Beginning of Oxf 2486.143a
[78] יקים Oxf 2628.53b
[79] פרוע אצולהם Oxf 2628.53a + Oxf 2486.143a
[80] וידאכל Oxf 2628.53b + Oxf 2486.143a
[81] אלמלך Spiegel
[82] וידכל Morag > L
[83] חצונה Spiegel + Morag
[84] חתי Oxf 2628.53b + Oxf 2486.143a
[85] אנייתהם Morag | אנחתהם Spiegel
[86] ידכלהמא Oxf 2628.53b + Oxf 2486.143a
[87] סנין Morag

אלאקרב פי קולה **ולקץ שנים יתחברו** (דניאל 11:6) אן יכון אלי סבע סנין כקולה **מקץ שבע שנים תעשה שמטה** (דב׳ 15:1). וקולה **ובת**[88] **מלך**[89]

הנגב (דניאל 11:6) גמאעה מן שיעתה עלי מא קדמנא תציר אלי אלעראק פי צלח, אן תוטיה או חילה. לאן לפטה **מישרים** (דניאל 11:6) תחתמל ד̇לך למשארכתהא **מישור** אלד̇י הו סהל ווטא מן אלארץ̇. ואכברהא באן אלחילה לא תתם ללשאמי עלי אלעראקי אד̇ קאל **ולא תעצר כח הזרוע** (דניאל 11:6), **ולא תעמד הבת, ולא יעצר זרועו** (ע׳ דניאל 11:6). ינוב אלחרף אלאול עלי אלת̇אני. **תנתן היא** (דניאל 11:6) יעני אלגמאעה. **ומביאיה** (דניאל 11:6), אדלתהא אללד̇ין דלוהא עלי אלטריק והם קום ליס מן רהט **מלך הצפון** ולא מן רהט **מלך הנגב**. ובעד ד̇לך תסלם אסתאדהא הו **היולדה** (דניאל 11:6) כקולך **ולאֶבן אַתְּ ילִדְתני** (ירמ׳ 2:27). ויסלמון אלמשירין עליהא הם אצחאב אלעתים כמא קדמנא **ויאמר המלך לחכמים ידעי העתים** (אסתר 1:13). וקאל איצ̇א **ועת ומשפט ידע לב חכם**[90] (קהלת 8:5). פהאולי[91] כלהם יסלמון אלי מלך אלעראק. ולכן יקום בעדהם מן אלעאמה פי מכאן **מלך הנגב** מן יט̇פר באלעראקי לקולה **ועמד מנצר שרשיה** (דניאל 11:7) הו כקולך או **לעקר משפחת גר** (ויק׳ 25:47).

וקולה **כנו** (דניאל 11:7) יט̇מר **על כנו**. וקולה **ויבא אל החיל** (דניאל 11:7) יעני ידאכ̇ל אלגיש פיאמר פיהם וינהא נט̇יר מא קאל הנאך **ויבא סגנים כמו חמר וכמו יוצר ירמס טיט** (יש׳ 41:25). ת̇ם **ויבא במעוז** (דניאל 11:7). חצ̇ין עלי מא קדמת. **ועשה בהם** (דניאל 11:7) יעני **ביושביהם ועשה כרצונו**. **והחזיק** (דניאל 11:7) **בארץ הצפון** חתי אן אלמעבודאת ואלנאס ואלמאל ואלאת̇את יאת בד̇לך סביא אלי מצר. יעני מן צלח מנהם אן יקאל אלסבי עליה נסיביהם כ̇אצה. וקולה **והוא שנים יעמד ממלך הצפון** (דניאל 11:8) יעני יעיש בעדה מדה נט̇יר מא קאל **ולא עצר כח**[92] **ירבעם**[93] **עוד בימי אביהו וימת** (דהי״ב 13:20). ת̇ם קאל

[88] ובת End of Oxf 2486.143a
[89] מלך Beginning of Oxf 2486.143b
[90] חכם End of Oxf 2486.143b
[91] פהאולי Beginning of Oxf 2486.144a
[92] כח End of Oxf 2486.144a
[93] ירבעם Beginning of Oxf 2486.144b

Dn 11:9

ובא במלכות מלך הנגב ושב אל אדמתו.

תֿם ידכֿל פי ממלכה[94] מלך אלגנוב וירגע אלי בלדה.

Dn 11:10

ובניו ותגרו ואספו המון חילים רבים ובא בו ושטף ועבר וישב ויתגרה עד מעוזו.

ובניה יתחרשון[95] בה פיגמעון עליה גמהור[96] גיש עטֿים[97] פידכֿלון בלדה דכֿולא וינסאבון ענה ויעברון תֿם יעודון ויתערצֿון לחצונה.[98]

Dn 11:11

ויתמרמר מלך הנגב ויצא ונלחם עמו עם מלך הצפון והעמיד המון רב ונתן ההמון בידו.

ויחתר[99] חיניד֗ מלך אלגנוב פיכֿרג[100] ויחארב מלך אלשמאל ויגמע גישא[101] עטֿימא[102] ויסלם[103] דֿלך[104] אלגמהור בידה.[105]

Dn 11:12

ונשׂא ההמון ורם לבבו והפיל רבאות ולא יעז.

ויספיה ספיא[106] ויעטֿם[107] קלבה ויוקע מעה[108] רבואת ולא יעתז בהא.[109]

94 ממלכת Spiegel + Morag

95 פיתחרשון Oxf 2628.54a

96 גמהור Morag > L

97 עצים Spiegel + Morag

98 בחצונה Oxf 2628.54a + Oxf 2486.144b

99 ויחתד Oxf 2628.54a

100 ויכֿרג Spiegel

101 כתֿירא Oxf 2628.54a + Oxf 2486.144b | כתֿירא End of Oxf 2486.144b

102 עצימא Spiegel + Morag | עטֿימא Oxf 2628.54a + Oxf 2486.144b > L

103 ויסלם Beginning of Oxf 2486.145a

104 דֿאלך Spiegel + Morag

105 פי ידה Oxf 2628.54a + Oxf 2486.145a

106 ספיאן Morag

107 ויעצם Spiegel + Morag

108 מנה Oxf 2628.54a + Oxf 2486.145a

Dn 11:13
ושב מלך הצפון והעמיד המון מלך רב מן הראשון ולקץ העתים שנים יבוא בו בחיל גדול וברכוש רב.

ת̇ם יעוד מלך אלשמאל[110] ויגהז[111] גמהורא[112] אכת̇ר מן אלאול[113] ואלי מדה[114] אוקאת מן אלסנין ידכ̇ל בלדה[115] דכ̇ולא וירגע בגיש כביר[116] וסרח כת̇יר.[117]

Dn 11:14
ובעתים ההם רבים יעמדו על מלך הנגב ובני פריצי עמך ינשׂאו להעמיד חזון ונכשלו.[118]

ופי[119] ד̇לך[120] אלעצר אלכת̇ירין יקאומון[121] מלך[122] אלשאם[123] ואחדאת̇[124] קומך אלמתג̇רין[125] יתחאמלון[126] עלי אקאמה נבוה[127] פיעת̇רון.

Dn 11:15
ויבא מלך הצפון וישפך סללה ולכד עיר מבצרות וזרועות הנגב לא יעמדו ועם מבחריו ואין כח לעמד.

109 יעתד בהם Oxf 2486.145a
110 ויגמע + Oxf 2628.54a
111 ויגהז Oxf 2628.54a > L ׀ ויגהז Beginning of TS Ar 24.22a
112 גמהור Oxf 2628.54a + Oxf 2486.145a ׀ [ג]מוהור TS Ar 24.22a
113 אלאולי TS Ar 24.22a ׀ אלאוול Spiegel
114 [מ]דה TS Ar 24.22a > D
115 בלדהם TS Ar 24.22a ׀ בלדח Spiegel
116 כתיר Morag
117 כביר Morag ׀ כת̇י[ר] TS Ar 24.22a > D
118 ונכשלו End of Oxf 2486.145a
119 ופי Beginning of Oxf 2486.145b
120 דאלך Spiegel + Morag
121 יקומון פי Oxf 2486.145b ׀ יקימאן פי Oxf 2628.54a
122 מלך Oxf 2628.54a and Oxf 2486.145b > L
123 [א]לשאם TS Ar 24.22a > D
124 אחתאת Morag
125 אלמתג̇ריין Morag ׀ אלמתג̇ירין Oxf 2486.145b ׀ אלמתגרין Oxf 2628.54a ׀ אלמג̇תארין TS Ar 24.22a > L
126 יתחאמלו Morag
127 נבווה Spiegel + Morag

תֿם יקבל[128] מלך אלעראק וילקי אלחסך ויפתח מדינה מן אלחצון וסלאטין[129] אלשאם לא תקום בין ידיה וכֿיאר אלקום פלא קוה[130] פיהם[131] ללקיאם.[132]

קולה אולא ען מלך הצפון **ובא במלכות**[133] **מלך הנגב** (דניאל 11:9) יחתמל מענאיין. אחדהמא אן יכון אלעראקי ידכֿל[134] בלד אלשאמי ליגסה כקצה אלמרגלים. ואלאכֿר אן יכון[135] יטא[136] בלדה מגתאזא ליחארב[137] קום[138] אכֿרין[139] כקצה פרעה נכו. ועלי אלחאלין גמיעא יסלם וירגע אלי בלדה. ולכן אולאד **מלך הנגב** יתערצֿו **במלך הצפון** כמא פעל יהונתן בן שאול בפלשתים[140] **ויך את**[141] **יהונתן**[142] **את נציב פלשתים אשר בגבע**[143] (שמ״א 13:3). פיגמעון **בני מלך הנגב, המון חילים רבים** (דניאל 11:10). פיכון מנהם סאיר אלאעמאל אלמנסובה אלי פראד[144] אד̇ יקול **ובא בוא ושטף ועבר וישב ויתגרה**[145] (דניאל 11:10) ינבגֿי אן תרד כלהא אלי גמע. פיקול[146] **נבאו בו ושטפו ועברו וישבו ויתגרו עד מבצריו**. ולעל ואחד[147] מנהם יבתדי ולדֿלך יכתב **ובנו**[148] (דניאל 11:10) מפרדא. פידכֿלון[149] בלד **מלך**[150]

[128] יקבול TS Ar 24.22a
[129] וצלאטין Morag
[130] קווה Spiegel + Morag
[131] פיהא TS Ar 24.22a
[132] לאלקיאם Spiegel + Morag | ללקואם TS Ar 24.22a + Oxf 2628.54a
[133] במלכ TS Ar 24.22a
[134] ידכל אלעראקי TS Ar 24.22a
[135] + פי TS Ar 24.22a
[136] יטא < L TS Ar 24.22a
[137] מגתאזא פיחארב TS Ar 24.22a
[138] קום End of Oxf 2486.145b
[139] אכֿרין Beginning of Oxf 2486.146a
[140] בפלשתים < L TS Ar 24.22a
[141] את < L MT
[142] יונתן MT
[143] אשר בגבע < L TS Ar 24.22a
[144] אלפראד TS Ar 24.22a
[145] וישב ויתגרה < L TS Ar 24.22a
[146] פיקאל TS Ar 24.22a
[147] [ו]א[ח]ד < D TS Ar 24.22a
[148] יוכתב ובניו ובָנו TS Ar 24.22a
[149] מפר[דא פי]דכלון < D TS Ar 24.22a
[150] בלד מלך בלד מלך TS Ar 24.22a

הצפון וינסאבון מנה[151] ויכ̇לצון אלי בלדהם. ת̇ם יעודון ת̇אניה ויתערצ̇ון בחצונה.[152] פאד̇א ראי **מלך הנגב** אן בניה קד ת̇ם להם ד̇לך גרד הו אלמחארבה[153] מע[154] **מלך הצפון**. כמא אן שאול[155] חין[156] ראי אן אלפתוח קד תם ליהונתן אבנה גרד הו[157] אלחרב מע **פלשתים** כמא קאל[158] **ויזעק שאול וכל העם אשר אתו ויאבו עד המלחמה**[159] (שמ״א׳ 14:20). וכד̇לך איצ̇א סאיר אלעבראניין אלד̇ין[160] כאנו מכ̇תפיין ט̇הרו ורגעו פאנצ̇אפו[161] אלי אלקום אלד̇ין מע שאול ויהונתן כמא קאל[162] **והעברים היו לפלשתים**[163] **כאתמול**[164] **שלש**[165] **אשר היו עמם במחנה סביב**[166] (שמ״א׳ 14:21). יעני כאנו עלי חאלהם מן אלכ̇וף כמא[167] כאנו. ת̇ם קאל באצ̇מאר[168] כלמה **וגם המה שבו**[169] **להיות עם ישראל אשר את שאול ואת**[170] **יונתן**[171] (שמ״א׳ 14:21). פהַכְדֵי ההנא[172] איצ̇א אד̇א ראי **מלך הנגב** מא קד תם לבניה **ויתמרמר מלך הנגב** (דניאל 11:11) חיניד̇ **ויצא ונלחם עם מלך הצפון** (דניאל 11:11). ואנמא זאד **עמו** (דניאל 11:11) לילא יתשאבה[173] בד̇כר ואלדה.

[151] וינס[אבון מנה] TS Ar 24.22a > D
[152] פיתעא[רצון בח]צונה TS Ar 24.22a > D
[153] אלמחארבה End of Oxf 2486.146a
[154] מע Beginning of Oxf 2486.146b | מע TS Ar 24.22a > L
[155] למא + TS Ar 24.22a
[156] חין TS Ar 24.22a > L
[157] הו TS Ar 24.22a > L
[158] כק TS Ar 24.22a
[159] ויאבו עד המלחמה TS Ar 24.22a > L
[160] אללדין Oxf 2486.146b
[161] ואנטאפו [א]לי אלק[ום] TS Ar 24.22a > D
[162] כק TS Ar 24.22a
[163] לפלשתים End of TS Ar 24.22a
[164] כאתמול Beginning of TS Ar 24.22b
[165] שלשים TS Ar 24.22b
[166] אשר ... סביב TS Ar 24.22b > L
[167] במא TS Ar 24.22b
[168] בעצמאר TS Ar 24.22b
[169] שבו TS Ar 24.22b > L
[170] ואת TS Ar 24.22b > L
[171] ויהונתן TS Ar 24.22b
[172] האהנא Oxf 2486.146b | ההונא TS Ar 24.22b
[173] יתשַבה Oxf 2486.146b

תֹם[174] **והעמיד מלך הצפון**[175] **המון רב** (דניאל 11:11) פיספיה ספיא ויקוי קלבה.

וקולה **ונשׂא ההמון** (דניאל 11:12) כמא קדמנא **ונשׂא אתכם בצנות** (עמוס 4:2). ואמא מעני **והפיל רבאות** (דניאל 11:12) פאנה יריד בה אנה לא ירי לדׄלך מקדארא כמא קאל הנאך **הנני מעיר עליהם את מדי אשר כסף לא יחשבו וזהב לא יחפצו בו** (יש׳ 13:17). תֹם בעד דׄלך דׄכר טׄפרא ללעראקי בקולה **ושב מלך הצפון והעמיד המון** (דניאל 11:13) וסאיר אלפסוק. וקד אטׄמר פיה (**וישׁוב**) **בחיל גדול וברכוש רב** (דניאל 11:13) אדׄ ליס פי אלעאדה אלמחארבין אן יחמלון מעהם **רכוש רב** אלי מוצׄע אלדׄי יחארבונה. ואנמא מן אלעאדה אן יקאל דׄלך למן יטׄפר פיגׄנם **וישוב ארצו** (דניאל 11:28) **בחיל גדול וברכוש רב** (דניאל 11:13). והדׄה אלחואדתׄ גרת פימא בין זׄ מלוך אליונאניין אלמתקדמין ומא כאן חדאהם מן מלוך ולפרס. ואמא[176] אלחׄ מנהם פקאל פיהם אן ישׂראל יקאומונה. והו קולה **ובעתים ההם**[177] **רבים יעמדו על מלך הנגב** (דניאל 11:14) ועלי אלאצל אלדׄי קאל [...][178] אן ילקב ישׂראל **רבים**. והדׄה קצה מקאומה [...][179] בני חשמונאי גׄ דפעאת. אלדפעה אלאולי יקתלון ניקנור וזירה. ופי אלתׄאניה יכסרון עסכרהם אלמקבל אליהם מע בגדיס וזירה וימלכון הם. ואמא קולה **ובני פריצי עמך** (דניאל 11:14) פאנה ישיר בה אלי אצחאב ישו אלדׄין אקאמה[180] מקאם נבי. פתחאמלו אן יקימו לה נבוה פיעתׄדון פיה ויזהקו. ודׄלך אן אלרגל פי חיותה[181] ....

....

....

....

.... עלי דׄלך ....כלאמא ....

....

............ואמא ....קום ....

....

[174] תם End of Oxf 2486.146b

[175] מלך הצפון MT > L

[176] ואנמא TS Ar 24.22b

[177] ובע[תים הה]ם TS Ar 24.22b > D

[178] ק[אל ...] TS Ar 24.22b > D

[179] [...] TS Ar 24.22b > D

[180] [א]קאמה TS Ar 24.22b > D

[181] חיותה End of TS Ar 24.22b

.... סנה .... לם יכן עלי ....
....

....
.....

.... מלך ....
....

.... אלאול ....
....

....
....

.... אופא ופי דלך ....
....

....[182] עליהא[183] הי אנטאכיה ב... לא יתֿבת לה קום אליונאני בל יהרבון כמא פי כֿברנא אנה גלס פי מרכב והרב אלי אלרובואת. וכדֿאך קואדה ובטארקתה. **ואין כח לעמד** (דניאל 11:15) פהו נטֿיר קולך **חוריה ואין שם מלוכה קראו וכל שׂריה היו אפס** (יש׳ 34:12), בזיאדה אולא פי **ואין** (דניאל 11:15).

ואדֿ קד שרחנא אליגֿ פסוקא אלאכֿר פי מלוך יון פינבגֿי אן נשרח אלאן אללֿ פסוק אלדֿי פי אדום ושריכתה. ונקול אן הדֿה אכבאר אלמלוך אלמדֿכורה כלהא איאת ועלאמאת לבני יסראיל חתי אדֿא שאהדוהא אהל גיל מנהם וגב עליהם אלתצדיק באמר אלישועה כמא שרחנא פי אמר כורש. פלא יראהא אנסאן בעין אכבאר פארגה או פצֿול ולא מעני לה. הודֿא תרי מא ה..אקל (?) מנהא פי אלמ...ראר. כיף געלהא[184]

Dn 11:16

ויעשׂ הבא אליו כרצנו ואין עומד לפניו ויעמד בארץ הצבי וכלה בידו.

[182] Oxf 2486.156a > D [... ...]

[183] עליהא Beginning og Oxf 2486.156b

[184] געלהא End of the readable part of Oxf 2486.156b

תֹם יצנע אלמסלט[185] עליה כמא ירצֹאה[186] ולא מקאום[187] לה ויתֹבת[188] פי בלד אלשאם ואלסיף בידה.[189]

Dn 11:17

וישֵׂם פניו לבוא בתקף כל מלכותו וישרים עמו יעשׂה ובת הנשים יתן לו להשחיה ולא תעמד ולא לו תהיה.

ויקצד[190] אלי אותֹק מא פי מלכה ואלמסתאמנין מעה פיצנע[191] וריסה[192] אלמדן יסלמהא אליה ליהלכהא[193] אפלא[194] תתֹבת ולא תכון לה.

Dn 11:18

וישב פניו לאיים ולכד רבים והשבית קצין חרפתו לו בלתי חרפתו ישיב לו.

ויקצד איצֹא אלגזיריין[195] ויפתח מנהא כתֹירין פיעטל מא עירה[196] בה דֹלך[197] אלמלך בעד אן יכאפיה עלי פעלה.

Dn 11:19

וישב פניו למעוז ארצו ונכשל ונפל ולא ימצא.

תֹם ירד וגהה אלי חצון בלדה תֹם יעתר פיקע[198] ולא[199] יוגד.

[185] אלמצלט Morag
[186] ירצֹא Spiegel + Oxf 2628.54b
[187] מקים Morag
[188] פיתֹבת Spiegel
[189] פי ידה Spiegel
[190] אלדכול + Oxf 2628.55a
[191] ויצנע Spiegel
[192] ורייסה Spiegel + Morag
[193] פיהלכהא Oxf 2628.55a | ויהלכהא Spiegel
[194] ולא Oxf 2628.55a
[195] אלגזירין Oxf 2628.55a | אלגזיריון Spiegel
[196] עיידה Morag | עיירה Spiegel
[197] דאלך Spiegel + Morag | ודלך Oxf 2628.55a
[198] ויקע Spiegel
[199] פלא Spiegel

Dn 11:20

ועמד על כנו מעביר נגש הדר מלכותו ובימים אחדים ישבר ולא באפים ולא במלחמה.

ויקום פי מרתבתה[200] מא[201] יקתצ̇י גלאוזה[202] אלקום[203] ואנמא ד̇אך לבהגה אלמלך ופי איאם יסירה ינכסר מן ג̇יר ג̇צב ולא מלחמה.

Dn 11:21

ועמד על בנו נבזה ולא נתנו עליו הוד מלכות ולא בשלוה והחזיק מלכות בחלקלקות.

ויקום פי מרתבתה[204] רגל זרי[205] לם יגעל[206] עליה בהא אלמלך פיאתי באטמנאן[207] ויחוז אלמלך באלחילה.

Dn 11:22

וזרעת השטף ישטפו מלפניו וישברו וגם נגיד ברית.

ואגלא אלמנסאבין[208] ינסאבון מן בין ידיה וינכסרון חתי ילי[209] אלעהד[210] פיהם.

Dn 11:23

ומן התחברות עליו יעשה מרמה ועלה ועצם במעאט גוי.

ומן אלמלתפין מעה מן יעאמלה בארב[211] חתי יצעד ג̇ירה פיעטם[212] בקום קלילין.

[200] מרתבה Spiegel + Oxf 2628.55a
[201] מן Spiegel + Oxf 2628.55a
[202] גלאוזה Oxf 2628.55a > L
[203] אלקום End of Oxf 2628.55a
[204] מרתבה Spiegel
[205] זרי Spiegel > L
[206] יגעלו Spiegel
[207] באטמאן Morag
[208] אלמנסאבון Morag
[209] ולי Spiegel
[210] עהד Morag
[211] כארב Spiegel
[212] פיעצם Morag ׀ פיתעצם Spiegel

Dn 11:24

בשלוה ובמשמנה מדינה יבוא ועשה אשר לא עשו אבותיו ואבות אבותיו בזה ושלל ורכוש להם יבזר ועל מבצרים יחשב מחשבותיו ועד עת.

וידכ̇ל מדינתה ופי נעמתהא בהדו פיצנע בהא מא לם יצנעה[213] אבאה ואבא אבאה ויגיז אצחאבה מן גנימתה וסלבהא וסרחהא וידבר תדבירא עלי אלחצון אלי וקת אכ̇ר.

Dn 11:25

ויער כחו ולבבו על מלך הנגב בחיל גדול ומלך הנגב יתגרה למלחמה בחיל גדול ועצום עד מאד ולא יעמד כי יחשבו עליו מחשבות.

ויט̇הר[214] קותה[215] וקצדה עלי מלך אלגנוב בגיש כביר ומלך אלגנוב יתערץ̇ למחארבתה בגיש כביר עט̇ים[216] גדא ולא יתׄבת ממא ידברון[217] עליה אלתדאביר.

Dn 11:26

ואכלי פתבגו ישברוהו וחילו שפט ונפלו חללים רבים.

חתי אכלי וצ̇איפה מן כ̇בז וראם יכסרונה פינסאב[218] בגישה ויקע מעה צרעא[219] כת̇ירין.

Dn 11:27

ושניהם המלכים לבבם למרע ועל שלחן אחד כזב ידברו ולא תצלח כי עוד קץ למועד.

וד̇אנך[220] אלמלכאן יתפק ראיהמא פי אלאסאה ויתכלמון[221] באלבאטל בסבב מאידה ואחדה[222] ולא ינגח להמ אד̇ קד[223] בקת מדה ללוקת.[224]

[213] יצנע Spiegel

[214] ויצהר Spiegel + Morag

[215] קוותה Morag

[216] עצים Spiegel + Morag

[217] ידברו Spiegel

[218] ואדם יכסרנה פינסאב Spiegel

[219] מנה צרעו Spiegel

[220] ודאניך Spiegel

Dn 11:28
וישב ארצו ברכוש גדול ולבבו על ברית קדש ועשׂה ושב לארצו.

ולכן ירגע אחדהמא אלי בלדה בסרח כביר[225] ופי קלבה אלאסאה עלי דׄוי עהד אלקדס ואלאכׄר[226] יקצׄי חרבה וירגע אלי בלדה.

Dn 11:29
למועד ישוב ובא בנגב ולא תהיה כראשונה וכאחרונה.

ואלי אלחול[227] יעוד פידכׄל[228] אלי אלגנוב ולא[229] תכון וקעה כאלאולי ולא כאלתׄאניה.

Dn 11:30
ובאו בו צִיים כתיים ונכאה ושב וזעם על ברית קדש ועשה ושב ויבן על עזבי ברית קדש.

וידאכׄלה אלמפאזיון[230] ובחריון[231] ויציר מגׄתאלא ויעוד ויסכׄט עלי גמיע[232] דׄוי עהד אלקדס ויצנע דׄלך[233] תׄם יעוד ויחאמל[234] תארכי עהד אלקדס.

Dn 11:31
וזרעים ממנו יעמדו וחללו המקדש המעוז והסירו התמיד ונתנו השקוץ משמם.

ואגלא יקמון מנה פיבדׄלון[235] אלקדס אלחצין ויזילון אלדאים ויגעלונה רגסא.

[221] ויתכלמאן Spiegel
[222] מא ירה ואחוה Spiegel
[223] קת Spiegel
[224] לאלוקת Spiegel + Morag
[225] עצׄים Spiegel
[226] ואלכר Spiegel
[227] חול Morag
[228] (ויבסט) וידכל Spiegel
[229] לא Spiegel
[230] אלמפאזיין Morag ׀ מפאזיון Spiegel
[231] ובחריין Morag
[232] גמיע < L Spiegel
[233] דאלך Spiegel + Morag
[234] ויתאמל Morag

Dn 11:32
ומרשיעי ברית יחניף בחלקות ועם יודעי אלוהיו יחזיקו ועשו.

וט̇אלמי[236] אלעהד ידחיהם באלחייל ואלקום אלטאיעי[237] מעבודה יתמכנון ויצנעון ד̇אלך.[238]

Dn 11:33
ומשׂכילי עם יבינו לרבים ונכשלו בחרב ובלהבה ובמלחמה בשבי ובבזה ימים.

ועלמא כל אמה יעלמון גמהור יבתלון[239] בסיף וחריק וסבי וג̇נימה מדה.

Dn 11:34
ובהכשלם יעזרו עזר מעט ונלוו עליהם רבים בחלקלקות.

וענד[240] אבתלאהם יעינון[241] עונא יסירא וינצ̇אפון[242] אליהם כת̇ירין באלחייל.

Dn 11:35
ומן המשׂכילים יכשלו לצרף בהם ולברר וללבן עד עת קץ כי עד למועד.

ומן אלעלמא יפתקרון[243] לכי יסבכון ויחררו[244] וינצפו אלי וקת[245] אלאגל אד̇ קד[246] בקי אלוקת אלי[247] מדה.

[235] פיבדלו Spiegel
[236] וצאלמי Spiegel + Morag
[237] אלמטיעי Spiegel
[238] דלך Spiegel + Morag
[239] גמהורהא ויבתלון Spiegel
[240] ובעד Spiegel
[241] יענון Spiegel
[242] וינצמון Spiegel
[243] יתפקון Spiegel
[244] ויפחררו Spiegel
[245] וקת Spiegel > L
[246] בקת לה Spiegel +
[247] בקי אלוקת אלי Spiegel > L

[...][248] דלך[249] אלאבן אלפארסי מן אלעראקי לה **ועצם במעט גוי** (דניאל 11:23). קאל ענה גבריאל **אשר לא עשׂו אבתיו** (דניאל 11:24), יעני אללדין

כאנו בחצ̇רה **מעביר נוגש** (דניאל 11:20). וקולה **ואבות אבתיו** (דניאל 11:24) יעני אללדין כאנו בחצ̇רה **[ב]תקף כל מלכותו** (דניאל 11:17). פאולאיך אלמחאדון לם ינתצ̇רו והד̇א אלג̇ אנתצ̇ר. וקולה **ועל מבצרים יחשב מחשבתיו ועד עת** (דניאל 11:24) יעני פכר פיהם פכרא בעידא. אלי סנתין וכניפה[250] ועשרין. וקולה **ויער כחו ולבבו** (דניאל 11:25) יריד בה באלקוה ואלחיל.[251] [...][252] בה **ועל[253] מלך הנגב** (דניאל 11:25) לאנה יריד קתלה

וחדא לא אכ̇ר מעה כמא קאל הנאך **ומלך ארם צוה את שׂרי הרכב אשר לו, לא תלחמו את הקטן ואת הגדול כי אם את מלך ישראל לבדו** (דהי״ב׳ 18:30). וכמא קאל אחיטפל **והחרדתי אתו ונס כל[254] העם[255] אשר אתו והכית את המלך לבדו** (שמ״ב׳ 17:2). ואמא קולה **ולא יעמד כי יחשבו עליו מחשבות** (דניאל 11:25) פג̇יר מחתאג אן נמת̇ל מת̇אלאת לתלך אלתדאביר ולא לג̇ירהא אד לם אלום נפסי אן אתכ̇לף שיא מן ד̇לך לסעתה וכת̇רה חיל אלמלוך ואלסלאטין. וקלה[256] פאידה הד̇א אלכתאב מנה. ובעד ד̇לך אחתאל[257] עלי מלך אדום בעץ̇ נדמאה חתי יג[י]אה מלך אלפרס כמא קאל **ואכלי פדבגו ישברוהו** (דניאל 11:26). פאמא לשרהם או לתקצירה בהם או לצ̇לע להם מע עדוה או לרגא או לכוף.

ואמא קולה **ושניהם המלכים לבבם למרע** (דניאל 11:27) אעני **מלך הצפון ומלך הנגב** יעציאן פי ד̇לך אלוקת עלי אלאסאה לישׂראל. וקולה **ועל שלחן אחד כזב ידברו[258]** (דניאל 11:27) אד̇[259] הו מנבר והו סריר והו מאידה וסאיר

[248] Oxf 2486.156b > D [...]
[249] דלך Beginning of Oxf 2486.157a
[250] וכני[פה] Oxf 2486.157a > D
[251] ו[א]ל[חי]ל Oxf 2486.157a > D
[252] וק[...] Oxf 2486.157a > D
[253] [ו]על Oxf 2486.157a > D
[254] כל End of Oxf 2486.157a
[255] העם Beginning of Oxf 2486.157b
[256] [ואן] לה Oxf 2486.157b lesson uncertain
[257] [א]חתמאל Oxf 2486.157b > D
[258] ידברו End of the readable part of Oxf 2486.157b
[259] אד Beginning of Oxf 2486.158a

אלקאב אלתכ̇ציץ. ומעני **כזב ידברו** (דניאל 11:27) ליס הו כד̇ב פי אלכלאם. ואנמא הו טמע כאד̇ב לא יחצל מנה שי. ואלעלה פי אן לא יתם להם מא טמעו בה פי בית אלמקדס. **כי עוד קץ למועד** (דניאל 11:27) לאנה קד בקית סנין כת̇ירה מן מדה עמדאנה. וכאן הד̇ה כאן פי אלד̇ו̇[260] סנין אלתי הי בית חשמנאי ומואליהם. ואקול האהנא **כזב** (דניאל 11:27) הו מת̇ל קול **מיכיהו בן ימלא לאחאב הנה נתן יוי רוח שקר בפי נביאיך** (מל״א 22:23) ליס הו כלאם **כזב**. [ו]לכן הו מא לא יתם ולא יצח. והו כקולה **שקר הסוס לתשועה** (תה׳ 33:17). ואיצ̇א **שקר החן והבל היפי** (משלי 31:30). ואיצ̇א **שוא עמלו בניו בו** (תה׳ 127:1). ואיצ̇א **שוא שקד שומר** (תה׳ 127:1). [...][261] **שוא**[262] **לכם**[263] (תה׳ 127:2). פאד̇א[264] לם יתם ד̇לך להד̇א ולא להד̇א רגע כל ואחד אלי בלדה כמא קאל **וישב ארצו ברכוש גדול** (דניאל 11:28) ען אחדהמא.

וקאל **ועשה ושב לארצו** (דניאל 11:28) ען אלאכ̇ר. ופסרת **למ֗ועד ישוב** (דניאל 11:29) מת̇ל **למועד אשוב אליך בעת חיה** (בר׳ 18:14). וקולה **ישוב** (דניאל 11:29) יעני **מלך הצפון** לתמאמה **ובא בנגב** (דניאל 11:29). וקולה **ולא תהיה כראשנה** (דניאל 11:29) יעני גזאתה וחדה. **וכאחרונה** (דניאל 11:29) תצ̇אפרה מע אלגנובי. וקולה **ובאו בו ציים כתים** (דניאל 11:30) יעני ידאכ̇לון **מלך הנגב** קום בדויין הם **ציים** (דניאל 11:30) וקום בחראניין הם **כתים** (דניאל 11:30). פאד̇א אגתמע מעה האולי אלקום יציר מג̇תאלא ומכארא כמא קאל **ונכאה** (דניאל 11:30). והו מת̇ל קולה הנאך **יאספו על נכים** (תה׳ 35:15). וקולה **ושב ויבן וזעם על ברית קדש** (דניאל 11:30) יעני בה[265] [...][266] כקצה[267] **ותשלך אמת ארצה ועשתה והצליחה** (דניאל 8:12) ומא פי סאיר אלקצה. וקולה **ומשׂכילי עם יבינו לרבים** (דניאל 11:33) יעני בה אלחכמים, **זכרוניהם לברכה**, אללד̇ין הם פי אלגלות פי מוצ̇ע אללוים אללד̇ין קיל פיהם **וידבר יחזקיהו על לב כל הלוים המשׂכילים שׂכל טוב ליוי** (דהי״ב׳ 30:22). וקאל פי בעצ̇הם **ויביאו לנו כיד אלהינו הטוב עלינו איש שכל מבני מחלי** (עזרא 8:18). וקאל פי בעצ̇הם **ויפל הגורל מזרחה**

[260] אלד̇ו̇ Oxf 2486.158a lesson uncertain

[261] Oxf 2486.158a > D [...]

[262] שוא Oxf 2486.158a lesson uncertain

[263] לכם End of the readable part of Oxf 2486.158a

[264] פאד̇א Beginning of Oxf 2486.158b

[265] בה End of the readable part of Oxf 2486.158b

[266] Oxf 2486.158b > D [...]

[267] כקצה Beginning of Oxf 2486.159a

לשלמיהו וזכריהו בנו יועץ בשׂכל (דה״א׳ 26:14) והם רבן יוחנן ור̇ אליעזר ור̇ יהושע ורבן גמליאל ור̇ עקיבא וזמ[ר]תהם ושיעתהם. לאן צנאעה אללוים **יורו משפטיך ליעקב ותורתך לישראל** (דב׳ 33:10). והדׄה בעצ̇הא[268] צנאעה אלרבונין אלאולין ואלאכ̇רין. וקולה **יבינו לרבים**[269] (דניאל 11:33) כמא[270] קאל ען אללוים **מבינים את העם לתורה** (נחמיה 8:7). וקולה איצ̇א **והלוים המבינים את העם** (נחמיה 8:9). וקאל איצ̇א **וליריב ולאלנתן מבינים** (נחמיה 8:16). ואשבאה ד̇לך. ת̇ם ערפה מא יגרי עליהם מן אלצרות בקולה **ונכשלו בחרב ובלהבה בשבי ובבזה ימים** (דניאל 11:33). פאמא **בחרב** (דניאל 11:33) פכמא קתל ר̇ עקיבא באלסיף [...][271] ר̇ יהודה בן בבא [...][272] ואמא **ובלהבה** (דניאל 11:33) פכמא אחרק ר̇ חנניה בן תרדיון והו מלפוף בספר תורה בעד מאשרת גזה צוף מבלולה באלמא עלי צדרה לילא תכ̇רג נפסה בסרעה בל [... ...].[273] ואמא **בשבי ובבזה** (דניאל 11:33) פכמא סבי ר̇ מאיר והו צבי פלמא[274] קאל ר̇ ישמעאל **מי נתן למשסה**[275] **יעקב**[276] **וישראל לבזזים** (יש׳ 42:24) אגאבה אלצבי וקאל **הלא יוי זו חטאנו לו** (יש׳ 42:24).

פסבק גבריאל אלי תעריף דניאל הדׄה אלחואדת̇ חתי אד̇א ואפתנא לא תצ̇יק צדורנא וניאס[277] מן אלישועה בל תכון **אותות ומופתים** לצחת אלישועה עלי מא קדמנא. וקולה לה **ובהכשלם יעזרו עזר מעט** (דניאל 11:34) יעני בעד תקצ̇י **הכשלם** תכון להם מעונה יסירה מן **מלכי אדום**. וד̇לך [...][278] כאן **לרבינו הקדוש** מן אנטונינוס בן אסירוס אד כאן רצ̇יעה והו בשרה באלמלך. וג̇רי עלי ידה אחסאן כת̇יר לישראל מת̇ל **חרות עזה וקלוניא טבריה** וג̇יר ד̇לך. וקולה **ונלוו עליהם רבים בחלקלקות** (דניאל 11:34) הו צ̇רוב אלמראראה אלתי קאסאהא אלאבא מן מלוך[279] אדום[280] [... ...][281] עליהם[282]

[268] ב[ע]צ[ה]א Oxf 2486.159a > D

[269] לרבים End of Oxf 2486.159a

[270] כמא Beginning of Oxf 2486.159b

[271] ובעג[...] Oxf 2486.159b > D

[272] ובעגא[...] Oxf 2486.159b > D

[273] טוו[...] ע[...]אבה Oxf 2486.159b > D

[274] פל[מא] Oxf 2486.159b > D

[275] [למ]שסה Oxf 2486.159b > D | למשסה End of Oxf 2486.159b

[276] יעקב Beginning of Oxf 2486.160a

[277] [ו]ניאס Oxf 2486.160a > D

[278] [...] Oxf 2486.160a > D

[279] מן מלוך Uncertain lesson

דינהם ומן בעדהם. ואכ̇ד̇ רבהם מן אלסמא באידיהם כמא קאל **וגם בימים ההמה נאם יוי לא אעשׂה אתכם כלה** (ירמ׳ 5:18). פלו כאנו כאלנאר לם יחרקונא. ולו צארו כאלמא לם יג̇רקונא כמא קאל **כי תעבר במים אתך אני ובנהרות לא ישטפוך כי תלך במו אש לא תכוה ולהבה לא תבער בך** (יש׳ 43:2). ולכנה ג̇זר עלי אכת̇ר אלאמה אלפקר ואלפאקה כמא קאל **ומן המשכילים יכשלו** (דניאל 11:35). ומעני ד̇לך יפתקרון כמא קאל **ויוציאם בכסף וזהב ואין בשבטיו כושל** (תה׳ 105:37). ת̇ם כשף אלסבב כיף אוג̇בת אלחכמה ד̇לך עליהם פעללה בת̇לת̇ עלל, **לצרף בהם ולברר וללבן** (דניאל 11:35). פאמא עלה **לצרף** (דניאל 11:35) פלימתחנהם כמא ימתחן אלאוליא. פאד̇א צברו עלי ד̇לך[283] עוצ̇הם[284] כ̇ירא כמא קאל פי יוסף **עד עת בוא דברו**

אמרת יוי צרפתהו (תה׳ 105:19). ואמא **לברר** (דניאל 11:35) פי צחון צנאעתהם כמא קאל **וישׂימני לחץ ברור** (יש׳ 49:2). ואיצ̇א **ודעת שׂפתי ברור מללו** (איוב 33:3). לילא יכון להם מאל פיתשאג̇לון ויתרכון עלם אלפקה ואלטאעאת וסאיר מא תחתאג אליה אלאמה. ואמא **וללבן** (דניאל 11:35) פליכונו טואעא תג̇פר ד̇נוב אלאמה עלי אידיהם כמא קאל **אם יהיו חטאיכם כשנים כשלג ילבינו** (יש׳ 1:18). וד̇לך בקבולהם קולהם ובברהם להם ובדעא האולי להם. [... ...][285] ואבטל בהד̇ה אלג̇ עלל אלעלה אלתי יג̇עלהא אלמנג̇מין לקלה מאל אלעלא [...][286] יקולון לאן ביתי [...][287] לביתי[... ...][288] פאנא[289] קד שאהדנא שלמה מלך ישראל ובטלמיוס אליונאני ובעצ̇ מלך אלערב וג̇ירהם עלמא. פתרי הד̇ה אלד̇ ביות לא תכון מתקאבלה פי זמאנהם. וקולה **עד עת קץ** (דניאל 11:35) יריד בה אנהם לם יזלו כד̇אך אלי אכ̇ר אלקץ. ותמאמה **כי עד למועד** (דניאל 11:35) יריד בה אנה ליס אכ̇ר

[280] אדום End of the readable part of Oxf 2486.160a

[281] [... ...] Oxf 2486.160a > D

[282] עליהם Beginning of Oxf 2486.160b

[283] דלך End of Oxf 2486.160b

[284] עוצ̇הם Beginning of Oxf 2486.161a

[285] [... ...] Oxf 2486.161a > D

[286] [...] Oxf 2486.161a > D

[287] [...]בלין Oxf 2486.161a > D

[288] אל[...] אל[...]ן לא[...] Oxf 2486.161a > D

[289] פאנמא Beginning of Oxf 2486.161b

מלכות אדום הו אכ׳ר אלשעבוד. בל להם שריך בעד ד׳לך והו מא סיד׳כר עיון אכ׳בארה פי אלפואסיק אלאכ׳ירה. ואד׳ קד אסתופינא שרוח אלכ׳ פסוק אלד׳י לאדום פנפסר נץ אלעשרה פואסיק אלתי לשריכה ונקול אולהא

Dn 11:36

ועשה כרצונו המלך ויתרומם ויתגדל על כל אלוה ועל אל אלים ידבר נפלאות והצליח עד כלה זעם כי[290] נחרצה[291] נעשתה.

ת׳ם יצנע אלמלך אלאכ׳ר כמא ירצ׳א[292] וירתפע[293] ויתכבר עלי כל אלמד׳אהב[294] ועלי רב אלארבאב ויתכלם[295] באלעגאיב[296] וינגח פי אמרה אלי אן יפנא אלסכ׳ט כמא וקע בה אלאנבתאר.

Dn 11:37

ועל אלהי אבתיו לא יבין ועל חמדת נשים ועל כל אלוה לא יבין כי על כל יתגדל.

ואלי מעבודי אבאה לא ילתפת ואלי מעבודי אמהאתה לא ילתפת בל ירתפע עלי אלכל.

Dn 11:38

ולאלוה מעוזים על כנו יכבד ולאלוה אשר לא ידעוהו אבתיו יכבד בזהב ובכסף ובאבן יקרה ובחמודות.

ומעבוד עזיז פי מכאנה וכרמה ומעבוד לם[297] יערפה אבאה[298] יכרם בד׳הב[299] ופצ׳ה וגואהר[300] ות׳יאב פאכ׳רה.

[290] כי End of Oxf 2486.161b

[291] נחרצה Beginning of Oxf 2486.162a

[292] ירצ׳יה Spiegel + Oxf 2486.162a

[293] ויתרפע Spiegel

[294] מדהב Oxf 2486.162a | אלמדהאב Spiegel

[295] יתכלם Spiegel + Oxf 2486.162a

[296] בעגאיב Oxf 2486.162a

[297] ליס Oxf 2486.162a

[298] אב[אה] Oxf 2486.162a > D | אבאה End of the readable Oxf 2486.162a

[299] בדהב Beginning of Oxf 2486.162b

[300] [וג]ו[א]הר Oxf 2486.162b > D

Dn 11:39

ועשה למבצרי מעוזים עם אלוה נכר אשר יביר ירבה כבוד והמשילם ברבים ואדמה יחלק במחיר.

ויצנע כד̇א[301] כת̇ירא לחצון אלמעבוד אלג̇ריב אלד̇י אעתרף לה ויסלט[302] עלי אלאמה אהלהא[303] ויקטעהם אלצ̇יאע בת̇מן.[304]

Dn 11:40

ובעת קץ יתנגח עמו מלך הנגב ויסתער עליו מלך הצפון ברכב ובפרשים ובאניות רבות ובא בארצות ושטף ועבר.

ובעד ינאטחה מלך אלרום וינתקל אליה מלך אלפרס בכ̇יל[305] ופרסאן וספן כת̇ירה[306] פידכ̇ל פי[307] בלדאנהם[308] וינסאב[309] ויגוז.

Dn 11:41

ובא בארץ הצבי ורבות יכשלו ואלה[310] ימלטו[311] מידו אדום ומואב וראשית בני עמון.

ואד̇א[312] דכ̇ל בלד אלשאם יהלך אכת̇רה ויפלת מן ידה בלד אדום ומואב וטרף[313] בלד[314] בני עמון.

Dn 11:42

וישלח ידו בארצות וארץ מצרים לא תהיה לו לפליטה.

301 כדי Morag
302 ויצלט Morag
303 אדלהא Spiegel
304 באלתמן Spiegel
305 בכיל Beginning of Oxf 3109.6
306 כתיר Spiegel
307 פי Spiegel > L
308 [בלדא]נהם Oxf 2486.162b > D
309 וינ[סא]ב Oxf 3109.6 > D
310 ואלה End of Oxf 2486.162b
311 ימלטו Beginning of Oxf 2486.163a
312 ואדי Spiegel + Morag
313 [וט]רף Oxf 3109.6 > D
314 בלד Oxf 3109.6 > L

ובסט ידה פי סאיר אלבלדאן ובלד מצר לא תפלת[315] מנה.[316]

Dn 11:43

ומשל במכמני הזהב והכסף ובכל חמודות מצרים ולובים וכושים במצעדיו.

ויתסלט[317] עלי מעאדן[318] אלד̇הב ואלפצ̇ה[319] וגמיע דק[320] מצר ויכון[321] בעץ̇[322] אלנובה[323] ואלחבשה פי כ̇טא קדמיה.[324]

Dn 11:44

ושמועות יבהלוהו ממזרח ומצפון ויצא בחמה גדולה להשמיד ולהחרים רבים.[325]

ופי[326] וקת תדהשה אלאכ̇באר מן אלמשרק ומן אלשמאל פיכ̇רג[327] בחמיה[328] כבירה[329] לינפד̇ אלכת̇יר[330] ויתלפהם.

Dn 11:45

ויטע אהלי אפדנו בין ימים להר צבי קדש ובא עת קצו ואין עוזר לו.

ויצ̇רב כבאה ופסטאמה בין אלבחר[331] וגבל[332] אלשאם חתי[333] יאתיה[334] אגלה[335] פלא מעין לה.

[315] יפלת Oxf 2486.163a

[316] מן ידה Spiegel + Oxf 2486.163a

[317] ויתצלט Morag

[318] מ[עא]ן Oxf 2486.163a > D

[319] [וא]ל[פצה] Oxf 2486.163a > D

[320] דק Oxf 2486.163a > D

[321] ויכון Oxf 2486.163a > L

[322] ובעץ Oxf 2486.163a

[323] אלנו[ב]ה Oxf 3109.6 > D

[324] [אלנובה ואלחבשה] פי [כטא קדמיה] Oxf 2486.163a > D | קדמה Oxf 3109.6 + Spiegel

[325] רבים End of Oxf 2486.163a

[326] ופי Beginning of Oxf 2486.163b | והו פי Oxf 3109.6 | פי Spiegel

[327] יכרג Oxf 2486.163b | י[כרג] Oxf 3109.6 > D | פיכרה Spiegel

[328] בחמייה Spiegel + Morag | עטימה + Oxf 2486.163b

[329] כבירה Spiegel + Oxf 2486.163b > L

[330] אלכתירין Spiegel

ואד׳ קד אסתתממנאהא נעוד עליהא בשרוח ונקול אמא אבתדאהא בקולה[336] **ועשה כרצונו המלך** (דניאל 11:36) ולם יקל[337] **מלך הנגב** ולא[338] **מלך הצפון** פאנה יומי בד׳לך אלי אנהא[339] אלממלכה אלאכ׳רה. ויכון הד׳א נט׳יר[340] קולה[341] אכ׳ירא **ויהי ערב ויהי בכר יום הששי** (בר׳ 1:31). והו אלמלך אלשריר[342] לאדום עלי[343] מא[344] שרחנא פימא[345] תקדם. וקולה[346] **ויתרומם ויתגדל על כל אל**[347] (דניאל 11:36) מא שוהד מנה מן אלטלול[348] עלי גמיע אלמד׳אהב בחגג אכ׳תרהא חק [...] **ועל אל אלים ידבר נפלאות** (דניאל 11:36) פאד׳א בקי אלמד׳הב אלחק אלואחד[349] תכלם פיה בעגאיב[350] אכ׳תצר גבריאל דון ד׳כרהא ואכ׳תצר אנא דון שרחהא. אלא אני אקול אן גמלה הד׳ה[351] אלקצה הי קצה **ופֻם**[352] **ממלל**[353] **רברבן** (דניאל 7:8.20) בעינהא. והי אלתי[354] שרחהא **עתיק יומיא**, **ומלין לצד עלאה ימלל** (דניאל 7:25) ועלי מא קדמנא.

[331] ובלד + Oxf 3109.6

[332] גבאל Oxf 2486.163b ׀ גבל L < Oxf 3109.6

[333] יגיה + Spiegel

[334] יאתיה L < Spiegel ׀ יאתיה End of Oxf 3109.6

[335] אגלה Beginning of Oxf 3109.7

[336] בקולה Beginning of Oxf 2659.40a ׀ בק[ו]לה D < Oxf 2486.163b ׀ בקול Oxf 2659.40a

[337] יקול Oxf 2659.40a

[338] מלך הנגב ולא D < Oxf 2486.163b

[339] אנהא L < Oxf 2659.40a

[340] ויכון ... נטיר D < Oxf 2486.163b

[341] קו Oxf 2659.40a

[342] אכ׳ירא ... אלשריר D < Oxf 2486.163b

[343] עלי End of Oxf 2486.163b

[344] מא Beginning of Oxf 2486.164b

[345] שרחנא פימא L < Oxf 2659.40a

[346] כק Oxf 2659.40a

[347] אל L < Oxf 2659.40a

[348] אל[טל]ול D < Oxf 2659.40a

[349] אלואחד אלחק Oxf 2659.40a

[350] בעגיב Oxf 2659.40a

[351] גמלה אן הדה Oxf 2486.164b ׀ גמלה הדה Oxf 2659.40a

[352] ופום Oxf 2659.40a

[353] ממליל Oxf 2486.164b

[354] אלדי Oxf 2659.40a

ופסרת[355] **ועל חמדת**[356] **נשים** (דניאל 11:37) "מעבוד אלאמהאת" אד̇ קד תקדם קבלה **ועל אלהי אבתיו**[357] **לא יבין ועל חמדת נשים ועל**[358] **כל אלוה לא יבין**[359] (דניאל 11:37). ואחתיג אלי הד̇ה אלתצריף אד̇א[360] כאן מעבודאת אבא אלקום מת̇ל אלהי מואב ומעבודאת אמהאתהם[361] מת̇ל[362] אלהי בני עמון עלי מא משאהד מן אכ̇תלאף אלאמם פי אלתזויג ופי אלעבאדה. ואסמי[363] ד̇לך **חמדות**[364] (דניאל 11:37) לאן אלכפאר הכד̇א[365] סבילהם, אית צורה ראוהא[366] פאשתהוהא,[367] עבדוהא. והכד̇א[368] מוגוד אלי אלאן פי בלד אלהנד[369] ולד̇לך[370] יסמיהם[371] **שקוצי עיניו** (יח' 20:7). פערפנא[372] אנהם[373] יתרכון מעבודאת[374] אלאבא ואלאמהאת ואן אכ̇תלפת. ויעני[375] בקולה **ולאלוה מעזים**[376] **על כנו יכבד** (דניאל 11:38) אן שריך אדום יתדרבו בעץ̇ תלך אלמעבודאת פי מואצ̇עהא אלתי וגדהא. פהו לא ינקלהא מנה ומע ד̇אך פהו יכרם ד̇לך אלמוצ̇ע ויפצ̇לה ולא יקצר פיה. ומעני קולה **ולאלוה אשר לא ידעוהו אבתיו** (דניאל 11:38) הו מא שהר (?) מן

[355] ופס Oxf 2659.40a

[356] חמודות Oxf 2659.40a

[357] אבות Oxf 2659.40a

[358] ועל חמדדת נשים ועל Oxf 2486.164b > D

[359] ועל חמדת ... יבין Oxf 2659.40a > L | יבין End of the readable part of Oxf 2486.164b

[360] אד̇א Beginning of Oxf 2486.164a

[361] אמהאתהא Oxf 2659.40a

[362] מתל Oxf 2659.40a > L

[363] וסמי Oxf 2659.40a

[364] חמודות Oxf 2659.40a

[365] הכדי Oxf 2486.164a

[366] ראוהא Oxf 2659.40a > L

[367] אשתהוהא Oxf 2659.40a

[368] [והכד]א Oxf 2486.164a > D

[369] אל[ה]נ[ד] Oxf 2486.164a > D

[370] ולדלך End of Oxf 2659.40a

[371] יסמון Beginning of Oxf 2659.40b

[372] [פער]פנ[א] Oxf 2486.164a > D

[373] אנהם Oxf 2659.40b > L

[374] מעב[וד]את Oxf 2486.164a > D

[375] אל[אבא ... יעני] Oxf 2486.164a > D

[376] מעזים End of the readadble part of Oxf 2486.164a

אטהאר[377] דין לם יערפה אבאיהם ווקע אלבר ואלאכראם לדׄלך אלדין. ופסרת[378] **ובחמדות**[379] (דניאל 11:38) ״תׄיאבא״ עלי מא קיל **את בגדי עשׂו בנה הגדול החמדות**[380] (בר׳ 27:15). וכדׄא[381] סביל אלהנד ואלכפאר, יכרמון מעבודאתהם בדׄהב ופצׄה וגוהר ותׄיאב.[382]

וקולה[383] **ועשׂה למבצרי מעזים**[384] **עם אלוה נכר** (דניאל 11:39) יעני אלקום[385] אלדׄין[386] ידׄכׄלון[387] פי דינהם דׄאך אלגׄריב יכתׄר[388] להם אלבר ואלכראמה כמא כׄלע[389] יהוא עלי עבדה אלבעל אדׄ קאל **ויאמר לאשר על המלתחה הוצא לבוש**[390] (מל״ב׳ 10:22). וקולה **והמשילם ברבים** (דניאל 11:39) פיסלטהם עלי אלנאס,[391] יגעל[392] להם עליהם אמרא ונהיא כמא[393] געל פרעה[394] ללכנהים[395] אדׄ קאל[396] **רק אדמת הכהנים**[397] **לא קנה** (בר׳ 47:22) וסאיר[398] אלקול.[399] וקולה **ויחלק במחיר** (דניאל 11:39) הו אן יגי אלי[400] אלארץׄ[401] אלמבקאת,[402] יביעהא ביעא[403] שביהא במא עמל[404] יוסף,

[377] אטׄהאר Beginning of Oxf 2486.165a
[378] ופ[סר]ת Oxf 2486.165a > D | ופס Oxf 2659.40b
[379] ובחמודות Oxf 2659.40b
[380] הגׄ הא (המדות אשר) Oxf 2659.40b
[381] וכדׄי Oxf 2486.165a
[382] ותׄיאב וגוהר Oxf 2659.40b
[383] וק Oxf 2659.40b
[384] מעזים Oxf 2486.165a > D
[385] י[עני] אלק[ום] Oxf 2486.165a > D
[386] אללדׄין Oxf 2486.165a
[387] [יד]כׄלון Oxf 2486.165a > D
[388] [דׄא]ך אלגׄ[ריב] י[כתׄר] Oxf 2486.165a > D
[389] כמא כׄלע Oxf 2486.165a > D
[390] הוצא לבוש Oxf 2486.165a > L
[391] אלנאס Beginning of TS Ar 28.1a | [אלנ]אס TS Ar 28.1a > D
[392] [עלי ...יג]על Oxf 2486.165a > D
[393] כמא Oxf 2486.165a > D
[394] [פר]עה TS Ar 28.1a > D
[395] ללכה[ני]ם Oxf 2486.165a > D | גק + Oxf 2659.40b
[396] אדׄ קאל Oxf 2659.40b > D
[397] הכהנׄ TS Ar 28.1a
[398] וסאיר Oxf 2486.165a > D | [וסא]יר TS Ar 28.1a > D | אלקצה + Oxf 2659.40b
[399] אלקול Oxf 2659.40b > D
[400] אלי TS Ar 28.1a > D

ויקן יוסף[405] **את**[406] **כל אדמת מצרים**[407] (בר׳ 47:20) וסאיר אלקול.[408] וליס יוגד דֿלך עכסה[409] אן יכון כל מן לם יעבד מעבודה קתלה או אחרקה[410] כמא פעל נבוכֿדנצר.[411] וערפה לדניאל אן[412] בעד מדה יתפק מלך אלפס ומלך אלרום גמיעא עלי מחארבתה,[413] בקולה[414] **ובעת קץ יתנגח עמו**[415] (דניאל 11:40). ופסרנו[416] **וישתער** (דניאל 11:40) "ינתקל אליה" מתֿל **וישׂערה ממקומו** (איוב 27:21), **כמוץ יסוער מגרן**[417] (הושע 13:3), **ואֵסָעֲרֵם על כל הגוים** (זכריהו 7:14) ומא מאתֿל דֿלך. ומן קולה[418] **ובאניות רבות** (דניאל 11:40) ידל עלי אן בינהם בחרא או בחארא. תֿם לא יסאוי תטֿאפרהמא[419] עליה שיא בל יטא בלדאנהם וינסאב ויגוז לקולה[420] **ובא בארצות ושטף ועבר** (דניאל 11:40). תֿם ערפה אן אכתֿר אהל אלשאם יהלכון פי דֿלך אלוקת.[421] ואנמא יסלם בלד אדום ובלד מואב ובעץֿ בלד בני עמון.

תאמלנא איצֿא הדֿה אלחואדתֿ פוגדנא פי אלסיר ואלפתוח, אן בלד מואב[422] ובעץֿ מגאוריהא[423] פתחת עלי[424] אמאן[425] פסלמת מן אלנהב ואלאנתסאף.[426]

401 במחיד ... אלארץ Oxf 2486.165a > D

402 אלמב[קאת] Oxf 2486.165a > D | אלמבקאת End of the readable part of Oxf 2486.165a

403 ביעא Beginning of Oxf 2486.165b

404 [עמ]ל TS Ar 28.1a > D

405 וג׳ + TS Ar 28.1a

406 את Oxf 2486.165b > D

407 את ... מצרים TS Ar 28.1a and Oxf 2659.40b > L

408 אלקול End of Oxf 2659.40b

409 [עכס]ה TS Ar 28.1a > D

410 א[חר]קה Oxf 2486.165b > D

411 נבוכדנׄ TS Ar 28.1a

412 אנה TS Ar 28.1a

413 מחארב[תה] Oxf 2486.165b > D

414 בקו TS Ar 28.1a

415 עמו Oxf 2486.165b > D

416 ופס TS Ar 28.1a

417 כמוץ ... מגרן TS Ar 28.1a > L

418 קול TS Ar 28.1a

419 תצאפרהמא Oxf 2486.165b

420 לקו TS Ar 28.1a

421 אלוקת End of the readadble part of Oxf 2486.165b

422 מואב Beginning of the readadble part of Oxf 2486.166a | [מו]אב Oxf > D

ואמא סאיר אלבלד פמנהוב[427] מתלוף כמא קאל[428] **וישלח ידו בארצות**[429] (דניאל 11:42) פי באקי אלארצות. ובלד מצר איצֿא[430] ידכֿל פי אלאמאן לקולה **וארץ מצרים**[431] **לא תהיה לו**[432] **לפליטה**[433] (דניאל 11:42) אי לא תפלת מן אן תכון[434] תחת[435] ידה בל יגוז אן תפלת מן אלנהב.[436] ופסרת[437] **במכמני**[438] **הזהב** (דניאל 11:43) ״מעאדן״ אד[439] פי מצר מעאדן דֿהב. ואמא **מכמני הכסף**[440] פליס[441] פיהא. לאכן פי אללגֿה יגוז[442] ידֿכר אלפצֿה עלי אנה יצרף בדֿהב[443] כמא עלמנא אן דויד[444] קאל **ושבעת אלפים**[445] **ככר כסף מזקק לטוח קירות הבתים**[446] (דהי״א 29:4). ולם[447] תטֿל תלך אלביות[448] בפצֿה[449]

[423] [מג]אוריה Oxf 2486.166a > D

[424] פ[תחת עלי] Oxf 2486.166a > D | עלי End of TS Ar 28.1a

[425] אמאן Beginning of TS Ar 28.1b

[426] ואלאנתס[אף] Oxf 2486.166a > D

[427] פמנה[וב] Oxf 2486.166a > D

[428] כמק TS Ar 28.1b

[429] באר TS Ar 28.1b

[430] איצ TS Ar 28.1b

[431] מצ TS Ar 28.1b

[432] מ[צרים ...לו] Oxf 2486.166a > D | לו TS Ar 28.1b > L

[433] לפ TS Ar 28.1b

[434] פי + TS Ar 28.1b

[435] תחת TS Ar 28.1b > L

[436] מן אלנהב Oxf 2486.166a > D

[437] ופס TS Ar 28.1b

[438] [מ]כמני Oxf 2486.166a > D

[439] אד Oxf 2486.166a > D

[440] דהֿ[ב ... ה]כסף Oxf 2486.166a > D

[441] ליס TS Ar 28.1b

[442] פיה[א ... יגוז] Oxf 2486.166a > D

[443] אנ[ה ... בדהב] Oxf 2486.166a > D

[444] [דוי]ד Oxf 2486.166a > D | דוד TS Ar 28.1b

[445] ושבעת Oxf 2486.166a > D

[446] קי' ה TS Ar 28.1b

[447] קירות ... ולם Oxf 2486.166a > D

[448] אל[ביות] Oxf 2486.166a > D | אלביות End of Oxf 2486.166a

[449] בפצה Beginning of Oxf 2486.166b | ב[פ]צה Oxf 2486.166b > D

בל ליס סביל אלנאס עלי טול[450] אלזמאן אן יפעלו ד֗לך. ואנמא יעני[451] אנה ד֗הב מצרוף[452] ען קימה סבעה אלאף[453] בדרה ורק. ופסרת **חמדת**[454] **מצרים** (דניאל 11:43) "דק מצר" אד֗ הו אלבז אלמשהור הנאך. ורצד[455] מא קאלה **ולובים וכושים במצעדיו**[456] (דניאל 11:43) פאד֗א בה אלדליל[457] אלד֗י דל עלי בלד מצר כאן מן[458] נובה[459] ואלחבשה. פעדנא[460] מעתקדין אן מעני **במצעדיו** (דניאל 11:43) אצחאב **כטא קדמה** אלד֗י יתכ֗טא ויסעי בקולהם. וקולה[461] בעד ד֗לך **ושמועות יבהלוהו ממזרח**[462] **ומצפון**[463] (דניאל 11:44) יעני[464] ינאלה ד֗לך אד֗א אנתקל[465] ען[466] אלמשרק ואלשמאל. פיציר חיניד֗ אלי מוצ֗ע הו[467] בין אלבחר וגבאל אלשאם. וקריבה אן תכון מדינה עכא אד֗ הי בין אלבחר וגבל אלגליל . פאד֗א תמת[468] הד֗ה אלחואדת֗ פהו[469] אכ֗ר מדה ד֗לך אלשריך כמא קאל[470] **ובא עד קצו**[471] (דניאל 11:45). והו מקאם[472] קולה[473] יואפיה אגלה בזיאדה **עד**[474] כמא קאל[475] ללאבא **ותקרבו ימיך ותבוא עד שנותיך**[476] (יח׳

[450] לי[ס סבי]ל אל[נאס עלי טול] Oxf 2486.166b > D
[451] יע׳ TS Ar 28.1b
[452] ואנמ[א יעני אנ]ה [ד֗ה]ב [מצרו]ף Oxf 2486.166b > D
[453] ז׳ אלאף TS Ar 28.1b | סבעה אלף Oxf 2486.166b
[454] חמודות TS Ar 28.1b
[455] ורצדנא TS Ar 28.1b
[456] [במ]צעדיו Oxf 2486.166b > D | במצ׳ TS Ar 28.1b
[457] [א]ל[ד]ל[י]ל Oxf 2486.166b > D
[458] מן Oxf 2486.166b > D
[459] אלנובה TS Ar 28.1b
[460] פערפנא TS Ar 28.1b
[461] וקו׳ TS Ar 28.1b
[462] ממ׳ TS Ar 28.1b | ממזרח End of TS Ar 28.1b
[463] ומצפון Beginning of TS Ar 28.1c | ומ׳ TS Ar 28.1c
[464] יע׳ TS Ar 28.1c
[465] [אנ]תקל Oxf 2486.166b > D
[466] מן TS Ar 28.1c
[467] הו TS Ar 28.1c > L
[468] תמת End of Oxf 2486.166b
[469] פהו Beginning of the readable part of Oxf 2486.172a
[470] [אלשריך ... קא]ל Oxf 2486.172a > D | כמק׳ TS Ar 28.1c
[471] קצ[ו] Oxf 2486.172a > D
[472] [מ]קאם Oxf 2486.172a > D
[473] קול׳ TS Ar 28.1c
[474] עד Oxf 2486.172a > D
[475] כק׳ TS Ar 28.1c

22:4). פהד֗ה גמלה[477] געלהא גבריאל דלאילא מן חואדת֗ מדה אלשעבוד עלי אלישועה. ומן אול מא אבתדי בד֗כר אחואל הד֗א[478] אלשריך ערפנא אנה לא ממלכה[479] אכ֗רי בעדה לתקדמתה **והצליח עד כלה**[480] **זעם** (דניאל 11:36).

והכד֗א[481] אסמי אלשעבוד **שבעים שנה**[482] כמא[483] קאל[484] אלמלאך[485] **אשר זעמתה זה שבעים שנה**[486] (זכריהו 1:25). וקולה[487] **כי נחרצה נעשׂתה** (דניאל 11:36) יעני[488] אנהא גזירה גזארה רב אלעאלמין בחכמתה. לאנא וגדנא[489] קטע אלחכם יקאל לה **חריצה** אד֗ קאל **כן**[490] **משפטיך אתה חרצת** (מל״א׳ 20:40).

ואעלם עלמך אללה אנה למא[491] צחת לנא הד֗ה אלאותות פראינא ג֗לבה ישׂראל[492] למלך יון וג֗לבה אדום עלי אלשאם[493] ומא גזר מן אלגזירות[494] עלי ישׂראל[495] ומן קתל מנהם ומן אחרק[496] ומן סבי[497] **בימי**[498] **שמד** וצלאח חאלהם[499] פי איאם רבינו בעדמא כאן מן אמר אספסינוס[500] ואמתאלה

[476] ותבא עד ש TS Ar 28.1c
[477] גמלא Oxf 2486.172a
[478] [הד]א Oxf 2486.172a > D
[479] מ[מ]ל[כה] Oxf 2486.172a > D
[480] לתק[דמ]תה [והצליח עד כלה] Oxf 2486.172a > D
[481] והכדי TS Ar 28.1c + Oxf 2486.172a
[482] ע סנה TS Ar 28.1c
[483] אלשעבוד ... כמא Oxf 2486.172a > D
[484] כמק TS Ar 28.1c
[485] אלמלאך TS Ar 28.1c > L
[486] ש ש TS Ar 28.1c
[487] וקו TS Ar 28.1c
[488] נעש יע TS Ar 28.1c
[489] זעמתם ... וגדנא Oxf 2486.172a > D
[490] כן End of the readable part of Oxf 2486.172a
[491] למא Beginning of Oxf 2486.172b
[492] יש TS Ar 28.1c
[493] ומגאזי + TS Ar 28.1c
[494] אלגזרות TS Ar 28.1c
[495] יש TS Ar 28.1c
[496] מנהם + TS Ar 28.1c
[497] סבי End of TS Ar 28.1c
[498] בימי Beginning of TS Ar 28.1d
[499] [ומ]לאח חאל[הם] TS Ar 28.1d > D

ואלמדׄהב אלדׄי אטׄהרתה משארכה[501] אדום ותרכהא עבאדה מעבודאתהא ותבקיתהא מכאנהא ותכׄלץ בלד[502] אדום ומואב מן נהבהא[503] וכון בעץׄ אלחבשה דׄלילהא וסאיר[504] מא וצפנא קד צחת כלהא וכאנת ולם יבק מנהא אלא קצה[505] **ויטע אהלי אפדנו** (דניאל 11:45) אזדאדת קלובנא[506] קוה באן אלישועה כאינה בעקב דׄלך לא מחאלה. וכמא קיל פי קום שמואל **וידע כל ישראל מדן ועד**[507] **בארשבע כי**[508] **נאמן**[509] **שמואל** (שמ״א׳ 3:20). וכמא קאל[510] יהוא[511] **דעו אפוא כי לא יפל מדבר יוי ארצה אשר**[512] **דבר יוי על בית אחאב** (מל״ב׳ 10:10). וכמא קאל לחבקוק בסבב מלך[513] בבל **כי עוד חזון למועד**[514] **ויפח לקץ לא יכזב אם יתמהמה הכה לו כי בוא יבוא ולא יאכר**[515] (חבקוק 2:3). פלמא[516] בלג גבריאל אלי הדׄא אלאצל[517] קאל לדניאל[518] אלי האהנא אכׄר עלמי[519] ומא ענדי. ובעד הדׄא[520] אלפצל[521] למיכאל. כמא[522] אתבע דׄלך בתׄלתׄה פואסיק אלישועה. פקאל [פי] אלפסוק אלאול[523]

500 אספ[סינו]ס TS Ar 28.1d > D

501 מ[שאר]כה Oxf 2486.172b > D

502 ו[תכלץ ב]לד TS Ar 28.1d > D

503 [נהבה]א TS Ar 28.1d > D

504 אלח[בשה דלילהא וסאיר] TS Ar 28.1d > D

505 קצה TS Ar 28.1d > L

506 אפדנו ... קלובנא TS Ar 28.1d > D

507 ו[ע]ד Oxf 2486.172b > D

508 כי End of Oxf 2486.172b

509 נאמן Beginning of Oxf 2486.170a

510 וכק TS Ar 28.1d

511 יה[וא] Oxf 2486.170a > D

512 אשר Oxf 2486.170a > D

513 אפוא ... מלך TS Ar 28.1d > D

514 וג׳ + TS Ar 28.1d

515 ויפח ... יאכר TS Ar 28.1d > L

516 ול[א י]אכר [פלמ]א Oxf 2486.170a > D

517 [א]ל[אצ]ל Oxf 2486.170a > D

518 ל[דני]אל Oxf 2486.170a > D

519 אכר עלמי Oxf 2486.170a > D

520 ובע[ד הד]א Oxf 2486.170a > D

521 [אל]פצל TS Ar 28.1d > D

522 [כמ]א Oxf 2486.170a > D

523 [פקא]ל אלפסוק [א]ל[או]ל Oxf 2486.170a > D | אלאול End of the readable part of Oxf 2486.170a

Dn 12:1

ובעת ההיא יעמד מיכאל השר הגדול העמד על בני עמך והיתה עת צרה אשר לא נהיתה מהיות גוי ועד העת ההיא ובעת ההיא ימלט עמך כל הנמצא כתוב בספר.

ופי ד̇לך[1] אלוקת[2] ינתצב מיכאל אלריס[3] אלכביר[4] אלמוכל[5] בקומך פיכון[6] וקת[7] שדה מא לם[8] יכן[9] מת̇להא מד̇ כאנת אלאמה[10] אלי ד̇לך[11] אלוקת ופיה יתכ̇לץ קומך כל מן וגד[12] מכתובא פי אלכתאב.[13]

אול מא נחתאג אן נשרחה אי שי מעני קולה **יעמד**[14] **מיכאל** (דניאל 12:1). והל הו[15] קאעד[16] או נאים? ונגב[17] באנה[18] יריד[19] בד̇לך נהצ̇תה[20] בקומה

[1] דאלך Spiegel + Morag

[2] אלוקת Oxf 3109.7 > L

[3] אלדייס Spiegel + Morag

[4] אלכביר Beginning of Oxf 2486.170b

[5] אלמווכל Spiegel + Morag

[6] [ב]ק[ו]מך [פיכון] Oxf 3109.7 > D ׀ דלך + Oxf 3109.7

[7] אלוקת Oxf 3109.7

[8] מ[א] ל[ם] Oxf 3109.7 > D

[9] יך Oxf 2486.170b ׀ יכון Spiegel + Morag + Oxf TS Ar 28.1d

[10] אלמלה Morag ׀ לאמה Spiegel

[11] דאלך Spiegel + Morag

[12] כל מן וגד Spiegel + Oxf TS Ar 28.1d + Morag ׀ כל וגד Oxf 3109.7

[13] מכת פי אלכת̇ Oxf TS Ar 28.1d

[14] יע[מד] Oxf 2486.170b > D

[15] הו End of Oxf TS Ar 28.1d

[16] ק[אעד] Oxf 2486.170b > D

[17] ו[נג]ב Oxf 2486.170b > D

[18] באנה Beginning of Oxf 2659.41a

[19] באנ[ה יריד] Oxf 2486.170b > D

[20] [נה]צתה Oxf 2486.170b > D

וקיאמה באמרהם. והכדי יקאל לכל מן[22] הו[23] קאים בקום כמא[24] קאל[25] הנאך **עד שקמתי[26] דבורה[27] שקמתי[28] עם[29] בישראל[30]** (שופטים 5:7). ואיצ̇א **כי הקים יוי[31] להם[32] שפטים** (שופטים 2:18). ואיצ̇א **נביא אקים להם** (דב׳ 18:18). ואיצ̇א **והקימתי לי כהן[33] נאמן[34]** (שמ״א׳ 2:35). ואיצ̇א **ואת דוד מלכם אשר אקים להם** (ירמ׳ 30:9). וכד̇י קאל לגמלה אלאמה **קומי שבי ירושלם** (יש׳ 52:2). ואיצ̇א **קומי אורי כי בא אורך[35]** (יש׳ 60:1). ובעכסה יקול פי וקת אלכ̇דלאן ואלאנחטאט **רדי ושבי על עפר בתולת בת בבל** (יש׳ 47:1). ואיצ̇א **רדי מכבוד ושבי בצמא ישבת בת דיבן[36]** (ירמ׳ 48:18) ומא מאת̇להמא גמיעא. ותסמיתה לה **השר הגדול** (דניאל 12:1) אד̇ הו אלמוכל באלקום[37] אלמסמאין **גוי גדול** (דב׳ 4:7.8), אלטאיעין למן יסמי **האל הגדול** (דב׳ 10:17), אלמצדקין **ביום יוי הגדול** (יואל 3:4), אלמפצלין **להבית אשר אני בונה גדול[38]** (דהי״ב׳ 2:4), אלד̇ין[39] ועדו **אור גדול** (יש׳ 9:1), וסמעו **קול גדול** (דב׳ 5:19), וירת̇ו[40] **האדם הגדול[41]** (יהושע 14:15),

[21] וק[יאמה] ב[אמרה]ם [ו]הכדי Oxf 2486.170b > D
[22] ל[כ]ל [מ]ן Oxf 2486.170b > D
[23] הו Oxf 2659.41a > L
[24] [כ]מא Oxf 2486.170b > D
[25] כמק Oxf 2659.41a
[26] ע[ד שקמת]י Oxf 2486.170b > D
[27] דברה Oxf 2659.41a
[28] שקמ̇ וג׳ Oxf 2659.41a | אל + Oxf 2486.170b
[29] אל MT | אם Oxf 2486.170b > L
[30] עם בישראל Oxf 2659.41a > L
[31] וכי ... יוי Oxf 2486.170b > D | לו + Oxf 2486.170b
[32] להם Oxf 2486.170b > D
[33] ואיצ̇א ... כהן Oxf 2486.170b > D
[34] נאמן End of the readable part of Oxf 2486.170b
[35] אורך Beginning of Oxf 2486.168a | כי בא אורך Oxf 2659.41a > L
[36] דיבון MT | ישבת ... דיבון Oxf 2659.41a > L
[37] בקום Oxf 2659.41a
[38] גוי גדול [... גדול] אלטאיעין Oxf 2659.41a > L homeoteleuton
[39] אללדין Oxf 2486.168a | אלדי Oxf 2659.41a
[40] [ויר]תו Oxf 2486.168a > D
[41] והם + Oxf 2659.41a

ויתעדנו בטוב הגדול (נחמיה 9:25), ומבשרין[42] **וצבא גדול**[43] (דניאל 10:1), אלמתוקעין[44] **יתקע**[45] **בשופר גדול** (יש׳ 27:13). ואלעמידה אלמדׄכורה[46] לה אדׄ קאל **העמד**[47] **על בני עמך** (דניאל 12:1) ליס הי מתׄל קולה[48] **ויאמר**[49] **יואש לכל אשר עמדו עליו** (שופטים 6:31) לאן[50] תלך מקאומה. ולא מתׄל **ויעמדו על עזיהו**[51] **המלך** (דה״ב׳ 26:18) לאן תלך ממאנעה.[52] ולא מתׄל[53] **יתיצבו**[54] **מלכי ארץ** (תה׳ 2:2) לאן תלך מחארבה. ולכן מתׄל[55] **וכל**[56] **צבא השמים עמדו**[57] **עליו**[58] (מל״א׳ 22:19) אלתי הי תשריף[59] ואגלאל עמך ושביה[60] במא קאל איצׄא **אלה שני בני היצהר העמדין על**[61] **אדון כל הארץ**[62] (זכריהו 4:14) יעני[63] בה אהל אלדהן אלממסוחין בה **בית אהרון ובית המלך**. הכדׄי מנזלה מיכאל בין ידי ישׂראל[64] לתשריפהם כמא יקום אלמצׄאף בין ידי אלסלטאן יקומון[65] בין ידיהם. וכמא יחוטון בסלטאנהם[66]

[42] באמת הדבר + Oxf 2659.41a
[43] והתקעים + Oxf 2659.41a
[44] אלמ[תו]קעין Oxf 2486.168a > D
[45] אלמתוקעין יתקע Oxf 2659.41a > L
[46] [וא]ל[עמיד]ה אלמ[דכו]רה Oxf 2486.168a > D | הונא + Oxf 2659.41a
[47] [קא]ל [העמד] Oxf 2486.168a > D
[48] קו Oxf 2659.41a
[49] ויאמר Oxf 2486.168a > D
[50] עמדו ... לאן Oxf 2486.168a > D
[51] ויעמד על עזיהו Oxf 2486.168a > D
[52] [ממאנע]ה Oxf 2486.168a > D
[53] מ[תל] Oxf 2486.168a > D | מתל End of Oxf 2486.168a
[54] יתיצבו Beginning of Oxf 2486.168b
[55] מתל End of Oxf 2659.41a
[56] וכל Beginning of Oxf 2659.41b
[57] השׁ עמ Oxf 2659.41b
[58] עליו Oxf 2659.41b > L
[59] תשרף Oxf 2659.41b
[60] ושביהה Oxf 2659.41b
[61] הע ע Oxf 2659.41b
[62] אדון כל הארץ Oxf 2659.41b > L
[63] יע Oxf 2659.41b
[64] ישׂר Oxf 2659.41b
[65] יקימון Oxf 2659.41b
[66] [יחו]טון [בסלטאנ]הם Oxf 2659.41b > D

כד'אך[67] יחוטונהם **חנה**[68] **מלאך יוי סביב ליראיו**[69] **ויחלצם**[70] (תה׳ 34:8). וכמא יחמלונה עלי אלאיאדי[71] יחמלונהם[72] **כי מלאכיו יצוה לך**[73] **לשמרך**[74] **בכל דרכיך**[75] **על כפים ישאונך**[76] **פן תגף באבן רגליך**[77] (תה׳ 91:11-12).

וקולה[78] **והיתה**[79] **עת צרה** (דניאל 21:1) יריד בה מבאדי אחואל אלישועה[80] אלתי יקאל להא **חבלי משיח**. ואנמא[81] קאל[82] להא[83] **חבלי משיח**[84] לאנהא אסם משתק[85] מן אלטלק. וכמא[86] הו[87] מעלום אנה לא וקת מן[88] אלאוקאת אצעב עלי אלאמראה מן אלטלקה אלקריבה[89] אלי[90] אלולאדה.[91] ובעקבהא יולד[92] אלולד סואא. פלד'לך שבהת אלקצה[93] עט'ם[94] תלך אלשדה פקאל[95] **אשר**

[67] בדאך Oxf 2659.41b
[68] חננה Oxf 2659.41b
[69] ל[יר]איו Oxf 2659.41b > D
[70] ויחלצם Oxf 2659.41b > L
[71] אלאידי Oxf 2486.168b
[72] יח[מ]לונה Oxf 2659.41b > D
[73] וג׳ + Oxf 2659.41b
[74] כי ... לשמרך Oxf 2486.168b > D
[75] לשמרך בכל דרכיך Oxf 2659.41b > L
[76] וג׳ + Oxf 2659.41b
[77] פן ... רגליך Oxf 2659.41b > L
[78] וק Oxf 2659.41b
[79] וקולה והיתה Oxf 2486.168b > D
[80] [מבאד]י [אחוא]ל אלי[שו]עה Oxf 2486.168b > D
[81] וא[נמ]א Oxf 2486.168b > D
[82] קאל End of Oxf 2486.168b
[83] להא Beginning of Oxf 2486.169a
[84] חבלי משיח [ואנמא ... חבלי משיח] לאנה Oxf 2659.41b > L homeoteleuton
[85] מ[שתק] Oxf 2486.169a > D
[86] מן + Oxf 2659.41b
[87] הו Oxf 2659.41b > L
[88] אוקאת אלטלק אצעב + Oxf 2486.169a
[89] מן + Oxf 2659.41b
[90] אלי Oxf 2659.41b > L
[91] אלולאד Oxf 2486.169a ׀ אלולד Oxf 2659.41b
[92] יולד Oxf 2486.169a > L
[93] שבהת אלקצה Oxf 2486.169a > L
[94] עטם Oxf 2659.41b > L
[95] פק Oxf 2659.41b

לא נהיתה מהיות גוי עד העת ההיא (דניאל 12:1). והדֿא אלמתֿל בעינה צֿרבה **ירמיה הנביא**[96] ען אללה, **כי כה אמר יוי**[97] **קול הרדה**[98] **שמענו**[99] **פחד ואין שלום**[100] (ירמ׳ 30:5). וינבגֿי אן נעלם מן הו אלדֿי יקול[101] **שמענו** (ירמ׳ 30:5). פנגֿיב באנה יתואעדהם באנכם[102] סתקולון[103] **קול הרדה שמענו** (ירמ׳ 30:5). פכֿאנה קד אצֿמר [... ...][104] **קול הרדה שמענו** (ירמ׳ 30:5) לאן אלכלאם ללקום[105] אדֿ [...][106] ואולה **ואלה הדברים אשר דבר יוי אל ישראל ואל יהודה** (ירמ׳ 30:4). פאיצֿא אדֿ במתֿל[107] הו בעינינא וקאל[108] שאלו[109] **נא וראו אם יולד זכר מדוע ראיתי כל גבר ידיו על כלציו כיולדה ונהפכו כל פנים לירקון** (ירמ׳ 30:6). תֿם עטֿם דֿלך אליום בקולה **הוי כי גדול היום ההוא מאין כמהו** (ירמ׳ 30:7). ואכֿבר באן אלישועה עקיבתה סואא בקולה **ועת צרה היא ליעקב וממנו יושע** (ירמ׳ 30:7).

ויחתמל **כל הנמצא כתוב בספר** (דניאל 12:1) כֿמס מעאני, תֿלתֿה פרדיה ואתֿנין גאמעין. פאמא אלתֿלתֿה אלפראד פהיה אולא[110] אן **ימלט עמך** (דניאל 12:1) מן יכון **נמצא כתוב בספר** (ע׳ דניאל 12:1), מן תֿבת עלי דינה פי **עת צרה** כמא קאל הנאך **אז אמרתי הנה באתי במגלת ספרכתוב עלי** (תה׳ 40:8). ואיצֿא כל מן אוגבת אלחכמה חיותה פהו כאל....ב פיהא כמא קאל הנאך **כל הכתוב לחיים בירושלם** (יש׳ 4:3). ואיצֿא יחתמל אן יכון דיואן כֿראג[111] אלסלטאן[112] כמא קאל הנאך פי אלכתאב אל[מקדס] **איה סופר איה**

[96] הנביא Oxf 2659.41b > L
[97] כה אמר יוי Oxf 2486.169a > D
[98] [הרד]ה Oxf 2659.41b > D
[99] [הרדה] שמ[ענ]ו Oxf 2486.169a > D
[100] פחד שלום Oxf 2659.41b > L
[101] נעל[ם ... יקו]ל Oxf 2486.169a > D
[102] אנכם Oxf 2659.41b
[103] סתקולון End of Oxf 2659.41b
[104] [... ...] Oxf 2486.169a > D
[105] ללקו[ם] Oxf 2486.169a > D
[106] [...] Oxf 2486.169a > D
[107] במתל Uncertain lesson
[108] בעינינא וקאל Uncertain lesson ו וקאל End of Oxf 2486.169a
[109] שאלו Beginning of Oxf 2486.169b
[110] פ[היה אול]א Oxf 2486.169b > D
[111] כראג End of Oxf 2486.169b
[112] אלסלטאן Beginning of Oxf 2486.171a

שוקל איה סופר את המגדלים (יש׳ 33:18). ואלתכ֗ריגאן אלגאמעאן יריד פיהמא גמלה אלאמה ויצ֗מר כף דאירה. יעני יתכ֗לץ גמיע אלאמה במת֗ל מא כתיב להם פי אלספר מן אלנחמות. פאלאול **נחמות** אלתוריה והו אלעשרה פואסיק אלד֗י קאלהא משה פי קצה **והיה כי יבאו עליך כל הדברים האלה** (דב׳ 30:1) וכפי בהא גמעא [...][113] ואצולהם (?). ואלתאני אלנחמות אלמכתובה פי גמיע ספור אלאנביא כמא קאל **נחמו נחמו עמי דברו על לב ירושלם** (יש׳ 40:1-2) [...][114] קאל **כל הנמצא כתוב בספר** (דניאל 12:1). אלפסוק[115] אלת֗אני[116]

Dn 12:2

ורבים מישיני אדמת עפר יקיצו אלה לחיי עולם ואלה לחרפות לדראון עולם.[117]

וכת֗יר מן אלניאם[118] פי אלתראב יסתיקט֗ון[119] פהאולי[120] לחיוה אלדהר והאולי[121] לעאר[122] ועברה אלדהר.

קולה **ורבים מישני** (דניאל 12:2) ליס הו כל אלמותי ואנמא הם בעצ֗הם כמא קאל הנאך **ורבים מהכהנים והלוים וראשי האבות הזקנים אשר ראו**[123] (עזרא 3:12). ויחתאג אן יכון להם עשר סנין חתי יעקלון כיף **ראו את הבית הראשון** (עזרא 3:12). ומעלום אן בני [...][124] ענה .ל.ל וגיאעהם פיטאבק לבאס. ונט֗יר קולה איצ֗א **ורבים מעמי הארץ מתיהדים** (אסתר 8:17) הם אקל. ומן לם [...][125] ומא אשבה ד֗לך [...][126] ללמותי **בישנים** (ע׳ דניאל 12:2)

[113] [...] Oxf 2486.171a > D

[114] [...] Oxf 2486.171a > D

[115] אלפסוק Uncertain lesson

[116] אלת֗אני End of the readable part of Oxf 2486.171a

[117] עולם Beginning of Oxf 2486.171b

[118] [אל]ניאם Oxf 3109.7 > D

[119] פיסתיקט֗ון Oxf 2486.171b > D | יסתיקצ֗ו Morag | יסתיקצון Spiegel

[120] פהולאי Spiegel + Morag

[121] והולאי Morag

[122] ל[עאר] Oxf 2486.171b > D

[123] אשר ראו Oxf 2486.171b > D

[124] [...] Oxf 2486.171b > D

[125] [...] Oxf 2486.171b > D

[126] [...] Oxf 2486.171b > D

ול.....חאהם בקול **יקיצו** (דניאל 12:2) למעני. מנהא אן אחיא [... ...][127] אלבאיס[128] [... ...][129] פיה[130] קבל ד̇לך כמא יד̇כר אלמנתבה. ומנהא אנהם לם יזלו יתוקעון ד̇לך כתוקע אלנאים אליקט̇ה. ומנא לאן אלמות לם יכן יהולהם כמא לא יהול אלנום אלאנסאן. ווגדנאה יקול הנאך **והעליתי אתכם מקברתיכם עמי** (יח׳ 37:12). פתצפחנא מן יסמי **עמי** פוגדנא אלמוחדין בד̇אך אד̇ קאל **שמעה עמי ואדברה ישראל ואעידה בך אלהים אלהיך אנכי** (תה׳ 50:7). ומן יצדק באלתוריה יקאל לה **עמי** כמא קאל **האזינה עמי תוארתי** (תה׳ 78:1). ומן יתוב קבל מותה יקאל לה **עמי** כמא קאל **ויכנעו עמי אשר נקרא שמי עליהם ויתפללו ויבקשו פני וישובו** (דה״ב 7:14). ואמא קולה **אלה ואלה** (ע׳ דניאל 12:2) פהו יעני בה **אלה אשר יקיצו לחיי עולם** (ע׳ דניאל 12:2) **ואלה אשר לא יקיצו לחרפות לדראון עולם** (ע׳ דניאל 12:2). והו יואפק מא נקל אלאבא[131] מן[132] **להם מתים שעתיד הקב̇ה̇ להחיותם שוב אינן חזרין לעפראן** מן מאת עלי ג̇יר תובה פלא שפיע[133] לה פי אלישועה ולא פי דאר אלאכ̇רה. והו כמן קאל פיה **במות אדם רשע תאבד תקוה ותוחלת אונים אבדה** (משלי 11:7). וקד[134] אשבעת **תחית המתים** שרחא פי אלמקאלה אלסאבעה[135] מן כתאב אלאמאנאת ופי קול מפרד אלפתה להד̇א אלמעני. ואלפסוק אלת̇אלת̇[136]

Dn 12:3

והמשׂכילים יזהירו כזוהר הרקיע ומצדיקי הרבים ככוכבים לעולם ועד.

ואלעלמא[137] יזהרון[138] כנור אלסמא ומסתצלחי אלנאס כאלכואכב[139] אלי אלדהר אבדא.[140]

[127] Oxf 2486.171b > D [...]אל ע[...]
[128] End of the readable part of Oxf 2486.171b אלבאיס
[129] Oxf 2486.171b > D [... ...]
[130] Beginning of Oxf 2486.173a פיה
[131] Oxf 2486.173a > D אלא[ב]א
[132] Beginning of Oxf 2486.173b מן | Uncertain lesson מן
[133] Uncertain lesson שפיע
[134] Beginning of TS Ar 24.22c וקד
[135] TS Ar 24.22c אלז̇
[136] TS Ar 24.22c אלג̇
[137] Oxf 2486.173b > D וא[ע]ל[מא]
[138] TS Ar 24.22c + Oxf 3109.7 פיזהרון
[139] Oxf 2486.173b > D יזהרון ... אלכואכב
[140] Oxf 3109.7 > D אבד[א] | Oxf 2486.173b > D אבדא

למא כאן אלנור עלי צ̇רבין, נור ד̇את אלסמא אלקאבלה מן אלכואכב. והי נור[141] אלכואכב אנפסהא[142] אלד̇י בעצ̇ה קאבלה מן אלשמס ובעצ̇ה מן ד̇אתה. וכאן אלעלמא[143] עלי צ̇רבין. פמנהם אלמתפהם לנפסה וליס[144] יחסן אן יפהם אחדא.[145] ומנהם מן יפהם לנפסה[146] ויחסן אן[147] יפהם ג̇ירה. געל גבריאל[148] תשביה אלאצ̇עפין מנהם באלאצ̇עף מן אלנור. ותשביה[149] אלקויין מנהם באלקוי מן אלנור. פצאר אלמשׂכילים[150] לאנפסהם[151] מת̇ל אלרקיע. ומסתצלחי ג̇ירהם כאלשמס ואלכואכב.[152] ועלי אן אלחכמא ינקסמון[153] להד̇ין אלקסמין.[154] פאן ד̇וי כל[155] קסם מנהם יתפאצ̇לון פי חאלהם.[156] כמא[157] אן כל מצ̇י ומניר מן אלקסמין יתפאצ̇ל[158] פי חאלה. פפי אלסמא דרג אקבל ללנור אכת̇ר[159] מן דרג אכ̇ר. ולד̇לך תסמי אלמנירה ואלמט̇למה[160] ואלמתוסטה. וכד̇אך[161] מן יתעלם לנפסה ג̇ צ̇רוב. וכמא אן אלכואכב מנהא מניר לא[162] מסתניר, והי אלשמס. ומנהא מסתניר לא מניר, [והו] אלקמר. ומניר ומסתניר והי אלבאקי מן [אלכואכב] כד̇אך פי מן יעלם ג̇ירה ג̇ צ̇רוב. ואד̇ [... ...] להד̇א[163] ולהד̇א[164]

[141] נור TS Ar 24.22c > L | נור End of Oxf 2486.173b

[142] אנפסהא Beginning of the readable part of Oxf 2486.174a

[143] אלעלמא Oxf 2486.174a > D

[144] ולא TS Ar 24.22c

[145] [אן יפ]הם אח[דא] TS Ar 24.22c > D

[146] נפסה TS Ar 24.22c | מן + TS Ar 24.22c

[147] יחסן אן TS Ar 24.22c > L

[148] גבריאל TS Ar 24.22c > D

[149] [ותש]ביה TS Ar 24.22c > D

[150] אלמשׂכילים TS Ar 24.22c > L

[151] לאנ[פסהם] TS Ar 24.22c > D

[152] ואל[כואכ]ב TS Ar 24.22c > D

[153] יוקסמון TS Ar 24.22c

[154] אלקס[מי]ן TS Ar 24.22c > D

[155] דו[י כ]ל TS Ar 24.22c > D

[156] פי + TS Ar 24.22c > D

[157] כמא TS Ar 24.22c > L

[158] ליתפאצל TS Ar 24.22c

[159] אכת̇ר TS Ar 24.22c > L

[160] ואלמ[ט]למה TS Ar 24.22c > D

[161] וכדלך TS Ar 24.22c

[162] לא End of Oxf 2486.174a

[163] [...ל]הדא TS Ar 24.22c > D

[164] להדא Beginning of the readable part of Oxf 2486.174b

אמתֿאלא מן אלנביין. אד֞ אלורע יוקפני מן[165] אלדכֿול פי תפאצֿלהם ולא פאידה איצֿא פי[166] דלך. ולכנא נגעל אלתמתֿיל מן אלחכמים[167] ונקול מתֿל רב ורבי חייה,[168] מתעלמין ומעלמין. ומתֿל בן עזאי ובן זומא, מתעלמין[169] לא מעלמין. וצאר תֿואב אלגמיע נורא כמא שרחנא פי תֿואב אלאכֿרה פי אלמקאלה אלתאסעה[170] מן כתאב[171] אלאמאנאת.[172] תֿם קאל[173]

Dn 12:4

ואתה דניאל סתום הדבארים וחתום הספר עד עת קץ ישוטטו רבים ותרבה הדעת.

ואנת יא דניאל[174] אחפט[175] הד֞א[176] אלכלאם[177] ואכֿתם הד֞א[178] אלכתאב אלי וקת אלאגל[179] יטוף פיה[180] אלכתֿירין[181] ותכתֿר[182] אלד֞האנהם.[183]

אנא אקול[184] [אן] קול גבריאל עלי מא נוקל אלינא ולם יריד בקולה [לה] **סתום הדבארים** (דניאל 12:4) כֿתמאן הד֞ה אלנבואת [...][185] יריד [...][186] לאן[187]

[165] אד ... מן TS Ar 24.22c > D

[166] פאיד[ה איצֿא פי] TS Ar 24.22c > D

[167] אלחכמ TS Ar 24.22c

[168] מתֿל רב ורב חייה TS Ar 24.22c > D

[169] [מת]עלמין TS Ar 24.22c > D

[170] אלאכֿר[ה ... אלת]סעה Oxf 2486.174b > D ׀ אלט TS Ar 24.22c

[171] כתאב End of TS Ar 24.22c

[172] אלאמאנאת Beginning of TS Ar 24.22d

[173] [תֿם קא]ל Oxf 2486.174b > D ׀ ק[א]ל TS Ar 24.22d > D

[174] וא[נת] יא ד[ניאל] TS Ar 24.22d > D

[175] אחפץ Spiegel + Morag

[176] הדי Morag

[177] אלכלאם End of Oxf 2486.174b

[178] הדי Morag

[179] [הדא אלכתא]ב אלי [וקת אלאגל] TS Ar 24.22d > D

[180] פיה TS Ar 24.22d > D

[181] אלכתֿיר Oxf 3109.7 + TS Ar 24.22d

[182] ותכתֿר End of Oxf 3109.7

[183] אדאבה[ם] TS Ar 24.22d > D ׀ אראהם Spiegel

[184] אקו[ל] TS Ar 24.22d > D

[185] [...] TS Ar 24.22d > D

[186] [...] TS Ar 24.22d > D

[187] [לא]ן TS Ar 24.22d > D

אלאמר לו כאן כד̇אך לם יגוז לדניאל תדוינהא לא[188] חל [...][189] תעלימהא וכיף תציר **אותות** [ינ]תפע[190] בהא. ולכנה[191] יריד בקולה **סתום** (דניאל 12:4) אחפט̇הא [בקל]בך[192] כק̇ הנאך **ובסתום חכמה תודיעני** (תה׳ 51:8). ויסתקים אן [...][193] סתרהא [אלי] אלאמות. וען אשראר יעו..אמי [...][194] באן [...][195] אלפאט̇ גבריאל מתשאבהם כק̇ לה חת [... ...][196] אלנאס ותנאזעהא. ולם יחצלהא [...][197] מקצוד[198] אלכל מקצודא ואחדא. ת̇ם קאל

Dn 12:5

וראיתי אני דניאל והנה שנים אחרים עומדים[199] אחד הנה לשפת היאר ואחד הנה לשפת היאר.

ואנא דניאל ראית[200] פאד̇א[201] באת̇נין[202] אכ̇רין[203] ואקפין[204] עלי שאטי אלדגלה ימנה[205] ויסרה.

Dn 12:6

ויאמר לאיש לבוש הבדים אשר ממעל למימי היאר עד מתי קץ הנפלאות.

[188] [ו]לא TS Ar 24.22d > D

[189] [...] TS Ar 24.22d > D

[190] [ינ]תפע TS Ar 24.22d > D

[191] ולכ[נה] TS Ar 24.22d > D

[192] [בקל]בך TS Ar 24.22d > D

[193] [...]ל TS Ar 24.22d > D

[194] [...] TS Ar 24.22d > D

[195] וג[...] TS Ar 24.22d > D

[196] [... ...] TS Ar 24.22d > D

[197] במ[...] TS Ar 24.22d > D

[198] [מ]קצוד TS Ar 24.22d > D

[199] עומדים Beginning of TS Ar 21.35a

[200] רא[ית] TS Ar 24.22d > D ׀ ונטרת אנא דניאל TS Ar 21.35a

[201] פאדי Morag

[202] באת̇נאן Morag ׀ את̇[נ]ין TS Ar 21.35a > D

[203] אכ̇רין Morag > L

[204] אכ̇ראן ואקפאן Spiegel

[205] [ש]אטי אלדג[לה י]מנה TS Ar 24.22d > D

פקאל[206] ללמלך [207] אללאבס[208] אלעשר אלמתעלק[209] פוק[210] מא אלדגלה אלי מתי אגל אלכ̇פיאת.[211]

Dn 12:7

ואשמע את האיש לבוש הבדים אשר ממעל למימי היאר וירם ימינו ושמאלו אל השמים וישבע בחי העולם כי למועד מועדים וחצי וככלות נפץ יד עם קדש תכלינה כל אלה.

פסמעת[212] אלמלך אללאבס אלעשר[213] אלמתעלק[214] פוק מא אלדגלה רפע ימינה ויסארה אלי אלסמא[215] וחלף[216] בחיוה[217] אלעאלם אנה אלי וקת אוקאתהם ונצפהא וענד[218] פנא תבדיד יד[219] קום אלקדס[220] תפנא גמיע הד̇ה.[221]

Dn 12:8

ואני שמעתי ולא אבין ואמרה אדני מא אחרית אלה.

ואנא סמעת ד̇לך[222] ולם אפהמה פקלת יא סידי[223] מא אכ̇ר[224] ד̇לך.[225]

[206] אן מן קאל מנהמא + TS Ar 21.35a + TS Ar 24.22d
[207] לאלמלך Spiegel + Morag | ללמ[ל]ך TS Ar 24.22d > D
[208] לאבס Spiegel
[209] אלמתעלך Spiegel
[210] פ[וק] TS Ar 24.22d > D
[211] אלכפאיאת Morag
[212] וסמעת Morag
[213] אללאבס אלעשר Morag > L
[214] אל[מת]עלק TS Ar 24.22d > D
[215] ויס[ארה אלי אלסמא] TS Ar 24.22d > D | אלסמא End of TS Ar 21.35a
[216] וחלף Beginning of TS Ar 21.35b
[217] ב[ח]יוה TS Ar 24.22d > D
[218] [ונצפהא וענ]ד TS Ar 24.22d > D
[219] יד TS Ar 24.22d > L
[220] [אלקד]ס TS Ar 24.22d > D
[221] הדה TS Ar 24.22d > D | הדא Spiegel
[222] דאלך Spiegel + Morag
[223] סיידי Spiegel + Morag
[224] ול[ם] אפהמ[ה] פ[ק]לת [יא סידי מא א]כר TS Ar 24.22d > D
[225] דאלך Spiegel + Morag

Dn 12:9
ואמר לך דניאל כי סתומים וחתומים הדברים עד עת קץ.

קאל[226] אמץׄ יא דניאל פאן[227] אלכלאם מחפוט[228] מכׄתום אלי וקת אלאגל.[229]

Dn 12:10
יתבררו ויתלבנו ויצרפו רבים והרשיעו רשעים ולא יבינו כל רשעים והמשׂכילים יבינו.

פיתחרר ויתנצׄף[230] וינסבך אלכתׄירין[231] ויטׄלמהא[232] אלטׄאלמין[233] ולא[234] יפהמונהא[235] ואלעלמא יפהמונהא.[236]

פלמא קאל **לבוש הבדים** (דניאל 12:6), הדׄא אלקול אעני [... ...][237] סמעה מנה אלמלכאן וקנעא בה ופהמהא [...][238] ואמא דניאל[239] [... ...][240] וקולה[241] **בחי העולם** (דניאל 12:7) [...][242] גל גלאלה אדׄ הו חיות אלעאלם ובה יקום אלעאלם[243] [...][244] ואלתכׄציץ. וקד כאן בעץׄ אלעלמא יסמי[245] [...][246] ואלכׄץ

[226] קא]ל[TS Ar 24.22d > D
[227] אמץ ... פאן TS Ar 24.22d > D
[228] מחפוץ Spiegel + Morag
[229] אלאהל Spiegel
[230] ויתנצף Spiegel
[231] אלכת]ירין[TS Ar 24.22d > D | אלכתיר Spiegel + TS Ar 21.35b
[232] ויטלמהא TS Ar 24.22d > D
[233] יצלמהא Spiegel + Morag
[234] ולם TS Ar 24.22d
[235] יפהמונה Morag | יפהמונא Spiegel
[236] יפהמונה Morag
[237] [... ...] TS Ar 24.22d > D
[238] [...] TS Ar 24.22d > D
[239] דניאל End of TS Ar 24.22d
[240] [... ...] Yeirin 217 > D
[241] קולה Beginning of the readable part of Yeirin (Str. BNU 5138.15)
[242] [...] Yeirin 217 > D
[243] אלע]אלם[Yeirin 217 > D
[244] [...] Yeirin 217 > D
[245] יסמ]י[Yeirin 217 > D
[246] [...] Yeirin 217 > D

יקול הו עקל אלעאלם אד̇ אלעקל [... ...][247] חיוה פי מענאהא ולכן כתבנא ועלננא[248] [... ...][249] ת̇ם אתאה [...][250] אלקץ פקאל **כי למועד** (דניאל 12:7) [... ...][251] פלפט̇ה **מועד** (דניאל 12:7) [...][252] כקולך **למועד**[253] [...][254] להם[255] **בביתי ובחומותי יד ושם טוב** (יש׳ 56:5) [...][256] בדיד אלגלות כקולך **ואפיץ אותם בגוים** (יח׳ 36:19) [...][257] קאל **לבוש הבדים** (דניאל 12:7) הד̇א אלקול, אעני **מועד**[258] [...][259] [...]לכאן[260] וקנעא בה ופהמאה. ואמא [...][261] עלי [...][262] ולם יפהמאה לאנה[263] קאל **ואני שמעתי** (דניאל 12:8) [... ...][264]

Dn 12:11
ומעת הוסר התמיד ולתת שקוץ ימים אלף מאתים ותשעים.[265]

ומן[266] וקת זואל[267] אלדאים וירגע אלרגס אלמוחש[268] אלף סנה מאיתין ותסעין[269] סנה.

Dn 12:12
אשרה המחכה ויגיע לימים אלף שלש מאות שלשים וחמשה.

[247] [... ...] Yeirin 217 > D
[248] ועלל[נא] Yeirin 217 > D
[249] [... ...] Yeirin 217 > D
[250] [...] Yeirin 217 > D
[251] [... ...] Yeirin 217 > D
[252] [...] Yeirin 217 > D
[253] למוע[ד] Yeirin 217 > D
[254] [...] Yeirin 217 > D | End of the readable upper part of Yeirin 217
[255] להם Beginning of the readable part of Yeirin 234 (Str. BNU 5138.16)
[256] [...] Yeirin 234 > D
[257] [...] Yeirin 234 > D
[258] מוע[ד] Yeirin 234 > D
[259] [...] Yeirin 234 > D
[260] [...]לכאן Yeirin 234 > D
[261] [...] Yeirin 234 > D
[262] לם Yeirin 234 > D
[263] ל[אנ]ה Yeirin 234 > D
[264] [... ...] Yeirin 234 > D | End of the readable upper part of Yeirin 234
[265] ותשעים End of TS Ar 21.35b
[266] ומן Beginning of TS Ar 21.35c
[267] זאל Spiegel
[268] מדה + Spiegel
[269] ר צ TS Ar 21.35c

פטובא[270] למן ינתט̇ר[271] ויבלג̇ ד̇כר[272] אלף סנה ת̇לאת̇ מאיה וכ̇מסה ות̇לאת̇ין[273] סנה.

Dn 12:13
ואתה לך לקץ ותנוח ותעמד לגורלך לקץ הימין.

ואנת פאמץ̇ אלי אלאגל פאנך תתואפא[274] ותקום בקצטך[275] ענד אגל[276] אלאיאם.[277]

[270] פטובה Spiegel
[271] ינתצר Spiegel + Morag
[272] אכר TS Ar 21.35c ׀ דכר Spiegel > L
[273] ש̇ל̇ה̇ TS Ar 21.35c
[274] תתואפא TS Ar 21.35c ׀ תתופא Spiegel
[275] בקצדך Morag ׀ לקצטך Spiegel
[276] אגאל Spiegel
[277] תם דניאל קרא ותפסיר + TS Ar 21.35c

Rabbi Saadia's Commentary on the Book of Daniel

Chapter 1

[…].[1] Because he said: *thus says the Lord to His anointed about Cyrus etc.* (Is 45:1)[2] till the end of the story. Therefore, when Cyrus reigned and ordered the building of the Temple,[3] they[4] had to gather and meditate on all the signs of the salvation. Similarly, Cambyses,[5] *the king of the north and the south* and all that was added to the story [are to be considered] in their totality as miraculous signs relative to salvation. [They are to be understood] by mutual elucidation. In the sense that, if the first event happened according to the king's order, that indicates the truth of the remaining events and the salvation [itself]. When the second event corroborates as well his[6] discourse, we have two proofs of the [truth] of the remaining events and the [authenticity] of the salvation. When the third event passes, three events become proofs for us of the remaining events and the [authenticity] of the salvation. And with time the proofs of the salvation multiply until its full realization. At that point, all that happened, plus the salvation and its miraculous signs, become proofs of the reality of the last world, as it has been said: *the sun will turn to darkness and the moon into blood at the coming of the great and terrible day of the Lord* (Jl 3:4).[7]

Thus, it becomes clear that the benefits of this book cannot be enumerated quickly. They are in its text and divided into ten parts. Five of them deal with

1 The first manuscript for this edition of R. Saadia's commentary on Daniel does not coincide with the beginning of the commentary. That is why it starts with the last two words of a previous quotation: ישׂראל ומשׂיחם. We are most probably at the end of Saadia's introduction to his commentary and in the middle of a discussion about the truthfulness of what happened in Babylon.

2 לאן כדא קאל אללה למסיחה ען כורשׁ is R. Saadia's translation of the quoted part of Is 45:1. Cf. the footnote concerning the same quotation in R. Saadia's commentary on Dn 7:7 and how, according to him, God speaks to the messiah about Cyrus, who is thus dissociated from the person of the messiah.

3 Lit. "The house."

4 Or the Jews of Babylon.

5 Uncertain reading of this word whose last part is damaged. Notice that Cambyses (or Canbuzi, 530–522 B.C.E), the son of Cyrus is not mentioned in the Bible. Some historians, however, think that the return of the Jews from Babylon took place under his reign rather than the reign of his father.

6 "His" designates either the king Cyrus, or Daniel.

7 The end of this paragraph shows that it is the conclusion of reasoning about the truth of the promise concerning salvation and the reality of the world to come.

kingship and the other five deal with the benefits and the advantages of the nation.[8] That is why he[9] arranged them in ten parts.[10] The first part deals with the Exile and the painful mistreatment by the nations.[11] The second part deals with what he reveals to Nebuchadnezzar about the four kingdoms and their representations by metaphors before he reveals to Daniel what pertains to him is the fifty-two years.[12] The third part deals with the prohibition from worshiping idols.[13] The fourth part deals with the manner in which calamity struck Belshazzar.[14] The fifth part deals with the manner in which Belshazzar was killed.[15] The sixth part deals with attachment to prayer during the Exile.[16] The seventh [part] deals with the category of discourses relative to the portrayal of kingdoms by animals. The eighth part deals with the particular discourse.[17] The ninth deals with explanation of the seventy weeks[18] which are for the rebuilding of the second [temple].[19] The tenth part deals with the kings' wars and the limit of the other ends.[20]

The four parts following the second one form the five parts relative to the kingdoms. The remaining five deal with considerations and benefits. And since I presented their names let me start explaining their text and meaning with the help of the God of mercy.

8 "The nation" in R. Saadia's vocabulary means always Israel. The word "nations", similar to its biblical disparaging interpretation, designates all the others, but Israel.

9 "He" is ambiguous: It could designate Daniel, the author of the Book of Daniel, or the Bible.

10 The consequential relation between this sentence and the previous one is difficult to apprehend. The meaning may well be because the number of benefits regarding the kingship is five; therefore the number of the benefits of the nation should be five.

11 Cf. Dn 1:1–21.

12 Cf. Dn 2:1–49.

13 Cf. Dn 3:1–30.

14 Cf. Dn 5:1–29.

15 Cf. Dn 5:30–6:10. This is the only verse dealing with the murder of Belshazzar. It is possible that the short title of the fifth part means that the fifth part starts from the murder of Darius.

16 With the double meaning: during the Exile and outside the Holy Land.

17 אלקול אלמוצוף, literally: "the qualified discourse" deals most probably with Daniel's vision in Dn 8.

18 Lit: "which are for the clarification of [+ corrupted word] and the rebuilding of the second [temple]."

19 Cf. Dn 9:1–27.

20 Cf. Dn 10–12.

Dn 1:1

In the third year of the reign of the king Jehoiakim of Judah, king Nebuchadnezzar came to Jerusalem and besieged it.

The first thing we have to investigate is the meaning of his expression *in the third year* (Dn 1:1). The Bible,[21] in fact, mentioned in the book[22] of Kings that Jehoiakim reigned eleven years.[23] Therefore, if Nebuchadnezzar captured him in the third year, how is it possible that he reigned eleven years? He could, accordingly, reign only three years. Then we inquire and ask: did the reign of Nebuchadnezzar start at the third year of Jehoiakim's [reign], or did he start, instead, at the fourth year of Jehoiakim's [reign], according to the verse: *the word which came to Jeremiah about all the people of Judah, in the fourth year of Jehoiakim son of Josiah, king of Judah, which was the first year of Nebuchadnezzar, king of Babylon* (Jer 25:1).[24]

We answer both questions in saying that the beginning of the reign of Nebuchadnezzar was at the fourth year of Jehoiakim;[25] that Jehoiakim ruled eleven years of which three were before Nebuchadnezzar and eight after him. That was the reason he said about Jehoiachin: *and he*[26] *took him*[27] *captive in the eight year of his reign* (2 Kgs 24:12). [...] Years after resisting him and confronting him, as it is said: *and he became his vassal for three years. Then he turned and rebelled against him* (2 Kgs 24:1). If, in fact, [we] put together two years before

21 אלכתאב literally "the book" most of the time means the Bible.

22 ספר "book" a common word in Hebrew and Arabic, is less emphatic than כתאב. It does not designate the Bible, but a book inside the Bible, similar to its meaning here.

23 Cf. 2 Kgs 23:36.

24 Yefet ben Eli explains the chronology of Jehoiakim's reign as follows: Four years under the domination of the Egyptian king; three years under the domination of the Babylonian king, plus three years of independence. According to Yefet, the total of Jehoiakim's reign is ten years.

25 Ibn Ezra advanced a solution to the difference between Jer 25:1, where Nebuchadnezzar attacked Jerusalem at the fourth year of Jehoiakim's reign, and Dn 1:1 where the same event is ascribed to Nebuchadnezzar, while Jehoiakim was in his third year. Ibn Ezra thinks that the Babylonians counted three years of Jehoiakim's reign when they attacked him, while the Hebrews counted four, because he just completed his three years (because he was enthroned in Adar). He started the fourth when he was captured in the month of Nissan. This partial year was counted a full one in Jer 25:1.

26 "He" designates Nebuchadnezzar.

27 "Him" designates Jehoiachin.

his victory, plus the three years of submission [by Jehoiakim], plus the three years of rebellion, the result is eight.[28] Then he said

Dn 1:2

God gave Jehoiakim, the king of Judah, into his hand with some of the vessels of the house of God. He brought them to the land of Shinar to the house of his god and the vessels he brought into the treasury of his god.[29]

His expression: *God gave into his hand* (Dn 1:2) without adding *they lament his murder*, if paralleled with his expression in the [other passage of the Bible]: *he bound him with shackles to convey him to Babylon* (2 Chr 36:6) without adding *he conveyed him to Babylon*, both demonstrate for us that [Jehoiakim] died while [Nebuchadnezzar] was binding him. He, nevertheless, gave the order to pull him while he was still inside the boundaries of Jerusalem according to his expression in the other passage: *he shall have the burial of an ass, dragged out and left lying outside the gates of Jerusalem* (Jer 22:19). His burial was forbidden according to his expression: *and his corpse shall be cast out, to the heat during the day, and to the cold during the night* (Jer 36:30). Furthermore, he should not be buried at all, because of what the Bible mentioned as a punishment measure for the burning of [Jeremiah's] scroll.[30] [About] his expression: ... *some of the vessels of the house of God* (Dn 1:2) we ask: how many? And we answer: one thousand four hundreds ninety-nine.[31] This is a detail that we obtained from the Bible, which mentions the number of the vessels when Cyrus returned them [to the Temple]. [...] Their number is five thousand four hundred. [The ones that Nebuchadnezzar took to Babylon] are divided into three parts [...] distributed as following: *thirty golden basins* (Ezr 1:9) which are [...]; *one thousand silver basins* (Ezr 1:9) which are similar to the [golden basins]; twenty-nine knives. They are the knives [which are deposited according to] the Mishna in *the House of the slaughter-knives, for there they used to keep the knives* (Middoth 4:7). [Plus] *thirty golden bowls* (Ezr 1:10) which are in differ-

28 R. Saadia places the siege of Jerusalem at the end of Jehoiakim's reign. Ibn Ezra place the same event at the beginning of Jehoiakim's reign or the same as the event mentioned in 2 Kgs 24:1.

29 Yefet ben Eli: "And introduced them to the house of his god."

30 Cf. Jer 36:23. R. Saadia explains Jehoiakim's violent death as a punishment. Another tradition looks positively at the same event and considers Jehoiakim's suffering as a sign of his resistance against the Babylonian invaders and his total opposition to the transfer of the Temple vessels.

31 Yefet ben Eli notes that we know neither the number of the vessels, nor their kind, nor the material of which they are made. This may be directed against R. Saadia's observation about the number and the kind of the vessels.

ent sizes, and *four hundred and ten silver double bowls* (Ezr 1:10) similar to the [golden bowels]. The total is one thousand four hundred and forty-nine.

There are also one thousand vessels in total, without any specification, according to his expression: *one thousand other vessels* (Ezr 1:10). It forms the second part. Then what remained to complete the five thousand four hundred, according to his expression: *in all there were five thousand four hundred golden and silver vessels* (Ezr 1:11). Their number is two thousand nine hundreds and one, in total and without specification. And if we examine who according to the Bible carried Jerusalem's vessels to Babylon we found that it happened on three occasions. The first one with Jehoiakim: *Nebuchadnezzar also brought some of the vessels of the House of the Lord, and set them in his temple in Babylon* (2 Chr 36:7). The second [time] with Jehoiachin. The third [time] with Zedekiah: *and all the vessels of the house of the Lord, large and small, with the treasures of the house of the Lord and the king and his officers were all brought to Babylon* (2 Chr 36:18). Thus, it is plausible that the vessels detailed [according to the expression]: *this is the inventory* (Ezr 1:9) were the [vessels brought] with Jehoiakim. The second part, *the other one thousand vessels* (Ezr 1:10) [were the vessels brought] with Jehoiachin. The remaining of the five thousand four hundred were [the vessels brought] with Zedekiah. That is why he did not add the [last] two parts,[32] because they were [brought to Babylon] on two occasions. His expression: *He brought them to the land of Shinar to the house of his god* (Dn 1:2), [indicating] the Israelites who were [brought] with Jehoiakim and the vessels, demonstrates that the vessels were brought during the deportation.

Dn 1:3

The king gave the order to Ashpenaz, the chief of his officers, to bring from the children of Israel, from the king's descent and the nobility.

Dn 1:4

Young men without any impediment, good looking, knowledgeable in every science, they know wisdom[33] and understand it and are strong enough to stand in the king palace, and to teach them the script of the Chaldeans and their language.

32 "The two parts" are the two collections of vessels without specification: the first collection is the unspecified 1000 vessels (Ezr 1:10). The second collection is what remains from the 5400, according to R. Saadia's interpretation of 2 Chr 36:18.

33 R. Saadia render the two Hebrew words דעת and מדע by one Arabic word מערפה 'knowledge, wisdom.' He translated the Hebrew word חכמה 'wisdom' by the Arabic word עלם 'science.'

Dn 1:5

The king assigned to them a daily portion from his bread, his food and his wine;[34] that they have to be nurtured in this way three years, after which they have to stand between the king's hands.

Dn 1:6

There were among them, from the children of Judah, Daniel, Hananyah, Mishael and Azaryah.

Dn 1:7

The chief officer gave them nicknames.[35] To Daniel [he gave the nickname] Belteshezzar; to Hananyah, Shadrak; to Mishael, Mishak, and to Azaryah, Abed Nego.

Dn 1:8

Daniel decided in himself not to be defiled by the king's bread neither by his food nor by his wine and prayed the chief officer not to force him to [defile himself].[36]

Dn 1:9

And God granted him favor and mercy in the eyes of the chief officer.[37]

Dn 1:10

The chief officer said to Daniel: 'I am afraid of the king, my master, who determined your food and your drink and who, looking at you, will find your faces more depressed than the youths of your generation, and so you imperil my life[38] before the king.'

Dn 1:11

Daniel answered the steward whom the chief officer assigned to Daniel, Hananyah, Mishael and Azaryah.

Dn 1:12

'Test your servants for ten days in which we will be given only grain to eat and only water to drink.

34 כמר שרבה literally 'the wine of his drinking.'

35 אלקאבא 'nicknames' and not אסמאא 'names' like in the translation of Yefet ben Eli.

36 Lit. "Not to do so." Most probably R. Saadia wanted to avoid the repetition of the expression לא יתגאל.

37 Lit. "That is why God granted him favor and mercy within him."

38 Lit. "My head."

Dn 1:13

Then it will become clear to you our appearance in comparison to the appearance of the youths who eat the king's plates and his food.[39] Then treat your servants according to what you see.'

Dn 1:14

He agreed to what they said and tested them for ten days.

Dn 1:15

Once the ten days passed, their look appeared to be better and their bodies fatter than the youths who ate the king's plates and food.

Dn 1:16

Therefore the housekeeper would take for himself[40] their bread, food and their wine and gave them grain.

Dn 1:17

God bestowed on those four youths knowledge and intelligence in all the book of wisdom, but Daniel surpasses[41] them in all in dreams and visions.

Dn 1:18

At the end of the days that the king assigned to them in order to be brought, the chief officer brought them between Nebuchadnezzar's hands.

Dn 1:19

The king spoke to them and found no one in all of them[42] like Daniel, Hananyah, Mishael and Azaryah, therefore he ordered them to remain in his presence.

39 פת־בג which was never written with *maqqef* (־) in the manuscripts used in this edition, is normally rendered in two words by R. Saadia. It is translated by one word by Yefet ben Eli who, in his commentary of Dn 1:16, explains that these two words mean "bread and meat".

40 יאכד לנפסה "take for himself" is added by R. Saadia and has no masoretic background.

41 הבין is understood by R. Saadia as comparison to show Daniel's superiority over his companions. Yefet ben Eli translates: "And Daniel was knowledgeable in every inspiration and dreams."

42 The expression "of them מכלם" designates either the Babylonian men of wisdom and astrologers, or the Israelites who were deported to Babylon. R. Saadia favors the first interpretation when he compares Daniel's wisdom to the Babylonian men's

Dn 1:20

And in any matter pertaining to wisdom and understanding he inquired of them he found them ten times superior to all men of wisdom and astrologers.[43]

Dn 1:21

And Daniel stayed until the first[44] **year of the king Cyrus.**

[...].[45] [He answered] their request then He weakened their bodies (Ps 106:15).[46] In the same way were the Jewish youths how ate the bread and the food of the king (cf. Dn 1:15).[47] But those who eat grain [...] more than all of them.[48] His expression: At the end of the days that the king assigned to them in order to be brought (Dn 1:18) refers to three years that he mentioned previously: they have to be nurtured in this way three years, after which they have to stand between the king's hands (Dn 1:5).

Perhaps we need to explain what happened to the Levites who need five full years [of preparation] and are then [be able] to serve, according to his expression: *From the age of twenty-five age up he shall join the legion [of the service of the Tent of Meeting]* (Nm 8:24).[49] Those [...]. We say this is literally the

---

wisdom. Yefet ben Eli, in his commentary of Dn 1:19, favors the second interpretation.

43 "Astrologers" designates those who, reading the constellations, can predict the future. Their predictions were of capital importance and were consulted regularly prior to big events, such as war.

44 The majority of manuscripts have the number "eleven" instead of "one". This translation is in harmony with the massoretic text.

45 The following text does not present the normal following to the end of R. Saadia's translation. The commentary of Dn 1:3–14 is missing. We join our commentator at the end of his explanation of Dn 1:15.

46 פאעטאהם סואלהם, ובעת֗ אלהזאל פי גסמהם is R. Saadia's translation of Ps 106:15. Literally: "He answered their request and imposed thinness on their bodies."

47 There is most probably a parallel that R. Saadia establishes between the Israelites who were rebellious against God in the desert during the Exodus and the Jewish youths who, during the exile became rebellious by accepting the Babylonian manners, particularly their eating and drinking customs.

48 It is easy to understand the missing part of this sentence: R. Saadia is trying to demonstrate that those who refused the Babylonian manners concerning the eating and drinking are better off than those who thought of improving their condition by accepting the new manners. The hidden question in all this discussion is faithfulness to God's commandments.

49 מן אבן כ֗מס ועשרין סנה פצאעדא ידכל ללגיש לכ֗דמה כ֗בא אלמחצר is R. Saadia's translation of Nm 8:24.

king's choice. Then we say that the Levites [...] for the service [...] before the five years [... ...] the wisdom before three years, according to the expression: *knowledgeable in every field* (Dn 1:4).[50]

[His expression] *He found them ten times superior to all men of wisdom and astrologers* (Dn 1:20) means multiple times more, that no [one can count them]. Of course, every man of wisdom had reached a high degree of knowledge. In fact, if the degree they [had reached] is not superior, its multiplication is not superior either. Then we say [...] Daniel [...] three years into the kingship of Cyrus, as it is said: *in the third year of Cyrus, the king of Persia something was revealed to Daniel* (Dn 10:1) how is it possible then to say here *And Daniel stayed until the first year of the king Cyrus* (Dn 1:21)? I have two answers for this question. The first, that he lived in Babylon until the first year of Cyrus' kingship, then he [...]. The second, that he remained at the ruler's service until the first year of Cyrus,[51] because the reason of the decline of the Babylonian kingdom[52] [... ...] Nebuchadnezzar in saying: *at the third year of Belshazzar* (Dn 8:1) *then I arose and attend to the king's business* (Dn 8:27). But Darius added [to his importance] by naming him *ruler of one third of his kingdom* (cf. Dn 5:7.16) until the coming of Cyrus who deposed him. The second [interpretation] is that he remained in Babylon until the third year of Cyrus.

50 The corrupted text of this portion of R. Saadia's commentary makes it difficult to grasp the real meaning of the comparison between the three years of formation imposed on Daniel and his companions in order to reach the necessary level of wisdom in order to stand before the king, and the five years necessary for the Levites in order to be able to serve liturgically. We can postulate that the Levites need more years either because of the complexity of the liturgy, or because liturgical service involves a higher degree of the religious activity.

51 According to Yefet ben Eli, the first year of Cyrus is the year that the Israelites were authorized to leave Babylon and go back to the Holy Land. It is according to Yefet, the year that Daniel either returned to Jerusalem, or decided to devote his life to prayer and adoration, or was simply too old to start new activity.

52 Most probably the manuscript interrupts here the reasoning of R. Saadia's argument. What comes next is a discussion of different problem.

Chapter 2

The text of the second chapter

Dn 2:1
In the second year of the reign of Nebuchadnezzar, he saw a dream[1] that saddened his spirit and disturbed his sleeping.

Dn 2:2
He commanded that the wise men, astrologers, magicians and Chaldeans be summoned to tell him the vision.[2] So they came and stood between his hands.

The first thing we have to examine is his expression: *In the second year of the king Nebuchadnezzar* (Dn 2:1). We start by saying that the beginning of Nebuchadnezzar's reign was clearly at the fourth year of Jehoiakim; that Daniel and his companions were deported at the eleventh year of Jehoiakim, which coincide with the eighth year of [Nebuchadnezzar's reign]. How is it then that [this event] happened at the second year of his reign, while they were not yet deported, nor was Jehoiakim obedient to him? We answer that it is *the second year of the war against Jerusalem* (cf. Dn 2:1.9:2).[3] In fact, the Bible registers the years according to Babylon, but also according to Jerusalem. Therefore, it was the thirteenth year of Daniel's staying in Babylon.[4] That is why we mentioned in the title of this book, I mean in its commentary, that it contains events

1 The word twmlj "dreams" is being translated as singular for a reason that R. Saadia explains in his commentary of this verse. In doing so he refrains from repeating the inelegant masoretic expression: "He dreamed dreams."

2 From Dn 2:2 and until the and of the chapter, R. Saadia will substitute the word "vision" אׄלרויה for the word "dream" חלם.

3 R. Saadia's interpretation is mentioned, without referring to his name, in Yefet's commentary on this verse. He characterizes it as "probable". Yefet's interpretation is that "the second year of Nebuchadnezzar" refers to the second year of Nebuchadnezzar's reign over the whole world, not before, according to Dn 2:38.

4 Lit. "It was the thirteenth year of Daniel by him (=Nebuchadnezzar)."

relative to one thousand three hundred and eighty six years.[5] Because he revealed the events, first from *the second year to the war against Jerusalem* (cf. Dn 2:1.9:2), which is fifty two[6] years before [what is meant by his expression]: *Blessed is the one who waits* (Dn 12:12).

His expression: *Nebuchadnezzar had dreams* (Dn 2:1) refers to a single vision.[7] Yet, since it was divided into four parts, he called it *dreams* (Dn 2:1).[8] His enumeration of the Chaldeans among the group of the learned men demonstrates that this name has the function of a scientific title as if to speak of "scholars."[9] His expression: *That they tell him his dreams*[10] (Dn 2:2) is to be taken literally as [the meaning] of what he asked from them, because he was not looking only for an interpretation, but for what the vision is, its essence. [He did not ask them] because he forgot it, but in order to test them. For if he did forget it, he would not be sure whether they would be truthful or they would invent something just to please him, while hiding their true feeling.[11] And when we inquire about those three kings we find that the wise men in everyone's city[12]

5 This part of R. Saadia's commentary belong to the beginning that is no longer extant.

6 This number is uncertain. At least three numbers reached us: four hundred ת׳, fifty two נ״ב and the erroneous number nb). Unfortunately we do not have the last part of R. Saadia's commentary on the last part of Dn 12:5–13 which makes difficult any further explanation of his interpretation. It is also possible that the number fifty two is a deformation of another number. In fact, the lesson that reads fifty two is unclear.

7 This same explanation of the plural *dreams* (Dn 2:1) is adopted by Yefet ben Eli. It goes without saying that he did not dignify his source, (R. Saadia, who was his major rabbinical opponent) by mentioning his name. It is also true that mentioning all the references is not common in the mediaeval period. However, R. Saadia's name will be mentioned whenever his interpretation is contested. This is the case, for example, in Yefet's interpretation of Dn 12:13.

8 The only difference between R. Saadia's interpretation and Yefet's is that *dreams* has five parts according to the latter: the four concerning the nations, plus the part concerning Israel. The last part is not mentioned explicitly. That is why R. Saadia does not take it into consideration as an independent part.

9 אצחאב אלרואק literally "the men of the portico", which is the part of the mosque reserved for teaching.

10 חלמותיו is being rendered here "dreams" since R. Saadia refers to the Hebrew text, and not to his translation which is "vision."

11 A difficult and uncertain reading. The meaning seems to be that Nebuchadnezzar insisted that they tell him what was his dream in the fullness of its meaning, because he suspected his wise and learned men of fearing him to the point that they would please him by an interpretation that does not reflect their true thinking.

12 The city is Babylon, capital of king Nebuchadnezzar, his son Belshazzar and Darius the Median.

try to outbid each other in their [explanation] of the vision. In the case of Pharaoh, he told them the vision and asked for its explanation, according to the expression: *And Pharaoh told them his dream* (Gn 41:8).[13] Nebuchadnezzar, however, diminished the importance of the interpretation, and asked for the vision itself, as it is said: *That they tell him his dreams* (Dn 2:2). [… …][14] that is why he diminished the importance of the interpretation. He asked […] a man from […] he has a vision during his sleep, before he sees it. And when he did not [… …] news from that time, Samuel used part of the dream and told him [about] what is disturbing him. […] worried him to the point that he became attached to it and did see it. If he had said […] then he took him into himself out of fear […].[15]

Dn 2:3
The king told them: I saw a vision and my spirit is agitated until I know it.[16]

Dn 2:4
They spoke to him in Aramaic:[17] 'O king, may God give you long life[18]! Tell the vision to your servants, and we will recount to you its interpretation.'

Dn 2:5
He answered them and said: 'I already decided the thing, if you do not make known to me the vision and its interpretation you will be torn in pieces and your houses will be reduced to stones.[19]

13 פקץ עליהם רויאה is R. Saadia's translation of the quoted part of Gn 41:8.
14 A damaged passage in the manuscript. It reads as follow: until […] that […] to Daniel, if it is taken […].
15 A very obscure passage because of the partial and damaged reading of the manuscript. Most probably it deals with a second example of a vision to underline the specific type of Nebuchadnezzar's vision.
16 לדעת את החלום is being understood by R. Saadia as "until the time I know it" and not " my spirit is anxious to know it", which is the common understanding of this verse. Yefet ben Eli has an imprecise translation that could mean: 'My soul is sad for knowing it.'
17 באלאנבטייה literally "the Nabatean language". Yefet ben Eli has a more bizarre translation: the Armenian language. He also mentioned the possibility that their conversation could be carried on in more than one language.
18 A translation preferred to the usual "long lives the king" where God does not appear explicitly as the subject of the action.
19 Its very difficult to understand the real meaning of צואפי in this verse which R. Saadia does not comment on. Is it "reduced to stones" or "empty" as in Yefet ben Eli's translation, which uses the same word?

Dn 2:6
But if you tell the vision and its interpretation, gifts, prices, dignity and great honor shall be given to you before me; therefore tell me the vision and its interpretation.'

Dn 2:7
They answered him again and said: 'May the king tell the vision to his servants and we will relate to him its interpretation.'

Dn 2:8
He answered them and said: 'I know with certainty that you are buying[20] time because you see that I have already decided the matter.

Dn 2:9
That if you do not make the vision known to me, your will have only one destiny, if you have prepared false and inaccurate discourse between my hands until the hour changes and passes; but tell me the vision itself in order that I know that you are truthful in telling me its interpretation.'[21]

Dn 2:10
The Chaldeans answered in his presence and said: 'No man on earth is capable of answering what the king wishes; in fact no great king, neither a ruler has ever requested a thing similar to your request from any wise man or an astrologer, or a Chaldean.

Dn 2:11
The matter[22] that the king investigates is precious and no one other than us is qualified to inform the king about what he said, except the angels who do not live with human beings.'

Dn 2:12
At that, the king got angry and intensely furious; he then ordered that all the wise men of Babylon be put to death.

20 Yefet ben Eli: "Buying or selling time."
21 Yefet ben Eli's translation is more literal: "Tell me the dream and I will know whether it is its interpretation that you give me."
22 Yefet ben Eli: "The word."

Dn 2:13

The decree was issued, that the Chaldeans will be put to death, and Daniel with his friends were almost killed.[23]

All those conversations have a clear meaning, which spares us its explanation, particularly since we translated with words[24] that demonstrate its purpose. The most important part is its Aramaic[25] discourse, which is difficult to be understood for someone unfamiliar with it. And because it has no similar discourse, we [decided] to make this commentary.[26] With all that we say what is the difference between the [two answers] of the group whose first [answer]: *Tell the vision to your servants, and we will recount its interpretation* (Dn 2:4) and the second: *May the king tell the vision to his servants and we will relate its interpretation* (Dn 2:7)? We say that they spoke to him, first, about his own future. Then they spoke to him without [referring the subject] to the future. They wanted to say that the usual way for any king is to narrate the vision then it is explained to him. We ask again why is it that he started [his discourse] to them by evil before the good? I mean [he started by]: *If you do not make known to me the vision* (Dn 2:5) before *if you tell the vision and its interpretation* (Dn 2:6). We say that the motif of his demand is a trial that he impose on them.[27] As to *almost* (Dn 2:13)[28] it is the parallel of *the ship was almost breaking up* (Jon 1:4) in the language of the Targum. It is a word of possibility and is translated accordingly.[29] Then he said:

Dn 2:14

At that moment, Daniel raised the matter to Aryoch the chief of the king's executioners who was about to kill the Babylonian wise men.

23 Yefet ben Eli: "And Daniel and his friends were commanded to be killed."

24 Lit. "And I include in it letters that demonstrate its purpose."

25 נבטי "Nabatean" is the same word that R. Saadia uses in Dn 2:4.

26 A sentence too unclear to be translated with certainty. Does R. Saadia mean that he will comment on this part of Daniel because of the difficulty of its language? Or, because of this difficulty that he comments on the book of Daniel?

27 This brief commentary seems to indicate that for R. Saadia the usual way to test someone is to start by danger of failure and end by the benefit of succeeding.

28 ובעו in the text.

29 Lit. "It has, in the language of the Targum, the function of rbvhl hbvj hynahw *and the ship was almost breaking up* (Jon 1:4), among the expressions of possibility, and its translation is *and the ship was almost breaking up* (Jon 1:4) arbtal ay[b aplaw. Its meaning: it was about to be broken." Our English translation avoids the repetition by translating one time Jon 1:4.

Dn 2:15

He asked him[30] saying: 'Why is it that the matter is precipitated by the king.' Then Aryoch made known the story to him.[31]

Dn 2:16

Daniel succeeded[32] to ask the king to receive him immediately[33] in order to make known to him the vision and its interpretation.

Dn 2:17

Then Daniel reached his house and informed his companions Hananyah, Mishael and Azaryah about the story.

Dn 2:18

And they were united[34] to ask for mercy from the Lord about this secret to prevent Daniel and his companions from being put to death with the rest of the wise men of Babylon.

Dn 2:19

Thereupon God revealed this secret to them in a night vision, then Daniel praised the Lord of heaven.

Dn 2:20

In saying: 'may the name of God be blessed from the beginning of the universe till its end, to whom belong wisdom and might.

Dn 2:21

He alters times and periods,[35] deposes and establishes kings,[36] gives wisdom to the wise men and science to the knowledgeable in cognition.

30 Lit. "He asked Aryoch."

31 Lit. "Then Aryoch made known the story to Daniel."

32 פחסבב lit. "he motivated" or "inspired" or "pushed" in order that the question be put to the king.

33 אגלא 'immediately' has no origin in the masoretic text.

34 'And they were united' has no origin in the masoretic text.

35 אלאוקאת ואלאזמאן translated by 'times and periods' are almost synonymous and render into Judeo-Arabic the Aramaic עידניא וזמניא. Yefet ben Eli's translation is similar. However, he understands עידניא 'seasons' and וזמניא as 'day and night.' He adopts later, still, R. Saadia's interpretation. Most of the modern translations read 'times and seasons.'

36 Yefet ben Eli has: "Suppresses and establishes kingdoms."

Dn 2:22
He reveals deep and hidden matters, knows what is in the dark and the light dwells with him.

Dn 2:23
To you, O God of our fathers, I give thanks and praise, because you assist me with wisdom and might. Now, make known to me what I asked from you, which is the question of the king.

Dn 2:24
Thereupon, Daniel reached Aryoch whom the king appointed to put to death the wise men of Babylon. He told him: 'Kill no one of them; introduce me to the king, that I make known to him the vision[37] and its interpretation.'

Dn 2:25
At that point Aryoch took the initiative to introduce Daniel to the King and told him: 'I found one from among the Jewish deported who said that he will make known to the king the vision[38] and its interpretation.'

Dn 2:26
The king started and said: 'Daniel, whose byname is Belteshazzar, are you able of informing me about the vision I saw and its interpretation.'

Dn 2:27
Daniel answered and said: 'What the king required of the wise men, the astrologers and the Chaldeans, they are not capable of narrating.[39]

Dn 2:28
However, God who is in heaven and who reveals secrets, made known to Nebuchadnezzar what will happen at the end of time about your vision and what your eyes contemplate on your bed is what I am saying.'

37 The MT has: "that I make known to him the interpretation." R. Saadia adds the vision in harmony with what the king requested, but with no basis in the text. The same observation applies to R. Saadia's translation of Dn 2:25.

38 אלרויא 'vision' is added by R. Saadia to his translation and has no masoretic background.

39 R. Saadia omits to add: "Narrating it *to the king*."

I interpreted החיב עטא וטעם (Dn 2:14) as *raised the matter*, similar to the expression טעם בעל רחום (Ezr 4:8). This means that he raised the matter. However, concerning Daniel, he[40] added החיב (Dn 2:14)[41] because he belongs to the king followers and can possibly be described by this word,[42] since it has been said: *In spite of that the lazy thinks that he is wiser than many good advisers* (Pr 26:16).[43] And his interrogation *why is it that the matter is precipitated [by the king]* (Dn 2:15) demonstrates that did not explain to the wise men that [the king] kills whom he [thinks that he] was guilty, because they did not all go before the king. And his mention of [the word] *interpretation* in three passages of this story designates *the vision and its interpretation*. He just abridged. They are *[to receive him] immediately in order to make known to him the interpretation* (Dn 2:16); *introduce me to the king, that I make known to him the interpretation* (Dn 2:24); *that he will make known to the king the interpretation* (Dn 2:25). However, when he was between the king's hand, the result was that he told the king [in his words] *the vision I saw and its interpretation* (Dn 2:26). And we ask [why is it] that Daniel dared request the postponement, without knowing whether the secret will be revealed to him or not? We answer that there are two reasons for that. The second, his trust in his Lord.

As to the name he gave to his Lord in this book (Dn 2:19) and in the [book] of Ezra (Ezr 1:2) *the Lord of heaven*,[44] it is according to our tradition that we explain it by the fact that before Israel[45] became a big [nation] it used to call God *the Lord of heaven*. For example, his expression: *The lord of heaven who took me* (Gn 24:7).[46] Then, when [Israel] became numerous it [started] to call [God] *the Lord of heaven and earth*. But when [Israel] was deported he returned the symbol back to *the Lord of heaven*.[47] That is why we said, Nehemiah, Cy-

40 "He" designates either the Bible or the scribe, the author of the Book of Daniel.

41 The Aramaic byth here is translated by the Arabic verb רפע 'raised' in the expression 'raised the matter.'

42 The word טעם:

43 ומע דׄאך פהו ענד נפסה אעקל מן וזרא כתׄירין is R. Saadia's translation of Pr 26:16. His translation is far from being a literal rendering of the masoretic text. Literally: 'In spite of that he (the lazy person) believes that he is wiser than many ministers.' In fact the Hebrew word טעם is not translated, but implied in the Arabic word וזרא 'who give good advice to the king.' טְעֵם translated by R. Saadia as "matter" or "story" as in Dn 2:14 and (Ezr 4:8) is being equated with "advice" or "good sense".

44 According to R. Saadia's translation of this expression, God is *the Lord of heaven*, רב אלסמא, and not God of heaven. Yefet ben Eli translates: God of heaven.

45 Lit. "The nation."

46 אללה רב אלסמא אכׄרגני מן בית אבי is R. Saadia's translation of the quoted part of Gn 24:7.

47 Lit. אלהי השמים ואלה שמיא: The Lord of heaven (in Hebrew) and the Lord of heaven (in Aramaic). It seems that R. Saadia ties the expression: "Lord of heaven and e-

rus, Artaxerxes and others with the praise of Daniel using those eight meanings, are similar to the situation of exile and penury.[48] Plus, there are different meanings that intersect, because the dirt is similar to the penury and the exile.[49] Therefore his expression: *He alters times and periods* (Dn 2:21) is parallel to what he observed about the replacement of the kingdom of Israel by the kingdom of the Chaldeans. Hence, his expression: *Deposes and establishes kings* (Dn 2:21) is by reason of what he observed of the fall of Zedekiahu and the crowning of Nebuchadnezzar. And his expression: *He gives wisdom to the wise men* (Dn 2:21) means that those whom he called wise men it is God who gave them the wisdom[50] which consequently allow them to become wise men. Similarly to some one who says: "I built this house". He does not mean that he built it while it was a house. What he means is that he built it on a site that consequently[51] became a house.[52] And as Aliphaz says: *You strip some of their cloths and they become naked* (Jb 22:6).[53] What he asked for is the clothing of the clothed [individuals], who consequently[54] become naked.[55] There is also Amos' expression: *fixing our scale for cheating* (Am 8:5). He explained how the scale

---

arth" to the times when Israel was an independent political entity. As if when Israel is not independent the Lord is deprived from being recognized as Lord on earth. In other word, it is Israel alone when it is master of its destiny that gives praise to the Lord.

48 Lit. "the situation of exile and the situation of penury." A difficult sentence to be understood in its minute details, because of the complexity of its textual tradition. R. Saadia's idea seems to be that the Babylonian exile modifies or impoverishes the biblical style, returning it back to the time of a poor and small Israelite community.

49 A difficult sentence that represents, probably, the summary of a comparison between dirt and exile.

50 Lit. "Those whom he (= Daniel or God) called wise men it is he (= God) who gave them wisdom". The first "he" may also be the biblical scribe.

51 Lit. "In a second degree."

52 What R. Saadia wants to say, with the help of many examples, is that calling someone a "wise man", before he receives wisdom from God is metaphorical and inaccurate chronologically, since the individual was not wise before receiving the wisdom.

53 ותסלך ת'יאב קום פיצירון עראה is R. Saadia's translation of the quoted part of Jb 22:6. In his commentary of Jb 22:6 R. Saadia refers to Dn 2:21 as well as to Am 8:5.

54 Lit. "In a second degree."

55 While the meaning is clear, the sentence structure is imprecise. Aliphaz is asking for cloths from the naked, which is an improper question according to R. Saadia. Because if someone is naked that means that the person is already without cloths, and the question has its own answer included.

[is modified] in order to be *dishonest.*[56] There is Isaiah's expression as well: *Who (= God) gave breath to the people upon it (= the earth)* (Is 42:5).[57] [The word "people" is to be understood] in a second degree. *[The expression: He gives] science to the knowledgeable in cognition* (Dn 2:21) designates someone who is capable of understanding and making known to someone else. Because "understanding" and "making known" are equal in the Hebrew language.[58] Since the Bible said about the understanding: *And Eli understood* (1 Sm 3:8). And about "making known": *He made me known, because he spoke to me [and said]* (Dn 9:21). Furthermore, we have to explain what Daniel meant by *wisdom and science* (cf. Dn 2:21). We say that wisdom designates what is inside the creatures, and that science designates what comes from the creatures. Moreover, it is our custom to attribute *wisdom* to what is in the past,[59] according to the expression: *All this I probed by wisdom*[60] (Ecc 7:23), *what exist, is far-reaching etc.* (Ecc 7:24).[61] As to the *understanding,*[62] [it applies] to what will happen, as the Bible says: *I came to make you understand what will happen [to your people]* (Dn 10:14). The fifth [action] is *He reveals deep and [hidden] matters* (Dn 2:22)[63] designates what is in the heart of the people, according to his ex-

56 Lit. "Then he explained the scale which becomes dishonest in the second situation.". In other words, if it is a scale delivering measure, you can not set it for cheating. If the scale is being set up for cheating you can not call it a scale anymore.

57 מעטי אלנסמה אלקום אלדין עליהא is R. Saadia's translation of the quoted part of Is 42:5.

58 R. Saadia refers to the verb בין in his two forms: Qal, to understand; Hiphil, to make known, to teach.

59 Does R. Saadia want to say that by wisdom it is possible to explain what happened alone and had impact on what will happen? Or does he want to say that wisdom is the fruit of human experience, the lessons that the wise accumulate from past experience? There is no clear indication of one or the other explanation.

60 R. Saadia does not indicate whether בחכמה should be translated "by wisdom", "in wisdom" or "with wisdom." The three translations are possible.

61 The sense of quoting Ecc 7:24 is that what already exists and remains unreachable by a human being is possible to reach only by wisdom.

62 R. Saadia started by establishing a parallel between חכמה and ומנדעא. He ended by explaining בינה instead of ומנדעא. Therefore, while it is possible to conclude that according to him hnyb and ומנדעא are synonymous, it is possible as well to read this text without trying to find a coherent meaning because of the many lacunae in the manuscripts relative to this passage of the commentary. Cf. the Judeo-Arabic text.

63 This fifth point shows that R. Saadia was enumerating God's action, revealing the inner side of the human being and demonstrating that nothing that pertains to the human existence can be hidden from God. Most probably R. Saadia is counting the aspects of God's action in Dn 2:21–22. Hypothetically, we can say with him that the first aspect is that *He alters times and periods* (Dn 2:21); the second, that He *deposes and establishes kings* (Dn 2:21); the third, that He *gives wisdom to the*

pression: *Their inside, their hearts were with deep thoughts* (Ps 64:7).[64] The sixth [action] is *the hidden matters* (Dn 2:22) by which he[65] designates what is under the soil, as he says: *How I would like to be hidden in the earth* (Jb 14:13)[66] and what is [hidden] in the seas, as the Bible says: *And if they hide from my sight in the bottom of the sea* (Am 9:3). The seventh [action]: *He knows what is in the dark* (Dn 2:22), following its obvious meaning. The eighth, *the light dwells with him* (Dn 2:22). He means that God helps by being comparable to the light; He enlightens the eyes and the brains, in conformity with the proverb by which [His action] is illustrated: *His instructions are pure, [they enlightens the eyes]* (Ps 19:9).[67] Moreover we have to know why it is that he attributed *wisdom and might* (Dn 2:23) to the description of God, since he already said: *To whom belong wisdom and might* (Dn 2:20) and to his own portrayal in saying: *You assist me with wisdom and might* (Dn 2:23). We say, respecting God, great is his glory,[68] the reason is that He is victorious like the wise man, as it has been said: *Among the wise men of the nations and among all their royalty there is none like you* (Jer 10:7). Regarding Daniel's own portrayal,[69] it is because his wisdom exceeds [the wisdom] of all the wise men of the king, as it is attested [by the expression]: *And no one in all of them is like Daniel Hananyah, Mishael and Azaryah* (Dn 1:19). That is why he followed it by his expression: *Now, make known to me what I asked from you* (Dn 2:23).[70] He means the vision and its interpretation. Concerning "the vision", it is about something in the past, since it has already happened. Therefore, he called it

---

wise men (Dn 2:21); the fourth, that He gives *science to the knowledgeable in cognition* (Dn 2:21). After that we reach the fifth point that we found in the text.

64 ובואטנהם וקלובהם דואת ראי עמיק is R. Saadia's translation of the quoted part of Ps 64:7.

65 "He" could designate God, or the biblical scribe as well.

66 פליתני פי אלת׳רי כ׳זנת is R. Saadia's translation of the quoted part of Jb 14:13.

67 ווצאיאה נקיה is R. Saadia's translation of the quoted part of Ps 19:9. From time to time R. Saadia's quotations are elliptic, and the part he intended to introduce as witness to what he is not mentioned, but supposed. This is, for example, the case in quoting Ps 9:9. Such cases typically deal with well known passages of the Bible.

68 גל גלאלה is a common exclamation concerning God in the Arabic language and in Islam. Its translation is uneasy, since it is a locution employing two words from the same origin: a verb (imperative) and a substantive. Its literal translation would be "may His splendor be splendid".

69 Lit. "His own portrayal."

70 R. Saadia's reasoning seems unclear. As a sign of Daniel's superiority to all the wise men of the kingdom, he quotes this part of Dn 2:23: *now, make known to me what I asked from you.* The only plausible conclusion is that Daniel's wisdom is superior to the others, because he had obtained it directly from God.

wisdom.[71] As to the interpretation, it deals with the future, since it has not already happened. That is why he called it *understanding.*[72] Regarding *thereupon* (Dn 2:24)[73] by which he joins one story with the other; its first meaning is *with.*[74] However, because it does not suit the explanation, we said: Thereupon. [... ...][75] before he says: *[What the king required] the wise men, the astrologers and the Chaldeans are not capable of narrating* (Dn 2:27) is similar to what the prophets used to accomplish: Before they confirm the prophetic discourse they deprecate the discourse of the swindlers[76], according to what we have explained in the story of *[it is I]who bring to naught the omens of the diviners* (Is 44:25),[77] *but confirm the word of His servant* (Is 44:26)[78] with all the verses. Soon after he refuted them[79] he attributes the power to his Lord, as he says: *However, God who is in heaven [and who reveals secrets]* (Dn 2:28). Then he said to the king:[80]

Dn 2:29

O king, your thoughts before your sleeping[81] were about what will happen after these days, and the revealer of secrets assisted by informing you about it.

Dn 2:30

As for me, it is not because I am wiser than any other that this secret was revealed to me, but in order that they make known to the king the interpretation and in order that you know your own purpose.

71 The wisdom is what allowed Daniel to tell the dream and its meaning. Since wisdom applies to what had already happened.

72 It is not the interpretation that is called understanding. The understanding is what allowed the interpretation.

73 In his commentary R. Saadia (or the scribe who writes the manuscript) writes כל קבל while in his direct translation we have כל קביל.

74 באזא is difficult to translate in one word. It means facing someone, being in company of someone, being adjacent to someone.

75 What is lost is the commentary on Dn 2:25–26.

76 אלמתברטין is dialectal form of אלמתברטמין. Its dialectal form has the meaning of someone who is not serious, while his original form describes someone who is manifesting anger in his expression.

77 אלפאסך איאת אלמשעודין is R. Saadia's translation of the quoted part of Is 44:25.

78 אלמקים כלאם עבדה is R. Saadia's translation of the quoted part of Is 44:26.

79 Soon after Daniel refuted the wise men of Babylon.

80 Lit. "To him."

81 R. Saadia, at least in his translation, seems to accredit the idea that the king had a vision a part from his dream.

Dn 2:31
O king, you saw that you were looking, and behold! A huge statue. And this statue was big, his brightness was immense. It was facing you and had a great fright.

Dn 2:32
This statue has a head of pure gold; its chest and arms were of silver; its belly and thighs of copper.

Dn 2:33
Its legs of iron and its feet, partially of iron and partially of clay.

Dn 2:34
Then you saw as a stone was cut off by the hand of no one and hit this statue in its feet that are of iron and clay; it smashed it and the statue fell down.[82]

Dn 2:35
Thereupon the iron, the clay, the copper, the silver and the gold were smacked together and became like little pieces of the summer seed. Then the wind scattered them and no trace of them at all[83] **was found. Thereafter the stone that hit the statue became a huge mountain and filled the whole earth.**[84]

Dn 2:36
This being the vision, we will tell its interpretation between the king's hands.

Dn 2:37
O king, you are the king of kings, because[85] **the Lord of heaven gave you the kingdom, the assurance, the assistance and the glory.**

82 "And the statue fell down" has no Hebrew background and is added by R. Saadia as a necessary complement to the meaning. He will try to justify this addition while commenting on Dn 2:34.

83 אלבתה "at all" is added by R. Saadia and has no masoretic origin.

84 Lit. "The whole of that earth" while the masoretic text reads "the whole earth."

85 yd is translated by R. Saadia as an adverb, 'because' introducing a subordinate causal sentence, while Yefet ben Eli translates it as a relative pronoun 'who.'

Dn 2:38
Wherever all human beings, the wild beast and the bird of the sky dwell He has submitted them to you; He has given you dominion over them all; that is why it is you who are represented by the head of gold.

Dn 2:39
However, after you shall raise another kingdom, lower than you. The third kingdom is similar to copper, and rules over the whole earth.

Dn 2:40
The fourth kingdom is as hard as iron, as iron smashes everything, crushes and bruises it, the fourth kingdom[86] smacks and bruises everything.

Dn 2:41
What you observed about the feet[87] and the fingers, which were partially of potter's clay, partially of iron, indicates a divided kingdom that contains part of iron origin, inasmuch as you did see iron that amalgamates with clay and mud.

Dn 2:42
The interpretation of the fingers, partially of iron and partially of clay, is that part of the kingdom will be stable and part will be broken.

Dn 2:43
As to what you have seen of their mixture[88], its interpretation is that those will intermingle by means of generation, but they do not amalgamate completely, like the iron that does not amalgamate with the clay.

Dn 2:44
After the time of those two kingdoms, God of heaven will raise a kingdom that will never be corrupted and will not be left to another nation; it will smash all those kingdoms, destroy them and will stand forever.

Dn 2:45
As you were looking, a stone was cut off from the mountain, not by a hand, and smashed the iron, the copper, the clay, the silver and the gold. To sum

86 Lit. "It."
87 Lit. "The two feet."
88 R. Saadia does not translate literally this part of Dn 2:43. Instead of "iron amalgamates with clay" we have their "mixture."

up the matter: The great God made known to the king what will happen at the last days. Thus the vision is complete and its interpretation trustworthy.

Beginning by the expression: *Your thoughts came while you were on your bed* (Dn 2:29)[89] does not weaken the vision.[90] In fact, there are four reasons to the vision, according to us. Three of them are futile and can be called "confusion". The fourth, is what escape [the kind of the first] three; it is the true one. The first of the three [futile reasons] is the result of too many thoughts and exhaustion.[91] And it is to [this futile reason] that refers the proverb that deals with the interdiction points,[92] as Koheleth has said: *For nightmares come from too much worrying, and a fool's utterance from too much speaking* (Ecc 5:2).[93] The second [futile reason] is the abundance, or the scarcity of food. And it is to [this futile reason] also that point the proverb about the interdiction points, according to the expression of Isaiah: *It shall be as when a hungry man dreams that he is eating, then he awakes and, behold, his soul is empty. Or, as when a thirsty man dreams that he is drinking, and he awakes, then, behold, he is faint and his soul yearns for water so shall be the multitude of all nations who are battling against mount Zion* (Is 29:8).[94] The third [reason for a vision] is motivated by pain and suffering. It is again a futile reason, following Job's expression: *When I said my bed shall relieve me, my couch shall ease my lament, you scare me with dreams and with visions you terrify me* (Jb 7:13–14).[95] But [the reason]

89 R. Saadia's translation of this part of Dn 2:29 is peculiar: "Your thoughts before your sleeping."

90 Lit. "is not that he weakens the vision in his soul." Which contains the difficulty of identifying the "he". Furthermore what is the meaning of the expression "weakening the vision in his soul"? Does it mean that the king pays no attention to his vision, since having a dream while sleeping is normal? Or, does it mean that the reader has to pay no further attention to just an ordinary dream?

91 Lit. the tiredness of the spirit.

92 אלאבטאל literally means "nullification" or "annulment". Normally, the word bears a complement: the nullification of something. R. Saadia does not specify the object of this nullification.

93 החלום is rendered here by "nightmare", since it has the meaning of a bad dream, according to R. Saadia. ענין is being rendered by "worries", not "cares", because, following R. Saadia's reasoning, it does not indicate positive thinking.

94 פיכון כמא ירי אלגאיע פי חלמה כאנה יאכל פיסתיקט פאדא בנפסה פראגה וכמא ירי אלעטשאן פי חלמה כאנה ישרב פיסתיקט פאדא בה לגב ונפסה מתלטיה כדאך יכון גמיע גמהור אלאמם אלמתגישין עלי גבל ציון is R. Saadia's translation of Is 29:8.

95 ואן קלת יעאזיני סרירי ויחתמל מן שכואי מצנעי אדערתני באלאחלאם ומן אלרויאת תהולני is R. Saadia's translation of Jb 7:13–14.

that escapes those three [futile reasons] is from God, following the expression: *In a dream, a night vision, when deep sleep falls en men* (Jb 33:15),[96] *then He advances toward them and ties on them their rope* (Jb 33:16)[97] and all the discourse, similar to what is in the book of the Philosophic Doctrines.[98] And, since Nebuchadnezzar, before sleeping, speculated about who will reign after him which, according to the erudite men, infects the vision and turns it to confusion, Daniel needed to start by an introduction to the king[99] telling him that the vision is not corrupted and your thoughts are similar to that vision, but the vision itself is undefiled, otherwise I would not have interpreted for you. This is in fact the meaning of the addition to the discourse: *Thus the vision is complete and its interpretation is trustworthy* (Dn 2:45). His explanation of the disclosure of the secret, because of [the expression] *that they make known to the king the interpretation* (Dn 2:30) means that I have to start [my interpretation,] otherwise those miserable [individuals] who were trying to make known the interpretation to the king will perish, while their intention was [to deliver] wisdom.[100]

I rendered חדוהי (Dn 2:32) by "its chest", because the Targum of "wave chest" חזה התנופה (Nm 6:20)[101] is חדיא דארמותא. I rendered כְּעור מן אדרי קיט (Dn 2:35) "little pieces", because its Targum is כמוץ. I rendered וחשׁל (Dn 2:40) "crushes", because its root is "to be feeble" similar to [the expression]: *All the feeble in your rear* (Dt 25:18).[102] I rendered מרעע (Dn 2:40) "bruises", because its Targum is קנה רצוץ.

Concerning the form of the statue itself, it is well known from the text that it is an imaginary form. We withhold its repetition; I mean the form [of the statue], for fear of being too long. What is needed, though, is to explain very well the interpretation of the vision. Hence, we say [Daniel's] expression: *O king,*

96 פי מנאם או רויא אלליל פי וקוע אלסבאת עלי אלנאס ונומהם עלי מצֿאגעהם is R. Saadia's translation of Jb 33:15.

97 חיניד ויתקדם קום ויכתם עליהם רבאהם is R. Saadia's translation of Jb 33:16. R. Saadia quotes Jb 33:16 in manner opposite to the verse order: 16b + 16a. In his commentary on Jb 33:16 he explains that he translates the Hebrew expression אז יגלה as 'he advances' which gives us an unusual translation of the verse.

98 ספר האמונות והדעות ורבה נ :כתאב אלאמאנאת ואלאעתקאדאת. A philosophical book by R. Saadia containing ten articles or treatises. Most probably R. Saadia refers to the second article of his book: The One who brings things into existence, blessed be he and exalted.

99 Lit. "To him."

100 In commenting on Dn 2:30 Yefet ben Eli, too, insists on the fact that one of Daniel's intentions is to deliver the wise men of the kingdom from their tragic end as a consequence of their incapacity to interpret the king's dream.

101 מע קץ אלתחריך is R. Saadia's translation of the quoted part of Nm 6:20.

102 נמיע אלמזחפין וראך is R. Saadia's translation of the quoted part of Dt 25:18.

you are the king of kings[103] (Dn 2:37) and not *kings' king*[104] is because he is king of kings, according to what Ezekiel had said: *Nebuchadnezzar king of Babylon from the north, king of kings* (Ez 26:7). Thus, he is not the kings' king, because this name is [reserved] to the Lord of the universe.[105] His expression: *Where all [human beings] dwell* (Dn 2:38) is similar to Jeremiah's expression: *I now have given all these lands to my servant Nebuchadnezzar, king of Babylon, I even give him the wild beasts to serve him* (Jer 27:6).[106] However, he added here *the wild beast* (Dn 2:38) as explanation. Though, it is not by virtue of reverence that Daniel said this to the king, but because it is wise that every classification starts by the most important fact.[107] Then we ask: what is the wisdom [in depicting] Nebuchadnezzar looking after all the kingdoms? We answer that he reigns over them, as if they were his possession. Hence, he was looking after them like someone who looks after his own house. That is why Daniel continues: *Where all [human beings] dwell* (Dn 2:38). And, moreover, in order that the news of his vision reach all the boundaries. What accredit this [interpretation] are the facts relative to the defeat of the wise men and their condemnation to death, because it is the more effective [event] to spread the news.

As to the small king, he looks after his kingdom alone, similar to Pharaoh who looked after *the land of Egypt and the land of Canaan* alone. Concerning the individuals, if only he establishes justice in his caring for his follow citizens! The prophet, on the other hand, must take care of everyone in the world, since his friend is the Lord of the universe, owner of the whole. Then we ask: what is the wisdom of representing the nations by a statue and Israel by a stone. We answer that the statue is made by human beings. Their administrations, likewise, are worldly. The stone, inversely, is created by God. Their kingdom, similarly, I mean the kingdom of Israel, is religious, following what he had said about the whole: *Who rules over men must be just, fearing God he rules* (2 Sm 23:3). And what benefit is there in incorporating all that they mean in one body? We answer that it is because the servitude over us is the same, whether [our enemies] are united or dispersed; they are like one messenger.[108] Don't you

103 מלך מלכיא

104 מלך די מלכיא

105 R. Saadia's idea is that מלך מלכיא expresses the partial dominion over some kings, rather than over all kings, which is the kind of dominion exercised exclusively by God.

106 Yefet ben Eli quotes the last part of Jer 26:6 in the same context.

107 Lit. "Starts from the head", which correlates with the "golden head" of Dn 2:38.

108 The reason that Yefet ben Eli gives for employing one symbol, the statue, to represent all the enemies of Israel is that all those enemies are known to be unjust. Such interpretation does not seem far from R. Saadia's reasoning that the adoration of a statue by all the enemies of Israel unites them because of the similarity of the servi-

see that the Torah calls the totality of our enemies *your enemy, in a singular form* [every time they are called] in the *second Torah*?[109] And why didn't he say *after you will rise another kingdom, of silver, lower than you,* similar to what he told him *it is you who are represented by the head of gold* (Dn 2:38)? We answer that the four Persian kings that came after the king of Babylon were very violent. Evidence of this is that their followers overcame him. That is why they pointed to Darius which [the king of Babylon] could not refuse.[110] Daniel himself tried to flee them, but he could not, as we will explain.

Concerning the king of Babylon, he was free to decide whatever pleases him, according to the expression: *He raises whom he wishes and puts down whom he wishes* (Dn 5:19). As to the third kingdom, I mean *Greece*, he overlooked it completely and mentioned nothing about it, except that *it rules over the whole earth* (Dn 2:39). This demonstrates to us that his intention is not to deal with one of the three kingdoms. His intention was [to deal with] the division in the fourth kingdom, according to what he will later say: *Then I wanted to know the truth about the fourth individual*[111] (Dn 7:19). Likewise, in his interpretation to Nebuchadnezzar he abridged the description of the three kingdoms, but expand on the fourth. He first said that it will be by itself for a longtime, parallel to what he already said: *Its legs of iron* (Dn 2:33) alone.[112] Then there is its association with Adom, the other kingdom, for a short time, similar, proportionately, of a foot to the leg, because of what he said: *Its feet, partially of iron and partially of clay* (Dn 2:33). It does not mean, however, that one foot of iron and the other of clay. He means that every foot is partially of iron and partially of clay.[113] By measure of the same proportion, the reign belongs to Adom for five hundred fifty years. Then a partner associates himself with him for circa three hundred fifty solar years. Therefore, the proportion of three hun-

---

tude they impose upon the Israelites. Hence, it is not totally irrelevant to think that Yefet ben Eli, who knew R. Saadia's commentary on Daniel, wanted to express the same idea, using other words.

109 The second Torah or the book of Deuteronomy (Gn R. s.3). However, if the book of Deuteronomy does not contain אויבים or אויבי it does contain אויביך (eleven times), לאויביך (two times) and אויביכם (four times).

110 Unclear sentence. Most probably it means that Daniel and his companions pointed to Darius as proof of the violence and strength of the Persian kings after the king of Babylon.

111 אלשכץ "the individual" or undetermined person, according to R. Saadia rendering of חיותא, not "beast" which would be חיואן.

112 R. Saadia sees parallel between the fact that the fourth beast's legs are of iron, not a mixture of two or more metals, and the fact that the fourth kingdom stand by itself, without being part of another kingdom.

113 The same explanation about the iron and the clay which are being separated, not being a mixture, is found in Yefet ben Eli's commentary on Dn 2:41.

dred fifty years to five hundred fifty years becomes similar to seven parts out of eleven[114] and the total proportion is eighteen.

As to his enumeration of the three actions by which the iron is represented, *smashes [any thing], crushes and bruises it* (Dn 2:40), we say that it depends on the different ways by which the nations were ruled. The nation whose religion looses strength to the point of being ineffective resembles something that the iron files: It is the action of smashing (חשל).[115] The nation that was dispersed in different horizons is represented by a crushed [matter] whose remnant is dispersed. The nation that it[116] placed under its obedience alone is the nation portrayed by the action of bruising. While this nation is represented by those three forces the Israelites[117] are still represented by what is stronger than they are, since he said about them: *It will smash all those kingdoms, destroy them* (Dn 2:44). That the iron scatter gold, silver or copper, is not a marvel, but that a stone smashes iron and what comes with it, that is a marvel.

Concerning his representation of the associate,[118] Adom, by the clay, its explanation does not to be found in [the clay], considered lower in its standing or its derivation or its power, but because of the people's arrangement of the plates: first they set forward the gold, then the silver, then the copper, then the iron and, last of all the clay. That is why he portrayed the kingdoms by those metaphors, since they came in order, one after the other. [And what is] the reason why he made the clay in three degrees: ordinary *clay* (Dn 2:33); *pottery clay* (Dn 2:41); and *clay of mud* (Dn 2:41.43)? We answer: Since what is made out of mud comes in three fashions, either wet, neither dry nor roasted, or dry, but not roasted, or [dry] and roasted. The people, likewise, are in three degrees: Those who are completely outside of religion; those who are in religion with a condition or conditions; and those who are completely in their religion.[119] The

114 "Eleven" is the total of the body parts mentioned about the statue: head, chest, two hands, belly, two thighs, two legs, and two feet. All the proportions which indicate the duration of the various kingdoms are to be measured by reference to the number of the statue body parts.

115 The action of the iron is compared to a file that by passing over a surface reduces it and produces small particles. According to R. Saadia's commentary, such negative result is the product of the action of the iron parallel in its consequence to the ineffectiveness of that nation's religion.

116 The nation represented by the iron.

117 Lit. "Israel", but the verb that follows is plural, indicating what was meant are the Israelites. Such figure of style is common in Judeo-Arabic.

118 Lit. "His representation of his associate." The first "his" belongs to the scribe, the writer of the book of Daniel, or to Daniel himself. The second "his" belongs to the first kingdom.

119 The "religion" in question here is Judaism. In this case, "their religion" means the religion of the Israelites. It remains possible to say that "religion" here designates

whole statue, whose basis is of clay, stands because of the will of its maker. If He wishes, he can destroy it quiet easily. He had already said: *Behold, like clay in the hands of the potter, so are you in my hands, house of Israel* (Jer 18:6). And also, if the foot is broken all the body falls apart and disintegrates. Furthermore, to apply [the sentence]: *Then they broke together etc.* (Dn 2:35). As to his expression: *Those will intermingle by mean of generation, but they do not amalgamate completely* (Dn 2:43), it refers to what is noticeable in marriages and in cohabitation of one with the other, but not to the degree that the two nations become one.[120]

His expression: *In their days* (Dn 2:44) means after *their days*. Similar to what he already said in another place: *In your feast of the week* (Nm 28:26)[121] meaning after *your feast of the week*. His expression: *Those two kingdoms* (Dn 2:44)[122] means: *Those two kingdoms, Adom* and its associate.[123] We will explain such interpretation in *four kings arise from the earth* (Dn 7:17). He means four kingdoms arise from the earth.[124] His expression: *It will smash all those kingdoms, destroy them* (Dn 2:44) does not intend two alone, but all the five. His expression: *And the kingdom will not be left to another nation* (Dn 2:44) after the disappearance of the four [kingdoms] proves that something of the first [kingdom] subsists until the beginning of the second [kingdom]. Something from the third [kingdom], likewise, will subsist until the third kingdom.[125]

---

any religion, because the word is unspecified. It is, however, of a lesser probability, since it supposes a category of people who are without religion, which is unheard – of in R. Saadia's time. Furthermore, the expression "religion" indicates Judaism alone in Judeo-Arabic literature.

120 The marriages and cohabitation of concubines stigmatized here are between members of different nations and religions.

121 אסאביעכם is R. Saadia's translation of Nm 28:26.

122 MT: די מלכיא אנון "those kings." R. Saadia understands and translates: "those two kingdoms." He also has מלכיא אלין in his lemma, while in his commentary, he has מלכיא אנון.

123 R. Saadia starts the sentence in Aramaic and finishes it in Judeo-Arabic.

124 Lit. "He means four kings arise from the earth" which is a simple repetition. Most probably the scribe missed the meaning that R. Saadia wanted to illustrate by quoting Dn 7:17. What he tried to demonstrate is that the word מלכין has the meaning of מלכיא which he translates in Dn 7:17 by "kingdoms."

125 It is not clear how the expression: *And the kingdom will not be left to another nation* (Dn 2:44) leads to the conclusion that the first kingdom will subsist till the beginning of the second. Maybe R. Saadia attributes to the verb לא תשתבק the meaning that the kingdom refuses to be left aside or to resist the coming of the new kingdom.

As to putting forward in his explanation *iron, copper, clay* it is following the breaking procedure, from the lower degree to the higher degree, contrary to what is usual. That is why he put *the copper* before *the clay.*[126] There is also a hidden statement in his expression: *It smashes it* (Dn 2:34) which is: *And the statue fell down, then was broken …* (Dn 2:34).[127] His expression: *Became like little pieces of the summer seed* (Dn 2:35) is similar to the representation of the heretics' princes by the chaff, since he says: *Like the chaff of mountains before the wind and like whirling before a storm* (Is 17:13).[128] His addition of the summer[129] is because in the winter the chaff becomes wet, due to the humidity of the air, and the wind does not carry it speedily. His expression: *And no trace of them was found* (Dn 2:35) is parallel to his expression: *And what remains of the beasts,*[130] *their dominion was taken away* (Dn 7:12). He, then, concluded the story by *thereafter the stone that hit the statue became a huge mountain* (Dn 2:35) whose explanation is: *God of heaven will raise a kingdom that will never be corrupt* (Dn 2:44). He compared it to a stone because [the stone] is his creation.[131] Likewise, Israel, his creation and his shoot: *The shoot that I panted, the work of my hands that I may be glorified* (Is 60:21).[132]

He represented the kingdom of Israel by the solid and stable stone, as he said already: *Behold! I will establish in Zion a stone* (Is 28:16).[133] [He also] characterized it by six descriptions: *A solid stone in a fortified corner, built in a palace* (Is 28:16).[134] As to the reason of his comparison to a stone, it is accord-

126 A complicated way to say that what breaks first, the clay, is being mentioned last. The order followed is chronological, the iron being the representation of the first kingdom, the clay being the representation of the last.

127 "And then the statue fell down" is the addition to Dn 2:34 which R. Saadia calls the hidden statement.

128 ויכלבון כהריס פי אלגבאל בין ידי אלריח אלג̇רבאלה is R. Saadia's translation of the quoted part of Is 17:13.

129 Lit. "His addition of the mention of the summer."

130 Lit. "The individuals."

131 R. Saadia repeats briefly the explanation that he gave at the start of his commentary of this section of Dn 2. His idea is that a statue is made by human hands, unlike stones, which are the creation of God, since they are not the product of the human hands.

132 סנך̇ ג̇רוסי וצנעה קדרתי ללאפתכ̇אר is R. Saadia's translation of the quoted part of Is 60:21.

133 האנא מאסס פי ציון חג̇רא is R. Saadia's translation of the quoted part of Is 28:16.

134 חג̇ר צנאם פי זאויה עזיזה פי איואן מבני is R. Saadia's translation of the quoted part of Is 28:16. Unclear biblical text: אבן בחן פנת יקרת מוסד מוסד. R. Saadia finding of six descriptions is based on the fact that he quotes this part of Is 28:16 that contains six words. It is very difficult to translate word for word this part of the verse.

ing to what we already mentioned. The meaning of בחן is "solid"[135] more than the absolute stone, and similar to *they erected its towers* (Is 23:13). The meaning of פנת is that the builders choose the solid stone for the angels, since it bears most of the effort. The higher [the solidity of the stone], the more reliable it is, according to what he has already said there: *The stone which the builders had rejected became the head stone of the corner* (Ps 118:22).[136] The meaning of מוּסָד is "building", because if stones are not built, they are valueless. The meaning of מוסד is "established", because a building without foundation is worthless. In fact, the two words of building and foundation belong to the *vocabulary of the groundwork.*[137] Most of the foundation, however, is in the darkness, similar to the expression:[138] *When the builder establishes the foundation of the Temple of the Lord* (Ezr 3:10).[139] His expression: *By the hand of no one* (Dn 2:34) points to the destruction, which will be acknowledged by [the statement] *he shall be broken by hand with no strength* (Dn 8:25). His expression: *[The statue became a huge mountain] and filled the whole earth* (Dn 2:35). For some interpreters it designates the country that belongs to the king.[140] Metaphorically, however, it designates all the earth. That is what He promised in implementing the messiah's kingship in the whole world, by saying: *His dominion [will extend] from sea to sea and from the river to the limits of the earth* (Zec 9:10). He also said: *May he rule from sea to sea...etc. let the desert-dwellers bow before him and his enemies lick the dust, let the kings of Tarshish and the islands bring presents, kings of Sheba and Seba offer gifts, let all kings fall down before him and all the nations serve him* (Ps 72:8–11).[141]

Learn, and may God increase your knowledge, that our benefit from this story[142] is not to be instructed about the circumstances of *the four kingdoms* and the salvation alone. In fact, it is one of the Israelites' greatest miracles. The truth is that the fathers validated the prophecy of Daniel with no possibility whatsoever to know how many kingdoms will arise on the earth: one or ten, or fifty or

135 צנאם plural (?) of צנים which means "hard, solid."

136 ואלחגר אלדי זהד פיה אלבנאאון צאר ראס זאויה is R. Saadia's translation of Ps 118:22.

137 בלשון יסידה

138 Lit. "As if you say."

139 R. Saadia compares the foundation of a building, hidden in the ground, and the visible base of a statue. Both can be designated by the same word in Hebrew, in spite of the difference that R. Saadia underlines.

140 Lit. "It designates the earth that was in his presence."

141 ויסתולי מן אלבלאד מן שרק וגרב ובחר ונהר ואלי אקטאר אלארץ: בין ידיה יגתון חתי אלמפאזיון ואעדאה ילחסון אלתראב: ומלוך אלבחר וגזאירהא הדאיא יגלבון ומלוך שבא וסבא תחפא יקדמון לה: ויגסד לה גמיע אלמלוך וכל אלאמם תטיעה is R. Saadia's translation of Ps 72:8–11.

142 In other words: Nebuchadnezzar's vision and Daniel's interpretation.

more.[143] And greater than that is the association of Adom, who is the fourth [kingdom], with [the first kingdom].[144] Moreover, it is not from the beginning of the [first] kingdom that [the fourth kingdom] becomes its associate. It is only at the end that [the fourth kingdom] becomes the associate of the [first kingdom]. And the most startling of all is how they realized that the time of the association [of the two kingdoms] will be in proportion of seven out of eleven parts from the time of the independence of Adom, which is the proportionate size of the *his feet* to *his legs* (Dn 2:33).[145] Therefore, I know of nothing [...] on earth more surprising, neither greater than this.[146] In no way [...] belongs to it of all the reasons only [the one] in our language. Nothing else is mentioned in history, but four hundred years.[147] That is why he said [...] that he knows that he [...] ended [...] always [...] the association [...] the period that [... ...] that the history in this prophecy is of one thousand four years and fraction [...] or for all the nations. [... ...].[148] We should never have the illusion that another kingdom will come after them, because the two legs and the two feet do not [...] in the statues.[149] Beside, we should never have this illusion, because we learned from [...] Yefet and Shem [... ...] since *all of them are fathers of the nations that Babylon ruled*,[150] according to what he said about Nimrod: *And the beginning of his kingdom was Babylon* (Gn 10:10.22).[151] And the *kingdoms of Media* are similar to Shem, according to his expression: *The sons of Shem are*

143 The implication of such assertion is that the book of Daniel was written at the time of Nebuchadnezzar (604–562), according to R. Saadia. Today the majority of scholars believe that the book of Daniel was written between 200–150 B.C.

144 The association designated here is symbolized by the mixture between the iron, representing the first kingdom, and the clay, representing the fourth kingdom. Cf. Dn 2:33.

145 As if R. Saadia is saying that the first kingdom (represented by the iron) was alone during four measures, before the appearance of the last kingdom, Adom, (represented by the clay) and its association with it.

146 Lit. "Therefore, I know nothing [...] on earth more surprising, neither greater, nor surprising than this."

147 Incoherent passage because of the lacuna in the manuscript.

148 Incoherent passage because of the many lacunae in the Ms Oxf 2629.43a from which this passage is quoted.

149 The lacuna in this sentence prevents us from fully understanding R. Saadia's reasoning. Most probably R. Saadia is building his reasoning by analogy: the foot being the last part of the body, the kingdom symbolized by it (Adom) is the last one.

150 Uncertain translation of a sentence in a defective passage, especially at the end: (?) אבות גוים מלכות בבל לחמה:

151 וכאן אול מלכה באביל is R. Saadia's translation of the quoted part of Gn 10:10.

Elam and Ashur (Gn 10:22).[152] And Daniel said: *As if I am in Sus the capital which is in the country of khuzestan* (Dn 8:2).[153] *The kingdom of Greece* [… …]. *The kingdom of Adom and Ishmael* are together from *the sons of Abraham*. Then he said:

Dn 2:46
At that point the king Nebuchadnezzar fell down on his face, prostrated himself to Daniel and ordered that gifts and perfumes be offered to him.[154]

Dn 2:47
Then he said to him: 'The complete truth is that your Lord is the God of gods,[155] the Master of kings and the Revealer of secrets, since He made you reveal this secret.'

Dn 2:48
Then the king magnified Daniel[156] and offered him precious and imposing gifts and made him ruler over the city[157] of Babylon and prince over all the wise men of Babylon.

Dn 2:49
Thereafter Daniel asked the king to appoint Shadrak, Mishak and Abed-Nego over the affairs of Babylon, and he himself [stood] at the gate of the king.

[… …] that Nebuchadnezzar changed[158] [… …] in his acceptance of something from him.[159] Because it is legitimate in our religion that someone bow down to

152 ובנו שם כ֗וזסתאן ואלמוצל is R. Saadia's translation of the quoted part of Gn 10:22. R. Saadia uses local geographical names of his time to rename Elam (כוזסתאן) and Ashur (אלמוצל).

153 שׁושׁן in the MT is rendered by סוס and עילם is rendered by כוזסתאן.

154 Yefet ben Eli: "Gifts and offerings be poured for him." In order to explain the king's gesture Yefet ben Eli adds that the king had seen in Daniel what Christians see in Jesus. This represents one of the very few mentions of Christianity in Yefet's commentary on Daniel.

155 Yefet ben Eli: "God of divinities."

156 Yefet ben Eli: "Then the king appointed Daniel noble man or master."

157 While מדינה is regularly rendered by "province" R. Saadia translates it according to the Arabic usage of the same word, which is "city".

158 From בדל "to change" or בדׄל "to give, to produced an effort".

159 In spite of the lacuna, it is clear that R. Saadia is discussing the opportunity of receiving a gift from people who are not Israelites. An opportunity that R. Saadia

the other, a bow out of reverence, not out of worship, as it is explained in the sentence. Concerning the offerings, Daniel[160] did not accept them. That is why he put in the text *and ordered that gifts and perfumes be offered to him* (Dn 2:48). This has [to be understood] as speech, not as action.[161] I also transposed the explanation of *since He made you reveal this secret* (Dn 2:47) from Daniel's activity to the Creator's activity. That is why I said: "He made you," because giving Him thanks is suitable for His action alone.[162] I also rendered ורב סגנין (Dn 2:48) "princes" since סגנים "caliphs".[163] In this case [Daniel] was greater than all of them. The explanation of the second part is completed.

---

refuses. Nevertheless, such gift can be accepted when there is an order to receive it, like the order that the king addressed on Daniel.

160 Lit. "He."

161 The end of R. Saadia's reasoning concerning gestures that are due to God alone, such as presenting offerings, which leads our commentator to conclude that Daniel refused such things from the king. An interpretation with no basis in the text. Yefet ben Eli resolves the problem by saying that Nebuchadnezzar saw in Daniel a divine presence, similar to what the Christians see in the person of Jesus Christ. He adds that Daniel forbade him from presenting the offerings. We are in the presence of the same reasoning as R. Saadia's, with a slight difference in its conclusion and without any textual justification.

162 R. Saadia tries to shift the thanksgiving from Daniel's action to God's action.

163 Two remarks may be recorded about R. Saadia's commentary on Dn 2:48. First, in the lemma he translates of ורב סגנין by "prince" and not "the greater of the princes" as his explanation seems to suggest. Secondly, the relationship between the two words סגנין and סגנים remains unclear. Are they synonymous? In this case, "prince" and "caliph" are not. Are they different in their degree of dignity? What is, then, the point of comparing them?
נ שׁנרפ הת :ללא ט תסהגה הת דנא סנתשׁנט יראתדרה נא ס ת :נ נ יב דתנפפא ס הפלאשׁ הת רס ב ת
ר גנכ הת מה נאהת רהגה ס הו נ יב דתנפפא ס דנא סנתשׁנט ללא ט תסהגה הת תנ ס דנאה רהת הת
רב דרו הת ט נתנמ הת נ סס ל נב תטי :הפלאשׁ הת applied to Daniel proof that Nebuchadnezzar became Daniel's disciple.

Chapter 3

The text of the third chapter

Dn 3:1
Then the king Nebuchadnezzar prepared a statue of gold that he raised sixty cubits, six [cubits] broad and set it in the plain of Dura, in the city[1] of Babylon.

Dn 3:2
Nebuchadnezzar then sent to gather jointly the satraps, the princes, the governors, the rulers, the workers, the scribes and the officers and all the commanders of the provinces to the inauguration of the statue that he had set up.[2]

Dn 3:3
Thereafter, the satraps, the princes, the governors, the rulers, the workers, the scribes and the officers and all the commanders of the provinces were

1 The Aramaic word מדינה exists in Arabic with the same spelling and almost the same meaning. In fact, while the Aramaic meaning of מדינה is large 'city' or 'province' the Arabic meaning is 'city' alone, without the connotation of 'province.'

2 The titles of the dignitaries mentioned in Dn 3:2 are translated differently by R. Saadia and Yefet ben Eli. The following is the list of Aramaic names and their translation by both writers. מכנש R. Saadia: אלבטארקה 'the satraps,' Yefet ben Eli: אלאמרא 'the princes.' אחשדרפניא (R. Saadia writes אכשדרפניא) R. Saadia: אלאמרא 'the princes,' Yefet ben Eli: אלרוסא 'the lords.' סגניא R. Saadia: אלכלפא 'the governors,' Yefet ben Eli: אלעמאל 'the workers.' פחותא R. Saadia: אלחכאם 'the rulers,' Yefet ben Eli: אצחאב אלשרט 'officers.' אדרגזריא R. Saadia: אלעמאל 'the workers,' Yefet ben Eli: אלגהאדה 'the money-changers.' דתבריא גבריא R. Saadia: אלכתאב ואלשרטיין 'the scribes and the officers,' Yefet ben Eli: אלכתאב ואהל אלעלם ואלפקה 'the scribes the learned and the judges.' מדינתא כל שלטוני R. Saadia: סאיר סלאטין אלבלדאן 'all the commanders of the provinces,' Yefet ben Eli: וכל סלאטין אלמדן 'all the commanders of the cities.'

gathered jointly at the inauguration of the statue that Nebuchadnezzar had set up and they stood between his hand.[3]

Dn 3:4
Then a herald proclaimed in a loud voice: 'To you, populations, nations and tongues.

Dn 3:5
When you hear the sound of the trumpet, the whistle, the tambourine, the drum, the cymbal, the flute[4] **and all kinds of amusements**[5] **you prostrate yourselves and kneel to the golden statue that Nebuchadnezzar the king had set up.**

Dn 3:6
And whom of you who does not prostrate himself and kneel to it from its base will be thrown into the burning fiery furnace.'

Dn 3:7
When all the populations hear the sound of the trumpet, the tambourine, the drum, the cymbal and all kinds of amusements, at that time all peoples, nations and tongues prostrate themselves and kneel to the golden statue that Nebuchadnezzar the king had set up.

Dn 3:8
Thereupon a certain group of Kasdians started to intrigue and calumniate the Jews.

Dn 3:9
They started by saying to Nebuchadnezzar the king: 'May God give long life to the king.[6]

3 The expression "between his hands" is ambiguous in R. Saadia's translation and could mean "between Nebuchadnezzar's hands" or "in front of the statue," which the MT clearly intends.

4 Here is Yefet ben Eli's enumeration of the instruments contained in Dn 3:5: Horn, trumpet, pipe, zither, lyre, flute, and the צרנאי (?), which has no parallel in the MT text.

5 Yefet ben Eli: 'All colors of instruments.' Later, in Dn 3:10 Yefet will translate the same expression by 'all kinds of instruments of singing.'

6 אטאל אללה בקא אלמלך 'may God give long life to the king' is an Arabic and Islamic way to wish long life to someone. In fact, there is no mention of God in the MT.

Dn 3:10-11
O king, you ordered that everyone[7] who hears the sound of the trumpet, the whistle, the tambourine, the drum, the cymbal, the flute and all kinds of amusements prostrate himself and kneel to the golden statue, and those who do not prostrate themselves and kneel will be thrown into the burning fiery furnace.

Dn 3:12
There is a group of Jews whom you have appointed over the affairs of the city of Babylon: Shadrak, Mishak and Abed-Nego; this is a group who does not accept the king's order, refuses to worship his god and does not prostrate and kneel to the golden statue that you set up.'

Dn 3:13
Thereupon Nebuchadnezzar, shaking and angry, ordered that Shadrak, Mishak and Abed-Nego be brought; so they were brought between his hands.

Dn 3:14
He started by asking them: 'Shadrak, Mishak and Abed-Nego, is it true that you are not worshipping my god and are not kneeling to the golden statue that I set up you?

Dn 3:15
Now, be ready when you hear the sound of the trumpet, the whistle, the tambourine, the drum, the cymbal, the flute and all kind of amusements you prostrate yourself and kneel to the golden statue, but if you do not kneel immediately you will be thrown into the burning fiery furnace, and what lord can deliver you from my hand!

Dn 3:16
They[8] answered him and said: 'O Nebuchadnezzar, we do not need even a word to answer you about this.[9]

Yefet ben Eli has more literal understanding and does not mention the Islamic name of God or אללה.

7 Yefet ben Eli starts Dn 10 by a question: 'Did you not order.'

8 The MT mentions that 'Shadrak, Mishak and Abed-Nego answered and said.'

9 Yefet ben Eli: 'We do not need a discourse in order to answer.'

Dn 3:17

For our Lord that we worship is capable of delivering us from the burning fiery furnace, and from your hand, O king, He will deliver us.

Dn 3:18

If, however, He does not deliver us, know, O king, that we will never worship your god and will never kneel to the golden statue that you set up.'

Dn 3:19

At that, the king was filled with anger and the color of his face altered against Shadrak, Mishak and Abed-Nego and ordered that the furnace be heated seven times than it should.[10]

Dn 3:20

He commanded a group of strong men from his army to bind Shadrak, Mishak and Abed-Nego in order to throw them into the burning fiery furnace.

Dn 3:21

Thereupon, they were bound[11] with their trousers, their shirts, their outer garment[12] and all[13] their clothes and threw them into the midst of the burning fiery furnace.

Dn 3:22

The [king's] order being urgent and the furnace being heated excessively, the men who carried Shadrak, Mishak and Abed-Nego were killed by the flames.[14]

10 Yefet ben Eli: 'That the furnace be heated seven times to the point that he could see the fire in it.'

11 The edition of Morag and Spiegel, which usually follows Morag, has the verb כפת for the more correct כתף, with the doubled ת. כפת here has the Aramaic meaning. But while in Aramaic כפת means "to tie, to bound", it does not have this meaning in Arabic. It can be glossed with "to pick up" which is not far from its Aramaic meaning. The translation here follows the MT of Daniel.

12 There are differences in the translation of the clothes by which Shadrak, Mishak and Abed-Nego were bound. סרבליהון R. Saadia: סראוילאתהם their trousers, Yefet ben Eli: סראוילאתהם their trousers. פטשיהון R. Saadia: קמצאנהם their shirts, Yefet ben Eli: כ̇פאתינהם their coats. כרבלתהון R. Saadia: משמאלהם their outer garment, Yefet ben Eli: טיאלסתהם their head-bands.

13 כל is added by R. Saadia to his translation and has no Aramaic background.

14 Lit. "Flames of fires."

Dn 3:23
However, the three individuals Shadrak, Mishak and Abed-Nego fell, bound, into the midst of the burning fiery furnace.

Dn 3:24
At that point Nebuchadnezzar the king was astonished and, rising quickly, he addressed the generals: 'Didn't we throw three individuals, bound, into the midst of the fire.' They answered him and said: 'Surely, O king.'

Dn 3:25
He addressed them and said: 'here I am looking at four men, unbound,[15] walking in the midst of the fire, without any hurt, and the appearance of the fourth looks similar to the angels.'

Dn 3:26
Then Nebuchadnezzar approached the opining of the burning fiery furnace and called: 'Shadrak, Mishak and Abed-Nego, servants of God the Most High, get out and come here.' Thereupon, Shadrak, Mishak and Abed-Nego came out from the midst of the fire.

Dn 3:27
The straps, the princes, the prefects and the king's generals gathered and looked at those men and were astonished how the fire did not have any effect over their bodies, how the hair of their head did not burn, how their clothes did not change and how the smell of the smoke[16] did not impregnate them.

Dn 3:28
Then Nebuchadnezzar started and said: 'Blessed be the God of Shadrak, Mishak and Abed-Nego who sent His angel to deliver His servants who put their faith in Him and changed the king's order, yielding their bodies rather than worshipping or kneeling to another god than theirs.

Dn 3:29
I hereby issue an order that any group or nations or tongues utter blasphemy against the God of Shadrak, Mishak and Abed-Nego will be dis-

15 Lit. "Here I am looking at four unbound."
16 MT: "The smell of the fire."

membered and their houses[17] confiscated, for there is no other God who is capable to save in this manner.'

Dn 3:30

Thereafter, the king improved the condition of Shadrak, Mishak and Abed-Nego in the city of Babylon.[18]

The first beneficial information for us[19] from this story is that the name of God when He is worshiped is three [...] or [...] standing up or kneeling.[20] Similar to what he said there: ... *to the inauguration*[21] *of the statue* (Dn 3:2.3), kneeling and standing up.[22] As to the offering, it is according to what he said there [... ...] and the benefit of this knowledge. We say that the Bible[23] had mentioned about the Fathers that, in Solomon's time they [... ...] *the feast of the booths* (2 Chr 8:13). He also said: *For they made the consecration of the altar during seven days* (2 Chr 7:9). When the inauguration did not happen during the eating [... ...] and the men ate and drank [in] *Yom Kippur* which is part of the seven days [... ...] that the seven days are separated [one] from the other by a day. Hence, it remains open for us [...]. [And if] this discourse is the meaning of the consecration: standing, kneeling and the offering we have no need for distinguishing the seven days, or separating seven [days] from another seven [days]. [... ...] the offering together is permitted in *[Yom] Kippur.*

I rendered: שׂמו עליך מלכא טעם (Dn 3:12) that "they did not accept your order" [... ...] *they have pleasure in you.*[24] This is similar to *everyone who is in the record* (Ex 30:13.14),[25] *those who are in charge of the enrollment* (Nm 7:2).[26]

17 Lit. "Its house."

18 Dn 3:31–33 will be treated by R. Saadia as part of Dn 4.

19 Yefet, as well, uses the word "benefit" of this story, starting his commentary by the same consideration: the benefit of such story for the reader of his time.

20 Most probably we are at the end of R. Saadia's reasoning about God's names and the believer's disposition before him.

21 וכארה (the Arabic word by which R. Saadia render the Hebrew word חנכה) designates the festive meal at the end of a building work. It is translated here by "inauguration" when it deals with Nebuchadnezzar's statue. However, the same word is translated by "consecration" when it deals with the altar, as in 2 Chr 7:9, for example.

22 Nothing in the text suggests that one had to either kneel or standing before the statue. Once again the lacuna makes it difficult to follow R. Saadia's reasoning.

23 Lit. "The Book."

24 עליהון טעם מניך an extra biblical quotation.

25 כל מן נאז עליה אלעדד is R. Saadia's translation of the quoted part of Ex 30:13.

[… …] *that the leprous has been healed of his leprosy* (Lv 14:3).[27] Similar to *lest he find fortified towns and escape us* (2 Sm 20:6). [… …], *they burnt your sanctuary* (Ps 74:7)[28] which means *they set fire in your sanctuary*.[29] Like *you will burn their fortress* (2 Kgs 8:12). I rendered הצדא by *is it true* (Dn 3:14) similar to אזדא *is it true* (Dn 2:5). I rendered by "I already" [decided] and "it is certain" since those two letters are interchangeable.[30] And I rendered חשחין *we need* (Dn 3:16).[31] Because there are three words in [biblical] Aramaic: לא חשחן *we do not need* (Dn 3:16); ומן חשחן *and what they need* (Ezr 6:9);[32] ושאר חשחות בית אלהיך *what is more to be needed for the house of your God* (Ezr 7:20). In fact, there are many possible interpretations in their expression "we do not need to answer this" (Dn 3:16).[33] One of them is that obviously it is the Lord of the universe who is to be worshipped. Moreover, what is accidental and fabricated can not be worshipped. Furthermore, the Mighty One, who rules over everything, is capable of delivering us. One of those [interpretations] is that we do not know whether He actually will save us or not, because maybe He is probing His friends.[34] However, we answer you about the two parts together: delivered by [God] or not delivered, we do not kneel to the statue.[35]

By adding *and from your hand* (Dn 3:17) they indicate all kinds of sufferings. In other words, it is not from the fire alone that He will deliver us, but from the imprisonment, the binding, the sword, the lions, the suffering and whatever the emperor's hands use against those who infuriated him. There are also two matters to be considered in his expression: *If, however, He does not*

---

26 אלחאצרון עלי עדדהם is R. Saadia's translation of the quoted part of Nm 7:2. It is difficult to understand his use of the passages from Exodus and Numbers since the lacuna prevent us from understanding the sense R. Saadia gives to פקודים.

27 אן אלאברץ קד אשפי מן בלא אלברץ is R. Saadia's translation of the quoted part of Lv 14:3.

28 וקד כלו וקד אלנאר פי מקדסך is R. Saadia's translation of the quoted part of Ps 74:7.

29 R. Saadia is trying to explain that שלחו באש מקדשיך has the meaning of שלחו אש בקדשיך.

30 R. Saadia is explaining that the letter צ and the letter ז are interchangeable and the two words given as example have the same meaning. However, R. Saadia did not forget to translate הצדא as an interrogation "is it true"? So, the meaning that he gives to הצדא "is it true," does not take into consideration the interrogative form.

31 חשחין is in negative form in Dn 3:16: לא חשחין "we do not need." However, R. Saadia will quote Dn 3:16 in its full context as an illustration of the meaning he gives to this word.

32 MT ומה חשחן.

33 R. Saadia quotes his translation, not the MT.

34 R. Saadia put his commentary in the form of a direct discourse by characters in Daniel's book.

35 R. Saadia is speaking in the name of Shadrak, Mishak and Abed-Nego.

deliver us, know, O king (Dn 3:18). The first is that we have to sacrifice ourselves rather than worshipping the statues. It is one of three conditions where it is our obligation to sacrifice rather than preserve our lives. The first [condition is when we are asked] to worship other than our Lord, which is the case in this story. The second [condition is when we are asked] to commit what is prohibited, similar to what had happened in the story of Joseph: *How can I commit this great evil and sin against God* (Gn 39:9).[36] He endangered his life, since his master's wife was capable of killing him. The third [condition is when we are asked] to kill, like what happened in Saul's story: *The servants of the king would not raise their hands to strike down the Lord's priests* (1 Sm 22:17). Hence, those three [conditions], *idolatry, exposure of flesh, shedding of blood* require the sacrifice of our life rather than accomplishing them if unbelievers impose them on us. Concerning all the oral laws, if we realize that the angry man's intention is to push us out of our religion our behavior should be similar to that of the three [previous conditions].[37] Yet, if the angry man was looking for his personal profit, we should not sacrifice our lives because of his profit. For example, if there is an unbeliever who disturbs a Jewish man in the Sabbath and tells him: "cut some tree branches for me, and if you do not I will kill you." If he perceives that his intention is [to have] food for his animal, let him cut [some branches] for him. But if he tells him to throw the branches into the river, let him cut no [branches] for him.[38] The second benefit[39] is that if the believer sacrifices his life for one of those three [reasons], being certain that God must save

36 פכ֗יף אצנע הדה אלבליה אלעט֗ימה ואכ֗טא ללה is R. Saadia's translation of the quoted part of Gn 39:9.

37 It is probable that R. Saadia draw up a distinction between the "unbelievers" אלכפאר and the angry man אלמתהדר. While the "unbeliever" asks for immoral actions, transgressions for the Rabbanites and the Karaites alike, the "angry men" aim to oppose the oral laws, sacred for the Rabbanites alone. Hence, it appears justified at first to apply the word "unbelievers" to the Muslims, representative of the authority in R. Saadia's time, and the expression "angry man" to the Karaites whose theology opposes the oral law. However, the example that follows the action of the "angry man" calls the later כאפר "unbeliever", a synonymous. So we do not have a clear distinction between these two words. That is why it seems that R. Saadia address the Muslims, who are not known for their specific opposition to the oral law alone, and to the Karaites who had no power to impose death penalty at the time of R. Saadia.

38 By asking the Jewish man to work uselessly the unbeliever's intention is to force the Jewish man to transgress the Sabbath commandment.

39 It is the second benefit that R. Saadia sees in the expression *If, however, He does not deliver us, know, O king* (Dn 3:18). The first was divided in two sections: when sacrificing one's life is an obligation and when it is relative to the adversary's intention.

him, his sacrifice is not perfect. In fact, it is not a sacrifice at all. [Because] he has to believe in sacrificing [his life] even if he is not delivered [by God].

In fact, if we scrutinize the discourse of Hananyah, Mishael and Azaryah we will find it in accord [with what we have said]. That is why they said: *He is capable of delivering us* (Dn 3:17). They did not say that He would deliver them actually. For this [reason] the matter of the imprisonment introduced doubts about the [the liberation of the] believers.[40] In order that He deliver some of them from the hand of the unbelievers, unlike others that He does not deliver until the sacrifice of their lives become perfect. Because, if they are convinced that He will deliver them any way, their sacrifice is useless. This, too, is similar to our question about Abraham and Isaac.[41] Someone may retort against us that if Abraham felt secure about Isaac's life and his inheritance, because of the expression *for through Isaac your offspring shall be called* (Gn 21:12)[42] then his sacrifice and all the matter of the offering was because of his trust in this covenant. We answer and say it is possible that [Isaac's] slaughtering would be achieved, then he would be revived by his Lord and would have inheritance. To this objection too the Lord will give another answer, if the man in trial asks him why He makes him suffer, and will not say to him "I will repay you",[43] for fear that people lose their capacity to wait for Him.[44] Similar to the answer of Moses when he said: *Why did you bring harm to this people etc.* (Ex 5:22),[45] *now shall you see what I will do to Pharaoh* (Ex 6:1).[46] Comparable to when He answered

40 Lit. "The partisans of unity of God". This expression can be found in Judaism and Islam. However, here it designates the believers alone. It is highly improbable that R. Saadia, a citizen living in an Islamic country, is speaking about the Muslims that God probes by imprisonment in an Islamic country because of their faith.

41 In the following lines R. Saadia abridges his commentary on the sacrifice of Isaac in Gn 22. Cf. R. Saadia's commentary on Genesis by Moshe Zucker, the Jewish Theological Seminary of America, N.Y. 1984, pp. 141–142 (Judeo-Arabic text) 401–402 (Modern Hebrew translation).

42 פאן מן אסחק ידעי לך אלנסל is R. Saadia's translation of the quoted part of Gn 21:12.

43 Yefet ben Eli, contrary to R. Saadia, mentions compensation in the life to come as an incentive to the acceptance of suffering in this life. To this, R. Saadia answer by the example of Abraham whose acceptance of the command to offer his son Isaac came out of trust and faith in God and with no guarantee about a future compensation.

44 Lit. "For fear that His patience diminishes among the people." That I interpret as "the patience for him." The meaning seems to be that certainty of being answered may increase the believers' impatience and, as is the case in the example taken from Exodus, could become a motive for all kind of difficulties and sufferings.

45 לם אבלית הולאי אלקום is R. Saadia's translation of the quoted part of Ex 5:22.

46 אלאן תנטֹר מא אצנע לפרעון is R. Saadia's translation of the quoted part of Ex 6:1.

him: *why did you bring harm to your servant* (Nm 11:11)[47] *gather for Me seventy men* (Nm 11:16).[48] It is comparable to His answer to Job when he asked: *Inform me why you put me on trial* (Jb 10:2)[49] [and God's answer] *where were you when I laid the earth's foundations* (Jb 38:4).[50] Until the end of the two stories.[51]

The fact that they started their speech by the words *O Nebuchadnezzar we do not need* (Dn 3:16) does not mean that they belittle him, since [previously] we find them calling him "king".[52] In fact, calling him "Nebuchadnezzar" is just like calling him "king." Because [Nebuchadnezzar] is a title, the name being different. His expression: *The men who carried Shadrak, Mishak and Abed-Nego* (Dn 3:22) demonstrate that they were projected into the fire by a stone launcher,[53] similar to what the warriors do. And Nebuchadnezzar's statement: *Here I am looking at four [men],* (Dn 3:25) shows that Hananyah, Mishael and Azaryah were walking in the midst of the fire before the king and that he was behind them, since he did not say *their former vision*.[54] Moreover, from this [scene] we say that the rank of the righteous men is higher than the angels' rank. There are many passages [to illustrate this] that we will not mention here [for fear of being too long]. That is why Nebuchadnezzar said: *[The God of Shadrak,*

47 לם אבלית עבדך is R. Saadia's translation of the quoted part of Nm 11:11. According to R. Saadia's interpretation, Moses' complaint is based on the difficulties he faced in ensuring the manna regularly for the people who were between their memory of their material security in Egypt (Nm 11:5–6) and the promise of a material security and of peaceful times (Nm 10:9–10) in their promised land that they did not yet experience.

48 אגמע לי סבעין רגלא is R. Saadia's translation of the quoted part of Nm 11:16.

49 ערפני עלי מא דא תכאצמני is R. Saadia's translation of the quoted part of Jb 10:2.

50 ואין כנת חין אססת אלארץ is R. Saadia's translation of the quoted part of Jb 38:4.

51 While the reference to Exodus seems clear as illustration of the people's impatience with God's promise and the difficulty of the situation for Moses, the reference to Job appears unfitting in this context. Job's interrogation is the expression of his incomprehension of God's ways of ruling the universe rather than his impatience for the belated realization of a promise. There is one common element in the quotations taken from Exodus and Job: both speak about the man's limited perception of his destiny compared to God's limitless knowledge of man's future.

52 According to Yefet ben Eli the meaning of *O Nebuchadnezzar we do not need* (Dn 3:16) is: we do not need to give you any excuse for our refusal of kneeling to the statue.

53 The idea that Shadrak, Mishak and Abed-Nego were thrown by an engine is repeated by Yefet ben Eli in his commentary on this verse.

54 וריוה / ורוה די קמאה.

Mishak and Abed-Nego] who sent His angel to deliver His servants (Dn 3:28).[55] Yet, we have to know how did He deliver them. For there are two ways to their liberation. Either the fire gets cold or they are protected by an accidental [factor].[56] If we say that He cools the fire, there will be no surprise, since we know that the cold thing burns no one.[57] Nevertheless, He did not alter the nature of the fire, but saved them by an accidental [factor] in order that the fire have no effect on them. This, in fact, is the splendid miracle.[58]

In every commentary I put פחותא (Dn 3:27) ahead of סגניא (Dn 3:27), because פחה [means] "prince" as in the expression: *The prince of Judah* (Hg 1:1) while וסגן [that means] "prefect" according to the [fathers] expression: *R. Hananiah the prefect of the priests* (Pesahim 1:6).[59]

There is a problem that we have to discuss. It is true to us that Hananyah, Mishael and Azaryah did not kneel to the statue. [Still], what shall we say[60] about the whole of the Exiled in Babylon or the whole Israelites: did they kneel to it or not? If they all kneeled, it is a catastrophe, or they did not have prophets. If they did not kneel, they would have been burnt. We answer and say that Nebuchadnezzar did not constrain all the people to kneel to his to his god, but only the ones who had power.[61] It is for this reason that he[62] offers such an extensive

55 It seems that the mere fact that angels were sent in order to save human beings justifies R. Saadia's categorizing. However, passages in the Bible (Jb 1 for example) are witnesses of the difficulty of attributing higher category to human beings to the detriment of angels.

56 Lit "by accident". "Accident" here is to be understood in its philosophical acceptation. It designates an added factor that does not belong to the nature of thing.

57 This and all other "scientific" information remind us of R. Saadia's time and the impossibility of judging his scientific knowledge according to our own.

58 As if R. Saadia's preference of this solution (their safety because of an accidental factor) is because of its improbability, which gives a "miraculous" aspect to the solution. Yefet ben Eli's solution is that God put a curtain or something that prevented the fire from reaching their body.

59 R. Saadia tries to justify the superiority of the prince's function compared to that of the prefect. The examples he chooses instruct about his interpretation: the prince אמיר seems to be in charge of a region, while כליפה appears as responsible or ruler of a group of people. However, in Arabic and Islamic vocabulary, there is no one higher than the one who is considered to be the prophet Muhammad's deputy on earth. He is also called the "prince of the believers." In this case alone, the words אמיר and כליפה are synonymous.

60 Lit. "What have you to say."

61 This problem received the same solution by Yefet ben Eli in his commentary on Dn 3. Like R. Saadia, he sees that Hananyah, Mishael and Azaryah are men of influence as is demonstrated by the fact that they are singled out for questioning by

list: *The satraps, the princes, the governors, the rulers, the workers, the scribes and the officers* (Dn 3:2–3). Then he added to them *all the commanders of the provinces* (Dn 3.2–3). He mentions, nevertheless, *populations, nations and tongues* (Dn 3:4) in the middle of the story. He wants, in mentioning them, [to show] that they belong to different nations and various languages. As to the learned men from every population, he did not ask them to kneel to the statue, nor even to be present [at the inauguration]. In fact, the obligation of kneeling devolved on Hananyah, Mishael and Azaryah because they were men of power, as he said first: *[Then Daniel asked the king to] appoint Shadrak, Mishak and Abed-Nego over the affairs of Babylon* (Dn 2:49).

It is because of their superiority[63] that the Kasdians slandered them. It may be because at that moment they were powerful, which motivated the [Kasdians'] resentment over their higher rank or because of the people gratefulness to them. That is why [the Kasdians] said: *[There are certain Jews] whom you have appointed over the affairs of the city of Babylon* (Dn 3:12). Now that [the fact] became clear that the population were not asked [to kneel to the statue] and that the men of power alone were asked [to do so], the difficulty finds its own solution. Nevertheless, a part of Daniel's question remains: Was he required, or was he not, to kneel [to the statue]? If he was required to kneel, because he was a man of power, according to what have been said: *And [the king] made him ruler over the city of Babylon* (Dn 2:48), and since it is certain that he refused, why is it, therefore, that he was not thrown into the fire? We answer that for Nebuchadnezzar Daniel was one of the divinities, because it is not unheard-of among the unbelievers that they worship various gods. To some people in fact the Creator's light is in every wise counsel, in every human being, or in many of them. If this light [resides] in him he should be worshipped. That is why when Nebuchadnezzar heard of Daniel's wisdom he knelt to him and ordered that offerings be presented to him, according to what we have said.[64]

Perhaps we have doubts about Nebuchadnezzar's action; whether it constitutes adoration or not. That is why he said that he[65] called him Belteshazzar, the name of his god. The reason of that was because in him resides the spirit of the holy god, as he said: *At last Daniel one of them came in before me, whose name is Belteshazzar, following the name of my god, and in whom resides the spirit of*

Nebuchadnezzar. Unlike R. Saadia, however, Yefet ben Eli, cites Ex 20:5 in this context, a text explicitly prohibiting idolatry.

62 "He" here designates either Nebuchadnezzar or the writer of the Book of Daniel.

63 Lit. "Their presidency." This may be a reference to their function as supervisors of the affairs of the province of Babylon (Cf. Dn 2:49).

64 Cf. Dn 2:46.

65 The first "he" of this sentence designates either the Book of Daniel's writer, or Nebuchadnezzar himself, while the second "he" indicates Nebuchadnezzar alone.

the holy gods (Dn 4:5). [Therefore] it becomes clear to us that the kneeling and the presentations of the offerings [to Daniel] were considered by [Nebuchadnezzar] as worship action. Then, since Daniel is regarded as a god, similar to the statue, it does not suit Nebuchadnezzar to request one god to kneel to another god, because both are of the same rank. Then we explain how the name "Belteshazzar" became comparable to [Nebuchadnezzar's] god and whole the reason, which is the hidden presence of the Spirit of God in him. We say that it is well known to us that "Bel" בל is the name of the Babylonian god, according to the expression: *And I will punish Bel in Babylon* (Jer 51:44). He also said: *Bel is bowed, Nebo is stooped* (Is 46:1).[66] He said again: *Say, Babylon is captured, Bel is confounded, Merdoch is broken, her idols are confounded, her fetishes are broken* (Jer 50:2). Therefore Nebuchadnezzar [... ...] comparable to us when we put the name of our Lord at the beginning of the names and say: Eliazar, Elhnan, Elgabar. We also say: Jehuram, Joshua and similar [names]. Then he added to it two Aramaic[67] words: טשא צר. טשא means certainly "to veil and to hide." As to צר, certainly it has the meaning of "vigorous and firm." As if [Nebuchadnezzar] is saying that his god is hidden firmly in Daniel's body. In fact, if Nebuchadnezzar did not say: *Whose name is Belteshazzar, following the name of my god* (Dn 4:5) we would not have this explanation. So, we fully detailed the answer to this part as well.

Some elders answered that certain Israelites did kneel [to the statue] inadvertently and that is certainly the reason why they were threatened by death at the time of Haman.[68] This answer, nevertheless, remains limited, since his appeal [to kneel before the statue] did not specify one single nation and it is impossible to gather all men. Didn't you observe that during the prosperity we worshipped the statue [... ...].[69] *They have made for themselves molten images from their*

66 גתא בל ותשׂא נבו is R. Saadia's translation of the quoted part of Is 46:1.

67 בכלמתין נבטתין "two Nabatean words."

68 Cf. Est 3–7.

69 R. Saadia's reasoning is unclear because of the lacuna that forbids its full understanding. It is possible that R. Saadia is underlining the inconsistency of the elders interpretation: Nebuchadnezzar, in his order to kneel before the statue did not specify the people who had to perform such a gesture, his order being issued to all the peoples of his kingdom, while Haman's plot was directed against the Jews in particular. It is possible as well that R. Saadia's reference to the time when the people in the Sinai worshipped the statue of the calf means to emphasize the willingness of the Israelites to worship a statue, which led to their punishment, compared to the an order coming from an no-Israelite who forced them to kneel before a statue that he had made. This hypothesis finds its justification in the quotation of Hos 13:2 that follows. According to Hosea it is the Israelites themselves that sinned by making and worshipping idol.

silver (Hos 13:2). Moreover, they were longing after them like a father longing for his son.[70] But when the *servitude* fell on us we learned our lesson and chose to be burnt by fire rather than worship [the idols].[71] This [meaning] is part of the comparison [that says]: *I opened to my beloved, but my beloved had turned and was gone, my soul failed when he spoke* (Sg 5:6) until the end of the story.[72] As to his writing *utter blasphemy* (Dn 3:29) means not even one single slip of the tongue. It has been said that it is a slip of the tongue, comparable to his statement: *How terrifying the thing that is heard about him* (Jb 26:14).[73] We rendered his expression: *Thereafter, the king improved the condition of Shadrak, Mishak and Abed-Nego in the city of Babylon* (Dn 3:30) by "improving their condition." The reason is that the Kasdians considered them objectors to the king's order. Yet, [the three] being certified by the miracle, Nebuchadnezzar found himself obliged to entrust them with many civil affairs [which] show to the Kasdians the harm they inflected on the Jews. [...] that they were not [...] disobedient to the king [...] their condition that they did not disobey them. It goes the same for *then the condition of Daniel improved* (Dn 6:29). The [commentary] of the third chapter is finished.[74]

70 R. Saadia is describing the passion that the Israelites had for idols during different stages of their history. Ex 32:1–6 describes one of the most representative moments of this false liturgy. Yefet ben Eli refers to the same episode in Exodus to understand how after being converted to Daniel's God Nebuchadnezzar went back to worship an idol.

71 Lit. "To worship them." It is odd that R. Saadia's reasoning against kneeling to the idols did not mention the most expressive prohibition against such gesture in Ex 20:5 and its parallel Dt 5:9, which Yefet ben Eli does while commenting on the same passage in Dn 3.

72 This is R. Saadia usual way to refer to the whole of a quotation, partially mentioned by him. It is also a common procedure among the Arabic and Judeo-Arabic writers.

73 פאי׳ שי׳ מן אלאמור סמע בה is R. Saadia's translation of the quoted part of 26:14. The point of comparison between Dn 3:29 and Jb 26:14 is not clear. The fact that R. Saadia in his commentary on Job (ed. J. Derenbourg and H. Derenbourg) did not comment on this verse does not help us to understand the similarity between the two verses.

74 Dn 3:30 is the end of the chapter for R. Saadia. Yefet ben Eli also adds the remaining verses to the next chapter.

Chapter 4

[This is] the text of the fourth chapter.[1] [It is] a copy of the decree written by Nebuchadnezzar to all horizons about what happened to him, that the fathers who transmitted the Holy Books[2] included it in the Book of Daniel, because of their certainty of the truthfulness of its contents. And while the king's scribes may add or abridge the information about events, mark them by their styles or embellish them, this copy is denuded of such thing. We found that all its account, with exception of some verses in its midst,[3] are ascribed to him [… …]. There are meanings in all the copy that we will mention, once we finish [its interpretation], with the help of the Merciful and His determination. [Here is] the beginning of the copy:

Dn 3:31

Then Nebuchadnezzar the king wrote[4] to all the populations, nations and tongues living in every country:[5] 'May the peace of God and His blessings be on you.[6]

Dn 3:32

I thought[7] of telling you[8] about the miracles and the wonders[9] that God the most High had worked with me.

1 The fourth chapter starts by Dn 3:31–33 since it forms a unity by being the beginning of the king's decree that continues in Dn 4. Yefet ben Eli adopts the same division.

2 It is not certain that the expression "the Holy Books" designates the Bible alone. It may also refer to all the religious literature admitted by the Rabbanites, which embodies the Mishna, the Talmud and, perhaps, some liturgical prayers.

3 Like Dn 4:25 that Yefet ben Eli attributes to the scribe. The commentary of R. Saadia's of this verse did not reach us.

4 כתב 'wrote' is added by R. Saadia to his translation and has no MT original.

5 MT: "In all the earth."

6 After criticizing the king's scribes who are not faithful to the truthfulness of events, marking them by their imprint of style or embellishment, R. Saadia gives us an example of a non-literal translation of the Aramaic text, since he adopts the ritual Arabic beginning of a letter: 'May the peace of God and His blessings be on you'. Yefet ben Eli's translation is more faithful to the Aramaic text when he writes 'may your peace be multiplied.'

7 Mt: "It pleases me to tell."

Dn 3:33

His miracles, how numerous, His wonders, how great,[10] His kingdom is the universe kingdom, His dominion is from generation of generations.[11]

Dn 4:1

I, Nebuchadnezzar, was living serenely in my house and quietly in my temple.[12]

Dn 4:2

Until[13] I saw a dream[14] that frightened me, my thoughts[15] on my bed, and my vision[16] terrifies me.

Dn 4:3

I ordered that all the wise men of Babylon be brought before me to let me know its explanation.[17]

Dn 4:4

Therefore, the wise men, the astrologers, the Kasdians, the rulers,[18] and I narrated to them the vision, but they did not give me its interpretation.[19]

---

8 אכברכם 'telling you' is R. Saadia's translation of להחויה literally 'to tell.' The plural personal pronoun כם 'you' is added by R. Saadia to his translation.

9 Yefet ben Eli renders the Aramaic word תמהיא by 'demonstrations' or 'proofs.' Thus, instead of "how great are His wonders" of R. Saadia we have "how strong are His demonstrations" or the demonstration of his power.

10 Yefet ben Eli: 'His miracles, how big and great, His demonstrations, how founded.'

11 MT: "Generation and generation," which is Yefet ben Eli's translation.

12 היכל designates, in Aramaic and Arabic, first of all "a temple" where the altar stands. It may also designate 'a place.' But the second meaning is far from being obvious. It is interesting to notice Yefet's interpretation: 'Being quietly in my temple' has the meaning of 'being well physically.'

13 חתי 'until' has no source in the MT.

14 One of the very few times that R. Saadia calls Nebuchadnezzar's dream by the Arabic word (similar to the Aramaic) חלם 'dream.' Otherwise, he often translates the same word by רויא 'vision.'

15 Yefet ben Eli uses two Arabic words, אפכארי וחואטרי to render the Aramaic word הרהרין.

16 MT: "The vision of my head." Yefet ben Eli: "And the visions of my head."

17 MT: "The explanation of the dream." By following the masoretic text literally, Yefet ben Eli an inelegant translation of Dn 4:3.

18 The four categories of dignitaries, according to the MT text, who came before the king are translated in five categories by Yefet ben Eli. Unlike R. Saadia, the categories mentioned by Yefet include some 'lower class' groups. Following Yefet

Dn 4:5

Until the last Daniel one of them came before me, whose name is Belteshazzar, following the name of my god, and in whom resides the spirit of the Holy God,[20] then I narrated the vision to him.[21]

Dn 4:6

And told him: Belteshazzar, head of the wise men, in whom, as I know from you, resides the spirit of the Holy God, that there is no secret unknown to you, and who told me earlier the vision and its interpretation.[22]

Dn 4:7

Now, on my bed, I saw a vision[23] that a tree was in the midst of the earth, large, its stature was great.

Dn 4:8

Until[24] it grew and became huge; its height almost reached the sky[25] and its branches[26] [extend to] all the earth.[27]

---

translation, they are: Philosophers, witches, jugglers, Kasdians, brigands. With the exception of the Kasdians, there is no category in common between the two translations.

19 The Aramaic פשר is translated differently by R. Saadia: In Dn 4:3 he translates it by the Arabic word תפסיר 'explanation,' which deals with clarification of the obvious meaning. While in Dn 4:4 he translates the same Aramaic word by the Arabic תאויל 'interpretation' which refers to the clarification of the hidden meaning. Yefet ben Eli maintains the same translation תפסיר 'explanation' in both verses.

20 When word "god" is related to Daniel, as in Dn 4:5, R. Saadia translates it by אללה the usual word that he uses for God. In the case of Dn 4:5–6 we have 'holy gods' אלהין קדשין. Still, R. Saadia uses the word אללה in the two cases. Yefet ben Eli maintains the plural: 'Holy gods.'

21 Lit. "I told it to him."

22 'Who told me earlier the vision and its interpretation' differs noticeably from the usual understanding of this part of Dn 4:6. The main difference comes from R. Saadia's interpretation of אמר as Qal and not as imperative. Hens, Yefet ben Eli's translation: "Tell me the vision of my dream and its interpretation."

23 MT: "The visions of my head" which is also the translation of Yefet ben Eli.

24 חתי 'until' is added by R. Saadia and has no source in the MT.

25 "Reached almost the sky" is the modification that R. Saadia's introduces to the verse, perhaps out of reverence for the sky as God's habitation.

26 שעבהא literally 'the ramification of its branches.'

27 Lit. "All that earth." Yefet ben Eli has another understanding of the final part of Dn 4:8: 'And its vision [can be seen] until the end of the earth.'

Dn 4:9

Its branches[28] were beautiful, its fruits were abundant, food for all was in it, beneath it, the beasts of the desert found shade, in its branches the bird of the sky had refuge and from it every human being there[29] receive sustenance.

Dn 4:10

Then I saw the accomplishment of my night vision[30] as if a holy and divine angel came from heaven.[31]

Dn 4:11

Crying loudly and saying as follow: 'Hew down the tree, cut its branches, strip off its leaves,[32] scatter its fruit, let the beasts disappear from beneath it and the birds[33] from its branches.

Dn 4:12

However, leave the stump of its roots in the earth and tie it by string of iron and bronze in the grass of the desert; he will be covered by the dew of heaven;[34] his [portion] food with the beasts from the grass of the desert.[35]

28 אגצאנהא is rendered here by the same word that translated the Arabic שׄעבהא 'its branches.' Yefet ben Eli: "Its leaves."

29 "There" or "in that place" is added by R. Saadia in his translation and has parallel in the MT.

30 MT: "The vision of my head." R. Saadia translation: תמאם רויאיי פי אלליל could also be rendered as 'my complete night vision.'

31 According to R. Saadia there is only one holy and heavenly angel that came down from heaven. He was certainly eager to harmonize the translation of Dn 4:10 with the following verse whose initial verb קרא applied to the one who came from heaven implies that the subject is singular.

32 In Yefet ben Eli's translation, the expression אתרו עפיה is rendered by 'extirpate its trace', certainly because of the similarity between the Aramaic אתרו and the Arabic אתׄרהו, 'his trace.'

33 While the Arabic words וחש 'beast' and טאיר "bird" are in a singular form they express regularly the species. That is why they are translated here as plural.

34 Lit. "Colored by the dew of heaven."

35 The first 'grass of the desert' is a translation of כׄלא אלצחרא The second, is a translation of עשב אלצחרא. It should be noticed that the Arabic word כׄלא also means 'emptiness,' and 'wilderness.'

Dn 4:13

His reasoning[36] is made different from [the normal reasoning of the] human condition and is given the imagination of beasts,[37] and seven years[38] pass over him in this condition.[39]

Dn 4:14

The expression was decreed by the angels and the answer to the question was by the expression of the holy ones in order that the people realize that the Most High is sovereign over the human realm; to whom He wishes, He gives; He establishes for them whoever He wishes and He may establish the lowest of them.[40]

Dn 4:15

This is the vision that I, the king Nebuchadnezzar, saw; and you, O Belteshazzar, tell its interpretation, since the wise men of my kingdom could not make its interpretation known to me, but you are capable, because the Spirit of the Holy God resides in you.[41]

Dn 4:16

Then Daniel, whose name was Belteshazzar, was bewildered[42] for almost one hour and his thoughts started to frighten him until the king began and said: 'O Belteshazzar, do not let the vision and its interpretation terrify

36 לבבה literally 'his heart' is rendered by the Arabic word תמייזה 'his reasoning' in R. Saadia's translation; עקלה 'his reason' or 'brain' in Yefet ben Eli's translation.

37 ולבב חיוה literally 'animal heart,' which is Yefet ben Eli's translation as well, becomes 'imagination of beasts' in R. Saadia's interpretation.

38 The word עדנין does not by itself mean 'seasons.' but 'period.' The Arabic word אחואל (plural of חול) by which R. Saadia translate עדנין is the old Arabic word for 'years.' Yefet ben Eli renders the same Aramaic word by the Arabic word אוקאת or 'times,' which is less precise than 'year.'

39 'In this condition' a translation of the Arabic expression כד̇אלך is added by R. Saadia and has no parallel in the MT.

40 A very difficult verse to translate. Yefet ben Eli's translation of its beginning is almost incomprehensible. It should be noted that he translates 'He establishes for them whoever He wishes' and not 'He establishes over them whoever He wishes,' which is Yefet ben Eli's way of rendering this part of Dn 4:14, underlining the power and authority of whom God establishes over them.

41 Cf. the footnote concerning the same expression in Dn 4:5.

42 Yefet ben Eli translates the Aramaic אשתומם by two Arabic words, the first is אטרק 'bewildered' which is similar to R. Saadia's translation. The second is אסתוחש 'he was frightened.'

you.' Daniel answered him and said: 'The vision concerns those who hate you and its interpretation concerns your enemies.'

Dn 4:17

The interpretation[43] of the tree that you saw growing, and which became huge, whose height almost reached the sky[44] and its branches to the limits of that earth;[45]

Dn 4:18

Its branches[46] are beautiful, its fruit is abundant and there is food from it for all, beneath it the beasts of the desert find refuge and in its branches live the bird of the sky;

Dn 4:19

It is you, O king, who grew, became great and your sovereignty has grown to reach almost the sky and your dominion is to the regions of the earth.[47]

Dn 4:20

As to what the king has seen of the holy angel who came down from heaven and said: hew down the tree, cut it, but leave the stump of its roots in the earth, tied by string of iron and bronze in the grass of the desert; he will be colored by the dew of heaven; his food with the beasts of the desert, until the seven years[48] pass over him.

43 תאויל 'the interpretation' is added by R. Saadia and has no source in the MT.

44 ובלג̇ ארתפאעהא דון אלסמא 'whose height almost reached the sky' is R. Saadia's translation of a text that reads 'whose height reached the sky.' It is the kind of correction, by suppressing the exaggeration of the text that R. Saadia introduces in order to make it more credible to the reader.

45 אלי אקצי תלך אלארץ̇ 'to the limits of that earth' instead of 'to all the earth' which is the translation of the MT that Yefet ben Eli follows closely.

46 Yefet ben Eli: "Its leaves."

47 אלי אקטאר אלארץ̇ literally 'to the regions of the earth' instead of 'to all the earth' which is the translation of the MT that Yefet ben Eli follows closely.

48 אחואל (plural of חול) as we have said, means "years." However, it could also mean "conditions" plural of חאל. Yet, there is another word for "year," סנה that is more precise and usual than חול. R. Saadia will also mention in the commentary of Dn 4 the opinion of those who think that Nebuchadnezzar lost his mind for one day, one month, or one year, without criticizing their interpretation about the duration of the king's difficulty. That is why it is plausible to think that R. Saadia's choice of חול meant that he did not want to give a precise duration of Nebuchadnezzar's exile from the human society. This been said, we have to admit that R. Saadia's contemporaries understood his interpretation of שבעה עידנין as "seven years." Yefet ben Eli

Dn 4:21
This is its interpretation,[49] O king; it is the sentence of the Most High who pronounced His judgment over my lord the king.[50]

Dn 4:22
That[51] he will be driven away from men and find refuge with the beasts of the desert and be nourished with grass like cattle, he will be covered by the dew of heaven[52] and over him seven years will pass[53] in order that you recognize that the Most High is sovereign over the human realm, to whom He wishes, He gives.[54]

Dn 4:23
Concerning what they said about leaving the stump of the root of the tree, its interpretation[55] is that your reign will return to you, in order that you recognize the dominion of the One to who belongs heaven.[56]

Dn 4:24
Therefore, O king, may my counsel be agreeable to you that you may untie your sin by an act of justice and your iniquities by mercy for the weak; may this delay be for your consolation.'[57]

---

in his commentary on Daniel (D. S Margoliouth's edition vol. 1, p. 151, line 25) criticizes him by name for his interpretation of עידנין as "years." However, there is inconsistency in Yefet ben Eli's thinking, since in his interpretation of Dn 4:20 he notes precisely that the interpretation of עידנין as "years" is plausible (cf. his commentary on Daniel, the text volume, p. 48 line 25).

49 MT: "This is the interpretation."

50 Yefet ben Eli: "It is the sentence of the Most High that reached my lord the king."

51 Dn 4:22 is translated as the judgment that the Most High pronounced over the king mentioned in Dn 4:21.

52 Lit. "Colored by the dew of heaven."

53 R. Saadia does not follow the MT in translating the verbs as second person singular. He chooses the third person singular: "He will be driven away, he will be nourished" instead of "you will be driven away, you will be nourished."

54 The verbs in the translation of Dn 4:22 are passive according to R. Saadia: "He will be driven away … he will be nourished." They are active with subject expressed according to Yefet ben Eli translation: "They will drive you away … they will nourish you."

55 The expression: "Its interpretation" has no source in the MT.

56 'The dominion of the One to whom belongs heaven' is R. Saadia's translation of שליטין שמיא. Yefet ben Eli remains closer to the MT: "The gods that dominate heaven." R. Saadia's theological correction is to underline that 'gods' here is another name of the God of Daniel.

Dn 4:25
All this happened to Nebuchadnezzar the king.[58]

Dn 4:26
Twelve months later he was wandering in the temple[59] **of the kingdom in Babylon.**

Dn 4:27
He started and said: 'Is not this the great Babylon that I built, by my strength,[60] **my glory and my splendor**[61] **to be the stage of the king.'**

Dn 4:28
While the word was still in his mouth,[62] **a voice came from heaven, saying:**[63] **'It has been decreed to you, O Nebuchadnezzar, the king, that the reign has departed from you.**

Dn 4:29
You will be driven away from men[64] **and find refuge with the beasts of the desert and be nourished with grass like cattle and over you seven years**[65] **will pass like this**[66] **in order that you recognize that the Most High is sovereign over the human realm, to whom He wishes, He gives.'**[67]

Dn 4:30
Immediately the decree was applied upon Nebuchadnezzar; he was driven away from men and started to eat grass like cattle, he was colored by the

---

57 We do not have R. Saadia's commentary on Dn 4:24. The idea is that justice and mercy could delay the imminent punishment of the king. This is also the interpretation of Yefet ben Eli.

58 Yefet ben Eli notices that Dn 4:25 was said by the scribe and is not part of the discourse of Daniel. There is no commentary of R. Saadia on Dn 4:25.

59 Lit. "On the temple."

60 בשדה ותאקי 'by my firm agreement' or 'solid covenant.'

61 ליקר הדרי literally 'my splendid glory' is translated by R. Saadia in two words 'My glory and my splendor.' Yefet ben Eli: "My mighty splendor."

62 MT: "In the mouth of the king."

63 'Telling' or 'it says,' while Yefet ben Eli follows the Aramaic אמרין 'they say.'

64 MT: "They will drive you away from men." Yefet ben Eli is closer in his translation to the MT.

65 Yefet ben Eli: "Seven times."

66 בדאך 'like this' or 'in such condition.'

67 MT: "The Most High is sovereign over the human kingdom, He gives it to whom He wishes." It is also Yefet ben Eli's translation.

dew of heaven, so his hair grew and became similar to the eagle's feathers and his nails like [the claw of] the birds of prey.

Dn 4:31
When those days past, I, Nebuchadnezzar, lifted my eyes to heaven and my reason returned to me, so I gave thanks to the Most High and praised and glorified the Ever-Living One whose dominion is eternal and whose reign is from generation to generations.[68]

Dn 4:32
And all the inhabitants of the earth are of no count, while He realizes His will in the army of heaven and in the inhabitants of the earth and no one can limit His power,[69] neither asks Him: What did you do?[70]

Dn 4:33
At that time, my reason[71] came back to me with the glory of my reign, my joy and my splendor returned to me; my generals and noble men sought after me, I was established in my kingship and more honor was bestowed on me.

Dn 4:34
Now I, Nebuchadnezzar, praising, elevating and exalting the King of the nations[72] whose works are all just and His ways right,[73] who is able to put down any one who walks arrogantly[74] between His hands.[75]

Our faith in the truthfulness of what the scribe composed in this copy is similar to the faithfulness of the fortune that Joshua imposed in saying: *You shall come forward tomorrow morning by tribes* (Jos 7:14), *then he who is designated for*

68 MT: "For generation and generation."
69 Lit. "No one can hit His hand."
70 R. Saadia does not comment on Dn 4:32.
71 The Aramaic expression: מנדעי literally 'my knowledge,' which is Yefet ben Eli's translation, is translated by R Saadia by the Arabic expression: עקלי 'my reason' but also 'my brain.'
72 MT: "God of heaven."
73 The Aramaic word דין in the expression וארחתה דין is employed in Yefet ben Eli's translation, since the Arabic language has the same word that means 'judgment.' Thus the translation becomes 'His ways constitute judgement.'
74 מהלכין בגוה literally 'those who walk arrogantly' is rendered by R. Saadia in a singular form: The man who walks arrogantly.
75 'Between His hands' is added R. Saadia and has no source in MT.

proscription (Jos 7:15). Without that we could not believe it. In fact he did apply it on the population only because he knew that it would surely happen.[76]

At the beginning he concealed a word: *Then Nebuchadnezzar the king* wrote[77] *to all the populations* (Dn 3:31). I rendered רענן "living quietly" with the meaning of being alone.[78] And when he described how he brought up the erudite men [he did not mention] that he asked them to tell him both, the vision and its interpretation. There are two reasons for this. First, he probed them the first time about similar matter and they showed their incapacity.[79] The second [reason] is due to the fright and the horror that this vision put in him, according to his words: *I saw a dream that frightened me* (Dn 4:2). As if he had to put up with it because of something he did.[80] That is why he did not dare ask Daniel to tell him both: the vision and its interpretation. However, the situation being what it is and given that Nebuchadnezzar himself has narrated the vision to the wise men why is that they could not provide him with its interpretation, since that the same interpretation is well known by many in the populace, all the more so by the elite. For they know that the noble man whose protection secure the life of many is similar to a tree whose shadow is a shelter for animals; birds nest on its branches and many find their sustenance in its fruit. Furthermore [... ...] the prophecy of Ezekiel concerning the king of Tyre whom he compared to the king of Assur who in turn is compared to a tree with such conditions.[81] He insisted on that because of his high dignity, his boasting, his humiliation, since he said about all that: *Behold, Assur was a cedar in Lebanon with beautiful branches and shady forest; with high stature and his top among leafy trees; waters nourished it, the deep made it grow tall, with its stream running round the place where it was planted, sending out its channels to all the trees of the field. That is why its height was exalted above all the trees of the field, its branches multiplied*

76 The commonality between Dn 4 and Jos 7:13–21 is that in the two cases Joshua and Daniel were narrating something (the interpretation of the dream or the discovery of the sinner, designated by fortune) because of the certainty they had from God. The belief of the Bible that they were truthful comes from the facts that witness the truthfulness of their certainty.

77 The word כתב "wrote" is what the scribe concealed, according to R. Saadia. That is why he added it to his translation.

78 Uncertain reading. רענן בהיכלי according to Yefet ben Eli designates the integrity of his body and his well-being.

79 Cf. Dn 2:1–13.

80 Lit. "As if he attributed it to himself."

81 Does R. Saadia suggest that the following quotations from Ezekiel are well known by all, including those who are not Jews? Is he implying that the metaphor of the tree as image of the noble man is common to biblical literature and the literature of the nations surrounding Israel? No satisfying answer to these questions could be obtained from this passage, because of the manuscript lacuna.

and its boughs became long because of the abundant water that burst for it. All the birds of the sky nested in its branches; under its boughs all the beasts of the field bore their young, and under its shadow all great nations lived (Ez 31:3–6). In the chapter of immodesty he said: *Because you lifted yourself high and because he has driven its top among thick trees and his heart became arrogant* (Ez 31:10).[82] In the chapter of punishment, he said: *Strangers, the most terrible of nations, cut him off and abandoned it; on the mountains and in all the valleys its branches fell down; his boughs were broken in every watercourse of the earth departed from its shadow and have left him* (Ez 31:12).[83]

Furthermore, Nebuchadnezzar's vision indicates clearly that it deals with a human being, moreover a king, who is present in the text.[84] As to the fact that [the vision deals with] a human being, it is the conclusion of his expression: *tie it by string of iron and bronze* (Dn 4:12). How is it possible for a tree to be tied by string of iron and bronze? And also: *he will be covered by the dew of heaven* (Dn 4:12). The dew for a tree is useful [...] is negative in it.[85] In addition, how is it possible to suppose that its food is grass, which is a plant? There is as well [the expression]: *His reasoning is different from the [the reasoning of the] human condition* (Dn 4:13). Isn't it obvious that this vision refers to a man? And the most important of all reasons is his expression: *[Order that the people realize that the Most High] is sovereign over the human realm* (Dn 4:14). What expression can be more explicit than this [to demonstrate that] He is a sovereign king.[86] Therefore, given all those explications, what forbids the wise men from

82 Ez 31:10 starts by God addressing the immodest ruler directly (second person singular), then indirectly (third person singular).

83 The uncertain meaning of many expressions in R. Saadia's quotations from Ezekiel obstructs our full understanding of the text with, consequently, a translation marked by ambiguity, since we do not know R. Saadia's interpretation. However, those uncertainties do not altar the general meaning that illustrates R. Saadia's reasoning.

84 R. Saadia is criticizing the wise men and their incapacity to see the clear meaning of the vision as being a metaphor for a man, and not a simple image of a tree.

85 Most probably R. Saadia's interpretation of "he will be covered by the dew of heaven" (Dn 4:12) is a negative effect when it deals with a human being, which is the case here, since it is a punishment according to the context. While its application to a tree would remove all the negative interpretation and make it impossible to be understood as punishment.

86 It is difficult to understand R. Saadia's way of thinking in citing Dn 4:14 in this context. First of all, in his translation of Dn 4:14 the expression די שליט עלאה מלכות אנשא is applied to the "Most High." Here, in his commentary, we have this part of Dn 4:14 as applied to Nebuchadnezzar, in a way that shows a human being, the king, and nothing else (a tree, for example) as the subject of the vision. So we have two different interpretations of the same passage. As if taken by his ea-

giving the interpretation of this vision? We answer that most probably their incapacity does not come from their incompetence, but from their fear of the king. They are [...] face him with the disappearance of his reign. Particularly because they witnessed earlier his order of their execution by stoning them when they did not realize his wish of telling him *the vision and its interpretation.* How much more [they imperil their life if they tell him] about the disappearance of his reign! It is also possible that he treats them roughly and pushes them to gave him this particular interpretation because of what he had decided about them.[87] Similar to what we found about the *deportation survivors* who treated Jeremiah's friends badly because of what happened earlier, and said: *It is Baruch son of Neriah who set you against us so that we will be delivered into the hands of the Kasdians to kill us or to exile us to Babylon* (Jer 43:3).[88] Don't you see that Daniel too was perplexed for some time in order to discern the way to answer [the king], to the point that king Nebuchadnezzar told him: *Do not let the vision and its interpretation terrify you* (Dn 4:16).[89]

Let us then start to define the vision. We say: if there is one angel who came down from heaven, why is it then that he give his order to a group: *Hew down the tree, cut its branches* (Dn 4:11).[90] We answer: [he gives his order] to different angels who came down with him; [angels] that he will mention in saying: *angels and holy ones* (Dn 4:14).[91] We have another interrogation: what was the question implied in the vision that incited him to say: *The answer to the question was by the expression of the holy ones* (Dn 4:14)? We reply: The question was about the motivation. As if when the honorable first angel communicated to the remaining [angels] the order he received they asked him: Why do we have to

---

gerness to show the wise men's incapacity of interpreting the vision, R. Saadia started to quote passages without verifying the meaning of their original context.

87 In other word, because of his first decision when they failed to tell him his dream and its interpretation.

88 The point in common between the two situations (the wise men in Daniel 4 and Jeremiah in Jer 43) is that in the two cases there was anger motivated by something that happened earlier: the king's supposed anger because the wise men were not able to give him what he wanted (the dream and its interpretation) and Jeremiah's auditors anger because of what he told them earlier.

89 Yefet ben Eli's interpretation contrasts with that of R. Saadia. He thinks that the king purposely was looking to demonstrate the wise men's incapacity to give the vision interpretation in order to illustrate Daniel's superiority over them.

90 גדו וקציצו אתרו. The imperative used in the MT is plural, given not to a single person, which is impossible to translate into English. R. Saadia's question is this: If we have one angel why then was the order given to many?

91 עירין וקדישין. R. Saadia render עירין by "angels." Yefet ben Eli establishes a hierarchy between the two categories: For him עירין is a higher category of angels than קדישין.

do to the tree what we have to do?[92] He replied: "For the instruction of the population." This is contained in his expression: *in order that the people realize that the Most High [is sovereign over the human realm]* (Dn 4:14). It is possible that part of the vision's ending could be added to this question, which is the exact duration of the time. As if they inquire from him: "How long will the tree remain in this condition?" He answered, saying: *until the seven conditions pass over him* (Dn 4:20).[93]

His expression to him: … *who told me* (אֲמַרְת) *earlier the vision and its interpretation* (Dn 4:6) is as if it were with two *patach(s)*: אֲמַר. He means: "It is you who the last time told me the vision and its interpretation; now I ask of you the interpretation alone, which is easier for you." I rendered וחזותה (Dn 4:8) by "ramifications,"[94] similar to קרן חזות (Dn 8:5)[95] "horn with ramification," and ותעלינה חזות ארבע (Dn 8:8)[96] by "and four ramifications pushed at its place." I rendered לבבה מן אנשא (Dn 4:13) [… …]. I rendered לבב חיוה (Dn 4:13)[97] by "animal imagination" following the necessity of the context. In fact, men of science attribute discernment to human beings, no to animals. However, they attribute imagination to them.[98] They imagine the lion, the vulture, the fire, the food, the water and all that attracts and repulses them. Now that I finished theses introductory remarks the interpretation of the vision becomes clear, how it is truly, and in conformity to what Daniel advanced. At present we need to relate the incident that happened to Nebuchadnezzar. Because many think that from a human being he was altered into an animal. Others added that he was altered into a female in order to be subjected, moreover, to the humiliation of the weakness.[99] Others went further to say that he changed from one person to another in

92 The question of the angels, according to Yefet ben Eli, is the following: why do we have to leave the stumps of its roots in the earth (Dn 4:12)?

93 Without answering the question about the exact duration of the "seven conditions" that pass over the king, R. Saadia start answering another question with no coherent relevance to the one he just asked.

94 שׁעבה en Judeo-Arabic.

95 קרן מתשׁעב en Judeo-Arabic.

96 פנבת מכאנה ארבע שׁעב en Judeo-Arabic.

97 תכ̇ייל אלבהאים en Judeo-Arabic.

98 R. Saadia's reasoning is that לבב חיוה should be translated by "animal discernment," which is inappropriate, since animals, according to the science of R. Saadia's time, have no discernment.

99 אלג̇שיאן means "fainting" is translated here by "weakness." The verb ג̇שי nevertheless has also the meaning "to cover." It is then possible that R. Saadia was hinting to both, the physical weakness of a woman and her social condition, which forced her at that time to be second in social manifestations; to cover her face, or to answer to a man, her father or her husband. This second interpretation has all its im-

every year,[100] every month or every day. Certainly every interpreter[101] followed a comparison. They intend [to show] the big humiliation of the proud and conceited men between God's hands. The correct [interpretation] whoever, is that Nebuchadnezzar's physical aspect did not change. What changed was his mind.[102] This is similar to what happened to Saul: *[The spirit of the Lord had departed from Saul] and an evil spirit started to torment him* (1 Sm 16:14). Nothing in his physical aspect was altered. [The evil spirit] on Saul, however, had little effect, so that the music and the beautiful arrangement could calm him, as it is explained in his story.[103] As to Nebuchadnezzar, his difficulty was immense, which is the total disappearance of the human mind from him. That is why he said: *My reason came back to me* (Dn 4:33). He reached the point that he abandoned the human company, according to his words: *He was driven away from men* (Dn 4:30). He wandered round deserts and mountains, but our Lord accomplished great miracles by which he protected his life during those times.

The first miracle is that he ate grass,[104] the way that someone feed the cattle, following the expression: *started to eat grass like cattle* (Dn 4:30). The heart of the miracle is that if a human being wants to feed on grass he could not. The grain itself is not edible, only what is selected, like wheat and barley. What had been selected itself is not edible [when it is] raw. And what is molded and kneaded remains inedible except when they are baked. Moreover, except when they are fully cooked. All the more so when it comes to kings' food, particularly Nebuchadnezzar, since he was the highest among them. It is then very astonishing that he did not die from eating grass all that time, and from the bareness, which constitute the meaning [his expression] that his body was covered by the dew. That means that he had no clothes to cover him. Furthermore, human beings do not bear to be naked in the inhabited areas, how much more in the desert, in the case of a king, of Nebuchadnezzar himself who is the highest among them. It is truly astonishing how he preserved himself, in spite of his bareness, from the heat, the cold and what they imply. Furthermore, [God] protected him from lions, so they did not devour him, particularly if they look at his body that

---

portance if applied to the king, the most visible and celebrated figure of the kingdom who answers to no one.

100 פי כל חול in Judeo-Arabic. חול is the singular of what was translated by אחואל "years" in Dn 4:20.

101 Lit. "Everyone."

102 This same interpretation is found in Yefet ben Eli's commentary on Dn 4:13.

103 Cf. 1 Sm 16:23.

104 Yefet ben Eli has a definite understanding of all that happened to Nebuchadnezzar. Eating grass, being covered because of the dew, and the loss of his mind are the three events that should be taken literally, according to him, and all others are subject to interpretation.

was unparalleled with what they see in the desert.[105] The fact that [God] makes them to fear him is in itself the greatest of miracles. It was by a miracle similar to what he said: *And God put a mark on Cain, lest anyone who found him should kill him* (Gn 4:15).[106] However, much greater chance than this [miraculous safe-keeping] should be ours during the exile![107] If it is to instruct [us] that a pagan, subject to God's anger, being put in prison, was promised to be freed and God protected his life from danger, how much more for us, whom he put in servitude, but promised to bring us back [to our land] and to protect us from any danger! How much more with the clear texts that we have! If our wandering during the servitude is similar to the turning of the wheat in the sieve, with no part of it falls down on the ground, according to what he said: *For I am ordering that I will shake the house of Israel among all the nations as one shakes [wheat] in a sieve and no part of it will fall to the ground* (Am 9:9). If [our servitude] is similar to throwing us to lions, the lions will eat each other, but us, we will be saved as he says: *All you beast of the field, come to devour all the beasts of the forest* (Is 56:9).[108] If [our servitude] is similar to throwing us to the water, God will preserve us from drowning as he says: *When you pass through water I will be with you, and the rivers will not overwhelm you* (Is 43:2).[109] If [our servitude] is similar to throwing us to the fire, God will preserve us from being burnt as he says: *When you walk through fire you will not be scorched, neither shall the flame burn you* (Is 43:2).[110] [We have to consider] as well how the afflicted faithful are in prison like us until they reach the proper time, then they are liberated, following his expression: *Saying to the prisoners: 'Go free,' to those who are in darkness: 'Show yourself'* (Is 49:9).[111] Job, nonetheless, wished to be

105 What R. Saadia wants to express is, most probably, is that the good health of Nebuchadnezzar's body, means a well nourished body, which makes good prey for a wild animal in the desert, a place where the scarcity of food means that the usual preys are meager.

106 פגעל אללה לקין איה לילא יקתלה כל מן וגדה is R. Saadia's translation of the citation from Gn 4:15.

107 From this point until the end of the paragraph is an application of this part of Nebuchadnezzar's story to the exiled Israelites of R. Saadia's time: if a pagan, Nebuchadnezzar, was saved by God how much more the people of God will benefit from God's salvation.

108 גמיע וחש אלצחרא אלתי תאתי לתאכל גמיע וחש אלשערי is R. Saadia's translation of Is 56:9.

109 ולו גזת פי אלמא פאנא מעך ואלאנהאר לא תגרקך is R. Saadia's translation of the citation from Is 43:2.

110 ולו סרת פי אלנאר לא תנכוי ואללהיב לא ישתעל פיך is R. Saadia's translation of the citation from Is 43:2.

111 ותקול ללאסארי אכרגו וללדין פי אלטמאת אטהרו is R. Saadia's translation of the citation from Is 49:9.

imprisoned in the ground for the time necessary to the adversity to pass, but he was not answered, as he says: *O that someone hide me in Sheol, you keep me in secret until your anger passes, set me a fixed time and remember me* (Jb 14:13).[112]

We should not mistake the interpretation of *however, leave the stump of its roots in the earth* (Dn 4:12) as nothing but the preservation of the reign to the king's children after him, since he explained it to us as the recovery of his reign. [He expressed it] in saying: *Concerning what they said about leaving the stump of the tree root, its interpretation is that your reign will return to you* (Dn 4:23). Besides, his expression: *That heavens rule* (Dn 4:23) makes it acceptable for us the pretension of the Rabbanites who consider שמיא as a *plural*.[113] All this is right, following their expression: They guarded him from heaven, they established him [...] ruler [...].[114] There is before that the expression of R. Hananiah ben Terdion: *They have pity from heaven*. This the principle of every name by which the Merciful is called in every language. Whoever swears by it[115] is obligated. We also found that whoever worships by it will be gratified.[116]

As to Daniel's advice for Nebuchadnezzar[117] to give to the weak it is in order to postpone the emergency of the punishment. Daniel either invented or discovered the effectiveness of this advice in the Torah when it dealt with the oppression of the weak saying: *When he cries out for me, I will hear, for I am compassionate* (Ex 22:26).[118] And: *When he calls me, I will have pity of him, for I am compassionate*.[119] That is why he repeated the mercy at the place of the

112 פליתני פי אלתרי כונת פכאן יסתרני אלי אן ירגע גצבך עני פתגעל לי רסמא תדכרני is R. Saadia's translation of Jb 14:13.

113 די שלטן שמיא is translated by R. Saadia as "the dominion of the One to whom belongs the dominion" which is far from being literal. The translation "that heaven rules" is classic, next to another one, classic as well, "that heavens rule." Rashi explains that the expression "heaven rules" means that the heavenly being rule over the world. All this explanation is an attempt to resolve the contradiction between שַׁלִּטִן the plural and שמיא the singular.

114 A quotation with many lacunae: [...]לך נטרוהי מן שמיא וקימוהי וגברוהי ל[...] שלטן ואשמ[...]ת.

115 In other words: Whoever swears by heaven.

116 All this reasoning, that the lacunae made unclear, tends to demonstrate that 'heaven' as a word, can be taken for "God" and indicates his presence. In the liturgy, for example, the word 'heaven' could be considered as synonymous of the word 'God.' R. Saadia extends such affirmation to other languages, which, in his case, designate basically the Semitic languages.

117 Lit. "As to his advice for him."

118 פאן הו צרך אלי סמעת לה אני ראוף is R. Saadia's translation of the citation from Ex 22:26.

119 והיה כי יקרא אלי וחנותיו כי חנון אני from an extra-biblical text.

punishment. […] We have to examine whether […] Nebuchadnezzar accepted his advice or not. [… …] twelve, as he says: *Twelve months later* (Dn 4:26). If he did not […] accept it, he wouldn't grant him the delay.[120] This [… …] the remedy[121] for an affliction that we push away by an act of mercy and kindness. Then he informed us that the affliction happened simultaneously with the expression of arrogance that Nebuchadnezzar uttered: *Is not this the [great] Babylon etc.* (Dn 4:27).

In this, we have a considerable lesson: That we should not be arrogant when we are between our Lord's hands, following the words of the wise man: *Don't be rash with your mouth, and don't let your heart be quick to utter anything before God in heaven; because God is in heaven and you are on earth; that is why your words should be few* (Ecc 5:1). We also found that Pharaoh was punished for his arrogant utterance, according to the words: *So the land of Egypt shall be desolation and ruin; and they shall know that I am the Lord: Because he answered and said, the river is mine and I have made it* (Ez 29:9). The king of Aram too [was punished] for his expression: *[May the gods do so to me, and more] if the dust of Samaria shall be enough for all the people that follow me to have a handful* (1 Kgs 20:10). Sennacherib, also, [was punished] for his utterance: *By the strength of my hands, I have done it; and by my wisdom, for I am clever* (Is 10:13)[122] until the end of the story. The prince of Tyre, likewise, [was punished] for his arrogant expression: *[Thus] answered [the Lord], because your heart became so proud and you said 'I am a god, I sit enthroned like god, in the heart of the seas'* (Ez 28:2). It goes the same for all the proud men[123] that the affliction will hit speedily following what he said to Job, describing His lordly action: *Ornament yourself now with majesty and grandeur and cloth yourself in glory and splendor; scatter wide the rage of your anger, observe every proud man and bring him low; observe every proud man and humble him; bring down the wicked where they stand; hide them together in the dust, and*

120 The first "he" refers to Nebuchadnezzar, the second, to Daniel.

121 מעאגלה "anticipation" that I choose to consider a metathesis for מעאלגה "remedy."

122 לאנה קאל ידי צנעת דלך ובחכמתי אד דהנת לה is R. Saadia's translation of the citation from Is 10:13.

123 Yefet ben Eli mentions another reason for the punishment that will hit some men: Their injustice and violence inflicted on the weak in general, and on the Israelites particularly. However, the three examples that he gives, beside Nebuchadnezzar's punishment, are the generation before the flood, the population of Sodom and Gomorrah, and the population of Nineveh. No one deals with injustice inflicted to Israel. The important point is that Yefet ben Eli in his commentary on Daniel choose to enumerate nations punished by God for their violence, whereas R. Saadia choose to enumerate kings punished for their pride and arrogance against God.

confine their faces in a hiding place (Jb 40:10–13),[124] according to the explanation that we gave in the commentary of the Song of Moses.[125]

In the same way, [the affliction hit] Nebuchadnezzar, since he said: *While the word was still in the king's mouth* (Dn 4:28). Many heard, without any doubt, the voice that reached Nebuchadnezzar's ears, so that the miracle would be manifested. Certainly it is the voice of someone who is able to articulate, one of the angels. And I rendered עד די כנשרין רבה *similar to the eagle's feathers* (Dn 4:30).[126] Because the human hair, even thick, is not comparable to the eagle.[127] I also rendered וטפרוהי כצפרין *like the birds of prey* (Dn 4:30).[128] Because not all the birds have claws, but the ones that devour [meat] alone.

Then we say that the verses in the middle of the story, [from] *then Daniel was perplexed* (Dn 4:16) until *his nails like [the claw] of the birds of prey* (Dn 4:30) are not said by Nebuchadnezzar, but they relate to him,[129] as he says: *He was walking. He started and said: 'Is not this [the great Babylon]'* (Dn 4:26–27) and other comparable [sentences]. The first thing we have to mention is the metaphoric use of language. That He strengthens Reuben, for example, [means] that he did and performed [something himself]. And God rewarded Reuben, designates [Reuben himself]. Like[130] the expression of Samuel: *And the Lord sent Jerubbaal and Bedan and Japhthah and Samuel* (1 Sm 12:11). Like the expression of David: *Take with you the servants of your lord* (1 Kgs 1:33). Like the expression of Ahasurerus: *Write what you please about the Jews and seal it with the king's ring* (Est 8:8). Like the expression of Lamech: *O wives of Lamech, give ear to my speech* (Gn 4:23).[131] Like the expression of Balaam:

124 באלקדרה ואלשמך ואלבס ואלבהא ואלבהגה אגמעין ובדד עבראת גצבך ואנטר כל מקתדר וצעה ואנטר כל מקתדר ואהזמה ודק אלטאלמין פי מכאנהם ואדפנהם פי אלתראב וגוההם פיפתזין אלדפין is R. Saadia translation of Jb 40:10–13.

125 Lit. "In the commentary of *He has triumphed gloriously* (Ex 15:2)." In fact it is a reference to all the Song of Moses and the Israelites, Ex 15:2–18.

126 There is a slight difference between R. Saadia's translation of Dn 4:30 in his translation of the whole chapter and his quotation here: שביה בריש אלנסור "similar to the eagle's feathers" in his first translation. While, in his quotation here, we have בבעץ ריש אלנסור "like some of the eagle's feathers."

127 R. Saadia tries to say that the expression following literally the MT, "his hair like eagles" has no meaningful sense. That is why he introduces the word "feather."

128 The full translation is: His nails like [the claw] of the birds of prey (Dn 4:30).

129 This is the probable meaning of this unclear sentence that seems to be incomplete.

130 בקול שמואל "following the expression of Samuel" that I choose to read כקול שמואל "like the expression of Samuel." Otherwise we will have a quotation about Samuel illustrating the immediate earlier sentence where Reuben is mentioned, without any reference to Samuel.

131 יא נסא למך אנצתא מקאלתי is R. Saadia's translation of the citation from Gn 4:23.

Oracle of Balaam son of Beor (Nm 24:3).[132] Like the expression of David: *Oracle of David son of Jesse* (2 Sm 23:1). We need [to remember] those witnesses[133] in every verse where the name of our Lord is repeated. Like when you say: *The Lord rained upon Sodom [Gomorrah sulfurous fire] from the Lord* (Gn 19:24).[134]

It is also possible that there is another meaning to those verses that are not attributed to Nebuchadnezzar; that the scribes who were in charge where ashamed to attribute it to him. In fact, in some perspective, such thing is not desirable.[135] There is also another meaning, stronger than all the others: the catastrophe that hit him, when it altered his mind he could not determine the testimony [about the catastrophe]; neither how it hit [him], nor when it hit [him], nor when it ceased [to affect him]. Similar to the epileptic who does not recognize what happen to him. What must certainly not be attributed to Nebuchadnezzar is the expression: *Immediately the decree was applied upon Nebuchadnezzar* (Dn 4:30). Then what we described at the beginning of the commentary happened to him. When those verses reached their limit, the discourse started to be said again by Nebuchadnezzar himself.[136] That is why he said: *When those days past, I, Nebuchadnezzar etc.* (Dn 4:31). By his expression: *When those days past* (Dn 4:31) he designates *the seven years* (Dn 4:29)[137] already mentioned. He[138] said: when they passed his mind came back to him and he returned

132 קל יא בלעם אבן בעור is R. Saadia's translation of the citation from Nm 24:3. R. Saadia's translation is different from what we used to read as translation of the same expression. His translation is: "Speak, O Balaam, son of Beor." In this particular case, his translation is not followed.

133 "All the witnesses" here are quotations where someone (Samuel, David, Ahasuerus, Lamech, Balaam) is speaking about himself in the third person. All this being said to justify that the passage of Dn 4:16–30 where Nebuchadnezzar does not speak about himself in the first person, could be said by him in the third person. R. Saadia applies this rule to every verse that mentions God in the third person, as God himself speaking about himself.

134 ואללה אמטר עלי סדום ועלי עמרה כבריתא ונארא מן ענדה is R. Saadia's translation of the citation from Gn 19:24.

135 Most probably it is not considered fitting that the king be mentioned in situation of humiliation, such as the situation where he loses his mind.

136 Lit. "When those verses reached their limit, he returned the signal to Nebuchadnezzar." The "he" designates the scribes. As if the scribe took on himself to describe what happened to Nebuchadnezzar, then started to register what Nebuchadnezzar has to say, once he recovered his full capacity to rule.

137 "Seven conditions" or "seven years." While leaning toward "seven years" R. Saadia does not specify the duration here, preferring the quotation of the MT without translation.

138 "He" designates the scribe.

to his kingship, the princes, the generals and all his followers gathered around him.

God taught us, in this too, a lesson in our servitude; that we have certainly a parallel to every event mentioned by Nebuchadnezzar. [Thus,] To equate [his expression]: *Lift my eyes to heaven* (Dn 4:31) he told us: *Lift your hands toward him for the life of your infants* (Lam 2:19). Similar [to his expression]: *And my reason returned to me* (Dn 4:31) [we have]: *And those with wrong opinion will know how to understand* (Is 29:24).[139] Similar to his expression: *With the glory of my reign* (Dn 4:33) [we have]: *When the nations see your bounties and all the kingdoms your glory [they will call you by a new name]* (Is 62:2).[140] Similar to his expression: *My joy and my splendor* (Dn 4:33) [we have]: *For it was perfect through my splendor that I had bestowed upon you* (Ez 16:14). And also: *[Your people will be noble the day your army take place] in the country of Jerusalem splendor, from the lowest part of the Black Sea [you throw on him your sons' arrows]* (Ps 110:3).[141] Similar to his expression: *My generals and noble men sought after me* (Dn 4:33) [we have]: *His leader shall be one of his own and his ruler shall come from its midst* (Jer 30:21). Similar to his expression: *I was established in my kingship* (Dn 4:33) [we have]: *I will establish the throne of his kingdom forever* (2 Sm 7:13). Similar to his expression: *And more honor was bestowed on me* (Dn 4:33) [we have]: *He will bestow on you His mercy, and will increase you more than your fathers* (Dt 30:5).[142] Similar to his expression: *Praising, elevating and exalting [the king of the nations]* (Dn 4:34) [we have]: *Bring to God all you inhabitants of the earth, praise, sing, glorify* (Ps 98:4).[143]

139 ויערפון צׄאלי (צׄאלו Derenbourg) אלראי אלפהם in Derenbourg's edition.

140 פאדׄא ראי אלאמם חסנאתך וגׄמיע אלממאלך כראמתך סמוך באסם גדיד is R. Saadia's translation of the citation from 62:2. The particularity of R. Saadia translation of Is 62:2 is the ו in וראו is conditional (protases) and has its conditional answer (apodosis) in the ו of וקרא.

141 [ויכון קומך נבל פי יום יציר גנדך] פי בהא אלקדס פמן חציץ אלחר אלסוד [לך תלקי אסהם אולאדך] R. Saadia's translation is midrashic and form a unity. Between [ ] are the parts of Ps 110:3 that R. Saadia does not quote in his commentary on Daniel. Thus, it is difficult to quote the part that R. Saadia mentions here alone, without mentioning his whole Judeo-Arabic translation.

142 ויחסן אליך ויתׄמרך ויכׄתרך מן אבאיך is R. Saadia translation of the citation from Dt 30:5. Note that R. Saadia renders the Hebrew verb והרבך by the Arabic verbs: ויתׄמרך ויכׄתרך 'He will makes you fertile and will increases you.'

143 אנלבוא ללה יא מעאשר אהל אלארץׄ וסבחוא ורננוא ומגדוא; is R. Saadia translation of Ps 98:4.

Praise be the One who makes the most of [...] of old, strength for our hearts about salvation.[144]

He chose the expression: *Who is able to put down any one who walks arrogantly* (Dn 4:34) in order to apply to it the story of Belshazzar, by reason of their similarity in this subject: *And you Belshazzar, his son, you did not humble yourself, though you knew all this* (Dn 5:22). The reason is not that Belshazzar ruled after Nebuchadnezzar's death, for if this were the reason, the prophet's expression: *And the entire nation shall serve him, his son and his grandson* (Jer 27:7) would be untrue.[145] However, since [Jeremiah's expression] must come to realization, then Awil Merodach,[146] Nebuchadnezzar's son, must have ruled after his death, which makes Belshazzar Nebuchadnezzar's grandson. From that point, their reign came to its end. Nonetheless, no part of the Bible[147] tells how many years Awil Merodach ruled, nor how many years Nebuchadnezzar ruled. Thus, we obtain this entire conclusion by counting. We say: When the Bible mentioned that Merodach the Fool rules in the thirty seventh year to the deportation of Jeconiah and that Jeconiah was deported in the eighth year of Nebuchadnezzar's [reign], following what we have already demonstrated, it results that Nebuchadnezzar must have ruled forty five years. And since [the term] ascertained to the king of Babylon is seventy years, according to the expression: *All those nations shall serve the king of Babylon seventy years* (Jer 25:11), [and since] one must deduct forty four complete years and part of the forty fifth[148], from the beginning [of the seventy years] for Nebuchadnezzar, [and since] one must deduct three incomplete years from the end [of the seventy years] for Belshazzar, [the years] that remain necessarily to Awil Merodach are between the forty third and the incomplete fifty first year.[149] As to Belshazzar's [name,] it is similar to what we have explained about the reason for calling

144 The last sentence in the paragraph, unclear because of the lacuna, most probably deals with the prophecies of the past, contained in the Bible, which are considered by R. Saadia as reasons for hope in God's salvation.

145 R. Saadia's reasoning is the following: If Belshazzar were Nebuchadnezzar's son he would not be the last of his dynasty, contrary to what we know. Because, according to Jeremiah the last of the dynasty was the grandson, Belshazzar.

146 אויל מרודך in Hebrew.

147 Lit. "In the Book, there is no book (ספר) of the books (אלספור wrong plural for אלאספאר) that mentions..."

148 Lit. "And part of a year."

149 Cf. R. Saadia's commentary on Dn 1:1. It is not easy to follow R. Saadia's reasoning, particularly in deducting three years for Jeconiah. To obtain the numbers that R. Saadia is suggesting he needs to deduct nineteen years for Belshazzar. However, Yefet ben Eli too indicates that Belshazzar ruled three years, confirming the number that R. Saadia gave.

[Daniel] Belteshazzar, which is to venerate the name of Nebuchadnezzar's god[150] by naming [someone after him]. It is the same for Merodach-Baladan[151] [where the name of the divinity] is at the beginning and Awil Merodach [where the name of the divinity] is at the end. It is also the case of Nebuchadnezzar, Nebuzaradan,[152] Nebushazban,[153] [where the name of the divinity] is at the beginning, and Samgarnebo[154] [where the name of the divinity] is at the end. Because those two names, I mean Merodach and Nebu, are names for divinities. Likewise Bel is a name for a divinity. [The commentary of] chapter four is completed.

150 Lit. "His god."
151 Cf. 2 Kgs 20:12. Is 39:1.
152 Cf. 2 Kgs 24:8–11,18–21. Jer 39:1–14, 52:30.
153 Cf. Jer 39:13–14.
154 Cf. Jer 39:3.

Chapter 5

The text of the fifth chapter[1]

Dn 5:1

Then Belshazzar the king gave a great banquet[2] for a thousand[3] governors with him and he sat before them,[4] drinking wine.[5]

Dn 5:2

When the wine overwhelmed him he ordered that the gold and silver vessels that his father[6] Nebuchadnezzar had taken from the Temple of the city of Jerusalem[7] be brought so that the king and the governors, his consorts and concubines could drink by them.[8]

Dn 5:3

Thereupon they brought the golden vessels that they took from the Temple in Jerusalem[9] and the king, the governors, his consorts and concubines began to drink from them.[10]

1 Another possible reading: "The fifth chapter indicates" or "states." The word נץ means "text" or "chapter." It could also be a verb, meaning "to indicate" or "to state."

2 Lit: "Gave abundant food."

3 Yefet ben Eli: "To one thousand and more of one noblemen."

4 "With him and sat before them" is added by R. Saadia. The expression has no source in the MT. Yefet ben Eli: "Belshazzar the king made a lot of food for a thousand and more of his noblemen and was drinking wine."

5 Yefet ben Eli: "Belshazzar the king made a lot of food for a thousand and more of his noblemen and was drinking wine."

6 Yefet ben Eli: "His grandfather." However, Yefet specifies in his commentary that Nebuchadnezzar is the king's father.

7 מדינת אלסלאם. R. Saadia translates the name of Jerusalem.

8 R. Saadia: "In order that the king and the governors … drink by them." Yefet ben Eli: "And the king and his noblemen … drunk by them."

9 Yefet ben Eli: "From the temple of the house of God which is in Jerusalem."

10 TM. Yefet ben Eli: "And drunk from them."

Dn 5:4

They started to drink wine from them,[11] and then they praised the gods of gold, silver, bronze, iron, wood and stone.

Dn 5:5

At that moment, fingers having the form[12] of a human hand appeared and wrote near the candelabrum,[13] on the plaster of the wall of the king's temple, and the king was looking at the hand[14] while it writes.

Dn 5:6

Then his appearance deteriorated, his thoughts frightened him, the joints of his backbone loosened and his knees clung one to the other.[15]

Dn 5:7

He called loudly to bring the astrologers, the Kasdians and the wise men, and told them, "Whoever is capable of reading this writing and makes known to me its interpretation shall be clothed with scarlet, wear a golden chain on his neck, and rule over a third of the kingdom."

Dn 5:8

Thereupon, all the wise men of the kingdom appeared, but could not read the writing, much less make known its interpretation to the king.

Dn 5:9

At that point Belshazzar the king grew very perplexed, his color changed, and the governors[16] who were with him became agitated.

Dn 5:10

While the king and the governors were speaking the queen came in. She started to speak, saying: "May God give long life to the king;[17] don't let your thoughts distress you, neither your color change.

11 "From them" is added by R. Saadia and has no source in the MT.

12 בצורה "having the form" is added by R. Saadia to his translation and has no source in the MT.

13 "Candelabrum" seems preferable to "menorah" which is the Hebrew word, used in English, and indicates the candleholder in the synagogue. It is this reference to the Jewish liturgy that makes "menorah" inappropriate in a pagan context.

14 אלכף literally 'the palm of the hand.' Yefet ben Eli: אליד 'the hand.'

15 Yefet ben Eli: "And his knees knock together."

16 R. Saadia: אלריסא the governors. Yefet ben Eli: אגלאוה the noblemen.

Dn 5:11

There is a man in your kingdom, in whom is the spirit of the holy God; from the days of your father illumination, intelligence and a wisdom similar to the angels' wisdom[18] were found in him; that is why your father[19] Nebuchadnezzar[20] established him master of the wise men, the astrologers, the Kasdians and the rulers.

Dn 5:12

Because of the noble understanding, the knowledge and the intelligence that he carries he interprets dreams, narrates events,[21] explains enigmas; all this is found in Daniel whom your father called Belteshazzar; now let him be called[22] in order to make the interpretation known to you."[23]

Dn 5:13

Then Daniel came before the king. The king addressed him saying: "You are Daniel, one of the deportation of the Jews that my father[24] deported from Judah.[25]

Dn 5:14

I have heard about you, that the spirit of God is in you, and clarity,[26] intelligence and high wisdom are found in you.

---

17 Lit: "May God extend the permanence of the king." This is a well known Arabic and Islamic expression equivalent to the English expression, 'long live the king.' It introduces the word 'God' which is lacking in the MT. However it renders the same meaning as the MT.

18 TM: "God's wisdom" which is also Yefet ben Eli's translation.

19 Yefet ben Eli translates the first אבוך in Dn 5:11 by 'your father' while he translates the second אבוך by 'your grandfather.'

20 MT: "Your father the king Nebuchadnezzar."

21 Yefet ben Eli: "He narrates all kind of rare events."

22 Yefet ben Eli: "Let him immediately be called."

23 TM: "That he may read and give the interpretation."

24 Yefet ben Eli: "That my grandfather deported from Judah."

25 מן אלשאם lit. "from Syria" or "from Damascus." Yefet ben Eli follows the MT: "That my grandfather deported from the Jews."

26 The Aramaic word נהירו is translated by R. Saadia as איצאח 'clarity' which refers to a quality of a judgment. Yefet ben Eli renders the same Aramaic word by the Arabic רשד which indicates the right conduct.

Dn 5:15
Now the wise men and the astrologers have been brought to me so they may read this writing and make known to me its interpretation, but they could not interpret its expressions and report [it to me.]

Dn 5:16
And I have heard about you, that you are capable of clear interpretation[27] and of the elucidation of the enigma; now if you are capable of reading this writing and telling me its interpretation you will be clothed with scarlet, wear a golden chain on your neck, and rule over a third of the kingdom."

Dn 5:17
Then Daniel answered him saying:[28] "Your gifts, keep them, and your presents, give them to others. However, I will read the writing to the king and make known to him its interpretation.

Dn 5:18
I start before anything [by saying]:[29] You know, O king, that God the Most High gave Nebuchadnezzar, your father[30] kingship, honor, glory and splendor.

Dn 5:19
And because of the honor He bestowed on him all the populations, nations and tongues revered him and feared him; he put to death whom he wanted and let live whom he wanted,[31] raised whom he wanted and humbled whom he wanted.

Dn 5:20
But when his heart became proud and his soul arrogant to the point of being contemptuous, he was deposed from his royal throne and his glory disappeared from him.

27 תפסיר אלתפאסיר lit. "interpretation of interpretations."
28 TM: "Saying before the king."
29 ואקדם קבל ד̇לך lit. "I start, before that [by saying]". Added by R. Saadia with no source in the MT.
30 Yefet ben Eli: "Your grandfather."
31 Yefet ben Eli: "he put to death whom he wanted and hit whom he wanted."

Dn 5:21

He was driven away from men and his mind[32] was with the beast of the desert, his refuge was with the quarrelers;[33] he was fed grass like cattle and he was covered by the dew of heaven, until he had acknowledged that God is sovereign over the realm of men; He gives to whom He wishes and is capable of enthroning the lowly one over them.[34]

Dn 5:22

And you Belshazzar, his son, you did not humble yourself, though you knew all this.

Dn 5:23

On the contrary, you exalted yourself against the Lord of heaven in bringing before you His House vessels,[35] and you, your governors, your consorts and concubines drunk wine by it, and praised the gods of gold, silver, bronze, iron, wood and stone, that could neither see, nor hear, nor understand a thing, and you did not honor God in whose hands is your breath and all your fortunes depend on Him.

Dn 5:24

Thereupon, He sent from His presence this wrist[36] that drew this writing.

Dn 5:25

And this is the depicted writing: He numbered the numbers; He weighed the weight; He fractured the fraction.[37]

Dn 5:26

And this is the interpretation of these words: As to the numbering, God numbered the time of your reign and completed it.

32 TM: "His heart."

33 ערביד the Arabic word by which R. Saadia translates the Aramaic ערודיא. ערביד has the meaning of 'troublesome' and can be said of a drunk man, for example. Yefet ben Eli: "His refuge was with the wild asses."

34 MT: "He establishes over it whom He wishes."

35 Yefet ben Eli: "you exalted yourself against the Lord of heaven and brought before you His House vessels."

36 MT. "The wrist of the hand." R. Saadia does not use the Arabic word יד to translate the Aramaic ידא. Instead, he uses the Arabic word כף. the Yefet ben Eli: "The palm of a hand."

37 Yefet ben Eli: "He measured a number, a weight and fractions." Another possible reading: "Number, number, weight and fractions."

Dn 5:27
As to the weight: You were weighed in a balance and found incomplete.

Dn 5:28
As to the fracture:[38] Your kingdom was fractured and handed to the Medes and the Persians."

Dn 5:29
Thereafter Belshazzar gave the order to clothe Daniel with scarlet, and to put a golden chain on his neck, and he was called to rule over a third of the kingdom.

Dn 5:30
In that night Belshazzar, the Kasdian king was killed.

The first thing that we have to consider in this story is not to drink to the point that the alcohol overcomes our judgment.[39] In fact, what pushed Belshazzar to do what he did is clearly that he was overwhelmed by wine, as he said: *When the wine overwhelmed him* (Dn 5:2).[40] Similarly, what incited Ahasuerus to do many things is the excessive wine drinking, as he attested: *On the seventh day when the king's heart was cheered by wine* (Est 1:10). It is also the reason that induced the Philistines to bring Samson, that he may play before them. There is no other reason to their destruction but the excessive drinking of wine, as he said: *And when their heart was cheered by wine they said ["call Samson"]* (Jgs 16:25). And nothing but the excessive drinking of wine prevented Amnon from protecting himself against being killed by Absalom, as it was said: *Absalom gave the order to his men saying "watch, and when Amnon's heart is cheered by wine and I say to you "strike down Amnon," kill him* (2 Sm 13:28). Elah son of Baasha too was killed *when in Tirzah he was drinking excessively* (1 Kgs 16:9). Ben-Hadad also was overcome *when he was drinking at Succoth* (2 Kgs 20:12). And what happen to Lot, likewise, could not have happened without inebriation, as he said: *Let us make our father drink wine* (Gn 19:32).[41] What happen to Noah also was not possible without him being drunk, since it

38 'As to the fracture' is added by R. Saadia to his translation and has no source in the MT.

39 Lit. "to the point that the wine overcomes our mind and takes possession of it."

40 This same interpretation is briefly mentioned by Yefet ben Eli.

41 תעאלי נסקי אבנא כ̇מרא is R. Saadia's translation of the citation from Gn 19:32.

has been said: *When Noah started [laboring the earth he planted a vineyard]* (Gn 9:20).[42] And similar cases.

Then we have to take into consideration that every drunk commits a misdeed. He must be punished, nevertheless, as if he was sober, without distinction. In fact, it is a certainty for us that Belshazzar perpetrated his offense[43] while being drunk, and God punished him for that.[44] We also find in the jurisprudence that being drunk is not an excuse at all: *The objection was raised, the sale or purchase of an intoxicated man is valid; if he committed a transgression involving the penalty of death he is to be executed, and if he committed one involving flogging he is to be flogged; the general rule is being that he is regarded as a sober man in all aspects except that he is exempt from prayer* (Erubin 65a).[45] As to the gift *scarlet* (Dn 5:7) that Belshazzar [...]. And if they say that the are clothed with the scarlet they are exaggerating. Like the Arabs who say about [...] this man wear bracelets. His name by others [...] and following our interpretation of *there were red horses in the first chariot* (Zec 6:2) designating the kingdom of Babylon.[46]

As to the incapacity of the Babylonian wise men to read the writing [on the wall] it is because it is in Hebrew, that is why they refrained from its interpretation.[47] The six qualities that the queen ascribed to Daniel which are *the noble understanding, the knowledge and intelligence, he interprets dreams, narrates the events, explains enigmas* (Dn 5:12) could be briefly described.[48] Concerning *the noble understanding* (Dn 5:12). The erudite were unanimous that it does not relate to the three aspects [...] the forth aspect.[49] As to the meaning of *knowledge* (Dn 5:12) it is the demonstration of what is real, as it is, following the

42 ואד̇ אבתדי̇ נוח בפלאחה אלארץ̇ פג̇רס כרמא is R. Saadia's translation of the citation from Gn 9:20.

43 Lit. "He did what he did."

44 R. Saadia does not specify the reason for the king's festivity. Yefet ben Eli evokes the seventieth year of the establishment of the kingdom as possible reason for the king's rejoicing.

45 The translation is taken from Epstein English edition (B. Moed vol. II, p. 451).

46 The many lacunae in this passages make it difficult to understand the symbolism of colors, or, because of the reference to the Arabic language, with the metaphorical use of some expressions related to colors.

47 According to Yefet ben Eli the Babylonian wise men's incapacity to read what was written did not come from their ignorance of the Hebrew language, since it is not established that the Hebrew language was totally unknown in Babylon. The reason is that the words were written with inverted letters: the first becoming second, the second becoming first etc. Yefet ben Eli does not give any evidence for this opinion.

48 Cf. Dn 2:23.

49 The lacuna makes it impossible to understand R. Saadia's interpretation.

expression: *I know that you are truthful in telling me its interpretation* (Dn 2:9).[50] Regarding [his] *intelligence* (Dn 5:12) it designates the veracity of his observation and speculation, like in *while I was observing that horn* (Dn 7:8).[51] The meaning of *he interprets dreams* (Dn 5:12) is the investigation of the dreams' logic by means of the four causes: the material cause; the formal cause; the efficient cause and the final cause.[52] He added to it the tradition[53] and the Law. The meaning of אחוית אחידון (Dn 5:12) is that *he narrates the events.* [It indicates that Daniel] bring ideas closer, so that they become part of the old or new tradition as it has been said: *in order to teach the proverb and to understand the wise men's discourse and their sayings* (Pr 1:6).[54] The meaning of [the expression]: *he explains enigmas* (Dn 5:12) refers [to Daniel's explanation] when the fact becomes complicated and the experts incapable of finding a solution.[55] As if they say that this chapter is to be forbidden for this reason and the other chapter for another reason. But Daniel's solution is [to chose] one of them by his skillful knowledge, similar to what do who examine in appeal the judgments, those saying that [the matter] implies this and that.[56] Furthermore, there is a seventh quality,[57] which is נהירו (Dn 5:14) that indicates the clarity.[58] That is, his discourse is audible, intelligible, that it reaches the heart of his audience by the precision of the words, the thoughtfulness and the harmony. If commentaries of those seven meanings, mentioned briefly, were gathered in a book, it would be a masterpiece in wisdom applications.

I rendered נברשתא (Dn 5:5) by "candelabrum," because I found that its plural is the Aramaic translation of נרות.[59] [We found this in the Targum of] the expres-

50 This is R. Saadia's translation, somehow midrashic, of ואנדע די פשרה תהחווני (Dn 2:9). To Yefet ben Eli מנדע designates the philosophical disciplines.

51 The connection between "intelligence" (שכלתנו) in Dn 12 and "observation" (משתכל) in Dn 7:8 is established because of the common root of the two words. To Yefet ben Eli ושכלתנו designates the philosophical discipline of deduction.

52 Those are the four causes that Aristotle uses in his analysis of reality.

53 אלכ̇בר could mean "tradition" or "knowledge." However, since R. Saadia regularly uses the word מערפה for "knowledge" it seems suitable to render this word by "tradition."

54 לתפהים אלמתל ואלפטנה כלאם אלחכמא ואחאדיתהם is R. Saadia's translation of Pr 1:6.

55 To Yefet ben Eli ופשרא קטרין indicates the philosophical explanation of what seems ordinary to the simple mind.

56 The fact that Daniel explains the enigmas means, for R. Saadia, not only that he is capable of resolving complicated matters, but also that other judges were incapable of resolving the problems that are referred to him. As if Daniel, according to R. Saadia, is a judge of a higher court.

57 The first six qualities of Daniel are all in Dn 5:12.

58 Yefet ben Eli explains נהירו as bringing to light what was hidden in the darkness.

59 Lit. "Because its plural is Targum נרות."

sion: *I will search Jerusalem by candelabrums* (Zep 1:12). Its Targum is: יתיב בירושלם אפקיד בלושין ויבלשון ית like דבלשין בנברשאתא. As to the hand that appeared, it is certainly the hand of an angel. Moreover, because of his expression: *And human hands under their wings* (Ez 1:8). The angel was hidden [...] only his hands, like [... ...].

[...] *A voice came to you from heaven* (Dn 4:28). About Daniel's expression to Belshazzar: *God in whose hands is your breath* (Dn 5:23), it constitutes the beginning of an allusion to his murder, since [God] takes out his breath if he disobeys him. As to the statement to him: *and all your conditions depend on Him* (Dn 5:23) he indicates the earthly conditions: health, sickness, inheritance, sterility, prosperity, poverty, might, abasement, victory, humiliation and similar conditions. Then we ask: What is the meaning of having these three words by which Belshazzar's trial was narrated?[60] We answer: Because the normal summary is obtained by three means, weight, number, measure.[61] Hence our Lord, may He be glorified, told His warning to [...] of kings' nations by the three [means together] and comparable to what our erudite men[62] said about the offering: *To count the fruits is praiseworthy; to measure them is more praiseworthy, but to weigh them is the most praiseworthy of the three* (Terumoth 4.6).[63] Following the same principles he said: מנה תקל פרס (cf. Dn 5:25).[64] [... ...][65] did not bring the measure.[66] And also because a kingdom does not belong to one individual but to the Medes and the Persians. In [saying] this He[67] instructs us. Concerning the example of *He numbered the numbers* (Dn 5:25) we learn that He delimitates the duration of kingdoms. That no one interferes in the other's [matters], following what the wisdom of delimitating people's age implies, as he says: *The duration of my body is known by your science, all of them are written in your register; they are secured days, with neither addition, nor reduction* (Ps 139:16).[68] This is similar to [the expression]: *He weighed the weight*

60 Lit. "by which Nebuchadnezzar Belshazzar's trial was narrated?"

61 Like the measure that indicates the weight of the seed, for example.

62 R. Saadia's expression עלמאנא "our erudite men" refers normally to the Mishnah alone or to Talmudic literature.

63 Translation by Herbert Danby (Oxford 1977, p. 56).

64 R. Saadia's translation: "He numbered the numbers; He weighed the weight; He fractured the fraction."

65 Lit. [... ...] מנהא לשון [...] did not bring the measure.

66 The end of an unintelligible sentence because of the lacuna.

67 "He" here refers to the angel who wrote the inscription on the wall, or, by extension, to God.

68 קץ ועמר גסמי קד אטלע עליה עלמך, ופי דיואנך כלהא מכתובה והי איאם מחפוטה לא זאיד פיהא ולא נא is R. Saadia's translation of Ps 139:16. The translation proposed here is established on the base of his Judeo-Arabic version.

(Dn 5:25). He weighs by judgement the importance of people's work and rewards them according to the plus or minus [of their actions], as he says: *Because the measure of attribution and the just balances belongs to God and His work as He weighs by the scales* (Pr 16:11).[69] And the other master said: *May He weigh me in a just balance, because he knows my integrity* (Jb 31:6).[70] And following the same meaning of [the expression]: *He fractured the fraction* (Dn 5:25), is that he fractures with energy the proud men, as he said: *And the elevated arm shall be broken* (Jb 38:15).[71] He also said: *He who elevates his door asks for ruin* (Pr 17:19).[72] Then we spread [... ...] which are inside it.

[...] that Belshazzar and his people were pleased that Daniel read the inscription and that he was truthful in his interpretation. Since it was possible for Daniel[73] to treat them in a way comparable to the way that dishonest men [treat others], by remaining silent until all auditors say their last word, and when they exhaust all their reasons,[74] showing their incompetence, the dishonest men invite them to maintain their opinions and no one can object to what [those dishonest men] declare [afterward]. Especially after the auditors' admission that they do not know.[75] So maybe Daniel was tempted to imitate such people. We answer that the requirement of the meaning invalidates such insinuation against Daniel. Because the inscription remained visible until Daniel had read it and gave its interpretation. And only when he did read it and give its interpretation that the inscription disappeared. The point of all this is [the advent] of a messenger from

69 לאן (אלתסקים Derenbourg) אלתקסים ומואזין אלעדל ללה ועמלה כמא יוזן באלצנגאת is R. Saadia's Judeo-Arabic translation of Pr 16:11. R. Saadia's understanding of this verse moves the atnach (^) from under יהוה and places it under מעשׂהו. The translation proposed here is established on the base of the Judeo-Arabic version.

70 יזנני פי מיזאן עדל פאנה יעלם בצחתי is R. Saadia's translation of the citation from Jb 31:6. The translation proposed here is established on the base of his Judeo-Arabic version.

71 ואלדׄראע אלרפיעה תנכסר is R. Saadia's translation of the citation from Jb 38:15. The translation proposed here is established on the base of his Judeo-Arabic version.

72 ומן שׂמךׄ באבה פקד טלב אלכסר is R. Saadia's translation of the citation from Pr 17:19. In his commentary on Pr 17:19 R. Saadia gives two examples. The first is Adonyiah son of Haggith (1 Kgs 1:5) and Uzziah, the king of Judah (2 Chr 26). The translation proposed here is established on the base of the Judeo-Arabic version.

73 Lit: "He."

74 Lit: "All what they have."

75 The lacuna at the beginning, plus the alternate pronouns, masculine singular and plural, makes it difficult to grasp R. Saadia's reasoning in its entirety. The main idea, however, is clear: R. Saadia stigmatizes the dishonesty of those who are much more interested in showing their superiority by putting down others, than resolving the difficulty facing them. Daniel, unlike a dishonest interpreter, is not interested in demonstrating other's incapacity to interpret the inscription.

the Creator to inform Belshazzar about what will happen to him, following the expression: *Thereupon, He sent from His presence this wrist* (Dn 5:24). And who is messenger must stay until he conveys his message. [...]. And there is no sense in saying [... ...] Daniel, it would be possible that he remains for a year or years.[76] When reason made it necessary that [the inscription] disappear, once read and interpreted by Daniel, the people should have believed that he read it correctly and interpreted truthfully without any doubt, once they observed the disappearance of the inscription.[77] As to his addition *the Kasdian king* (Dn 5:30), it is to inform us that the Kasdian kingdom reached this point [in time] then ceased. In fact as it is customary for him to add an expression at the end, like in *while he was still in hiding because of Saul son of Kish* (1 Chr 12:1) to designate the end. And in *what he lacks yet is the kingship* (1 Sm 18:8) to designate the end. And in *while he was still arrested in the prison compound* (Jer 33:1) to indicate the end, and what is similar to those examples.[78] End of the interpretation of the fifth chapter.

76 Most probably this passage is an explanation of the disappearance of the hand, because of Daniel's presence, who, by his interpretation, permitted that the message reach its recipient.

77 The core of R. Saadia's reasoning is that any message, once it has reached its addressee, disappears. Since the inscription disappeared after Daniel's reading and interpretation, then it had reached its recipient. Hence the disappearance becomes the guaranty of the accuracy of Daniel's reading and interpretation. Therefore he should be believed.

78 There is no further explanation for what R. Saadia advances. He thinks that the expression "Kasdian king" is added to Dn 5:30 and his only function is to indicate the end of something: the Kasdian kingdom. He sees a parallel in עוד added to the three examples that he gives in order to indicate the end of something: The kingdom of Saul or the kingdom of Judah.

Chapter 6

The text of the sixth chapter

Dn 6:1

Then the kingship came to Darius the Mede[1] who was about sixty-two years old.[2]

Dn 6:2

He thought it is judicious to appoint a hundred-twenty satraps in his kingdom to be in charge of it all.[3]

Dn 6:3

There were three ministers over them,[4] of whom Daniel was one, in order that those ministers[5] advise all others,[6] so that the king may not be bothered.[7]

1 Instead of "Darius the Mede received the kingship" which follows closely the MT style.

2 R. Saadia adds the word שביה that has no source in the MT. This word, with the preposition ב, introduces lack of certainty to the number mentioned immediately afterward. Thus according to R. Saadia Darius was not sixty-two years old exactly. No such lack of certainty can be found in Yefet's commentary on the same verse.

3 Yefet ben Eli: "In order to be in all the kingdom."

4 According to R. Saadia Darius appointed one hundred-twenty satraps, בטריק, and three ministers, וזרא, that supervise them. According to Yefet ben Eli, Darius appointed one hundred-twenty princes, אמיר, and designated three satraps, בטריק, among them to supervise all others. To be noticed that R. Saadia does not translate the verb ועלא, (he writes ועילא), that could be translated by 'he (Darius) elevated.'

5 The difficulty of R. Saadia's translation is that אחשדרפניא and סרכין are both rendered by the word וזרא.

6 Yefet ben Eli: "In order that they command them."

7 Lit: "So that the king may not be hurt."

Dn 6:4

At that point Daniel was superior to the ministers and the satraps because of the good advice found in him[8] and the king was determined to establish him over all the kingdom.

Dn 6:5

Therefore the ministers and the satraps were looking for a pretext that they could find against Daniel with regard to the state, but they found neither fault nor misdeed, because he was faithful and neither deviation nor error could be found in him.

Dn 6:6

Then those people said "We found nothing wrong against this Daniel, but we can find something against him through the precepts of his religion."[9]

Dn 6:7

Then those ministers and satraps went to the king and said to him "May God give long life to the king Darius,

Dn 6:8

All the nobles of the kingdom, the princes, the satraps, the lords, the rulers[10] advise that the king promise firmly and pledge solidly[11] that anyone who request anything from any god or human being other than the king,[12] for thirty days, will be thrown to the lions' den.

8 Yefet ben Eli: "Because of the noble spirit found in him."

9 MT: "Through the legislation of his God."

10 The high ranking men of the kingdom are translated differently by R. Saadia and Yefet ben Eli. For R. Saadia they are: the noble men of the kingdom (סרכי מלכותא - אגלא אלממלכה) the princes (סגניא - אלאמרא) the satraps (אלבטארקה - ואשדרפניא) the lords (הדבריא - אלרויסא) the rulers (ופחותא- אלכלפא). For Yefet ben Eli the are: the satraps of the kingdom (סרכי מלכותא - בטארקה אלממלכה) the lords (סגניא - אלרויסא) the princes (ואשדרפניא - אלאמרא) the servants (הדבריא - אלכדמא) and the workers (ופחותא - אלעמאל).

11 Yefet ben Eli: "In order to establish firmly the king, or the kingdom, affair and to consolidate the alliance." Unlike R. Saadia's interpretation, the request made to the king is in order strengthen the kingdom, not in order that the king issue a firm decree. In so doing, they established the king higher than God, since he will be the recipient of the people's requests and prayers.

12 TM: "Other than from you, O king."

Dn 6:9

Now we want that you, O king, decree this ban and declare it in writing; that it may never change, similar to the ordinances[13] of the Medes and the Persians that will never be abrogated."

Dn 6:10

Thereupon[14] the king decreed the edict about the prohibition.[15]

Dn 6:11

When Daniel learned that this edict was decreed, he went to his house where there was a room[16] with a small window, opened, facing Jerusalem and three times a day he kneels, prays and gives thanks to his Lord, as he used to do before.

Dn 6:12

At that time those people were agitated concerning Daniel and found him imploring[17] and pleading between his Lord's hands.

Dn 6:13

Then they approached and spoke to the king about his ban, "did you not decree the ban, that anyone who request anything from any god or human being other than you for thirty days will be thrown to the lion's den"? The king answered them and said, "The matter stands firm like ordinances[18] of the Medes and the Persians, that nobody can abrogate."

Dn 6:14

Immediately they answered in the presence of the King and said,[19] "Daniel who is from the Jewish deportation did not accept the king's order and paid no attention to the ban that you decreed, and three times a day he presents his plea."

13 TM: "Ordinance."

14 כל קבל דנא is translated as the beginning of a temporal subordinate clause for R. Saadia: "Thereupon." For Yefet ben Eli, it is the start of causal subordinate clause: "Because of that."

15 TM: "Decreed the edict and the prohibition."

16 MT: "In his room."

17 MT: "At that time those people were agitated and found Daniel imploring."

18 TM: "Ordinance."

19 Yefet ben Eli: "Thereupon they advanced and spoke to the king about the king's prohibition."

Dn 6:15

When the king heard this matter he was very upset, however he was determined to save Daniel,[20] and till the sun set, he was eager to save him.

Dn 6:16

Therefore the ministers and the satraps excited the king and told him, "The king knows that according to the ordinances of Medes and the Persians no ban or decree promulgated by the king should be abrogated."

Dn 6:17

At that point the king order that Daniel be brought and thrown to the lion den. He said to him[21] "Your God that you always worship will save you."

Dn 6:18

Then a big stone[22] was brought, placed on the opining of the den and the king sealed it by his seal and the lords' seals, so that his opinion about Daniel does not change.

Dn 6:19

Soon after he went to his temple and spent the night fasting,[23] no table[24] was set for him and his sleep left him.

Dn 6:20

At dawn the king stood up and went in haste[25] to the lion's den.

Dn 6:21

When he reached it he called Daniel in a sad voice, saying,[26] "O Daniel, servant of the living God, did your God that you always worship deliver you from the lion"?[27]

20 Yefet Ben Eli: "He manoeuvred to save Daniel."

21 Lit. "He started saying to him."

22 MT: "a stone." Or "one stone."

23 טאויא literally "empty." It could also mean "bent" which can possibly be translated by depressed or sad. Yefet ben Eli, referring to unspecified source mentions that טאויא is the Targum of צלי אש literally, "roasted by fire." It is the translation that he adopts.

24 דחון is translated by R. Saadia as כואן a small table where one sets small dishes, probably after the main meal. Yefet ben Eli translates it as אלאת אלמלאהי "instruments for entertainment."

25 Yefet ben Eli adds: "with a candle."

26 Yefet ben Eli: "the king answered and he was saying to Daniel the following."

Dn 6:22

Then Daniel spoke to the king and said, "May God give long life to the king.

Dn 6:23

My Lord sent his angel and closed the lions' mouth that they not hurt me, because my good deeds were between his hands and I did not commit harm in your presence too."

Dn 6:24

When the king heard about this matter[28] he was pleased greatly and ordered to take Daniel from the den. He was brought up and no damage was found in him because he believed in his Lord.

Dn 6:25

And the king ordered that those who slandered Daniel be brought and they were thrown to the lions' den with their children and their wives. They hardly reached its bottom when the lions took hold of them and crushed all their bones.

Dn 6:26

Then Darius, the king, wrote to all populations, nations and tongues that live in all the countries,[29] "may the peace of God and His blessings be upon you."[30]

Dn 6:27

I commanded by a decree in all the territory of my kingdom that everyone should be pious, and frightened before the God of Daniel, because He is the living God who endures for ever; His kingship never vanishes and His dominion extends to the end of the universe.[31]

---

27 TM: "the lions." However, R. Saadia accords to the word 'lion' a plural meaning, since in Dn 6:23 the same word is followed by a verb in the plural.

28 "When the king heard about this matter" is added by R. Saadia and has no source in the MT.

29 MT: "In all the earth."

30 "The peace of God and His blessing be upon you" is an Arabic and typical Islamic idiom that R. Saadia uses; he does not translate the MT literally. Yefet ben Eli's translation: "May your peace be multiplied," which remains closer to the MT.

31 R. Saadia does not translate מן קדמי which has the literal meaning of 'before me' or 'in my presence.' Thus the beginning could be rendered as 'a decree is issued in my presence to all the territory of my kingdom."

Dn 6:28

He is the rescuer, savior, the miracles and the worker of wonders[32] in heaven and on earth, because he delivered Daniel from the power of the lion.[33]

Dn 6:29

Soon after, Daniel's condition was improved[34] in the reign of Darius and Cyrus[35] the Persian.

The first question we have to answer relating[36] to these verses is about the advantage of registering the number […] of the years until he reigned […]. If we count back the years […] this date, we find that the year of Darius' birth is the year in which Nebuchadnezzar conquered Jerusalem at the time of Jehoiakim.[37] He said about him: *He carried out from there all the treasures of the house of the Lord and the treasures of the king's house and cut in pieces all the golden vessels which Solomon had made* (2 Kgs 24:13).

The same thing is said of Jehoiada, the priest. The Bible did not explain the age of other priests, but did so with him, when it said: *And Jehoiada became old and full of days. He died at the age of a hundred and thirty years* (2 Chr 24:15). We answer that we scale back the years from that date to six years before the catastrophe[38] after Solomon's death. Thus, the birth of the reformer precedes the existence of what needs to be reformed. […] years. Likewise for the date [… …] and twenty *cities* […] announced in another passage […] *the desert of Israel* thirteen years until the time that the house of Judah acknowledged, which are seven years before the end of the twenty. The second,[39] is that the two years ascribed to king Saul are in fact years with Samuel. Therefore the settlement for Samuel is eleven years. Also that the house of Israel passed five years without

32 Yefet ben Eli: "Miracles and demonstrations."

33 Lit. "from the hand of the lion אלאסד." Yefet ben Eli usually translates אריותא with סבאע "lions."

34 Yefet ben Eli: "Daniel became successful."

35 Lit. "the reign of Darius and the reign of Cyrus."

36 Lit. "The first thing we have to reveal in these verses."

37 The same reasoning is found, almost literally, in Yefet ben Eli's commentary on Dn 6:1.

38 אלתכלים lit. "the mixture." This probably refers to Nebuchadnezzar's entry into Jerusalem.

39 The second reason or argument? R. Saadia's reasoning is unclear because of the lacunae in different places in the manuscripts. He is trying to establish the exact time of Darius' reign.

the kingship of Ish-Bosheth who reigned over them for two years out of those seven.[40]

His expression: *In order that those satraps advise all others* (Dn 6:3) is similar to [the expression:] *In order that those ministers advise all others.*[41] That is why he rendered it by "ministers." But they were described differently in order to distinguish their qualification.[42] Likewise, he described מלכיה "her kings," נביאיה "her prophets" because of the presidency. Since he says: *The conspiracy of her prophets in her midst is like a roaring lion ravening the prey; they devour human beings; they seize treasure and wealth; they multiplied her widows in her midst* (Ez 22:25). Its meaning is *The conspiracy of her kings in her midst.* And like when he called the *deaf blind* in saying: *There is no blind but during the punishment, and no deaf but during the reward of God's friends* (Is 42:19).[43] Because they are parallel if we consider the handicap.[44] Similar examples are too numerous to expand on them.

His expression: *And the king was determined to establish him* (Dn 6:4) demonstrates that their presentiment about Daniel, that he was perfect in his management in the king's eye, increased his enemies' jealously[45] against him, and that is because of what they harbor against him. Similar to Jacob's love for Joseph: *He made an ornamented tunic for him* (Gn 37:3).[46] Likewise [because of] *his dreams* (Gn 37:8)[47] which increased his brothers' jealousy because of what they are. The reason for the jealousy in all these cases[48] is the superiority of knowledge.[49]

40 Cf. 2 Sm 2:8-12.

41 Cf. the footnote relative to the difficulty of R. Saadia's translation of Dn 6:3.

42 ואנמא לקב האולי בהאולי למגאנבה אלריאסה. Lit. "But they were described, those by those, in order to separate the presidency." An enigmatic sentence by which R. Saadia tries to explain his translation of אחשדרפניא "satraps" and סרכין "ministers" by the word וזרא.

43 ולא מתעאמי אלא ענד אלעקובה ולא מתצאם אלא פי גזא אוליא אללה is the Judeo-Arabic translation by R. Saadia of Is 42:19b where the second עור "blind" is rendered by חרש "deaf." The English translation of Is 42:19b here follows R. Saadia's interpretation of this passage.

44 Since we have the pair blind-deaf in Is 42:19a we should have their parallel in Is 42:19b. However we have blind-blind in Is 42:19b. Hence the correction that R. Saadia introduces to the MT.

45 Lit. "Their jealousy."

46 פצנע לה תוניה דיבאג is the Judeo-Arabic translation of Gn 37:3 by R. Saadia.

47 אחלאמה is R. Saadia's translation of the citation of Gn 37:8.

48 Lit. "The former reason for the jealousy of all."

49 The superiority of Daniel's knowledge compared to the Babylonian wise men is the reason for their jealousy. However, Joseph's case is a bit different. He has been subjected to his brothers jealousy because of his father's preferential love for him

There are three הרגישו that I interpret in three different ways, according to what is fitting in each case.[50] I interpreted the first [הרגישו, Dn 6:7], which came in the form of an advice,[51] as "conversation."[52] I rendered the second [הרגישו, Dn 6:12], as "looking for information"[53] which is comparable to observing Daniel's prayer. I rendered the third [הרגישו, Dn 6:16], which is comparable to a request for Daniel's punishment, as "slander." Besides, we have to explain how it was possible for them to advise that the king forbid the population from [...] asking for thirty days [... ...]. As if they charged some people with the accusation, or accusations, that they are harmful to the kingdom. And this discovery became the justification for their request.[54] It is possible that the king[55] admitted this explanation.

We have received many benefits relating to the prayer from this story. First among them is that the perpetual prayers are three: *Three times a day* (Dn 6:11.14). [It inform us] too about the identical obligation of this prayer on the land of Israel as well as on the exile, because of his expression: *As he used to do before* (Dn 6:11). [It informs us] moreover that it is a prayer divided into the three parts of night and day, because of his expression: *[Three times] a day* (Dn 6:11.14). in fact, it is well known that the two parts of the day have two prayers. And since the middle of the night is unknown, the third prayer is in its first half.[56] [It tells us] also that the essence of the prayer is particular requests and demands, because he expressed it[57] by *he presents his pleas* (Dn 6:14). It is

---

and his "dreams" that reflect his foresight. It seems that Jacob's love for his son is the main reason for his brethren's hatred. Cf. Gn 37:4.

50 Cf. Dn 6: 7.12.16.

51 Lit. "Which came with advice."

52 מכאטבה which can be translated by "conversation" or "exchange of ideas." R. Saadia's translation of Dn 6:7 has no such word.

53 This meaning could easily be understood as "spying."

54 Lit. "Then they made the discovery of that appeal by this matter." R. Saadia's idea, explaining Daniel's accusers, is that praying to another god than the king's god is equal to betraying the country.

55 Lit. "He."

56 R. Saadia does not determine a precise time for praying, because he supposes that the days' prayers are known and most probably he did not want to decide a specific moment for the night prayer. Yefet ben Eli thinks that the three times are dawn, noon and sunset.

57 Lit. "Because he translated it." Either we have to render the Arabic verb תרגמהא (from the verb תרגם to translate) by 'he expressed it' or we have to suppose that R. Saadia means that there was a Hebrew background to the Aramaic text.

his expression: *have pity on us; bring us back; pardon us; heal us*[58] and what can be added to them. Plus, the individual who is praying must [...] delaying the petition [...] *imploring and pleading between his Lord's hands* (Dn 6:12). [It inform us] too that the man who prays must bend several times during his prayers, according to the expression: *He genuflects* (Dn 6:11). While it is genuflection, the Hebrews practice it as bending, following his expression: *Solomon had mad a bronze platform and had set in the middle, five cubits long and five cubits broad and three cubits high, and upon it he stood and genuflected* (2 Chr 6:13). Thus, you can not reunite [the two positions of] standing and to genuflecting, except through being bent. Once we finish the chapter of our pleas we have to give thanks to God, following the expression: *He prays and gives thanks to God* (Dn 6:11). It is similar to what one says after the petitions: *We praise you* (1 Chr 29:13). And he concludes: *The praise suit you.* The prayer in *the foreign lands*[59] must also be facing the land of Israel, following Solomon's expression: *And they prayed toward their land* (2 Chr 6:38). And on the land [to pray] toward Jerusalem. And in Jerusalem [to pray] toward the Temple, as he said: *And this House that you built for your name* (2 Chr 6:38). And in the House itself [to pray] toward the west, according to the expression: *That they pray toward this place* (2 Chr 6:21). Except if the direction toward the land of Israel and Jerusalem is directly the same as he said in Daniel: *There was a small opened window, facing Jerusalem* (Dn 6:11). Then we add 'if the prayer is authorized in a house which has no small window why is it then that he said: *There was a small opened window* (Dn 6:11)?' we answer: 'In order to add: *They were looking for information about Daniel and found him imploring and pleading* (Dn 6:12). As if the small window was the reason [of reporting his behavior to the king], or one of the reasons.[60]

His expression: *However, was determined to save Daniel* (Dn 6:15) proves that the king[61] had objections[62] against their discourse by which he intended to save Daniel until they succeeded in destroying all his objections.[63] In spite of all

58 It is possible to understand those expressions as quotations. However, and most likely, they are prayers expressions that reveal the state of mind of a Jewish believer living in exile.

59 חוצה לארץ.

60 The window allowed them to spy on Daniel. R. Saadia sees no reason in mentioning this detail other than a device serving the narration of the event.

61 Lit. "He."

62 אמכאנאת lit. "possibilities" which here has the meaning of "objections."

63 אלי אן פנו אלגאיז מן קולה lit. "until they destroyed what is licit in his discourse." As if Daniel's enemies succeeded in answering all the king's objections against putting Daniel to death. Yefet ben Eli "gives" the reason that Daniel's enemies provided to

that he started to resist them until they reached the point of denigrating Daniel.[64] At that moment the king[65] could not continue to resist them. And what is the meaning of *then a big stone was brought, placed on the opining of the den and the king sealed it by his seal and the lords' seals* (Dn 6:18), since the fait of anyone thrown into the den is to be devoured immediately by the lions[66]? Then what advantage is there in sealing the den? We answer: In order that the king does not change his mind and bring up Daniel. Isn't this useless[67]? We answer that this demonstrates that the den itself is a like a corridor [leading] to the lions. And the lions are deep inside, so that from the den one can get into them. When Daniel was thrown into the den in their presence and it was clear that the lions were not agitated and did not rush to him they attributed this to [the fact] that the lions were not hungry. They decided to leave him there until the lions become hungry. However, they wanted to seal the den entry so that Daniel does not come into the king's sight and that the king may bring him up from there. When they appealed for that he answered them [saying] that they have to seal it by their [own] seals in order that no one accuse the king of saving him.[68] Moreover, the king himself sealed it by his seal so that no ruse from them would be set up against Daniel.[69] That is why he said: *So that his opinion about Daniel does not change* (Dn 6:18). As to his expression: ובת טות (Dn 6:18) it has the [following] meaning: He added day to night without eating. His [expression]: ודחון (Dn 6:19) can be interpreted as small tables[70] in order that one can eat between his hands. It is possible to find such a word in the Tosefta Kelim: *The vessels of the small tables on which men can eat* (Tosefta Kelim B, m: V,3). However, it is also possible to interpret it as friends and familiars[71] from יחוון [to

---

the king: If he allows Daniel to escapes punishment, it will be impossible to apply such punishment to others.

64 Lit. "Him."

65 Lit. "He."

66 Lit. "lion" אלאסד which R. Saadia uses normally for "lions" אלאסוד with the verb in the plural form.

67 Nothing is mentioned about the reason that sealing the den is useless.

68 Lit. "In order that they declare the king innocent from bringing him up."

69 Yefet ben Eli seems to be repeating and expending on R. Saadia's reasoning: The king sealed the den opening because he knew of the evil intention against Daniel by those who slandered him. He also knew that God will save him, in opposition to Nebuchadnezzar who did not believe that God will save those whom he threw into the furnace. That is why he wanted to maintain him in life by forbidding his enemies from killing him, once they realize that the lions did not touch him.

70 כואנאת are small tables destined to receive small dishes for appetizers, not plates for the main meal.

71 מחאדתין friends with whom one can converse; מסאמרין friends with whom one can spend part of the night.

tell][72] ויהתוון [to discuss][73] all together. Its meaning: What takes the sleep away from him.[74]

Daniel's expression: *My Lord sent his angel and closed the lions' mouth that they not hurt me* (Dn 6:23), according to the natural principle,[75] [means] that God[76] does not erase the nature of the matter.[77] He may, however, prevent its action, similar to what we have mentioned in the story of *the burning fiery furnace* (Dn 3:26). His expression: *And in your presence too I did not commit harm* (Dn 6:23) is reprimand directed to him, because Daniel[78] did not deserve punishment from him. His expression: *And the king ordered that those [who rejected Daniel]* (Dn 6: 25) helps us to determine the lions number: Three hundred sixty-six. Since the group was one hundred twenty two and since he added *their children and their wives* (Dn 6:25)[79] their number[80] becomes [what we have mentioned] approximately.[81] The kings had gathered a similar [number of lions] and more.

As to Darius' expression: *The miracles and wonders' worker in heaven and on earth* (Dn 6:28) indicates the coming down of the angel from heaven to save Daniel on earth, according to his word *my Lord sent his angel etc.* (Dn 6:23). Nebuchadnezzar too had said: *He realizes His will by the army of heaven and the inhabitants of the earth* (Dn 4:32), in the manner of *a holy and heavenly angel came from the sky* (Dn 4:10) *crying loudly and saying as follows etc.* (Dn 4:11). And he concluded the story by saying: *Soon after, Daniel's condition was improved etc.* (Dn 6:29) which demonstrates that Darius[82] improved his conditions, and illustrates Daniel's[83] obedience to the king.[84] In this way the

72 חוי "to tell."
73 הוה "to discuss."
74 The meaning of ודחון is what prolongs the night either by conversation with friends or by continuing eating and drinking.
75 Lit. "The first principle."
76 Lit. "He." Which could be a reference to God or to the angel that he sent.
77 The nature of lions, that devour their pray, is maintained. It is the act of devouring that is stopped by closing the lions' mouth.
78 Lit. "He."
79 Yefet ben Eli gives a hypothetical reason for the punishment of the children and the wives, because they rejoiced at what happened to Daniel.
80 This could refer to the lions' number or the number of those who were thrown to the lions' den.
81 יציר מתאלהם באלתקריב זאיד מע נאקץ could be translated in different manners: "Their example becomes approximately, plus or minus." Also: "[the lions' number] become like their number approximately, plus or minus."
82 There is also the word כורש expunged by a supralinear point.
83 Lit. "His."
84 Lit. "in it, his obedience becomes manifest to him."

citizens who noticed his disobedience to the king would not see Daniel[85] serving him, which would make[86] Daniel and the king subject to their jokes. This is similar to the arrangement that we made earlier with Hananyah, Mishael and Azaryah.[87]

Having commented briefly the first six parts[88] we are ready to follow with the commentary of the four remaining parts,[89] with more explanation than what we have done,[90] because of the need to know the explanation of the appointed times[91] and the use of language, with help from the Merciful. [The commentary of] the sixth chapter is completed.

85 Lit. "See him."

86 Lit. "Which makes him."

87 Cf. Dn 2:49.

88 Cf. R. Saadia's introduction to his commentary, before commenting on Dn 1:1, and how he divided the book into ten parts.

89 The four remaining parts, following R. Saadia's division of the Book of Daniel, are: The seventh part (Dn 7) relates to the kingdom of animals; the eighth part (Dn 8) relates to Daniel's vision; the ninth part (Dn 9) deals with the explanation of the seventy weeks; the tenth part (Dn 10-12) relates to the wars between the kingdoms and the measures of the last times. There is an attempt by Yefet ben Eli to divide the remaining chapters of Daniel in his commentary of Dn 7:1.

90 Lit. "Than those commentaries" referring to the commentary of the first six chapters.

91 אלקצים. R. Saadia does not translate קץ consistently in the Book of Daniel. We will point out in loco the different translations.

Chapter 7

In the seventh chapter of the Book of Daniel, He[1] mentions the beginnings of the four intermediary kingdoms, the exile of the Israelites and their fathers. He said at the beginning:

Dn 7:1

In the first year of king Belshazzar, king of Babylon, Daniel saw a dream, as if he was looking while he was on his bed,[2] he then wrote the dream and said at the beginning of the discourse,

What we have to say, as something necessary for the explanation of the last four parts:[3] They have dates that belong to three kings. Two of [the four parts] pertain to Belshazzar. The first, in the first year of his kingship [and the second, in] the third [year] of his kingship. The other two [parts] belong to Darius and to Cyrus. One, in the first year of Darius' kingship, the other, in the third year of Cyrus' kingship.[4] The reason for that is that Belshazzar was the last of the Babylonian kings, that Darius was the first king from the Medes, and that Cyrus was the first Persian king.[5] Daniel knew of those hidden sciences[6] at the beginning and the end of the reign of every one. That is why he said: *In the first year of king Belshazzar, king of Babylon* (Dn 7:1); *in the third year of the reign of Bel-*

1 "He" refers either to Daniel or to the scribe.

2 R. Saadia's translation of וחזוי ראשה על משכבה is not a literal translation: פי מנצעה כמא תרא עינאה והו. Yefet ben Eli chooses the literal and somewhat awkward translation of the MT: "And the vision of his head on the bed."

3 Lit. "Those last four parts."

4 Lit. "One, in the first year of the kingship of this, the other, in the third year of the kingship of that."

5 It is not clear why it is that being the last of the Babylonian kings is a reason for attributing two of the last four parts of the Book of Daniel to Belshazzar and the last two parts to Darius and Cyrus. Is it because being the last, Belshazzar represents numerous kings that came before him, while Darius and Cyrus are the beginning of chain of kings? Is it a reference for the duration of those kingdoms? Is it because of the value, or the strength of each of those kings or kingdoms?

6 Yefet ben Eli specifies that Daniel was given this knowledge because of his love for his people and his sadness for seeing them struggling in their ordeal.

shazzar, the king (Dn 8:1); *in the first year of Darius* (Dn 9:1); *in the third year of Cyrus, the king of Persia* (Dn 10:1).[7]

His expression: *Daniel saw a dream* (Dn 7:1) is according to what we have already said,[8] is a prophecy which, here, has the form of a dream which, following the signs that we established briefly in the introduction of this book[9] and that we will explain with details in the middle of the chapter. We interpreted his expression: וחזוי ראשה על משכבה (Dn 7:1) "a vision by the eyes" since the Arabic language[10] does not apply the vision to the head, as the Aramaic language[11] does, but attributes it to the eyes. This in fact is our translation,[12] like our translation of ושמחת עולם על ראשם (Is 35:10) by "the joy of the century in their heart," since the Arabic language does not apply joy to the head, which the Hebrew language does.[13] And why is it that after saying: *Daniel saw a dream* (Dn 7:1) he needed to add: *Like his eyes looking while he was on his bed* (Dn 7:1)? [The answer is that he did so] in order to inform us that the dream is of two kinds. First, what is originated by something outside the soul, which comes in the three kinds we have already mentioned. I refer to what results from worrying,[14] from food and from suffering. There are [dreams,] however, which originate from inside the human soul. It comes from what [the human soul] grasps out of the light of wisdom which is over it. And we established a clear distinction between [theses two kinds of dreams]. [The dream] originating in the soul[15] is fashioned

7 Yefet ben Eli has the same introduction with the same division of the second part of the Book of Daniel, using the same quotations (Dn 7:1, 8:1, 9:1 quoting its translation alone, and 10:1). He adds, however, what Daniel saw in his dream, as an independent part; which allows him to speak of five parts, and not four, as in R. Saadia's commentary.

8 Maybe R. Saadia is referring to his commentary of Dn 2:29 where he determine the three reasons for a false vision and a forth for a truthful and divine inspiration.

9 This is probably a reference to the missing part of the introduction, since the manuscripts of this edition do not cover the totality of R. Saadia's introduction.

10 Lit. "The language of the Arabs."

11 Lit "The language of the Kasdians."

12 אכ̇ראגנא "our production, our translation," which here has the meaning of "our interpretation."

13 Lit. "like the language of the Hebrews applies it."

14 Lit. "Before the chyme." "Chyme" אלכימוס in Judeo-Arabic, (from the Greek χυμός). "Worrying" is mentioned here in harmony with R. Saadia's enumeration in his commentary on Dn 2:29. Maybe "before the chyme" according to R. Saadia has the same meaning as "worrying."

15 מן מעדן אלנפס means either "from the same matter as the soul" or "from the proper place of the soul."

in imitation of the wisdom, what is conceivable[16] or what is written. In contrast, what is not originated in the soul is confused and in disorder. The difference is what makes it possible for an individual [with a dream originating in his soul] to remember what was before the dream.[17] And because the dream that Daniel had originated in the soul and belongs to the substance of wisdom he introduced it by וחזוי ראשה (Dn 7:1). He means that the this vision belongs to the inner being[18] and that it is true, similar to his introduction to the two former dreams of Nebuchadnezzar.

His expression: *He then wrote the dream* (Dn 7:1) indicates that he registered it immediately, not believing that it is a prophecy until, awake, he saw the individual that interpreted [the prophecy] to him in his dream, as we will explain [when we examine] his expression: *I approached one of those who were standing* (Dn 7:16). His expression: ראש מלין (Dn 7:1) *the beginning of the discourse* is a theme with three possible interpretations. [According to the first interpretation] which is the weakest of [the three] this expression constitutes a possible reference to *as if the four sides of heaven were running, rejoining the big sea* (Dn 7:2).[19] In other words, it suited him to compare the universe to the sea after contemplating the four directions rejoining the sea. In this case *rejoining the big sea* (Dn 7:2) is [designated] by ראש מלין (Dn 7:1). And *raising from the sea* (Dn 7:3) becomes *the end of the discourse.*[20] [According to] the second [interpretation], which is of a higher probability[21] than [the first one], his expression: ראש מלין (Dn 7:1) becomes the principle and the rule of all the story. He means that he does not intend to explain the particular history[22] of every kingdom, neither the facts about each of their kings, nor their annals, for fear of being long and because he does not want to burden [his reader].[23] However, concerning the conditions of every kingdom, he will explain principles, foundations[24] and statements that overlap with the biggest part of the kingdom, according to the listener's and the speaker's capacity. [In its] third [interpretation], the expres-

16 אלמעקול "intelligible," different from written principles, refers to the part of wisdom that, without being codified, is part of reasonable principles that rule any normal existence.

17 Lit. "vision" which R. Saadia uses frequently for "dream."

18 אלדֿאת Lit. "Nature, substance, essence."

19 Cf. the footnote concerning R. Saadia's translation of Dn 7:2 characterized by "four directions" instead of "four winds."

20 סוף מלין.

21 אגל literally 'of a higher dignity.'

22 פרוע אכבארהם Lit. "The branches, or details, of their chronicles, or news."

23 וכֿרוגה ען אחתמאל אלתכליף Lit. "and in order to be outside the possibility of imposing on others."

24 עיונא Lit. "sources, springs."

sion: ראש מלין (Dn 7:1) indicates part of the first story. Hence, he says 'I will explain part of my story; the story of the servitude and the number of the kingdoms.'[25] As to its last part which pertains to the length of the end and sources of the salvation,[26] that constitutes *the end of the discourse,* he does not neglect it[27] completely. In fact, he had an integrated discourse that remained unnoticed in the first one, since he said: *A time, two times and half a time* (Dn 7:25). He also said: *And the kingdom, the dominion and the glory that belongs to the kingdom of all that is under heaven, was given to the group of eminent saints* (Dn 7:27). Then he added:

Dn 7:2

Daniel started and said: 'Through the limits of a nightly vision, I saw the four sides of heaven as if they were running, rejoining the big sea.[28]

I rendered his expression ענה דניאל ואמר (Dn 7:2) by "he started," because it is not an answer to a former discourse.[29] And by adding חזה חוית בחזוי to what he had said he wanted to indicate that it is a vision that belongs to Daniel[30] alone and no one ever heard about an individual having such vision. We too, if we hear about it, remain under the same impression. His expression: *As if the four sides of heaven were running, rejoining the big sea* (Dn 7:2) pertains to the Syrian sea[31] alone. Since the whole story is about a particular people and a par-

25 Yefet ben Eli had two interpretations for the expression ראש מלין (Dn 7:1). First, it may mean the source of the dream (עין אלמנאם) that is used as the frame of the comparison; the second interpretation is Daniel's discourse, beginning by "Daniel started and said" Dn 7:2.

26 כמיה אלקץ ועיון אלישועה lit. "The quantity" or "the measure" of the limit," or "the end, and the sources of salvation."

27 Lit. "The chapter."

28 R. Saadia translation of Dn 7:2 has three distinctive points: first, חזוי is translated impersonally, lit. "as one can see." However, in his commentary he reserves the vision to Daniel alone. The second point is his translation of וארו by "as if." The third distinctive mark is his translation of מגיחן by two words מצדרה אלי running to, מנצמה אלי rejoining, or joined to. Yefet ben Eli's translation is as follow: "Daniel answered and said 'I was looking in my meditations," (or visions), during the night, and suddenly the four winds of heaven were making the sea jump."

29 Yefet ben Eli's translation of Dn 7:2 begins with by "Daniel answered and said," which seems opposed to R. Saadia's remark.

30 Lit. "To him."

31 בחר אלשאם. Yefet ben Eli translates: אלבחר אלמחיט lit. "the oceanic sea." In translating by 'the oceanic sea' or 'the ocean' Yefet ben Eli's intention, perhaps, is to

ticular sea. The rushing of the four sides of heaven has three meanings. First, in all that he will mention about the possessions of every kingdom he does not refer to what it has in its possession in the far limits of the world and in its remote regions, but he refers to what it has in its possession in Syria[32] particularly. In fact, the Babylonians had great possessions during many years before they took over Syria. But it has been said that they conquered Syria in particular, only for seventy years. It has been said, equally, about the Persians that they took over Syria in particular only for fifty two years. As to what is before and after that [period] they were in possession of many different places. It is the same with the Greeks, the Romans and others. The second [meaning] is that every nation that takes over Syria does not maintain its independence for long, but once it takes control of the county it ends by being dominated by it.[33] The third [meaning] is that the Israelites must never imagine that a kingdom, other that the ones mentioned, will rule over them. Since there is no side that Daniel did not notice surrounding the sea. As to us, how to understand that Daniel can see the four sides surrounding the sea, we answer that as if he saw eastern side one with the sea, with no city or way or mountain, or anything [between them]. It is the same with the southern, the northern and the western sides.[34] It is also possible that he contemplates what was more elevated than this: That the southern and the northern stars, those who are surging between them and those who are invisible, all are joining the sea. There is no shore other than the place where Daniel and the individuals[35] stand. However, after the coming of the judge, which he will mention,[36] for whom the seat will be prepared, the ocean that [surrounds] the earth recovers its natural dimension and its contraction with the sea stopped. This enabled Daniel[37] to see *the river of fire, thousand of thousands, myriad of myriads* (Dn 7:10) and all that he described after that. Then he added:

---

make Daniel's vision, less particular or local, related to בלד אלשאם or Syria alone, which is R. Saadia's understanding of Daniel's dream.

32 בלד אלשאם lit. "The country of Sham."

33 A very complicated sentence that has the following literal meaning: "Every nation that rules by a country over Syria does not remain a nation neighboring that country, but it becomes under its control, once it governs Syria."

34 R. Saadia will refine this image by specifying that all the waters surrounding the earth rejoin the Syrian sea (בחר אלשאם), which allows Daniel to see all of the universe.

35 The individuals with Daniel are the attendants who will ask about the meaning of the vision. Cf. Dn 7:16.

36 Cf. Dn 7:9.

37 Lit. "Him."

Dn 7:3

Four mighty individuals[38] rose from the sea, each one different from the other.

I rendered חיון (Dn 7:3) by 'individuals,' since it is inconvenient that I say 'animals.'[39] Nevertheless, it is possible that we say 'beasts.'[40] His addition of the word רברבן (Dn 7:3) 'mighty' indicates that its interpretation should not be 'years,' like [in the expression of the] *seven cows* (Gn 41:26)[41] that Pharaoh saw; neither should it have the interpretation of "man" like when Joseph saw *eleven stars* (Gn 37:9).[42] It has the meaning of great kingdoms, if we follow what the angel told him: *They are four kingdoms that rise on earth* (Dn 7:17). Yet, if he did not add anything to this expression, they would become four kings.[43] But he specified afterward that it is not the name of separate men, when he said: *A fourth kingdom rises on the earth and will change the earlier kingdoms* (Dn 7:23). We are informed then that the fourth as well as the three before it were all nations and kingdoms having territories and exercising their dominion.[44] And there are many meanings to the expression: *Each one different from the other* (Dn 7:3). One of the differences has to do with their countries. The Babylonians, in fact, are ascribed to the north side, following the expression: *For here I am calling all the families of the kingdoms of the north* (Jer 1:15). As to the Persians, in spite of the fact that they might be ascribed to the north side, according to the expression: *For see I will raise and bring up against Babylon*

38 אשכ̇אץ literally, 'individuals, persons.' The word could also mean 'unidentified, or unspecific thing.' However, R. Saadia avoids rendering the word חיון by the similar word in Arabic חיואנאת "animals," which is Yefet ben Eli's translation. R. Saadia will explain immediately that the reason for his preference for 'individuals' is the inelegance of the word 'animals.' As if it is unfitting for prophecy to deal with realities or beings of a lesser status or dignity than human beings. Since the word 'individual' does not reflect a human being, I shall replace it by the pronoun 'it' every time that R. Saadia uses the pronoun referring to this word.

39 There is no other justification than R. Saadia's own sensitivity for his refusal to use of the word חיואנאת or 'animals' that is largely employed in the Bible.

40 The word 'beasts' is the usual translation of חיון in Dn 7:3.

41 אלסבע אלבקראת is R. Saadia's translation of the citation from Gn 41:26. The addition of the article אל to בקראת is a grammatical mistake and the translation should have been אלסבע בקראת.

42 אחד עשר כוכב is R. Saadia's translation of the citation from Gn 37:9.

43 It is possible that R. Saadia's reflection has its foundation in the fact that while none of the six uses of רברבן in the Bible (all in Daniel) applies to a "year" or "person," of such interpretation is not impossible.

44 Lit. "Nations and kingdoms having states and dominion."

an assembly of great nations from the land of the north (Jer 50:9) they could also be ascribed to the eastern side.[45] Furthermore, we notice the Greeks; they are from the west as he will say: *And here is a goat that comes from the west* (Dn 8:5).[46] We also know that Athena, Cecilia and France are in the western side. That Edom is in the southern side as he said: *Then starts for you the southern border, form the wilderness of Sin to the side of Edom* (Nm 34:3).[47]

They have also differences in their religions and beliefs and those, as we know are called שִׁינוּי 'laws,' since he says that among the Israelites [there are certain populations …] *their laws are different from all people* (Est 3:8). Moreover, they are different in the [colors] of their clothes; between red, white, yellow and black, as he said: *The one with the black horses goes to the north, the white ones go after them; and the spotted ones go to the region of the south* (Zec 6:6). They differ too in their unjust actions against Israel. Concerning Babylon, they imposed brutally the kneeling to the statue. Media [ordained] that there will be no prayer. Persia [commanded] *to destroy, to kill and to exterminate* (Est 3:13). Greece prohibited the Sabbath and the circumcision. Edom asked [the Jews] to leave the all religion[48] and proscribed the reading of the Torah. It is because of these facts and their similar that he said: *Each one different from the other* (Dn 7:3). Then he added:

Dn 7:4

The first individual[49] was comparable to a lion and had wings like an eagle, then I saw that his wings were plucked off and it was lifted off the ground and set up on two feet like a human being and was given the mind of a man.[50]

Since the angel did not explain to Daniel the identity of this individual, or the other two,[51] neither did he explain every aspect of their qualities and conditions. We need to explain it and clarify it. The angel did not, however, totally neglect the explanation;[52] he did it briefly and because Daniel asked him a question with no relation to events connected to the individual's conditions. That is why he

45 Lit. "The eastern side participate in them also."

46 According to Dn 8:21 the goat is the king of the Greeks.

47 פיבתדי לכם אלחד אלגנובי מן בריה צן אלי נאגב אדום is R. Saadia's translation of Nm 34:3.

48 אלדין 'the religion' is R. Saadia's superlative way of naming Judaism. It implies that other religions can not adequately be called religions.

49 MT: "The one in front" which is also Yefet ben Eli's translation.

50 Lit. "And was given men's mind." MT: "And was given a human heart" which is also Yefet ben Eli's translation.

51 The other two are the bear (Dn 7:5) and the leopard (Dn 7:6).

52 Lit. "The angel did not leave this as void."

explained it and clarified it [in this manner].[53] We say that this individual, compared to a lion, is the kingdom of Babylon, as he previously said of Nebuchadnezzar: *The lion comes up from his thicket* (Jer 4:7). His speed is comparable to the eagle's wings movement, following his expression: *The Lord will bring a nation against you from a far, from the end of the earth, which will swoop down like the eagle* (Dt 28:49).[54] He also said: *He shall come like an eagle against the House of the Lord* (Hos 8:1).

His expression: *Then I saw that his wings were plucked off and it was lifted off the ground* (Dn 7:4) indicates the complete immobility. Indeed, this king was given feet like a lion and wings like an eagle. If he wished to walk, he could; if he wished to fly, he could. If his wings are plucked off and left on the ground, he could still walk on his feet. If he is lifted from the ground, he could still fly with his remaining wings. But the two infirmities were in him: His wings were plucked off, so he was forbidden from flying; he was lifted from the ground, so he was forbidden from walking.[55] The explanation of this is what happened to Nebuchadnezzar: The confusion of his mind and his wandering in the desert during the period already mentioned.[56] His kingship, his dominion and his administration were taken away from him, according to what we have explained, and he became unlike any human being, or animal. The meaning of his expression: *[Set up] on two feet like a human being and was given a mind of a man* (Dn 7:4) indicates the restoration of Nebuchadnezzar's mind, the recovery of his kingship[57] and the coming back of his princes and generals to him, according to what he said: *At that time, my reason came back to me with the glory of my reign, my joy and my splendor returned to me; my generals and noble men sought after me* (Dn 4:33). That is why I rendered אנש לבב as 'the mind of a

53 Reading the manuscripts pertaining to this passage gives the impression that there is no logical connection between the sentence 'that is why he (= the angel) explained it and clarified it,' and the following sentence, which is the beginning of R. Saadia's explanation. The solution resides in a modification that no manuscript attests, which leads one to read the sentence as follows: "That is why I (= R. Saadia) will explain it and clarify it." In fact, the previous sentence that mentions the reason for the angel's brevity in his explanation cannot logically end by 'that is why he explained it and clarified it.' Furthermore, all R. Saadia's reasoning is made necessary because of the brevity of the angel's explanation.

54 יג׳יך אללה קבילא מן בעיד מן טרף אלארץ׳ כמא יתחלק אלנסר is R. Saadia's Judeo-Arabic translation of the citation from Dt 28:49.

55 Yefet ben Eli's interpretation is that the immobility of the beast hints at the travels and invasions of the king Nebuchadnezzar.

56 Cf. Dn 4:29–30.

57 Yefet ben Eli gives the same interpretation, but adds that, as a consequence of his recovery, he started to worship God and abandoned all injustice.

man.' There are many such interpretations in *Proverbs* [where] wisdom is called לב 'heart'.

Nevertheless, the story of Nebuchadnezzar was finished before the time of registering[58] this vision. But because the intention is to show that Daniel is knowledgeable of the facts of the kingdoms, according to our tradition,[59] he started by what happened to him in order to add to it what will appear. Similar to his expression: *God told him 'your name is Jacob'* (Gn 35:10)[60] so he might add: *It will not be called anymore Jacob alone* (Gn 35:10).[61] And comparable to what the angel said to Manoah's wife: *Behold, you are barren* (Jgs 13:3) in order to add: *You shall conceive and give birth to a son* (Jgs 13:3) and what is similar to those [examples]. Then he said:

Dn 7:5

There was another individual like a bear, raised to one side, and there were three ribs in its mouth, hung between his teeth and suchlike it was addressed: Arise and eat the abundant meat.

The interpretation of this second individual is the Persian kingdom that he likened to the bear because it is of a lower dignity[62] than the lion and according to what he said previously: *However, after you shall arise another kingdom, lower than you* (Dn 2:39). The reason is that the reign did not belong exclusively to

58 Lit. 'Before the time of archiving תאריך this vision' which may suggest that R. Saadia envisions a time between the writing of the Book of Daniel and its acceptance as part of the Bible.

59 עלי נֹצאמנא literally 'according to our order' or style, or arrangement.

60 וקאל לה אסמך יעקוב is R. Saadia's translation of Gn 35:10a.

61 לא יסמי אבדא יעקוב פקט is R. Saadia's translation of Gn 35:10b. R. Saadia's translation of Gn 35:10 is very particular, which makes the division of his translation impossible, since it is one sentence and should be read without separation. Thus וקאל לה אסמך יעקוב לא יסמי אבדא יעקוב פקט has the following translation: "Your name Jacob will not be called Jacob alone anymore." There are two specific points of R. Saadia's translation. First, he adds the word פקט "alone" to the text, a justification for using either Jacob or Israel, and not Israel alone. The second point is that discourse is shifted from Jacob to his name: from "you shall not be called" we pass to "your name will not be called."

62 R. Saadia does not specify in which manner the bear is lower than a lion: Its speed, its strength, its aggressivity? Yefet ben Eli gives a curious reason for the fact that the bear is lower than the lion: The bear is more ignorant, or more careless (אגהל) than the lion.

the Persians. The people of Hamadan[63] were associated with them, as he said: *The power of Persia and Media* (Est 1:3) He also said: … *of the kings of Media and Persia* (Est 10:2). And we found that the kings are four: Two interpreted of the Persians, which are Cyrus and Artaxerxes, another interpreted of [a king from] Media, who is Darius. The fourth is probably of [a king from] Media, who is Ahasuerus. Even if this is not being said clearly. It was about it that he said: *Raised to one side* (Dn 7:5) which applies either to Media or to Persia.[64] As to the meaning of *there were three ribs in its mouth, hung between his teeth* (Dn 7:5) it is an extraordinary meaning. As if there is a lion, standing; three ribs taken from the prey, are in its mouth, hanging between its teeth. They are neither eaten, since it did not swallow them, nor ejected, since it did not throw them out. They are somehow between the two situations.[65] Their interpretation is that there will be three cities[66] that do not belong to this or to that.[67] Yet for a time they are dominated by the Greeks,[68] and by the Persians, in other times. It is impossible to have the name of those cities[69] by other mean than the tradition.[70] They are Harran,[71] Nesibin[72] and Shahrezor.[73] According to what the elders have transmitted [the expression] *there were three ribs in its mouth, hung between his teeth* (Dn 7:5) *this refers to Harran Adiabene and Nesibin that the*

63 A historical city to the southwest of Teheran that, according to R. Saadia, seems to be the center of Media.

64 Lit. "Which is Media in the line and Persia in the line."

65 Lit. "It is between that."

66 בלדאן (plural of בלד) is imprecise in its meaning. It could mean countries, provinces or cities. It is translated here by "cities," because of אלמדן cities, towns, used as synonymous, in the next sentence. For Yefet ben Eli, the three ribs represent three sides of the world.

67 In other word: Neither to the Greeks, nor to the Persians.

68 אלרום lit. "the Romans" but in the old Arabic literature means the Greeks.

69 אלמדן lit. "cities."

70 אלנקל "the tradition" which refers to all the old religious literature beside the Bible, mainly the Talmud.

71 חראן is not clear that it is the same as חָרָן in Gn 11:31. It seems also that there are different traditional spellings for the same city. Yalkut Sh. (ad. loc.) calls it חרוֹן. Cf. also חָרָן in Ez 27:23 and its Targum חַרְוָן. It appears to have been a city in the southeast of Turkey.

72 נצִיבִין a city and a province at the northeast of Turkey and the country of the tanna R. Yehudah ben Beseira (B Pesachim 3b).

73 There will be no mention later of this name. Another name will appear in the quotation from the Talmud: הדיב which seems to be the other name of שהרזור since R. Saadia continues to mention the three cities without any explanation for the appearance of הדיב and the disappearance of שׁהרזור.

sinful kingdoms once throw out, once dominate over them (cf. B Kid 72a).[74] And according to the language of the fathers the sides of the earth could be called צלעות "ribs" of which the Targum is עלעין (Dn 7:5). They[75] also say: *To the side of the house* (Ex 26:20).[76] They say too: *Shimei walked alongside the hill* (2 Sm 16:13). As to his expression: *And suchlike he was addressed: Arise and eat the abundant meat* (Dn 7:5) it has an interpretation similar to the fact that it pleased Ahasuerus to destroy the Israelites.[77] Because [the expression]: *The abundant meat* (Dn 7:5) designates Israel, as he says: ... *and became there a big and great nation* (Dt 26:5).[78] There are many passages comparable to this one.[79] The meaning of *arise and eat* (Dn 7:5) is that he exterminated the people and destroyed them.[80] He also said: And you will destroy all the peoples (Dt 7:5).[81] He said again: *Because they have destroyed Jacob; they have destroyed him and consumed him* (Jer 10:25).[82] The meaning of *he was addressed* (Dn 7:5) is that Ahasuerus did not have the intention to do that. It is Haman who advised him to do that, according to the expression: *There is a certain people scattered abroad* (Est 3:8); *if it is pleased the king let it be written that they may destroyed* (Est 3:9).[83] It was not said in the vision that he ate something, but that someone told him: 'Arise and eat the abundant meat.'[84] Furthermore, Ahasuerus did not kill the Israelites; he was just told to kill them. Then he said.

74 זו חרן חריב ונציבין שׂפעמים פילטתן מלכות הרשעה ופעמים מולכת עליהן is R. Saadia quotation. While in the Talmud we have פולטתן זו חלזון חדייב ונציבין שׂפעמים בולעתן ופעמים (B Kid 72a).

75 After his reference to the "Fathers" while quoting the Targum, אלאבא קד תסמי R. Saadia continues to use the "Fathers" as reference while quoting the Bible כמא תקול. The use of the "Fathers" here is unusual, since he names them only for the religious literature outside the Bible.

76 ולגאנב אלמסכן is R. Saadia' translation of the quoted part of Ex 26:20. "The House" here designates the Tabernacle.

77 Cf. Est 3:9–11. Lit. "His interpretation is like his saying that it pleased Ahasuerus to destroy the Israelites."

78 פצאר תם אמה כבירה עטימה is R. Saadia' translation of the citation part of Dt 26:5.

79 Lit. "And what is similar to that."

80 Lit. "And their destruction."

81 פתפני גמיע אלשעוב is R. Saadia's translation of this part of Dt 7:16.

82 The verb אכל, lit. "to eat," in this passage, of which we have no Judeo-Arabic translation, is translated by "to destroy" in harmony with R. Saadia translation of the same verb in a similar context.

83 Yefet ben Eli quotes the same part of Est 3:9 in an explanation similar to that of R. Saadia.

84 R. Saadia quotes his translation and the massoretic text, as he usually does.

Dn 7:6

After that I saw another individual like a leopard,[85] it has four of the bird's wings on its back,[86] it has four heads and dominion was given to it.

The interpretation of this [individual] refers to the third kingdom, comparable to the leopard. It is the kingdom of Greece, because it has patience, stability and determination like the leopard, as he said: *A leopard shall watch their towns* (Jer 5:6).[87] The interpretation of the four wings on its back is the divisions that happened in the kingdom.[88] It was divided into four parts after the death of Alexander. He appointed a ruler from the population over every division. And this division is mentioned in the Book of Daniel[89] in three other passages: *And four ramifications grew at its place toward the four sides*[90] *of heaven* (Dn 8:8). Its interpretation: *It has four heads* (Dn 7:6) according to what has been observed about the Greeks; that they had four high places[91] during their time. One in Greece;[92] one in Antioch; one in Alexandria and one in Jerusalem.[93] Because the establishment of a column[94] in various places is called in the language of our fathers ראשים 'heads.' The Bible also said:[95] *And the raiding group came out of the Philistine camp in three columns* ראשים. *One column* הראש *is intended for Ophrah road, toward the land of Shual; the other column is intended for Beth Horon; and the last column is intended for the border road that overlooks the valley of Zeboim toward the desert* (1 Sm 13:17–18). His expression: *And dominion was given to it* (Dn 7:6) designates the fullness of dominion, as he said at the beginning: *The third kingdom, is similar to the copper, and rules over the*

85 For Yefet ben Eli, the leopard in Dn 7:6 is a collective figure representing all the Greek kings.

86 Yefet ben Eli does not mention the number of wings on the beast's back.

87 According to Yefet ben Eli, if the third kingdom is similar to a leopard it is because of its smaller size, when compared to the second kingdom likened to a bear.

88 For Yefet ben Eli, the four wings represent the four rulers that govern the Greek kingdom after the death of Alexander.

89 Lit. "In this Book."

90 רוחות השמים is not translated by R. Saadia according to its obvious meaning, 'the winds of heaven' but by the Judeo-Arabic expression: נהאת אלסמא 'sides of heaven.'

91 מנאבר (sing. מנבר) are high places, pulpits, chairs. It designates here regional centers of the Greek empire or the military group, camps or column that protect these centers.

92 רומיה lit. "romaine lower empire" or Greece.

93 בית אלמקדס

94 אלאנתצאב the establishment of a ruler, or the establishment of a column, or a camp.

95 Lit. "He also said."

whole earth (Dn 2:39). We did know too that the one who had two horns ruled over the biggest part of the universe.[96] Then he said:

Dn 7:7

I saw after that in the night vision that the fourth individual was frightening, fearsome, very powerful and has big iron teeth by which[97] it eats and crushes and tramples the remains by its feet; it is different from all the other individuals before it and it has ten horns.

The interpretation of the fourth kingdom is Edom.[98] He compared it to a huge body. He did not give [it] a definition as he did for the first three kingdoms that were like a lion, a bear and a leopard.[99] But the [fourth individual] was huge and great alone. As if he hints that it is comparable to an elephant. And we ask why?[100] In fact, if [the fourth individual] is comparable to the elephant it is because the Israelites in their relation to it are comparable to the rhinoceros, which is much more frightful and bigger than it as he says: *The powerful who brought them out of Egypt; He who is like the horns of the rhinoceros protects them* (Nm 23:22).[101] The power of the Israelites and their strength are [also] compared to the horns of the rhinoceros, according to the expression: *His horns are similar to the rhinoceros' horns, by which he gores the nations* (Dt 33:17).[102] He named it תועפת, the name of the high and towering mountains, similar to his expression: *In his hands are the ends of the earth and the peaks of the mountains belong to him* (Ps 95:4).[103] His qualification of [the fourth kingdom] as *frightening, fearsome* (Dn 7:7), which the is the targum[104] of נורא ואיום means

96 אלעמארה has also the meaning of tribe and culture.

97 'By which' is added by R. Saadia and has no source in the MT.

98 Lit. "The interpretation of this fourth kingdom is the kingdom of Edom."

99 According to Yefet ben Eli, if the animal compared to the fourth kingdom is undefined it is because the fourth kingdom, or Rome, did not have a definite religion or a definite law.

100 פנקול עלא הדא אלימא lit. "we say about this why?".

101 אלטאיק אלמכרגהם מן מצר בארק אלרים מאנע ענהם is R. Saadia's translation of Nm 23:22.

102 קרונה כקרון אלכרכדאן חתי ינטח בהא אלאמם is R. Saadia's translation from the citation of Dt 33:17.

103 אלדי פי ידה נהאיאת אלארץ ותחליק אלגבאל לה is R. Saadia's translation of Ps 95:4 where תועפת הרים is translated תחליק אלגבאל "the peaks of the mountains." While the expression in (Nm 23:22) כתועפת ראם is translated by בארק אלרים "the horn-sword of the rhinoceros." Thus the word has two different translations according to context.

104 The word "targum" used here means simply "translation." It does not refer to the translation of the Hebrew Bible into Aramaic or "Targum."

that [the fourth kingdom] is higher than Babylonian kingdom, of which he said: *They are frightening and fearsome, their law and majesty proceed from themselves* (Hb 1:7).[105] And the meaning of his expression: *powerful* (Dn 7:7), which is the targum of חזקה indicates [the fourth kingdom] is higher than the Persian kingdom, of which he said: *{Thus said the Lord to his anointed} about Cyrus 'the one whose right hand I grasp I will humiliate nations before him, untie the loins of kings* (Is 45:1).[106] As to the meaning of his expression: יתירה (Dn 7:7) "very" it indicates that [the fourth kingdom] is higher than the Greek kingdom about which he said: *It became very powerful in the side of the south wind, and the east and [the side] of Syria, which means the north* (Dn 8:9). All these meanings [are mentioned] after similar qualities in the body. [Thus,] דחילה (Dn 7:7) "frightening" is something strong and intentional that appears in the eyes. The meaning of אימתני (Dn 7:7) "fearsome" is anxiety in its form and its marks. The meaning of תקיפא (Dn 7:7) "powerful" is solidity and massiveness in its members.[107] As for יתירה (Dn 7:7) "very" it indicates more than what is usually admitted.

The interpretation of the teeth is strength and stability.[108] The fact that they are of iron designates higher density and firmness. The passage of such comparison is: *O God, smash their teeth in their mouth and wreck, O Lord, the lions' teeth from them* (Ps 58:7).[109] He also said earlier: *And you broke the teeth of my oppressors* (Ps 3:8)[110] and what is similar to that. Then he added [something] while relating the vision by the angel, because of the claws which were of bronze. It is his expression: *And its claws were of bronze* (Dn 7:19). This tells us that this part of [the fourth individual description] belongs to the vision, but was

105 It is probable that R. Saadia establishes a hierarchy between the fourth kingdom and the Babylonian kingdom because the former is qualified by three expressions while the later is qualified only by two. The qualification pertains to the terror of the two kingdoms.

106 לאן כדא קאל אללה למסיחה ען כורש אלדי אמסך ימינה אדל בין ידיה אלאמם ואחקא אלמלוך אחלהא ואפתח בין ידיה מצארעהם ואבואבהם לא תגלק. is R. Saadia's translation of Is 45:1. Its particularity is that it does not identify Cyrus and the Messiah. "Thus said the Lord to his anointed about Cyrus" introduces a preposition ען "about" that has no massoretic background. The whole translation follows this principle: It is a message that the Lord address to his Messiah and not to Cyrus.

107 Yefet ben Eli translates תקיפא as 'very solid.'

108 The fact that the beast's teeth were of iron allows Yefet ben Eli to identify the beast as the wicked Titus (טיטוס הרשע), with no further explanation. The teeth, according to Yefet, signal his frequent invasions.

109 אללהם פאהדם אסנאנהם מן פאההם ויא רב פאנקץ אניאב אלצ̇ראגמה מנהם is Rsg's translation of Ps 58:7.

110 וכסרת אסנאן אלט̇אמין לי is R. Saadia's translation of the citation from Ps 3:8.

abridged.[111] The interpretation is that there are claws and feet, smashing, as he said by comparison in another passage: *Arise and thresh, O daughter of Zion, because I will make your horn of iron and make your hoof of bronze so you will crush many peoples* (Mi 4:13). The interpretation of *it eats and crushes* (Dn 7:7) is the excessive exploitation and stealing of what falls in its hands from the enemy. It is similar to what he said to Israel: *He eats its enemies from the nation and gnaw their bones* (Nm 24:8).[112] The interpretation of *and tramples the remains by its feet* (Dn 7:7) designates what remains from the possessions of the towns and the kingdoms which are in war against [the fourth kingdom] that it did not invade directly or were subjected. It is either by fire that it hits [the remains] or by flooding or by another destructive way. It is similar to what he said to Israel: (Dt 20:12)[113] till the end of the verse.[114] It is also possible that his expression: *And tramples the remains by its feet* (Dn 7:7) designates pride and insolence as it is in *is it not enough for you that you have eaten up the good pasture, but you also trample with you feet what is left from pasture lands? And to have drunk of the clear waters, but you must also muddy what is left with your feet* (Ez 34:18)*?* The interpretation of [the expression]: *It is different from all the other individuals before him* (Dn 7:7) is that [the citizens of the fourth kingdom] are unlike [the citizens of the other kingdoms] in their ways of practicing their religion, their clothes, their buildings and the injustice they use against Israel as we have already mentioned.[115] It is possible too that he refers to the duration of its existence; that it exceeds the total of duration of the former three kingdoms. In fact, the total of the three is three hundred and two years: Seventy for Babylon, fifty two for Persia and one hundred eighty for the Greeks. The kingdom of Edom exceeds this total, since it existed during five hundred fifty two years.

The interpretation of [the expression]: *And it has ten horns* (Dn 7:7) is that first and evidently [it designates] 'kings,'[116] following what the angel explained to Daniel, saying: *And the interpretation of the ten horns is that from that kingdom arise ten kings* (Dn 7:24) and according to what he had said: *There, I will*

111 Lit. "This tells us that the expression was at the beginning, but he abridged it." "At the beginning" means that the mention of the claws which are of bronze belongs to the first description of the fourth individual in Dn 7:7–9.

112 פהו יאכל אעדאה מן אלאמם עטאמהם ינהש is R. Saadia's translation of the citation from Nm 24:8.

113 ואן לם תסאלמך is R. Saadia's translation of the citation from Dt 20:12.

114 Lit. "Till its end."

115 Lit. "Against the nation, that we have already mentioned."

116 For Yefet ben Eli the ten horns designates the ten thrones.

honor David (Ps 132:17).[117] He also said: *He shall exalt the horn of his anointed* (1 Sm 2:10). If someone objects [saying] that during the years already mentioned these arose more than thirty we answer that it is possible that he hinted to the more elevated ones among them, and left the others. It is also possible that he implied the fathers who are the beginning [of dynasties] and left the sons. It is possible too that he refers to the ones who belong to different tribes, and left those who are from the same family. It does not matter which one of those three ways of interpretation allows as to subtract from the total, the remaining is ten kings alone. Nevertheless, it is possible that by those horns, he points out to cities[118] that are inexpugnable, firm, similar to the solid place that we found to be called "horn," since he said: *My beloved had a vineyard in a very fruitful hillside* (Is 5:1).[119] Thus, the interpretation of קַרְנַיִן עֲשַׂר לַהּ (Dn 7:7) becomes that Edom conquered ten great cities.[120] This is an interpretation[121] that we took into consideration, to the point that we asked whom we trust then we inquired and founded it right.[122] Again, if there is someone who objects, [saying] that there were more than one hundred fifty great cities under the domination of Edom, we answer that it is possible that he wanted [to designate] the important ones that surround the borders and left the cities that are far away.[123] We also say that Joshua counted in Syria the villages and the cities that surrounded the border and left what is far away, as he said: And the fortified cities were Ziddim, Zer, Hammat, Raqqat, Kinneret (Jos 19:35). Then he said:

Dn 7:8

While I was observing those horns a small horn sprouted up among them and three of the first horns were uprooted before it; there were eyes comparable to the human eyes in that horn, and a mouth that says enormities.

117 והנאך ארפע שׂאנא לדאוד is R. Saadia's translation of the partial citation of Ps 132:17. Lit. "There, I will raise honor/dignity (קרן) to David."

118 בלדאן (plural of בלד) may also mean "countries."

119 כאן לודידי כרם רכן די סמן is R. Saadia's translation of the partial citation of Is 5:1. The Hebrew word קרן is translated by the Arabic word רכן which is the solid side of a house. It is rendered here by 'hillside'.

120 For Yefet ben Eli, the ten horns represent ten thrones.

121 Lit. "This is something."

122 Lit. "And founded it such."

123 Lit. "And left what is between them."

This small horn designates the other nation[124] which is associated with Edom and rules Syria after it. Our expression 'is associated with Edom' comes because of what he said here: *Among them* (Dn 7:8). Our expression 'after it' is because of what he said there: *[And another king] rises after them* (Dn 7:24). His addition of משתכל in the description, that we rendered by "While," means that Edom was made prisoner and in a very short time the [new] nation overcomes it.[125] A similar [expression] has been already said to Edom: *If thieves come to you, if robbers by night, how would you be ruined! Would not they have stolen until they have enough* (Ob 5)*?* The meaning of *and three of the first horns were uprooted before it* (Dn 7:8) is that, the [new] kingdom overcomes three kings, according to the first interpretation. According to the second interpretation, it conquers three of their cities.[126] And this is perceptible, since it has conquered from Edom Syria, Egypt and Africa.[127] As to the whole cities, it is from the Persians that it seized them. If anyone thinks that the second interpretation, where the "horns" are cities, is in contradiction with what the angel explained saying: *And he puts down three kings* (Dn 7:24) we answer that he called the kingdoms kings: *And four kings* (Dn 7:17).[128] He also said: *There will be a fourth kingdom on earth that will change the earlier kingdoms* (Dn 7:23).

The interpretation of [the expression]: *There were eyes comparable to the human eyes in that horn* (Dn 7:8) is that the "eyes" [designates] knowledge, divine law, judgments and wisdom, as he said: *The eyes of the wise man in his head* (Ecc 2:14). Representing the wisdom by the eyes, he also said: *It is pleasant for the eyes to see the sun* (Ecc 11:7). He said too about representing prophets by the eyes: *Because God poured out upon you from the wind of deep sleep what can close your eyes, prophets* (Is 29:10).[129] The [expression]: *And a mouth that says enormities* (Dn 7:8) has the meaning of an infamous and opprobrious

124 Lit. "The interpretation of this small horn is the other nation." It is curious that Yefet ben Eli refuses to speak of the identity of the little horn. All that he says about him, in his commentary on the passage that ends with Dn 7:25, is that his identity is well known.

125 Lit. "And on the verge of closing its [= Edom's eyes] the nation overcomes it."

126 In his commentary on Dn 7:7 R. Saadia gives to the word "horn" two distinct interpretations. Following his first interpretation, "horn" has the meaning of a "king." Following his second interpretation, it means "city."

127 "Africa" in R. Saadia explanation designates North Africa. According to Yefet ben Eli, the three horns that the little horn dislodges are Alexandria, Jerusalem and Aka. Three cities, not three countries.

128 In 7:17 R. Saadia translates Aramaic מלכין "kings" by the Judeo-Arabic ממאלך "kingdoms." When he transcribes Dn 7:17 the word מלכין is replaced מלכיא.

129 כאן אללה קד אפרג̇ עליכם מן ריח סבאת מא גמ̇ץ עיונכם אי אלאנביא is R. Saadia's translation of the citation from Is 29:10. "the wind of deep sleep" is literally: "The wind of immobility."

discourse that the unbelievers from Edom and its followers utter against the Israelites and their Lord.[130] Because this is the meaning of saying enormities, according to the example [mentioned in]: *O Lord, cut off all defamatory and hypocritical discourse and the tongue that says enormities* (Ps 12:4).[131] Speaking about pride had this same meaning according to the expression: *Don't speak with haughtiness; let no arrogance come out of your mouth* (1 Sm 2:3). Then he said:

Dn 7:9

Then I saw that thrones were set up[132] and an old man[133] sat on them; his dress was like white snow, the hair of his head was white like wool,[134] his throne was of fire with sparks and its wheels were of blazing fire.

Dn 7:10

And the river of fire streamed and came forth before him and thousands of thousands served him, and myriads of myriads stood before him; the judgement was set and the registers were spread.

I say, in interpreting those two verses, that the mention in them of thrones, fires, judgement and registers, led some people from our nation to think that they are descriptions of our Creator, may He be exalted and elevated, [in a discourse] denuded from abomination. Others, not from our nation,[135] disputed this with us, and considered it anthropomorphism[136] and assimilation.[137] Others applied it to

130 Lit. "Against the Lord of the Israelites and against them."

131 אללהם פאקטע כל נטק כׄסי לינא ולסאן מתכלם אלכבאיר is R. Saadia's translation of Ps 12:4. The specifics of R. Saadia's translation is that the word שׂפתי חלקות "lips" becomes "defamatory and hypocritical discourse."

132 Instead of 'the thrones were set up' Yefet ben Eli understands 'the kings were removed.' For him, 'thrones' has the meaning of kings. Most probably, he refers to the four animals of Dn 7:3.

133 R. Saadia render עתיק יומין by אלשׄיך "the old man" and not literally as "the ancient of Days" which is the translation of Yefet ben Eli קדים אלזמאן.

134 MT: "Like the pure wool."

135 The Mu'tezlites, Muslim theologians, known for their anti-anthropomorphic opinions in the interpretation of God in the Koran, are most probably those who are meant by "others not from our nations."

136 The objection of those "who are from outside the nation" does not appear clearly in R. Saadia's words. Do they protest against the fact that R. Saadia thinks that the descriptions related to the old man are qualities of the Creator, which is not his opinion. Or that that they think of R. Saadia as holder of an anthropomorphic interpretation, which is not the case. Most probable is that the expression שׄנעו עלינא

the nation of Israel and considered it as its description. We answer, with the help of God, that ascribing these qualities[138] to the Israelites is not right, because the old man in this story assigned the kingship and tied it to the savior (אלמושיע) that we await, since the old man is higher than him. In contrast, the nation cannot assign [the kingship] to the savior, because it is lower than him [in dignity] and under his power. In fact, ascribing these verses to the Creator, may His glory and strength be manifested, by anthropomorphism and assimilation is not appropriate, because He is the Creator of every form, essence and accident. It is impossible that something He created be in Him. There are also indications in the books[139] that nothing is similar to Him in heaven, like the expression: *That they say who in the heights is equal to God, or similar to him among the powerful* (Ps 89:7).[140] And nothing is similar to him on earth, as he says: *To whom you compare the Powerful and to what resemblance can you liken Him* (Is 40:18).[141] And the impossibility of applying accidents to Him is shown by the expression: *He does not wear out neither does He tire and there is no end to His knowledge* (Is 40:28).[142] And also his expression: *Behold! He neither sleeps nor slumbers, the Guardian of Israel* (Ps 121:4).[143] He is, in fact, imperceptible to the vision,

---

"disputed this with us" means that they disputed this opinion with the Israelites that hold this interpretation. However, their dispute was not directed against those who in Israel hold this opinion alone, but was generalized to include all the Israelites. Hence the expression of R. Saadia, as Israelite, "disputed this with us."

137 תשביה "assimilation" of God's qualities to human qualities. It is another word for anthropomorphism.

138 Lit. "This story.

139 "Books" here could designate either the different parts of the Bible, or different parts of the Jewish traditional scriptures, which include the Talmud.

140 באן יקולון מן פי אלשואהק יעאדל אללה, או ישבהה מן דוי אלטאקה is R. Saadia's translation of Ps 89:7. It is to be noted that the expression באן יקולון is added by R. Saadia in his translation. The translation of this quotation is founded on R. Saadia's understanding of this verse. Also to be noted is R. Saadia's translation of the Hebrew original into the Judeo-Arabic אלטאקה דוי literally "those who are powerful," by which he designates the angels, since Ps 89:7 is quoted as evidence that no creator in heaven is comparable to God.

141 פבמן תשבהון אלטאיק ואי שבה תצאפוה בה is R. Saadia's translation of Is 40:18. This verse, according to him designates the dissimilarity between God and earthy creators. In this case the Hebrew word דמות, translated by שבה, refers to earthly creators alone.

142 ולם יתעב ולא נהאיה לעלמה (Derenbourg לגב) לם ילגב is R. Saadia's translation of Is 40:28.

143 הודא לא ינאם ולא יוסן חאפט אלאסראיל is R. Saadia's translation of Ps 121:4. It is possible that by adding an article to Israel (אלאסראיל) R. Saadia wanted to say "the Guardian of the Israelites."

and perceptible by [His] acts,[144] following the expression: *You are truly a hidden Lord, the God of Israel, his savior* (Is 45:15).[145] Saying: *hidden* (Is 45:15) he designates the essence; saying: *savior* (Is 45:15) he designates the act.

The true interpretation[146] is that the individual mentioned in this story is a light[147] initiated by the Creator, by which He proves to his prophet that those sayings are from Him. This interpretation can be proven true to anyone looking for it by four introductions. The first introduction[148] is that every prophet needs a sign by which he verifies that the discourse he is hearing comes from God. Either the sign is a column of clouds standing closely, while all the sky is clear. That is [what the Bible calls] עמוד ענן like when it speaks about Moses, Aaron and Samuel: *He spoke to them through a column of cloud* (Ps 99:7).[149] Or the sign could also be a global light that proceeds neither from the sun nor from the moon, nor of any known luminary. It is also explained in many prophetic books[150] that they saw the *glory of the Lord*. This sign appears with the beginning of the [prophetic] discourse and ends at its end. At that moment the prophet becomes certain that [the sign] has appeared to him in order that he realizes that the voice he heard comes from his Lord.

The second introduction[151] is that when the prophet, or the assembly, sees that light they say 'we saw God' in a metaphorical use of the Hebrew language. However, they do not intend to say that they saw the essence of God. Because there is no relation[152] between His essence and the men of good will. What they want to say[153] is that they saw His miracles and observed His proofs.[154] We also found that the Torah declares metaphorically about the angels that they saw the

144 Lit. "Invisible by the vision and apparent by act."

145 ויקינא אנך לרב מחתגב ואלאה אסראיל מג׳יתה is R. Saadia's translation of Is 45:15.

146 לכן אלקול אלצחיח. Lit. "But the true expression," or the true expression of the interpreter, the commentator.

147 According to Yefet ben Eli, the light mentioned in Dn 7:10 is a fire by which the angel punishes the nations.

148 "Introduction" here has the meaning of an introductory sign that legitimates the prophet's authority and allow him to continue his mission.

149 בעמוד מן גמאם יכאטבהם is R. Saadia's translation of Ps 99:7. In explaining ענן עמוד R. Saadia uses two synonymous (סחאב, גמאם) for the same Hebrew word ענן.

150 Lit. "Explained in many prophets."

151 'Introduction' here has the meaning of a principle, or rule, of interpretation.

152 וצלה 'joining point.'

153 Lit. "What they want to say by their discourse."

154 The Arabic words איאתה "His miracles" and דלאילה "His proofs" both have the meaning of "sign." The "miracles" here refer to the miracles of His power, and the "proofs" are those of His existence.

Creator. Then it explains indirectly[155] [...] that they saw His Glory. That is [the meaning of] the expression: *Then Moses, Aaron, Nadab, Abihu and seventy from the elders of Israel ascended and contemplated the light of the God of Israel* (Ex 24:9–10).[156] Next, the Torah explains:[157] *The vision of the light of God* (Ex 24:17).[158] That is why he said [... ...]. And Micaiah said: *I saw the Lord* (1 Kgs 22:19).[159]

The third introduction is that this light [... ...] in the form of a living creature[160] as we have explained while [commenting on his] expression: *The vision of the light of God was like a consuming fire* (Ex 24:17).[161] He[162] also said [... ...]. He[163] also wishes to show it in the form of a human being, under whom [... ...] vested in cloths of light, as he said: *And his radiance fills the Temple* (Is 6:1).[164] It is not a tail to anything other than a garment. What is compared to a tail is the radiance of that light. He also represented the sun with a wing or wings, saying: *But for you who fear my name the sun of righteousness and healing on its wings* (Mal 3:20). It is possible too that angels appear at the right and the left of that throne, following the expression of Micaiah: *And all the host of heaven were standing at His right and left* (1 Kgs 22:19). Moreover, it possible that a platform appears under that seat[165] and four of the angels[166] carry it, as it

155 פי אלתוריה lit. "in theory, in a dissimulated manner." אלתוריה could also mean a rhythmic style of writing.

156 תם צעד מוסי והרון ונדב ואביהוא וסבעון מן שיוך אסראיל, טרו נור אללה אסראיל is R. Saadia's partial translation of Ex 24:9–10. It is to be noticed that R. Saadia, following his theory of the impossibility of God being seen by a creature, does not hesitate to add the word נור 'light,' that has no masoretic background. The translation of Ex 24:9–10 follows R. Saadia's interpretation.

157 Lit: "Then it said in explaining that."

158 רויא נור אללה (Derenbourg וכאן (ריא is R. Saadia's translation of the citation from Ex 24:17. It is to be noted that the Hebrew word כבוד 'glory' is translated by the Arabic word נור "light."

159 According to R. Saadia's understanding, this part of 1 Kgs 22:19 should be translated as follow: I saw the light of the Lord. However, we don't have R. Saadia's translation. That is why we maintain the translation from the masoretic text without any modification.

160 חיואן is translated here as 'living creature'. Its usual translation is 'animal.'

161 רויא נור אללה כנאר אכלה (Derenbourg וכאן (ריא is R. Saadia's translation of the citation from Ex 24:17. This passage refers to R. Saadia's commentary on the Book of Exodus, which remains unedited.

162 'He' here refers to the Bible.

163 'He' here refers to God.

164 ושעאעה מלא אלהיכל is R. Saadia's translation of the citation from Is 6:1.

165 ערשא תחת דלך אלכרסי literally "throne under that seat." The Arabic word ערש is the translation of the Hebrew word רקיע. However, in his translation of Gn 1:6.13

is mentioned by Ezekiel: *And there was on the heads of the living something similar to a firmament* (Ez 1:22). Then he added: *And above the firmament that was over their heads there was, similar to the sapphire, something like a throne* (Ez 1:26). It also possible that the individual[167] addresses the prophets, as in his expression*: And he said to me 'son of Adam, stand up on your feet that I may speak to you'* (Ez 2:1). And according to all the prophets, these individuals who are of light are created, for everyone who addressed a prophet is a creature, with the exception of Moses about whom it has been said in the explanation: *Because God knew him face to face* (Dt 34:10).[168] And since the consideration of a vision of the Creator is about a light that is created, not the vision of the essence [of God] it is the same for ordinary people and those who remain faithful to their religion. Because they rendered[169] [the expression]: *They looked at the God of Israel* (Ex 24:10)[170] [by] *they contemplated the magnificence of the God of Israel.*[171] They also translated: *I saw the Lord* (Is 6:1)[172] and *I saw the Lord* (1 Kgs 22:19) [by] *I contemplated the magnificence of the Lord.*[173] Yet, this individual[174] does not appear in any circumstances other than being created, as we have already described.

R. Saadia renders the Hebrew word רקיע by the Arabic word גלד. It is to be noted that in his edition of R. Saadia's translation of the Book of Genesis Derenbourg hesitates between the correct גלד (Derenbourg writes גֹלד) like in Gn 1:6.7 and the mistaken נֹלד (Gn 1:13.15.17).

166 Lit. "Four individuals from the angels."

167 In other words, one of the angel addresses the prophets.

168 לאן ערפה אללה משאפהה is R. Saadia's translation of the citation from Dt 34:10.

169 תרגמו literally "they translated, they rendered," a verb taken from the noun תרגום.

170 פנטרו נור אללה אסראיל is R. Saadia's translation of the partial citation from Ex 24:10. Its translation is: "And they contemplated the light of the God of Israel." The word נור "light" has no masoretic original. In order to show the difference between the masoretic text, in Hebrew, and the Targum, in Aramaic, the translation of the examples that R. Saadia quotes are made from the masoretic text and not, as usual, from R. Saadia's Judeo-Arabic translation.

171 וחזו תי יקר אלהא דישראל. The word יקר "magnificence" is added in the Aramaic and it has no masoretic original.

172 ראית נור אללה is R. Saadia's translation of partial citation from Is 6:1. The translation is: "I looked at the light of God."

173 חזיתי ית יקרא דיוי The word יקרא "magnificence" is added in the Aramaic and it has no masoretic original.

174 For R. Saadia, "the individual" here is synonymous to the created light, which is all that a human being can see of God.

The fourth introduction is that no prophet could see the beginning[175] of that light. Because the strength of any light resides habitually in its inner part.[176] If any one looks at its beginning his composition will disintegrate. It is about it that God says to Moses: *So you may see the ends of My light, but its beginning shall not be seen* (Ex 33:23).[177] It is impossible that by this expression the Creator intended His own essence. Because the vision of His essence is impossible for a man, living or dead. What He intended by this expression is the created light that could be seen. It remains to be known for us, however, whether the human being that sees it could or could not live. Thereupon we were informed[178] that the human being who looks at the beginning of that light or faces its element will disintegrate and he will die, according to the expression: *You are not capable to look at the beginning of My light, because no human being can look at it and remain in life* (Ex 33:20).[179] In spite of that, if the Creator wishes that a human being look at that created light and remain in life, He veils [it] by a cloud or something similar until the beginning of that light pass and go further. At that point He dissipates the cloud from it and the man can look at it and yet remains in life. Comparable to what he did with Moses, our master, since He said to him: *I will move away My clouds so you may see [the ends of My light]* (Ex 33:23).[180] Most of the [biblical] books mentioned such two situations: that whoever looks at the beginning of the light dies. Habakkuk, for example, says: *There is a brightness like the light etc.* (Hb 3:4), *before him walks the pestilence* (Hb 3:5). However, anyone who looks at its ends remains unharmed, following what Isaiah had said: And it is called the light of the king and your eyes will see his

175 אואיל 'beginnings' could be understood as a temporal beginning or the first moment of the eruption of that light. The same word could also be understood as 'sources' or what causes that light. the second interpretation is the more plausible, in light of the citation of Ex 33:23.

176 מסתקבלה literally "its inner part" or "the part that is facing us."

177 חתי תנטׄר אואכׄר נורי ואואילה לא תרא is R. Saadia's translation of the partial citation of Ex 33:23. The translation of the masoretic text is: 'So you may see my back, but may face shall not be seen.' R. Saadia's translation has two specifics. First, he inserts the word נורי "my light" and obtains 'the back of my light.' Secondly, he translates the Hebrew word ופני "but my face" by the Arabic ואואילה "its beginning" and obtains 'and its beginning.'

178 Lit. "It (= the Bible) made known to us."

179 לא תסתטיע אן תנטׄר אול נורי לאנה לא יראה אנסאן פיחיי is R. Saadia's translation of the citation from Ex 33:20. The translation of Ex 33:20 follows R. Saadia's Judeo-Arabic translation.

180 תׄם אזיל סחאבי חתי תנטׄר is R. Saadia's translation of the partial citation of Ex 33:23. Avoiding any anthropomorphism, R. Saadia translates והסרתי את כפי literally 'I will take away My hand' by תׄם אזיל סחאבי literally 'I move away My clouds.'

beauty like when they see a remote country (Is 33:17).[181] He means, as [you eyes] see a faraway country.

Now that we have finished [explaining] those four introductions, thus become clear that the lights appearing to the prophets are created. They may have the form of a human being, sometimes, and it is possible that [the same lights] have in some [other] times the form of an old man [sitting] on a throne. It is what Daniel had said here: *Thrones were set up and an old man sat on them* (Dn 7:9). The wise advantage of appearing as an old man could be that he will hand the reign to the savior as his superior,[182] as he will say: *He brought the young man in the presence of the old man* (Dn 7:13)[183] *and the old man gave him dominion* (Dn 7:14).[184] As to the savior, he was similar to the rising plant, the growing up, the beginner, as he said: *A rod will come forth from the stump of Jesse* (Is 11:1).[185] [the Bible] also said: *I will raise to David a righteous offshoot* (Jer 23:5). And: *I will pluck a tender one from his young twigs* (Ez 17:22) and what is similar to that.

He introduced at the beginning of his expression the one who will be his lord and his Master, like the old man,[186] the ancient one and the elder[187] in order that he represent him as a young man. Thus he said: *That a young man* (Dn 7:13)[188] so the images may match each other. Hence the old man invested the power to the young man, like Moses to Joshua, Samuel to David and David to Solomon and what is similar to that. As to his expression: *Thrones* (Dn 7: 9) in the plural, and that he did not say 'throne,' in the singular, the explanation could be that the throne is of multiple parts and sections. When all its pieces are put together it becomes one, for the reason that he gives in the middle of the verse: *His throne was of fire with sparks* (Dn 7:9) and did not say: *His thrones*. Now that we have elucidated the meaning of *thrones and the old man* (Dn 7: 9), we have to men-

181 ויקאל לה נור אלמלך וגמאלה תרא עינאך כמא תרא אלבלאד אלבעיד is R. Saadia's translation of Is 33:17. R. Saadia adds literally ויקאל לה נור 'and it is called' that has no masoretic original. Hence, the human eyes will not see the king (= God) but the light of the king.

182 Lit. "Maybe that he will hand the reign to the savior, like a superior handing [something to an inferior."]

183 Lit. "He brought him (= the young man) between his (= the old man) hands."

184 Lit. "And he (= the old man) gave him (= the young man) the dominion."

185 יכ̇רג קצ̇יב מן ענצר ישי is R. Saadia's translation of Is 11:1.

186 עתיק יומין for Yefet ben Eli is a king. It is not clear from his commentary on Dn 7:9 whether this king is God Himself.

187 כאלשׁיך ואלעתיק ואלקדים literally like an old man and an ancient one and an elder or an eternal.

188 R. Saadia renders the Aramaic expression: כבר אנשׁ literally 'like a son of man' by the Arabic expression שׁאב or 'young man.'

tion the interpretation of *his dress was white like snow* (Dn 7:9). Its apparent [meaning] refers to *the light* (Dn 7:9), which is comparable to what he has said there: *And his radiance fills the Temple* (Is 6:1).[189] With his expression: *And the court was full of the brightness of the Lord's glory* (Ez 10:4). There is also his expression before that: *The light of God fills the Tabernacle* (Ex 40:34).[190] Its interpretation is the promise that He made to the Israelites about the appearance of the light on the Temple at the time of salvation, standing from the earth to the heaven and the nations come forth to it, as he said: *Arise, shine* (Is 60:1),[191] *so that the nations walk toward your light* (Is 60:3).[192] As to the interpretation of *the hair of his head was white like wool* (Dn 7:9) […] that the faults of the nation and its sins become like darkness […] white like the pure wool, as he already said there: *If your sins are like the red color they become white like snow* (Is 1:18).[193] […] *He saves your people*[194] […] *and I will cleanse them from all their iniquity* (Jer 33:8). And the interpretation of *his throne was of fire with sparks and its wheels* (Dn 7:9) is that [… …] the extreme circumstances like burning fire [… …] *God will come by fire* (Is 66:15),[195] *God will punish by fire* (Is 66:16).[196] He also said: And I […] he said to different people than us when […] *and their wheels like whirlwind* (Is 5:28).[197] This is according to the customs of […] revenge and advance.[198]

It is possible that the interpretation of *the river of fire* (Dn 7:10) punishments [… …] against the apostates and the oppressors like a hot torrent as he said there: *Behold, the storm of the Lord* (Jer 23:19) [… …]. And the meaning of his obvious expression: *thousands of thousands* (Dn 7:10) is what we will describe about the contemplation [… …]. The meaning of *and myriads of myriads* (Dn 7:10) […] without service, in order that if it goes [… …] that his court may

189 ושעאעה מלא אלהיכל is R. Saadia's translation of the partial citation of Is 6:1.

190 ונור אללה מלא אלמסכן is R. Saadia's translation of the partial citation of Ex 40:34. To be noticed that the Hebrew expression: כבוד יי׳ literally 'glory of the Lord' is rendered in Judeo-Arabic by ונור אללה literally 'the light of God.'

191 אלא פקומי פאצ׳י is R. Saadia's translation of the quoted part from Is 60:1.

192 חתי תסעי אלאמם אלי צ׳יאך is R. Saadia's translation of the partial citation of Is 60:3.

193 אן כאנת כטאיאכם כאלחמרה אביצ׳ת כאלתלג׳ is R. Saadia's translation of the partial citation of Is 1:18.

194 יצל עמך while the words, in Hebrew, seem to refer to a biblical quotation, there is no such expression in the masoretic text.

195 אן אללה סיאתי באלנאר is R. Saadia's translation of the partial citation of Is 60:15. The expression: could be translated either 'come by the fire' or 'come with fire.'

196 אן אללה סיעאקב באלנאר is R. Saadia's translation of the partial citation of Is 60:16.

197 ובכרה כאלזואבע is R. Saadia's translation of the partial citation of Is 5:28.

198 אלקדום literally "the coming forth" or "the advance" does not seem fitting in the context which the lacunae make unclear. It could also mean 'the attack' which is more in harmony with the preceding word.

never be lacking. [the interpretation of] *the old man* (Dn 7:9) is similar to what we have said there:[199] *And all the host of heaven serving Him* (1 Kgs 22:19) [… …] of the arrival of the thousands and myriads from the nations [… …] as he said: *Thus, O Israel, there will be a nation that you do not know etc.* (Is 55:5).[200] He also said: So that the armies of the nation may (Is 60:11),[201] and: *And all the flocks of Kedar etc.* (Is 60:7),[202] and: *Kings will be nursing you* (Is 49:23)[203] with what is similar to that. The [expression]: *The judgement was set* (Dn 7:10) does not have the meaning of judging all the people, because *the day of salvation* is not the day of the resurrection. It has the meaning of judging the nations for […].[204] It is what Joel had already explained, saying: *Let the nations rouse themselves and come up etc.* (Jl 4:12).[205] The meaning of *the registers were spread* (Dn 7:10) […] the good and bad deeds of all the faithful, since this can be done in the future life.[206] In fact, the prophets have mentioned that the Creator preserves the deeds of His faithful, like the events we preserve in books and registers, since it has been said: *And a book of remembrance was written before Him concerning those who fear the Lord* (Mal 3:16). He also said: *Behold! It is written* (Is 65:6).[207] And Job[208] had said: *That my adversary may write a book* (Jb 31:35)[209] and what is similar to that. However, the books and the registers

199 This could be an indication of the existence of R. Saadia's commentary on the Book of Kings.

200 כדׄאך אנת יא אסראיל אמה לם תערפהא is R. Saadia's translation of the partial citation of Is 55:5. The expression: אנת יא אסראיל is added by R. Saadia and has no origin in the masoretic text.

201 לידכׄל אליך פיהא גנוד [אלאמם] is R. Saadia's translation of the partial citation of Is 60:11.

202 ונמיע גׄנם קדר is R. Saadia's translation of the partial citation of Is 60:7.

203 ויכון מן מלוכהם חאצׄנוך is R. Saadia's translation of the partial citation of Is 49:23.

204 Maybe the idea of R. Saadia, unclear because of the defective manuscript, is that in the day of salvation there will be judgement solely for those nations who mistreated Israel because of their injustice against the Israelites, leaving the universal judgement to the day of the resurrection.

205 Yefet ben Eli refers to Jl 4:2 in the same context as Jl 4:12 which is the judgment of the nations. Since R. Saadia specifies that the judgement of the nations is not the judgment of all people, which is reserved to the day of resurrection, we may conclude that he refers to the nations for their harsh treatment of the Israelites. The lacuna prohibits us from a full understanding of R. Saadia's interpretation. This is, however, Yefet ben Eli's interpretation.

206 Lit. "The last resting place."

207 הודׄא יה מכתובה is R. Saadia's translation of the partial citation of Is 65:6.

208 ולי literally 'friend."

209 ויכון דׄו כׄצמתי קד כתב כתאבא is R. Saadia's translation of the partial citation of Jb 31:35.

that are mentioned here, *the registers [that] were spread* (Dn 7:10), [include] what the population did against Israel[210] in order that God[211] punish them according to what He had told them: *And if you give retribution in my behalf* (Jl 4:4). He also said: *And I will pay back to Babylon and to all the inhabitants of Chaldea* (Jer 51:24). And: *According to what he gave them {He will remunerate them}* (Is 59:18)[212] and what is similar to this [meaning]. The proof that those books and the judgement that *the old man* (Dn 7:9) will exercise, regarding the conduct of the kingdoms and the nations,[213] is what he said after that about the judgement. When it happens part of the kingdoms deserve killings, anxiety and destruction. While the remaining [kingdoms] deserves the end of their reign, without disappearing. This was his discourse in the text of this chapter.

Dn 7:11

Then I looked: Because of the great words that the horn was saying the whole individual deserved to be killed, its body was destroyed and became fuel for the fire.[214]

Dn 7:12

As to the remaining individuals, their dominions disappeared[215] **and were given extension in life for a duration and a time.**

We already explained that the small horn represents the nation that came immediately after the kingdom[216] [... ...] what the atheists in its midst say against

210 Yefet ben Eli too considers that the conduct of the nations against Israel is the matter for God's judgment of the nations.
211 Lit. "He."
212 וכמא עלי אלאילא is R. Saadia's translation of the partial citation of Is 59:18. It is difficult to determine the precise meaning of אלאילא here. It could designate what God gave them, and the meaning becomes: He will punish them according to what He gave them. It could also designate the function in which He establish them, and the meaning becomes: He will punish them according to the function they occupy.
213 Lit: "Regarding what they did during the days of their reign."
214 Yefet ben Eli: "Then I was looking because of the voice that the horn was uttering, I was looking until I saw that it was killed and its body was delivered to the burning fire."
215 Yefet ben Eli: "And the dominion of all the individuals was removed."
216 The lacuna does not help in the attempt to discern the identity of those nations. In his commentary on Dn 7:8 R. Saadia mentions a nation that comes after Edom and was associated with it, as the nation represented by the small horn. He does not give a name to this nation, but most probably it is the kingdom of Islam. Maybe it

God and His nation. He clarified here that God will judge them and ask about it[217] then destroy them. In fact, He already said that he will lead those who are excessive among them to the mountain of the holy Temple, so that they may be destroyed there, some by fire and some by water, as he said: *And I will battle him with pestilence and blood; torrential rain, hailstones and sulfurous fire {I will pour upon him}* (Ez 38:22).[218] Some [will be destroyed] by afflictions in their flesh and their members according to his expression: *And this is the plague with which the Lord will bruise the peoples that fought against Jerusalem, their flesh shall rot away* (Zec 14:12). To the point that when one of them extends his hand to find strength in the hand of some one else, his hand disjoins his body,[219] as it was said: *And everyone shall lay hold on the hand of another and his hand shall rise up against the hand of his neighbor* (Zec 14:13). As to the others [... ...] they were not excessive against God and his nation by mortal intrigues [...] in the time of salvation, as he said to his beloved: *Ask from me* (Ps 2:8).[220] Some of them [... ...] they say: *You tell the remaining 'now, O kings, be clever, worship God with fear'* (Ps 2:10–11).[221] He also said: *Any nation and kingdom that does not {obey you}*(Is 60:12).[222] He explained that those who remain enter into

---

is because of this interpretation, and because he lived in an Islamic country that R. Saadia does not give a clear identity to the nation represented by the small horn.

217 It is unclear whether the expression 'the atheists in its midst' refers to a specific accusation against a particular group inside the hostile nations, that deserve a harsher punishment than the punishment reserved to the nations who are against God and against Israel. It is also possible that the same expression symbolizes the punishment of all hostile nations.

218 Yefet ben Eli interprets the destruction of the fourth animal's body as the killing of the king and the destruction of the rules that govern the kingdom represented by the fourth animal. As to its burning, or the burning of its body, it means, according to the same Yefet, the cessation of their laws and their worship.

219 Lit. "His hand, disjoined, will come with him." This very realistic, almost surgical understanding of Zec 14:13 is particular to R. Saadia. Others (Rashi, Radak) understand the extending the hands one to the other as attacking one another.

220 סאלני {אעטיך מן אלאמם נחלה} is R. Saadia's translation of the partial citation of Ps 2:8. The full translation of Ps 2:8a is mentioned here to show that R. Saadia does not understand this part as: 'Ask of me and I will give you the nations as inheritance,' but: 'Ask from me and I will give you inheritance from the nations.' It is not the nations that constitute the inheritance, but the inheritance will be taken from the nations.

221 ותקול אלבאקיין אלאן יא איה אלמלוך אעקלו, אעבדו אללה בכוף is the translation by R. Saadia's of the citation from Ps 2:10–11.

222 ואי אמה וממלכה לא {יטיעוך} is R. Saadia's translation of the partial citation of Is 60:12.

the religion[223] and direct their face to Jerusalem[224] and every year, they make the pilgrimage to the holy Temple, following his expression: *It will happen that the remaining from all the nations {that came up against Jerusalem will make the pilgrimage}* (Zec 14:16). Then he said:

Dn 7:13

Soon afterward[225] I saw among what man can see during the night that a young man was coming with clouds[226] until he reached the place of the old man. Then he brought the young man[227] in the presence of the old man.

Dn 7:14

The old man[228] gave him dominion glory and kingship and all peoples, nations and tongues show him obedience, his dominion is an eternal dominion that will never disappear and his kingship[229] will never change.[230]

The interpretation of *the young man* (Dn 7:13) is the savior. He described him as being young because of his growth, his prosperity, his excellency and his nobility.[231] That is why he imagines that his observer and the one who elevates him is an old man, so that the comparisons may be harmonious. The harmony, furthermore, comes from the fact that the one who saves is called בר אנש (Dn 7:13) *young man*. Because the first old man is one of the angels and in the language of the Kasdians the angel is called בר אלהין. That is the reason why the young has a name parallel to the old man, בר אנש (Dn 7:13).[232]

223 In other word, they convert to Judaism, usually called 'the religion.' According to Yefet ben Eli, the remaining nations, those represented by the first three horns, will be destroyed, not converted, when the reign of Israel appears.

224 ויסתקבלון אלקבלה literally: "The face the side toward which one must turn his face during the prayer." For Muslims, it is Mecca; for Jews, it is Jerusalem.

225 תם translated here by 'soon afterward' has no source in the MT.

226 TM: "With the clouds of the sky."

227 Yefet ben Eli: "Then they brought him."

228 Lit: "He."

229 ומלכה 'kingship' is R. Saadia's translation of ומלכותה which is normally translated by וממלכתה 'his kingdom."

230 Yefet ben Eli: "and his kingship will never be removed."

231 The particularity that Yefet ben Eli will put forward is the human figure of the savior, or the messiah's representation, in comparison to the animal figure of his enemies' representation.

232 Lit: "That is why this was called בר אנש parallel to that." That means that both have בר as part of their name: בר אלהין (= עתיק יומין) the old man, and the young man, which sharpens the contrast between them.

The reason why the young man does not appear with the Old man from the beginning of the story, but only when the old man is enthroned, chastising and beating the world, promising[233] it to the young man and bending its will, resides in the fact that one is an angel, while the other is a human being. The prophet made it clear in saying: *Behold, here I am sending my angel;*[234] *he shall clear the way before Me and suddenly the Lord whom you are seeking will come to His Temple; as to the angel of the covenant whom you delight in, behold, here he comes says the Lord of hosts* (Mal 3:1). Then he compared it to two salutary things. The first, highly positive: the fire that refines; the other, immediately useful: the ashes that wash. As he said after that:[235] *Who shall endure the day of his coming? Who shall stand his appearance? For he is like a refiner's fire and like the washer's product* (Mal 3:2). Thus he is *a refiner's fire* (Mal 3:2) for the excessive nations, as he said here: *And became fuel for the fire* (Dn 7:11). And [he is a refiner's fire] for the nation of Israel, as he told them: *I will refine your dross and remove all your untruthfulness* (Is 1:25).[236] And he is like *the washer's product* (Mal 3:2) for the sinners who did not exaggerate in their sin, as he said about them: *I will take away his blood from his mouth and the detestable things from between his teeth* (Zec 9:7). Concerning [the sinners] from the nation of Israel he said: *If God washes the dirt of all the family of Zion and cleans the rebellions of the family of Jerusalem* (Is 4:4).[237] When all these situations are in order [… …]. There are different meanings of him being in the

233 וימהרהא from the verb מהר "to settle a dowry for a marriage." As if the old man has the function of arranging the marriage of the young man. What is underlined in this image of marriage engagement, and following R. Saadia's mentality, is not the love between the two spouses but the obedience of the spouse (the world) to her husband (the young man).

234 מלאכי, ומלאך are translated here by 'my angel' 'angel' and not 'my messenger' and 'messenger,' following the interpretation of Dn 7:13 by R. Saadia.

235 Lit: "One of them, in the highest situations, is the fire that refines, the others, in a close situation, is the ashes from alkali salt (אלאשנאן) that washes."

236 ואסבך נקאא זיפך ואזיל גמיע סתוקך is R. Saadia's translation of the citation from Is 1:25. The word סתוק designates something false because it does not have the value that it should have, like false money. It is translated here by 'untruthfulness.'

237 אדא גסל אללה וסך אל ציון גמיעא ומעאצי אל ירושלם ינטפהא is the translation by R. Saadia of the citation from Is 4:4. His translation has three particularities. First, he translates אם by אדא 'if' the first part of a conditional proposition that he never completes. The usual translation is 'when.' The second particularity is that R. Saadia avoids the literal rendering of the Hebrew expression בנות ציון 'daughters of Zion.' His translation is אל ציון literally 'family of Zion'. The other Hebrew expression that R. Saadia avoids to translating literally is דמי ירושלם 'the blood of Jerusalem.' His translation is ומעאצי אל ירושלם 'and the rebellions of Jerusalem.'

clouds. One of them is honor,[238] similar to what Elijah explained when he said: *And Elijah went up in a storm of heaven* (2 Kgs 2:11).[239] [Another meaning] is the quickness with the appearing and disappearing as he said: *Who are those who fly like clouds* (Is 60:8)?[240] [Another meaning] is because there is the pardon with him, as he said: *I will erase your sins like a passing cloud and pass over your errors like mist* (Is 44:22).[241] [Another meaning] is that with him appears the inspiration: *In a pillar of cloud He speaks to them* (Ps 99:7).[242] [Another meaning] is the appearance of the Shekinah as he said: *The cloud filled the House of the Lord* (1 Kgs 8:10).

The meaning of [the expression]: *Until he reached the place of the old man* (Dn 7:13) is to demonstrate that he proceeds by energy other than his own or the energy of the old man,[243] until he reaches his position. It is the energy coming from the Lord of the universe, as he said to the nation: *I will strengthen them in the Lord, and they shall walk in His name, oracle of the Lord* (Zec 10:12). [His expression]: *Then he brought the young man in the presence of the old man* (Dn 7:13)[244] means that those who wait on the old man[245] receive the young man and present him between the hands of the old man in order that he give him the kingship, as he said after that: *The old man gave him dominion* (Dn 7:14). [The expression]: *And all peoples, nations and tongues show him obedience* (Dn 7:14) designates what we have described, that the population shows him the sixty elders.[246] Plus the eighty mentioned in the Torah and what comes after from the clans and tribes, as we have explained in commenting *here is the ex-*

238 The idea is that being in the clouds means being in a high position, which is synonymous with being honorable. Yefet ben Eli's interpretation of being in the clouds is that people will see him like they see clouds. He does not expand on his explanation.

239 The part of 2 Kgs 2:11 that R. Saadia quotes is not an explanation by Elijah, contrary to what he writes. It is a narrative report and not direct discourse by Elijah.

240 מן האולי כאלגיום יטירון is R. Saadia's translation of the citation from Is 60:8.

241 פאני אמחו דנובך כאלגים אלמאר אתאגאוז כטאיאך אלסחאב is R. Saadia's translation of the citation from Is 44:22. Note the translation of the Hebrew כעב literally 'a cloud,' by the Judeo-Arabic כאלגים אלמאר 'the passing cloud'.

242 בעמוד מן גמאם יכאטבהם is R. Saadia's translation of the citation from Ps 99:7.

243 It is not clear why the expression ועד עתיק יומיא מטא (Dn 7:13) is translated here by 'until he reached the place of the old man.' Is there anything particular in the meaning of the verb מטא 'to reach' that allows such interpretation? R. Saadia does not elaborate. For Yefet ben Eli it is the old man who brings the savior, or the messiah close to him.

244 This is R. Saadia's translation, not very literal, of וקדמוהי הקרבוהי (Dn 7:13).

245 Lit: "Him."

246 Uncertain reading.

planation of the generation of the sons of Noah (Gn 10:1).[247] And the meaning of the expression: *His kingdom is a kingdom forever* (cf. Dn 7:14)[248] designates the eternity of the kingship that our Lord promised him when the prophet said: *Israel too shall be saved by God, an eternal salvation* (Is 45:17).[249] [It is a salvation] that will never be removed as far as the universe exists: *That your sun shall set no more, nor shall your moon, but superior to that is that God becomes your eternal light, and that the days of your sadness disappear* (Is 60:20)[250] and similar passages. As to the expression of Daniel pertaining to the young man: *And all peoples, nations and tongues show him obedience* (Dn 7:14) it designates something that he sees in his dream. His expression: *His dominion is eternal* (Dn 7:14) does not designate something that he can see, but a voice that he had heard in his dream and he repeated it.[251] when the vision ended, he informed us how some angels explained it to him, saying:

Dn 7:15

When my spirit in my body[252] was grieved and the vision of my eyes[253] startled me[254]

Dn 7:16

I came forward to one of those who were standing[255] and asked him about the truth in all that, he communicated it[256] to me and made known to me the interpretation of the matter.

247 והדׄא שׄרח תאליד בני נוח is R. Saadia's translation of the quoted part of Gn 10:1. This quotation is meant to refer the reader to the whole of Gn 10.

248 In his translation of Dn 7:14 R. Saadia renders מלכות 'kingdom' by the Arabic מלך 'kingship.'

249 כדׄאך אסראיל מגׄאתׄ באללה גׄותׄ אלדהור is R. Saadia's translation of the citation from Is 45:17.

250 מן חיתׄ לא תגׄיב שׄמסך אבדא ולא קמרך לכן אפצׄל מנהא יכון אללה לך נור אלדהר ותפנא איאם חזנך is R. Saadia's translation of the citation from Is 60:20.

251 Lit. "But a voice that he had head heard then said 'his dominion is eternal' (Dn 7:14).

252 MT: "In the middle of my sheath." It is also the translation of Yefet ben Eli.

253 MT: "Visions of my head."

254 R. Saadia chooses to establish a relation of subordination conjunction (starting by *when* in v,15) between Dn 7:15–16. Yefet ben Eli does not see such relation between the two verses.

255 Yefet ben Eli: "One of the angels who were standing." R. Saadia will explain that, following interpreters that he does not name and in reference to Dn 10:13 'the one who is standing' could be the angel Michael.

256 MT: "He said to me."

Concerning the word אתכרית (Dn 7:15) *my spirit was grieved,* it is the targum of ותפעם רוחי. It was not suitable that this word be in another passage of the Bible.[257] The exact meaning of בגוא נדנה (Dn 7:15) is 'in the bottom of something deep'[258] as the Bible said: *And he put his sword into its sheath* נדנה (1 Chr 21:27). The frame of the spirit being the body, I interpreted נדנה as body. It is from this meaning that the saying derives: *I cannot be part of those people* (Gn 6:3).[259] The meaning is that he does not stay stable. He also explains [the expression]: *In my body* (Dn 7:15) as in the middle of the passage, the movement, the trouble, like in [the passage]: *Among them, those who were shaken like the guardian hut* (Is 24:20)[260] and what is similar to that. His expression: וחזוי ראשי (Dn 7:15)[261] is a vision of eye, as it possible [to say] in Aramaic.[262]

His expression: קרבת על חד *I came forward to one* (Dn 7:16) is similar to לחד קרבת. Like אל that could replace ועל. His expression: *Those who were standing* (Dn 7:16) designates those who were standing between the old man's hand, as he said [earlier]: *And myriads of myriads stood before him* (Dn 7:10). They are of higher dignity *than those who serve him* (Dn 7:10). It was said that the angel mentioned here is Michael, because of what Gabriel said afterward: *when Michael, one of the first lords, [came to my rescue]* (Dn 10:13). It is a credible [interpretation]. His expression: *I asked* (Dn 7:16) and his expression: *Made known to me* (Dn 7:16) seem to be in the future [form], while their [meaning belongs] to the past. They are comparable to the expression: *God came from Teman* (Hb 3:3),[263] and the expression: *They made a calf in Horeb*

257 R. Saadia's declaration about word אתכרית as hapax is expressed in a particular: It is because of its unsuitable meaning that such word should not be mentioned more than one time.

258 פי גוף אלגֹמר has the obvious following meaning: 'In the bottom of the mass of the water that covers a surface.' However, the example that R. Saadia will mention immediately after his explanation does not authorize such translation. Hence the translation of אלגֹמר here by 'something deep' since the depth is what is specific to this word.

259 לא ינגֹמד דאתי פי הולא אלנאס is R. Saadia's translation of the quoted part of Gn 6:3. Literally 'I can not immerge my identity in those people.'

260 נֹעֹ ונד והתנודדה. While it is a clear reference to Is 24:20 the first two words (with a supralinear point on the first two letters designating a mistake) are not clear enough and probably a misquote of Isaiah. ומנהם מן נאד כאלערזאל is R. Saadia's translation of the citation from Is 24:20. It should be noticed that אלערזאל 'the guardian hut,' taken here as example of something which could be shaken, is built sometimes among the branches of a tree.

261 Lit: "The vision of the head."

262 Lit: "In the language of the Targum."

263 יבוא is 'He comes' from 'to come' בוא having a past meaning.

(Ps 106:19),[264] *so the earth opened up then swallowed Datan* (Ps 106:17)[265] and what is similar. Then he continued the explanation.

Dn 7:17

Those great individuals are four kingdoms that rise on earth.

Dn 7:18

Then the elevated saints[266] receive the kingship and inherit it forever, forever and ever.

This what we have already said, that [the expression]: ארבעה מלכין (Dn 7:17) designate four kingdoms, not four persons. That is because of what he said thereafter: מלכו רביעאה (Dn 7:23) *There will be a fourth kingdom*. The lesson of all this here is that no other kingdom than those four shall enslave the Israelites. Because he adds: *Then the elevated saints receive the kingship* (Dn 7:18) which points to the Israelites whom God honors by those two words,[267] since he told them: *He will elevate you, and you will become a holy people* (Dt 26:19).[268] He also said: *God, your Lord, will elevate you* (Dt 28:1)[269] and: *God will establish you a holy people for Himself* (Dt 28:9).[270]

We have already explained in the commentary of the Book of Ester that the fathers of the nations are four: Shem, Ham and Yefet, as he said: *Those are the three sons of Noah, from them the people spread out on the earth* (Gn 9:19).[271] Plus Abraham, following his expression: *Because I made you the father of many*

264 וכאנוא יעמלון עגל פי חריב is R. Saadia's translation of the partial citation of Ps 106:19. יַעֲשׂוּ is 'they make' from עשׂא 'to make' translated here by וכאנוא יעמלון 'they made' or 'they were making.'

265 חתי אנפתחת אלארץ פבלעת דתן is R. Saadia's translation of the partial citation of Ps 106:17. תפתח 'it opens' from פתח 'to open' and תבלע 'it swallows' from בלע 'to swallow' are translated here in the past: אנפתחת פבלעת 'it opened up then swallowed.'

266 אלקדוסין אלמתעאליין 'the elevated or the high saints' and not 'the saints of the most high' as in Yefet ben Eli's translation and the usual one of קדישי עליונין. For R. Saadia the expression 'the elevated or the high saints' designates the Israelites.

267 The two words are קדישי עליונין. All the examples that follow have those two words, in Hebrew.

268 ואן יגעלך עליא, ואן תכון שעבא מקדסא is R. Saadia's translation of the quoted part of Dt 26:19.

269 יגעלך אללה רבך עאליא is R. Saadia's translation of the partial citation of Dt 28:1.

270 וינצבך אללה לה שעבא מקדסא is R. Saadia's translation of the partial citation of Dt 28:9.

271 האולי אלתלתה בנו נוח ומנהם תפרק אלנאס פי אלארץ is R. Saadia's translation of the partial citation of Gn 9:19.

nations (Gn 17:5).[272] The royal family of the first one who enslaved us belongs to Ham, and that is Nebuchadnezzar the king of Babylon. He said about Nimrod, son of Kush, son of Ham: *The beginning of his kingship was Babylon* (Gn 10:10).[273] The royal family of the second [of those who enslaved us] was in the country of Elam, son of Shem. They are the Persians as he said: *As if I was in Suza the fortress in the country of Elam* (Dn 8:2). The third [of those who enslaved us] are the Greek that the text explains[274] clearly, saying: The sons of Yefet, Gomer תרך, Magog ויאגוג, Maday ומאהאת and Yavan ואליונאניה (Gn 10:2).[275] The forth [of those who enslaved us] are Edom and the Ismaelites[276] who are sons of Abraham. He started by Edom, because he is the son of Abraham and Isaac all together. We should not imagine that there will be another kingdom that enslaves us, because there is no other father of the nations. That is why [once he said]: *Four kingdoms* (Dn 7:17) he added: *Then the elevated saints receive the kingship* (Dn 7:18). Then he said:

Dn 7:19

Then I wanted to ascertain the fact of the fourth individual who was different from all. In fact it was very frightful; its teeth are of iron and its claws were of bronze; it devours, crashes and tramples what remain by its feet.[277]

Dn 7:20

The ten horns which are on its head and the other that rose and three that fell before it;[278] **that horn**[279] **was standing upright; it has eyes and a mouth saying enormities; its appearance is greater than its counterparts.**

Dn 7:21

And I saw that the horn was fighting the holy men and overpowering them.[280]

272 לאני געלתך אבא גמהור אלאמם is R. Saadia's translation of the partial citation of Gn 17:5.

273 וכאן אול מלכה באביל is R. Saadia's translation of the partial citation of Gn 10:10.

274 פצחת אלתוריה literally 'that the theory or the words in their hidden meaning mean.'

275 בנו יפת תרך ויאגוג ומאהאת ואליונאניה is R. Saadia's translation of the partial citation of Gn 10:2.

276 Lit: "Ishmael."

277 Yefet ben Eli: "And kicks what remains by its feet."

278 The sentence does not seem complete, since it starts by ואמא 'as to the ten horns…' with no second part answering the first.

279 Lit: "The horn."

Dn 7:22

Until the coming of the old man, then the judgement became in favor of the eminent saints;[281] the end of the time had come and the saints inherited the kingship.

Daniel added here three points that he did not mention in the earlier text of the vision. He completed it here, in order to achieve it and to explain it. The first point is that the fourth individual has claws of bronze, as he said: *And its claws were of bronze* (Dn 7:19). This is appropriate for animals [designating] their increasing strength in trampling and lashing out something. It is a meaning that helps [him to say]: *And tramples what remain by its feet* (Dn 7:19). However, if we transpose the interpretation to human beings the meaning of the claws designates the act of writing and of being stable.[282] And because the situation is negative, the act of writing designates hatred from sins[283] and conservation of the offenses. It designates too the pardon of the sin, as he said metaphorically: *The sin of Judah is written with pen of iron, with the point of a diamond* (Jer 17:1). The second point pertains to what was mentioned about the small horn, that his appearance became greater than its counterparts, because he said: *Its appearance is greater than its counterparts* (Dn 7:20). It is what is obvious about the fourth kingdom, Edom: Its appearance is greater [than the appearance of the prior three kingdoms]. The third point is the fight against the Israelites, as he said: *The horn was fighting the holy men* (Dn 7:21). It remains victorious over them until the advent of the time of salvation: *[It was] overpowering them* (Dn 7:21) *until the coming of the old man* (Dn 7:22).

We already know that his expression: *Then the judgement became in favor [of the eminent saints]* (Dn 7:22) concerns *the old man* (Dn 7:22), that he examines requests from the people. Why is it then that he says: *The judgement became in favor of [the eminent saints]* (Dn 7:22) without any investigation by the Israelites of [those requests]? We answer that he does not mean that they examine the request of others.[284] What he wants to say is that the old man examines

280 The misuse of pronouns of in Yefet ben Eli's translation of Dn 7:21 alters the meaning of the verse and makes it possible to understand that the saints overcome the horn in their fight against it.

281 Yefet ben Eli: קדיסין אלעאלי literally 'the saints of the most high.

282 'Claws' transposed to human beings designate fingers that help to write or to seize something. This could explain the two meanings of writing and being stable that R. Saadia deduces from the mention of claws.

283 חקדא ללדנוב could also be understood as 'hatred of sins.'

284 The objection that R. Saadia answers does not seem clear, since he establishes from the beginning that the old man alone is the one who judges. Is there another reading

the request [of the Israelites] and pronounces the sentence in their favor and against their oppressors as we already explained [in commenting on the expression]: *And there I will contend with them for My people and My heritage Israel* (Jl 4:2). And As we know, God[285] said to Abraham: *I will judge too the people that enslave them* (Gn 15:14).[286] He also told Moses: *I saw the pressure that the Egyptians apply on them* (Ex 3:9).[287] And He said about the kingdom of Babylon: *Because if you become angry against My nation and waste My chosen ones whom I delivered into your hand, you will show mercy toward them* (Is 47:6).[288] And about the Persian Kingdom he said: *I am very angry with those nations who are at ease, for I was a little angry, but they increased the affliction* (Zec 1:15). And he said concerning all the nations: *God will judge in favor of His people and will pardon His servants* (Dt 32:36).[289] He also said: *And gives back revenge to My enemies and reward to those who hate Me* (Dt 32:41);[290] and also: *Because He avenges the blood of His servants and bring back that vengeance against His enemies* (Dt 32:43).[291] Then he answers the question saying:[292]

---

of this passage that allows another interpretation (That the Israelites are the ones who examine the requests of other people)? In this case, the eminent saints designate all the Israelites. Nothing is being specified about the origin of this objection.

285 Lit: "He."

286 ואיצא אלקום אלדין יסתכדמונהם פאחכם עליהם is R. Saadia's translation of the partial citation of Gn 15:14.

287 ראית אלצגט אלדי אלמצריין יצאגטונהם is R. Saadia's translation of the partial citation of Ex 3:9.

288 לאנך אדא סכטת עלי אמתי ובדלת צפותי ואסלמתהא פי ידך לם תצירי רחמה להם is R. Saadia's translation of the partial citation of Is 47:6. R. Saadia's interpretation is very peculiar. He does not read the verbs as first person singular קצפתי and חללתי, but reads them as second person feminine, like שמת which describes the action of the daughter of Zion. Hence, the particular translation of this quotation which illustrates, according to R. Saadia, the injustice that the daughter of Zion inflict on the Israelites, and not the Lord's anger. However, this harmonization puts R. Saadia in a new difficulty: there is nothing in the verse that explains why the Lord put the Israelites in the hands of the daughter of Zion. Derenbourg in his translation of R. Saadia's rendering of the Book of Isaiah does not pay attention to his particular interpretation and translates Is 47:6 directly from the masoretic text.

289 אד יחכם אללה לשעבה וען עבידה יצפח is R. Saadia's translation of the partial citation of Dt 32:36. There is a particular understanding of the Hebrew verb חנן 'to be merciful' translated by the Arabic verb צפח 'to pardon.'

290 וארד אלאנתקאם לאעדאיי ואלמכאפה עלי שאניי is R. Saadia's translation of the partial citation of Dt 32:41.

291 לאנה ינתקם דם עבידה פירד תלך אלנקמה עלי אדאיה is R. Saadia's translation of the partial citation of Dt 32:43.

292 Lit. "Then he answers the answer after the question and said."

Dn 7:23
And this is what he said: The interpretation of the fourth individual is that there will be a fourth kingdom on earth that will change the earlier kingdoms,[293] as if it devours all the country,[294] tramples it and knocks it.

Dn 7:24
And the interpretation[295] of the ten horns is that ten kings arise from that kingdom and another king arises after them; he will change what was made by the former ones, and puts down three kings.[296]

Dn 7:25
He will speak against the Most High,[297] lies about the eminent saints,[298] and aspires to change their feasts and laws. They remain in his hand a period, two periods and a half [of a period].

His introduction: *And this is what he said* (Dn 7:23) does not refer to *the old man*, even if it is in the continuation of his mention.[299] Because *the old man* does not explain anything to Daniel. In fact, what he designates by *And this is what he said* (Dn 7:23) is *one of those who were standing* (Dn 7:16) of whom he solicited the interpretation. I mean the interpretation of *the fourth individual* (Dn 7:23). We already established all this. I mean [the interpretation] of *as if it devours all the country, tramples it and knocks it* (Dn 7:23). [As to the interpretation] of *the ten horns* (Dn 7:24) and all what follows, he mentioned it briefly, according to what is right and avoiding a further illicit explanation. However, he

293 תגׄיר מא תקדם מן אלממאלך does not mean that the individual or the beast is different from what was before him, which is Yefet ben Eli's translation and the usual modern translation, but for R. Saadia, it means that the individual or the beast changes the kingdoms that were before it.

294 R. Saadia translates Aramaic ארעא 'earth' by the Arabic אלבלאד 'the country.' He also adds וכאנהא 'as if' transforming the fact that the beast or the individual eats all the earth into comparison: it exercises such violence as if it is devouring the earth or the country.

295 'And the interpretation of' is added by R. Saadia to his translation and has no source in the MT.

296 יגׄיר מא תקדם מן אלאולין יצׄע תׄלאתה מלוך. Once again R. Saadia is different in his translation. The last king is not different, according to him, but he changes others and puts down three kings. In his translation, Yefet ben Eli is closer to the masoretic text.

297 Yefet ben Eli: "He speaks about the Most High."

298 Yefet ben Eli: "the saint of the Most High."

299 In other words: Even if the precedent verse Dn 7:22, speaks about the 'old man.'

explained more about the conditions of the kingdom related to Edom. He had already said: *[The horn] was fighting the holy men and overpowering them* (Dn 7:21). And he made known here what was the reason for the war saying that it was in order that they leave Judaism[300] and in order to alter [the appointed times of] their feasts and their laws. That is what he asserted [by saying]: *And he aspires to change their feasts and laws* (Dn 7:25).

As to ויסבר (Dn 7:25) *and he aspires*, it is the targum of *I did not think of seeing your face* (Gn 48:11).[301] Concerning זמנין (Dn 7:25) *a time* it designates feasts, like in the expression תלת זמנין which is the targum of *three times* (Ex 23:17).[302] Concerning דת (Dn 7:25) it designates the laws of the Torah, as he said: *And from His right hand He brought to the multitude of Jerusalem the Law of light* (Dt 33:2).[303] And their enemy said: *And their laws were different from all people* (Est 3:8). And their friend told Ezra: *According to the law of your God which is in your hand* (Ezr 7:14). His intention then is to change their laws fabricating lies, as he said: *He lies about the eminent saints* (Dn 7:25).

Having already said: וזמנא מטא (Dn 7:22), which designates the end of the time or the extremity, he explained its duration, saying: *They remain in his hand a period, two periods and a half [of a period]* (Dn 7:25) which bears four harmonious explanations that lead to the same point. Two of these explanations put together the duration of the last kingdom and the [the duration] of the former kingdoms. He says: *They remain in his hand* (Dn 7:25) until the completion of *a period, two periods and a half [of a period]* (Dn 7:25) which does not mean that all of [those kingdoms] are in the hand of the last one. But, one under the power of the other, successively. Thus, the measure עדן according to the first explanation is four hundred years, similar to [the duration] of the Israelites' slavery in Egypt.[304] Because קץ וזמן ועדן are comparable in that they mean duration and times. Therefore, the measure of עדן is four hundred years; the measure of עדנין is eight hundred years, and the measure of ופלג עדן is two hundred years.[305]

300 Lit. "In order to leave the religion."

301 אלנטר ונהך לם אטן בה is R. Saadia's translation of the citation from Gn 48:11. In fact, what R. Saadia wants to indicate is that the Aramaic יסבר has the same meaning as the Hebrew פללתי which is translated by R. Saadia as the Arabic אטן which has the original meaning of 'I think.' The same verb in Gn 48:11 has the meaning of 'I hope.'

302 שלש פעמים is R. Saadia's translation of the partial citation of Ex 23:17.

303 {ואתי רבואת אלקדס} בשריעה נור מן ימינה להם is R. Saadia's translation of the partial citation of Dt 33:2.

304 Lit. "Similar to the slavery that retained the people in Egypt."

305 For Yefet ben Eli, while עדן designates a specific period, עדנין does not mean twice the period designated by עדן. According to his commentary of Dn 7:25 עדנין means more than the period designated by עדן. While פלג עדן means less than a period des-

That makes one thousand four hundred years. This is from *the deportation of Jehoiakim* until the time of salvation. In fact, this discourse was addressed to Daniel *in the first year of king Belshazzar* (Dn 7:1) which is the fifty second year of the Jehoiakim's deportation, because his deportation was at the eighth year from the kingship of Nebuchadnezzar, as he said: *And he took him in the eighth year of his reign* (2 Kgs 24:12). Nebuchadnezzar ruled forty five years, and what remained then is thirty eight years.[306] Evil-Merodach his son ruled twenty three [years]. Belshazzar, his grand son, [ruled] one year. That makes sixty two years. Two uncompleted years remain to Belshazzar. One belongs to Cyrus. That makes sixty three; plus two years that belong to Cyrus which makes [the total sixty five] years. Then in the third year of the reign of Cyrus, Daniel was told that one thousand three hundred thirty five years.[307] That makes the total one thousand four hundred years.

According to the second of the two explanations which considers the servitude[308] globally,[309] עדן ועדנין ופלג עדן (Dn 7:25) is similar to his expression למועד מועדים וחצי (Dn 12:7).[310] The ו added to ועדנין is to mark the succession, as in the expression: *The sons of Elah and Kenaz* (1 Chr 4:15),[311] and in the expression: *There were the heads of the houses of their fathers: Efer and Ishi* (1 Chr 5:24), and in the expression: *[From the east sides fifty cubits]* (Ex 27:14) *of which fifteen cubits of hangings on the one flank* (Ex 27:14).[312] The complete form would be: עד עדן ועדנין ופלג עדן. It is similar to [the expression]: למועד מועדים וחצי (Dn 12:7). In this case the first מועד is helper [to understand] the discourse. Like when you say: In the laps of time of fifty days,[313] and ac-

---

ignated by עדן and not the exact half of the duration signified by עדן as it is the case for R. Saadia.

306 Forty five years minus eight, the years before the deportation, makes thirty eight, the years being incomplete.

307 This way of reasoning by R. Saadia is disputed and his name and the school of the Rabbanites are mentioned by Yefet ben Eli in his commentary on Dn 12:13.

308 In other word, the domination of the Israelites and the disappearance of their political institutions.

309 Lit. "That consider the servitude from its beginning until its end."

310 עדן ועדנין ופלג עדן (Dn 7:25) is translated by R. Saadia as 'a period מדה, two periods and half a period.' As to his translation of מועד מועדים וחצי (Dn 12:7) his translation is as follows: 'Time of their times and a half [of a time].' Which indicates that R. Saadia understands מועדים as 'their time', reading the ם as the remnant of the third person plural pronoun הם. Hence the difficulty of comparing the expression of Dn 7:25 and Dn 12:7.

311 תעקיב succession, which in Arabic is signified by the letter 'פ' and 'תם.'

312 מנהא כמס עשרה דראעא קלוע ללכם is R. Saadia's translation of the citation from Ex 27:14.

313 באגל נ׳ יום.

cording to my interpretation of this verse in its place.[314] We also say that מועדים designates the duration of the state of Israel, from their departure of Egypt until the destruction of the Temple, which makes eight hundred ninety years. Out of them four hundred eighty until the construction of the Temple. And four hundred ten is the duration of the frequentation of the Temple. The half of this period is four hundred forty five. That makes one thousand three hundred thirty five, which is the period mentioned in the verse: *Happy is he who waits* (Dn 12:12). Thus the Israelites will be under the domination of *the other king that rises after them* (cf. Dn 7:24) until the completion of what remains from the *their time and the half [of the time]* (Dn 12:7), starting from the beginning of the servitude.

The other two interpretations pertain to the servitude that is under the last [kingdom] alone. According to one of them, the third interpretation, עדן [designates] one hundred years; ועדנין [designates] two hundred years, and עדן ופלג [designates] fifty years. The total is three hundred fifty years, which is approximately what remains from the one thousand three hundred thirty five years that belong to *the other king that rises after them* (cf. Dn 7:24). According to the second of those particular interpretations עדן [designates] the duration of the reign of Babylon, which is seventy years; ועדנין [designates] the duration of the two kingdoms, the Persian and the Greek; which is two hundred thirty two years. Because the Persian reign [lasted] fifty two [years] then the Greek reign started and their kingdom remained one hundred eighty years. The total is three hundred two years.[315] As to [the expression] *a half of a period* (Dn 7:25) it designates half the first period which is [the duration] of the Babylonian reign. That is thirty five years. The total globally comes close to three hundred forty years. It is licit and accurate if any of those four interpretations has been retained. One of them, namely the second, has more veracity than the others. Then he said:

Dn 7:26

Once he established the judgement his dominion was taken away from him, was ended, destroyed until the end of time.[316]

Dn 7:27

And the kingdom, the dominion and the glory that belong to the kingdom of all what is under heaven, was given to the group of eminent saints,[317] their reign is forever and all the empire listen to them and obey [them].[318]

314 In other words: According to R. Saadia's commentary on Dn 12:7.

315 The total of עדן 70 plus ועדנין 232.

316 R. Saadia reads Dn 7:26 as a temporal clause, which is not the reading of Yefet ben Eli, for example.

Dn 7:28

Here is the end of the story[319] and I, Daniel, was very terrified by thoughts, my aspect changed, and I conserved the story in my heart.

His expression: *When he established the judgement his dominion was taken away from him* (Dn 7:26) is similar to what we have already specified, that when the judgment was established, the dominion of all the kingdoms was taken away. It is same as in the expression: *I will overturn the throne of kingdoms and destroy the strength of the kingdoms of the nations* (Hg 2:22) and comparable [passages]. As to his expression: *And the kingdom, the dominion and the glory that belong to the kingdom of all that is under heaven was given to the group of eminent saints* (Dn 7:27), it is like his expressions: *And the kingdom shall belong to the Lord* (Ob 21), *and the Lord shall be king over all the earth, on that day the Lord shall be one and His name one* (Zec 14:9). His expression: *Here is the end of the story* (Dn 7:28) means that the limit and the ends of this prophecy and the prophecies of all the prophets [is directed] toward the days of salvation. As to the explanations of what will happen in the last resting place, it is not yet revealed to us. As the sages, of blessed memory, told us: *All the prophets prophesied only for the days of the Messiah, as to the world to come* (bBerk 34b), *no eye did see another god than you accomplishing something like that for him that solicits him* (Is 64:3).[320] The explanations about what will happen in the last resting place, however, will be revealed during the time of salvation, as he said: *And it shall happen that I will pour out My spirit on all flesh, and your sons and your daughters shall prophesy* (Jl 3:1) and the [meaning of what] is remaining of the passage.[321] The [commentary] of chapter seven is completed.

---

317 Yefet ben Eli: "Was given to the people of the saint of the Most High." His normal translation of עליון is the Most High or God. He mentions, however, the possibility that עליון could be said of the people of Israel, in reference to Dt 26:19.

318 Yefet ben Eli's ending of Dn 7:27 is very peculiar. He finishes his translation by 'and all the rulers obey him and gather ויגתמעון.' There is no reason to have 'and gather' as a translation for וישתמעון other than the phonetic similarity between this Aramaic word and the Arabic word by which it is translated. In fact the similarity is such that there is one single letter that differentiates the two words. All this, however, has nothing to do with their meaning.

319 R. Saadia uses the Arabic word קצה to translate the Aramaic מלתא, while Yefet ben Eli uses the Arabic word אלקול to translate the same Aramaic word.

320 לם תר עין מעבודא סואך צנע מתל דלך למן ירגוה is R. Saadia's translation of the citation from Is 64:3. These words of Is 64:3 are quoted in Berk 34b.

321 Lit. "The remaining of the story."

Chapter 8

The explanation of the eighth chapter of this book, that contains clarifications of what is relative to the four kingdoms and was already mentioned.[1] Daniel said in its beginning:

Dn 8:1

In the third year of the reign of Belshazzar I, Daniel, was shown a vision following what was shown to me earlier.[2]

He added the expression: *Following what was shown to me earlier* (Dn 8:1). We know, however, [that this vision] came later, since the first [vision] was in *the first year {of the king Belshazzar}* (Dn 7:1) and this one is *in the third year of the reign of Belshazzar* (Dn 8:1). In fact, what he wanted to say by his expression: *Following what was shown to me earlier* (Dn 8:1) is that sources of this dream are part of the meanings of the former vision: Each one represent the completion of the former one.[3] There is another meaning to his expression: *Following what was shown to me earlier* (Dn 8:1). It indicates that the nations establish peaceful truce with the Israelites, after [the time] when they used to frighten and terrify them. The kingdoms, in the first vision, had been compared to the lion, the bear, the leopard and the elephant. These are all terrifying [elements]. While in the second vision [the nations] are comparable to the ram and to the goat, which are both clean[4] and inoffensive. That is what He promised the nation [of Israel]; that He soften their enemies and decrease their harm as he said: *He put mercy for them in all those who deported them* (Ps 106:46).[5] He said about the king of Babylon: *I will have mercy on him, that he may show you mercy* (Jer 42:12). And about the king of the Persians he said: *Who are you, great mountain? Before Zerubbabel become plain* (Zec 4:7). He also said, glob-

1 Lit. "That contains clarifications of what remains between the parts of the four kingdoms already mentioned."

2 Yefet ben Eli: "Following what appeared to me at the beginning."

3 Uncertain reading. Lit: "The sources of this dream enter in the meanings of starting by the closest, and being its complement." The passage is also unclear because this part of the manuscript is damaged.

4 עפיפאן literally 'chaste' or 'moderate in his use of pleasurable things.'

5 ונעל להם רחמה ענד גמיע סאביהם is R. Saadia's translation of Ps 106:46.

ally, if [Israel] confront fire or water God will preserve us from its heat and its cold, as He said: *If you pass through waters, they will not submerge you, and if you walk through fire it will not burn you* (Is 43:2).[6] Then he added:

Dn 8:2

And I saw in my sleep[7] as if I was in Shushan the fortress in the country of Elam,[8] and I was on the shore[9] Ulay.[10]

Dn 8:3

I lifted up my eyes and saw a ram standing on the shore,[11] with two horns; the two horns were great, one greater than the other, and greater than them is the one that rose later.

Dn 8:4

I saw it butting whoever it found[12] westward, northward, southward, and no beast could stand in its presence and no one could deliver from its hand; thus it accomplishes in them[13] what it pleases and exaggerates.[14]

Dn 8:5

While I was trying to understand, here comes a goat from the west, running[15] over the face of the earth and it did not touch it because of velocity its running,[16] it has a horn with ramification[17] between its eyes.

6 ולו גזת פי אלמא פאנא מעך ואלאנהאר לא תגרקך ולו סרת פי אלנאר לא תנכוי ואללהיב לא ישתעל פיך is R. Saadia's translation of Is 43:2.

7 Yefet ben Eli: "I was contemplating the vision and in my vision I was as if I am in Shushan the fortress." In his commentary, however, he mentions that the vision happened while he was sleeping.

8 Yefet ben Eli: "Which is in the country of Khuse."

9 שט has the meaning of both river and shore. As a river, it designates the Tigris specifically. Yefet ben Eli translates this word by 'river.' However, in his commentary R. Saadia will distinguish between שט and נהר. And since the usual word for 'river' is נהר the word שט is translated by 'shore.'

10 R. Saadia does not translate ואראה בחזון which can be translated by 'and contemplated the vision' Yefet ben Eli: "I looked in the vision," or "I saw by vision."

11 Yefet ben Eli: 'Standing before קדאם the river נהר.' While R. Saadia's translation is 'standing on the shore עלי שט.'

12 מן וגד 'whoever it found' is added by R. Saadia and has no trace in the MT.

13 "In them" is added by R. Saadia and has no source in the MT.

14 הגדיל is translated by R. Saadia by the Arabic word אסרף 'he exaggerates in his wrongdoing.' While Yefet ben Eli translates the same Hebrew verb by the Arabic word כבר which has the meaning of 'becoming great.'

15 "Running" is added by R. Saadia and has no source in the MT.

Dn 8:6

It reached the ram with two horns that I saw[18] standing on the shore and charged at it with the strength of its ferocity.

Dn 8:7

And I saw that when the goat reached the ram,[19] it raged against it, hit it, broke its two horns and the ram did not have enough strength to stand between its hands; so it threw the ram[20] to the ground, trampled it, and the ram had no one to deliver it from its hand.[21]

The introduction of this discourse demonstrates that Daniel in fact was in Babylon. However, he was looking at Shushan, like someone in Baghdad looking as if he was in Basra. Concerning אובל אולי (Dn 8:2) our friends think unanimously that it is a river.[22] Still, they exchange words. Some consider that אובל is the name of the shore and אולי is the name of the river. Some consider that אובל is the name of the river and אולי is the name of the shore. As to those who abandoned its meaning as 'river' and said [that it means] 'buildings' 'time' 'energies' [their interpretations] are eccentric and we do not mention them along with those [who form] the common consent.

The continuous interpretation of this vision is part of the explanation that Gabriel gave to Daniel. That the ram represents kings of Medes and Persians, as he will say: *The ram with two horns that you saw represents the kings of the Medes and the Persians* (8:20). Daniel has this vision the year of the disappearance of the Belshazzar's reign, who was the last king of Babylon, and the beginning of the Persian reign. The meaning of the ram standing on the shore of

---

16 "Because of the velocity of its run" is added by R. Saadia and has no source in the MT.

17 Yefet ben Eli: "With a vision between his eyes." Most probably he read the expression קרן חזות as קרן חזון.

18 ראיתי "That I saw" is not translated by Yefet ben Eli.

19 Lit: "When I saw it (= the goat) reaching it (= the ram)."

20 Lit: "So it (= the goat) threw it (= the ram)."

21 R. Saadia's translation of Dn 8:7 is almost unintelligible because of his excessive use of the third person singular pronoun for both the ram and the goat. His translation is as follow: And I saw that when it (the goat) reached it (the ram), raged against it, hit it, broke its two horns and it (the ram) did not have enough strength to stand between its hands; so it threw it (the ram) to the ground, trampled it, and it (the ram) had no one to deliver it from its hand.

22 אצחאבנא 'our friends' designates most probably the rabbanites. There is no trace, however, of any discussion about the name of the river in Yefet ben Eli's commentary on this passage of Daniel.

the river, and not on [the shore] of the great sea, as it was in the first [vision where it was said that *the four sides of heaven were running,*] *rejoining the big sea* (Dn 7:2), is, as we have already mentioned, because of the diminution of their aberrations against the Israelites. Thus their situation becomes like crossing a river after it was similar to sailing in the sea.

The interpretation of the two horns is leadership and honor,[23] as we have explained in the first vision and similar to the [meaning] of *the seven horns* that may become *ten horns* if considered as reward. It is the horn of Israel (קרן ישׂראל) as he says: *He exalts the honor of His people* (Ps 148:14).[24] The horn of prophecy (קרן נבוה), as he says: *{Herman} the seer of the king according to the word of God in order to lift up His horn* (1 Chr 25:5). The horn of garland (לויה קרן) as he said: *My horn is exalted in the Lord* (1 Sm 2:1). The horn of priesthood (כהנה קרן), as he said: *By Your good will our honor is exalted* (Ps 89:18).[25] The horn of the kingdom, as he said: *And by My name his honor will be exalted* (Ps 89:25).[26] The horn of the righteous (קרן צדיקים), as he said: *Exaltation of the dignities of the upright* (Ps 75:11).[27] The horn of the Temple (קרן המקדש), as he said: *My beloved had a vineyard in fertile part of the land* (Is 5:1).[28] Three other [meanings] that are different. The horn of Abraham ((קרן אברהאם), because [of the expression]: *{A ram} whose two horns were caught in the branches of a tree* (Gn 22:13).[29] The horn of Moses, because [of the expression]: *Behold, his face*

23 Lit. "The two horns also, their interpretation is leadership and honor."

24 וקד רפע שאן קומה is R. Saadia's translation of the partial citation of Ps 148:14. In his translation R. Saadia avoids mention of the literal translation of קרן 'horn' that he renders by 'honor.' The English translation here reflects R. Saadia's interpretation.

25 וברצ̇אך ירתפע שאננא is R. Saadia's translation of the citation from Ps 89:18. קרננו is translated by 'our honor.' Since this citation is to illustrate the notion of קרן כהנה, the expression שאננא 'our honor' refers to the priests.

26 ובסמי ירתפע שאנה is R. Saadia's translation of the citation from Ps 89:25. The expression קרננו translated by שאנה 'his honor' designates the kingdom.

27 ארתפאע שאון אלצאלחין is R. Saadia's translation of the citation from Ps 75:11. The expression קרנות צדיק translated by שאון אלצאלחין 'honors' or dignities of the upright.'

28 כאן לודידי כרם פי רכן ד̇י סמן is R. Saadia's translations of the citation from Is 5:1. The word קרן is rendered by רכן 'place, corner, principle part of a land.' R. Saadia applies this chapter of Isaiah to the Temple, since he uses this passage to illustrate the expression קרן המקדש.

29 מלתחמה פי שעב אלשגרה קרנאה is R. Saadia's translation of the citation from Gn 22:13.

shone (Ex 34:30).[30] And the *horn of the altar*, as something named, not visually established.[31]

How suitable is that after saying: *The two horns were great* (Dn 8:3), he says: *One greater than the other* (Dn 8:3)? We answer that it is as suitable as after saying: *And God made the two great luminaries* (Gn 1:16)[32] he says: *The greater luminary to illuminate during the day, and the smaller luminary to illuminate during the night* (Gn 1:16).[33] We represent this as a group of one thousand persons, among them two are oldest in the group. Then one of the two old men is older than the other; say one is one hundred years old and the other is ninety. The situation of the kings of Media and Persia is similar. The explanation of his expression: *And greater than both of them is the one that rose later* (Dn 8:3) is that Cyrus who came after Darius[34] was of a sharper thorn and a larger kingdom than Darius. Since Darius ruled for two years and Cyrus for three.[35] And that Artaxerxes who came after Ahasuerus was of a sharper thorn and [ruled] for a longer time. Since Ahasuerus ruled for fourteen years and Artaxerxes ruled for thirty four years.[36]

The explanation of his expression: *I saw it butting whoever it found* (Dn 8:4) is the war that the Persian kings engaged against the kings of the world, as he has established clearly in this book [saying]: *After that the king of the Greeks shall lock horns with him* (Dn 11:40), and according to what he said to Israel: *That by them he may butt the nations* (Dt 33:17).[37] And according to what they said themselves: *By You we strike our enemies* (Ps 44:6)[38] and what is similar to that. As to his contraction of the four sides into three, since he said: *Westward, northward, southward* (Dn 8:4) without adding *eastward*, it is because the back of the ram is in the east. So it cannot butt backward; it butts up front, to its right and to its left. And his expression: *No beast could stand in its presence* (Dn 8:4) the totality of this verse could be interpreted [designating] the power that God

30 פאר̇א קד בין וגהה is R. Saadia's translation of the citation from Ex 34:30. R. Saadia does not translate the Hebrew expression קרן אור פניו literally, but as 'his face shone.'

31 R. Saadia does not give an example for קרן המזבח. In fact none of the fourteen examples in the Bible, mainly in Exodus and Leviticus, has קרן 'horn' in its singular form. All the examples are in the plural קרנות.

32 פצנע אללה אלנירין אלעט̇ימין is R. Saadia's translation of the citation from Gn 1:16.

33 אלניר אלאכבר ללאצ̇אה פי אלנהאר ואלניר אלאצג̇ר ללאצ̇אה פי אלליל is R. Saadia's translations of the citation from Gn 1:16.

34 Lit: "Cyrus who was one of them after Darius."

35 Lit: "Since that one ruled for two years and this for one three."

36 Lit: "Since that one ruled for fourteen and this for one thirty four."

37 חתי ינטח בהא אלאמם is R. Saadia's translation of the citation from Dt 33.17.

38 פאנא בך נצדם אעדאינא is R. Saadia's translation of the citation from Ps 44:6.

bestowed on the four Persian kings. We already know that he said about Darius [that he] *wrote to all populations nations and tongues that live in all the countries 'the peace of God and His blessing be upon you'* (Dn 6:26)[39] which is comparable to what he said about Nebuchadnezzar. He also said in his explanation of Cyrus' [situation]: *I will humiliate nations before him, and I will open before him the gate-wings and their doors will not be closed* (Is 45:1).[40] And he said: *The Lord, God of heaven, gave me all the kingdoms of the earth* (Ezr 1:2). About Ahasuerus he said: *And the king Ahasuerus imposed tribute on the land and on the islands* (Est 10:1). And he said about the fourth: Artaxerxes the king of kings (Ezr 7:12), comparable to what he said about Nebuchadnezzar: *Behold! I will bring against Tyre Nebuchadnezzar, king of Babylon, king of kings, from the north* (Ez 26:7).

The meaning of his expression: *While I was trying to understand* (Dn 8:5) is that he was reflecting on the manner [the goat] fiercely struck the ram. *The goat* (Dn 8:5) designates the first king that rose over the Greeks, as Gabriel explained to him: *And the goat*[41] *is the king of the Greek* (Dn 8:21). His expression: *Came from the west* (Dn 8:5) is because the Greek are from the west. I mean, from the French country and its surroundings with the surroundings of the Andalusia until Africa and Cecile, and until Athena, the country of Wisdom. What subsist of them now is in the French [country]. His expression: *Over the face of the earth* (Dn 8:5) [describes his] great condition in the besieging and the attack; that all the earth is level for it: Plain, mountain, valley, hill, precipice, marshland, and much more than that. None of that stopped it, nor slow the his quick attack. The meaning of his expression: *And did not touch [the earth] because of its running* (Dn 8:5)[42] means that it does not touch the ground because of the high speed. Like what has been said about the camel's steps that do not appear on the soil because of speed. In fact it has been mentioned that in one day it runs forty parasang.[43] And I rendered: קרן הזות (Dn 8:5) [Horn] 'with ramification' similar to what has been said about the tree that Nebuchadnezzar saw: *And its*

39 R. Saadia's translation of Dn 6:26 is far from being literal. The translation into English follows his own interpretation. Cf. the footnotes concerning Dn 6:26.

40 אדל בין ידיה אלאמם ואפתח בין ידיה מצארעהם ואבואבהם לא תגלק is R. Saadia's translation of the citation from Is 45:1. R. Saadia's interpretation of Is 45:1 is very peculiar. Cf. the footnote about Is 45:1 in the commentary on Dn 7:7.

41 R. Saadia translates הצפיר השׂעיר by one word: 'Goat.'

42 R. Saadia's translation: 'And did not touch it because of its run' (Dn 8:5) of the Hebrew expression: ואין נוגע בארץ is far from being literal. The expression 'because of its run' has no Hebrew original, and the word ארץ is translated by the pronoun, in English, 'it.'

43 פרסך 'parasang' or about 18,000 feet.

ramifications [reaches] all the earth (Dn 4:8) according to what we have explained.

His expression: *It reached the ram* (Dn 8:6), *and I saw that when the goat reached the ram etc.* (Dn 8:7) designates the victory of the first king of the Greeks, I mean Alexander, over the Persian kingdom. So the meaning of *and hit it* (Dn 8:7) indicates their flight.[44] And [the expression]: *Broke its two horns* (Dn 8:7) is a reference to his defeat of their armies. [The expression]: *So it threw the ram to the ground* (Dn 8:7) designates the dispersion of their association. [The expression]: *Trampled it* (Dn 8:7) indicates his humiliation of those of them who remain. The interpretation of [the expression]: *And the ram had no one to deliver it from its hand* (Dn 8:7) is that they tried to find help, however, the was nothing, since he did not say ואין מציל but ולא היה מציל.[45] Then he said:

Dn 8:8

Then I saw[46] the goat exaggerating greatly[47] and in its haughtiness the biggest horn broke and four ramifications grew at its place toward the four sides[48] of heaven.

Dn 8:9

A small horn rose from one of them.[49] It became very powerful in the side of the south wind, and the east and [the side] of Syria, which means the north.[50]

Dn 8:10

It rose until the stars of heaven[51] so it cast down on the ground stars[52] and planets and trampled them.

44 The flight of the Persians.

45 It is possible to translate the expression: ואין מציל 'they did not find any help.' The expression: ולא היה מציל means that there was no help.

46 תֹם ראית 'Then I saw' is added by R. Saadia and has no source in the MT.

47 Yefet ben Eli: "The goat became very mighty."

48 רוחות השמים is not translated by R. Saadia according to its obvious meaning, 'the winds of heaven' but by the Judeo-Arabic expression: נהאת אלסמא 'sides of heaven.' Such is also the translation of the same expression by Yefet ben Eli.

49 Yefet ben Eli: "A small horn appeared from one of them, from the small one."

50 The expression: "Which means the north" is added by R. Saadia and has no source in the MT.

51 Yefet ben Eli: גיש אלסמא 'the army of heaven.' However, he indicates in his commentary of Dn 8:10 that this expression may probably mean 'the stars of constellations."

Dn 8:11

Then it rose until the head of the stars[53] and took the daily sacrifice[54] away from him and cast down the place where its sacrifice is prepared.

Dn 8:12

And because of the daily sacrifice the stars became guilty; they cast down the right on the ground, they committed their deed and succeeded immediately in it.[55]

Introducing [this part] by the expression: *Then I saw the goat exaggerating greatly and in its haughtiness* (Dn 8:8) is to indicate the extravagance. He informed us that the reason for the revenge against every dominator and mighty one is his extravagance, as he said about Nebuchadnezzar: *But when his heart became proud and his soul became arrogant to the point of being contemptuous, he was deposed from his royal thrown and his glory disappeared from him* (Dn 5:20). And as he said about Sennacherib: *Once God achieved all His work in mount Zion and Jerusalem He said 'I will ask the king of Assure about the pride of his heart and the haughtiness of his eyes* (Is 10:12).[56] And [he said] about all the people: *And once his portion is full, he will be in distress and the punishment of all those he afflicted with misery will be upon him* (Jb 20:22)[57] and what is similar to that. And the meaning of [the expression]: *And in its haughtiness the biggest horn broke and four ramifications grew at its place* (Dn 8:8) is that, once he is dead the leadership of the Greek disappears, and belongs to one man, they become four groups having four lords, according to what he will explain in the tenth chapter of this book. It is possible that Alexander was called 'the man with two horns' because of Daniel's expression: *The ram with two horns* (Dn 8:6). However, he did not apply [this expression] to one

52 R. Saadia will explain in his commentary that the Hebrew expression מן הצבא, translated here by the Arabic נגום 'stars', designates the 'common people' אלאמה עואם.

53 Yefet ben Eli: ראייס אלגיש 'the head of the army.'

54 אלשׄיא אלדאים literally 'the permanent thing.' Yefet ben Eli: 'the permanent [thing],' with no further explanation in his commentary.

55 Here is Yefet ben Eli's translation of this obscure verse: וגׄיש תסלם מע אלדאים בגרם ותלקי אלחק אלי אלארץׄ ותעמל ותנגח. 'An army had an agreement with the permanent unlawfully, cast down the right to the ground, accomplished and was successful.'

56 פאע עיניה פיכון אדׄא תמם אללה גמיע מא יצנעה פי גבל ציון וירושלם קאל אטאלב מלך אשור עלי תׄמר עטׄם קלבה ופכׄר ארת is R. Saadia's translation of Is 10:12.

57 ואדׄא אמתלא קפיזה יצׄיק בה ועקובה כל שׄקי אשׄקאה תאתיה is R. Saadia's translation of Jb 20:22.

particular king, but to all their kings. And we found that the Greek kings were eight. It is then possible that they come by two from every opposed country in the four directions of the earth, as he said: *Toward the four sides of heaven* (Dn 8:8).[58] It is also possible that at certain time the dispersion of the eight, they come from the four sides of the earth.[59]

His expression: *A small horn rose from one of them* (Dn 8:9) designates Seleucus[60] and how weak he was at the beginning of his reign.[61] His expression: *It became very powerful* (Dn 8:9) indicates that he became powerful at the end of his kingdom. As to the reason of his mentioning the three sides when he said: *In the side of the south wind, and the east and [the side] of Syria* (Dn 8:9) without adding in the west is that he rose from the west, as he said already in the beginning of his narration: *Here came a goat from the west* (Dn 8:5). Which means that it aimed rightward, leftward, forward, not backward, as had explained about his expression: *I saw it butting* (Dn 8:4). His expression: הצבי ואל (Dn 8:9) is the side of Syria, following his expression: *Splendor of all the lands* (Ez 20:6)[62] which is in the northward. [...] as he said: *Mount Zion, the corner of Syria* (Ps 48:3).[63] [...] over the nations.

[...]. The interpretation of *until the stars of heaven* (Dn 8:10) is the Israelites who are compared to the stars, as in his expression: *Behold! Today you are as numerous as the stars of heaven* (Dt 1:10).[64] His expression: *So it cast down on the ground* (Dn 8:10) indicates their humiliation and submission, as we have explained about: *So it threw the ram to the ground and trampled it* (Dn 8:7). It is parallel to the expression: *He has thrown from heaven to earth the majesty of Israel* (Lam 2:1).[65] His expression: *And trampled them* (Dn 8:10) represent additional humiliation, in comparison to the expression: *By two feet the crowns of the proud men will be trampled* (Is 28:3).[66] There is also what he said about

58 רוחות is neither translated by R. Saadia as 'directions' and nor as 'winds.'

59 Lit. "It is possible that more or less after the dispersion of the eight it [comes] from the four sides of the earth." The meaning is unclear. Does it pertain to the kingdom of the Israelites who will gather from the different countries? Is there another kingdom (ממלכה since the subject of תציר must be feminine) that will come?

60 נסקלנס. Probably Seleucus III who ruled four years and was assassinated.

61 Lit: "beginning of his matter,"

62 Ez 20:6 speaks about the Exodus from Egypt and installation in the holy land which is at the north.

63 גבל ציון רכן אלשאם is R. Saadia's translation the partial citation of Ps 48:3.

64 פהודאכם אליום ככואכב אלסמא כתרה is R. Saadia's translation of the partial citation of Dt 1:10.

65 While R. Saadia apply Dn 8:7 to the nations and their association, he quotes, as its parallel, Lam 2:1 which refers to the humiliation of Israel.

66 חתי תציר באלרגלין תדאס תיגאן אלמקתדרין is R. Saadia translation of the partial citation of Is 28:3.

Moab: *Feet started to trample it, all the feet of the humble and their steps* (Is 26:6).[67] It is similar to what David had said: *I crushed them like windswept dust and like the mud of the marketplace mashed them* (Ps 18:43).[68] It is toward this interpretation that his expression hint: מן הצבא (Dn 8:10) 'the common people' as in the expression: *Joab was over the common people of Israel* (2 Sm 20:23). About his expression: הכוכבים (Dn 8:10) it is similar to what he had already said: *There will emerge a star from the family of Jacob and a scepter will rise from the family of Israel in them* (Nm 24:17).[69]

His expression: *Then it rose until the head of the stars* (Dn 8:11), according to the vision itself[70] [has the meaning of rising] to the sun, since it is the mightiest [of the stars]. Or to the Saturn. As to its interpretation, it means that the catastrophe Seleucus reached the head of Israel. Among their heads it affects the High Priest because he ends the verse saying: *Took the daily sacrifice away from him* (Dn 8:11). The meaning is the revocation of the daily burnt-offering and other [ceremonies] from the High Priest. The meaning of *and cast down the place where its sacrifice is prepared* (Dn 8:11) is the refusal of the altar which is *the place of the daily sacrifice* and the place for the preparation of the sacrifice.[71] Thus, there is something special that pertains to the vision with no comparison during the clear vision: the revocation of the place of the sun. In fact, this is a saying mentioned for the *High Priest*. The meaning of the daily sacrifice because of which Israel[72] committed sin and transgression, as he said: *And because of the daily sacrifice the stars became guilty* (Dn 8:12)[73] is that it contains the offering, like in the [the expression] *perpetual offering* (Nm 28:10).[74] It is followed by all the laws, because its recitation is forever, since he said: *Recite it day and night* (Jos 1:8). He also said: *They will never cease the presentation of the daily sacrifice* (Is 62:6)[75] and what is similar to that. And how did Israel[76]

67 פצארת אלארגל תדוסהא בל ארגל אלמסאכין ואקדאמהם is R. Saadia's translation of the partial citation of Is 26:6.
68 וסחקתהם כאלתראב אלמדרא קבאלת אלריאח וכטין אלאסואק דקקתהם is R. Saadia's translation of the partial citation of Ps 18:43.
69 יטלק כוכב מן אל יעקוב ויקום קצ׳יב מן אל אסראיל פיוהן is R. Saadia's translation of the partial citation of Nm 24:17.
70 Lit: "the apparent vision."
71 Lit. "The refusal of the altar which is מכון התמיד and its place that prepares for it."
72 Lit: "The nation."
73 תמיד is interpreted by Yefet ben Eli as a place. The meaning of the expression becomes: There was a place that belonged to the head of the army, in which a special seat was reserved to him and that seat was thrown to the earth and was broken.
74 אלקרבאן אלדאים is R. Saadia's translation of the partial citation of Nm 28:10.
75 דאימא מא יסכתון is R. Saadia's translation of the partial citation of Is 62:6. The word תמיד is translated by R. Saadia as an adverb דאימא 'forever' or 'perpetually.' Hence, the meaning according to R. Saadia becomes: 'They (the guardians) will never be

sin concerning the daily sacrifice? In that when the infidels tell the Israelites that by leaving their religion they succeed in life, as it has been said: *They cast down the right* (Dn 8:12) by which he designates the Torah, according to his expression: *Your laws are right* (Ps 119:142),[77] with the wisdom and the good manners,[78] as he said: *Acquire the right and do not sell wisdom, good manners and understanding* (Ps 23:23).[79] [The expression]: *They committed their deed and succeeded* (Dn 8:12) designates the earthly matters,[80] like the order to kneel to the statue that Nebuchadnezzar communicates to Hananyah, Michael and Azaryah. It is similar to what the friends of Darius asked Daniel [...] and the prayers. And Nicanor, who is a Greek, said to Yuhanan*: Slaughter of a pork, slaughter according to tyrannical laws, having the garment of a king, or the horse of a king or being one of the king's familiars* (Beit HaMidrash 6:5–6). Then he said:

Dn 8:13

Then I heard one of the angels[81] speaking and another angel said to the one who was speaking 'for how long is the vision of the daily sacrifice,[82] and the sin and the desolation,[83] and the sanctuary and its army trampled'?[84]

Dn 8:14

He answered me: 'until two thousand three hundred nights and days,[85] [then] the sanctuary will be purified and prosper.[86]

---

silent.' In his quotation, however, the interpretation is 'they will never cease the presentation of the daily sacrifice.'

76 Lit: "The nation."

77 ושראיעך חק is R. Saadia's translation of the citation from Ps 119:142. The particularity of R. Saadia's translation is the that he renders the Hebrew תורתך 'your Torah,' singular, by the Arabic plural . The quotation, Ps 119:142 as well as the text, (Dn 8:12), mention the word אמת, 'right, truthfulness.' Yefet ben Eli refers to the righteous as those who are cast down according to Dn 8:12.

78 The Hebrew word מוסר is translated by the Arabic word אלאדב which has the meaning of 'literary education', beside its meaning as 'good manners.'

79 אשתר חקא ולא תבע אלחכמה ואלאדב ואלפהם is R. Saadia's translation of Ps 23:23.

80 אמור אלדניא 'the earthly matters' has a particular meaning here. It designates the matters opposed to the true adoration of God.

81 Yefet ben Eli: "One of the saints." However, he joins R. Saadia in calling 'the saints' angels in his commentary of Dn 8:13.

82 Yefet ben Eli: "The perpetual vision."

83 MT reads הפשע שמם and not הפשע ושמם. So if we use R. Saadia's words, the translation must be 'the sin of desolation' and not 'the sin and the desolation.'

84 MT: "The sanctuary and the army."

His expression: ואשמעה אחד קדוש מדבר (Dn 8:13) designates an angel, because such is the name of the angels in the Hebrew language, following the example: *The holy of all the angels is with you* (Zec 14:5).[87] The same can be said of the Kasdians' language,[88] as in his expression: *Holy and divine angel came from heaven* (Dn 4:10). This first angel is the master [of all the angels], since he is the one who was asked and he did not justify any thing he was saying. The only thing he mentioned [about him] is *he said* (Dn 8:13). Most probably he was praising [God], since the normal and well known discourse of the angels is the praise, as he says: *They call each other saying 'holy, holy, holy the Lord of armies, His glory has filled all the universe'* (Is 6:3).[89] The second angel is of a lower rank, that is why he asked him about the limit of time, since he declares: *And another angel said* (Dn 8:13). His expression: לפלמוני (Dn 8:13) is a word composed of two. In fact, if someone in the Hebrew language wants to designate a person in particular, he says: פלני אלמני as in the expression of David[90] as well as in the expression of Boaz[91] and the story of Elisha.[92] It is then possible that they contract the two words in one saying: לפלמוני (Dn 8:13).

The words about which he questioned him relate to four meanings. *The vision* אלרויא (Dn 8:13) here has the same meaning it is in its earlier place: *I saw in my sleep* אלמנאם (Dn 8:2). He also said in its middle: *For the interpretation of the vision is for the end* (Dn 8:17).[93] Which is the targum of המראה. And there are four things in this vision. [First] is the story of the daily offering. Its interpretation is the elevation of the offerings, as he said: *And took the daily sacrifice away from him* (Dn 8:11). [Second] is the story of the transgression when the nation was asked to leave Judaism[94] as he said: *And because of the daily sacri-*

---

85 Yefet ben Eli: 'Until the evening and the morning of one thousand three hundred days.'

86 R. Saadia translates the Hebrew verb נצדק by two Arabic verbs יזכי 'to be purified' and ויפלג 'to prosper, be victorious.'

87 Zechariah's expression: ובא יוי אלהי כל קדשים עמך (Zec 14:5) is normally translated as 'the Lord my God (אֱלֹהַי) will come and all the holy ones with you.' However, R. Saadia's understanding of the quotation favors the translation of the expression אלהי כל קדשים 'the God of all the holy men' with the particular interpretation of כל קדשים as 'all the angels.'

88 Kasdians' language or the Aramaic.

89 ויגאדי בעצהם בעץ ויקולון קדוס קדוס קדוס רב אלגיוש וכרמה מלא גמיע אלעאלם is R. Saadia's translation of Is 6:3.

90 Cf. 1 Sm 21:3.

91 Cf. Ru 4:1.

92 Cf. 2 Kgs 6:8.

93 R. Saadia's rendering of Dn 8:17 is not literal. The word תפסיר 'interpretation' has no Hebrew origin in MT.

94 Lit. "To leave the religion."

fice the stars became guilty (Dn 8:11). [Third] is the story of solitude שומם which is the home sickness for the country [and the sadness because] of its destruction. [Fourth] is the story of [how] *the sanctuary and its army were trampled* (Dn 8:13) which is the abasement of Jerusalem and the humiliation of the nation. The inquirer gathered all these conditions[95] and asked about them saying 'until when they endure.' The one who answered replied: 'Until two thousand three hundred days and nights.' If you put them together, I mean the day and the night, you have to divide the number by two, following [the interpretation] of [the expression]: *What was spent of the evening and the morning was one day* (Gn 1:5).[96] In fact, there are three measures in the whole of this book. [The first] measure is one thousand two hundred ninety, qualified by *days*: *One thousand two hundreds ninety years*[97] (Dn 12:11). [The second] measure is one thousand three hundreds thirty five qualified [in the expression]: *{Happy is who waits and reaches the mention} of one thousand three hundred thirty five years*[98] (Dn 12:12). And here he would also say: ימים אלפים ואלש מאות עד [which means] two thousand three hundreds years,[99] with the understanding that the 'year' is called ימים 'days' as it is in the text of some commercial transactions in the Torah: *Its redemption will be one year* (Lv 25:29).[100] And also: *If he does not redeem it before a complete year* (Lv 25:30).[101] Therefore, having replaced *days* by *nights and days* (Dn 8:14), which are parts of days, we ought then to divide them by two. So, the total of the days and the nights being two thousand three hundred, the days that unite them must be one thousand one hundred fifty.[102] What derive from this expression is that the time during which these events happen to the nation, I mean the daily offerings תמיד, the transgression הפשע, the desolation שומם and the trampling מרמס, ends after one thousand

95 Yefet ben Eli mentions the same reasons as a pretext for the question by the angel. However, they are three according to him, not four, as they are for R. Saadia, since he does not speak about the cessation of the daily offering as a motive for the angel's inquiry.

96 ולמא מצי מן אלליל ואלנהאר יום ואחד is R. Saadia's translation of the partial citation of Gn 1:5.

97 R. Saadia translates ימים (literally 'days') by the Arabic סנה (סנין) 'year.'

98 R. Saadia translates the expression בימים לימים (literally 'days of days') by the Arabic סנה (סנין) 'year.'

99 Cf. Dn 8:14.

100 פיכון פכאכה חולא is R. Saadia's translation of the citation from Lv 25:29. The Arabic word חול used by R. Saadia is synonymous with סנה.

101 פאן לם יפכה אלי אן כמלת סנה תאמה is R. Saadia's translation of the partial citation of Lv 25:30.

102 The basic idea of R. Saadia that the expression 'day and night' equals one day. That is why the numbers of 'days and nights' must be divided by two in order to obtain the exact numbers of 'days.'

one hundred fifty years. The emergence of all these events begins one hundred eighty five years after the time when it was said to Daniel: *Happy is who waits* (Dn 12:12). This coincides with the Greek State. In fact if we measure these years[103] they reach a point in time that synchronizes with the time of [the expression]: *Happy is who waits* (Dn 12:12), no more no less.

There was only one incident about the daily offering תמיד in the thirty two years of Artaxerxes' reign, which is forty five years after the time when it was said: *Happy is who waits* (Dn 12:12). In which he said: *And from the time of the disappearance of the daily offering one thousand two hundred ninety years* (Dn 12:11). If this period too is counted from the year [of its beginning] it ends by agreeing with the total.[104] Therefore, if the one thousand one hundred fifty are completed, then *the sanctuary will be purified and prosper* (Dn 8:14). It is also possible that its interpretation becomes 'to be victorious' since he has said: *And you shall be victorious over every tongue that contends with you at law* (Is 54:17).[105] It is also possible that its [interpretation] is purity and prayers, as he said: *And when my justice becomes near* (Is 51:5),[106] *and your people, all of them, are righteous* (Is 60:21)[107] and all [the passages] having the same meaning.

Furthermore, it came to my knowledge the some commentators consider that this period is a complete two thousand three hundred years. They consider that its beginning started twenty years before the Israelites' exodus from Egypt, which coincides, according to their view, with [the following event]: *The king of Egypt died and the Israelites sighed* (Ex 2:23).[108] Then [the same commentators] synchronize the end [of that period] with the end [of the period described in the expression]: *Happy is who waits* (Dn 12:12). Some of them continue to consider that the period is two thousand three hundred years, but they make its beginning start at [the time when] God told Abraham: *As about Ishmael, I heard you* (Gn 17:20).[109] And [they made] it [coincide] with the beginning of the kingdom of Ishmael.[110] Some consider it as only days, which makes it six years that they

103 In other word, the years of the Greek State.
104 Uncertain reading, thus, uncertain translation.
105 וכל לסאן יקאומך פי אלחכם תפלגין עליה is R. Saadia's translation of the partial citation of Is 54:17.
106 וכמא עדלי יקרב is R. Saadia's translation of the partial citation of Is 51:5.
107 וקומך כלהם צאלחון is R. Saadia's translation of the citation from Is 60:1.
108 מאת מלך מצר פתנהדו בנו אסראיל is R. Saadia's translation of the citation from Ex 2:23.
109 ופי אסמאעיל קד סמעתך is R. Saadia's translation of the partial citation of Gn 17:20.
110 In other words, the Islamic kingdom of the Arabs. It is difficult to point to one specific Arabic kingdom. In fact, it is almost impossible to sustain that Ishmael started a kingdom, once he was separated from his father Abraham, in spite of

apply to the period of Gessius Florus.[111] Some take into consideration half [of this number] similar to what we have mentioned in our conclusion about *nights and days* (Dn 8:14). However, they think that they are only days, which makes it three years, that they apply to the time of his devastation of the nation.[112] What satisfies me is the interpretation that I already explained. Then he narrated the interpretation of the story, saying:

Dn 8:15
Then when I, Daniel, did see this vision,[113] I sought to understand it[114] and, behold, there was an individual, similar to the appearance of a man, standing before me.

Dn 8:16
And I heard something like a human voice[115] from the side of the river,[116] calling the one to whom he spoke:[117] Gabriel, make this [man] perceive the interpretation of the vision.'[118]

Dn 8:17
He came close to where I stood and with his coming I became afraid and fell on my face. He then said to me 'understand, O son of man, the interpretation of the vision[119] because it is for the time of the end.'[120]

Dn 8:18
When he spoke to me I fell asleep on my face toward the ground, so he approach me until he set me upright.[121]

Gn 25:12–18 that credits Ishmael with relative importance. R. Saadia's time corresponds to the end of the glorious first period of the Abbasid dynasty.

111 גסקלנס.

112 The years 64–66.

113 Yefet ben Eli: 'While I Daniel was seeing the vision.' Which is closer to the masoretic text than R. Saadia's interpretation.

114 MT: "I sought to understand."

115 MT: "And I heard a human voice." This remark could be attributed to R. Saadia's effort to eliminate any anthropomorphism from God or the celestial creatures.

116 Yefet ben Eli's translation, literally is as follow: "And I heard a human voice between the river בין אלנהר.

117 MT: "Calling and saying."

118 MT: "Make this man understand the vision."

119 תפסיר אלרויא 'the interpretation of the vision' is added by R. Saadia and has no source in the MT.

120 Yefet ben Eli's translation could be rendered, following his commentary, as 'because the vision deals with the time of the end.'

Dn 8:19

Thereafter he said 'here I am making known to you what will happen at the end of this wrath,[122] because it is for the time of the end.'

Dn 8:20

'The ram with two horns that you saw represents the kings[123] of the Medes and the Persians.'

Dn 8:21

'And the goat[124] represents the kings[125] of the Greek. The great horn between his eyes represents their first king.'[126]

Dn 8:22

'The broken ones, in place of which four [horns] came up are four kingdoms arising from one nation,[127] but not by its power.'

Dn 8:23

'And at the end of their reign, when transgressions reach their full,[128] an impudent king arises who understands the sayings.'[129]

Dn 8:24

'His power will be great, but not by his own power, he will defile extraordinarily[130] and he will complete its making, he will destroy the mighty and the holy people.'[131]

---

121 R. Saadia and Yefet ben Eli avoid the translation of the verb נגע 'to touch' here 'touched me.' Both translate the same Hebrew verb by the Arabic verb דני 'to come near.' However, Yefet ben Eli renders the end of Dn 8:18 by 'he made me stand' which implies 'he touched me.' The end of R. Saadia's translation of the same verse lessens the meaning of a direct physical contact.

122 MT: "At the end of the wrath."

123 Another translation attested by a Ms: "The kingdom of the Medes." Yefet ben Eli: "The kings of the Medes and the Persians."

124 הצפיר השׂעיר is translated by R. Saadia as אלתיס.

125 MT: The king.

126 MT: "The great horn between his eyes represents the first king."

127 MT: "Four kingdoms arise from the nation."

128 כהתם הפשׁעים is rendered by R. Saadia as כמאל אלגרום translated here by 'when transgressions reach their full.' Yefet ben Eli: אנתיהא אלעאצין 'the end of the rebels.'

129 אלאחאדית̇ literally 'the conversations.' Yefet ben Eli: אלרואיאת literally 'the stories.'

130 Yefet ben Eli: ואלעג̇איב יפסד 'he will defile the marvels' or 'the miracles.'

131 Yefet ben Eli: "He will succeed, he will achieve, he will corrupt the strongmen and group of saints."

Dn 8:25

'With his malice there is also the success of the ruse in his hands,[132] therefore he magnifies his heart, destroys many and becomes calm,[133] he will stand against the lord of lords, but he will be broken, once the power disappears.'[134]

Dn 8:26

'The vision that lasts the evening and the day,[135] which was told, is true. As to you, retain the vision,[136] for it is for a long period.'[137]

Dn 8:27

And I, Daniel, was disheartened and became sick for days, until I rose up and did the king's business, and I was absorbed, thinking about the vision,[138] and found no one who explains.

He started by the expression: *I sought to understand* (Dn 8:15) in order to inform us that because he was bewildered, he asked for the interpretation, and the individual that he described as *similar to the appearance of a man* (Dn 8:15) appeared to him. When the individual appeared he heard a voice like a human voice enjoining the individual to inform Daniel about the interpretation, as he said: *And I heard something like a human voice* (Dn 8:16). The one whose voice he heard was of a higher dignity than the individual and closer [...] in the rank of *the old man* עתיק ימין (Dn 7:9) compared to *a young man* בר אנש (Dn 7:13). And as the rank of the *angel who was speaking* פלמוני המדבר (Dn 8:13) to *one of the angels* אחד קדוש (Dn 8:13).[139] However, Daniel did see *the old man* עתיק ימין (Dn 7:9), but he did not see *angel who {was speaking* המדבר*}*

132 שׂכלו is rendered by R. Saadia as כבחתה 'malice.' Yefet ben Eli: אקבאלה 'his success.' Yefet ben Eli's translation becomes: "With his prosperity the ruse succeeds in his hand." By using the word 'malice' R. Saadia wants to say that 'his success' is the fruit of his malice. In his commentary on this word he quotes Jer 4:22 to explain that there is a way of being clever in doing what is evil.

133 Yefet ben Eli: "By amusement and calmly, he will destroy many."

134 Yefet ben Eli: "He will be broken without [the intervention] of a hand."

135 Lit: "The vision of the duration of the night and the day."

136 Yefet ben Eli: 'close the vision.'

137 Yefet ben Eli: "For it is for many days."

138 Yefet ben Eli: 'I was bewildered because of the vision.'

139 The translation of the expressions mentioned in this comparison follows R. Saadia's understanding. Yefet ben Eli too thinks that the voice belong to an angel of higher rank than the one who will explain the interpretation to Daniel. however, he does not compare him to others, as R. Saadia does.

פלמוני (Dn 8:13) neither did he see this man.[140] His expression: *Calling {the one to whom he spoke:} 'make this [man] understand* (Dn 8:16) designates Daniel. The meaning of בין אולי is *from the side of the river* (Dn 8:16), because of the similarity of this [...] the story of [the angel who] *was suspended over the water of the Tigris* (Dn 12:6) [...] that he will describe in what will follow. [...] in the interrogation of some angels [... ...] the end. And the order of some of them [...] to Daniel, so he may become precious for us. [...] the roots and the diversities of the expression, then he explains it when we hear it [...] meanings about which the angel asks [...].[141]

[...] *{I will give} the land into the hand of evil men* (Ez 30:12) and what is similar to that. I interpreted his expression: *An impudent king* (Dn 8:23) as [belonging] to someone that does not have pity, nor is he afraid, as in the expression: *A group of insolent faces who do not show respect before old man's face, neither have pity on a young* (Dt 28:50).[142] As to the meaning of [the expression]: *Who understands the sayings* (Dn 8:23), he informs [...] the kings who were before them and their life. Thus, he needs to say about every action he achieves, and how he achieves it, that he performed like such or such king performed it.[143]

His power will be great, but not by his own power (Dn 8:24) has a meaning similar to what we have already explained.[144] The meaning of [his expression]: *And he will defile extraordinarily* (Dn 8:24) is that he will be overwhelmed over his corruption, because this overwhelming pertains to things that no one ever witnessed. I mean [witnessed in] two times. The meaning of [his expression]: *Destroy the mighty and the holy people* (Dn 8:24) is that he kills from Israel's elects. The meaning of [his expression]: *With his malice, there is also the success of the ruse in his hands* (Dn 8:25) [...] with right mind, because only the right mind promulgates justice. However, it is to be clever and to be wise, as he said: *They are clever at wrong doing* (Jer 4:22). That is why I rendered it[145] by 'malice.' Likewise, I rendered every הצליח (Dn 8:24.25) in this book by 'fullness' and not 'righteousness.'[146] Because the malice is not the righteousness.

140 The man to whom belongs the human voice mentioned in Dn 8:16.

141 R. Saadia's commentary on Dn 8:17–22 is lacking.

142 קבילא וקיח אלונה מן לם יהאב וגה שיך ולא יראף עלי צבי is R. Saadia's translation of Dt 28:50.

143 It is difficult to grasp the precise meaning of the last two sentences, because of the lacuna in the manuscripts. Probably it deals with a comparison between Daniel's actions and the various kings' actions.

144 R. Saadia is referring to an explanation that is probably part of the lost part of his commentary that deals with Dn 8:17–22.

145 The word שׂכלו.

146 תמאם fullness, אצלאח righteousness.

The meaning of [his expression]: *He magnifies his heart, destroys many* (Dn 8:25) is, first, he gives the Israelites the assurance of security, so that they me feel secure and protected. Then he looks down on them and destroys. It is also possible that he does the same thing to others. The meaning of [his expression]: *He will stands against the lord of lords* (Dn 8:25) is probably that he is on the two lands, referring to the most important of kings or princes, in other words, *the high priest*, and those who are of similar rank. It is also possible that it pertains to those who are mentioned.[147] As if he means by his discourse to call either Michael or Gabriel, or one of a similar rank. As to the meaning of [his expression]: *But he will be broken, once the power disappears* (Dn 8:25) deals with the time of the loss of his ruling and his power. Like what he said about Moab: *Because the grass does not grow anymore, no more pastures, and there is no greenery at all* (Is 15:6).[148] He also said: *Because the quarreler does not exist any more and the spoiler was destroyed together with the one who tramples the land with violence* (Is 16:4).[149] And [all the passages] in harmony with this [meaning].

The meaning of [his expression]: *As to you, retain the vision* (Dn 8:26)[150] is not 'close [the vision]' because if this is the meaning, Daniel would not be able to fix it and put it in writing. In fact, its meaning is 'retain it, store it, save it' as he said: *Secretly you taught me wisdom* (Ps 51:8)[151] and according to what we will say at the end of this book. The word ונהייתי *disheartened* (Dn 8:27) is possibly derived from נהי[152] or הוה.[153] Both in their acceptation of 'sorrow and grief.' The addition to this expression of: *Until I rose up and did the kings business* (Dn 8:27) means that what happened to him was so enormous that without the necessity of accomplishing the ruler's business he would not wake up from his sorrow. His expression: *Thinking about the vision and finding no one to explain* (Dn 8:27) does not mean the interpretation of the vision, since Gabriel had al-

147 Uncertain reading: אל[מ]סמאין.

148 ממא כׄלא אלחשיש ופני אלכלא ואלכׄצׄר לם כתן אצלא is R. Saadia's translation of the citation from Is 15:6.

149 במא קד כׄלא אלמנאצׄי ופני אלנאהב ומן כאן ידוס אלארץׄ ענפא is the translation of the citation from Is 16:4 by R. Saadia.

150 R. Saadia's interpretation pertains to the verb סתם whose first meaning is to 'seal, to stop, to close' like in 2 Chr 32:4.30.

151 ופי סרא קד ערפתני אלחכמה is R. Saadia's translation of the citation from Ps 51:8. Note that the Arabic word סרא by which R. Saadia renders the Hebrew word סָתֻם , has the meaning of 'secretly and by night.' Note also that Yefet ben Eli translate the Hebrew verb סתם by the expression that R. Saadia rejects: 'to close' to which he gives two meanings: That the vision suffers no doubt, or to close the chapter.

152 Cf. Am 5:16.

153 Cf. Ez 7:26.

ready elucidated it to him, as he said: *Understand, O son of man* (Dn 8:17). What he means is that he did not know whether he was a prophet or not until the apparition of Gabriel to him after that, while he was awake, as he will explain immediately afterward. So Daniel[154] left believing that this vision was a prophecy. By this, the explanation of the eighth chapter is completed.

154 Lit: "He."

Chapter 9

Dn 9:1

In the first year of Darius, son of Ahasuerus, of a Median descent, who was made king after the reign of the Kasdians.[1]

His expression here continues what he already advanced, that when Belshazzar was killed Darius rose after him as he said: *In that night Belshazzar, the Kasdian king was killed* (Dn 5:30), and: *Then the kingship came to Darius the Mede* (Dn 6:1). However, he did not explain whose son is he. So he explained here that he is Ahasuerus' son. But it is not the same Ahasuerus as the friend of Haman.[2] In fact there are still four years to the beginning of the reign of Ahasuerus the friend of Haman and eighteen years until the end of his reign, since he was [king] for fourteen years. This Ahasuerus,[3] yet, is different and was not qualified at all, neither as king nor as a simple man. Then he said:

Dn 9:2

In that first year of his reign I Daniel inquired in the books concerning the number of years, that God inspired to Jeremiah[4] about the fulfillment of the seventy years to the destruction of Jerusalem.

Dn 9:3

I turned to God my Lord imploring prayer[5] and supplication with fasting, sackcloth and ashes.

1 Yefet ben Eli: "How reigned over the Kasdians' kingdom."

2 Cf. Est 3:1–15. Yefet ben Eli mentions the same points in his commentary of Dn 9:1.

3 Or Ahasuerus that is mentioned in Dn 9:1. Yefet ben Eli remarks that Ahasuerus of the Book of Esther is Persian, while this one is Mede.

4 MT and Yefet ben Eli: "In the discourse of God to Jeremiah."

5 לבקש תפלה is translated literally by R. Saadia: 'To implore, or ask, prayer and supplication.' In his commentary of the same verse, Yefet ben Eli understands the expression as לבקש בתפלה, 'imploring by the prayer' which is the usual understanding of this expression. Such is not the explanation of R. Saadia when he comments this part of Dn 9:3.

He started first by [mentioning] the reason that made it necessary for him to initiate the supplication in that year for the building of the Jerusalem. He informed us that when he counted the seventy[6] [years] and concluded that they are completed he thought the end needs to be hastened by supplication and prayers. So he did that, like the end[7] that the cries of the people hastened, as it was said: *The children of Israel sighed from because of their servitude, they cried and their cry because of the servitude rose up to God* (Ex 2:23).[8] He started the enumeration here by the *destruction of Jerusalem* (Dn 9:2). Thus we have to know that [this enumeration] refers to *the kingdom of Babylon*, because God spoke to Jeremiah like this: *After the accomplishment of seventy years I will take care of you* (Jer 29:10). And Daniel hoped that the beginning of the seventy [years] coincides with the beginning of the reign of Nebuchadnezzar. That is why he said that, according to this calculation, the seventy years are accomplished. In fact, Nebuchadnezzar ruled forty five years, his son ruled twenty three years and his grand son Belshazzar ruled three years, which makes [the total] seventy years. How do we know that Nebuchadnezzar ruled forty five years? From the expression of the Bible[9] stating that Evil-Merodach reigned in the thirty seventh year of *the exile of Jeconiah*, since [the Bible] had already said: *In the thirty seventh year of the exile of Jehoiachin the king of Judah {on the twenty seventh day of the twelfth month} Evil-Merodach, the king of Babylon, lifted up {the head of Jehoiachin}* (2 Kgs 25:27). At the time of *the exile of Jeconiah* the of Nebuchadnezzar's reign was of eight years as he said: *Jehoiachin, the king of Judah, along with his mother, his servants, his princes and his officers, but the king of Babylon, in the eighth year of his reign, captured him* (2 Kgs 24:12). And this agrees with what the Bible stated, that Nebuchadnezzar started his reign in the fourth year of Jehoiakim, since it said: *The word that came to Jeremiah concerning all the people of Judah in the fourth year of Jehoiakim, the son of Josiah the king of Judah, that was the first year of Nebuchadnezzar the king of Babylon* (Jer 25:1). Thus, it became clear that Nebuchadnezzar reigned forty five years and Belshazzar three years because of what Daniel had said: *In the third year of the reign of Belshazzar* (Dn 8:1). What has been said leads necessarily to the conclusion that Evil-Merodach ruled between Nebuchadnezzar and Belshazzar, because of Jeremiah's expression: *And these nations shall serve the king of Babylon seventy years* (Jer 25:11).[10] He also said:

6 Lit. "Counted the count."

7 The end of the slavery time in Egypt.

8 פתנהדו בנו אסראיל מן כֿדמתהם וצרכֿו פצעד שֿהיקהם אלי אללה מן אלכֿדנה is R. Saadia's translation of the citation from Ex 2:23.

9 Lit. "The Book."

And these nations shall serve him, his son and his son's son (Jer 27:7). Therefore his son is Evil-Merodach and his son's son is Belshazzar, according to what we have explained.

About the dating of the incomplete years, [his expression]: *The first year of Darius* (Dn 9:1) [designates] the seventy first year of the kingdom of Babylon. That is why he considered it as the year when Belshazzar showed the vessels of Jerusalem, as we have explained.[11] Therefore [...] to Jerusalem is cancelled. And if the incomplete year is deducted, *the first year of Darius* (Dn 9:1) becomes the seventieth year. That is why [...] to Cyrus, as he said: *In the first year of Cyrus, king of Persia, when the word of the Lord by the mouth of Jeremiah was fulfilled* (Ezr 1:1). The reason of that is the deduction of three years from the count: A year between Nebuchadnezzar and Evil-[Merodach], a year between Evil-[Merodach] and Belshazzar and a year between Belshazzar and Darius. Hence, the fulfilment of the seventieth year coincides with [the expression]: *In the first year of Darius* (Dn 9:1). That does not designate, however, the achievement of the construction, because it came at the end of *seventy years to the destruction of Jerusalem* (Dn 9:2).

As to the time after the fulfilment of the seventieth year for Babylon, He only guaranteed taking care of them, as he said: *I will take car of you* (Jer 29:10). In fact, there are eighteen years between the [fulfilment] seventieth year for Babylon and the seventieth year *to the destruction of Jerusalem* (Dn 9:2) following his expression: *In the fifth month, on the tenth day of the month, which was the nineteenth year of Nebuchadnezzar, the king of Babylon* (Jer 52:12), *he burned the house of the Lord* (Jer 52:12). Those nineteen[12] [years] are three years to the king Cyrus, fourteen years to the king Ahasuerus, and two years to the king Artaxerxes who is [also] called Darius as it is stated in the prophecy of Haggai and Zechariah: *In the second year of Darius* (Hg 1:1. Zec 1:1). It was also said that [the time of] Ahasuerus too has to be counted like [the time] of Belshazzar. Thus he[13] said 'I see that there is a mistake of eight

---

10 The same reference to Jer 25:11 is cited by Yefet ben Eli in the same context. However, and unlike R. Saadia, Yefet ben Eli, does not expand on the explanation of the exact timing of the seventy years, starting by the destruction of Jerusalem.

11 The beginning of this sentence is uncertain because of a damaged in MS Oxf 2486.121a.

12 Lit. "And those יח." Which means 'those eighteen.' Most probably because the beginning of the reign in the first year and its end in the last years did not happen in the first month of the year and, thus, we do not have tow full years. Therefore they are counted one year, which gives us a total of eighteen years instead of nineteen.

13 Who is the person represented by the pronoun 'he'? The passage is not clear and a mistake, or a missing expression from the manuscript, is not totally excluded. Most probably the 'he' designates Hananiah son of Azzur who prophesied against

years in the counting of Belshazzar's [time]. That is why his [...] was hastened. They are the eight years at the beginning of Nebuchadnezzar's reign until the deportation of Jeconiah, like the explanation we presented.[14] Then Ahasuerus realized that they were completed *in the third year oh his reign* (Est 1:3). Which is two years for Darius, three for Cyrus, and three incomplete for Ahasuerus. And that makes [the total] seventy.[15] That is the reason why *he made a feast for all his servant* (Est 1:3) for joy because [he thought that] the end of [the exile of] Israel was untrue,[16] following what we have said in the commentary of the Book of Ester. Then it happened to him what we all know.[17]

It has been said, too, that Hananiah son of Azzur[18] enumerated these years[19] before anyone else. In doing so he made a mistake, because he begun to count the seventy years starting by the thirty fifth year into Manasseh, which is the time when [the king of Assure] ruled over Israel, as he said: *The Lord brought upon them the generals of the king of Assure* (2 Chr 33:11). He also said: *And he took him captive to* Babylon (2 Chr 33:11). Thus, twenty years remain to the reign of Manasseh,[20] two years to Amon,[21] thirty one year to Josiah[22] and eleven years to Jehoiakim.[23] Then when four years passed to [the reign of] Zedekiah[24] as he said: *In that year, at the beginning of the reign of the king Zedekiah, the king of Judah, in the fifth month of the fourth year, the prophet Hananiah son of Azzur said to me* (Jer 28:1) *in two years I will bring back all the vessels of the house of the Lord* (Jer 28:3), which completes six years to [the reign] of Zedekiah. That gave him the illusion that the [total of] seventy years is fulfilled. Therefore Daniel said: 'When I hoped that the term [of the exile] is fulfilled I started to hasten [its advent] by supplication and prayer.' He divided [his effort]

Jeremiah and whose name will be soon mentioned as the author of this particular manner of counting.

14 כמא שרחנא נחן literally: 'Like we, we have explained.' The expression insists on R. Saadia's explanation in opposition to the explanation he just presented and whose author does not appear clearly from the lesson of Oxf 2486.121b.

15 it is an explanation for the eight missing years in the first manner of counting that R. Saadia refutes here.

16 The fact that the seventieth year passes without seeing the predicted end of the of the Israelites' exile, is a reason for celebration for Ahasuerus.

17 Lit. "It happened to him what happened to him."

18 Hananiah son of Azzur is the false prophet who prophesied against Jeremiah. Cf. Jer 28:1–17.

19 Lit. "Counted this count."

20 Cf. 2Kgs 20:21–21:18.

21 Cf. 2Kgs 21:18–26.

22 Cf. 2Kgs 21:26–22:3, 23:1–23:30.

23 Cf. 2Kgs 23:34–24:6.

24 Cf. 2Kgs 24:17–25:6.

in to five [acts of devotion]: prayer תפלה, supplication תחנונים, fasting צום, sackcloth שׂק, ashes אפר.

Concerning תפלה, it is the repetition of the parts of God's commandment that are optional for the learned.[25] As to the תחנונים it is the supplication and the yearning that the faithful utter after the prayers, as he said: *They offer prayer and supplication before you in this house* (1 Kgs 8:33). As for the fasting, it has the meaning that we explained in the laws relative to the *day of Atonement.*[26] Concerning the *sackcloth and ashes* (Dn 9:3) they deal with the reasons that we demonstrated in the commentary on [the Book of] Lamentations and the Book of Ester.[27] All these [acts of devotions] have no benefit if they do not proceed from the pure heart of the servant of God, since they are introduced by the expression: *I turned to God my Lord* (Dn 9:3) which designates the [pure] intention.[28]

Dn 9:4

When[29] I prayed the God my Lord I acknowledged my transgressions[30] and said 'O my Lord, powerful, great and awesome, who keep the covenant and the favor for those who love Him and keep His commandments,

Dn 9:5

We have sinned, committed transgression, we were unjust,[31] we rebelled and deviated from your laws and judgments,

25 In his commentary of Dn 9:4, Yefet ben Eli, specifies the meanings of praying, which, according to him, are four: The praise of the Lord, enumerating sins and transgressions, mentioning what happened to the Israelites because of their sins and, finally, asking him to renounce his punishment of Israel. He also remarks that תפלה may reunite three of the four meanings above mentioned.

26 יום הכפורים

27 According to Yefet ben Eli Dn 9:3 means that he prayed while he was fasting, dressed with sackcloth and covered with ashes. For him, the three later acts of devotions are conditions of Daniel's prayer.

28 Lit: "I faced God my Lord" which is the attitude of someone having nothing to hide or be blamed for. In other word, someone who is not afraid of facing the Lord, since his intentions and deeds are pure.

29 R. Saadia understands the ו in ואתפללה as a consecutive ו and translates it by ולמא 'when' introducing a temporal circumstance. The majority of translators (Yefet ben Eli, for example) understand the ו here as 'and' connecting two realities.

30 "My transgressions" is added by R. Saadia to his translation and has no source in the MT.

31 The Hebrew verb מרדנו is translated by R. Saadia as ט̇למנא which is rendered here by 'we were unjust.' The same Arabic verb may be translated by 'we oppressed' since is we have ט̇לם as Arabic word for 'oppression.' According to his understand-

Dn 9:6

We did not listen to Your messengers[32] the prophets who in your name addressed our kings, our lords, our fathers and all the people,

Dn 9:7

To you, O Lord, belongs the justice, and to us belongs the shame[33] in this day,[34] to the men of Judah and the men of Jerusalem,[35] to all the Israelites, near and far, in all the countries where You spread them because of their betrayal of Your religion,[36]

Dn 9:8

And as it is for us, O Lord, to our kings, our lords and fathers too belongs the shame,[37] because we sinned against You,

Dn 9:9

To God our Lord, however, belongs mercy and forgiveness,[38] since we rebelled against Him,

Dn 9:10

And we did not receive the command of our Lord[39] to follow in his laws that His messengers the prophets recited to us,[40]

---

ing, others are the first victims of such act. Yefet ben Eli renders the same Hebrew verb by a an Arabic verb, פסקנא, that directs us toward acts of immorality or impurity. According to his translation, we are the first victims of our own act.

32 ולם נקבל מן רסלאך אלנבי׳א. Lit. 'We did not receive from Your messengers the prophets.' Yefet ben Eli: "We did not receive the discourse of Your servants the prophets" which is a literal translation of the MT.

33 בשת הפנים literally, 'the shame or confusion of faces' is rendered by R. Saadia in one word: אלכ׳זא 'the shame.'

34 Yefet ben Eli: "And to us belong the shame, like in this day."

35 לאיש יהודה ולישבי ירושלם literally, 'men of Judah and inhabitants of Jerusalem' (which is Yefet ben Eli's translation) is translated by R. Saadia as 'the men of Judah and the men of Jerusalem.' The two words איש and ישבי are translated by the same Arabic word אל.

36 Another possible translation: "Because of their betrayal in their obedience to you." MT: "Because of the betrayal by which they betrayed you," which is Yefet ben Eli's translation.

37 בשת הפנים literally, 'confusion of faces' is rendered by R. Saadia in one word: אלכ׳זא 'the shame.'

38 MT: "Mercies and remissions."

Dn 9:11

All the Israelites transgressed Your Torah, deviated and did not receive Your command,[41] so was poured upon us what was written in the Torah of Moses,[42] the messenger of God,[43] because we have sinned against Him,

Dn 9:12

Therefore He accomplished the threat that He made against us and against the judges that ruled over us,[44] by carrying out against us a great calamity that did nothing under haven[45] similar to what it did to Jerusalem,

Dn 9:13

As it was written in the Torah of Moses,[46] because all this happened to us without imploring God our Lord, that we may turn way from our sins and meditate His principles.

Dn 9:14

Therefore God decreed the calamity and inflicted it on us, because it is Him who is just in all the works He accomplishes, as for us,[47] we refused his command,

---

39 ולא שמענו בקול יהוה literally, we did not listen to the discourse of Our Lord' (which is Yefet ben Eli's translation) is translated by R. Saadia as רבנא ולם נקבל אמר literally, 'and we did not receive the command of our Lord.'

40 אשר נתן לפנינו ביד עדיו הביאים is translated freely by R. Saadia as עלינא רסלאה אלאנביא אלתי תלאהא literally, 'that His messengers the prophets recited to us.' Yefet ben Eli: "That he put before us by the hand of His servants, the prophets" which is closer than R. Saadia to the MT.

41 MT: "And ceased from hearing your discourse" which is also Yefet ben Eli's translation.

42 האלה והשבעה אשר כתובה בתורת משה is translated by R. Saadia as תוראת מוסי מא מכתוב פי literally, 'what was written in the Torah of Moses.' In fact, R. Saadia does not translate האלה the curse, והשבעה the oath. He uses the neutral word מא 'what is.' Yefet ben Eli uses the words אלחראמה 'the anathema' and אלקסאנה 'the oath' for his translation of the two Hebrew words.

43 MT: "The servant of God."

44 ויקם את דבריו that is traditionally translated by 'He confirmed the word He spoke to us and to the judges who ruled over us' (such is the translation of Yefet ben Eli) is rendered here by פואפא בועידה 'therefore He accomplished His threat.'

45 'Under heaven' and not 'under all heaven.' R. Saadia does not translates the Hebrew word כל 'all.'

46 As if the beginning of Dn 9:13 'as it was written in the Torah of Moses' belongs to Dn 9:12. R. Saadia does not comment this part of Dn 9:13.

Dn 9:15

And now, O God our Lord,[48] who has brought Your people out of the Land of Egypt by a strong hand and has mad a great name for Yourself,[49] as to this day we have sinned and we were unjust,[50]

Dn 9:16

God, according to all your kindness, I beg You[51] to turn away Your anger and Your fury from Your city Jerusalem, the mountain of Your holiness, that by our sins and the transgressions of our fathers with Your people, became a disgrace to all those who surround us,

Dn 9:17

And now hear, O Lord, the prayers of Your servant and his supplications and turn the light of Your face toward Your desolated sanctuary, for Your sake,

Dn 9:18

Hear us completely and look[52] on us thoroughly, on our desolation, on the city that was called after Your name, for it is not because of our righteousness that we present our supplication between Your hands, but because of Your immense mercy,[53]

---

47 ונחנו 'as for us' is added by R. Saadia to his translation and has no source in the MT.

48 Yefet ben Eli: "O Lord our God."

49 MT: "And has made a name for Yourself" which is also the translation of Yefet ben Eli.

50 רשענו is translated by R. Saadia by טׄלמנא literally, 'we were unjust' or 'we committed acts of injustice.' Yefet ben Eli renders the same word by פסקנא which can be translated as 'we committed acts of immorality.'

51 אסאלך 'I beg you' is added by R. Saadia to his translation and has no source in the MT.

52 וראה is not translated by R. Saadia as simple imperative: ואנטׄר 'and look.' He translates the one Hebrew verb by ואנטׄר נטׄרא כאמלא literally 'and look in a perfect' or 'complete look.' Hence, its translation here: "And look thoroughly."

53 Yefet ben Eli follows closely the MT in translating the final expression in its plural form: 'Your many acts of mercy.'

Dn 9:19

O God hear us, O God forgive us, O God answer us and accomplish our needs,[54] do not delay it, for Your sake,[55] O Lord, because Your city and Your people are called after You.[56]

Now that we have translated the verses of this prayer we have to go back and briefly examine its meanings. We speak first about the righteous manner of interceding in favor of a group or a nation, with the hope of being approved. If the intercessor[57] is a priest, there will be no surprise, since God, may He be exalted and honored, established him for this reason, as He said: *Between the porch and the alter, let the priests weep and say: 'Spare Your people O Lord, and let not Your heritage become a mockery, to be subjected by nations, why should they say among the people where is their God?'* (Jl 2:17). But, how should someone, who is not priest,[58] hope that his intercession in favor of the nation be approved? We answer: Aren't there explanations already given by Him that some acts are to be considered as an obligation for the whole nation?[59] Thus, any one comes first in accomplishing them does it in the name of all the nation. Like what did Phinehas[60] in Shittim. Therefore, the supplication must be in a similar way, with contriteness and humility. In a similar way Daniel said: *When I prayed the God my Lord I acknowledged my transgressions* (Dn 9:4).[61]

54 The expression חואיגנא 'our needs' is added by R. Saadia in his translation, as a complement to the verb אעשׂה.

55 The Hebrew expression כי שמך נקרא literally 'it is to Your name that we appeal' is translated here by במא אנת אהלה literally 'what You are capable of' and rendered by 'for Your sake.' The word 'name' does not appear in R. Saadia's translation.

56 MT: "Because your name designates your city and your people," which is also Yefet ben Eli's translation.

57 Lit: "He."

58 Lit. "Who is not one of the priests."

59 A rhetorical question. R. Saadia wants to say that there are many instructions from God for any Israelite to behave in the name of all the nation. Their existence seems so obvious that R. Saadia does not need to enumerate them.

60 Cf. Nm 25:1–15. Whoever, Phinehas was the son of Eleazar, son of Aaron the priest. Cf. Nm 25:7.

61 MT: "When I prayed the God my Lord I acknowledged." The expression 'my transgressions' is being added by R. Saadia who does not understand it as Daniel' admission for his own sins, but as the Israelites' transgressions, since Daniel is praying in their name. Yefet ben Eli's interpretation of Dn 9:4 appears to be completely different. By the expression 'I acknowledge' he understands the recognition of the marvels that God had accomplished, which is the traditional introduction to some prayers in the Bible. He quotes Dt 3:24 as example of such introduction to a prayer.

And why is it that he said: *Powerful, great and awesome* (Dn 9:4) and did not say: *Mighty*? There is also Jeremiah who said: *Powerful, great and Mighty* (Jer 32:18) and did not say: *Awesome*. And as to Ezra, he says: *God the great* (Neh 8:6) and did not say neither *the mighty* nor *awesome*. As for *our master* Moses, he said: *The powerful, the great, the mighty, the awesome* (Dt 10:17).[62]

There are two answers to this [question].[63] The first [answer] pertains to the whole. It is the fact that all those [qualities] are descriptions of our Lord, blessed is His name. Hence, when one, two or three of those [qualities] are said of [God] it is as if all of them are being said of [Him]. The second [answer] is partial. It is possible that Daniel used *awesome* speaking about [God], because his request relates to the rebuilding of the Temple. In fact, it was said about it: *How awesome is this place* (Gn 28:17).[64] It is because of it that [the expression]: *He inspires fear in His holy place* (Ps 68:36) was said.[65] The Bible[66] also said: *The Lord will be terrible against them, because He will destroy all the gods of the earth* (Zep 2:11). As to Jeremiah, he emphasized in his discourse the [expression]: *mighty* because he was looking for revenge of the country's besiegers, saying: *Here is the siege works raised against the city to take it* (Jer 32:24). It was also said in a similar situation: *God appears like a mighty, like a warrior He stirs up ardor, He overcomes, roars and appears mighty against His enemies* (Is 42:13).[67] Concerning our master Moses, his intention was to inform his people that the Creator is eternal. Therefore he said: *The great* הגדול, because the old man, by us, being called *ancient* הגדול the characteristic of being ancient increases with the time until it becomes comparable to the Eternal who has no beginning. He also wanted to tell them that God punishes and rewards. That is why he said: *the mighty, the awesome* (Dt 10:17) according to what we have explained. As to Ezra, he did not intend [to speak] about punishment and reward. He was reciting the Torah and the wisdom,[68] which is the first creator, as

62 אלטאיק אלכביר אלגבאר אלמכיף is R. Saadia's translation of the citation from Dt 10:17.

63 The question deals with the multiplicity and variety of the qualities applied to God.

64 מא אכוף הדא אלנוצע is R. Saadia's translation of the citation from Gn 28:17. 'The place' in which Jacob had his vision is described in the same verse as 'house of God' and gate of heaven.'

65 והו מכוף פי מקדסה is R. Saadia's translation of the citation from Ps 68:36. R. Saadia modifies the meaning of the Hebrew expression ממקדשך 'Your holy place' and translates it by the Arabic expression פי מקדסה which is 'in His holy place.' As if he read the Hebrew expression ממקדשהו.

66 Lit. "He."

67 אד יטהר אללה כאלגבאר וכדי אלמלאחם יתיר יגלב ויצרך ועלי אעדאה יתגבר is R. Saadia's translation of the citation from Is 42:13.

68 The expression 'Torah and the wisdom' here designates the Torah alone.

it[69] has said: *God invented me at the beginning of His creation* (Pr 8:22).[70] And it does not disappear, because no one could look at it. that is why he said: הגדול *the great* (Neh 8:6) alone.[71]

His expression: *We have sinned, committed transgression, we were unjust, we rebelled* (Dn 9:5) indicates different manners of committing sins. Their order is from the most important to the less important[72] as we have explained in the commentary of another [passage where it is question of being] *deviated from your laws* (Dn 9:5) that we received by tradition,[73] *and from judgments* (Dn 9:5) that we elaborate.[74] I explained [the expression]: *In your name* (Dn 9:6) according to the well known four meanings of *the name.*[75] As to [the expression]: כיום הזה *in this day* (Dn 9:7) which is in the verse: *To you, O Lord, belongs the justice* (Dn 9:7) it should be written כהיום because it is possible that it refers to four verses in which there is [the expression]: כהיום each of which is similar in part to this supplication. The first is: *And it happened that in one day* כהיום הזה *Joseph went to the house to do something* (Gn 39:11).[76] That is similar to the *shame* (Dn 9:7) mentioned here and following the expression: *They should have been ashamed because they committed abomination* (Jer 6:15). The second [passage where we find the same expression] is: *And we become alive as it is in this day* כהיום הזה (Dt 6:24).[77] This is similar to [the expression]: *To you, O Lord, belongs the justice* (Dn 9:7). Because we find immediately after it: *Benefits will reach us* (Dt 6:25).[78] The third [passage where we find the same expression] is: *In about this day*[79] *you find him* (1 Sm 9:13). Similar to his ex-

69 'It' designates the Torah.

70 אללה אכתרעני אול כלקה is R. Saadia's translation of the quoted part of Pr 8:22.

71 It is unclear how the fact that the unseen quality of the Torah or wisdom can lead the word 'great' as description of the same Torah. Because if its hidden nature forbids it to be called 'mighty' or 'awesome' the same aspect should make impossible to call it great.

72 Lit. "From the less important to the lesser important."

73 אלסמעיה literally, 'that we received by hearing.'

74 אלעקליה literally, 'that are mental' or 'rational.'

75 Lit. "According to what is known that the divisions of the 'name' are into four meanings."

76 כאן פי בעץ̇ אלאיאם דכל יוסף אלי אלבית ליצנע צנאעה is R. Saadia's translation of the citation from Gn 39:11.

77 ונחיא כיומנא הדֿא is R. Saadia's translation of the citation from Dt 6:24.

78 וחסנאת תכון לנא is R. Saadia's translation of the citation from Dt 6:25. חסנאת 'benefits' is R. Saadia's translation of the Hebrew word הצדקה applied to men. When the same Hebrew word is applied to God R. Saadia translates it by אלעדל 'justice.'

79 כהיום and not כהיום הזה.

pression: *To our kings, our lords and fathers too belongs the shame* (Dn 9:8).[80] The forth [passage where we find the expression כהיום הזה] is: *Therefore your land will become ruin, a desolation and a curse, without inhabitants as it is in this day* (Jer 44:22). Similar to his expression: *Your desolated sanctuary* (Dn 9:17), *and look on us thoroughly, on our desolation* (Dn 9:18). After [these] four passages there is a book that has [the expression]: כהיום. It is the book of Ezra, since it deals with the construction of the *second Temple*.[81] His expression: *Near* (Dn 9:7) [designates events] like *the exile of Babylon and Egypt*. [His expression]: *And far* (Dn 9:7) [designates events]: לחלח וחבור וגוזן.[82]

His repetition [of the expression]: *And as it is for us, O Lord, to our kings, {our lords and fathers too belongs the shame}* (Dn 9:8) refers to the elite of the population. Their transgression, in fact, is multiple.[83] His expression: *But to God our Lord belongs the mercy and the forgiveness* (Dn 9:7) means that 'while our sin is big, Your forgiveness is bigger still.' It is similar to what we find in the discourses of the prophets: *And our guilt mounted until heaven* (Ezr 9:6), *because your kindness is greater than heaven* (Ps 108:5).[84] His expression: *That did nothing under haven similar to what it did to Jerusalem* (Dn 9:12) refers to the story of the sons that ate the flesh of the fathers and like what Ezekiel said: *That is why the fathers will eat the sons in your middle and the sons will eat the fathers* (Ez 5:10).[85] Because something similar to the fathers eating flesh of the sons happened in Samaria at the time of Jehuram son of Ahab.[86] It is also possible that the two quotations reflect exaggeration for the severe hunger. However, since we found that *the fathers will eat the sons* (Ez 5:10) is possible, the fact that *the sons will eat the fathers* (Ez 5:10) too becomes plausible.

His expression: *Without imploring* (Dn 9:13) designates that [particular] time, as it was said there: *I will deprive them from having children, I will destroy My people, since they did not return from their way* (Jer 15:7). I inter-

80 The similarity between 1 Sm 9:13 and Dn 9:8 is not clear and no explanation is given to how the situation of Samuel choosing Saul as a ruler of Israel can be related to the prayer of Daniel.

81 Cf. Ezr 9:7.15. However, there is another passage where the expression כהיום הזה occurs. That is Neh 9:10.

82 Uncertain reading of the damaged manuscript.

83 R. Saadia does not expand on the reason for the particular importance of the elite's sins. Most probably because their knowledge of the consequences of their acts made their transgressions more conscious and more intentional.

84 לאן אחסאנך אעטם עלווא מן אלסמא is R. Saadia's translation of the quoted part of Ps 108:5.

85 It remains unclear how R. Saadia establishes a relation between Dn 9:12 and Ez 5:10.

86 Cf. Ex. R. s. 31.

preted his expression: *Therefore God finally decreed the calamity* (Dn 9:14) as a 'final decision' since we saw Him threatening for a longtime. When they refused He finally decided [the calamity]. In spite of that *it is Him who is just* (Dn 9:14).[87] It is Him who is just and kind, since He bestowed His kindness on us for eighteen years before the Exile of Jehoiachin, in which the Israelites[88] build and plant, as he said: *They built houses and dwelled [in them] and planted gardens* (Jer 29:5). In order that, when they prosper, they give to their neighbors and their families, so that may ease their distress.

As for his supplication, using the story: *Who has brought Your people out of the Land of Egypt by a strong hand* (Dn 9:15) in spite of the fact that there are almost one thousand years between them, his intention was [to say] 'that Your power is still the same, notwithstanding the longtime.[89] His addition [of the expression]: *According to all your kindness* (Dn 9:16) is comparable to what Samuel said: *All the kindness of the Lord that He accomplished in your favor and in favor of Your fathers* (1 Sm 12:7), *when Jacob went to Egypt* (1 Sm 12:8). His intention is saying: *And turn the light of Your face toward Your {desolated} sanctuary* (Dn 9:17) is to allow the reconstruction of Jerusalem and that He may bring back the Shekinah which is light, according to what Ezekiel has said: *And the earth was enlightened by His glory* (Ez 43:2). And similar to what will be said at the time of salvation in the story of *arise then shine, O Jerusalem, because your light has come* (Is 60:1)[90] until its end. His expression: *For Your sake* (Dn 9:17) is the same as for God's sake. Like his expression: *To You, O Lord* אליך יי' *I cried* (Ps 30:9) has the same meaning as the expression: *To the Lord* אל יי' *I made my supplication* (Ps 30:9).[91] Similar cases are many.

I rendered: הטה אלהי אזנך ושמע (Dn 9:18) *hear us completely* as I found that the people usually approach their ears if they want to hear fully. I also rendered: פקח עיניך וראה (Dn 9:18) *and look on us thoroughly* as I found that if they want

87 R. Saadia does not translate literally the MT. A more literal translation would be: 'Because the Lord our God is just.'

88 Lit: "They."

89 Yefet ben Eli: "Because by bringing Your people out of Egypt, by ten plagues, and You manifested their strength and their honor, over all the other nations. Thus, You have no other nation, but Israel." The meaning is: Don't destroy You only nation.

90 אלא פקומי פאצ'י יא דאר אלסלאם לאן נורך קד אקבל is R. Saadia's translation of the citation from Is 60:1. It is to be noted that R. Saadia adds to his translation דאר אלסלאם or Jerusalem, which does not exist in the MT. According to J. Derenbourg's edition of R. Saadia's commentary on Isaiah, he follows in this the targum which applies the same discourse to Jerusalem.

91 פאליך יא רב אדעו ואליך אתחנן is R. Saadia's translation of Ps 30:9. R. Saadia applies in his translation of Ps 30:9 what he is trying to explain here: That the Hebrew expression: אליך יי' is synonymous to the expression: אל יי'.

to look carefully, they normally insist in their look. And his intercession, using the expression: *It is to Your name that we appeal* (Dn 9:19) is by way of attribution, as it is in the expression of Joshua: *And what will You do for Your great name?* (Jos 7:9) since the population and the land belong to You? If You refuse to have mercy on them Your name will be despised among the nations. The prophets continually appealed to [God] using this meaning until He answered Ezekiel saying: *I do not do this for your sakes, O house of Israel, but because of My holly name which you have profaned among the nations to which you have come* (Ez 36:22), *and I will sanctify My holy name which was profaned among the nations* (Ez 36:23). He also said: *And I will make My name known among My people Israel and I will not let My name be profaned* (Ez 39:7).[92] Then he added:

Dn 9:20

Once again[93] I was appealing, praying and acknowledging my sin and the sins of my people the Israelites and placing my supplication between the hands of God my Lord about His holy mountain,

The discourse of Daniel proves that he did not register here all what he prayed for and appealed for. In fact, of his [discourse] he registered headlines alone, as its principles and apothegms. However, his intercession in favor of the people and Jerusalem is much more than that. [that is what we conclude] from his expression: *Once again* (Dn 9:20).[94]

Dn 9:21

While I am in my supplication, after the prayers,[95] the angel[96] Gabriel that I saw in my first vision, flying quickly reached me during the evening prayer.[97]

92 Yefet ben Eli: "Because Your name have been said of your city [Jerusalem]."

93 The Hebrew word ועוד at the beginning of Dn 9:20 and Dn 9:21 is translated differently by R. Saadia. In Dn 9:20 he translates it by ואיצׄא 'again.' In Dn 9:21 the same word is translated by ובינמא 'while.' His translation of Dn 9:20 'again' is in harmony with R. Saadia's interpretation that the prayer of Daniel is much longer than what is transmitted in Dn 9. Yefet ben Eli translates the same word by ובעד אנא מתכלם 'while I am speaking still.'

94 R. Saadia avoids the explanation of 'Daniel's sin.' Yefet ben Eli attributes this sin to the time when Daniel was living according to the instructions he received from his parents, before living according to God's law. He, therefore, introduces a conversion to God's law in the middle of Daniel's life.

95 MT: "During the prayer" which also Yefet ben Eli's translation.

Dn 9:22

He instructed me, because he spoke to me, saying:[98] 'O Daniel, I came forth now to instruct you how to understand,

Dn 9:23

In fact, from the beginning of your supplication, an order was issued for you[99] and I came to tell you, since it is you who are chosen[100] who understand the matter and who contemplate the vision.

His expression: *While I am in my supplication* (Dn 9:21) indicates that he was answered before the end of his appeal, which is the condition of being righteous [according to the expression of the prophet Isaiah]: *And while they are still speaking I already heard them* (Is 65:24).[101] And from what we have learned from our master Moses, God told him: *Why do you cry to Me? Ordain that the Israelites leave* (Ex 14:15).[102] [We know this too] from Eliezer, about whom it was said: *Before he finished his discourse...* (Gn 24:15)[103] and what is similar to such [meaning]. His expression: *The angel Gabriel that I saw in my first vision* (Dn 9:21) testifies that he believed now that what he had saw in his sleep was a prophecy, since the individual whom he saw while being awake [... ...] sleep, in the condition of the vision [...] the intention of the message is to answer his appeal in favor of his people and Jerusalem.[104] He informed him about what will happen to both: The destruction of the first Temple and the destruction of the second Temple and that there will be four hundred ninety years between [the two events]. Therefore he said:

---

96 האיש literally 'the man' is translated by R. Saadia and Yefet ben Eli as 'angel' מלאך.

97 MT: "During the evening offering" which also Yefet ben Eli's translation.

98 Yefet ben Eli: "He made me understand and said to me."

99 לך 'for you' is added by R. Saadia and has no source in the MT.

100 Yefet ben Eli: "A man of desires."

101 ובינאהם יתכלמון קד סמעת להם is R. Saadia's translation of the citation from Is 65:24. R. Saadia seems to indicate that the righteous has, as an correlative to his being righteous, the benefit of being heard before the end of his prayer.

102 מא תצרך אלי מר בני אסראיל אן ירחלו is R. Saadia's translation of the citation from Ex 14:15. The understanding of R. Saadia is this: 'Why are you crying to me, telling Me something that I already know.'

103 פהו קבל אן יפרג׳ מן כלאמה is R. Saadia's translation of the citation from Gn 24:15.

104 While the Ms is damaged the meaning remains clear: the angel Gabriel being a messenger of God to tell Daniel a prophecy in his second appearance to him, the first time that Daniel saw him must also be to tell him a prophecy.

Dn 9:24

They are seventy weeks decreed concerning your people and your holy city, in order to terminate transgression[105] and sin and to forgive the iniquity, to bring eternal justice, to seal inspiration[106] and prophecy[107] and the anointing of the most holy place,

Dn 9:25

Learn and understand that from the time the order was issued until the return and the construction of Jerusalem with[108] the anointed and leader,[109] there will be seven weeks, then in sixty two weeks[110] its alleys and its sections will be rebuilt, but there will be groaning sometimes,[111]

Dn 9:26

After the sixty two weeks the anointed will be cut off the place[112] and nothing of him [will remain], the city and the sanctuary will be corrupted by the people of the coming leader, its end will be by drowning, and until the end of the war, it will be marked by desolation,

Dn 9:27

He shall establish a covenant to the many for one week, in its middle, however, he will break the rest of the sacrifice[113] and the offering and in his

105 Yefet ben Eli adds another interpretation: To contain the transgression.

106 R. Saadia renders the Hebrew word חזון literally 'vision' by the Arabic word אלוחי 'inspiration.'

107 R. Saadia renders the Hebrew word נביא literally 'prophet' by the Arabic word אלנבוה literally 'prophecy.'

108 R. Saadia translates Hebrew word עד literally 'until, to the point of' by the Arabic word מע 'with'. This translation allows him to place the period mentioned in Dn 9:25, seven weeks, between the time the decree was issued and the coming back, and not between the coming back from the exile and the arriving of the anointed.

109 The Hebrew נגיד is rendered by R. Saadia as אלמדבר literally 'the one who is in charge' and by Yefet ben Eli as חליפה literally 'the hire' or 'the one who comes afterward.'

110 Yefet ben Eli: "There will be seven weeks which are sixty two weeks."

111 Yefet ben Eli renders the last expression of Dn 9:25 בצוק העתים by the Arabic expression ענין אלאוקאת literally 'the kneaded times.' He explains it as reference to the time of trial concerning the high priest.

112 "Off the pace" is added by R. Saadia and has no source in the MT.

113 ינכת פי עטל אלדבח literally 'he breaks the repose of the sacrifice.' As if he does not prohibit the sacrifice itself, but by breaking the repose necessary to perform the sacrifice. Yefet ben Eli" "He will stop the sacrifice."

expansion[114] of the abomination there will be desolation until he is destroyed and cut off, and they will remain desolated.'[115]

[...] years, since he said: *I will count seven rest years for you* (Lv 25:8) and also: *Seven days-weeks of rest years* (Lv 26:8).[116] In fact there are two exceptions in the Torah, *weeks and days*, according to what we have explained. His expression: *Concerning Your people* (Dn 9:24) does not indicates all the nation, which is the whole of the people of Daniel. What he meant is *the tribes of Judah and Benjamin* which are the particular people of Daniel, since he is from Judah. The request of Daniel, explicitly and implicitly, certainly pertains to the nation as a whole. However, the objective being relative to the construction of the second Temple and to the return to it of the people who, according to the explanation of the Book of Ezra, were in their majority from the tribes of Judah and Benjamin, the answer must be particular, and refers to the immediate people of Daniel. Such is the explanation of [the Book] of Ezra: *These are the children of the province who came up from the captives of the exile, whom Nebuchadnezzar, king of Babylon deported to Babylon* (Ezr 2:1). He counts their number, which is thirty thousands in detail, that becomes in total more than forty two thousands. This demonstrates those who are counted in detail are from Judah and Benjamin and what is added to them [and appears] in the total comes from all the tribes.

Now that we answered this big question, let us add an answer to another big question. That is that repetition by Nehemiah the population count, already counted by Ezra, without obtaining the same number.[117] There are people mentioned by Ezra that Nehemiah did not mention. There are others that Nehemiah mentioned and that Ezra did not mention. With all that, Nehemiah said: *And my God put into my heart to gather the nobles, the prefects and the people in order to register them by family and I found a register of genealogy of those who were first to come up and found written there* (Neh 7:5). This supposes agreement

114 כנף literally 'wing' is rendered by מבסוט literally 'expended.'

115 Yefet ben Eli: "And over the wing of abominations he will desolated" or " he will spread desolation, until the time of the end, then God's fury will be poured out on the one who spreads desolation."

116 סנה] תֹם אחץ לך סבע סנין עטלה [ודלך סבע סנין סבע מראר] פתציר גמלה [דלך תסע ארבעין is R. Saadia translation of Lv 26:8. In fact R. Saadia does not translate the Hebrew part on this verse והיו לך ימי שבע שבתות שנים. He got rid of the difficulty by translating it as פתציר גמלה דלך literally 'and the total of all this becomes.' It is to be noted that the Hebrew word שבתות is translated by עטלה 'rest.' We are here in the determination of the jubilee year. The translation suggested tries to be in harmony with R. Saadia's understanding.

117 Lit: "We find them with plus and minus."

[between Ezra and Nehemiah], but there is disagreement instead.[118] That is why we say that there must be a hidden part. *I found* in the *register* (Neh 7:5) that the children of such [tribe] remain the same, that the [number of the] children of such another [tribe] increased, that the [number of the] children of such another diminished, that the children of such another vanished. Someone, with no mention at the beginning [for example], was found by Nehemiah in his time. In fact, there are thirty six years between the time of Nehemiah and the time of Ezra. Because the time of Ezra [starts] *at the first year of Cyrus* (Ezra 1:1) and there sixteen years between his [time] and the beginning of Artaxerxes. While the time of Nehemiah [starts] *at the twentieth year of Artaxerxes the king* (Neh 2:1). In those thirty six years, some were born, others died, some increased, others diminished. Thus, his expression: *Concerning Your people* (Dn 9:24) pertains to the house of Judah and Benjamin together.

He made it possible that the events of those seventy weeks gather facts [...] some are joyful and others are sad. They are seven events: *To finish the transgression, the sin and to forgive iniquities, to bring eternal justice* (Dn 9:24). These four [events] are joyful. But among there are also: *To seal inspiration and prophecy and the anointing of the most holy place* (Dn 9:24). These three are sad. In saying: *To bring eternal justice* (Dn 9:24) he does not mean something left alone without interruption, because of the word עולמים *eternity* (Dn 9:24) that hints to centuries and universe. What he wants to designate is a particular century and a particular period of time. It is the time of justice that He will establishes [during] the second Temple. Investigating, we found that [the word] *eternity* (Dn 9:24) [indicates] a past time, following what Koheleth had said: *There is something about which one say 'look, this one is new' it happened long since, in ages* עולמים *that went by before us* (Ecc 1:10). And, hence the time before us is already gone, thus it becomes clear that עולמים designates a partial time. That is why the Bible[119] [expressing the idea] of eternity says: עד עולמי עד *to all eternity* (Is 45:17)[120] and what is similar to that. Among those three hundred ninety years there was the promise for the house of Judah *to finish the transgression, the sin and to forgive iniquities* (Dn 9:24). It is what he promised them according to Jeremiah's expression: *Thus said the Lord, the God of Israel 'like these good figs I will look favorably to the Judean exiles that I have sent away from this place to the land of the Chaldean. I will look upon them favorably and brig them back to this land, I will build them and not pull them*

118 The fact that there is a register containing names and numbers of the deported families is a reason to find the same number in the book of Ezra and the book of Nehemiah. We have a disagreement, whoever, between the two books.

119 Lit. "I say that is why he says.'

120 אלי עואלם אלדהר is R. Saadia translation of the citation from Is 45:17. Literally 'to the ages of eternity.'

down, I will plant them and not uproot them, I will give them a heart to know Me, for I am the Lord, and they shall be My people and I will be their God, for they shall return to Me with all their heart (Jer 24:5–7) which happens at the beginning of the construction of the second Temple. At that time, at the period of Nehemiah, it will be right for them *to bring eternal justice* (Dn 9:24). You also know that the judgement and the justice appeared at the time of Ezra, following the expression: *And you Ezra, by the wisdom of your God in your hand, appoint magistrates and judges* (Ezr 7:25) *and whoever refuses to obey the law of your God* (Ezr 7:26) and the rest of the passage. Nehemiah too described His justice and His mercy for the people: *But I did not do saw, because of the fear of God* (Neh 5:15), *remember in my favor, O God, all what I did for this people* (Neh 5:19).[121]

During some of the three hundred ninety years the prophecy ceased and the inspiration was sealed, attested by his expression: *To seal inspiration and prophecy* (Dn 9:24) [and] according to Ezekiel has said: *Because the vision concerning the whole does not return* (Ez 7:13). The Bible[122] also said: *Her prophets find no vision from the Lord* (Lam 2:9). In fact seventy years to the construction and at its achievement the ceasing of the anointing happened to them as he said: *and the anointing of the most holy place* (Dn 9:24). No one from the family of Aaron remained in order to be *high priest and common priest* who are called holy among holy of holies as he said: *The sons of Amram are Aaron and Moses, and Aaron was separated, he and his sons in order to be sanctified for ever, holy of holies, to offer burnt offerings to the Lord, to minister to Him and to bless in His name for ever* (1 Chr 23:13). Therefore Gabriel gathered all these events and told Daniel that there Duration is three hundred ninety years as we have already explained.

Then he divided for him the three weeks into three parts. The first part is seven weeks [indicated] by his expression: Learn and understand that from the time the order was issued until the return and the construction of Jerusalem with the anointed and leader, seven weeks (Dn 9:25). The second part is sixty two weeks, about which he told him: Then in sixty two weeks its alleys and its sections will be rebuilt (Dn 9:25). The third part is one week, about which he told him: He shall establish a covenant to the population for one week (Dn 9:27). The total is seventy weeks. Yet, he mad an exception for half of the last week, saying: In its middle, however, he breaks the rest of the sacrifice and the offering (Dn 9:27) in order not to expand [the number] seventy. We will fully explain these three parts.

121 The two passages from taken from the end of the prayers of Nehemiah describe how the people and the governor were observant of the divine law.

122 Lit: "He also said."

The explanation of the first part, which is of seven weeks, [is this]. Gabriel had determined it *from the time the order was issued* (Dn 9:25) until the time of *the return and the construction of Jerusalem* (Dn 9:25). His expression: *from the time the order was issued* (Dn 9:25) does not mean *from the time the order was issued for Daniel.* I mean [he does not refer] to what Gabriel said to Daniel: *From the beginning of your supplication, an order was issued* (Dn 9:23). Because [the order mentioned here] concerns the time of his conversation with him.[123] What he wants to say is *from the time the order was issued for Jeremiah* about their return. [All this is contained in] what he said to them: *When the seventy years at Babylon are accomplished, I will take note of you and I will fulfill my good word for you* (Jer 29:10). Thus, his expression: *my good word* (Jer 29:10) is *the order* [that] *was issued* (Dn 9:25). In fact, there are fifty years from before the ruin of the first Temple until the time when Cyrus gave the permission of *the return and the construction of Jerusalem* (Dn 9:25), according to what we have explained [while commenting the expression]: *The number of years* (Dn 9:2). Whoever, seven weeks means forty nine years, but he did not want the added year, because it was not a half week. Then in the fifty first year reigned and appeal for *the return and the construction of Jerusalem* (Dn 9:25) in saying: *{Anyone of you His people} may his God be with him and let him go up to Jerusalem which is in Judah and build the house of the Lord* (Ezr 1:3). And it is possible that his expression: *with the anointed and leader* (Dn 9:25) designate anyone of the leaders, the one who gives order, as well as the one who receives order. I mean Cyrus and Jeshua son of Jozadak. As for Jeshua son of Jozadak, he could be called *anointed* because he was *high priest*, since the Bible[124] said: *If the anointed priest* {sins} … (Lv 4:3),[125] *then the anointed priest takes …* (Lv 4:5),[126] *the [anointed] priest from his sons that comes after him* (Lv 6:15).[127] He calls *leader* (Dn 9:25) as it is in *Jehoiada the leader of the house of Aaron* (1 Chr 12:28). He also said: *Azaryah the leader in the house of the Lord* (2 Chr 31:13). As for Cyrus, he is called anointed, as it is for any established monarch, anointed or not, as it was said for the king of Tyre: *You are the far anointed Cherub* (Ez 28:14).[128] And he calls *leader* (Dn 9:25) as it is in *son of man say to the leader of Tyre: 'Because your heart is lifted up …* (Ez 28:2).

123 The time in which Daniel addressed God. Or the time in which Gabriel was speaking with Daniel.

124 Lit: "He."

125 אן אכטא אלמאם אלממסוח is R. Saadia's translation of the citation from Lv 4:3.

126 ויאכד אלמאם אלממסוח is R. Saadia's translation of the citation from Lv 4:5.

127 וכדך אלמאם [אלממסוח] אלמסתכלף בעדה מן בניה is R. Saadia's translation of the quoted part of Lv 6:15. To be noted that in his translation of Lv 6:15 R. Saadia omits to translate the Hebrew word המשיח.

128 Uncertain meaning of the Hebrew text.

You also know that God tolled Elijah: *You go and anoint Hazael the king of Aram* (1 Kgs 19:15). But we have no trace of him, neither [a trace of] Elisha anointed him. Elisha, however, addressed him: *The lord made me see that you become king of Aram* (2 Kgs 8:13).

Thus, it became clear that the word anointed pertains to every of leadership, in Israel or among the nations.[129] The Bible[130] also said about Abraham Isaac and Jacob: *He said 'do not harm my anointed ones and do not hurt my prophets* (Ps 105:15)[131] without having any one anoint them by oil or any thing else. It is possible that someone indicate Cyrus in particular was designated and called *His anointed* by God, since He had established him leader saying: *Thus said the Lord to His anointed Cyrus* (Is 45:1).[132] Yet, tow other interpretations [for this passage] remain possible. First, that by [the expression] the Bible[133] alludes to Isaiah by its expression *His anointed* (Is 45:1) since he is one of the prophets and God[134] may tell him this or that about Cyrus. The other [interpretation], that the Bible[135] hints to the redeemer that we are expecting, by its expression *His anointed* (Is 45:1), implying אות משיחו. As if He made of the story of Nebuchadnezzar a wonder and a proof the salvation events. And because the events concerning Nebuchadnezzar were verified, the events of the redeemer will be verified, and according to what we have explained in the commentary of Isaiah.

He explained of the second part[136] which is of sixty two week saying: *Then in sixty two weeks {its alleys and its sections} will be rebuilt* (Dn 9:25). The total

129 In his commentary of Dn 9:26 Yefet ben Eli offers two hypothesis about the interpretation of the Hebrew expression: עד המשיח נגיד. Either the המשיח and נגיד designate the same individual. In this case the indicates the high priest. Or, in case they designate two different individuals, the המשיח indicates the messiah and נגיד indicates Zerubabel son of Shealtiel (cf. Ezr 3:2.8).

130 Lit. "He."

131 קאל לא תודו מסיחאי ולא תסוא אלי אנביאי is R. Saadia's translation of Ps 105:15. The Arabic קאל 'he said' and is added by R. Saadia in his translation and has no Hebrew origin.

132 לאן כדא קאל אללה למסיחה ען כורש is R. Saadia's translation of Is 45:1. It is very important to notice that R. Saadia quotes Is 45:1 in manner that contradict his translation, since the literal rendering of his translation is: 'Because this is what God told His anointed about Cyrus.' He does not apply the Hebrew word משיחו to Cyrus. This is the meaning that he will explain immediately in giving tow interpretations for this passage, that do not apply משיחו to Cyrus. This is the one exception where R. Saadia's translation of the quoted part of Is 45:1 is not followed in the English translation here.

133 Lit. "He."

134 Lit. "He."

135 Lit: "He."

136 The second part of the seventy weeks.

of this four hundred thirty four years.[137] If take this into consideration the second Temple will stand for four hundred thirty four years. But when he added: *Its alleys and its sections {will be rebuilt} but there will be groaning sometimes* (Dn 9:25) two interpretations became possible. The first is that וחרוץ רחוב (Dn 9:25) designate the alleys of the city and sections. It has the same meaning as in *harrow of Iron* (2 Sm 12:31) and *pieces of cheese* (1 Sm 17:18) and similar cases. The second interpretation[138] is that the construction was done, once easily, and once with difficulty. I consider this as the meaning of the expression: *But there will be groaning sometimes* (Dn 9:25).[139] The fact that there are stay and quickness sometimes [means] that the four hundred thirty four years should not be considered [years of] full construction. There must be among them interruption, interdiction, stay and quickness, which is [what he witness] in saying: *Then the work of the house of the Lord at Jerusalem was interrupted, until the second year of the reign of king Darius of Persia* (Ezr 4:24). So the work was interrupted sixteen years, in a way, or eighteen years in another way, if we add the incomplete years, according to what we have explained [in commenting the expression]: *The number of years* (Dn 9:2).

Then he informed us that after these sixty two weeks there will be no more anointing for any human being, saying: *The anointed will be cut off the place and nothing of him will remain* (Dn 9:26). Neither from the family of Aaron, nor from the family of David. Because his expression: *The anointed will be cut off* (Dn 9:26) has the meaning of all the anointed will be cut off, without hinting to a particular individual. This can be demonstrated in conjunction with the beginning of the story when he said: *In order to terminate the transgression, the sin and to forgive the iniquity* (Dn 9:25), while it is untrue that there is one *transgression*, one *sin* and one *iniquity*. What he meant is *every transgression*, *every sin* and *every iniquity*. There is also his expression: *To seal inspiration and prophecy* (Dn 9:24) that does not designate one *inspiration* and one *prophecy*. What it means is *every inspiration* and *every prophecy*. His expression: *He breaks the rest of the sacrifice and the offering* (Dn 9:27) refers to *every sacrifice* and *every offering*, and not one sacrifice. Thus, his expression: *The anointed will be cut off* (Dn 9:26) does not designate one *anointed*, but *all the anointed*. Such [examples] are measureless in short time in the language of the Hebrews, like when they say: *Horse and rider He has thrown into the sea* (Ex 15:1).[140] What they wanted to say is: *All the horses and all the riders He thrown them*

137 The result of 62 weeks (where every day is a year) multiplied by 7 days of every week.

138 Lit: "The other."

139 Lit: "I apply to that but there will be groaning sometimes"

140 אלכ̇יל ורכאבהא רמא בהם פי אלבחר is R. Saadia's translation of the citation from Ex 15.1. to be noticed that R. Saadia translates in a plural form.

into the sea. They say too: *Since the woman of Benjamin has been killed off* (Jgs 21:16). What they mean is *all the women*, not one women. They also say: *Be ashamed, you farmers, wail, you vine dressers over the wheat and over the barley* (Jl 1:11). They want to say: *All the wheat and all the barley*. There are many cases like this. Therefore, the group that insisted on this [passage], applying it to their master, did not consider these proofs at all.[141] They also neglected the context of the language because the expression *cut off* applies to the person who is liable to be put to death, as it was said: *Spirit of human beings are in their bodies, who ever eat them shall be cut off* (Lv 17:14).[142] And also: *This man will be cut off completely; his iniquity will be upon him* (Nm 15:31).[143] And when they saw that their master was born one hundred thirty five years before the destruction of the second Temple, they considered that these four hundred thirty four years started at the time [the vision] was told to Daniel.[144] Therefore, they added the fifty years earlier to that to the one hundred thirty five years after the birth of their master. The total was close to two hundred years that they added in the chronology between the Persian and the Greek reign. They pretended that from the time the vision was told to Daniel until the beginning of the reign of the one with the two horns there are a bit more than two hundred forty years. And, unsatisfied with that, they attacked us pretending that we deducted from the count two hundred years, out of prejudice against their master. The did the same concerning the date of *the creation*. In fact, they learned by hearing that the messiah comes in the fifth thousands of the creation. Yet, when the counted and found that their master had come in the forth thousands [of the creation] they added one thousand year to the chronology in order that [the coming of their messiah] coincides with the fifth thousands. We inquired about them and found that they pretend that Adam lived two hundred thirty years before the

141 the grope that R. Saadia does not mention by name, could be one of the following three: The Karaites, another dissident Jewish group, the Christians. To be noticed that Yefet ben Eli, for example, does not pay particular attention to the messiah in Dn 9:6. In fact, it is impossible for him to see in the messiah of Dn 9:26 the one the Karaites expect, since in Dn 9:26 he is 'cut off.' We will see shortly that the group whom R. Saadia refutes here is the Christian church.

142 אד׳ נפוס כל אלבשרין אלדם מסכנהא וכל מן אכלה ינקטע is R. Saadia's translation of the citation from Lv 17:14. To be noticed that R. Saadia in his translation renders the Hebrew expression: נפש כל בשר which is in a singular form, by the Judeo-Arabic expression: נפוס כל אלבשרין which has a plural form.

143 פינקטע ד׳לך אלאנסאן אנקטאעא ווזרה עליה is R. Saadia's translation of the citation from Nm 15:31.

144 It is clear now that the 'master' designated here is Jesus Christ and that the group being under R. Saadia's attack is the Christian Church.

birth of Shet.[145] Then [Shet] lived two hundred five years before the birth of Enosh.[146] And Enosh lived one hundred ninety years before the birth of Kenan.[147] And Kenan lived one hundred seventy years before the birth of Mahalalel.[148] In such way, they added one thousand years from Adam to the Flood. Worse than that, they pretend that it is us who deducted [the numbers] out of prejudice against their master. *God save my soul from the false discourse and from the malicious tongue* (Ps 120:2).[149] The strange thing is that the chronology of the copies of the Torah that they have is the same as the chronology we have. Nonetheless, they pretend that they found a copy containing this chronology in the coffer of the *wicked* Ptolemy[150] that different scribes had transmitted. However, they do not correct their copies according to its contents.[151] They are truly blind in what they pretend.

We examined his expression: *The city and the sanctuary will be corrupted by the people of the coming leader* (Dn 9:26) and found that it refers to Titus the Roman,[152] because the title *leader* pertains more to him than to all other kings[153] about whom Daniel said: *Until the covenant rule over them* (Dn 11:22).[154] He is the one who reached and destroyed Jerusalem and its region, according to the tradition of our nation. His expression: *Its end will be by drowning* (Dn 9:26)[155]

145 Cf. Gn 5:3 where it is mentioned that Adam lived one hundred thirty years before the birth of Shet.

146 Cf. Gn 5:6 where it is mentioned that Shet lived one hundred five years before the birth of Enosh.

147 Cf. Gn 5:9 where it is mentioned that Enosh lived ninety years before the birth of Kenan.

148 Cf. Gn 5:12 where it is mentioned that Kenan lived seventy years before the birth of Mahalalel.

149 אללהם כדׄאך נגי נפסי מן קול אלבאטל ומן לסאן אלארב is R. Saadia's translation of Ps 120: 2. To be noticed that R. Saadia translates the Hebrew expression: שקר משפת literally 'from the lying lips' by the Judeo-Arabic expression: קול אלבאטל 'the false discourse.'

150 According to the legend, Ptolemy II Philadelphus (283–247 B.C.) wishing to have the law of the Jews in his library was at the origin of the Greek version of the Old Testament, or the LXX.

151 In another word, in spite of their assertion that their Greek chronology, different from the chronology of the Hebrew text, is the right one, they do not dare correct the Hebrew text of Genesis.

152 Cf. Targ. Lam 1:19. bGitt. 56b.

153 Lit. "Because he is leader over the naming of all the kings."

154 Translated according to R. Saadia's interpretation. His translation will be discussed ad. loc.

155 Yefet ben Eli' interpretation of 'its end will be by drowning' is that the remaining few of the Israelites will be deported.

means that his army will inundate the land completely, as it was said about Pharaoh: *Behold! Waters are rising from the north, they shall become a raging flood, they shall inundate the land and its creatures, town and its inhabitants* (Jer 47:2). He also said that the Assyrian king: *He shall pass through the family of Judah sweep and go over, after that the water had reached the neck* (Is 8:8).[156] The use of this word[157] by Daniel is multiple: *The noble men among the deported will be deported in his presence* (Dn 11:22)[158] and similar cases. We examined the Bible again about his expression: *And until the end of the war, it is marked by desolation* (Dn 9:26) and found that *the end of the war* (Dn 9:26)[159] is three years, which is the half of a week. The meaning of *marked {by desolation}* (Dn 9:26) refers to the two ways in which a war ends: Either in favor of the people or against them. This war, however, ended against them. It meant more of desolation and destruction of their country, than being [their physical destruction].

His expression: *He shall establish a covenant to the many for one week* (Dn 9:27) means that he establishes a pact and a covenant with them for one week. Yet, he betrays them in the middle of that week, engaging the war against them and prohibiting them from presenting the offering of the meat and the seed, which is the same as forbidding *the daily burnt offering*. His expression: *And in his expansion of the abomination there will be desolation* (Dn 9:27) designates the statue that they introduced to Jerusalem, as he said: *And {he built an altar} for Molech, the abomination of the Ammonites* (1 Kgs 11:7),[160] *you have seen their abominations* (Dt 29:16)[161] and similar cases. He also said in the *Geziroth*: *He established a statue in the Temple.* In narrating this he used the word כנף (Dn 9:27)[162] wanting to say that he expanded it and the place was covered by it. like his expression: *So {the water} filled its farthest regions completely* (Is 8:8).[163] In fact this the word כנף has five meanings. The first, is its

156 וימצ׳י פי אל יהודה וינסאב וימר בעד אן יאלג׳ אלמא אלי אלענק the citation from Is 8:8 as translated by R. Saadia.

157 Out of thirty seven uses of the verb שָׁטַף, and noun שֶׁטֶף (sixteen of them in the prophetic books) Daniel uses the verb four times and the noun two times. With the exception of Dn 9:26 all the other uses are in Dn 11.

158 Translated according to R. Saadia's interpretation. His translation will be discussed ad. loc.

159 Yefet ben Eli specifies that it is the war against Gog. He also notice that it is the case of the Jerusalem of his time.

160 The altar that Salomon built to Molech, the divinity of the Ammonites.

161 וראיתם ארג׳אסהם is R. Saadia's translation of the citation from Dt 29:16.

162 The same Hebrew word in Dn 9:27 designates the Greek army, for Yefet ben Eli. He also mention that their army is normally labeled by שׁקוצים.

163 פיכון מאל אקטארה מלא is R. Saadia's translation of the citation from Is 8:8.

obvious meaning: Wing. [like in the expression]: *And every bird having a wing* (Gn 7:14).[164] The second [meaning] is 'a corner in the house' as in [the expression]: *The four corners of the house* (Jb 1:19).[165] The same [meaning may be applied] to the whole earth, as in [the expression]: *From the farthest regions of the earth* (Is 24:16),[166] *from the four farthest regions of the earth* (Is 11:12).[167] The same thing [may be said] about the veil [as in the expression]: *In the four ends of your garment* (Dt 22:12),[168] *and tie them in your skirts* (Ez 5:3). The third [meaning] is the radiance of the sun as the Bible[169] said: *Righteousness and healing in its radiance* (Mal 3:20).[170] The forth [meaning] is the first light of dawn, as in the expression:[171] *And if I wished to look to the apparition of dawn* (Ps 139:9).[172] The fifth [meaning pertains] to the expansion that someone operates, [like in the expression]: *And in his expansion of the abomination* (Dn 9:27). It is also possible that כנף may be used metaphorically to depict the protection of God for His friends, as the Bible[173] said: *He protects you by His wings like a bird who covers by its feather* (Ps 91:4)[174] and similar cases.

He concluded the discourse by: *Until he is destroyed and cut off, and they will remain desolated* (Dn 9:27). By his expression: *He is destroyed* (Dn 9:27) he refers to the sword, the whip. [His expression]: *Cut off* (Dn 9:27) [indicates] the disease. So he states that these two [calamities] merge over the land, in addition to the desolation. In fact, in the language [of the book] of Daniel the sword is called כלה [as in the expression]: *He shall remain firm in the land of Syria and a sword* כלה *was in his hand* (Dn 11:16). As for נחרצה 'disease' it [has a meaning] similar to [the meaning of] the expression: *Or his age is shortened*

164 כל טאיר די גנאח is R. Saadia's translation of the citation from Gn 7:14.

165 ארבע זואיא אלבית is R. Saadia's translation of the citation from Jb 1:19.

166 מן אקטאר אלארץ׳ is R. Saadia's translation of the citation from Is 24:16. When it refers to the earth the Hebrew word כנף is translated by the Arabic word that means 'side, region' with the connotation of the 'end of the earth' or 'the farthest regions.'

167 מן ארבע אקטאר אלארץ׳ is R. Saadia's translation of the citation from Is 11:12.

168 פי ארבעה אטראף אזארך is R. Saadia's translation of the citation from Dt 22:12.

169 Lit: "He."

170 R. Saadia seems to understand Mal 3:20 as follow: 'But to you who fear my name the sun shall arise, righteousness and healing in its radiance בכנפיה.' Another traditional understanding is this: 'But to you who fear my name the sun of righteousness shall arise, with healing in its wings.'

171 Lit: "As when you say."

172 ואן עסית אן אתחאמל נחו מטלע אלפגר is R. Saadia's translation of the citation from Ps 139:9.

173 Lit: "He."

174 ויחגבך כאלטאיר אלד׳י יסתרברישה ויכן באגנחתה is R. Saadia's translation of the citation from Ps 91:4.

(Jb 14:5).[175] This condition does not change until God drive them out of the land, as the Bible[176] says: *They shall dwell in it, there will be no more destruction and Jerusalem will remain secure* (Zec 14:11). [the commentary] of the ninth chapter is completed.

175 או יבתר עמרה is R. Saadia's translation of the citation from Jb 14:5. The translation of this part of Jb 14:5 by R. Saadia does not reflect his idea of חרוצים as 'diseases.' However, in his commentary on this verse he explains that the expression: ימיו אם חרוצים is an aspect of the human weaknesses. Hence its reference to the disease that shortens the human life.

176 Lit: "He."

Chapter 10

Dn 10:1

In the third year of Cyrus the king of Persia a matter was appeared[1] to Daniel whose name is Belteshazzar, this matter is true and its intention is big,[2] he understood the matter and was enlightened about the vision.[3]

The first thing that need to be explained in this verse is the meaning of his expression: *Daniel whose name is Belteshazzar* (Dn 10:1). We say that this name is noble in Nebuchadnezzar's eyes, since it carries the name of his god Bel. That is why he honored Daniel [by bestowing on him this name] as he said: *Daniel whose name is Belteshazzar, following the name of my god* (Dn 4:5). However, the Jews and the angels did not call him by a name other than Daniel. The Book will show, in its middle, that Gabriel called him Daniel several times.[4] In fact, in the first vision he called him by a neutral [name]: *Make this [man] understand the interpretation of the vision* (Dn 8:16). And also: *Understand, O son of man* (Dn 8:17). Then we ask, what is the meaning of [the expression]: *This matter is true* (Dn 10:1)? Is there any doubt that *[this matter] is true* (Dn 10:1), since it is [part of] a revealed discourse?[5] It is because that he intends to say that it in-

1 Yefet ben Eli: "A discourse" or "a saying was revealed to Daniel."

2 וצבא גדול is rendered by R. Saadia as אלמראד לה כביר literally 'the desire for him is big' or 'its intention is great,' follow the Aramaic meaning of the verb צבא 'to choose, to desire' or צבי 'desirable thing' as he will explain in his commentary. While Yefet ben Eli translates the same expression by 'big army' following the Hebrew meaning of צבא 'army' explaining that it belongs either to the Romans or to the Arabs.

3 ובינה לו במראה is understood by R. Saadia as pertaining to the part of the vision that he did not understand by himself, so he needed to be informed, which is exactly what Gabriel the angel did. Thus the translation follows closely his commentary on this part of Dn 10:1. Yefet ben Eli: "He was instructed by vision."

4 Lit: "It will also be described in the middle of the story that Gabriel called him Daniel many times." Yefet ben Eli, commenting Dn 10:1 makes a distinction between אשר נקרא שמו בלטשאצר (MT) 'who was called Belteshazzar' and the usual way of naming someone אשר שמו בלטשאצר 'whose name is Belteshazzar.' He concludes that the MT hints to the fact that Daniel was called Belteshazzar during the Kasdians' time alone.

5 Lit. "Since he had said a revealed discourse, are we going to doubt that it is true."

cludes neither condition nor exception.[6] In fact, many prophecies, as you may know, does not contain any clear exception. However, by mental deduction or judgment exception or exceptions may be found, like in the declaration: *Forty more days and Nineveh will be overthrown* (Jon 3:4).

I rendered צבא by 'intention' because I estimate it according to the Aramaic meaning,[7] [like the expressions]: די לא תשׂנא צבו בדניאל *because his intention about Daniel did not change*; צבית *desired*; ליצבא *in order to desire*; ולמן די יצבא *to the man who wishes*. His description of the intention that it is big is because it unites the conditions of four kingdoms, plus the explanation of the end, the purpose of the salvation, *the resurrection of the dead,* and the reward *in the world to come*. What a prophecy, the one that unites all these matters! His repetition of the expressions: *He understood* ובין *the matter and was informed* ובינה לה *about the vision* (Dn 10:1) indicates that he understood by himself the biggest part of the vision.[8] He did not, yet, understand a part of it until he was enlightened by Gabriel, as he will say at the end [of the book]: *I heard it and did not understood* (Dn 12:8) until the angel enlightened him later. That is why I wrote 'he understood' ופהם and 'he was enlightened' ואפהם. Then he said:

Dn 10:2
At that time I was sad for three weeks-days.

Dn 10:3
I did not take a delicious nourishment, meat and drinks did not go into my mouth[9] and did not anoint myself until the accomplishment of three weeks-days.

The advanced reason for his sadness this time is that he beseeched and prayed in *the first year of Darius* (Dn 9:1) and was answered in the *seventy weeks* (Dn 9:24). It is noticeable also that in the second year he pleaded with Cyrus for the construction of the Temple. But a year later the construction was interrupted. All those years are incomplete, as we have explained, and that those five years, two years of Darius and the three years of Cyrus, plus the three years of Belshazzar, are equal to only five [years]. Thus, when the interruption occurred

6 Yefet ben Eli: "ואמת הדבר means that the discourse should be understood in its obvious signification, since it is neither a dream nor a vision." in other word, it is a discourse that suffers no interpretation and should be taken in its apparent meaning.
7 Lit. "According to the language of the Targum."
8 Lit. "The story."
9 Yefet ben Eli: "I did not take bread of delicacy, meat and wine did not go into my mouth."

after [the beginning] of the construction, Daniel became sad and said because of it: *I was sad* (Dn 10:2).[10] Similar to what Nehemiah said because of his grief about Jerusalem: *And it happened that when I heard these words I sat down and wept and mourned* (Neh 1:4) until the end of the whole story.

His expression: *I did not take a delicious nourishment, meat and drinks did not go into my mouth* (Dn 10:3) instructs us that during the exile the Israelites were not forbidden neither from consuming meats, nor from drinking wine, nor [from eating] allowed delicacy, because of the destruction of Jerusalem. If the Torah had prohibited them from such thing, Daniel and his friends would be the first to abide by this prohibition. And since we found him reserving twenty one days without eating these aliments we knew that he ate them before and after those twenty one days. Especially after being specific [and saying]: *Until the accomplishment {of three weeks-days}* (Dn 10:3). It goes the same for the anointing and similar [marks of prosperity]. It is also possible that *delicious nourishment* (Dn 10:3) [designates] the food of the kings, following the expression of Nehemiah: *I did not eat the governor's food* (Neh 5:14). This is a confirmation of the general meaning. It is also possible to believe that those twenty one days starts from July seventeen until August nine. This is wrong for many reasons. One of them is that[the period] of July seventeen and August nine are decrees of the destruction of the second Temple. As to the decrees of the destruction of the first Temple they are July nine and August ten. Because *{in the fourth month} the ninth {the famine had become severe in the city and there was no food for the people. Then the city was breached}* (Jer 52:6),[11] *in the fifth month, the tenth day of the month* (Jer 52:12) *he burnt the House of the Lord* (Jer 52:12). Therefore, thirty days were between the two dates.[12] But about Daniel he said: *In the twenty fourth of the first month I was standing at the bank of the great river* (Dn 10:4). So [the name of] the month is clear [...].[13] However, from the three [remaining] days of Nisan until our day there are undoubtedly the days of the feast of Pesah. Then he said:

10 According to Yefet ben Eli, the reason of the sadness of Daniel and his self imposed interdiction of enjoying delicious meals and drinks, is similar to that of David in Ps 132:3. It is a pledge that they decided until God reveal to them what they needed to know about the future of the nation.

11 One single word בתשעה reached us from this quotation of Jeremiah. It is a word used two times in the book of Jeremiah. The first time is in Jer 39:2. The second, in Jer 52:6. Both quotations deal with the same event: The breach of the wall of Jerusalem by the army of Nebuchadnezzar. The choice Jer 52:6 over is motivated by the fact the two other quotations from the same chapter follow immediately.

12 Lit: "Between them."

13 Uncertain reading of this unclear and damaged part of the MS Oxf 2486.135b.

Dn 10:4

In the twenty fourth of the first month I was standing at the bank of the great river, the Tigris.

Dn 10:5

I extended my look and saw an angel in the appearance of a man[14] dressed with linen[15] and his two loins were girded by joints of Ufaz.[16]

Dn 10:6

I saw[17] his body, [it was] like a blue jewel, his face similar to the manifestation of a thunder, his eyes like torches of fire,[18] his hands and legs has the color of the burnished bronze and the sound of his discourse like the sound of a crowed.[19]

Dn 10:7

And I Daniel alone saw this vision, the men who were with me did not see it. However, they were disturbed greatly, so they fled and hid themselves.[20]

Dn 10:8

I remained alone and saw this great vision, no more strength left in me, my joy[21] was altered in me and I could not retain my strength.[22]

14 MT: "A man" which is also the translation of Yefet ben Eli. Most probably R. Saadia translated the Hebrew expression איש אחד because of what will be said in the next verse as a description of this 'man.'

15 לאבס עשר literally 'dressed with the tenth of a dress.' It seems that R. Saadia attributes the meaning of a precious tissue to the Arabic word עשר. Yefet ben Eli too has an unclear translation of the same expression: מלבס מקדאריה literally 'dressed with measure' or 'appropriately dressed' and explains that because he was a warrior his was dressed accordingly. R. Saadia too will described the angel's dress as the dress of a warrior. Since Yefet ben Eli had in hands R. Saadia's commentary on Daniel, the conclusion is that in this verse, like many others, he follows the interpretation of R. Saadia. Yet in this case he follows him partially, since he differs with him when by not retaining R. Saadia's idea of a dress made of light.

16 R. Saadia renders the Hebrew word אופז par the Arabic word אלפאיז. Yefet ben Eli uses another Arabic word to translate the same Hebrew word, אבריז which designates, for him, a name of a locality. This same Arabic word means as well a 'pure gold.'

17 וראית literally 'and I saw' is added by R. Saadia to his translation and has no Hebrew original.

18 כפלאיל נאר literally 'like lines of fire.'

19 Yefet ben Eli: "Like the sound of an army crowed."

20 Yefet ben Eli: "And they fled into a hidden place."

The first thing we have to ask is why is it that the Bible called Tigris *the great river* (Dn 10:4) while in the Torah we have *the great river, the Euphrates* (Gn 15:18).[23] We answer that the Euphrates in the Torah and in the Book of Joshua is located in Syria and there it is the biggest river. Because all the rivers, like the Jordan, the Yarmok, the Berda, the Fijah, the Arnat, the Jihan, and others, there, are small rivers. As to Daniel, he located Tigris in Iraq, and according to the description, it is the biggest river in Iraq. Then he described the disposition of the angel without mentioning that he was suspended over the water. This he mentioned at the end of the story, saying two times: *Who was suspended over the water of Tigris*[24] (Dn 12:6.7). His representation of the angel[25] as *dressed with linen* (Dn 10:5) does not mean that he was really dressed with cloths of linen.[26] What he was wearing was a light that looks like linen. The meaning of *his two loins were girded* (Dn 10:5) is that he was a messenger sent to Daniel in the manner of a military in charge or a head of a division.

The reason for his representation of his members by many colors, saying that *his body was like a blue jewel etc.* (Dn 10:6) is to show them clearly by attributing different color to every one.[27] The color of the body is of incandescent fire, blue, because of his expression: *His body was like a blue jewel* (Dn 10:6). He designates תרשיש the jewel. The face,[28] [similar] to a yellow fire, because he says: *His face similar to the manifestation of a thunder* (Dn 10:6).[29] His eyes like red fire, since he says: *His eyes like torches of fire* (Dn 10:6). His hands and legs are of a bright copper color, because he says: *His hands and legs has the color of the burnished bronze*[30] (Dn 10:6). All these arrangements, stripes are similar to the changing of living creatures, wheels, the firmament, the garment,

---

21 Lit: "and my joy was altered on me." Yefet ben Eli: "And the splendor of my face."

22 MT: "And I could not retain any strength." It also the translation of Yefet ben Eli.

23 אלנהר אלכביר נהר אלפראת is R. Saadia's translation of the quoted part of Gn 15:18.

24 According to R. Saadia's translation of Dn 10:4 and Dn 12:6.7 נהר הדקל and מימי היאר are both the river Tigris.

25 Lit. "Of him."

26 Yefet ben Eli mentions specifically that this angel was dressed in a military garment, because he came from a war.

27 For Yefet ben Eli, the reason for the colors that characterize the different part of the messenger's body is to impress any one who sees him.

28 Lit: "Faces."

29 R. Saadia supposes, as an well-known reality, that the light of the thunder is yellow. He will continue his description of the different colors of the fire, as evidences that do not need to be discussed.

30 R. Saadia uses two Arabic words נחאס and צפר to translates the Hebrew word נחשת. While the Arabic נחאס renders the Hebrew נחשת, having both the same old Semitic root, the Arabic word צפר designates a particular yellow copper. To be noticed that the Arabic word for yellow is אצפר.

the human appearance, and the entire circles that Ezekiel observed. All this was created subject for changing in order to be present to him[31] [as such] in the vision, the mind and the narration. Here we bridge and avoid explaining any of these matters. As to his expression: *And the sound of his discourse like the sound of a crowed* (Dn 10:6) it means that when he speaks it appears to the hearer as if there is a crowed who speaking. It is like what Ezekiel had said about the sound of the wings of the living creatures: *A voice like the noise of an army* (Ez 1:24).

The most probable interpretation [concerning the expression]: *The men who were with me* (Dn 10:7) is that it designates Hananiah, Michael, Azaryah.[32] And what indicates that what Daniel did see happening was while he was awake is his astonishment about [the fact that] *they did not see the vision* (Dn 10:7).[33] Had it happened during his sleeping, he would be like someone in a group of ten each one sees something different in his dream and no one could know what did the other nine see in their dreams.[34] And also, if this had happened while [he was] sleeping, the men [who were with him] would not flee, since they would not be able to feel what Daniel did see. As if when Ruben in his sleep sees that he is beaten by stronger than him, Simon would not feel the same event. His expression: *No more strength left in me* (Dn 10:8) about [his own] strength bears some exaggeration.[35] [His expression]: *And my joy was altered in me* (Dn 10:8) [refers] to the countenance of his face. [His expression]: *And I could not retain my strength* (Dn 10:8) [means] that there was nothing he could do to retain his strength.[36] Then he added:

31 Unclear sentence. It remains unsettled wither 'him' here refers to Ezekiel or to Daniel.

32 For Yefet ben Eli, the men that were with him are a group of individuals that followed him for a reason, that the Book did not mention. They are not, according to Yefet ben Eli, Hananiah, Michael, Azaryah. R. Saadia gives no reason why is it that the men with Daniel were Hananiah, Michael, Azaryah.

33 According to Yefet ben Eli, the reason of the reason for the fear that overcame Daniel's companions is voice of the messenger during the vision. His interpretation is that while it was said that they did not see, nothing has been said about the fact that they did not hear.

34 While the meaning of this sentence is clear its grammatical construction is somehow obscure.

35 Yefet ben Eli: "He couldn't move anymore."

36 Lit: "And I could not retain my strength (Dn 10:8) by action." The meaning is that there wasn't any action to accomplish in order to retain his vanishing strength.

Dn 10:9

Then I heard his discourse,[37] and when I heard his speech[38] I prostrated on my face,[39] and my face was toward the ground.

Dn 10:10

A hand touched me and me and set me on my knee and on my palm.[40]

Dn 10:11

He said to me 'Daniel, the chosen one,[41] understand the discourse I am telling you and stand on your feet,[42] because I was sent to you.'[43] When he told me so, I stood up, shaking.

Dn 10:12

He also told me 'do not be afraid, Daniel, for from the first day you set up your mind to repent and to fast[44] between the hands of your Lord He answered your appeal[45] and I came because of your appeal.[46]

37 MT: "The voice of his discourse."

38 The same Hebrew expression קול דבריו mentioned two times in Dn 10:9 is translated differently by R. Saadia. The first time: כלאמה 'his discourse.' The second time: כטאבה 'his speech.'

39 There are two distinct lessons of this part of R. Saadia translation of Dn 10:9. The first (Morag): כנת מסבחא עלי וגהי 'I was prostrated on my face' or 'I fell asleep on my face.' The second lesson (Oxf 2486.138b) וקעת עלי וגהי 'I fell on my face.' Yefet ben Eli's translation: כנת סאבת עלי וגהי 'I was asleep on my face.'

40 'My knee and my palm' and not 'my knees and my palms' as it is in MT. Yefet ben Eli: "A hand go toward me and hit my on my knees and the palms of my feet."

41 Yefet ben Eli: "Man of desire" or "desired man."

42 MT: "And stand on your standing," which is also Yefet's translation.

43 Yefet ben Eli: "because I was sent to you immediately" which is closer to the Mt that has עתה 'now.'

44 Yefet ben Eli: "To understand and do penance."

45 MT: "Your words were heard." Yefet ben Eli: "Your discourses were heard." R. Saadia translates in a singular form: "Your discourse was heard."

46 We have tow distinct lessons about R. Saadia translation of Dn 10:12. Usually, R. Saadia's translation of the book of Daniel follows Morag's edition, used here because of its completeness, compared to other MSS of R. Saadia's translation of the book of Daniel. Oxf 2486.139a has another Judeo-Arabic translation and R. Saadia's commentary follows the lesson of Oxf 2486.139a. That is why, exceptionally, it is the lesson of the MS of Oxf 2486.139a rendered in the English translation. Here is the translation of Morag's lesson: "He told me 'do not be afraid, Daniel, for from the first day you set your mind to understand and to worship before your God your discourse was heard and I came because of your discourse."

Dn 10:13

The head of the Persian kingdom was standing before me for twenty one days when Michael, one of the first lords,[47] came to my rescue, then I was took away[48] and the Persian kings were crashed.[49]

Dn 10:14

I came to instruct you about what will happen to your population at the end of the time, since there is revelation for the time.'[50]

Dn 10:15

When he told me such discourse, I bent toward the ground and remained still.[51]

Dn 10:16

And soon after an individual like human being reached my lips, then I opened my mouth and spoke to the one who was standing before me 'my lord, I was in pain because of the vision of the individual,[52] and could not retain my strength.[53]

Dn 10:17

How could this servant of my lord speak[54] and I, because of his vision, had lost my strength and almost[55] lost my breath.'

47 Yefet ben Eli: "One of the first angels."

48 The Hebrew expression: ואני נותרתי is rendered by R. Saadia and Yefet ben Eli in two opposite ways. For R. Saadia: ואנא פצלת literally 'and I was separated.' While for Yefet ben Eli the translation of the same expression is: ואנא תבקית literally 'and I stayed.'

49 Lit. "And the Persian kings were cleaved." Yefet ben Eli almost has the same translation: Instead of the Arabic לזק verb 'to cleave' (R. Saadia) he has the synonymous Arabic verb לצק 'to cling.'

50 Yefet ben Eli: "Because the revelation is for the time too."

51 MS Morag has וסבתת literally 'I remained still.' Oxf 2486.138b has וכ̇רסת literally 'and I became dumb.' Yefet ben Eli has the same lesson: "I prostrated my face to the ground and remained dumb ונכ̇רסת."

52 MT: "Because of his vision."

53 MT: "And could not retain any strength." The same as Yefet ben Eli's translation.

54 MT: "Speak with my lord." In his translation R. Saadia omits to renders 'with my Lord.' The expression: "This servant of my lord" refers to Daniel himself.

55 MT: "And had lost my breath." R. Saadia introduced 'almost' as a kind of a logical correction, since the 'losing the breath' means death, which is illogical for someone who is still speaking. Yefet ben Eli, closer in his translation to the MT has: "And had lost my breath."

Dn 10:18

Then the angel with the human form[56] came again and touched me and strengthened me.[57]

Dn 10:19

He said 'do not be afraid Daniel, the chosen one, peace be to you,[58] be strong and resolute.'[59] When he told me this[60] I became strong and said 'may my lord say to me what he wants,[61] because you strengthened me.'

Dn 10:20

He said 'do you know why I have come to you? Know that I will restart the fight[62] with the king[63] in charge of Persia.' Then I will leave and the king in charge of the Greece will come.[64]

Dn 10:21

'But I will tell what was instated in the book of truth[65] and no one helped me against these,[66] except Michael who is in charge of you.'[67]

We start again the explanation of this story, saying: Daniel had stated first that *the sound of his discourse like the sound of a crowed* (Dn 10:6) without falling on his face. What is then the meaning of his expression: *And when I heard his*

56 MT: "Then he came again." R. Saadia renders the 'he' by 'the angel with human form'.

57 MT: "And strengthened me." R. Saadia added 'and touched me' to his translation.

58 Yefet ben Eli renders the Hebrew שלום by the Arabic סלאמה which means 'protection.' His translation of this part of Dn 10:19 could be 'there will be protection for you.'

59 MT: "Be strong and strengthen" which also Yefet ben Eli's translation.

60 Yefet ben Eli: "While speaking with me."

61 MT: "May my lord speak to me." R. Saadia added 'any thing he wants' to his translation.

62 Yefet ben Eli: "I will fight again immediately." R. Saadia does not translate the word עתה 'now' that Yefet ben Eli renders by 'immediately.'

63 The Hebrew word שׂר is translated by R. Saadia as אלמלך 'the king.' While the same word is translated by ראייס 'lord' by Yefet ben Eli.

64 Yefet ben Eli: "And while I was leaving and here comes the lord of Greece."

65 'But I will tell what was instated in the book of 'the book of righteousness' כתאב אלחק becomes in Yefet ben Eli's translation: "But truly I will tell you what was instated in the book of is right פי אלכתאב חק."

66 Yefet ben Eli: "Against the falsehood of theses."

67 Yefet ben Eli: "Michael who is your lord" or "your master."

speech I prostrated on my face (Dn 10:9)? We say that, first, it is possible that his second expression is the explanation of his former one. It is also possible that the first voice was not directed to him, which is the reason why it did not frighten him. However, when he directed his speech to him, he terrified him and panicked him.[68] It is the hand of the angel that set him on his hands and knees is to help him standing up so he may help himself by posing his hand on the ground. That is why he told him *stand on your feet* (Dn 10:11).[69] I rendered דניאל איש חמדות (Dn 10:11) by 'the chosen one' as I already said about the interpretation of [the expression]: *Because God reserved*[70] *a mountain of them to inhabit it* (Ps 68:17).[71] I rendered להבין (Dn 10:12) by 'repentance'[72] which is the same meaning as in [the expression]: *There hearts will understand and they will comeback* (Is 6:10).[73] And I translated להתענות (Dn 10:12) by 'fasting' in accordance with [the expression]: *Because you will fast yourselves* (Lv 16:31).[74] The expression of the angel: *For from the first day, the Lord answered your appeal* (Dn 10:12)[75] means that 'your appeal was heard [by the Lord] from its beginning and He sent me as a reply, but I was late during all these twenty one days, because I had to deal with matter of the king of Persia.[76] Once I finished with it I came to you.'

We need to set aside here three questions. The first, why is it that Gabriel, who was sent from the first day, was late for twenty one days? The second, is there in heaven an angel for every nation that sustains it and strengthens it? If such is the case, the reinforcement of their religions and their impiety come from the Creator. The third, are there quarrels and wars between these angels? If this is the case, is it by an order from their Lord or by their own choice? We answer the first question and say that when Gabriel having said: *The head of the Persian kingdom was standing before me for twenty one days* (Dn 10:13) he

68 Yefet ben Eli interprets the expression: "I prostrated on my face" (Dn 10:9) as if Daniel passed out when he heard the voice of the angel.

69 For Yefet ben Eli Daniel was on his hand and knees because of his fear.

70 In the Judeo-Arabic expression כ'ץ אללה literally 'God reserved' or 'God choose' that R. Saadia uses to translates the Hebrew expression חמד אלהים in Ps 68:17 is likened to the Hebrew expression: איש חמדות literally 'the chosen one.' In one case, Ps 68:17, we have a verb, in the other case, Dn 10:11, we have a noun.

71 אד' כ'ץ אללה גבלא מנהא ליסכנה is R. Saadia translation of the citation from Ps 68:17.

72 Or 'to repent' as it is rendered in the translation given in the footnote of Dn 10:12 and following the lesson of Oxf 2486.139a.

73 פתפהם קלובהם וירגעון is R. Saadia translation of the quoted part of Is 6:10.

74 אד' תניעון אנפסכם is R. Saadia translation of the quoted part of Lv 16:31.

75 Cf. R. Saadia's particular translation of this part of Dn 10:12.

76 Yefet ben Eli's commentary of Dn 10:12 is almost, word by word, the same as R. Saadia's. The only difference is that, unlike R. Saadia, he did not specify the reason for which the angel was late in his coming to Daniel.

demonstrated to us that his Lord directed him to answer Daniel from the first day. But He also added: 'Do not deliver [the answer] to him before finishing what I ordered you about the king of Persia.' So Gabriel remained [dealing with this order] for twenty one days. This was equal to [the time] that Daniel offered for fasting and praying. We answer the second question saying that if there is a nation manifested to the population, the wisdom implies that the Lord of the universe establishes one of the angels in order to strengthen it and consolidate it from its beginning until the end of its time. Similar to what Gabriel had said: *And I, since the first year of Darius the Mede, was standing to strengthen him and to fortify him* (Dn 11:1). That means that his Lord made set him in order to consolidate his matter.[77] The meaning [of his expression]: *In the first year* (Dn 11:1) is *since the first year* of having his reign. It goes the same for every nation. Coming from God, this is a consolidation of its reign, and not of its religion. Likewise, He strengthens the kingship of kings, not their impiety. He also [reinforces] in the population its capacity to choose, without anyone saying that He strengthens […] this obedience and nothing else.[78] We answer the third question saying that the quarrel between the angels is neither rivalry nor competition in order that someone win. It is a change, by an order from God, that touches some of them, so that the weak kingdom remain with no king[79] that sustain it, finish its concerns and discontinue its sovereignty. The fact he called this [quarrel] *fight* (Dn 10:20) is metaphorical and by similarity to the acts of kings and emperors. Don't you see that such [way of speaking] is applied to the God. To his action in Egypt: *God will fight for you* (Ex 14:14).[80] And at the time of Joshua: *Because the Lord fought for Israel* (Jos 10:14). Nehemiah too has said: *Our God will fight for us* (Neh 4:14). And Zechariah has said: *And the Lord will come forth and fight against those nations, as when he fought in the day of battle* (Zec 14:3). He also told as when were sent away from the country: *And I, myself will fight against you with an outstretched hand and a powerful arm, with anger and fury and great wrath* (Jer 21:5). So, since the wars attributed to the Creator are neither a brawl nor a battle, but having the genuine meaning of a calamity [for a group] and the ascendancy for another, those wars attributed to the angels too represent the calamity for a nation and the ascendancy of another.

77 In other word: God sent Gabriel to strengthen the reign of Darius.

78 The lacuna forbids the full understanding of R. Saadia's illustration. However, the idea seems to be that God consolidate the capacity to choose, not the possible erroneous choice.

79 מלך literally 'king' could also be a possible writing for מלאך literally 'angel.' In which case the meaning becomes: There will be no angel in heaven to sustain the kingdom by strengthening its king.

80 אללה יחארב ענכם is R. Saadia's translation of the citation from Ex 14:14.

Now that we finished the answer of the three questions we go back to complete the explanation of the chapter.[81] We say that the expression of Gabriel to Daniel: *The head of the Persian kingdom was standing before me for twenty one days* (Dn 10:13) demonstrates that his Lord said to him: 'Answer Daniel once you finish with what I instructed you to do about Persia.'[82] His expression to him: *When Michael, one of the first lords, came to my rescue* (Dn 10:13) proves that Michael helped him in most of the matter dealing with the population.[83] His expression: *One of the first lords* (Dn 10:13) demonstrates that Michael[84] is one of the lords of Israel. Similar to the angel that appeared to Jacob and gave him the name Israel. [And like the angel that appeared] to Moses: *The angel of God appeared to him in a flame of fire* (Ex 3:2).[85] [And similar to the angel that appeared] Joshua: *I am the head of the host of the Lord and now I come* (Jos 5:14) as well as all the angels that appeared to the prophets of Israel. It is possible that they are many, but it is also possible that they are only one. His expression: *One of the first lords* (Dn 10:13) is because of his appearance in different times and forms.

His expression: *What will happen* יקרה *to your population at the end of the time* (Dn 10:14) designates the end of the servitude that started at the time of Daniel and that we live its ending now. It is possible to write יקרה (Dn 10:14) which means to happen[86] either with ה or א. This [is similar] to the expression of Jacob: *I tell what will happen* יקרא *to you* (Gn 49:1).[87] This is too similar to [the expression]: *meeting* וקרהו {*his end*}(Gn 44:29),[88] [and]: {And if his end} meets him וקראהו (Gn 42:38).[89] All of those [forms] are possible. Daniel also said: *I bent toward the ground and remained still* (Dn 10:15) without having the inten-

81 Lit. "The explanation of the story."

82 R. Saadia had already treated this theme at the beginning of the section when he answered the three questions mentioned above.

83 Uncertain lesson of a damaged passage in the MS.

84 Lit. "He."

85 פתגלי מלאך אללה בצרים נאר is R. Saadia's translation of the citation from Ex 2:3.

86 In his translation of Dn 10:14 R. Saadia renders the Hebrew verb יקרה by the Arabic יצאדף, but here he renders the same Hebrew word by the Arabic יערץ which is its synonymous.

87 [אכברכם] במא ינאלכם is R. Saadia's translation of the citation from Gn 49:1. R. Saadia translates by יקרא אתכם by במא ינאלכם. That means that he translates קרא by נאל another verb, synonymous of צאדף and ערץ.

88 [אלמניה] וואפתה is R. Saadia's translation of the citation from Gn 44:29. Here too we have the Hebrew verb וקרהו by ואפי another verb synonymous of צאדף, ערץ and נאל.

89 [אלמניה] ואן ואפתה is R. Saadia's translation of the quoted part of Gn 42:38. The Hebrew verb וקראהו is rendered by the Arabic verb ואפי.

tion to say that he falls on his face like the first time.[90] He bent to the ground and remained still until the angel fortified him. His intention of [mentioning] the expression: *With the human form* (Dn 10:18) [and] *an individual like human being* (Dn 10:16) is to elate him,[91] since a human being is not elated other than by […] and his form.[92] His expression: *I was in pain because of the vision of the individual* (Dn 10:16) [and] *how could this servant etc.* (Dn 10:17) has the following meaning: How is possible for him to speak to the angel when was greatly frightened by his vision!

I rendered חזק וחזק *be strong and resolute* (Dn 10:19) as if it is in חזק ואמץ *be strong and resolute* (Dt 31:7)[93] because of the repetition.[94] [and what is the reason] in telling him in the second discourse *do you know why I have come to you* (Dn 10:20) since he already informed him in the first discourse *I came to instruct you about what will happen to your population at the end of the time* (Dn 10:14)? The reason is that when he saw him terrified as Daniel[95] had attested [saying] '*I stood up, shaking*' (Dn 10:11) he thought that may be Daniel did not understand his discourse. That is why he needed to ask him *do you know why I have come to you* (Dn 10:20).[96] Therefore he may repeat the first discourse in case he did not remember it. in fact the angels do not know what is the people's heart. It is the Creator Himself who knows that, as it was said: *For you alone know that the heart of human beings* (2 Chr 6:30). So when Daniel kept silent, or may be he had said 'yes' without pursuing about what he knows,[97] Gabriel completed [telling] the story to him and said: *Know that I will restart the fight with the king in charge of Persia* (Dn 10:20) because of the necessity

90 Yefet ben Eli who had an ample knowledge of R. Saadia's commentary on Daniel states exactly the opposite opinion: According to him Daniel fall on his face.

91 ליונסה translated here by 'to elate him' is the same word that Yefet ben Eli chooses to explain the reason why the angel that appeared to Daniel had a human form.

92 The lacuna does not forbid us from clearly perceiving R. Saadia's reasoning: A human being is disturbed by any image other than a human image, which is his own.

93 תשדד ותאיד is R. Saadia's translation of the citation from Dt 31:7.

94 Otherwise the translation would be 'be strong and make strong.' A repetition that R. Saadia avoided.

95 Lit: "He."

96 The angel according to R. Saadia wants to inquire whether Daniel was in state of understanding what he did hear; whether the frightening seen of the angel addressing him affected his capacity of grasping the meaning of the vision he is witnessing or not. Yefet ben Eli's understanding of the same angel's question is whether Daniel was capable of perceiving all the details of what he was told.

97 או קאל לה נעם ואכתצר אתבאתה uncertain meaning because of the two pronouns used with the verbs קאל and ואכתצר. They could represent either Daniel or the angel.

[to resolve] the remaining matters of the population.[98] In this way, Gabriel leaves the help [he is giving to king of Persia] and the Greek kingdom comes.[99] That is signified by his expression: *Then I will leave and the king in charge of the Greece will come* (Dn 10:20). His expression to him: *But I will tell what was instated in the book of truth* (Dn 10:21) [has to be taken] following our commentary of the expression: *This matter is true* (Dn 10:1).[100] He means unconditionally and unexceptionally, similar to what the Bible[101] said about David: *God swore to David by a truth that He will never deny* (Ps 132:11),[102] that your first born will succeed you inevitably: *You will have a successor from your children* (Ps 132:11)[103] who is Solomon. As to those who came after Solomon[104] they lived according to their obedience to God,[105] as He said: *If your sons keep my covenant and my testimony that I teach them, they too will be to the end your successors* (Ps 132:12).[106] That is why, when he sinned, Solomon was not disgraced, unlike his son. It goes the same for those of the second temple, they were granted, unexceptionally, the return to the land as He said: *I will truly plant them in this land* (Jer 32:41). Same for us, He unexceptionally granted us

98 According to Yefet ben Eli, the angels interrupted his war with the Persian kings and came to tell Daniel about the meaning of the vision and that, once he finishes telling him, he has to go back to the war he left. According to R. Saadia's commentary on Dn 11:1, the war with the Persian king should be understood as a war beside him not against him.

99 למוֹצע מא כאן בקי מן אמור אלקום חתי ינצרף גברראל ען אלמעאונה ותאתי דולה אליונאניין is unclear. Thus, the translation is uncertain.

100 The main point of R. Saadia's commentary on the expression: "This matter is right (Dn 10:1)" means that there is no exception for the prophecy that the angel is revealing to Daniel. Yefet ben Eli interprets the same expression as an invitation to consider the obvious meaning of the vision and not to look for other explanation.

101 Lit. "This is similar to what he said to David."

102 כמא אקסם אללה לדאוד בחקיקה לא ירגע ענהא is R. Saadia's translation of the citation from Ps 132:11.

103 אן מן ולדך אגעל לך כֹלפא is R. Saadia's translation of the citation from Ps 132:11. R. Saadia gives first his interpretation then the quotation in Hebrew of the remaining part of Ps 132:11. May be he did so because of his particular interpretation of this verse, since nothing in Ps 132:11 mention that David successor is his first born, neither that the succession is without exception, or inevitably.

104 Lit. "Him."

105 Lit. "Him."

106 ואן חפט בניך עהדי ושהאדתי אלתי אעלמהם פיכונוא הם איצא אלי אלאבד יקומון לך כֹלפא is R. Saadia's translation of the citation from Ps 132:12. Unlike the unconditional pledge to Solomon, his sons were promised to be his successors with the condition that they keep the Lord's covenant and testimony.

the salvation as He said: *You will show truth to Jacob* (Mi 7:20).[107] Likewise, the angel said to Daniel: *What was instated in the book of truth* (Dn 10:21). He also said about the truthfulness of salvation: *I swore by my name, from my mouth a word with purity that will not return, because every knee shall bend to me and every tong shall swear by my name* (Is 45:23).[108] And also: *In God my purity and my strength* (Is 45:24)[109] and the whole story. Then Gabriel told him:[110]

107 The whole Mi 7:20 is: "You will show truth to Jacob, love to Abraham, as you have sworn to their fathers from the days of old." Thus, the promise is unconditional since it is an oath from God.

108 וקד אקסמת באסמי וכ̇רג מן קולי אמר בזכוה לא ירגע לאן כל רכבה תג̇תו לי ולסאן תחלף כד̇א באסמי is R. Saadia's translation of the citation from Is 45:23.

109 באללה זכותי ועזי is R. Saadia's translation of the citation from Is 45:24.

110 Follows the first verse of Dn 11. R. Saadia reaches the conclusion of Dn 10 at the end of his commentary of Dn 11:1 which thematically appears as the true end of Dn 10.

Chapter 11

Dn 11:1

And I, since the first year of Darius the Mede, was standing to strengthen him and to fortify him.

This prince, that demonstrate the establishment of *princes* for each nation in order to have them under control […] it is what Ezekiel had said: *I will strengthen the arms of the king of Babylon* (Ez 30:24).[1] As to [the expression]: *To fortify him* (Dn 11:1) it has the same [meaning] as [the meaning] of the expression of Isaiah: *A strong king dominates over them* (Is 19:4).[2] Therefore, Gabriel remained to instruct and to strengthen the Persian kingdom until the end of the day when *the king in charge of Persia* (Dn 10:20) stood between his hands.[3] As if he was instructing him about the kingdom, opens his eyes, and shows him the ways for the consolidation. So when Michael came, Gabriel handed him *the king in charge of Persia* (Dn 10:20) in order to instruct him and consolidate him. He himself[4] went to Daniel and made known the answer to him, as he told him: *{Michael, one of the first lords} came to my rescue* (Dn 10:13) and: *I came to instruct you* (Dn 10:14). Once he finish to answer him, he came back to help *the king in charge of Persia* (Dn 10:20) in his war against his enemies, as he said: *I will restart the fight with the king in charge of Persia* (Dn 10:20). This is similar to the expression: *Will you come with me to battle Ramoth-Gilead* (1 Kgs 22:4). And when the kingdom of Persia ceased, Gabriel abstained from rescuing, as he said: *Then I leave and the king in charge of the Greece will come* (Dn 10:20), since he was not ordered to help the Greeks, but to help the Persians, according to what we have explained.

Know and may God instruct you, that we reached […] the purpose of the tenth chapter that gives information about the kings that arise at the time of

1 It is impossible, because of the lacuna, to fully understand the reasoning of R. Saadia and the context in which Ezekiel is quoted.

2 ומלך עזיז יתסלט עליהם is R. Saadia's translation of the citation from Is 19:4.

3 Unclear sentence containing crossing-word. Hence, it is an uncertain translation. The erroneous grammatical construction in itself is a mark of such obscurity of the meaning. Here is the erroneous part of the sentence:
אלדֹי וקף שׂר פרס בין ידיה ואכֹר דלך פי אלכֹא יומא.

4 In other words, Gabriel himself.

Daniel until the time of salvation. It does not deal, however, with all the events that happen in one thousand three hundred thirty five years. Because if you want to gather extensively, the events of one single year fill all the registers. In fact, they are the mains events and the leading information that need to be known. You may find among them an event that takes twenty years, another that takes ninety years, more or less. The total forms the contents of forty seven verses. Among them, there is the first verse that deals with final episode of the Persian kings. Then thirteen verses that pertain to the Greek kings. And twenty verse about the Kings of Edom. Plus ten verses concerning the kings of Ishmael. The total is forty four verses. It remains the last three verses. The first is about the salvation. It is: *At that time stands Michael etc.* (Dn 12:1). The second, about honoring the *dead*. It is: *Many of those who are sleeping in the dust etc.* (Dn 12:2). The third, deals with the reward of the world to come. It is: *And the knowledgeable will shine like the heavenly light etc.* (Dn 12:3).

I need to start by this introduction in order that the general public do not misunderstand that Gabriel explained to Daniel every event, big or small, that happened during the time of slavery. So I say it is not as they think. Had he dealt with the events of one single year, it would be in the same proportion of the Torah or more. Therefore he abridged that, so it may be comparable to the Torah.[5] Because, as you know, the events of one thousand seven hundred fifty five years are contained in one [biblical] section.[6] It goes the same for the events of Egypt, dealt in two verses alone, for equal necessity. Likewise, the facts of those kings were mentioned for us by selected examples. Some of them relate to us, like [his expression]: *The knowledgeable of every nation will instruct many, yet they will be tested by the sword, the flame, the deportation and the spoil for a period* (Dn 11:33). And: *The young and conceited among your people, they oppose the fulfilment of a vision, but they stumble* (Dn 11:14). Some others [are mentioned] so they may become for us signs of the good news that he will proclaim to us. Like the story of Cyrus, as sign of the salvation. There is also the story [described in the expression]: *[His kingdom] disintegrates into the four sides of heaven* (Dn 11:4). And the story of *the land of Edom and Moab and the extremity of the land of the sons of Amon will skip his hand* (Dn 11:41). Plus the story: *The Nubians and the Cushites will follow at his heel* (Dn 11:43). This and what is similar to it are signs, according to what we will explain, to the Israelites

5 It is difficult to understand the intention of R. Saadia' in comparing the revelation that Gabriel made to Daniel to the Torah. Probably, the length of time, or the number of events, that the revelation of the angel to Daniel and some revelations in the Torah, is the point in common to which hints R. Saadia. In his commentary on Dn 11:1 Yefet ben Eli to the fact the message of the angel to Daniel may be compared to messengers and their message in the Torah.

6 פרשה a section or a biblical division.

for the truthfulness of the salvation and the consolations when they observe them. Gabriel, yet, was extensive [in relating the] information about kings. Thus, he reserved to them forty four verses. Then he shortened [the information] about the salvation, mentioning only three verses about it. Because the prophets had spoke at length and large about it. Like the discourse of Isaiah, Jeremiah, Ezekiel and others. As for the matter of the four kingdoms, the prophets did not speak about it, other than by insinuation. That is the reason why Gabriel was extensive in what [his predecessors] treated briefly, and abridged what [his predecessors] treated extensively.

Now that I finished introducing to these verses, I think that I should introduce to the strange words abundantly used in this story. I will translate them, so that they may be used in the explanation of the whole story. In translating them, I will refer to their parallel in the whole Bible. On that account I found thirteen [particular] words. Among them, there is the naming of 'the sons' אחרית. He said here: *[And his kingdom] shall not belong to his descendant* (Dn 11:4). The definition of the word is 'posterity' and 'offspring.'[7] Like the expression of Amos: *And your* ואחריתכון *offspring in fish basket* (Am 4:2). In Aramaic we have ובנתכון.[8] And following the expression of Ezekiel: *Your offspring shall fall by the sword* (Ez 23:25). And according to Jeremiah's expression: *Among his offspring there will be a fool* (Jer 7:11).[9] The second [word] is the naming of 'the stronghold' מעוז when he said: *Then they will comeback and confront his strongholds*[10] (Dn 11:10). This is comparable to the expression of Amos: *He shall brig down your stronghold*[11] (Am 3:11). The third [word] is the naming of the sword by כלה, since he says: *He shall remain firm in the land of Syria*[12] *and a sword* כלה *was in his hand* (Dn 11:16). This is similar to his expression: *{Until} he is destroyed and cut off* (Dn 9:27).[13] The forth [word] is בת [and it designates] the

7 עקב 'posterity' כלף 'offspring.' עקב 'posterity' is the translation that choose Yefet ben Eli, which corroborate R. Saadia's interpretation of the same word.

8 Lit: "And the translator to the Aramaic אלמתרגם said: ובנתכון.

9 This is the translation that R. Saadia's interpretation suggests. There is a much common translation where אחרית is taken as 'consequence,' 'immediately after,' 'result' or 'the next thing.' Which gives us the following translation: And at the end of his life he will become a fool (Jer 17:11).

10 While the MT has מעוזו 'stronghold' R. Saadia render the same singular word by the plural 'strongholds.'

11 עזך according to R. Saadia's understanding has to be rendered by 'your stronghold' while the same word is usually rendered, in the this context, by 'your strength' or 'your splendor.'

12 Lit. "The land of Sham." Others translate by 'beautiful land' or 'coveted land.'

13 In his translation of Dn 9:27 R. Saadia does not translate the Hebrew word כלה by 'sword' but by 'destroyed and cut off.' However, he explains in his commentary of

'crowd.'[14] He said: *And the group of the king of Syria join {the king of Iraq}* (Dn 11:6). This is comparable to the expressions: *Crowd of Zion* (Is 1:8),[15] *crowd of Sidon* (Is 23:12),[16] *crowd of Babylon* (Ps 137:8),[17] *the crowd of the people of Babylon* (Is 47:1)[18] and the like. The fifth [word] is נשים [and it designates] the 'cities.'[19] [Like its meaning in the expression]: *O cities comparable to women, stand up and hear my voice, and you who are similar to confident girls, listen to my discourse* (Is 32:9).[20] The sixth [word] is רבים [and it designates] 'Israel.' This is [what we conclude from] his expression: *{The knowledgeable of every nation} will instruct many*[21] (Dn 11:33), and *the reformers of the people* (Dn 12:3).[22] The seventh word is מישרים [that has the meaning of] 'reconciliation' since he said: *To work a reconciliation* (Dn 11:6). It is from this [word] that comes ישרים 'those who are protected'[23] because he said: *Those who are protected being with him he acts* (Dn 11:17). This is comparable to what Achish had told David: *You are an upright man* (I Sm 29:6). He also said: *From the day he defected to this day* (1 Sm 29:3).[24] The eighth [word] is חלקות (Dn 11:32) and

---

the same verse, at the very last paragraph his commentary of Dn 9, that כלה means 'sword.'

14 גמאעה literally 'crowd.'

15 גמע ציון is R. Saadia's translation of the citation from Is 1:8. To be noticed that בת is translated not by גמאעה, but by גמע. Obviously, the two words, coming from the same root, are synonymous for R. Saadia.

16 גמע צידון is R. Saadia's translation of the citation from Is 23:12.

17 גמאעה בבל is R. Saadia's translation of the citation from Ps 137:8.

18 גמאעה אהל בבל is R. Saadia's translation of the citation from Is 47:1. 'The people of Babylon' is R. Saadia translation of כשדים.

19 It is the second and figurative meaning of נשים is 'cities.' The first meaning is 'women.' The translation of the quotation from Isaiah shows that R. Saadia does not ignore the obvious meaning of the word.

20 יא איהא אלמדן אלשביהה קמן פאסמען צותי ויא אלממתלה בבנאת ואתקאת אנצתן מקאלתי באלנסא אלמטמאנאת is R. Saadia's translation of the citation from Is 32:9.

21 In his translation of Dn 11:33 R. Saadia does not render the Hebrew word רבים by 'Israel' but by the Arabic word גמהור literally 'the principle part of a majority' and translated into English by many. This too is the case of רבים in Dn 12:3 that R. Saadia will quote immediately after Dn 11:33.

22 Lit. "The reformers of many." Whoever, in his translation renders this part of Dn 12:3 by 'the reformers of the people.'

23 אלמסתאמנין literally 'the foreigners or those of different faith who are under the protection of the emperor or the law of the land.' This word designates, for example the Christians who lived under the Calif. protection in the Islamic kingdom. R. Saadia does not comment this part of Dn 11:17.

24 The quotation of 1 Sm 29:3 does not add information about R. Saadia's interpretation of מישרים. By this quotation R. Saadia seems eager to justify Achish descrip-

חלקלקות (Dn 11:21.34) 'tricks' replacing חחבלות as we will mention. The ninth [word] is the שטיפה 'spreading of an army in the land'[25] which is used many times in the book of Daniel.[26] Similar [to the expression]: *He goes through the population of Judah, spreads then passes over* (Is 8:8).[27] The tenth [word] is עתים, since he says: *Those who sustain them by their advice* (Dn 11:6). This is comparable to the expression: *Then the king told the wise men who know the advice'* (Est 1:13). The eleventh [word] is חרפה [that means] 'deportation' as in his expression: *And the king shall put an end to his insult against him after paying him back for his action* (Dn 11:18).[28] It is similar to the [expression]: *those who are left of the captivity in the province in great affliction and insult, and the wall of Jerusalem is beached and its doors destroyed by fire* (Neh 1:3). The twelfth [word] is נשיאה, dispersion and destruction,[29] since he says: *And he disperse greatly* (Dn 11:12). It is parallel [to the expression]: *They will be dispersed with hooks* (Am 4:2). The thirteenth [word] is [which designates] what leads to nothing. It is his expression: *They will utter lies at one table* (Dn 11:27). Which is similar to the expression of Michayehu: *Behold! The Lord put a spirit of lie the mouth of all those prophets of yours* (1 Kgs 22:23). Those thirteen words are used in this chapter[30] [in a particular way], as if they were [written] purposely for it. It is similar to the use of the expression: *Under the sun* (Ecc 1:3) by Koheleth at the place of under the heaven. Like the use of 'light' אור by Elijah at the place of מטר 'rain.'[31] Such is too the use by the Torah of: שלה 'what belong to him' (Gn 49:10)[32] and שליתה her membrane (Dt 28:57)[33] in the meaning of *his son and her son*. Plus every particular word in a [biblical]

tion of David as an upright man, witnessing that he found no fault in him 'From the day he defected to this day' (1 Sm 29:3).

25 Cf. Dn 11:10.22.26.40. To be noticed that the while we have the verb שָׁטַף and the noun שֶׁטֶף the noun שְׁטִיפָה mentioned in R. Saadia's commentary does not exist in the Bible.

26 Lit. "Which is used many times in the story."

27 וימצי פי אל יהודה וינסאב וימר is R. Saadia's translation of the citation from Is 8:8. To be noticed that in his translation R. Saadia adds אל to יהודה, changing the meaning into 'the population of Judah.'

28 R. Saadia's commentary of Dn 11:18 did not reach us. Therefore, it is uneasy to expand on R. Saadia's interpretation of the Hebrew word חרפה.

29 ספי אנתסאף translated here by 'dispersion and destruction.' The fact that R. Saadia does not comment ונשא ההמון (Dn 11:12) makes it difficult to understand the exact meaning that R. Saadia sees in the word ונשא.

30 Lit: "In this story."

31 R. Saadia does not give an example for this last meaning of אור. It is possible to see this meaning in Is 18:4.

32 אלדי הו להו is R. Saadia's translation of the citation from Gn 49:10.

33 במשימתהא is R. Saadia's translation of the citation from Dt 28:57.

book, either for a especial reason or in order to multiply [the effect]. Now that I put forward [some specific] word used in this chapter[34] I start by [the explanation] of the first verse that deals with the end of the Persian kingdom. Then Gabriel said to him:[35]

Dn 11:2

Now the truth I tell you,[36] three kings remained for the Persians and the fourth will become greatly riche, richer than all of them,[37] and once he grows strong in his riches all could see the kingdom of the Greek.[38]

This decree starts from [the time of] Darius the Median. He was the first Persian king over Syria. Three different kings [ruled] after him: Cyrus, Ahasuerus and Artaxerxes according to what we have explained in *the books concerning the number of years* (Dn 9:2). The fourth that becomes richer than the [former] three is Artaxerxes. That is why he was described as *king of kings* (Ezr 7:12).[39] Similar to the description of Nebuchadnezzar as *king of kings* (Ez 26:7). This fourth king is the *third* of those remaining [kings]. In fact he is *the fourth, starting by Darius the Median.* Thus, by this expression appears the falsehood of the allegation of those who pretend that there were more than four kings between the Kasdian and the Greek kingdoms. He also said: *And once he grows strong in his riches all could see the kingdom of the Greek* (Dn 11:2). This is a refutation of the Christians and some sectarians who pretend that there were seventeen kings to the Persians. His expression: *All could see [the kingdom]* (Dn 11:2) does not mean that some princes and armies alone could see the establishment of the Greek [king], but all, with no exception. This will be after thirty four years according to our observation of the king.[40] Then there was one year for Artaxerxes, the fourth [king]. He did not mention here that the construction of the Second Temple was in his time, because he has fully explained it in [the passage] *they are seventy weeks* (Dn 9:24).[41]

34 Lit: "In this story."
35 Lit: "I say that Gabriel has told him."
36 Yefet ben Eli: "Now I tell you truly." Then Yefet ben Eli adds: "In other word, the discourse according to its obvious meaning."
37 MT: "Richer than all."
38 Yefet ben Eli: "And in his strength all will rush to the king of the Greek."
39 Yefet ben Eli repeats, almost word for word, the beginning of R. Saadia's commentary on Dn 11:2. However, he differs in citing Est 1:4 to as witness for Artaxerxes' riches.
40 Another possible reading: "According to our observation of the kingdom."
41 R. Saadia adds: "In the ninth chapter."

After that I want to mention the text of the forty three verses of which thirteen deal with the Greeks, twenty to Edom and ten to Ishmael.[42] Furthermore, I say that at the beginning of each kingdom he states that *he accomplishes what pleases him* (Dn 11:3.16.36). Similar to what he said about the Kasdian: *He put to death whom he wanted etc.* (Dn 5:19).[43] He also said at the beginning of the Persian kingdom: *I saw it [the ram] butting, it accomplishes in them what it pleases and exaggerates* (Dn 8:4). Likewise, [he mentions the same expression is] at the opening of the thirteen verses reserved to the Greeks: *A mighty king shall arise for them and establish his dominion with great power and accomplishes what pleases him* (Dn 11:3); *{and the other king shall do what pleases him} and shall ascends etc.* (Dn 11:36).[44] Now that I achieved this introduction I will start by the verses pertaining to the Greeks, that starts by:[45]

Dn 11:3

A mighty king shall arise for them;[46] he shall establish his great dominion and accomplish what pleases him.

Dn 11:4

But once he finishes establishing himself his kingdom shall break down, disintegrate into the four sides of heaven and shall not belong to his descendant, nor to the dominion that he founded. His kingdom shall be cut off and belong to others than these.

Dn 11:5

The king of the south shall become strong, with some of his officers,[47] and overcome him; he shall apply a powerful dominion.[48]

We examined what already passed and found that his expression: *A mighty king shall arise* (Dn 11:3) refers to the one with two horns. I mean Alexander.[49] His expression: *He shall establish his great dominion* (Dn 11:3) means [that he

42 Edom represent the Romans. Ishmael represent the Arabs and the Muslims.
43 Yefet ben Eli too quotes Dn 5:19 in his explanation of ועשה כרצונו. However he does it in his commentary on Dn 11:3.
44 R. Saadia renders the Hebrew verb עשה in Dn 11:16.36 by the Arabic verb צנע. However, he renders the same Hebrew verb by the Arabic verb עמל in Dn 11:3.
45 Lit: "And I say at its beginning."
46 "For them" is added by R. Saadia in his translation and has no Hebrew origin.
47 Yefet ben Eli: "From some of his officers."
48 Lit: "And from his dominion there will be a powerful dominion that rules."
49 Yefet ben Eli too identifies the king mentioned in Dn 11:3 as Alexander.

ruled] over the big part of the world. His expression: *And accomplish what pleases him* (Dn 11:3) [indicates] that he destroys, builds and displaces nations from one country to the other. Similar to what Sennacherib had said: *I erased the borders of the nations, I abruptly took away their provisions and put down many inhabited places* (Is 10:13).[50] His expression: כעמדו (Dn 11:4) means once his establishment was completed, which happens after his death.[51] That was [after] twelve years. Then *his kingdom shall break down* (Dn 11:4) and be divided into four parts, starting from Syria, the country mentioned in this story. likewise [his expression]: *And I will bring upon Elam four winds from the four limits of heaven* (Jer 49:36); starting from Elam.[52] No part of it will belong to his children, because of his expression: *Shall not belong to his descendant* (Dn 11:4) which designates his descendant as we have explained about the meaning of the words.[53] The meaning of [the expression]: … *neither to the dominion that he founded* (Dn 11:4) is that [his dominion] will not belong to anyone from his religion or his followers.[54] His expression: *His kingdom shall be cut off* (Dn 11:4). Similar to his expression: *So God cut them off his land* (Dt 29:27).[55] His expression: … *and belong to others than these* (Dn 11:4) means that [the kingdom] will not belong to those that he is about to mention. They are *the king of Syria and the king of Iraq*. In fact the kingdom will be divided between two kings different from [the of Syria and the king of Iraq]. They are *the king of the east and the king of the west* that [the story] didn't specify.[56] Thus the total becomes four. As to *the king of the east and the king of the west* that, their time was not long. It is the king of Syria that takes possession [of the kingdom] after them, as it has been said: *The king of the south shall become strong* (Dn 11:5) in the like of the expression: *The people who followed Omri became stronger than those who followed Tibni, son of Ginath* (1 Kgs 16:22).

50 פאזלת תכ֗ום אלשעוב ומא אסתעדוה אט֗טלמתה וחטטת כת֗ירא {מן אלעמארה} is R. Saadia's translation of Is 10:13.

51 Yefet ben Eli has the same explanation.

52 R. Saadia's idea is that Syria in Dn 11:4 is as central as Elam in Jer 49:36.

53 Reference to his explanation following his commentary on Dn 11:1.

54 כמשלו has a different interpretation according to Yefet ben Eli. He understands כמשלו as 'like Alexander's way of governing his empire.' That leads to his interpretation that no one of the four parts of the empire after its division will be governed in the manner in which Alexander used to govern his empire.

55 פקלעהם אללה מן בלדה is R. Saadia's translation of Dt 29:27. In his translation the Hebrew expression אדמתם literally 'their land' is rendered by בלדה literally 'his land.' The translation quoted follows R. Saadia's interpretation.

56 Yefet ben Eli gives two reasons for the absence of news related to the king of the east and the king of the west. First, because there were no war between them. Secondly, because their power was absorbed by the king of Syria and the king of Iraq.

But the king of the north invaded him a time after his establishment with some of his followers [as it is has been said] at the end of the verse: … *and shall overcome him* (Dn 11:5). Like a strong man *he shall apply a powerful dominion* (Dn 11:5). Thereafter the two kings become strong alone, the king of the south, the king of Syria, and the king of the north, the king of Iraq. Then he said:

Dn 11:6

For years they join their force.[57] And the group[58] of the king of Syria reach the king of Iraq[59] to work a reconciliation and submission.[60] But their arm[61] will not retain strength and their group does not grow firm neither strong. They will surrender with those who are familiar with them, their master and those who sustain them by their advice.[62]

Dn 11:7

Then [some one] from a branch of his roots[63] shall arise on his throne[64] and infiltrates the army of the king of Iraq and permeates his fortification. He shall do with its population whatever he wants and dominate them.[65]

57 Lit: "For years they become acquainted one with the other."

58 The Hebrew word בת literally 'daughter' is rendered here by the Arabic word גמאעה according to R. Saadia's interpretation explained immediately after Dn 11:1.

59 מלך הצפון that R. Saadia renders by 'the king of Iraq' is not translated by Yefet ben Eli who maintains the Hebrew expressions in his Arabic text. Which means that, unlike R. Saadia, he refuses to identify both kings.

60 The Hebrew word מישרים literally 'agreement' or 'reconciliation' is rendered by two Arabic words: צלח 'reconciliation' and וטאה 'submission.'

61 In other word, 'the arm of the group' following R. Saadia's interpretation of the Hebrew word בת.

62 Lit: "And his arm does not retain strength and his arm will not be stable, but will surrender together with the one who brought it and made it grow and made it strong during sometimes" which is also Yefet ben Eli's translation. R. Saadia renders the Hebrew word עתusually understood here as 'time,' by the Arabic word אלמשורה 'advice' basing his interpretation on a citation from Est 1:13 where we find the Hebrew word עתים with the meaning of 'advice.'

63 R. Saadia will explain in his commentary that the branch that arises represents some individual from the followers of the king or Syria or the king of the south.

64 The Arabic word מנבר literally means 'chair, pulpit, platform'. Yefet ben Eli choose the Arabic word כרשי 'chair' in his translation.

65 Lit: "And infiltrates the army then permeates the fortification of the king of the north, he shall deal with them and become strong" which is also Yefet ben Eli's translation.

Dn 11:8

Their gods with their favorites,[66] with their precious golden and silver vessels he will bring in captivity to Egypt. He will live years after the king of Iraq.

The probable interpretation of his expression: *For years they join their force* (Dn 11:6) is seven years,[67] similar to his expression: *At the end of every seven years you make a release* (Dt 15:1).[68] His expression: *And the group of the king of Syria* (Dt 15:1) designates a group of his partisans, according to what we have explained, that will arrive to Iraq [in a mission] of reconciliation, a submission or a stratagem. Because the word מֵישָׁרִים bears such [meaning] for its participation [at the meaning] of מִישׁוֹר which designates 'a plain' or 'a low ground.' He informed him that the stratagem of the Syrian will not prevail against the Iraqi, since he said: *But their[69] arm will not retain strength* (Dn 11:6).[70] *[However] the group will not stand up and their hand will not grow [strong].*[71] The first letter replaces the second.[72] [The expression]: *They will surrender* (Dn 11:6) pertains to the group [of the Syrian king]. *Those who are familiar with them* (Dn 11:6) refers to the guides who guided [the group] in [their] way. They belong neither to the partisans of *the king of the south* nor to the partisans of *the king of the north*. Thereafter, they will surrender היולדה (Dn 11:6) their master. Similar to the expression: *For a stone you gave birth to me* (Jer 2:27).[73] They will also surrender their advisers. They are the ones entitled to give advice, according to what we have explained: *The king spoke to the wise men who know the advice* (Est 1:13). He also said: *The heart of the wise man knows advice and judgment*

66 עם נסכיהם 'with their favorites' is not translated by Yefet ben Eli. However, he renders this word in his commentary by 'lords and princes.'

67 Yefet ben Eli mentions the impossibility of having a specific number for these years.

68 פי כל סבע סנין אצנע סייבא is R. Saadia translation of Dt 15:1.

69 The arm of the group of the Syrian king.

70 For Yefet ben Eli, the word 'arm' designates the arm of the of the king of the south

71 In Hebrew. The word בת is translated here as 'group' following R. Saadia's interpretation explained in his commentary of Dn 11:1.

72 ולא תעמד הבת ולא יעצר זרועו. The ת which is the first letter of the first verb תעמד replaces the י which is the first letter of the second verb יעצר. In this case the two verbs has הבת or the group of the Syrian king as subject.

73 The point of comparison between Dn 11:6 and Jer 2:27 remains unclear. Most probably the point of comparison is היולדה in Dn 11:6 and ילדתני in Jer 2:27. However, R. Saadia translates היולדה by the Arabic word אסתאד̇ 'master.' While the normal translation ילדתני of is 'gave me birth' or 'bring me forth.'

(Ecc 8:5).[74] All these will be surrendered to the king of Iraq. Afterward, taking the place of *the southern king*, will arise from the populace, those who will overcome the Iraqi [king]. [this will happen] because of the expression: *Then [some one] from a branch of his roots* (Dn 11:7). Similar to the expression: … *or to the offshoot of the tribe of the alien* (Lv 25:47).[75]

[The meaning of] the expression: כנו (Dn 11:7) *his throne* implies על כנו *on his throne*. His expression: … *and infiltrates the army* (Dn 11:7) means that he passes through the army giving and exercise his power over it.[76] He said similarly: *He passes among princes like an artist who works the argil and the potter who treads the clay* (Is 41:25).[77] Then *he permeates his fortification* (Dn 11:7). [The word מעוז means] 'fortification' following what I have said.[78] [His expression:] *He shall do with its population* (Dn 11:7) means that *he shall do with its inhabitants whatever he wants.* [His expression:] … *and dominate them* (Dn 11:7) *on the land of the north* in order that he deport to Egypt [statues of their] divinities, population, wealth and furniture. That means that whoever escapes death will be deported. [The meaning is] that they will be expressly deported. His expression: *He will live years after the king of Iraq* (Dn 11:8) means that he will survive him for a period.[79] Similar to he had said: *Jeroboam did not recover his strength in the days of Abijah and he died* (2 Chr 13:20). Then he said:

Dn 11:9

Thereafter he will enter the kingdom of the king of the south[80] then he will go back to his land.

74 The translation of עתים, עת mentioned in the quotation of Est 1:13 and Ecc 8:5 is according to R. Saadia's interpretation of the word עתים as משורה 'advice.'

75 או לאצל עשׁירה אלג̇ריב is R. Saadia's translation of the quoted part of Lv 25:47. The context of Lv 25:47 (the Lord words to Moses on mount Sinai) seems different from what is described in Dn 11:7 and does not appear to be the point of comparison in this quotation.

76 Lit: "Giving permission and forbidding."

77 ויתוסט אלכ̇לפא כדכ̇ול אלמצור פי אלטין וכמא ידוס אלפכ̇ראני אלחמאה is R. Saadia's translation of the citation from Is 41:25.

78 Following the explanation of the same word in his commentary of Dn 11:1.

79 Yefet ben Eli interprets this part of Dn 11:8 as the king of the north will be obedient to the king of the south.

80 R. Saadia translates מלך הנגב by 'the king of the south' or the king of Syria.' He does the same for the expression מלך הצפון translated once by 'the king of Iraq' once by 'the king of the north.' Yefet ben Eli: "He comes under the king of the south."

Dn 11:10

His sons will stand against him.[81] They will assemble a big army against him[82] and invade strongly his country.[83] They will leave him alone and pass, then comeback and confront his strongholds.[84]

Dn 11:11

The king of the south shall become angry, he shall come out and fight against the king of the north.[85] He shall assemble great army and the multitude shall be given to his hand.

Dn 11:12

And he shall disperse greatly.[86] His heart shall be proud, he shall cast down myriad with him, but shall not be stronger by them.[87]

Dn 11:13

Then the king of the north shall come back and put together bigger multitude than the first one.[88] Afterward, he shall certainly invade his country.[89] Then he will come back with great army and large supply.

Dn 11:14

At that time[90] many resist the king of Syria. The young and conceited among your people, they oppose the fulfillment of a vision, but they stumble.[91]

81 Yefet ben Eli: "His sons will fight" or "will be quarrelsome." Unlike R. Saadia, he does not add 'against him' to his translation which follows closely the Hebrew text.

82 R. Saadia adds 'against him' to his translation, that has no source in the MT.

83 R. Saadia adds 'his country' to his translation, that has no source in the MT. Yefet ben Eli: "His sons will assemble big army, but he will come strongly, invade then pass away."

84 The singular Hebrew word מעזו is rendered by the plural Arabic word חצונה 'Strongholds.' R. Saadia soon will explain the reason why he choose to translate Dn 11:10b as if its subject is plural and not singular as it is in the text.

85 Yefet ben Eli is more literal in his translation: "He shall come out and fight him, the king of the north."

86 Yefet ben Eli translates the MT. Literally: "He carries the army."

87 Yefet ben Eli: "And no one will be strong before him."

88 Yefet ben Eli: "Bigger army than the former armies."

89 Yefet ben Eli: "And there will be years for the end of times."

90 The plural Hebrew expression בעתים literal 'in those times' is rendered by the singular Arabic expression בדלך אלעצר 'at that age' or 'time.' Yefet ben Eli: 'In those times."

91 Yefet ben Eli: "They will arise to confirm the inspiration, but they will stumble."

Dn 11:15

Then the king of Iraq shall arrive and establish a siege and invade a fortified city.[92] The rulers of Syria will show no resistance before him and the best of the people will have no strength to resist.[93]

His expression earlier about *the king of the north* that *he will enter the kingdom of the king of the south* (Dn 11:9) bears two meanings. One of them is that the Iraqi [king] enters the land of the Syrian [king] in order to examine him as it is the case in the story of the Roglim.[94] The other is that he walks over his country in his way to fight others as it is the case of the Pharaoh Neco.[95] In both cases he remains unharmed and returns to his country.[96] But the sons of *the king of the south* will attack the *king of the north* similar to what Jonathan did to the Philistines: *Jonathan struck down the prefect of the Philistines who was at Geba* (1 Sm 13:3). Then *the sons of the king of the south assemble a big army* (Dn 11:10). They accomplish all the actions attributed [in the text] to one individual, in the like of his expression: *He shall leave him alone and pass then comeback and confront his strongholds* (Dn 11:10). All this must be treated as plural. What he intends is *they will leave him alone and pass, then comeback and confront his strongholds*. It is possible that one of the sons starts which allows him to write *his son* (Dn 11:10) in singular form.[97] They will enter the land of the king of the north then leave it to go back to their land. Afterward they will comeback and fight his strongholds.[98] When the king of the south realizes that his sons succeed [in their attack] he shall reserve to himself the fight against the king of the north. Similar to Saul who realizing that the invasion was accomplished by his son Jonathan he reserved to himself the fight against the Philistines: *Saul and the people who were with him assembled and rushed to the battle* (1 Sm 14:20). All the Hebrews who were hidden appeared,

92 Yefet ben Eli: "And besiege the king's city."

93 The Hebrew text does not specify that 'the people will have no strength to resist' but 'that there is no strength to resist'. Yefet ben Eli: "The hands of the king of the south will not resist, with his chosen group, and there will be no strength to resist."

94 Cf. 2 Sm 19:32–39 where the king in his passage to the Jordan was testing the aptitude of Barzillai.

95 Cf. Jer 46:2–28. The Pharaoh Neco was defeated by Nebuchadrezzar after crossing the Euphrates

96 According to Yefet ben Eli's interpretation, the king of the north will be under the power of the king of the south.

97 MT: ובנו 'his son.' Whoever, in his transcription of the Hebrew text, R. Saadia text (Morag) has ובניו 'his sons.'

98 במצוזנה could be translated as the strongholds of the king (his strongholds) or the stronghold of the land (its strongholds).

came back and joined the group who was with Saul and Jonathan, as he said: *And the Hebrew who were with the Philistines before that time they turned with them into the neighboring camp* (1 Sm 14:21). He means that they were afraid at the beginning. After that he briefly said: *Likewise they joined Israel who was with Saul and Jonathan* (1 Sm 14:21). We have the same thing here. The king of the south realizing the accomplishment of his sons *the king of the south shall become angry* (Dn 11:11). At that time *he shall come out and fight against the king of the north* (Dn 11:11). However, he added *against him* (Dn 11:11)[99] in order to prevent any confusion.[100] Then: *The king of the north set forth a multitude* (cf. Dn 11:11). But he strongly dispersed him.

His expression: *And he shall disperse greatly* (Dn 11:12) [has the meaning] that we already mentioned: *You will be dispersed with baskets* (Am 4:2).[101] As to the meaning of *he shall cast down myriad* (Dn 11:12) it points to the limitlessness[102] as he said: *Here I am stirring up the Medians against them, who have no consideration for money and disdain gold* (Is 13:17).[103] Afterward he mentions a victory for the Iraqi [king], saying: *Then the king of the north shall come back and put together bigger multitude [than the first one]* (Dn 11:13) and the rest of the story. Which implies that *he will come back with great army and large supply* (Dn 11:13). In fact it is not customary for fighters to carry *large supply* to the site where the fight takes place. This could be said, however, about the [the fighter] who obtains victory, captures spoils and *goes back to his country, with great army and large supply* (cf. Dn 11:28). These events happened between the seven former kings of the Greek and their counter part of the kings of Persia. As to the eighth [king] he mentioned that the Israel will resist him. This is [indicated by] his expression: *At that time many resist the king of Syria* (Dn 11:14). According to the principle he emitted [...] Israel is called many. It is the story of the resistance [...] the sons of the Hasmonean for three times. The first time, they kill Nicanor, his minister.[104] In the second time they defeated their army with Bacchides and they take possession [of them].[105] Concerning his

99 עמו 'against him' is no translated by R. Saadia.

100 Lit: "In order to prevent any comparison with his father."

101 The Arabic verb by which R. Saadia renders the Hebrew verb נשׂא is כפא that means 'taken off, carried out' or ' being dispersed.' Hens the translation of Am 4:2 'you will be dispersed.'

102 Lit: "... by which he means that he sees no measure for that."

103 והאנא מֹטהר עליהם אלהמדאניין אלדֿין לא יחסבון אלורק שׄיא ואלדֿהב לא ירידונה is R. Saadia's translation of Is 13:17. To be noticed that R. Saadia translate כסף by אלורק literally paper.

104 The general (וזיר literally 'minister') under Antioch Epiphanes and Demetrius I that was killed by Judah Maccabi. Cf. 1 Mc 7:39; 2 Mc 15:30.

105 Cf. 1 Mc 7:1–24.

expression: *The young and conceited among your people* (Dn 11:14) refers to the followers of Jesus who established him in the rank of a prophet. They tried to invent a prophecy for him, but they will stumble by him and die. In fact, in his life the man […] the Greek did not remain faithful to him.[106] On the contrary, they run away from him. According to the information we have he took place in a boat and escaped to high places.[107] It goes the same for his rulers and patriarchs and.[108] [The expression:] … *will have no strength to resist* (Dn 11:14) is parallel to the expression:[109] *No one of its noble men shall be there; how possible to call some one to rule? All its leaders shall become nothing* (Is 34:12)[110] in putting the negation at the beginning.[111]

Now that we have explained the other thirteen verses relative to the Greek kings, we must explain the thirty verses pertaining to the [kingdom] of Edom and its associate. We say that the entire information relative to the cited kings is signal and marks destined to the Israelites in order that observed by any of their generations they may have faith in the reality of the salvation as we have explained about Cyrus…[112]

Dn 11:16

Then the one who overcomes[113] shall do according to his will, and no one will resist him; he shall remain firm in the land of Syria[114] and a sword was in his hand.[115]

106 Dn 11:14 is normally used to refute the Christian claim about Jesus as Christ. It is the case of Rambam and Ibn Ezra. R. Saadia's refutation seems to reach Jesus and his disciples, since the lacuna is preceded by an attack on the truthfulness of Jesus and is followed by an attack on Paul. Yefet ben Eli, too, applies Dn 11:14 to the Christians, especially to the four evangelists, implying that all of them were Jews that turned against their religion. Their major act of rebellion against Judaism is their attempt to attribute a vision to Jesus.

107 'High places' uncertain reading. The sentence probably pertains to St. Paul, the apostle of Jesus Christ to the nations.

108 It could be the rulers and Patriarchs that St. Paul installed or the rulers and Patriarchs that belong to Jesus.

109 Lit: "… to your expression."

110 ליס פיהא מן אחרארהא אחד פכיף ידעא להם באלמלך וגמיע ריסאהא יצירון כלוא is R. Saadia's translation of Is 34:12.

111 Lit. "In adding אין at the beginning."

112 The remaining part of Oxf 2486.156b is partially readable and does not represent a coherent meaning.

113 MT: "The one who comes" which is also Yefet ben Eli's interpretation.

114 ארץ הצבי is usually interpreted as 'the land of Israel' in reference to Jer 3:19 and Ez 20:6.15. Yefet ben Eli: "The land of joy" or the land of Israel.

Dn 11:17

He goes toward the most trustful in his kingdom, those who are protected being with him,[116] then he acts; to his master he shall hand the cities[117] for destruction; they will neither resist nor will they belong to him.

Dn 11:18

He shall face the islanders[118] and invade many of them[119] and he shall put an end to the insult by this king against himself after paying him back for his action.[120]

Dn 11:19

Then he shall return to face the strongholds of his land, afterward he shall stumble then fall and shall not be found.

Dn 11:20

In his place shall stand someone who direct the officers among the people for the splendor of the kingdom,[121] but he shall be put down in few days, without anger, nor fight.[122]

Dn 11:21

A detestable man, on whom there is no splendor of the kingdom,[123] shall stand up in his place; he shall come quietly[124] and obtain the kingdom by stratagem.[125]

---

115 Yefet ben Eli: "And he shall be destroyed by his hand." That means that, unlike R. Saadia, he does not understand כלה as name for 'sword', but as a verb: 'to finish, to perish.'

116 Yefet ben Eli: "He direct his intention to invade resolutely all his kingdom and will bring with him those who are righteous."

117 R. Saadia renders בת הנשים by מדן 'cities.' Doing so, he renders in plural what is singular in the MT. Yefet ben Eli: "The daughter of women" as it is usually translated. Yefet ben Eli translation, therefore is: "He shall hand him the daughter of women to corrupt her."

118 Lit: "Islands" and not the islands' inhabitants.

119 The expression 'of them' is added by R. Saadia to his translation and has no source in the MT.

120 Yefet ben Eli: "And this prince shall put an end to the insult against him, but the insult shall return to him."

121 Yefet ben Eli: "And on his place someone who causes the follower of the king's joy to pass."

122 Yefet ben Eli: "But he shall beak down in few days, without encounter nor war" or "sword."

Dn 11:22

The noble men among the deported will be deported in his presence. They will be broken until the covenant rule over them.[126]

Dn 11:23

Among those who are familiar with him there will be some who will treat him with malice until another than him[127] **arise and become great over few people.**

Dn 11:24

He shall enter quietly in his city and shall do what neither his fathers nor his forefathers did;[128] **he shall reward his friends**[129] **from its riches, its spoils and its herds; he shall set up schemes against the strongholds, but for another time.**[130]

Dn 11:25

He shall show up his strength[131] **and intention, by a big army, against the king of the south, and the king of the south shall stir up to fight him with a big and great army,**[132] **but he will not resist because of the schemes they set up against him.**

Dn 11:26

Even[133] **the eaters of his portions of bread and meat**[134] **will put him down, his army shall be dispersed and many, overwhelmed, will fall will him.**[135]

---

123 MT: "The splendor of the kingdom don't bestow on him" which is also Yefet ben Eli's translation.

124 Yefet ben Eli: "He shall come with pride."

125 Instead of R. Saadia' translation of חילה 'stratagem' which implies malice, Yefet ben Eli render the same Hebrew word חלקות by מלאטאה which implies flattery.

126 Yefet ben Eli: "And the armies of the coast will be deported out of his presence; they will be broken and also what remains from the covenant."

127 "Another than him" is added by R. Saadia and has no Hebrew background in Daniel's text.

128 Another possible reading: "His father and his father's fathers."

129 'His friends' is added by R. Saadia and has no source in the MT.

130 MT: "But for a time" which is also Yefet ben Eli's translation.

131 Yefet ben Eli: "He shall excite his strength."

132 MT: "shall stir up to the fight with a big and great army" which also Yefet ben Eli's translation.

133 חתי could be translated by 'even' or 'until.'

134 "Bread and meat" has no Hebrew background in Daniel's text.

135 MT: "And many, dead, will fall" which is also Yefet ben Eli's translation.

Dn 11:27

Those two kings will agree in wrongdoing and they will utter lies at one table, but no success will be for them,[136] because there is an appointed time that remains for the end.[137]

Dn 11:28

One of them shall comeback with big herds and the harm in his heart against those of Jerusalem covenant.[138] The other[139] shall finish his fight and go back to his land.[140]

Dn 11:29

He shall return in the appointed time and invade the south; the battle[141] shall not be similar to the first one, nor to the second.[142]

Dn 11:30

The men of the desert and the men of the littoral[143] will come in and join him;[144] he shall assail and come back with anger against those of Jerusalem covenant; he shall accomplish that[145] and return to treat harshly those who abandoned Jerusalem covenant.[146]

Dn 11:31

Nobel men among them will rise,[147] defile the fortified sanctuary, take away the daily sacrifice and make it abomination.[148]

136 "For them" has no Hebrew background in Daniel's text.

137 MT: "Because there is an end to the time" which is also Yefet ben Eli's translation.

138 MT: "He Shall comeback with big herds and his heart was set against the covenant of Jerusalem" which is also Yefet ben Eli's translation.

139 "The other" has no Hebrew background in Daniel's text. The Hebrew text attributes all the verbs to one subject. R. Saadia, instead, has two subjects: One of them and the other.

140 MT: "He shall accomplish then go back to his land" which is also Yefet ben Eli's translation.

141 "The battle" added by R. Saadia and has no and has no source in the MT.

142 Lit: "Shall not be similar to the first one, nor to the last."

143 Yefet ben Eli: "The men of the desert and אלקברסיין the men of Cyprus."

144 "And join him" is added by R. Saadia to his translation and has no source in the MT.

145 "That" added by R. Saadia and has no Hebrew background in Daniel's text.

146 Yefet ben Eli: "And remember ויפטן – for the Hebrew ויבן – those who abandoned the covenant of Jerusalem."

147 Lit: "Arms among them will rise." Yefet ben Eli chooses the literal meaning in his translation.

Dn 11:32

He will overcome the oppressors of the covenant by stratagems and those who show obedience to his divinity[149] will become powerful and will accomplish that.[150]

Dn 11:33

The learned of every nation[151] will instruct many, yet they will be tested by the sword, the flame, the deportation and the spoil for a period.[152]

Dn 11:34

During their trial they will be helped a little and many will join them by stratagems.

Dn 11:35

Among the learned some will be impoverished[153] to refine, to polish[154] and to justify; until the time of the end for it remains a period until the appointed time.[155]

[...][156] the Persian son from the Iraqi: *He shall become great over few people* (Dn 11:23).[157] Gabriel said about him: *What his fathers did not do* (Dn 11:24). He designates those who were in the presence of *someone who directs the officers* (Dn 11:20). His expression: ... *nor his forefathers* (Dn 11:24) designates those who were in the presence of *the most trustful in his kingdom* (Dn 11:17). This third [king] shall obtain victory.[158] His expression: *He shall set up schemes*

148 ותנו השקוץ משמם is rendered by R. Saadia as "and make it abomination." That means that משמם is not translated. Yefet ben Eli: "And make the abomination aberrant."

149 Yefet ben Eli: "And those who know God."

150 "That" added by R. Saadia and has no Hebrew background in Daniel's text.

151 "Every" is added by R. Saadia. The MT has 'the learned of the nation' which also Yefet ben Eli's translation.

152 Yefet ben Eli: "By the sword, the deportation, the flame, and the spoil for days."

153 Yefet ben Eli: "Among the learned some will stumble."

154 וללבן 'to make white' is translated by to liberate or to declare some one innocent.

155 Yefet ben Eli does not translate the final part of Dn 11:35: כי עוד למועד.

156 R. Saadia's commentary on Dn 11:16–22 did not reach us.

157 Yefet ben Eli applies Dn 11:23 as well as Dn 11:25 to Omer, the third Caliph after Muhammed, whom he called איש הרוח or 'the man of the wind.' Yefet ben Eli sees in the remaining part of Dn 11 a prophecy relative to the struggle between Muslims and Christians or the Greek, the triumph of the Islamic army in the Middle East and their oppressive behavior against the Israelites.

158 Uncertain lesson for a very damaged manuscript.

against the strongholds, but for another time (Dn 11:24) means that he had a long term thought about them. something more than twenty two years.[159] His expression: *He shall show up his strength and intention* (Dn 11:25) means by strength and stratagem. [...] *against the king of the south* (Dn 11:25) because his intention is to kill him alone, and no other than him, as he already said: *The king of Aram had ordered the captains of the chariots that belong to him, saying, do not fight with small or big, but only with the king of Israel* (2 Chr 18:30). Similar to what Ahitophel had said: *I will make him afraid and when all the people who are with him flee, I will kill the king alone* (2 Sm 17:2). As to his expression: *But him will not stand because of the schemes they set up against him* (Dn 11:25) there is no need to show examples of those schemes or others if I don't want to blame myself for such endeavor, because of the big number of the schemes from kings and rulers, not to mention of the no profit of such [effort] for [the understanding] of the Book. Then some of the king's familiars plotted against him in order to be invaded by the Persian king, as he said: *The eater of his portions of bread and meat...* (Dn 11:26), because of their ill-will, of his injustice against them, of their connivance with [king's] enemy, of an expectation [for better life] or of being afraid.

His expression: *Those two kings will agree in wrongdoing* (Dn 11:27) indicates that the king of the north and the king of the south[160] insist in their wrongdoing against Israel. His expression: *They will utter lies at one table* (Dn 11:27) [could be from] of a pulpit,[161] bed, table and all the particular [names of the table]. The meaning of *They will utter lies* (Dn 11:27) is not lies in words. It is a deceitful ambition that leads to nothing. The justification [for such meaning] is their inconclusive ambition about the Temple. [The expression:] *Because there is an appointed time that remains for the end* (Dn 11:27) [means] that there are many remaining years for the period of its standing up.[162] It is possible that [this passage] pertains to the years of the Hasmonean House and their allies. I also say that *lies* (Dn 11:27) here are comparable to the expression of Micaiah, son of Imlah to Ahab: *Behold, The lord has put a lying spirit in the mouth of all your prophets* (1 Kgs 22:23). It is not lying in words. It is about what will not be achieved, what will not be rightful. Which is similar to his expression: *Useless*

159 Yefet ben Eli applies Dn 11:24 to Muhammed.

160 According to Yefet ben Eli the two kings are a Greek and an Arabic kings, or the Christian and the Islamic kingdoms in their oppression of the Jews.

161 Yefet ben Eli mentions that a possible interpretation of the 'one table' could be Israel, because of their particular way of eating. The others, Edom and Ishmael, could not be described as 'one table' since they eat the same plates, according to Yefet ben Eli. Thus, they could not be described 'one table.'

162 Uncertain lesson: עמדאנה its standing up, or עמראנה being built. Both seems to be relative to the same reality: the no destruction of the Temple.

is the salvation by the horse (Ps 33:17).[163] And also: *The grace is vain and the beauty illusory* (Pr 31:30).[164] And also: *Falsity is what its builder did in it* (Ps 127:1).[165] And also: *Falsely the watchman stays awake* (Ps 127:1).[166] [...] *In vain for you {to rise up early}* (Ps 127:2).[167] When [the fallacious enterprise] is not completed for both [kings] they went back to their respective countries, as he said: *One of them shall come back with big herds* (Dn 11:28). About the other he said: The other *shall finish his fight and go back to his land* (Dn 11:28).[168] I interpreted [the expression:] *He shall return in the appointed time* (Dn 11:29)[169] similar to [the expression:] *I shall come back to you at this time from the coming year* (Gn 18:14).[170] His expression: *He shall return* (Dn 11:29)[171] pertains to the *king of the north* whose achievement is *to invade the south* (Dn 11:29). His expression: *The battle shall not be similar to the first one* (Dn 11:29) means that he engage the battle alone.[172] [His expression:] *nor to the second* (Dn 11:29) [means] his request for help from the [king] of the south.[173] His expression: *The men of the desert and the men of the littoral* (Dn 11:30) indicates that a group from the Bedouins becomes familiar with the king of the south. They are *the men of the desert* (Dn 11:30). They are others: *The men of the littoral* (Dn 11:30). When these men rejoin him he becomes alert and agile in his attack, as he witnessed: *He shall assail* (Dn 11:30).[174] This is similar to his expression: *They gathered against me quickly* (Ps 35:15).[175] His expression: *He shall come back with anger against those of Jerusalem covenant* (Dn 11:30) means [... ...].[176]

163 ובאטל גׄיאתֿ אלפרס is R. Saadia's translation of the citation from Ps 33:17.
164 פאלחטׄא באטל ואלגמאל גׄרור is R. Saadia's translation of the citation from Pr 31:31.
165 פזור מא עמל פיה באניה is R. Saadia's translation of the citation from Ps 127:1.
166 פזור מא ראבט אלהראס פיהא is R. Saadia's translation of the citation from Ps 127:1.
167 וזור לכם is R. Saadia's translation of the citation from Ps 127:2.
168 Yefet ben Eli specifies that the king that will comeback to his land is the Islamic king after his triumph over the Greek king.
169 According to Yefet ben Eli, starting Dn 11:29 the vision deals with the end of the Islamic kingdom, or the kingdom of Ishmael.
170 סארגע אליך פי מתל הדא אלוקת מן קאבל is R. Saadia's translation of the citation from Gn 18:14.
171 Yefet ben Eli specifies that starting Dn 11:29 the text deals with the end of the kingdom of Ishmael.
172 Uncertain lesson.
173 Uncertain lesson.
174 For Yefet ben Eli, the two groups of the Israelites that either accept the Islam or accept to be submitted to the Islamic authority while remaining faithful to the religion of Israel.
175 אנתמעו עלי מגתאין is R. Saadia's translation of the citation from Ps 35:15.
176 The commentary of R. Saadia on Dn 11:31–32 is missing.

[...] *they cast down the right on the ground, they committed their deed and succeeded* (Dn 8:12).[177] His expression: *The learned of every nation will instruct many* (Dn 11:33) designates the wise men, of blessed memory, whose function in the Diaspora is the same as the Levites about whom it was said: *Heyekiah spoke to the heart of all the Levites who displayed cleverness in the service of the Lord* (2 Chr 30:22).[178] He also said about some of them: *They brought us, by the hand of our God, a wise man from the sons of Mahli* (Ezr 8:18). And about some others: *The lot eastward fell to Shelemiahu, then for Zekariahu his son, a wise counselor* (1 Chr 26:14). They are Roben Jonathan, Eleazar, Joshua, Gemalial and Akiba, with their friends and followers. Because the function of the Levites is *to advice the sons of Jacob in judgment and the sons of Israel in the Torah* (Dt 33:10).[179] His expression: *They will instruct many* (Dn 11:33) is similar to what the Bible[180] had said about the Levites: *They lead the people to understand the Torah* (Neh 8:7). There is also his expression: *The Levites who teach the people* (Neh 8:9) and similar expressions. Then he[181] informed him about the distress that will face him: *They will be tested by the sword, the flame, the deportation and the spoliation for a period* (Dn 11:33). As to [the expression:] *By the sword* (Dn 11:33) it is in the like of the death of R. Akiba by the sword [...] R. Yehudah ben Papa [...]. About [his expression:] *By the flame* (Dn 11:33) it is similar to the burning of R. Hananiah ben [...] while wrapped by the Scroll of the Torah[182] and after covering his chest by a humid liar of wool in order that his spirit do not leave quickly. However [... ...]. Concerning [the expression:] *By the deportation and the spoil* (Dn 11:33) it is similar to the manner in which R. Meyer, still youngster, was deported. When R. Ishmael said: *He who gave the people of Jacob to the spoliation and the people of Israel to plunderer* (Is 42:24)[183] he answered saying: *Isn't he God against whom we have sinned* (Is 42:24)?[184]

Gabriel had anticipated the information to Daniel about these events in order that, once they happened, we won't be depressed and lose the hope of being

177 The quotation from Dn 8:12 seems to conclude R. Saadia's commentary on Dn 11:32.

178 "The learned in the nation" according to Yefet ben Eli' commentary on Dn 11:33, designates, the 'masters' among the Karaites, or the משׂכילים.

179 והם יפתון פי אחכאמך לאל יעקוב ופי תוראתך לאל אסראיל is R. Saadia's translation of the citation from Dt 33:10.

180 Lit: "What he said about the Levites."

181 The individual who has a human appearance. Cf. 10:18.

182 Lit: 'The Book of the Torah."

183 מן געל אל יעקוב אטטלאמא ואל אסראיל ללגאנמין is R. Saadia's translation of the citation from Is 42:24.

184 אליס הו אללה אלדי אכטאנא לה is R. Saadia's translation of the citation from Is 42: 24.

saved. On the contrary, [these events] should be considered as *signs and evidences* for the truthfulness of salvation, according to what we have said. And in saying to him: *During their trial they will be helped a little* (Dn 11:34) he means that *during their trial* there will be a little help from *the king of Edom.*[185] Because [...] was to our holly Rabbi from Antoninus, son of Asirus[186] who was his foster-brother. He gave him the good news that he will be king. Many good things were done to Israel through his hand. Like *the draining of Gaza and the declaration of Tiberias as Roman colony.* His expression: *And many will join them by stratagems* (Dn 11:34) designates the different kinds of bitterness that the fathers suffered from the kings of Edom [... ...] their religion and their descendant. Their Lord guided them from heaven, following the expression: *Even in those days I will not make the end of you* (Jer 5:18). So if they were like fire, they wouldn't yet be able to burn us. And if they were like water we wouldn't be submerged by them, as he said: *Even if you had to pass through water I will be with you and the rivers will not overflow you and should you walk through the fire the flames will not burn you* (Is 43:2).[187] But on the big part of the nation he multiplied poverty and misery, as it has been said: *Among the learned some will be impoverished* (Dn 11:35) the meaning is that they will become poor.[188] Similar to his expression: *He will bring them forth with gold and silver ant there will be no indigent in their tribes* (Ps 105:37).[189] Then he uncovered why the wisdom imposed such thing on them. He refers it to three reasons: *To refine, to polish and to justify* (Dn 11:35). *To refine* (Dn 11:35) [means] to test them the way the faithful should be tested. If they remain faithfully patient they will be rewarded by the good, as he had said about Joseph: *Until the time His salvation become near, the discourse of God stand for a test* (Ps 105:19).[190] *To polish* (Dn 11:35) in their crucible of their work, as he said: *He made me a polished arrow* (Is 49:2).[191] And also: *My lips express a pure knowledge* (Jb 33:3).[192] In order to be deprived of possessions that occupy them to the point of leaving aside the study of law, the observances and all the need of the nation. [His ex-

185 Yefet ben Eli evokes two means by which God will help the Israelites: Either by rising a savior, like the queen Esther, or by destroying the king that subjects them or harms them.

186 A roman emperor frequently mentioned as friend of R. Judah Ha-Nassi.

187 ולו גזת פי אלמא פאנא מעך ואלאנהאר לא תגרקך ולו סרת פי אלנאר לא תנכוי ואללהיב לא ישתעל פיך is R. Saadia's translation of Is 43:2.

188 For Yefet ben Eli, 'among the learned some will stumble' by leaving Judaism. He gives the disciples of Jesus as an example of those who stumble.

189 ואכרגהם בפצה ודהב וליס פי אסבאטה מעוז is R. Saadia's translation of Ps 105:37.

190 אלי וקת דנא פרגה אקאם קול אללה סבכה is R. Saadia's translation of Ps 105:19.

191 וצירני כסהם ינתקי is R. Saadia's translation of the citation from Is 49:2.

192 ושפתי במערפה נקיה תכלמת is R. Saadia's translation of the citation from Jb 33:3.

pression:] *To justify* (Dn 11:35) [means] that they should be observant; the nation sins are forgiven by their intermediary, as he said: *If your sins are red like scarlet they shall be as white as snow* (Is 1:18).[193] This [will happen] if the nation receive the discourse of [the faithful] and trust them and if the [these faithful] intercede in their favor. [... ...]. The negation of these three reasons occurs by the intermediary of the astrologers' reasoning [... ...]. We have observed the zodiacs of Solomon, the king of Israel, of Ptolemy[194] the Greek, of some of the Arabic kings and others.[195] They observe that these four zodiacs are not in accordance in their time. His expression: *Until the time of the end* (Dn 11:35) means that they remained in such condition until the coming of the end. His conclusion by [the expression:] *For it remains a period until the appointed time* (Dn 11:35) means that the end of Edom's kingdom does not coincide with the end of the slavery. In fact, they will have an associate afterward, whose where about will be mentioned in the last verses. Now that we have explained the twenty verses pertaining to Edom let us explain the ten verses relative to his associate. We say that its beginning is

Dn 11:36

And the other king[196] shall do what pleases him and shall ascends and magnify himself over every religion and against the Lord of lords and shall speak of astonishing things[197] and he will prosper in his affair[198] until the end of the anger, because upon him is the verdict.[199]

193 פאנה אן כאנת כטאיאכם אלחמרה אביצ׳ת כאלתלג׳ is R. Saadia's translation of the citation from Is 1:18.

194 R. Saadia does not specify which king Ptolemy he intends.

195 We are at the end of the astrologers reasoning by which they the faithful trust in the Daniel's vision. The mss lacuna does not help us fully understand their thinking. It appears clearly, yet, that the negative point resides in replacing the faith in Daniel's vision by astrological predictions.

196 MT: "The king."

197 על כל אל written in R. Saadia's Hebrew text of Daniel as על כל אלוה is translated by his as 'over every religion.' Yefet ben Eli: 'against every almighty and against the God of noblemen shall speak of astonishing things.' R. Saadia reads וידבר instead of the MT. In this way the 'speaking of astonishing things' is not directed against 'the Lord of lords' but becomes an independent act. Thus we have the king 'magnifying himself over every religion and over God, then saying outrageous things' instead of 'magnifying himself over every religion and saying outrageous things against God.'

198 פי אמרה 'in his affair' is added by R. Saadia and has no source in the MT.

199 אלאנבתאר will be called by R. Saadia קטע אלחכם by which he means a definitive and negative judgment. He will illustrate this meaning by reference to 1 Kgs 20:40 where we have the verb חרץ with his meaning of to cut and to decide.

Dn 11:37
He shall not turn his face[200] toward the gods of his fathers and he shall not turn his face toward the gods of his mothers,[201] but he shall rise over all.[202]

Dn 11:38
A mighty god shall take his place and his glory. A god that his fathers did not know he shall honor by gold, silver, precious stones and priceless cloths.[203]

Dn 11:39
He shall accomplish such thing many times against the strongholds of the foreign god whom he acknowledged. He shall make that the nation is ruled by his people. He shall divide for them lands for a price.[204]

Dn 11:40
Thereafter[205] the king of the Greeks shall lock horns with him and the Persian king[206] shall join him[207] with horses, horsemen and big fleet;[208] he shall invade their lands and shall overflow and pass over.[209]

Dn 11:41
When[210] he invades Syria the majority of its population shall perish, but the land of Edom and Moab and the extremity of the land of the sons of Amon will skip his hand.[211]

200 Yefet ben Eli: "He shall not bear differentiate the god of his fathers."
201 חמדת נשים is translated by Yefet ben Eli as שהות אלנאס 'the people desire.'
202 Yefet ben Eli: "But he shall raise himself over every god."
203 Yefet ben Eli: "And he shall give glory to the god of the mighty and to the god that his fathers that he did not know he shall give glory by the means of gold, silver and by precious jewels and desirable objects."
204 Yefet ben Eli: "He accomplishes against the strongholds of the powerful with a foreign god who is stable. The glory will be multiplied and he shall make them rule over many and divide the land by the price."
205 Yefet ben Eli: "At the time of the end." Which closer to the massoretic text.
206 For Yefet ben Eli the two kings are not identified. They are the king of the south and the king of צפון that he mentions with the Hebrew name in his commentary.
207 Yefet ben Eli: "Shall storm against him."
208 Yefet ben Eli: "Big ships."
209 Yefet ben Eli: "At the time of the end the king of the south shall lock against him and the king צפון of shall run over him like a storm, by chariots, horsemen and big ships. He shall invade the lands, submerge and pass over."
210 R. Saadia reads the ו in ובא as a conditional, 'when' or 'if.'

Dn 11:42

He shall extend his hands over all[212] the lands and the land of Egypt shall not escape him.

Dn 11:43

He shall rule over the mines of gold and silver[213] and all the precious tissue from Egypt and the Nubians and the Cushites will follow at his footsteps.

Dn 11:44

But in a time, the news from the east and the north[214] will surprise him. Therefore he shall go forth with great anger to destroy many and exterminate them.[215]

Dn 11:45

He shall plant his camp and his tent[216] between the sea and the mountain of Syria[217] until his end reaches him, then he shall have no help.

Now that we have finished [the translation of the last part of this chapter] let us go back to explain it. We say that he started by his expression: *And the other king shall do what pleases him* (Dn 11:36) and did not say *the king of the south* nor *the king of the north*. Doing so he indicates that it is the other kingdom. This is similar to his expression at the end: *And when a night and a day had passed it was the sixth day* (Gn 1:31).[218] He is the wicked king from Edom as we have already explained.[219] His expression: *And shall ascends and magnify himself over every religion* (Dn 11:36) according to what have been observed of his

---

211 Yefet ben Eli: "He shall invade the joyful land and many will stumble, but these lands will skip his evil hand with Moab and the extremity of the sons of Amon".

212 "All" is added by R. Saadia to his translation and has no source in the MT.

213 Yefet ben Eli: "The treasures of gold and silver."

214 Yefet ben Eli: "From the east and from Iraq."

215 MT: "To destroy and exterminate many" which also Yefet ben Eli's translation.

216 MT: "The tent of his camp" which is also Yefet ben Eli's translation.

217 Yefet ben Eli: "The mountain of Jerusalem."

218 ולמא מצי מן אלליל ואלנהאר יום סאדס is R. Saadia's translation of the citation from Gn 1:31. R. Saadia does not elucidate the point of comparison between Dn 11:36 and Gn 1:31. It is possible that he alludes to the orders given by the Creator during the six days and that encounter no resistance. Another possibility could be contained in the expression: וירא אלהים כי טוב that punctuates the days of the creation as signals of God's satisfaction.

219 For Yefet ben Eli, this part of Dn 11:36 deals with Ishmael or the Islamic kingdom.

domination over every religion by reasons [...][220] in their majority. [He added:] *And over the Lord of lords and shall speak of astonishing things* (Dn 11:36). And when the only rightful religion subsist he will utter astonishing things against it.[221] Things that Gabriel spares their mention and I spare their explanation. I say, yet, that the total of this story refers to the exact fact of *the mouth that says enormities* (Dn 7:8.20) that the *old man* explained [saying]: *He will speak against the Most High* (Dn 7:25) and following what we have said.

I rendered [the expression] חמדת נשים (Dn 11:37) by *the gods of his mothers* because it was preceded by *he shall not turn his face toward the gods of his fathers* (Dn 11:37). This interpretation became necessary because the gods of the fathers are similar to the gods of Moab and the gods of the mothers are similar to the gods of the sons of Amon, according to the observation of the difference between the nations in marriages and worship.[222] This was named חמדות because this the way of the apostates: They desire, then worship any form they observe.[223] This exist until now in the country of India. This is why the Bible[224] calls them *the abominations of his eyes* (Ez 20:7).[225] So he informed us that they will leave the gods of the fathers and the gods of the mothers, in spite of their difference. As to his expression: *Another mighty god shall take his place and his glory* (Dn 11:38) he means that the associate of Edom [...] in the place where he found them.[226] He will not move them from their. On the contrary, he will venerate the place and favor it and will make sure that nothing will be lacking in it. The meaning of his expression: *He is a god that his fathers did not know* (Dn 11:38) it is what will be known of an immerging religion that their

220 ... חק could be the beginning of the adjective חקירה 'despicable.'

221 Yefet ben Eli repeats the same opinion and specifies that the other religions are the ones that they do not know the true God.

222 For Yefet ben Eli, the expression: חמדת נשים designates Jerusalem. Yet, in his translation he renders the same expression by שהות אלנאס 'the desire' or 'the aspiration of the people.' He also adds a second curious interpretation: 'the desire of a form.' This, according to Yefet, justify the use of the expression, because it refers to a desire similar to that of a women for a sexual encounter with a man. This second interpretation is partially similar to R. Saadia's interpretation, since the later was the first to mention the desire of a form.

223 After translating חמדות by 'gods' understood as false gods, R. Saadia goes back to the original meaning of this word: What is desired or things desired.

224 Lit: "He."

225 "The abominations of his eyes" in Ez 20:7 is given here as synonymous of חמדות.

226 It is difficult to understand the reasoning of R. Saadia because of the lacuna in the MS. For Yefet ben Eli ולאלוה מעזים refers either to a particular god or to the god of a population whose name is מעזים.

fathers did not experience, with the devotion and the glory that surround it.[227] I rendered ובחמדות (Dn 11:38) *cloths*[228] following the example *then Rebecca took the precious cloths of hers son first borne Esau* (Gn 27:15).[229] This is equally the life style of the Hindus[230] and the apostates: They honor their gods by gold, silver, jewels and precious cloths.

His expression: *He shall accomplish such thing many times against the strongholds of the foreign god* (Dn 11:39) designates the people who join their strange religion. Their riches and their glory will be magnified, in the like of Jehu who dress the worshipers of Baal: *He said to the man in charge of the wardrobe 'bring out garments {for all the worshipers of Baal}* (2 Kgs 10:22). His expression: *He shall make that the nation is ruled by his people* (Dn 11:39) means that he shall appoint them rulers over the people, capable to establish their authority, in the like of the priests that Pharaoh appointed: *With exception of the fields of their priests that they did not buy* (Gn 47:22)[231] till the end of the story. His expression: *He shall divide for them the lands for a price* (Dn 11:39) means that he shall the remaining land and sell it in the manner Joseph proceeded: *Then Joseph bought all the fields of the Egyptians* (Gn 47:20)[232] till the end of the story. There will be opposition to it, that he kills or burns every one who does not worship his god, similar to what Nebuchadnezzar did. He also informed Daniel that after a time the king of the Persians shall join the king of the Greek in order to battle him, by saying that *thereafter the king of the Greeks shall lock horns with him* (Dn 11:40). I rendered וישׂתער[233] by (Dn 11:40) *shall join him*, similar to *it driven him away from his place* (Jb 27:21),[234] *like a chaff driven away from the floor* (Hos 13:3), *I will scatter them among the nations* (Zec 7:14) and similar examples. And it is possible to conclude from his expression: *Big fleet* (Dn 11:40) that there was a sea or seas between them. Their victory against him shall be deceptive. On the contrary he shall submit their coun-

227 It is possible that this explanation of Dn 11:38 hints to the immerging karaite movement that R. Saadia considers as a new religion, unfaithful to the Rabbinical Jewish religion, or the religion of the fathers.

228 R. Saadia renders ובחמדות by ת׳יאב פאכ׳רה 'precious cloths' and not 'cloths' alone as he does in his commentary.

229 ת׳ם אכ׳דת רבקה ת׳יאב עשׂו אבנהא אלאכבר אלפאכ׳רה is R. Saadia's translation of the citation from Gn 27:15.

230 Lit. "India."

231 עדא ריאץ׳ אימתהם פאנה לם ישתרהא is R. Saadia's translation of the citation from Gn 47:22.

232 פאשתרי יוסף גמיע ריאץ׳ אלמצריין is R. Saadia's translation of the citation from Gn 47:20.

233 In Morag text: ויסתער.

234 נקלה מן מוצ׳עה is R. Saadia's translation of the quoted part of Jb 27:20.

try, overflow and pass over, as he said: *And he shall invade their lands, shall overflow and pass over* (Dn 11:40). Then he informed him that the majority of the inhabitants of Syria will perish at that time. Yet the land of Edom, the land of Moab and part of the land of the sons of Amon will be safe.

We meditate again these events and found that in the biographies and the conquest narration the land of Moab was invaded without war, which spares it the spoliation and disorder. As to the rest of the land, it shall be spoiled, ruined, as he said: *He shall extend his hands over all the lands* (Dn 11:42). [Which means] in the remaining lands. The land of Egypt, too, shall know peace, because he said: *Egypt shall not escape him* (Dn 11:42). The meaning is that it will not succeed in its effort to be out of his domination. It is possible, however, that it will escape the spoliation. I rendered במכמני הזהב (Dn 11:43) by mines. Because there are mines of gold in Egypt. However, no mines of silver can be found there. Yet it is possible to mention in Hebrew[235] the silver, since it could be refine by gold as we knew from David when he said: *Seven thousand talents of refined silver* (1 Chr 29:4). These houses, however, were not daubed with silver. In fact it was never the practice of the people to do so. What he means is that it is a refined gold which has the value of seven thousand seed of a plate. I rendered חמודות מצרים (Dn 11:43) *the precious tissue from Egypt* because it designates their famous silk. The observation of his expression: *And the Nubians and the Cushites will follow at his footsteps* (Dn 11:43) represent the proof that the land of Egypt is made of the Nubians and the Cushites. That is why we believe again that the meaning of *his footsteps* (Dn 11:43) refers to the his friends[236] whose opinion lead his footsteps.[237] His expression afterward: *But in a time, the news from the east and the north will surprise him* (Dn 11:44) means that this will happen to him if he moves from the east or from the north. At that time he joins a place between the sea and the mountain of Syria. It is possible that it designates the city of Akka[238] because it is between the sea and the mountain of Galilee. When these events happened it is the end of this associate, as he said: *Until his end reaches him* (Dn 11:45).[239] It is as if he is saying that his end will reach him with the addition of עד. Like his expression to the fathers: You have made your days drew near and have reached your years (Ez 22:4).[240] These is a sentence of events from [the time] of slavery, that Gabriel placed as signals of the salvation. And from the beginning of his mention of the conditions per-

235 Lit: "In the language."

236 Lit: "The friends of his footsteps."

237 A difficult reasoning that the uncertainty of the lesson represents no help for its full understanding.

238 Akko or St. John of Acre, a city on the north of Israel.

239 ובא עד קצו.

240 ותקרבו ימיך ותבוא עד שנותיך.

taining to this associate we knew that there will be no other kingdom after him. This is because of he had said: *He shall prosper in his affair until the end of the anger* (Dn 11:36).[241] Such is the name of the time of slavery of *seventy years*, following the expression: *{Jerusalem and the towns of Judah} that you placed under anger for seventy years* (Zec 1:25). His expression: *Because upon him is the verdict* (Dn 11:36)[242] means that he shall be cut off in the manner the Lord of the universe choose by His wisdom. Because we found that the mutilation by wisdom is called חר׳צה. That is why the Bible says: *Such is your verdict* (1 Kgs 20:40).

Know, and may God be your help, that when these signs were verified, that we saw the victory of Israel over the king of the Greek, and the victory of Edom over Syria, and the persecutions to which Israel was submitted, with some who were killed, others who were burnt and still others who were deported in *the days of forced apostasy*[243] and their reparation at the time of *our teacher*,[244] after what happened to Vespasian and the like, and the religion that demonstrate the association of Edom, with the abandon of the worship of its gods and its permanent staying in its place, and the escape of Edom and Moab from its spoliation and the fact that some of the Cushites are submitted to it, with all what we have described which was verified and took place, with nothing remaining if not the story [signified by his expression:] *He shall plant his camp and his tent* (Dn 11:45)[245] our hearts will rejuvenate, because it is inevitable that the salvation will come afterward.[246] Similar to what Jehu had said: *Know now that nothing of the word that the Lord has said about the house of Ahab will fall on the ground* (2 Kgs 10:10). And similar to what the he had said to Habakkuk about the king of Babylon: *There is still a vision for the appointed time; it speaks about the end; it does not lie. If it does not come soon wait for it for it will certainly come, without delay* (Hb 2:3). Having attained this principle Gabriel said to Daniel 'I reached the limit of what I know and what I have.' What is remaining after this chapter belongs to Michael. He then added the three verses of salvation, saying at the beginning:

241 The name of the slavery time is זם according to R. Saadia.

242 כי נחרצה נעשׂתה.

243 בימי שׂנד.

244 The title of Judah ha-Nasi.

245 Yefet ben Eli identify the place where the victorious camp will be established: Four hours running by a horse from Jerusalem.

246 One of the longest and most difficult to understand sentence in R. Saadia's commentary on Daniel. The massive use of pronouns makes it very uncertain to identify the nations whose events are described by R. Saadia. Such conclusion is reached by Yefet ben Eli at the end of his commentary on Dn 11:39.

Chapter 12

Dn 12:1

At that time stands Michael[1] the great chief who is in charge of your people. It will be a time of incomparable distress, from the beginning of the nation[2] until that time. During that time your people will be delivered, every one who shall be found written in the Book.[3]

The first thing we need to explain is the meaning of his expression: *Stands Michael* (Dn 12:1) whether he was sitting or laying down. We answer that the meaning is that he rises up your people and takes care of them.[4] In fact this is the way to speak of anyone who is in charge of your people in the like of what he already had said: *Until I, Deborah, rose, mother in Israel* (Jgs 5:7), *when the Lord raised up as judges for them* (Jgs 2:18), *I will raise up a prophet for them* (Dt 18:18),[5] *I will raise up a faithful priest for myself* (1 Sm 2:35), *and David their king that I will raise up for them* (Jer 30:9). He also said to the whole nation: *Stand up, sit down Jerusalem* (Is 52:2),[6] *arise, shine, O Jerusalem, for your light is advancing* (Is 60:1).[7] In opposition to that he said about the time of humiliation and disgrace: *Get down and sit in the dirt, assembly of the people of Babylon* (Is 47:1),[8] get down from glory and sit with thirst, inhabitant of the

1 Yefet ben Eli: "Michael the great chief who serves your people will be firm."

2 Yefet ben Eli: "From the beginning of any nation."

3 Yefet ben Eli: "At that time every one written in the book will be delivered." 'Your people are delivered' is omitted in his translation.

4 One of the two reasons, according to Yefet ben Eli, that justifies the fact that Michael was standing, or taking car of the Israelites. The other reason that R. Saadia does not mention is the fact that the other kingdoms are destroyed. As if, following Yefet reasoning, the standing of Michael is out of relief, once he accomplished his what he had to do about the other kingdoms.

5 ואני אנצבה נבי להם is R. Saadia's translation of the citation from Dt 18:18.

6 וקומי ואגלסי יא ירושלם is R. Saadia's translation of the citation from Is 52:2.

7 אלא פקומי פאצׄי יא דאר אלסלאם לאן נורך קד אקבל is R. Saadia's translation of the citation from Is 60:1. The expression 'O Jerusalem' is an addition by R. Saadia to his translation and has no origin in the MT.

8 אנחדרי ואגלסי עלי אלתראב יא גמאעה אהל באבל is R. Saadia's translation of the citation from Is 47:1.

assembly[9] of Dibon (Jer 48:18) plus what is similar to all of them.[10] The fact that the Bible[11] calls him *the great chief* (Dn 12:1) is because he is in charge of the people named *great nation* (Dt 4:7.8.),[12] who are obedient to whose name is *the great mighty* (Dt 10:17),[13] who believe in *the great day of the Lord* (Jl 3:4), who venerate [about which it was said that] *the house that I built is great* (2 Chr 2:4), to whom *a great light* (Is 9:1)[14] was promised, who had heard a great voice (Dt 5:19),[15] who will inherit from *the biggest man* (Jos 14:15), *and will be delighted in the great bounty* (Neh 9:25), who will proclaim that *{the matter is true} and its intention is great* (Dn 10:1),[16] who expect *{the time} in which the great ram's horn shall be blown* (Is 27:13).[17] The standing up related to Michael,[18] sine he said: *Who is in charge* (יעמד על) *of your people* (Dn 12:1) is different from the expression: *Yoash said to all those who stand against him* (יעמדו עליו) (Jgs 6:31) because [the meaning] is to resist.[19] It is different from [the meaning of the expression:] *They confronted* (ויעמדו על) *the king Uzziah* (2 Chr 26:18), because [the meaning] is to oppose. It is different from [the meaning of the expression:] *The kings of the earth stood up...* (Ps 2:2),[20] because [the meaning] is to battle. Yet it is the same as [the meaning of the expression:] *All the host of heaven are standing by Him* (1 Kgs 22:19) which means giving [Him] honor and veneration. It is also similar to his expression: *They are the two anointed ones that stand by the Lord of the whole earth* (Zec 4:14) which designates the men of oil, by which are anointed, *the house of Aaron and the house of the king*. It goes the same for Michael in his relation to Israel, to honor them. Comparable to the visitors who are in the presence of the emperor,

9 בת is rendered by 'assembly' in conformity with R. Saadia's understanding of this word as it is explained in his commentary of Dn 11:1 and as it is rendered in his quotation of Is 47:1.

10 Either what is similar to the examples of Is 47:1 and Jer 48:18 or to the both categories of examples surrounding the verb קום 'raise up' and ירד 'get down.'

11 Lit: "He."

12 אמה כבירה is R. Saadia's translation of the citation from Dt 4:7.8.

13 אלטאיק אלכביר is R. Saadia's translation of the citation from Dt 10:17.

14 נורא עטימא is R. Saadia's translation of the citation from Is 9:1.

15 צות עטים is R. Saadia's translation of the citation from Dt 5:19.

16 "The matter is true and its intention is big" or "great" follows the interpretation of R. Saadia of this expression in his commentary of Dn 10:1.

17 יצרב פיה בבוק עטים is R. Saadia's translation of the citation from Is 27:13.

18 Lit: "Related to him."

19 R. Saadia is reflecting on the different understandings of the expression: על עמד which in Dn 12:1 means 'being in charge of,' a positive meaning, while in the examples that follow the same expression has negative meanings.

20 אנתצאב מלוך אלארץ is R. Saadia's translation of the citation from Ps 2:2.

the angels stand in the presence of the Israelites.[21] In their like when they surround their emperor *the angle of God coming down surrounds those who fear Him, delivering them* (Ps 34:8).[22] And as they carry him by hands they will carry them, *because He gives order to His angels in your favor that they protect you in all your ways, that they carry you on both hands so that your foot do not hurt a stone* (Ps 91:11–12)[23]

His expression: *It will be a time of distress* (Dn 12:1) designates the beginning of the salvation which described as *the messianic tribulations.*[24] They are called *messianic tribulations* because their meaning derives from labor pains.[25] In fact, it is well known that no time is more difficult for a women than the time form the beginning of the birth labor to the delivery. Thereafter, the infants' birth is the same.[26] That is the reason for this comparison of the of the distress in this story: *Incomparable distress, from the beginning of the nation until that time* (Dn 12:1). In fact, this is the same comparison that the prophet Jeremiah in the name of God: *Thus said the Lord 'we have heard voice of panic, terror without peace'* (Jer 30:5). We have to know who are these who say: *we have heard* (Jer 30:5)? We answer that the Lord[27] is threatening them: You will say: *We have heard voice of panic* (Jer 30:5). As if the Bible[28] supposes [… …] *we have heard voice of panic* (Jer 30:5), because the discourse belongs to the people, since […]. Its beginning is: *These are the words that the Lord said concerning Israel and Judah* (Jer 30:4). So it is by a comparison that [He speaks to them:] *Ask and see whether a man bear a child? Why then do I see every man with his hands on his loins like a woman in labor and all faces turned paleness* (Jer 30:6)? Then He speaks about the greatness of that day saying: *Ah, that day is great; there is none like it* (Jer 30:7). Then He informed that the salvation no

21 Lit. "Comparable to the visitors who are in the presence of the emperor, they stand in their presence."

22 וכדֹאך מלך אללה נאזל מחיט באתקיאה יכלצהם is R. Saadia's translation of Ps 34:8.

23 בחגר אדֹ יאמר לך במלאיכתה יחפטונך פי גמיע טרקך יחמלונך עלי אלכפין כלא תצדם רגלך is R. Saadia's translation of Ps 91:11-12.

24 חבלי משיח. The Hebrew word חבלי means also the labor pangs. For Yefet ben Eli the reason for these tribulation is that an army from the Israelites, represented by the זרעים of Dn 11:31, will try to abolish the Islamic cult and forbid the mention of their prophet, Muhammed, that Yefet ben Eli calls 'the man of the wind.'

25 Lit. "Because it is a name that derives from labor pains."

26 ובעקבהא יולד אלולד סואא literally 'after that the infants are born equally.' R. Saadia seems to suggest that there is difference between women in enduring the labor pains, while the coming of the child to the world happens in the same way.

27 Lit: "He."

28 Lit: "he."

doubt will come after it: *It is a time of distress for Jacob, but he shall be saved from it* (Jer 30:7).

It is possible that the expression: *Every one who shall be found written in the Book* (Dn 12:1) bear five meanings; three are having individual dimension and two are with collective dimension. The three with the individual dimension mean, first, that among *your people will be delivered* (Dn 12:1) every one *who shall be found written in the Book* (Dn 12:1). Every one who remained firm on his religion during *the time of distress*. Similar to what was said in the Psalm:[29] *Then I said to the people*[30] *'behold! I came to you with a scroll, written in a book I have with me* (Ps 40:8).[31] Likewise, every one whose life by wisdom [...] as he said there: *All who were written for life in Jerusalem* (Is 4:3).[32] It is also possible that it is the register that belongs to the emperor, as he said there about the register [...]: *where is the scribe? Where is the tax collector? Where is who count the houses* (Is 33:18)?[33] The two collective interpretations pertain to the nation as a whole[34] and have a general meaning.[35] It means that the whole nation shall be saved, according to the consolations that have been written to them in the Book.[36] First, the consolation of the future vision which are the ten verses that Moses had said in the story: *When all these things happen to you* (Dt 30:1).[37] [These verses] satisfy the whole [...] and their principles. The second is the consolation registered in all the books of the prophets as he said: *comfort My People, comfort them again, appease the community of Jerusalem*

29 Lit: "Similar to what was said there."

30 The expression לאלקום 'to the people' is added by R. Saadia to his translation and has no Hebrew origin in the MT.

31 חיניד קלת לאלקום הודא קד תיתכם בצחיפה מכתובה פי כתאב מעי is R. Saadia's translation of Ps 40:8.

32 כל מן כתב ללחיוה פיהא is R. Saadia's translation of the citation from Is 4:3. Lit. "All who were written for life in her (= Jerusalem)." Yefet ben Eli cites the same verse of Isaiah in the same context.

33 אין אלכאתב ואין אלואזן ואין מחצי אלמנאזל is R. Saadia's translation of the citation from Is 33:18.

34 Yefet ben Eli does not retain any collective interpretation.

35 ויצמר כף דאירה literally 'presupposes a round palm.'

36 Yefet ben Eli thinks that those who will be saved are those who cleaned themselves from the filthiness of being acquainted with the nations, or those who adopted the pagans' behavior. Will be also saved the Israelites who are not sinners.

37 ויכון אדא חלת בך גמיע הדה אלאמור is R. Saadia's translation of the citation from Dt 30:1. Form time to time the mention of the first verse of a chapter in the Bible has no other meaning than the designation of the chapter itself. As if R. Saadia is saying: The thirtieth chapter.

(Is 40:1).[38] […] he said: *Every one who shall be found written in the Book* (Dn 12:1). The second verse:

Dn 12:2

Many of those who are sleeping in the dust shall wake up,[39] some to the life eternal and some to the dishonor and everlasting lesson.[40]

His expression: *Many of those who are sleeping* (Dn 12:2) does not concern all the dead, but some of them, as he has said in the Bible: *Many from the priests and the Levites and the chiefs of the fathers' houses old men who had seen...* (Ezr 3:12). They need to be ten years old in order to reach the age of reason, so how *did they see the first Temple* (Ezr 3:12)? It is well known that the sons of [… …] all of them, with similar clothing. It is also comparable to his expression: *And many of the people of the land became Jews* (Est 8:17). They were smaller number. And these who were not […] and what is similar to that.[41] [He called] the dead *those who are sleeping* (Dn 12:2). [About them] he said: *shall wake up* (Dn 12:2) for [many] reasons. One of them is that reviving [… …] the broken-hearted. [… …] before that, as the attentive man mentions. Another [reason] is that they are yet expecting [the salvation] like a sleeper is expecting the wake up. Another [reason] still is that the death does not frighten them, like the sleep does not frighten people. We also found Him saying in anther place [of the Bible]: *O my people, I will lift you out your graves* (Ez 37:12). Then we investigate [in order to know who is called *my people*. We found [that those who are called by such name] are those who professing the unity of God.[42] because He had said: *Hear, O My people, the voice of what I say to you, what I recite to you, O Israel, I am God your Lord* (Ps 50:7).[43] Who believe in the God's prediction is called *My people*, as he said: *Listen, O My people to My prediction* (Ps 78:1).[44] Who repent before dying is also called *My people*, as he said: *When My*

38 עזו קומי תם עזוהם יקול רבכם ודארו גמאעה מדינה אלסלאם is R. Saadia's translation of the citation from Is 40:1-2.

39 Yefet ben Eli: "Many shall rise from the dust" which exclude the comparison with the individuals who sleeps that R. Saadia will use.

40 Yefet ben Eli: "… and some to the shame, an everlasting lesson."

41 The end of a difficult reasoning to be understood, because of the lacuna in the manuscript.

42 אלמוחדין 'those who are professing the unity of God' are mentioned here, probably by opposition to the Christens.

43 בקול אסמע יא שעבי מא אכלמך בה ויא אסראיל מא אנאשדך אנא אללה רבך is R. Saadia's translation of Ps 50:7. The Arabic word 'voice' is added by R. Saadia to his translation and has no Hebrew origin in the MT.

44 אנצתוא יא קומי אלי דלאלתי is R. Saadia's translation of the citation from Ps 78:1.

people, who are called by My name, humble themselves, pray, seek My face and return {from their wicked ways}... (2 Chr 7:14). As to his expression: *Some ... and some* (Dn 12:2) it designates *those who shall wake up to the life eternal* (cf. Dn 12:2) and *those who shall not wake up [and are destined to be] to the dishonor and everlasting lesson* (cf. Dn 12:2).[45] It is also in accordance with what the fathers have transmitted: *The curse for those who are eternally dead, may they never return to be alive, but may they come back to be dirt.*[46] And who dies without atonement, there shall be no helper for him, neither in the salvation, nor in the eternal habitation. It is similar to what had been said: *When the impious dies there is no hope, and the hope of the unjust will perish* (Pr 11:7).[47] I also treated extensively the question of the revival of the death in the seventh article of *the Book of the Philosophic Doctrines and Religious Beliefs*,[48] plus in an article that I wrote for this purpose. The third verse:

Dn 12:3

knowledgeable men will shine like the heavenly light and the reformers of the people like stars for ever and eternally.

Since the light is of two kinds, the light of the sky itself that receives from the stars and the light of the stars that receive from the sun or that they produce by themselves, and because the knowledgeable people are of two kinds, the kind that understand by themselves without being able to make others understand,

45 According to Yefet ben Eli those who are destined to the dishonor and to be a lesson to consider for generations are those who do not mourn the of Israel in its deportation. Furthermore, they are the same that ridicule the righteous who spend their time mourning and praying for the salvation and the restoration of the glory of old.

46 להם מתים שעתיד הקבה להחיותם שוב אינן חזין לעפראן.

47 אדא מאת אלאנסאן אלפאסק פקד אנקטע אלרגא כמא אן רגא אלמגלין יביד is R. Saadia's translation of Pr 11:7.

48 כתאב אלאמאנאת ואלאעתקאדאת (Ed. S. Landauer, Brill 1880), in its Hebrew translation: ספר האמונות והדעות. The seventh article (pp. 211–229) deals with the revival of the dead during the salvation time which coincides with coming of the Messiah in order to restore Israel's glory. The hidden question is the difference between the resurrection at the end of time and the resurrection during the messianic time. R. Saadia's answer is that the resurrection during the messianic time is a privilege reserved to the pious Israelites: Those who remained faithful until death and thus who amended their life before dying. The nations are not concerned by this privilege and the resurrection of the just among them will take place at the end of time. The compensation of the Israelites who observed the Lord's Law implies an anticipated eternal life that until the time of the general resurrection. To be noticed that R. Saadia quotes Dn 12:1–3 in his treatment of this subject (pp. 215–216).

and the kind that is capable to understand and to make others understand, that is why Gabriel compared the weakest among them with the weakest light and the stronger among them with the stronger light. Therefore the knowledgeable for themselves are compared to the [light] of the dome of the sky. As to those who are reformers for others they are compared to the sun and the stars.[49] Even if the men of knowledge are in two categories they still compete among themselves in each category. In the like of the luminaries and stars that compete among themselves.[50] In fact there are paths in the sky that receive more light than others. That is why they are called the bright the obscure and the middle. In the same way, the individuals who learn for the benefit of himself are of three kinds. Like the stars who are lightening without being enlightened, which is the case of the sun, and enlightened without lightening, which is the case of the moon, and lightening and enlightened, which is the case of the remaining [stars], those who instruct others are of three kinds. [... ...] for this [kind] and this [kind] there many examples among the prophets. Whoever, the fear stop me from starting to detail there respective superiority. Beside there is no benefit in doing so. That is why we take examples from among the wise men. We say then that similar to Rab[51] and Rabbi Hiyya[52] there are those who are knowledgeable and who instruct. And similar to Ben Azzai[53] and Ben Zoma[54] there are those who are

49 Yefet ben Eli's comparison between the wise men and light in the sky is opposed, in a way, to the same comparison here. According to Yefet ben Eli the light of the dome of the sky is brighter than the light of the stars. This is following his interpretation of the משׂכילים 'the masters' as the highest degree among the knowledgeable people. For R. Saadia, the highest degree comes not only by knowledge, משׂכילים, but by sharing the knowledge with the people מצדיקי הרבים. It is also useful to know that a karaite master is called משׂכיל.

50 The light that shines from the face of the knowledgeable men is compared by Yefet ben Eli to the light that shined from Moses' Face after his encounter with the Most High.

51 Rabbi Judah ha-Nasi, from the second century, the redactor of the Mishnah.

52 R. Hiyya is compiler of beraitot, and the author of some of them, known later as the Tosefta, and pupil of Judah ha-Nasi. He was born near Sura, in Babylonia, at the end of the second century and is considered the second teacher in Judaism after R. Judah ha-Nasi.

53 Simeon Ben Azzai, from the early second century, was a tanna contemporary to R. Akiba. Although he was unmarried, which contradict some of the obvious teaching of the Judaism, he was known for his saintly life. Some of his sayings are quoted in the Mishna (Avot 4:2). He did not write or teach and his name is usually quoted without the title of 'rabbi.'

54 Like Rab and R. Hiyya, Simeon Ben Zoma is a tanna from the second century who studied under Joshua ben Hananiah. However, unlike his contemporaries he did not write or teach. Meanwhile his was famous for his discussions with his master and

knowledgeable without instructing. The reward for all of them is light, as we have explained about the reward of the life to come in the ninth article[55] of the book of *the Book of the Philosophic Doctrine.* Then he said:

Dn 12:4

And you, O Daniel, retain this discourse[56] and seal this Book until the time of the end in which many will turn around[57] and their knowledge shall be increased.[58]

I say that the discourse of Gabriel is directed to us. In fact, he did not intend, while saying: *Retain this discourse* (Dn 12:4) the confinement of this prophecy [...] he wants to say [...]. Because if such was the matter, Daniel would not be able to write it down and it would not be lawful [...] to teach it and how it becomes signs in which benefit may be found.[59] What he truly intended by his expression: *Retain this discourse* (Dn 12:4) is know it by heart. Similar to his expression elsewhere: (Ps 51:8).[60] It also right to say [...] that he kept it secret [until] death. About the wicked men [... ...] the words of Gabriel are comparable, as he already said to him: [... ...] the people and their quarrels. [... ...] the intention in all is the same. Then he said:

---

many of his sayings were registered in the Mishna (Avot 4:1) and Tosefta (Hag 2:5).

55 In the ninth article of his כתאב אלאמאנאת ואלאעתקאדאת (Ed. S. Landauer, Brill 1880 pp. 255–280) R. Saadia discuses the reward and punishment in the life to come. He mentions thirteen reasons, six already discussed in the third article, and seven that he adds in the ninth article. He ends his article by eleven points about the nature of such reward and punishment.

56 Yefet ben Eli: "Close the discourse."

57 We have a very tendentious interpretation by Yefet ben Eli to Dn 12:4. The many that will turn around are the משׂכילים or 'the karaite masters.' They travel in order to explain the karaite doctrine of reference to the Hebrew Bible alone. In doing so the demonstrate the falsehood of the rabbinical doctrine founded, according to Yefet, on the human tradition of the Mishna and Talmud. Yefet ben Eli mention the name of R. Saadia Gaon as representative of the rabbinical interpretation. Himself and other rabbis are accountable of the tragedy of Israel and the Jews' lack of knowledge of their duty toward God.

58 Lit: "And the knowledge shall increase."

59 "To seal the Book" has the meaning, according to Yefet ben Eli, of telling Daniel not to ask for more than what was explained to him by the angel.

60 ופי סרא קד ערפתני אלחכמה is R. Saadia's translation of the citation from Ps 51:8.

Dn 12:5

And I Daniel looked and there are two others[61] standing on the river of Tigris,[62] at the left and the right.[63]

Dn 12:6

So I said to the angel dressed with linen[64] suspended over the water of Tigris, 'until when is the end of the rewards.'[65]

Dn 12:7

Then I heard the angel dressed with linen suspended over the water of Tigris raising his right and his left to the sky and swore by the One who lives forever that it shall be for a time of their times and a half [of a time],[66] and at the end of the destruction of the hand that belongs to the people of Jerusalem all this shall be finished.

Dn 12:8

I heard it and did not understand so I said, 'My lord, what shall be the end of this?[67]

Dn 12:9

He answered: 'Pass away Daniel, because the discourse is kept secret and sealed until the time of the end.'

Dn 12:10

Then many will be freed, cleaned[68] and refined, the oppressors will oppress them, but they will not understand; the knowledgeable men will understand.[69]

61 Yefet ben Eli: "Two other angels."
62 Yefet ben Eli, following the MT refuses to identify the river, while R. Saadia add to the MT the name of Tigris, the biggest river of Iraq.
63 MT: "One to one side of the river, one to one side of the river" which is also Yefet ben Eli's translation.
64 Cf. the footnote relative to the same expression in Dn 10:5.
65 אלכפאיאת literally 'the skills.' Yefet ben Eli: "The miracles."
66 MT and Yefet ben Eli: "For a time, two times and a half." R. Saadia reads the ם in מועדים as a suffix 'their.' Which gives us the Arabic translation אוקאתהם 'their time.'
67 Another possible translation: "What will come after this?"
68 MT and Yefet ben Eli: "Become white."

When the *angel dressed with linen* (Dn 12:6) pronounced these words, I mean [... ...] the two angels heard it from him, they became convinced and understood it [...]. As to Daniel [... ...]. *By the One who lives forever* (Dn 12:7) [...] may He be glorified, since He is the life of the world and by whom the world stands [...] in particular. Some of the learned call [...] what is particular is the brain of the knowledgeable man [... ...] life in its meaning [... ...] the end. So he said: *That it shall be for a time* (Dn 12:7). [...]. The word *time* (Dn 12:7) as you say *for a time* [...]. *I will give them in My house and My walls dignity and good names* (Is 56:5)[70] [...] the dispersion of the deportation, as if you say: *And I disperse them among the nations* (Ez 36:19) [...]. He said: *Dressed with linen* (Dn 12:7). This expression, I mean *time* [...] they were convinced and they understood it [... ...] they did not understand it because he said: *I heard it* (Dn 12: 8) [... ...].

Dn 12:11

And from the time of the disappearance of the daily offering, the abomination that inspires fear will come back for one thousand two hundreds ninety years.[71]

Dn 12:12

Happy is the man who waits and reaches the mention of a thousand three hundred thirty five years.[72]

---

69 Yefet ben Eli: "And many will become rebellious, but the wicked will not understand, but the masters will understand."

70 פי ביתי ואסוארי אתארא ואסמא כ׳יר is R. Saadia's translation of the citation from Is 56:5. It is difficult to determine the exact meaning for which R. Saadia quotes Is 56:5.

71 Yefet ben Eli: "The abomination, empty inspiring fear, will be established for one thousand two hundreds ninety days."

72 Yefet ben Eli: "Happy is the man who observes and reach days which are one thousand three hundred thirty five days."

Dn 12:13

As for you, go proceed until the end[73] you shall be rewarded and stand by your portion at the end of the days.[74]

73 According to Yefet ben Eli, the expression לך לקץ that he translates by 'pass to the end' means 'put your worries aside and die in peace like your fathers.'

74 At the end of his commentary on Daniel, Yefet ben Eli criticizes the interpretation of קץ הימין by the Rabbanites in general and R. Saadia in particular. Their they understand this expression as 'the end of the years' instead of its literal understanding as 'the end of the days.' After citing Benjamin Alnahawendi who interprets ימים as years, he sides with Salmon ben Yeruham who interprets it as days. The particularity of Yefet ben Eli's interpretation is that he interprets ימים as days, and that he underlines the impossibility of knowing the exact time of the end.

Bible Index[1]

1 Bible references in pp. 75–420 are to the Judeo-Arabic text. Bibles references to pp. 423-665 are to the English translation.

Joshua

Judges

1 Samuel

2 Samuel

1 Kings

2 Kings

Bible in History

Series List

Vol. 1 Joseph Alobaidi: *Le commentaire des psaumes par le qaraïte Salmon ben Yeruham. Psaumes 1–10. Introduction, édition, traduction.* 1996.

Vol. 2 Joseph Alobaidi: *The Messiah in Isaiah 53. The commentaries of Saadia Gaon, Salmon ben Yeruham and Yefet ben Eli on Is 52:13–53.12. Edition and translation.* 1998.

Vol. 3 Emmanuel Uchenna Dim: *The Eschatological Implications of Isa 65 and 66 as the Conclusion of the Book of Isaiah.* 2005.

Vol. 4 Se-Hoon Jang: *Particularism and Universalism in the Book of Isaiah. Isaiah's Implications for a Pluralistic World from a Korean Perspective.* 2005.

Vol. 5 Michael Avioz: *Nathan's Oracle (2 Samuel 7) and Its Interpreters.* 2005.

Vol. 6 Joseph Alobaidi: *The Book of Daniel. The Commentary of R. Saadia Gaon. Edition and Translation.* 2006.

Vol. 7 Pnina Galpaz-Feller: *Samson: The Hero and the Man. The Story of Samson (Judges 13–16).* Forthcoming.